Walter Benjamin

SELECTED WRITINGS

Michael W. Jennings
General Editor

Marcus Bullock, Howard Eiland, Gary Smith
Editorial Board

Walter Benjamin

SELECTED WRITINGS
VOLUME 2
1927–1934

Translated by Rodney Livingstone
and Others

Edited by Michael W. Jennings,
Howard Eiland, and Gary Smith

THE BELKNAP PRESS OF HARVARD UNIVERSITY PRESS

Cambridge, Massachusetts, and London, England   1999

This work is a translation of selections from Walter Benjamin, *Gesammelte Schriften, Unter Mitwirkung von Theodor W. Adorno und Gershom Sholem, herausgegeben von Rolf Tiedemann und Hermann Schweppenhäuser,* copyright © 1972, 1974, 1977, 1982, 1985, 1989 by Suhrkamp Verlag. Some of the pieces in this volume were previously published in English, as follows: "On the Image of Proust," "Unpacking My Library," and "Franz Kafka" apppeared in Walter Benjamin, Illuminations, edited by Hannah Arendt, English translation copyright © 1968 by Harcourt Brace Jovanovich, Inc. "Moscow," "Surrealism," "Marseilles," "Karl Kraus," "The Destructive Character," "A Berlin Chronicle," "Hashish in Marseilles," "On the Mimetic Faculty," and "The Author as Producer" appeared in Walter Benjamin, *Reflections,* English translation copyright © 1978 by Harcourt Brace Jovanovich, Inc. Published by arrangement with Harcourt Brace Jovanovich, Inc. "From the Brecht Commentary" and "A Family Drama in the Epic Theater" appeared in Walter Benjamin, *Understanding Brecht* (London: NLB/Verso, 1973). "Little History of Photography" appeared in Walter Benjamin, *"One-Way Street" and Other Writings* (London: NLB/Verso, 1979, 1985). "Theories of German Fascism" and "Doctrine of the Similar" appeared in *New German Critique* 17 (Spring 1979). "Goethe" appeared in *New Left Review* 133 (May–June 1982). "Left-Wing Melancholy" appeared in *Screen* 15, no. 2 (Summer 1974). "The Rigorous Study of Art" appeared in *October* 47 (Winter 1988), translation © 1988 by October Magazine Ltd. and the Massachusetts Institute of Technology.

Publication of this book has been aided by a grant from Inter Nationes, Bonn.

Frontispiece: Walter Benjamin, Berlin, 1929. Photo by Charlotte Joël. Courtesy of the Theodor W. Adorno Archiv, Frankfurt am Main.

Library of Congress Cataloging in Publication Data

Benjamin, Walter, 1982–1940.
[Selections. English. 1999]
Selected writings / Walter Benjamin; edited by Michael W. Jennings, Howard Eiland, and Gary Smith
   p. cm.
"This work is a translation of selections from Walter Benjamin, Gesammelte Schriften . . . copyright 1972 . . . by Suhrkamp Verlag"—T.p. verso.
Includes index.
Contents: v. 1. 1913–1926.—v. 2. 1927–1934.
ISBN 0-674-94585-9 (v. 1: alk. paper)   ISBN 0-674-94586-7 (v. 2: alk. paper)
I. Jennings, Michael William. II. Title.
PT2603.E455A26   1996
833'.91209—dc20   96-23027

Designed by Gwen Nefsky Frankfeldt

Contents

THE RETURN OF THE *FLANEUR*, 1929

CRISIS AND CRITIQUE, 1930

THE DESTRUCTIVE CHARACTER, 1931

IBIZAN SEQUENCE, 1932

THOUGHT FIGURES, 1933

THE AUTHOR AS PRODUCER, 1934

Moscow, 1927

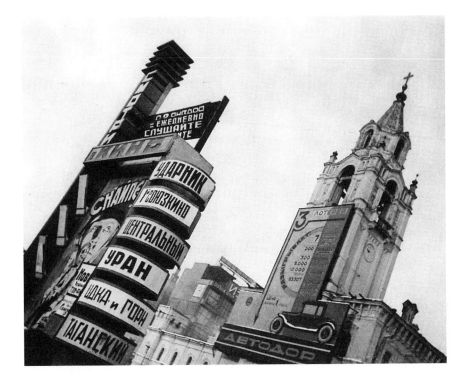

Cinema kiosk in front of the Strastnoy monastery, Moscow, 1932. Photo by Alexander Rodchenko. Courtesy Alexander Lavrentiev, Moscow.

Dream Kitsch

Gloss on Surrealism

No one really dreams any longer of the Blue Flower.[1] Whoever awakes as Heinrich von Ofterdingen today must have overslept.[2] The history of the dream remains to be written, and opening up a perspective on this subject would mean decisively overcoming the superstitious belief in natural necessity by means of historical illumination. Dreaming has a share in history. The statistics on dreaming would stretch beyond the pleasures of the anecdotal landscape into the barrenness of a battlefield. Dreams have started wars, and wars, from the very earliest times, have determined the propriety and impropriety—indeed, the range—of dreams.

No longer does the dream reveal a blue horizon. The dream has grown gray. The gray coating of dust on things is its best part. Dreams are now a shortcut to banality. Technology consigns the outer image of things to a long farewell, like banknotes that are bound to lose their value. It is then that the hand retrieves this outer cast in dreams and, even as they are slipping away, makes contact with familiar contours. It catches hold of objects at their most threadbare and timeworn point. This is not always the most delicate point: children do not so much clasp a glass as snatch it up. And which side does an object turn toward dreams? What point is its most decrepit? It is the side worn through by habit and patched with cheap maxims. The side which things turn toward the dream is kitsch.

Chattering, the fantasy images of things fall to the ground like leaves from a Leporello picture book, *The Dream*.[3] Maxims shelter under every leaf: "Ma plus belle maîtresse c'est la paresse," and "Une médaille vernie pour le plus grand ennui," and "Dans le corridor il y a quelqu'un qui me veut à la mort."[4] The Surrealists have composed such lines, and their allies among the artists have copied the picture book. *Répétitions* is the name that Paul Eluard gives to one of his collections of poetry, for whose frontispiece Max Ernst has drawn four small boys. They turn their backs to the reader, to their teacher and his desk as well, and look out over a balustrade where a balloon hangs in the air. A giant pencil rests on its point in the windowsill. The repetition of childhood experience gives us pause: when we were little, there was as yet no agonized protest against the world of our parents. As children in the midst of that world, we showed ourselves superior. When we reach for the banal, we take hold of the good along with it—the good that is there (open your eyes) right before you.

For the sentimentality of our parents, so often distilled, is good for providing the most objective image of our feelings. The long-windedness of their speeches, bitter as gall, has the effect of reducing us to a crimped picture puzzle; the ornament of conversation was full of the most abysmal entanglements. Within is heartfelt sympathy, is love, is kitsch. "Surrealism is called upon to reestablish dialogue in its essential truth. The interlocutors are freed from the obligation to be polite. He who speaks will develop no theses. But in principle, the reply cannot be concerned for the self-respect of the person speaking. For in the mind of the listener, words and images are only a springboard." Beautiful sentiments from Breton's *Surrealist Manifesto*. They articulate the formula of the dialogic misunderstanding—which is to say, of what is truly alive in the dialogue. "Misunderstanding" is here another word for the rhythm with which the only true reality forces its way into the conversation. The more effectively a man is able to speak, the more successfully he is misunderstood.

In his *Vague de rêves* [Wave of Dreams], Louis Aragon describes how the mania for dreaming spread over Paris. Young people believed they had come upon one of the secrets of poetry, whereas in fact they did away with poetic composition, as with all the most intensive forces of that period.[5] Saint-Pol-Roux,[6] before going to bed in the early morning, puts up a notice on his door: "Poet at work."—This all in order to blaze a way into the heart of things abolished or superseded, to decipher the contours of the banal as rebus, to start a concealed William Tell from out of wooded entrails, or to be able to answer the question, "Where is the bride?" Picture puzzles, as schemata of the dreamwork, were long ago discovered by psychoanalysis. The Surrealists, with a similar conviction, are less on the trail of the psyche than on the track of things. They seek the totemic tree of objects within the thicket of primal history. The very last, the topmost face on the totem pole, is that of kitsch. It is the last mask of the banal, the one with which we adorn ourselves, in dream and conversation, so as to take in the energies of an outlived world of things.

What we used to call art begins at a distance of two meters from the body. But now, in kitsch, the world of things advances on the human being; it yields to his uncertain grasp and ultimately fashions its figures in his interior. The new man bears within himself the very quintessence of the old forms, and what evolves in the confrontation with a particular milieu from the second half of the nineteenth century—in the dreams, as well as the words and images, of certain artists—is a creature who deserves the name of "furnished man."

Written in 1925; published in *Die neue Rundschau*, January 1927. *Gesammelte Schriften*, II, 620–622. Translated by Howard Eiland.

Notes

1. The subtitle, "Gloss on Surrealism," was used as the title of the published article in 1927.
2. *Heinrich von Ofterdingen* is the title of an unfinished novel by Novalis, first published in 1802. Von Ofterdingen is a medieval poet in search of the mysterious Blue Flower, which bears the face of his unknown beloved.
3. Leporello is Don Giovanni's servant in Mozart's opera *Don Giovanni*. He carries around a catalogue of his master's conquests, which accordians out to show the many names. In the mid-nineteenth century, there was a German publishing house, Leporello Verlag, which produced such pop-out books.
4. "My loveliest mistress is idleness." "A gold medal for the greatest boredom." "In the hall, there is someone who has it in for me."
5. Reference is to the years 1922–1924. *Une vague de rêves* was first published in the fall of 1924.
6. Pseudonym of Paul Roux (1861–1940), French Symbolist poet.

The Political Groupings of Russian Writers

What distinguishes the stance of the Russian writer most strikingly from that of all his European colleagues is the absolutely public nature of his activity. This makes his opportunities incomparably greater and the external supervision incomparably stricter than in the case of Western literati. This public supervision of his activities by the press, the public, and the party is political in nature. For the books that are published, the actual official censorship—which is, as is well known, preventive—is no more than a prelude to the political debate that constitutes most of the reviews that appear. Under these conditions, it is vital for the Russian writer to show his political colors.

The process of grappling with the political slogans and problems of the day can never be intensive enough, to the point where every important decision of the party confronts the writer with the most immediate challenge, and novels and stories in many cases come to acquire a relationship to the state not unlike that which a writer's works used to have to the convictions of his aristocratic patron in former times. In a few brief years, this situation has necessarily engendered unambiguous and highly visible political groupings among writers. These group formations are authoritative; they are exclusive and unique. Nothing can shed more light on them for the Western writer than the realization that artistic schools and *cénacles* have almost entirely vanished from Russian soil.

VAPP, the All-Union Association of Proletarian Writers, is the leading organization.[1] It has 7,000 members. Its position: with the conquest of political power, the Russian proletariat has established its right to intellectual and artistic hegemony. On the other hand, since, thanks to a centuries-long process of development, the organizational and productive means for the creation of art are still decidedly in the hands of the bourgeoisie, a dictatorship is currently essential if the rights of the proletariat are to be asserted in the fields of art and literature. It was not until quite recently that this program was able to prevail in the public sphere, albeit only to a very limited extent. The severe setback in cultural policy that followed the liquidation of War Communism[2] and almost toppled the "left-wing cultural front," initially prevented the official recognition of a "proletarian literature" by the party. A year ago VAPP was able to chalk up its first public successes. Within this group, the extreme but also dominant wing consists of the Napostovtsi, who take their name from their journal, *Na postu* [On Guard].[3] Under the leadership of Averbakh, they represent current party orthodoxy. At the level of theory, this group is led by Lelevitch and Besymensky.[4] Or rather it was. Not long ago Lelevitch, who had openly declared his sympathy for the opposition (Zinoviev, Kamenev) and had committed the sin of a "left deviation," was stripped of his influence and banished from Moscow.[5] For all that, this former locksmith remains the leading art theorist of the new Russia. In his work he has sought to build on the foundations of the materialist aesthetic established by Plekhanov.[6] Of the leading creative writers of the group, the best-known are Demyan Bedny, the first great popular revolutionary lyric poet, and the novelists Libedinski and Serafimovitch.[7] These last should perhaps more properly be called "chroniclers." Their chief works, *Nedelya* [A Week] and *Zhelezny Potok* [The Iron Flood], which are also known in Germany, are accounts of their experiences during the Russian civil war. Their method of writing is Naturalist through and through.

This new Russian Naturalism is interesting in more than one respect. Its predecessors lie not merely in the social Naturalism of the 1890s, but even more curiously and remarkably in the pathetic Naturalism of the Baroque period. "Baroque" is the only fitting way to describe the heaped-up crassness of its subject matter, the unconditioned presence of political detail, the predominance of content. Problems of form did not exist for the German Baroque, any more than for contemporary Russia. Debate has raged for two years over whether the true value of a new literary work should be determined by its revolutionary form or its revolutionary content. In the absence of a specific revolutionary form, this debate was recently resolved in favor of revolutionary content.

It is a remarkable fact that all the radical "leftist" formal trends that made their appearance in the posters, written works, and processions of "heroic Communism" actually stem directly from the last Western bourgeois slogans of the prewar period—from Futurism, Constructivism, Unanimism, and so on. Even today, traces of these movements still survive in the second of the three major groups, the Left Poputchiki.[8] This group—literally, the Left

Fellow-Travelers—is not an organized association like VAPP, even though it had its roots in one. LEF—the "Left Front"—was an association of artists who set out to develop revolutionary forms. Their focal point was Vladimir Mayakovsky.[9] Mayakovsky had also been the leading spirit in the first Proletcult groups. Furthermore, it is the members of this school whose works and personalities are best-known in Germany: Babel, Seifullina, and the theater director Meyerhold.[10] One of Meyerhold's greatest successes took place over a year ago; it was his production of *Ritchi Kitai!* [China, Roar!]. The writer Tretyakov[11] should also be included in this group, which whole-heartedly supports the Soviet state but does not acknowledge the literary hegemony of the proletariat.

The standpoint of the third group could be described as qualified approval of the new regime—de facto, but not de jure. This is the Right Poputchiki,[12] a nationalist and even chauvinist group that includes in its ranks people as dissimilar as Yesenin and Ehrenburg.[13] It can be said that ever since he took his own life, Yesenin has continued to keep the literary public under his spell. Less than a month ago, Bukharin, who rarely intervenes in literary matters, wrote a long essay on Yesenin for *Pravda*. It is easy to understand why. Yesenin is the shining and influential personification of an "old" Russian type—that of the tortured and turbulent dreamer with a profound and confused attachment to the Russian soil. Such a man is incompatible with the new man who has brought about the revolution in Russia. The attack on the huge shadow cast by Yesenin has a distant echo in the highly topical efforts to combat hooliganism. What is at stake in both cases is the annihilation of an asocial type in which Russia can descry the specter of its own past, a specter that blocks the path to the new industrialized Eden. The great majority of the 6,000 Russian peasant writers belong to this right-wing trend. Their theoretical leaders are Voronsky and Efros.[14] Voronsky has adopted Trotsky's theory, which for a long time was official party policy. According to this, the proletariat has not yet in any sense transformed society to the point where it can be meaningful to talk in terms of "proletarian" literature. That spells the end of the proletarian claim to cultural hegemony. As noted, this has ceased to be the party's position. Last, we should also mention the writers of the "New Bourgeoisie" who have grown out of the NEP.[15] To mention a few names, they include the novelist Pilnyak and the well-known dramatists Alexander Tolstoy and Mikhail Bulgakov.[16] Two plays by Bulgakov are running in Moscow at the moment: *Zoykina Quartira* [Zoyka's Apartment], a play set in a brothel, and *Dni Turbini* [Days of the Turbine], a civil war drama. This play has been a fixture in Stanislavsky's program for months, and has received publicity that can stem only from a scandal. Its tendency is purely counterrevolutionary. The public, the old bourgeoisie—the "has-beens," as one puts it so nicely in Russia today—express their gratitude by filling the theater night after night. The play was banned several times by the censor, and numerous changes had to be made to the text. Even so, the first performance caused an uproar in the theater. But the radical elements in the audience were unable to prevail, with the result that Moscow now has a reactionary historical play that would be hard put to survive even on the Berlin stage, given its inferiority in terms of theatrical competence and message.

Yet all this counts for little. The particular instance matters less in Soviet literature than in any other. There are times when things and thoughts should be weighed and not counted. But also—though this often escapes notice—there are times when things are counted and not weighed. In our time, Russia's literature is—rightly—more important for statisticians than for aesthetes. Thousands of new authors and hundreds of thousands of new readers want above all to be counted and mobilized into the cadres of the new intellectual sharpshooters, who will be drilled for political command and whose munitions consist of the alphabet. In today's Russia, reading is more important than writing, reading newspapers is more important than reading books, and laboriously spelling out the words is more important than reading newspapers. If Russian literature is what it ought to be, its best products can only be the colored illustrations in the primer from which peasants learn to read in the shadow of Lenin.

Published in *Die literarische Welt*, March 1927. *Gesammelte Schriften*, II, 743–747. Translated by Rodney Livingstone.

Notes

1. Soviet literary organization founded in October 1920. By 1928 it was the leading association for writers in the USSR.
2. "War Communism" is the term used to describe the first period of state-dominated economic and social policy, between 1918 and 1921. It was superseded by the New Economic Policy.
3. This journal became the organ of VAPP and, after 1928, of RAPP, the Russian Association of Proletarian Writers.
4. Leopold Averbakh (1903–1939), was the leader of RAPP, which assumed a dominant position on the literary scene in the Soviet Union after 1929, when it attained official approval for its program of establishing the Soviet First Five-Year Plan as the sole theme of Soviet literature. Grigory Lelevitch (pseudonym of Labori Gilelevich Kalmanson), a poet and critic, was one of the editors of the magazine *Na postu*. Expelled from the party, he died in a camp in 1928. Aleksandr Ilyich Besymensky (1898–1973), poet and official in VAPP, produced tendentious poetry consistent with current party doctrine.
5. Grigory Evseyevich Zinoviev (originally Ovsel Gershon Aronov Radomyslsky; 1883–1936) and Lev Borisovich Kamenev (originally Lev Borisovich Rosenfeld;

1883–1936) were Russian Communist revolutionaries and members of the original post-Lenin triumvirate (along with Joseph Stalin). Both were executed at the beginning of the Great Purge.

6. Georgy Valentinovich Plekhanov (1857–1918), Russian political philosopher and Menshevik revolutionary, founded the first Communist organization in Russia. He is generally considered the father of Russian Marxism.

7. Demyan Bedny (pseudonym of Efim Alekseyevich Pridvorov; 1883–1945) wrote verse in an accessible and popular mode; his work was known for its inflammatory tone. Yury Nikolayevich Libedinski (1898–1959) was a novelist; his *Nedelya* (A Week) attempted to fuse Andrei Bely's symbolism and a reportorial style that portrayed the lives of Communists in connection with their party work. Aleksandr Serafimovich Serafimovich (pseudonym of A. S. Popov; 1863–1949) was a novelist and the editor of the journal *Oktyabr*. His novel *Zhelezny Potok* (The Iron Flood) of 1924 depicts the retreat of the Bolshevik army.

8. The Left Poputchiki (Levy front iskusstva, or Left Front of Art), known as LEF, was a Marxist literary group that arose in Moscow at the end of 1922; it included much of the Russian avant-garde. LEF's rational aesthetic aspired to a union between art and production. It was attacked by the proletarian groups Oktyabr and VAPP.

9. Vladimir Vladimirovich Mayakovsky (1893–1930) was Russia's leading poet; he was considered the poet of the October Revolution and the model for Socialist Realist poetry. Mayakovsky gradually became disillusioned with the course of the postrevolutionary Soviet Union, and committed suicide in 1930.

10. Isaac Emmanuilovich Babel (1894–1941?), Jewish prose writer and dramatist known for the 1926 short-story collection *Konarmiya* (Red Cavalry) and the 1931 *Odesskiye rasskazy* (Tales of Odessa). Purged in 1939, his death was announced on March 17, 1941. Lydia N. Seifullina (1889–1954) was a prolific writer; most of her work is prose. Vsevolod Emilevich Meyerhold (1874–1942), preeminent Russian actor and director, opposed the Naturalism of the Moscow Art Theater and was the first theater director to offer his services to the new government after the Revolution. In 1923 he was given his own theater, the Teatr imeni Meyerhold (TIM).

11. Sergei Mikhailovich Tretyakov (1892–1939?) was a Futurist playwright, novelist, and poet. A member of LEF, he fought for revolutionary experimentation in art.

12. "Right Poputchiki" originally referred to writers in the Soviet Union who had neither supported nor opposed the revolution. Trotsky's use of the term in *Literature and Revolution* (1925) recognized artists' need for intellectual freedom and their dependence on links with the cultural traditions of the past. Fellow travelers such as Osip Mandelstam, Leonid Leonov, Boris Pilnyak, Isaac Babel, and Ilya Ehrenburg were officially recognized in the early 1920s. They met bitter opposition, however, from champions of a new proletarian art, and by the end of the decade the term came to be practically synonymous with "counterrevolutionary."

13. Sergei Aleksandrovich Yesenin (1895–1925), poet and member of a literary group known as the Imagists, was an early supporter of the Revolution, to which he attributed utopian and messianic potential. Ilya Grigoryevich Ehren-

burg (1891–1967) was a prose writer, journalist, and diplomat. Arrested for his revolutionary activities, he emigrated to Paris in 1908. He is best-known for his journalism, propaganda, and autobiographical works, especially his *Lyudi, gody, zhizn* (translated as *People and Life: Memoirs, 1891–1917*). Nikolai Ivanovich Bukharin (1888–1938) was a leading Communist theoretician. After the Revolution, he was appointed editor of the official party organ *Pravda* and leader of the Communist International (Comintern). He was stripped of his party posts in 1929 and fell victim to Stalin's purges.

14. Aleksandr Konstantinovich Voronsky (1884–1943) was a critic, revolutionary, and prose writer who established himself as a leading figure in Soviet cultural politics by rejecting the idea of the Proletcult. As part of the transition to Socialist Realism, Voronsky was arrested and expelled from the party in 1927. He died while in prison. Abram Markovich Efros (1888–1954) was a literary critic, art historian, poet, and translator.

15. The New Economic Policy (NEP) was the economic policy of the Soviet Union from 1921 to 1928 which revised the original emphasis on centralization and planning. The NEP included the return of most agriculture, retail trade, and light industry to private ownership, while the state retained control of heavy industry, transport, banking, and foreign trade.

16. Boris Andreyevich Pilnyak (pseudonym of B. A. Vogau; 1894–1938/41?), a prose writer who depicted the Revolution as a struggle between elemental and rational forces, was one of the first victims of the government purges in 1937. Mikhail Afanasyevich Bulgakov (1891–1940) was a playwright, prose writer, and satirist best-known for his posthumously published works, including *Master i Margarita* (The Master and Margarita).

On the Present Situation of Russian Film

The greatest achievements of the Russian film industry can be seen more readily in Berlin than in Moscow. What one sees in Berlin has been pre-selected, while in Moscow this selection still has to be made. Nor is obtaining advice a simple matter. The Russians are fairly uncritical about their own films. (For example, it is a well-known fact that *Potemkin* owes its great success to Germany.) The reason for this insecurity in the matter of judgment is that the Russians lack European standards of comparison. Good foreign films are seldom seen in Russia. When buying films, the government takes the view that the Russian market is so important for the competing film companies of the world that they really have to supply it at reduced prices with what are in effect advertising samples. Obviously, this means that good, expensive films are never imported. For individual Russian artists, the resulting ignorance on the part of the public has its agreeable side. Iljinsky[1] works with a very imprecise copy of Chaplin and is regarded as a comedian only because Chaplin is unknown here.

At a more serious, general level, internal Russian conditions have a depressing effect on the average film. It is not easy to obtain suitable scenarios, because the choice of subject matter is governed by strict controls. Of all the arts in Russia, literature enjoys the greatest freedom from censorship. The theater is scrutinized much more closely, and control of the film industry is even stricter. This scale is proportional to the size of the audiences. Under this regimen the best films deal with episodes from the Russian Revolution; films that stretch further back into the Russian past constitute the insignificant average, while, by European standards, comedies are utterly irrelevant. At the heart of the difficulties currently facing Russian producers is the fact that the public is less and less willing to follow them into their true domain: political dramas of the Russian civil war. The naturalistic political period of Russian film reached its climax around a year and a half ago, with a flood of films full of death and terror. Such themes have lost all their attraction in the meantime. Now the motto is internal pacification. Film, radio, and theater are all distancing themselves from propaganda.

The search for conciliatory subject matter has led producers to resort to a curious technique. Since film versions of the great Russian novels are largely ruled out on political and artistic grounds, directors have taken over well-known individual types and built up new stories around them. Characters from Pushkin, Gogol, Goncharov, and Tolstoy are frequently taken over in this way, often retaining their original names.[2] This new Russian film is set by preference in the far eastern sections of Russia. This is as much as to say, "For us there is no 'exoticism.'" "Exoticism" is thought of as a component of the counterrevolutionary ideology of a colonial nation. Russia has no use for the Romantic concept of the "Far East." Russia is close to the East and economically tied to it. Its second message is: we are not dependent on foreign countries and natures—Russia is, after all, a sixth of the world! Everything in the world is here on our own soil.

And in this spirit the epic film of the new Russia, entitled *The Soviet Sixth of the Earth,* has just been released. It must be admitted that Vertov,[3] the director, has not succeeded in meeting his self-imposed challenge of showing through characteristic images how the vast Russian nation is being transformed by the new social order. The filmic colonization of Russia has misfired. What he has achieved, however, is the demarcation of Russia from Europe. This is how the film starts: in fractions of a second, there is a flow of images from workplaces (pistons in motion, laborers bringing in the harvest, transport works) and from capitalist places of entertainment (bars, dance halls, and clubs). Social films of recent years have been plundered for fleeting individual excerpts (often just details of a caressing hand or dancing feet, a woman's hairdo or a glimpse of her bejeweled throat), and these have been assembled so as to alternate with images of toiling workers. Unfortunately, the film soon abandons this approach in favor of a description of Russian peoples and landscapes, while the link between these and their modes of production is merely hinted at in an all too shadowy fashion. The uncertain and tentative nature of these efforts is illustrated by the simple fact that pictures of cranes hoisting equipment and transmission systems are accompanied by an orchestra playing motifs from *Tannhäuser* and *Lohengrin.* Even so, these pictures are typical in their attempts to make film straight from life, without any decorative or acting apparatus. They are produced with a "masked" apparatus. That is to say, amateurs adopt various poses in front of a dummy set, but immediately afterward, when they think that everything is finished, they are filmed without being aware of it. The good, new motto "Away with all masks!" is nowhere more valid than in Russian film. It follows from this that nowhere are film stars more superfluous. Directors are not on the lookout for an actor who can play many roles, but opt instead for the characters needed in each particular instance. Indeed, they go even further. Eisenstein,[4] the director of *Potemkin*, is making a film about peasant life in which he intends to dispense with actors altogether.

The peasants are not simply one of the most interesting subjects for a film; they are also the most important audience for the Russian cultural film. Film is being used to provide them with historical, political, technical, and even hygienic information. Up to now, however, the problems encountered in this process have left people feeling fairly perplexed. The mode of mental reception of the peasant is basically different from that of the urban masses. It has become clear, for example, that the rural audience is incapable of following *two simultaneous narrative strands* of the kind seen countless times in film. They can follow only a single series of images that must unfold chronologically, like the verses of a street ballad. Having often noted that serious scenes provoke uproarious laughter and that funny scenes are greeted with straight faces or even genuine emotion, filmmakers have started to produce films directly for those traveling cinemas that occasionally penetrate even the remotest regions of Russia for the benefit of people who have seen neither towns nor modern means of transport. To expose such audiences to film and radio constitutes one of the most grandiose mass-psychological experiments ever undertaken in the gigantic laboratory that Russia has become. Needless to say, in such rural cinemas the main role is played by educational films of every kind. Such films range from lessons in how to deal with plagues of locusts or use tractors, to films concerned with cures for alcoholism. Even so, much of the program of these itinerant cinemas remains incomprehensible to the great majority and can be used only as training material for those who are more advanced—that is to say, members of village soviets, peasant representatives, and so on. At the moment, the establishment of an "Institute for Audience Research" in which audience reactions could be studied both experimentally and theoretically is being considered.

In this way, film has taken up one of the great slogans of recent times: "With our faces toward the village!" In film as in writing, politics provides the most powerful motivation: the Central Committee of the party hands down directives every month to the press, the press passes them on to the clubs, and the clubs pass them on to the theaters and cinemas, like runners passing a baton. By the same token, however, such slogans can also lead to serious obstacles. The slogan "Industrialization!" provided a paradoxical instance. Given the passionate interest in everything technical, it might have been expected that the slapstick comedy would be highly popular. In reality, however, for the moment at least, that passion divides the technical very sharply from the comic, and the eccentric comedies imported from America have definitely *flopped*. The new Russian is unable to appreciate irony and skepticism in technical matters. A further sphere denied to the Russian film is the one that encompasses all the themes and problems drawn from bourgeois life. Above all, this means: *They won't stand for dramas about love. The dramatic and even tragic treatment of love is rigorously excluded from the whole of Russian life.* Suicides that result from disappointed or unhappy love still occasionally occur, but Communist public opinion regards them as the crudest excesses.

For film—as for literature—all the problems that now form the focus of debate are problems of subject matter. Thanks to the new era of social truce, they have entered a difficult stage. The Russian film can reestablish itself on firm ground only when Bolshevist society (and not just the state!) has become sufficiently stable to enable a new "social comedy" to thrive, with new characters and typical situations.

Published in *Die literarische Welt*, March 1927. *Gesammelte Schriften*, II, 747–751. Translated by Rodney Livingstone.

Notes

1. Igor Vladimirovich Iljinsky (1901–1987) was a Russian film and dramatic actor, well known for his comic portrayals of buffoons, vagabonds, rogues, and urban hustlers.
2. Ivan Alexandrovich Goncharov (1812–1891) was a Russian novelist whose works include *Oblomov* (1859) and *The Precipice* (1869).
3. Dziga Vertov (pseudonym of Denis Arkadyevich Kaufman; 1896–1954) was a Soviet director whose best-known film is *Man with the Movie Camera*. His *kino-glaz* ("film-eye") theory—that the camera is an instrument much like the human eye and is best used to explore the actual happenings of real life—had an international impact on the development of documentaries and cinema realism during the 1920s.
4. Sergei Mikhailovich Eisenstein (1898–1948) was a Russian (Latvian-born) film director whose works include *October, Strike, Alexander Nevsky,* and *Battleship Potemkin*.

Reply to Oscar A. H. Schmitz

There are replies that come close to being an act of impoliteness toward the public. Shouldn't we simply allow our readers to make up their own minds about a lame argument full of clumsy concepts? In this instance, they would not even need to have seen *Battleship Potemkin*. Any more than Schmitz did.[1] For whatever he knows about the film he could have gleaned from the first newspaper notice that came to hand. But that is what characterizes the cultural Philistine: others read the notice and think themselves duly warned; he, however, has to "form his own opinion." He goes to see the film and imagines that he is in a position to translate his embarrassment into objective knowledge. This is a delusion. *Battleship Potemkin* can be objectively discussed either as film or from a political point of view. Schmitz does neither. He talks about his recent reading. Unsurprisingly, this leads him nowhere. To take this rigorous depiction of a class movement that has been wholly shaped according to the principles of the film medium and try to see how it measures up to bourgeois novels of society betrays an ingenuousness that is quite disarming. The same cannot quite be said of his onslaught on tendentious art. Here, where he marshals some heavy artillery from the arsenal of bourgeois aesthetics, plain speaking would be more appropriate. We may well ask why he makes such a fuss about the political deflowering of art, while faithfully tracking down all the sublimations, libidinous vestiges, and complexes through two thousand years of artistic production. How long is art supposed to act the well brought-up young lady who knows her way around all the places of ill-repute yet wouldn't dream of asking about politics? But it's no use: she has always dreamed about it. It is a truism that political tendencies are implicit in every work of art, every artistic epoch—since, after all, they are historical configurations of consciousness. But just as deeper rock strata emerge only where the rock is fissured, the deep formation of "political tendency" likewise reveals itself only in the fissures of art history (and works of art). The technical revolutions are the fracture points of artistic development; it is there that the different political tendencies may be said to come to the surface. In every new technical revolution the political tendency is transformed, as if by its own volition, from a concealed element of art into a manifest one. And this brings us at long last to the film.

Among the points of fracture in artistic formations, film is one of the most dramatic. We may truly say that with film a *new realm of consciousness* comes into being. To put it in a nutshell, film is the prism in which the spaces of the immediate environment—the spaces in which people live, pursue their avocations, and enjoy their leisure—are laid open before their eyes in a comprehensible, meaningful, and passionate way. In themselves these offices, furnished rooms, saloons, big-city streets, stations, and factories are ugly, incomprehensible, and hopelessly sad. Or rather, they were and seemed to be, until the advent of film. The cinema then exploded this entire prison-world with the dynamite of its fractions of a second, so that now we can take extended journeys of adventure between their widely scattered ruins. The vicinity of a house, of a room, can include dozens of the most unexpected stations, and the most astonishing station names. It is not so much the constant stream of images as the sudden change of place that overcomes a milieu which has resisted every other attempt to unlock its secret, and succeeds in extracting from a petty-bourgeois dwelling the same beauty we admire in an Alfa Romeo. And so far, so good. Difficulties emerge only with the "plot." The question of a meaningful film plot is as rarely solved as the abstract formal problems that have arisen from the new technology. And this proves *one* thing beyond all others: the vital, fundamental advances in art are a matter neither of new content nor of new forms—the technological revolution takes precedence over both. But it is no accident that in film this revolution has not been able to discover either a form or a content appropriate to it. For it turns out that with the untendentious play of forms and the untendentious play of the plot, the problem can be resolved only on a case-by-case basis.

The superiority of the cinema of the Russian Revolution, like that of the American slapstick comedy, is grounded on the fact that in their different ways they are both based on tendencies to which they constantly recur. For the slapstick comedy is tendentious too, in a less obvious way. Its target is technology. This kind of film is comic, but only in the sense that the laughter it provokes hovers over an abyss of horror. The obverse of a ludicrously liberated technology is the lethal power of naval squadrons on maneuver, as we see it openly displayed in *Potemkin*. The international bourgeois film, on the other hand, has not been able to discover a consistent ideological formula. This is one of the causes of its recurrent crises. For the complicity of film technique with the milieu that essentially constitutes a standing rebuke to it is incompatible with the glorification of the bourgeoisie. The proletariat is the hero of those spaces that give rise to the adventures to which the bourgeois abandons himself in the movies with beating heart, because he feels constrained to enjoy "beauty" even where it speaks of the annihilation of his own class. The proletariat, however, is a collective, just as these spaces are collective spaces. And only here, in the human collective, can the film complete the prismatic work that it began by acting on that milieu. The epoch-making impact of *Potemkin* can be explained by the fact that it made this clear for the first time. Here, for the first time, a mass movement acquires the wholly architectonic and by no means monumental (i.e., UFA) quality that justifies its inclusion in film.[2] No other medium could reproduce this collective in motion. No other could convey such beauty or the currents of horror and panic it contains. Ever since *Potemkin,* such scenes have become the undying possession of Russian film art. What began with the bombardment of Odessa in *Potemkin* continues in the more recent film *Mother* with the pogrom against factory workers, in which the suffering of the urban masses is engraved in the asphalt of the street like running script.[3]

Potemkin was made systematically in a collective spirit. The leader of the mutiny, Lieutenant Commander Schmidt, one of the legendary figures of revolutionary Russia, does not appear in the film. That may be seen as a "falsification of history," although it has nothing to do with the estimation of his achievements. Furthermore, why the actions of a collective should be deemed unfree, while those of the individual are free—this abstruse variant of determinism remains as incomprehensible in itself as in its meaning for the debate.

It is evident that the character of the opponents must be made to match that of the rebellious masses. It would have been senseless to depict them as differentiated individuals. The ship's doctor, the captain, and so on had to be types. Bourgeois types—this is a concept Schmitz will have nothing to do with. So let us call them sadistic types who have been summoned to the apex of power by an evil, dangerous apparatus. Of course, this brings us face to face with a political formulation. An outcome which is unavoidable because it is true. There is nothing feebler than all the talk of "individual cases." The individual may be an individual case—but the uninhibited effects of his diabolical behavior are something else; they lie in the nature of the imperialist state and—within limits—the state as such. It is well known that many facts gain their meaning, their relief, only when they are put in context. These are the facts with which the field of statistics concerns itself. If a Mr. X happens to take his own life in March, this may be a supremely unimportant fact in itself. But it becomes quite interesting if we learn that suicides reach their annual peak during that month. In the same way, the sadistic acts of the ship's doctor may be isolated incidents in his life, the result of a poor night's sleep, or a reaction to his discovery that his breakfast egg is rotten. They become interesting only if we establish a relationship between the medical profession and the state. During the last years of the Great War, there was more than one highly competent study of this topic, and we can only feel sorry for the wretched little sadist of *Potemkin* when we compare his actions and his just punishment with the murderous services performed—unpunished—a few years ago by thousands of his colleagues on the sick and crippled at the behest of the general staff.

Potemkin is a great film, a rare achievement. To protest against it calls for the courage born of desperation. There is plenty of bad tendentious art, including bad socialist tendentious art. Such works are determined by their effects; they work with tired reflexes and depend on stereotyping. This film, however, has solid concrete foundations ideologically; the details have been worked out precisely, like the span of a bridge. The more violent the blows that rain down upon it, the more beautifully it resounds. Only if you touch it with kid gloves do you hear and move nothing.

Published (along with Oscar A. H. Schmitz's "Potemkin and Tendentious Art") in *Die literarische Welt*, March 1927. *Gesammelte Schriften*, II, 751–755. Translated by Rodney Livingstone.

Notes

1. Oscar Adolf Hermann Schmitz (1873–1931), a playwright and essayist, maintained close contact with the circle around Stefan George. Benjamin's reply to Schmitz exemplifies the tenor of the arguments over *Battleship Potemkin.*
2. UFA (Universum-Film AG), the largest firm in the German film industry, was founded in 1917. Vertically integrated, UFA owned everything from machine shops and film laboratories to production and distribution facilities. It was acquired by the Hugenberg Group in 1927, nationalized by the German Reich in 1936–1937, and dismantled by the Allies in 1945.
3. The film *Mother* was made in 1925 by the Russian director and film theorist Vsevolod Pudovkin (1893–1953).

Introductory Remarks on a Series for *L'Humanité*

I belong to the generation that is now between thirty and forty years old.[1] The intelligentsia of this generation will presumably be the last for a long time to have enjoyed a completely unpolitical education. The war caught its most left-leaning elements in the camp of a more or less radical pacifism. The history of Germany in the postwar period is in part the history of the revolutionary education of this original left-bourgeois wing of the intelligentsia. It may confidently be asserted that the revolution of 1918, which was defeated by the petty-bourgeois, parvenu spirit of German Social Democracy, did more to radicalize this generation than did the war itself. In Germany, it is increasingly the case—and this is the feature of particular importance in this entire process—that the status of the independent writer is being called into question, and one gradually realizes that the writer (like the intellectual in the wider sense), willy-nilly, consciously or unconsciously, works in the service of a class and receives his mandate from a class. The fact that the economic basis of the intellectual's existence is becoming ever more constricted has hastened this realization in recent times. The political counterpressure of the ruling class in Germany, which has led, especially in this past year, to ruthless censorship and literary trials [reminiscent of the age of the Holy Alliance],[2] has had a comparable effect. Given these circumstances, the sympathy of the German intelligentsia for Russia is more than abstract fellow-feeling; they are guided by their own material interests. They want to know: How does the intelligentsia fare in a country where their patron is the proletariat? How does the proletariat shape their conditions of life, and what sort of environment confronts them? What can they expect from a proletarian government? Guided by the sense of crisis that looms over the fate of the intelligentsia in bourgeois society, writers like Ernst Toller, Arthur Holitscher, and Leo Matthias, painters like Vogeler-Worpswede, and theater directors like Bernhard Reich have all studied Russia and established contacts with their Russian colleagues.[3] In the same spirit, I myself visited Moscow early this year and lived there for two months. For the first time in my life I found myself in a city where I enjoyed privileges of a material and administrative nature simply because I am a writer. (I know of no city apart from Moscow where a writer can obtain a reduced price for a hotel room at the behest of the state—for the hotels are all run by the Soviets.) The following pieces are excerpted from a diary I kept there regularly over a period of eight weeks. In them I have attempted to convey the image of proletarian Moscow that you can understand only when you have also seen it in snow and ice. Above all, I have tried to reproduce the physiognomy of its workday and the new rhythm that permeates the life of worker and intellectual alike.

Paris; May 1, 1927

Written in 1927; unpublished in Benjamin's lifetime. *Gesammelte Schriften*, VI, 781–782. Translated by Rodney Livingstone, on the basis of a prior version by Richard Sieburth.

Notes

1. Benjamin composed this short text as an introduction to a series that was to appear in *L'Humanité: Journal Socialiste*. (Published between 1904 and 1940, this periodical appeared clandestinely under the Occupation as the central organ of the French Communist party.) It is unclear whether the series was to consist of reworked excerpts from the essay "Moscow" (see next page) or from the *Moskauer Tagebuch*. See *Moscow Diary*, trans. Richard Sieburth, ed. Gary Smith (Cambridge, Mass.: Harvard University Press, 1986).
2. Bracketed material is crossed out in the manuscript.
3. Ernst Toller (1893–1939), a pacifist, left-liberal Jewish writer active in the Bavarian Council Republic of 1919, was imprisoned for his political agitation. He went into exile in 1933 and committed suicide in 1939. His 1919 play *Masse Mensch* is his best-known work; his plays were frequently performed on Soviet stages in the 1920s. Arthur Holitscher (1869–1941) was a dramatist and essayist whose works were on the first list of books banned by the Nazis. Leo Matthias (1893–1970), dramatist, travel essayist, and sociologist, emigrated to Mexico in 1933, moved to the United States in 1939, and returned to Germany in 1950. Heinrich Vogeler (1872–1942), painter, printmaker, and architect, was the cofounder of the important artists' colony at Worpswede. His utopian leftism led him to spend his last years in the Soviet Union. Bernhard Reich was a prominent German theater critic working in Moscow. He was also Benjamin's rival for the attentions of Asja Lacis.

Moscow

1

More quickly than Moscow itself, one learns to see Berlin through Moscow. To someone returning home from Russia, the city seems freshly washed. There is no dirt, but no snow either. The streets seem in reality as desolately clean and swept as in the drawings of George Grosz. And how true-to-life his types are has become more obvious. What is true of the image of the city and its people applies also to the intellectual situation: a new optics is the most undoubted gain from a stay in Russia. However little you may know Russia, what you learn is to observe and judge Europe with the conscious knowledge of what is going on in Russia. This is the first benefit to the intelligent European in Russia. But, equally, this is why the stay is so exact a touchstone for foreigners. It obliges everyone to choose his standpoint. Admittedly, the only real guarantee of a correct understanding is to have chosen your position before you came. In Russia above all, you can see only if you have already decided. At the turning point in historical events that is indicated, if not constituted, by the fact of "Soviet Russia," the question at issue is not which reality is better or which has greater potential. It is only: Which reality is inwardly convergent with truth? Which truth is inwardly preparing itself to converge with the real? Only he who clearly answers these questions is "objective." Not toward his contemporaries (which is unimportant) but toward events (which is decisive). Only he who, by decision, has made his dialectical peace with the world can grasp the concrete. But someone who wishes to decide "on the basis of facts" will find no basis in the facts.—Returning home, he will discover above all that

Berlin is a deserted city. People and groups moving in its streets have solitude about them. Berlin's luxury seems unspeakable. And it begins on the asphalt, for the breadth of the pavements is princely. They make the poorest wretch a *grand seigneur* promenading on the terrace of his mansion. Princely solitude, princely desolation hang over the streets of Berlin. Not only in the West End. In Moscow there are three or four places where it is possible to make headway without that strategy of shoving and weaving that you learn in the first week (thus, at the same time as you learn the technique of achieving locomotion on sheet ice). Stepping onto the Stolechnikov, you breathe again: here at last, you may stop without compunction in front of shopwindows and go on your way without partaking in the loitering, serpentine gait to which the narrow pavements have accustomed most people. But what fullness this street has, which overflows with more than just people, and how deserted and empty Berlin is! In Moscow, goods burst everywhere from the houses; they hang on fences, lean against railings, lie on pavements. Every fifty steps stand women with cigarettes, women with fruit, women with sweets. They have their wares in a laundry basket next to them, sometimes a little sleigh as well. A brightly colored woolen cloth protects apples or oranges from the cold, with two prize examples lying on top. Next to them are sugar figures, nuts, candy. One thinks: before leaving her house a grandmother must have looked around to see what she could take to surprise her grandchildren. Now she has stopped on the way to have a brief rest in the street. Berlin streets know no such places with sleighs, sacks, little carts, and baskets. Compared to those of Moscow, they are like a freshly swept, empty racecourse on which a field of six-day cyclists hastens comfortlessly on.

2

The city seems already to deliver itself at the train station. Kiosks, arc lamps, buildings crystallize into figures that will never return. Yet this impression is dispelled as soon as I seek words. I must be on my way. . . . At first there is nothing to be seen but snow, the dirty snow that has already installed itself, and the clean slowly moving up behind. The instant you arrive, the childhood stage begins. On the thick sheet ice of the streets, walking has to be relearned. The jungle of houses is so impenetrable that only brilliance strikes the eye. A transparency with the inscription *Kefir* glows in the evening. I notice it as if the Tverskaia, the old road to Tver on which I now am, were really still the open road, with nothing to be seen far and wide except the plain. Before I discovered Moscow's real landscape, its real river, found its real heights, each thoroughfare became for me a contested river, each house number a trigonometric signal, and each of its gigantic squares a lake. For every step you take here is on named ground.

And where one of these names is heard, in a flash imagination builds a whole neighborhood about the sound. This will long defy the later reality and remain brittlely embedded in it like glass masonry. In the first phase, the city still has barriers at a hundred frontiers. Yet one day the gate and the church that were the boundary of a district become without warning its center. Now the city turns into a labyrinth for the newcomer. Streets that he had located far apart are yoked together by a corner, like a pair of horses reined in a coachman's fist. The whole exciting sequence of topographical deceptions to which he falls prey could be shown only by a film: the city is on its guard against him, masks itself, flees, intrigues, lures him to wander its circles to the point of exhaustion. (This could be approached in a very practical way: during the tourist season in great cities, "orientation films" would run for foreigners.) But in the end, maps and plans are victorious: in bed at night, imagination juggles with real buildings, parks, and streets.

3

Moscow in winter is a quiet city. The immense bustle on the streets takes place softly. This is because of the snow, but also because the traffic is behind the times. Car horns dominate the orchestra of great cities. But in Moscow there are only a few cars. They are used only for weddings and funerals and for accelerated governing. True, in the evening they switch on brighter lights than are permitted in any other great city. And the cones of light they project are so dazzling that anyone caught in them stands helplessly rooted to the spot. In the blinding light before the Kremlin gate, the guards stand in their brazen ocher furs. Above them shines the red signal that regulates the traffic passing through the gate. All the colors of Moscow converge prismatically here, at the center of Russian power. Beams of excessive brilliance from the car headlights race through the darkness. The horses of the cavalry, which has a large drill ground in the Kremlin, shy in their light. Pedestrians force their way between cars and unruly horses. Long rows of sleighs haul snow away. Single horsemen. Silent swarms of ravens have settled in the snow. The eye is infinitely busier than the ear. The colors do their utmost against the white. The smallest colored rag glows out of doors. Picture books lie in the snow; Chinese vendors sell artfully made paper fans and, still more frequently, paper kites in the form of exotic deep-sea fish. Day in, day out, children's festivals are provided for. There are men with baskets full of wooden toys, carts, and spades; the carts are yellow and red, yellow or red the children's shovels. All these carved wooden utensils are more simply and solidly made than in Germany, their peasant origin clearly visible. One morning, at the side of the road stand tiny houses that have never been seen before, each with shining windows and a fence around the front garden: wooden toys from Vladimir province. That is to say, a new consignment of goods has arrived. Serious, sober utensils become audacious in street trading. A basket seller with all kinds of brightly colored wares, such as can be bought everywhere in Capri, two-handled baskets with plain square patterns, carries at the end of his pole glazed-paper cages with glazed-paper birds inside them. But a real parrot, too—a white ara—can sometimes be seen. In the Miasnitskaia stands a woman with linen goods, the bird perching on her tray or shoulder. A picturesque background for such animals must be sought elsewhere, at the photographer's stand. Under the bare trees of the boulevards are screens showing palms, marble staircases, and southern seas. And something else, too, reminds one of southern climes. It is the wild variety of the street trade. Shoe polish and writing materials, handkerchiefs, dolls' sleighs, swings for children, ladies' underwear, stuffed birds, clothes hangers—all this sprawls on the open street, as if it were not twenty-five degrees below zero but high Neapolitan summer. For a long time I was mystified by a man who had in front of him a densely lettered board. I wanted to see him as a soothsayer. At last I succeeded in watching him at work: I saw him sell two of his letters and fix them as initials to his customer's galoshes. Then there are the wide sleighs with three compartments for peanuts, hazelnuts, and *semitchky* (sunflower seeds, which now, according to a ruling of the Soviet, may no longer be chewed in public places). Cookshop owners gather in the vicinity of the labor exchange. They have hotcakes to sell, and sausage fried in slices. But all this goes on silently; calls like those of every trader in southern regions are unknown. Rather, the people address the passer-by with words, measured if not whispered words, in which there is something of the humility of beggars. Only one caste parades noisily through the streets here: the ragpickers, with sacks on their backs. Their melancholy cry rings out one or more times a week in every neighborhood. Street trading is in part illegal and therefore avoids attracting attention. Women, each with a piece of meat, a chicken, or a leg of pork resting on a layer of straw in her open hand, stand offering it to passers-by. These are vendors without permits. They are too poor to pay the duty for a stall and have no time to stand in line many hours at an office for a weekly concession. When a member of the militia approaches, they simply run away. The street trade culminates in the large markets, on the Smolenskaia and the Arbat. And on the Sucharevskaia. This, the most famous of all, is situated at the foot of a church that rises with blue domes above the booths. First, one passes the neighborhood of the scrap-iron dealers. The people simply have their wares lying in the snow. One finds old locks, meter rulers, hand tools, kitchen utensils, electrical goods. Repairs are carried out on the spot; I saw someone soldering over a pointed flame. There are no seats anywhere; everyone stands up, gossiping or trading. At this market the architectonic function of wares is perceptible: cloth and fabric form buttresses and columns; *valenki* (felt boots), hanging threaded on strings across the counters, become the roof of the booth; large *garmoshkas* (accordions) form sounding walls—thus, in a sense, Memnon's walls.[1] Whether, at the few stalls with pictures of saints, one can still secretly buy those strange icons that it was already punishable under czarism to sell, I do not know. There is the Mother of God with three hands. She is half-naked. From her navel rises a strong, well-formed hand. At right and left the two others spread in the gesture of blessing. This threesome of hands is deemed a symbol of the Holy Trinity. Another devotional picture of the Mother of God shows her with open belly; clouds come from it instead of entrails; in their midst dances the Christ child holding a violin in his hand. Since the sale of icons is considered a branch of the paper-and-picture trade, these booths with pictures of saints stand next to those with paper goods, so that they are always flanked by portraits of Lenin, like a prisoner between two policemen. The street life does not cease entirely even at night. In dark gateways you stumble against furs built like houses. Night watchmen huddle inside on chairs, from time to time bestirring themselves ponderously.

4

In the street scene of any proletarian neighborhood, the children are important. They are more numerous there than in other districts, and move more purposefully and busily. Moscow swarms with children everywhere. Even among them there is a Communist hierarchy. The "Komsomoltsy," as the eldest, are at the top. They have their clubs in every town and are really trained as the next generation of the party. The younger children become—at six—"Pioneers." They, too, are united in clubs, and wear a red tie as a proud distinction. Last, "Octobrists" *(Oktyabr)*—or "Wolves"—is the name given to little babies from the moment they are able to point to the picture of Lenin. But even now one also comes across the derelict, unspeakably melancholy *besprizornye*, war orphans. By day they are usually seen alone, each one on his own warpath. But in the evening they join up before the lurid façades of movie houses to form gangs, and foreigners are warned against meeting such bands alone when walking home. The only way for the educator to understand these thoroughly savage, mistrustful, embittered people was to go out on the street himself. In each of Moscow's districts, children's centers have already been in existence for years. They are supervised by a female state employee who seldom has more than one assistant. Her task is, in one way or another, to make contact with the children of her district. Food is distributed, games are played. To begin with, twenty or thirty children come to the center, but if a superintendent does her work properly, it may be filled with hundreds of children after a couple of weeks. Needless to say, traditional pedagogical methods never made much impression on these infantile masses. To get through to them at all, to be heard, one has to relate as directly and clearly as possible to the catchwords of the street itself, of the whole collective life. Politics, in the organization of crowds of such children, is not tendentious, but as natural a subject, as obvious a visual aid, as the toyshop or dollhouse for middle-class children. If one also bears in mind that a superintendent has to look after the children, to occupy and feed them, and in addition to keep a record of all expenses for milk, bread, and materials, that she is responsible for all this, it must become drastically clear how little room such work leaves for the private life of the person performing it. But amid all the images of childhood destitution that is still far from being overcome, an attentive observer will perceive one thing: how the liberated pride of the proletariat is matched by the emancipated bearing of the children. Nothing is more pleasantly surprising on a visit to Moscow's museums than to see how, singly or in groups, sometimes around a guide, children and workers move easily through these rooms. Nothing is to be seen of the forlornness of the few proletarians who dare to show themselves to the other visitors in our museums. In Russia the proletariat has really begun to take possession of bourgeois culture, whereas on such occasions in our country they have the appearance of planning a burglary. Admittedly, there are collections in Moscow in which workers and children can quickly feel themselves at home. There is the Polytechnic Museum, with its many thousands of experiments, pieces of apparatus, documents, and models relating to the history of primary production and the manufacturing industry. There is the admirably run toy museum, which under its director, Bartram, has brought together a precious, instructive collection of Russian toys, and serves the scholar as much as the children who walk about for hours in these rooms (around midday there is also a big, free puppet show, as fine as any in the Luxembourg). There is the famous Tretiakov Gallery, in which one understands for the first time what genre painting means and how especially appropriate it is to the Russians. Here the proletarian finds subjects from the history of his movement: *A Conspirator Surprised by the Police*, *The Return from Exile in Siberia*, *The Poor Governess Enters Service in a Rich Merchant's House*. And the fact that such scenes are still painted entirely in the spirit of bourgeois art not only does no harm—it actually brings them closer to this public. For education in art (as Proust explains very well at various points) is not best promoted by the contemplation of "masterpieces." Rather, the child or the proletarian who is educating himself acknowledges, rightly, very different works as masterpieces from those selected by the collector. Such pictures have for him a very transitory but solid meaning, and a strict criterion is necessary only with regard to the topical works that relate to him, his work, and his class.

education in art...

"eye of the beholder"

5

Begging is not aggressive as in southern climes, where the importunity of the ragamuffin still betrays some remnant of vitality. Here it is a corporation of the dying. The street corners of some neighborhoods are covered with bundles of rags—beds in the vast open-air hospital called Moscow. Long, beseeching speeches are addressed to the people walking past. There is one beggar who always begins, at the approach of a promising-looking passer-by, to emit a soft, drawn-out howling; this is directed at foreigners who cannot speak Russian. Another has the exact posture of the pauper for whom Saint Martin, in old pictures, cuts his cloak in two with his sword: he kneels with both arms outstretched. Shortly before Christmas, two children sat day after day in the snow against the wall of the Museum of the Revolution, covered with a scrap of material and whimpering. (But outside the English Club, the most genteel in Moscow, to which this building earlier belonged, even that would not have been possible.) One ought to know Moscow as such beggar children know it. They know of a corner beside the door of a certain shop where, at a particular time, they are allowed to warm themselves for ten minutes; they know where one day each week at a certain hour they can fetch themselves crusts, and where a sleeping place among stacked sewage pipes is free. They have developed begging to a high art, with a hundred schematisms and variations. They watch the customers of a pastry cook on a busy street corner, approach one, and accompany him, whining and pleading, until he has relinquished to them a piece of his hot pie. Others keep station at a streetcar terminus, board a vehicle, sing a song, and collect kopecks. And there are places, admittedly only a few, where even street trading has the appearance of begging. A few Mongols stand against the wall of Kitai Gorod. Each stands no more than five paces from the next, selling leather briefcases, and each offers exactly the same article as his neighbor. There must be some agreement behind this, for they cannot seriously intend such hopeless competition. Probably in their homeland the winter is no less harsh and their ragged furs are no worse than those of the natives. Nevertheless, they are the only people in Moscow whom one pities on account of the climate. Even priests who go begging for their churches can still be seen. But you very seldom see anyone give. Begging has lost its strongest foundation, the bad social conscience, which opens purses so much wider than does pity. Beyond this, it appears as an expression of the unchanging wretchedness of these beggars; perhaps, too, it is only the result of judicious organization that, of all the institutions in Moscow, they alone are dependable, remaining unchanged in their place while everything around them shifts.

6

Each thought, each day, each life lies here as on a laboratory table. And as if it were a metal from which an unknown substance is by every means to be extracted, it must endure experimentation to the point of exhaustion. No organism, no organization, can escape this process. Employees in their factories, offices in buildings, pieces of furniture in apartments are rear-ranged, transferred, and shoved about. New ceremonies for christening and marriage are presented in the clubs, as if the clubs were research institutes. Regulations are changed from day to day, but streetcar stops migrate, too. Shops turn into restaurants and a few weeks later into offices. This astonishing experimentation—it is here called *remonte*—affects not only Moscow; it is Russian. In this ruling passion, there is as much naive desire for improvement as there is boundless curiosity and playfulness. Few things are shaping Russia more powerfully today. The country is mobilized day and night—most of all, of course, the party. Indeed, what distinguishes the Bolshevik, the Russian Communist, from his Western comrade is this un-conditional readiness for mobilization. The material basis of his existence is so slender that he is prepared, year in, year out, to decamp. He would not otherwise be a match for this life. Where else is it conceivable that a distinguished military leader could one day be made director of a great state theater? The present director of the Theater of the Revolution is a former general. True, he was a man of letters before he became a victorious commander. Or in which other country can one hear stories like those told me by the porter at my hotel? Until 1924 he was employed in the Kremlin. Then one day he was afflicted by severe sciatica. The party had him treated by their best doctors, sent him to the Crimea, had him take mud baths and try radiation treatment. When all proved in vain he was told, "You need a job in which you can look after yourself, keep warm, and not move!" The next day he was a hotel porter. When he is cured he will go back to the Kremlin. Ultimately, even the health of comrades is a prized possession of the party, which, against the person's wishes if necessary, takes such mea-sures as are needed to conserve it. This is the way the situation is presented, at any rate, in an excellent novella by Boris Pilnyak.[2] Against his will a high official undergoes an operation, which has a fatal outcome. (A very famous name is mentioned here among the dead of the last few years.) There is no knowledge or faculty that is not somehow appropriated by collective life and made to serve it. The specialist is a spearhead of this increasingly practical approach and the only citizen who, outside the political sphere, has any status. At times, the respect for this type verges on fetishism. Thus, the Red military academy employed as a teacher a general who is notori-ously for his part in the civil war. He had every captured Bolshevik unceremoni-ously hanged. For Europeans such a point of view, which intransigently subordinates the prestige of ideology to practical demands, is barely com-prehensible. But this incident is also characteristic of the opposing side. For it is not only the military of the czarist empire who, as is known, placed themselves at the service of the Bolsheviks. Intellectuals, too, return in time as specialists to the posts they sabotaged during the civil war. Opposition, as we would like to imagine it in the West—intellectuals holding themselves aloof and languishing under the yoke—does not exist, or, better, no longer exists. It has—with whatever reservations—accepted the truce with the Bolsheviks, or it has been annihilated. There is in Russia—particularly outside the party—only the most loyal opposition. For this new life weighs on no one more heavily than on the outsider observing from a distance. To endure this existence in idleness is impossible because, in each smallest detail, it becomes beautiful and comprehensible only through work. The integration of personal thoughts with a preexisting force field; a mandate, however virtual; organized, guaranteed contact with comrades—to all this, life here is so tightly bound that anyone who abstains or cannot achieve it degenerates intellectually as if through years of solitary confinement.

7

Bolshevism has abolished private life. The bureaucracy, political activity, the press are so powerful that no time remains for interests that do not converge with them. Nor any space. Apartments that earlier accommodated single families in their five to eight rooms now often lodge eight. Through the hall door, one steps into a little town. More often still, into an army camp. Even in the lobby, one can encounter beds. Indoors one only camps, and usually the scanty inventory is merely a residue of petty-bourgeois possessions that have a far more depressing effect because the room is so sparsely furnished. An essential feature of the petty-bourgeois interior, however, was completeness: pictures must cover the walls, cushions the sofa, covers the cushions; ornaments must fill the mantelpiece, colored glass the windows. (Such petty-bourgeois rooms are battlefields over which the attack of commodity capital has advanced victoriously; nothing human can flourish there again.) Of all that, only a part here or there has been indiscriminately preserved. Weekly the furniture in the bare rooms is rearranged; this is the only luxury indulged in with them, and at the same time a radical means of expelling "coziness"—along with the melancholy with which it is paid for—from the house. People can bear to exist in it because they are estranged from it by their way of life. Their dwelling place is the office, the club, the street. Of the mobile army of officials, only the baggage train is to be found here. Curtains and partitions, often only half the height of the walls, have had to multiply the number of rooms. For each citizen is entitled by law to only thirteen square meters of living space. He pays for his accommodations according to his income. The state—all house ownership is nationalized—charges the unemployed one ruble monthly for the same area for which the better-off pay sixty or more. Anyone who lays claim to more than this prescribed area must, if he cannot justify his claim professionally, make manifold amends. Every step away from the preordained path meets with an immeasurable bureaucratic apparatus and with impossible costs. The member of a trade union who produces a certificate of illness and goes through the prescribed channels can be admitted to the most modern sanatorium, be sent to health resorts in the Crimea, enjoy expensive radiation treatment, without paying a penny for it. The outsider can go begging and sink into penury if he is not in a position, as a member of the new bourgeoisie, to buy all this for thousands of rubles. Anything that cannot be based on the collective framework demands a disproportionate expenditure of effort. For this reason, there is no "homeyness." But neither are there any cafés. Free trade and the free intellect have been abolished. The cafés are thereby deprived of their public. There thus remain, even for private affairs, only the office and the club. Here, however, transactions are under the aegis of the new *byt*—the new environment, for which nothing counts except the function of the producer in the collective. The new Russians say that milieu is the only reliable educator.

8

For each citizen of Moscow the days are full to the brim. Meetings, committees are fixed at all hours in offices, clubs, and factories, and often have no site of their own, being held in corners of noisy editorial rooms, or at a cleared table in a canteen. There is a kind of natural selection and a struggle for existence among these events. Society projects them to some extent, plans them; they are convened. But how often must this be repeated until finally one of the many is successful, proves viable, is adapted, takes place. That nothing turns out as intended and expected—this banal expression of the reality of life here asserts itself in each individual case so inviolably and intensely that Russian fatalism becomes comprehensible. If civilizing calculation slowly establishes itself in the collective, this will, in the first place, only complicate matters. (A person is better provided for in a house that has only candles than in one where electric light has been installed but the supply of current is interrupted hourly.) A feeling for the value of time, notwithstanding all "rationalization," is not met with even in the capital of Russia. Trud, the trade-union institute for the study of work, under its director, Gastiev, launched a poster campaign for punctuality. From earliest times a large number of clockmakers have been settled in Moscow. Like medieval guilds, they are crowded in particular streets, on the Kuznetsky Bridge, on Ulitsa Gertsena. One wonders who actually needs them. "Time is money"—for this astonishing statement posters claim the authority of Lenin, so alien is the idea to the Russians. They fritter everything away. (One is tempted to say that minutes are a cheap liquor of which they can never get enough, that they are tipsy with time.) If on the street a scene is being shot for a film, they forget where they are going and why, and follow the camera for hours, arriving at the office distraught. In his use of time, therefore, the Russian will remain "Asiatic" longest of all. Once I needed to be wakened at seven in the morning: "Please knock tomorrow at seven." This elicited from the *Schweizar*—as hotel porters are called here—the following Shakespearean monologue: "If we think of it we shall wake you, but if we do not think of it we shall not wake you. Actually we usually do think of it, and then we wake people. But to be sure, we also forget sometimes when we do not think of it. Then we do not wake people. We are under no obligation, of course, but if it crosses our mind, we do it. When do you want to be wakened? At seven? Then we shall write that down. You see, I am putting the message there where he will find it. Of course, if he does not find it, then he will not wake you. But usually we do wake people." The real unit of time is the *seichas*. This means "at once." You can hear it ten, twenty, thirty times, and wait hours, days, or weeks until the promise is carried out. By the same token, you seldom hear the answer no. Negative replies are left to time. Time catastrophes, time collisions are therefore as much the order of the day as *remonte*. They make each hour superabundant, each day exhausting, each life a moment.

9

Travel by streetcar in Moscow is more than anything else a tactical experience. Here the newcomer learns perhaps most quickly of all to adapt himself to the curious tempo of this city and to the rhythm of its peasant population. And the complete interpenetration of technological and primitive modes of life, this world-historical experiment in the new Russia, is illustrated in miniature by a streetcar ride. The conductresses stand fur-wrapped at their places like Samoyed women on a sleigh. A tenacious shoving and barging during the boarding of a vehicle usually overloaded to the point of bursting takes place without a sound and with great cordiality. (I have never heard an angry word on these occasions.) Once everyone is inside, the migration begins in earnest. Through the ice-covered windows, you can never make out where the vehicle has just stopped. If you do find out, it is of little avail. The way to the exit is blocked by a human wedge. Since you must board at the rear but alight at the front, you have to thread your way through this mass. But conveyance usually occurs in batches; at important stops the vehicle is almost completely emptied. Thus, even the traffic in Moscow is to a large extent a mass phenomenon. So one can encounter whole caravans of sleighs blocking the streets in a long row, because loads that require a truck are being stacked on five or six large sleighs. The sleighs here take the horse into consideration first and then the passenger. They do not know the slightest superfluity. A feeding sack for the nags, a blanket for the passenger—and that is all. The narrow bench can fit two at the most, and since it has no back (unless you are willing so to describe a low rail), you must keep a good balance on sudden corners. Everything is based on the assumption of the highest velocity; long journeys in the cold are hard to bear, and distances in this gigantic village immeasurable. The *izvozshchik* drives his vehicle close to the sidewalk. The passenger is not enthroned high up; he looks out on the same level as everyone else and brushes the passers-by with his sleeve. Even this is an incomparable experience for the sense of touch. Whereas Europeans, on their rapid journeys, enjoy superiority, dominance over the masses, the Muscovite in the little sleigh is closely mingled with people and things. If he has a box, a child, or a basket to take with him—for all such things the sleigh is the cheapest means of transport—he is truly wedged into the street bustle. No condescending gaze: a tender, swift brushing along stones, people, and horses. You feel like a child gliding through the house on his little chair.

10

Christmas is a feast of the Russian forest. With pines, candles, tree decorations, it settles for many weeks in the streets, for the Advent of Greek Orthodox Christians overlaps with the Christmas of those Russians who celebrate the feast by the Western—that is, the new—official calendar. Nowhere does one see Christmas trees more beautifully decorated. Little boats, birds, fishes, houses, and fruit crowd the street stalls and shops, and every year about this time the Kustarny Museum for Regional Art holds a kind of trade fair for all this. At a crossroads, I found a woman selling tree decorations. The glass balls, yellow and red, glinted in the sun; it was like an enchanted apple basket in which red and yellow were divided among different fruits. Pines are drawn through the streets on slow sleighs. The smaller ones are trimmed only with silk bows; little pines with blue, pink, and green ribbons stand on the corners. But to the children the Christmas toys, even without a Santa Claus, tell how they come from deep in the forests of Russia. It is as if only under Russian hands does wood put forth such luxuriant greenness. It turns green—and then reddens and puts on a coat of gold, flares sky-blue and petrifies black. "Red" and "beautiful" are *one* word in [old] Russian. Certainly the glowing logs in the stove are the most magical metamorphosis of the Russian forest. Nowhere does the hearth seem to glow with such splendor as here. But radiance is captured in all the wood that the peasant carves and paints. And when varnished, it is fire frozen in all colors. Yellow and red on the balalaika, black and green on the little *garmoshka* for children, and every shade in the thirty-six eggs that fit one inside another. But forest night, too, lives in the wood. There are the heavy little boxes with scarlet interiors; on the outside, on a gleaming black background, a picture. Under the czars, this industry was on the point of extinction. Now, besides new miniatures, the old, gold-embellished images

Christmas

are again emerging from peasant life. A troika with its three horses races through the night, or a girl in a sea-blue dress stands at night beside green flaring bushes, waiting for her lover. No night of terror is as dark as this durable lacquer night—everything that appears in it is enfolded in its womb. I saw a box with a picture of a seated woman selling cigarettes. Beside her stands a child who wants to take one. Pitch-black night here, too. But on the right a stone and on the left a leafless tree are discernible. On the woman's apron is the word *Mossel'prom*. She is the Soviet "Madonna with the Cigarettes."

11

Green is the supreme luxury of the Moscow winter. But it shines from the shop in the Petrovka not half as beautifully as the paper bunches of artificial carnations, roses, lilies on the street. In markets they are the only wares to have no fixed stall and appear now among groceries, now among textile goods and crockery stalls. But they outshine everything—raw meat, colored wool, and gleaming dishes. Other bouquets are seen at New Year's. As I passed through Strastnaia Square, I saw long twigs with red, white, blue, green blooms stuck to them, each stalk of a different color. When speaking of Moscow flowers, one must not forget the heroic Christmas roses, or the gigantically tall hollyhock made of lampshades that the trader carries through the streets. Or the glass cases full of flowers with the heads of saints looking out among them. Or what the frost here inspires: the peasant cloths with patterns embroidered in blue wool, imitating ice ferns on windows. Finally, the glistening candy-icing flower beds on cakes. The Pastry Cook from children's fairy tales seems to have survived only in Moscow. Only here are there structures made of nothing but spun sugar, sweet icicles with which the tongue indemnifies itself against the bitter cold. Most intimately of all, snow and flowers are united in candy icing; there at last the marzipan flora seems to have fulfilled entirely Moscow's winter dream: to bloom out of the whiteness.

12

Under capitalism, power and money have become commensurable qualities. Any given amount of money can be converted into a specific power, and the market value of all power can be calculated. So things stand on a large scale. We can speak of corruption only where this process is mastered too hastily. In the smooth interplay of press, boards, and trusts, there is a system of gears within whose limits the process remains entirely legal. The Soviet state has severed this communication between money and power. It reserves power for the party, and leaves money to the NEP man.[3] In the eyes of any party functionary, even the highest, to put something aside, to secure the "future," even if only "for the children," is quite unthinkable. To its members the Communist party guarantees the bare minimum for material existence—it does so practically, without actual obligation. On the other hand, it controls their further earnings and sets an upper limit of two hundred fifty rubles on their monthly income. This can be increased solely through literary activity alongside one's profession. To such discipline the life of the ruling class is subjected. But the power of the ruling authorities is by no means identical with their possessions. Russia is today not only a class but also a caste state. "Caste state"—this means that the social status of a citizen is determined not by the visible exterior of his existence—his clothes or living place—but exclusively by his relations to the party. This is also decisive for those who do not directly belong to it. To them, too, employment is open, to the extent that they do not overtly repudiate the regime. Between them, too, the most precise distinctions are made. But however exaggerated—or obsolete—the European conception of the official suppression of nonconformists in Russia may be, no one living abroad has any idea of the terrible social ostracism to which the NEP man is here subjected. The silence, the mistrust, perceptible not only between strangers, is otherwise inexplicable. If you ask a superficial acquaintance here about his impressions of however unimportant a play, however trivial a film, you may expect stock phrases in reply: "One says here . . ." or "The conviction is prevalent here . . ." A judgment is weighed innumerable times before being uttered to more distant contacts. For at any time, the party can casually, unobtrusively change its line in *Pravda*, and no one likes to see himself disavowed. Because a reliable political outlook, if not the only good, is for most people the only guarantee of other goods; everyone uses his name and his voice so cautiously that the citizen with a democratic turn of mind cannot understand him.—Two close acquaintances are having a conversation. In the course of it one of them says: "That fellow Mikhailovich was in my office yesterday looking for a job. He said he knew you." "He is an excellent comrade, punctual and hardworking." They change the subject. But as they part, the first says, "Would you be kind enough to give me a few words on that Mikhailovich in writing?"—Class rule has adopted symbols that serve to characterize the opposing class. And of these, jazz is perhaps the most popular. That people also enjoy listening to it in Russia is not surprising. But dancing to it is forbidden. It is kept behind glass, as it were, like a brightly colored poisonous reptile, and so appears as an attraction in revues. Yet always a symbol of the "bourgeois." It is one of the crude stage sets with the aid of which, for propaganda purposes, a grotesque image of the bourgeois type is constructed. In reality the image is often merely ridiculous, the discipline and competence of the adversary being overlooked. In this distorted view of the bourgeois, a nationalist impulse is present. Russia was the possession of the czar (indeed, anyone walking past the endlessly piled-up valuables in the Kremlin collections is tempted to say "*a* possession"). The people, however, have overnight become his immeasurably wealthy heirs. They now set about drawing up a grand inventory of their human and territorial wealth. And they undertake this work with the awareness that they have already performed unimaginably difficult tasks, and built up, against the hostility of half the world, the new system of power. In admiration for this national achievement all Russians are united. It is this reversal of the power structure that makes life here so heavy with content. It is as complete in itself and rich in events, as poor and in the same breath as full of prospects, as a gold digger's life on the Klondike. From early till late, people dig for power. All the combinations of our leading figures are meager in comparison to the countless constellations that here confront the individual in the course of a month. True, a certain intoxication can result, so that a life without meetings and committees, debates, resolutions, and votes (and all these are wars, or at least maneuvers of the will to power) can no longer be imagined. What does it matter—Russia's next generation will be accustomed to this existence. Its health, however, is subject to one indispensable condition: that never (as one day happened even to the Church) should a black market of power be opened. Should the European correlation of power and money penetrate Russia, too, then perhaps not the country, perhaps not even the party, but Communism in Russia would be lost. People here have not yet developed European consumer concepts and consumer needs. The reasons for this are above all economic. Yet it is possible that in addition an astute party stratagem is involved: to achieve, at a freely chosen moment, a level of consumption equal to that of Western Europe—the trial by fire of the Bolshevik bureaucracy, steeled and with absolute certainty of victory.

13

In the Red Army Club at the Kremlin, a map of Europe hangs on the wall. Beside it is a handle. When this handle is turned, the following is seen: one after the other, at all the places through which Lenin passed in the course of his life, little electric lights flash. At Simbirsk, where he was born, at Kazan, Petersburg, Geneva, Paris, Krakow, Zurich, Moscow, up to the place of his death, Gorki. Other towns are not marked. The contours of this wooden relief map are rectilinear, angular, schematic. On it Lenin's life resembles a campaign of colonial conquest across Europe. Russia is beginning to take shape for the man of the people. On the street, in the snow, lie maps of the SFSR,[4] piled up by street vendors who offer them for sale. Meyerhold[5] uses a map in *D.E.* (*Here with Europe!*)—it shows Western Europe as a complicated system of little Russian peninsulas. The map is almost as close to becoming the center of the new Russian iconic cult as Lenin's portrait. Quite certainly the strong national feeling that Bolshevism has given all Russians, regardless of distinction, has conferred a new reality on the map of Europe. They want to measure, compare, and perhaps enjoy that intoxication with grandeur which is induced by the mere sight of Russia; citizens can only be urgently advised to look at their country on the map of neighboring states, to study Germany on a map of Poland, France, or even Denmark; but all Europeans ought to see, on a map of Russia, their little land as a frayed, nervous territory far out to the west.

14

What figure does the man of letters cut in a country where his employer is the proletariat?—The theoreticians of Bolshevism stress how widely the situation of the proletariat in Russia after this successful revolution differs from that of the bourgeoisie in 1789. At that time the victorious class, before it attained power, had secured for itself in struggles lasting decades the control of the cultural apparatus. Intellectual organization, education, had long been pervaded by the ideas of the Third Estate, and the mental struggle for emancipation was fought out before the political. In present-day Russia it is quite different. For millions upon millions of illiterates, the foundations of a general education have yet to be laid. This is a national, Russian task. Prerevolutionary education in Russia was, however, entirely unspecific, European. The European moment in higher education, and the national moment on the elementary level, are in Russia seeking an accommodation. This is one side of the educational question. On the other, the victory of the Revolution has in many areas accelerated the process of Europeanization. There are writers like Pilnyak who see in Bolshevism the crowning of the work of Peter the Great. In the technical area this tendency, despite all the adventures of its earliest years, is presumably sure of victory sooner or later. Not so in the intellectual and scientific areas. It is now apparent in Russia that European values are being popularized in just the distorted, desolating form that they owe finally to imperialism. The second academic theater—a state-supported institution—is putting on a performance of the *Oresteia* in which a dusty Greek antiquity struts about the stage as untruthfully as in a German court theater. And since the marble-stiff gesture is not only corrupt in itself, but also a copy of court acting in revolutionary Moscow, it has a still more melancholy effect than in Stuttgart or Anhalt. The Russian Academy of Science has for its part made a man like Walzel—an average specimen of the modern academic *bel esprit*—a member. Probably the only cultural conditions in the West for which Russia has a lively enough understanding for disagreement with it to be profitable are those of America. In contrast, cultural rapprochement as such (without the foundation of the most concrete economic and political community) is an interest of the pacifist variety of imperialism; it benefits only gossiping busybodies, and is for Russia a symptom of restoration. The country is isolated from Western Europe less by frontiers and censorship than by the intensity of an existence that is beyond all comparison with the European. Stated more precisely: contact with the outside world is through the party and primarily concerns political questions. The old bourgeoisie has been annihilated; the new is neither materially nor intellectually in a position to establish external relations. Undoubtedly Russians know far less about the outside world than foreigners (with the possible exception of the Romance-language countries) know about Russia. If an influential Russian mentions Proust and Bronnen in the same breath as authors who take their subject matter from the area of sexual problems, this shows clearly the foreshortened perspective in which European matters appear from here. But if one of Russia's leading authors, in conversation, quotes Shakespeare as one of the great poets who wrote before the invention of printing, such a lack of training can be understood only from the completely changed conditions affecting Russian writing as a whole. Theses and dogmas that in Europe—admittedly only for the past two centuries—have been regarded as alien to art and beneath discussion by men of letters are decisive in literary criticism and production in the new Russia. Message and subject matter are declared of primary importance. Formal controversies still played a not inconsiderable part at the time of the civil war. Now they have fallen silent. Today it is official doctrine that subject matter, not form, decides the revolutionary or counterrevolutionary attitude of a work. Such doctrines cut the ground from under the writer's feet just as irrevocably as the economy has done on the material plane. In this, Russia is ahead of Western developments—but not as far ahead as is believed. For sooner or later, with the middle classes who are being ground to pieces by the struggle between capital and labor, the "freelance" writer must also disappear. In Russia the process is complete: the intellectual is above all a functionary, working in the departments of censorship, justice, and finance, and, if he survives, participating in work—which, however, in Russia means power. He is a member of the ruling class. Of his various organizations the most prominent is VAPP, the general association of proletarian writers in Russia.[6] It supports the notion of dictatorship even in the field of intellectual creation. In this it takes account of Russian reality. The transfer of the mental means of production into public ownership can be distinguished only fictitiously from that of the material means. To begin with, the proletarian can be trained in the use of both only under the protection of a dictatorship.

15

Now and again one comes across streetcars painted all over with pictures of factories, mass meetings, Red regiments, Communist agitators. These are gifts from the personnel of a factory to the Moscow Soviet. These vehicles carry the only political posters still to be seen in Moscow, but they are by far the most interesting. For nowhere are more naive commercial posters to be seen than here. The wretched level of pictorial advertising is the only similarity between Paris and Moscow. Countless walls around churches and monasteries offer on all sides the finest surfaces for posters. But the constructivists, suprematists, abstractionists who under War Communism[7] placed their graphic propaganda at the service of the Revolution have long since been dismissed. Today, only banal clarity is demanded. Most of these posters repel the Westerner. But Moscow shops are inviting; they have something of the tavern about them. The shop signs point at right angles into the street, as otherwise only old inn signs do, or golden barber-basins, or a top hat before a hatter's. Also, the last charming, unspoiled motifs that remain are most likely to be found here. Shoes falling out of a basket; a Pomeranian running away with a sandal in his mouth. Pendants before the entrance to a Turkish kitchen; gentlemen, each with a fez adorning his head and each at his own little table. Catering to a primitive taste, advertising is still tied to narrative, example, or anecdote. In contrast, the Western advertisement convinces first and foremost by the expense of which it shows the firm capable. Here almost every ad also specifies the commodity in question. The grand, showy logo is alien to commerce. The city, so inventive in abbreviations of all kinds, does not yet possess the simplest—brand names. Often Moscow's evening sky glows in frightening blue: one has unwittingly looked at it through one of the gigantic pairs of blue spectacles that project from opticians' shops like signposts. From the gateways, on the frames of front doors, in black, blue, yellow, and red letters of varying sizes—as an arrow, a picture of boots or freshly ironed washing, a worn step or a solid staircase—a silently determined, contentious life accosts the passer-by. One must ride through the streets on a streetcar to perceive how this struggle is continued upward through the various stories, finally to reach its decisive phase on the roof. This height only the strongest, youngest slogans and signs attain. Only from an airplane does one have a view of the industrial elite of the city, the film and automobile industries. Mostly, however, the roofs of Moscow are a lifeless wasteland, having neither the dazzling electric signs of Berlin, nor the forest of chimneys of Paris, nor the sunny solitude of the rooftops of great cities in southern lands.

16

Anyone entering a Russian classroom for the first time will stop short in surprise. The walls are crammed with pictures, drawings, and pasteboard models. They are temple walls to which the children daily donate their own work as gifts to the collective. Red predominates; they are pervaded by Soviet emblems and heads of Lenin. Something similar is to be seen in many clubs. Wall newspapers are, for grownups, schemata of the same collective form of expression. They came into being under the pressure of the civil war, when in many places neither newsprint nor printing ink was available. Today they are an obligatory part of the public life of factories. Every Lenin niche has its wall newspaper, which varies its style among factories and authors. The only thing common to all is the naive cheerfulness: colorful pictures interspersed with prose and verses. The newspaper is the chronicle of the collective. It gives statistical reports but also jocular criticism of comrades, mingled with suggestions for improving the factory or appeals for communal aid. Notices, warning signs, and didactic pictures cover the walls of the Lenin niche elsewhere, too. Even inside a factory, everyone is as if surrounded by colored posters all exorcising the terrors of the machine. One worker is portrayed with his arm forced between the spokes of a driving wheel, another, drunk, causing an explosion with a short circuit, a third with his knee caught between two pistons. In the lending room of the Red Army bookshop hangs a notice, its short text clarified by many charming drawings showing how many ways there are of ruining a book. In hundreds of thousands of copies a poster introducing the weights and measures normal in Europe is disseminated throughout the whole of Russia. Meters, liters, kilograms, and so on must be stuck up in every pub. In the reading room of the peasant club on Trubnaia Square, the walls are covered with visual aids. The village chronicle, agricultural development, production technique, cultural institutions are graphically recorded in lines of development, along with components of tools, machine parts, retorts containing chemicals displayed everywhere on the walls. Out of curiosity, I went up to a shelf from which two Negro faces grimaced at me. But as I came nearer, they turned out to be gas masks. Formerly, the building occupied by this club had been one of the leading restaurants in Moscow. Today, the erstwhile *séparées* are bedrooms for peasants of both sexes who have received a *komandirovka* to visit the city. There they are conducted through collections and barracks, and attend courses and educational evenings. From time to time, there is also pedagogical theater in the form of "legal proceedings." About three hundred people, sitting and standing, fill the red-draped room to its farthest corners. In a niche, a bust of Lenin. The proceedings take place on a stage in front of which, on the right and the left, painted proletarian types—a peasant and an industrial worker—symbolize the *smychka,* the clasping together of town and country. The hearing of evidence has just finished; an expert is called on to speak. He and his assistant have one table; opposite him is that of the defense; both tables face sideways to the public. In the background, facing front, the judge's table. Before it, dressed in black, with a thick branch in her hand, sits the defendant, a peasant woman. She is accused of medical incompetence with fatal results. Through incorrect treatment, she caused the death of a woman in childbirth. The argumentation now circles around this case in monotonous, simple trains of reasoning. The expert gives his report: the incorrect treatment was to blame for the mother's death. The defense counsel, however, pleads against harshness; in the country, there is a lack of sanitary aid and hygienic instruction. The final word of the defendant: *nichevo,* people have always died in childbirth. The prosecution demands the death penalty. Then the presiding judge turns to the assembly: Are there any questions? But only a Komsomol[8] appears on the stage, to demand severe punishment. The court retires to deliberate. After a short pause comes the judgment, for which everyone stands up: two years' imprisonment with recognition of mitigating circumstances. Solitary confinement is thus ruled out. In conclusion, the president points to the necessity of establishing centers of hygiene and instruction in rural areas. Such demonstrations are carefully prepared; there can be no question of improvisation. For mobilizing the public on questions of Bolshevik morality in accordance with party wishes, there can be no more effective means. On one occasion, alcoholism will be disposed of in this way; on others, fraud, prostitution, hooliganism. The austere forms of such educational work are entirely appropriate to Soviet life, being precipitates of an existence which requires that a stand be taken a hundred times each day.

17

In the streets of Moscow, there is a curious state of affairs: the Russian village is playing hide-and-seek in them. If you step through one of the high gateways—they often have wrought-iron gates, but I never found them closed—you stand on the threshold of a spacious settlement. Opening before you, broad and expansive, is a farmyard or a village. The ground is uneven; children ride about in sleighs; sheds for wood and tools fill the corners; trees stand here and there; wooden staircases give the backs of houses, which look like city buildings from the front, the appearance of Russian farmhouses. Frequently churches stand in these yards, just as on a large village green. So the street is augmented by the dimension of landscape. Nor is there any Western city that, in its vast squares, looks so rurally formless and perpetually sodden from bad weather—thawing snow, or rain. Scarcely one of these broad spaces bears a monument. (In contrast, there is hardly one in Europe whose secret structure was not profaned and destroyed by a monument in the nineteenth century.) Like every other city, Moscow uses names to build up a little world within itself. There is a casino called the Alcazar, a hotel named the Liverpool, a Tirol boardinghouse. From there it still takes half an hour to reach the centers of urban winter sports. True, skaters and skiers are encountered throughout the city, but the toboggan track is closer to the center. There sleighs of the most diverse construction are used: from a board that runs at the front on sleigh rails and at the back drags in the snow, to the most comfortable bobsleds. Nowhere does Moscow look like the city itself; at the most, it resembles its outskirts. The wet ground, the wooden booths, long convoys carrying raw materials, cattle being driven to the slaughterhouse, and indigent taverns are found in the busiest parts. The city is still interspersed with little wooden buildings in exactly the same Slavonic style as those found everywhere in the surroundings of Berlin. What looks so desolate in Brandenburg stone is attractive here, with the lovely colors of warm wood. In the suburban streets leading off the broad avenues, peasant huts alternate with Art Nouveau villas or with the sober façades of eight-story blocks. Snow lies deep, and if all of a sudden silence falls, one can believe oneself in a village in midwinter, deep in the Russian interior. Nostalgia for Moscow is engendered not only by the snow, with its starry luster by night and its flowerlike crystals by day, but also by the sky. For between low roofs the horizon of the broad plains is constantly entering the city. Only toward evening does it become invisible. But then the shortage of housing in Moscow produces its most astonishing effect. If you wander the streets in the dusk, you see in the large and small houses almost every window brightly lit. If the light coming from them were not so unsteady, you would believe you had a festive illumination before your eyes.

18

The churches are almost mute. The city is as good as free of the chimes that on Sundays spread such deep melancholy over our cities. But there is still perhaps not a single spot in Moscow from which at least *one* church is not visible. More exactly: at which you are not watched by at least *one* church. A Russian under the czars was surrounded in this city by more than four hundred chapels and churches—that is to say, by two thousand domes, which hide in the corners everywhere, cover one another, spy over walls. An architectural *okhrana* surrounded him. All these churches preserve their incognito. Nowhere do high towers jut into the sky. Only with time do you become accustomed to putting together the long walls and crowds of low domes into complexes of monastery churches. It then also becomes clear why in many places Moscow looks as tightly sealed as a fortress: the monasteries still bear traces today of their old defensive purpose. Here Byzantium with its thousand domes is not the wonder that the European dreams it to be. Most of the churches are built on an insipid, sickly sweet pattern: their blue, green, and golden domes are a candied Orient. If you enter one of these churches, you first find a spacious anteroom with a few sparse portraits of saints. It is gloomy, the half-light lending itself to conspiracy. In such rooms one can discuss the most dubious business—even pogroms, if the occasion demands. Adjoining the anteroom is the only room for worship. In the background it has a few small steps leading to a narrow, low platform along which one advances past pictures of saints to the iconostasis. At short intervals, altar succeeds altar, a glimmering red light denoting each. The side walls are occupied by large pictures of saints. All parts of the wall that are not thus covered with pictures are lined with shining gold-colored tin plate. From the trashily painted ceiling hangs a crystal chandelier. Nevertheless, the room is always lit only by candles, a drawing room with sanctified walls against which the ceremony unrolls. The worshiper greets the large pictures by making the sign of the Cross and kneeling down to touch the ground with the forehead; then, with renewed signs of the Cross, the worshiper, praying or doing penance, goes on to the next. Before small, glass-covered pictures lying in rows or singly on desks, the genuflection is omitted. One bends over them and kisses the glass. On such desks, beside the most precious old icons, series of the gaudiest oil paintings are displayed. Many pictures of saints have taken up positions outside on the façade and look down from the highest cornices under the tinny eaves, like birds sheltering there. From their inclined, retort-shaped heads, affliction speaks. Byzantium seems to have no church-window form of its own. A magical but uncanny impression: the profane, drab windows looking out onto the street from the assembly rooms and towers of the church, as if from a living room. Behind them the Orthodox priest is ensconced like a Buddhist monk in his pagoda. The lower part of Saint Basil's Cathedral might be the ground floor of a fine boyar house. But if you enter Red Square from the west, its domes gradually rise into the sky like a pack of fiery suns. This building always holds something back, and could be surprised only by a gaze coming from an airplane, against which the builders forgot to take precautions. The inside has been not just emptied but eviscerated, like a shot deer. (And it could hardly have turned out differently, for even in 1920 people still prayed here with fanatical fervor.) With the removal of all the furniture, the colorful vegetal convolutions that proliferate as murals in all the corridors and vaults are hopelessly exposed, distorting with a sad rococo playfulness the much older decoration that sparingly preserves in the interior the memory of the colorful spirals of the domes. The vaulted passageways are narrow, suddenly broadening into altar niches or circular chapels into which so little light falls from the high windows above that isolated devotional objects which have been left standing are scarcely discernible. Many churches remain just as untended and empty. But the glow that now shines only occasionally from the altars into the snow has been well preserved in the wooden cities of the commercial booths. In their snow-covered, narrow alleyways it is quiet. You hear only the soft jargon of the Jewish clothiers in their stalls next to the junk of the paper dealer, who, enthroned and concealed behind silver chains, has drawn tinsel and cotton-wool-tufted Father Christmases across her face like an oriental veil.

19

Even the most laborious Moscow weekday has two coordinates that sensuously define each of its moments as expectation and fulfillment. One is the vertical coordinate of mealtimes; the other, which intersects it, is the evening horizontal of the theater. You are never very far from either. Moscow is crammed with pubs and theaters. Sentries with sweets patrol the street; many of the large grocery stores do not close until about eleven at night; and on the corners, tearooms and beerhouses open. *Chainaia, pivnaia*—but usually both are painted on a background where a dull green from the upper edge gradually and sullenly merges into a dirty yellow. Beer is served with curious condiments: tiny pieces of dried white bread, black bread baked over with a salt crust, and dried peas in salt water. In certain taverns one can dine on this fare and enjoy, in addition, a primitive *intsenirovka*. This is the term for an epic or lyrical subject that has been adapted for the theater. It is often a folksong crudely scored for a choir. In the orchestra of such folk music, alongside accordions and violins, abacuses used as instruments are sometimes heard. (They can be found in every shop and office. The smallest calculation is unthinkable without them.) The intoxicating warmth that overcomes the guest on entering these taverns, on drinking the hot tea and enjoying the sharp *zakuska*, is Moscow's most secret winter lust. Therefore, no one knows the city who has not known it in snow. Each region must be visited during the season in which its climatic extreme falls, for to this it is primarily adapted, and it can be understood only through this adaptation. In Moscow, life in winter is richer by a dimension. Space literally changes according to whether it is hot or cold. People live on the street as if in a frosty chamber of mirrors; each pause to think is unbelievably difficult. It needs half a day's resolution even to mail an already addressed letter, and despite the severe cold it is a feat of willpower to go into a shop and buy something. Yet when you have finally found a restaurant, no matter what is put on the table—vodka (which is here spiced with herbs), cakes, or a cup of tea—warmth makes the passing time itself an intoxicant. It flows into the weary guest like honey.

20

On the anniversary of Lenin's death, many people wear black armbands. For at least three days, flags throughout the city are at half-mast. Many of the black-veiled pennants, however, once hanging, are left out for a few weeks. Russia's mourning for a dead leader is certainly not comparable to the attitudes adopted by other nations on such days. The generation that was active in the civil wars is growing old in vitality, if not in years. It is as if stabilization had admitted to their lives the calm, sometimes even the apathy, that is usually brought only by old age. When the party one day called a halt to wartime Communism with the NEP, there was a terrible backlash, which felled many of the movement's fighters. At that time, many returned their membership books to the party. Cases are known of such total demoralization that trusty pillars of the party became defrauders within a few weeks. For Bolsheviks, mourning for Lenin means also mourning for heroic Communism. The few years since its passing are, for Russian consciousness, a long time. Lenin's activity so accelerated the course of events in his era that he is receding swiftly into the past; his image is quickly growing remote. Nevertheless, in the optic of history—opposite in this to that of space—movement into the distance means enlargement. Today other orders are in force than those of Lenin's time, admittedly slogans that he himself suggested. Now it is made clear to every Communist that the revolutionary work of this hour is not conflict, not civil war, but canal construction, electrification, and factory building. The revolutionary nature of true technology is emphasized ever more clearly. Like everything else, this (with reason) is done in Lenin's name. His name grows and grows. It is significant that the report of the English trade union delegation, a sober document sparing with prognoses, thought it worthwhile to mention the possibility "that, when the memory of Lenin has found its place in history, this great Russian revolutionary reformer will even be pronounced a saint." Even today the cult of his picture has assumed immeasurable proportions. One finds shops in which it can be bought in all sizes, poses, and materials. It stands as a bust in the Lenin niches, as a bronze statue or a relief in the larger clubs, as a life-size portrait in offices, as a small photo in kitchens, washrooms, and storage rooms. It hangs in the vestibule of the armory in the Kremlin, as in formerly godless places the Cross was erected by converted heathens. It is also gradually establishing its canonical forms. The well-known picture of the orator is the most common, but another one speaks perhaps more intensely and directly: Lenin at a table, bent over a copy of *Pravda*. When he is thus immersed in an ephemeral newspaper, the dialectical tension of his nature appears: his gaze is turned, certainly, to the far horizon; but the tireless care of his heart, to the moment.

Published in *Die Kreatur*, 1927. *Gesammelte Schriften*, IV, 316–348. Translated by Edmund Jephcott.

Notes

1. Benjamin may have been thinking of "Memnon's Colossos" in Thebes—two monumental seated figures of King Amenhotep III which were later mistakenly identified as representations of the legendary Ethiopian king Memnon.
2. Boris Andreyevich Pilnyak (pseudonym of B. A. Vogau; 1894–1938/41?) was a prose writer who depicted the revolution as a struggle between elemental and rational forces. He was one of the first victims of the government purges in 1937.
3. The New Economic Policy (NEP) was the economic policy of the Soviet Union from 1921 to 1928 which revised the original emphasis on centralization and planning. The NEP included the return of most agriculture, retail trade, and light industry to private ownership, while the state retained control of heavy industry, transport, banking, and foreign trade.
4. Soviet Federated Socialist Republic.
5. Vsevolod Emilevich Meyerhold (1874–1942), preeminent Russian actor and director, opposed the Naturalism of the Moscow Art Theater and was the first theater director to offer his services to the new government. In 1923 he was given his own theater, the Teatr imeni Meyerhold (TIM).
6. VAPP (All-Union Association of Proletarian Writers) was a Soviet literary organization founded in October 1920. By 1928 it was the leading association for writers in the USSR.
7. "War Communism" is the term used to describe the first period of state-dominated economic and social policy, between 1918 and 1921. It was superseded by the New Economic Policy.
8. A member of the oldest Soviet youth organization, the Kommunisticheskiy Soyuz Molodezhi.

Review of Gladkov's *Cement*

Fyodor Gladkov, *Cement: A Novel,* translated from the Russian by Olga Halpern (Berlin: Verlag für Literatur und Politik, 1927), 464 pages.

Gladkov[1] inaugurated a new epoch in Russia. His masterpiece, *Cement,* was the first novel of the period of reconstruction. At a stroke, the environment that he depicts became visible; starting as prose, the work soon conquered the stage, and has enjoyed a run that has lasted for months. Dramatic versions of successful novels are nothing new in Russia, but the transition has never been more appropriate than here. For the strength of the novel lies in its dialogue. It imported the argot of the Bolsheviks into literature. It is this linguistic achievement—one that is even more important than its content—that constitutes the book's information value. Through the medium of an unusually perfect translation, the reader becomes conversant with the manners and the language, the procedures and the debating tactics that have developed in the congresses and commissions. At the same time, he makes the acquaintance of the human types created in the workers' struggle for freedom. God knows, many of them are far from being leaders. They include people who were struck down—as if by apoplexy—in their thought and speech by the power that suddenly fell into their hands; sinister bureaucrats who lurk slyly in their forest of paragraphs like foxes in their burrows; agitators who flee from ideas; secret agents whose effectiveness remains a mystery even to themselves. But there are also young functionaries who are prepared at any moment to transform not just their lives, but the day, the hour, and even the minute into the executive organ of a higher will, wherever it points them; fanatics who promise nothing, reveal nothing of themselves, and silently, unexpectedly turn up at the riskiest places on the front; reformers who, thanks to their revolutionary self-confidence, promote the cause of the proletariat even in the face of obstacles thrown up by committees and soviets. The chief character is such a person: the Red Army man who returns to his home on the Black Sea after fighting at the front during the civil war. The economic key to this town is the great cement factory that is lying idle, decaying, and dragging the entire town down with it. He is the man who gets the factory going again after months of bitter conflict, a conflict that divides the camp of comrades in two. In the process, he loses his wife; no one can say why. The novel tells us, and indeed she tells us herself, that it is her work that estranges her from the family—and she is an outstanding worker. But this explanation says nothing to the reader, because the depiction of their marital relations is such that all possible side issues are invalidated by its unconstruable truth. A great experience has here found a valid form. It is not just the bonds uniting couples that have canonical forms, which change over time and often bear the features of their age in ways that are as difficult to express as the forms of love itself. The same is true of what separates couples. The true features of the emancipation of women are gradually taking shape, but in ways that differ from what was expected by the enlightened Philanthropists[2] (and this applies to Russia as much as to Europe). If the forces of command and domination really become feminine, this will bring about change in those forces, in the age, and even in the Feminine itself. Moreover, it does not mean a change into a vague humanity in general, but will present us with a new, more mysterious countenance, a political enigma, if you like, a sphinx-like expression, compared to which all the old secrets of the boudoir are no more than outworn riddles. This countenance projects itself into this book, which would have been a great work of literature if the writer had allowed it to grow out of this image. But the book suffers from the absence of a narrative focal point. The man's struggle to restore the fortunes of the cement factory is not so much the internal scaffolding of the action as a connecting thread linking the numerous events. In other words, the tension in his struggle remains external; it fails to become the central force field of the action. To make it so would have called above all for a larger context, a freer panorama. The vision of the sea and mountains closes off the horizon in a false idyll. A cement factory has to be shown against an economic background, not against a landscape. Here it is shown in miniature. This weakness of construction makes itself clearly felt at the end. The moment of apotheosis, the typical effect with which so many Russian novels seek to secure official approval, distorts a work in which the primacy of the political has asserted itself so vigorously that it has left its external justification lagging behind. Admittedly, only someone who understands nothing of the conditions affecting Russian literature could make such a fuss about such signs of insecurity. Many efforts will be needed before new forms bring a new self-assurance. Together with Boris Pilnyak's *The Naked Year* and Konstantin Fedin's *Cities and Years* (a German edition is now being prepared by Malik Verlag), Gladkov's *Cement* is one of the crucial works of modern Russian literature.[3] For anyone who is following its development, particularly if he is able to do so only in German translation, a knowledge of it is utterly indispensable.

Published in *Die literarische Welt*, June 1927. *Gesammelte Schriften*, III, 61–63. Translated by Rodney Livingstone.

Notes

1. Fyodor Vasilyevich Gladkov (1883–1958) was a Russian writer best known for *Tsement* (1925), the first postrevolutionary novel to dramatize Soviet industrial development.
2. Philanthropism was a pedagogical reform movement of the late eighteenth century which derived many of its ideas from Rousseau. Its main theorist was Johann Bernhard Basedow (1723–1790), whose school—the Philanthropin, in Dessau—became the model for a number of similar institutions throughout Germany, Switzerland, and Russia.
3. Boris Andreyevich Pilnyak (pseudonym of B. A. Vogau; 1894–1938/41?), a prose writer who depicted the revolution as a struggle between elemental and rational forces, was one of the first victims of the government purges in 1937. Konstantin Aleksandrovich Fedin (1892–1977) was a Soviet writer best known for a series of early novels that examine the situation of the intellectual in Soviet Russia. *Goroda I gody* (Cities and Years), published in 1924, details the reactions of the intelligentsia to the Revolution.

Journalism

Alongside all the solemnity that frames Lindbergh's flight across the Atlantic, we may allow ourselves the arabesque of a joke—the amusing pendant to the regrettable frivolity with which the Paris evening papers prematurely announced the triumph of Nungesser and Coli.[1] The same papers are now exposed for the second time. They owe this to an idea conceived by a student at the Ecole Normale—an idea that Karl Kraus might envy. As is well known, this Ecole Normale is the celebrated French state school that every year admits only an elite group of applicants, after the stiffest entrance examinations. On the afternoon of the first day Charles Lindbergh spent in Paris, someone telephoned all the newspaper editors with the news that the Ecole Normale had resolved to declare the aviator "a former student." And all the papers printed the announcement. Among the medieval Scholastics, there was a school that described God's omnipotence by saying: He could alter even the past, unmake what had really happened, and make real what had never happened. As we can see, in the case of enlightened newspaper editors, God is not needed for this task; a bureaucrat is all that is required.

Published in *Die literarische Welt,* June 1927. *Gesammelte Schriften,* IV, 454. Translated by Rodney Livingstone.

Notes

1. François Coli (1881–1927) and Charles Nungesser (1892–1927) were French aviators whose plane, L'Oiseau Blanc, disappeared over the North Atlantic during their attempt to fly nonstop from New York to Paris.

Gottfried Keller

In Honor of a Critical Edition of His Works[1]

> We may give lovers of the so-called "good things of life" the assurance that here
> they are truly in the presence of one.
> —Gottfried Keller on Heinrich Leuthold's poetry

The story is told of Haydn that on one occasion he found himself unable
to finish a symphony. In order to make further progress, he imagined a story:
A businessman in financial difficulties is striving in vain to keep his head
above water; he goes bankrupt—Andante; he resolves—Allegro ma non
troppo—to emigrate to America; once there—Scherzo—things take a turn
for the better; and—Finale—he returns home in triumph to his family and
friends. This, roughly, is the prehistory and opening of *Martin Salander*.[2]
And it would be nice to discover a formula with which to sum up the
indescribable sweetness of Keller's prose style, with its rich harmonies, by
inventing a story to complement this one and explain how he was inspired
by melodies when writing his works. But since we have no such story, we
must resort to cruder instruments. This is not the place to explain the
unmistakable fact that some ten years ago the affection of the Germans at
long last turned toward Stifter.[3] No sound from Keller's panpipes has ever
penetrated the stillness of Stifter's winter and summer landscapes. But the
Germans had just—after the end of the war—forsworn the political dances
whose rhythm can be heard quite faintly in Keller's works, and instead
sought out the noble Stifter landscape, more as a therapeutic clinic than as
a new home.

However that may be, the old but novel truth that would include Keller
among the three or four greatest prose writers in the German language has
a tough time of it. It is too old to interest people, and too new to command

their support. In this respect their situation is like that of the entire nine-teenth century, in whose "summery midst" Seldwyla—a *civitas dei helvetica*—has erected its towers.[4] For valid insight into Keller's work, we would need to arrive eventually at a revaluation of the nineteenth century as a whole. For only this could clear up the embarrassments of the literary historians. Who can have failed to observe the radically different assess-ments of this century in the bourgeois and the materialist literature? And who would not be certain that Keller's work should be reserved for a viewpoint that can claim as its own legacy the historical soil on which it has been built? Bourgeois literary history can hardly make this claim for Keller's atheism and materialism. Or rather can do so no longer. For it must be admitted that his atheism—something he acquired from Feuerbach[5] in his Heidelberg years—was not subversive. On the contrary, it fitted in with the attitudes of a strong, victorious bourgeoisie, although not a bourgeoisie on its way to imperialism. The founding of the Reich signals an ideological rupture in the history of the German bourgeoisie. Materialism disappears, in both its philistine and poetic versions. The upper strata of Swiss society were probably the last to abandon the features of a preimperialist bourgeoi-sie. (And they retain them even today. They lack, for example, the oppor-tunistic savoir vivre that has enabled the imperialist states to grant de jure recognition to the Soviet Union.) Moreover, the Swiss character may well possess more love of country and less of the nationalistic spirit than any other. Toward the end of Keller's life, the clarion call of Nietzsche's warnings about the spirit of the new Reich issued from Basel. And Keller, who had found himself forced in his Munich period to earn more of his livelihood from work with his hands than he would have liked, represents a class that had not yet completely cut its links to craft methods of production. It is astonishing to see the perseverance with which the Zurich patriciate strove, over a period of years and at a cost of many sacrifices, to turn this man into a respected fellow-citizen and ultimately into one of the leading officials—clerk of the canton. For years, there was something like a joint stock company for the education and promotion of Gottfried Keller; and follow-ing his unproductive early career, its capital had to be renewed time and again, until he finally paid back his sponsors with interest and compound interest. When he was at long last and very suddenly appointed cantonal clerk, this news item, which no one had foreseen, was commented on exhaustively in the city press. On September 20, 1861, the *Zürchersche Freitagszeitung* wrote: "It is generally known that until recently Mr. Keller had not familiarized himself with politics in general, and even less with the details of administrative questions . . . More recently, however, he seems to have felt the need to write in various papers and to criticize and deride political developments in the Canton of Zurich, albeit with more wit and eloquence than expert knowledge acquired from serious study." This exalted bureaucratic post suited a character that was burdened by fundamental inhibitions and passionate reservations. Pedagogic activity was as dear to his heart as to the hearts of the majority of the great writers of his nation, and the opportunity to engage in it indirectly but on a grander scale fitted in with his nature. In his public persona he could not be a teacher, but only a legislator. (Keller was involved in writing the new constitution of the Canton of Zurich.) It is reported that the office was safe in his hands. The effect of his duties on himself was to concentrate his efforts and thus shield him entirely from the idealist movement sweeping the Reich. In this respect it allied itself to his materialism. It is well known that Keller defended the principles of materialism—in particular, those insisting on the utter mortality of man—not as a self-righteous rationalist but as a passionate hedonist who was unwilling to permit his rendezvous with this life to be diminished by any afterlife. His work is the breakwater from which the tide of bourgeois ideas once more retreats, revealing the treasures of its own and every past, before gathering up and unleashing the idealistic floodwaters that will devastate Europe. For we have to remind ourselves how close Keller already stands to a doomed, sterile generation—and how only a fine linguistic line, a mere nothing, an obstinate spinning-out of his stories in a process obscure even to him, separates them from the decadent works of Heyse or Auerbach and makes them stand out as enigmatically perfect in comparison.[6] That Thumann, Vautier, and others of the same kind should have been commissioned to illustrate *Romeo und Julia auf dem Dorfe* [A Village Romeo and Juliet] tells us everything.[7] Keller's strict worldliness, however, did not turn him into a freethinker. His radicalism preserved him from that. The most astounding evidence of this is documented in his debates with Gotthelf.[8] Anyone to whom it means little that in a review of Gotthelf's writings Keller takes a book prize as his starting point should note his remarks at another point: "Nowadays everything is political—everything from the leather on our shoes to the tile on the rooftop. The very smoke that rises from the chimney is political, and it remains suspended in incriminating clouds above huts and palaces alike, and drifts hither and thither above towns and villages." He focuses his comments on Gotthelf's worldly-wise, uplifting manner and utters the astounding words: "The people, the peasant above all, know only black and white, night and day, and care nothing for any tear-filled, emotional twilight, where no one knows who is the cook and who the waiter. If the old natural religion no longer satisfies someone, he turns without more ado to its direct opposite, for he wishes above all to remain a human being and not turn into a bird or amphibian."

Keller's liberalism—which is as remote from the modern variety as is every thought-out attitude—had the most exacting standards of what was imperative and what reprehensible. And it sounds monstrous to say that on the whole it was that of bourgeois constitutionality. But you need only look at

it closely. In Goethe's *Wahlverwandtschaften* [Elective Affinities], an anni-
hilating fate proceeds from a marriage bond shaken to its roots. Likewise,
in Keller's immortal novella *Romeo und Julia auf dem Dorfe,* the catastrophe flows from the violation of the rights of ownership to a field. In his old
age, in the story of *Martin Salander,* Keller maintained the most stringent
links between bourgeois constitutional forms of existence and those of the
ethical human order. This would presumably secure him his place—let us
say, between Dahn and Marlitt;[9] a place that even today God knows how
many Germans are willing to grant him at the center of their educated
hearts. So far so good. But this is precisely the point at which we cross the
threshold into that "questionable" system of grottoes and caverns that by
imperceptible stages tends—the more deeply it enters into Keller himself—to
constrain and ultimately to repress the rhythmic babble of bourgeois voices
and opinions in favor of the cosmic rhythms it captures within the bowels
of the earth. If we seek a name for this miracle of grottoes and caves, it can
be none other than "humor." Keller's gentle and melodious laughter is as
much at home in these subterranean vaults as Homer's is in the heavenly
ones. But it has repeatedly been found that to call a writer a humorist is to
block any access to him. And Keller's humor is not a superficial gilded
polish, but the unpredictable ground plan of his half-melancholic, half-
choleric nature. This is expressed in the elaborate arabesques of his vocabulary. And if he shows his respect for bourgeois rules and regulations, he has
learned it in the arbitrary world of internal experience; shame, Keller's most
passionate emotion, lies at the root of both. In its own way, humor is itself
a kind of judicial system. It is the universe of enforcement without verdict,
a universe in which both verdict and pardon express themselves through
laughter. This is the great reservation that stands at the source of Keller's
silence and utterance. He thought little of speech, verdict, and condemna-
tion—to say nothing of moral judgment, as we can see from the concluding
words of his love story.[10] In its honor, he erected Seldwyla on the southern
slope of the hills and forests on whose northern slope the town of Ruechenstein could be found. Ruechenstein's inhabitants liked to have "an agreeable,
windless day . . . for their executions, burnings at the stake, and drown-
ings"; thus, "there was always something happening on really fine summer
days." He was in no doubt that "if need arises, an entire town of unjust or
frivolous people can survive the vicissitudes of time," but that "three righteous men are incapable of living under the same roof without getting in
each other's hair." The sweet and bracing skepticism that ripens with a
concentrated gaze and that, like a powerful aroma of people and things,
takes possession of the sympathetic observer has never entered into any
prose as it has Keller's. It is inseparable from the vision of happiness that
animates it. In it—and this is the secret skill of the narrative writer, who

alone is able to communicate happiness—the most minuscule cell of the world weighs as much as the rest of reality. The hand that came down with such a resounding thud in the saloon never slipped up in weighing the most delicate and fragile things. The task of apportioning the right amounts both in sound and substance was one assigned to the officialese that makes its presence felt from time to time in Keller's prose. A spoonful of soup in the hand of an honest man is more valuable, at the crucial moment, than grace before meals and talk of salvation in the mouth of a crook. "In every situation in life where there was a soup, it was Martin Salander's custom to set to and enjoy it without delay, as soon as it was put in his plate."

Nothing illustrates more convincingly the thoroughly unromantic nature of his works than the unsentimental, epic settings of his stories. Conrad Ferdinand Meyer[11] succeeds in conveying the flavor of this when he writes to Keller in July 1889, for his seventieth birthday, with almost biblical phrasing: "Since you love the earth, the earth will refuse to part with you for as long as it can." Keller's hedonistic atheism does not allow him to festoon "nature with the tendrils of Christian faith," as Gotthelf did. "The nature that supplies him with the most fruit, and disturbs and worries him least, is the most beautiful of all." What Hehn says of the old Latinist holds good for Keller. Sunday sermons and the interpretation of nature are not his cup of tea. Only as a process does the landscape with its natural forces intervene in the economy of human existence. This confers on the narrative events something of the flavor of Antiquity. In the early Renaissance, painters and poets frequently imagined that they were portraying Antiquity when they were only depicting their own age. For Keller, almost the reverse is true. He thought he was giving us his own age, while in it he gave us Antiquity. But he treats the experiences of humanity—and antiquity is a human experience—just as he treats the individual. Its formal law is a law of shrinkage; its laconic manner is not that of ingenuity but that of the wizened dryness of old fruit, old human faces. The soothsaying, orphic head has contracted into the hollow doll's head from which the buzzing of trapped flies can be heard—as we see in one of Keller's novellas.[12] Keller's writings are filled to the brim with this kind of authentic and shriveled Antiquity. His earth has become compressed into a "Homeric Switzerland"; it is the landscape from which his similes are drawn. "She realized that she no longer had a church now, and in her woman's mind, thanks to the power of habit, she felt like a bee that had strayed from the hive and flown out over the endless ocean waves in a cold autumn night." In Keller's homesickness for his native Switzerland you can hear the echo of his yearning for distant ages. For a good half of his life Switzerland was a distant memory for him, like Ithaca for Odysseus. And when he did return home, the Alps, which he had never explored, remained beautiful, remote images. Keller the writer liked the *Odyssey* above all other books, while the would-be painter found again and again that his studies of nature were blocked by a fantastic paraphrase of his native landscape.

The spirit in which Keller presides over this space of nineteenth-century Antiquity is palpable in his language. Keller's deliberate whittling away at the form of the language is indeed inhibited; he was quite timid in reading his own works. We can see from the textual apparatus of the *Complete Works* how for the most part it was the desire for decorum, correctness, that led him to make changes, and only rarely the wish for greater imaginative precision. It is all the more important that we now have access to what he crossed out. Nevertheless, even without this assistance his vocabulary and usage everywhere point to a Baroque strand in his homey fictional universe. The unique character of his prose is something he owes, as no other writer has since Grimmelshausen,[13] to the fact that he knows so much about the margins of the language, and that he can use both the earthiest dialect expression and the most recent foreign loanword with the greatest facility. The thesaurus of dialect is a set of token coins that circulate in the forms in which they have been minted over the centuries. And whenever the writer requires a particularly heartfelt, joyous expression, he instinctively turns to this linguistic legacy. Keller is as generous in his use of these as his sister was miserly with the metallic treasure—that same Regula of whom he said that "as a spinster, she had found herself in the less fortunate half of the nation." By way of contrast, words of foreign origin in his works are like bills of exchange, a precarious document from far away that needs to be handled with vigilant caution. He tends to use them by preference in letters. From these letters we can see beyond the shadow of a doubt that the most important and beautiful statements occur to him, even more than to other writers, in the course of writing. It is for this reason that he demanded less of himself than he might have in terms of quality, while in terms of quantity he expected more. This is why he so often yielded to the "majesty of indolence." He did not believe that there was much to be said, but his hand possessed a need to communicate that his mouth knew nothing of. "It is freezing today; the little garden beneath the window is trembling with the cold; 762 rosebuds are on the point of creeping back into the branches." Such passages with their small sediment of nonsense (something which Goethe once declared obligatory for verse) are the most tangible proof of the wholly unpredictable nature of his writing, which informed the publishing history of his work.

What fills Keller's books is the sensuous pleasure not of gazing but of describing. Describing is sensuous pleasure because the object returns the gaze of the observer, and every good description captures the pleasure with which two gazes seek each other out and find one another. It is in Keller's prose that the interpenetration of the narrative and the poetic—the essential contribution of the post-Romantic age in Germany—has been most consummately achieved. In almost all the products of the Romantic school, these two elements appear separately. On the one side stand works like E. T. A. Hoffmann's *Serapionsbrüder;* on the other, novels like Clemens Brentano's *Godwi.*[14] For Keller, these two impulses are in equilibrium. This is why the most mundane activities of his characters possess the rounded, canonical, sensuous reality that they must have had for a Roman. According to Walter Calé, one of the very few critics who have spoken of Keller in distinctive tones: "A further characteristic along these lines is the fact that it is often impossible to describe the 'idea' in his stories. To have an idea would mean limiting oneself to a single set of symbolic meanings developed in a particular direction. But as a true imitator of nature, Keller reproduces it as it is, *infinita infinitis modis:* with countless meanings that spring up almost disturbingly at every point and that cannot be compressed into a single word, so that for this very reason they appear able to express everything and every deep truth." To reflect reality—this, of course, can never prove in theory to be the content of art. But this does not mean that it cannot be a valid description of the aspirations of great writers. Indeed, this mirroring of reality may be described as the special province of the prose writer. The unfolding of nature's plan in its fullest extent is as fundamental a creative principle as the dramatist's desire to provide a cross-section of the structure of action, and the lyric poet's attempts to achieve an infinite concentration in his verse. The world of Keller's writings is a mirror world—even down to the fact that something in it is back to front, that left and right are reversed. While the active and weighty elements of life are seemingly unaffected and are present in their true proportions, the male imperceptibly changes into the female and vice versa. Even during Keller's own lifetime, there were readers who perceived in the pale reflexes of his humor an illusory world that seemed to them uncanny. Theodor Storm wrote to him concerning the end of "Die arme Baronin" [The Poor Baroness],[15] "How the devil, Master Gottfried, can such a sensitive and tender poet portray such a callous action—all right, just let me finish—as something delightful? How can you give us a man who presents his beloved with her former husband and brothers as clowns who have come down in the world so terribly, and how can he do this to increase her pleasure at her wedding feast?"

There is an uncertain flicker in the conciliatory light that is meant to be cast on a life gone awry in "Der Landvogt von Greifensee" [The Governor of Greifensee], something demented about the old man's laugh.[16] Only as a lyric poet was it given to Keller to purify this faint, unsteady flame into a few poems—albeit poems of such perfection!

Slowly, shimmeringly fell the rain
into which the evening sun shone down.
Beneath, the wanderer strode on narrow paths
with darkness in his soul.

In such an evening sun stand the distant images that the poet, conscious of the approach of death, invokes with his mention of the scythe. His smiling face is furrowed with the strain of renunciation, comparable only to that in the Houri poems of Goethe's *Westöstlicher Divan:*[17]

Let me not be punished, guilty though I am,
for the loveliest of poetic sins:
that of inventing dear images of women
such as are not found on the bitter earth!

Among his characters we must include Judith, the most deeply desired woman, the same woman who he said was "a fantasy image, not clouded by any reality." Nor is it irrelevant that of the few women Keller loved, one ended in madness and another committed suicide. Last, those two lines in the Swiss national anthem that characterize Keller's vision as nothing else does—the rose on this shore, the rose that is Switzerland, which because the pedant cannot pluck it is anything but a sterile piece of flowery rhetoric: "Loveliest rose, although all others faded / you still smell sweetly on my barren shore." The "quiet underlying sadness" to which he confesses is the bottom of the well in which his *humor* collects again and again. To express it in graphological terms, the curious hollows and oval forms of this script are—notwithstanding all psychoanalytic investigations—in their concave aspect, the image of the "miserable den" that constituted his inner being, and, in their convex aspect, the visible equivalent of his cranky idiosyncrasies. Keller refused to approve the portrait of him drawn by Stauffer-Bern. But the weary Keller whom this artist captured in an etching at an unguarded moment was the true one: the sonorous, echoing interior of the exhausted man was his. "Often, when I lie awake in bed at night," Keller said on his deathbed to Adolf Frey,[18] "I feel as if I were already buried inside a huge vault, and above me I hear a voice constantly echoing, 'I am guilty, I endure.'" But when we encounter such sentiments in a few isolated passages in his writings, it is, significantly, always in the shape of a woman. He sees himself in the figure of a nixie[19] vainly beating against the icy surface of the water on a winter's night. He recognizes himself "in sadness" as a Danaid:

And as the weary Danaid
let fall her sieve and gazed around her curiously,
so do I gaze after you perplexed,
concerned to see how you adjust and accept.

But even in jest, which sometimes comes quite close to sadness, such utterances come easily to him. "I could readily see myself," he observes in a Berlin letter, "presiding with dignity over a respectable milliner's shop, thanks to the detailed studies I have been making, between the acts, of bonnets and ruffs of every kind." And if anyone were to conclude from such statements that Keller's gloomy composure is based on the profound equilibrium that the masculine and feminine sides of his being have reached, he would have put his finger on Keller's facial appearance, too. The hermaphrodite is not the only androgynous type recognized by Antiquity. Its pleasing forms are of late origin and owe more to Roman and Alexandrian fancy than to the Greeks. And even if it is not true that Antiquity was led by physiognomic speculation to posit a mature androgynous type, or that the Aphroditos—in other words, the bearded Aphrodite—is as real a cultic image as was the custom of Argive women to adorn themselves with a false beard on their wedding night, nevertheless the idea of such faces brings us closer than anything else to the face of this poet.

The inner world into which the observer—the Swiss citizen and politician—poured reality on rivers of good wine was no sunlit hermit's cell, but a magic space circumscribed by two slow-moving rivers of life from which visions constantly arose. Keller's *Traumbuch* [Dream Book] is an anthology of such visions. In his writings, they press up against and intertwine with one another as in coats of arms. His style of writing has something heraldic about it. He often puts the words together with a baroque defiance, just as a coat of arms joins up halves of things. In a letter written in his old age, expressing his thanks for an embroidered cushion, he says: "I cannot . . . really answer for the trouble your skillful fingers have taken to make such a beautiful setting for these two initials, particularly in the light of the fact that they will not hold together for all that much longer." The symbols of the bourgeois state laboriously gather together for one last time in his works, in this heraldic book of the cantons. As a young man he had once written:

Farewell myth, Nibelungs, Bible!
The ancient dreams have been interpreted enough,
The ancient dragon has been flayed enough . . .
Paint now a picture book of freedom!

A picture book is what his writings became. They appeared at a time when people began to forget the language they spoke, and instead the daughters of Switzerland, in whom his gaze discerned both Helen of Troy and Lucretia, began to learn the language of bookkeeping from that same America which he had so often conjured up in his novels.

Both the organization and the format of the already published volumes of the edition are remarkable. The critical apparatus includes the earlier versions of his texts, and has broken them down into certain stylistic categories. It is hard to say whether this procedure, which is rather bold from the traditional philological viewpoint, will establish itself as the norm. But we can say with some assurance that the appendix is among the few things of this sort that can be studied with pleasure. It restricts itself to essentials in a way that goes well with the austere appearance of the edition, which neither makes any concessions to snobbery nor attempts to ingratiate itself with the public. Of how many German editions of complete works can this be said? The problem of typeface and typesetting that is always especially difficult with Keller seems to me to have been satisfactorily resolved. The binding testifies to the same confident taste that can be seen in the typography.

Published in *Die literarische Welt,* August 1927. *Gesammelte Schriften,* II, 283–295. Translated by Rodney Livingstone.

Notes

1. *Gottfried Kellers Sämtliche Werke,* edited by Jonas Fränkel on the basis of Keller's unpublished papers. The edition is authorized by the administrators of the Gottfried Keller Estate, and has been published by Eugen Rentsch Verlag, Erlenbach-Zurich and Munich. [Benjamin's note]
2. Gottfried Keller (1819–1890) was one of the great German-language prose stylists of the nineteenth century. After his early attempts to establish himself as a painter in Munich were frustrated, he returned to Zurich and inaugurated a career in literature. *Der grüne Heinrich* (Green Henry; 1854–1855, revised version 1879–1880) and the story collection *Die Leute von Seldwyla* (The People of Seldwyla; first volume 1856, second volume 1874) are his best-known works. *Martin Salander* (1886) is his second, and last, novel.
3. Adalbert Stifter (1805–1868) was an Austrian writer whose short stories and novels are characterized by an unusually graceful style and a reverence for natural process.
4. Seldwyla is the imaginary Swiss town that provides the setting for many of Keller's stories. Ruechenstein is a rival town. *Civitas dei helvetica* means "Swiss city of God."
5. Ludwig Andreas Feuerbach (1804–1872) was a German philosopher and moralist who studied theology at Heidelberg and, later, philosophy with Hegel in Berlin. His most important work, *Das Wesen des Christenthums* (The Essence of Christianity; 1841), defined religion as nothing more than the consciousness of infinity. Feuerbach's work exerted an important influence on Karl Marx.
6. Paul Johann Ludwig von Heyse (1830–1914), a traditionalist German writer, received the Nobel Prize for literature in 1910. Berthold Auerbach (1812–1882) was a German novelist noted chiefly for his tales of village life.

7. Friedrich Paul Thumann (1834–1908), a German illustrator and painter, was celebrated for his illustrations of children's books and classics of German literature. Louis Benjamin Vautier (1829–1898) was a Swiss painter and illustrator known for his nature and peasant scenes.

8. Jeremias Gotthelf (pseudonym of Albert Bitzius; 1797–1854) was a Swiss novelist and short-story writer whose works, such as "The Black Spider," extol the traditional values associated with church and home life.

9. Felix Dahn (1834–1912) was a popular, nationalistic novelist. His best-known work, *Ein Kampf um Rom* (The Struggle for Rome), appeared between 1876 and 1878. Eugenie Marlitt (1825–1877) was known for her popular love stories and family novels.

10. Keller's *Romeo und Julia auf dem Dorfe* ends with an ironic commentary, in the form of a newspaper report, on the death of the lovers: "This event is presumably linked to the ship from that region which landed in the town, its cargo of hay intact but its crew vanished. It is believed that the young couple stole the ship in order to celebrate their desperate and godforsaken wedding on it—a further sign of the growing immorality and decadence of the passions."

11. Conrad Ferdinand Meyer (1825–1898) was a leading Swiss writer noted for his historical fiction and poetry.

12. This is a reference to the doll that Sali and Vrenchen play with as children in *Romeo und Julia auf dem Dorfe*.

13. Hans Jacob Christoph von Grimmelshausen (1621/22–1676) was the author of the most important novel of the German Baroque, *Der abenteuerliche Simplicissimus* (The Adventurous Simplicissimus), a satirical and partially autobiographical view of the Thirty Years' War.

14. *Die Serapionsbrüder* (The Serapion Brothers; 1819/20), by Ernst Theodor Amadeus Hoffmann (1776–1822), is a collection of stories with a frame narrative. A leading German Romantic, Hoffmann combined, in his work, wild flights of imagination with penetrating examinations of psychology and character. *Godwi* (1801), by Clemens Brentano (1778–1842), is a Romantic *Bildungsroman* with an eccentric structure and coruscating irony. Brentano, an exceptionally gifted writer, produced influential poetry, prose, and dramas.

15. "Die arme Baronin" is one of the stories in *Das Sinngedicht* (1881–1882), a novella by Keller with a cyclical, thirteen-chapter structure.

16. "Der Landvogt von Greifensee" is part of Keller's collection *Zürcher Novellen* (Zurich Novellas).

17. Goethe's *West-Easterly Divan* (1819) is a verse cycle inspired by the Persian poet Hafiz (1320–1389). Written when Goethe was almost seventy, it contains some of his most memorable love poems.

18. Adolf Frey (1855–1920) was a Swiss novelist and poet whose best-known works are his literary biographies of Swiss writers.

19. A water sprite of Germanic folklore.

Diary of My Journey to the Loire

August 12, 1927. I shall confine myself to notes. The familiar torment of loneliness that afflicts me particularly when traveling has for the first time assumed the features of growing old. L. has not come with me.[1] The likelihood that this is because of a misunderstanding is no greater than 10 percent. The likelihood that I have been deceived in the ordinary way is about 90 percent. Admittedly, I myself intentionally created this possibility. That now turns out to be a mistake. If she had come, that would have been the basis for enjoying this trip.

I can be certain that I shall now, alone, find all the places which would have been sheer delight with her. Here I am, for example, sitting in a very quiet and very good restaurant, the Hôtel St. Cathérine in Orléans. The table is precisely the right width for sitting opposite someone. The electric lights are so faint that I can barely see to write.

Until midday I was uncertain whether I should travel on my own. If Scholem hadn't been arriving today, I probably would not have done so. But I took flight. At the time, I simply did not think I could bear his sometimes ostentatious self-assurance.

This afternoon I saw Orléans Cathedral: modern colored-glass windows that mean nothing. Yet above, in the choir, plain glass. The rose window above the entrance, too, is plain: a polar sun. Behind the plain glass of the aisle windows the buttresses can be seen in the half-light, like a shoreline in banks of mist. In the transept the rose windows are in harsh, barbaric yellows and reds.—The exterior is incredibly beautiful. Outside, the chancel has a stone foundation from which the shafts and pilasters rise up. It is as if they are rooted in the stone walls.

While I was walking through the cathedral, the organist was practicing.

Everything, especially every trivial thing on this journey, makes me want to burst into tears. For example, the fact that on this trip I do not speak French. (At all!) I weep when I think about the rue de Reuilly, a magic name for me, one that I can no longer use.

August 13. At the station in Orléans, in the train to Blois. I slept better than I had expected. From the hotel I went back to the cathedral again. This time I approached it from the Hôtel de Ville, which is faced by some older houses rising up on a beautiful slope. In the cathedral I heard the story of the red hat that hangs from the ceiling. It belonged to a cardinal (probably Cardinal Touchet, who is seated at the feet of the statue of Joan of Arc) and will hang there until it falls of its own accord.—From a distance, from the boulevard St. Vincent, the buttresses look like fragments of Christ's crown of thorns. Never have I seen such a thorny cathedral as this one, with its icy cold rose window.

While I was walking through the town and visiting all the churches listed in the guidebook, it occurred to me that it is quite possible L. really had gone away; in other words, that she may well have gone on a trip with him. Considered perhaps calling at her apartment again shortly before leaving for Berlin, or at the hotel in the rue de la Chapelle, and observing her if possible.

Orléans is a center for fishing. A very alluring shop with all sorts of equipment for anglers, "Le Pêcheur Moderne," on the rue de Bourgogne.

In Blois. Here you have to sit on the terrace behind the Cathédrale St. Louis if you want to see the famous French *clarté,* the French *limpidité,* total harmony of landscape, architecture, and the art of gardening. Thank God the sky is heavily overcast; the sun has disappeared. I still feel bitterness within me, churned-up emotions that refuse to settle down. It was an infallible instinct that bid me make precisely this journey with L., a Parisian. The absent one retreats from me for the second time—like a landscape, at every moment drawing farther away. I place landscapes, courtyards, around her as frames, all of which remain empty. And the whole situation is made worse by my vanity's whispered insistence that all this happened by accident, not design. Even so, when I return to Paris, I will not let my efforts to find her again go too far. In Paris I can survive without her, and indeed cannot really make use of her, as matters stand. It was during the guided tour through the castle of Blois that I suffered most. This was where her astonishment would have made everything bearable, if not agreeable. As it was, as I gazed around the empty rooms, whose walls are painted in imitation of the Gobelins tapestries or Cordoba leather that used to hang there, I could see that I was almost the only person who was alone. I am not far from tears. What was the point of it all—not just of all these preparations, but of having made this huge change in my life—if I cannot contrive to carry out the simplest little planned journey that any traveling salesman could manage? Am I never again to travel anywhere with a woman I desire?

August 15. To my surprise, I see that comfort is having an effect on my gloomy mood. Since I . . .

The same day, evening. In short, I have an excellent, luxurious room that will have to make up for L.'s absence as far as possible. I shall presumably not see her again, and I shall make only modest attempts to do so. But I have caught myself trying to conjure up her face, specifically to recall that expression (that coldness, that refusal to make contact with me) which is no doubt the source of my present situation. I made this effort this afternoon beneath the trees in front of the Café Universel, behind the big statue of Balzac which shows the master in his dressing gown.

Only the sight of the buildings really gives me the feeling of having arrived here in Tours, or wherever it may be, and nowhere else. I stood behind the chancel of St. Gatien. My gaze turned to the dead, gray, nondescript exterior view of the famous stained-glass windows. A moment before, I had been sitting on a bench, looking at the façade; now I was looking at the back of the church, leaning against a wall. It gave me a shock. Compared to this peace, this immediate sense of presence that comes with gazing at great works of architecture, all our ordinary activity is like traveling on a train that suddenly stops with a jerk. Here we are: nothing will take us any further. Tours has the most cheerful, most childlike rose windows I have ever seen, especially the one over the main portal. After that I took a walk behind the cathedral, through little streets with low squat buildings. But with what names! Rue Racine, rue Montaigne. And this square is the place St. Grégoire de Tours. A woman was delivering newspapers, and she blew a horn—a last vestige of the medieval town crier, probably. The houses have two stories, but much lower still are the courtyard walls with the doors in them.

In the cathedral I suddenly cheered up. It occurred to me that a month previously I had been in Chartres—it was not yet a month since I had met L.—and she had been marvelously planted (this Parisian rose) between these two cathedrals. And that was as it should be. She had her place.

August 16. I went back to St. Gatien. The stained glass must have had this appearance of faded velvet cloth right from the start. Incidentally, this rose window is an unsurpassable symbol of the Church's way of thinking: from the outside, all slaty, scaly, almost leprous; from the inside, blossoming, intoxicating, and golden. When you walk over to the other side of the Loire, St. Gatien does not stand out, as it should, in Gothic splendor above many gables, but rises above the leaves of the trees on the Loire islands and the riverbank promenade.—Yesterday I saw two chimney stacks on a roof high above the town: a new paradise that Virgil shows with a dramatic gesture to a Dante who recoils with a shiver.—From the front the cathedral looks out onto the place du Quatorze Juillet, and from behind onto the place St. Grégoire de Tours. It looks as if it is resting its head on a cushion and has its feet in the water. Concerning street names: on the sign for the rue Auguste Comte, together with his dates, appears the word *Positiviste*. What must the good townsfolk think that means?—(Behind the cathedral: rue du Petit Cupidon.)

I would have had a photograph of L. made on this trip. Apart from that, I find I have been able to restore my equanimity by imagining that her failure to come was due to the influence of someone else. For my vanity, and the probabilities of the situation, do not allow me to consider the possibility that she deceived me from start to finish. And to contemplate the thought that we may have missed each other as a result of a misunderstanding would drive me mad.

Before coming to Tours I had never seen a town (other than Heidelberg) that allows the landscape to come so much into its own. There is scarcely more than a ribbon of gray along the banks of the Loire as they pass through the town. And the boulevard Grammont passes into the countryside as if through festively built-up, inhabited meadows. The great stone bridge is shallowly suspended above the river, like a hand stroking it. Everything is low, apart from a few lofty towers. It is a town *à la portée des enfants;* it gives me pleasure to reflect that the great Catholic children's-book publisher Mame is based in Tours.

Written August 1927; unpublished in Benjamin's lifetime. *Gesammelte Schriften,* VI, 409–413. Translated by Rodney Livingstone.

Notes

1. The identity of Benjamin's friend has not been established.

Review of Soupault's *Le coeur d'or*

Philippe Soupault, *Le coeur d'or* [The Heart of Gold] (Paris: Bernard Grasset, 1927), 260 pages.

For all its renown, Surrealism as a theory is now precisely three years old. As a practice it is significantly older. This ancient practice of complete relaxation, which is what it prescribes as the foundation of literature, constitutes the entire interest of the theory. One immediately understands why it could be formulated only under the influence of Freud, who made a late appearance in France but had an enduring effect. And indeed Surrealism made its entry into Paris on a *vague de rêves,*[1] an epidemic of dream-ridden sleep to which both the movement's leaders and their acolytes succumbed. Yet they overlooked the fact that it may be much harder for artists than for amateurs to follow the precepts of an art based on a relaxed psyche, a stock of ideas from the unconscious, and that the entire task of the "artist" is to dredge them to the surface. We realize that the dilettante sticks much closer to the stereotypes of writing or painting than the professional artist, because he is less able to grasp them or see through them. We realize that such a dilettante is necessarily unfree, because in certain matters freedom springs exclusively from knowledge and practice. It is the artist who possesses this freedom. But he is exposed to a threat of quite a different kind. The fortunate constellation and the evidence of imagination that are to be found at these deepest levels manifest themselves only intermittently. Any practice that tries to mold the mind to make it more flexible, more prompt, more adept in appropriating them runs the risk of falsifying the most important data: the time, place, and circumstances in which they become audible. This is not a technical necessity but a vital one—in other words, the most precise specification among all the incidentals in time and space that gives the amateurish products of children, dilettantes, or the insane an autonomy amid the banalities, a freshness amid horror, that is often absent from Surrealism, for all its efforts. And if the content of these dreams is very detailed, as would be the case with the depiction of a place, the narration of an experience, or the exploration of an idea (since in reality it ought to be all these things simultaneously), then the unwilled, relaxed process of recollection would have to be highly concentrated to capture the quality of dreams. If, on the other hand, we are dealing with conscious memories that the author transposes subsequently into the unconscious, then the dreary consequences will not be long in coming. In that case, events will unfold without clarity, without fantasy, monotonously and in a nondreamlike way. Regrettably, Soupault's latest book furnishes proof of this. Nothing is good about it—and this deserves emphasis—but the dust jacket. There we read, "'Coeur d'or—coeur solitaire' (proverbe de Montrouge)." The story deals with loneliness, which it presents in a long series of images. Interspersed among these, and framed by them, we see glimpses of the woman he loves. To read this book is agonizing; to live through it was even more agonizing; to write it was not hard at all. The man who endured the sufferings described in this book has, as author, comfortably slid down the slope that, as lover, he was forced to climb laboriously. And the reader comes away empty-handed. Paul Valéry recently found an apt formula for the perceived dangers of the new literary school. It alludes to the gambling booths in large fairgrounds and marketplaces that put up huge posters to attract the public. They say, "Chaque coup gagne"—in other words, "Every throw a winner." He claims that this is the basic principle of the new school. It is only a minor bon mot, but it is just enough to offset a feeble book.

Published in *Internationale Revue* (Amsterdam), 1927. *Gesammelte Schriften*, III, 72–74. Translated by Rodney Livingstone.

Notes

1. The allusion is to *Une vague de rêves* (Wave of Dreams; 1924), by the Surrealist writer Louis Aragon (pseudonym of Louis Andrieux; 1897–1982).

The Idea of a Mystery

To represent history as a trial in which man, as an advocate of dumb nature, brings charges against all Creation and cites the failure of the promised Messiah to appear. The court, however, decides to hear witnesses for the future.[1] Then appear the poet, who senses the future; the artist, who sees it; the musician, who hears it; and the philosopher, who knows it. Hence, their evidence conflicts, even though they all testify that the future is coming. The court does not dare to admit that it cannot make up its mind. For this reason new grievances keep being introduced, as do new witnesses. There is torture and martyrdom. The jury benches are filled with the living, who listen to the human prosecutor and the witnesses with equal distrust. The jury members pass their duties on to their heirs. At last, the fear grows in them that they might be driven from their places. At the end, the entire jury has fled; only the prosecutor and the witnesses remain.

Written ca. November 1927; unpublished in Benjamin's lifetime. *Gesammelte Schriften,* II, 1153–1154. Translated by Rodney Livingstone.

Notes

1. This short text accompanied a letter from Benjamin to Gershom Scholem of November 1927. Scholem suggests that it represents a first reaction to Kafka's novel *Der Prozeß* (The Trial).

Review of Hessel's *Heimliches Berlin*

Franz Hessel, *Heimliches Berlin* [Unknown Berlin], a novel (Berlin: Ernst Rowohlt Verlag, 1927), 183 pages.

The short flights of steps, the pillared porticoes, the friezes and architraves of the villas in the Tiergarten have been taken at their face value in this book.[1] The "old" West of Berlin has become the West of Antiquity—the source of the westerly winds that fill the sails of the boatmen whose vessels pass slowly up the Landwehr Canal, laden with the Apples of the Hesperides, and tie up at the Bridge of Hercules. This neighborhood distinguishes itself from Berlin's sea of houses as unmistakably as if the entrance to it were guarded by thresholds and gateways. Its author is an expert on thresholds in every sense of the word, except for the dubious thresholds of the experimental psychology he dislikes. But the thresholds that separate situations, hours, minutes, and words from each other are something he feels more sharply beneath the soles of his feet than anyone else.

And precisely because he responds to the city in this way, it would be a mistake to expect descriptions or mood paintings here. What is "unknown," secret, about this Berlin is no windy whispering, no tiresome flirting, but simply this strict classical image-being of a city, a street, a house, even a room that, as a *cella,* holds within itself the yardstick for the events in this book, just as it does for the figures in a dance.

Every architecture worthy of the name ensures that it is the spatial sense as a whole, and not just the casual gaze, that reaps the benefits of its greatest achievements. Thus, the narrow embankment between the Landwehr Canal and Tiergarten Street exerts its charm on people in a gentle, companionable manner—hermetically guiding them on their way. Engrossed in conversation, they stride from time to time across the stony embankment. And just as the author caused the Roman heart to beat and the Greek tongue to speak in the fourteen imagined characters of his *Sieben Dialoge*,[2] something comparable can be seen here, in these frail children of the world. They are not Greeks and Romans in modern costume, and even less are they our contemporaries in humanist carnival dress. Instead, this book is technically close to photomontage: housewives, artists, fashionable women, businessmen, scholars are all intercut contrastively with the shadowy outlines of Platonic and comic masks.

For this unknown Berlin is the stage of an Alexandrian *Singspiel*.[3] It borrows the unity of time and place from Greek drama: in twenty-four hours the love story experiences its crisis and resolution. From philosophy it has borrowed the great Greek Socratic morality that the author had previously treated in a verse play—a classical formulation of the story of the Matron of Ephesus.[4] From the Greek language it has taken its musical instrumentation. There is no writer living today who has a greater or more sympathetic understanding of the Greco-German tendency to create compound words. In his mouth, words become magnets that irresistibly attract other words. His prose is shot through with such magnetic threads. He knows that a beautiful woman can be a "Nordic blond," a cashier a "seated goddess," a hairdresser's widow "cake-beautiful," a dull prig a "do-no-harm," and a dwarf a "bound-to-be-little."

In another way, however, the novel is peopled by loving couples who are never on their own and always accompanied by friends; they are nothing but links in a well-soldered magnetic chain. And whether we are reminded of the story of Swan-Stick-On or the Pied Piper of Hamlin—in this instance the Pied Piper is called Clemens Kestner—it remains true that this procession of young Berliners, however unadmirable they may be individually, and however unenviable their fate, nevertheless draws the reader behind it, past the "river landscape with the curved footbridge, the forked chestnut branches, and the three weeping willows" that "have something of the Far East about them, as do some of the little Berlin lakes at certain moments."

Where does the narrator obtain his mysterious talent for investing the tiny territory described in his story with such a sense of temporal and spatial distance? In a generation of writers who have virtually all been affected by the phenomenon of Stefan George,[5] Hessel spent the years when others were busy spreading dogmas and wasting time on the already tottering edifice of education devoting himself to mythological studies, to Homer, and to the task of translation. Those who know how to read his books can sense how they conjure up classical Antiquity between the walls of aging big cities, and among the ruins of the past century. But even though he casts his net so widely, embracing Greece, Paris, and Italy in its sweep, the center of this activity always comes back to his room in the Tiergarten—a room which his friends rarely enter without sensing that they are in danger of being transformed into heroes.

Published in *Die literarische Welt,* December 1927. *Gesammelte Schriften,* III, 82–84. Translated by Rodney Livingstone.

Notes

1. Franz Hessel (1880–1941) was a writer, as well as a translator of Proust, Stendhal, and Balzac. He produced the most important works of his career between 1924 and 1933, when he worked for Rowohlt Verlag in Berlin. He emigrated to Paris in 1938. "Tiergarten" here refers to the neighborhood of Berlin centered on the Tiergarten park (Berlin's equivalent of New York's Central Park) and the zoo from which it takes its name.
2. Franz Hessel, *Sieben Dialoge* (Seven Dialogues), with seven etchings by Renée Sintenis (Berlin, 1924).
3. The *Singspiel* is a simple form of opera with songs and spoken dialogue. Both Goethe and Wieland wrote *Singspiele,* but Mozart's *Zauberflöte* remains the apogee of the form.
4. Franz Hessel, *Die Witwe von Ephesos* (The Widow of Ephesus), dramatic poem in two scenes (Berlin, 1925). Hessel based his play on one of the tales in Petronius' *Satyricon.*
5. Stefan George (1868–1933) was a German neo-Romantic poet and the editor of the influential *Blätter für die Kunst,* published from 1892 to 1919. His school, the "George circle," was held together by his authoritarian personality and self-consciously backward-looking aesthetics.

A State Monopoly on Pornography

Spain probably has the most beautiful newspaper kiosks in the world. Strolling along the streets of Barcelona, you find yourself flanked by these wind-ruffled, brightly colored structures—dancing masks, beneath which the youthful goddess of information performs her provocative belly dance. A few weeks ago the authorities removed the glittering headband from this mask. They prohibited the sale of the five or six explicit series that treat of love without ". . ." or "——," the universal Morse code used in literature to represent the language of love. As is well known, this emancipation from the Morse code in the description of sexual acts is labeled "pornography." However that may be, the pastel-colored Spanish magazines were indistinguishable from such books as our *Memoirs of a Milliner, Boudoir and Racetrack*, and *Her Older Girlfriend*. What was instructive about them was something else. The list of authors contained the names of respected writers, including even such prestigious names as that of Gómez de la Serna.[1] There is undoubtedly material enough for a commentary that would eagerly consume its object in the pure flame of moral indignation. Rather than trying something of that sort, let us dwell on the object for a few moments.

In one respect, pornographic books are like other books: they are all based on language and writing. If language did not contain elements in its vocabulary that are obscene in themselves, pornography would be robbed of its best instruments. Where do such words come from?

Language in the various phases of its historical development is a single great experiment that is conducted in as many laboratories as there are peoples. And everywhere we see the striving for instant, unambiguous communication through a liberating, suggestive mode of expression. (What the speakers of a language think it worthwhile to say depends on their opportunities for expression, what modes of discourse are generally available to them.) For this huge process of experimentation, great poetry provides what might be thought of as a formulary, while the demotic language supplies the materials. The experimental arrangements are in continual flux, and the entire corpus of knowledge has to be kept constantly under review. By-products of every kind are inevitable. They include all the idioms and fixed expressions, whether written or spoken, that stand outside normal usage: nicknames, company names, swear words, oaths, devotional expressions, and obscenities. These may be excessive, lacking in expression, sacred, a fermentation of cultic language, or else overexplicit, shameless, and depraved. The waste products of daily usage, these same elements acquire a crucial value in other contexts—in scientific contexts, above all—since there these astonishing linguistic splinters can be understood as fragments from the primeval granite of the linguistic massif. We know how precisely these extremes correspond to each other in their polar tension. And one of the most interesting subjects of study would be the role of scatological wit in the monastery language in the Middle Ages.

But, one might object, if the production of such words is so grounded in the nature of language that all words which lecherously indulge in the excesses of communicative energy already find themselves on the boundaries of the obscene, then it is all the more important to banish them from writing.

On the contrary. It is society's duty to put these natural—not to say profane—processes in the life of language into service as natural forces. Just as Niagara Falls feeds power stations, in the same way the downward torrent of language into smut and vulgarity should be used as a mighty source of energy to drive the dynamo of the creative act. What poets should actually live on is a question as shameful as it is ancient, and one that up to now has been answered only with embarrassed evasiveness. Whether they look after themselves or whether the state assumes that task, the result is the same: their starvation.

For this reason, we call for a state monopoly on pornography. We demand the socialization of this not inconsiderable source of power. The state should administer this monopoly and should ensure that this literary genre is the exclusive prerogative of an elite group of important authors. Instead of a sinecure, the writer should be given a license to supply the authorities with a specified percentage of the statistically calculated demand for pornographic works. It is in the interest of neither the public nor the state to depress the price of this commodity excessively. The writer should produce in order to supply a fixed, demonstrable need in return for cash payment, which is designed to protect him from the completely unforeseeable vagaries of the market that afflict his true writing. This enterprise will be much cleaner than a situation in which he serves—directly or indirectly, consciously or unconsciously—a party or other interest group. As an expert he will be superior to the amateur, and will help to counteract the intolerable dilettantishness that prevails in this field. Moreover, the more he does this kind of work, the less he will despise it. He is not a sewer worker, but a pipe layer in a comfortable new Babel.

Published in *Die literarische Welt*, December 1927. *Gesammelte Schriften*, IV, 456–458. Translated by Rodney Livingstone.

Notes

1. Ramón Gómez de la Serna (1891–1963) was a Spanish writer whose highly associative poetic fragments *(greguerias)* were widely read in Europe and Latin America.

Image Imperatives, 1928

Maidenhair fern *(Adiantum pedatum),* magnified eight times. Photo by Karl Blossfeldt. From Blossfeldt, *Urformen der Kunst: Photographische Pflanzenbilder,* 2nd ed. (Berlin: Verlag Ernst Wasmuth, 1929), plate 55. Copyright © 1999 Karl Blossfeldt Archiv, Ann and Jürgen Wilde / Artists Rights Society (ARS), New York.

Curriculum Vitae (III)

I was born in Berlin on July 15, 1892. My father was a businessman. I went to a classically oriented grammar school, interrupting my studies there for a two-year period to become a boarder at Haubinda School in Thuringia.

I entered university in the summer semester of 1912 to study philosophy. The first and third semesters, I studied in Freiburg im Breisgau; the second, fourth, and subsequent semesters, in Berlin. In 1916 I went to the University of Munich, and in the winter semester of 1917–1918 I moved to the University of Berne. I completed my studies there in June 1919 and was awarded my doctorate *summa cum laude.*

The title of my dissertation was "Der Begriff der Kunstkritik in der deutschen Romantik" [The Concept of Criticism in German Romanticism]. I majored in philosophy and also passed exams in my minor subjects: history of German literature, and psychology. In particular, I read and reread Plato and Kant, then the philosophy of Husserl and the Marburg school. Gradually, my interest came to focus on the philosophical content of imaginative literature and artistic form, and ultimately found expression in my dissertation.

This tendency also dominated my subsequent work, in which I strove to concentrate ever more narrowly on concrete detail, both for greater precision and as a result of the content of my literary investigations. The idea of casting light on a work by confining my attention purely to the work itself was one I attempted to carry out in my essay "Goethes Wahlverwandtschaften" [Goethe's Elective Affinities]. My next piece of work, *Ursprung des deutschen Trauerspiels* [Origin of the German Trauerspiel] was devoted to exploring the philosophical significance of a vanished and misunderstood form of art: allegory.

From the very beginning, my studies were marked by an intensive preoccupation with French literature. This led to a number of translations—Baudelaire, Proust—but above all to a recurrent interest in problems of translation associated with the philosophy of language. I attempted to engage these in an essay entitled "Die Aufgabe des Übersetzers" [The Task of the Translator]—the preface to my Baudelaire translations.

Just as Benedetto Croce opened the way to the individual concrete work of art by destroying the theory of artistic form, I have thus far directed my efforts at opening a path to the work of art by destroying the doctrine of the territorial character of art. What our approaches have in common is a programmatic attempt to bring about a process of integration in scholarship—one that will increasingly dismantle the rigid partitions between the disciplines that typified the concept of the sciences in the nineteenth century—and to promote this through an analysis of the work of art. Such an analysis would regard the work of art as an integral expression of the religious, metaphysical, political, and economic tendencies of its age, unconstrained in any way by territorial concepts. This task, one that I had already undertaken on a larger scale in *Ursprung des deutschen Trauerspiels,* was linked on the one hand to the methodological ideas of Alois Riegl, especially his doctrine of the *Kunstwollen,*[1] and on the other hand to the contemporary work done by Carl Schmitt, who in his analysis of political phenomena has made a similar attempt to integrate phenomena whose apparent territorial distinctness is an illusion.[2] Above all, however, any such approach seems to me to be a precondition for any effective physiognomic definition of those aspects of artworks that make them incomparable and unique. To that extent, I believe it is closer to an eidetic way of observing phenomena than to a historical one.

At the center of my plans for the coming years are two subjects that link up with my latest book, albeit in different ways. First, having attempted to lay bare the philosophical, moral, and theological content of allegory, I would now like to perform the same task for the fairy tale as an equally fundamental and originary repository of certain traditional themes—namely, as the disenchantment of the sinister powers embodied in the saga. The second subject for which I have been making preparatory studies for some time now is an account of classical French comedy; it will be a companion piece to my treatment of German Baroque drama. In addition, I have been planning a book on the three great metaphysical writers of our day: Franz Kafka, James Joyce, and Marcel Proust. Finally, I hope that I shall have the opportunity to expand upon the picture of Goethe that I drew in my work on *The Elective Affinities* with two further studies, one on *Pandora,* the other on "Die neue Melusine" [The New Melusine].[3]

Written in early 1928; unpublished in Benjamin's lifetime. *Gesammelte Schriften,* VI, 217–219. Translated by Rodney Livingstone.

Notes

1. Alois Riegl (1858–1905) was an influential Austrian art historian who argued that different formal and stylistic orderings of art gradually emerge as expressions of different historical epochs. Riegl defines the *Kunstwollen* as the manner in which a given culture at a given time wants to see its cultural objects; his assertion that each epoch's art is informed by its own, inherently legitimate *Kunstwollen* posed a significant challenge to reigning theories of art derived from the notion of a classical ideal.
2. Carl Schmitt (1888–1985) was a German legal scholar. His work is characterized by an emphasis on the necessity of authoritative decision in moments of constitutional crisis, a deep skepticism toward the liberal premises of the Weimar constitution, and an inherent anti-Semitism. After the Nazi assumption of power, Schmitt joined the party; certain of his ideas formed the legal-theoretical basis for the Nazi suspension of parliamentary law.
3. *Pandora* is a verse play that Goethe wrote in 1810. "Die neue Melusine" is a story embedded in his novel *Wilhelm Meisters Wanderjahre* (Wilhelm Meister's Wanderings).

André Gide and Germany

A Conversation with the Writer

A few weeks ago I asked one of France's leading critics, "Which of the great French writers seems to you to be most like us in his work and his general persona?" He replied, "André Gide." I won't deny that I had hoped for this answer, though I hadn't expected it. But let us begin by clearing up a possible misunderstanding. If Gide has a certain affinity with the German mind, both as a man and a thinker, this does not mean that as an artist he has made overtures to the Germans, or that he makes things easy for them. He does not make things easy either for them or for his own countrymen.

The Paris he comes from is not that of the countless novelists and the international marketplace for new comedies. His disposition and family bind him less to Paris than to the North, to Normandy and above all to Protestantism. You have to read a work like *La porte étroite* [Strait Is the Gate] to realize the love Gide feels for this landscape, and the extent to which the ascetic passion of his young heroine has internalized it.

There was a moralistic, Protestant strain in his work right from the outset; productive energy and critical energy have hardly ever been so closely intertwined in any writer as in him. Thirty years ago there was the protest of the youthful Gide against the primitive, sterile nationalism of Barrès; more recently, his latest novel, *Les Faux-monnayeurs* [The Counterfeiters], undertook to provide a creative corrective to the current novel form in the spirit of the Romantic philosophy of reflection. But whatever he did, he remained true to himself in one respect: his need to reject the given, whether he found it outside or inside himself.

If we have captured the essence of this author, whose significance is as much that of a moralist as that of a writer, we must add that there were two great men who pointed him in the direction of self-discovery: Oscar Wilde and Nietzsche. The European spirit in its Western form has perhaps never defined itself more clearly than in this triad—in contrast, that is, to its Eastern manifestation, with Tolstoy and Dostoevsky. But if later, in an account of his debt to German literature, Gide omits the name of Nietzsche, this may be explained by the fact that to talk about Nietzsche would imply talking about himself in an overly pointed and responsible way. For anyone who was unaware that Nietzsche's ideas meant more to him than the outline of a philosophical *Weltanschauung* would know very little about Gide. "Nietzsche," Gide remarked once in conversation, "created a royal road where I could only have beaten a narrow path. He did not 'influence' me; he helped me."

It is out of modesty if he says nothing of all this today. Modesty: this virtue has two faces. One is the ostensible, cramped, or false modesty of the small-minded person; the other is the heart-warming, tranquil, true modesty of the great one. The latter type radiates convincingly from Gide's every gesture. You feel that he is accustomed to move at his ease in the royal court of ideas. Here, in the society of queens, is the origin of the subdued voice, the hesitant yet imposing gestures, the unobtrusive, attentive gaze. And when he assures me that he is normally an awkward conversationalist—shy and fierce at the same time—I realize that for him it is both a danger and a sacrifice for him to emerge from that courtly ambience, from his accustomed, isolated existence. He quoted to me one of Chamfort's aphorisms: "If a man has created a masterpiece, people will have nothing better to do than prevent him from creating another one."[1] Gide is second to none in his ability to shake off the honors and dignities of fame. "It is true that according to Goethe," he said, "only scoundrels are modest. But there was no genius," he went on, "who was more modest than he. What does it mean to have had the patience, in extreme old age, to take up Persian literature? For such a man, in the evening after a prodigious workday the mere act of reading was modesty itself."

A rumor has long been circulating in France to the effect that Gide wanted to translate *Die Wahlverwandtschaften* [The Elective Affinities]. And since his recent *Voyage au Congo* [Travels in the Congo] also speaks of his rereading the book, I asked him about his intentions in this regard.[2] "No," said Gide, "I am less interested in translation at present. Of course, I would still be attracted by Goethe even now." After a characteristic hesitation he added, "And there can be no doubt that *The Elective Affinities* contains the whole of Goethe. But if I were to translate anything now, it would be his *Prometheus,* some passages from *Pandora,* and some less obvious prose works, such as his essay on Winckelmann."[3]

I then recollected Gide's recent translation of a chapter from Gottfried Keller's *Der grüne Heinrich* [Green Henry].[4] What had induced him to undertake this? Something that Jacques Rivière, Gide's late friend, had once said passed through my mind.[5] He had spoken of "the magic garden of hesitation" in which Gide had lived his whole life. Keller, likewise a writer of fundamental inhibitions and passionate reservations, had lived in a similar garden, and it is perhaps this that brought about the encounter of the two great novelists.

But there was no opportunity to explore this matter with Gide. The conversation took a sudden turn.

I'd like to tell you briefly about my intention in coming to see you. My plan was to give a lecture in Berlin. I had wanted to devote the first week of my stay there to preparing it in peace and quiet. But things turned out otherwise. The kindness of the Berliners, their friendly interest in me, proved to be so great that the leisure I had counted on never arrived. Meetings and conversations monopolized my time. On the other hand, I was firmly resolved to give only a lecture that had been fully thought out. *Je voulais faire quelque chose de très bien.* I would be greatly pleased if you could make this known, and if you could add that my resolution has not been abandoned—just that its execution has been postponed. I shall return, and next time I shall bring the lecture with me. It will perhaps have a different subject from the one I envisaged this time. I shall say only that it was not my intention, nor is it now, to talk about French literature, as has been the case a number of times recently. I have frequently discovered in the course of conversations in Berlin how very well informed people who take an interest in it actually are.

I thought I would speak about something quite different. I wanted to talk about those aspects of your literature that have been the most seminal and helpful for me as a French writer. You would have heard me discuss the role played in France, particularly in my work, by Goethe, Fichte, and Schopenhauer. I would also have used the opportunity to mention the new and intense interest that the French now take in matters German. When I compare French intellectuals of today to those of the previous generation, I can make one observation: they have become more inquisitive. Their horizon is about to expand beyond the cultural and linguistic frontiers of their native land. Compare this attitude with Barrès' statement: "Learn languages! What for? So as to say the same idiotic thing in three or four different ways?"[6] Did you notice the astonishing aspect of this statement? Barrès thinks only about speech; reading a foreign language, immersion in a foreign literature, is of no interest to him at all. What motivated Barrès was a predominantly nationalistic complacency. At around the same time there was something similar in Mallarmé, only in his case he was content not to go beyond a world of spiritual interiority that converted every gaze at the outside world, every thought of traveling or learning foreign languages, into something exotic. Wasn't it perhaps the philosophy of German idealism that induced its French disciples to adopt this attitude?

And Gide related the charming anecdote about the way in which Hegel's philosophy had gained access to the circle around Mallarmé through Villiers de l'Isle-Adam. As a young man, Villiers had once bought some hot potatoes wrapped in paper from a street-corner vendor. The bag consisted of a page translated from Hegel's *Aesthetics*. It was in this way, and not the official route via the Sorbonne and Victor Cousin, that German idealism met up with the Symbolists.[7]

"Ne jamais profiter de l'élan acquis"—never make use of an acquired élan. In the *Journal des "Faux-monnayeurs"* [Journal of *The Counterfeiters*], Gide declares this to be one of the principles of his literary technique. But it is far more than a rule governing his writing; it is the expression of an attitude of mind that treats every question as if it were the first—indeed the only—question in a world that has just arisen from the void. And if, as we may hope, Gide is soon to address German listeners as the representative of the French intelligentsia, he will do so in the hope of a fresh start, in a spirit that owes nothing to the moods and fashions of public opinion on either side of the frontier. No one is more aware than he that the community of nations is something that can be created only where national characters achieve their highest, most precise forms, but also only where they achieve their most stringent spiritual purification. No one knows this better than the man who wrote many years ago: "The only works we recognize as valuable are those that at their most profound are revelations of the soil and race from which they sprang." Semi-darkness and haziness, of whatever kind, are alien to him; it is no accident that Gide has always claimed to be a fanatic lover of line drawing, of sharp contours.

It is in this spirit that we shall wait expectantly and with pleasure to welcome back to Germany such a great Frenchman, a man whose efforts, passion, and courage have combined to lend his physiognomy a particularly European cast.

Published in the *Deutsche allgemeine Zeitung*, January 1928. *Gesammelte Schriften*, IV, 497–502. Translated by Rodney Livingstone.

Notes

1. Nicolas-Sébastien Roch de Chamfort (1740–1794), French man of letters, was the author of the caustic and world-weary *Pensées, maximes, et anecdotes,* published posthumously in 1803.
2. Gide's diary of a trip through Equatorial Africa in 1925–1926 was published in 1927.
3. Goethe's *Prometheus,* a "dramatic fragment in two acts," was written in the 1770s but published only in 1830. His verse play *Pandora* dates from 1810. His essay on the German archaeologist and art historian Johann Joachim Winckelmann (1717–1768) emphasizes Winckelmann's embodiment of a cultural ethos that privileges form and intellect over nature and feeling.
4. *Der grüne Heinrich,* first published in 1854–1855, then in a substantially revised

version in 1879–1880, is one of the most important examples of the German *Bildungsroman,* or novel of self-formation.

5. Jacques Rivière (1886–1925), French man of letters, edited the *Nouvelle Revue Française* from 1919 until his death.

6. Maurice Barrès (1862–1923) was a French writer and politician whose individualism and nationalism were influential in the early twentieth century.

7. Victor Cousin (1792–1867), a French philosopher, wrote books on Kant and Pascal, as well as several histories of philosophy.

Main Features of My Second Impression of Hashish

Written January 15, 1928, at 3:30 P.M.

The memories are less rich, even though the immersion was less profound than it was the previous time.[1] To put this more precisely, I was less immersed, but more profoundly inside it.

Moreover, it is the murky, alien, exotic aspects of the trance that remain in my memory, rather than the bright ones.

I recollect a satanic phase. The red of the walls was the deciding factor for me. My smile assumed satanic features, even though it was the expression of satanic knowledge, satanic satisfaction, and satanic calm, rather than satanic destructiveness. The people became more deeply entrenched in the room. The room itself became more velvety, more aflame, darker. I uttered the name of Delacroix.

The second powerful perception was the game with the next room. You start to play around with rooms in general. You start to experience seductions with your sense of orientation. In a waking state, we are familiar with the sort of unpleasant shift we can voluntarily provoke when we are traveling in the back of a train at night and imagine that we are sitting in the front—or vice versa. When this is translated from a dynamic situation into a static one, as here, it can be thought of as a seduction.

The room dons a disguise before our eyes, assumes the costume of each different mood, like some alluring creature. I experience the feeling that in the next room events such as the coronation of Charlemagne, the assassination of Henri IV, the signing of the Treaty of Verdun, and the murder of Egmont might have taken place.[2] The objects are only mannequins; even the great moments of world history are merely costumes beneath which they exchange understanding looks with nothingness, the base, and the common-place. They reply to the ambiguous wink from Nirvana.

To refuse to be drawn into this understanding is what constitutes the "satanic satisfaction" of which I have spoken. It is at this point that the roots of addiction, the collusive knowledge about nonbeing, can be bound-lessly intensified by increasing the dose.

It is perhaps no self-deception if I say that in this state you become hostile to free space—one might even call it "Uranian" space—and that the thought of an "outside" becomes almost a torture. It is no longer, as it was the first time, a friendly, sociable lingering in a room, out of sheer pleasure in the situation as it is; it is rather like being wrapped up, enclosed in a dense spider's web in which the events of the world are scattered around, sus-pended there like the bodies of dead insects sucked dry. You have no wish to leave this cave. Here, furthermore, the rudiments of an unfriendly attitude toward everyone present begin to take shape, as well as the fear that they might disturb you, drag you out into the open.

But this trance, too, has a cathartic outcome, despite its basically depres-sive nature, and even if it is not as ecstatic as the previous trance, it is at least resourceful and not without charm. Except that this charm emerges only as the drug wears off and the depressive nature of the experience becomes clearer, leading one to conclude that the increase in the dose is after all partly responsible for this depressive character.

The dual structure of this depression: on the one hand, anxiety; on the other, an inability to make up one's mind on practical matters. I finally mastered the sense of indecision; suddenly tracked down a very deeply concealed aspect of a compulsive temptation, and thereby gained the ability to pursue it a certain distance, with the prospect of eliminating it.

Hunger as an oblique axis cutting through the system of the trance.

The great hope, desire, yearning to reach the new, the untouched, in a state of trance scarcely takes wing on this occasion; instead they are attained only in a submerged, relaxed, indolent, inert stroll downhill. In this act of strolling downhill, I thought I was still able to generate some friendliness, some attractive qualities, the ability to take friends along with a smile that had a dark edge to it, half Lucifer, half Hermes *transducens*,[3] very remote from the spirit and the man I was last time.

Less human being, more daemon and pathos in this trance.

The unpleasant feeling of wanting simultaneously to be alone and to be with others, a feeling that manifests itself in a deeper sense of fatigue and has to be acquiesced in: this feeling grows in intensity. You have the feeling of needing to be alone, so as to give yourself over in deeper peace of mind to this ambiguous wink from Nirvana; and at the same time, you need the presence of others, like gently shifting relief-figures on the plinth of your own throne.

Hope as a pillow beneath your head, but only now, with an enduring effect.

Through the first trance, I became acquainted with the fickle nature of doubt; the doubt lay in myself as a kind of creative indifference. The second trance, however, made objects appear dubious.

Operation on my tooth. Remarkable trick of memory. Even now I cannot rid myself of the idea that the operation was on the left side.

On my return home, when the chain on the bathroom door proved hard to fasten, the suspicion: an experiment was being set up.

You hear the "Tuba mirans sonans,"[4] but push against the tombstone in vain.

It is well known that if you close your eyes and lightly press on them, you start to see ornamental figures whose shape you cannot control. The architectures and configurations of space you see in a hashish trance are somewhat similar in origin. At what point and in what form they manifest themselves is at first involuntary, so swiftly and unexpectedly do they make their appearance. Then, once they are there, a more conscious play of the imagination takes over and they can be treated with greater freedom.

In general, it can be said that the feeling of "beyond" is connected with a certain feeling of displeasure. But it is important to make a sharp distinction between the "outside" and a person's visual space, however extended it may be—a distinction that has the same significance for the person in a hashish trance as the relationship between the stage and the cold street outside has for the theatergoer. Yet, to extend the image, on occasion something rather like a proscenium stage intervenes between the person in a trance and his visual space, and through this a quite different wind blows—the wind from outside.

The idea of the closeness of death came to me yesterday, in the formula: death lies between me and my trance.

The image of automatic connections: certain intellectual things articulate themselves of their own accord—just like a violent toothache, for example. All sensations, especially mental ones, have a steeper gradient and drag the words along with them as they hurtle downward.

This "ambiguous wink from Nirvana" has probably never been expressed so vividly as by Odilon Redon.

The first serious sign of damage is probably the inability to deal with future time. When you look into this more closely, you realize how astonishing it is that we can exercise control over the night, or even individual nights—that is to say, over our usual dreams. It is very hard to control the dreams (or the trance) resulting from hashish.

Bloch wanted to touch my knee gently. I could feel the contact long before it actually reached me. I felt it as a highly repugnant wound to my aura. In order to understand this, it is important to realize that this happens because, with hashish, all movements seem to gain in intensity and intentionality, and are therefore unpleasant.

Aftereffect: perhaps a certain weakening of the will. But the sense of elation gains the upper hand, though with diminishing effect. Despite my recurring depression, my writing has recently displayed a rising tendency, something I have never before observed. Can this be connected with hashish? A further aftereffect: on returning home, I tried to fasten the chain, and when this proved difficult my first suspicion (quickly corrected) was that an experiment was being set up.

Even if the first trance stood on a higher plane morally than the second, the climax of intensity was on a rising curve. This should be understood roughly as follows: the first trance loosened the objects, and lured them from their accustomed world; the second inserted them quite quickly into a new one—far inferior to this intermediate realm.

The constant digressions under the influence of hashish. To start with, the inability to listen. This seems incongruent with the boundless goodwill toward other people, but in reality they share the same roots. No sooner has the person you are talking to opened his mouth than you feel profoundly disillusioned. What he says is infinitely inferior to what we would have expected from him before he opened his mouth, and what we confidently, happily assumed him to be capable of. He painfully disappoints us through his failure to focus on the greatest object of our interest: ourselves.

As for our own inability to focus, to concentrate on the subject under discussion, the feeling resembles an interrupted physical contact and has roughly the following features. What we are on the verge of talking about seems infinitely alluring; we stretch out our arms full of love, eager to embrace what we have in mind. Scarcely have we touched it, however, than it disillusions us completely. The object of our attention suddenly fades at the touch of language. It puts on years; our love wholly exhausts it in a single moment. So it pauses for a rest until it again appears attractive enough to lead us back to it once more.

To return to the dime-novel aspect of the room: we simultaneously perceive all the events that might conceivably have taken place here. The room winks at us: What do you think may have happened here? The connection between this phenomenon and cheap literature. Cheap literature and subtitles. To be understood as follows: think of a kitschy oleograph on the wall, with a long strip cut out from the bottom of the picture frame. There is a tape running through the batten, and in the gap there is a succession of subtitles: "The Murder of Egmont," "The Coronation of Charlemagne," and so on.

In this experiment I often saw cathedral porches with Gothic windows and once said, "I can see Venice, but it looks like the upper part of the Kurfürstenstrasse."

"I feel weak" and "I know I am weak" imply fundamentally different meanings. Perhaps only the first statement has expressive validity. But in a hashish trance we can almost speak of the despotism of the second, and this may explain why, despite an intensified "inner life," facial expression is impoverished. The distinction between these two statements should be explored further.

Moreover, there is a functional displacement. I have borrowed this expression from Joël. Following is the experience that led me to it. In my satanic phase someone gave me one of Kafka's books, *Betrachtung* [Meditation]. I read the title. But then the book at once changed into the book-in-the-poet's-hand, which it becomes for the (perhaps somewhat academic) sculptor who confronts the task of sculpting that particular poet. It immediately became integrated into the sculptural form of my own body, hence far more absolutely and brutally subject to me than could have been achieved by my most derogatory criticism.

But there was also something else. It was as if I were in flight from Kafka's spirit, and now, at the moment he touched me, I was transformed into stone, like Daphne turning into ivy at Apollo's touch.

The connection between cheap fiction and the profoundest theological intentions. They reflect it through a glass darkly, transpose into the space of contemplation what is of value only in the space of active life. Namely, that the world always remains the same (that all events could have taken place in the same space). Despite everything, that is rather a tired, faded truth in the realm of theory (for all the sharpness of perception it contains); but it is spectacularly confirmed in the lives of the pious, for whom all things turn out for the *best,* much as the space of the imagination subserves the *past.* So profoundly is the realm of theology submerged in that of cheap fiction. We might even say that, far from having arisen from the dull, brutish side of mankind, the profoundest truths possess the great power of being able to adapt to mankind's dull, baser side, and even of being reflected in their own way in the irresponsible dreamer.

Written January 1928; unpublished in Benjamin's lifetime. *Gesammelte Schriften,* VI, 560–566. Translated by Rodney Livingstone.

Notes

1. This is the most extensive of Benjamin's drug protocols; he also kept records of his first hashish session, in 1927, and several subsequent sessions—in 1928, 1930, and 1934. Records of these drug sessions were also kept by other participants and supervisors: physicians Ernst Joël and Fritz Fränkel, and Benjamin's cousin

the neurologist Egon Wissing. Benjamin offers a brief account of several other sessions in a letter to Gershom Scholem dated January 30, 1928.

2. Charlemagne was crowned emperor in Rome in A.D. 800; Henri IV of France was assassinated in 1610; the Treaty of Verdun of 843 ratified the breakup of the Carolingian Empire; and Count Egmont, one of the leaders of the Flanders nobility, was executed by the Spaniards under the Duke of Alba in 1568.

3. The god Hermes in his function as guide (e.g., of the three goddesses to Paris, of the souls of the dead down to Charon the Ferryman, and of Persephone back from the underworld).

4. From the Requiem Mass. The text actually reads, "Tuba mirum spargens sonum / Per supulcra regionum" ("The trumpet, scattering a wondrous sound / through the tombs of every land").

Conversation with André Gide

It is wonderful to talk to André Gide in his hotel room. I know he owns a country house in Cuverville and an apartment in Paris, and there can be no doubt that to meet him among his books, in the very places where he conceived and carried out great works, would be an unforgettable experience. But it would not be this one—namely, to encounter this great traveler amid his bundled possessions, *omnia sua secum portans,* on the alert in the bright morning light of his spacious room on Potsdamer Platz. Admittedly, the interview, a format that has been created by diplomats, financiers, and film people for their own purposes, is not the one in which we might initially expect a writer—and the most subtle writer alive, at that—to reveal himself. But if we take a closer look, the situation appears differently. Question and answer articulate Gide's ideas in sharp focus. I like to compare his thinking to a fort: vast in its overall structure, replete with protective ramparts and protruding bastions, and above all with highly strict forms and perfect in its deliberate dialectical construction.

And even the most helpless amateur knows full well that trying to take photographs in the vicinity of a fort is dangerous and fraught with complications. Paper and pencil must be put aside, and if the following words are authentic they owe this to the soft, inspired voice that uttered them.

Scarcely any of the questions I wanted to ask Gide were those that normally turn up in an interview—ones that are posed more out of habit than genuine interest. For as he sat there in front of me on a step leading to his bay window, his back resting against the seat of his armchair, a brown silk scarf around his neck, and his hands burying themselves in the carpet or clasped around his knees, he was interviewer and interviewee simultaneously. From time to time a glance from his prominent horn-rimmed spectacles fell on me, when one of my rare questions aroused his attention. It is fascinating to watch his face, even if only to follow the alternation of kindness and malice that seem to inhabit the same furrows, siblings sharing his expressions. And there are moments, by no means the worst ones, when pure pleasure in a malicious anecdote lights up his features.

No European writer living today has given as cold a reception to his own fame as he did, when his finally arrived, toward the end of his forties. No Frenchman has ever barricaded himself more securely against the Académie Française. Gide and D'Annunzio: you need only juxtapose these names to realize what action a man may take for and against his own fame.[1] "How do you deal with your fame?" And then Gide told me how little he had sought it, to whom he owed the fact that he finally found it, and how he resisted it.

Until 1914 he was firmly convinced that he would be read only after his death. This was not resignation—it was trust in the enduring power of his work. "Ever since I began to write, Keats, Baudelaire, and Rimbaud have been my models, in the sense that, like them, I have wanted to owe my name only to my work and to nothing else." When a writer has adopted this view, it is not uncommon for an enemy to intervene, like Balaam's ass. In this instance it was the novelist Henri Béraud.[2] He spent so much time bombarding French newspaper readers with the assurance that there was nothing more stupid, more boring, and more corrupt than the books of André Gide, that people finally started to take notice and asked themselves, who exactly was this André Gide whom decent people should avoid reading under any circumstances? Some years later Béraud wrote in one of his outbursts that, in addition to everything else, Gide was also ungrateful toward his benefactors; whereupon Gide resolved to take the sting out of this rebuke and sent him a box of the best Pihan chocolates, together with a card saying, "Non, non, je ne suis pas un ingrat."

What really irritated the young Gide's enemies was the knowledge that Gide was held in greater esteem abroad than they were. They thought this created a completely false impression. And it is perfectly true that their own books would have given a better picture of the average novel of the day. Gide was translated into German quite early on, and he remained on friendly terms with his first translators—that is to say, with Rilke until his death, and with Kassner and Blei to this day.[3] This brings us to the topical question of translation. Gide himself did what he could as translator to popularize Conrad, and as translator he engaged critically with Shakespeare. We've heard of his masterly translation of *Antony and Cleopatra*. Quite recently, Pitoëff, the director of the Théâtre de l'Art, approached him with the request that he translate *Hamlet*.[4] "The first act took me months. When it was finished I wrote to Pitoëff, 'I can't do any more—it costs me too much.' 'But you will publish the first act?' 'Perhaps; I do not know. At the moment, I have mislaid it. It is somewhere among my papers in Paris, or in Cuverville. I have been traveling so much, my papers have all fallen into disarray'" He intentionally diverts the conversation to Proust. He knows about the plans for a German translation, as well as the darker pages of its prehistory. All the kinder are his hopes for a favorable outcome. And because it is my experience that everyone who becomes closely involved with Proust finds that this relationship moves in phases, I ventured to inquire into his. It turned out to be no exception. As a young man, Gide had been a first-hand observer during those memorable days when Proust, the dazzling *causeur*, had first made his appearance in the salons. "Whenever we met in society, I thought him the most outrageous snob. I think he must have thought much the same of me. At that time neither of us had an inkling of the close friendship that would bind us together." And when one day the meter-high pile of student-composition books landed on the desk of the *Nouvelle Revue Française*, everyone was initially flabbergasted. At first Gide did not dare to immerse himself in the world of Proust's novel. But once he had made a start, he succumbed to its fascination. Ever since, Proust has been in his eyes one of the greatest pioneers of that latest conquest of the mind—psychology.

This word, too, opened the door to one of those endless galleries in whose corridors the eye risks losing itself when you speak with Gide. Psychology as the cause of the decline of the theater. The psychological drama as the death of the theater. Psychology as the realm of the subtle, the isolating, the disconcerting. The theater as the realm of unanimity, closeness, fulfillment, love, enmity, fidelity, jealousy, courage, and hatred: for the theater, these are all constellations, predictable and established scenarios—the opposite of what they are for psychology, which reveals hatred in love and cowardice in courage. "Le théâtre, c'est un terrain banal."

We return to Proust. Gide gives the now classic account of Proust's sickroom, of that invalid in his perpetually darkened room lined with cork to shut out the noise—even the window shutters were insulated with cushions. He seldom saw visitors. Reclining on his legless bed, surrounded by heaps of paper covered with scribbling, he wrote and wrote; instead of reading his corrected pages, he filled them with additions, "bien plus que Balzac" (even more than Balzac). For all Gide's admiration, however, he says: "I have no contact with his characters. *Vanité*—that's the stuff they are made of. I think there was much in Proust that he never expressed, buds that never opened. In his later work a certain irony gained the upper hand over the morality and religion that are evident in his earlier writings." Gide also seems to have detected an ambiguity in Proust which had been veiled by his irony—an ambiguity that was manifest in a basic element of his technique: his mode of composition. "People talk about Proust's being a great psychologist—which he certainly was. But when they keep pointing to the artful way in which he depicts the development of his characters over the lifespan, they often overlook one factor. Each of his characters, down to the least important, was based on a single model. But this model did not always remain the same. In the case of Charlus, for example, there were always at least two. The later Charlus was based on someone completely different from the proud model of the earlier one." Gide talks of a composite image, a *fondu*. As in a film, one character dissolves imperceptibly into another.

"I came here," Gide said after a pause, "to give a lecture. But Berlin life did not give me the peace of mind I needed to work out what I had actually wanted to say. I will come back again and will bring my lecture with me. But even at this stage, I would like to tell you something about my relationship with the German language. After a lengthy, intensive, and exclusive preoccupation with German—this was in the years of my friendship with Pierre Louÿs,[5] when we read *Faust, Part II* together—I abandoned everything German for about ten years. My entire attention had been captured by English. Then, last year, in the Congo, I finally opened a German book again. It was *The Elective Affinities*. I made a curious discovery: I found reading German after this ten-year interval not harder, but easier. It is," and here Gide's tone became insistent, "not the affinity between German and English that made it easier for me. What gave me the élan enabling me to master a foreign tongue was the fact that I had felt repelled by my own mother tongue. The crucial thing when learning languages is not which language to choose; it is the ability to abandon one's own language. In principle, one begins to understand only at that point." Gide then quoted a sentence from the explorer Bougainville's account of his travels: "When we left the island, we gave it the name Ile du Salut."[6] And then he added the wonderful sentence, "Ce n'est qu'en quittant une chose que nous la nommons." (Only after taking leave of something do we give it a name.)

"If I have had any influence on the younger generation," Gide continued, "it lies in the fact that the French are now beginning to show an interest in foreign countries and languages, whereas previously they displayed only indifference and indolence. Read Barrès' *Voyage de Sparte* [Travels in Sparta] and you'll know what I mean.[7] What Barrès sees in Greece is really France, and where he does not see France, he pretends he has seen nothing at all." We have thus come around to one of Gide's pet topics: Barrès. His critique of Barrès' novel *Les Déracinés* is now some thirty years old, but it is more than a sharp repudiation of that epic of attachment to the soil.[8] It is the masterly profession of faith of a man who refuses to accept the claims of a thoroughgoing nationalism, and who recognizes French national identity only if it includes the tension-filled area of European history and the European family of nations.

"Men who have lost their roots" [*les déracinés*]—Gide has nothing but tolerant scorn for a poetic metaphor that has so completely lost touch with the reality of nature. "I have always said it's a shame that Barrès has botany against him. As if a tree really restricted itself, instead of instinctively spreading its boughs everywhere into space, in every direction. It's unfortunate when writers don't know the first thing about natural science." Before me sat the man who once wrote, "I will have nothing to do with anything that is not nature. A vegetable cart conveys more truth than the most beautiful Ciceronian periods." Even today, Gide is in thrall to this realm of imagery.

> I spoke earlier of Proust, and of the fact that many of his buds failed to blossom. It has been different with me. My aim is to make sure that everything I have inherited should be revealed, and to discover its appropriate form. This may have had its drawbacks. My work seems a little like a thicket from which my distinguishing features emerge only with difficulty. I accept this patiently. *Je n'écris que pour être relu.* (I write only to be reread.) I have confidence in the future that will follow my death. Only death will drive the figurations in my work out into the open. Only then will its unity become unmistakable. It is true that I have not made matters easy for myself. I know that there are writers who strive from the outset to confine their work within ever narrower limits. A man like Jules Renard achieves what he has achieved not by allowing his talents to develop, but by ruthlessly cutting back his instincts.[9] And Renard's achievement is far from trivial. Do you know his diaries? A most fascinating document . . . But that sort of thing can sometimes assume grotesque features. My situation is quite different. I know what a torture Stendhal's books were for me when I first encountered them—how alien his world was to me. Yet I felt myself inspired by it for that very reason. I later learned much from Stendhal.

Gide has been a great learner. If we look more closely, we may feel that this has protected him to a much greater extent from alien influences than stubborn reserve might have done. It is mainly the indolent who find themselves "influenced," whereas the learner sooner or later succeeds in taking possession of what may be of use to him, integrating it as a technique into his own work. In this sense there are few authors who have been better or more dedicated learners than Gide. "Once I had taken a particular direction, I followed it through as far as it would go and followed this up by advancing in the opposite direction with the same resoluteness." This principled rejection of every golden mean, this commitment to extremes— what else is it but dialectic, not as intellectual method but as life's breath and as passion. Gide shows no desire to contradict me (or so it seems to me) when I detect in this the basis for all the misunderstandings and much of the hostility that he has encountered. "Many people have quite made up their minds," he went on, "that I am able to write only about myself; and then, when my books make use of the most varied characters, they conclude ingeniously that the author must be quite characterless, vacillating, and unreliable."

"Integration": this is Gide's intellectual and literary passion. His growing interest in "nature"—which appears as a mature trend in many great writers—means in his case that even in its extreme aspects the world is still whole, still healthy, still natural. And what drives him toward these extremes is not curiosity or apologetic zeal, but the highest form of dialectical insight.

It has been said of Gide that he is the "poète des cas exceptionels"—the poet of the exceptional case. Gide: "*Bien entendu,* that is true. But why? Day after day, we encounter modes of behavior and people who through their very existence invalidate our existing norms. A large share of our ordinary everyday decisions, as well as our extraordinary ones, are not susceptible to judgment by traditional moral values. And because this is so, it is necessary to focus on such cases, to scrutinize them, without cowardice and without cynicism." Whatever Gide has conveyed of such things in novels like *Les Faux-monnayeurs* [The Counterfeiters], in his essays, in his important autobiography, *Si le grain ne meurt* [If It Die]—his enemies would have forgiven him, if only they had contained the small dose of cynicism that reconciles snobs and philistines with the world. What gets on their nerves is not his "immorality" but his seriousness. Yet seriousness is an essential part of Gide, for all the maliciousness in his conversation, and for all the masterful irony to be found in *Prométhée mal enchaîné* [Prometheus Misbound], in *Les nourritures terrestres* [Fruits of the Earth], and in *Les caves du Vatican* [The Vatican Cellars].[10] As Willy Haas pointed out a few weeks ago, he is the latest Frenchman in the tradition of Pascal. In the line of French moralists that runs through La Bruyère, La Rochefoucauld, and Vauvenargues, none is more like him than Pascal, a man who would quite certainly have been described as a *cas particulier,* a sick man, if they had possessed the superficial clinical terminology of our age. This places Gide alongside Pascal in the ranks of the great French educators. For the withdrawn, eccentric German loner, the model educator will always be someone who in his character or his teaching represents the typical German of the sort attempted in our day by Borchardt or Hofmannsthal.[11] For the French, however, with their richer national character, based on its diversity of tribal types, and with a more powerful but also more precarious national and literary identity, it is the great moral exception who is the highest pedagogic authority. This is what Gide is. That countenance, which at times conceals rather than reveals the great writer, represents his undeviating and even threatening challenge to both moral indifference and lax complacency.

Published in *Die literarische Welt,* February 1928. *Gesammelte Schriften,* IV, 502–509. Translated by Rodney Livingstone.

Notes

1. Benjamin refers here to the vanity and ostentatiousness often seen as characterizing the life and work of Gabriele D'Annunzio (1863–1938), literary virtuoso of decadence and heroic vitalism and enthusiastic supporter of Mussolini.
2. Henri Béraud (1885–1958) was a prolific French writer. His novel *Le vitriol de lune* (Moon-Vitriol; 1921) won the Goncourt Prize. "Balaam's ass": In II Peter 2:16, the prophet Balaam is "rebuked for his iniquity" by his donkey.
3. Rudolf Kassner (1873–1959), a German writer and friend of Rilke and Hofmannsthal, translated Tolstoy, Gogol, and Pushkin as well as Gide. Franz Blei (1871–1942) was an Austrian novelist and playwright.
4. Georges Pitoëff (1888–1939) was a Russian actor and director. He established his "poetic theater" in Paris in 1918.
5. The French writer Pierre Louÿs (1870–1925) published novels, stories, and poems celebrating fin-de-siècle decadence, voluptuousness, and sensual-aesthetic refinement.
6. Louis-Antoine de Bougainville (1729–1811) led the first French expedition to circumnavigate the globe. He also attempted, unsuccessfully, to colonize the Falkland Islands.
7. This account of a trip from Athens to Sparta in 1900 was published in 1906. It contrasts the "voice of blood" and "dream of death" associated with Sparta with the sterile republicanism of Athens, and so reveals Barrès' ultranationalist, medico-determinist political and aesthetic creed.
8. Barrès' book *Les Déracinés* (Men without Roots), one of the first sociological novels, was intended as an indictment of the Third Republic; it extols the virtues of attachment to blood and soil and condemns cosmopolitan modernism and the purportedly arid intellectualism of the "uprooted." Gide's "A propos des *Déracinés*" first appeared in 1897. It opens with the words: "I was born in Paris to a father who was from Uzès and a mother who was from Normandy. Where, Monsieur Barrès, do you wish me to be rooted? I thus made the decision to travel."
9. Jules Renard (1864–1910), French man of letters, was one of the founders of *Mercure de France,* the influential journal of politics and the arts which published its first issue in 1890.
10. Gide referred to his mock-mythic *Prométhée mal enchaîné* (1899) and his novel *Les caves du Vatican* as *soties*—that is, new versions of a fourteenth-century genre of French farce. Both texts privilege spontaneity and the "exceptional moment" over social and moral convention. *Les nourritures terrestres* (1897) similarly refuses any morality that is imposed by tradition and alien to the individual's emotional-erotic needs.
11. Rudolf Borchardt (1877–1945) was a German-Jewish essayist and poet. His essays were national-conservative in tenor; his poetry is marked by great formal refinement.

Old Toys

The Toy Exhibition at the Märkisches Museum

Over the past few weeks an exhibition of toys has been on view at the Märkisches Museum in Berlin. It occupies only a medium-sized room; this tells us that the curators' focus is not on the splendid or the monstrous: life-size dolls for royal children, vast train sets, or giant rocking horses. Their aim is to show, first, the sort of toys Berlin produced during the eighteenth and nineteenth centuries, and, second, what a well-stocked toy cupboard in an ordinary Berlin home might have looked like. They have therefore concentrated on pieces that can be shown to have survived in the possession of old established Berlin families. Items owned by collectors are of secondary importance.

Let us start by explaining what is special about this exhibition: it includes not just "toys," in the narrower sense of the word, but also a great many objects on the margins. Who knows where one might otherwise find such a profusion of wonderful parlor games, building sets, Christmas pyramids, and peep shows, to say nothing of books, posters, and wall charts for teaching. All of this often inaccessible detail gives a far more vivid overall picture than a more systematically compiled exhibition ever could. And the same sure touch can be found in the catalogue. It is no dead list of objects on display, but a coherent text full of precise references to the individual exhibits as well as detailed information on the age, make, and distribution of particular types of toys.

Of these, the tin soldier must be the most thoroughly researched, ever since Hampe of the Germanisches Museum published a monograph on the subject. Here you can see them posed in front of charming backdrops, such as handbills from Berlin puppet theaters; but there are also other tin figures from town and country, arranged in genre scenes. They were not manufactured in Berlin until relatively late; in the eighteenth century it was the ironmongers who stocked goods of this kind, made in southern Germany. This itself is enough to tell us that actual toy sellers emerged only gradually during a period in which there was a strict division of labor among tradesmen.

The toy sellers' predecessors included, on the one hand, turners, ironmongers, paper merchants, and fancy-goods sellers, and, on the other hand, door-to-door peddlers in towns and at fairs. There is even a special kind of figurine in a niche labeled "Cakes and Pastries." Here one finds the gum-resin doll familiar from Hoffmann's stories, together with parodies of monuments made from sugar and old-fashioned gingerbread. This sort of thing has vanished from Protestant Germany. In contrast, the attentive traveler in France, even in the quieter suburbs of Paris, may easily come across two of the main examples of old-style confectionery: babies in their cradles, which used to be given to older children on the birth of a brother or sister; and confirmation children, posed on blue or pink sugar pillows and holding a candle and prayer book, performing their acts of devotion, sometimes in front of a prayer stool made of the same icing. But the most fanciful specimens of this type seem to have been lost today. These were flat sugar dolls (or hearts or similar objects) which could be easily divided lengthways so that in the middle, where the two halves were joined together, there was a little piece of paper with a brightly colored picture and a motto. An uncut broadsheet is on display with examples of such confectioners' mottoes. For instance: "I have danced away / My weekly wage today." Or: "Here, you little flirt, / This apricot won't hurt." Such lapidary two-liners were called "devices" because you had to divide the figurine into two parts in order to uncover the motto. Thus, a Berlin advertisement from the Biedermeier period reads: "Zimmermann's Confectionery in Königsstrasse supplies a full range of candy figures as well as confectionery of other kinds, together with devices, at a reasonable price."

But you can also find quite a variety of texts. Natke's great Baths-and-Basins Theater Saloon, Palisadenstrasse 76, advertised "Entertainment through humor and tasteful wit of well-known quality." Julius Linde's mechanical marionette theater issued the following invitation to its latest productions: "The Robber Knight Flayed Alive, or Love and Cannibalism, or Roast Human Heart and Flesh . . . Concluding with a Great Ballet of Metamorphoses. In this ballet several dancing figures and metamorphoses, very true to life, will entertain the public's eye very agreeably with their delightful and skillful movements. In conclusion, Pussell the Wonder Dog will distinguish himself." The peep shows along with the dioramas, myrioramas, and panoramas, whose pictures were manufactured in Augsburg for the most part, lead the observer even more deeply into the mysteries of the world of play than do the marionettes. "You can't find toys like that anymore" is what you often hear adults saying when they encounter old toys. Actually, most adults just think this; in fact they have become indifferent to such things, whereas children notice them at every turn. But here, gazing at the panoramas, they are right for once. Panoramas were products of the 1800s; they vanished with the century and are inseparable from its most curious features.

Today, old toys are important from a number of viewpoints. Folklore, psychoanalysis, art history, and the new education all find it a rewarding subject. But this alone does not explain why the little exhibition room is never empty and why, in addition to whole classes of schoolchildren, hundreds of adults have passed through it in recent weeks. Nor can its popularity be due to the amazingly primitive specimens, even though these would be reason enough for a snob to attend the exhibition.

These include not only jumping jacks, woolen sheep clearly produced by poor domestic workshops remote from modern manufacturing, and Neuruppin broadsheets with their famous garishly colored scenes,[1] but also (to mention only one item) a set of pictures recently discovered in the attic of a school in the Mark Brandenburg. They are the work of a certain Wilke, a deaf-mute teacher, and were intended to be used for instructing deaf-mute children. Their crude vividness is so oppressive that the normal person, seeing this airless world for the first time, runs the risk of losing his own hearing and voice for a few hours. There are painted carvings that were made in the mid-nineteenth century by a shepherd in the Altmark. The subjects are taken from both secular and biblical life, and in every case stand midway between miniature models of characters from Strindberg's *Dance of Death* and lifeless cloth figures of the kind seen at fairgrounds, where they perch in the rear of booths and act as targets for wooden balls.

As we have said, all this is enticing for adults, but it is not the only attraction. Or the decisive one. We all know the picture of the family gathered beneath the Christmas tree, the father engrossed in playing with the toy train that he has given his son, the latter standing next to him in tears. When the urge to play overcomes an adult, this is not simply a regression to childhood. To be sure, play is always liberating. Surrounded by a world of giants, children use play to create a world appropriate to their size. But the adult, who finds himself threatened by the real world and can find no escape, removes its sting by playing with its image in reduced form. The desire to make light of an unbearable life has been a major factor in the growing interest in children's games and children's books since the end of the war.

Not all the new impulses that have given fresh impetus to the toy industry have been beneficial. The prissy silhouettes of the varnished wooden figures that represent the modern age do not stand out to advantage among so many old objects. On the contrary, they tend to show what adults under-stand by toys rather than what children expect from them. They are curi-osities. Here they are useful for purposes of comparison, but have no place in the nursery.

More captivating are the older curiosities, among them a wax doll from the eighteenth century that strikingly resembles a modern character doll. But there is probably some truth in the suggestion made to me in the course of conversation by Mr. Stengel, the museum's director and the organizer of this special exhibition: that the doll's face should be seen as the wax portrait of a baby. It took a long time before people realized, let alone incorporated the idea into dolls, that children are not just men and women on a reduced scale. It is well known that even children's clothing became emancipated from that of adults only at a very late date. Not until the nineteenth century, in fact. It sometimes looks as if our century wishes to take this development one step further and, far from regarding children as little men and women, has reservations about thinking of them as human beings at all. People have now discovered the grotesque, cruel, grim side of children's life. While meek and mild educators still cling to Rousseauesque dreams, writers like Ringel-natz[2] and painters like Klee have grasped the despotic and dehumanized element in children. Children are insolent and remote from the world. After all the sentimentality of a revived Biedermeier, Mynona is probably right in his views of 1916:[3]

> If children are ever to grow up into first-rate people, they must not be spared the sight of anything human. Their innocence instinctively ensures that the necessary boundaries are not crossed; and later, when these boundaries are gradually extended, new experiences will encounter minds that have been prepared. The fact that little children laugh at everything, even the negative sides of life, is a glorious extension of radiant cheerfulness into all the spheres of life it had so shamefully neglected and that are so utterly dreary as a result . . . Wonderfully successful little bomb plots, with princes who just fall apart but are easily put back together again. Department stores with automatic outbreaks of arson, break-ins, thefts. Victims who can be murdered in a multitude of ways and with every appropriate weapon . . . My children would not like to be without their guillotines and gallows, at the very least.

Such things should not be expected in this exhibition. But we must not forget that the most enduring modifications in toys are never the work of adults, whether they be educators, manufacturers, or writers, but are the result of children at play. Once mislaid, broken, and repaired, even the most princely doll becomes a capable proletarian comrade in the children's play commune.

Published in the *Frankfurter Zeitung*, March 1928. *Gesammelte Schriften*, IV, 511–515. Translated by Rodney Livingstone.

Notes

1. The popular Neuruppin prints appeared from 1831 in a series of single sheets with humorous or sarcastic subject matter. The early ones were based on colored woodcuts; the later sheets were lithographs.
2. Joachim Ringelnatz (pseudonym of Hans Bötticher; 1883–1934) directed the Berlin cabaret Schall und Rauch (Noise and Smoke) during the Weimar Republic. His satirical, scurrilous poems and songs brought attacks on middle-class convention with a sharp political edge.
3. Mynona was the pseudonym of the German-Jewish philosopher Salomo Friedländer (1871–1946). A collaborator on the important Expressionist journals *Der Sturm* and *Die Aktion,* he published a number of satires.

Hugo von Hofmannsthal's *Der Turm*

Written following its premieres in Munich and Hamburg.

In recent weeks Hugo von Hofmannsthal's *Der Turm* [The Tower] has begun to make its way through Germany's theaters. The stage version differs significantly from the original, which appeared in the *Neue deutsche Beiträge* in 1925; the fourth and fifth acts have been completely rewritten. But this does not in itself justify a comparison of the two versions—not here, at any rate. No, what justifies our taking a second look at the play, even after our notice in *Die literarische Welt* (vol. 15, no. 2), are the extraordinary insights that his progress from one version to the other gives us into the author's method of writing and the structure of his work. We know that he took his subject from Calderón's *La vida es sueño* [Life Is a Dream].[1] This formulaic title, which gave powerful expression to the dramatic impulses of the age, has a double meaning for Calderón. On the one hand it means that life is nothing more than a dream, that its possessions are like chaff in the wind. This is his secular wisdom. But he also asserts: just as a mere nothing—this life—decides our salvation, and is weighed and judged by God, we cannot escape God even when we dream, in the illusory world of dream. Dreaming and waking—in God's eyes they are no more distinct from each other than life and death. The Christian dimension is equally present in both. This second motif of the title—dream as a theological paradigm—is one that a modern writer like Hofmannsthal could have no desire to appropriate for himself. And with compelling logic, the complete reworking of the dream motif seems to have resulted in an entirely new drama. In the first version of *Der Turm*, the dream bore all the marks of its chthonic origins. In particular, the last act of the first version shows the prince, Sigismund, as the master who conjures up the dark forces to which he finally succumbs in the fight to the finish. In a sense we might say that the prince has been the victim of forces that rose up against him from within himself. Such an action has tragic overtones, but we should note that Hofmannsthal was careful to call his play a *Trauerspiel* [mourning play], not a *Tragödie* [tragedy]. And it will not have escaped readers that in the later version the outlines of the patient martyr in the tradition of Christian tragic drama emerge in their purity, pushing the original dream motif into the background and significantly enhancing the aura surrounding Sigismund.

The fact that on the lips of this youth every sound necessarily became a sound of lamentation—because lamentation is the primal sound of nature's creatures—was the source of one of the most touching effects of the first version. But also one of the riskiest. For to liberate the expression of suffering from the bonds of verse is an unprecedented procedure, or at any rate has not been attempted since the prose of the *Sturm und Drang*.[2] And it is far from clear whether it can be done successfully within the constraints of the drama. To be sure, even the quieter, more sharply defined Sigismund of this revised version forms a link in the chain that is constantly taken up by writers who wish to find words for the secret connection between silent suffering and all the earliest experiences of childhood, now lost in the mists of the past. Even in his revised form, the prince comes from the same stock as Kaspar Hauser.[3] In the new version, too, the hero's utterances surface only fleetingly from the turbulent sea of sounds and gaze around like naiads seeing the world for the first time. It is the same gaze that touches us so deeply in the language of children, visionaries, and the mentally disturbed. The poet has summoned up the most potent forces of language—not in its most exalted, most consummate, yet also most dependent forms, but in its primitive sounds, as auxiliaries in their struggle, which is also his. The difference is that the natural immediacy of the speech with which he endowed his first Sigismund tended, near the end, to move in the direction of the chthonic, of primitive menace. In the new version, by contrast, where the serene silence of the prince seems to dispel the morning mists, the undistorted speech of the natural Christian soul seems to strike our ears like the song of a lark. The chthonic element, whose power vanished with the disappearance of the dream motif, can be heard only as a faint echo. Nothing is more revealing about the author's rigorous and dispassionate approach to the new version than the change in meaning undergone even by the most terrible symbol of the natural: the slit-open pig's belly which Sigismund remembered seeing with horror, long before, nailed to the door lintel in the house of his peasant foster-father: "The morning sun shone into the interior, where it was dark; for my soul had been called away and had flown off somewhere. These are all joyful signs, but I cannot tell you what they mean."

In complete contrast to the focus in the first version, the emphasis of the drama now falls on the political action. For all but two scenes the setting is the king's castle. This change is not only justified by the much tighter plot structure; it also makes the portrayal of the rebellion much more convincing. For the audience, this now has something of the features of a palace revolt, and hence situates the action much more firmly than before "in the atmosphere of the seventeenth century." The conspiracy in which the action culminates now combines political and eschatological elements. The play of forces illustrates a permanent, providential element of all revolutions. By the same token, it may be that in modern history recurring political configurations have never found clearer, more permanent expression than in the seventeenth century. But in the first version, it was the power of the violent fanatics—with their visionary figurehead, the Children's King—that had the last word. The second version ends with the triumph of Olivier, the soldier. What this means is that the figure of the Children's King has now been merged with that of Sigismund. His conflict between willing and not willing has been resolved by the author, and only now do we grasp the whole meaning of what he wishes to say to his master, the leader of the rebellion and the precursor of his own power: "You placed me in straw, like an apple, and I have become ripe. Now I know my place. But it is not where you wanted me to be." Sigismund dies not in the army camp, as the commander of troops and princes, but as a wanderer on the highroad that leads to "a large, open country." "It smells of earth and salt. That is where I shall go."

What can his dying words—"I am much too well to hope"—mean, if not the same as Hamlet's "The readiness is all: since no man knows aught of what he leaves, what is't to leave betimes"? For this reason, it is perhaps not unreasonable to regard the poetic space filled by these two versions of *Der Turm* as ruled by the same forces that transform the bloody fatalities of pre-Shakespearean tragedy into the world of Christian suffering that is portrayed in *Hamlet*. A great poet has the ability to compress into a few years a transformation of forms and subjects that originally required decades for their fulfillment.

Published in *Die literarische Welt*, March 1928. *Gesammelte Schriften*, III, 98–101. Translated by Rodney Livingstone.

Notes

1. Pedro Calderón de la Barca (1600–1681), dramatist and poet, was one of the major playwrights of Spain's Golden Age. Among his best-known secular dramas are *El médico de su honra* (The Surgeon of His Honor; 1635), *La vida es sueño*

(Life Is a Dream; 1635), *El alcalde de Zalamea* (The Mayor of Zalamea; c. 1640), and *La hija del aire* (The Daughter of the Air; 1653). He also wrote operas and plays with religious and mythological themes.

2. *Sturm und Drang* refers to a literary movement in Germany between 1770 and 1780. The young authors, centered around Goethe, produced a number of dramas remarkable for their formal innovation and especially their expression of feeling. *Sturm und Drang* prose is exemplified, in particular, by Goethe's novel *Die Leiden des jungen Werther* (The Sorrows of Young Werther).

3. Kaspar Hauser was the most famous case of a "wild child" in Germany in the nineteenth century. A foundling, he was brought before a magistrate in Nuremberg on May 26, 1828, bewildered and incoherent; he had apparently been kept in virtual isolation for years. His origins remained a mystery, though some suspected he was of royal blood. He lived under the protection of educational reformers and noblemen, finally assuming a position in the court of appeals in Ansbach. He died from a wound that was either self-inflicted or, as he claimed, the result of an attack by a total stranger. The case has inspired many creative works, including Paul Verlaine's poem "Je suis venu, calme orphelin," in his collection *Sagesse* (1881); novels by Jakob Wassermann (1908), Sophie Hoechstetter (1925), and Otto Flake (1950); a play by Erich Ebermayer (1928); and a film directed by Werner Herzog (1974).

Moonlit Nights on the Rue La Boétie

At first, it is like entering an aquarium. Along the wall of the huge darkened hall, you see what appears to be a strip of illuminated water behind glass, broken at intervals by narrow joints. The play of colors in deep-sea fauna could not be more fiery. But what we see here are supraterrestrial, atmospheric miracles. Seraglios are mirrored in moonlit waters; nights in abandoned parks expose themselves to your gaze. In the moonlight you can recognize the château of Saint Leu, where a hundred years ago the body of the last Condé was discovered hanged in a window frame.[1] Somewhere a light is burning behind the curtains. A few shafts of sunlight fall at intervals. In the purer rays of a summer morning, you can peer into the *stanze* of the Vatican; they look just as they must have appeared to the Nazarenes.[2] Not far off, you can see the whole of Baden-Baden; and if the sun were not dazzling, you might be able to pick out Dostoevsky on the casino terrace from among the doll-like figures on a scale of 1:10,000. But even candlelight comes into its own. In the twilit cathedral, wax candles form a sort of *chapelle ardente* surrounding the murdered duc de Berry;[3] and the lamps in the silken skies of an island of love almost put chubby Luna to shame.

This is a unique experiment in what the Romantics called the "moonlit night of magic." It emerges triumphantly in its noble essence from every conceivable test to which its specific form of poetry has been subjected to here. It is almost frightening to think of the impact it must have had in its cruder, more massive state—in the magic pictures of the annual fairs and in dioramas. Or was this watercolor painting never popular because the technique was always too expensive? (It was done on paper that was scraped and rubbed, cut out in different places, given an underlay, and finally covered with wax in order to achieve the desired transparency.) We do not know the answer. For these forty transparencies are unique. We know of nothing like them and knew nothing even of these until recently, when they were discovered in someone's estate. They belonged to a collection assembled by a wealthy connoisseur, the great-grandfather of their present owner. Every piece was made for him individually. Great artists like Géricault, David, and Boilly are said to have been involved to a greater or lesser degree. Other experts believe that Daguerre worked on these plates before he created his famous diorama (which burned down in 1839, after seventeen years).

Whether the greatest artists really were involved or not is important only for the American who sooner or later will cough up the one and a half million francs that will be needed to buy the collection. For this technique has nothing to do with "art" in the strict sense—it belongs to all the arts. Its place is alongside that group of arts which is reckoned inferior at the moment but will not necessarily remain so, and which ranges from early techniques of the observer right down to the electronic television of our own day. In the nineteenth century, when children constituted the last audience for magic, these practical arts all converged in the dimension of play. Their intensity was not thereby diminished. Anyone who takes the time to dwell upon the transparency of the old spa of Contrexéville soon feels as if he had often strolled along this sunny path between the poplars, and as if he had brushed up against that very stone wall: modest magical effects for domestic use, of a sort only rarely seen—in Chinese soapstone groups, for example, or Russian lacquer paintings.

Published in *Die literarische Welt,* March 1928. *Gesammelte Schriften,* IV, 509–511. Translated by Rodney Livingstone.

Notes

1. "The last Condé" is the traditional name for Louis Henri-Joseph, duc de Bourbon (1756–1830). Having played a minor role on the side of the aristocracy in the French Revolution, he led a dissolute life in England and returned to France with his mistress, Sophie Dawes, in 1814. After he was found hanged in his château, Dawes was suspected of the murder; she was, however, released by order of Louis-Philippe, and the crime remained unsolved.

2. The Nazarenes were a group of painters roughly contemporary with the late Romantic movement who produced a body of spiritualizing work, comparable to that of the Pre-Raphaelites, though with a more explicitly religious content. The best-known artist of the group was Peter Cornelius.

3. In Catholicism, a *chapelle ardente* is a darkened room, illuminated with candles,

in which the body of a deceased person lies until placed in a casket. Charles Ferdinand de Bourbon, duc de Berry (1778–1820), served in the prince de Condé's army against the French Revolution, was exiled to England, and, after his return to France in 1815, was assassinated by Louis-Pierre Louvel, a worker obsessed with, in his own words, "exterminating the Bourbons."

Karl Kraus Reads Offenbach

Karl Kraus reads Offenbach. The orchestral music is replaced by an arrangement for piano, the French text by Treumann's translation, the troupe of costumed actors by himself in a business suit. And of himself we see only the head, arms, and torso. The rest has disappeared behind the little table which is covered by a cloth reaching down to the floor, rather like the tables used by conjurers to facilitate their acts. He thus devotes himself entirely to the business at hand, absolutely renouncing the use of any material props; but what he provides in these circumstances is unforgettable and unrepeatable in a higher sense than even the world premiere sixty years ago in the Théâtre du Palais-Royal could have been. The miracle of this evening did not spring from the fact that the work of Offenbach was being celebrated by the voice of one of the most inspired performers, the hand of one of the most indefatigable benefactors, and the gaze of one of the most courageous tamers of men. The miraculous thing about it was that it was brought about by the man who had devoted his life's work to *Die Fackel*,[1] with its world of pandemonium and paradise, whose inhabitants have now paired off and have plunged into the round dance of Offenbach's characters that opens up in delight and closes ranks behind them.

So the events on the stage stand completely outside the stubborn opposites of productive or reproductive achievement that apply only to the more or less vain or servile maneuverings of virtuosos. Kraus is no more of a "virtuoso" as a lecturer than he is a "master of language" as an author.[2] He is the same in both roles: on the one hand, the interpreter who catches out the rogue by printing his own words—often with commentary—between red covers, and, on the other hand, the man who makes a work of Offenbach's seem like a fairy tale merely by reading it aloud. But the fact is that he does not so much express Offenbach's words as speak from inside Offenbach. And every now and then he casts a breathtaking, half-blank, half-glinting procurer's glance at the crowd before him, inviting them to an unholy wedding with the masked figures in which they fail to recognize themselves, and invoking here too the evil privilege of the demon: the right to ambiguity.

Offenbach's works here undergo a mortal crisis. They contract, shed all superfluous trappings, venture the risky passage through this life and re-emerge at the end, redeemed and more real than before. For where this unpredictable voice is heard, the lightning shafts of illuminated advertisements and the thunder of the Métro cleave the air of the Paris of omnibuses and gaslights. And the works pay all this back with interest. At times they are transformed into a curtain; and like a fairground showman whose wild gestures accompany the entire performance, Karl Kraus tears this curtain aside, exposing the contents of their and our own chamber of horrors to our gaze. We glimpse Schober and Bekessy; and at its center point this evening, in honor of our city, we see Alfred Kerr on a lofty podium.[3]

At this point Kraus—intentionally, rightly—explodes the framework of the entire evening. Anarchically, he turns directly to the audience during an interval in a brief speech that applies to Berlin the refrain we have just heard: "I bring out the worst in every town." And in so doing he affects his listeners directly, in the same way he does with the texts he reads—that is to say, he assaults them unexpectedly, destructively, disrupting the prepared "mood," attacking the audience where they least anticipate it. In this respect he can only be compared to a puppeteer. It is here, not in the style of the operetta star, that his mimicry and his gestural language have their origin. For the soul of the marionette has entered his hands.

None of Offenbach's works fulfills the requirements of operetta as completely as *La vie parisienne*;[4] nothing in *La vie parisienne* is as Parisian as the transparent nature of that nonsensical nightlife through which not the logical but certainly the moral order makes its appearance. Of course, it does not come to judge; it comes as protest and evasion, as cunning and as mollifying gesture: in a word, as music. Music as preserver of the moral order? Music as the police of a world of pleasure? Yes, that is the splendor that falls on the old Paris ballrooms—the Grande Chaumière, the Bal Mabille, the Clôserie des Lilas—during his performance of *La vie parisienne*. "And the inimitable duplicity of this music, which simultaneously puts a plus sign and a minus sign before everything it says, betraying idyll to parody, mockery to lyricism—the abundance of musical devices ready to perform every service, uniting pleasure and pain: this gift is here developed to its purest pitch."[5] Anarchy, the only international constitution that is moral and worthy of man, becomes the true music of these operettas. The voice of Kraus speaks, rather than sings, this inner music. It whistles bitingly about the peaks of dizzying stupidity, reverberates shatteringly from the abyss of the absurd, and in Frascata's lines hums, like the wind in the chimney, a requiem to our grandfathers' generation.

Published in *Die literarische Welt,* April 1928. *Gesammelte Schriften,* IV, 515–517. Translated by Rodney Livingstone.

Notes

1. *Die Fackel* (The Torch) was the satirical magazine edited by Karl Kraus from 1899 to his death in 1936.
2. Kraus, whose satire focused on the defects in the language and style of his opponents, always claimed to be the true servant of language, not its master.
3. Johann Schober (1874–1932), Austrian politician and Vienna's chief of police, was responsible for the bloody suppression of workers' demonstrations. Alfred Kerr (pseudonym of Alfred Klemperer; 1867–1948) was Berlin's most prominent and influential theater critic.
4. *La vie parisienne,* a farcical opera in four acts with music by Jacques Offenbach and libretto by Henri Meilhac and Ludovic Halévy, premiered at the Palais Royal in 1886.
5. Karl Kraus, "Offenbach Renaissance," *Die Fackel* 557–558 (April 1927): 47.

The Cultural History of Toys

Karl Gröber, *Kinderspielzeug aus alter Zeit: Eine Geschichte des Spielzeugs* [Children's Toys from Olden Times: A History of Toys] (Berlin: Deutscher Kunstverlag, 1928), 68 pages, with 306 black-and-white illustrations and 12 color plates.

At the beginning of Karl Gröber's book *Kinderspielzeug aus alter Zeit,* we find a self-denying ordinance. The author declares that he will not discuss children's games, so as to be able to focus more on his physical material and devote himself exclusively to the history of toys. The extraordinary density not so much of his topic as of his own method has led him to concentrate on the European tradition. If this meant Germany was at the geographic center, then in this sphere it is also the spiritual center. For a good proportion of the most beautiful toys that we still encounter in museums and homes may be described as a German gift to Europe. Nuremberg is the home of the tin soldier and the well-kept collection of animals from Noah's ark. The oldest known dollhouse comes from Munich. Even people who have no patience with claims to priority, claims that are of little consequence in this context anyway, will readily agree that they are presented with unsurpassable examples of simple beauty in Sonneberg's wooden dolls (Illustration 192), the trees made of wood shavings from the Erzgebirge (Illustration 190), the spice shops and bonnet shops (Illustrations 274 and 275, Plate X), and the harvest festival scene in pewter from Hanover.

Of course, such toys were not originally the invention of toy manufacturers, but were produced in the workshops of wood carvers, pewterers, and so forth. Not until the nineteenth century did toymaking become the province of a branch-industry of its own. The particular style and beauty of toys of the older kind can be understood only if we realize that toys used to be a by-product of the many handicrafts that were all subject to the rules and regulations of the guilds, so that each member could manufacture only products that fell within the definition of his own trade. In the course of the eighteenth century, when manufacturing began to be specialized, producers everywhere came up against the restrictions imposed by the guilds. The guilds forbade turners to paint their own dolls, and they compelled workers in various trades who made toys from all sorts of different materials to divide the simplest work among themselves and so made the goods more expensive.

It obviously follows from this that sales, particularly retail sales in toys, were not the province of special toy sellers. You could find carvings of animals at the woodworker's shop, tin soldiers at the boilermaker's, gum-resin figurines at the confectioner's, and wax dolls at the candlemaker's. The picture was rather different at the wholesale level. Here too the middlemen, the so-called *Verlag,* originated in Nuremberg, where exporters began to buy up toys from the urban handicraft industry and above all from the homeworkers and distribute them among retailers. At around the same time, the advance of the Reformation forced many artists who had formerly worked for the Church "to shift to the production of goods to satisfy the demand for craftwork, and to produce smaller art objects for domestic use, instead of large-scale works." This led to a huge upsurge in the production of the tiny objects that filled toy cupboards and gave such pleasure to children, as well as the collections of artworks and curiosities that gave such pleasure to adults. It was this that created the fame of Nuremberg and led to the hitherto unshaken dominance of German toys on the world market.

If we survey the entire history of toys, it becomes evident that the question of size has far greater importance than might have been supposed. In the second half of the nineteenth century, when the long-term decline in these things begins, we see toys becoming larger; the unassuming, the tiny, and the playful all slowly disappear. It was only then that children acquired a playroom of their own and a cupboard in which they could keep books separately from those of their parents. There can be no doubt that the older volumes with their smaller format called for the mother's presence, whereas the modern quartos with their insipid and indulgent sentimentality are designed to enable children to disregard her absence. The process of emancipating the toy begins. The more industrialization penetrates, the more it decisively eludes the control of the family and becomes increasingly alien to children and also to parents.

Of course, the false simplicity of the modern toy was based on the authentic longing to rediscover the relationship with the primitive, to recuperate the style of a home-based industry that at this very time was locked in an increasingly hopeless struggle for survival in Thuringia and the Erzgebirge. Anyone who has been following the statistics on wages knows that these industries are heading toward their demise. This is doubly regrettable, particularly when you realize that of all the available materials none is more suitable than wood, thanks to its resilience and its ability to take paint. And in general it is this external point of view—the question of technology and materials—that leads the observer most deeply into the world of toys. Gröber brings this out in a highly illuminating and instructive way. If we look beyond the question of materials and glance at the child playing, we may speak of an antinomian relationship. It looks like this: On the one hand, nothing is more suitable for children than playhouses built of harmonious combinations of the most heterogeneous materials—stone, plasticine, wood, and paper. On the other hand, no one is more chaste in the use of materials than children: a bit of wood, a pinecone, a small stone—however unified and unambiguous the material is, the more it seems to embrace the possibility of a multitude of figures of the most varied sort. And when adults give children dolls made of birchbark or straw, a cradle made of glass, or boats made of pewter, they are attempting to respond in their own way to the children's feelings. In this microcosm, wood, bones, wickerwork, and clay are the most important materials, all of which were already used in patriarchal times, when toys were still a part of the production process that found parents and children together. Later came metals, glass, paper, and even alabaster. The alabaster bosom that seventeenth-century poets celebrated in their poems was to be found only in dolls, whose fragility often cost them their existence.

A review like this can only hint at the riches of Gröber's work, the thoroughness of its underlying research, the beguiling objectivity of its presentation. This completely successful collection of illustrations is perfect at the technical level, too. Anyone who fails to read it attentively will scarcely know what toys are, let alone their importance. This last question leads, of course, beyond the framework of the book to a philosophical classification of toys. As long as the realm of toys was dominated by a dour naturalism, there were no prospects of drawing attention to the true face of a child at play. Today we may perhaps hope that it will be possible to overcome the basic error—namely, the assumption that the imaginative content of a child's toys is what determines his playing; whereas in reality the opposite is true. A child wants to pull something, and so he becomes a horse; he wants to play with sand, and so he turns into a baker; he wants to hide, and so he turns into a robber or a policeman. We are also familiar with a number of ancient playthings that were presumably once cult objects but that scorn the function of masks: balls, hoops, tops, kites—authentic playthings; "the more authentic, the less they meant to adults." Because the more appealing toys are, in the ordinary sense of the term, the further they are from genuine playthings; the more they are based on imitation, the further away they lead us from real, living play. This is borne out by the different kinds of dollhouses that Gröber includes. Imitation (we may conclude) is at home in the playing, not in the plaything.

But of course, we would penetrate neither to the reality nor to the conceptual understanding of toys if we tried to explain them in terms of the child's mind. After all, a child is no Robinson Crusoe; children do not constitute a community cut off from everything else. They belong to the nation and the class they come from. This means that their toys cannot bear witness to any autonomous separate existence, but rather are a silent signifying dialogue between them and their nation. A signifying dialogue to the decoding of which this work provides a secure foundation.

Published in the *Frankfurter Zeitung,* May 1928. *Gesammelte Schriften,* III, 113–117. Translated by Rodney Livingstone.

Toys and Play

Marginal Notes on a Monumental Work

Karl Gröber, *Kinderspielzeug aus alter Zeit: Eine Geschichte des Spielzeugs* [Children's Toys from Olden Times: A History of Toys] (Berlin: Deutscher Kunstverlag, 1928), 68 pages, with 306 black-and-white illustrations and 12 color plates.

It will be a while before you are ready to read this book, so fascinating is the sight of the endless variety of toys that its illustrated section unfolds before the reader. Battalions of soldiers, coaches, theaters, sedan chairs, sets of dishes—all in Lilliputian format. The time had to come when someone would assemble the family tree of rocking horses and lead soldiers, and write the archaeology of toyshops and dolls' parlors. This has been done here in a scholarly and conscientious manner and without any archival pedantry in the book's text, which stands on a par with the illustrations. The book is cast in a single mold, and the reader can detect nothing of the labor involved in producing it. Now that the book lies before us, it is hard to imagine how it could ever have been otherwise.

But it must be said that research of this kind is in tune with the age. The German Museum in Munich, the Toy Museum in Moscow, the toy department of the Musée des Arts Décoratifs in Paris—all creations of the recent past or the present—point to the fact that everywhere, and no doubt for good reason, there is growing interest in honest-to-goodness toys. Gone are the days of character dolls, when adults pandered to childish needs under the pretext of satisfying childlike ones. The schematic individualism of the arts-and-crafts movement and the picture of the child given by the psychology of the individual—two trends that understood each other all too well— were undermined from within. At the same time, the first attempts were made to escape from the influence of psychology and aestheticism. Folk art and the worldview of the child demanded to be seen as collectivist ways of thinking.

On the whole, the work under review corresponds to this latest state of research, if indeed it is possible to tie a standard work of a documentary kind to a theoretical stance. For in reality the stage reached here must form a transition to a more precise definition of our knowledge of the subject. The fact is that the perceptual world of the child is influenced at every point by traces of the older generation, and has to take issue with them. The same applies to the child's play activities. It is impossible to construct them as dwelling in a fantasy realm, a fairy-tale land of pure childhood or pure art. Even where they are not simply imitations of the tools of adults, toys are a site of conflict, less of the child with the adult than of the adult with the child. For who gives the child his toys if not adults? And even if he retains a certain power to accept or reject them, a not insignificant proportion of the oldest toys (balls, hoops, tops, kites) are in a certain sense imposed on him as cult implements that became toys only afterward, partly through the child's powers of imagination.

It is therefore a great mistake to believe that it is simply children's needs that determine what is to be a toy. It is nonsense to argue, as does an otherwise meritorious recent work, that the necessity of, say, a baby's rattle can be inferred from the fact that "As a rule it is the ear that is the first organ to clamor for occupation"—particularly since the rattle has always been an instrument with which to ward off evil spirits, and this is why it has to be put in the hand of a newborn baby. And even the author of the present work is surely in error when he writes, "The child wants from her doll only what she sees and knows in adults. This is why, until well into the nineteenth century, the doll was popular only when dressed in grown-up clothing; the baby in swaddling clothes that dominates the toy market nowadays was completely absent." No, this is not to be laid at the door of children; for the child at play, a doll is sometimes big and sometimes little, and as an inferior being it is more often the latter. We may say instead that until well into the nineteenth century the idea of an infant as a creature shaped by a spirit of its own was completely unknown; on the other hand, the adult was the ideal in whose image the educator aspired to mold the child. This rationalism, with its conviction that the child is just a little adult, makes us smile today, but it had the merit of declaring seriousness to be the child's proper sphere. In contrast to this, the inferior sense of "humor" manifests itself in toys, alongside the use of larger-scale objects, as an expression of the uncertainty that the bourgeois cannot free himself of in his dealings with children. The merriment that springs from a sense of guilt sits admirably with the silly distortions of size. Anyone who wishes to look the hideous features of commodity capital in the face need only recollect toyshops as they typically were up to five years ago (and as they still often are in small towns today). The basic atmosphere was one of hellish exuberance. On the lids of the parlor games and the faces of the character dolls, you found grinning masks; they gaped at you alluringly from the black mouth of the cannon, and giggled in the ingenious "catastrophe coach" that fell to pieces, as expected, when the train crashed.

But scarcely had this militant viciousness made its exit than the class character of this toy reappeared elsewhere. "Simplicity" became the fashionable slogan of the industry. In reality, however, in the case of toys simplicity is to be found not in their shapes but in the transparent nature of the manufacturing process. Hence, it cannot be judged according to an abstract canon but differs in different places, and is less a matter of formal criteria, because a number of methods of processing—carving, in particular—can give free rein to their imagination without becoming in the least incomprehensible. In the same way, the genuine and self-evident simplicity of toys was a matter of technology, not formalist considerations. For a characteristic feature of all folk art—the way in which primitive technology combined with cruder materials imitates sophisticated technology combined with expensive materials—can be seen with particular clarity in the world of toys. Porcelain from the great czarist factories in Russian villages provided the model for dolls and genre scenes carved in wood. More recent research into folk art has long since abandoned the belief that "primitive" inevitably means "older." Frequently, so-called folk art is nothing more than the cultural goods of a ruling class that have trickled down and been given a new lease on life within the framework of a broad collective.

Not the least of this book's achievements is that Gröber decisively shows how the economic and particularly the technological culture of the collective have influenced toys. But if to this day toys have been far too commonly regarded as objects created for children, if not as the creations of children themselves, then with play it is the other way around: play has been thought about altogether too exclusively from the point of view of adults, and has been regarded too much as the imitation of adults. And it cannot be denied that we needed this encyclopedia of toys to revive discussion of the theory of play, which has not been treated in this context since Karl Groos published his important work *Spiele der Menschen* [People at Play] in 1899.[1] Any novel theory would have to take account of the "*Gestalt* theory of play gestures"—gestures of which Willy Haas recently listed (May 18, 1928) the three most important.[2] First, cat and mouse (any game of catch); second, the mother animal that defends her nest and her young (for example, a goalkeeper or tennis player); third, the struggle between two animals for prey, a bone, or an object of love (a football, polo ball, and so on). Going beyond that, one would have to investigate the enigmatic doubles of stick and hoop, whip and top, marble and king-marble, as well as the magnetic attraction generated between the two parts. In all probability the situation is this: before we transcend ourselves in love and enter into the life and the often alien rhythm of another human being, we experiment early on with basic rhythms that proclaim themselves in their simplest forms in these sorts of games with inanimate objects. Or rather, these are the rhythms in which we first gain possession of ourselves.

Last, such a study would have to explore the great law that presides over the rules and rhythms of the entire world of play: the law of repetition. We know that for a child repetition is the soul of play, that nothing gives him greater pleasure than to "Do it again!" The obscure urge to repeat things is scarcely less powerful in play, scarcely less cunning in its workings, than the sexual impulse in love. It is no accident that Freud has imagined he could detect an impulse "beyond the pleasure principle" in it. And in fact, every profound experience longs to be insatiable, longs for return and repetition until the end of time, and for the reinstatement of an original condition from which it sprang. "All things would be resolved in a trice / If we could only do them twice." Children act on this proverb of Goethe's. Except that the child is not satisfied with twice, but wants the same thing again and again, a hundred or even a thousand times. This is not only the way to master frightening fundamental experiences—by deadening one's own response, by arbitrarily conjuring up experiences, or through parody; it also means enjoying one's victories and triumphs over and over again, with total intensity. An adult relieves his heart from its terrors and doubles happiness by turning it into a story. A child creates the entire event anew and starts again right from the beginning. Here, perhaps, is the deepest explanation for the two meanings of the German word *Spielen:* the element of repetition is what is actually common to them.[3] Not a "doing as if" but a "doing the same thing over and over again," the transformation of a shattering experience into habit—that is the essence of play.

For play and nothing else is the mother of every habit. Eating, sleeping, getting dressed, washing have to be instilled into the struggling little brat in a playful way, following the rhythm of nursery rhymes. Habit enters life as a game, and in habit, even in its most sclerotic forms, an element of play survives to the end. Habits are the forms of our first happiness and our first horror that have congealed and become deformed to the point of being unrecognizable. And without knowing it, even the most arid pedant plays in a childish rather than a childlike way; the more childish his play, the more pedantic he is. He just does not recollect his own playing; only to him would a book like this have nothing to say. But when a modern poet says that everyone has a picture for which he would be willing to give the whole world, how many people would not look for it in an old box of toys?

Published in *Die literarische Welt,* June 1928. *Gesammelte Schriften,* III, 127–132. Translated by Rodney Livingstone.

Notes

1. Karl Groos (1861–1946), German philosopher, wrote a number of pioneering works on the psychology of human and animal play.
2. Willy Haas (1891–1973), German-Jewish author and critic, founded the periodical *Die literarische Welt,* which he edited until 1933.
3. The German word *Spielen* means both "to play" and "games."

Everything Is Thought

Everything is thought [*gedacht*]. The task is to make a stopover at every one of these many little thoughts. To spend the night in a thought. Once I have done that, I know something about it that its originator never dreamed of.

Fragment written ca. June 1928. *Gesammelte Schriften*, VI, 200. Translated by Rodney Livingstone.

Books by the Mentally Ill

From My Collection

A sense of embarrassment often goes unnoticed as the source of a successful enterprise.

When I began, ten years ago, to create a more satisfactory order among my books, I soon came across volumes that I could not bring myself to get rid of but that I could no longer bear to leave where they were.

Hermann von Gilm's poems are among the curiosities of German literature, but I know that at the time I was experiencing Hölderlin as a revelation, I had no wish to include them in the section on German poetry.[1] Emil Szittya's first publication, *Ecce-Homo-Ulk* [Ecce Homo Trick], is something I would not want to be without, any more than many another revealing piece of juvenilia by better-known writers. Yet I drove it from one section to another, until it finally found a refuge not far from Gilm's poetry. And Blüher's *Aristie des Jesus von Nazareth* [The Heroic Ballad of Jesus of Nazareth] was a work I did not wish to include in my books on the philosophy of religion. Nevertheless, its contribution to the pathology of anti-Semitic resentment seemed too valuable for me to dispose of it.[2]

In this way a motley collection came together over the years, a "Library of Pathology," long before I thought to actively build a collection of writings by the mentally ill—indeed, long before I even knew that books by the mentally ill existed.

Then, in 1918, in a small antiquarian bookshop in Berne, I came across Schreber's famous *Denkwürdigkeiten eines Nervenkranken* [Memoirs of My Nervous Illness], published by Oswald Mutze in Leipzig. Had I already heard of this book? Or did I read about it a few weeks later in the essay on it by Freud in volume 3 of his *Kleine Schriften zur Neurosenlehre* [Shorter

Writings on the Theory of the Neuroses], published in Leipzig in 1913? No matter. I was at once spellbound by it.

The publisher of Schreber's memoirs had built something of a reputation for specializing in the quaintest spiritualist writings. It is readily understandable that such an enterprise might be the most likely to agree to publish a theological system in which "only God might approach corpses without danger," or whose author "could be in no doubt that God is familiar with the concept of railways," or which develops a theory to the effect that God's language, the so-called "basic language, is a somewhat old-fashioned, but vigorous German." In this language God is called "that which is and will be," and the patient's former comrades from his dueling fraternity are referred to as "those suspended beneath Cassiopeia." And equally remarkable and succinct are the turns of phrase this paranoid finds at different stages of his illness to describe everyday facts that have become inexplicable to him. The idea of the end of the world, not uncommon among paranoids, obsesses him to such a degree that he can conceive of other people's existence only as a frivolous delusion. To enable him to come to terms with it, his writings abound in references to "casually improvised men," "miracle dolls," people who have been "magicked away," and so forth. The book also contains a number of other extraordinary coinages. The patient's compulsion to shout, the "shouting miracle," he contemptuously calls a "psychic throat-clearing." Similarly, references to the "countermeaning of primal words," a theme treated sporadically by Freud, also appear in this remarkable document. "Juice" is called "poison," "poison" is called "food," "reward" is called "punishment," and so on.

The entire work was originally dedicated by the author to his wife, as a guide to the religious ideas he developed during his illness. Not without a concrete reason. After being hospitalized for ten years, Presiding Judge Schreber was declared fit and able to return to his duties and was restored to his family, the result of his frequent and highly intelligent reports, which he later published as appendixes to his memoirs. The various stages of his illness, right down to the remarkably rigorous and successful process of containing his delusions, cannot be discussed here of course, any more than there is room to give a psychiatric account of his case or the others mentioned below.

This much is clear: the universe constructed by the Royal Bavarian Government and District Medical Counselor Carl Friedrich Anton Schmidt, Doctor of Philosophy, Medicine, Surgery, and Midwifery and member of several learned societies, scarcely provides a clinical picture of paranoia or any other psychosis. Psychiatry has long since progressed beyond the time when every symptom was misused to characterize a particular form of insanity; if this were not the case, we might well speak of a "cataloguing psychosis." The learned and perhaps highly esteemed author of *Leben und*

Frontispiece from C. F. Schmidt, *Leben und Wissenschaft in ihren Elementen und Gesetzen.* The eye in the center of the image symbolizes God, whose life-giving gaze encompasses the four main areas of human endeavor: religion, jurisprudence, medicine, and art. These four fields appear in the corners of the illustration as (respectively) a virgin at prayer, a female judge, Aesculapius, and a hovering Apollo, all represented with the symbols of their activities. The figures grouped around the centerpoint suggest, on one side, the stages of individual existence—man, angel, seraph—and, on the other, the higher material world, in the form of stars, moon, and sun. Beneath the eye is the sun of being, which shines down on the earth (with its symbols of time and transience). We cannot here enter into the extremely complex details of these symbols, all of which come together in various triads.

Haus

	Zurichtung						Einrichtung					
	Gestaltung			**Zugänge**			**Hauptpunete des häuslichen Bedürfnisses**			**Nebenpunete des häuslichen Bedürfnisses**		
	Grundtheile	Verbindungstheile	Schlusstheile	Hauptöffnungen	Nebenöffnungen	Lichte Räume	Wohnorte	Bereitungs- u. Verwahrungs- Orte in erster Reihe	Feuerungsplätze	Nebenorte des Aufenthaltes u. allgemeiner Aufbewahrung in zweiter Reihe	Specielle Bereitungs- u. Aufbewahrungs- Orte in zweiter Reihe	Für Unterbringung von Thieren, Abfällen u. dgl.
	Grundmauern	Fußböden	Giebel	Thore	Kellerlöcher	Vorplatz	Zimmer	Küche	Oefen	Altane	Waschhaus	Stallung
	Umfassungsmauern	Decken	Dach	Thüren	Bodenlöcher	Gänge	Saal	Keller	Heerde	Mezane	Holzlager	Dungstätten, Abtritte u. dgl.
	Verbindungsmauern	Treppen	Schläue	Fenster	Oberlichter	Hof	Kabinet	Boden	Kamine	Kammer	Remisen	Reservoirs

Hauptbaumaterial			**Hülfsbau material**			**Bauhaltpunete**		
Stein	Holz	Eisen	Ziegel oder Schiefer	Mörtel und Farbe	Glas	Gewölbe und Tragbogen	Tragsteine und Tragbalken	Säulen und Pfeiler.

Tabular breakdown of the house. From C. F. Schmidt, *Leben und Wissenschaft in ihren Elementen und Gesetzen*, illustration 6. [The table divides and subdivides the house in a seemingly rational manner, listing not merely furnishings and construction methods, but rooms, roofs, walls, cellars, and arches, ending with a list of support structures. *Zurichtung* = "Preparation"; *Einrichtung* = "Arrangement." Major categories, from left to right and from top to bottom, are "Shaping," "Apertures," "Primary sites of domestic need," "Secondary sites of domestic need," "Primary building materials," "Accessory building materials," and "Load-bearing points."—*Trans.*]

Wissenschaft in ihren Elementen und Gesetzen [The Elements and Laws of Life and Science], published in Würzburg in 1842, was perhaps entirely sane in the ordinary sense of the term. The text of his book betrays nothing of his obsessive idea. At most, readers might be puzzled by the excessive space devoted to model psychiatric reports in the section entitled "Anthropology and Medicine." The reports he discusses were obviously written by him. This man seems to be more like a reincarnation of an early surgeon, or rather a contemporary of the doctor in Büchner's *Woyzeck*.[3] A glance at the illustrations instantly makes clear the manic character of his worldview.

If the realm of delusion had four faculties, like the realm of knowledge, the works of Schreber and Schmidt would be a compendium of their theology and worldly wisdom, respectively. We turn now to jurisprudence. Take, for example, *Der Ganz-Erden-Universal-Staat* [The Whole-Earth Universal State]. The prodigal author has written a handbook for use by heads of state, particularly "the King of England, London," and has dedicated it to various saints, notably "H. P. Blavatsky of the Great and Universal Theosophical Society."[4] The work was presumably published at his own expense. A small rubber-stamped notice reading "Ganz-Erden-Universalstaats-Edition, Brno 2—Brünn 2, P.O. Box 13," and the label stuck on by a commissioned publisher, constitute all the bibliographic information we can glean about this book. The printer's credit gives the year 1924.

No closer examination of it is called for. If ever a lunacy was harmless, the work of this Slavic author, imbued as it is with the spirit of vagabond Russian monks, is a prime example.

Last: a document testifying to a psychosis of the most serious kind, a medical work with which we will conclude for the moment. Carl Gehrmann, a doctor practicing in Berlin, wrote *Körper, Gehirn, Seele, Gott* [Body, Brain, Soul, God], four parts in three volumes, published in Berlin in 1893. The following are from volume 4, which contains the medical histories:

Case 1. The broken reed is raised up again.

Case 7. Stimulation of the nubes—the ear of corn becomes a reed—reduction in size as the starting point for perfecting the form of a blueberry—stimulation of the "pneuma" and "mother of God" centers—forget me not—the water level of the day of the Lord—the gulf between "religion and yearning" is concerned with clandestine love and how it bears on conflict.

Case 13. Effect of sweaty feet on the sexual and respiratory systems—a cure implies the harmonious unfolding of the "stocking" [*Strümpfe*] centers—the well of the sacraments.

Case 30. The crucifix behind the green, veil-like window curtains—*pneuma and Mother of God*—the abstract window dominates the will—the scar as symbol of piety heals the crucifix *tactile*.

Deshalb können *gegenwärtig* die Lohnverhältnisse *gutherzig, liebevoll, vernünftig* und *zweckmäßig-segensreich* nur auf diese Art geregelt werden (selbstverständlich unter noch bedeutend vorteilhafteren und besseren Approvisationsverhältnissen als vor dem Kriege!) und zwar:

1. Dienende Bürger	1000	Kronen
2. Hoffnungs-Bürger	1500	"
3. Ehrenbürger mit 4 höheren Volksschulklassen	2000	"
4. Ehrenbürger mit Matura	3000	"
5. Ehrenbürger mit 2facher Universitätsbildung	4000	"
6. Ehrenbürger mit 3f. Univ. b.	4500	"
7. Ehrenbürger mit 4f. Univ. b.	5000	"
8. Ehrenbürger mit 5f. Univ. b.	5500	"
9. Ehrenbürger mit 6f. Univ. b.	6000	Kronen
10. Ehrenbürger mit 7f. Univ. b.	6500	"
11. Ehrenbürger mit 8f. Univ. b.	7000	"
12. Ehrenbürger mit 9f. Univ. b.	7500	"
13. Ehrenbürger m. 10f. Univ. b.	8000	"
14. Hervorragende Künstler, Komponisten, Maler, Dichter, Erfinder usw. (Ehrenbürger!) sollen jährlich mit einem *Ehrenhonorar* belohnt werden.	9000	"
15. Könige ausnahmsweise	10000	"
16. Herren	6000	"
17. HErren	5000	"
18. HERRen	4000	"
19. HERREN (Asketen)	3000	"
20. HEILIGE im aktiven Stand	2000	"
21. KAISER	—	"

Salary categories. From *Der Ganz-Erden-Universal-Staat*, illustration 7. [Categories 1 and 2 give wages for "Citizens in domestic service" and "Hope citizens," respectively. Categories 3–13 give wages for workers at various ascending levels of education. Category 14 gives wages for distinguished artists, composers, painters, poets, and inventors. Category 15 = "Kings (special case)." Categories 16–19 list salaries for various levels of "Gentlemen." Category 20 = "Currently active saints."—*Trans.*]

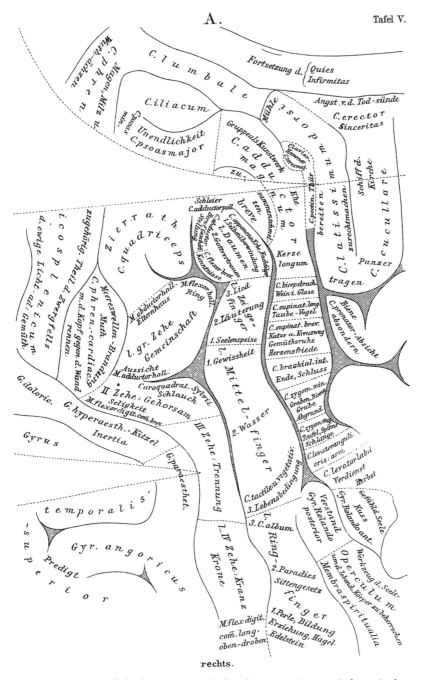

Diagram of a region of the brain. From Carl Gehrmann, *Körper, Gehirn, Seele, Gott*, illustration 8. [Gehrmann claims to identify not only areas of the brain associated with physical attributes ("Middle finger," "Index finger") but also areas associated with spiritual states and functions ("Fear of moral sin," "Implements of the soul," "Feeling of the soul," "Infinity," "Abyss").—*Trans.*]

Case 32. The millwheel in the hot-air balloon of the church (the *red currant*).

Case 40. Lying in the forest stream of the blessing is homologous with sleeping in the bed of the church—the blue rocky pinnacle bathed in light.

Gehrmann's theological medical science, which is illustrated by 258 cases of this sort, is concerned principally with menstruation and is based on the assumption that all the organs, nerves, blood vessels, and parts of the body correspond to specific parts of the brain. To these he has given the fantastic names that are referred to in the titles to his "cases." Reproduced here is an example of the countless diagrams the sick man has included in his book.

The mere existence of such works has something disconcerting about it. So long as we habitually regard writing as—despite everything—part of a higher, safer realm, the appearance of insanity, especially when it enters less noisily than elsewhere, is all the more terrifying. How could this happen? How did it manage to slip past the passport control of the city of books, this Thebes with a hundred doors? The publishing history of such works must often be as bizarre as their contents. Nowadays, one would like to think, the situation is different. Interest in the manifestations of madness is as universal as ever, but it has become more fruitful and legitimate. The writings of the insane, so we might suppose, would have no trouble obtaining a valid passport today. Yet I know of a manuscript that is finding it as difficult as ever to obtain the approval of a respected publishing house, even though it is at least the equal of Schreber's in both human and literary terms, and far superior in intelligibility. If this brief essay should arouse interest in it, and if these all too brief excerpts could stimulate the reader to turn his attention to the posters and leaflets of the insane, then these lines would have fulfilled a twofold purpose.

Published in *Die literarische Welt,* July 1928. *Gesammelte Schriften,* IV, 615–619. Translated by Rodney Livingstone.

Notes

1. Hermann von Gilm (1812–1864) was the author of many poems, including the cycle *Sonette aus Wälschtirol* (Sonnets from the Italian Tirol).
2. Hans Blüher (1888–1955) was a German theorist of the Youth Movement and the author of *Die deutsche Wandervogelbewegung als erotisches Phänomen* (The German Youth Movement as Erotic Phenomenon; 1912). The *Aristie* was published in 1922.
3. The doctor in Georg Büchner's play hopes to cure Woyzeck of his mental delusions by prescribing a diet consisting solely of peas.
4. Helena Petrovna Blavatsky (1831–1891) founded the Theosophical Society. Her most important work is *The Secret Doctrine* (1888).

Review of the Mendelssohns' *Der Mensch in der Handschrift*

Anja and Georg Mendelssohn, *Der Mensch in der Handschrift* [Man in His Handwriting] (Leipzig: E. A. Seemann, [1928–]1930), 100 pages.

Does this book need a recommendation? I think not. It will be a great success. One thoroughly well deserved.

It represents the science of graphology at its very best. It represents graphological intuition at its very best. It is also scientific exposition at its very best.

Furthermore, it is tactful in the extreme—a factor worth mentioning in books with a psychoanalytic bent. At any rate, the brevity and precision of this book may in a sense be interpreted as tact. It nowhere says too much, and says nothing too often. Hence, its tone is as stimulating as it is instructive. Last, it has the rare creative modesty typical of the person who lives wholly inside his subject and who is utterly incapable of viewing it complacently from the outside.

If there is anything about the activities of graphologists that might give offense to the plain-thinking person, it is the complacency with which vulgar practitioners have appealed to the philistines' curiosity and passion for gossip by offering to reveal the "truth" about Tom, Dick, and Harry, and a whole gallery of revelations about everyone from their ancestors to the housewife. The more recent scientific experiments of Klages, Ivanovic, and others have of course nothing in common with any of that. But it is unlikely that anyone has ever fought so tenaciously to grasp the integral riddle of mankind—a riddle that seems to survive all analysis unscathed in its purity.

This is the laudable expression of a methodology of which the aforementioned tact is only an outer manifestation. Not that the methodology is so very new. But what is crucial in this instance is the seriousness with which it is applied. It represents a systematic attempt to construe the handwriting of even civilized people as a set of hieroglyphs. And the authors have managed to preserve contact with the world of images to a hitherto unprecedented degree. People have always regarded the distinction between strokes—right and left, top and bottom, straight and sloping, heavy and light—as crucial. But these qualities always contained a vague remnant of analogy and metaphor. In the case of a person with cramped handwriting, it would be said that "he keeps his possessions close together—that is to say, he is parsimonious." This was doubtless accurate, but it was the language that had to bear the cost of this graphological insight. The same holds true for the "spiritual vision" that Klages invokes as judge of the general formal level [*Formniveau*] of someone's handwriting, of the greater or lesser amount of wealth, plenitude, weightiness, warmth, density, or depth.[1] At decisive moments it comes up against the image that we encapsulate in our handwriting as we write. This gives us some justification for arguing, against Klages, that the idea of handwriting as "fixed expressive movement" is inadequate. For the idea "claims that writing is determined by gesture—but this theory can be extended: gesture in its turn is determined by the *inner* image."

It would be an easy matter to show how this link with the image has the power to strengthen the graphologist's reluctance to make moral judgments on handwriting—something that he is always called on to do and that will no doubt continue for the foreseeable future. It would be even better if he were to take the initiative and refrain from saying any more on such matters than a man of honor can justify today—namely, anything at all. Or, to quote the authors: "Observation . . . teaches that a person carries both the light and dark sides of his character within himself." Nothing moral is ever apparent in physiognomy. Moral character is a thing without expression [*ein Ausdrucksloses*]; it emerges, invisibly or dazzlingly, from the concrete situation. It can be confirmed, but never has any predictive force. Where ignoring it can lead to is something demonstrated by Klages' own major contribution to graphology. If the authors retreat from his basic concept—that of the "formal level," which he believes affords him an ethical yardstick for assessing the character of the person writing—this retreat can be justified by reference to the abstruse arguments that Klages' vitalism [*Lebensphiloso-phie*] imposes on his graphology: "The vitality and plenitude of humanity and the expressive power of their precipitates in men's spirit have been in decline ever since the Renaissance, and have been hurtling toward total collapse ever since the French Revolution. It has now reached the point where the richest and most talented person of our day partakes of an incomparably impoverished medium, and can achieve at best no more in terms of wealth of personality than what had been the *average* some four or five hundred years before." Such ideas have their place and their justification in Klages' polemics, and there is nothing new in this. But it would be intolerable to have to think of graphology as a playground for such life philosophies [*Lebensphilosophien*] or occult teachings. Its ability to free itself from sectarianism of every kind is a question of life and death for it at the present time. And it is evident that far from being conclusive, its only possible reply is for it to take the form of a creative indifference, of an *extrême milieu*.[2]

Such creative indifference can never of course be found in the golden middle way. It is an unceasingly renewed dialectical compromise; it is no geometric location, but the focal point of a process, the force field of a discharge. In terms of its contribution to a theory of handwriting, one might sketch the outlines of this realm by defining it as the dynamic (nonmechanistic) compromise between the theories of the Mendelssohns and those of Klages, something that contributes toward the theory of interpreting handwriting. The antagonism between the two is important because it is so rich in possibilities. It is rooted in the opposition of body [*Leib*] and language.

Language has a body and the body has a language. Nevertheless, the world is founded on that part of the body which is not language (the moral sphere), and on that part of language which is not body (the expressionless [*dem Ausdruckslosen*]). In contrast, graphology is concerned with the bodily aspect of the language of handwriting and with the expressive aspect of the body of handwriting. Klages' starting point is language, expression. The Mendelssohns' is the body—that is to say, the image.

Illuminating signposts lead us into the hitherto scarcely suspected richness of this pictorial dimension. In much of this, the authors have learned from Freud and Bachofen. But they are sufficiently open-minded to look for a stock of images even in inconspicuous material—anywhere, in fact, where they could discover value and expressive force for our feeling for life. Nothing is more revealing yet more appropriate to the subject, for example, than the following comparison between handwriting and children's drawings, in which the ground is represented by a straight line: "At a certain point in children's development, the letters . . . stand on the line, just as their models—people, animals, and objects—stand on the ground. The fact that the tails extend below ground level must not deter us from looking for the legs *on* the line when we translate the letters back into bodily postures. In other letters, heads, eyes, mouths, and hands can be found at the same height and next to one another, just as in the drawings of young children who have not yet learned how to draw the parts of the body in proportion or in the correct relationship to each other." Just as revealing are the sketchy outlines of a cubic graphology. Handwriting is only apparently a surface phenomenon. We can see from the impression made in the paper during printing that there is a sculptural depth, a space behind the writing plane for the writer; on the other hand, interruptions in the flow of writing reveal the few points at which the pen is drawn back into the space in front of the writing plane, so as to describe its "immaterial curves." Could the cubic pictorial space of writing be a copy in microcosm of a clairvoyant space? Is this the source of the insights of telepathic graphologists like Rafael Scherman? Whatever the answer, the cubic theory of writing opens up the prospect that one day it may be possible to exploit graphology to investigate telepathic events.

It goes without saying that a theory which takes such an advanced position feels able to dispense both with polemics and with the need for the sort of apologias that characterized older works. The book develops its argument from its own internal logic. Even illustrations of different types of handwriting are less numerous here than is customary in such books. The authors focus so intently on their graphological inspiration that they might well have ventured to expound the elements of their science—or rather, their craft—by referring to a single specimen of handwriting. Anyone able to share their way of seeing would be able to take any scrap of paper covered with writing and discover in it a free ticket to the great *theatrum mundi*. It would reveal to him the pantomime of the entire nature and existence of mankind, in microcosmic form.

Published in *Die literarische Welt,* August 1928. *Gesammelte Schriften,* III, 135–139. Translated by Rodney Livingstone.

Notes

1. Ludwig Klages (1872–1956), psychologist and anthropologist, exerted a wide influence in the first half of the twentieth century. His central thesis—most exhaustively expressed in *Der Geist als Widersacher der Seele* (The Intellect as Opponent of the Soul; 1929–1933, 3 vols.), but also evident in his graphological treatise *Handschrift und Charakter* (Handwriting and Character; 1917)—was that an originary unity of soul and body has been destroyed by the human rational capacity. Strongly influenced by Nietzsche, Bergson, and Bachofen, Klages' ideas have gained notoriety because of their absorption into the mystagogic stream of Nazi ideology, whose anti-Semitism Klages shared.
2. A reference to the influential book *Schöpferische Indifferenz* (Creative Indifference), by Salomo Friedländer (1918).

Food Fair

Epilogue to the Berlin Food Exhibition

After the Neapolitans have celebrated Piedigrotta, on one of the days following the eighth of September, a herald goes around the city proclaiming through all the major thoroughfares how many pigs, calves, goats, and chickens, how many eggs, and how many barrels of wine were consumed that year during the night's feasting. The public waits expectantly to learn whether or not it has broken the previous record. The Berlin Food Exhibition resembled the gaping mouth of this herald; it was a splendid, shameless, lip-smacking maw. We discovered to our astonishment and delight the achievements of mankind in the realm of gourmandizing, down to our own time. And like the Piedigrotta herald, behind the resounding Berlin mask this giant orifice remained tuned to the tastes of the masses. It is greatly to its credit that there was very little evidence of eccentric private dining extravagance, and that this entire exuberant, witty proclamation rang out in honor of the plain fare of all lands, ages, and peoples.

Until a few years ago, popularization was a dubious region on the margins of science, a sphere of activity for joyless missionaries. More recently it has emancipated itself, thanks to the great exhibitions—in other words, the assistance of industry. In fact, the extraordinary improvements that have been introduced in the art of display are merely the counterpart to the progress that has been made in advertising.

Exhibitions like these are the most advanced outposts in the realm of display methods. And since it is the Golem of Industry that has made these conquests, the fact that all sorts of ugly messes have remained at the scene is not to be wondered at. At the Berlin Food Exhibition, the mess has consisted mainly of empty beer bottles. The Golem has turned this into a gigantic tree of questionable value that has climbed up one wall of the exhibition hall. Elsewhere a Buddhist rice temple executed in the best grocery style also testifies to industry's influence. And in other places, too, you keep stumbling over traces of giant activity: sacrificial loaves of bread as tall as a man on the altar of statistics, or a huge, gaping orifice, ostensibly the model of an open mouth but in fact a display cabinet for Pantagruelesque banquets: the "whale pie complete with scales and fins" and the "Great Tower of Dorten" that Aschinger has created according to medieval recipes. What these things mean for science escapes me entirely. But their meaning to children is perfectly obvious. There is scarcely a single stand in the entire exhibition that you could not take children to. At one booth the Dual Monarchy of Giants and Dwarfs, over which the child reigns, pays homage to its ruler. Next to the giant dowry stand unambiguous, comforting toy models: miniature pies and pasties; tiny cabinets in which toy models of great physiologists like Sanctorius, Lavoisier, Liebig, and Pettenkofer perform their tasks;[1] transparent northern coastlines, with their cod fishermen; and indefatigable puppet workers that seem to have been transported from dainty mechanical mines-in-a-bottle to a didactic otherworld.

The masses do not wish to be "instructed." They can absorb knowledge only if it is accompanied by the slight shock that nails down inwardly what has been experienced. Their education is a series of catastrophes that befall them at fairs, in darkened tents, where anatomical discoveries enter their very bones, or in the circus ring, where the sight of their first lion is inseparable from the image of the lion tamer putting his fist between its jaws. It takes genius to extract such traumatic energy, the small, specific *frissons*, from things in this way. Our exhibition managers must never cease to learn from such itinerant people, the unsurpassed masters of these countless tricks of the trade.

At the Berlin Food Exhibition, they have done so. Here is a vegetable oracle, a very Delphi, where you need only aim a pointer at a particular month for a colored sign to pop up prophesying the menus to come. Here you can plunge into a sultry gloom in which nothing of the universe can be discerned, other than a process that goes "from the Atlantic Ocean to smoked eel." Next door the gates of Hades open to reveal the Lethe, a brown river flowing "from the primeval forest to the coffee table." There are resplendent wooden charts with little lights going on and off, illustrating crop cultivation in different seasons or the process of metabolism in the human body. Their red is that of a thermometer of love in which ethyl alcohol rises and falls, and their precipitate movement is the same as that in shooting galleries, where huntsmen, devils, and mothers-in-law spring to life at the moment of the fatal shot.

Manifestations of a culinary afterlife: the gustatory pleasures of the peoples of the past. Egyptians, Greeks, Romans, the Germanic tribes of the Frankish period, and Renaissance Italians dine in illuminated niches but consume nothing, like spirits meeting for a midnight feast. Or caring for infants in the next world of the Christians: in the foreground, the kind sisters. They test the temperature of the bottles, pour a drop on their hands to make sure, cradle a baby in the right way for feeding, and wash out the bottle. Their countless virtues could only be described in a didactic poem. In the background, bathed in a murky, sulphurous red, are the bad nurses, along with the unfortunate children they are responsible for. They put the bottle to their own mouths, hold the drinking child head-down, chatter all the while to another one of the damned, and produce a picture that is enough to warm the heart of any devil.

On a pedestal, a splendid Alpine landscape. But the inscription underneath reads: "The end of the summer peak in infant mortality." The distant background shows the steep July peak in fatalities dating from some gray year before the war. Contrasting with this: layers of mountains, one after the other, with lower and lower peaks, an entire mountain range vanishing into the plain of sheer astonishment with which the observer perceives it. When he gradually comes to himself, the only thing that surprises him is the absence of the touring medical expert who conquered this statistical Matterhorn—there's no model of the fellow clambering about the massif. And next to this there is a different topographic display, as unprecedented as the others: a transport model. You see a milk delivery on its way from the producer to the consumer. It arrives at its destination in the upper half of the scene, with an endless series of stops en route. This is why the milk had to be sterilized before it could be transported. Precious vitamins were lost in the process. Thick clouds and a rainbow loom above a sterile flat landscape. In the lower half of the display, however, a fast-moving car passes through a fertile plain beneath a cloudless sky without stopping. How out-of-date the dry charts of old-fashioned statistics seem to us now, with their unattractive mess of lines. The whole earth, with its bushes and trees and fields, houses and homes, men and beasts, is all just good enough to enter into the vocabulary of this wonderful new and unspoiled sign language. We ourselves, and everything that is appropriate or congenial to us, can discover ourselves in it any time and can come into our own from our least-known side, the fourth or fifth dimension that we did not even know existed—namely, as providers of yardsticks. In the same way, the Brandenburg Gate is constantly forced to enter the arena to do battle in heroic competitions with cabbages, apples, loaves of bread, potatoes, and other consumer goods.

All these things make the fair what it is. In every corner and in a thousand different forms, food performs its somersaults and does all its other tricks. We move from one thing to the next—from a display of babies' pacifiers to medieval feeding bottles, and from the medieval feeding bottles to the medical incunabula in which they were first depicted. In short, we come across so many things at every moment, that this fairground could dispense with the free film shows, free guides, and free amusement-park refreshments because it is an amusement park itself. And all of this is merely the obverse of the successful but tightly organized management, which could operate with a light hand because it did not lose sight of its objective: to promote an interest in rational, hygienic, and enjoyable eating.

The exhibition's political angle: the section devoted to food in wartime. I think this section has witnessed classical scenes of recognition as shattering as any in a Greek amphitheater. "Ah, that's the marvelous sausage we had in those days!" And: "I can still remember the evening Uncle Oskar opened the Lusatian beer, and we all . . ." Or again, at the sight of "blood sausage made of fish": "Well, I never made any of that." But they used to serve "Gloria," the Imperial German coffee substitute, and guests who were invited for "after dinner" would be offered a big cup of "cocoa tea," perhaps with a drop of "Bomb-and-Grenade Rum Substitute," while the children would have a glass of "Alcohol-Free" and they themselves sooner or later indulged in a glass of "War Bitters." And while the husband watched his colleagues playing cards, he could satisfy the minimum demands of German decency by downing a foaming cup of "Wartime Pearl."—This large, price-less collection is on loan from the Dresden Museum of Hygiene, and it has been displayed in a manner worthy of it. It deserves to make the rounds of all the housewives' associations throughout Germany. The Red Cross or the national women's associations would do well to send this exhibition on tour. Only it would have to be supplemented by copies of all the opinions of the medical authorities who helped to make these diabolical drinks and disgust-ing synthetic foods acceptable to the people. Aside from this, the exhibition provides the essentials. Nor have the well-preserved labels on the bottles and packets been forgotten. There they all are: the sadistic dried milk "DrinkOnly," "Fruitogen" jam, and the apocalyptic-sounding wartime cake "Astro"—all of them registered trademarks in which the unaccommodated truth of the day found refuge, as if in ultimate linguistic exile. When will these things return to haunt us? And when nothing is left of our generation, who will come and unearth the remnants of the first "guaranteed gas-proof" foodstuffs?

Riepenhausen's famous engraving after Hogarth's etching *Tailpiece* is well known. It is an important work that was designed to attack the spirit of allegorical painting, but that ended up confirming it magnificently. It shows Saturn resting on a ruined heap of emblems; in his hand is a will in which he declares: "Over each and every Atom thereof [i.e., of the world], I appoint Chaos my sole executor. Witnesses: Clotho, Lachesis, Atropos"—the Three Fates.[2] The end of the world can be imagined in a less dramatic, more spacious, more peaceable and provincial manner. And it is in this sense that the end of the food exhibition would be no bad model of the place where the world gets boarded up and nailed shut. At the far end of the show, to one side of the exhibition halls and at the end of a garden path, is a shed. To the right, in the foreground, is a giant battery of tin milk churns: 3,000 liters. To the left, in the background, we can see how much food is given to the cows so that they produce milk in such quantities. We see twelve sacks containing 650 kilos of concentrated feedstuff, 900 kilos of straw, 2,700 kilos of hay in two cartloads, and 11,000 kilos of turnips in five heavy cartloads. Who wouldn't find solace in the thought that here, where everything is going downhill, the solution to the riddle of the universe is to be found where we would least expect it—casually, the way you give a picture postcard to a child. And to be found here in the shape of a few figures drifting gently in the wind above the peaceful, unknown life that lies between fodder and milk: the mystery of chewing the cud.

When we were young, we all leafed through *Robinson Crusoe* time after time, looking with beating heart for that terrifying thrill that overcame us at the sight of the picture in which Robinson gazes in horror at the traces left by cannibals. This was not simply an episode from his life; it was the Ultima Thule of food that appeared to us in that stretch of beach littered with human bones. Why have we been deprived of this sight at a show that has brought us face to face with the most exotic sights? And why are people who in a few short hours have become veritable connoisseurs of food denied the opportunity to experience the greatest artistic gratification of all—the chance to see how the circle is completed and how the mysterious serpent of the eating instinct bites its own tail?

Published in the *Frankfurter Zeitung*, September 1928. *Gesammelte Schriften*, IV, 527–532. Translated by Rodney Livingstone.

Notes

1. Sanctorius, or Santorio Santorio (1561–1636), was an Italian physician whose research on basal metabolism constituted the first use of quantitative experimental procedures in medicine. Antoine Lavoisier (1743–1794), French scientist, introduced quantitative experimental procedures to chemistry; his theory of oxidation replaced then-prevalent phlogiston theories of combustion. Justus Liebig (1803–1873), German chemist, was responsible for the first synthesis of many materials important for manufacturing. Max von Pettenkofer (1818–1901), German chemist and medical researcher, did pioneering work on the control of typhus and cholera through proper hygiene.
2. William Hogarth's *Tailpiece, or The Bathos* is an etching and engraving of 1764 depicting the end of time.

Paris as Goddess

Fantasy on the Latest Novel by Princess Bibesco

Marthe Bibesco, *Cathérine-Paris,* translated into German by Käthe Illich (Vienna and Leipzig: F. G. Speidl'sche Verlagsbuchhandlung, 1928), 365 pages. (This is a good translation.)

A bibliographic allegory: The goddess of the capital of France resting dreamily in her boudoir. A marble chimney, cornices, bulging cushions, animal skins spread over divans and floors. And knickknacks, knickknacks everywhere. Models of the Pont des Arts and the Eiffel Tower. On plinths, reminders of so many forgotten things—the Tuileries, the Temple, and the Château d'Eaux in miniature.[1] In a vase, the ten lilies from the city's coat of arms. But all this colorful bric-à-brac is intensified, outdone, buried beneath the overwhelming quantity of books of every shape and size—in sextodecimo, duodecimo, octavo, quarto, and folio in every conceivable color—held out by illiterate amoretti swooping down from above, scattered by fauns shaking out the Horn of Plenty from the hangings, spread out before her by kneeling genies: signs of poetic homage from every corner of the globe. Chaste street directories covered in shrunken leather and secured with a lock dating back to the city's youth—far more seductive for the true connoisseur than the illustrated atlases, which sumptuously reveal all; *Les mystères de Paris,* shamelessly laid bare in all the black luster of its copper-plate engravings;[2] vain volumes that speak to the city of nothing but their author, of his astuteness, his distinction, if not indeed of the moments of happiness he has enjoyed with her; and books with the aristocratic modesty of crystalline mirrors, in which the object of veneration can view herself in all the shapes and poses she has adopted over the centuries. To say nothing of the most important sign of the Baroque emblem that we are constructing here *post festum:* the sight of the flood of books in the foreground, pouring out over the curved ramp of the boudoir and landing at the feet of a committee of reviewers, who have their hands full catching them and sharing them out among themselves.

Princess Bibesco's book has the basic ingredients of all the things that may be washed ashore here. This novel has succeeded in integrating the history, statistics, and topography of Paris. Seldom has homage been paid to the city in a more imaginative and demure form. A passion comes to the surface such as only foreigners experience. For Princess Bibesco is a Romanian. Her heroine likewise, for that matter. If this conveys the impression that we are the recipients of a confession and that we should seek the key to the other characters, the impression is strengthened by internal factors. The heroine, with her divine impertinence, might well have the makings of a writer of *romans à clef* if she decided to take up her pen—and who is to say that this was not the case here? And we could perhaps gain a greater appreciation of the charm and importance of the book if we could make up our minds, hypothetically as it were, to regard the *roman à clef* as a genuine artistic genre. One would then not have to be a high-born Polish magnate, like the author's first husband, to admit that this novel is a success. But in Poland they do not waste much time on such theoretical subtleties, and instead identified the moral of the story in line with an experience of its author: "On n'épouse pas un Polonais" [You don't marry a Polish fellow]. This is a counterpart to the resigned epigraph to Chapter 4: "On n'épouse pas une ville" [You don't marry a city]—namely Paris, which she does end up marrying, in the form of an air force lieutenant.

However that may be, the *roman à clef* is a genuine romantic variant of the novel; the fact that the princess obviously learned her craft from the most romantic of contemporary writers is very much in line with this. It is only when we look at her work that we can see what a great literary tutor of princes this Giraudoux really is. And rightly so. No exponent of romantic absolutism displays such virtuosity as he. Giraudoux is the source of that remarkable wealth of nuances which was hitherto unknown in the modern novel. He is worth the effort of a closer look. His work contains none of the polished speech of Oscar Wilde's characters. Instead we find the polished angularity and multifaceted transparency of the characters themselves. The author treats them as prisms that refract his feelings into the most startling hues. This is enough to highlight the lyricism of this new type of novel. It appears in its most radiant form in *Eglantine,* one of his latest, most eccentric books. In another sense, however, we should take note of *Bella.*[3] It is no accident that this, too, is a *roman à clef*—or, as Horatio would say, "a piece of him."[4] For that is the other side of Giraudoux: his topicality, the presence of the sporting element, the political and the worldly. On this side these books are threatened by snobbery, just as on the other side their lyricism runs the risk of descending into preciosity. These new novels are a kind of explosive compromise between these two poles. Or, to choose an image that does greater justice to such writers: the leading article and the love poem are the twin posts anchoring the tightrope on which the authors move backward and forward, with the aid of the balancing pole of cleverness to help them keep their footing. And Princess Bibesco really is very clever. In her, the wisdom of the heart and the experiences of court life merge into a Baroque ensemble that is a distant descendant of the great writers of the seventeenth century, who were also men of affairs. "He may have discovered what all ambitious men realize once they have achieved their goal—namely, that the possession of power knows only one pleasure, the pleasure of despising power." Isn't that worthy of Vauvenargues?[5]

In this spirit Princess Bibesco might relish a Baroque apotheosis—a pendant to one of the favorite subjects of the Old Masters. Don't they often depict the victorious general, in an imperial pose, receiving the keys to the city he has conquered? Here, with an equally grandiose gesture, a vanquished heart surrenders its keys to the goddess of the city.

Published in *Die literarische Welt*, September 1928. *Gesammelte Schriften*, III, 139–142. Translated by Rodney Livingstone.

Notes

1. Three Parisian landmarks. The Tuileries, the royal residence on the Right Bank of the Seine, was destroyed by arson in 1871. The Temple was originally built as the monastery for the order of the Templars, but later served as a sanctuary for artists and debtors and as a prison; it was razed in 1811. The variety theater of the Château d'Eaux, founded in 1867, had room for 4,000 spectators.
2. Published in ten volumes in 1842–1843, *Les mystères de Paris* (The Mysteries of Paris), by Eugène Sue (1804–1857), was enormously successful. The novel, in addition to its highly melodramatic plot, depicts the suffering of ordinary Parisians and life in the city's underworld during the July Monarchy.
3. *Bella* (1926), *Eglantine* (1927), and *Les aventures de Jérôme Bardini* (1930) make up Jean Giraudoux's trilogy of sociopolitical novels that—in contrast to his dramas—have received little critical acclaim.
4. *Hamlet*, I.1.19.
5. Vauvenargues (the marquis de Luc de Clapiers; 1715–1747), French moral essayist, combined a Plutarchian ethos with elements of late neoclassicism and early romanticism.

The Path to Success, in Thirteen Theses

1. There is no great success without authentic achievements. But it would be a fallacy to imagine that these achievements are its foundation. The achievements are themselves a consequence—a consequence of the increased self-confidence and working pleasure of the person who finds himself recognized. This is why a great challenge, a shrewd repartee, an advantageous transaction are the genuine achievements on which great successes are built.

2. Satisfaction with the reward paralyzes success. Satisfaction with the achievement increases it. Reward and achievement balance each other out; they lie in the pans of a set of scales. The entire weight of self-respect must lie in the pan that contains the achievement. This means that the pan containing the reward will always fly into the air.

3. Only people who seem to be or really are guided in their behavior by straightforward, transparent motives will obtain success in the long run. The masses destroy every success as soon as it seems to become opaque, or to be devoid of any instructive, exemplary value. That is to say, transparent in its own terms; such success has no need to be intellectually transparent. Any priestly rule demonstrates that. Success only has to conform to an idea, or more accurately an image, whether of a hierarchy, militarism, plutocracy, or any other. Thus, the priest has his confessional, the general his medals, the financier his mansion. Anyone who refuses to pay tribute to the masses' collection of images must fail.

4. People have no conception of the hunger for clarity. This is the supreme emotional need of any public. *One* center, *one* leader, *one* slogan. The more unambiguous an intellectual phenomenon, the greater its radius of action will be and the more the public will flock to it. People's "interest" in an

author grows; that is to say, they begin to seek his formula—in other words, the most basic, unambiguous expression of his writing. From that moment on, his every new work becomes the raw material in which his readers strive to test that formula, and to refine and prove its worth. Strictly speaking, the public has an ear only for the message that the author would just have time and strength enough to utter on his deathbed with his last breath.

5. A writer cannot remind himself too often how modern our concept of "posterity" is. It dates from the era in which the independent writer made his appearance and stems from the fact that his place in society was insecure. The reference to posterity was a form of pressure on his contemporaries. As late as the seventeenth century, it would not have occurred to any writer to appeal to posterity as a weapon against his own age. All previous ages were unanimous in their conviction that their own contemporaries held the keys that would open the doors to future fame. And how much truer this is today, when every new generation finds itself with even less time or inclination to revise already established judgments, and as its need to defend itself against the sheer mass of what the past has bequeathed it is assuming ever more desperate forms.

6. Fame, or rather success, has become obligatory and is no longer the optional extra it formerly was. In an age when every wretched scrap of paper is distributed in hundreds of thousands of copies, fame is a cumulative condition. Quite simply: the less successful the writer, the less available his works.

7. A condition of victory: the enjoyment of the trappings of success as such. A pure, disinterested enjoyment, which proclaims itself best when someone just enjoys success, even if it belongs to someone else, and especially if it is "undeserved." A pharisaical self-righteousness is one of the greatest obstacles to advancement.

8. Much is innate, but much can be improved by training. This is why success will not come to anyone who saves himself up, who exerts himself only on the most important occasions, and who is incapable of occasionally making a supreme effort for trivial goals. For the most important factor even in a crucial negotiation can be learned only through these means: the pleasure in negotiation that extends even to taking a sporting interest in your opponent, the great capacity for temporarily taking your eye off the ball (the Lord provides for his own in their sleep), and, last and most important, charm. Not the softening, straightforward, comfortable kind, but the surprising, dialectical charm that is full of verve, a lasso that unexpectedly enables you to bring your opponent into line. And isn't society full of people from whom we can learn the secret of success? Just as in Galicia pickpockets use straw dolls, little figurines covered all over with little bells, to teach their trade to their pupils, so too we have waiters, porters, officials, and managers on whom we can practice the art of giving orders with charm.

The "Open Sesame" of success is the formula begotten from the marriage between Fortuna and the language of command.

9. "Let's hear what you can do!"[1]—this is what they say in America to everyone applying for a job. But they are less interested in hearing what he says than in seeing how he behaves. Here we touch on the secret of examinations. Any examiner normally wants nothing more than to be persuaded of the suitability of the person he is testing. We have all learned by experience that the more frequently you use a piece of information, an opinion, a formula, the more it seems to lose its suggestive power. Our conviction will scarcely ever persuade others as completely as it persuaded the person who witnessed its birth in our mind. It follows that in every examination the greatest chance of success lies not with the person who is well prepared, but with the one who is best at improvising. And for the same reason, it is almost always the incidental questions and events that prove decisive. The inquisitor we have before us desires above all that we hide from him the nature of his own position. If we succeed in this, he will be grateful to us and turn a blind eye to our deficiencies.

10. Cleverness, a knowledge of human nature, and similar talents are far less important in real life than we imagine. Despite this, there is genius of some sort in every successful person. But we should not try to find it, any more than we should try to find the erotic genius in a Don Juan when he is alone. Success, too, is a rendezvous: it is no small thing to be in the right place at the right time. Because it means understanding the language in which luck makes its arrangements with us. How can anyone who has never in his life heard this language pass judgment on the genius of the successful? He has no conception of it. In his eyes it is all a matter of chance. It does not occur to him that, in the grammar of success, chance plays the same role that irregular verbs do in ordinary grammar. It is the surviving trace of primeval energy.

11. The structure of all success is basically the structure of gambling. To reject one's own name has always been the most thorough way to rid oneself of one's inhibitions and feelings of inferiority. And gambling is precisely a sort of steeplechase over the hurdles of one's own ego. The gambler is nameless; he has no name of his own and requires no one else's. For he is represented by the chips he places on specific numbers on the table—which is said to be green, like the golden tree of life, but which in reality is as gray as asphalt.[2] And what intoxication it is in this city of opportunity, in this network of good fortune, to multiply oneself, to make oneself ubiquitous and be on the lookout for the approach of Lady Luck at any one of ten different street corners.

12. A man may swindle as much as he likes. But he must never feel like a swindler. Here the confidence man is the model of creative neutrality. His inherited name is the anonymous sun around which his adopted names

revolve like planets. Pedigrees, honors, titles—they are all so many little worlds emanating from the radiant core of that sun, dispensing a gentle light and warmth over the world of ordinary people. Indeed, they are his achievement, his gift to society, and hence are evidence of the bona fides that the sharp-witted swindler always possesses but that the poor sucker almost never has.

13. The secret of success does not lie in the mind; it is revealed by language itself in the term "presence of mind." The question is not whether mind is present, or what form it takes, but only *where* it is. That it happens to be present here, at this very moment, is possible only if it enters into a person's intonation, his smile, his conversational pauses, his gaze, or his gestures. For only the body can generate presence of mind. And in the case of the highly successful person, the body keeps such a tight rein on the reserves of the mind that the latter seldom has the opportunity to let off fireworks. This explains why the success achieved by financial wizards in their careers is of the same kind as that of an Abbé Galiani in the salon.[3] For nowadays, as Lenin has remarked, what must be overcome are not people, but things. This is the source of that dullness which so often characterizes the presence of mind of great captains of industry.

Published in the *Frankfurter Zeitung,* September 1928. *Gesammelte Schriften,* IV, 349– 352. Translated by Rodney Livingstone.

Notes

1. In English in the original.
2. An allusion to Mephistopheles' lines in Goethe's *Faust:* "My friend, all theory is gray, and green / The golden tree of life." *Faust, Part I,* trans. David Luke (Oxford: Oxford University Press, 1987), p. 61.
3. Ferdinando Galiani (1728–1787), Italian man of letters and economist, was a friend of the Encyclopedists. His book *Della moneta* (On Money) appeared in 1750.

Weimar

I

In small German towns, it is impossible to imagine the windows without windowsills. But seldom have I seen such wide sills as in the marketplace in Weimar, in "The Elephant,"[1] where they turned the entire room into a theater box affording me a view of a ballet which surpassed anything that the stages of Neuschwanstein and Herrenchiemsee could offer Ludwig II. For it was an early-morning ballet. Toward 6:30 A.M. the players started to tune their instruments: builders' beams on the bass, protective-umbrella violins, flower flutes, and fruit drums. The stage was still almost empty: market women, no buyers. I fell back to sleep. When I awoke again, toward 9:00, it was an orgy. Markets are the orgies of the early morning; and, as Jean Paul would have said, hunger rings in the day, as love rings it out. The syncopated clink of coins can be heard everywhere, and girls with net shopping bags, inviting the observer to enjoy their rounded shapes, slowly push and pull. But when I dressed and went downstairs, ready to make my entrance on the stage, its entire freshness and glory vanished. I realized that all the gifts of the morning hours are like the sunrise: best enjoyed from a height. And wasn't the light that had just been shining on these delicately checkered cobblestones the faint red sunrise of commerce? Now it all lay buried beneath paper and rubbish. Instead of dancing and music, there was now nothing but exchange and trade. Nothing can vanish as irretrievably as a morning.

II

In the Goethe and Schiller Archive the stairs, rooms, display cases, and bookshelves are all white. There isn't a single square inch where the eye might rest. The manuscripts lie propped up like patients in hospital beds. But the longer you expose yourself to this harsh light, the more you imagine you can discern a logic in the organization of these collections—a logic of which the archive itself is unaware. Whereas a lengthy period of confinement to a sickbed makes people's faces seem spacious and still, and turns them into the mirror of impulses that a healthy body would express in decisions, in a thousand different actions—in short, whereas a sickbed causes a human being to regress to an imitation of himself, these sheets of paper do not lie around aimlessly in their repositories like patients. The fact that everything which we know today as Goethe's *Works,* and which confronts us consciously and sturdily in countless published volumes, once existed in this unique, fragile handwritten form, and the fact that what emanated from it can only be the austere, purifying atmosphere which surrounds patients who are dying or recovering and which is perceptible to the few who are close to them—this is something we do not care to dwell on. But didn't these manuscript sheets likewise find themselves in a crisis? Didn't a shudder run through them, and no one knew whether it was from the proximity of annihilation or that of posthumous fame? And don't they embody the loneliness of poetry? And the place where it took stock of itself? And don't its pages include many whose unnameable text only rises as a glance or a breath of air from their silent, ravaged features?

III

The primitive nature of Goethe's study is well known. Its ceiling is low; it has no carpet and no double window. The furniture is unprepossessing. He could easily have done things differently. Leather armchairs and cushions existed even then. This room is not in any way ahead of its time. It was his decision to keep things within limits. No one need be ashamed of the candlelight by which the old man sat and studied in his housecoat in the evening at the table in the middle of the room, with his arms resting on a faded cushion. To think that today the quietness of such hours can be found only at night. But if we could overhear it, we would understand the pattern of existence as it was destined and created, the never-repeated blessing of having gathered the richest harvest of the past few decades, in which the wealthy man had yet to experience the harshness of life in his own body. Here the old man celebrated the vastness of the nights with his anxieties, guilt, and despair, before the hellish dawn of bourgeois comfort began to cast its light in at the window. We still await a philology that could open our eyes to this clearly delineated and far from distant world—the true Antiquity of the poet. This study was the cell of the small house that Goethe had dedicated exclusively to two purposes: sleep and work. We cannot possibly gauge the importance of this tiny bedroom, with both its closeness to and its separation from his study. Only the threshold separated him and his work, like a step, from the towering bed. And when he slept, his work awaited him in the next room to plead nightly with the dead for his liberty. Anyone who has had the good fortune to be able to collect his thoughts in this space will have experienced in these four little rooms, in which Goethe slept, read, dictated, and wrote, the forces that bade a world give him answer when he struck the sounding-board of his innermost being. We, however, have to make an entire world resound in order to cause the feeble overtone of our inner being to ring out.

Published in the *Neue schweizer Rundschau,* October 1928. *Gesammelte Schriften,* IV, 353–355. Translated by Rodney Livingstone.

Notes

1. A renowned hotel and restaurant in Weimar.

The Fireside Saga

We are familiar with the lonely country manors of North America from which Poe derived the gloomy fairy castles of the Arnheims, Landors, and Ushers.[1] Now, once again, and as if for all eternity, we can see the emergence of a new building of this kind, enclosed by fir trees, and commanding a view over the park and forest right up to the blue hills in the distance. And no one who enters it as a reader can say what he has seen. For there can scarcely be any novels that are harder to retell, and were harder to retell right from the start, than the novels of Julien Green. None, in other words, for which it would be anything but perverse or superficial to search for a "key" or an "experience" through which to interpret them. None that resist the observer more rigorously. None more classical. Where, then, are we to look for the vital principle animating such works?

This particular work is not the product of an experience. Rather, it is an experienceable reality in itself. A sudden break in the weather overwhelms the reader. What we see here is a meteorological compromise between a climate of human primal history and that of the present day, but one that can occur only as the result of a catastrophe. How to retell the story? It would be just as easy or difficult to tell the story of last night's storm.

When shafts of lightning sunder the night sky, the sudden light projects our gaze into the furthest distances in thousandths of a second. In like manner, we glimpse pale and fleeting clearings in history, one after the other. This house—"in the simplest style of American dwellings, chest-shaped, with a colonnaded porch that extends over almost the whole of the façade"—quickly becomes as transparent as the night sky in a storm, and turns into a vista of caverns, chambers, and galleries extending back into the primeval past of mankind.

"To dwell": Does this still mean barely having a roof over one's head, a process full of fear and magic, one that was perhaps never so voracious as it has been under the cover of civilization and the small-minded bourgeois-Christian world? For beneath the surface, things glow and smoulder; the cold flames of miserliness lick at the walls of the icy house. When at the end a fire lights up its windows and blazes from the roof, it will have been properly warm for the first time.

The primal history of the nineteenth century, whose monuments have become ever more audible since the Surrealists, have been enriched by one further unforgettable document. One of the profoundest, most legitimate features of the new schools of architecture may well be seen in their efforts to liquidate the magical powers that we are inevitably and unconsciously subject to in the rooms and furniture of our dwellings. These efforts strive to transform us from the inhabitants of houses into their users, from proud owners into practical critics. If this is the case, it is no more than the reverse side of the illuminations which have inspired this work. Here the bed really is still the throne occupied by dreamers or the dying; the fireplace really is the flame of the eternal hearth, kept alight by the dread vestal, the heroine of the book; sewing really is still concerned with the magic of destiny that the lowliest maid shares with the three Fates. And once we have listed these primitive possessions, the inventory of the house and the author's vocabulary are exhausted. The moral concepts of the catechism and the object world of the primer—these are the runes from which the three women whom the author has invited into his circle gather up their destiny, rigorously, heedlessly, as in a dream.

This world of the saga lies as far beneath the earth's surface as the fairy-tale world lies above it. Emily is the fairy-tale child—but as if in a mirror. In a fairy tale the Sunday child stands there in all his grace, helpless and victorious at the same time. Here, however, the heroine of the novel stands threatening, terrible, yet defeated. If there were a weekday that stood out above all others, if the gray of all the weekdays were concentrated into one, that would be her birthday—indeed, it would be the day of her life. In fact, that is what it is, the day that casts its pall over Mont-Cinère year in, year out. This everyday, work-a-day child of toil reaches old age in a few years, unpurified and via disreputable paths, while losing nothing of the terrible folly of early life. She stands between her mother and her grandmother; and by nature and age, she is much closer to the latter than to the former. The mother is the pious, poor, faithfully caring widow of fairy tales. But as in a mirror image: she is as pious as she is heartless, as faithful and careful with the linen, household possessions, and firewood as she is faithless and uncaring toward her mother and her child; she is as poor and as wealthy as only a miser can be. The former—the grandmother—tells stories to her grandchild on long winter evenings, a pattern we know from fairy tales; but these stories are of the kind that paranoia inspires in the insane, and the child surrenders to them merely because the fireplace in the sickroom is the only one that has a fire in it. And then there is Stevens, the gardener's lad, the foolish prince in disguise who redeems the princess. But as in a mirror image: for only now, after the wedding, does the true story begin; and if they have not been burned to death, they are burning still. It is the fairy-tale world reflected in the pitch-black water of death. "Alas, Mother, alas!" sang the young Brentano when he glanced into the same mirror.

Emily sits in her rocking chair, at the window. She gazes out into the landscape. She studies it intently, as if it were a picture. "Her gaze slid incessantly from one point to another. You could sense that this was one of the many little distractions of which a life without major activities is full. And it was one that had become a habit." It is a day like a thousand others. Or perhaps not. Perhaps it is the mysterious day of which a great contemporary philosopher, Franz Rosenzweig, has written: "One day the self falls upon a person like an armed man, and takes possession of all that he owns in his house." The profoundly tight-lipped, truculent self, the legacy of all this author's characters, enters into this heroine as mute pride-in-possession. And gradually we perceive that in her sullen pretensions this child has become as inflexible as Oedipus in his delusion, Antigone in her sense of duty, Electra in her desire for vengeance. In the final analysis, it is the composition as a whole that provokes these comparisons. A race of men, a legendary race, that in Greek tragedy finally breaks through the imprisonment in myth for the first time—for Greek tragedy is nothing other than this breakthrough—resurfaces here amid the spectral brightness and sobriety of the nineteenth century and vanishes once more into its darkest, most ensnared, and utterly hopeless existence. This is why the extraordinary could happen—why a novel could achieve the necessity of classical tragedy, indeed a tragedy that is even more hopeless and inexorable. Because there are no gates through which the chorus might force its way in.

But ultimately is this not Germanic rather than Greek classicism, the death-defying Germanic women whose meanspiritedness is disastrously intertwined with that crooked, atrophied world of objects? Truculence has thrown itself on the most denatured things and turned possessiveness into character. This is why the heroine of Mont-Cinère has become wooden, overgrown, and smothered with passion from early childhood. In all her activities, she is a breathtaking antithesis to the innocent, matter-of-fact child found in fairy tales. Such a child finds all objects at his service. He has the right knack. How different things are here. How brilliantly this child passes the fairy-tale test with the six shirts for the poor; and despite this, the fairy, the brave Methodist sister that looks after her, creates nothing but poverty and death with her blessing. For miserliness is always at death's door; for the miser, everything becomes a straw at which he clutches in panic. The miser always finds the bottom of the chest. In his eyes the world is threadbare from the outset. He is always at his last gasp. Giotto omitted miserliness in his allegories of vice in Padua. But with every one of their gestures, the characters in this novel declare their readiness to enter the eternal cycle of his frescoes.

Published in *Die literarische Welt*, November 1928. *Gesammelte Schriften*, III, 144–148. Translated by Rodney Livingstone.

Notes

1. This essay is Benjamin's review of Julien Green's novel *Mont-Cinère* (1926). The German title of the review, *Feuergeiz-Saga*, suggests a pun on John Galsworthy's *Forsyte Saga*. The German also combines a reference to fire with another to the miserliness *(Geiz)* that Benjamin discerns in Green's universe.

News about Flowers

Karl Blossfeldt, *Urformen der Kunst: Photographische Pflanzenbilder* [Originary Forms of Art: Photographic Images of Plants], edited and with an introduction by Karl Nierendorf (Berlin: Ernst Wasmuth, 1928), 120 pages.

Criticism is a sociable art.[1] A healthy reader mocks the reviewer's judgment. But what pleases that reader most deeply is the delicious bad taste of taking part uninvited when someone else reads. Opening a book so that it beckons like a table already set, a table at which we are about to take our place with all of our insights, questions, convictions, quirks, prejudices, and thoughts, so that the couple of hundred readers (are there that many?) in this society disappear and just for that reason allow us to enjoy life—this is criticism. Or at least the only form of criticism that gives a reader an appetite for a book.

If we can agree on this, then the table is set with the one hundred twenty plates in this book, inviting countless observations from countless observers. Yes, we really wish this rich book (poor only in words) that many friends. The silence of the scholar who presents these images must really be honored; perhaps his knowledge is of the kind that makes the one who possesses it mute. And here, doing is more important than knowing. The person who created this collection of plant photos can eat more than bread. He has done more than his share of that great stock-taking of the inventory of human perception that will alter our image of the world in as yet unforeseen ways. He has proven how right the pioneer of the new light-image, Moholy-Nagy, was when he said: "The limits of photography cannot be determined. Everything is so new here that even the search leads to creative results.

Technology is, of course, the pathbreaker here. It is not the person ignorant of writing but the one ignorant of photography who will be the illiterate of the future." Whether we accelerate the growth of a plant through time-lapse photography or show its form in forty-fold enlargement, in either case a geyser of new image-worlds hisses up at points in our existence where we would least have thought them possible.

These photographs reveal an entire, unsuspected horde of analogies and forms in the existence of plants. Only the photograph is capable of this. For a bracing enlargement is necessary before these forms can shed the veil that our stolidity throws over them. What is to be said of an observer to whom these forms already send out signals from their veiled state? Nothing can better portray the truly new objectivity of his procedure than the comparison with that highly personal but ever so brilliant procedure by means of which the equally revered and misunderstood Grandville, in his *Fleurs animées,* made the entire cosmos emanate from the world of plants. Grandville took hold of the procedure—God knows, not gently—from the opposite end. He stamped the punitive mark of creatureliness, the human visage, directly onto the blossom of these pure children of nature. This great pioneer in the field of the advertisement mastered one of its fundamental principles, graphic sadism, as hardly any other of its adepts has done. Isn't it odd now to find here another principle of advertisement, the enlargement of the plant world into gigantic proportions, gently healing the wounds opened by caricature?

Originary Forms of Art—certainly. What can this mean, though, but originary forms of nature? Forms, that is, which were never a mere model for art but which were, from the beginning, at work as originary forms in all that was created. Moreover, it must be food for thought in even the most sober observer that the enlargement of what is large—the plant, or its buds, or the leaf, for example—leads us into a wholly different realm of forms than does the enlargement of what is small—the plant cell under the microscope, say. And if we have to tell ourselves that new painters like Klee and even more Kandinsky have long been at work establishing friendly relations between us and the realms into which the microscope would like to seduce us—crudely and by force—we instead encounter in these enlarged plants vegetal "Forms of Style."[2] One senses a gothic *parti pris* in the bishop's staff which an ostrich fern represents, in the larkspur, and in the blossom of the saxifrage, which also does honor to its name in cathedrals as a rose window which breaks through the wall. The oldest forms of columns pop up in horsetails; totem poles appear in chestnut and maple shoots enlarged ten times; and the shoots of a monk's-hood unfold like the body of a gifted dancer. Leaping toward us from every calyx and every leaf are inner image-imperatives [*Bildnotwendigkeiten*], which have the last word in all phases and stages of things conceived as metamorphoses. This touches on one of the deepest, most unfathomable forms of the creative, on the variant that was always, above all others, the form of genius, of the creative collective, and of nature. This is the fruitful, dialectical opposite of invention: the *Natura non facit saltus* of the ancients.[3] One might, with a bold supposition, name it the feminine and vegetable principle of life. The variant is submission and agreement, that which is flexible and that which has no end, the clever and the omnipresent.

We, the observers, wander amid these giant plants like Lilliputians. It is left, though, to fraternal great spirits—sun-soaked eyes, like those of Goethe and Herder—to suck the last sweetness from these calyxes.

Published in *Die literarische Welt*, November 1928. *Gesammelte Schriften*, III, 151–153. Translated by Michael Jennings.

Notes

1. Karl Blossfeldt (1865–1932) was a German photographer and art teacher whose entire photographic output was devoted to the representation of plant parts: twig ends, seed pods, tendrils, leaf buds, and so on. These he meticulously arranged against stark backgrounds and photographed with magnification, so that unfamiliar shapes from the organic world were revealed as startling, elegant architectural forms. Blossfeldt originally produced his work as a study aid for his students at the Berlin College of Art; he believed that the best human art was modeled on forms preexisting in nature.
2. Benjamin is referring to *Stilfragen* (1893), a work by Alois Riegl. It traces the influence of natural forms such as the acanthus through a series of stylistic periods in the ancient world.
3. *Natura non facit saltus:* Latin for "nature does not make a leap." In rationalist philosophy, the phrase expresses the notion that God leaves no gaps in nature.

Review of Green's *Adrienne Mesurat*

Julien Green, *Adrienne Mesurat* (Paris: Plon, 1927), 355 pages.

Paul Léautaud, the outstanding Parisian novelist and chronicler, once said, "The books that count are written from start to finish in the same tone, without showpieces or purple passages. Showpieces and purple passages are the mark of inferior books."[1] The homogeneous simplicity of narrative cannot be taken further than it is by the young Julien Green in his first two novels. Now, we all know that nothing is more difficult than such a uniform, undifferentiated mode of writing, a writing that offers no threshold. And the difficulty in question is not one of style. It is easy to understand Green when he says that style is something he hates. What he means by "style" is a technique that enables a writer to take impoverished and mundane thoughts and experiences and imbue them with the sheen of originality. The less striving for effect there is, the simpler and more comprehensible a narrative is, the denser and more extraordinary the world must be from which it sprang. If not, it will merely seem trivial, for all its matter-of-factness. In short, simplicity, if it is to stand the test, must push forward to the foundations of reality. A superficial naturalism, if stylized, may in a pinch appear readable. (Examples would fill pages, and not with the most contemptible of names.) But a work of the linguistic austerity of *Adrienne Mesurat* must be rooted in the basic metaphysical stratum of reality if it is to have substance and meaning.

And in reality the novel has never been further from naturalism than here. This is the source of this book's inner truth, something that in art always contradicts external appearance. Art means to go against the grain of reality.

Smoothing and polishing is the work of interior decorators. Books in which one thing follows another "in logical sequence," or in which "the characters are so true to life and vividly depicted"—these are the petty-bourgeois art of upholstery. But *art* is hard. It does not want one thing "to follow logically from another"; it wants much to come from little. Like Meyerhold's Russian theater, it allows us a glimpse of what is happening in the machinery of passion behind the scenes, and shows us the simple cogwheels at work: the loneliness, fear, hatred, love, or defiance that underpins every action. And these forces should be understood not as "psychological motives" propelling the actors but as forces that find expression in their destiny.

Green's distance from novelists of the normal variety is represented by the gulf between imagination [*Vergegenwärtigung*] and depiction [*Schilderung*]. Green does not depict people; he imagines them in fateful moments. That is to say, they behave as if they were apparitions. Adrienne Mesurat, who pauses in her dusting to gaze at the family portraits; old Mesurat, stroking his beard; Madame Legras, who flees, taking Adrienne's necklace with her—these would be their gestures if they were compelled to relive these moments as poor souls beyond the grave. Green's insight into the drearily stereotyped nature of all fateful moments is something he shares with but one other writer: it is the same gaze that Pirandello fixes on his six characters in search of an author. The same gaze, except that it comes from the motionless, passionless eye of a Nordic man. A Nordic man who is also a painter. Born in the United States, Green was a painter until his twenty-third year. He then wrote his first novel, *Mont-Cinère,* in five months. By way of an experiment, as he puts it, and with the near certainty that it would be received with total indifference.

"My inclination is to imagine what lies furthest from me. Whatever has not been thought out is worthless for me. And I would be incapable of describing the most trivial accident that I had witnessed." This is completely in accord with the strange impression that all his works make. Despite their precision of detail, and despite the drastic nature of the catastrophes they contain, they convey the impression that they may, or rather must, have been written by someone who has hardly experienced anything at all, let alone the events described. It sounds like a poor paradox, but only the purest, most powerful works are capable of making such an impression on the reader. (Or do *Don Quixote* and *War and Peace* read even remotely as if they had been "experienced"?) But the astonishing aspect of the book goes beyond even this. Just as this work—*Adrienne Mesurat*—seems to have arisen from a vision rather than an experience, so too we may say that it is not a contemporary novel, a novel of our time. It reads like an unassuming yet essential piece of evidence in a historical legal process that has not been launched. Like Stendhal's novels, *Adrienne Mesurat* belongs to a genre of works whose contemporary relevance is latent only at the time they are published, so that scarcely anyone recognizes their significance; only later, in the light of their fame, does it become apparent just how central they are to their age. Everything in this novel appears timeless, from the elemental forces at work in its characters to the no less primeval nature of their world, so that we are barely able to imagine that in later times it will be immediately obvious that it was written in our day. Unless, that is—and we must conclude by at least hinting at the fundamental motif of the book—we admit to ourselves that the vision of love that dominates it could have arisen only in our day: a character who is half cleaning-woman, half Fury, wringing out the damp cloth, the human body, with her mighty hands until the last drop of life in it has been squeezed out.

Published in *Internationale Revue* (Amsterdam), December 1928. *Gesammelte Schriften*, III, 153–156. Translated by Rodney Livingstone.

Notes

1. Paul Léautaud (1872–1946) was secretary of *Mercure de France* from 1908 to 1941.

Goethe

When Johann Wolfgang Goethe came into the world on August 18, 1749, in Frankfurt am Main, the town had 30,000 inhabitants. In Berlin, the largest town in Germany at the time, there were 126,000, whereas both Paris and London had already surpassed 500,000. These figures are an important gauge of the political situation in Germany, for throughout the whole of Europe the bourgeois revolution depended on the big cities. On the other hand, it is a significant fact about Goethe that during his entire life he never lost his powerful dislike of living in big towns. He never visited Berlin,[1] and in later years he paid only two reluctant visits to his native Frankfurt, passing the larger part of his life in a small princely town with 6,000 inhabitants. The only cities he ever became more familiar with were the Italian centers Rome and Naples.

Goethe was the cultural representative and, initially, the political spokesman of a new bourgeoisie, whose gradual rise can be clearly discerned in his family tree. His male ancestors worked their way up from artisan circles and married women from educated families or families otherwise higher in the social scale than themselves. On his father's side, his great-grandfather was a farrier; his grandfather was first a tailor and then an innkeeper; and his father, Johann Caspar Goethe, began as an ordinary lawyer. Within a short time, however, Johann acquired the title of imperial councilor, and when he had succeeded in winning the hand of Katharina Elisabeth Textor, the daughter of the mayor, he definitively established his position among the ruling families of the city.

Goethe's youth, which he spent in a patrician household in a Free Imperial City, developed and consolidated in him a trait traditionally found in the

Rhenish Franconian region: reserve toward any political commitment and a correspondingly lively appreciation of what was appropriate and advantageous to the individual. The tight family circle—Goethe had only one sister, Cornelia—soon permitted him to concentrate on himself. Despite this, the attitudes prevailing in the household prevented him from contemplating an artistic career. His father forced him to study law. With this end in view, he went first to Leipzig University at the age of sixteen, and, in the summer of 1770, to Strasbourg. He was then twenty-one.

It is in Strasbourg that we first get a clear picture of the cultural milieu from which Goethe's early poetry emerged. Goethe and Klinger from Frankfurt, Bürger and Leisewitz from Central Germany, Voss and Claudius from Holstein, Lenz from Livonia. Goethe was the patrician; Claudius was a burgher. There were the sons of teachers or parsons, like Holtei, Schubart, and Lenz; members of the petty bourgeoisie, like Maler Müller, Klinger, and Schiller; the grandson of a serf (Voss); and, finally, noblemen like Counts Christian and Friedrich von Stolberg.[2] They all worked together in an effort to "renew" Germany by means of ideology. But the fatal weakness of this specifically German revolutionary movement was its inability to reconcile itself with the original program of bourgeois emancipation: the Enlightenment. The bourgeois masses, the "Enlightened," remained separated from their vanguard by a vast abyss. German revolutionaries were not enlightened, and German enlighteners were not revolutionary. The ideas of the first centered on revolution, language, and society; those of the latter focused on the theory of reason and of the state. Goethe subsequently took over the negative side of both movements: together with the Enlightenment, he opposed violent change, while with the *Sturm und Drang* he resisted the state. It is in this division within the German bourgeoisie that we find an explanation for its failure to establish ideological contact with the West; Goethe, who subsequently made a detailed study of Diderot and Voltaire, was never further from an understanding of France than when he was in Strasbourg. Particularly revealing is his comment on that celebrated manifesto of French materialism, Holbach's *Système de la nature,* a book in which the icy draft of the French Revolution can already be felt.[3] He found it "so gray, so Cimmerian, so lifeless," that it startled him as if he had seen a ghost. He thought it "unpalatable, insipid—the very quintessence of senility." It made him feel hollow and empty in "this melancholy atheistic gloom."

These were the reactions of a creative artist, but also of the son of a Frankfurt patrician. Goethe subsequently presented the *Sturm und Drang* movement with its two most powerful manifestos, *Götz von Berlichingen* and *Werther.* But it is to Johann Gottfried Herder that these two works owe the universal form which made it possible to fuse their disparate elements into a single ideological whole.[4] In his letters and conversations with Goethe,

Hamann, and Merck,[5] he provided the program for the movement: the "original genius"; "Language: the revelation of the spirit of the people"; "Song: nature's first language"; "the unity of human and natural history." During the same period Herder was busy assembling material for his great anthology, *Stimmen der Völker in Liedern* [Voices of the Peoples in Song], a collection of poems from countries ranging from Lapland to Madagascar which had the greatest influence on Goethe. For in his own early poetry we find him using the folk song as a means of revitalizing the lyric, in combination with the great liberation that had been effected by the poets of the Göttinger Hain.[6] "Voss emancipated the marshland peasantry for poetry. He expelled the conventional figures of the Rococo from poetry with pitchforks, flails, and the Lower Saxon dialect, which only half doffs its cap to the squire." But since the basic mode of Voss's poetry is still descriptive (just as for Klopstock poetry is still conceived in terms of the rhetoric of the hymn),[7] it was left to Goethe's Strasbourg poems—"Willkommen und Abschied" [Welcome and Farewell], "Mit einem gemalten Band" [With a Colored Ribbon], "Mailied" [May Song], "Heidenröslein" [Rose on the Heath]—to liberate German poetry from the realms of description, didactic message, and anecdote. This liberation, however, could still not be anything more than a precarious, transitory phenomenon, and one that would lead German poetry into a decline in the course of the nineteenth century, whereas in the poetry of his old age, in the *West-Östlicher Divan* [West-Easterly Divan], Goethe himself had already introduced conscious restrictions. In 1773, together with Herder, Goethe produced the manifesto *Von deutscher Art und Kunst* [On German Style and Art] containing his study in praise of Erwin von Steinbach, the builder of Strasbourg Cathedral—an essay whose very existence made Goethe's later fanatical classicism an additional source of irritation to the Romantics in their efforts to rehabilitate the Gothic.

This milieu also supplied the matrix for *Götz von Berlichingen* (1772). The divided nature of the German bourgeoisie is clearly dramatized in this work. The towns and courts, as the representatives of a principle of reason which has been reduced to a coarse expression of Realpolitik, stand for the host of unimaginative Enlighteners; they are opposed by the *Sturm und Drang,* in the person of the leader of the insurgent peasantry. The historical background to this work, the German Peasants' War, could easily convey the impression that Goethe had a genuine revolutionary commitment.[8] This would be a mistake, for at bottom what Götz's rebellion expresses are the grievances of the old seigneurial class, the Imperial Knights, who are in the process of surrendering to the growing power of the princes.[9] Götz fights and dies in the first instance for himself, and then for his class. The core idea of the play is not revolution, but steadfastness. Götz's actions are redolent of reactionary chivalry. They are the fine, charming deeds of a seigneur; they are the expression of an individual impulse and are not to be seen in the same light as the brutal destructive deeds of the peasant robbers with whom he joins forces. We see in this work the first instance of a process which is to become typical for Goethe: as a dramatist, he repeatedly succumbs to the seduction of revolutionary themes, only to deflect them or to abandon them as fragments. Examples of the first procedure are *Götz* and *Egmont;* an example of the second is *Die natürliche Tochter* [The Natural Daughter]. Goethe's essential withdrawal from the revolutionary energy of the *Sturm und Drang* movement in his very first important play emerges very clearly from a comparison with the plays of his contemporaries. In 1774 Lenz published *Der Hofmeister, oder Vortheile der Privaterziehung* [The Tutor, or The Advantages of Private Education], a work which mercilessly exposes the social constraints pressing upon the world of letters— constraints of consequence for Goethe's career, too. The German middle class was far too weak to be able to support an extensive literary life from its own resources. In consequence, literature's dependence on feudalism persisted even when the writer's sympathies had gone over to the middle class. His penury compelled him to accept free board, to act as tutor to the children of the nobility, and to accompany young princes on their travels. His state of dependence went so far as to jeopardize his literary earnings, since only works expressly named by government decree were protected from pirate editions produced in the various states of Germany.

In 1774, after Goethe's appointment to the Imperial Supreme Court of Appeals in Wetzlar, *Die Leiden des jungen Werthers* [The Sorrows of Young Werther] appeared in print. This book may well be the greatest success in the history of literature. Goethe here perfected the portrait of the writer as "genius." For if the great writer is someone who transforms his inner life into a matter of public interest from the very outset, and simultaneously makes the questions of the day into matters of immediate concern for his own personal thought and experience, then it is in Goethe's early works that we find the most consummate avatar of this kind of author. In *Werther* Goethe provided the bourgeoisie of his day with a perceptive and flattering picture of its own pathology, comparable in its way to the one supplied by Freud for the benefit of the modern bourgeoisie. Goethe knitted the story of his unhappy love for Charlotte Buff, the fiancée of a friend,[10] into his account of the adventures in love of a young writer, whose suicide had caused a sensation. In Werther's moods we see the *Weltschmerz* of the period unfolding in all its nuances. Werther is not just the unhappy lover whose unhappiness drives him to find a solace in nature which no lover had looked for since the appearance of Rousseau's *Nouvelle Héloïse;* he is also the burgher whose pride is wounded by battering at the barriers of class, and who demands recognition for himself in the name of the rights of man and even of the rights due to any living creature. This is the last occasion for a very long time on which Goethe allows the revolutionary element in his youth to have its say. In an early review of a novel by Wieland, he had written: "The marble nymphs, the flowers, the vases, the colorfully embroidered cloth on the tables of these nice people—what a high degree of refinement they presuppose, what inequality among the classes, what want where there is so much pleasure, what poverty where the wealth is so great." In *Werther,* however, he had already softened his attitude a little: "Many things can be said in defense of the Rules [of classical drama]—the same things, more or less, that can be said in praise of bourgeois society." In *Werther* the bourgeoisie finds the demigod who sacrifices his life for them. They feel redeemed, without being liberated; hence the protest of Lessing, whose class-consciousness was incorruptible. He missed the presence of bourgeois pride as a counterweight to the nobility and called for a cynical conclusion to the book.

After the hopeless complications of Goethe's love for Charlotte Buff, the prospect of a bourgeois marriage to a beautiful, impressive, and respected Frankfurt girl appeared as a welcome solution. "It was a strange decision on the part of the powers whose will governs our lives that the remarkable twists and turns of my life should include the experience of what it feels like to be engaged." But the engagement to Lili Schönemann turned out to be no more than a tempestuous incident in that war against marriage which he conducted for over thirty years.[11] The fact that Lili Schönemann was probably the most significant woman, and certainly the most liberated one, ever to have had a close relationship with him could ultimately only increase his resistance to being bound to her. In 1775 he fled, traveling to Switzerland in the company of Graf Stolberg. The outstanding feature of the journey was his meeting with Lavater.[12] In the latter's physiognomic studies, a sensation of the period, Goethe discovered something of his own understanding of nature. In later years, Goethe came to dislike the way Lavater found it necessary to synthesize this study of the creaturely world with his own Pietistic beliefs.

On the return journey, chance brought about a meeting with Karl August, the crown prince and subsequently duke of Saxe-Weimar.[13] A little after this, Goethe accepted the prince's invitation to his court. What was intended as a visit turned out to be a lifelong stay. Goethe arrived in Weimar on November 7, 1775. In the same year he was made a privy councilor, with a seat and vote on the Council of State. From the outset, Goethe himself viewed his decision to enter into the service of Karl August as a commitment that would change the course of his life. Two factors influenced his acceptance. In an age when the German bourgeoisie harbored increased political expectations, his position at court afforded him close contact with the realities of politics. On the other hand, as a high official in a bureaucratic apparatus he was relieved of the need to make any radical decisions. For all his inner uncertainty of mind, this position did at the very least provide him with an outward support for his self-confidence and his actions. The heavy price he had to pay was something he could have learned about easily enough from the questioning, disappointed, and indignant voices of his friends, had his own incorruptibly alert self-knowledge not kept it permanently before his mind. Klopstock and even Wieland,[14] like Herder later on, took offense at the generous spirit in which Goethe acceded to the demands of his position, and even more to the demands made on him by the personality and mode of life of the grand duke. For, as the author of *Götz* and *Werther,* Goethe represented the bourgeois *Fronde.* And his name meant all the more as the tendencies of the age were barred from almost every means of expression other than the personal and individual. In the eighteenth century an author was still a prophet, and his works were the keystone to a gospel which seemed most perfectly expressed by his life. The immeasurable personal prestige which Goethe's first works had brought him—they were received as revelations—evaporated in Weimar. But since people were unwilling to think of him as being anything other than larger than life, the most nonsensical legends about him began to take shape. He was said to be getting drunk on brandy every day; Herder was alleged to be preaching in boots and spurs and riding three times round the church after the sermon. This was how people imagined the wild escapades of those first months in Weimar. Of greater consequence, however, was the friendship between Goethe and Karl August, the foundations for which were laid during this period and which subsequently provided Goethe with the guarantee of a comprehensive intellectual and literary sovereignty—the first such universal European dominion since Voltaire. "As for the judgment of the world," the nineteen-year-old Karl August wrote at the time, "which might disapprove of my installing Dr. Goethe in my most important council without his having already achieved the status of magistrate, professor, chamberlain, or state councilor—none of that will deter me in the least."

The suffering and the inner conflict of these first Weimar years were given new shape and sustenance in Goethe's love for Charlotte von Stein.[15] An examination of the style of the letters he wrote to her in the years from 1776 to 1786 reveals the steady transition from Goethe's earlier revolutionary prose—a prose "which cheated language of its privileges"—to the great composed rhythms of the letters which he dictated for her in Italy between 1786 and 1788. As for their content, they are the most important source of our knowledge of the difficulties the young poet experienced in coming to terms with the business of administration and, above all, with court society. By nature, Goethe was not always very adaptable.

He wished to become so, however, and kept a close watch on "the so-called men of the world, to see how they did it." And in fact it was impossible to conceive of a harder school than his relationship with Charlotte, which, given the small-town environment, was inevitably highly exposed. An added factor was that Charlotte von Stein, even in the years when she was in such profoundly intimate communion with Goethe's world, was never prepared to flout the rules of courtly decorum. It took years before she could acquire such an unshakable and propitious place in his life that her image could enter his work in the figures of Iphigenia and Eleonore d'Este, Tasso's beloved. The fact that he proved able to put down roots in Weimar the way he did is very closely bound up with his relationship to Charlotte von Stein. Through her he came to know not just the court, but also the town and the countryside. Alongside all the official memoranda, there is a constant stream of more or less hasty notes to Frau von Stein in which Goethe appears, as was his practice as a lover, in the full range of his talents and activities: as sketcher, painter, gardener, architect, and so on. When, in the course of his account of Goethe's life in 1779, Riemer relates how Goethe spent a month and a half traveling around the duchy, inspecting the roads by day, helping to recruit young men for military service in the evenings, and resting at small inns and working on *Iphigenie* at night, he provides us with a miniature portrait of this critical and in many ways threatened phase of Goethe's life.

The poetic yield of these years includes the beginnings of *Wilhelm Meisters theatralische Sendung* [Wilhelm Meister's Theatrical Mission], *Stella*, *Clavigo*, *Werthers Briefe aus der Schweiz* [Werther's Letters from Switzerland], *Tasso*, and above all a large part of his most powerful lyric poetry: "Harzreise im Winter" [Journey to the Harz in Winter], "An den Mond" [Ode to the Moon], "Der Fischer" [The Fisherman], "Nur wer die Sehnsucht kennt" [Only the One Who Knows Longing], "Über allen Gipfeln" [Over All the Summits], "Geheimnisse" [Secrets]. Goethe also did some work on *Faust* during these years, and even laid the inner foundations for parts of *Faust, Part II*, to the extent at least that it was in the experiences of these first Weimar years that we find the origins of Goethe's nihilistic view of the state, which was to be so bluntly expressed later in Act 2. In 1781 we find him saying: "Our moral and political world is undermined by subterranean galleries, cellars, and sewers, as often occurs in a great city when there is no one to think about and concern himself with its needs and with the conditions of the inhabitants. Only, for anyone who has got wind of the situation it will come as no very great surprise if one day the earth caves in, if smoke . . . rises up in one place and strange voices are heard in another."

Every step which strengthened Goethe's position in Weimar increased the distance between himself and the friends and associates of his youth in Strasbourg and Wetzlar. The incomparable authority which had accompanied him to Weimar and which he had brought to bear to such effect in the court, was based on his role as leader of the *Sturm und Drang*. In a provincial town like Weimar, however, this was a movement which could make only a brief appearance and, since it was prevented from bearing any fruit, it was forced to remain at the level of tumultuous extravaganza. Goethe saw this quite clearly from the outset and did everything in his power to prevent any attempts to transplant Strasbourg ways to Weimar. In 1776, when Lenz appeared in Weimar and behaved at court in the style of the *Sturm und Drang*, Goethe had him expelled. That was political expediency. But to an even greater degree it was an instinctive reaction against the boundless impulsiveness and emotional extravagance implicit in the lifestyle of his youth—a style which he felt himself unable to contain in the long run. Among his associates at that time, he had seen the most egregious examples of scandalous behavior; a statement of Wieland's from that period gives us a glimpse of the devastating effects on him of his association with such people. Wieland wrote to a friend saying that he would not like to purchase Goethe's fame if the price he had to pay was the latter's physical suffering. In later years, then, the poet took the strictest prophylactic measures to protect his constitutional sensitivity. Indeed, when we observe the precautions Goethe took to avoid certain tendencies—all forms of nationalism and most of Romanticism, for example—we are forced to conclude that he was afraid they might be directly contagious. The fact that he wrote no tragic work is something he himself attributed to that same frailty of constitution.

The more Goethe's life in Weimar approached a certain state of equilibrium—in external terms, his acceptance into court society was completed in 1782 by his elevation into the nobility—the more unbearable he found the town. His impatience took the form of a pathological irritation with Germany. He talked of writing a work which the Germans would hate. His antipathy went even deeper. After a two-year youthful enthusiasm for German Gothic, landscape, and chivalry, Goethe began to discover in himself a resistance to the climate, landscape, history, politics, and nature of his own people—a resistance which came from his innermost being. This mood began to take shape vaguely and unclearly when he was twenty-five; it gradually became clearer, and then a matter of passionate conviction, culminating in a definite view systematically rationalized. It found dramatic expression in 1786 in Goethe's abrupt departure for Italy. He himself described his journey as a flight. He was so oppressed by tensions and superstitious feelings that he had not ventured to divulge his plans to anyone.

In the course of this journey—which lasted two years and which took him to Verona, Venice, Ferrara, Rome, and Naples and down to Sicily—two issues were resolved. The first was that Goethe renounced his hopes of committing himself to a life based on the visual arts. This was an idea he had repeatedly entertained. If Goethe had unconsciously acquired the image of a dilettante in the eyes of the nation, an image which he was long reluctant to discard, one of the reasons for this, as well as for the many instances of uncertainty and carelessness in his literary works, was his hesitation about the nature of his gifts. In order to smooth his way as a poet, he all too often allowed his genius to degenerate to a mere talent. His experience of the great art of the Italian Renaissance—which Goethe, since he was gazing at it through Winckelmann's eyes,[16] was unable to distinguish clearly from that of Antiquity—on the one hand laid the foundation for his conviction that he was not meant to be a painter, while on the other it supplied the basis for that narrow classicist theory of art which is perhaps the only sphere of thought in which Goethe lagged behind his age, rather than taking the lead. There was yet another sense in which Goethe may be said to have rediscovered his true self. In a letter home, he says, referring to the Weimar court: "The illusion that the fine seeds which are ripening in my life and in those of my friends had to be sown in this ground, and that those celestial jewels could be made to fit into the earthly crowns of these princes, has now been completely dispelled, and I find my youthful happiness wholly restored."

In Italy, the prose draft of *Iphigenie* gave way to the definitive version. The following year, 1788, Goethe completed *Egmont*. *Egmont* is no political drama, but a character study of the German tribune that Goethe, as the spokesman of the German bourgeoisie, might at a pinch have become. The only trouble with it is that this portrait of the fearless man of the people is all too idealized, and this in turn lends greater force to the political realities uttered by Alba and William of Orange. The concluding phantasmagoria— "Freedom clad in a celestial gown, bathed in light, rests upon a cloud"— unmasks the supposedly political ideas of Count Egmont and reveals them as the poetic inspiration they fundamentally are. Goethe inevitably had a very limited view of the revolutionary freedom movement which broke out in the Netherlands in 1566 under the leadership of Count Egmont. His vision was obscured, in the first place, by a social milieu and a personal temperament for which the conservative notions of tradition and hierarchy were inalienable; and, in the second place, by his basic anarchistic attitude, his inability to conceive of the state as a factor in history. For Goethe, history represented an unpredictable sequence of cultures and forms of rule in which the only fixed points were great individuals such as Caesar and Napoleon, Shakespeare and Voltaire. He was never able to bring himself to believe in national or social movements. It is true that he was unwilling on principle to make a general statement about such matters, but this is the view that emerges both from his conversations with Luden, the historian, and also from *Wilhelm Meisters Wanderjahre* [Wilhelm Meister's Wanderings] and *Faust*. It is such convictions as these that determined his relationship with the dramatist Schiller. For Schiller, the problem of the state had always been a matter of central importance. The state in its relations to the individual was the subject of his early plays; the state in its relations to the representatives of power was the theme of the works of his maturity. In contrast, the driving force in Goethe's dramas is not conflict but a process of unfolding.—The chief lyrical product of his Italian period was the *Römische Elegien* [Roman Elegies], a collection of poems which preserve the memory of many Roman nights of love in verses remarkable for their classical definition and perfection of form. The heightened sensual intensity of his nature now drove him to the decision to concentrate his energies and henceforth to confine himself to more limited commitments. While still in Italy, Goethe wrote the duke a letter which shows his diplomatic style at its best, asking to be relieved of all his political and administrative duties. His request was granted, but despite this it was only after lengthy detours that Goethe found his way back to intensive literary production. The chief cause of the delay must be sought in his preoccupation with the French Revolution. In order to understand his attitude here—as well as his scattered, disconnected, and impenetrable utterances on political matters—it is less important to make a synthesis of his theoretical improvisations than to consider their function.

It is beyond all doubt that after his experience as a privy councilor in Weimar and long before the outbreak of the French Revolution, Goethe found the enlightened despotism of the eighteenth century problematic in the extreme. Nevertheless, he proved unable to reconcile himself to the Revolution. This was not just because of his temperamental attachment to the feudal regime, or even because of his fundamental opposition to any violent upheavals in public life, but because he found it difficult and even impossible to arrive at any considered views on political issues. If he never made the clear statement on the "limits of the efficacy of the state" that we find, for example, in Wilhelm von Humboldt,[17] the reason was that his political nihilism was too extreme to enable him to do more than drop inconclusive hints. It is enough to note that Napoleon's intention of dividing the German people up into its original tribes held no terrors for Goethe, who regarded such perfect fragmentation as the outward manifestation of a community in which great individuals could demarcate their own spheres of activity—a realm in which they could exercise patriarchal sway and communicate with one another down the ages and across the frontiers of the state. It has been rightly said that for Goethe, who was himself the quintessence of a gallicized Franconia, the Germany of Napoleon supplied the environment that suited him best. But in his relationship to the Revolution, we must also take note of the effects of his hypersensitivity, the pathological state of shock induced in him by the great political events of his age. This shock, the effect of certain episodes in the French Revolution as well as of personal blows of fate, made the idea of reordering the world of politics purely on the basis of principles as inconceivable to him as applying such principles in order to regulate the private existence of individuals.

In the light of the class antagonisms existing in Germany at the time, we may interpret this in the following way: unlike Lessing,[18] Goethe felt himself to be less the champion of the middle classes than their deputy—their ambassador to German feudalism and the princes. His constant vacillation may be explained in terms of the conflicts arising from his position as representative. The greatest representative of classical bourgeois literature— the only indisputable claim of the German people to the honor of being admitted to the ranks of modern cultured nations—was himself unable to conceive of bourgeois culture outside the framework of a perfected feudal state. Of course, if Goethe rejected the French Revolution, this was not just so as to defend feudalism—the patriarchal idea that every culture, including bourgeois culture, could thrive only under the protection of and in the shadow of the absolutist state. Of equal importance was the petty-bourgeois motive, the efforts of the private individual who anxiously seeks to seal off his life and protect it from the political upheavals all around. But neither the spirit of feudalism nor that of the petty bourgeoisie sufficed to make his rejection absolute and unequivocal. It is for this reason that not a single one of the literary works in which he sought over a period of ten years to come to terms with the Revolution can be assigned a central place in his overall output.

Between 1792 and 1802, there are no fewer than seven works in which Goethe attempted again and again to arrive at a compelling formula or a definitive portrait. Primarily these included occasional pieces such as *Der Grosskophta* [The Great Magician] or *Die Aufgeregten* [The Agitated], which mark the nadir of Goethe's achievement, or else, as in *The Natural Daughter,* efforts that were doomed to remain fragments. In the end, however, Goethe came closest to his goal in two works that both treat the Revolution, as it were, *en bagatelle. Hermann und Dorothea* reduces it to a sinister background which serves as a useful foil to an attractive German small-town idyll; *Reineke Fuchs* [Reynard the Fox] dissolves the pathos of the Revolution into a verse satire in which it is no coincidence that Goethe reverts to the medieval genre of the animal epic. The Revolution as background to a moralistic genre scene—this is the method of *Hermann und Dorothea;* the Revolution as comic intrigue, as an intermezzo in the animal history of mankind—this is his approach in *Reynard the Fox.* It is by such methods that Goethe overcomes the traces of resentment that are evident in his earlier attempts in this direction, above all in the *Unterhaltungen deutscher Ausgewanderten* [Conversations of German Emigrés]. But the notion that has the last word here is the hierarchical, feudal belief that the high point of human history finds mankind assembled around the person of the monarch. Despite this, it is the king in *The Natural Daughter* who makes Goethe's failure to comprehend political history so palpably plain. He is King Thoas of *Iphigenie* in a new garb, the king as "the good man," who, when transported into the upheavals of the Revolution, must inevitably be found wanting.

The political problems which the 1790s imposed on Goethe's writing explain why he made a series of efforts to escape from literature. His chief refuge was the study of science. Schiller clearly perceived the escapist character of Goethe's scientific preoccupations in these years. In 1787 he wrote to Körner:[19] "Goethe's mind has molded all the people who belong to his circle. A proud philosophical contempt for all speculation and investigation, together with an attachment to nature bordering on affectation and a retreat to knowledge as vouchsafed by his five senses—in short, a certain childlike simplicity of mind characterizes him and his whole sect here. They prefer looking for herbs or studying mineralogy to empty theorizing. This can be quite wholesome and good, but it can also be greatly overdone." His study of natural history could only estrange Goethe still further from politics. He understood history only as natural history, and comprehended it only insofar as it remained bound to creatureliness. This is why the educational theory he later developed in *Wilhelm Meister's Wanderings* represented the most advanced position he was able to adopt in the realm of the historical. His scientific bent went against the grain of politics, but it must be added that it was equally hostile to theology. In this respect it represents the most positive fruit of Goethe's anticlerical Spinozism. It explains why he took offense at the Pietistic writings of Jacobi,[20] his former friend, because the latter had argued that nature conceals God, whereas for Goethe the crucial aspect of Spinoza's thought lay in his assertion that both nature and spirit are a visible aspect of the divine. This is what Goethe means when he writes to Jacobi, saying, "God has punished you with metaphysics . . . ; whereas He has blessed me with physics."—Goethe's master concept in describing the revelations of the physical world is the "primal phenomenon" [*Urphänomen*]. It developed originally out of his botanical and anatomical studies. In 1784 Goethe discovered that the bones of the skull were the morphological development of changes in the bones of the spine; a year later he discovered the "metamorphosis of plants." What he meant by this was the idea that all the organs of plants, from the roots to the stamen, are nothing but leaves in a modified form. This led him to the concept of the "primal plant" [*Urpflanze*], which Schiller, in his celebrated first conversation with him, declared to be an "idea," whereas Goethe insisted on endowing it with a certain sensuous reality. The place occupied in Goethe's writings by his scientific studies is the one which in lesser artists is commonly reserved for aesthetics. This aspect of Goethe's work can be appreciated only when one realizes that, unlike almost all other intellectuals in this period, he never really made his peace with the idea of art as "beautiful appearance" [*der schöne Schein*]. What reconciled poetry and politics in his eyes was not aesthetics, but the study of nature. And precisely because of this it is vital to note even in his scientific writings how obstinately Goethe opposed certain innovations in the realm of technology, just as much as in politics. On the very threshold of the scientific age, which was destined to extend the range and precision of our sense-perceptions in such a radical and unprecedented way, he reverted once more to old forms of scientific explanation and could therefore write: "Man himself, when he makes use of his own sound senses, is the greatest and most precise physical apparatus that can exist; and the great catastrophe of modern physics is that in it experiments have, as it were, been separated off from man, and aim . . . to know Nature simply by virtue of what artificial instruments can reveal." According to his way of thinking, the immediate natural purpose of science is to bring man in his thought and actions into harmony with himself. Changing the world by means of technology was not really his concern, even though as an old man he was astonishingly clear about its immeasurable implications for the future. To his mind, the greatest benefit of scientific knowledge was determined by the form it gives to one's life. This conviction was something he developed into a strict pragmatic maxim: "Only what is fruitful is true."

Goethe belongs to the family of great minds for whom there is basically no such thing as an art separated from life. In his eyes, the theory of the "primal phenomenon" in science was also a theory of art, just as scholastic philosophy had been for Dante and the technical arts for Dürer. Strictly speaking, his only genuine scientific discoveries were in the field of botany. His research in anatomy was also important and has received recognition: this was his work on the intermaxillary bone, which admittedly was no original discovery.[21] His *Meteorologie* received little attention, and his *Farbenlehre* [Theory of Colors], which for Goethe represented the crowning point of his entire scientific work—and indeed, according to a number of statements, of his whole life—became the subject of fierce dispute. In recent times the controversy surrounding this, the most comprehensive of Goethe's scientific writings, has flared up once more. The *Theory of Colors* takes up a position diametrically opposed to Newton's optics. The basic disagreement underlying Goethe's often bitter polemic, prolonged over many years, is this: whereas Newton explained white light as the composite of the different colors, Goethe declared it to be the simplest, most indivisible and homogeneous phenomenon known to us. "It is not a compound . . . least of all, a compound of colored lights." The *Theory of Colors* regards the colors as metamorphoses of light, as phenomena which are formed in the course of the struggle between light and darkness. Together with the idea of metamorphosis, the concept of polarity, which runs like a thread through

Goethe's entire scientific enterprise, is of decisive importance here. Darkness is not merely the absence of light—for then it would not be discernible—but a positive counter-light. In his old age we even find him entertaining the idea that perhaps plants and animals evolved from their primal condition through the agency of light or darkness.—A peculiar feature of his scientific studies is that in them Goethe comes as close to the spirit of the Romantic school as he remains remote from it in his aesthetics. It is much harder to explain Goethe's philosophical position in terms of his poetic writings than to explain it in terms of his scientific ones. Ever since that youthful moment of illumination which is recorded in Goethe's celebrated fragment "Die Natur" [Nature], Spinoza remained the guiding light in his morphological studies. It was these that subsequently provided the basis for his relationship with Kant. While he could not find any point of contact with Kant's main critical oeuvre—the *Critique of Pure Reason* and the *Critique of Practical Reason* (i.e., ethics)—he held the *Critique of Judgment* in the greatest possible esteem. For in that work Kant repudiates the teleological explanation of nature which had been one of the chief supports of enlightened philosophy and of deism. Goethe had to agree with him on this point, particularly since his own anatomical and botanical researches represented very advanced positions in the campaign of bourgeois science against the teleological outlook. Kant's definition of the organic as a purposiveness whose intent lay inside and not outside the purposive being was in harmony with Goethe's own concepts. The unity of the beautiful—natural beauty included—is always independent of purpose. In this, Goethe and Kant are of one mind.

The more Goethe was affected by developments in Europe, the more vigorous were his efforts to achieve security in his private life. It is in this context that we have to consider the fact that very shortly after his return from Italy he ended the relationship with Charlotte von Stein. Goethe's association with Christiane Vulpius,[22] whom he met soon after he came back from Italy and who later became his wife, continued to outrage the citizens of the town for fifteen years. Nevertheless, it would be an error to think of this relationship with a proletarian girl, who worked in a flower nursery, as evidence of Goethe's emancipated views. Even in such matters of private life, Goethe held no fixed principles, let alone revolutionary ones. At the start, Christiane was no more than his mistress. The remarkable feature of the relationship was not its beginnings but its later development. Even though Goethe was never able, and perhaps never even tried, to bridge the enormous cultural gap between himself and Christiane, even though Christiane's lowly birth inevitably gave offense to the petty-bourgeois society of Weimar and her way of life proved unacceptable to more liberal-minded and intelligent people, and even though neither partner regarded marital fidelity as sacrosanct—all this notwithstanding, Goethe dignified this union and with it Christiane by his unswerving loyalty and by a wholly admirable perseverance in an extremely delicate situation. And with a church wedding in 1807, fifteen years after their first meeting, he forced both court and society to accept the mother of his son. As for Frau von Stein, a lukewarm reconciliation was achieved only much later, after years of profound antipathy.

In 1790, as minister of state, Goethe assumed responsibility for culture and education, and a year later he was put in charge of the court theater. His activities in this sphere are simply immeasurable. They grew in scope from one year to the next. All scientific institutes, all the museums, the University of Jena, the technical schools, the voice-training academies, the academy of art—all these were placed under the poet's immediate direction, and he frequently concerned himself with the most minute details. Hand in hand with this went his efforts to expand his own household into an institute of European culture. His activities as a collector extended to every area of study and interest. These collections have formed the basis of the Goethe National Museum in Weimar, with its picture gallery, its galleries of drawings, porcelain, coins, stuffed animals, bones and plants, minerals, fossils, and chemical and physical apparatus, to say nothing of the collections of books and manuscripts. His universality knew no bounds. In areas in which he could not achieve anything as an artist, he wished at least to be a connoisseur. At the same time, these collections provided a framework for a life which increasingly was enacted publicly on the European stage. They also endowed him with the authority which he required in his role as the greatest organizer of princely patronage that Germany had ever known. Voltaire was the first man of letters to secure a reputation on a European scale and to make use of intellectual and material resources of equal magnitude to defend the prestige of the bourgeoisie vis-à-vis the aristocracy. In this respect, Goethe is Voltaire's immediate successor. And as with Voltaire, Goethe's position must be thought of in political terms. Hence, despite his rejection of the French Revolution it remains true that he more than anyone else made purposeful and ingenious use of the increase in power which that revolution brought to men of letters. Whereas Voltaire acquired wealth on a princely scale in the second half of his life, Goethe never achieved comparable financial status. But in order to understand his remarkable obstinacy in business matters, notably in his dealings with the publishing house of Cotta, we must bear in mind that from the turn of the century onward he looked upon himself as the founder of a national heritage.

Throughout this decade it was Schiller who time and again recalled Goethe from the distractions of his political activities and his immersion in the observation of nature and brought him back to literary work. The first meeting between the two poets took place soon after Goethe's return from Italy, and was not a success. This was very much in tune with the opinion each held of the other. Schiller, who had made his name with such plays as *Die Räuber* [The Robbers], *Kabale und Liebe* [Intrigue and Love], *Fiesko,* and *Don Carlos,* had committed himself to class-conscious statements of a directness that stood in the sharpest possible contrast to Goethe's efforts at moderate mediation. Whereas Schiller wanted to take up the class struggle all along the line, Goethe had long since retreated to that fortified position from which only a cultural offensive could be launched and any political activity on the part of the bourgeoisie had of necessity to be defensive. The fact that these two men could reach a compromise is symptomatic of the unstable character of the class consciousness of the German bourgeoisie. This compromise was brought about under the aegis of Kantian philosophy. In the interests of aesthetics, Schiller, in his letters concerning *Über die ästhetische Erziehung des Menschen* [The Aesthetic Education of Man], had stripped the radical formulations of Kantian ethics of their subversive bite and converted them into an instrument of historical construction. This paved the way for a rapprochement—or, better, an armistice—with Goethe. In reality, the association between the two men was always marked by the diplomatic reserve which was the price of this compromise. The discussions between them were almost anxiously confined to formal problems of writing. Admittedly, on this plane their exchanges were epoch-making. Their correspondence is no doubt a balanced document, carefully edited to the last detail, and for ideological reasons it has always enjoyed a greater prestige than the deeper, freer, livelier correspondence which the aged Goethe conducted with Zelter.[23] The Young-Germany critic Gutzkow[24] has rightly drawn attention to the "hairsplitting discussions about aesthetic trends and artistic theories" which go round and round in circles throughout the correspondence. And he was also right to lay the blame for this at the door of the hostility—indeed, the utter incompatibility—of art and history which we encounter here. And even when it came to their greatest works, the poets could not always rely on each other for a sympathetic reception. "He was," Goethe says of Schiller in 1829, "like all people who base themselves too much on ideas. He had no peace of mind and could never be finished with a thing . . . I had my work cut out to hold my own, and protect his work and mine and keep them safe from such influences."

Schiller's influence was important primarily for Goethe's ballads: "Der Schatzgräber" [The Treasure Seeker], "Der Zauberlehrling" [The Sorcerer's Apprentice], "Die Braut von Korinth" [The Bride of Corinth], and "Der Gott und die Bajadere" [The God and the Bayadere]. The official manifesto of their literary alliance, however, was *Die Xenien.* The almanac containing these satirical epigrams appeared in 1795. Its thrust was directed at the enemies of Schiller's *Die Horen*[25]—namely, the vulgar rationalism centered on Nicolai's circle in Berlin. The onslaught was effective. The literary success was heightened by a personal interest: both poets had put their names to the whole collection, without revealing the authorship of the individual couplets. But all the verve and elegance of their campaign could not conceal an underlying note of desperation. The era of Goethe's popular acclaim was over; and even if his authority grew from one decade to the next, he never again achieved true popularity. The later Goethe in particular displays that resolute contempt for the reading public which is characteristic of all the classical writers with the exception of Wieland, and which receives its strongest expression at certain points in the Goethe-Schiller correspondence. Goethe had no relationship with his public. "Although he had a powerful impact, it remains true that he never lived or continued to live in that realm in which he created those first works which set the world alight." He remained unaware of the extent to which he was himself a kind of gift to Germany. And least of all was he able to commit himself to any trend or tendency of the age. His attempt to represent his alliance with Schiller as such a trend ultimately proved illusory. The destruction of this illusion was a legitimate need, and one which repeatedly led the German public in the nineteenth century to contrast Goethe and Schiller and measure each against the other. The influence of Weimar on the great mass of Germans was not that of the two poets, but that of the periodicals of Bertuch[26] and Wieland: the *Allgemeine literarische Zeitung* and the *Teutscher Merkur.* "We do not desire the upheaval," Goethe had written in 1795, "which could pave the way for classical works in Germany." The upheaval in question—that would have been the emancipation of the bourgeoisie, which came too late to give birth to any classical works. Germanness, the genius of the German language—those were undoubtedly the strings on which Goethe played his great melodies. Yet the sounding-board of this instrument was not Germany, but the Europe of Napoleon.

Goethe and Napoleon shared a similar vision: the social emancipation of the bourgeoisie within the framework of political despotism. This was the "impossible," the "incommensurable," and the "inadequate" that was the deepest source of their unease. It brought Napoleon down. Of Goethe, however, it can be said that the older he became, the more his life assumed the shape of this political idea, consciously acquiring the form of the incommensurable and the inadequate, and turning itself into a miniature model of that political idea. If we could draw clear lines of demarcation, then we could think of poetry as providing a metaphor for the bourgeois freedom of this micro-state, whereas in its private affairs the regime corresponds perfectly to the rule of despotism. But in reality, of course, it is equally essential to pursue the interweaving of these irreconcilable aspirations in both life and poetry: in life, as a freedom of erotic breakthrough and as the strictest regime of "renunciation"; in poetry, nowhere more than in the second part of *Faust,* whose political dialectics provide the key to Goethe's position. Only in this context is it possible to understand how Goethe could spend his last thirty years subordinating his life to the bureaucratic categories of compromise, mediation, and procrastination. It is senseless to judge his actions and his stance in terms of any abstract standard of morality. It is such abstraction that is responsible for the touch of absurdity we see in the attacks Börne launched against Goethe in the name of Young Germany.[27] It is precisely when we come to examine his maxims and the most remarkable aspects of his conduct that we find that Goethe becomes comprehensible only in the context of the political position which he created and in which he installed himself. The subterranean but all the more profound kinship with Napoleon is so decisive that the post-Napoleonic age, the power that toppled Napoleon, is no longer capable of understanding it. The son of bourgeois parents rises in the world, outstrips everyone, becomes the heir to a revolution whose power in his hands is such that it makes everyone tremble (French Revolution; *Sturm und Drang*); and at the very moment he dealt the most grievous blow to the power of superannuated forces, he established his own dominion within the selfsame archaic, feudal framework (empire; Weimar).

Within the political constellation that governed his life, the animosity Goethe felt for the Wars of Liberation, an animosity highly offensive to bourgeois literary historians, becomes entirely comprehensible. In his eyes, Napoleon had been the founder of a European public even before he had established a European empire. In 1815 Goethe let himself be persuaded by Iffland[28] to write one last play, *Des Epimenides Erwachen* [The Awakening of Epimenides], in celebration of the entry of the victorious troops into Berlin. But he could bring himself to renounce Napoleon only by simultaneously refusing to relinquish the chaotic and dark manifestations of the same elemental power which Napoleon embodied and which had once shaken the world. He could muster no sympathy for the victors. And on the other hand, we find the same kind of idiosyncrasy in the pained determination with which he fends off the patriotic spirit which moved Germany in 1813—something we also see in the way he could not bear to remain in the same room with sick people or in the vicinity of the dying. His dislike of everything military is not so much a rejection of army discipline or even drill, as a horror of everything which is calculated to detract from the appearance of the human being—everything from the uniform to the wound. In 1792 his nerves were subjected to a severe test when he had to accompany the duke in the invasion of France by the allied armies. On this occasion Goethe was forced to display all his art in concentrating on the observation of nature, optical studies, and sketching, in order to insulate himself from the events he was witnessing. The "Kampagne in Frankreich" [Campaign in France] is just as vital for an understanding of the poet as it is a melancholy and vague response to the problems of world politics.

The change of direction toward Europe and toward politics—this is the mark of the final stage of Goethe's poetic work. But it was only after the death of Schiller that he could feel this as the firmest of all ground beneath his feet. In contrast, the great prose work which was taken up again after a long pause and completed under Schiller's influence, *Wilhelm Meisters Lehrjahre* [Wilhelm Meister's Apprenticeship], shows Goethe still tarrying in the antechambers of idealism, in that German humanism from which he later emerged after much struggle to enter into an ecumenical humanism. The ideal of the *Appenticeship* (education) and the social milieu of the hero (the world of actors) are indeed strictly related to each other, since they are both the exponents of that specifically German realm of "beautiful appearance" that seemed so empty of meaning to the bourgeoisie of the West, which was just in the process of entering on its period of hegemony. In fact, it was almost a poetic necessity to place actors in the center of a bourgeois German novel. It enabled Goethe to avoid a confrontation with the contingencies of politics, only to take them up again with a correspondingly greater vigor twenty years later in the sequel to the novel. The fact that in *Wilhelm Meister* Goethe's hero was a quasi-artist was what guaranteed the novel's decisive influence, precisely because it was a product of the German situation at the end of the century. It led to the series of artist-novels of Romanticism, from the *Heinrich von Ofterdingen* of Novalis and Tieck's *Sternbald* down to Mörike's *Maler Nolten*.[29] The book's style is in harmony with its content. "There is no sign anywhere of logical machinery or a dialectical struggle between ideas and subject matter; instead, Goethe's prose offers a theatrical perspective. It is a thought-out piece that has been learned by heart, a work in which gentle prompting has led to a creative structure of thought. In it, things themselves do not speak but, as it were, seek the poet's permission to speak. This is why its language is lucid and yet modest, clear but without obtruding itself, diplomatic in the extreme."

It lay in the nature of both men that Schiller's influence functioned essentially as a formative stimulus on Goethe's production, without basically modifying its direction. The fact that Goethe turned toward the ballad and resumed work on *Wilhelm Meister* and the *Faust* fragment may perhaps be put down to Schiller's influence. But the actual exchange of ideas about these works almost always confined itself to questions of craft and technique. Goethe's inspiration remained undiverted. His friendship was with Schiller the man and the author. But it was not the friendship of two poets, as has often been claimed. The extraordinary charm and force of Schiller's personality nevertheless revealed themselves to Goethe in their full magnitude, and after Schiller's death Goethe left a memorial to them in the poem "Epilog zu Schillers, 'Glocke,'" [Epilogue to Schiller's "Bell"].

After Schiller's death, Goethe reorganized his personal relationships. Henceforth he would not have anyone in his immediate circle whose stature was even remotely comparable to his own. And there was hardly anyone in

Weimar who could be said to have been taken into his confidence in any special way. On the other hand, in the course of the new century his friendship with Zelter, the founder of the Berlin voice-training academy, grew in importance for Goethe. In time, Zelter came to assume the rank of a sort of ambassador for Goethe, representing him in the Prussian capital. In Weimar itself Goethe gradually acquired an entire staff of assistants and secretaries, without whose help the vast inheritance that he prepared for publication could never have been organized. In an almost mandarin way, the poet ended up putting the last thirty years of his life in the service of producing the written word. It is in this sense that we have to regard his great literary press office with its many assistants, from Eckermann, Riemer, Soret, and Müller down to clerks like Kräuter and Kohn.[30] Eckermann's *Conversations with Goethe* are the main source for these last decades, and are moreover one of the finest prose works of the nineteenth century. What fascinated Goethe about Eckermann, perhaps more than anything else, was the latter's unrestrained attachment to the positive—a quality never found in superior minds and which is rare even in lesser men. Goethe never had any real relationship with criticism in the narrower sense. The strategy of the art business, which did fascinate him from time to time, always expressed itself in dictatorial ways—in the manifestos he drafted with Schiller and Herder, or in the regulations he drew up for actors and artists.

More independent than Eckermann, and for that very reason, of course, less exclusively useful to the poet, was Chancellor von Müller. But his *Conversations with Goethe* are likewise one of the documents that have helped to shape the image of Goethe as it has come down to posterity. These two should be joined by Friedrich Riemer (a professor of classical philology), not because of his gifts as a conversationalist but by virtue of his great and perceptive analysis of Goethe's character. The first great document to emerge from this literary organism which the aging Goethe created for himself was the autobiography. *Dichtung und Wahrheit* [Poetry and Truth] is a preview of Goethe's last years in the form of a memoir. This retrospective account of his active youth provides access to one of the most crucial principles of his life. Goethe's moral activity is in the last analysis a positive counterpole to the Christian principle of remorse: "Seek to give a coherent meaning to everything in your life." "The happiest man is one who can establish a connection between the beginning of his life and the end." In such statements we see an expression of the desire to give shape to and make manifest the image of the world he had accommodated himself to in his youth: the world of the inadequate, the compromised, the contingent; of erotic indecision and political vacillation. It is only against this background that we can see the Goethean credo of "renunciation" in its right sense, in all its terrible ambiguity: Goethe renounced not just pleasure, but also greatness and heroism. This is perhaps why his autobiography breaks off before its hero has achieved a position in society. The reminiscences of later years are scattered through the *Italienische Reise* [Italian Journey], the *Campaign in France,* and the *Tag- und Jahreshefte* [Diaries]. In his description of the years 1750–1775, Goethe has included a series of vignettes of the most important contemporaries of his youth; while Günther, Lenz, Merck, and Herder have partly entered literary history in the same formulas that Goethe devised for them. In portraying them Goethe depicted himself at the same time, and shows himself adopting a hostile or sympathetic stance toward the friends or competitors with whom he had to deal. We see here the same compulsion at work that inspired him as a dramatist to confront William of Orange with Egmont, the courtier with the man of the people; Tasso with Antonio, the poet with the courtier; Prometheus with Epimetheus, the creative man with the elegiac dreamer; and Faust with Mephisto—the ensemble of personas at work in his own personality.

Beyond this more immediate group of assistants, a further circle grew up in these later years. There was the Swiss artist Heinrich Meyer,[31] Goethe's expert on questions of art, strictly classicist in outlook, a reflective man who helped Goethe with the editing of the *Propyläen* and with the later periodical *Kunst und Altertum* [Art and Antiquity]. There was Friedrich August Wolf, the classical philologist, whose demonstration that the Homeric epics were the product of a whole series of unknown poets which were harmonized by a later editor and only then became known as the works of Homer evoked very mixed feelings in Goethe.[32] Wolf, together with Schiller, was drawn into Goethe's attempt to write the *Achilleis* as a sequel to the Homeric epics, a work that remained a fragment. We should also mention Sulpiz Boisserée, the discoverer of the German Middle Ages in painting, the inspiring advocate of German Gothic, and, as such, a friend of the Romantics, who chose him to act as spokesman for their views on art.[33] (His labors in this direction, which were spread over many years, had to rest content with a half-victory: Goethe finally allowed himself to be persuaded to submit a collection of documents and plans concerning the history and completion of Cologne Cathedral to the court.) All these relationships, and countless others, are the expression of a universality in the interests of which Goethe consciously blurred the dividing lines between the artist, the researcher, and the amateur. No poetic genre or language acquired popularity in Germany without Goethe at once turning his attention to it. Everything he achieved as translator, writer of travel books, biographer, connoisseur, critic, physicist, educationalist, and even theologian, as theatrical producer, court poet, companion, and minister—all this served to enhance his reputation for universality. But it was a European as opposed to a German arena which increasingly became the focus of these interests. He felt a passionate admiration for the great European minds who emerged toward the end of his life—for Byron, Walter Scott, and Manzoni.[34] In Germany, on the other hand, he would often give advancement to mediocrities, and he failed to appreciate the genius of such contemporaries as Hölderlin, Kleist, and Jean Paul.[35]

In 1809, at the same time as *Poetry and Truth,* Goethe also wrote *Die Wahlverwandtschaften* [Elective Affinities]. His work on this novel coincided with his first real experience of the European nobility, an experience which gave him an insight into that new, self-assured worldly public to whom, twenty years previously in Rome, he had resolved to address his writings. *Elective Affinities* is in fact directed at a public consisting of the Silesian-Polish aristocracy, lords, émigrés, and Prussian generals who congregated in the Bohemian spas around the empress of Austria. Not that this prevents the poet from giving a critical view of their mode of life. For *Elective Affinities* provides a sketchy but very incisive picture of the decline of the family in the ruling class of the period. Yet the power which destroys this already disintegrating institution is not the bourgeoisie, but a feudal society which, in the shape of the magic forces of fate, finds itself restored to its primordial state. Fifteen years before, in his drama of the French Revolution, *The Agitated,* Goethe had made the schoolmaster say of the nobility, "For all their superciliousness, these people cannot rid themselves of the mysterious feeling of awe that permeates all the living forces of nature; they cannot bring themselves to deny the eternal bond that unites words and effects, actions and their consequences." And these words provide the magical patriarchal ground-motif of this novel. It is a mode of thought we find repeated in *Wilhelm Meister's Wanderings,* in which even the most resolute attempts to construct the image of a fully developed bourgeoisie lead him back inexorably to the pastiche of mystical, medieval organizations—the secret society of the Tower. Goethe understood the emergence of bourgeois culture more fully than any of his predecessors or successors, but he was nonetheless unable to conceive of it otherwise than from within the framework of an idealized feudal state. And when he found himself even further estranged from Germany by the mismanagement of the German Restoration, which coincided with the last twenty years of his working life, he emphasized this idealized feudalism still further by amalgamating it with the patriarchal features of the East. We witness the emergence of the oriental Middle Ages in the *West-Easterly Divan.*

Not only did this book create a novel type of philosophical poetry; it was also the greatest expression of the love poetry of old age to be found in German and European literature. It was more than political necessity that led Goethe to the Orient. The powerful late blossoming of Goethe's erotic passion in his later years made him regard old age itself as a rebirth, as a sort of fancy-dress which merged in his mind with the world of the Orient and which transformed his encounter with Marianne von Willemer into a brief, intoxicating festival.[36] The *West-Easterly Divan* is the epode of this love. Goethe could understand the past, history, only to the extent to which he could integrate it into his life. In the succession of passionate relationships, Frau von Stein represented for him the reincarnation of Antiquity, Marianne von Willemer the Orient, and Ulrike von Levetzow, his last love, the symbiosis of these with the fairy-tale images of his youth.[37] This is the message of his last love poem, the *Marienbader Elegie*. Goethe underlined the didactic strain in the *West-Easterly Divan,* in the notes he appended to the volume; there basing himself on Hammer-Purgstall and Diez, he presented the fruits of his oriental studies to the public. Amid the expanses of the Middle Ages in the East, amid princes and viziers, in the presence of the splendor of the imperial court, Goethe assumes the mask of Hatem, a vagabond and drinker, a man without needs, and thereby commits himself in his poetry to that hidden aspect of his nature which he once confided to Eckermann: "Magnificent buildings and rooms are all right for princes and wealthy men. When you live in them, you feel at your ease . . . and want nothing more. This is wholly at odds with my nature. When I live in a splendid house, like the one I had in Karlsbad, I at once become lazy and inactive. A lowlier dwelling, on the other hand, like the wretched room we are in now, a little disorderly in its order, a little gipsy-like—that is the right thing for me; it leaves my inner being with the complete freedom to do what it wishes and to create from within myself." In the figure of Hatem, Goethe, who had by then become reconciled to the experience of his adult years, allows free rein to the unstable and untamed elements of his youth. In many of these poems he was able to use all his genius to give the wisdom of beggars, tavernkeepers, and tramps the finest poetic expression they have ever received.

In *Wilhelm Meister's Wanderings* the didactic quality of the later writings is at its most deliberate. The novel, which had long lain fallow, was then completed in a great hurry. Teeming with contradictions and inconsistencies, it was finally treated by the poet as a storehouse in which he got Eckermann to record the contents of his notebooks. The numerous stories and episodes which form the basis of the work are only loosely connected. The most important of them concern the "Pedagogical Province," a very remarkable hybrid in which we can see Goethe coming to grips with the great socialist writings of Sismondi, Fourier, Saint-Simon, Owen, and Bentham.[38] It is unlikely that his knowledge of them derived from his own reading; their influence among his contemporaries was powerful enough to induce Goethe to try to combine feudal tendencies with those of the bourgeois praxis which are so prominent in these writings. This synthesis is achieved at the expense of the classical ideal of education, which retreats here all along the line. Very typical is the fact that farming is held to be obligatory, whereas instruction in the dead languages goes unmentioned. The "humanists" of *Wilhelm Meister's Apprenticeship* have all turned into artisans: Wilhelm is a surgeon, Jarno a mining engineer, Philine a seamstress. Goethe took over the idea of

vocational education from Pestalozzi.[39] Earlier, he had sung the praises of
handicraft in *Werther's Letters from Switzerland,* and now he does so again.
Since at this time economists were already beginning to confront the problems of industry, we may regard this as a rather reactionary stance. But that
aside, the socioeconomic ideas which Goethe supports here fit well enough
into an extreme utopian version of the ideology of bourgeois philanthropy.
"Property public and private" is the slogan proclaimed by one of the
inscriptions on the uncle's model estates. And another motto runs: "From
the useful via the true to the beautiful." The same syncretism is to be found,
typically, in religious instruction. While on the one hand Goethe is the sworn
enemy of Christianity, on the other he respects religion as the strongest
guarantee of any hierarchical form of society. He even goes so far as to
reconcile himself to the image of the sufferings of Christ, something which
had provoked a violent antipathy in him for decades. The social order in
the Goethean sense—that is, an order governed by patriarchal and cosmic
norms—finds its purest expression in the figure of Makarie. The experience
Goethe gained of practical, political activity failed to modify his basic
attitudes, even though it frequently contradicted them. In consequence, his
attempt to reconcile his experience and his convictions in a work of art was
inevitably doomed to remain as fissured as the structure of this novel. And
we even see ultimate reservations in Goethe himself, when he looks to
America to provide his characters with a happier, more harmonious future.
That is where they emigrate to at the end of his novel. It has been described
as an "organized, communist escape."

If in the years of his maturity Goethe frequently avoided literature to
follow his whims or inclinations more freely in theoretical work or administrative duties, the major phenomenon of his later years can be said to lie
in the fact that the boundless circle of his continuing study of natural
philosophy, mythology, literature, art, and philology, his former involvement
in mining, finance, the theater, freemasonry, and diplomacy, was now all
drawn together concentrically into a final, monumental work of literature:
the second part of *Faust.* By his own admission Goethe spent over sixty
years working on both parts of *Faust.* In 1775 he brought the first fragment,
the *Urfaust,* with him to Weimar. It already contained some of the principal
features of the later work. There was the figure of Gretchen, who was the
naive counterpart to Faust, the prototypical reflective man; but she was also
the proletarian girl, the illegitimate mother, the child-murderer who is
executed and whose fate had long fueled the fierce social criticism in the
poems and plays of the *Sturm und Drang* writers. There was the figure of
Mephistopheles, who even then was less the devil of Christian teaching than
the Earth Spirit from the traditions of magic and the Kaballah. And finally
Faust himself, who was already the titan and superman, the twin brother

of Moses about whom Goethe had also planned to write and who likewise
was to attempt to wrest the secret of creation from God/Nature. In 1790,
Faust: A Fragment appeared. In 1808, for the first edition of his works,
Goethe sent the completed Part I to Cotta, his publisher.[40] Here, for the first
time, we find the action clearly defined. It is based on the "Prologue in
Heaven," where God and Mephisto make a wager for the soul of Faust.
When the devil comes and offers his services, however, Faust makes a pact
with him to the effect that he will forfeit his soul only if he says to the
moment:

> Ah, linger on, thou art so fair!
> Then may your fetters on me lay
> I'll gladly perish then and there.
> Then may the death-bell toll, recalling
> That from your service you are free;
> The clock may stop, the pointer falling,
> And time itself be past for me!

But the crux of the work is this: Faust's fierce and restless striving for the
absolute makes a mockery of Mephisto's attempts at seduction. The limits
of sensual pleasure are soon reached, but are insufficient to cost Faust his
soul: "Thus from desire I reel on to enjoyment / And in enjoyment languish
for desire."[41] With the passage of time Faust's longing grows and grows,
surpassing all bounds. The first part of the play ends in Gretchen's dungeon,
amid cries of woe. Taken on its own, this first part is one of Goethe's darkest
works. And it has been said that the Faust saga articulates—as a world
legend of the German bourgeoisie in the sixteenth century and as its world
tragedy in the eighteenth—how this class, in each case, lost the game it was
playing. The first part concludes Faust's existence as a bourgeois. The
political setting of Part II consists of imperial courts and classical palaces.
The outlines of Goethe's own Germany, which are still discernible through
the veil of the Romantic Middle Ages in Part I, have disappeared entirely
in Part II. Instead, the whole vast movement of thought is ultimately imaged
in terms of the German Baroque, and it is through the eyes of the Baroque
that Goethe views Antiquity. Having labored his whole life long to imagine
classical Antiquity ahistorically and, as it were, suspended freely in space,
Goethe now constructs, in the classical-romantic phantasmagoria of the
Helen scenes, the first great image of Antiquity as seen through the prism
of the German past. Around this work, which was to become Act 3 of *Faust
II*, the rest of the poem is assembled. It can hardly be overemphasized how
much these later parts, above all the scenes at the imperial court and in the
military camp, constitute a political apology and represent a political sum-
ming-up of Goethe's former activities at court. If his period of duty as a

minister had ended in a mood of profound resignation and with his capitulation to the intrigues of a mistress of the prince, he nevertheless creates at
the end of his life, in the setting of an ideal Baroque Germany, a screen on
which he projects a magnified image of the world of the statesman in all its
ramifications, and at the same time shows all its defects intensified to the
point of grotesqueness. Mercantilism, Antiquity, and mystical scientific experiments: the perfection of the state through money, of art through Antiquity, of nature through experiment. These provide the signature of the epoch
of the German Baroque which Goethe here invokes. And it is ultimately not
a dubious aesthetic expedient but the innermost political necessity of the
poem when, at the close of Act 5, the heaven of Catholicism is unveiled to
disclose Gretchen as one of the penitent. Goethe saw too deeply to allow
his political regression toward absolutism to rest content with the Protestant
courts of the eighteenth century. Soret has made the penetrating observation
that "Goethe is liberal in an abstract sense, but in practice he inclines toward
the most reactionary principles." In the crowning stage of Faust's life,
Goethe gives expression to the spirit of his practice: the reclaiming of land
from the sea, an activity which nature prescribes to history and in which
nature is itself inscribed—that was Goethe's conception of historical action,
and any political formation was justified in his eyes only if it could protect
and guarantee such action. In the mysterious, utopian interplay between
agrarian and technological activity on the one hand with the political
apparatus of absolutism on the other, Goethe glimpsed the magic formula
which would dissolve the realities of social conflict into nothingness. Bourgeois agricultural methods operating under the dominion of feudal tenure—
that was the discordant image in which Faust's greatest moment of fulfillment was to be crystallized.

Shortly after bringing the work to completion, Goethe died, on March
22, 1832. By that time, industrialization in Europe was proceeding at a
furious pace. Goethe foresaw future developments. In a letter to Zelter in
1825, for example, he says: "Wealth and speed are what the world admires
and strives for. Railways, express mail, steamships, and all possible facilities
for communication are what the cultivated world desires in order to over-
cultivate itself and thereby to stick fast in mediocrity. The concept of the
general public has also led to the spread of a medium-level culture: this is
the goal of the Bible Societies, the Lancastrian method, and God knows
what else.[42] The fact is that this is the century for able minds, for quick-
thinking, practical men with a certain dexterity which enables them to feel
superior to the crowd, even though their gifts do not put them in the first
rank. Let us try to remain true to the principles with which we came; along
with perhaps a few others, we shall be the last members of an era which
may not return so quickly." Goethe knew that in the short run his work

would have little impact, and in fact the bourgeoisie in whom the hopes of a German democracy were burgeoning once more preferred to look up to Schiller as their model. From the circle of Young Germany came the first weighty literary protests.[43] Börne, for example, wrote as follows: "Goethe always paid homage only to egoism and coldness; hence, it is only the cold who like him. He has taught educated people how to be educated, broad-minded, and unprejudiced, while remaining egoistic; how to possess every vice without becoming coarse, every foible without becoming ridiculous; how to keep a pure mind uncontaminated by the filth of the heart, how to sin with decorum and to make use of artistic form to beautify anything reprehensible or base. And because he taught all this, he is revered by educated people." Goethe's centenary in 1849 passed unnoticed, whereas that of Schiller, ten years later, was made the occasion for a great demonstration by the German bourgeoisie. Goethe did not come to the fore until the 1870s, after the establishment of the empire, at a time when Germany was on the lookout for monumental representatives of national prestige. The chief milestones are as follows: the foundation of the Goethe Society under the aegis of German princes; the publication of the Weimar edition of his works, under princely patronage; the establishment of the imperialist image of Goethe in the German universities. But despite the never-ending flood of literature produced by Goethe scholars, the bourgeoisie has never been able to make more than a limited use of his genius, to say nothing of the question of how far they have understood his intentions. His whole work abounds in reservations about them. And if he founded a great literature among them, he did so with face averted. Nor did he ever enjoy anything like the success that his genius merited; in fact, he declined to do so. And this was so that he could pursue his purpose of giving the contents [Gehalte] that fulfilled him the form which has enabled them to resist their dissolution at the hands of the bourgeoisie—a resistance made possible because they remained without effect and not because they could be deformed or trivialized. Goethe's intransigence toward the cast of mind of the average bourgeois and hence a new view of his work acquired new relevance with the repudiation of Naturalism. The Neo-Romantics (Stefan George, Hugo von Hofmannsthal, and Rudolph Borchardt)[44]—the last bourgeois poets of any distinction to attempt to rescue bourgeois ideology, if only on the plane of culture and under the patronage of the enfeebled feudal authorities—provided a new, important stimulus to Goethe scholarship (Konrad Burdach, Georg Simmel, Friedrich Gundolf).[45] Their work was above all concerned with the exploration of the works and the style of Goethe's last phase, which nineteenth-century scholars had ignored.

Written 1926–1928; condensed version published in *Die literarische Welt* in December 1928. *Gesammelte Schriften*, II, 705–739. Translated by Rodney Livingstone.

Notes

1. Benjamin was in error here: Goethe visited Berlin in 1778.
2. Friedrich Maximilian von Klinger (1752–1831) was a dramatist and novelist. His play *Der Wirrwarr, oder Sturm und Drang* (Confusion, or Storm and Stress; 1776) gave the *Sturm und Drang* movement its name. Gottfried August Bürger (1747–1794) was one of the first poets to translate the new interest in European folk song into new forms, especially the ballad. His best-known work is the ballad "Leonore" (1773). Johann Anton Leisewitz (1752–1806) was a dramatist; his one important work, *Julius von Tarent* (1776), served as a model for many *Sturm und Drang* plays that followed it. Johann Heinrich Voss (1751–1826) was a poet remembered chiefly for his translations of Homer. Matthias Claudius (1740–1815), poet and editor, was a prominent opponent of the rationalist and neo-classical spirit that had dominated German letters for much of the eighteenth century. His journal, *Der Wandsbecker Bote*, published work by Herder, Klopstock, and Lessing, among many others. Jakob Michael Reinhold Lenz (1751–1792), Russian-born poet and dramatist, was, after Goethe, the most important of the *Sturm und Drang* writers. His plays from his Strasbourg years—a didactic comedy, *Der Hofmeister, oder Vortheile der Privaterziehung* (The Tutor, or The Advantages of Private Education; published 1774, performed 1778, Berlin); and the bourgeois tragedy *Die Soldaten* (The Soldiers; performed 1763, published 1776)—have exerted a lasting influence on German literature. He ended his life as a vagabond, and finally in insanity. Although Benjamin wrote "Holtei," he undoubtedly meant "Hölty": Ludwig Christoph Heinrich Hölty (1748–1776) was a poet and an original member of the circle known as the Göttinger Hainbund (Union of the Göttingen Grove), a group of poets who sought to return poetry to its natural and national roots. Christian Friedrich Daniel Schubart (1739–1791), poet and editor, became famous through his journal *Die deutsche Chronik;* his writings earned him ten years of imprisonment without trial. Friedrich Müller, known as Maler ("Painter") Müller (1749–1825), was a poet, dramatist, and painter; his play *Fausts Leben dramatisiert* (Faust's Life, Dramatized; 1778) brought him closest to the feeling and style of the *Sturm und Drang.* Friedrich Leopold, Graf zu Stolberg (1750–1819), a poet, was, along with his brother Christian, associated with Göttinger Hainbund. After 1772, he composed a series of poems striking for their revolutionary ardor.
3. Paul-Henri Dietrich, baron d'Holbach (1723–1789), French encyclopedist and philosopher, published *Système de la nature* in 1770 under the pseudonym J. B. Mirabaud. He championed an atheistic, deterministic materialism.
4. Johann Gottfried von Herder (1744–1803) was a critic, theologian, and philosopher. His innovations in the philosophy of history and culture lent the initial impulse to the young writers gathered around him in Strasbourg who went on to form the core of the *Sturm und Drang* movement.
5. Johann Georg Hamann (1730–1788), philosopher and theologian, produced a series of innovative, hermetic texts that sought to reconcile philosophy and Christianity on an intuitive, antirationalist basis. His *Sokratische Denkwürdigkeiten* (Socratic Notable Thoughts; 1759) and *Aesthetica in Nuce* (Aesthetics in a Nutshell; 1762) were key texts for Herder and the *Sturm und Drang*

writers. Johann Heinrich Merck (1741–1791), writer and critic, served as an early adviser to and supporter of several writers of the younger generation, including Herder and Goethe. His journal, the *Frankfurter gelehrte Anzeigen*, published biting social and aesthetic criticism of friend and foe alike.

6. The Göttinger Hain or Göttinger Hainbund (Union of the Göttingen Grove) was a literary association that stressed the reintroduction of national and natural themes into German poetry. Members included the young poets (mostly students at the University of Göttingen) H. C. Boie, J. H. Voss, Ludwig Hölty, J. F. Hahn, K. F. Cramer, the Stolberg brothers, and J. A. Leisewitz. The group dissolved in 1774.

7. Friedrich Gottlieb Klopstock (1724–1803) was the greatest lyric poet of the eighteenth century before Goethe. His remarkable linguistic gifts and prosodic inventiveness enabled Klopstock to virtually reinvent German poetry, pointing the way to a more natural and expressive use of language.

8. "The German Peasants' War" is a loose designation for a series of peasant uprisings in south and middle Germany that lasted from 1524 to 1526. The decisive victory of the princes eliminated the peasantry from the political life of Germany for centuries.

9. The Imperial Knights were direct vassals of the Holy Roman Emperor. Each knight had holdings that ranged in size from part of a single village to a small independent state.

10. Charlotte Buff (1753–1828), the model for Lotte in *Werther*, married J. C. Kestner (a Hannover administrator and friend of Goethe's) in 1773. Werther himself is modeled in part on the law student Karl Wilhelm Jerusalem (1747–1772).

11. Her full name was Anna Elisabeth Schönemann (1758–1817).

12. Johann Kaspar Lavater (1741–1801) was a Swiss writer and Protestant pastor whose theories of physiognomy were widely influential in the late eighteenth century. His *Physiognomische Fragmente zur Beförderung der Menschen-kenntnis und Menschenliebe* (4 vols., 1775–1778; translated as *Essays on Physiognomy*, 1789–1798) were founded on the conviction that the spirit leaves its mark on people's physical features.

13. Karl August, grand duke of Saxe-Weimar-Eisenach (1757–1828), was a liberal, enlightened ruler who made his court and the University of Jena leading intellectual centers of Germany during the late eighteenth and early nineteenth centuries. After he repeatedly sided with the allies against Napoleon, Weimar's territories were increased at the Congress of Vienna (1815); but he protested the congress' reactionary spirit. In 1819 he granted his state a liberal constitution, becoming the first German ruler to do so.

14. Christoph Martin Wieland (1733–1813) was a poet, novelist, dramatist, and man of letters whose work helped define each of the major trends of his age, from rationalism and the Enlightenment to classicism and pre-Romanticism. His journal, *Der teutsche Merkur* (The German Mercury), was a leading cultural focus for thirty-seven years.

15. Charlotte von Stein (1742–1827) was a writer and woman of letters.

16. Johann Joachim Winckelmann (1717–1768) was an archaeologist and art historian whose writings on classical art, and especially the art of ancient Greece,

exerted a powerful influence on Western painting, sculpture, literature, and philosophy in the eighteenth century. His major work is *Gedanken über die Nachahmung der griechischen Werke in der Malerei und Bildhauerkunst* (1755; translated as *Reflections on the Painting and Sculpture of the Greeks,* 1765), in which he promulgated the idea that classical art is characterized by an "edle Einfalt und stille Grösse" (a noble simplicity and quiet grandeur).

17. Karl Wilhelm, Freiherr von Humboldt (1767–1835), German philologist, philosopher, diplomat, and educational reformer, is best-known for his work on the development of language and for being the founder of the modern university system.

18. Gotthold Ephraim Lessing (1729–1781), German dramatist, critic, and writer, led the struggle to found a German national literature based on indigenous models. His plays—*Nathan der Weise* (1779), *Minna von Barnhelm* (1767), and *Emilia Galotti* (1772)—form the first body of German dramatic work of lasting importance.

19. Christian Gottfried Körner (1756–1831) was a civil servant and a close friend of Schiller's.

20. Friedrich Heinrich Jacobi (1743–1819) was a novelist and philosopher whose writings champion feeling at the expense of reason. His best-known work is the novel *Woldemar* (1779).

21. The intermaxillary bone (a bone between the upper and lower jaws) played a role in the pre-Darwinian debates on evolution. Contemporary theologians insisted that humans were anatomically different from primates; Goethe, almost simultaneously with the French anatomist Vicq-d'Azyr, of whose work he was ignorant, showed that this bone, which is present in animals, also survives vestigially in humans, who therefore could not be considered generically unique.

22. Christiane Vulpius (1765–1816), Goethe's companion and, after 1806, his spouse, bore five children. Only one, their son August, survived infancy.

23. Carl Friedrich Zelter (1758–1832), a composer, founded numerous musical institutions, including the Royal Institute for Sacred Music (Berlin). He served as Goethe's musical adviser and set many of his texts.

24. Karl Ferdinand Gutzkow (1811–1878), novelist, dramatist, and social critic, was a leader of the Young Germany movement which revolted against Romanticism.

25. Schiller's journal *Die Horen* [The Hours] appeared from 1795 to 1798. Friedrich Nicolai (1733–1811) was an early advocate of the Enlightenment who became intolerant of change. He attacked Goethe, Herder, and Kant in widely read parodies.

26. Friedrich Justin Bertuch (1747–1822) was a writer, translator, and editor.

27. Ludwig Börne (originally Löb Baruch; 1786–1837), writer and social critic, lived in exile in Paris after 1830. A member of the Young Germany movement, he was one of the first writers to use the feuilleton section of the newspaper as a forum for social and political criticism.

28. August Wilhelm Iffland (1759–1814), actor, dramatist, and stage manager, was a major voice in the German theatrical world.

29. Novalis (pseudonym of Friedrich Leopold, Freiherr von Hardenberg; 1772–

1801) was a poet and theorist of the early German Romantic period. His novel *Heinrich von Ofterdingen* (1802), set in an idealized vision of the European Middle Ages, recounts the mystical quest of a young poet; the central image of his visions, a blue flower, became a widely recognized symbol of Romantic longing among Novalis' fellow Romantics. Johann Ludwig Tieck (1773–1853), a writer and critic, produced a huge corpus of fanciful work in many genres. *Franz Sternbalds Wanderungen* (2 vols., 1798) follows the life of an artist in the late Middle Ages. Eduard Friedrich Mörike (1804–1875), a lyric poet and novelist, was perhaps the greatest of the late Romantics. *Maler Nolten* (Painter Nolten; 1832) is peopled by an unusual number of mentally unbalanced characters; like many other Romantic novels, it has dramas and poems interspersed throughout.

30. Johann Peter Eckermann (1792–1854) was a writer who is remembered chiefly as Goethe's amanuensis. His *Gespräche mit Goethe in den letzten Jahren seines Lebens* (3 vols., 1823–1832; translated as *Conversations with Goethe in the Last Years of His Life,* 1836–1848), is often compared to James Boswell's *Life of Johnson.* Friedrich Riemer (1774–1845), philologist and literary historian, was, like Eckermann, a literary assistant to Goethe. He edited, with Eckermann, the final version of *Faust* (1832). Frédéric Soret (1795–1865), French natural scientist and educator, was tutor to the prince's children in Weimar between 1822 and 1836. He noted his conversations with Goethe in a series of journals, some of which Eckermann used in the third part of his *Gespräche.* The texts were published in full only in 1932.

31. Heinrich Meyer (1760–1832), an artist, was a student of the Anglo-Swiss painter Henry Fuseli. He met Goethe in Rome and in 1791 came to Weimar, where he became the director of the Ducal Drawing School. He served as Goethe's adviser on art.

32. Friedrich August Wolf (1759–1824), German classical scholar, is considered one of the founders of modern philology. He is best-known for his *Prolegomena ad Homerum* (Prolegomena on Homer; 1795).

33. Sulpiz Boisserée (1783–1854) was an art historian and collector. His collection of old German and Dutch paintings played a central role in the rediscovery of the Middle Ages by the Romantic generation.

34. Alessandro Manzoni (1785–1873), Italian poet and novelist, is best-known for the novel *I promessi sposi* (The Betrothed; 1852).

35. Benjamin here names three major authors whose style resisted any easy absorption into a period paradigm. Johann Christian Friedrich Hölderlin (1770–1843) was a German lyric poet, novelist, and dramatist whose poetry succeeds in integrating the rhythm and syntax of classical Greek verse into German. His major works include the novel *Hyperion* (1797) and the poems "Brot und Wein," "Hälfte des Lebens," "Der Rhein," "Wie wenn am Feiertage," and "Patmos." Bernd Heinrich Wilhelm von Kleist (1777–1811), dramatist and short-story writer, produced in the course of his restless and tortured life a remarkable number of major works. These include the plays *Der zerbrochene Krug* (The Broken Pitcher; 1811) and *Penthesilea* (1808), and the stories "Michael Kohlhaas," "Die Marquise von O," and "Das Erdbeben in Chile," all of

which appeared in the two-volume *Erzählungen* in 1810–1811. Jean Paul Richter (1763–1825) produced a series of wildly extravagant, highly imaginative novels that are characterized by their combination of fantasy and realism.

36. Marianne von Willemer (1784–1860) was the wife of Goethe's friend J. J. von Willemer, a Frankfurt banker. She distinguished herself from many of the women who served as models for figures in Goethe's verse in that she was the coauthor of several of the poems in the two cycles that seek to merge East and West: the *Chinesisch-Deutsche Jahres- und Tageszeiten* (Chinese-German Hours and Seasons; 1830) and the *West-Östlicher Divan* (West-Easterly Divan; 1819).

37. Ulrike von Levetzow (1804–1899) met Goethe at the spa at Marienbad in 1821. In 1823, at the age of seventy-four, Goethe made a kind of indirect proposal to Levetzow, who was then nineteen. She responded to it evasively.

38. Jean-Charles-Léonard Simonde de Sismondi (1773–1842), Swiss economist and historian, was a prominent early critic of the societal transformations that followed from industrialism. His theories of economic crises and the dangers of limitless competition, overproduction, and underconsumption were taken up by such later economists as Karl Marx and John Maynard Keynes. François-Marie-Charles Fourier (1772–1837), French social theorist, called for a reorganization of society based on communal associations known as *phalanges* (phalanxes). In each community, the members would continually change roles within different systems of production. Henri de Saint-Simon (1760–1825), French social theorist, is credited with founding Christian socialism. His most important work, *Le nouveau Christianisme* (1825), insisted that human fraternity must accompany any scientific restructuring of society. Robert Owen (1771–1858), Welsh manufacturer turned reformer, was one of the most influential socialists of the early nineteenth century. His mills in Lanarkshire, which operated under a wholly reconceived social and industrial system, became a model for utopian communities in Europe and the United States. Jeremy Bentham (1748–1832), English philosopher, economist, and theoretical jurist, was the founder and a major theorist of Utilitarianism.

39. Johann Heinrich Pestalozzi (1746–1827), Swiss educational reformer, formulated a teaching regimen centered on each student's abilities and needs. He also advocated education of the poor.

40. Johann Friedrich Cotta, Baron von Cottendorf (1764–1832), took over the family business in Tübingen and turned it into one of the leading publishing houses in Europe. Cotta eventually published Goethe, Herder, both Humboldts, Hegel, Fichte, Wieland, A. W. Schlegel, Tieck, Jean Paul, and Kleist.

41. Goethe, *Faust*, trans. G. M. Priest (New York: Covici, Friede, 1932).

42. Joseph Lancaster (1778–1838), British educator, formulated an educational system intended to reach a broad societal base. The "Lancastrian" method was based on the idea that children who were more proficient could teach other children under the supervision of an adult.

43. Young Germany (Junges Deutschland) was a movement in Germany that, between about 1830 and 1850, advocated social and literary reform. Its principal members were Ludolf Wienbarg, Karl Gutzkow, and Theodor Mundt, although Heinrich Laube, Georg Herwegh, Ludwig Börne, and Heinrich Heine were also involved. All of these writers, at one time or another, set themselves in virulent

opposition to the prevailing social and literary norms: nationalist monarchy and Romanticism. Although they attained only limited popular success, their writings were formally banned by the Diet of the German Confederation on December 10, 1835.

44. Stefan George (1868–1933), German lyric poet, attempted in his verse and through his remarkable personal influence to "purify" German language and culture around the turn of the twentieth century. See "Stefan George in Retrospect" (1933), in this volume. His conservative-nationalist ideas exerted a powerful influence on many German intellectuals. Hugo von Hofmannsthal (1874–1929), Austrian poet, dramatist, and essayist, made his reputation with lyrical poems, stories, and plays in the last decade of the nineteenth century. His operatic collaborations with the German composer Richard Strauss made him world famous. See "Hugo von Hofmannsthal's *Der Turm*," in this volume. Rudolf Borchardt (1877–1945) was a German prose writer and essayist whose works combined a polished personal style and conservative ideas; he promoted, as literary models, classical antiquity and the Middle Ages.

45. Konrad Burdach (1859–1936), German literary historian, was a main proponent of intellectual history as a mode of cultural analysis. Georg Simmel (1858–1918), German sociologist and neo-Kantian philosopher, developed a theory of modernity, starting with his *Philosophie des Geldes* (Philosophy of Money; 1900) and continuing through classic essays such as "Die Großstadt und das Geistesleben" (The Metropolis and Mental Life). His work exerted an enormous influence on the next generation of social philosophers, some of whom were his students: Georg Lukács, Ernst Cassirer, Ernst Bloch, Siegfried Kracauer, and Benjamin. Friedrich Gundolf (pseudonym of Friedrich Gundelfinger; 1880–1931) was a disciple of Stefan George, a prominent literary critic, and, after 1920, a professor at Heidelberg. See Benjamin's essays "Comments on Gundolf's *Goethe*" and "Goethe's Elective Affinities," in Volume 1 of this edition.

Karl Kraus (Fragment)

In Karl Kraus we find the most magnificent irruption of halachic writing into the massif of the German language. You understand nothing about this man if you do not recognize that everything without exception, words as well as things, is necessarily acted out within the realm of law. It is not enough that every day the newspaper brings a bundle of denunciations into his house; his eyes know how to read between the lines and cannot fail to notice that the nameless informers with their accusations, however well-founded these may be, are themselves not without guilt. His entire fire-eating, sword-swallowing philological scrutiny of the newspapers is actually concerned not with language but with justice. His linguistic investigations are incomprehensible unless they are perceived as contributions to the code of criminal procedure, unless the word of others in his mouth is regarded as nothing but a *corpus delicti,* and an issue of *Die Fackel* as only a hearing.[1] The court cases pile up around him. Not those that he has to conduct in the Viennese courts, but those whose place of jurisdiction is *Die Fackel.* Kraus, however, as public prosecutor, takes every case to appeal. Of the sentences he has handed down, none can satisfy him. He provides an unprecedented, ambiguous, genuinely demonic spectacle of the accuser eternally calling for justice, the public prosecutor who becomes a Michael Kohlhaas because no justice can satisfy his accusation and none of his accusations can satisfy him.[2] His linguistic and ethical quibbling is not a form of self-righteousness; it belongs to the truly desperate justice of a proceeding in which words and things concoct the most implausible alibi simply to save their own skin, and must be incessantly refuted by the evidence of one's eyes or straightforward calculation. The fact that this man is one of the very few who have a vision of freedom and can further it only by assuming the role of chief prosecutor is a paradox that most purely reveals the powerful dialectic at work. His life is one that embodies the most fervent prayer for salvation that passes Jewish lips in our age.

Published in *Internationale Revue*, December 1928. *Gesammelte Schriften*, II, 624–625. Translated by Rodney Livingstone.

Notes

1. *Die Fackel* (The Torch) was the satirical magazine edited by Karl Kraus from 1899 to his death in 1936. Although it initially included contributions from other authors, after December 1911 Kraus was its sole writer and editor.
2. Michael Kohlhaas is the eponymous hero of a story by Heinrich von Kleist from 1810. After a horse is stolen from him, he tries repeatedly but in vain to obtain justice; as his efforts escalate, he becomes an outlaw and a rebel, and ends on the gallows.

The Return of the *Flâneur,* 1929

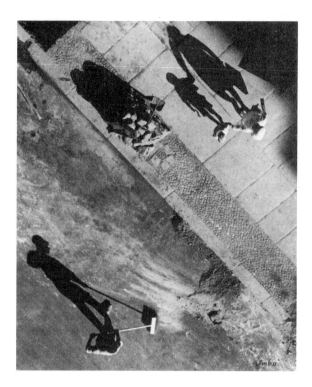

Chaplin

After a showing of *The Circus*. Chaplin never allows the audience to smile while watching him. They must either double up laughing or be very sad.

Chaplin greets people by taking off his bowler, and it looks like the lid rising from the kettle when the water boils over.

His clothes are impermeable to every blow of fate. He looks like a man who hasn't taken his clothes off for a month. He is unfamiliar with beds; when he lies down, he does so in a wheelbarrow or on a seesaw.

Wet through, sweaty, in clothes far too small for him, Chaplin is the living embodiment of Goethe's *aperçu:* Man would not be the noblest creature on earth if he were not too noble for it.

This film is the first film of Chaplin's old age. He has grown older since his last films, but he also acts old. And the most moving thing about this new film is the feeling that he now has a clear overview of the possibilities open to him, and that he is resolved to work exclusively within these limits to attain his goal.

At every point the variations on his greatest themes are displayed in their full glory. The chase is set in a maze; his unexpected appearance would astonish a magician; the mask of noninvolvement turns him into a fairground marionette. The most wonderful part is the way the end of the film is structured. He strews confetti over the happy couple, and you think: This must be the end. Then you see him standing there when the circus procession starts off; he shuts the door behind everyone, and you think: This must be the end. Then you see him stuck in the rut of the circle earlier drawn by poverty, and you think: This must be the end. Then you see a close-up of his completely bedraggled form, sitting on a stone in the arena. Here you think the end is absolutely unavoidable, but then he gets up and you see him from behind, walking further and further away, with that gait peculiar to Charlie Chaplin; he is his own walking trademark, just like the company trademark you see at the end of other films. And now, at the only point where there's no break and you'd like to be able to follow him with your gaze forever—the film ends!

Fragment written in 1928 or early 1929; unpublished in Benjamin's lifetime. *Gesammelte Schriften*, VI, 137–138. Translated by Rodney Livingstone.

Program for a Proletarian Children's Theater

Prefatory Remarks

Every proletarian movement, whenever it has for once escaped the format of parliamentary debate, finds itself confronting many different forces for which it is unprepared. The most powerful of these, as well as the most dangerous, is the younger generation. The self-confidence of parliamentary tedium springs from the fact that a parliament is a monopoly of adults. Mere catchphrases have no power over children. True, in a year you can make sure that children are parroting them throughout the country. But the question is how to make sure that the party program is acted on in ten or twenty years. And catchphrases will not have the slightest effect on this.

Proletarian education must be based on the party program—or, more precisely, on class consciousness. But the party program is no instrument of a class-conscious education, because the element of ideology, important though it is, reaches the child only as a catchphrase. We are calling for, and shall not cease to call for, instruments for the class-conscious education of proletarian children. In what follows, we shall ignore the question of the teaching curriculum as such, because long before children need to be instructed (in technology, class history, public speaking, and so on), they need to be brought up in a proletarian manner. We shall take, as our starting point, the age of four.

In line with the class position of the bourgeoisie, the bourgeois education of little children is unsystematic. This does not mean that the bourgeoisie has no system of education. But the inhumanity of its content betrays itself in its inability to provide anything at all for the youngest children. On children of this age, only truth can have a productive effect. The education of young proletarian children should distinguish itself from that of the bourgeoisie primarily by its systematic nature. "System" here means a framework. For the proletariat, it would be quite intolerable if every six months a new method were to be introduced with all the latest psychological refinements, as in the nursery schools of the bourgeoisie. Everywhere—and the realm of education is no exception here—the preoccupation with "methodology" is a symptom of the authentic bourgeois attitude, the ideology of laziness and muddling through. Proletarian education needs first and foremost a framework, an objective space *within* which education can be located. The bourgeoisie, in contrast, requires an idea *toward* which education leads.

We shall now explain why the framework of proletarian education from the fourth to the fourteenth year should be the proletarian children's theater.

The education of a child requires that *its entire life be engaged.*

Proletarian education requires *that the child be educated within a clearly defined space.*

This is the positive dialectic of the problem. It is only in the theater that the whole of life can appear as a defined space, framed in all its plenitude; and this is why proletarian children's theater is the dialectical site of education.

Scheme of Tension

Let us set aside the question whether the children's theater of which we shall speak has a connection with the ordinary theater at the high points in its history. Yet we must state firmly that this theater has nothing at all in common with that of the modern bourgeoisie. Economically, the theater of the modern bourgeoisie is determined by the profit motive; sociologically, both in front of the curtain and backstage, it is primarily an instrument of sensation. The proletarian children's theater is quite different. Just as the first action of the Bolsheviks was to hoist the Red flag, so their first instinct was to organize the children. In this organization the proletarian children's theater, the basic motif of Bolshevist education, has a central place. There is a way of cross-checking this. In the view of the bourgeoisie, nothing presents a greater danger to children than the theater. This is not just a vestige of the old bogey—the myth of traveling actors who steal children. What we find expressed is the fear that the theater will unleash in children the most powerful energies of the future. And this fear causes bourgeois education theory to anathematize the theater. We may easily imagine how it would react once the fire came too close—the fire in which, for children, reality and play coincide and are fused so that acted sufferings can merge with real sufferings, acted beatings can shade into real beatings.

Nevertheless, the performances of this theater—unlike those of the great bourgeois theater—are not the actual goal of the concentrated collective labor that is performed in the children's clubs. One might say that here performances come about incidentally, as an oversight, almost as a children's prank, and in this way the children interrupt the course of study that they have never actually completed. The leader is relatively unconcerned about whether or not the course has been completed. He is more interested in the tensions that are resolved in such performances. The tensions of collective labor are the educators. The overhasty, unrelaxed process of educational labor that the bourgeois director performs—far too late—on the bourgeois actor no longer applies in this system. Why? Because in the children's club no leader would survive if he attempted in the authentic bourgeois spirit to influence the children directly as a "moral personality." There is no process of moral influence here. There is no direct influence either. (And it is on this that directing in the bourgeois theater is based.) What counts is simply and solely the indirect influence of the director on the children as mediated by subject matter, tasks, and performances. The inevitable moral processes of compensating and providing correctives are undertaken by the children's collective itself. This explains why children's theater productions inevitably strike adults as having authentic moral authority. There is no superior standpoint that an audience can adopt when witnessing children's theater. Everyone who has not quite sunk into feeblemindedness will perhaps even feel ashamed.

But even this does not take us much further. To have a positive effect, proletarian children's theaters make a collective audience quite indispensable. In a word: they need the class as audience. Just as only the working class has an infallible intuition for the existence of collectives. Such collectives may be public meetings, the army, or the factory. But the child, too, is such a collective. And it is the prerogative of the working class to have a completely fresh eye for the children's collective, whereas the bourgeoisie is unable to perceive it. This collective radiates not just the most powerful energies, but also the most relevant ones. In fact, the relevance of childlike forms and modes of conduct is unsurpassed. (We draw attention here to the well-known exhibitions of the latest children's art.)

The neutralization of the "moral personality" in the leader unleashes vast energies for the true genius of education—namely, the power of observation. This alone is at the heart of unsentimental love. No pedagogic love is worth anything unless in nine-tenths of all instances of knowing better and wanting better it is deprived of its courage and pleasure by the mere observation of children's lives. It is sentimental and vain. For the true observer, however—and this is the starting point of education—every childhood action and gesture becomes a signal. Not so much a signal of the unconscious, of latent processes, repressions, or censorship (as the psychologists like to think), but a signal from another world, in which the child lives and commands. The new knowledge of children that has been developed in the Russian children's clubs has led to the theory that the child inhabits his world like a dictator. For this reason, the "theory of signals" is no mere figure of speech. Almost every childlike gesture is a command and a signal in a world which only a few unusually perceptive men, notably Jean Paul, have glimpsed.[1]

The task of the leader is to release children's signals from the hazardous magical world of sheer fantasy and apply them to materials. This happens in the various theatrical workshops. To take an illustration from painting, we know that in this sphere of childhood activity, too, gesture is all-important. Konrad Fiedler is the first to have shown in his *Writings on Art* that the painter is not a man who sees more naturalistically, more poetically, or more ecstatically than other people. He is, rather, a man who sees more accurately with his hand when his eye fails him, who is able to transfer the receptive innervation of the eye muscles into the creative innervation of the hand. What characterizes every child's gesture is that creative innervation is exactly proportioned to receptive innervation. The development of these gestures in the different forms of expression—the making of stage props, painting, recitation, music, dance, or improvisation—is the task of the different workshops.

In all of them improvisation is central, because in the final analysis a performance is nothing but an improvised synthesis of all of them. Improvisation predominates; it is the framework from which the signals, the signifying gestures, emerge. And the synthesis of these gestures must become performance or theater, because they alone have the unexpected uniqueness that enables the child's gesture to stand in its own authentic space. The kind of "fully rounded" performance that people torment children to produce can never compete in authenticity with improvisation. The aristocratic dilettantism that is eager to make its poor pupils produce such "artistic achievements" ended up by filling cupboards and memory with junk, which was piously preserved so that our mementos of early youth might survive to enable us to torment our own children. But childhood achievement is always aimed not at the "eternity" of the products but at the "moment" of the gesture. The theater is the art form of the child because it is ephemeral.

Scheme of Resolution

Educational work in the different workshops stands in the same relationship to the performance as a tension to its resolution. For no pedagogic wisdom can foresee how children will fuse the various gestures and skills into a theatrical totality, but with a thousand unexpected variations. Even for the professional actor, the first performance can often serve as the trigger that enables him to introduce genuine improvements into a well-rehearsed role.

But in the case of a child, it brings the genius of variation to a peak of perfection. In relation to the process of schooling, the performance is like the radical unleashing of play—something which the adult can only wonder at.

The embarrassments of bourgeois education theory and of the rising bourgeois generation in general have expressed themselves recently in the "Youth Culture" movement.[2] The conflict that this new movement is destined to hush up lies in the claims that bourgeois society (like every political society) makes on the energies of young people, which can never be activated directly in a political way. And on the energies of children above all else. Now Youth Culture attempts to achieve a hopeless compromise: it drains the enthusiasm of young people by a process of idealistic self-reflection, so as gradually and imperceptibly to replace the formal ideologies of German idealism by the contents of the bourgeois class. The proletariat must not pass on its own class interest to the next generation with the tainted methods of an ideology that is destined to subjugate the child's suggestible mind. The discipline the bourgeoisie demands from *children* is its mark of shame. The proletariat *disciplines* only the proletarians who have grown up; its ideological class education starts with puberty. Proletarian education theory demonstrates its superiority by guaranteeing to children the fulfillment of their childhood. There is no need, therefore, for the realm in which this occurs to be isolated from the realm of class struggles. At the level of play, the themes and symbols of class struggle can—and perhaps must—have a place in this realm. But these themes and symbols cannot lay claim to a formal dominance of the child. Nor will they do so. Hence, the proletariat has no need of the thousand little words which the bourgeoisie uses to disguise the class nature of its education theory. It will be possible to dispense with "unbiased," "sympathetic" practices and with teachers who are "fond of children."

The performance is the great creative pause in the process of upbringing. It represents in the realm of children what the carnival was in the old cults. Everything was turned upside down; and just as in Rome the master served the slaves during the Saturnalia, in the same way in a performance children stand on the stage and instruct and teach the attentive educators. New forces, new innervations appear—ones that the director had no inkling of while working on the project. He learns about them only in the course of this wild liberation of the child's imagination. Children that have learned about theater in this way become free in such performances. Through play, their childhood has been fulfilled. They carry no superfluous baggage around with them, in the form of overemotional childhood memories that might prevent them later on from taking action in an unsentimental way. Moreover, this theater is the only usable one for the child spectator. When grownups act for children, the result is archness.

This children's theater contains a force that will annihilate the pseudorevolutionary gestures of the recent theater of the bourgeoisie. For what is truly revolutionary is not the propaganda of ideas, which leads here and there to impracticable actions and vanishes in a puff of smoke upon the first sober reflection at the theater exit. What is truly revolutionary is the *secret signal* of what is to come that speaks from the gesture of the child.

Written in late 1928 or early 1929; unpublished in Benjamin's lifetime. *Gesammelte Schriften,* II, 763–769. Translated by Rodney Livingstone.

Notes

1. Jean Paul Richter (1763–1825) is remembered for a series of wildly extravagant, highly imaginative novels that combine fantasy and realism.
2. A reference to the various movements and ideas that were prevalent between 1895 and 1920 and that are known today as the "Youth Movement." The movement embraced a wide spectrum of ideas—from tame and pragmatic revisions in pedagogy, through the nature worship of young people tramping through the countryside (the *Wandervögel*), to the virulent nationalism and anti-Semitism of the radical Right. On Benjamin's involvement in the movement and his indebtedness to his teacher Gustav Wyneken, one of the main ideologues of the movement, see the Chronology in Volume 1 of this edition.

Surrealism

The Last Snapshot of the European Intelligentsia

Intellectual currents can generate a sufficient head of water for the critic to install his power station on them. The necessary gradient, in the case of Surrealism, is produced by the difference in intellectual level between France and Germany. What sprang up in 1919 in France in a small circle of literati—we shall give the most important names at once: André Breton, Louis Aragon, Philippe Soupault, Robert Desnos, Paul Eluard—may have been a meager stream, fed on the damp boredom of postwar Europe and the last trickle of French decadence.[1] The know-it-alls who even today have not advanced beyond the "authentic origins" of the movement, and even now have nothing to say about it except that yet another clique of literati is here mystifying the honorable public, are a little like a gathering of experts at a spring who, after lengthy deliberation, arrive at the conviction that this paltry stream will never drive turbines.

The German observer is not standing at the source of the stream. This is his opportunity. He is in the valley. He can gauge the energies of the movement. As a German he has long been acquainted with the crisis of the intelligentsia, or, more precisely, with that of the humanistic concept of freedom; and he knows how frantically determined the movement has become to go beyond the stage of eternal discussion and, at any price, to reach a decision; he has had direct experience of its highly exposed position between an anarchistic Fronde and a revolutionary discipline, and so has no excuse for taking the movement for the "artistic," "poetic" one it super-ficially appears.[2] If it was such at the outset, it was, however, precisely at the outset that Breton declared his intention of breaking with a praxis that presents the public with the literary precipitate of a certain form of existence while withholding that existence itself. Stated more briefly and dialectically, this means that the sphere of poetry was here exploded from within by a closely knit circle of people pushing the "poetic life" to the utmost limits of possibility. And they can be taken at their word when they assert that Rimbaud's *Saison en enfer* [A Season in Hell] no longer had any secrets for them.[3] For this book is indeed the first document of a movement like this (in recent times; earlier precursors will be discussed later). Can the point at issue be more definitively and incisively presented than by Rimbaud himself in his personal copy of the book? In the margin, beside the passage "on the silk of the seas and the arctic flowers," he later wrote, "There's no such thing."

Just how inconspicuous and peripheral a substance the dialectical kernel that later grew into Surrealism was originally embedded in was shown by Aragon in 1924—at a time when its development could not yet be foreseen—in his *Vague de rêves* [Wave of Dreams]. Today it can be foreseen. For there is no doubt that the heroic phase, whose catalogue of heroes Aragon left us in that work, is over. There is always, in such movements, a moment when the original tension of the secret society must either explode in a matter-of-fact, profane struggle for power and domination, or decay as a public demonstration and be transformed. At present, Surrealism is in this phase of transformation. But at the time when it broke over its founders as an inspiring dream wave, it seemed the most integral, conclusive, absolute of movements. Everything with which it came into contact was integrated. Life seemed worth living only where the threshold between waking and sleeping was worn away in everyone as by the steps of multitudinous images flooding back and forth; language seemed itself only where sound and image, image and sound, interpenetrated with automatic precision and such felicity that no chink was left for the penny-in-the-slot called "meaning." Image and language take precedence. Saint-Pol-Roux, retiring to bed about daybreak, fixes a notice on his door: "Poet at work."[4] Breton notes: "Quietly. I want to pass where no one has yet passed, quietly!—After you, dearest language." Language takes precedence.

Not only before meaning. Also before the self. In the world's structure, dream loosens individuality like a bad tooth. This loosening of the self by intoxication is, at the same time, precisely the fruitful, living experience that allowed these people to step outside the charmed space of intoxication. This is not the place to give an exact definition of Surrealist experience. But anyone who has perceived that the writings of this circle are not literature but something else—demonstrations, watchwords, documents, bluffs, forgeries if you will, but at any rate not literature—will also know, for the same reason, that the writings are concerned literally with experiences, not with theories and still less with phantasms. And these experiences are by no means limited to dreams, hours of hashish eating, or opium smoking. It is a cardinal error to believe that, of "Surrealist experiences," we know only the religious ecstasies or the ecstasies of drugs. Lenin called religion the opiate of the masses, and brought the two things closer together than the Surrealists could have liked. I shall refer later to the bitter, passionate revolt against Catholicism in which Rimbaud, Lautréamont, and Apollinaire brought Surrealism into the world.[5] But the true, creative overcoming of religious illumination certainly does not lie in narcotics. It resides in a *profane illumination,* a materialistic, anthropological inspiration, to which hashish, opium, or whatever else can give an introductory lesson. (But a dangerous one; and the religious lesson is stricter.) This profane illumination did not always find the Surrealists equal to it, or to themselves; and the very writings that proclaim it most powerfully, Aragon's incomparable *Paysan de Paris* [Peasant of Paris] and Breton's *Nadja,* show very disturbing symptoms of deficiency. For example, there is in *Nadja* an excellent passage on the "delightful days spent looting Paris under the sign of Sacco and Vanzetti"; Breton adds the assurance that in those days the boulevard Bonne-Nouvelle [Boulevard of Good Tidings] fulfilled the strategic promise of revolt that had always been implicit in its name. But Madame Sacco also appears—not the wife of Fuller's victim but a *voyante,* a fortuneteller who lives at 3 rue des Usines and who tells Paul Eluard that he can expect no good from Nadja. Now, I concede that the breakneck career of Surrealism over rooftops, lightning rods, gutters, verandas, weathercocks, stucco work (all ornaments are grist to the cat burglar's mill) may have taken it also into the humid backroom of spiritualism. But I am not pleased to hear it cautiously tapping on the windowpanes to inquire about its future. Who would not wish to see these adoptive children of revolution most rigorously severed from all the goings-on in the conventicles of down-at-heel dowagers, retired majors, and *émigré* profiteers?

In other respects, Breton's book illustrates well a number of the basic characteristics of this "profane illumination." He calls *Nadja* "a book with a banging door." (In Moscow I lived in a hotel in which almost all the rooms were occupied by Tibetan lamas who had come to Moscow for a congress of Buddhist churches. I was struck by the number of doors in the corridors that were always left ajar. What had at first seemed accidental began to be disturbing. I found out that in these rooms lived members of a sect who had sworn never to occupy closed rooms. The shock I had then must be felt by the reader of *Nadja.*) To live in a glass house is a revolutionary virtue par excellence. It is also an intoxication, a moral exhibitionism, that we badly need. Discretion concerning one's own existence, once an aristocratic virtue, has become more and more an affair of petty-bourgeois parvenus. *Nadja* has achieved the true, creative synthesis between the art novel and the *roman à clef.*

Moreover, one need only take love seriously to recognize in it, too—as

Nadja also indicates—a "profane illumination." "At just that time" (i.e., when he knew Nadja), the author tells us, "I took a great interest in the epoch of Louis VII, because it was the time of the 'courts of love,' and I tried to picture with great intensity how people saw life then." We have from a new author quite exact information on Provençal love poetry, which comes surprisingly close to the Surrealist conception of love. "All the poets of the 'new style,'" Erich Auerbach points out in his excellent *Dante: Poet of the Secular World,* "possess a mystical beloved; they all have approximately the same very curious experience of love. To them all, Amor bestows or withholds gifts that resemble an illumination more than sensual pleasure; all are subject to a kind of secret bond that determines their inner and perhaps also their outer lives." The dialectics of intoxication are indeed curious. Is not perhaps all ecstasy in *one* world humiliating sobriety in the world complementary to it? What is it that courtly *Minne* seeks (and it, not love, binds Breton to the telepathic girl), if not to make chastity, too, a transport? Into a world that borders not only on tombs of the Sacred Heart or altars to the Virgin, but also on the morning before a battle or after a victory.

The lady, in esoteric love, matters least. So, too, for Breton. He is closer to the things that Nadja is close to than to her. What are these things? Nothing could reveal more about Surrealism than their canon. Where shall I begin? He can boast an extraordinary discovery: he was the first to perceive the revolutionary energies that appear in the "outmoded"—in the first iron constructions, the first factory buildings, the earliest photos, objects that have begun to be extinct, grand pianos, the dresses of five years ago, fashionable restaurants when the vogue has begun to ebb from them. The relation of these things to revolution—no one can have a more exact concept of it than these authors. No one before these visionaries and augurs perceived how destitution—not only social but architectonic, the poverty of interiors, enslaved and enslaving objects—can be suddenly transformed into revolutionary nihilism. To say nothing of Aragon's *Passage de l'Opéra,* Breton and Nadja are the lovers who convert everything that we have experienced on mournful railway journeys (railways are beginning to age), on godforsaken Sunday afternoons in the proletarian neighborhoods of great cities, in the first glance through the rain-blurred window of a new apartment, into revolutionary experience, if not action. They bring the immense forces of "atmosphere" concealed in these things to the point of explosion. What form do you suppose a life would take that was determined at a decisive moment precisely by the street song last on everyone's lips?

The trick by which this world of things is mastered—it is more proper to speak of a trick than a method—consists in the substitution of a political for a historical view of the past. "Open, graves! You, the dead of the picture galleries, corpses behind screens, in palaces, castles, and monasteries! Here stands the fabulous keeper of keys holding a bunch of the keys to all times, who knows where to press the most artful lock and invites you to step into the midst of the world of today, to mingle with the bearers of burdens, the mechanics whom money ennobles, to make yourself at home in their automobiles, which are beautiful as armor from the age of chivalry, to take your places in the international sleeping cars, and to weld yourself to all the people who today are still proud of their privileges. But civilization will make short work of them." This speech was attributed to Apollinaire by his friend Henri Hertz.[6] Apollinaire originated this technique. In his volume of novellas, *L'Hérésiarque,* he used it with Machiavellian calculation to blow Catholicism (which he inwardly embraced) to smithereens.[7]

At the center of this world of things stands the most dreamed-about of their objects: the city of Paris itself. But only revolt completely exposes its Surrealist face (deserted streets in which whistles and shots dictate the outcome). And no face is surrealistic to the same degree as the true face of a city. No picture by de Chirico or Max Ernst can match the sharp elevations of the city's inner strongholds, which one must overrun and occupy in order to master their fate and—in their fate, in the fate of their masses—one's own.[8] Nadja is an exponent of these masses and of what inspires them to revolution: "The great living, sonorous unconsciousness that inspires my only convincing acts—in the sense that I always want to prove that it commands forever everything which is mine." Here, therefore, we find the catalogue of these fortifications, from Place Maubert, where as nowhere else dirt has retained all its symbolic power, to the Théâtre Moderne, which I am inconsolable not to have known. But in Breton's description of the bar on the upper floor ("it is quite dark, with arbors like impenetrable tunnels—a drawing room on the bottom of a lake") there is something that brings back to my memory that most uncomprehended room in the old Princess Café. It was the back room on the first floor, with couples sitting in the blue light. We called it the "anatomy school"; it was the last restaurant designed for love. In such passages in Breton, photography intervenes in a very strange way. It makes the streets, gates, squares of the city into illustrations of a trashy novel, draws off the banal obviousness of this ancient architecture to inject it with the most pristine intensity toward the events described, to which, as in old chambermaids' books, word-for-word quotations with page numbers refer. And all the parts of Paris that appear here are places where what is between these people turns like a revolving door.

The Surrealists' Paris, too, is a "little universe." That is to say, in the larger one, the cosmos, things look no different. There, too, are crossroads where ghostly signals flash from the traffic, and inconceivable analogies and connections between events are the order of the day. It is the space on which the lyric poetry of Surrealism reports. And this must be noted, if only to counter the obligatory misunderstanding of *l'art pour l'art.* For "art for art's sake" was scarcely ever to be taken literally; it was almost always a flag under which sailed a cargo that could not be declared because it still lacked a name. This is the moment to embark on a work that would illuminate as has no other the crisis of the arts that we are witnessing: a history of esoteric poetry. Nor is it by any means fortuitous that no such work yet exists. For written as it demands to be written—that is, not as a collection to which particular "specialists" all contribute "what is most worth knowing" from their fields, but as the deeply grounded composition of an individual who, from inner compulsion, portrays less a historical evolution than a constantly renewed, primal upsurge of esoteric poetry—written in such a way, it would be one of those scholarly confessions that find their place in every century. The last page would have to show an X-ray image of Surrealism. Breton indicates in his "Introduction au discours sur le peu de réalité" [Introduction to a Discourse on the Small Bit of Reality] how the philosophical realism of the Middle Ages was the basis of poetic experience. This realism, how-ever—that is, the belief in a real, separate existence of concepts whether outside or inside things—has always very quickly crossed over from the logical realm of ideas to the magical realm of words. And it is as magical experiments with words, not as artistic dabbling, that we must understand the passionate phonetic and graphic transformational games that have run through the whole literature of the avant-garde for the past fifteen years, whether it is called Futurism, Dadaism, or Surrealism. How slogans, magic formulas, and concepts are here intermingled is shown by the following words of Apollinaire's from his last manifesto, "L'esprit nouveau et les poètes" [The New Spirit and the Poets]. He says, in 1918: "For the speed and simplicity with which we have all become used to referring by a single word to such complex entities as a crowd, a nation, the universe, there is no modern equivalent in literature. But today's writers fill this gap; their synthetic works create new realities whose plastic manifestations are just as complex as those referred to by the words standing for collectives." If, however, Apollinaire and Breton advance even more energetically in the same direction and complete the linkage of Surrealism to the outside world with the declaration, "The conquests of science rest far more on surrealistic than on logical thinking"—if, in other words, they make mystification, the culmination of which Breton sees in poetry (which is defensible), the foun-dation of scientific and technical development, too—then such integration is too impetuous. It is very instructive to compare the movement's overpre-cipitous embrace of the uncomprehended miracle of machines—"the old fables have for the most part been realized; now it is the turn of poets to create new ones that the inventors on their side can then make real again" (Apollinaire)—to compare these overheated fantasies with the well-ventilated utopias of a Scheerbart.[9]

"The thought of all human activity makes me laugh." This utterance of

Aragon's shows very clearly the path Surrealism had to follow from its origins to its politicization. In his excellent essay "La révolution et les intellectuels" [The Revolution and the Intellectuals], Pierre Naville, who originally belonged to this group, rightly called this development dialectical.[10] In this transformation of a highly contemplative attitude into revolutionary opposition, the hostility of the bourgeoisie toward every manifestation of radical intellectual freedom played a leading part. This hostility pushed Surrealism to the left. Political events, above all the war in Morocco, accelerated this development. With the manifesto "Intellectuals against the Moroccan War," which appeared in *L'Humanité*, a fundamentally different platform was gained from that which was characterized by, for example, the famous scandal at the Saint-Pol-Roux banquet.[11] At that time, shortly after the war, when the Surrealists, who deemed the celebration for a poet they worshiped compromised by the presence of nationalistic elements, burst out with the cry "Long live Germany!" they remained within the boundaries of scandal, toward which, as is known, the bourgeoisie is as thick-skinned as it is sensitive to all action. There is remarkable agreement between the ways in which, under such political auspices, Apollinaire and Aragon saw the future of the poet. The chapters "Persecution" and "Murder" in Apollinaire's *Poète assassiné* [The Poet Assassinated] contain the famous description of a pogrom against poets. Publishing houses are stormed, books of poems thrown on the fire, poets beaten to death. And the same scenes are taking place at the same time all over the world. In Aragon, "Imagination," in anticipation of such horrors, marshals its forces for a last crusade.

To understand such prophecies, and to assess strategically the line arrived at by Surrealism, one must investigate the mode of thought widespread among the so-called well-meaning left-wing bourgeois intelligentsia. It manifests itself clearly enough in the present Russian orientation of these circles. We are not of course referring here to Béraud, who pioneered the lie about Russia, or to Fabre-Luce, who trots behind him like a devoted donkey, loaded with every kind of bourgeois ill will.[12] But how problematic one finds even the typical mediating book by Duhamel. How difficult it is to bear the strained uprightness, the forced animation and sincerity of the Protestant method, dictated by embarrassment and linguistic ignorance, of placing things in some kind of symbolic illumination. How traitorous his résumé: "the true, deeper revolution, which could in some sense transform the substance of the Slavic soul itself, has not yet taken place." It is typical of these left-wing French intellectuals—exactly as it is of their Russian counterparts, too—that their positive function derives entirely from a feeling of obligation not to the revolution but to traditional culture. Their collective achievement, as far as it is positive, approximates conservation. But politically and economically they must always be considered a potential source of sabotage.

Characteristic of this whole left-wing bourgeois position is its irremediable coupling of idealistic morality with political practice. Only in contrast to the helpless compromises of "sentiment" can certain central features of Surrealism, indeed of the Surrealist tradition, be understood. Little has happened so far to promote this understanding. The seduction was too great to enable one to regard the satanism of a Rimbaud or a Lautréamont as a pendant to "art for art's sake" in an inventory of snobbery. If, however, one resolves to open up this romantic dummy, one finds something usable inside. One finds the cult of evil as a political device, however romantic—a device that can be used to disinfect and isolate against all moralizing dilettantism. Convinced of this, and coming across the scenario of a horror play by Breton that centers on a violation of children, one might perhaps go back a few decades. Between 1865 and 1875 a number of great anarchists, without knowing of one another, each worked on their infernal machine. And the astonishing thing is that independently of one another they set its clock at exactly the same hour, and forty years later in Western Europe the writings of Dostoevsky, Rimbaud, and Lautréamont exploded at the same time. One might, to be more exact, select from Dostoevsky's entire work the one episode that was actually not published until about 1915: "Stavrogin's Confession," from *The Possessed*. This chapter, which touches very closely on the third canto of Lautréamont's *Chants de Maldoror* [Songs of Maldoror], contains a justification of evil in which certain motifs of Surrealism are more powerfully expressed than by any of its present spokesmen. For Stavrogin is a Surrealist *avant la lettre*. No one else understood, as he did, how naive philistines are when they say that goodness, for all the manly virtue of those who practice it, is God-inspired, but that evil stems entirely from our spontaneity, and in it we are independent and self-sufficient beings. No one else saw inspiration, as he did, in even the most ignoble actions, and precisely in them. He considered vileness itself as something preformed, both in the course of the world and also in ourselves, to which we are disposed if not called, as the bourgeois idealist sees virtue. Dostoevsky's God created not only heaven and earth and man and beast, but also baseness, vengeance, cruelty. And here, too, he gave the devil no opportunity to meddle in his handiwork. That is why all these vices have a pristine vitality in his work; they are perhaps not "splendid," but eternally new, "as on the first day," separated by an infinity from the clichés through which sin is perceived by the philistine.

The pitch of tension that enabled the poets under discussion to achieve their astonishing long-range effects is documented quite scurrilously in the letter Isidore Ducasse addressed to his publisher on October 23, 1869, in an attempt to make his poetry look acceptable. He places himself in the line that descends from Mickiewicz, Milton, Southey, Alfred de Musset, and Baudelaire, and says:[13] "Of course, I somewhat swelled the note to bring something new into this literature that, after all, sings of despair solely in order to depress the reader and thus make him long all the more intensely for goodness as a remedy. So that in the end one really sings only of goodness; but the method is more philosophical and less naive than that of the old school, of which only Victor Hugo and a few others are still alive."[14] Yet if Lautréamont's erratic book has any lineage at all, or, rather, can be assigned one, it is that of insurrection. Soupault's attempt, in his edition of the complete works in 1927, to write a political curriculum vitae for Isidore Ducasse was therefore a quite understandable and not unperceptive venture. Unfortunately, there is no documentation for it, and that adduced by Soupault rests on a confusion. On the other hand, and happily, a similar attempt in the case of Rimbaud was successful, and it is the achievement of Marcel Coulon to have defended the poet's true image against the Catholic usurpation by Claudel and Berrichon.[15] Rimbaud is indeed a Catholic, but he is one, by his own account, in the most wretched part of himself, which he never tires of denouncing and consigning to his own and everyone's hatred, his own and everyone's contempt: the part that forces him to confess that he does not understand revolt. But this is the confession of a communard dissatisfied with his own contribution who, by the time he turned his back on poetry, had long since—in his earliest work—taken leave of religion. "Hatred, to you I have entrusted my treasure," he writes in *Une saison en enfer*. This is another dictum around which a poetics of Surrealism might grow like a climbing plant, to sink its roots deeper than the theory of "surprised" creation originated by Apollinaire—sink them to the depth of the insights of Poe.

Since Bakunin, Europe has lacked a radical concept of freedom.[16] The Surrealists have one. They are the first to liquidate the sclerotic liberal-moral-humanistic ideal of freedom, because they are convinced that "freedom, which on this earth can be bought only with a thousand of the hardest sacrifices, must be enjoyed unrestrictedly in its fullness without any kind of pragmatic calculation, as long as it lasts." And this proves to them that "mankind's struggle for liberation in its simplest revolutionary form (which is nevertheless liberation in every respect), remains the only cause worth serving." But are they successful in welding this experience of freedom to the other revolutionary experience, which we must acknowledge because it has been ours—the constructive, dictatorial side of revolution? In short, have they bound revolt to revolution? How are we to imagine an existence oriented solely toward the boulevard Bonne-Nouvelle, in rooms designed by Le Corbusier and Oud?[17]

To win the energies of intoxication for the revolution—this is the project on which Surrealism focuses in all its books and enterprises. This it may call its most particular task. For them it is not enough that, as we know, an intoxicating component lives in every revolutionary act. This component is identical with the anarchic. But to place the accent exclusively on it would be to subordinate the methodical and disciplinary preparation for revolution entirely to a praxis oscillating between fitness exercises and celebration in advance. Added to this is an inadequate, undialectical conception of the nature of intoxication. The aesthetic of the painter, the poet, *en état de surprise,* of art as the reaction of one surprised, is enmeshed in a number of pernicious romantic prejudices. Any serious exploration of occult, surrealistic, phantasmagoric gifts and phenomena presupposes a dialectical intertwinement to which a romantic turn of mind is impervious. For histrionic or fanatical stress on the mysterious side of the mysterious takes us no further; we penetrate the mystery only to the degree that we recognize it in the everyday world, by virtue of a dialectical optic that perceives the everyday as impenetrable, the impenetrable as everyday. The most passionate investigation of telepathic phenomena, for example, will not teach us half as much about reading (which is an eminently telepathic process) as the profane illumination of reading will teach us about telepathic phenomena. And the most passionate investigation of the hashish trance will not teach us half as much about thinking (which is eminently narcotic) as the profane illumination of thinking will teach us about the hashish trance. The reader, the thinker, the loiterer, the *flâneur,* are types of illuminati just as much as the opium eater, the dreamer, the ecstatic. And more profane. Not to mention that most terrible drug—ourselves—which we take in solitude.

"To win the energies of intoxication for the revolution"—in other words, poetic politics? "We've tried that beverage. Anything, rather than that!" Well, it will interest you all the more to see how much an excursion into poetry clarifies things. For what is the program of the bourgeois parties? A bad poem on springtime, filled to bursting with metaphors. The socialist sees that "finer future of our children and grandchildren" in a society in which all act "as if they were angels" and everyone has as much "as if he were rich" and everyone lives "as if he were free." Of angels, wealth, freedom, not a trace—these are mere images. And the stock imagery of these poets of the social-democratic associations? Their *gradus ad parnassum?* Optimism. A very different air is breathed in the Naville essay that makes the "organization of pessimism" the call of the hour. In the name of his literary friends, Naville delivers an ultimatum in the face of which this unprincipled, dilettantish optimism must unfailingly show its true colors: Where are the conditions for revolution? In the changing of attitudes or of external circumstances? This is the cardinal question that determines the relation of politics to morality and cannot be glossed over. Surrealism has come ever closer to the Communist answer. And that means pessimism all along the line. Absolutely. Mistrust in the fate of literature, mistrust in the fate of freedom, mistrust in the fate of European humanity, but three times mistrust in all reconciliation: between classes, between nations, between individuals. And unlimited trust only in IG Farben and the peaceful perfecting of the air force.[18] But what now? What next?

Here, due weight must be given to the insight which in the *Traité du style* [Treatise on Style], Aragon's last book, required a distinction between metaphor and image, a happy insight into questions of style that needs extending. Extension: nowhere do these two—metaphor and image—collide so drastically and so irreconcilably as in politics. For to organize pessimism means nothing other than to expel moral metaphor from politics and to discover in the space of political action the one hundred percent image space. This image space, however, can no longer be measured out by contemplation. If it is the double task of the revolutionary intelligentsia to overthrow the intellectual predominance of the bourgeoisie and to make contact with the proletarian masses, the intelligentsia has failed almost entirely in the second part of this task because it can no longer be performed contemplatively. Yet this has hindered scarcely anybody from approaching it again and again as if it could, and calling for proletarian poets, thinkers, and artists. To counter this, Trotsky had to point out—as early as *Literature and Revolution*—that such artists would emerge only from a victorious revolution.[19] In reality, it is far less a matter of making the artist of bourgeois origin into a master of "proletarian art" than of deploying him, even at the expense of his artistic activity, at important points in this image space. Indeed, mightn't the interruption of his "artistic career" perhaps be an essential part of his new function?

The jokes he tells will be better for it. And he will tell them better. For in the joke, too, in invective, in misunderstanding, in all cases where an action puts forth its own image and exists, absorbing and consuming it, where nearness looks with its own eyes, the long-sought image space is opened, the world of universal and integral actualities, where the "best room" is missing—the space, in a word, in which political materialism and physical creatureliness share the inner man, the psyche, the individual, or whatever else we wish to throw to them, with dialectical justice, so that no limb remains untorn. Nevertheless—indeed, precisely after such dialectical annihilation—this will still be an image space and, more concretely, a body space. For in the end this must be admitted: metaphysical materialism, of the brand of Vogt and Bukharin—as is attested by the experience of the Surrealists, and earlier by that of Hebel, Georg Büchner, Nietzsche, and Rimbaud—cannot lead without rupture to anthropological materialism.[20] There is a residue. The collective is a body, too. And the *physis* that is being organized for it in technology can, through all its political and factual reality, be produced only in that image space to which profane illumination initiates us. Only when in technology body and image space so interpenetrate that all revolutionary tension becomes bodily collective innervation, and all the bodily innervations of the collective become revolutionary discharge, has reality transcended itself to the extent demanded by the *Communist Manifesto*. For the moment, only the Surrealists have understood its present commands. They exchange, to a man, the play of human features for the face of an alarm clock that in each minute rings for sixty seconds.

Published in *Die literarische Welt*, February 1929. *Gesammelte Schriften*, II, 295–310. Translated by Edmund Jephcott.

Notes

1. André Breton (1896–1966), French poet, essayist, critic, and editor, was one of the founders of the Surrealist movement and became its dominant voice. In 1924 Breton's *Manifeste du surréalisme* defined Surrealism as "pure psychic automatism, by which it is intended to express . . . the real process of thought. It is the dictation of thought, free from any control by the reason and of any aesthetic or moral preoccupation." Breton's chief works include the novel *Nadja* (1928), the prose experiments *Les vases communicants* (The Communicating Vessels; 1932) and *L'amour fou* (Mad Love; 1937), and the critical essays "Le surréalisme et le peinture" (Surrealism and Painting; 1926), "Qu'est-ce que le surréalisme?" (What Is Surrealism?; 1934), and "La clé des champs" (The Key to the Fields; 1953). In the late 1920s Breton and many of his Surrealist colleagues came to a new political engagement; Breton joined the Communist party, but broke with it in 1935, espousing his own brand of Marxism. Louis Aragon (pseudonym of Louis Andrieux; 1897–1982), French poet, novelist, and essayist, was one of the most politically active Surrealists. His novel *Le paysan de Paris* (The Nightwalker; 1926) was a key text in Benjamin's early thinking about *Das Passagen-Werk* (The Arcades Project). Aragon joined the French Communist party in 1927, visited the Soviet Union in 1930, and broke with the Surrealists in 1933 over issues of party orthodoxy. Philippe Soupault (1897–1990) was a French poet and novelist whose book *Les champs magnétiques* (The Magnetic Fields; 1920), written jointly with Breton, is regarded as the first major Surrealist work. As the Surrealist movement became increasingly dogmatic and political, Soupault grew dissatisfied with it and eventually broke with it and Breton. Robert Desnos (1900–1945), French poet, emerged as a key figure in early Surrealism because of his susceptibility to hypnotism, under which he could recite his dreams, write, and draw. His works include *La liberté ou l'amour!* (Liberty or Love!; 1927), *Corps et biens* (Bodies and Goods; 1930), and, after the inevitable break with Breton and Surrealist orthodoxy, the successful screenplay *Complainte de Fantomas* (Fantomas' Lament; 1933). Paul Eluard (pseudonym of Eugène Grindel; 1895–1952), French poet, was an early Surrealist and one of the leading lyric poets of the century. His major collections include *Capitale de la douleur* (Capital of Sorrow; 1926), *La rose publique* (The Public Rose; 1934), and *Les yeux fertiles* (The Fertile Eyes; 1936). After the Spanish Civil War, Eluard abandoned Surrealist experimentation.

2. The "Fronde" is the collective name for the series of civil wars that raged in France between 1648 and 1653, during the minority of Louis XIV. The term, meaning "sling," is derived from the toy catapults that were used in a children's game played in the streets of Paris in defiance of the civil authorities. The wars arose in part in an attempt to check the growing power of royal government; their failure prepared the way for the absolutism of Louis XIV's reign.

3. Arthur Rimbaud (1854–1891), Symbolist poet, published *Une saison en enfer,* a series of prose poems, in Brussels in 1873.

4. Saint-Pol-Roux (pseudonym of Paul Roux; 1861–1940) was a French Symbolist poet whose highly original but extravagant figurative language found a late echo among the Surrealists.

5. The comte de Lautréamont (pseudonym of Isidore-Lucien Ducasse; 1846–1870) was a French poet whose major work was the prose poem *Les chants de Maldoror* (1868–1869). The Surrealists recognized in the work's startling imagery an important precedent for their own literary practice. Guillaume Apollinaire (pseudonym of Wilhelm Apollinaris de Kostrowitzki; 1880–1918), French poet and critic, was the driving force in the French avant-garde until his early death. His most important works include the pioneering essay "Peintures cubistes" (Cubist Painters; 1913), the poem collections *Alcools* (1913) and *Calligrammes* (1918), the story "Le poète assassiné" (The Poet Assassinated; 1916), and the play *Les mamelles de Tirésias* (The Breasts of Tiresias; staged in 1917). Apollinaire described the play as "surrealist," the first use of the term.

6. Henri Hertz (1875–1966), French poet, novelist, essayist, and journalist, was an important left-liberal voice in France after about 1910. He moved easily between the avant-garde circles around Apollinaire and the world of international politics.

7. Apollinaire's volume of novellas, *L'Hérésiarque,* appeared in Paris in 1910.

8. Giorgio de Chirico (1888–1978) was an Italian painter who, with Carlo Carrà and Giorgio Morandi, founded the *pittura metafisica* style of painting. De Chirico's paintings, with their harsh juxtapositions of oddly disparate objects in deep, barren perspectives, exerted a strong influence on the Surrealists. Max Ernst (1891–1976), German painter and sculptor, moved easily from Dada in Cologne to Surrealism in Paris. His experimentation with automatism in painting formed an important parallel to the writing practices of the movement.

9. Paul Scheerbart (1863–1915), German author, produced poetry and prose oriented toward a gently fantastic science fiction. In 1919, Benjamin wrote an unpublished review of his novel *Lesabéndio* (1913).

10. Pierre Naville's pamphlet "La révolution et les intellectuels" publicly challenged the political engagement of his fellow Surrealists.

11. *L'Humanité,* the daily paper founded in 1904 by Jean Jaurès as the organ of the Socialist party, became the organ of the Communist party in 1920.

12. Henri Béraud (1885–1958), French novelist and journalist, was an active right-wing pamphleteer. During World War II, he was a collaborator of the Vichy regime and edited the weekly newspaper *Gringoire.*

13. Adam Mickiewicz (1798–1855) was one of the greatest poets of Poland and a lifelong advocate of Polish national freedom. His exalted patriotism, mystical feeling, and passionate appreciation of the positive aspects of Polish life stood

as a model for succeeding generations of Polish writers. John Milton (1608–1674), English poet and advocate of civil and religious liberty, produced a number of important political tracts ("Of Education," 1644; "Areopagitica," 1644; "The Second Defence of the English People," 1654), as well as the long poems for which he is best-known (*Paradise Lost*, 1667; *Paradise Regained*, 1671; *Samson Agonistes*, 1671). Robert Southey (1774–1843), English poet and prose writer, was an early and outspoken champion of the French Revolution, in such works as the long poem *Joan of Arc* (1796) and the verse drama *The Fall of Robespierre* (1794), which he coauthored with Samuel Taylor Coleridge. After about 1797, Southey's views became increasingly conservative, and his pen turned to support of the Tories. Alfred de Musset (1810–1857) was a French Romantic poet and playwright. Though always associated with the Romantic movement, Musset often caricatured its excesses. Charles Baudelaire (1821–1867) was a French poet whose collection *Les Fleurs du Mal* (1857) is generally recognized as the most important and influential volume of poetry of the nineteenth century. Although his political affiliations and activities remain somewhat obscure, recent studies have suggested that his radical political views led to his participation in the February 1848 riots that overthrew King Louis-Philippe and installed the Second Republic, as well as in the resistance to the Bonapartist military coup of December 1851.

14. Victor Hugo (1802–1885), French dramatist, novelist, and poet, was the most important of the Romantic writers. While his novels (*Les Misérables*, 1862; *Notre-Dame de Paris*, 1831) remain his best-known works, his legacy to the nineteenth century was his lyric poetry.

15. Paul Claudel (1868–1955), poet, playwright, and essayist, was an important force in French letters at the turn of the century. The tone and lyricism of his work owe much to his deeply felt Catholicism. Paterne Berrichon (pseudonym of Pierre Dufour; 1855–1922), French editor and man of letters, married Rimbaud's sister Isabelle. Berrichon and his wife oversaw the early editions of the poet's work and produced a quantity of biographical writing; the thrust of all of this was to present Rimbaud as a Christian author who had strayed from the true path but had reconverted near the end of his life.

16. Mikhail Aleksandrovich Bakunin (1814–1876) was the chief proponent of anarchism in the nineteenth century. He was engaged equally as a revolutionary agitator and as a prolific political writer. A quarrel with Karl Marx over the direction of the International split the European revolutionary movement for many years.

17. Le Corbusier (pseudonym of Charles-Edouard Jeanneret; 1887–1965) was a Swiss architect and city planner whose work combined a modernist functionalism with a bold, sculptural expressionism. In addition to buildings and drawings, Le Corbusier produced a large body of theoretical writings; he was perhaps the most effective public advocate of the first generation of the International school of architecture. Jacobus Johannes Pieter Oud (1890–1963), Dutch architect, founded, together with Theo van Doesburg, the influential review *De Stijl* in 1917. Oud soon became the chief proponent of the austere, geometric style identified with the circle around the journal; his best-known works include a

series of massive housing projects. Oud's book *Höllandische Architektur* (1926) solidified his international reputation.

18. IG Farben (in full: Interessengemeinschaft Farbenindustrie Aktiengesellschaft, or Syndicate of Dye-Industry Corporations) was the world's largest chemical concern, or cartel, between its founding in 1925 and its dissolution by the Allies after World War II. The IG (Interessengemeinschaft—literally, "community of interests"), partly patterned after earlier U.S. trusts, grew out of a complex merger of German manufacturers of chemicals, pharmaceuticals, and dyestuffs *(Farben)*. The major members were the companies known today as BASF, Bayer, Hoechst, Agfa-Gevaert, and Cassella.

19. Leo Trotsky (pseudonym of Lev Davidovich Bronshtein; 1879–1940), Communist theorist and agitator, was a leader in the October Revolution of 1917, and later, under Lenin, was commissar of foreign affairs and of war (1917–1924) in the Soviet Union. In the struggle for power following Lenin's death, however, Joseph Stalin emerged as victor, while Trotsky was removed from all positions of power and later exiled (1929). He remained the leader of anti-Stalinist opposition abroad, until his assassination in Mexico, allegedly by a Stalinist agent. His *Literatura i revoljucja (Literature and Revolution)* was published in 1922.

20. Nikolai Ivanovich Bukharin (1888–1938) was an early Bolshevik, a Marxist theoretician and economist, and a prominent member of both the Politburo and the Communist International (Comintern). He was stripped of his party posts in 1929 and fell victim to one of the last of Stalin's purge trials. Johann Peter Hebel (1760–1826), German journalist and prose stylist, remained one of Benjamin's favorite authors (see the essay "Johann Peter Hebel," in Volume 1 of this edition). His "Calendar Stories," composed in a lapidary style, combine humor, didacticism, and folk wisdom. Georg Büchner (1813–1837), German dramatist, has emerged as one of the great playwrights of the nineteenth century. His three plays—*Dantons Tod* (Danton's Death; 1835), *Leonce und Lena* (1836), and *Woyzeck* (1836)—combine a harshly episodic structure with extreme naturalism and materialism. Friedrich Wilhelm Nietzsche (1844–1900), German philosopher, psychologist, and moralist, composed a body of work notable for its adherence to an extreme materialism.

Chaplin in Retrospect

The Circus is the first product of the art of film that is also the product of old age. Charlie has grown older since his last film. But he also acts old. And the most moving thing about this new film is the feeling that Chaplin now has a clear overview of his possibilities and is resolved to work exclusively within these limits to attain his goal. At every point the variations on his greatest themes are displayed in their full glory. The chase is set in a maze; his unexpected appearance would astonish a magician; the mask of noninvolvement turns him into a fairground marionette . . .

The lesson and the warning that emerge from this great work have led the poet Philippe Soupault to attempt the first definition of Chaplin as a historical phenomenon. In November the excellent Paris review *Europe* (published by Rieder, Paris), to which we shall return in greater detail, presented an essay by Soupault containing a number of ideas around which a definitive picture of the great artist will one day be able to crystallize.[1]

What he emphasizes there above all is that Chaplin's relation to the film is fundamentally not that of Chaplin the actor, let alone the star. Following Soupault's way of thinking, we might say that Chaplin, considered as a total phenomenon, is no more of an actor than was William Shakespeare. Soupault insists, rightly, that "the undeniable superiority of Chaplin's films . . . is based on the fact that they are imbued with a poetry that everyone encounters in his life, admittedly without always being conscious of it." What is meant by this is of course *not* that Chaplin is the "author" of his film *scripts*. Rather, he is simply the author of his own films—that is to say, their director. Soupault has realized that Chaplin was the first (and the Russians have followed his example) to construct a film with a theme and variations—in short, with the element of composition—and that all this stands in complete opposition to films based on action and suspense. This explains why Soupault has argued more forcefully than anyone else that the pinnacle of Chaplin's work is to be seen in *A Woman of Paris*. This is the film in which, as is well known, he does not even appear and which was shown in Germany under the idiotic title *Die Nächte einer schönen Frau* [Nights of a Beautiful Woman]. (The Kamera Theater ought to show it every six months. It is a foundation document of the art of film.)

When we learn that 125,000 meters of film were shot for this 3,000-meter work, we get some idea of the capital that this man requires, and that is at least as necessary to him as to a Nansen or an Amundsen[2] if he is to make his voyages of discovery to the poles of the art of film. We must share Soupault's concern that Chaplin's productivity may be paralyzed by the dangerous financial claims of his second wife, as well as by the ruthless competition of the American trusts. It is said that Chaplin is planning both a Napoleon-film and a Christ-film. Shouldn't we fear that such projects are no more than giant screens behind which the great artist conceals his exhaustion?

It is good and useful that at the moment old age begins to show itself in Chaplin's features, Soupault should remind us of Chaplin's youth and of the territorial origins of his art. Needless to say, these lie in the metropolis of London.

> In his endless walks through the London streets, with their black-and-red houses, Chaplin trained himself to observe. He himself has told us that the idea of creating his stock character—the fellow with the bowler hat, jerky walk, little toothbrush moustache, and walking stick—first occurred to him on seeing office workers walking along the Strand. What he saw in their bearing and dress was the attitude of a person who takes some pride in himself. But the same can be said of the other characters that surround him in his films. They, too, originate in London: the shy, young, winsome girl; the burly lout who is always ready to use his fists and then to take to his heels when he sees that people aren't afraid of him; the arrogant gentleman who can be recognized by his top hat.

Soupault appends to this portrait a comparison between Dickens and Chaplin that is worth reading and exploring further.

With his art, Chaplin confirms the old insight that only an imaginative world that is firmly grounded in a society, a nation, and a place will succeed in evoking the great, uninterrupted, yet highly differentiated resonance that exists between nations. In Russia, people wept when they saw *The Pilgrim;* in Germany, people are interested in the theoretical implications of his comedies; in England, they like his sense of humor. It is no wonder that Chaplin himself is puzzled and fascinated by these differences. Nothing points so unmistakably to the fact that the film will have immense significance as that it neither did nor could occur to anyone that there exists any judge superior to the actual audience. In his films, Chaplin appeals both to the most international and the most revolutionary emotion of the masses: their laughter. "Admittedly," Soupault says, "Chaplin merely makes people laugh. But aside from the fact that this is the hardest thing to do, it is socially also the most important."

Published in *Die literarische Welt*, February 1929. *Gesammelte Schriften*, III, 157–159. Translated by Rodney Livingstone.

Notes

1. Philippe Soupault, "Charlie Chaplin," in *Europe: Revue mensuelle* [Paris] 18 (November 1928): 379–402.
2. Fridtjof Nansen (1861–1930) and Roald Amundsen (1872–1928) were Norwegian explorers of the Polar regions. Nansen won the Nobel Peace Prize in 1922 for his work with refugees. Amundsen, having led the expeditions that first reached the South Pole (1911) and flew over the North Pole (1926), disappeared while attempting to rescue his colleague Umberto Nobile in the Arctic in 1928.

Chambermaids' Romances of the Past Century

Chambermaids' romances? Since when are works of literature categorized according to the class that consumes them? Unfortunately, they are not—or all too seldom. Yet how much more illuminating this would be than hackneyed aesthetic appreciations! Nevertheless, such a categorization would pose problems. Above all, because we so rarely obtain any insight into the relations of production. They used to be more transparent than they are in our day. This is why a start should be made with cheap fiction, with colportage, if indeed literary history is ever going to explore the geological structure of the book-alps, rather than confining itself to a view of the peaks.

Before the development of advertising, the book trade was dependent on itinerant colporteurs or booksellers for distribution of its wares among the lower classes. It is amusing to imagine the complete literary traveling salesman of that age and those classes, the man who knew how to introduce ghost stories and tales of chivalry into the servants' quarters in the cities and the peasants' cottages in the villages. To a certain extent he must have been able to become part of the stories he was selling. Not as the hero, of course, not the banished prince or the knight errant, but perhaps the ambiguous old man—warner or seducer?—who appears in many of these stories and who, in the first illustration shown here, is about to make himself scarce at the sight of a crucifix.

It is not surprising that this entire body of literature has been despised for as long as the superstitious belief in absolute "art" has existed. The concept of the document, however, which we nowadays apply to the works of primitives, children, and the sick, has also provided essential contexts within which to consider these writings. People began to recognize the value

"Swear!"

This illustration is from a medieval tale of ghosts and chivalry entitled *Adelmar von Perlstein, the Knight of the Golden Key; or, The Twelve Sleeping Maidens, Protectors of the Enchanting Young Man.*

Lady Lucie Guilford,

die

Fürstin der Rache,

genannt:

die Hyäne von Paris.

Seitenstück zu der Antonetta Czerna.

Von

O. G. Derwicz.

Dresden,
Verlag von I. Bremer.

Ich schwöre es, wie dieser sollen Alle fallen!

The Princess of Vengeance, Known as the Hyena of Paris

"I swear it: they shall all suffer the fate of this man!" The beauty portrayed here is a collector of preserved human heads, which she keeps on the shelves of a cupboard in her house.

"My Curse upon You!"

This illustration comes from a story of recent times by O. G. Derwicz, entitled *Antonetta Czerna, the Princess of the Wild; or, The Vengeance of a Woman's Wounded Heart* (Pirna, n.d.). These smartly dressed ladies have turned up for the shooting of the young man as if for a garden party.

"Stand Back, Base Scoundrel!"

This is the notorious "Black Knight," who has just conquered York Castle and is about to overpower the beautiful Rebecca. One might say that the two figures are dancing a kind of country waltz of horror.

of typical stories [*Stoffe*—literally, subjects] and became interested in studying the few truly living ones that continue to have an impact and are capable of constant renewal. They perceived that the artistic ideals of various generations and classes were embodied just as definitively in formal idioms of these groups as in the ways in which they differed. The archive of such eternal stories is the dream, as Freud has taught us to understand it.

Works that pander so directly to the public's hunger for stories are interesting enough in themselves; but they become even more so when the same spirit is expressed graphically and colorfully through illustrations. The very principle of such illustrations testifies to the close connection between reader and story. The reader wants to know exactly what their place is. If only we had more such pictures! But where they were not protected by the stamp of a lending library—like two of those shown here—they have followed their predestined path: from the book to the wall and from the wall to the rubbish bin.

These books raise many questions. Apart from external ones, such as matters of authorship, influence, and so on, there is the question of why, in stories that were written in the heyday of the bourgeoisie, moral authority is always tied to a lady or gentleman of rank. Perhaps because the servant classes still felt a certain solidarity with the middle class and shared its most secret romantic ideals.

Many of these novels have a motto in verse at the head of each of their bloodthirsty chapters. There you can encounter Goethe and Schiller, and even Schlegel and Immermann, but also such leading poets as Waldau, Parucker, Tschabuschnigg, or the simple B.,[1] to whom we owe these lines:

Alone she strays, abandoned,
through the endless city streets,
Every instant to fear
the enemies she might meet.

We are still clumsy in our efforts to approach these clumsy works. We feel it is strange to take seriously books that were never part of a "library." But let us not forget that books were originally objects for use—indeed, a means of subsistence. These were devoured. Let us use them to study novels from the point of view of their food chemistry!

Published in *Das illustrierte Blatt,* April 1929. *Gesammelte Schriften,* IV, 620–622. Translated by Rodney Livingstone.

Notes

1. Benjamin probably refers here to Friedrich Schlegel (1772–1829), the prominent Romantic theorist, translator, scholar, critic, and novelist. Karl Leberecht Immer-

mann (1796–1840) was a German author whose novels of contemporary social analysis and village life were widely read. Max Waldau (pseudonym of Richard Georg Spiller von Hauenschild; 1825–1855) was a poet and novelist active in East Prussia; he is best-known for the novels *Nach der Natur* (After Nature; 1850) and *Aus der Junkerwelt* (From the World of the Country Squires; 1850). Adolf Ritter von Tschabuschnigg (1809–1877) was an Austrian writer and politician; after a long political career, he became minister of justice in 1870–1871. His novels *Die Industriellen* (The Industrialists; 1854) and *Sünder und Toren* (Sinners and Fools; 1875) were oriented toward societal analysis and critique.

Marseilles

The street . . . the only valid field of experience.
—André Breton

Marseilles: the yellow-studded maw of a seal with salt water running out between the teeth. When this gullet opens to catch the black and brown proletarian bodies thrown to it by ship's companies according to their timetables, it exhales a stink of oil, urine, and printer's ink. This comes from the tartar baking hard on the massive jaws: newspaper kiosks, lavatories, and oyster stalls. The harbor people are a bacillus culture, the porters and whores products of decomposition with a resemblance to human beings. But the palate itself is pink, which is the color of shame here, of poverty. Hunchbacks wear it, and beggarwomen. And the faded women of the rue Bouterie are given their only tint by the sole pieces of clothing they wear: pink shifts.

Les Bricks, the red-light district is called, after the barges moored a hundred paces away at the jetty of the old harbor. A vast agglomeration of steps, arches, bridges, turrets, and cellars. It seems to be still awaiting its designated use, but it already has it. For this depot of wornout alleyways is the prostitutes' quarter. Invisible lines divide up the area into sharp, angular territories like African colonies. The whores are strategically placed, ready at a sign to encircle hesitant visitors, and to bounce the reluctant guest like a ball from one side of the street to the other. If he forfeits nothing else in this game, it is his hat. Has anyone yet probed deeply enough into this refuse heap of houses to reach the innermost place in the gynaeceum, the chamber where the trophies of manhood—boaters, bowlers, hunting hats, trilbies, jockey caps—hang in rows on consoles or in layers on racks? From the interiors of taverns the eye meets the sea. Thus, the alleyway passes between rows of innocent houses as if shielded from the harbor by a bashful hand. On this bashful, dripping hand, however, shines a signet ring on a fishwife's hard finger, the old Hôtel de Ville. Here, two hundred years ago, stood patricians' houses. The high-breasted nymphs, the snake-ringed Medusa's heads over their weather-beaten doorframes have only now become unambiguously the signs of a professional guild. Unless, that is, signboards were hung over them as the midwife Bianchamori has hung hers, on which, leaning against a pillar, she turns a defiant face to all the brothelkeepers of the quarter, and points unruffled to a sturdy baby in the act of emerging from an egg.

Noises. High in the empty streets of the harbor district they are as densely and loosely clustered as butterflies on a hot flower bed. Every step stirs a song, a quarrel, a flapping of wet linen, a rattling of boards, a baby's bawling, a clatter of buckets. Only you have to have strayed up here alone, if you are to pursue them with a net as they flutter away unsteadily into the stillness. For in these deserted corners all sounds and things still have their own silences, just as, at midday in the mountains, there is a silence of hens, of axes, of cicadas. But the chase is dangerous, and the net is finally torn when, like a gigantic hornet, a grindstone impales it from behind with its whizzing sting.

Notre Dame de la Garde. The hill from which she looks down is the starry garment of the Mother of God, into which the houses of the Cité Chabas snuggle. At night, the lamps in its velvet lining form constellations that have not yet been named. It has a zipper: the cabin at the foot of the steel band of the rack railway is a jewel, from whose colored bull's-eyes the world shines back. A disused fortress is her holy footstool, and about her neck is an oval of waxen, glazed votive wreaths that look like relief profiles of her forebears. Little chains of streamers and sails are her earrings, and from the shady lips of the crypt issues jewelry of ruby-red and golden spheres on which swarms of pilgrims hang like flies.

Cathedral. On the least frequented, sunniest square stands the cathedral. This place is deserted, despite the proximity at its feet of La Joliette, the harbor, to the south, and a proletarian district to the north. As a reloading point for intangible, unfathomable goods, the bleak building stands between quay and warehouse. Nearly forty years were spent on it. But by the time all was complete, in 1893, place and time had conspired victoriously in this monument against its architects and sponsors, and the wealth of the clergy had given rise to a gigantic railway station that could never be opened to traffic. The façade gives an indication of the waiting rooms within, where passengers of the first to fourth classes (though before God they are all equal), wedged among their spiritual possessions as if between suitcases, sit reading hymnbooks that, with their concordances and cross references, look very much like international timetables. Extracts from the railway traffic regulations in the form of pastoral letters hang on the walls, tariffs for the discount on special trips in Satan's luxury train are consulted, and cabinets where the long-distance traveler can discreetly wash are kept in readiness as confessionals. This is the Marseilles religion station. Sleeping cars to eternity depart from here at Mass times.

The light from greengrocers' shops that is visible in the paintings of Monticelli[1] comes from the inner streets of his city, the monotonous residential neighborhoods of the long-standing inhabitants, who know something of the sadness of Marseilles. For childhood is the divining rod of melancholy, and to know the mourning of such radiant, glorious cities one must have been a child in them. The gray houses of the boulevard de Longchamps, the barred windows of the cours Puget, and the trees of the allée de Meilhan give nothing away to the traveler if chance does not lead him to the cubiculum of the city, the passage de Lorette, the narrow yard where, in the sleepy presence of a few women and men, the whole world shrinks to a single Sunday afternoon. A real-estate company has carved its name on the gateway. Doesn't this interior correspond exactly to the white mystery ship moored in the harbor, *Nautique,* which never puts to sea, but daily feeds foreigners at white tables with dishes that are much too clean, as if they've been surgically rinsed?

Shellfish and oyster stalls. Unfathomable wetness that swills from the upper tier, in a dirty, cleansing flood over dirty planks and warty mountains of pink shellfish, bubbles between the thighs and bellies of glazed Buddhas, past yellow domes of lemons, into the marshland of cresses and through the woods of French pennants, finally to irrigate the palate as the best sauce for the quivering creatures. Oursins de l'Estaque, Portugaises, Maremmes, Clovisses, Moules marinières—all this is incessantly sieved, grouped, counted, cracked open, thrown away, prepared, tasted. And the slow, stupid agent of inland trade, paper, has no place in the unfettered element, the breakers of foaming lips that forever surge against the streaming steps. But over there, on the other quay, stretches the mountain range of "souvenirs," the mineral hereafter of seashells. Seismic forces have thrown up this massif of paste jewelry, shell limestone, and enamel, where inkpots, steamers, anchors, mercury columns, and sirens commingle. The pressure of a thousand atmospheres under which this world of images writhes, rears, piles up, is the same force that is tested in the hard hands of seamen, after long voyages, on the thighs and breasts of women; and the lust that, on the shell-covered caskets, presses from the mineral world a red or blue velvet heart to be pierced with needles and brooches is the same lust that sends tremors through these streets on paydays.

Walls. Admirable, the discipline to which they are subject in this city. The better ones, in the center, wear livery and are in the pay of the ruling class. They are covered with gaudy patterns and have sold their whole length many hundreds of times to the latest brand of aperitif, to department stores, to "Chocolat Menier," or to Dolores del Rio. In the poorer neighborhoods they are politically mobilized, and post their spacious red letters as the forerunners of red guards in front of dockyards and arsenals.

The down-and-out fellow who, after nightfall, sells his books on the corner of the rue de la République and the Vieux Port, awakens bad instincts in the passers-by. They feel tempted to make use of so much fresh misery. And they long to learn more about such nameless misfortune than the mere image of catastrophe that it presents to us. For what extremity must have brought a man to spill out such books as he has left on the asphalt before him, and to hope that a passer-by will be seized at this late hour by a desire to read? Or is it all quite different? And does a poor soul here keep vigil, mutely beseeching us to lift the treasure from the ruins? We hasten by. But we shall falter again at every corner, for everywhere the southern peddler has so pulled his beggar's coat around him that fate looks at us from it with a thousand eyes. How far we are from the sad dignity of our poor, the war-disabled of competition, on whom tags and tins of boot blacking hang like braid and medals.

Suburbs. The farther we emerge from the inner city, the more political the atmosphere becomes. We reach the docks, the inland harbors, the warehouses, the poor neighborhoods, the scattered refuges of wretchedness: the outskirts. Outskirts are the state of emergency of a city, the terrain on which incessantly rages the great decisive battle between town and country. It is nowhere more bitter than between Marseilles and the Provençal landscape. It is the hand-to-hand fight of telegraph poles against agaves, barbed wire against thorny palms, the miasmas of stinking corridors against the damp gloom under the plane trees in brooding squares, short-winded outside staircases against the mighty hills. The long rue de Lyon is the powder conduit which Marseilles has dug in the landscape so that in Saint-Lazare, Saint-Antoine, Arenc, Septèmes it can blow up this terrain, burying it in the shrapnel of every national and commercial language. Alimentation Moderne, rue de Jamaïque, Comptoir de la Limite, Savon Abat-Jour, Minoterie de la Campagne, Bar du Gaz, Bar Facultatif—and over all this lies the dust that here conglomerates out of sea salt, chalk, and mica, and whose bitterness persists longer in the mouths of those who have pitted themselves against the city than the splendor of sun and sea in the eyes of its admirers.

Published in *Neue schweizer Rundschau,* April 1929. *Gesammelte Schriften,* IV, 359–364. Translated by Edmund Jephcott.

Notes

1. Adolphe Monticelli (1824-1886) was a French painter whose dreamlike courtly revels are washed with radiant light and deep shadow.

On the Image of Proust

I

The thirteen volumes of Marcel Proust's *A la recherche du temps perdu* are the result of an unconstruable synthesis in which the absorption of a mystic, the art of a prose writer, the verve of a satirist, the erudition of a scholar, and the self-consciousness of a monomaniac have combined in an autobiographical work. It has rightly been said that all great works of literature establish a genre or dissolve one—that they are, in other words, special cases. Among these cases, this is one of the most unfathomable. From its structure, which is at once fiction, autobiography, and commentary, to the syntax of boundless sentences (the Nile of language, which here overflows and fructifies the plains of truth), everything transcends the norm. The first revealing observation that strikes one is that this great special case of literature at the same time constitutes its greatest achievement in recent decades. The conditions under which it was created were extremely unhealthy: an unusual malady, extraordinary wealth, and an abnormal gift. This is not a model life in every respect, but everything about it is exemplary. The outstanding literary achievement of our time is assigned a place at the heart of the impossible, at the center—and also at the point of indifference—of all dangers, and it marks this great realization of a "lifework" as the last for a long time. The image of Proust is the highest physiognomic expression which the irresistibly growing discrepancy between literature and life was able to assume. This is the lesson which justifies the attempt to evoke this image.

We know that in his work Proust described not a life as it actually was [*wie es gewesen ist*] but a life as it was remembered by the one who had lived it. Yet even this statement is imprecise and far too crude. For the important thing to the remembering author is not what he experienced, but the weaving of his memory, the Penelope work of recollection [*Eingedenken*]. Or should one call it, rather, a Penelope work of forgetting? Is not the involuntary recollection, Proust's *mémoire involontaire*, much closer to forgetting than what is usually called memory? And is not this work of spontaneous recollection, in which remembrance is the woof and forgetting the warp, a counterpart to Penelope's work rather than its likeness? For here the day unravels what the night has woven. When we awake each morning, we hold in our hands, usually weakly and loosely, but a few fringes of the carpet of lived existence, as woven into us by forgetting. However, with our purposeful activity and, even more, our purposive remembering, each day unravels the web, the ornaments of forgetting. This is why Proust finally turned his days into nights, devoting all his hours to undisturbed work in his darkened room with artificial illumination, so that none of those intricate arabesques might escape him.

The Latin word *textum* means "web." No one's text is more of a web or more tightly woven than that of Marcel Proust; to him nothing was tight or durable enough. From his publisher Gallimard we know that Proust's proofreading habits were the despair of typesetters. The galleys always came back covered with writing to the edge of the page, but not a single misprint had been corrected; all available space had been used for fresh text. Thus, the laws of remembrance were operative even within the confines of the work. For an experienced event is finite—at any rate, confined to one sphere of experience; a remembered event is infinite, because it is merely a key to everything that happened before it and after it. There is yet another sense in which memory issues strict regulations for weaving. Only the *actus purus* of remembrance itself, not the author or the plot, constitutes the unity of the text. One may even say that the intermittences of author and plot are only the reverse of the continuum of memory, the figure on the back side of the carpet. This is what Proust meant, and this is how he must be understood, when he said that he would prefer to see his entire work printed in one volume in two columns and without any paragraphs.

What was it that Proust sought so frenetically? What was at the bottom of these infinite efforts? Can we say that all lives, works, and deeds that matter were never anything but the undisturbed unfolding of the most banal, most fleeting, most sentimental, weakest hour in the life of the one to whom they pertain? When Proust in a well-known passage described the hour that was most his own, he did it in such a way that everyone can find it in his own existence. We might almost call it an everyday hour; it comes with the night, a lost twittering of birds, or a breath drawn at the sill of an open window. And there is no telling what encounters would be in store for us if we were less inclined to give in to sleep. Proust did not give in to sleep. And yet—or, rather, precisely for this reason—Jean Cocteau was able to say in a beautiful essay that the intonation of Proust's voice obeyed the laws of night and honey. By submitting to these laws, Proust conquered the hopeless sadness within him (what he once called "l'imperfection incurable dans l'essence même du présent"),[1] and from the honeycombs of memory he built a house for the swarm of his thoughts. Cocteau recognized what really should be the major concern of all readers of Proust. He recognized Proust's blind, senseless, obsessive quest for happiness. It shone from his eyes; they were not happy, but in them lay happiness, just as it lies in gambling or in love. Nor is it hard to say why this heart-stopping, explosive will to happiness which pervades Proust's writings is so seldom comprehended by his readers. In many places Proust himself made it easy for them to view this oeuvre, too, from the time-tested, comfortable perspective of resignation, heroism, asceticism. After all, nothing makes more sense to the model pupils of life than the notion that a great achievement is the fruit of toil, misery, and disappointment. The idea that happiness could have a share in beauty would be too much of a good thing, something that their *ressentiment* would never get over.

There is a dual will to happiness, a dialectics of happiness: a hymnic form as well as an elegiac form. The one is the unheard-of, the unprecedented, the height of bliss; the other, the eternal repetition, the eternal restoration of the original, first happiness. It is this elegiac idea of happiness—it could also be called Eleatic—which for Proust transforms existence into a preserve of memory. To it he sacrificed in his life friends and companionship, in his works plot, unity of characters, the flow of the narration, the play of the imagination. Max Unold, one of Proust's more discerning readers, fastened on the "boredom" thus created in Proust's writings and likened it to "idle stories." "Proust managed to make the idle story interesting. He says: 'Imagine, dear reader: yesterday I was dunking a bit of cake in my tea when it occurred to me that as a child I had spent some time in the country.' For this he takes eighty pages, and it is so fascinating that you think you are no longer the listener but the daydreamer himself." In such stories—"all ordinary dreams turn into idle stories as soon as one tells them to someone"— Unold has discovered the bridge to the dream. No synthetic interpretation of Proust can disregard it. Enough inconspicuous gates lead into it—Proust's frenetic study, his impassioned cult of similarity. The true signs of its hegemony do not become obvious where he unexpectedly and startlingly uncovers similarities in actions, physiognomies, or speech mannerisms. The similarity of one thing to another which we are used to, which occupies us in a wakeful state, reflects only vaguely the deeper similarity of the dream world in which everything that happens appears not in identical but in similar guise, opaquely similar to itself. Children know a symbol of this world: the stocking which has the structure of this dream world when, rolled up in the laundry hamper, it is a "bag" and a "present" at the same time. And just as children do not tire of quickly changing the bag and its contents into a third thing—namely, a stocking—Proust could not get his fill of emptying the dummy, his self, at one stroke in order to keep garnering that third thing, the image which satisfied his curiosity—indeed, assuaged his homesickness. He lay on his bed racked with homesickness, homesick for the world distorted in the state of similarity, a world in which the true surrealist face of existence breaks through. To this world belongs what happens in Proust, as well as the deliberate and fastidious way in which it appears. It is never isolated, rhetorical, or visionary; carefully heralded and securely supported, it bears a fragile, precious reality: the image. It detaches itself from the structure of Proust's sentences just as that summer day at Balbec—old, immemorial, mummified—emerged from the lace curtains under Françoise's hands.

II

We do not always proclaim loudly the most important thing we have to say. Nor do we always privately share it with those closest to us, our intimate friends, those who have been most devotedly ready to receive our confession. If it is true that not only people but also ages have such a chaste—that is, such a devious and frivolous—way of communicating what is most their own to a passing acquaintance, then the nineteenth century did not reveal itself to Zola or Anatole France, but to the young Proust, the insignificant snob, the playboy and socialite who snatched in passing the most astounding confidences from a declining age as if from another bone-weary Swann. It took Proust to make the nineteenth century ripe for memoirs. What before him had been a period devoid of tension now became a force field in which later writers aroused multifarious currents. Nor is it accidental that the most significant work of this kind was written by an author who was personally close to Proust as admirer and friend: the memoirs of the princesse de Clermont-Tonnerre. And the very title of her book, *Au temps des équipages*, would have been unthinkable prior to Proust. This book is the echo which softly answers Proust's ambiguous, loving, challenging call from the Faubourg Saint-Germain. In addition, this melodious performance is shot through with direct and indirect references to Proust in its tenor and its characters, which include him and some of his favorite objects of study from the Ritz. There is no denying, of course, that this puts us in a very feudal milieu, and, with phenomena like Robert de Montesquiou, whom the princesse de Clermont-Tonnerre depicts masterfully, in a very special one at that. But this is true of Proust as well, and in his writings, as we know, Montesquiou has a counterpart. All this would not be worth discussing, especially since the question of models would be secondary and unimportant for Germany, if German criticism were not so fond of taking the easy way out. Above all, it could not resist the opportunity to descend to the level of the lending-library crowd. Hack critics were tempted to draw conclusions about the author from the snobbish milieu of his writings, to characterize Proust's works as an internal affair of the French, a literary supplement to the *Almanach de Gotha.*[2] It is obvious, though, that the problems of Proust's characters are those of a satiated society. But there is not one that would be identical with those of the author, which are subversive. To reduce this to a formula, it was to be Proust's aim to construe the entire structure of high society as a physiology of chatter. In the treasury of its prejudices and maxims, there is not one that is not annihilated by his dangerous comic treatment. It is not the least of Léon Pierre-Quint's many services to Proust that he was the first to point this out. "When humorous works are mentioned," he wrote, "one usually thinks of short, amusing books in illustrated jackets. One forgets about *Don Quixote, Pantagruel,* and *Gil Blas*—fat, ungainly tomes in small print." The subversive side of Proust's work appears most convincingly in this context. Here, though, it is less humor than comedy that is the real source of his power; his laughter does not toss the world up but flings it down—at the risk that it will be smashed to pieces, which will then make him burst into tears. And unity of family, unity of personality, of sexual morality and class honor, are indeed smashed to bits. The pretensions of the bourgeoisie are shattered by laughter. Their retreat and reassimilation by the aristocracy is the sociological theme of the work.

Proust did not tire of the training which moving in aristocratic circles required. Assiduously and without much constraint, he conditioned his personality, making it as impenetrable and resourceful, as submissive and difficult, as it had to be for the sake of his mission. Later on, this mystification and fussiness became so much a part of him that his letters sometimes constitute whole systems of parentheses, and not just in the grammatical sense—letters which despite their infinitely ingenious, flexible composition occasionally call to mind that legendary example of epistolary art: "My dear Madam, I just noticed that I forgot my cane at your house yesterday; please be good enough to give it to the bearer of this letter. P.S. Kindly pardon me for disturbing you; I just found my cane." Proust was most resourceful in creating complications. Once, late at night, he dropped in on the princesse de Clermont-Tonnerre and made his staying dependent on someone's bringing him his medicine from his house. He sent a valet for it, giving him a lengthy description of the neighborhood and of the house. Finally he said: "You cannot miss it. It is the only window on the boulevard Haussmann in which there is still a light burning!" Everything but the house number! Anyone who has tried to get the address of a brothel in a strange city and has received the most long-winded directions, everything but the name of the street and the house number, will understand what is meant here and what the connection is with Proust's love of ceremony, his admiration for Saint-Simon, and, last but not least, his intransigent Frenchness. Isn't it the quintessence of experience to find out how very difficult it is to learn many things which apparently could be told in very few words? It is simply that such words are part of an argot established along lines of caste and class and unintelligible to outsiders. No wonder the secret language of the salons excited Proust. When he later embarked on his merciless depiction of the *petit clan,* the Courvoisiers, and the "esprit d'Oriane," he had already— through his association with the Bibescos—become conversant with the improvisations of a code language to which we too have now been introduced.

In his years of life in the salons, Proust developed not only the vice of flattery to an eminent—one is tempted to say, to a theological—degree, but the vice of curiosity as well. We detect in him the reflection of the laughter which like a flash fire curls the lips of the Foolish Virgins represented on the intrados of many of the cathedrals which Proust loved. It is the smile of curiosity. Was it curiosity that made him such a great parodist? If so, we would know how to evaluate the term "parodist" in this context. Not very highly. For though it does justice to his abysmal malice, it skirts the bitterness, savagery, and grimness of the magnificent pieces which he wrote in the style of Balzac, Flaubert, Sainte-Beuve, Henri de Régnier, the Goncourts, Michelet, Renan, and his favorite Saint-Simon, and which are collected in the volume *Pastiches et mélanges.*[3] The mimicry of a man of curiosity is the brilliant device of these essays, as it is also a feature of his entire creativity, in which his passion for vegetative life cannot be taken seriously enough. Ortega y Gasset was the first to draw attention to the vegetative existence of Proust's characters, which are planted so firmly in their social habitat, influenced by the position of the sun of aristocratic favor, stirred by the wind that blows from Guermantes or Méséglise, and inextricably enmeshed in the thicket of their fate. This is the environment that gave rise to the poet's mimicry. Proust's most accurate, most conclusive insights fasten on their objects the way insects fasten on leaves, blossoms, branches, betraying nothing of their existence until a leap, a beating of wings, a vault, show the startled observer that some incalculable individual life has imperceptibly crept into an alien world. "The metaphor, however unexpected," says Pierre-Quint, "forms itself quite close to the thought."

The true reader of Proust is constantly jarred by small frights. In the use of metaphor, he finds the precipitate of the same mimicry which must have struck him as this spirit's struggle for survival under the leafy canopy of society. At this point we must say something about the close and fructifying interpenetration of these two vices, curiosity and flattery. There is a revealing passage in the writings of the princesse de Clermont-Tonnerre: "And finally we cannot suppress the fact that Proust became intoxicated by the study of domestic servants—whether it be that an element which he encountered nowhere else intrigued his investigative faculties or that he envied servants their greater opportunities for observing the intimate details of things that aroused his interest. In any case, domestic servants in their various embodiments and types were his passion." In the exotic shadings of a Jupien, a Monsieur Aimé, a Célestine Albalat, their ranks extend from Françoise—a figure with the coarse, angular features of Saint Martha that seems to be straight out of a book of hours—to those grooms and *chasseurs* who are paid for loafing rather than working. And perhaps the greatest concentration of this connoisseur of ceremonies was reserved for the depiction of these lower ranks. Who can tell how much servant curiosity became part of Proust's flattery, how much servant flattery became mixed with his curiosity, and where this artful copy of the role of the servant on the heights of the social scale had its limits? Proust presented such a copy, and he could not help doing so, for, as he once admitted, *voir* and *désirer imiter* were one and the same thing to him. This attitude, which was both sovereign and obsequious, has been preserved by Maurice Barrès in the most apposite words that have ever been written about Proust: "Un poète persan dans une loge de portière."[4]

There was something of the detective in Proust's curiosity. The upper ten thousand were to him a clan of criminals, a band of conspirators beyond compare: the *camorra* of consumers.[5] It excludes from its world everything that has a part in production, or at least demands that this part be gracefully and bashfully concealed behind the kind of manner that is sported by the polished professionals of consumption. Proust's analysis of snobbery, which is far more important than his apotheosis of art, constitutes the apogee of his criticism of society. For the attitude of the snob is nothing but the consistent, organized, steely view of life from the chemically pure standpoint of the consumer. And because even the remotest as well as the most primitive memory of nature's productive forces was to be banished from this satanic fairyland, Proust found an inverted relationship more serviceable than a normal one, even in love. But the pure consumer is the pure exploiter—logically and theoretically—and in Proust he is this in the full concreteness of his actual historical existence. He is concrete because he is impenetrable and elusive. Proust describes a class which is everywhere pledged to camouflage its material basis and which for this very reason is attached to a feudalism lacking any intrinsic economic significance but all the more serviceable as a mask of the upper middle class. This disillusioned, merciless deglamorizer of the ego, of love, of morals—for this is how Proust liked to view himself—turns his whole limitless art into a veil for this one most vital mystery of his class: the economic aspect. It is not as if he thereby serves his class; he is merely ahead of it. That which this class experiences begins to become comprehensible only with Proust. Yet much of the greatness of this work will remain inaccessible or undiscovered until this class has revealed its most pronounced features in the final struggle.

III

In the 1800s there was an inn by the name of "Au Temps Perdu" at Grenoble; I do not know whether it still exists. In Proust, too, we are guests who enter through a door underneath a suspended sign that sways in the breeze, a door behind which eternity and rapture await us. Ramón Fernandez rightly distinguished between a *thème de l'éternité* and a *thème du temps* in Proust. But Proust's eternity is by no means a platonic or a utopian one; it is rapturous. Therefore, if "time reveals a new and hitherto unknown kind of eternity to anyone who becomes engrossed in its passing," this certainly does not enable an individual to approach "the higher regions which a Plato or Spinoza reached with one beat of the wings." It is true that in Proust we find rudiments of an enduring idealism, but it is not these elements which determine the greatness of his work. The eternity which Proust opens to view is intertwined time, not boundless time. His true interest is in the passage of time in its most real—that is, intertwined—form, and this passage nowhere holds sway more openly than in remembrance within and aging without. To follow the counterpoint of aging and remembering means to penetrate to the heart of Proust's world, to the universe of intertwining. It is the world in a state of similarity, and in it the *correspondances* rule; the Romantics were the first to comprehend them and Baudelaire embraced them most fervently, but Proust was the only one who managed to reveal them in our lived life. This is the work of *la mémoire involontaire,* the rejuvenating force which is a match for the inexorable process of aging. When that which has been is reflected in the dewy fresh "instant," a painful shock of rejuvenation pulls it together once more as irresistibly as the Guermantes Way and Swann's Way become intertwined for Proust when, in the thirteenth volume, he roams about the Combray area for the last time and discovers the intermingling of the roads. In an instant the landscape turns about like a gust of wind. "Ah! que le monde est grand à la clarté des lampes! / Aux yeux du souvenir que le monde est petit!"[6] Proust has brought off the monstrous feat of letting the whole world age a lifetime in an instant. But this very concentration, in which things that normally just fade and slumber are consumed in a flash, is called rejuvenation. *A la Recherche du temps perdu* is the constant attempt to charge an entire lifetime with the utmost mental awareness. Proust's method is actualization, not reflection. He is filled with the insight that none of us has time to live the true dramas of the life that we are destined for. This is what ages us—this and nothing else. The wrinkles and creases in our faces are the registration of the great passions, vices, insights that called on us; but we, the masters, were not home.

Since the spiritual exercises of Loyola, Western literature has scarcely seen a more radical attempt at self-absorption. Proust's writing, too, has as its center a solitude which pulls the world down into its vortex with the force of a maelstrom. And the overloud and inconceivably hollow chatter which comes roaring out of Proust's novels is the sound of society plunging into the abyss of this solitude. Proust's invectives against friendship have their place here. It was a matter of perceiving the silence at the bottom of this crater, whose eyes are the quietest and most absorbing. What is manifested irritatingly and capriciously in so many anecdotes is the combination of an unparalleled intensity of conversation with an unsurpassable aloofness from one's interlocutor. There has never been anyone else with Proust's ability to show us things; Proust's pointing finger is unequaled. But there is another gesture in friendly togetherness, in conversation: physical contact. To no one is this gesture more alien than to Proust. He cannot touch his reader, either; he couldn't do this for anything in the world. If one wanted to group literature around these poles, dividing it into the deictic kind and the touching kind, the core of the former would be the work of Proust; the core of the latter, the work of Péguy.[7] This is basically what Fernandez has formulated so well: "Depth, or rather intensity, is always on his side, never on that of his interlocutor." This is demonstrated brilliantly and with a touch of cynicism in Proust's literary criticism, the most significant document of which is an essay that came into being on the high level of his fame and the low level of his deathbed: "A propos de Baudelaire." The essay is jesuitical in its acquiescence in his own maladies, immoderate in the garrulousness of a man who is resting, frightening in the indifference of a man marked by death who wants to speak out once more, no matter on what subject. What inspired Proust here in the face of death also shaped him in his intercourse with his contemporaries: an alternation of sarcasm and tenderness which was so spasmodic and harsh that its recipients threatened to break down in exhaustion.

The provocative, unsteady quality of the man affects even the reader of his works. Suffice it to recall the endless succession of "soit que . . ." ["whether it be . . ."] by means of which an action is shown—exhaustively, depressingly—in the light of the countless motives upon which it may have been based. Yet these paratactic flights reveal the point at which weakness and genius coincide in Proust: the intellectual renunciation, the tested skepticism with which he approached things. After the self-satisfied inwardness of Romanticism, Proust came along—determined, as Jacques Rivière puts it, not to give the least credence to the "Sirènes intérieures" ["internal Sirens"]. "Proust approaches experience without the slightest metaphysical interest, without the slightest penchant for construction, without the slightest tendency to console." Nothing is truer than that. And thus the basic feature of this work, too, which Proust kept proclaiming as having been planned, is anything but the result of construction. But it is as planned as the lines on the palm of our hand or the arrangement of the stamen in a calyx. Completely worn out, Proust, that aged child, fell back on the bosom of nature—not to suckle from it, but to dream to its heartbeat. One must picture him in this state of weakness to understand how felicitously Jacques Rivière interpreted the weakness when he wrote: "Marcel Proust died of the same inexperience which permitted him to write his works. He died of ignorance of the world, and because he did not know how to change the conditions of his life which had begun to crush him. He died because he did not know how to make a fire or open a window." And, to be sure, of his neurasthenic asthma.

The doctors were powerless in the face of this malady; not so the writer, who very systematically placed it in his service. To begin with the most external aspect, he was a perfect stage director of his illness. For months he connected, with devastating irony, the image of an admirer who had sent him flowers with their odor, which he found unbearable. Depending on the ups and downs of his malady he alarmed his friends, who dreaded and longed for the moment when the writer would suddenly appear in their drawing rooms long after midnight—"brisé de fatigue" and for just five minutes, as he said—only to stay till the gray of dawn, too tired to get out of his chair or interrupt his conversation. Even as a writer of letters he extracted the most singular effects from his ailment. "The wheezing of my breath is drowning out the sounds of my pen and of a bath which is being drawn on the floor below." But that is not all, nor is the fact that his sickness removed him from fashionable living. This asthma became part of his art—if indeed his art did not create it. Proust's syntax rhythmically, step by step, enacts his fear of suffocating. And his ironic, philosophical, didactic reflections invariably are the deep breath with which he shakes off the crushing weight of memories. On a larger scale, however, the threatening, suffocating crisis was death, which he was constantly aware of, most of all while he was writing. This is how death confronted Proust, and long before his illness assumed critical dimensions—not as a hypochondriacal whim, but as a "réalité nouvelle," that new reality whose reflections on things and people are the marks of aging. A physiology of style would take us into the innermost core of this creativeness. No one who knows with what great tenacity memories are preserved by the sense of smell—but by smells that are not at all in the memory—will be able to call Proust's sensitivity to smells accidental. To be sure, most memories that we search for come to us as images of faces. Even the free-floating forms of *la mémoire involontaire* are still in large part isolated—though enigmatically present—images of faces. For this very reason, anyone who wishes to surrender knowingly to the innermost sway of this work must place himself in a special stratum—the bottommost—of this involuntary remembrance, a stratum in which the materials of memory no longer appear singly, as images, but tell us about a whole, amorphously and formlessly, indefinitely and weightily, in the same way the weight of the fishing net tells a fisherman about his catch. Smell—this is the sense of weight experienced by someone who casts his nets into the sea of the *temps perdu*. And his sentences are the entire muscular activity of the intelligible body; they contain the whole enormous effort to raise this catch.

For the rest, the closeness of the symbiosis between this particular creativity and this particular illness is demonstrated most clearly by the fact that in Proust there never was a breakthrough of that heroic defiance with which other creative people have risen up against their infirmities. And therefore one can say, from another point of view, that so close a complicity with life and the course of the world as Proust's would inevitably have led to ordinary, indolent contentment on any basis but that of such great and constant suffering. As it was, however, this illness was destined to have its place in the great work process—a place assigned to it by a furor devoid of desires or regrets. For the second time, there arose a scaffold like the one on which Michelangelo, his head thrown back, painted the Creation on the ceiling of the Sistine Chapel: the sickbed on which Marcel Proust held aloft the countless pages covered with his handwriting, dedicating them to the creation of his microcosm.

Published in *Die literarische Welt*, June–July 1929; revised 1934. *Gesammelte Schriften*, II, 310–324. Translated by Harry Zohn.

Notes

1. "The incurable imperfection in the very essence of the present."
2. The *Almanach de Gotha* is a journal that chronicles the social activities of the French aristocracy.
3. Henri de Régnier (1864–1936) was a prominent French poet. Ernest Renan (1823–1892) was a French philosopher, historian, and scholar of religion. Louis de Rouvroy, duc de Saint-Simon (1675–1755), was a soldier, statesman, and writer, whose *Mémoires* depict the French court under Louis XIV and Louis XV.
4. Maurice Barrès (1862–1923) was a French writer and politician whose individualism and nationalism were influential in the early twentieth century. The phrase translates: "A Persian poet in a porter's lodge."
5. The *camorra* was a secret Italian criminal society that arose in Naples in the nineteenth century.
6. "Ah! How big the world is by lamplight, / But how small in the eyes of memory!" Charles Baudelaire, "Le Voyage."
7. Charles Péguy (1873–1914) was a French poet and philosopher whose work brought together Christianity, socialism, and French nationalism.

The Great Art of Making Things Seem Closer Together

The great art of making things seem closer together. In reality. Or from where we are standing; in memory. "Ah! que le monde est grand à la clarté des lampes! / Aux yeux du souvenir que le monde est petit!"[1] This is the mysterious power of memory—the power to generate nearness. A room we inhabit whose walls are *closer* to us than to a visitor. This is what is homey about home. In nurseries we remember, the walls seem closer to each other than they really are, than they would be if we saw them today. The sight of them tears us apart because we have become attached to them. The great traveler is the person who passes through cities and countries with anamnesis; and because everything seems closer to everything else, and hence to him, since he is in their midst, all his senses respond to every nuance as truth. The distanced Romantic is as ignorant of this as the Positivist.

Fragment written no later than mid-1929; unpublished in Benjamin's lifetime. *Gesammelte Schriften*, VI, 203. Translated by Rodney Livingstone.

Notes

1. "Ah! How big the world is by lamplight, / But how small in the eyes of memory!" Charles Baudelaire, "Le Voyage."

Milieu Theoreticians

If we reflect how long the belief in disguises survived—how farce throughout the ages, Shakespeare's high comedy, and even the detective story of the late nineteenth century found it quite unproblematic to work with the confusions that result from disguises—it must be a matter of considerable astonishment to see how reluctant people are to accept such devices in more recent times. When it comes to disguises, they refuse to see the joke, and in the modern novel such mistaken identities are frowned on. Yet this dogged insistence on the unmistakable, unique singularity of the body comes at precisely the moment when philanthropists, the disciples of Proust, and psychoanalysts assure us that all possibilities dwell within each of us, and that nothing could be more out-of-date and philistine than the belief in the unity of personality. What can be behind this?

Fragment written in 1929; unpublished in Benjamin's lifetime. *Gesammelte Schriften,* VI, 203–204. Translated by Rodney Livingstone.

Children's Literature

Dear invisible listeners!

You've all heard people say, "Lord! In my childhood, we weren't so well off! We were all afraid of getting poor marks. We weren't even allowed to walk on the beach barefoot!" But have you ever heard anyone say, "Lord! When I was young, we didn't have such nice games to play!" Or, "When I was little, there weren't such wonderful story books!" No. Whatever people read or played with in their childhood not only seems in memory to have been the most beautiful and best thing possible; it often, wrongly, seems unique. And it is very common to hear adults complaining about the disappearance of toys they used to be able to buy without difficulty in the nearest shop. Remembering *these* things, everyone becomes a *laudator temporis acti,* a reactionary. So there must be something special about them. And without going into this for the moment, we should bear in mind that for children books, like everything else, can contain very different things from what adults see in them.

How much one could say—to start with the first reading book—about the child's relationship with the ABC's! From the earliest stages, when each sign is a yoke under which hand and tongue have to humble themselves, to the later stages, when the child masters the sounds with ease and creates his first secret society in the playground jungle of the language of robbers and games counting peas. There can be no doubt that no pirate stories or ghost stories will grip the adolescent boy as powerfully as his ABC-book did when he was little. It is true that the earliest reading primers approached children with naive pedagogic skill. These "voice books" were based on onomatopoeia. The O rang out in the mouth of a drayman urging his horses on in the illustration; the *Sh* comes from a woman shooing the hens in another picture; the *R* is a dog growling; and the *S* is a hissing snake. But this onomatopoeia soon gave way to other things. After the Counter-Reformation, we find primers in which the startled child is presented with the majesty of script, full of clouds of arabesques and high falutin phrases. This was followed by the fans and the caste system of the eighteenth century, in which the words to be read were placed grimly together in military rank-and-file and the capital letters were sergeants issuing orders to their nouns. From this period date primers with covers that hold out the promise of 248 pictures. When you look at them more closely, you find that the whole book has only eight pages and the pictures stand packed together in tiny frames. Of course, no primer can be so eccentric as to prevent a child from taking what it needs from it, as Jean Paul shows in his delightful description of his schoolmaster Wuz: "He wrote the alphabet in beautiful copperplate, merrily and without interruption. Between all the black letters he put red ones, so as to attract attention; this is why most German children can still remember the pleasure with which they fished the ready-cooked red letters out from among the black ones like boiled crabs, and enjoyed them."[1]

Of course, schoolteachers soon discovered that not only did children have problems with the primer, but the primer had problems with children. The obvious solution was to separate the visual as far as possible from the word, and even more from the letter. In 1658 the first attempt of this sort appeared: the *Orbis Pictus* of Amos Comenius.[2] It displays all the objects of daily life—including the abstract ones—simply and crudely, in several hundred card-size illustrations. The text was restricted to a German-Latin table of contents. This work is one of the rare great successes in the field of educational children's books; and if you think about it, you can see that it stands at the beginning of two and a half centuries of development—a process that is by no means concluded. Today less than ever. The extraordinary contemporary relevance of a visually based method of instruction stems from the fact that a new, standardized and nonverbal sign system is now emerging in the most varied walks of life—transport, art, statistics. At this point, an educational problem coincides with a comprehensive cultural one, which could be summed up in the slogan: Up with the sign and down with the word! Perhaps we shall soon see picture books that introduce children to the new sign language of transport or even statistics. Among the older books, the milestones are Comenius' *Orbis Pictus,* Basedow's *Elementarwerk* [Elementary Work], and Bertuch's *Bilderbuch für Kinder* [Picture Book for Children]. The latter consists of twelve volumes, each with a hundred colored engravings; it appeared under Bertuch's direction from 1792 to 1847. The care lavished on its production shows the dedication with which books were produced for children at the time. To provide a picture book with text, to give it a basic textual form without turning it into a primer, is a difficult, almost impossible task. It has seldom been solved. All the more remarkable is the brilliant picture book by Johann Paul Wich, *Steckenpferd und Puppe* [Hobbyhorse and Doll], which appeared in Nördlingen in 1843. It contains the following verses:

> Before the little town there sits a little dwarf,
> Behind the little dwarf there stands a little hill,
> From the little hill there flows a little stream,
> Upon the little stream there swims a little roof,
> Beneath the little roof there is a little room,
> In the little room there sits a little boy,
> Behind the little boy there stands a little bench,
> Upon the little bench there stands a little chest,
> In the little chest there lies a little box,
> In the little box there sits a little nest,
> Before the little nest there sits a little cat,
> For certain I'll remember to note the little spot.

If there is any field in the whole world where specialization is bound to fail, it must be in creating things for children. And the beginning of the decline in children's literature can be seen at the moment it fell into the hands of the specialists. I mean the decline of children's *literature,* not of children's *books.* For it was a stroke of good luck that for a long time the educational experts paid only cursory attention to the books' illustrations, or at least proved unable to set valid norms for them. So in this sphere we see maintained something that became increasingly rare in literature— namely, the pure seriousness of mastery and the pure playfulness of the dilettante, both of which create for children *without doing so deliberately.* Rochow's *Kinderfreund* [The Child's Friend] of 1772, the first reader, is at the same time the beginning of "literature for young people." It is important to distinguish two phases: the edifying, moral Age of Enlightenment, which came to meet the child, and the sentimental period of the nineteenth century, which insinuated itself into his mind. The first was certainly not as boring and the second not as mendacious as the upstart educational theory of our own day claims, but both are characterized by a sterile mediocrity. A delightful, linguistically catastrophic example that stands on the frontiers of both genres will illustrate the point:

> Having arrived home, Emma at once set to work, for she had promised Auguste to embroider the letters *A.v.T.* on six handkerchiefs . . . Auguste and Wilhelmine sat on either side of her; Charlotte and Sophie, who had brought their own sewing with them, did likewise. It was most agreeable to see the four young girls so diligently at work, each eager to surpass the others.
> As they sat working, Auguste wished to make use of the time for further instruction. So she asked Emma:

"What day is it today?"

"I think it is Tuesday."

"You are mistaken, child. Yesterday was Sunday."

"In that case it is Monday."

"Correct: Monday. How many days are there in a week?"

"Seven."

"And how many in a month?—Do you know?"

"How many?—I think you have told me several times that, with respect to the days, the months are not all alike."

"That is so. Four months have thirty days, seven thirty-one, and a single one has twenty-eight and sometimes twenty-nine days."

"Thirty days is a very long time."

"Can you count as far as that?"

"No."

"How many fingers do you have?"

"Ten."

"Count your fingers three times and that gives you thirty, as many as there are days in four of the months of the year."

"That's a century."

"A century?—Where did you pick that word up?—Do you know what a century is?"

"No, I do not."

"Yet you use a word you do not understand?—That smacks of boasting! You wish to be thought cleverer than you are. A century consists of one hundred years, each year consisting of twelve months. The months, as I have already told you, have either thirty or thirty-one days, with one exception. A day has twenty-four hours, the hours are divided into minutes, and these are divided into seconds. There are sixty minutes in an hour."

"A second is very small, isn't it?"

"A second flies away like lightning—it is a moment."

"So a person's life consists of an infinite number of seconds?"

"And it still flies past very quickly. And quick as it is, we should never forget our transition into the next world. In other words, we should always be mindful of our duty toward God, our fellow human beings, and ourselves, so that when the Creator and Ruler of the universe resolves in His wisdom to summon us from here, we shall be found worthy to enter Heaven, where we will find our reward for having been pious and righteous here on earth."

"What will happen to little girls who have been naughty?"

"They will go to Hell."

"Will they be unhappy there?"

"Of course! They experience the torments of remorse for their offenses forever."

"Forever?"—Oh, I shall take good care not to be naughty!"

Auguste saw full well that Emma could not understand this as clearly as she, since she had read it in her catechism and had had it thoroughly explained to her. She would have been better advised to frighten her young pupil by telling her about caning or about Ruprecht the farmhand, instead of explaining to her about Hell."[3]

While this could scarcely be surpassed in absurdity, there are many works that are superior in quality. Nevertheless, it is significant that despite Johanna Spyri's beautiful and justly famous *Stories for Children and Those Who Love Children,* subsequent trends in children's literature have produced no masterpiece. Yet we do possess a masterpiece of morally edifying literature that is also a masterwork of the German language. This is Hebel's *Treasure Chest.*[4] Of course, strictly speaking, it is not intended for young people as such but is a product of the Philanthropist interest in the masses, particularly the rural reading public.[5] If we may attempt briefly to define this incomparable prose stylist who combines in an almost unfathomable unity the expansiveness of the epic writer with the brevity of the legislator, we might say that the crucial feature of Hebel is the way in which he overcomes the abstract morality of the Enlightenment through a political, theological morality. Yet since this is never done in general terms but always case by case, it is scarcely possible for us to give an idea of it except in concrete terms. To use a metaphor: when he tells his stories, it is as if a clockmaker were showing us his clock, explaining the springs and the cogwheels individually. Suddenly (Hebel's moral always comes suddenly), he turns it around and we see what the time is. And these stories further resemble a clock in that they arouse our earliest childhood astonishment and never cease to accompany us our whole life long.

Some years ago a literary magazine hit upon the idea, as happens from time to time, of asking a number of well-known people what their favorite childhood book had been. The answers undoubtedly included children's literature. But what was remarkable was that the great majority named works like the *Leather-Stocking Tales, Gulliver's Travels, Treasure Island, Baron Münchhausen,* the *1001 Nights,* Andersen, Grimm, Karl May, and Wörishöffer. Many of them named forgotten works whose authors they no longer knew. But when we try to put some sort of order into their varied responses, it turns out that hardly any of the books mentioned were expressly written for children or young people. Almost all of them are great works of world literature, cheap novels, or fairy tales. Among the respondents was Charlie Chaplin. His choice was *David Copperfield.* This provides us with a great example to study just what a children's book—or rather, a book that is read by a child—can mean. *David Copperfield* paved the way for that great man's intuition. A French critic has in fact made a very acute comparison between the art of Dickens and that of Chaplin. And Chaplin himself "has told us that the idea of creating his stock character—the fellow with the bowler hat, jerky walk, little toothbrush moustache, and walking stick—first occurred to him on seeing office workers walking along the

Strand." And how close other typical figures in his films are to the gloomy London of Oliver Twist or David Copperfield: "the shy, young, winsome girl; the burly lout who is always ready to use his fists and then to take to his heels when he sees that people aren't afraid of him; the arrogant gentleman who can be recognized by his top hat."

But it must not be imagined that young people growing up can obtain substantial, healthy sustenance only from the masterpieces of Cervantes, Dickens, Swift, or Defoe. It is also available in certain, though by no means all, works of cheap literature, of that colportage which emerged simultaneously with the rise of technological civilization and the leveling of culture which was not unconnected with it. The dismantling of the old, hierarchical spheres of society had just been completed. This meant that the noblest and most refined substances had often sunk to the bottom, and so it happens that the person who can see more deeply can find the elements he really needs in the lower depths of writing and graphic art rather than in the acknowledged documents of culture. Quite recently Ernst Bloch wrote a charming essay along these lines in which he attempted a vindication of the much disparaged Karl May. And one could mention many other books that one was almost ashamed to ask for on borrowing day in the school library, or even in the local paper shop: *Die Regulatoren in Arkansas, Unter dem Äquator, Nena Sahib.*[6] And if these books tend to transcend the horizon of their young readers, that only made them more exciting and impressive. For such concepts and turns of phrase seemed to contain the talisman that would guide young people as they successfully crossed the threshold from childhood into the Promised Land of adulthood. And this is why everyone has always devoured them.

"Devouring books." A strange metaphor. One that makes you think. It is true that in the world of art no form is so affected in the course of enjoyment, is so deformed and destroyed, as narrative prose. Perhaps it really is possible to compare reading and consuming. Above all, we should bear in mind that the reasons we need nourishment and the reasons we eat are not perhaps identical. The older theory of nourishment is perhaps so instructive because eating is its starting point. It claimed that we obtain nourishment by absorbing the spirits of the things we have eaten. Now, it is true that we do not obtain nourishment in that way, but we do eat via a process of absorption that is rather more than a matter of absorbing what we need to live. And our reading, too, involves such a process of absorption. That is to say, not to increase our experience, our store of memories and experiences. Such psychological substitution theories are the theories of nourishment which maintain that from the blood we consume we obtain our blood, from the bones we devour come our bones, and so forth. But matters are not as simple as that. We do not read to increase our experiences; we read to increase ourselves. And this applies particularly to children who always read in this way. That is to say, in their reading they absorb; they do not empathize. Their reading is much more closely related to their growth and their sense of power than to their education and their knowledge of the world. This is why their reading is as great as any genius that is to be found in the books they read. And this is what is special about children's books.

Radio talk broadcast by Südwestdeutschen Rundfunk, August 1929. *Gesammelte Schriften*, VII, 250–257. Translated by Rodney Livingstone.

Notes

1. Jean Paul Richter (1763–1825) wrote a series of wildly extravagant, highly imaginative novels that combine fantasy and realism. The story "Das Leben des vergnügten Schulmeisterlein Maria Wutz in Auenthal" (The Life of the Satisfied Little Teacher Maria Wutz in Auenthal) appeared in 1793. It recounts the search for happiness of the pleasantly eccentric teacher named in the title.
2. The full title is *Orbis Sensualium Pictus* (The Visible World in Pictures).
3. *Wie Auguste und Wilhelmine ihre Puppe erzogen: Von einer Kinderfreundin* (How Auguste and Wilhelmine Educated Their Doll: By a Children's Friend) was published in Berlin in 1837.
4. Johann Peter Hebel's *Schatzkästlein des rheinischen Hausfreunds* (Treasure Chest of the Rhenish Family Friend) is a compendium of his poetry and prose published in the *Badischer Landkalendar,* an annual publication not unlike the American *Old Farmer's Almanac.*
5. Philanthropism was a pedagogical reform movement of the late eighteenth century. Its main theorist was Johann Bernhard Basedow (1723–1790), whose school—the Philanthropin, in Dessau—became the model for a number of similar institutions throughout Germany and Switzerland.
6. *Die Regulatoren in Arkansas* (The Pendulums in Arkansas) and *Unter dem Äquator* (Under the Equator) are by Friedrich Gerstacker. *Nina Sahib* is by Sir John Retcliffe (Hermann Ottomar Friedrich Goedsche).

Robert Walser

We can read much by Robert Walser, but nothing about him.[1] What in fact do we know about the few people among us who are able to take the cheap satirical gloss[2] in the right way—in other words, who do not behave like the hack who tries to ennoble it by "elevating" it to his own level? For the real challenge is to take advantage of the contemptible, unassuming potential of this form to create something which is alive and has a purifying effect. Few people understand this "minor genre," as Alfred Polgar[3] termed it, or realize how many butterflies of hope are repelled by the insolent, rock-like façade of so-called great literature, seeking refuge instead in its unpretentious calyxes. And others never guess the extent of their debt to a Polgar, a Hessel,[4] or a Walser for the many tender or prickly blooms that flourish in the barren wastes of the journalistic forests. In fact, the name Robert Walser is the last that would occur to them. For the first impulse of their meager store of cultural knowledge—their sole asset in literary matters—tells them that what they regard as the complete insignificance of content has to be compensated for by their "cultivated," "refined" attention to form. And in this respect what we find in Robert Walser is a neglect of style that is quite extraordinary and that is also hard to define. For the idea that this insignificant content could be important and that this chaotic scatteredness could be a sign of stamina is the last thing that would occur to the casual observer of Walser's writings.

They are not easy to grasp. For we are accustomed to ponder the mysteries of style through the contemplation of more or less elaborate, fully intended works of art, whereas here we find ourselves confronted by a seemingly quite unintentional, but attractive, even fascinating linguistic wilderness.

And by a self-indulgence that covers the entire spectrum from gracefulness to bitterness. Seemingly unintentional, we said. Critics have sometimes disagreed about whether this is really so. But it is a fruitless quarrel, as we perceive when we recall Walser's admission that he never corrected a single line in his writing. We do not have to believe this, but would be well advised to do so. For we can set our minds at rest by realizing that to write yet never correct what has been written implies both the absence of intention and the most fully considered intentionality.

So far so good. But this cannot prevent us from trying to get to the bottom of this neglect of style. We have already asserted that his neglect makes use of every conceivable form. We should now add: with a single exception. And this exception is one of the most common sort—namely, one in which only content and nothing else counts. Walser is so little concerned with the way in which he writes that everything other than what he has to say recedes into the background. We could claim that what he has to say is exhausted in the process. This calls for explanation. And further investigation alerts us to a very Swiss feature of Walser's writing: his reticence [*Scham*]. The following story has been told of Arnold Böcklin, his son Carlo, and Gottfried Keller.[5] One day they were sitting in an inn, as they frequently did. Their regular table was well known for the taciturn, reserved habits of the drinking companions. On this occasion the group sat together in silence. The young Böcklin finally broke the lengthy silence with the words, "It's hot"; and after a further quarter of an hour had passed, his father added, "And there's no wind." As for Keller, he waited for a while, but finally got up and left, saying, "I won't drink with chatterboxes." The peasant linguistic reticence [*Sprachscham*] that is captured in this eccentric joke is typical of Walser. Scarcely has he taken up his pen than he is overwhelmed by a mood of desperation. Everything seems to be on the verge of disaster; a torrent of words pours from him in which the only point of every sentence is to make the reader forget the previous one. When in the course of a virtuoso piece he transforms Schiller's monologue "Along this narrow pathway must he come" into prose, he begins with the classic words, "Along this narrow pathway." But then his Wilhelm Tell is overcome by self-doubt, appears weak, insignificant, lost. He continues, "Along this narrow pathway must he come, I think."[6]

No doubt, such writing has its precedents. This chaste, artful clumsiness in all linguistic matters is heir to a tradition of folly. If Polonius, the model for all windbags, is a juggler, then Walser is a Bacchus who wreathes himself in linguistic garlands that then trip him up. The garland is in fact the proper image for his sentences. But the idea that stumbles around in them is a thief, a vagabond and genius—like the heroes of his writings. He is unable, incidentally, to depict anyone who is not a "hero"; he cannot free himself from his main characters and has contented himself with three early novels so that he can henceforth consort exclusively with his hundred favorite rascals.[7]

It is well known that the Germanic languages are particularly rich in heroes who are windbags, wastrels, and thieves, and who in general have gone to the dogs. Knut Hamsun, a master of such characters, has recently been discovered and celebrated. Eichendorff who created his Ne'er-do-well and Hebel his Firebrand Fred are others.[8] How do Walser's characters fare in such company? And where do they spring from? We know where Eichendorff's Ne'er-do-well comes from: he comes from the woods and dales of Romantic Germany. Firebrand Fred comes from the rebellious, enlightened petty bourgeoisie of the Rhenish cities around the turn of the nineteenth century. Hamsun's characters come from the primeval world of the fiords—they are drawn to the trolls by their homesickness. And Walser's? Perhaps from the Glarn Alps? Or the meadows of Appenzell, where he hails from? Far from it. They come from the night at its blackest—a Venetian night, if you will, illuminated by the faint lamps of hope—with a little of the party spirit shining in their eyes, but distraught and sad to the point of tears. The tears they shed are his prose. For sobbing is the melody of Walser's loquaciousness. It reveals to us where his favorite characters come from—namely, from insanity and nowhere else. They are figures who have left madness behind them, and this is why they are marked by such a consistently heartrending, inhuman superficiality. If we were to attempt to sum up in a single phrase the delightful yet also uncanny element in them, we would have to say: *they have all been healed.* Admittedly, we are never shown this process of healing, unless we venture to approach his "Schneewittchen" [Snow White], one of the profoundest products of modern literature, and one which is enough on its own to explain why this seemingly most fanciful of all writers should have been a favorite author of the inexorable Franz Kafka.

These tales are quite extraordinarily delicate—everyone realizes that. But not everyone notices that they are the product not of the nervous tension of the decadent, but of the pure and vibrant mood of a convalescent. "I am horrified by the thought that I might attain worldly success," he says, in a paraphrase of Franz Moor's speech.[9] All his heroes share this horror. But why? Not from horror of the world, moral resentment, or pathos, but for wholly Epicurean reasons. They wish to enjoy themselves, and in this respect they display a quite exceptional ingenuity. Furthermore, they also display a quite exceptional nobility. And a quite exceptional legitimacy. For no one enjoys like a convalescent. The enjoyment of the convalescent has nothing of the orgy about it. His reinvigorated blood courses toward him from mountain streams, and the purer breath on his lips flows down from the treetops. Walser's characters share this childlike nobility with the characters in fairy tales, who likewise emerge from the night and from madness—

namely, from the madness of myth. It is commonly thought that this process of awakening took place in the positive religions. If that is the case, it did not do so in any very straightforward or unambiguous way. The latter has to be sought in that great profane debate with myth that the fairy tale represents. Of course, fairy-tale characters are not like Walser's in any simple manner. They are still struggling to free themselves from their sufferings. Walser begins where the fairy tales stop. "And if they have not died, they live there still." Walser shows *how* they live. His writings—and with this I shall finish, as he begins—are called stories, essays, poetic works, short prose pieces, and the like.

Published in *Das Tagebuch*, September 1929. *Gesammelte Schriften*, II, 324–328. Translated by Rodney Livingstone.

Notes

1. Robert Walser (1878–1956), Swiss author, was a native of Biel (Bern canton). In his youth he was a wanderer; he later worked briefly in a bank, a publisher's office, and a library, but was unemployed for most of his life. After 1933 he was in a series of mental institutions. His work includes three novels but is made up largely of stories, sketches, glosses, and miniatures. It is characterized by a deceptively simple, fluid style that is balanced with irony and absurd elements.

2. The satirical gloss is a recognized literary form in German, more familiar than in English, where the term "gloss" refers mainly either to the interlinear gloss of medieval texts or to marginal comments of the kind Coleridge provides in "The Ancient Mariner." In German the gloss was developed into high art by Karl Kraus, who practiced it throughout his career in his commentaries on other writers and journalists in his periodical *Die Fackel*.

3. Alfred Polgar (1873–1955) was a Viennese journalist and a gifted literary critic and commentator on cultural trends. Many of his essays were collected and published in book form during his lifetime. He was famous for his elegant, ironic style.

4. Franz Hessel was a close friend of Benjamin and had worked with him both on the translation of Proust's *A la recherche du temps perdu* and in the early stages of Benjamin's *Passagen-werk* (Arcades Project). For Benjamin's evaluation of Hessel's importance, see "The Return of the *Flâneur*" and "Review of Hessel's *Heimliches Berlin*," both in this volume.

5. Arnold Böcklin (1827–1901), the Swiss painter, was known for his Romantic treatment of mythological subjects. Gottfried Keller (1819–1890), also a Swiss, was the major exponent of literary realism in German. See Benjamin's essay "Gottfried Keller" in this volume.

6. The quotation comes from the classic monologue in Schiller's *Wilhelm Tell*, Act 4, scene 3. As Tell lies in wait for the tyrant Gessler, he reflects on the moral justification of the murder he is about to commit.

7. The three novels are *Die Geschwister Tanner* (The Tanner Siblings; 1907), *Der Gehülfe* (The Assistant; 1908), which is his best-known work, and *Jacob von Gunten* (1909).

8. Knut Hamsun (1859–1952) was a Norwegian novelist who criticized the American way of life and idealized the farmer's existence. He supported the German invasion of Norway and in 1947 was condemned for treason. His most famous—and extremely popular—novel was *Hunger* (1890). Joseph von Eichendorff (1788–1857) was one of the leading figures of German Romanticism. Known mainly for his lyric poetry, he also wrote the classic novella *Aus dem Leben eines Taugenichts* (Adventures of a Ne'er-do-well; 1826). Johann Peter Hebel (1760–1826) was a journalist and author; he was much esteemed for the use of dialect in his writings, a practice that had fallen prey to eighteenth-century enlightened universalism. As editor and chief writer of the *Badischer Landkalendar,* an annual publication not unlike the American *Old Farmer's Almanac,* Hebel produced an enormous volume of prose and poetry. A typical calendar would include a cosmology embellished with anecdotes and stories, practical advice for the homeowner and farmer, reports on crime and catastrophe, short biographies, riddles, and, finally, political observations on the year just past. Hebel's narrative persona, the "Rhenish Family-Friend," narrates and comments; Sterne-like ironic interjections are not infrequent. See Benjamin's essays on Hebel in Volume 1 of this edition.

9. Franz Moor is the villain in Schiller's play *Die Räuber* (The Robbers).

The Return of the *Flâneur*

Franz Hessel, *Spazieren in Berlin* [On Foot in Berlin] (Leipzig and Vienna: Verlag Dr. Hans Epstein, 1929), 300 pages.

If we were to divide all the existing descriptions of cities into two groups according to the birthplace of the authors, we would certainly find that those written by natives of the cities concerned are greatly in the minority. The superficial pretext—the exotic and the picturesque—appeals only to the outsider. To depict a city as a native would calls for other, deeper motives— the motives of the person who journeys into the past, rather than to foreign parts. The account of a city given by a native will always have something in common with memoirs; it is no accident that the writer has spent his childhood there. Just as Franz Hessel has spent his childhood in Berlin. And if he now sets out and walks through the city, he has nothing of the excited impressionism with which the travel writer approaches his subject. Hessel does not describe; he narrates. Even more, he repeats what he has heard. *Spazieren in Berlin* is an echo of the stories the city has told him ever since he was a child—an epic book through and through, a process of memorizing while strolling around, a book for which memory has acted not as the source but as the Muse. It goes along the streets in front of him, and each street is a vertiginous experience. Each leads downward, if not to the Mothers,[1] then at least to a past that is all the more spellbinding as it is not just the author's own private past. As he walks, his steps create an astounding resonance on the asphalt. The gaslight shining down on the pavement casts an ambiguous light on this double floor. The city as a mnemonic for the lonely walker: it conjures up more than his childhood and youth, more than its own history.

What it reveals is the endless spectacle of *flânerie* that we thought had been finally relegated to the past. And can it be reborn here, in Berlin of all places, where it never really flourished? We should point out in reply that Berliners have changed. Their problematic national pride in their capital has started to yield to their love of Berlin as a hometown. And at the same time, Europe has witnessed a sharpening of the sense of reality, the awareness of chronicle, document, and detail. In this situation we see the arrival of someone who is just young enough to have experienced this change, and just old enough to have been personally acquainted with the last classics of *flânerie*: Apollinaire and Léautaud. The *flâneur* is the creation of Paris. The wonder is that it was not Rome. But perhaps in Rome even dreaming is forced to move along streets that are too well-paved. And isn't the city too full of temples, enclosed squares, and national shrines to be able to enter undivided into the dreams of the passer-by, along with every paving stone, every shop sign, every flight of steps, and every gateway? The great reminiscences, the historical *frissons*—these are all so much junk to the *flâneur*, who is happy to leave them to the tourist. And he would be happy to trade all his knowledge of artists' quarters, birthplaces, and princely palaces for the scent of a single weathered threshold or the touch of a single tile—that which any old dog carries away. And much may have to do with the Roman character. For it is not the foreigners but they themselves, the Parisians, who made Paris into the Promised Land of *flâneurs,* into "a landscape made of living people," as Hofmannsthal once called it. Landscape—this is what the city becomes for the *flâneur.* Or, more precisely, the city splits into its dialectical poles. It becomes a landscape that opens up to him and a parlor that encloses him.

"Give the city a little of your love for landscape," Fritz Hessel tells Berliners. They wanted only to see the countryside in their city. After all, didn't they have the Tiergarten, that sacred grove of *flânerie* with its views of the sacred façades on the Tiergarten villas; of the tents from which you can see the leaves falling to the ground even more mournfully during the jazz than usual; and of the Neuer See, whose bays and wooded islands are engraved in the mind—the lake "where in winter we artfully traced big figure-eights in the ice like Dutchmen, and in autumn clambered down into a canoe from the wooden bridge by the boathouse with the lady of our choice, who took over the rudder"?[2] But even if none of this existed, the city would still be full of landscape. Berliners would need only to see the sky stretched out above the arches of the elevated railway, as blue as over the mountain chains of the Engadine; to see how silence arises from the din as from the surf; to see how the little streets in the inner city reflect the times of day like a mountain hollow. Of course, the true life of the inhabitants— which fills the city to the brim and without which this knowledge would not exist—does not come cheaply. "We Berliners," says Hessel, "must inhabit our city much more fully." He undoubtedly wants this to be under-stood literally, and to be applied less to the houses than to the streets. For it is they that are the dwelling place of the eternally restless being who is eternally on the move, the being that experiences, learns, knows, and imag-ines as much between the houses as the individual between his four walls. For the masses as well as the *flâneur,* glossy enameled corporate nameplates are as good a wall-decoration as an oil painting is for the homebody sitting in his living room, or even better; the fire walls are their desks, the news-paper kiosk their library, letterboxes their bronze statuettes, benches their boudoir, and the café terrace the bay window from which they can look down on their property. Wherever asphalt workers hang their coats on iron railings, that's their hall; and the gateway that leads from the row of courtyards into the open is the entrance into the chambers of the city.

Even in Hessel's earlier, masterly "Vorschule des Journalismus" [Primer of Journalism],[3] the question of what "dwelling" means could be seen as an underlying motif. Just as every tried-and-true experience also includes its opposite, so here the perfected art of the *flâneur* includes a knowledge of "dwelling." The primal image of "dwelling," however, is the matrix or shell—that is, the thing which enables us to read off the exact figure of whatever lives inside it. Now, if we recollect that not only people and animals but also spirits and above all images can inhabit a place, then we have a tangible idea of what concerns the *flâneur* and of what he looks for. Namely, images, wherever they lodge. The *flâneur* is the priest of the genius loci. This unassuming passer-by, with his clerical dignity, his detective's intuition, and his omniscience, is not unlike Chesterton's Father Brown, that master detective.[4] You have to follow the author into the "Old West" of Berlin to get to know this side of him and see how he sniffs out the *lares* beneath the threshold, how he celebrates the last monuments of an ancient culture of dwelling.[5] The last, because the cult of "dwelling" in the old sense, with the idea of security at its core, has now received its death knell. Giedion, Mendelssohn, and Le Corbusier are converting human habitations into the transitional spaces of every imaginable force and wave of light and air.[6] The coming architecture is dominated by the idea of transparency—not just of space but also of the week, if we are to believe the Russians, who intend to abolish Sundays in favor of leisure-time shifts.[7] But it should not be thought that a single reverential glance at traditional buildings is enough to reveal the entire antiquity of the "Old West" to which Hessel introduces his readers. Only a man in whom modernity has already announced its presence, however quietly, can cast such an original and "early" glance at what has only just become old.

Among the *plebs deorum* of the caryatids and Atlases, Pomonas and putti, that Hessel reveals to the reader, his favorites are those once dominant figures that have now been reduced to *penates*—unassuming household gods on dusty landings, in nameless hall niches, the guardians of rites of passage who once served as presiding spirits every time someone stepped over a wooden or metaphorical threshold.[8] He is unable to tear himself away from them, and their power wafts over him even when their images have long since vanished, or have become unrecognizable. Berlin has few gates, but he is familiar with the lesser transitions, those that separate the city from the surrounding lowland, or one district from another: building sites, bridges, urban railway overpasses, and squares. They are all honored here and recorded, to say nothing of the transitional hours, the sacred twelve minutes or seconds of microcosmic life, that correspond to the Twelfth Nights of the macrocosm and can seem the opposite of sacred at first sight. "The tea dances of Friedrichstadt also have their instructive hour before opening time—the hour when the lights are dimmed, the instruments are still in their cases, and the ballet mistress is eating a snack and chatting with the wardrobe girl or the waiter."

Baudelaire is the source of the cruel *aperçu* that the city changes faster than a human heart. Hessel's book is full of consoling leave-taking formulas for Berlin's inhabitants. It is a genuine manual of leave-taking. And who would not be inspired to take his departure if his words could strike to the heart of Berlin, as Hessel does with his Muses from Magdeburger Strasse? "They have long since vanished. Like quarry stones, they stood there decorously holding their ball or pencil, those that still had hands. Their white, stone eyes followed our footsteps, and the fact that these heathen girls gazed at us has become a part of our lives."

And: "We see only what looks at us. We can do only . . . what we cannot help doing." The philosophy of the *flâneur* has never been more profoundly grasped than in these words of Hessel's. Once, when he was walking through Paris, he saw women concièrges sitting and sewing in the cool doorways in the afternoon. He felt they looked at him like his nurse. Nothing is more revealing about the difference between the two cities—Paris, his late, mature hometown, and Berlin, his early, strict home—than the fact that this great city walker was soon noticed and regarded with suspicion by Berliners. This is why he entitles the first chapter of his book "The Suspect." In it we can gauge the extent of the prevailing resistance to *flânerie* in Berlin, and see with what bitter and threatening expressions both things and people pursue the dreamer. It is here, not in Paris, where it becomes clear to us how easy it is for the *flâneur* to depart from the ideal of the philosopher out for a stroll, and to assume the features of the werewolf at large in the social jungle—the creature of whom Poe has given the definitive description in his story "The Man of the Crowd."

So much for the "Suspect." Chapter 2, however, is entitled "I Am Learning." Now, "learning," too, is one of the author's favorite words. Writers mostly call it "studying," when they describe their attitude to a city; yet a whole world separates these words. Anyone can study, but learning is something you can only do if you are there for the duration. Hessel has an overriding love of the enduring, an aristocratic distaste for nuances. There is a kind of experience that craves the unique, the sensational, and another kind that seeks out eternal sameness.[9] "Paris," it was said years ago, "is the narrow latticework balcony in front of a thousand windows; the red, tin cigar in front of a thousand *tabacs;* the zinc counter in the little bar; the concièrge's cat." In much the same way, the *flâneur* memorizes lists like a child, insisting like an old man on the truth of what he knows. We now have a similar register for Berlin, a comparable Egyptian Dream Book for those who are awake. And if a Berliner is willing to explore his city for any treasures other than neon advertisements, he will grow to love this book.

Published in *Die literarische Welt,* October 1929. *Gesammelte Schriften,* III, 194–199. Translated by Rodney Livingstone.

Notes

1. A reference to Goethe's *Faust, Part II,* Act 1, in which Faust visits "the Mothers," vaguely defined mythological figures, in search of the secret that will enable him to discover Helen of Troy. The phrase has now entered into proverbial speech, evoking the search for the ultimate mysteries of life.
2. "Tiergarten" refers to the large park in the center of Berlin, to the neighborhood surrounding it, and to the zoo which gives the park its name. The Neuer See is a large lake in the park.
3. Franz Hessel, "Vorschule des Journalismus," in Hessel, *Nachfeier* [Belated Celebration] (Berlin: Ernst Rowohlt, 1929). [Benjamin's note]
4. The English author G. K. Chesterton (1874–1936) was best-known for his "Father Brown" novels, which use the figure of the sleuthing priest to mix detective fiction and social analysis.
5. The "Old West" is the west-central area of Berlin that was built up before the city expanded into the wealthier sections of the "New West." *Lares,* in the ancient Roman pantheon, were household protective deities.
6. Sigfried Giedion (1888–1968) was a Swiss architect and theorist whose book *Bauen in Frankreich* (Construction in France) exerted a deep influence on Benjamin. Erich Mendelssohn (1887–1953) was a German architect best known for his "expressionist" work in northern Germany. Le Corbusier (pseudonym of Charles-Edouard Jeanneret; 1887–1965) was one of the twentieth century's most influential architects. Born in Switzerland, he became part of the first generation of practitioners of the International Style. His work combined stark functionalism with bold, expressionistic elements.
7. A reference to the revision, in autumn of 1929, of the Soviet calendar: the week was abolished as a unit of temporal measurement and replaced by staggered four-day shifts for workers. The revision failed to have the desired effect on

industrial production, and the Soviet Union returned to the Gregorian calendar in 1940.

8. *Plebs deorum* is Latin for "the mob of the gods"—that is, the multitude of lesser deities. Pomona is the Roman goddess of fruit.

9. Benjamin here distinguishes *Erlebnis,* a single, noteworthy experience, from *Erfahrung,* "experience" in the sense of learning from life over an extended period.

Short Shadows (I)

Platonic Love. The nature and character of a love is most sharply defined by the fate that links it to someone's name—the person's *first* name. Marriage takes a woman's original surname from her and replaces it with the man's, but this does not leave her first name unaffected—and this holds good for almost every sexual encounter. Her original name is surrounded and veiled by pet names that conceal it, often for years or even decades. In this broad sense—and only with respect to the destiny of a name, not of a body—marriage stands in contrast to Platonic love in its only authentic, significant meaning: that of the love which does not satisfy its desire in the name but which loves the beloved in her name, possesses her through the name, and worships her name. The fact that Platonic love preserves and guards the name—the first name—without changing it is the true expression of the tension, the love from afar, that is its distinguishing mark. Like rays from a glowing nucleus, the existence of the loved one proceeds from her name, and even works created by the lover proceed from the same source. In this sense the *Divine Comedy* is nothing but the aura surrounding the name of Beatrice, the most powerful representation of the idea that all the forces and figures of the cosmos arise from the name born of love.

Once Is as Good as Never. The truth of this dictum is demonstrated most surprisingly in the realm of the erotic. So long as you have pursued a woman in constant uncertainty as to whether your pleas will be heard, fulfillment can come about only amid these doubts—namely, as redemption, resolution. But scarcely have your desires been fulfilled in this way when a new and unbearable yearning—for naked, bare fulfillment in itself—takes their place in an instant [*im Nu*]. In memory, the first fulfillment is canceled out more or less in the process of resolution—that is to say, in its function vis-à-vis doubt. It becomes abstract. So this once becomes never, when measured against a naked, absolute fulfillment. Conversely, it can also devalue itself erotically as a naked, absolute event. Such is the case when a mundane adventure gets under our skin, when it takes us brutally by surprise; and we annul that first time and call it never, because we are searching for the vanishing-lines of expectation in order to experience how the woman rises up before us as their point of intersection. In Don Juan, the lucky child of love, the secret is the way he simultaneously achieves—in a flash—resolution and the sweetest pursuit in all his adventures, the way he repeats the expectation in the midst of ecstasy and anticipates the resolution in the act of wooing. This once-and-for-all of pleasure, this interlacing of different time frames can be expressed only in music. Don Juan requires music as the magnifying glass of love.

Poverty Always Has to Foot the Bill. No gala loge is as prohibitively expensive as the entrance ticket to God's own nature. And even nature—which surrenders so readily, as we've all learned, to vagabonds and beggars, scoundrels and ne'er-do-wells—maintains its most consoling, peaceful, and pure countenance for the rich when it passes through the large French windows into their cool, shaded rooms.—This is the inexorable truth that the Italian villa teaches anyone entering its gates for the first time in order to get a view of lake and mountains—a view next to which everything he has seen outside pales, like a Kodak photograph next to the work of a Leonardo. Indeed, the landscape hangs for him in the window frame, and only for him has God's master hand added His signature.

Too Close. I dreamed I was on the Left Bank of the Seine, in front of Notre Dame. I stood there, but saw nothing that resembled Notre Dame. A brick building loomed, revealing the extremities of its massive shape, above a high wooden fence. But I *was* standing in front of Notre Dame, overwhelmed. And what overwhelmed me was yearning—yearning for the very same Paris in which I found myself in my dream. So what was the source of this yearning? And where did this utterly distorted, unrecognizable object come from?—It was like that because I had come too close to it in my dream. The unprecedented yearning that had overcome me at the heart of what I had longed for was not the yearning that flies to the image from afar. It was the blissful yearning that has already crossed the threshold of image and possession, and knows only the power of the name—the power from which the loved one lives, is transformed, ages, rejuvenates itself, and, imageless, is the refuge of all images.

Keeping Mum about One's Plans. Few kinds of superstition are as widespread as the one that keeps people from talking to each other about their most important intentions and projects. Not only is this type of behavior seen in all classes of the population, but all manner of human motives, from the most humdrum to the most complex, seem to be affected by it. Indeed, what is closest to us seems so sensible and commonplace that many people will regard talk of superstition as pointless. Nothing, one might think, is more readily understandable than that a person should wish to keep his failures to himself, and should say nothing about his intentions so as to make sure of this. But that is really the upper layer of motivation, the surface varnish that conceals the deeper factors. Underneath is the second layer: the obscure knowledge that resolve weakens through the mere fact of physical release, the physical substitute satisfaction in talking about something. People have rarely taken the destructive character of speech—revealed to us in the simplest experiences—as seriously as it deserves. If you reflect how almost every important plan is linked to a name, indeed is inseparable from it, then you see how costly uttering that name can be. There can be no doubt, however, that this second layer is succeeded by a third one. This is the idea of using other people's ignorance—above all, the ignorance of one's friends—to achieve a superior position, like someone climbing the steps of a throne. And as if that weren't enough, there is a final layer, the bitterest one, whose depths Leopardi plumbs when he says: "The admission of one's own suffering produces not compassion but pleasure, and arouses not sadness but joy—not just in enemies but in everyone who learns of it, because it provides confirmation that the person affected is less valuable, and that we ourselves are more valuable." But how many people could believe themselves if word of Leopardi's *aperçu* ever reached them? How many wouldn't rather spit it out, repelled by the bitterness of such knowledge? At this point, superstition makes its entrance—the pharmaceutical distillation of the bitterest ingredients whose taste no one would be able to endure in isolation. Man far prefers to obey the dark mysteries embodied in popular customs and proverbs, rather than allow anyone to preach to him of all the harshness and suffering of life, in the language of ordinary common sense.

How to Recognize Your Strengths. By your defeats. Where we failed through weakness, we despise and are ashamed of ourselves. Where we are strong, however, we despise our defeats; we put our misfortune to shame. Should we recognize our strengths through our victories and good fortune!? Who doesn't know that nothing reveals our foibles as much as they? Who hasn't once felt a kind of ecstatic shiver of weakness after a victory in a fight or in love, and wondered: Did I do that? Did victory fall to me, the weakest? It is otherwise with a series of defeats, in which we learn all the tricks of survival and bathe in shame as if it were dragon's blood. Whether it be fame, alcohol, money, or love—wherever someone has his strong point, he knows nothing of honor; he has no fear of disgrace and no inner composure. No Jew haggling with a customer could be more insistent than Casanova with Madame Charpillon. Such people dwell in their strength. It is, of course, a special and monstrous kind of dwelling; that is the price of any strength. It is life inside a tank. If we live inside it, we are stupid and unapproachable, fall into all the ditches, stumble over all the obstacles, churn up a lot of dirt, and violate the earth. But only where we are so besmirched are we unconquerable.

On Belief in Things That Have Been Prophesied. To investigate the circumstances of someone who appeals to dark powers is one of the quickest and surest ways of understanding these powers and learning how to criticize them. For every miracle has two sides: one for the person who performs it, and another for the person to whom it happens. And the second is often more illuminating than the first, because it contains the latter's secret within itself. If someone has had his handwriting analyzed, his palm read, or his horoscope cast, what we would like to ask is: What is happening to him? You would think that the person concerned would start by comparing and examining—by sifting more or less skeptically one assertion after another. But far from it. If anything, you see the opposite—above all, a curiosity about the result, a curiosity as urgent as if he were waiting for information about a matter of great importance, but of which he knew nothing. The fuel for this burning curiosity is vanity. Soon it has become a sea of flames, because now he has come across his own name. Putting forth a person's name has one of the most powerful effects on its owner that can be imagined (Americans have made practical use of this by addressing Smith and Brown in neon lights). But in the case of prophecy, it is natural to combine exposition of the name with the content of what is predicted. The situation here is as follows: The so-called inner image of oneself that we all possess is a set of pure improvisations from one minute to the next. It is determined, so to speak, entirely by the masks that are made available to it. The world is an arsenal of such masks. But the impoverished and desolate human being seeks out the image as a disguise within himself. For we are generally lacking in internal resources. This is why it makes us so happy when someone approaches us with a whole boxful of exotic masks, offering us the more unusual kinds, such as the mask of the murderer, the magnate, or the round-the-world sailor. We are fascinated by the opportunity of looking out through these masks. We see the constellations, the moments in which we really were one or another of these things, or all of them together. We yearn for this game with masks as a kind of intoxication, and it is this that enables fortunetellers and palm-readers and astrologers to earn a living even today. They know how to transport us into one of those silent pauses of fate that only subsequently turn out to have possessed the seed for quite a different lot in life from the one given us. The fact that fate may stop beating, like a heart—this is something we sense with profound, ecstatic terror in those seemingly so meager, seemingly so distorted images of ourselves that the charlatan holds out to us. And we hasten all the more to confirm his predictions, the more thirstily we feel the shadows of the lives we never lived welling up within us.

Short Shadows.   Toward noon, shadows are no more than the sharp, black edges at the feet of things, preparing to retreat silently, unnoticed, into their burrow, their secret being. Then, in its compressed, cowering fullness, comes the hour of Zarathustra—the thinker in "the noon of life," in "the summer garden." For it is knowledge that gives things their sharpest outline, like the sun at its zenith.

Published in *Neue schweizer Rundschau,* November 1929. *Gesammelte Schriften,* IV, 368–373. Translated by Rodney Livingstone.

A Communist Pedagogy

Psychology and ethics are the poles around which bourgeois education theory revolves. One should not assume that it is stagnating. It has assiduous and occasionally important contributors at work. But they can do nothing to mitigate the fact that in this field, as in all others, the thinking of the bourgeoisie is badly riven and divided in an undialectical manner. On the one hand, there is the question of the nature of the child (psychology of childhood and adolescence), and on the other, the goal of education: the complete human being, the citizen. Official education theory is the attempt to harmonize these two elements—the abstract natural disposition and the chimerical ideal—and it progresses by a gradual process of replacing force with cunning. Bourgeois society hypostatizes an absolute childhood or adolescence for whose benefit it postulates the nirvana of the Wandervögel and the Boy Scouts.[1] It hypostatizes a no less absolute concept of adulthood and citizenship which it tricks out with the attributes of idealist philosophy. In reality, each is attuned to the other and they amount to no more than the masks of the useful, socially dependable, class-conscious citizen. That is the unconscious character of this education, and it relies on a strategy of insinuation and empathy. "Children need us more than we need them" is the tacit maxim of this class, underlying everything from the subtle speculations of education theory to its reproductive practice. The children of the bourgeoisie confront it as its heirs; to the disinherited, they are helpers, avengers, liberators. This is the sufficiently drastic distinction. Its educational consequences are incalculable.

In the first place, proletarian education theory is predicated not on two abstract pieces of data but on one concrete reality. The proletarian child is born into his class—more precisely, into the next generation of his class—rather than into a family. From the outset, this is a feature of the younger generation. What determines the child's future is not any doctrinaire educational goal, but the situation of his class. This situation, like life itself, takes possession of him from the very first moment—indeed, while he is still in the womb. Contact with it is wholly aimed at sharpening his consciousness, from an early age, in the school of poverty and suffering. It develops class consciousness. For the proletarian family does not protect the child from the harsh lessons of social knowledge any more than his frayed summer jacket protects him from the biting winter wind. Edwin Hoernle gives numerous examples of revolutionary children's organizations, spontaneous school strikes, children's strikes during the potato harvest, and so on.[2] What distinguishes his views from those of even the best and most honest thinkers in the bourgeois camp is that he devotes serious attention not just to the child and the child's nature, but also to his social situation, something which the "educational reformers" can never allow themselves to see as problematic. Hoernle has devoted the powerful concluding chapter of his book to this problem. He takes issue there with "Austro-Marxist" school reformers and proponents of a "pseudorevolutionary educational idealism." But—as Hoernle shows—what are the hidden but precise functions of elementary and vocational schools, militarism and Church, youth organizations and Boy Scouts, if not to act as the instruments of an antiproletarian education for proletarians? Communist education opposes them, not defensively but as a function of class struggle. It is class struggle on behalf of the children that belong to this class and for whom it exists.

Education is a function of class struggle, but it is not only this. In terms of the Communist creed, it represents the thoroughgoing exploitation of the social environment in the service of revolutionary goals. Since this environment is a matter not just of struggle but also of work, education is also a revolutionary education for work. Offering a program for this, the book is at its best. In the process, it meets up with a point of crucial importance for the Bolsheviks. In Russia, during the Lenin years, the important debate over single-subject or polytechnic education took place. Specialization or universal labor? Marxism's response is: universal labor. Only if man experiences changes of milieu in all their variety, and can mobilize his energies in the service of the working class again and again and in every new context, will he be capable of that universal readiness for action which the Communist program opposes to what Lenin called the "most repulsive feature of the old bourgeois society": its separation of theory and practice. The bold, unpredictable personnel policy of the Russians is wholly the product of this new, nonhumanist, and noncontemplative but active and practical universality; it is the product of universal readiness. The immeasurable versatility of raw human manpower, which capital constantly brings to the consciousness of the exploited, returns at the highest level as the polytechnical—as opposed to the specialized—education of man. These are basic principles of mass education—principles whose seminal importance for young people growing up is utterly obvious.

Nevertheless, it is scarcely easy to accept without reservation Hoernle's claim that the education of children does not differ in essentials from that of the adult masses. Such bold assertions make us realize how desirable, indeed necessary it would have been to supplement the political exposition he has given us with a philosophical one. But of course the Marxist dialectical anthropology of the proletarian child is a neglected field of research. (Moreover, since Marx, there have been no significant new discoveries about adult workers either.) Such an anthropology would be nothing other than a debate with child psychology, which would have to be replaced with detailed records—prepared according to the principles of materialist dialectics—of the actual experiences of working-class children in kindergartens, youth groups, children's theaters, and outdoor groups. These should be introduced as soon as possible to supplement the present handbook.

It is in fact a handbook, but it is also something more. In Germany, there is no orthodox Marxist literature apart from economic and political writings. This is the chief reason for the astonishing ignorance on the part of intellectuals, including left-wing intellectuals, about matters concerning Marxism. Hoernle's book gives us an authoritative and incisive account of education theory. By demonstrating its relevance to a question of fundamental importance, he shows us what orthodox Marxist thought is and where it leads. We should take this book to heart.

Published in *Die neue Bücherschau*, December 1929. *Gesammelte Schriften*, III, 206–209. Translated by Rodney Livingstone.

Notes

1. The Wandervögel were organized groups of young boys who took walks through the countryside. Their activities represented the beginnings of the German Youth Movement, which embraced a wide spectrum of ideas ranging from pragmatic suggestions for pedagogical reform through nature worship and on to the virulent nationalism and anti-Semitism of the radical Right.
2. See Edwin Hoernle, *Grundfragen der proletarischen Erziehung* [Basic Questions of Proletarian Education] (Berlin: Verlag der Jugendinternationale, 1929), 212 pages. [Benjamin's note]

Notes on a Conversation with Béla Balász (End of 1929)

It began quite harmlessly. Some philosophical question or other. Only what irritated me from the outset was that he represented as an extraordinary discovery the fact that words in different languages with the same conceptual values signify in different ways (needless to say, this was not how he expressed it). I felt at once that this man could produce nothing but false ideas. Now, here's my old tactic in such circumstances. *Either* you can contradict at all costs. Thus, I developed an entire theory of poetry from the point of view of the philosophy of language. This was workable only because the fellow uttered the clichés of mystical philosophies of language—clichés that I found it both difficult and useful to refute. *Or* you can steal the ideas of such a man (if they turn out to be correct) and make off with them, as you would abscond with his girlfriend. And this is how I started. He made a very true observation about foreign words: foreign words are always torn from their natural linguistic context and become inflexible. This reminded me, in a not very precise way, of Polgar's statement to the effect that I use even German words as if they were foreign[1] (an astounding intuition that starts with a reflection on my style, but proceeds to penetrate to my very core), and I went on to endorse Balász's statement with exaggerated enthusiasm, taking advantage of the subsequent conversational confusion to make off with the idea in a completely impenetrable disguise (although one very characteristic of myself): the notion that foreign words are little linguistic burial chambers.—The theory of poetry that I opposed to his banal language mysticism turned on the contrast between, on the one hand, the magic, metaphorical, cosmic sphere in which the word emerged originally from image, and, on the other, the incorporating, intentionalist, anthropological idea of poetry, which I presented as the conqueror—the irenic, pacifying, victorious power that overcomes myth and magic. The discovery of the intentional character of the word takes place much later than that of its magic, executive nature, which constitutes the oldest form of practice. And this intentional nature of the word develops only in the sentence, and appears first, perhaps, in poetry.

Record of a conversation from 1929; unpublished in Benjamin's lifetime. *Gesammelte Schriften*, VI, 418. Translated by Rodney Livingstone.

Notes

1. Alfred Polgar (1873–1955), Viennese journalist and theater critic, was known for his elegant, ironic essays. In 1938 he escaped across the Pyrenees and spent the World War II years in the United States. Béla Balász (pseudonym of Herbert Bauer; 1884–1949) was a prominent Hungarian film theorist, scriptwriter, and director.

Some Remarks on Folk Art

Folk art and kitsch ought for once to be regarded as a single great movement that passes certain themes from hand to hand, like batons, behind the back of what is known as great art. They both depend on great art at the level of detail, but apply what they have taken in their own way and in the service of their own "goals," their *Kunstwollen.*[1]

What is the direction of this *Kunstwollen?* Well, certainly not toward art, but toward something far more primitive, yet more compelling. If we ask ourselves what "art" in the modern sense means to folk art on the one hand and to kitsch on the other, the answer would be: all folk art incorporates the human being within itself. It addresses him only so that he must answer. Moreover, he answers with questions: "Where and when was it?" The idea surfaces in him that this space and this moment and this position of the sun must have existed once before. To throw the situation that is imagined here around one's shoulders, like a favorite old coat—this is the deepest temptation awakened by the refrain of a folk song, in which a basic feature of all folk art may be perceived.

It is not just that our image of our character is so discontinuous, so much a matter of improvisation, that we are eager to fall in with every suggestion made by the graphologist, the palm-reader, and similar practitioners. Rather, our destiny may be said to be governed by the same intensive imagination that illuminates in a flash the dark corners of the self, of our character, and creates a space for the interpolation of the most unexpected dark or light features. When we are in earnest, we discover our conviction that we have experienced infinitely more than we know about. This includes what we have read, and what we have dreamed, whether awake or in our sleep. And who knows how and where we can open up other regions of our destiny?

What we have experienced but do not know about echoes, after its own fashion, when we enter the world of primitives: their furniture, their ornaments, their songs and pictures. "After their fashion"—this means in quite a different way from great art. As we stand in front of a painting by Titian or Monet, we never feel the urge to pull out our watch and set it by the position of the sun in the picture. But in the case of pictures in children's books, or in Utrillo's paintings, which really do recuperate the primitive, we might easily get such an urge. This means that we find ourselves in a situation of the kind we are used to, and it is not so much that we compare the position of the sun with our watch as that we use the watch to compare this position of the sun with an earlier one. The *déjà vu* is changed from the pathological exception that it is in civilized life to a magical ability at whose disposal folk art (no less than kitsch) places itself. It can do so because the *déjà vu* really is quite different from the intellectual realization that the new situation is identical to the old one. It would be more accurate to say: *basically* identical to the old one. But even this is wide of the mark. For the situation is not one experienced by a bystander; it has been pulled over our heads—we have wrapped ourselves up in it. However you think of it, it ends up as the fundamental fact of the mask. In this way the primitive, with all its implements and pictures, opens up for our benefit an infinite arsenal of masks: the masks of our fate—the masks with which we emerge from unconsciously experienced moments and situations that have now, at long last, been recuperated.

Impoverished, uncreative man knows of no other way to transform himself than by means of disguise. Disguise seeks the arsenal of masks within us. But for the most part, we are very poorly equipped with them. In reality, the world is full of masks; we do not suspect the extent to which even the most unpretentious pieces of furniture (such as romanesque armchairs) used to be masks, too. Wearing a mask, man looks out on the situation and builds up his figures within it. To hand over these masks to us, and to form the space and the figure of our fate within it—this is where folk art comes to meet us halfway. Only from this vantage point can we say clearly and fundamentally what distinguishes it from "more authentic" art, in the narrower sense.

Art teaches us to look into objects.

Folk art and kitsch allow us to look outward from within objects.

Fragment written in 1929; unpublished in Benjamin's lifetime. *Gesammelte Schriften*, VI, 185–187. Translated by Rodney Livingstone.

Notes

1. Benjamin adopts the term *Kunstwollen* from the Austrian art historian Alois Riegl. Riegl defines it as the manner in which a given culture at a given time wants to see its cultural objects.

Tip for Patrons

The wretched state of German book criticism is a secret to no one. Unlike the reasons for it. But chief among these are the absence of comradeship, of opposition, and of *clarity* in the commerce between writers. Hence the astoundingly wishy-washy nature of trends and their representatives, and the sterile dignity of a criticism that is merely the expression of the stiflingly narrowminded spirit in which it is practiced. Humor needs elbow room and space. A shrewd patron who wished to do something for German literature should abandon the notion of discovering fresh talent, or of launching Kleist and Schiller prizes. Instead, he should adopt the following proposal: he should set up a fairground for German literature. The terrain does not need to be very large. Its possibilities are unlimited: a roller-coaster ride through the peaks and troughs of the German novel, starting off in the Kafka grotto, plunging suddenly into the Ludwig wolf's lair, hurtling past Samiel Fischer and Hauptmann the sharpshooter.[1]

Literary stalls: Nietzsche, Goethe, Brecht . . .

After this ceremony, a choir leader will step forward and say something to this effect: nothing of importance.

Fragment written in 1929; unpublished in Benjamin's lifetime. *Gesammelte Schriften,* VI, 168–169. Translated by Rodney Livingstone.

Notes

1. Benjamin plays here on Carl Maria von Weber's opera *Der Freischütz* (The Sharpshooter) with his reference to the wolf's lair (the word "wolf" here referring

perhaps to Ludwig Wolff, the author of popular novels serialized in the *Berliner Illustrierte,* or perhaps to Emil Ludwig, the no less popular author of romanticized biographies of Bismarck, Wilhelm II, and others), as well as his allusion to the diabolical figure of Samiel (for the publisher Samiel Fischer). The sharpshooter himself refers to Gerhart Hauptmann, whose dramas and prose made him the central figure in German Naturalism.

Crisis and Critique, 1930

"Ich bin ein Kohlkopf" ("I Am a Cabbagehead"), 1930. Rotogravure by John Heartfield, from *Arbeiter Illustrierte Zeitung,* vol. 9, no. 6 (1930), page 103. Copyright © 1999 Artists Rights Society (ARS), New York / VG Bild-Kunst, Bonn. The image expresses the Communists' hostility to the Social Democratic Party. It was accompanied by a caption that said: "Whoever reads bourgeois newspapers becomes blind and deaf. Away with stultifying bandages!" And superimposed on the image was a parody of the Prussian nationalist song, "Ich bin ein Preusse. Kennt ihr meine Farben?" ("I am a Prussian. Do you know my colors?"):

I am a cabbagehead. Do you know my leaves?
I'm nearly out of my mind with worries,
But I keep my mouth shut and hope for a savior.
I want to be a black-red-and-gold cabbagehead!
I don't want to see anything, or hear anything,
Or get mixed up in public affairs.
And you can take everything, even the shirt on my back,
Yet I won't let the Red press into my home!

Notes (II)

The so-called immortal works just flash briefly through every present time. *Hamlet* is one of the very fastest, the hardest to grasp.

Child before the goodnight kiss in bed . . .

A writing child
  The writing hand is suspended in the scaffolding of the lines like an athlete in the giddy-making wall-bars of the arena (or of the theater-flies). Mouse, hat, house, twig, bear, ice, and egg fill the arena—a pale, glacial audience. They watch their dangerous tricks.
  Salto mortale of the *s* / Watch how the hand seeks the place on the page where it should make a start. The threshold before the realm of writing. When the child writes, its hand sets off on a journey. A long journey with pauses for it to spend the night. The letter disintegrates into pauses. Panic and paralysis of the hand. The pain of leaving the accustomed landscape of space, because from now on it may move only along the surface.

The hierarchy of the senses from the point of view of consolation.

Criticism in the form of stories: Thomas Mann / Hamsun

Reading: in order to know what a book contains; to know what someone has written and how; to inform oneself about a given subject; to criticize criticisms; to read.

For the writer, it can sometimes be dangerous or unnecessary to pick a quarrel with his public. There are instances where he can dispense with doing so. But what is quite indispensable is for every writer who wishes to be effective in any way at all to adopt a precise strategic position in his own generation. For even though he may have passionate opponents among younger or older writers, only those of his own age will know his weak points. To construct a typology of critical lives, we must distinguish between literary names that have been made by older writers, those that have been made by writers of the same age, and those that have been made by younger ones. Of course, such a classification will not bring out differences of value.

Sainte-Beuve draws a distinction between *intelligence-glaive* and *intelligence-miroir*.[1]

A postscript to the case of Borchardt.[2] If we wanted to solve the problem of explaining Borchardt's writings from that curious experience of semblance [*Schein*] which hardly ever proclaims itself so vociferously, so desperately, but by the same token hardly ever so perfectly or with such consciousness of its perfection, it would mean inserting it into contexts that are anything but those of literary history. Who—we would have to inquire—knew this kind of experience in such sensuous clarity and plenitude? We might suggest Hofmannsthal, who for that very reason had been Borchardt's great teacher. But ultimately we would also have to propose Goethe. And this points to a quite astonishing historical phenomenon: it implies the claim that the Goethean conquest of a world of semblances has discovered, in Hofmannsthal and Rudolf Borchardt, successors who are both frighteningly quick to learn and frighteningly inflexible. This Goethean world—which is merely one of the Master's many worlds, although it is the *only* one in the eyes of these disciples—usurps the place of the effective and truly developing one in their minds, through a kind of temporal hallucination. Their version of his world neither has any effect nor undergoes any development, and for this very reason they not unreasonably confuse it with the world of the early Greeks, in a way that Goethe himself would never have done. It is likewise significant that neither Hofmannsthal nor Borchardt is willing to concede even the smallest space to irony. Unobtrusive reversals, voluntary parings of things: only these methods are inconceivable in their world of semblances. This also explains Hofmannsthal's hostility to Keller. The claim that they are having an impact—a claim Borchardt in particular makes all the more insistently the more he imperialistically extends the hegemony of appearance to include the realm of science—is itself a revealing sign. For nowadays, *in the realm of forms and as form,* the only art that can claim to be unpolitical in the strictest sense of the word is what is hidden, what is unassuming, what seems to—and to a certain extent really does— renounce effect.

Depiction of the southern night, based on the idea that beneath the moonlight the earth passes once again through all the past stages of its life. And also, perhaps, anticipates in a dream the stages to come.

Thought and style. Style is the rope that a thought must vault over if it is to advance to the realm of writing. The thought must gather up all its strength. But style must come toward it halfway and go slack, like a rope in the hands of children when one of them makes ready to jump.

Dialectics of happiness: a twofold will—the unprecedented, that which has never existed before, the pinnacle of bliss. Also: eternal repetition of the same situation, eternal restoration of the original, first happiness.

We wish to enjoy our rest when it is poured out for us from a jug that is painted in the most garish colors.

Books, too, begin like the week—with a day of rest in memory of their creation. The preface is their Sunday.

Karl Valentin's comic art: diversionary marches in order to mount a flank attack on Jewish wit.[3]

Effect and productiveness are incompatible. Dampness, closeness, vagueness in productiveness; dryness, outline, distance in effectiveness.

Fragment written 1928, 1929, or 1930; unpublished in Benjamin's lifetime. *Gesammelte Schriften*, VI, 200–203. Translated by Rodney Livingstone.

Notes

1. "Sword-like intelligence" and "mirror-like intelligence."
2. Rudolf Borchardt (1877–1945) was a German poet, essayist, and translator. Politically and aesthetically conservative, he adopted a writing style marked by a highly self-conscious formal mastery.
3. Karl Valentin (pseudonym of Valentin Ludwig Fey; 1882–1948) was an enormously popular German cabaret artist.

Notes (III)

People stick roses, violets, and chrysanthemums on furs. I know of nothing that is more apt to assign women a place between animals and flowers, instead of the false, banal positioning between angel and beast. Indeed, women are creatures in flowery furs, a raging flowerbed, a heap of blood-filled calyxes with makeup on. The clock with its ebony casing that gazes like a fruit from a golden wreath of plants and precociously knows more than the seasons themselves.

Ortega y Gasset. The further Nietzsche's ideas travel around the world, the more provincial they become.

Fragment written 1928, 1929, or 1930; unpublished in Benjamin's lifetime. *Gesammelte Schriften*, VI, 205. Translated by Rodney Livingstone.

Program for Literary Criticism

1. Annihilatory criticism must retrieve its good conscience. This means that the function of criticism in general has to be returned to the level of consciousness. By a gradual process, it has degenerated into sheer exhaustion and harmlessness. In such circumstances, even corruption has its good side: at least it still has a face, a definite physiognomy.

2. A principal source of error is the illusion that the corruption can be stemmed by an appeal to the personal integrity of the reviewer. Under present conditions, it is extremely rare for the noxious parasite to pursue his activities in good faith; and the greater the bribe, the less he feels he is being bought.

3. Honest criticism from the standpoint of unprejudiced taste is uninteresting and basically lacking in substance. What is crucial about any critical activity is whether it is based on a concrete sketch (strategic plan) that has its own logic and its own integrity.

4. This is missing almost universally nowadays, because political and critical strategies coincide only in the most outstanding cases. Nevertheless, such a coincidence should be the ultimate goal.

5. In this connection, the following critical work of enlightenment should be deployed. Germany's reading public has a highly peculiar structure. It can be divided into two roughly equal parts: "the public" and "the literary circles." There is scarcely any overlap between the two. The public regards literature as an instrument of entertain-

ment, animation, or the deepening of sociability—a pastime in a higher or lower sense. The literary circles regard books as books of life, as sources of wisdom, as the statutes of their small groups— groups that alone bring bliss. Hitherto, criticism has concerned itself almost exclusively—and very wrongly—with what catches the attention of the public.

6. To trace the literature of the circles would be a terrible and by no means risk-free job of enlightenment. At the same time, it would be a preliminary study for the history of sectarianism in Germany in the twentieth century. At first glance, it is difficult to discover the source of this highly potent and rapid development of sectarianism. We can only predict that it will be the authentic form of the barbarism to which Germany will succumb if Communism fails to conquer. But we should regard it as certain that what underlies this sudden outbreak of ritual complexes is the attempt to release the body from traditional collectives and to insert it into new ones, and that what makes them symptoms of madness is precisely the absence of any relationship to collective activity.

7. Furthermore, criticism has to secure its own power by developing a more effective attitude toward the relations of production in the book market. It is well known that far too many books are published. What is worse, a consequence of this is that too few good books appear. And those that have appeared have made too little impact. Until now, when critics wished to reject a book, they directed their fire at the author. It is obvious that they have not achieved very much by this procedure. Their judgments cannot be followed up by executions. Not to mention that for every bad writer who is demolished in this way, nine new ones spring up in his place. A different approach is when the critic insists, within certain limits, on the principle of the publisher's (economic) responsibility, and denounces the publisher of bad books as the squanderer of the already small capital that is available for producing books. The aim here, of course, is not to attack the commercial aspect of publishing—to criticize the publisher who makes money from bad books, just as other businessmen make money from inferior merchandise—but to appeal to the misguided idealist whose patronage supports dangerous products.

8. Good criticism is composed of at most two elements: the critical gloss and the quotation. Very good criticism can be made from both glosses and quotations. What must be avoided like the plague is rehearsing the summary of the contents. In contrast, a criticism consisting entirely of quotations should be developed.

9. The theory of the unrecognized genius should be inserted here.

10. Causes of tolerance in criticism until today.

11. Prognosis for the universities. In ten years, university chairs will have been completely divided up between the charlatans and the sectarians. The conquest of chairs by the George school was the first symptom.[1] It turns out (as I learned from a conversation with Christiane von Hofmannsthal) that there are still university teachers who possess exact knowledge and exact skills, but it has already become impossible for them to transmit this knowledge further. "The students learn nothing, but they know how to cross the street as well as their teachers." And this illustrates the truth that the transmissibility of knowledge does not depend just on its wealth and exactness. On the contrary, we can perceive its moral structure here more clearly than anywhere else.

12. What would happen if one of the twelve people whose voices carry weight with the German public were to speak out against his fellow conspirators? Everything is based on the certainty that no one will refuse to play the game.

13. Historical retrospect: the decay of literary criticism since the Romantic movement. A contributory factor is the absence of a collective authority that could judge great objects and slogans. Every cohort of critics has seen itself as a "generation" in all its limitations, as a puny guardian of "posterity." In this way, caught between productive writers and posterity, it didn't dare to move a muscle, and so foundered in epigonism. Friedrich Theodor Vischer the ultimate stage.[2]

14. The stronger a critic is, the more comprehensively he is able to digest the entire personality of his adversary, right down to the details of his character.

15. Critical procedures. The danger of their multiplicity.

    1. Speak only of the author—speak only of the work.
    2. Consider the work in relation to other works by the same author—consider the work in isolation.
    3. Place the work in a literary-historical context and compare it in terms of style or content with other works in the tradition.
    4. Treat the work—polemically, prognostically, analytically—according to its effect on its public.
    5. The work as representative of a thesis—the thesis as representative of a work.

16. The function of criticism, especially today: to lift *the mask of "pure art"* and show that there is no neutral ground for art. Materialist criticism as an instrument for this.

17. The risk in bestowing praise: the critic forfeits his credit. Looked at strategically, every expression of praise is a blank check.

18. There is fine art in giving praise. But it is also a fine art to bring out the importance of something apparently peripheral through negative criticism.

19. The critic must know how to give the public the feeling that it will know where to expect him. When he will speak out and in what way.

20. The question of space. Under this rubric the question of the critic's style should be treated. Take up the ideas from my conversations with Bernhard Reich.

21. We do not know what Hofmannsthal, Thomas Mann, and Wassermann think of each other.[3] Indeed, we do not even know what the spokesmen of the younger generation—Leonhard Frank, Alfred Döblin, Arnolt Bronnen—think of their elders.[4] Not that this would be very interesting or crucial, or that we could not imagine it for ourselves if need be. But it would clear the air. It would articulate the utterly amorphous mass of people who "live by their pen" to the point where partisanship and debate could emerge, things which are absent from our literature to an absolutely incomprehensible degree. There is a contrast here with theatrical criticism, which occupies an important place in the public eye for this reason—and for this reason *alone,* since the theater is otherwise unimportant.

22. The false and unsustainable fiction that literary criticism today can still expect to derive its standards from pure aesthetics, and that criticism is basically nothing but the application of those standards. Criticism has failed to notice that the time for aesthetics in every sense, and especially in the sense practiced by Friedrich Theodor Vischer, is gone forever.

23. "The gift of judgment is rarer than the gift of creativity" (Oskar Loerke).[5]

24. *Stefan Zweig in Böttcherstrasse* (Bremen; edited by Ludwig Roselius) I,1.[6]

25. Criticism via images (*Prochainement Ouraitre* [?]);[7] criticism via narrative *(The Magic Mountain).*

26. Topical critical themes: the war novel in Germany (Arnold Zweig, Ernst Gläser, Ludwig Renn, Erich Maria Remarque).[8] The unmasking of Jakob Wassermann.

27. The division into groups, or rather parties, that is taking place in Germany. The authors who made their debut under Expressionism, as well as others.

28. The question of war novels. The right-wing parties have been able to cash in immediately on the experience of the Great War. Their world view has not been shaken by it. Neither has that of the Communists. The situation is different with the parties occupying the middle ground, especially those of the grand bourgeoisie and, in a different way, of the petty bourgeoisie. We must bear this in mind when confronting the question: What (or whose) interest is served by the fashion for war novels? The more the "objectivity" and the "documentary nature" of these novels are emphasized, the more closely we should scrutinize the deeply hidden tendencies they serve. Of course, not all these tendencies are deeply hidden. For example, the pacifist element is strikingly obvious. And it is this that cries out for closer analysis.

29. More on the war novel. What is *hidden* about this pacifism is the fact that—and the way in which—it subserves capitalist interests at their present stage. And hard though it is to think of pacifism as an instrument of imperialism, it is no easier to trace its connection with the apparently "objective" and "documentary" reality of the war. This ideology is concealed in the "objective" [*sachlichen*] representation the way Easter eggs are hidden in the crevices of a sofa. We could sum it up in this formula: The ostensible reality of the war in these new novels is related to its true (and this means its present, contemporary) reality much as pacifist ideology is related to the necessities of the contemporary economy. In both cases, the convergence between the two is more apparent than real.

30. Further comments on the war novel. The books on the war that are appearing now were written in part immediately after the war. At that time, no one was interested. They were incompatible with the mood of the day, to which the great volumes of memoirs made a stronger appeal. On the other hand, Expressionism was—on a formal plane—the expression of life at the time (the inflation). The critique of the new war books would be contained implicitly in an account of the transition from Expressionism to the New Objectivity.[9] Such a trajectory would reveal that the New Objectivity represented the consolidation of the debt incurred by Expressionism. It

incurred this debt with its borrowings from metaphysics. The New Objectivity is the interest required to service the debt.

31. Book criticism must be based on a program. As a form of criticism that improvises the standards it applies, immanent criticism can lead to satisfying results in individual cases. But what is needed more urgently is a program. Its starting point must be the perception that the aesthetic categories (criteria) are, without exception, completely devalued. Nor can they be resurrected from the old aesthetics by any "reformulation," however ingenious. On the contrary, what is required now is a detour through materialist aesthetics, which would situate books in the context of their age. Such criticism would lead to a new, dynamic, dialectical aesthetics. Even the old aesthetics included the most profound insights into the contemporary world. But the modern critic thinks of these old concepts and schemata in absolute terms, much as he regards the works. He is firmly convinced that everything must be possible at every moment.

32. Atomization of contemporary criticism. The book regarded outside the context of the age, the author, current trends. But that is no more than a hypothetical working basis for certain lucky instances of an improvising, immanent criticism.

33. The relation of book criticism to film criticism the reverse of what it should be. Book criticism should learn from film criticism. Instead, film criticism mainly apes book criticism.

34. Writers abuse their own names and influence. When we compare this with the situation in France, it is scandalous how our best-known writers refuse to lift a finger to improve the status of book criticism.

35. "Quand on soutient un mouvement révolutionnaire, ce serait en compromettre le développement que d'en dissocier les divers éléments au nom du goût."[10] Apollinaire in conversation.

36. The atomization of criticism is connected with the demise of the art of critical portraiture.

37. One should adopt as a maxim: never write a critique without at least *one* quotation from the work under review.

38. A metaphor for criticism: Take the plants from the garden of art and transplant them to the alien soil of science, in order to obtain a detailed picture of the minute changes in color and form that appear there. The most important thing is the gentle touch, the care with which the work is taken out with its roots, for it is this that

then improves the soil of knowledge. Everything else happens of its own accord, since it is the work's merits themselves that alone deserve the title of criticism in the highest sense.

39. How times have changed. A hundred years ago Börne wrote, "What the Germans like most of all is a book about a book; . . . Whoever wishes to lead them down the path of virtue need do nothing but write, and whoever wishes for certain success should become a critic." Ludwig Börne, *Gesammelte Schriften: Vollständige Ausgabe,* edited by Karl Grün, vol. 6 (Vienna, 1868), page 3.

40. Highly symptomatic of modern criticism: it never compromises an author more than when it bestows praise. And on the whole, that is right and proper, since the critics prefer to praise worthless books. But significant works are not treated any differently. Consider Hofmannsthal, for example.

Fragment written in 1929 or 1930; unpublished in Benjamin's lifetime. *Gesammelte Schriften,* VI, 161–167. Translated by Rodney Livingstone.

Notes

1. "George school" refers to the circle around the lyric poet Stefan George (1868–1933), which included a number of influential writers and especially academics. It was held together as much by the force of George's charismatic, authoritarian personality as by his ideas, which centered on a conservative restoration of the German language and through it of the German nation.
2. Friedrich Theodor Vischer (1807–1887), a leading critic and liberal politician, is best-known for his championing of literary realism at mid-century.
3. Jakob Wassermann (1873–1934) was a German novelist best-known for his work on the mysterious foundling Kaspar Hauser and for a series of historical novels published in the 1920s.
4. Leonhard Frank (1882–1961) was a German novelist and playwright working in the wake of Expressionism. Alfred Döblin (1878–1957), a leading German novelist and essayist, is best-known for *Berlin Alexanderplatz* (1929). Arnolt Bronnen (1895–1959) was a German dramatist who combined leftism and Expressionism in a series of controversial plays.
5. Oskar Loerke (1884–1941), a German lyric poet, was best-known for his nature poetry.
6. Stefan Zweig (1881–1942) was a German biographer, poet, essayist, dramatist, and novelist. He explored a series of imagined and historical figures in a number of fictional and nonfictional genres.
7. "*Prochainement Ouraitre*" is probably a garbled reference to Henri Guilac's book

Prochainement Ouverture (Paris, 1925). It contains drawings by Guilac which caricature contemporary French books.

8. Arnold Zweig (1887–1968) was a German novelist whose book *Der Streit um den Sergeanten Grischa* (The Case of Sergeant Grischa; 1927) caused a sensation; the encounter of the Russian prisoner of war Grischa and the Prussian military machine proved a potent allegory of state power during the Weimar Republic. Ernst Gläser (1902–1962) was a German journalist and author of realist novels. Ludwig Renn (pseudonym of Arnold von Golssenau; 1889–1979) was a German novelist best-known for *Krieg* (War; 1928), which was based on his own wartime experiences. Erich Maria Remarque (1898–1970), a German novelist, is chiefly remembered for *Im Westen nichts Neues* (All Quiet on the Western Front; 1929), the best-known novel of World War I.

9. Benjamin refers here to the last throes of German Expressionism in the period after World War I; Expressionism in the visual arts and literature had arisen and reached full maturity already in the years leading up to the war. The German inflation began as early as 1914, when the imperial government began financing its war effort with a series of fiscally disastrous measures. The economic situation deteriorated rapidly in the years following the end of the war, as an already crippled economy was further burdened by war reparations. The inflation reached its critical phase—that of hyperinflation—in late 1922 and 1923. If we compare late 1913 (the last year before the war) with late 1923 using the wholesale price index as the basis for the comparison, we find that one German mark in 1913 equaled 1.26 trillion marks by December 1923. *Neue Sachlichkeit* (New Objectivity) was the term originally applied by the museum curator G. F. Hartlaub to an emergent figuration in German postwar painting. It gradually came to designate the Weimar "period style" in art, architecture, design, literature, and film: cool, objective, analytical.

10. "When you support a revolutionary movement, you would compromise its development if you were to dissociate it from certain elements in the name of taste."

Notes on a Theory of Gambling

Certain matters are clear. What is decisive is the level of motor innervation, and the more emancipated it is from optical perception, the more decisive it is. From this stems a principal commandment for gamblers: they must use their hands sparingly, in order to respond to the slightest innervations. The gambler's basic approach must, so to speak, adumbrate the subtlest network of inhibitions, which lets only the most minute and unassuming innervations pass through its meshes.—It is also an established fact that the loser tends to indulge in a certain feeling of lightness, not to say relief. Conversely, the experience of having won weighs on the gambler's mind. (This refers to his state of mind after the game, not during it.) We may say of the winner that he has to do battle with the feeling of hubris which threatens to overwhelm him. He falls, perhaps not unintentionally, into a state of depression.— Another fact: the genuine gambler places his most important bets—which are usually his most successful ones, too—at the last possible moment. He could be said to be inspired by a certain characteristic sound made by the roulette ball just before it falls on a specific number. But one could also argue that it is only at the last moment, when everything is pressing toward a conclusion, at the critical moment of danger (of missing his chance), that a gambler discovers the trick of finding his way around the table, of reading the table—if this, too, is not just an expression from the realm of optics.— The gambler may form the impression that the winning numbers are hiding from him. This happens because—we may hypothesize—he knows every winning number in advance, except for the one that he (accidentally) bet on with an optical or rational consciousness. In the case of the others, there is a twofold possibility: either he bet on them correctly, relying on his motor innervations (inspiration), or else he knew them in advance but was unable to discover (reveal, make manifest) this knowledge in terms of motor stimuli. Hence the feeling that the number was hiding.—When a winning number is clearly predicted but not bet on, the man who is not in the know will conclude that he is in excellent form and that next time he just needs to act more promptly, more boldly. Whereas anyone familiar with the game will know that a single incident of this kind is sufficient to tell him that he must break off instantly. For it is a sign that the contact between his motor stimuli and "fate" has been interrupted. Only then will "what is to come" enter his consciousness more or less clearly as what it is.—Also established is the fact that no one has so many chances of betting on a winning number as someone who has just made a significant win. This means that the correct sequence is based not on any previous knowledge of the future but on a correct physical predisposition, which is increased in immediacy, certainty, and uninhibitedness by every confirmation, such as is provided by a win.— The happiness of the winner: the winner's highly remarkable feeling of elation, of being rewarded by fate, of having seized control of destiny. Comparison with the expression of love by a woman who has been truly satisfied by a man. Money and property, normally the most massive and cumbersome things, here come directly from the hands of fate, as if they were the caressing response to a perfect embrace.—Furthermore, one should note the factor of danger, which is the most important factor in gambling, alongside pleasure (the pleasure of betting on the right number). It arises not so much from the threat of losing as from that of *not winning*. The particular danger that threatens the gambler lies in the fateful category of arriving "too late," of having "missed the opportunity." We could learn something from this about the character of the gambler as a type.—Last, the best that has thus far been written about gambling focuses on the factor of acceleration, acceleration and danger. What Anatole France has said on pages 14ff. of *Le jardin d'Epicure* [The Garden of Epicurus] must be combined with what has been noted here: gambling generates by way of experiment the lightning-quick process of stimulation at the moment of danger, the marginal case in which presence of mind becomes divination— that is to say, one of the highest, rarest moments in life.

See, on this subject, "The Path to Success, in Thirteen Theses" [in this volume]; and Alain, *Les idées et les âges* (Paris, 1927), under "Le jeu."

Fragment written in 1929 or 1930; unpublished in Benjamin's lifetime. *Gesammelte Schriften*, VI, 188–190. Translated by Rodney Livingstone.

The Crisis of the Novel

Alfred Döblin, *Berlin Alexanderplatz: Die Geschichte von Franz Biberkopf* [Berlin Alexanderplatz: The Story of Franz Biberkopf] (Berlin: S. Fischer Verlag, 1929), 530 pages.

From the point of view of epic, existence is an ocean. Nothing is more epic than the sea. One can of course react to the sea in different ways—for example, lie on the beach, listen to the surf, and collect the shells that it washes up on the shore. This is what the epic writer does. You can also sail on the sea. For many purposes, or none at all. You can embark on a voyage and then, when you are far out, you can cruise with no land in sight, nothing but sea and sky. This is what the novelist does. He is the truly solitary, silent person. Epic man is simply resting. In epics, people rest after their day's work; they listen, dream, and collect. The novelist has secluded himself from people and their activities. The birthplace of the novel is the individual in his isolation, the individual who can no longer speak of his concerns in exemplary fashion, who himself lacks counsel and can give none. To write a novel is to take that which is incommensurable in the representation of human existence to the extreme. Simply to think of the works of Homer and Dante is to sense what separates the novel from the genuine epic. The oral tradition, the stuff of epic, is different in kind from what forms the stock-in-trade of the novel. What distinguishes the novel from all other forms of prose—folktale, saga, proverb, comic tale—is that it neither originates in the oral tradition nor flows back into it. And this is what distinguishes it above all from storytelling, which in the prose tradition represents the epic form at its purest. Indeed, nothing contributes more to the dangerous falling silent of the inner human being, nothing kills the spirit of storytelling more thoroughly, than the outrageous proportions that the reading of novels has undergone in all our lives. It is therefore the voice of the born storyteller that makes itself heard here, in opposition to the novelist: "Nor do I wish to mention that I consider the emancipation of the epic from the book . . . to be advantageous—advantageous above all for language. The book spells the death of real languages. The most important, creative energies of language elude the epic author who only writes." Flaubert could never have written this. This thesis is Döblin's. He has given a very comprehensive account of it in the first yearbook of the Section for Literature of the Prussian Academy of Arts; his "Structure of the Epic Work" is a masterly document of the crisis of the novel, which was initiated by the reinstatement of epic that we now encounter everywhere, even in drama. Anyone who thinks carefully about this lecture of Döblin's will have no need to concern himself with the external signs of this crisis, this reinforcement of radical epic. The flood of biographical and historical novels will cease to astonish him. The theoretician Döblin, far from resigning himself to this crisis, hurries on ahead of it and makes its cause his own. His latest book shows that his theory and practice are one.

Nothing is more illuminating than to compare Döblin's position with the one that André Gide has recently revealed in his *Journal des "Faux-monnayeurs"* [Journal of *The Counterfeiters*], which is equally magisterial, equally precise, and equally spirited in its praxis, but nonetheless opposed to Döblin's on every point.[1] In the clash of these two critical minds the contemporary situation of epic finds its sharpest expression. In this autobiographical commentary to his latest novel, Gide develops the doctrine of the *roman pur*. With the greatest subtlety imaginable, he has set out to eliminate every straightforward, linear, paratactic narrative (every mainline epic characteristic) in favor of ingenious, purely novelistic (and in this context that also means Romantic) devices. The attitude of the characters to what is being narrated, the attitude of the author toward them and to his technique—all this must become a component of the novel itself. In short, this *roman pur* is actually pure interiority; it acknowledges no exterior, and is therefore the extreme opposite of the purely epic approach—which is narration. In strict contrast to Döblin's notions, Gide's ideal is the novel as pure writing. He is perhaps the last to uphold Flaubert's views. And no one will be surprised to discover that Döblin's speech contains the sharpest repudiation imaginable of Flaubert's achievement. "They will throw up their hands in despair when I advise their authors not to shrink from introducing lyrical, dramatic, and even reflective elements into their narratives. But I insist on it."[2]

His lack of inhibition in implementing this program is revealed in the perplexity of many of the readers of this latest book. Now, it is true enough that narrative has seldom been handled in such a manner as this. It is rare indeed for the waves of incident and reflection to sweep over the reader and destabilize his comfort to this degree, and the spray of actual spoken speech has never given him such a soaking as here. But this does not mean that we must operate with technical terms, such as *dialogue intérieur*, or refer the reader to James Joyce. In reality, something quite different is at work. The stylistic principle governing this book is that of montage. Petty-bourgeois printed matter, scandalmongering, stories of accidents, the sensational incidents of 1928, folk songs, and advertisements rain down in this text. The montage explodes the framework of the novel, bursts its limits both stylistically and structurally, and clears the way for new, epic possibilities. Formally, above all. The material of the montage is anything but arbitrary. Authentic montage is based on the document. In its fanatical struggle with the work of art, Dadaism used montage to turn daily life into its ally. It was the first to proclaim, somewhat uncertainly, the autocracy of the authentic. The film at its best moments made as if to accustom us to montage. Here, for the first time, it has been placed at the service of narrative. Biblical verses, statistics, and texts from hit songs are what Döblin uses to confer authenticity on the narrative. They correspond to the formulaic verse forms of the traditional epic.

The texture of this montage is so dense that we have difficulty hearing the author's voice. He has reserved for himself the street-ballad-like epigraphs to each chapter; otherwise, he is in no great hurry to make his voice heard. (Even though he is determined to have his say in the end.) It is astounding how long he trails behind his characters before risking any challenge to them. He approaches things in a relaxed way, as befits an epic writer. Whatever happens—even when it happens suddenly—seems to have been prepared well in advance. In this attitude, he has been inspired by the spirit of Berlin dialect—a dialect that moves at a relaxed pace. For the Berliner speaks as a connoisseur, in love with the way things are said. He relishes it. Whether he is swearing, mocking, or threatening, he takes his time, just as he takes his time over breakfast. Glassbrenner dramatically highlighted the qualities of Berlinish.[3] Here we see it in its epic profundity. The ship of Franz Biberkopf's life is heavily laden, yet never runs aground. The book is a monument to the Berlin dialect because the narrator makes no attempt to enlist our sympathies for the city based on any sort of regional loyalty. He speaks from within Berlin. It is his megaphone. His dialect is one of the forces that turn against the reserved nature of the old novel. For this book is anything but reserved. It has its own morality, one that is relevant even to Berliners. (Tieck's "Abraham Tonelli" had earlier unleashed the power of the Berlin dialect, but no one had previously attempted to find a cure for it.)[4]

It is rewarding to follow the cure that is prescribed for Franz Biberkopf.

What happens to him?—But first, why is the novel called *Berlin Alexander-platz,* with *The Story of Franz Biberkopf* only a subtitle? What is Alexanderplatz in Berlin? It is the site where for the last two years the most violent transformations have been taking place, where excavators and jackhammers have been continuously at work, where the ground trembles under the impact of their blows and under the columns of omnibuses and subway trains; where the innards of the metropolis and the backyards around Georgenkirchplatz have been laid bare to a greater depth than anywhere else; and where districts built in the 1890s have managed to survive more peacefully than elsewhere in the untouched labyrinths around Marsiliusstrasse (where the secretaries of the Immigration Police are crammed into a tenement block) and around Kaiserstrasse (where the whores make their rounds in the evening). It is no industrial district; commerce above all—petty bourgeoisie. And then, there is its sociological negative, the crooks who obtain their reinforcements from the unemployed. One of these is Biberkopf. He is released from Tegel prison, and finds himself without work; he remains respectable for a time, starts selling goods on street corners, gives it up, and joins the Pums gang. The radius of his life is no more than one thousand meters. Alexanderplatz governs his existence. A cruel regent, if you like. An absolute monarch. For the reader forgets everything else around him, learns to feel his life within that space and how little he had known about it before. Everything turns out to be different from what the reader expected to find in a book he has taken out of the mahogany bookcase. It did not seem to have the feel of a "social novel." No one sleeps under the trees. They all have a room. Nor do you see them looking for one. Even the first of the month seems to have lost its terrors in the area around Alexanderplatz. These people are certainly miserable [*elend*]. But they are miserable in their rooms. What does this mean, and how does it come about?

It has two meanings. A broad one and a limiting one. A broad one, for misery is in fact not what little Moritz had imagined. *Real* misery, at least—in contrast to the kind imagined in your nightmares. It is not just people who have to cut their coat according to their cloth, and cope as best they can; this is something that holds good for poverty and misery, too. Even its agents, love and alcohol, sometimes rebel. And nothing is so bad that you cannot live with it for a time. In this book, misery shows us its cheerful side. It sits down at the same table with you, but this does not put an end to the conversation. You adjust to the situation and keep on enjoying yourself. This is a truth that the new low-life Naturalism refuses to acknowledge. This is why a great storyteller had to come and help it gain credence. It is said of Lenin that he hated only one thing more than misery: making a pact with it. There is in fact something bourgeois about this—not just in the mean, petty kinds of slovenliness, but also in the large-scale forms of

wisdom. In this sense Döblin's story is bourgeois, and it is so in its origin—
that is to say, in a much more limiting way than in its ideology and intention.
What we find here once again, in a beguiling form and with undiminished
force, is the reemergence of the magic of Charles Dickens, in whose works
bourgeois and criminals fit each other like a glove because their interests
(however opposed to each other they may be) inhabit one and the same
world. The world of these crooks is homologous with the world of the
bourgeoisie. Franz Biberkopf's road to pimp and petty bourgeois is no more
than a heroic metamorphosis of bourgeois consciousness.

The novel, we might reply to the theory of the *roman pur*, is like the sea.
Its only source of purity is its salt. Now, what is the salt in this book? Salt
in the epic is like a mineral: it makes things last when it is alloyed with
them. And duration is a criterion of epic writing far more than of other
types of literature. Duration not in time, but in the reader. The true reader
reads an epic in order to "retain" it. And it is quite certain that he will retain
two incidents from this book: the story about the arm and the events
concerning Mieze. How does it come about that Franz Biberkopf gets
thrown under a car and thus loses an arm? And that his girlfriend is taken
from him and killed? The answer can be found as early as the second page.
"Because he wants more from life than bread and butter." In this instance,
not rich food, money, or women, but something far worse. His big mouth
longs for something less tangible. He is consumed by a hunger for destiny—
that's what it is. This man is always asking for trouble in a big way; no
wonder it keeps coming to him. The way in which this hunger for destiny
is satisfied for the whole of his life, and the way he learns to be content with
bread and butter—in short, the way in which the crook becomes a sage—is
the nature of the sequence of events. At the end, Franz Biberkopf loses his
sense of destiny; he becomes "clear-headed," as the Berliners put it. Döblin
made this great process of maturation unforgettable by means of a great
artistic device. Just as at a Bar Mitzvah Jews reveal to the child his second
name, which up to then has remained a secret, so too Döblin gives Biberkopf
a second name. From now on, he is Franz Karl. At the same time, something
strange has happened to this Franz Karl, who is now working as assistant
doorman in a factory. And we would not swear that this has not escaped
Döblin's attention, even though he keeps a pretty sharp eye on his hero. The
point is that Franz Biberkopf has now ceased to be exemplary, and has been
whisked away into the heaven for characters in novels. Hope and memory
will console him in this heaven, the little porter's lodge, for his failure in
life. But we do not follow him into his lodge. This is the law governing the
novel: scarcely has the hero discovered how to help himself than he ceases
to be capable of helping us. And if this truth becomes manifest in its grandest
and most inexorable form in Flaubert's *L'éducation sentimentale,* we may

think of Franz Biberkopf's history as the "sentimental education" of the crook. The most extreme and vertiginous, the last and most advanced stage of the old bourgeois *Bildungsroman*.

Published in *Die Gesellschaft*, 1930. *Gesammelte Schriften*, III, 230–236. Translated by Rodney Livingstone.

Notes

1. André Gide, *Journal des "Faux-monnayeurs"* (1926).
2. Alfred Döblin, "Der Bau des epischen Werks" (The Structure of the Epic Work), in *Jahrbuch der Sektion für Dichtkunst* (Berlin, 1929), p. 262.
3. Adolf Glassbrenner (1810–1876) was a radical journalist who wrote satirical and comic vignettes of Berlin life in the local dialect. His writings include *Berlin, wie es ist—und trinkt* (Berlin, As It Is—and Drinks; 1832–1850) and *Buntes Berlin* (Colorful Berlin; 1837–1841).
4. Ludwig Tieck (1773–1853), a leading German Romantic writer, wrote the whimsical story "Merkwürdige Lebensgeschichte Sr. Majestät Abraham Tonelli" (Remarkable Life Story of His Majesty Abraham Tonelli) in 1798.

An Outsider Makes His Mark

S. Kracauer, *Die Angestellten: Aus dem neuesten Deutschland* [White-Collar Workers: The Latest from Germany] (Frankfurt am Main: Frankfurter Societätsdruckerei, 1930), 148 pages.

The malcontent is a type as old as the hills, perhaps as old as writing itself. Thersites, Homer's cynic; the first, second, and third conspirators in Shakespeare's histories; the Faultfinder from the only great drama of the World War—all of these are the changing faces of this one figure.[1] But the literary fame of the archetype does not seem to have given heart to its incarnations in real life. They tend to pass through existence nameless and tight-lipped, and for the physiognomist it is undoubtedly an event when one of the breed suddenly draws attention to himself and declares in public that he is not going to play the game. The writer in question here likewise appears reluctant to make free with his own name. A laconic "S." in front of his surname warns us not to take too many liberties. The reader is made aware of this laconic stance through other, more internal means as well—as in the way humanity is born from the spirit of irony. S. glances at the proceedings in the labor courts, and the merciless light reveals to him "not so much wretched human beings, as human beings made wretched by circumstances." What is clear is that this man refuses to play the game. He declines to don a mask for the carnival mounted by his fellow human beings. He has even left his Doctor of Sociology cap at home. And he rudely pushes his way through the throng, so as to lift the masks of the most impudent here and there.

It is easy to understand why he repudiates the term "reportage" as a description of his own enterprise. In the first place, he finds modern Berlin radicalism and the New Objectivity—both of which acted as godparents to reportage—equally repugnant.[2] In the second place, a troublemaker who unmasks others has no desire to be thought of as a portrait painter. Unmasking others is this writer's passion. He forces a dialectical entry into the lives of office workers not because he is an orthodox Marxist, even less a practical agitator, but because "unmasking" is what is meant by "forcing a dialectical entry." Marx asserted that social existence determines consciousness. But he also claimed that only in a classless society would consciousness be adequate to that existence. It follows that in a class society social existence is inhuman to the degree to which the consciousness of the different classes, far from being adequate, is highly mediated, inauthentic, and displaced. And since such a false consciousness on the part of the lower classes is in the interest of the upper classes, and since that of the upper classes is explained by the contradictions of its economic situation, the creation of a true consciousness—primarily in the lower classes, who have everything to gain from it—must be the chief task of Marxism. In this sense, and originally only in this sense, the author can be said to think as a Marxist. Of course, his project leads him all the more deeply into the overall system of Marxism because the ideology of white-collar workers represents a unique combination: on the one hand it comes very close to that of the proletariat, in the sense that it reflects the given social reality, while on the other it bears the imprint of the wishes and memories of the bourgeoisie. Today, there is no class of people whose thoughts and feelings are more alienated from the concrete reality of their everyday lives than those of white-collar workers. In other words, the process of adaptation to the inhuman side of the contemporary social order has made greater strides among white-collar workers than among blue-collar ones. The white-collar worker's more indirect relations to the production process go hand in hand with a more direct involvement in the forms of human interaction that correspond to that process. And since the medium in which this reification of human relations actually takes place is that of the organization—the only medium, incidentally, in which reification could be overcome—the author arrives inevitably at a critique of the trade unions.

   This critique is not carried out in terms of party politics or wage policy. Nor can it be found in a single place; rather, it is something that emerges at every point. Kracauer is not concerned with what the union achieves for its members. Instead he asks: How does it educate them? What does it do to liberate them from the spell of the ideologies that hold them in thrall? His consistent outsider status greatly helps him in formulating answers to such questions. He has no commitments that might allow authorities to trump his assertions and force him to hold his tongue. No commitment to the idea of community, for example. He unmasks this idea as a variant of economic opportunism. What about the higher educational qualifications of the white-collar worker? Kracauer dismisses these as illusory, and demonstrates how the exaggerated claims to education increase the white-collar worker's impotence when it comes to defending his rights. What about cultural goods, then? To fix them once and for all means, in his view, to pander to the belief that "the disadvantages of mechanization can be evened out by spiritual values that can be taken like medicines." This entire ideological cast of mind "is itself the expression of the reification whose effects it is trying to counteract. It is founded on the belief that values represent ready-made realities that can be delivered to your home like commodities." Such statements do more than comment on a problem. The entire book is an attempt to grapple with a piece of everyday reality, constructed here and experienced now. Reality is pressed so closely that it is compelled to declare its colors and name names.

The name is Berlin. In the author's view, it is the quintessential white-collar worker's city—to the point where he is fully aware that he has made an important contribution to the physiology of the capital. "Today, Berlin is the city of white-collar culture par excellence; that is to say, a culture which has been made by white-collar workers for white-collar workers, and which most white-collar workers regard as culture. Only in Berlin, where the links with origins and roots have been pushed so far into the background that the weekend can become a great fashion, can the reality of white-collar workers be fully grasped."[3] Sports are an essential aspect of the weekend. The author's critique of the popularity of sports among white-collar workers shows how disinclined he is to compensate for his ironic treatment of cultural ideals by an even more passionate defense of nature. Far from it. The instinctual insecurity fostered by the ruling class is countered here by a writer who defends uncorrupted *social* instincts. He plays to his own strengths—and these consist in his ability to see through bourgeois ideologies, if not totally, then at least in every matter where they are still connected with the petty bourgeoisie. "The increased popularity of sports," Kracauer writes, "does not eliminate complexes, but is, among other things, an instrument of social repression on a grand scale. Far from promoting social change, it is a chief means of depoliticization."[4] And even more explicitly, in another passage: "A supposed natural law is erected as a counterweight to the present economic system, but no one realizes that Nature, which is also incorporated into the capitalist economy of desires, is one of its most powerful allies, and that the unqualified glorification of Nature stands in the way of the planned organization of economic life."[5] This hostility to Nature means that the author denounces it precisely at the point where traditional sociologists would talk of "decadence." What he regards as "Nature," on the other hand, is a certain traveling salesman in tobacco products who is remarkable for his expertise and jaunty attitude. Kracauer's thorough grasp of the economy leads him to perceive the basic—not to say barbaric—character of the forces and relations of production even in their contemporary, abstract forms. We need hardly add that he sees the much-vaunted process of mechanization in a very different light from the way it is viewed by our social pastors. How much more promising in the eyes of this critic is the soulless mechanized action of the unskilled worker than the wholly organic "moral rosiness"[6] that, in the priceless words of a personnel manager, is typical of the complexion of the good white-collar worker. "Morally rosy"—this is the color of the white-collar worker's existence.

The personnel manager's flowery speech shows how the white-collar worker's jargon communicates with the author's own language, and reveals the rapport that has been established between this outsider and the language of the collective he is targeting. Quite without effort, we learn about *Blut-orangen* and *Radfahrer, Schleimtrompeten* and *Prinzessinnen*.[7] And the better we become acquainted with all this, the more easily we can see how knowledge and humanity seek refuge in metaphors and nicknames in order to avoid the broad-brush vocabulary of professors and trade-union functionaries. Or should we say that in all these articles concerned with reforming, humanizing, and deepening wage labor, what we find is not so much a mode of discourse as the perversion of language itself—a perversion that uses the most heartfelt words to conceal the shabbiest reality, the most elevated words for the basest reality, and the most peaceable words for the most inhospitable reality? However that may be, Kracauer's analyses, particularly of academic, Taylorist studies, contain elements of the most scathing satire—a satire that has long since retreated from the realm of humorous political magazines in order to claim a space on an epic scale appropriate to the immeasurable scope of its subject.[8] Unfortunately, this epic scope is that of a land laid waste. And the more completely it is repressed in the minds of the social classes concerned, the more creative it turns out to be—in accordance with the laws of repression—at producing images. One might suggest a comparison between the processes in which an unbearably tense economic situation produces a false consciousness, and the situations that lead neurotics and the mentally ill along the path from unbearable private conflicts to their false consciousness.

As long as we persist in refusing to supplement the Marxist theory of the superstructure with an urgently needed theory about the origins of false consciousness, we will be unable to dispense with the concept of repression as an answer to the question: How can the contradictions of an economic situation give rise to a form of consciousness inappropriate to it? The products of false consciousness resemble picture puzzles in which the true subject peeks out from among clouds, foliage, and shadows. And the author has even descended into the advertising sections of white-collar newspapers in order to discover those true subjects that appear embedded like puzzles in the phantasmagoria of radiance and youth, education and personality. That is to say, encyclopedias, beds, crepe soles, pens that prevent writer's cramp, good-quality pianos, rejuvenation potions, and white teeth. But the higher reality does not rest content with a fantasy existence, and so makes its presence felt in everyday life in puzzle-picture form, just as poverty does in the bright lights of distraction. Thus, in the neo-patriarchal office, where one performs work that ultimately amounts to unpaid overtime, Kracauer detects the model of the mechanical organ that emits old-fashioned musical phrases; and in the typist's manual dexterity, he sees the petty-bourgeois sterility of the piano étude. The true symbolic centers of this world are the "pleasure barracks," the white-collar worker's pipe dreams in stone, or rather in stucco.[9] In his explorations of these "refuges for the homeless," the author's language, with its sensitivity to the logic of dreams, displays its full cunning. It is astounding to see how it molds itself to fit all these artsy, atmospheric cellars, all these cosy alcazars and intimate mocha parlors, only to expose them mercilessly to the light of reason like so many carbuncles and abscesses. An infant prodigy and enfant terrible all in one, the author tells tales from the school of dreams. And he is much too clearly in the picture to caricature these institutions as nothing more than the instruments used by the ruling class for keeping people stupid, and to load the entire responsibility onto that class. Radical though his criticism of the entrepreneurial class may be, he thinks it too much like the class it dominates, too subaltern in its outlook, for us to acknowledge it as the truly shaping power and the responsible intellectual force in the general economic chaos.

Because of this evaluation of the entrepreneurial class, although not for that reason alone, his book will have to renounce any ambition to political impact, as this is understood today; in other words, it will have to give up all hope of demagogic effect. The author's awareness of this, not to say his self-assurance on this score, sheds some light on his dislike of everything connected with reportage and the New Objectivity. This left-radical wing may posture as much as it likes—it will never succeed in eliminating the fact that the proletarianization of the intellectual hardly ever turns him into a proletarian. Why? Because from childhood on, the middle class gave him a means of production in the form of an education—a privilege that establishes his solidarity with it and, perhaps even more, its solidarity with him. This solidarity may become blurred superficially, or even undermined, but it almost always remains powerful enough to exclude the intellectual from the constant state of alert, the sense of living your life at the front, which is characteristic of the true proletarian. Kracauer has taken this insight absolutely seriously. This is why his book is a milestone on the road toward the politicization of the intelligentsia, in sharp contrast to the fashionable radicalism of the writings of the latest school. There we see the horror of theory and knowledge that commends it to the sensation-seeking of the snobs; here we find a constructive theoretical schooling that addresses neither the snob nor the worker, but is able to promote something real and demonstrable—namely, the politicization of the writer's own class. This indirect impact is the only one a revolutionary writer from the bourgeoisie can aim at today. A direct effect can proceed only from practice. When confronted with parvenu colleagues, he will keep Lenin in mind, for Lenin's writings are the best proof of how far the literary value of political practice, direct impact, is removed from the crude fact-finding and reportage that nowadays poses as such.

Thus, in the end this writer rightly stands alone. A malcontent, not a leader. No pioneer, but a spoilsport. And if we wish to gain a clear picture of him in the isolation of his trade, what we will see is a ragpicker, at daybreak, picking up rags of speech and verbal scraps with his stick and tossing them, grumbling and growling, a little drunk, into his cart, not without letting one or another of those faded cotton remnants—"humanity," "inwardness," or "absorption"—flutter derisively in the wind. A ragpicker, early on, at the dawn of the day of the revolution.

Published in *Die Gesellschaft*, 1930. *Gesammelte Schriften*, III, 219–225. Translated by Rodney Livingstone.

Notes

1. The last reference is to Karl Kraus's mammoth, sweepingly apocalyptic drama *Die letzten Tage der Menschheit* (The Last Days of Humankind). The play was published in final form in 1923; due to its great length (it has 220 scenes and approximately 500 characters), it was first performed in Vienna only in 1964— and even then in a shortened version. "The Faultfinder" (Der Nörgler), who engages in conversations with "the Optimist," is the play's stand-in for Kraus himself.
2. *Neue Sachlichkeit* (New Objectivity) was the term originally applied by the museum curator G. F. Hartlaub to an emergent figuration in German postwar painting. It gradually came to designate the Weimar "period style" in art, architecture, design, literature, and film: cool, objective, analytical.
3. Kracauer, *Die Angestellten*, p. 20.
4. Ibid., p. 129.
5. Ibid., pp. 145–146.
6. Ibid., p. 32.
7. *Blutorangen* (literally, "blood oranges") are people who are yellow on the outside and red on the inside—in other words, people who hypocritically conceal their opinions in order to succeed in the workplace. *Radfahrer* ("bicycle riders") are people who bow to those above them while kicking down hard on those below. *Schleimtrompeten* ("slime-trumpets") are official company newsletters. And *Prinzessinnen* ("princesses") are office girls who regard themselves as superior to the

salesgirls behind the counter, although the outsider can discern no difference in status. Only the term "bicycle rider" still survives in contemporary German.

8. Benjamin is alluding to the theories of Frederick Winslow Taylor (1856–1915), who established the modern discipline of business administration and pioneered in the study of rationalization and management efficiency. He is best-known for *The Principles of Scientific Management* (1911). "Taylorism" and "Taylorization" were buzzwords for a more general industrial modernization in Weimar Germany.

9. In the passage to which Benjamin refers, Kracauer describes these "pleasure barracks"—which offered stylish ambience, food, and entertainment—as "gigantic nightclubs, in which (as a gossip once put it in a Berlin paper), 'people can get a whiff of the wide world for little money,'" in the process satisfying their "hunger for glamor and distraction."

Theories of German Fascism

On the Collection of Essays *War and Warriors,* edited by Ernst Jünger

Léon Daudet, the son of Alphonse Daudet and himself an important writer, as well as a leader of France's Royalist party, once gave a report in his *Action Française* on the Salon de l'Automobile—a report that concluded, in perhaps somewhat different words, with the equation: "L'automobile, c'est la guerre."[1] This surprising association of ideas was based on Daudet's perception that there had been an increase in technological artifacts, in power sources, in tempo, and so on that private lives could neither absorb completely nor utilize adequately but that nonetheless demanded justification. They justified themselves in that they abstained from any harmonious interplay in war, whose destructive power provided clear evidence that social reality was not ready to make technology its own organ, and that technology was not strong enough to master the elemental forces of society. Without going too deeply into the significance of the economic causes of war, one might say that the harshest, most disastrous aspects of imperialist war are in part the result of the gaping discrepancy between the gigantic means of technology and the minuscule moral illumination it affords. Indeed, according to its economic nature, bourgeois society cannot help insulating everything technological as much as possible from the so-called spiritual [*Geistigen*], and it cannot help resolutely excluding technology's right of determination in the social order. Any future war will also be a slave revolt on the part of technology. Today factors such as these determine all questions of war, and one would hardly expect to have to remind the authors of the present volume of this, nor to remind them that these are questions of imperialist war. After all, they were themselves soldiers in the World War and, dispute what one may, they indisputably proceed from the experience of this war. It is therefore quite astonishing to find, and on the first page at that, the statement: "It is of secondary importance in which century, for which ideas, and with which weapons the fighting is done." What is most astonishing about this statement is that its author, Ernst Jünger,[2] thus adopts one of the principles of pacifism—indeed, the most questionable and most abstract of all its principles. Though for him and his friends this is based not so much on some doctrinaire schema as on a deep-rooted and—by all standards of male thought—really rather impious mysticism. But Jünger's mysticism of war and pacifism's clichéd ideal of peace have little to accuse each other of. Even the most consumptive pacifism has, for the moment, one thing over its epileptically frothing brother—namely, a certain contact with reality, and not least some conception of the next war.

The authors like to speak—emphatically—of the "First World War." Yet how little their experience has come to grips with that war's realities (which they refer to with alienated exaggeration as the "worldly-real") is shown by the utterly thoughtless obtuseness with which they view the idea of future wars without any conception of them. These trailblazers of the *Wehrmacht* could almost give one the impression that the military uniform represents their highest end, their heart's desire, and that the circumstances under which the uniform later attains its validity are of little importance by comparison. This attitude becomes more comprehensible when one realizes, in terms of the current level of European armaments, how anachronistic their espoused ideology of war is. These authors nowhere observe that the new warfare of technology and matériel [*Materialschlacht*], which appears to some of them as the highest revelation of existence, dispenses with all the wretched emblems of heroism that here and there have survived the World War. Gas warfare, in which the contributors to this book show conspicuously little interest, promises to give the war of the future a face which will permanently replace soldierly qualities by those of sports; all action will lose its military character, and war will assume the countenance of record-setting. For the most prominent strategic characteristic of such warfare consists in its being waged exclusively and most radically as an offensive war. And we know that there is no adequate defense against gas attacks from the air. Even individual protective devices, gas masks, are of no use against mustard gas and Levisit. Now and then one hears of something "reassuring," such as the invention of a sensitive listening device that registers the whir of propellers at great distances. And a few months later a soundless airplane is invented. Gas warfare will be based on annihilation records, and will involve an absurd degree of risk. Whether its outbreak will occur within the bounds of international law—after prior declarations of war—is debatable, but its end will no longer be concerned with such limitations. Since gas warfare obviously eliminates the distinction between civilian and military personnel, the most important principle of international law is abolished. The most recent war has already shown that the total disorganization imperialist war entails, and the manner in which it is waged, threaten to make it an endless war.

More than a curiosity, it is symptomatic that something written in 1930 about "war and warriors" overlooks all this. It is symptomatic that the same boyish rapture that leads to a cult of war, an apotheosis of war, is here heralded particularly by von Schramm and Günther. The most rabidly decadent origins of this new theory of war are emblazoned on their foreheads: it is nothing other than an uninhibited translation of the principles of *l'art pour l'art* to war itself. But if, even on its home ground, this theory tends to become a mockery in the mouths of mediocre adepts, its outlook in this new phase is disgraceful. Who could imagine a veteran of the Marne or of Verdun reading statements such as these: "We conducted the war on very impure principles . . . Real fighting from man to man, from company to company, became rarer and rarer . . . Certainly the front-line officers often conducted war without style . . . For through the inclusion of the masses, the lesser blood, the practical bourgeois mentality—in short, the common man—especially in the officers' and noncommissioned officers' corps, the eternally aristocratic elements of the soldier's trade were increasingly destroyed." Falser notes could hardly be sounded; more inept thoughts could not be written; more tactless words could not be uttered. The authors' absolute failure precisely here is the result—despite all the talk about "the eternal" and "the primeval"—of their unrefined, thoroughly journalistic haste to seize control of the actual present without having grasped the past. Yes, there have been cultic elements in war. They were known in theocratically constituted communities. As harebrained as it would be to want to return these submerged elements to the zenith of war, it would be equally embarrassing for these warriors on their flight from ideas to learn how far a Jewish philosopher, Erich Unger,[3] has gone in the direction they missed. And it would be embarrassing for them to see to what extent his observations—made, if in part with questionable justice, on the basis of concrete data from Jewish history—would cause the bloody schemes conjured up here to evaporate into nothingness. But these authors are incapable of making anything clear, of calling things by their names. War "eludes any economy exercised by the understanding; there is something inhuman, boundless, gigantic in its Reason, something reminiscent of a volcanic process, an elemental eruption, . . . a colossal wave of life directed by a painfully deep, cogently unified force, led to battlefields already mythic today, used up for tasks far exceeding the range of the currently conceivable." Only a suitor who embraces his beloved awkwardly is so loquacious. And indeed these authors are awkward in their embrace of thought. One has to bring them back to it repeatedly, and that is what we will do here.

And the point is this: War—the "eternal" war that they talk about so

much here, as well as the most recent one—is said to be the highest manifestation of the German nation. It should be clear that behind their "eternal"
war is concealed the idea of cultic war, just as behind the most recent war
hides the idea of technological war; and it should also be clear that these
authors have had little success in perceiving these relationships. But there is
something rather special about this last war: it was not only one of matériel
but also one that was lost. And thus, admittedly, it was the German war in
a special sense. To have waged war out of their innermost existence is
something that other peoples could claim to have done. But to have lost a
war out of their innermost existence—this they cannot claim. What is special
about the present and latest stage in the controversy over the war, which
has convulsed Germany since 1919, is the novel assertion that it is precisely
this loss of the war that is tied to Germanness. One can call this the latest
stage because these attempts to come to terms with the loss of the war show
a clear pattern. These attempts began with an effort to pervert the German
defeat into an inner victory by means of confessions of guilt, which were
hysterically elevated to the universally human. This political position, which
supplied the manifestos for the course of the decline of the West, was the
faithful reflection of the German "revolution" by the Expressionist avant-
garde. Then came the attempt to forget the lost war. The bourgeoisie turned
over, to snore on its other side—and what pillow could have been softer
than the novel? The terrors endured in those years became the down filling
in which every sleepyhead could easily leave his imprint. What finally
distinguishes this latest effort from earlier ones in the process involved here
is the tendency to take the loss of the war more seriously than the war
itself.—What does it mean to "win" or "lose" a war? How striking the
double meaning is in both words! The first, manifest meaning certainly refers
to the outcome of the war, but the second meaning—which creates that
peculiar hollow space, the sounding board, in these words—refers to the
totality of the war and suggests how the war's outcome also alters the enduring significance it holds for us. This meaning says, so to speak, the victor
retains the war; the vanquished misplaces it. It says, the victor annexes the
war for himself, makes it his own property; the vanquished no longer
possesses it and must live without it. And he must live not only without the
war per se but without every one of its slightest ups and downs, every
subtlest one of its chess moves, every one of its remotest actions. To win or
lose a war reaches so deeply (if we follow language) into the fabric of our
existence, that our whole lives become that much richer or poorer in symbols, images, and sources. And since we have lost one of the greatest wars
in world history, one which involved the whole material and spiritual
substance of a people, one can assess the significance of this loss.

Certainly one cannot accuse those around Jünger of not having taken this
into account. But how did they approach it, monstrous as it was? They have

not yet stopped fighting. They continued to celebrate the cult of war when there was no longer any real enemy. They complied with the desires of the bourgeoisie, which longed for the decline of the West, the way a schoolboy longs for an inkblot in place of his wrong answer. They spread decline, preached decline, wherever they went. Not even for a moment were they capable of holding up to view—instead of doggedly holding onto—what had been lost. They were always the first and the bitterest to oppose coming to one's senses. They ignored the great opportunity of the loser—which the Russians had taken advantage of—to shift the fight to another sphere until the moment had passed and the nations of Europe had sunk to being partners in trade agreements again. "The war is being *administered,* not *led* anymore," one of the authors complains. This was to be corrected by the German "postwar war" [*Nachkrieg*]. This *Nachkrieg* was as much a protest against the war that had preceded it, as it was a protest against the civilian character they had discerned in it. Above all, that despised rational element was to be eliminated from war. And, to be sure, this team bathed in the vapors rising from the jowls of the Fenriswolf. But these vapors were no match for the mustard gases of the yellow-cross grenades. This arch-Germanic magical fate acquired a moldy luster when set against the stark background of military service in army barracks and impoverished families in civilian barracks. And without subjecting that false luster to materialist analysis, it was possible even then for a free, knowing, and truly dialectical spirit such as Florens Christian Rang[4]—whose biography exemplifies the German better than whole hordes of these desperate characters—to counter their sort with enduring statements:

> The demonic belief in fate, the belief that human virtue is in vain; the dark night of defiance which burns up the victory of the forces of light in the universal conflagration of the gods; . . . this apparent glorying of the will in this belief in death in battle, without regard for life, flinging it down for an idea; this cloud-impregnated night that has hovered over us for millennia and which, instead of stars, gives us only stupefying and confusing thunderbolts to guide the way, after which the night only envelops us all the more in darkness; this horrible world view of world-death instead of world-life, whose horror is made lighter in the philosophy of German idealism by the notion that behind the clouds there is after all a starry sky: this fundamental German spiritual tendency in its depth lacks will, does not mean what it says, is a crawling, cowardly know-nothingness, a desire not to live but also a desire not to die either . . . For this is the German half-attitude toward life; indeed, to be able to throw it away when it doesn't cost anything, in a moment of intoxication [*Rausch*], with those left behind cared for, and with this short-lived sacrifice surrounded by an eternal halo.

But in another statement in the same context, Rang's language may sound familiar to those around Jünger: "Two hundred officers, prepared to die, would have sufficed to suppress the revolution in Berlin—as in all other places; but not one was to be found. No doubt many of them would actually have liked to come to the rescue, but in reality—not actuality—nobody quite wanted to begin, to put himself forward as the leader, or to proceed individually. They preferred to have their epaulets ripped off in the streets." Obviously the man who wrote this knows from his very own experience the attitude and tradition of those who have come together here. And perhaps he continued to share their enmity to materialism until the moment they created the language of material warfare.

If at the beginning of the war supplies of idealism were provided by order of the state, the longer the war lasted the more the troops had to depend on requisitions. Their heroism turned more and more gloomy, deadly, and steel-gray; glory and ideals beckoned from ever more remote and nebulous spheres; and those who saw themselves less as the troops of the World War than as the executors of the *Nachkrieg* increasingly adopted a stance of obstinate rigor. Every third word in their speeches is "stance." Who would deny that the soldier maintains a stance? But language is the touchstone for each and every position taken, and not just, as is so often assumed, for that of the writer. Yet those who have conspired here do not pass the test. Jünger may echo the noble dilettantes of the seventeenth century in saying that the German language is an originary language, but he betrays what he means when he adds that, as such, it inspires an insurmountable distrust in civilization and in the cultivated world. Yet this linguistic distrust cannot equal that of his own countrymen when the war is presented to them as a "mighty reviser" that "feels the pulse" of the times, that forbids them "to do away with" "a tried and proven conclusion," and that calls on them to intensify their search for "ruins" "behind gleaming varnish." Far more shameful than these offenses, however, is the smooth style of these purportedly rough-hewn thoughts which could grace any newspaper editorial; and more distressing yet than the smooth style is the mediocre substance. "The dead," we are told, "went, in death, from an imperfect reality to a perfect reality, from Germany in its temporal manifestation to the eternal Germany." This Germany "in its temporal manifestation" is of course notorious, but the eternal Germany would really be in a bad way if we had to depend on the testimony of those who so glibly invoke it. How cheaply they purchased their "solid feeling of immortality," their certainty that "the terrors of the last war have been frightfully exaggerated," and their symbolism of "blood boiling inwardly"! At best, they have defeated the war that they are celebrating here. However, we will not tolerate anyone who speaks of war, yet knows nothing but war. Radical in our own way, we will ask: Where do you come from? And what do you know of peace? Did you ever encounter peace in a child, a tree, an animal, the way you encountered a sentry in the field? And without waiting for you to answer, we can say No! It is not that you would then not be able to celebrate war more passionately than now; but to celebrate it *the way* you do would be impossible. How would Fortinbras have borne witness to war? One can deduce how he would have done it from Shakespeare's technique. Just as he reveals Romeo's love for Juliet in the fiery glow of its passion by presenting Romeo in love from the outset, in love with Rosalinde, he would have had Fortinbras begin with a passionate eulogy of peace so enchanting and mellifluously sweet, that when at the end he raises his voice all the more passionately in favor of war, everyone would have wondered with a shudder: What are these powerful, nameless forces that compel this man, wholly filled with the bliss of peace, to commit himself body and soul to war?—But there is nothing of that here. These are professional freebooters speaking. Their horizon is fiery but very narrow.

What do they see in their flames? They see—here we can entrust ourselves to F. G. Jünger[5]—a transformation:

> Lines of psychic decision cut across the war; transformations undergone by the war are paralleled by transformations undergone by those fighting it. These transformations become visible when one compares the vibrant, buoyant, enthusiastic faces of the soldiers of August 1914 with the fatally exhausted, haggard, implacably tensed faces of the 1918 veterans of machine warfare. Looming behind the all too sharply arched curve of this fight, their image appears, molded and moved by a forceful spiritual convulsion, by station after station along a path of suffering, battle after battle, each the hieroglyphic sign of a strenuously advancing work of destruction. Here we have the type of soldier schooled in those hard, sober, bloody, and incessant campaigns of attrition. This is a soldier characterized by the tenacious hardness of the born fighter, by a manifest sense of solitary responsibility, of psychic abandonment. In this struggle, which proceeded on increasingly deeper levels, he proved his own mettle. The path he pursued was narrow and dangerous, but it was a path leading into the future.

Wherever precise formulations, genuine accents, or solid reasoning are encountered in these pages, the reality portrayed is that of Ernst Jünger's "total mobilization" or Ernst von Salomon's "landscape of the front." A liberal journalist who recently tried to get at this new nationalism under the heading "Heroism out of Boredom" fell, as one can see here, a bit short of the mark. This soldier type is a reality, a surviving witness to the World War, and it was actually this "landscape of the front," his true home, that was being defended in the *Nachkrieg*. This landscape demands that we linger.

It should be said as bitterly as possible: in the face of this "landscape of total mobilization," the German feeling for nature has had an undreamed-of upsurge. The pioneers of peace, who settle nature in so sensuous a manner, were evacuated from these landscapes, and as far as anyone could see over the edge of the trench, the surroundings had become the terrain of German

Idealism; every shell crater had become a problem, every wire entanglement an antinomy, every barb a definition, every explosion a thesis; by day the sky was the cosmic interior of the steel helmet, and at night the moral law above. Etching the landscape with flaming banners and trenches, technology wanted to recreate the heroic features of German Idealism. It went astray. What it considered heroic were the features of Hippocrates, the features of death. Deeply imbued with its own depravity, technology gave shape to the apocalyptic face of nature and reduced nature to silence—even though this technology had the power to give nature its voice. War, in the metaphysical abstraction in which the new nationalism believes, is nothing other than the attempt to redeem, mystically and without mediation, the secret of nature, understood idealistically, through technology. This secret, however, can also be used and illuminated via a technology mediated by the human scheme of things. "Fate" and "hero" occupy these authors' minds like Gog and Magog, yet they devour not only human children but new ideas as well. Everything sober, unblemished, and naive that has been considered regarding the improvement of human society ends up between the worn teeth of these Molochs, who react with the belches of 42-cm. mortars. Linking heroism with machine warfare is sometimes a bit hard on the authors. But this is by no means true for all of them, and there is nothing more revealing than the whining digressions exposing their disappointment in the "form of the war" and in the "senselessly mechanical machine war" of which these noble fellows "had evidently grown bored." Yet when one or another of them attempts to look things squarely in the eye, it become obvious how very much their concept of the heroic has surreptitiously changed; we can see how much the virtues of hardness, reserve, and implacability they celebrate are in fact less those of the soldier than those of the proven activist in the class struggle. What developed here, first in the guise of the World War volunteer and then in the mercenary of the *Nachkrieg,* is in fact the dependable fascist class warrior. And what these authors mean by "nation" is a ruling class supported by this caste, a ruling class—accountable to no one, and least of all to itself, enthroned on high—which bears the sphinx-like countenance of the producer who very soon promises to be the sole consumer of his commodities. Sphinx-like in appearance, the fascists' nation thus takes its place as a new economic mystery of nature alongside the old. But this old mystery of nature, far from revealing itself to their technology, is exposing its most threatening feature. In the parallelogram of forces formed by these two—nature and nation—war is the diagonal.

It is no surprise that the question of "governmental checks on war" arises in the best, most well-reasoned essay in this volume. For in this mystical theory of war, the state naturally plays no role at all. These checks should not for a moment be understood in a pacifist sense. Rather, what is demanded of the state is that its structure and its disposition adapt themselves to, and appear worthy of, the magical forces that the state itself must mobilize in the event of war. Otherwise it will not succeed in bending war to its purpose. It was this failure of the powers of state in the face of war that instigated the first independent thinking of the authors gathered here. Those military formations ambivalently hovering between comradely brotherhoods and regular government troops at the end of the war very soon solidified into independent, stateless mercenary hordes. And the captains of finance, the masters of the inflation to whom the state was beginning to seem a dubious guarantor of their property, knew the value of such hordes.[6] They were available for hire at any time, like rice or turnips, by arrangement through private agencies or the *Reichswehr.* Indeed, the present volume retains a resemblance to a slogan-filled recruiting brochure for a new type of mercenary, or rather *condottiere*. One of its authors candidly declares: "The courageous soldier of the Thirty Years' War sold himself life and limb, and that is still nobler than simply selling one's politics or one's talents." Of course, when he adds that the mercenary of Germany's *Nachkrieg* did not sell himself but gave himself away, this is of a piece with the same author's comment on the comparatively high pay of these troops. This was pay which shaped the leadership of these warriors just as clearly as the technical necessities of their trade: as war engineers of the ruling class, they were the perfect complement to the managerial functionaries in their cutaways. God knows their designs on leadership should be taken seriously; their threat is not ludicrous. In the person of the pilot of a single airplane full of gas bombs, such leadership embodies all the absolute power which, in peacetime, is distributed among thousands of office managers—power to cut off a citizen's light, air, and life. This simple bomber-pilot in his lofty solitude, alone with himself and his God, has power-of-attorney for his seriously stricken superior, the state; and wherever he puts his signature, the grass will cease to grow—and this is the "imperial" leader the authors have in mind.

Until Germany has exploded the entanglement of such Medusa-like beliefs that confront it in these essays, it cannot hope for a future. Perhaps the word "loosened" would be better than "exploded," but this is not to say it should be done with kindly encouragement or with love, both of which are out of place here; nor should the way be smoothed for argumentation, for that wantonly persuasive rhetoric of debate. Instead, all the light that language and reason still afford should be focused upon that "primal experience" from whose barren gloom this mysticism of the death of the world crawls forth on its thousand unsightly conceptual feet. The war that this light exposes is as little the "eternal" one which these new Germans now worship as it is the "final" war that the pacifists carry on about. In reality, that war is only this: the one, fearful, last chance to correct the incapacity of peoples to order their relationships to one another in accord with the relationship they possess to nature through their technology. If this corrective effort fails, millions of human bodies will indeed inevitably be chopped to pieces and chewed up by iron and gas. But even the habitués of the chthonic forces of terror, who carry their volumes of Klages in their packs, will not learn one-tenth of what nature promises its less idly curious but more sober children, who possess in technology not a fetish of doom but a key to happiness.[7] They will demonstrate this sobriety the moment they refuse to acknowledge the next war as an incisive magical turning point, and instead discover in it the image of everyday actuality. And they will demonstrate it when they use their discovery to transform this war into civil war, and thereby perform that Marxist trick which alone is a match for this sinister runic nonsense.

Published in *Die Gesellschaft*, 1930. *Gesammelte Schriften*, III, 238–250. Translated by Jerolf Wikoff.

Notes

1. Alphonse Daudet (1840–1897), French author, was known for his gentle portrayals of life in the French countryside. His son, Léon Daudet (1867–1942), edited the right-wing Catholic journal *L'Action Française*, organ of the eponymous nationalist political movement that he founded with Charles Maurras in 1898. The journal was noted for its antidemocratic and anti-Semitic views.
2. Ernst Jünger (1895–1998), German novelist and essayist, was perhaps the leading voice of the intellectual radical Right in the Weimar Republic. His ideas and writing took a dramatic turn after World War II, when he began to espouse peace and European union.
3. Erich Unger (1887–1952), German-Jewish author, was a member of the circle around the esoteric thinker Oskar Goldberg. He was a student of the Kaballah, and criticized empiricism from a magical and mystical viewpoint.
4. Florens Christian Rang (1864–1924), conservative German intellectual and author, was perhaps Benjamin's most important partner in intellectual exchange in the mid-1920s.
5. Friedrich Georg Jünger (1898–1977), German writer and Ernst Jünger's brother, published poems, novels, and stories. He is best-known for his memoirs and his essays on political, cultural, philosophical, and literary topics.
6. The German inflation began as early as 1914, when the imperial government began financing its war effort with a series of fiscally disastrous measures. The economic situation deteriorated rapidly in the years following the end of World War I, as an already crippled economy was further burdened by war reparations. The inflation reached its critical phase—that of hyperinflation—in late 1922 and 1923. If we compare late 1913 (the last year before the war) with late 1923 using the wholesale price index as the basis for the comparison, we find that one German mark in 1913 equaled 1.26 trillion marks by December 1923.
7. Ludwig Klages (1872–1956), German philosopher and psychologist, attempted to found a "metaphysical psychology" which would study human beings in their relationship to reality—a reality which he saw as composed of archetypal images. Klages became the darling of the radical Right in the course of the 1920s.

Demonic Berlin

Today I will begin with an experience that occurred when I was fourteen. At the time, I was a pupil in a boarding school. As is customary in such places, the children and teachers met together in the evenings several times a week, and made music, or else someone gave a talk, or there was a poetry reading. One evening, the music teacher was in charge of the "chapel," as these evenings were called. He was a funny little man, with an unforgettable expression in his serious eyes, and the shiniest bald pate I have ever seen, surrounded by a semicircular wreath of tightly curled dark hair. His name is known to German music-lovers: he was August Halm.[1] This August Halm came to the chapel to read to us from the stories of E. T. A. Hoffmann, the very writer I wish to discuss with you today. I no longer remember what he read to us, nor is it of any importance here. But what I did note was a single sentence from the speech in which he introduced his reading. He described Hoffmann's writings—his liking for the bizarre, the cranky, the eerie, and the inexplicable. I think his words were calculated to raise our expectations about the stories we were going to hear. He then concluded with the sentence that I have not forgotten to this day: "Why anyone should tell stories like this is something I shall tell you in the near future." I am still waiting for that "in the near future." And since the good man has died in the meantime, this explanation would now have to reach me, if at all, via such an uncanny route that I would prefer to anticipate it; and so I shall attempt today to fulfill a promise that was made to me twenty-five years ago.

If I wanted to cheat a little, I could easily do so. I would need only to replace the words "For what purpose?" with "Why?" and the answer would be very straightforward. Why does a writer write? For a thousand reasons.

Because it is fun to invent something; or because ideas, images take possession of him and he can rest only when he has written them down; or because he is preoccupied with questions and doubts for which he seeks answers in the fates of imagined people; or simply because he has learned to write; or—and this is unfortunately very common—because he has not learned anything at all. It is not hard to explain why Hoffmann wrote. He is one of those writers who are obsessed with their characters. *Doppelgänger,* horrific figures of every kind—when he wrote, he really felt surrounded by them. And not only while he was writing, but even during an innocent conversation at table in the evening, over a glass of wine or punch, he would see things; and on more than one occasion he would interrupt one or other of his companions with the words:

> Forgive me, my dear friend, if I interrupt you. But don't you see over there in the corner, to the right, that accursed little squirt pulling himself from under the floorboards? Just watch the devil of a fellow! Look, look, now he's gone! Oh, please don't be shy on our account, dear Tom Thumb—please stay with us! Pray listen to our good-humored conversation—you can't imagine how delighted we would be to enjoy your highly esteemed company. Ah, there you are again. Won't you do us the honor of coming nearer? Really—you *will* agree to partake of a little something? What did you say? Oh, you are leaving. Our humble respects!

And so on. And no sooner had he uttered all this gibberish, his eyes fixed on the corner in which he saw the vision, than he would come to his senses with a start, turn to his companions and calmly ask them to proceed. This is how Hoffmann's friends have described him for us. And we feel ourselves infected by his character when we read such stories as "The Deserted House," "The Deed of Entail," "The Doubles," or "The Golden Pot." And if the circumstances are favorable, the effect of these ghost stories can be intensified to an astounding degree. I have experienced this myself, and in my case the favorable circumstance was that my parents had forbidden me to read Hoffmann. When I was little, I could read him only on the sly, on evenings when my parents were away from home. And I can remember a particular evening, when I was sitting alone under the lamp at the giant dining-room table—it was in Carmerstrasse—and there was not a sound to be heard in the entire house. And as I sat there reading "The Mines of Falun," all the horrors gradually gathered around me at the table edge in the surrounding gloom, like fish with blank expressions, so that my eyes remained fixed on the pages of the book from which all this horror emerged, as if redemption might come from them. Another time, earlier in the day—I can still remember—I was standing right by the bookcase that was open just a crack, ready to throw the book into the case at the first noise. I stood there reading "The Entail," with hair on end, and so frozen with the twofold horror of the terrors of the book and the risk of being caught that I failed to grasp a single word of what I was reading.

"The devil himself could not write such diabolical stuff," Heine said of Hoffmann's writings. And in fact, there is something satanic that goes hand in hand with the ghostly, eerie, uncanny aspect of these stories. If we try to explore this a little further, we shall soon progress from the answer to the question of why Hoffmann wrote his stories, and from there to the answer to the more mysterious question: For what purpose? The devil—alongside his many other peculiarities—is also an ingenious and knowing fellow. Anyone who is acquainted with Hoffmann's stories will understand me at once when I say that the narrator in these stories is always a very perceptive, sensitive fellow who detects spirits even in their most subtle disguises. Indeed, this narrator insists with a certain stubbornness that all the honest archivists, senior medical counselors, students, apple-sellers, musicians, and genteel daughters are no more what they seem to be than Hoffmann himself was a pedantic legal counselor at the court of appeals which was the source of his income. But, in other words, this means that the eerie, spectral figures who appear in Hoffmann's stories are not characters dreamed up by their author in the stillness of his own little room. Like many other great writers, he found the extraordinary not somehow floating freely in mid-air, but in quite specific people, things, houses, objects, and streets. As you may have heard, people who judge other people by their face, their walk, or their hands, or judge their character, their profession, or even their fate by the shape of their head, are known as physiognomists. In this sense, Hoffmann was not so much a seer as someone who looked at people and things. And that is quite a good definition of the term "physiognomy." One of the main things he looked at was Berlin, both the city and the people who inhabit it. In his introduction to *The Deserted House* (which in reality was a house on Unter den Linden), he speaks with a certain bitter humor of the sixth sense he had been endowed with, of the gift of being able to look at every manifestation—whether a person, an action, or an event—and perceive what was unusual about it, the sort of thing to which we have no access in our everyday life. He had a passion for wandering alone through the streets and observing the people he met, even casting their horoscopes in his mind's eye. For days on end, he would follow people unknown to him because they had something that struck him in their walk, clothing, voice, or glance. He felt he was in constant contact with the suprasensual, and the spirit world pursued him even more than he pursued it. It barred his way in the clear light of day in this rational Berlin; it pursued him amid the bustle of Königstrasse, and even to the few surviving remnants of the Middle Ages around the decaying Town Hall. On Grünstrasse it caused him to smell a mysterious scent of roses and carnations, and it cast a spell on him on Unter den Linden, the elegant street that was the meeting place of high society.

Hoffmann could be called the father of the Berlin novel. The traces of the city were subsequently submerged in generalities when people began to call Berlin the "capital," the Tiergarten the "park," and the Spree the "river"; until in our own time it sprang to life once more—in such works as Döblin's *Berlin Alexanderplatz*. He makes one of his characters say to another, standing in for himself: "You had a definite reason for setting the scene in Berlin, and calling streets and squares by their proper names. But in my opinion it is not a bad idea in general to describe the scene precisely. Apart from the fact that the whole story gains the illusion of historical truth and thus bolsters a limp imagination, it also gains uncommonly in vividness and freshness for anyone familiar with the setting."

I could certainly list the many stories in which Hoffmann thus proves himself the physiognomist of Berlin. I could name the buildings that appear in his writings, starting with his own home on the corner of Charlottenstrasse and Taubenstrasse, down to the Golden Eagle on Dönhoffplatz, to Lutter & Wegner in Charlottenstrasse, and so on. But I think we would do better to look more closely at how Hoffmann studied Berlin and what impression this has left in his stories. The writer was never a particular friend of the solitude of nature. People—communicating with them, observing them, merely looking at them—were more precious to him than anything. If he went out walking in the summer, as he did every evening if the weather was fine, it was always to public places where he might meet people. And even on the way to these places, there were few wine bars or cafés that he failed to enter, to see whether people were there and who they were. Not that he looked in at such places only to discover new faces that would give him strange new ideas. Rather, the wine bar was a kind of poetic laboratory, a place for experimentation in which he could try out the complications and effects of his stories every evening on his friends. Hoffmann was not a novelist but a storyteller; and even in book form, many of his stories—if not the majority—are told from the point of view of one of the characters. To be sure, it is really always Hoffmann himself who is the narrator, sitting around the table with his friends, each of whom tells a story in turn. One of Hoffmann's friends tells us explicitly that he was never idle in the wine bar, like the many people you see sitting there who do nothing but sip their wine and yawn. On the contrary, he would sit there gazing around with eagle eyes; whatever he saw that was ridiculous, striking, or even touching among the other customers became fodder for his work. Or else he quickly sketched it with a few bold strokes of his pen—for he had great dexterity in drawing. But woe betide the people in the wine bar if they were not to his liking, if they were narrow-minded philistines sitting around the table. On those occasions he must have been quite unbearable, making frightening use of his talent for pulling faces, embarrassing people, and intimidating them. But the epitome of horror, to his mind, were the arty tea parties that were fashionable at the time. These were meetings of aesthetes—actually ignorant and unintelligent people who were far too conceited about their interest in art and literature. He has given a very droll account of such a party in his *Phantasiestücke* [Weird Tales].

In drawing this discussion to a close, we will not allow anyone to reproach us with having forgotten our original question about the purpose of his writing. Far from forgetting it, we have in fact already provided an unobtrusive answer to it. For what purpose did Hoffmann write his stories? Needless to say, he did not have any deliberate aims in mind. But we can undoubtedly read the tales as if he did have some. And these aims can be none other than physiognomic ones: the desire to show that this dull, sober, enlightened, commonsensical Berlin was full of things calculated to stimulate a storyteller—things that were to be found lurking not only in its medieval corners, remote streets, and dreary houses, but also in its active citizens of all classes and districts, if only you knew how to track down such things and look for them in the right way. And as if Hoffmann really had intended his works for the edification of his readers, one of his very last stories, one that he dictated on his deathbed, is in fact nothing but a textbook of physiognomic seeing. This story is entitled "Des Vetters Eckfenster" [My Cousin's Corner Window]. The cousin is Hoffmann himself; the window is the corner window in his apartment and looks out onto Gendarmenmarkt. The story is actually a dialogue. Hoffmann, paralyzed, sits in an armchair, gazing down onto the weekly market, and proves to his cousin, who is there on a visit, how much you can infer—and, even more, spin out and imagine—simply by looking at the clothes, tempo, and gestures of the market women and their customers. And now that we have said so much in praise of Hoffmann, we ought to end by pointing out something quite unknown to the majority of Berliners: he is the only writer to have made Berlin famous abroad. The French read him and loved him at a time when in Germany and in Berlin no dog would have accepted a piece of bread from him. Now all that has changed. There are a host of very affordable editions, and there are even more parents who allow their children to read Hoffmann than there were in my day.

Radio talk delivered on Berliner Rundfunk, February 1930. *Gesammelte Schriften*, VII, 86–92. Translated by Rodney Livingstone.

Notes

1. August Halm (1869–1929), German musicologist and composer, was the author of several popular introductions to music.

Hashish, Beginning of March 1930

A divided, contradictory experience. On the positive side: the presence of Gert, who, thanks to her apparently very extensive experiments of this kind (even though hashish was new to her), had the effect of intensifying the power of the poison.[1] More later on the extent of this. On the negative side: inadequate effect on her and Egon, perhaps because of the inferior quality of the drug, which was different from the one I was taking. As if that were not enough, Egon's tiny room was far too small for my imagination, and it provided such poor sustenance for my dreams that for the first time I kept my eyes shut during the entire procedure. This led to experiences that were entirely new to me. If the contact with Egon was nil, or even negative, that with Gert was rather too sensual to make possible a purely distilled intellectual outcome.

Despite these reservations, I see from certain subsequent statements of Gert's that the trance was so profound that the words and images of certain stages have escaped me. Since, in addition, contact with others is indispensable for the person in the trance if he is to succeed in formulating his thoughts in language, it will be evident from what has been said that on this occasion the insights yielded were disappointing in relation to the depth of the trance and, so to speak, the enjoyment. All the more reason to emphasize the core of this experiment as it appeared in Gert's statements and my own recollections. These statements concerned the nature of aura. Everything I said on the subject was directed polemically against the theosophists, whose inexperience and ignorance I find highly repugnant. And I contrasted three aspects of genuine aura—though by no means schematically—with the conventional and banal ideas of the theosophists. First, genuine aura appears in all things, not just in certain kinds of things, as people imagine. Second, the aura undergoes changes, which can be quite fundamental, with every movement the aura-wreathed object makes. Third, genuine aura can in no sense be thought of as a spruced-up version of the magic rays beloved of spiritualists and described and illustrated in vulgar works of mysticism. On the contrary, the characteristic feature of genuine aura is ornament, an ornamental halo, in which the object or being is enclosed as in a case. Perhaps nothing gives such a clear idea of aura as Van Gogh's late paintings, in which one could say that the aura appears to have been painted together with the various objects.

From another stage: my first experience of *audition colorée*. I did not fully appreciate what Egon said to me, because my apprehension of his words was instantly translated into the perception of colored, metallic sequins that coalesced into patterns. I explained it to him by comparing it to the beautiful colored knitting patterns that we had liked so much as children in the *Herzblättchens Zeitvertreib*.

Even more remarkable perhaps was a later phenomenon linked to the sound of Gert's voice. It came at the point when she herself had taken morphine, and I, who had no knowledge of the effects of this drug apart from what I had read, was able to give her an accurate and penetrating account of her condition—on the evidence, as I myself remarked, of her intonation. Apart from that, this turn of events—Egon's and Gert's excursion into morphine—was in a certain sense the end of the experiment for me, although it was also the climax. It was the end because, given the enormous sensitivity induced by hashish, every moment of not being understood threatens to turn into acute unhappiness. How I suffered from the feeling that "our ways had parted." This was how I formulated it.—The climax because, as Gert busied herself with the syringe (an instrument that gives me a certain feeling of revulsion), the subdued but constant sensual relationship I had with her seemed to me to be colored black, undoubtedly a result of the black pyjamas she was wearing. And without her frequent and persistent attempts to induce me to try morphine, she might easily have appeared to me as a kind of Medea, a poisoner from Colchis.

Some attempt to characterize the image zone. An example: when we are conversing with someone and at the same time can see the person we are talking to smoking his cigar or walking around the room and so on, we feel no surprise that despite the effort we are making to speak to him, we are still able to follow his movements. The situation is quite different when the images we have before us while speaking to someone have their origins in ourselves. In a normal state of consciousness, this is of course quite impossible. Or rather, such images do arise—they may even arise constantly—but they remain unconscious. It is otherwise in a hashish trance. As this very evening proved, there can be an absolutely blizzard-like production of images, independently of whether our attention is directed toward anyone or anything else. Whereas in our normal state free-floating images to which we pay no heed simply remain in the unconscious, under the influence of hashish images present themselves to us seemingly without requiring our attention. Of course, this process may result in the production of images that are so extraordinary, so fleeting, and so rapidly generated that we can do nothing but gaze at them simply because of their beauty and singularity. For example, as I was listening to Egon, every word he uttered deprived me of a long journey; I have now acquired a certain skill in imitating—when my head is clear—the formulations that have arisen under the influence of hashish. About the images themselves I cannot really say very much, because of the tremendous speed with which they arose and then vanished again; moreover, they were all on a very small scale. In the main, they were images of objects. Often, however, with strongly ornamental features. Objects easy to ornament are the best: walls, for instance, or vaulting, or certain plants. Right at the start, I formed the term "knitting palms" to describe something I saw—palm trees with the sort of stitching you see in pullovers. But then also quite exotic, indecipherable images of the kind we know from Surrealist paintings. For example, a long gallery of suits of armor with no one in them. No heads, but only flames playing around the neck openings. My "Decline of the *pâtissier*'s art" unleashed a gale of laughter in the others. This had the following explanation. For a time I had visions of gigantic cakes, larger than life, cakes so huge that it was like standing in front of a mountain and being able to see only part of it. I went into detailed descriptions of how these cakes were so perfect that it wasn't necessary to eat them, because the mere sight of them was enough to quench all desire for them. And I called that "eyebread." I can no longer recollect how the previously mentioned coinage came about. But I may not be far off if I reconstruct it this way: the fact that we have to eat cakes nowadays is attributable to the decline of the *pâtissier*'s art. I had the same attitude to the coffee I was given. I held the cup of coffee motionless in my hand for a good quarter of an hour, declared it beneath my dignity to drink it, and transformed it, as it were, into a scepter. In a hashish trance, you can certainly talk about the hand's need for a scepter. This trance was not very rich in great coinages. I remember *Haupelzwerg*,[2] which I tried to explain to the others. More comprehensible is my reply to a statement of Gert's that I received with my usual boundless contempt. The formula for this contempt was, "What you are saying is as much use to me as a Magdeburg roof."

It was strange at the beginning, when I could just sense the approach of the trance and I compared objects to the instruments of an orchestra that was just tuning up before the start of the performance.

Drug protocol from March 1930; unpublished in Benjamin's lifetime. *Gesammelte Schriften*, VI, 587–591. Translated by Rodney Livingstone.

Notes

1. Participating in this session were Egon and Gert Wissing, who took part in a number of Benjamin's drug experiments. Egon, a neurologist, was Benjamin's cousin.
2. A nonsense word, although *Zwerg* means "dwarf."

Julien Green

"Nous qui sommes bornés en tout, comment le sommes-nous si peu lorsqu'il s'agit de souffrir?"[1] This question of Marivaux's is one of those brilliant formulations with which the mind is sometimes rewarded by distance, detachment, from the matter in hand. For no age was further removed from the contemplation of suffering than the French Enlightenment. It was this distance that led Marivaux to such a compelling formulation. Julien Green, however, who used this quotation as an epigraph for his *Adrienne Mesurat,* is well aware of what is at stake in the idea of the Passion. And this applies not just to this novel but to his writing as a whole, in which suffering is the dominant if not the sole theme. But anyone who starts to inquire how suffering can become such an exclusive concern of a writer will soon realize how alien to Julien Green Marivaux's analytical psychology must be—or indeed any psychological view of human beings, for that matter. Anyone who wishes to study human beings from a humane, humanist standpoint—we might almost say, from the standpoint of the layman—would try to portray people in the round, as the phrase goes, but also as pleasure-loving, healthy, dominating beings. For the theological mind, however, it is suffering alone that holds the key to the deepest insights into the essence of humanity. Not, of course, without taking into account the powerful ambiguity of the Latin word *passio*—that intertwining of suffering and passion which helps *passio* become the world-historical massif, the watershed of religions. It is on these inhospitable heights that the disturbing, forbidding work of Green has its origins. Here we find the source of both tragic myth and Catholic myth—the pious heathen passion of King Oedipus, Electra, and Ajax, as well as of the pious Christian Jesus. Here, at the point of indifference, at the mountain pass where all myths meet, the writer makes ready to delineate the situation of modern man through the traces of his *passio*.

Creaturely suffering as such is timeless. But this is not the case with the passions on which *passio* feeds. Avarice, the thirst for power, inertia of the heart, pride—each of these vices emerges in his writing in allegorically incisive figures, yet the passions that scourge his characters inwardly are not found in the old Christian canon of the deadly sins. On the other hand, anyone who wished to describe the genius and the curse of people alive today in theological terms would undoubtedly encounter impatience, the newest vice, a modern and most hellish vice. Emily Fletcher, Adrienne Mesurat, Paul Guéret—avid tongues of flame that flicker in the breeze of fate. Does Green wish to show (we might thus sympathetically interpret his writings) what would have become of this generation if it had not been able to sate its consuming impatience on enormous torrents of movement, communication, and pleasure? Or does he wish to invoke the dangerous energies that are lodged in the heart of this generation and produce its proudest achievements, and that only await the opportunity to increase their speed a thousandfold to break out in destructive processes of unprecedented rapidity? For passion—and this is a basic motif of *passio*—does not just violate God's commandments, but also offends against the natural order. This is why it arouses the destructive forces of the entire cosmos. And what passion brings down upon itself is not so much divine judgment as the revolt of Nature against whoever disturbs its peace and distorts its countenance. This profane doom is passion's lot, the consequence of its own action. Moreover it is the work of chance. In his latest and most mature work, *Léviathan*, Green presents us with the annihilation of the sufferer in a less inward way, more as the result of a tragic entanglement. He has thus done homage to this extreme of externality in much the same way as Calderón, the master of dramatic passion who constructed his plays on the most baroque of complications, the most contrived interventions of fate. Chance is the figure of Necessity abandoned by God. This is why, in Green, the depraved interiority of passion is in reality so completely in the grip of externality. So much so that passion is basically nothing but the agent of chance in the created being. Speed is the portion of chance that transmits despair to his characters' various destinies. Hope is the ritardando of fate. His characters are incapable of hope. They have no time for it; they are exasperated.

"Patience" is the word that embraces all the virtues of this author; at the same time, it contains all that his characters lack. The man who understands so much about these raving lunatics stares unblinkingly with large eyes. His face has the regular features and pale olive complexion of the Spaniard. In the unsullied nobility of his voice, there is something that seems to fend off too many words; and like his voice, his handwriting—with its transparent, unadorned letters—advances almost in silence. One is tempted to speak of letters that have learned renunciation. The hardest part, however, is to convey a sense of the childlike composure expressed in his confession that it was not given to him to describe even the simplest incident he had experienced himself. Nothing can be more incomprehensible for anyone who is looking for some sort of bridge to the commonplace idea of the novel—that preposterous amalgam of thought and experience. Green stands beyond that deaf, sterile combination. He writes nothing that has been experienced. His experience [*Erlebnis*] is writing itself. Nor does he think anything up. For what he writes leaves no latitude. He goes on to say that nothing is more dubious than a straightforward plot, the progress of the story. These things cannot simply be thought out. He works on his manuscript in order to continue the lives of his characters as far as is required by the succeeding pages. And without thinking about it or explaining it to himself in the interval, he returns the following day to where he left off. We are not speaking loosely if we describe this procedure as visionary, and as the origin of the excessively stringent, hallucinatory clarity with which his characters move. Green's distance from novelists of the usual sort can be defined as the gulf between making present [*Vergegenwärtigung*] and depicting.

Making present: it is not the magical side of the phrase but its temporal aspect that must first be addressed. It compels us to distinguish two varieties of Naturalism: that of Zola, who depicts people and conditions such as only his contemporaries might see them; and that of Green, who imagines them in a way that they would never have appeared to a contemporary. Where does he do it?—In our imagination?—This tells us little. He does it in our temporal space, which is alien to them and which encloses them in a vault of hollow years that echoes back their whispered words and screams. Only this second present immortalizes what existed; and this is why this form of making present is a magical act. Green does not depict people; he makes them present at fateful moments. That is to say, they behave as if they were apparitions. Adrienne Mesurat standing at the window and gazing at Maurecourt's villa; old Mesurat stroking his beard; Madame Legras making off with Adrienne's necklace—each and every one of their gestures was of this kind, and as poor souls beyond the grave they are compelled to relive these moments anew. They stand before the reader in that desperate stereotypicality of all truly fateful moments, like the figures of Dante's Inferno, the embodiments of an irrevocable existence after the Last Judgment. This stereotypicality is the mark of Hell. If you get to the bottom of these moments, you understand what fate is—namely, the rule of chance in its consummate, merciless form. And its most despairing form. For consummate despair is despair in its consummate, perfected form. Just as Pascal saw in the starry heavens the archetype of mathematical perfection, nothing but the sterility of eternal silence, in the same way Green, as the great interpreter of fate, discerns in the perfect concatenation of individual destinies nothing but the desolate abandonment of all creatures.

Yet the visionary aura that surrounds them is the very opposite of "vivid, true-to-life characterization." Such a stereotyped notion of vision likes to think in terms of dreams, of the evidence and vividness of faces. But assume that a person has a nightmare and is experiencing one of the terrifying images that are so abundant in Green's books. What will he do when he awakes? Put on the light and breathe a sigh of relief. It is quite different if you have a vision: however terrible it may be, the moment you wake up, the climax, the terror of terrors, will always lie beyond your visual horizon. For the here and now is the seal of authenticity that clings to every vision— the here and now that we find conquered, populated, colonized now and forever by its faces. A phased submerging and awakening—this is how we should envisage Green's work. A process of being shaken to the core by a thousand terrors, each one of them the terror of giving birth. The surrounding world lies there in an unwelcome light, with deep, jagged shadows. A "vale of tears" reveals itself to the waker. And perhaps this means that when a man has long ceased to shed a tear, the world around becomes moistened by the sweat or dew of misery. There are three huge heaps of coal mounded in the storage area of a coal dealer's yard, and Guéret lands in them after clambering over a wall. Green provides a very precise description of these black hillocks shimmering in the moonlight. I was familiar with it when I asked him one day whether he knew the origins of his works. A character? An experience [Erfahrung]? An idea? But his only answer was, "I can tell you the origin of my latest book quite precisely. It was a heap of coal I came across one day." In his works everything is assembled around such images, the way they appear to the startled gaze of a person waking up. Nowhere is this more obvious than at the beginning of his books. In all his novels, the first character readers meet is the protagonist. He or she is always absorbed by something: Guéret by his clock, Adrienne by the daguerreotypes of her ancestors, Emily by the landscape in front of her window. It is the moment of a strange absentmindedness, a commonplace moment of absorption at the point when fate enters and afflicts the characters like an illness. This is how Green sees them—just as we see ourselves after many years in our memory (a seeing which is also an awakening), engaged in pursuits of no real significance. These are moments for eternity. It is these and these alone that Green fixes on. "Toujours, semblait-il, murmura la rivière, toute la vie de même, toute la vie."[2] This is the lifelong song of these people, for their moments of destiny accompany them to the very end. They do not develop. Unless you want to call it a "development" that they stumble from one misfortune to the next, like a body falling down a stone staircase that doesn't miss a single step.

So they fall to their deaths. And they thus experience the earthly doom of *passio:* the destruction of body and life. Impotence, sleep, and finally death—it is always the answer of the body that stands at the ultimate end of suffering. In the eyes of this novelist the bed is the hereditary site, the throne, of the living creature. "Une passion par personne, cela suffit."[3] It suffices because passion means a life of hardship, and the regular sequence of its stations is already laid down in advance. But can this rule be formulated? Does it really apply to contemporary man? Green's characters are anything but modern. Inflexible as the mask-like personae of tragedians, they live out their lives in small French towns. Their clothes and their daily lives are stunted and old-fashioned, but in their gestures survive age-old rulers, evildoers, fanatics. Amid woodcarvings and plush, their ancestors still lodge in their rooms, as if in dead tree-stumps or sedge. The merging of the old-fashioned with primal history [*Urgeschichte*], the trauma of seeing one's parents in a dual perspective—one that is both historical and part of primal history—is the abiding motif of this author. From the twilight in which the world is here embedded emerge houses and rooms in which the members of our fathers' generation passed their lives. Indeed, looked at rightly, Green's three principal works are all set in the same house, whether it belongs to Mrs. Fletcher, old Mesurat, or Mme. Grosgeorges. In the same way, the tragedies of Antiquity were all acted out before the façade of the same palace, which belonged now to Agamemnon, now to Creon or Theseus. "Having a place to live": Does this still mean barely having a roof over one's head, a process full of fear and magic—one that was perhaps never so voracious as it has been under the cover of civilization and the everyday bourgeois Christian world? The house of the fathers, which stands in the twofold darkness of what has only just happened and the unthinkably remote past, is here momentarily illuminated by the lightning shafts of destiny, and is as transparent as the night sky in a storm. It has been transformed into a vista of caverns, chambers, and galleries extending back into the primeval past of mankind. It is certain that for every generation a piece of primal history is fused with the existence, the life forms, of the immediately preceding one; thus, for the generation alive now, such a fusion takes place with the middle and end of the previous century. Nor is Green the only one to feel this. Cocteau's book *Les enfants terribles* is an expedition, equipped with all modern techniques, into the submarine depths of the nursery—to say nothing of Proust's work, dedicated as it is to time past and its cells in which we were children. Proust conjures up the magical time of childhood; Green brings order to our earliest terrors. In the cleared-out home of our childhood, he sweeps together the traces left by the existence of our parents. And from the pile of suffering and horror that he has heaped up, their unburied corpses suddenly appear to us with as much force as, centuries ago, the human body appeared to the pious man, whom it stigmatized.

Published in *Neue schweizer Rundschau,* April 1930. *Gesammelte Schriften,* II, 328–334. Translated by Rodney Livingstone.

Notes

1. "We are limited in all things; why are we limited so little when it comes to suffering?" Pierre de Marivaux, *La vie de Marianne,* part 9.
2. "Always, it seemed, the stream kept murmuring, one's whole life long in the same way, the whole of one's life."
3. "One passion per person—that suffices."

Paris Diary

December 30, 1929. No sooner do you arrive in the city than you feel rewarded. The resolve not to write about it is futile. You reconstruct the preceding day just like children who reconstruct the table full of presents on Christmas Day. This, too, is a way of expressing your gratitude. Still, I'm holding to my plan that someday soon I will do more than just this. For the moment, at least, the plan prevents me—as does the space for reflection that I need in order to work—from abandoning my willpower and surrendering myself to the city. For the first time I elude it; I fail to turn up at the rendezvous to which loneliness, that old pimp, invites me, and arrange matters so that on many days I fail to see Paris for the Parisians. Of course—what an easy matter it is to overlook this city! It is as easy as overlooking health and happiness. You can't imagine how uninsistent it is. There are perhaps few cities in which so little is—or can be—overlooked as in Berlin. This may be the effect of the organizational and technical spirit that prevails there, for good or ill. Contrast this with Paris. Just think how the streets here seem to be inhabited interiors, how much you fail to see day after day, even in the most familiar parts, and how crucially important it is, more so than anywhere else, to keep crossing from one side of the street to the other.—You need to have lived in Paris a long time to know these things. What is the source of this unassuming exterior that seems oriented toward the needs and talents of the most insignificant members of society? Perhaps it is to be found in a way of thinking that is both conservative and urban, a synthesis quite alien to us. It's not just the Aragon who wrote the book who is a *paysan de Paris*—the real peasants are the concierge, the *marchand de quatre saisons,* and even the *flic.*[1] All of these are people who cultivate their *quartier*, as constant and peace-loving as peasants. It goes without saying that the history of the city's construction was no less turbulent, no less full of violent ruptures than others. But just as nature heals the wounds of old castles with greenery, so here a bustling bourgeoisie has settled down and calmed the strife of the metropolis. If some out-of-the-way squares enclose their space so inwardly—as if a convention of houses had founded them—then the feeling for peacefulness and permanence that created them has, in the course of centuries, been passed on to their residents. And all this was echoed in the greeting I received from the old cashier in my money-exchange office, when I returned after a long interval: "Vous avez été un moment absent."—With a single tug he drew the moments of my absence together, like a sack in which he might hand me three years' savings.

January 6, 1930. In the first few days of January I saw Aragon, Desnos, Green, Fargue.[2] Fargue turned up in Le Bateau Ivre. The latter has bridges, portholes, loudspeakers, lots of brass, and white enameled walls. The latest fashion is for night spots to be owned by ladies from the nobility. This one belonged to a princesse d'Erlanger. Moreover, since the gin fizz costs 20 francs, the nobility can also make money on the side—and can even do so with a good conscience because a large proportion of those who are inspired by their cocktails are writers, so that the cultural capital of the nation is thereby increased. Here, then, is where I encountered Léon-Paul Fargue one evening, long past midnight, as he was emerging, boiling hot, as it were, from the cauldron. When he suddenly appeared, I just had time to whisper to Dausse, who sat next to me, "Here is the greatest living poet in France." Apart from the fact that Fargue is in fact a great poet, we discovered that evening that he was also one of the most enchanting of storytellers. Scarcely had he heard that I had been much preoccupied with Proust than he made it a point of honor to conjure up the most colorful and contradictory picture of his old friend. It was not just the physiognomy of the man that, to our amazement, his voice contrived to bring to life; not just the loud, exaggerated laugh of the young Proust, the socialite, his whole body in paroxysms, holding his white-gloved hands up to his gaping mouth, while his square monocle danced in front of him, dangling from a broad black ribbon; not just the invalid Proust living in a bedroom that could barely be distinguished from the furniture storeroom of an auction house, lying in a bed that had not been made for days on end, a bed that was really more like a cave filled with manuscripts, sheets of paper both blank and scribbled on, writing pads and books, all piled up, caught in the gap between the bed and the wall, and heaped up on the bedside table. It was not just this Proust that he conjured up. He also sketched the history of their twenty-year friendship, the outpourings of heartbreaking affection, the fits of insane mistrust, those "Vous m'avez trahi!" at the slightest pretext; not to mention his remarkable account of the dinner he had given for Marcel Proust and James Joyce, who met each other then for the first and only time.[3] "To keep the conversation going," said Fargue, "was like lifting a deadweight. And I had even taken the precaution of inviting two beautiful women, to soften the force of the collision. But this did not prevent Joyce from vowing, as he took his leave, that he would never again enter a room where he might risk encountering Proust." And Fargue imitated Joyce's gesture of revulsion when Proust, his eyes wide with enthusiasm, declared of some imperial or royal highness, "C'était ma première altesse!"[4]—This early Proust of the late 1890s stood at the beginning of a road whose end he himself could not yet descry. In those days, he was seeking identity in the individual human being. It seemed to him the truly deifying element. This was how the greatest scourge of the idea of personality in modern literature had started out.—"Fargue," wrote Léon-Pierre Quint[5] in November 1929,

> is one of those people who write as they speak; he constantly utters works that remain unwritten—perhaps from indolence, perhaps from contempt for writing. An endless sequence of unforced flashes of wit and puns—this was the only way he was capable of speaking. He has a childlike love of Paris, with its godforsaken little cafés, its bars, its streets, and its nightlife that never ends. He must be in robust health and have a highly resilient character. During the day he works as an industrialist, and at night he is always on the move. He is constantly seen with elegant women, Americans. He is close to fifty years of age, yet leads the life of a gigolo by night, hypnotizing everyone he meets with the charm of his speech."

This describes him exactly as he appeared to me. We stayed together, amid a mini–fireworks display of reminiscences and epigrams, until they threw us out at around 3 A.M.

January 9. Jouhandeau.[6] The space in which he received me is a perfect synthesis of atelier and monk's cell. An unbroken row of windows runs along two walls. In addition, there was a skylight in the ceiling. Heavy green curtains everywhere. Two tables, both of which could rightly be described as desks. In front of them, chairs that seemed lost in space. Five in the afternoon: the light comes from a small chandelier and a tall standing lamp. Conversation about the magic of work conditions. Jouhandeau talks about the inspirational power of light that comes from the right. After this, a lot of autobiographical information. When he was thirteen or fourteen, he fell under the decisive influence of two charming sisters who lived in the Carmelite convent school of his hometown. Under their guidance he was overwhelmed by Catholicism, which up until then had been nothing but an object of education and instruction. The sight of a porcelain crucifix above his bed, on my first glance around his room, told me that his religion now meant much more to him. Yet I confessed to him that after I had read his first book I was still uncertain whether he approached Catholicism as a believer or merely as an explorer. He was delighted with this description. As he sat opposite me, talking insistently and animatedly, a very distinguished, somewhat fragile presence, I felt some regret that I was only now coming closer to him, at a time when so many of the forces that threatened his world had sprung to life in me. He went on talking about his life, and especially about the night—the one following Déroulède's[7] funeral—when he had burned all his writings, an endless pile of notes and speculations that had finally come to seem to him nothing but an obstacle on the path to a true life. This is when his writing had started to lose its lyrical and speculative side. It was only afterward that he had begun to create the world of characters that in fact all originated, as Jouhandeau told me, from a single street in his hometown, the street he had lived on. It is important to him to describe the world of these characters—a cosmos whose laws can be decoded only from one central point. That central point is Godeau, a new Saint Anthony, whose devils, whores, and beasts spring from speculative theology.—Furthermore: "What fascinates me most about Catholicism are the heresies." In his view, every individual is a heretic. And what excites him are the countless individual distortions of Catholicism. He lives with his characters (many of whom have never appeared in his books) for a long while, until they become real enough for him to describe them. Often it takes a great deal of time before a small gesture or mannerism reveals to him their particular heresy. I talk to him about the magnificent and abstruse playfulness of his characters, and the fact that they distract themselves not with the objects of daily life—knives or forks, matches or pencils—but with dogmas, incantations, and illuminations. My expression *jouets menaçants*[8] pleases him greatly. Ermeline and Noëmie Bodeau are mentioned. And Mademoiselle Zéline, whose history I like to represent in the allegorical image of a vice that does not seduce her but that seizes her by the scruff of the neck and pushes the stupefied woman along the path of virtue. It goes without saying that I tell him my ideas about the magnificently illuminating description of madness in "Le marié du village." One critic has compared the author with Blake. I believe this is justified: think of the cruelty with which Jouhandeau exposes his characters to religious experience, an exposure that is expressed in the abrupt contours of his sentences. "Vos personnages sont tout le temps à l'abri de rien."[9]—The end of our conversation was marked by the passage he showed me in the beautiful deluxe edition of his *Monsieur Godeau intime.* He himself described it as the crucial point of the book; it contains the account of God's sojourn in Hell and His struggle with it.

January 11. Breakfast with Quint. He is planning a book on Gide. Stressed how disconcerted the reading public had been by Gide's recent books, and how poorly they had sold—with the exception of *L'école des femmes.*[10] The

French public had no interest in the debate on sexual questions, and even now was closer to the *retroussés*[11] of *Le Sourire* and *La vie parisienne* than to the Oscar Wilde phenomenon. My own view is that the most noticeable defect in Gide's treatment of homosexuality is his attempt to establish it as a purely natural phenomenon—in contrast to Proust, who took sociology as his starting point for his study of this tendency. But this, too, is connected with the man's makeup, which increasingly seems—to my mind—to lie in the contrast between his belated puberty, his tortured and divided disposition, on the one hand, and the pure, astringent, graphic line of his writings, on the other.

January 16. Théâtre des Champs-Elysées. Giraudoux's *Amphitryon 38,* the only play worth going to in Paris at the present time, since the talented Pitoëff has filled his stage with a production of *Les Criminels.*[12] The "38" means that it is the thirty-eighth treatment of this material. You need only reflect on that word a little to see the essence of his achievement. In fact, Giraudoux regards the story as a uniquely precious piece of material that has not lost any of its value from having passed through so many hands. On the contrary, its value has been enhanced by the aura of a radiant old age; it has set the writer the fashionable challenge of finding an elegant new shape for it and of displaying it from an unexpected angle. It is being compared with Cocteau's *Orpheus,*[13] another reworking of a classical subject: whereas Cocteau is said to have reconstructed the myth according to the latest architectonic principles, Giraudoux has understood how to renew it in line with fashion. We might perhaps equate Cocteau with Le Corbusier, and Giraudoux with Lanvin.[14]

In fact, the great fashion house of Lanvin did provide the costumes; and Valentine Tessier,[15] the actress playing Alcmena, gives a performance in which ruches, sashes, flounces, and fichus are partners with at least as much talent and vivacity as Mercury, Sosie, Zeus, and Amphitryon. Add to this the fact that the moral that insinuates itself into the spectator's mind so virtuously and seductively is one that defends marital fidelity against all the erotic sophistries of Olympus, and you have grasped the entire fashionable, conservative, and—in a word—eminently French tendency of the play. Walking home pensively on one of those mild winter evenings, you feel closer to the forces that for centuries have enabled this city to devote itself to the comprehensive economic and intellectual organization of fashion. Giraudoux, too, conveys the certainty that fashion suits the Muses as well as women.

January 18. Berl.[16] This primitive system is still the best: before meeting someone unknown to you, spend half an hour reading through his writings. My efforts were not in vain. In *La mort de la pensée bourgeoise* I came across the following passage, which not only shed light on Berl in advance, but also illuminated retrospectively my conversation with Quint about Lautréamont. The passage dealt with sadism:

> What does Sade's work teach us, if not to recognize the extent to which a truly revolutionary mind is alienated from the idea of love? Insofar as his writings are not straightforward repressions, as would be natural for a prisoner, and insofar as they did not spring from the desire to give offense—and in Sade's case I do not think they did, since that would have been a foolish aspiration for an inmate of the Bastille—insofar as such motives are not involved, his works have their roots in a revolutionary negation developed to its ultimate logical extreme. What indeed would be the purpose of a protest against the powerful, once you have accepted the dominance of nature over human exist-ence, with all the indignities that this implies? Isn't "normal love" the most repulsive of all prejudices? Is conception anything but the most contemptible way of underwriting the fundamental design of the universe? Aren't the laws of nature, to which love submits, more tyrannical and hateful than the laws of society? The metaphysical meaning of sadism lies in the hope that the revolt of mankind might become so intensely violent that it would force nature to change its laws, and that once women have developed the resolve to cease tolerating the injustice of pregnancy and the dangers and pain of giving birth, nature would find itself compelled to find other ways of ensuring the survival of the human race on earth. The strength that says no to the family or the state must also say no to God; and just like the regulations of officials and priests, the ancient law of Genesis, too, must be broken: "In the sweat of thy face shalt thou eat bread; in pain shalt thou bring forth children." For what constitutes the crime of Adam and Eve is not that they provoked this law, but that they endured it.

—And now I am in the room inhabited by the author of this passage. Low chairs, apart from a desk chair. Along the shorter wall to the right, an aquarium that can be illuminated. Above the aquarium, a painting by Picabia. All the walls are colored green, circled by a gilt border. The book-shelves are covered in green leather: Courier, Sainte-Beuve, Balzac, Staël, the *Thousand and One Nights,* Goethe, Heine, Agrippa d'Aubigné, Meilhac, and Halévy.[17] Not hard to see that he is one of the people who like nothing better than to be allowed to descant on their favorite topic and who then recite what they have to say without brooking much interruption. His main concern now is to continue his polemical work by expelling pseudo-religi-osity from its very last hiding-places. These he discovers not in Catholicism, with its hierarchies and sacraments, nor even in the state, but in individu-alism, with its faith in the incomparable nature, the immortality, of the individual—the conviction that one's own interiority is the stage for a unique, unrepeatable tragic action. He discerns the most fashionable form of this conviction in the cult of the unconscious. That he has Freud on his side in the fanatical struggle he has instigated against this cult—that is to say, against Surrealism, which celebrates it—is something I would have known even if he had not assured me of it. And with a glance at the copy of *Le Grand Jeu* that I had just bought (the magazine put out by some dissident members of the group): "They are seminarists, nothing more." This was followed by a few curious comments on the lifestyle of these young people—their *refus*, as Berl called it. We might translate this as "sabotage." To turn down an interview, reject the chance of a collaboration, refuse to allow a photograph to be taken—these things they view as so many proofs of their talent. Berl ingeniously connects this with the ingrained tendency toward asceticism typical of Parisians. On the other hand, there is still a vestige here of the idea of the unrecognized genius—an idea that we are just in the process of demolishing so thoroughly. A person who is a failure still has something of a halo here, and the snobs are on the point of gilding it anew. For example, the financiers who have formed a club to buy paintings and have agreed not to put them back on the market until ten years have elapsed. Their chief principle: no more than 500 francs may be paid for any single painting. Any painter whose works cost more has already succeeded; anyone who succeeds is no good. I listen to him without contradiction. But I find neither the attitude of those young people nor that of these old snobs so completely incomprehensible. How many ways there are, after all, to succeed as an artist, and how few of them have even the remotest connection with art!

January 21. M. Albert.[18] D. appeared at my hotel in the morning; asked me to keep the evening free. He will call for me at seven and introduce me to M. Albert. He will, as he puts it, visit M. Albert in his *établissement*. He claims that this is a perfectly extraordinary place. Now, this establishment— a public bathhouse in the Quartier Saint-Lazare—is indeed remarkable. But far from picturesque. The serious, genuine—in other words, socially dangerous—vices appear unassuming and try to avoid giving any impression of business; they can even seem rather touching. M. Albert's friend Proust may have known all about that. Hence, the atmosphere of this bathhouse is difficult to describe. Let us say, a pervasive family mood, but behind the scenes all the genuine vices. What is really striking, right through the evening, is the honest family intimacy of these boys, with which their amazing candidness does not conflict at all. At any rate, those I saw, for all their ostentatious and precious manner, had a naïveté, boyish rebelliousness, playfulness, and defiance that secretly reminded me of my time at boarding school.—First comes the courtyard that you have to cross: a landscape of cobblestones and peace. Lights in only a few of the windows that overlook it. But there is light behind the frosted glass of Albert's office and in a garret on the left that rises up like battlements. There were three of us: Hessel and I had to put up with being introduced by D. as translators of Proust.[19] I was astonished to see confirmed what Hessel had said to me about him a few days earlier: he is something of a sea-god, merging with everything, flowing off everything. Incidentally, you can see this most clearly in the porcelain figurines. Porcelain is the most licentious material for depicting loving couples; I picture D. as a whoremongering porcelain river-god. Chief among the bit players was Maurice Sachs.[20] His vivacious manner and the obviously well-rehearsed precision of his anecdotes had the effect of making certain episodes and pieces of information appear suspect. Scarcely was he stuffed into the car with Hessel and myself than he began to regale us with a sort of catalogue of the main stories about Albert that gave me the uneasy feeling I was witnessing a *tournée des grands-ducs*. Behind the frosted-glass panes, the reception room was sealed off by blinds from all the adjoining rooms, where offensive scenes might be taking place. And M. Albert behind the counter, or the till—a contrivance consisting of washcloths, perfumes, *pochettes surprise,* tickets to the baths, and tarty dolls. Very polite and discreet in his manner of greeting, and agreeably occupied on the side by the backlog of daily chores. If I remember rightly, Proust met him first in 1912. He could not have been more than twenty at the time. And you can see from his present appearance that he must have been very handsome in the days when he was a personal valet to Prince von Radziwill and, before that, to Prince Orloff. The complete fusion of utter obsequiousness and absolute decisiveness that characterizes the lackey—as if the master caste took no pleasure in ordering around people they had not drilled into becoming generals—has entered into his features through a sort of fermentation, so that at times he looks like a gym teacher. The evening program was planned on a large scale. At least, the intention was to follow up dinner by reinforcing the new friendship with a visit to M. Albert's second establishment, the Bal des Trois Colonnes. There appeared to be some uncertainty, perhaps out of excessive politeness, about where to go for dinner. They quickly settled on the place on the rue de Vaugirard that Hessel and I had once walked past three years previously without even glancing inside. Today there were some astoundingly beautiful boys there. Including a presumably authentic Indian prince, who interested Maurice Sachs so profoundly that he was distracted from carrying out his intention of luring M. Albert into parting with some of his most cherished secrets. But I'm not sure they would have interested me any more than some very unimportant, almost involuntary comments that inadvertently cropped up in our conversation. For I am almost wholly indifferent to the question of what would emerge if someone were to use Proust's passions—some of which strongly resemble a famous scene with Mademoiselle Vinteuil—as an aid to the interpretation of his works. Conversely, however, Proust's works appear to me to point to general sadistic characteristics in him, although they are well concealed. My starting point here would be Proust's insatiable compulsion to analyze the most trivial incidents.

Also his curiosity—something which is very close to it. We know from experience how curiosity in the shape of repeated questions, constantly probing the same issue, can become an instrument in the hands of the sadist—the same instrument that is so innocent in the hands of children. Proust's relationship to existence has something of this sadistic curiosity. There are passages where his questioning may be said to provoke life to extremes; and in other passages, he stands before a fact of the heart like a sadistic teacher before an intimidated child, forcing it to reveal a suspected, perhaps not even genuine secret with ambiguous gestures, a tweaking and pinching that lies halfway between endearment and torment. Yet we can see a convergence of his two great passions—curiosity and sadism—in another of his traits: his inability to rest satisfied with any information, his compulsion to scent out in every secret an even more minute secret contained in it, and so on to infinity, but with the effect that as their size decreases, their importance grows.—All this went through my mind while M. Albert sketched the course of their acquaintance. It is generally known that some time after they had met, Proust set up a *maison de rendezvous* for him. This became a *pied-à-terre* and laboratory at the same time. Here he informed himself, partly through the evidence of his own eyes, about all the varieties of homosexual experience; this was where he made the observations that were subsequently incorporated into his depiction of the bondage of Charlus; this was where he deposited the pieces of furniture belonging to an aunt who had died, only to lament (in *A l'ombre des jeunes filles en fleur*) their unseemly end in a brothel.—It grew late. I could barely filter out M. Albert's faint voice from the noise of a gramophone, which was constantly being supplied with new records by an elegiac beauty who was unable to dance because he had a hole in his trousers and felt put out by the successful competition from the Indian prince. We were too tired to give M. Albert the opportunity of returning our hospitality *chez lui,* that is to say, at the Trois Colonnes. D. drove us home in his car.

January 26. Félix Bertaux. Despite his southern appearance, he is from Lorraine. But presumably has some French blood. Here is a nice anecdote from his time as a young teacher in Poitiers. There was an evening meeting of Action Française—this was before the war.[21] Bertaux had gone to it with some friends, in a spirit of opposition. After a recruitment address, the chairman invited comments from the floor from those who were not in agreement. To Bertaux's astonishment, no one came forward. Quickly making up his mind, he leaped from his seat at the back, stormed down the length of the hall with giant strides to the podium, and mesmerized the audience for three quarters of an hour. His speech produced a complete change of heart among this audience of Action Française fellow travelers. *Il a renversé la salle,* as they say. And the aftermath in his classroom the next day. He dropped a piece of chalk while writing something on the blackboard. Ten boys rushed from their seats to pick it up. Bertaux was taken aback, thought about it, and dropped something else, apparently by chance. This time, twenty boys jumped up. Such was the passionate response to his speech of the previous evening. He could have made the most brilliant career as a politician—he might have become a prefect, or a member of parliament. But he prefers to spend his spare time working at a French-German dictionary which has preoccupied him for the past fifteen years and which is eagerly awaited. Our conversation turns mainly on Proust. Proust and Gide—in 1919 their ranking may have been momentarily in doubt. But not for Bertaux, even then. The canonical objections and reservations: Proust failed to enrich the substance of mankind; he did not enhance or purify the concept of *l'humanité*. Bertaux cites Gide's description of Proust's treatment of everyday reality: a piece of cheese under the microscope. You say to yourself, "Eh bien, c'est ça ce que nous mangeons tous les jours?!"[22]— My reaction. Of course, he has not elevated humanity, but only analyzed it. His moral greatness lies quite elsewhere. The task he has made peculiarly his own and that he has pursued with a passion unknown in any previous writer is that of describing with unprecedented fidelity the things that have crossed our path. His fidelity to an afternoon, a tree, a stain from the sun on the wall; his fidelity to a gown, furniture, perfumes, or landscapes. (I would say the discovery in the last volume—that the roads to the Guermantes and to Méséglise meet up—represents allegorically the greatest moral that Proust can vouchsafe.) I concede that, at bottom, Proust *peut-être se range du côté de la mort.*[23] *Jenseits des Lustprinzips* [Beyond the Pleasure Principle], Freud's late work of genius, is probably the fundamental commentary on Proust. Bertaux is willing to admit all of this, but is not won over, *se range du côté de la santé.*[24] I end up saying that if there was any health which Proust had sought and loved in his works, it was not the vigorous health of the man but the defenseless and tender health of the child.

February 4. Adrienne Monnier.[25] Shortly after three, I open the door of Aux Amis des Livres, 7 rue de l'Odéon. I sense a certain difference from other bookshops. This seems to be no second-hand bookshop. Evidently, Adrienne Monnier deals only in new books. But it all looks a little less colorful, less agitated, and less unfocused than other shops. A pale, warm ivory tone lies spread over the broad tables. Perhaps it comes from the transparent jackets on many of the books—all modern first editions, all de luxe editions. I walk up to the woman closest to me. She has given me the feeling that if this should turn out to be Adrienne Monnier, it would mean the greatest possible disappointment of my fleeting, superficial expectation of meeting a pretty, young girl. A stolid, blond woman with very clear gray-blue eyes and clad in a dress of coarse gray wool of a severe, nun-like cut. In front, a row of inlaid buttons, old-fashioned edgings. It is she. I feel instantly that she is one of those people to whom one can never show enough respect, and who without seeming to expect that respect in any way, do nothing to reject or deprecate it. It is remarkable that this woman only twice crossed Rilke's path, as she put it, even though he lived in Paris for such a long time. I could imagine that he would have felt the deepest interest [*Neigung*] in a being of such rustic purity, in such a cosmically monastic creature. Incidentally, she speaks very beautifully of him and says, "He seems to have given everyone who knew him the feeling that he was profoundly involved in everything they did." And during his life he was able to give them this feeling quite without words, simply by virtue of his existence. We are sitting at her narrow desk, which is covered with books and right at the front of her shop. Needless to say, I.M.S. is our first topic of conversation;[26] this is followed by the wise and the foolish virgins. She talks about the different forms assumed by the *vierge sage;* such as the virgin of Strasbourg, who inspired her to write the play I had read, and the virgin of Notre Dame de Paris, "qui est si désabusée, si bourgeoise, si parisienne— ça vous rappelle ces épouses qui ont appris à se faire à leur mari et qui ont cette façon de dire, 'Mais oui, mon ami'; qui pensent un peu plus loin."[27] "And now," Paulhan[28] apparently said to her, once he had seen the *vierge sage,* "you must write us a *vierge folle*." But not at all! There is only one *vierge sage,* even though there is a group of seven—but the *vierge folle,* well there are many of them, it's really the whole group. Moreover, her *servante en colère* was herself such a foolish virgin. And then she said something that even if I had read none of her works would have given me an insight into the nature of her world. She was speaking of the virginity of the wise virgins, and how this virginity was not entirely devoid of a hint, a shimmer, of hypocrisy. The wise and foolish virgins—of course, what she said about them was not really in line with the Church's view, but it differed by only a minute amount; they were extremely close to each other, or so she said. And as she spoke, her hands made such a winning and compelling swing-like gesture that I suddenly saw a portal in my mind's eye, with all fourteen virgins resting on their round, movable stone pedestals; and as they all swayed toward each other they perfectly echoed the meaning of her words. This naturally led us to talk about the *coincidentia oppositorum* [coincidence of opposites], without explicitly mentioning the term itself. I try to steer the conversation to Gide, since I know that she was, or is, close to him, and that here within these rooms the famous auction took place in which Gide solemnly parted company with those of his friends who had rejected his *Corydon,*[29] and did so by selling off the copies of their works that they had dedicated to him. "No, not under any circumstances"—she does not want Gide spoken of here. Gide does indeed possess both affirmation and negation, but in succession and in time, not in the great unity, the great peace, in which they can be found in the mystics. Then she mentions— and this really does interest me—Breton. She does a character sketch of

Breton: a tense, explosive person in whose vicinity life is impossible—
"quelqu'un d'inviable, comme nous disons."[30] But she thought his first
Surrealist Manifesto extraordinary, and the second contained some magnificent things as well. I confess to her that it was the turn to the occult that
had struck me about the second one, and rather unpleasantly. She, too, is
impatient with the idealization of telling fortunes from cards—in Breton's
Lettre aux voyantes.[31] She recalls the time Breton appeared in her shop with
Apollinaire. How obsequious he was toward Apollinaire, at his every beck
and call. "Breton, faites cela, cherchez ceci."[32] Many customers appear. I
have no wish to prolong this situation at the table unnaturally, and I am
also worried that I might be interfering with her work. But I then found
myself fascinated to see how eagerly she leaped to the defense of photographs of works of art—an old bête noire of mine. At first she seemed struck
by my statement about how much easier it was to "enjoy" a painting—and
especially a piece of sculpture, and even architecture—in a photograph than
in reality. But when I went on to call this kind of preoccupation with art
impoverishing and nerve-racking, she resisted. "Great creations," she said,
"cannot be thought of as the works of individuals. They are collective
objects, so powerful that a condition of enjoying them is to reduce them in
stature. In the last analysis, the methods of mechanical reproduction are a
technique for reducing them. They enable people to obtain the degree of
domination over the works without which they cannot enjoy them." In this
way I exchange a photograph of the *vierge sage* of Strasbourg, which she
had promised me at the beginning of our conversation, for a theory of
reproduction that may be even more valuable to me.

February 7. Bernstein's *Mélo* at the Gymnase.[33] The architecture of this
theater is found nowadays only in the façades of old spa casinos. When it
is floodlit, as at the beginning and the end, in the style of the Paris Opéra—
so that all the projecting ties and beams become ramps from which spot-
lights show the primadonna-columns to their best advantage, while the
darkness of the night sky forms an arch in the niches above them—the
outside theater of the façade becomes immeasurably superior to the indoor
stage.

February 10. Adrienne Monnier for the second time. In the meantime I have
become more familiar with the topography of the rue de l'Odéon. In her
forgotten volume of poetry, *Visages,* I have read the beautiful lines about
her friend Sylvia Beach, who owned the little boutique opposite hers that
witnessed the turbulent events surrounding the first publication of Joyce's
Ulysses in English. "Déjà," she wrote, "Déjà midi nous voit, l'une en face
de l'autre / Debout devant nos seuils, au niveau de la rue / Doux fleuve de
soleil qui porte sur ses bords / Nos libraires."[34] She enters the shop toward
3:30, precisely one minute after me, enveloped in a fleecy gray coat, like a

Cossack grandmother, shy and very determined. And scarcely are we sitting in the same place as before than she waves to someone through the shop window. He enters the shop. It is Fargue. And since it is a heavenly day in Paris, somewhat cold, but sunny, and we are all full of the beauty of the scene outside, and I too tell them how I had strolled around Saint-Sulpice, Fargue confides that he would like to live there. And then the two of them produce a wonderful duet about the priests of Saint-Sulpice, a duet that reverberates with the warmth of their old friendship. Fargue: "Ces grands corbeaux civilisés."[35] Monnier: Whenever I cross the square, it is so beautiful, even though the wind cuts through you in the winter; and when the priests come out of the church I feel that the storm will catch in their cassocks and sweep them up into the air." In order to grasp the key to this incomparable neighborhood, and especially the square, which stands at its heart, you have to have seen this black throng coming and going with your own eyes, pausing and surging to and fro in the *quartier* and merging noiselessly with the sheer silence of the many bookshops. The two then resume their amicable quarrels, which must have been going on for years. Fargue is berated for his indolence, his failure to write. "Que voulez-vous, j'ai pitié de ce que je fais. Ces pauvres mots, je les vois, à peine écrits, qu'ils s'en vont, traînant, boitant, vers le Père Lachaise."[36] Our subsequent conversation is dominated by the Joyce translation she published. She reports on the circumstances leading up to this rare success.—Some mention of Proust: she talks of the revulsion he evoked in her with his transfiguring of high society, of the rebellious protest that prevented her from loving him. And then she speaks with fanaticism, almost hatred, of Albertine, who was so absurdly like *ce garçon du Ritz*—Albert—whose burly body and masculine gait she could always sense in Albertine. Proust's moral side prevented her from liking him, or even wanting to like him. What she says gives me an opening to tell her of the problems encountered in introducing Proust to the German public, of pointing out how such problems make penetrating studies of the writer indispensable, how rare such studies have been in Germany, and basically even in France. Her astonishment at my words is enough to persuade me to give a brief sketch of my interpretation of Proust. What has remained undiscovered, I say, is not the psychological side of Proust, not the analytical aspect, but the metaphysical element of his writings. The hundred doors that offer an entry into his world have remained unopened: the idea of aging, the affinity between human beings and plants, his portrait of the nineteenth century, his feeling for decay, for residues, and the like. And how I have become increasingly convinced that, in order to understand Proust, it is vital to realize that his true subject is the reverse side: *le revers—moins du monde que de la vie même.*[37]

Later the same afternoon a conversation with Audisio, to whom I am able to talk in some detail about his *Héliotrope,* which delights him.[38] He tells

me about the circumstances in which he wrote the book, and this leads to
the subject of working in a southerly climate. We are in complete agreement
about the absurdity of the belief that the southern sun is the foe of intellectual concentration. Audisio reveals his plan to write a *Défense du soleil*. We
embark on a discussion of the different kinds of mystical contemplation to
be found beneath the northern midnight heavens and the southern midday
sky. Jean Paul on the one hand, oriental mysticism on the other.[39] The
Romantic stance of the northerner, who seeks to align his dream world with
infinity; and the rigor of the southerner, who, perhaps defiantly, attempts to
compete with the infinity of the blue skies at noon in order to create
something equally enduring. The conversation makes me think of my stay
on Capri, when I wrote the first forty pages of my book on mourning
drama,[40] in the middle of July: I had nothing but pen, ink, paper, a chair,
a table, and the noonday heat. This competition with infinite duration—
whose image is so compellingly evoked by the midday sky of the south, just
as the night sky conjures up the picture of infinite space—characterizes the
hermetic, constructive nature of southern mysticism of the kind expressed
in the architecture of Sufi temples.

February 11. Breakfast with Quint. I would not have broached the topic
of the latest developments in Surrealism so directly, had I recollected that
Editions Kra—of which Quint is one of the directors—is publishing the
Second Surrealist Manifesto. He thinks the parts that take issue with former
members of the group are the weakest. This aside, his statement that the
original movement is now at an end is something I needed to have confirmed. But it is the right moment to look back at the movement and
establish some of the facts. The first one is also the most laudable: Surrealism
reacted to that blend of poetry and journalism which has started to become
the formula for literary activity in Germany with a violence that does credit
to France and testifies to the vitality of its intellectuals. At a time when the
idea of *poésie pure* was threatening to peter out in sterile academicism,
Surrealism gave it a demagogic, almost political emphasis. It rediscovered
the great tradition of esoteric poetry that is actually quite removed from
l'art pour l'art and that is such a secret, salutary practice for poetry, a set
of prescriptions. It saw through the intimate interrelationship between dilettantism and corruption that forms the basis of journalism. It brought an
anarchistic passion to the task of destroying the concept of standards in
literature, the decent average. And it went even further in its efforts to
sabotage ever broader regions of public and private life, until finally the
political rightness of this stance—its analytical or, even better, eliminating
force—became evident and effective. We also agreed that one of the great
limitations of the movement lay in the laziness of its leaders. When you meet
Breton and ask him what he is doing, he answers, "Rien. Que voulez-vous

que l'on fasse?"[41] There is an element of affectation in this, but also much truth. Above all, Breton fails to realize that diligence has its magical side, as well as a bourgeois, philistine one.

Before that, a farewell walk down the Champs-Elysées. The unbroken surface of the days is like a mirror: as I approach their edges, they light up in all the colors of the prism. Spring has come with the cold, and when you come striding down the Champs-Elysées as if down a snowy mountain slope, with racing pulse and flushed cheeks, you suddenly call a halt in front of a small lawn behind the Théâtre Marigny—a lawn in which spring is in the air. Behind the Théâtre Marigny, an impressive building is in process of construction; a tall green fence surrounds the site, and behind it the scaffolding rises. Then I glimpsed this bit of magic: a tree growing in the fenced-off area, its bare branches extending out a little over the fence to one side. The rough-hewn fence nestled as snugly into these branches, with their delicate openwork, as a ruff around the throat of a young girl. Amid the gigantic joinery, this silhouette had been drawn by a cutter's sure hand. The sun's rays shone down dazzlingly from the right; and as the tip of the Eiffel Tower—my favorite symbol of self-assertiveness—almost dissolved in the luminous light, it became the image of the reconciliation and purification that comes with spring. The radiance of the sunshine melted the tenement blocks that barred the view to the rue La Boétie and the avenue Montaigne in the distance, and became masses of golden-brown impasto that the demiurge had spread over the palette that is Paris. And as I walked along, my thoughts became all jumbled up as in a kaleidoscope—a new constellation at every step. Old elements disappeared, and unknown ones came stumbling up—figures of all shapes and sizes. If one remained, it was called a "sentence." And among thousands of possible ones, I found this one, for which I had been waiting for many years—the sentence that wholly defined the miracle that the Madeleine—not the Proustian madeleine, but the real one[42]—had been from the first moment I saw it: in winter the Madeleine is a great furnace that warms the rue Royale with its shadow.

Published in *Die literarische Welt*, April–June 1930. *Gesammelte Schriften*, IV, 567–587. Translated by Rodney Livingstone.

Notes

1. Louis Aragon (1897–1992) wrote his *Paysan de Paris* at the time André Breton was writing his *Manifeste du surréalisme* (Surrealist Manifesto). Aragon's minute description of the Passage de l'Opéra, one of the Parisian arcades lined with restaurants and small shops, is a key document of Surrealism. His attempt to

liberate the imagination through a poetic focus on ordinary, often commercial objects spoke very directly to Benjamin, who referred to it repeatedly in the early years of his work on the *Passagen-Werk* (Arcades Project) in the late 1920s and early 1930s. A *marchand de quatre saisons* is a seller of fruits and vegetables; a *flic* is a policeman.

2. Robert Desnos (1900–1945), French poet, was one of the earliest adherents of Surrealism. He died in the Nazi concentration camp at Theresienstadt, having been deported for his Resistance activities. On Julien Green, see "The Fireside Saga" and "Julien Green" in this volume. Léon-Paul Fargue (1876–1947), poet, essayist, and critic, contributed to the *Nouvelle Revue Française* and edited (together with Paul Valéry and Valery Larbaud) the journal *Commerce,* which promoted the work of a number of Surrealist authors.

3. For a succinct account of the (mutually disappointing) encounter between Proust and Joyce, see Richard Ellmann, *James Joyce* (New York: Oxford University Press, 1959), ch. 30. "Vous m'avez trahi!" means "You've betrayed me!"

4. "That was my first Highness!"

5. Léon-Pierre Quint (1895–1958), French critic and friend of Benjamin's, was the author of the first major study of Proust's oeuvre (1925).

6. Marcel Jouhandeau (1888–1979) was the author of numerous works of auto-biographically based fiction; they were stamped with a strongly Catholic focus on sin and possible redemption. Benjamin's translation of Jouhandeau's "Mademoiselle Zéline, ou Bonheur de Dieu à l'usage d'une vieille demoiselle" (1924) appeared in an anthology of contemporary French writing, *Neue französische Erzähler,* in 1930; his translation of Jouhandeau's story "Le marié du village" was published in the February 1931 issue of the *Europäische Revue.* In 1917, Jouhandeau worked in Albert Le Cuziat's well-known male brothel, which was frequented by Proust; he would sometimes serve there as Proust's assistant in acts of sadistic voyeurism, which he then recorded. As this text makes clear, Benjamin also visited Le Cuziat's establishment.

7. Paul Déroulède (1846–1914), a poet and dramatist, was president of the French League of Patriots and an active supporter of Georges Boulanger's populist, antirepublican campaign.

8. "Threatening toys."

9. "Your characters are never safe for a single moment."

10. *L'école des femmes,* Gide's novel of a woman's disillusionment in marriage, was published in 1929.

11. "Raised skirts."

12. Jean Giraudoux's drama in three acts had its premiere at the Comédie des Champs-Elysées in November 1929; it was published the same year. *Les Criminels* may refer to Offenbach's one-act comic opera of this title.

13. Jean Cocteau's one-act "tragedy" was first performed at Georges Pitoëff's theater in June 1926; it was published in 1927.

14. The Swiss-born Le Corbusier (pseudonym of Charles-Edouard Jeanneret; 1887–1965) gained fame as France's leading avant-garde architect through structures such as the "Esprit Nouveau" pavilion in Paris (1925). Jeanne Lanvin (1867–1946), with her *haute couture* house in the Faubourg Saint-Honoré, was a prominent designer of clothing for the fashionable elite of Paris.

15. Valentine Tessier (1892–1981) was the actress of choice for the first performances of Giraudoux's plays. Her great beauty and acting talent won her a number of film roles, including the lead in Jean Renoir's *Madame Bovary* (1934).

16. Emmanuel Berl (1892–1976) was a French essayist. In both the text cited here (1930) and its companion volume, *La mort de la morale bourgeoise* (1929), Berl denounced the sociocultural petrification he saw as resulting from modern bourgeois culture.

17. Paul-Louis Courier (1772–1825), French pamphleteer, was a master of irony and invective; he was a passionate opponent of the Bourbon Restoration of 1814. Charles Augustin Sainte-Beuve (1804–1869), influential and prolific critic, novelist, and poet, is now best-known for his delineation of a literary-historical method which emphasizes authorial psychology and the role of the author's milieu. Madame de Staël (née Germaine Necker; 1766–1817) rose to fame after the publication of *De l'Allemagne* (1810), a wide-ranging survey of cultural activity in Germany; the book opened a crucial bridge between German Romanticism and postrevolutionary French culture. Théodore Agrippa d'Aubigné (1552–1630), was a French historian and a champion of the Protestant Reformation. Henri Meilhac (1831–1897) was a French dramatist and a virtuoso of boulevard theater. He collaborated with Ludovic Halévy (1834–1908) on a series of operetta librettos, many of which were set to Jacques Offenbach's music; *La vie parisienne* is perhaps the best-known of these.

18. Albert Le Cuziat served Proust as an important source on the homosexual underworld in Paris. He served as the model for Jupien, the waistcoat maker (Charlus' aide in *Sodome et Gomorrhe*) in *A la recherche du temps perdu;* and he served as one of the secondary models for Albertine (though not the principal model, as Benjamin claimed in a letter to Gershom Scholem of January 25, 1930). Le Cuziat opened his male brothel in the Hôtel Marigny, 11 rue de l'Arcade, in 1916.

19. On Franz Hessel's collaboration with Benjamin on a translation of Proust's *A la recherche du temps perdu,* see the chronology to Volume 1 of this edition, pp. 513–514. They would complete three volumes of the translation, including Benjamin's now-lost version of *Sodome et Gomorrhe.*

20. Maurice Sachs (pseudonym of Maurice Ettinghausen; 1906–1945), French novelist and satirical essayist, gained notoriety as a result of his chaotic and scandal-ridden life. A convert from Judaism to Catholicism, he went on to collaborate with the Gestapo; he was nonetheless deported and murdered in a Hamburg prison toward the end of World War II.

21. Action Française was France's most potent nationalist and right-wing political movement before World War II. Founded by Charles Maurras and Léon Daudet in 1898 within the larger context of the Dreyfus Affair, its struggle against parliamentary democracy, its militant Catholicism, and its anti-Semitism were propagated in its journal, likewise named *L'Action Française.*

22. "Well, so *that's* what we eat every day?!"

23. "Perhaps sides with death."

24. "Sides with health."

25. The Paris bookshop of Adrienne Monnier (1892–1968), actually called La

Maison des Amis des Livres, was located across from Sylvia Beach's Shakespeare and Company, at 7 rue de l'Odéon. The two shops served as an important forum for European modernists such as Paul Valéry, André Gide, and James Joyce.

26. I.M.S. was the pseudonym under which Adrienne Monnier published some of her shorter prose pieces.

27. "Who is so disillusioned, so bourgeoise, so Parisian—it makes you think of housewives who have become inured to their husbands and who have a way of saying, 'But of course, darling,' while they go on thinking their own thoughts."

28. Jean Paulhan (1884–1968), French critic and man of letters, became the editor of the *Nouvelle Revue Française* in 1925. He was the first to publish experimental writers such as Antonin Artaud, Francis Ponge, and Raymond Queneau in the journal.

29. Gide's *Corydon: Quatre dialogues socratiques* was published anonymously in excerpt form in 1911, and in a full version in 1920. The text appeared under his name only in 1924. It represents Gide's most explicit exploration of his homosexuality; its publication cost him many friends.

30. "An 'unviable person,' as we say."

31. The *Lettre aux voyantes* accompanied a new edition of the *Manifeste du surréalisme,* including a frontispiece by Max Ernst, published by Editions Kra in 1929.

32. "Breton, do this, look for that."

33. The work of the French dramatist Henry Bernstein (1876–1953)—plays such as *Félix* (1926) and *Mélo* (1929)—offer a record of the moral and erotic dilemmas of the secularized French bourgeoisie at the turn of the twentieth century.

34. "Already noon sees us, opposite one another / Standing before our doors, at street level / Gentle river of sun which carries on its banks / our booksellers."

35. "Those huge civilized crows."

36. "I simply can't help taking pity on what I've written. I look at the poor words and see how—scarcely having been written down—they hobble off, limping, to Père Lachaise cemetery."

37. "The reverse—less of the world than of life itself."

38. Gabriel Audisio (1900–1978), French poet and novelist, was a public official in both Algeria and France. His work celebrates the light and sun of the Mediterranean world; his novel *Héliotrope* was published in 1928.

39. Jean Paul Richter (1763–1825) wrote a series of wildly extravagant, highly imaginative novels that, in their combination of fantasy and realism, continue to defy categorization.

40. *Ursprung des deutschen Trauerspiels* (Origin of the German Trauerspiel).

41. "Nothing. What do you expect me to be doing?"

42. That is to say, not the little sponge cakes that triggered Proust's recollection of his childhood, but the neoclassical church off the Place de la Concorde in Paris.

Review of Kracauer's *Die Angestellten*

S. Kracauer, *Die Angestellten: Aus dem neuesten Deutschland* [White-Collar Workers: The Latest from Germany] (Frankfurt am Main: Frankfurter Societätsdruckerei, 1930), 148 pages.

Many people still have memories of the time when it was normal to give their books titles such as *Toward a Sociology of . . .* In those days, this book would have been called *Toward a Sociology of the White-Collar Worker*. Or rather, it would not have been written at all. For what such fashionable titles expressed was really only the fear of making clear political analyses, instead of enveloping them in a cocoon of academic clichés so that the awkward aspects of the subject could give no offense. This is not Kracauer's way. And he has not abandoned this old approach to replace it with his own form of obfuscation. In particular, he finds reportage, this modern method of evading political realities under the guise of left-wing phraseology, just as repugnant as the euphemistic maunderings of sociologists. "Reality," he says, "is a construct. No doubt, life must be scrutinized if it is to emerge before us. But it certainly does not reside in the more or less adventitious observations of reportage. On the contrary, it is to be found exclusively in the mosaic formed by the synthesis of individual observations that results from an understanding of their content."[1] In other words, sociological knowledge and the material of observation are the mere preconditions of his method, a method that rewards precise study because of both its originality and its explanatory power.

The fact that Kracauer goes his own way is revealed by his use of language. Stubbornly and aggressively, it seeks out its own coordinates with an obstinacy that an Abraham a Sancta Clara might have envied as he hammered out his own sermons in a series of puns.[2] The difference is that in *Die Angestellten* the role of wordplay has been replaced by that of the pictorial pun. Puns are of course anything but arbitrary; they are intimately bound up with the linguistic life of the Baroque. In the same way, Kracauer's pictorial wit is no chance affair, but is related to those composite Surrealist images that not only characterize dreams (as we have learned from Freud) and the sensual world (as we have learned from Paul Klee and Max Ernst), but also define our social reality. "In the evenings in Luna Park,"[3] we read in Kracauer, "they sometimes have fountain displays illuminated by fireworks. A whole sequence of different colored sprays—red, yellow, green— light up the darkness. Once the splendid illumination is over, you can see that it came from a tawdry jumble of pipes. This fountain display resembles the lives of many white-collar workers. They seek distraction as an escape from the shabbiness of their existence, experience a brief burst of fireworks, and, oblivious of its origins, sink back into obscurity."[4] Of course, this is more than a mere metaphor. For these fireworks dazzle the office worker himself. It is this that alerts us to the political clarity of vision that flashes from these composite images.

What is the source of this ability to interpret political dreams? We are not speaking here of literary influences. Nor need we concern ourselves with Kracauer's linguistic debt to the anonymous author of *Ginster*.[5] What is evident, however, is that his interpretive practice is solidly based on the exact study of his own most personal experience. (Just as white magic goes hand in hand with the rigorous, sober scrutiny of experience, while black magic never gets further than enchantment and mystery.) But the experience we are talking about here is the experience of the intellectual. The intellectual is the sworn enemy of the petty bourgeoisie, because he must constantly overcome the petty bourgeois in himself. Here he has played to his own strengths, which enable him to see through bourgeois ideologies, if not entirely, then at least to the extent that they are still linked with the petty bourgeoisie. In white-collar workers, we see the emergence of a more uniform, inflexible, drilled sort of petty bourgeoisie. It is incomparably poorer in types, in originals, in cranky yet conciliatory specimens of humanity. In exchange, it is infinitely richer in illusions and repressions. It is against these that the author takes aim. Not after the fashion of Gregers Wehrle, who mounts an assault against "life as a lie," much as Don Quixote does against windmills.[6] His concern is not with individuals, but with the composition of a homogeneous mass and the circumstances in which this mass is reflected. In his eyes, the sum of these circumstances is encompassed by the name "Berlin." "Today, Berlin is the city of white-collar culture par excellence—that is to say, a culture which is made by white-collar workers for white-collar workers, and which most white-collar workers regard as culture."[7] Joseph Roth is correct in his recent claim in these pages that the writer's task is not to transfigure, but to unmask.[8] Thus, we may say that the author of *Die Angestellten* has approached Berlin in a brilliant manner. That is not the least important achievement of this important book. At a time when the first signs of an active affection for the capital have begun to show themselves, we now see people starting to track down its failings. In his monumental work *Das steinerne Berlin*, Werner Hegemann has produced a political history of the tenement and explained its roots in landed property.[9] This is now followed by Kracauer's account of offices and pleasure palaces as the expression of the mentality of white-collar workers—a mentality that reaches deep into the private sector. Kracauer has also just taken up the post of Berlin correspondent for the *Frankfurter Zeitung*. It is good for the city to have its enemy within the walls. Let us hope that it will know how to silence him. In what way? Well, by making use of him in its own best interests.

Published in *Die literarische Welt*, May 1930. *Gesammelte Schriften*, III, 226–228. Translated by Rodney Livingstone.

Notes

1. Kracauer, *Die Angestellten*, p. 21.
2. Abraham a Sancta Clara (1644–1709) was a south German Catholic who became the most prominent preacher of his day. His sermons, mostly delivered in Vienna, were addressed to ordinary people and were famous for their earthy wit, their wealth of puns and metaphors, and their rhetorical power.
3. Luna Park was a fairground built in Berlin on reclaimed land at the end of the newly extended Kurfürstendamm. It has since become a generic term for "fairground."
4. Kracauer, *Die Angestellten*, p. 129.
5. Kracauer's novel of the time of the Great War, *Ginster von ihm selbst geschrieben* (Ginster Written by Himself), appeared anonymously in 1928. Benjamin was certainly aware that the debt to which Kracauer referred was to himself.
6. Wehrle is a character in Ibsen's play *The Wild Duck*.
7. Kracauer, *Die Angestellten*, p. 20.
8. A reference to Joseph Roth's article "Schluss mit der 'neuen Sachlichkeit'!" (Enough of the "New Objectivity"!), which appeared in *Die literarische Welt* in January 1930.
9. Werner Hegemann (1881–1936) was a German city planner and journalist. *Das steinerne Berlin: Geschichte der grössten Mietskasernenstadt der Welt* (Berlin in Stone: The History of the World's Biggest Tenement-City) appeared in early 1930. Hegemann's anti-Nazi activities forced him to flee Germany in 1933, initially for Prague and Paris, and finally for New York City.

Food

Fresh Figs

No one who has never eaten a food to excess has ever really experienced it, or fully exposed himself to it. Unless you do this, you at best enjoy it, but never come to lust after it, or make the acquaintance of that diversion from the straight and narrow road of the appetite which leads to the primeval forest of greed. For in gluttony two things coincide: the boundlessness of desire and the uniformity of the food that sates it. Gourmandizing means above all else to devour one thing to the last crumb. There is no doubt that it enters more deeply into what you eat than mere enjoyment. For example, when you bite into mortadella as if it were bread, or bury your face in a melon as if it were a pillow, or gorge yourself on caviar out of crackling paper, or, when confronted with the sight of a round Edam cheese, find that the existence of every other food simply vanishes from your mind.—How did I first learn all this? It happened just before I had to make a very difficult decision. A letter had to be posted or torn up. I had carried it around in my pocket for two days, but had not given it a thought for some hours. I then took the noisy narrow-gauge railway up to Secondigliano through the sun-parched landscape. The village lay in still solemnity in the weekday peace and quiet. The only traces of the excitement of the previous Sunday were the poles on which Catherine wheels and rockets had been ignited. Now they stood there bare. Some of them still displayed a sign halfway up with the figure of a saint from Naples or an animal. Women sat in the open barns husking corn. I was walking along in a daze, when I noticed a cart with figs standing in the shade. It was sheer idleness that made me go up to them, sheer extravagance that I bought half a pound for a few soldi. The woman gave me a generous measure. But when the black, blue, bright green, violet, and brown fruit lay in the bowl of the scales, it turned out that she had no paper to wrap them in. The housewives of Secondigliano bring their baskets with them, and she was unprepared for globetrotters. For my part, I was ashamed to abandon the fruit. So I left her with figs stuffed in my trouser pockets and in my jacket, figs in both of my outstretched hands, and figs in my mouth. I couldn't stop eating them and was forced to get rid of the mass of plump fruits as quickly as possible. But that could not be described as eating; it was more like a bath, so powerful was the smell of resin that penetrated all my belongings, clung to my hands and impregnated the air through which I carried my burden. And then, after satiety and revulsion—the final bends in the path—had been surmounted, came the ultimate mountain peak of taste. A vista over an unsuspected landscape of the palate spread out before my eyes—an insipid, undifferentiated, greenish flood of greed that could distinguish nothing but the stringy, fibrous waves of the flesh of the open fruit, the utter transformation of enjoyment into habit, of habit into vice. A hatred of those figs welled up inside me; I was desperate to finish with them, to liberate myself, to rid myself of all this overripe, bursting fruit. I ate it to destroy it. Biting had rediscovered its most ancient purpose. When I pulled the last fig from the depths of my pocket, the letter was stuck to it. Its fate was sealed; it, too, had to succumb to the great purification. I took it and tore it into a thousand pieces.

Café Crème

No one who has his morning coffee and rolls served up to him in his room in Paris on a silver platter, together with little pats of butter and jam, can know anything at all about it. You have to have it in a bistro where, among all the mirrors, the *petit déjeuner* is itself a concave mirror in which a minute image of this city is reflected. At no other meal are the tempi so varied, from the mechanical gesture with which the clerk sitting at the bar downs his café au lait, to the contemplative relish with which a traveler slowly empties his cup in the interval between trains. You may be sitting next to him—at the same table, on the same bench—yet be worlds away from him, absorbed in your own thoughts. You sacrifice your morning sobriety in order to have a little something. And what don't you have along with your coffee! The entire morning, the morning of this day, and sometimes also the missed mornings of life. If you had sat at this table as a child, countless ships would have sailed across the frozen sea of the marble table-top. You would have known what the Sea of Marmara looks like. With your gaze fixed on an iceberg or a sail, you would have swallowed one mouthful for your father and one for your uncle and one for your brother, until slowly the cream would have come floating up to the thick rim of your cup, a huge promontory on which your lips rested. How feeble your sense of revulsion has become! How quickly and hygienically you behave now! You drink; you don't crumble up your bread, or dunk it. You sleepily reach out to the breadbasket for a madeleine, break it in two, and do not even notice how sad it makes you not to be able to share it.

Falernian Wine and Stockfish

Fasting is an initiation into many secrets, not least the secrets of food. And if hunger is the best cook, fasting is the king of cooks. I made its acquaintance one afternoon in Rome, after wandering from one fountain to the next and clambering up one flight of steps after another. On my way home at around four o'clock, I found myself in Trastevere, where the streets are wide and the houses shabby. There were plenty of places to eat along the way. But I was on the lookout for a shaded room, a marble floor, snow-white linen, and silver cutlery—the dining room of a large hotel where at this hour I would have some prospect of being the solitary guest. The riverbed was dried out, and dust clouds passed over the Tiber island. Finding myself on the other side, I went down the Via Arenula. I did not count the *osterie* I left behind. But the hungrier I grew, the less inviting or even approachable they appeared. In one place I shied away from the customers, whose voices reached me out in the street; in another I recoiled from the dirtiness of the curtain billowing in the doorway. Finally, I even crept furtively past the more remote bars, so certain was I that a single glance would only increase my distaste. In addition, and quite apart from my hunger, my nerves felt increasingly on the alert; no place seemed safe enough for me, no food clean enough. Not that I was indulging in fantasies of the most exclusive delicacies—caviar, lobsters, or snipe. On the contrary, only the simplest, most basic foods would have seemed pure enough. I felt that here was an unrepeatable opportunity to unleash my senses into the folds and gorges of the most unassuming raw fruit and vegetables, melons, wine, ten varieties of bread or nuts, so as to identify a scent I had never before known. It had turned five o'clock by the time I found myself in a broad, uneven cobbled square, the Piazza Montanara. One of the narrow passages that led into the square seemed to me to point me in exactly the right direction. For by now I had decided that my best course of action was to go back to my room and buy something to eat nearby. At this moment I was struck by the light in a window, the first of the evening. It was an *osteria,* and the lights had been turned on earlier there than in the shops and houses. In the window a solitary guest could be seen. He was just standing up to settle his bill. It suddenly occurred to me that I had to take his place. I entered and sat down in a corner. Whereas a moment before I had been immeasurably choosy and indecisive, now I suddenly no longer minded where I sat. A waiter asked me merely how much I wanted to drink; there appeared to be no choice of wine. I began to feel lonely, and so I brought out my magic little black rod which had so often conjured up that bouquet of letters with the name in the middle, and which caused the scent that was now merged with the aroma of the Falernian wine to be wafted over to me in my solitude. And I became absorbed in all that—the bouquet, the name, the scent, and the wine—until a noise made me look up. The room had filled up. With workmen from nearby who came after work to eat their evening meal away from home, bringing their wives and even their children, many of them. For they were eating as well as drinking, and what they ate was cured stockfish, the only dish that was served here. I looked down and saw that there was a plateful of the same fish in front of me and a shudder of disgust ran down my spine. I then took a closer look at the people. They were the sharply defined, closely knit inhabitants of the neighborhood, and because it was a petty-bourgeois population, there was no one to be seen from the upper classes, let alone any foreigners. My clothes and appearance must have made me stand out. But curiously, no one glanced in my direction. Did no one notice me, or did I seem, as I sat there more and more immersed in the sweetness of the wine, to be one of them? A feeling of pride overcame me at this thought—a great sense of happiness. Nothing should henceforth distinguish me from the crowd. I put away my pen. As I did so, I felt something rustle in my pocket. It was the *Impero*, a Fascist newspaper that I had picked up on my walk. I ordered another carafe of Falernian wine, opened the paper, wrapped myself up in the dirty cloak it provided, lined with the events of the day, much as the Madonna cloaked herself in the mantle of the stars, and slowly put one piece of dried fish after another into my mouth until the pangs of hunger had been stilled.

Borscht

It starts by spreading a mask of steam over your features. Long before your tongue touches the spoon, your eyes have started to water and your nose is dripping with borscht. Long before your insides have gone on the alert and your blood has become a single wave that courses through your body with the foaming aroma, your eyes have drunk in the red abundance in your bowl. They are now blind to everything that is not borscht, or its reflection in the eyes of your table companion. It's sour cream, you think, that gives this soup its rich texture. Perhaps. But I have eaten it in the Moscow winter, and I know one thing: it contains snow, molten red flakes, food from the clouds that is akin to the manna that also fell from the sky one day. And doesn't the warm flow soften the pieces of meat, so that it lies inside you like a ploughed field from which you can easily dig up the weed Sadness by the root? Just leave the vodka next to it, untouched; do not start to cut up the piroshkis. It is then that you will discover the secret of the soup that alone among foods has the ability to satisfy you gently. It gradually pervades you entirely, while with other foods a sudden cry of "Enough!" abruptly causes a shudder to pass through your entire body.

Pranzo Caprese

She had been the Capri village cocotte, and was now the sixty-year-old mother of little Gennaro, whom she beat when she was drunk. She lived in the ocher-colored house in a vineyard on the steep mountainside. I came looking for my girlfriend, to whom she was renting the house. From Capri came the sound of the clock striking twelve. There was no one to be seen; the garden was empty. I reclimbed the steps I had just come down. Suddenly I could hear the old woman close behind me. She stood in the kitchen doorway dressed in a skirt and blouse, discolored items of clothing which you'd have searched in vain for any stains, so evenly, so uniformly was the dirt spread over them. "Voi cercate la signora. E partita colla pìccola."[1] And she was due back shortly. But this was just the start: it was followed by a flood of inviting words uttered in her shrill, high-pitched voice, accompanied by rhythmic movements of her imperious head, which decades previously must have had provocative power. I would have had to be an accomplished gentleman to decline her offer, and I was not even able to express myself in Italian. So much was comprehensible: it was an invitation to share her midday meal. I now caught sight of her wretched husband inside the cottage, taking something out of a dish with a spoon. She now went up to this dish. Immediately afterward, she reappeared in the doorway with a plate, which she held out to me without interrupting her flow of speech. I found myself bereft of the remnants of my ability to understand Italian. I felt instantly that it was too late for me to take my leave. From amid a cloud of garlic, beans, mutton fat, tomatoes, and onions, there appeared the domineering hand from which I took a tin spoon. I am sure you are thinking that I would have choked on this nauseating swill and that my sole thought would be to vomit it all up again as quickly as possible. How little you would understand of the magic of this food, and how little I understood it myself up to the moment I am describing now. To taste it was of no importance. It was nothing but the decisive yet imperceptible transition between two moments: first between the moment of smelling it, and then of being overwhelmed, utterly bowled over and kneaded, by this food, gripped by it, as if by the hands of the old whore, squeezed, and having the juice rubbed into me—

whether the juice of the food or of the woman, I am no longer able to say. The obligation of politeness was satisfied and so was the witch's desire, and I went on up the mountain enriched by the knowledge of Odysseus when he saw his companions transformed into swine.

Mulberry Omelette

I shall tell the following story for all those who would like to try figs or Falernian wine, borscht or a peasant meal in Capri. Once upon a time there was a king who could call all the power and the treasures of the earth his own, but who for all that was not happy and who became more and more despondent from one year to the next. One day he summoned his personal cook and said to him, "You have served me faithfully for many a year and have filled my table with the most marvelous foods, and I am well disposed toward you. Now, however, I wish to make a final trial of your art. You shall prepare for me a mulberry omelette just like the one I enjoyed fifty years ago in my childhood. At that time, my father was at war with his evil neighbor to the east. His neighbor had won and we had to flee. And so we fled day and night, my father and I, until we came to a dark forest. We wandered around in it and were close to perishing from hunger and exhaustion, when at long last we spied a hut. An old woman lived there and cordially bid us rest, while she busied herself at the hearth. It was not long before the mulberry omelette stood before us. Scarcely had I put the first bite in my mouth than I was overcome by a wonderful feeling of solace and new hope. In those days I was still a child, and it was not until long afterward that the memory of the blissful taste of that precious dish came back to me. But when, later on, I had my whole empire combed in search of the old woman, she was nowhere to be found, nor was there anyone who knew how to cook the mulberry omelette. If you are able to satisfy this last wish, I shall make you my son-in-law and heir to my empire. But if you are unable to gratify my desire, you shall die." The cook replied, "If that is so, Your Majesty, you should summon the executioner without delay. Of course I know the secret of the mulberry omelette and all the ingredients that are required, down to the common cress and the noble thyme. I also know the words you have to say while stirring, and know that you have to whisk the boxwood beater from left to right, for fear that otherwise all the labor will prove to have been in vain. But for all that, O King, I shall still forfeit my life. Despite all my efforts, my omelette would not taste right to you. For how could I spice it with all the tastes you enjoyed in it on that occasion: the dangers of battle, the vigilance of the pursued, the warmth of the hearth and the sweetness of rest, the strange surroundings and the dark future." Thus spake the cook. The king remained silent for a while, but not long afterward he is said to have allowed him to retire from his service, richly laden with gifts.

Published in the *Frankfurter Zeitung*, May 1930. *Gesammelte Schriften*, IV, 374–381. Translated by Rodney Livingstone.

Notes

1. "You are looking for the lady. She is out with the little girl."

Bert Brecht

There is always an element of dishonesty when someone sets out to talk in a serene, unbiased, objective manner about living writers. Not only a personal dishonesty, and perhaps even less a personal one than a scientific one—although nobody can avoid being affected by the atmosphere surrounding a contemporary, which may take a thousand different forms, hardly any of which are under his conscious control. This does not at all imply that when tackling such a subject you can just let yourself go and seek your fortune in a vague succession of associations, anecdotes, and analogies. On the contrary, if literary history proves inadequate to the task, criticism is the appropriate form. And as a form it is all the more rigorous, the more it distances itself from a facile tone of superiority and instead engages resolutely with the topical aspects of a writer's work. In the case of Brecht, for example, it would be folly to ignore the risks inherent in his work, the question of his political attitude, or even his so-called plagiarisms. To do so would be to deny oneself access to the nature of his work. In order to unpack these matters, it is more important to convey an idea of his theoretical convictions, his way of talking, or even his outward appearance than to reel off a list of his works in chronological sequence and give an account of their content, form, and public reception. It is for this reason that we do not scruple here to take his latest book as our starting point, a blunder no doubt for a literary historian, but all the more apposite for a critic as this latest work—which is called *Versuche* [Experiments] and has been published in Berlin by Kiepenheuer—is one of his most refractory, and compels us to make a frontal assault on the entire phenomenon of Brecht.[1]

If we were to invite the author as bluntly as he treats his own characters to make a statement about the nature of his commitment, we would hear him say, "I refuse to exploit my talent 'freely'; I exploit it as educator, politician, and organizer. There is no criticism of my literary activities—'plagiarist,' 'troublemaker,' or 'saboteur'—that I would not adopt for my unliterary, anonymous, yet systematic efforts and regard as a badge of honor." However this may be, it is certain that Brecht belongs to the very small minority of contemporary German writers who ask *where* they ought to apply their talents, who apply them only where they are convinced of the need to do so, and who abstain on every occasion that does not meet this standard. The *Versuche* are such chosen points at which Brecht applies his talents. What is new about them is that these points of application emerge there in their full significance; the writer takes leave of his *Works* for their sake, and, like an engineer who starts drilling for oil in the desert, he starts operations in carefully calculated sites in the desert of the present day. Such sites are the theater, the anecdote, and the radio—others are to be added at a later date. "The publication of the *Versuche*," the author begins, "takes place at a time when certain works are intended less as individual experiences (or as possessing the character of finished 'works') than as a means of using (transforming) certain institutes and institutions." Instead of proclaiming reform, he plans innovations. Literature here no longer expects anything from a feeling on the part of the author, other than one in which the will to change this world has allied itself to sobriety. It is fully aware that its only chance is to become a by-product in a highly ramified process designed to change the world. That is what it is here. An invaluable by-product. The principal product, however, is a new attitude. Lichtenberg says, "It is not a person's convictions that matter, but what they make him."[2] In Brecht's case, this "what" is his "stance" [*Haltung*]. This is something new, and what is new about it is that it can be learned. "The second *Versuch*, the *Geschichten vom Herrn Keuner* [Stories of Herr Keuner], represents an attempt to make gestures quotable." But it is not just Keuner's stance which is quotable; that of the pupil in *Der Flug der Lindberghs* [The Lindberghs' Flight] is, with some practice, no less so, as is also that of the egoist Fatzer. And what is quotable about them is not just their stance, but also the words that accompany them. Yet these words need to be practiced—that is to say, first noticed, and then understood. They have first a pedagogical effect, then a political one, and last a poetic one.

These few remarks give you—perhaps in an overly compressed form—all the important motifs in Brecht's work, and after this run-up we have probably earned the right to take a breather. "Breather" here means a pause to take a general view of the figures he has created, focusing on one or another in whom the author's intentions may be seen to their best advantage. I would like to give pride of place to the already-mentioned Herr Keuner, who first appears in Brecht's latest work. We need not inquire where his name originates. Let us assume with Lion Feuchtwanger, one of Brecht's former collaborators, that it is based on the Greek root χοινός [choinós]—the universal, that which concerns all, belongs to all.[3] And in fact, Herr Keuner is the man who concerns all, belongs to all, for he is the leader. But in quite a different sense from the one we usually understand by the word. He is in no way a public speaker, a demagogue; nor is he a show-off or a strongman. His main preoccupations lie light-years away from what people nowadays understand to be those of a "leader." The fact is that Herr Keuner is a thinker. I can remember Brecht once envisaging how Keuner might make his entrance on the stage. He would be brought in on a stretcher, because a thinker does not go to any pains. He would then follow—or perhaps would not follow—the events on the stage in silence. For it is symptomatic of so many situations today that the thinker is unable to follow them. His entire stance will prevent our confusing this thinker with Greek sages—the strict Stoics or the life-enjoying representatives of the school of Epicurus. He is rather more akin to Paul Valéry's character Monsieur Teste: a purely thinking man without any emotions. Both characters have Chinese features. They are infinitely cunning, infinitely discreet, infinitely polite, infinitely old, and infinitely adaptable. Herr Keuner, however, differs entirely from his French counterpart in that he has a goal he never forgets for a single minute. This goal is the new state. A state that has literary and philosophical foundations as deep as those of Confucius. But—abandoning the Chinese analogy—we may say that we can also discern Jesuitical features in Herr Keuner. This is anything but an accident. The more closely we analyze the types created by Brecht (we shall follow up our discussion of Herr Keuner with an examination of two other characters), the more clearly it emerges that for all their vigor and vitality, they represent political models, or, as the doctors would say, phantoms. What they all have in common is the desire to bring about rational political actions that spring not from philanthropy, love of one's neighbor, idealism, nobility of mind, or the like, but only from the relevant attitude. This attitude may be essentially dubious, unsympathetic, or self-interested. If only the man it belongs to does not delude himself, if only he clings fast to reality, the attitude will itself provide its own corrective. Not an ethical corrective: the man does not become any better. But a social one: his behavior makes him useful. Or, as we read elsewhere in Brecht: "'All vices are good for something,' / said [Baal], 'Only the man who practices them isn't.'"[4]

Herr Keuner's vice is cold and incorruptible thought. What is this good for? It is good for bringing people to the point where they become clear about the assumptions that have led them to the so-called leaders, the thinkers or politicians, their books or speeches, and then to subject these assumptions to as thorough a criticism as possible. It will turn out to be a whole bundle of assumptions that will all fall apart once you have loosened the string that binds them together. The string of fixed opinion: somewhere or other, people are certainly thinking—we can rely on this. Notables who have the right posts, and are paid for it, will think for everyone else, are conversant with the relevant procedures, and are permanently occupied in disposing of the doubts and obscurities that remain. If you were to deny this, if you could prove that this is not the case, the public would undoubtedly be overcome by a certain anxiety. Because it might run the risk of having to think for itself. Now, Herr Keuner concentrates his attention on showing that the plethora of problems and theories, theses and world views, is a fiction. And the fact that they all cancel each other out is neither accidental nor grounded in thought itself; rather, it is grounded in the interests of the people who have placed the thinkers in their posts.—Does this mean, the public will now want to know, that thinking corresponds to specific interests? Doesn't thought stand above all interests?—At this point, the public will undoubtedly start to feel uneasy. If people think in the service of specific interests, who will guarantee that these are the interests of the public? And with this the knot is untied and the bundle of assumptions falls apart, transforming itself into sheer question marks. Is thinking worthwhile? Should it be of use? What benefit is it in reality? And to whom?—Blunt questions all of them, no doubt. But we, or so says Herr Keuner, have nothing to fear from blunt questions; we have our most refined answers ready to hand for those blunt questions. For this is the nature of our relationship to these other people. They understand how to pose subtle and sophisticated questions, but they swamp the sewers of their questions with the tidal sludge of their answers—that unfiltered wealth which is beneficial for a few and detrimental to almost everyone. We, on the other hand, pose down-to-earth questions. But we let the answers through only if they have been screened three times over. Precise, clear answers in which the attitude of the speaker, as well as the substance of what is said, becomes transparent. So much for Herr Keuner.

This Herr Keuner is, as we have noted, the most recent of Brecht's characters. No sudden leap of logic is required for us to pass on to one of his earliest. You may perhaps remember that I spoke of the risks attached to Brecht's work. They are to be found in Herr Keuner. If he is a daily guest of the writer, he must inevitably—or so we must hope—encounter other visitors who are very unlike himself, and who will banish the dangers he brings with him. And in fact he meets Baal, Mack the Knife, Fatzer, and the entire horde of hooligans and criminals who people Brecht's plays and who above all are the true singers of his songs, the songs that have been collected in the astounding *Hauspostille* [Book of Family Devotions]. This entire business of songs and rowdiness goes back to Brecht's youth, to his life in Augsburg, where, in the company of his friend and collaborator Caspar Neher[5] and others, he traced the motifs of his later plays in strange melodies and uncouth, heartrending refrains. It is this world that gave birth to Baal, the drunken poet and murderer, and finally, as well, to the egoist Fatzer. It would be a great mistake to suppose, however, that these characters interested the author only as a warning. Brecht's true interest in Baal and Fatzer goes much deeper than this. They do indeed stand for egoism, for the asocial. But Brecht's constant effort is to describe these asocial figures and hooligans as virtual revolutionaries. What sways him in this is not just his own personal sympathy with this character type, but also a theoretical element. Marx, we may say, set himself the task of showing how the revolution could arise from its complete opposite, capitalism, without the need for any ethical change. Brecht has transposed the same problem onto the human plane: he wants the revolutionary to emerge from the base and selfish character devoid of any ethos. Just as Wagner produced a homunculus in a test tube from a magic brew, so Brecht hopes to produce the revolutionary in a test tube from a mixture of poverty and nastiness.[6]

For my third example, I have chosen Galy Gay. He is the hero of a comedy, *Mann ist Mann* [A Man's a Man].[7] No sooner has he walked out his own door to buy a fish for his wife, than he meets some soldiers belonging to the Anglo-Indian army who have lost the fourth man in their unit while plundering a pagoda. They all have an interest in finding a substitute as quickly as possible. Galy Gay is a man who is unable to say no. He follows the three of them without knowing what they want with him. Bit by bit, he assumes possessions, thoughts, attitudes, and habits of the kind needed by a soldier in a war. He is completely reassembled, ceases to recognize his wife when she comes looking for him, and ends up as a dreaded warrior and the conqueror of the fortress of Sir El Dchowr. The nature of this transformation is explained in the following statement:

Herr Bertolt Brecht maintains: A man's a man.
And this is something anyone can say.
But Herr Bertolt Brecht goes on to prove
That you can make as much of a man as you want.
This evening you'll see a man assembled like a car,
Without his losing anything by it.
The man is humanly approached;
He will be asked calmly, but with force,
To follow the world and its ways
And to let his private fish go for a swim.
Herr Bertolt Brecht hopes you will see the ground on which you stand
Melt beneath your feet like snow
And will learn from the packer Galy Gay
That it's easy in life to go astray.[8]

The process of reassembling which we learn of in this passage—we have already heard Brecht proclaim it as a literary form. What he writes is not a "work" but an apparatus, an instrument. The higher it stands, the more capable it is of reshaping, dismantling, and transforming. The study of the great canonical literatures, Chinese literature above all, has shown him that the supreme claim which can be made of the written word is that of its quotability. This suggests that we may find here the beginnings of a theory of plagiarism that will speedily reduce the quipsters to silence.

Anyone who wants to define the crucial features of Brecht in a few words could do worse than confine himself to the comment that Brecht's subject is poverty. How the thinker must make do with the few applicable ideas that exist; the writer, with the few valid formulations we have; the statesman, with the small amount of intelligence and energy man possesses: this is the theme of his work. "What they have made," the Lindberghs say of their machine, "must be enough for me."[9] Stick closely to the bare reality: this must be our watchword. Poverty, Herr Keuner thinks, is a form of mimicry that allows you to come closer to reality than any rich man can. This, of course, is not Maeterlinck's mystical view of poverty. Nor is it the Franciscan idea that Rilke has in mind when he writes, "For poverty is a great light from within."[10] This Brechtian poverty is more like a uniform and is calculated to confer a high rank on anyone who wears it. It is, in short, the physiological and economic poverty of man in the machine age. "The state should be rich; man should be poor; the state should be obliged to do much; man should be permitted to do little." This is the universal human right to poverty as Brecht has formulated it. He has explored its potential in his writings and has displayed it in public in his own slight, ragged appearance.

We will not offer any conclusions, but will just break off. You can, Ladies and Gentlemen, follow up these observations with the assistance of any good bookshop, but even more thoroughly without one.

Talk broadcast by Frankfurter Rundfunk, June 1930. *Gesammelte Schriften,* II, 660–667. Translated by Rodney Livingstone.

Notes

1. Bertolt Brecht, *Versuche 1–3* (Berlin: Kiepenheuer, 1930).
2. Georg Christoph Lichtenberg (1742–1799), writer and experimental psychologist. Although Lichtenberg was a feared satirist in his time, he is remembered today as the first great German aphorist. More than 1,500 pages of notes were published posthumously; alongside jokes, puns, linguistic paradoxes, and excerpts from other writers, they contain thousands of memorable aphorisms like this one.
3. Lion Feuchtwanger (1884–1958), a prominent German novelist, was best-known for his historical novel *Jud Süss* (Jew Süss; 1925). He collaborated with Brecht

on a translation of Christopher Marlowe's play *Edward II*. He was exiled in 1933 and spent the remainder of his life in California.

4. Bertolt Brecht, *Brechts "Hauspostille," mit Anleitungen, Gesangsnoten und einem Anhange* [Brecht's "Book of Family Devotions," with Instructions, Notes on the Songs, and an Appendix] (Berlin: Propyläen-Verlag, 1927), p. 117.

5. Caspar Neher (1897–1962), a prominent stage designer, was a close friend of Brecht's from their youth. Among many other projects, he designed the sets for Brecht's *Threepenny Opera* and *Man Is Man;* and the opera *Mahagonny,* by Brecht and Kurt Weill.

6. The Wagner referred to is Faust's assistant. The experiment referred to is performed in Goethe's *Faust, Part II,* Act 2, Laboratory.

7. Bertolt Brecht, *Mann ist Mann* (Berlin: Propyläen-Verlag, 1926).

8. Ibid., p. 62.

9. Brecht, *Versuche,* p. 6. Brecht's play *Der Flug der Lindberghs* (The Lindberghs' Flight) was first published and performed in 1929.

10. Rainer Maria Rilke, *Das Stundenbuch* (The Book of Hours), section 3: "Von der Armut und vom Tode" (Concerning Poverty and Death).

The First Form of Criticism That Refuses to Judge

I

The first form of criticism that refuses to judge. The initial task is to present the critic's own subjective viewpoint. In connection with the experience of reading. Sealsfield: there is nothing more beautiful than lying on a sofa and reading a novel.[1] The speechlessness of the great physiognomist. Read the highest achievements of traditional physiognomy. Very insistent on this. Then, however, objective truth as the antithesis to this subjective view. That is to say, Goethe's insight that classical works do not really allow for their criticism. Imperative to try to interpret this sentence. Various attempts: for example, that since classical works are the foundations of our judgments, they cannot be made its objects. But this is extremely superficial. Rather deeper: that the exegesis, the ideas, the admiration and enthusiasm of past generations have become indissolubly part of the works themselves, have completely internalized them and turned them into the mirror-images of later generations. Or something along these lines. And here, at this highest stage of the investigation, it is vital to develop the theory of the quotation—since hitherto quotation has been discussed only under the rubric of technique. What emerges at this highest stage is that strategic, polemical, scholastic criticism and an exegetical, commentating form of criticism are antitheses that sublate each other [*sich aufheben*] and merge in a criticism whose sole medium is the life, the ongoing life, of the works themselves.

II

Even though criticism must be divorced from literary history, the exclusive focus on the new and the topical must be no less lethal. Indicate that this theory of criticism as a manifestation of the life of works has a connection with my theory of translation.

Fragment written June 1930 or later; unpublished in Benjamin's lifetime. *Gesammelte Schriften*, VI, 170–171. Translated by Rodney Livingstone.

Notes

1. Charles Sealsfield (pseudonym of Karl Anton Postl; 1795–1864) was a Czech-German novelist and journalist who emigrated to the United States in 1823. His novels, written in English and in German, show a keen awareness of social crisis and economic change.

From the Brecht Commentary

Bert Brecht is a difficult phenomenon. He refuses to make "free" use of his great literary gifts. And there is not one of the slurs leveled against his style of literary activity—"plagiarist," "troublemaker," "saboteur"—that he would not claim as a compliment to his unliterary, anonymous, yet noticeable activity as educator, thinker, organizer, politician, and theatrical producer. In any case, he is unquestionably the only writer writing in Germany today who asks himself where he ought to apply his talent, who applies it only where he is convinced of the need to do so, and who abstains on every occasion that does not meet this standard. The writings assembled under the title *Versuche 1–3* are such points of application of his talent.[1] The new thing here is that these points emerge in their full importance; that the author, for their sake, takes temporary leave of his *Works* and, like an engineer starting to drill for oil in the desert, takes up his activity at precisely calculated places in the desert of the present day. Here these points are situated in the theater, the anecdote, and radio; others will be engaged at a later stage. "The publication of the *Versuche*," the author begins, "marks a point at which certain works are not so much meant to represent individual experiences (that is, to have the character of finished works) as they are aimed at using (and transforming) certain institutes and institutions." What is proposed here is not renovation but innovation. Here literature no longer trusts any feeling of the author's which has not, in the desire to change the world, allied itself with sober intelligence. Here literature knows that the only chance left to it is to become a by-product in the highly ramified process of changing the world. *Versuche 1–3* is such a by-product, and an inestimable one; but the principal product is a new attitude. Lichtenberg said: "It is not what a man is convinced of that matters, but what his convictions make him." This thing that a man's convictions make him Brecht calls "attitude." "The second *Versuch, Geschichten vom Herrn Keuner* [Stories of Herr Keuner]," says the author, "represents an attempt to make gestures quotable." Anyone who reads these stories will see that the gestures quoted are those of poverty, ignorance, and impotence. The innovations introduced—patents, so to speak—are only small ones. For Herr Keuner, a proletarian, stands in sharp contrast to the ideal proletarian of the humanitarians: he is not interiorized. He expects the abolition of misery to arrive only by the logical development of the attitude which poverty forces upon him. Herr Keuner's attitude is not the only one that is quotable; the same applies to the disciples in *Der Flug der Lindberghs* [The Lindberghs' Flight], and likewise to Fatzer the egoist. In each case what is quotable is not just the attitude but also the words which accompany it. These words, like gestures, must be practiced—which is to say, first noticed and later understood. They have their pedagogical effect first, their political effect second, and their poetic effect last of all. The purpose of the commentary from which a sample is reproduced below is to advance the pedagogical effect as much as possible and to retard the poetic one.

I

Leave your post.
The victories have been gained. The
   defeats have been gained:
Now leave your post.

"The defeats have been gained . . . ": less by him, Fatzer, than for him. The victor must not allow the defeated the experience of defeat. He must snatch this, too; he must share defeat with the defeated. Then he will have become master of the situation.

Plunge back into the depths, conqueror.
Jubilation resonates where the fighting
   was.
Be no longer there.
Expect the cries of defeat where they
   are loudest:
In the depths.
Leave your old post.

"Plunge back . . . ": "No glory to the victor, no pity for the defeated." Pokerwork inscription on a wooden plate, Soviet Russia.

Withdraw your voice, orator.
Your name is wiped off the tablets.
   Your orders
Are not obeyed. Allow
New names to appear on the tablets
   and
New orders to be carried out.

"Allow . . . ": Here a harshness bordering on cruelty is permeated with courtesy. The courtesy is persuasive because one senses why it is there. It is there to

(You who no longer command
Do not incite to disobedi-
    ence!)
Leave your old post.

You were not up to it.
You did not finish it off
Now you have had experi-
    ence and are up to it
Now you can start:
Leave your post.

You who ruled over offices
Stoke your oven.
You who had no time to eat
Cook yourself soup.
You about whom much is written
Study the ABCs.
Make a start at once:
Take up your new post.

One who is beaten does not escape
Wisdom.
Hold on tight and sink! Be afraid! Go
    on, sink! At the bottom
The lesson awaits you.
You who were asked too many ques-
    tions
Receive now the inestimable
Teaching of the masses:
Take up your new post.

induce the weakest and most worthless creature (to put it quite simply, man, in whom we recognize ourselves) to perform the greatest and most important action of all. It is the courtesy inherent in the act of sending a rope to someone committing hara-kiri, an act whose wordlessness still leaves room for pity.

"Now you can start . . . ": The "start" is dialectically made new. It manifests itself not in a fresh beginning but in a cessation. The action? The man must leave his post. Inward beginning = ceasing to do an outward thing.

"You who ruled . . . ": this is to emphasize the forces which the Soviet practice of moving officials around the various ministries releases in the person concerned. The command "Start all over again" means, in dialectical terms: (1) learn, for you know nothing; (2) occupy yourself with fundamentals, for you have grown wise enough (through experience) to do so; (3) you are weak; you have been relieved of your post. Take it easy now, so that you can get stronger; you have the time for it.

"Go on, sink!": Fatzer must find a foothold in his hopelessness. A foothold, not hope. Consolation has nothing to do with hope. And Brecht offers him consolation: a man can live in hopelessness if he knows how he got there. He can live in it because his hopeless life is then of importance. To sink to the bottom here means always: to get to the bottom of things.

II

The table is finished, car-
    penter.
Allow us to take it away.
Stop planing it now
Leave off painting it
Speak neither well nor ill of it:
We'll take it as it is.
We need it.
Hand it over.

"Carpenter . . . ": The carpenter we have to imagine here is an eccentric who is never satisfied with his "work," who cannot make up his mind to let it out of his hands. If writers are taking temporary leave of their *Works* (see above), then statesmen, too, are expected to show the same attitude. Brecht tells them: "You are amateur craftsmen; you want to make the State your *Work* instead of realizing that the State is supposed to be not a work of art, not an eternal value, but an object of practical use."

You have finished, statesman.
The State is not finished.
Allow us to change it
To suit the conditions of life.
Allow us to be statesmen, statesman.
Beneath your laws stands your name.
Forget the name
Respect your laws, legislator.

Submit to order, man of order.
The State no longer needs you
Hand it over.

"Hand it over": Here is what "the Lindberghs" say of their machine: "The thing they made will have to do for us." Keep hard by hard reality: that is the order of the day. Poverty, so the bearers of knowledge teach, is a mimicry which brings the poor man closer to reality than any rich man can ever be.

Published in the *Literaturblatt der Frankfurter Zeitung,* July 1930. *Gesammelte Schriften,* II, 506–510. Translated by Anna Bostock.

Notes

1. Bertolt Brecht, *Versuche 1–3* (Berlin: Kiepenheuer, 1930).

Against a Masterpiece

Max Kommerell, *Der Dichter als Führer in der deutschen Klassik* [The Poet as Leader in German Classicism]: *Klopstock, Herder, Goethe, Schiller, Jean Paul, Hölderlin* (Berlin: Georg Bondi, 1928), 486 pages.

If there were such a thing as a German conservatism worth its salt, it would have to regard this book as its Magna Carta. But none has existed for eighty years now. Hence, we are probably not far from the truth if we say that Kommerell is unlikely to have received a more comprehensive critique than this one, which comes from another direction. This book provides the critic with one of those rare and memorable occasions when no one questions him about the book's quality, its stylistic form, or the author's qualifications. We have no reservations about any of these things. Seldom has literary history been written like this: with the diverse approaches, the sharp-edged, impenetrable surface of that symmetrical, adamantine certitude which we have long since come to recognize as the George school's Black Stone of Kaaba.[1] From the praise of blood, the contempt for music, and the hatred of the mob, down to the love of young boys, there is not a single motif that is not invoked either aloud or in a whisper, and that has not grown in importance since we last encountered it. The critical maxims, the sense of values that even in Gundolf's[2] writings had been wheeled out in mastersinger style have here been thrown on the scrap heap, or rather melted down in the heat of an experience that can afford to renounce the hieratic separation of life and work because it approaches both with the same physiognomic and—in the strictest sense—unpsychological mode of seeing. For this reason, almost everything we find here about individual writers—not so much about themselves per se as about their friendships, feuds, meetings, and separations—is characterized by its singular precision and boldness. As is so often the case in horoscopes, chiromantic texts, and other esoteric writings, the wealth of authentic anthropological insights is astounding. Stefan George's theory of the hero should be counted among these occult disciplines. Here it throws light on the principal figures in the Weimar court of the Muses— sometimes on a prophetic aspect, other times on a Pan-like aspect, still others on a satyr-like or centaur-like aspect. You become aware of just how at ease the classical writers were on horseback.

What is the source of this dynamism in figures that so easily tend to lapse into the poses struck by their own monuments? The author does not confine himself to what has actually happened; he even uncovers what *didn't* happen. This does not mean that he invents it—say, as a vision. Rather, he simply and clearly discovers it—namely, as something that in truth did not actually happen. His picture of the past emerges against the background of what might have been, and it is against this background that what actually happened casts its shadow. It is in keeping with this that nothing aims at effects and highlights, and that the offbeat and the obscure detail seem to have been most consummately shaped. In this book, the great controversies have been reproduced for the first time—Jacobi's with the younger writers, Herder's with the Weimar Goethe, Schiller's with the Schlegels, Klopstock's with the king[3]—and it is in interaction with them that the friendships of the classical period acquire their firm contours. It can be neither expected nor desired that the historian of these controversies should abstain from taking sides. But the judgments that are made are symptomatic of the book and its hidden intention. Nothing happens by chance here, but few things are more illuminating than the annihilation of the two Schlegels in their confrontation with Schiller. It would be absurd to ask for "historical justice" here. Other things are at stake. Romanticism stands at the origin of that rebirth of German lyrical poetry accomplished by George. It stands also at the inauguration of the philosophical and critical development that has turned against that achievement today. Looked at strategically, to nudge Romanticism into the background is no idle enterprise, still less a guileless one. By denying the origins of its own attitudes, Romanticism simultaneously denies the forces that proliferate from its core. The Classicism we learn about here is a late and very statesmanlike discovery of the George circle. It is no accident that a student of Wolters has been the one to undertake the task.[4] Every dialectical analysis of George's poetry will have Romanticism at its heart, while every orthodox hagiography will be best advised to downplay Romanticism as much as possible.

And in fact, with a radicalism unattained by any of its predecessors in the George circle, this book constructs an esoteric history of German literature. Only the *profanum vulgus* will see this as literary history at all; in reality, it is a salvation history of the Germans. A history that is enacted in encounters, alliances, testaments and instructions, and that risks collapsing at every moment into the apocryphal, the ineffable, and the meretricious. A theory of true Germanness and the inscrutable paths of the ascent of Germany revolves, pregnant with the future, around the affinity between the genius of the Germans and that of the Greeks. Germans are the heirs to the mission of Greece; that mission is the birth of the hero. It goes without saying that this understanding of the Greeks has been wrenched from every historical context and inserted into a mythological force field. Nor is it mere coincidence that Kommerell echoes, albeit faintly, a famous passage in a letter of Hölderlin's about the spirit of Greece and Germany—a passage in which he calls for a patriotic literature that is imbued with the tradition of the tribe and at the same time inwardly stands at the opposite pole from it, and in which he declares that shame is the surest seal of its authenticity.[5] Words that give some idea of the culture that has set in motion the forces working here toward the twilight of the Teutonic gods. For runes, interpretation, eons, blood, fate[6]—now that Lechter's sun,[7] which once bathed them in its glow, has gone to its resting place, they all stand there like so many thunderclouds in the sky. It is they who give us the lightning flashes that serve as signposts according to which—in the words of Florens Christian Rang, the profoundest critic of the cult of the Teutonic since Nietzsche—"the night only embroiders us more darkly: this monstrous world view of universal death, instead of universal life."[8] How feeble, though, and how long-winded is the rhetorical thunder that follows! It booms throughout all the books of the George circle. It does not exactly win friends for its teachings; its arguments fail to carry conviction if you feel that the speakers never run out of breath. "The fact is that all preachers and propagandists—even if they are recruiting for the purest cause and preaching of nothing but love—leave you feeling empty because they treat everyone, even the richest man, as so much fodder for their intentions."—Something of this insight, which Kommerell formulates so magisterially and which Goethe was destined to learn from Lavater, is transmitted to the reader by Kommerell's own book.[9] The longer you read it, the more his image of Hellas fades in the dazzling light of a morning "in which youth senses the birth of a new nation in glowing unity and in the clanking of arms that were hitherto buried all too deeply." "Our word 'hero,'" we read in another passage, "has not yet passed through this reality . . . But something not yet real surrounds the word: if neighboring peoples borrow their word for 'hero' from the Greeks, it is *we* who possess the organic word-stem, and hence the claim to the thing it names. But if hero becomes demigod, who would then shy away from the hardest hammer and the hottest forge of our future fate?"

Grandiloquent imagery? Not at all. It is the clanking of steel runes, the dangerous anachronism of sectarian language. This book can be fully understood only by close observation of the relationship of the sects to history.

For them, history is never a subject of study; it is only an object of their claims. They attempt to coopt the past as the seal of their origins or as paradigm. In this instance, German Classicism becomes their model. The preeminent concern of the author is to construe Classicism as the first canonical German insurrection against time—a holy war of the Germans against the century, as George himself later proclaimed. It would be one thing to argue this thesis; another, to investigate whether this campaign was successful; a third, to discover whether it was truly paradigmatic. For the author, all these things are inseparable, but the third one has pride of place. In other words, he regards the campaign as paradigmatic, and hence declares it victorious; ultimately, he loses no sleep over its object, the position of the warring parties. But what is their position? Are we justified in reducing this complex process—a process that is, as Goethe shows, oppressive in its complexity—to the interplay and conflict between the heroic and the banal? There is heroism enough among the classical writers, but in itself it was anything but heroic. Its stance was one of resignation. And only Goethe proved able to sustain it to the end without being broken by it. Schiller and Herder were destroyed by it. And those who remained outside Weimar—Hölderlin not the least of them—hid their heads from this "movement." Goethe's opposition to his age was that of a born leader of conservative tendencies. Yet what he wished to restore stemmed not from any classical past but from a geological antiquity of pristine power—indeed, from the most ancient natural relations themselves. For his part, Schiller constructed his opposition in historical terms. His conservatism was a matter of moral sensibility, and far removed from any fundamental spontaneity. Kommerell knows all this as well as anyone. But it means nothing to him. It is as if Antiquity, and indeed the whole of history, had come to an end with Napoleon, the last hero.

The greatness of this book is of course wholly bound up with such anachronisms. For it revives the great Plutarchan style of biography once more. At the same time, Kommerell's distance from the more recent, fashionable form of biography as practiced by Emil Ludwig is even greater than from Gundolf's history of the poets.[10] Plutarch presents his heroes to the reader pictorially, even paradigmatically, but always externally. Ludwig attempts to interiorize them, for the sake of the reader, but even more for the sake of the writer. He incorporates them into himself; he consumes them, and nothing remains. This is the secret of their success: they provide every reader with an "inner Goethe," an "inner Napoleon." Yet just as it has been wittily but correctly claimed that there are few people who have not at some point in their lives just missed becoming a millionaire, we may also say that most people have not lacked the opportunity to become great men. Ludwig's cleverness consists in his ability to lead the reader back over slippery paths to these turning points, and to show them that their worn-out, colorless existence really has the great format of a heroic life. When Kommerell evokes the image of Goethe, it does not even breathe the same air as the reader, let alone share his mood. Thus, while giving an account of Goethe's early years, Kommerell can grant *Der Wanderer und seine Gesellen* [The Wanderer and His Companions] the status of a commentary on *Dichtung und Wahrheit* [Poetry and Truth]. To think of Goethe's early years as a process of coming to terms with contemporary forms of leadership is more than illuminating. Here we find the basis for his discussion of the poet's relationship with Karl August [duke of Weimar], which Kommerell has declared to be the exemplary case of education and personality formation in Goethe, and whose influence he still detects in Goethe's relations with Napoleon and Byron—a passage that ranks among the few inspired pieces that have been written about Goethe's life. No one will expect the relationship between the ruler and the poet to be given a historical treatment here, rather than a timeless, mythological one, nor will anyone call for a description of the specificities of the German state around 1780. What Kommerell provides is sufficient. The tone in which Schelling addresses the old Goethe in his letters is marked by such respect that it takes your breath away; even death failed to lift any of its burden. In such passages the "interpretation" has undergone an inversion and, at the pinnacle of its boldness and success, has achieved a simple, objective, incorruptible reading. This author collects lived hours the way another might collect antiques. Not that he talks about them; you see them because of the knowing, exploratory, reverent, involved, testing, inquiring way he turns each around in his hand, examining it from every side, conferring on it not the false life of empathy but the true life of tradition. Closely related to this is the author's own bent: that of a collector. For whereas with the systematic thinker the positive and negative are always cleanly separated, worlds apart from each other, here preferences and antipathies lie close together. The author picks out a single poem from a cycle, a single moment in an existence, and he makes very sharp distinctions between people and ideas that seem very closely related.

The extent of Kommerell's inability to venture a "redemption" of Classicism is best seen in the chapter "Legislation." Not for nothing does it show how absolutely we are estranged from what provided Goethe with his revelation of classical art on his Italian journey; it reveals just how much rococo lies concealed even in Goethe's work and how unacceptable are the model works of art on which he based his criticism, even if that criticism itself still stands up. Kommerell's picture of Classicism, insofar as it is of permanent value, lives on the basis of the claim to authority he recognizes in it. But the impotence of that claim is as much a part of that picture as its title. "To this day," the author writes, "the average educated person has failed to understand completely the essential features of Weimar culture, and his beggar's pride seeks to cover his shameful nakedness with the theological, philosophical, musical cloak that consists in declaring he is unconcerned about physical appearance." If this is true—and it is true—Weimar Classicism must contain great scope for misunderstanding, not to say ambiguity, at its heart. Scope for misunderstanding—to such a frightening degree that when the philistines resolutely turned their backs on the most precious heritage of the nation, they did so in the name of Schiller, and that it required a Nietzsche to raise doubts about the possibility of reconciling the spirit of Weimar and that of Sedan.[11]

It is consistent only if the author's concluding remarks about Classicism are consigned to the realms of destiny and the stars:

> Thus, we were endowed with a destiny difficult to decipher, more so than any other nation: dual authority and a dual moment, an open one and a secret one. The destruction of Hölderlin by the spirit of the age—although coinciding with this in terms of strict chronology—comes into a different eon: his moment is no less valid, but has a different focal point from Goethe's, and Jean Paul's dream figures appear anemic only until their terrestrial brothers actually tread our soil. All this amazing activity took place in Germany within two decades; and in our heavens can be seen, simultaneously, the sun, a dawn, and the eternal stars.

This is true, beautiful, and important. Nevertheless, confronted by this openly flowery—passionately flowery—gaze, we must declare our preference for the unvarnished truth, for a laconic conception of the seminal, of fertility; and this means opting for the realm of theory and bidding farewell to the world of "vision" [Schau]. If images are timeless, theories certainly are not. It is not tradition but their vitality that determines their worth. The authentic image may be old, but the authentic idea is new. It is of today. Admittedly, this "today" may be paltry. But whatever form it takes, our task is to seize it by the horns so that we can interrogate the past. It is the bull whose blood must fill the grave if the spirits of the departed are to appear at its edge. It is this deadly thrust of ideas that is absent from the works of the George circle. Instead of offering up sacrifices to the present, they avoid it. Every critique must contain some militant element; it, too, knows the daemon of battle. A critique that is nothing but vision loses its way, and deprives literature of the interpretation it owes it, and of the right to grow. Nor should we forget that if criticism is to achieve anything, it must absolutely affirm its own claims. Perhaps it must even claim the highest rank for itself—as do the Brothers Schlegel in their theories. Such claims are worlds away from this author. In his view, the critic is "forever denied the creative innocence of the artist." The disciple of Stefan George cannot admit the carefree verity that innocence never preserves creativity, but that creativity constantly produces innocence.

This salvation history of the Germans concludes with a chapter on

Hölderlin. The image of the man that unfolds here is a fragment of a new life of the saints, and can no longer be assimilated into any historiography. Its almost unbearably dazzling contours lack any of the shading or nuance that theory might have provided. But this is not its purpose. Kommerell's intention was to erect a warning about the future of Germany. Overnight, ghostly hands will write a sign saying "Too Late!" in huge letters. Hölderlin was not of the breed that is resurrected, and the country whose seers proclaim their visions over corpses is not his. This land can become Germany once again only when it is purified, and it cannot be purified in the name of Germany—let alone the "secret Germany" that ultimately is nothing but the arsenal of official Germany, in which the magic hood of invisibility hangs next to the helmet of steel.[12]

Published in *Die literarische Welt,* August 1930. *Gesammelte Schriften,* III, 252–259. Translated by Rodney Livingstone.

Notes

1. "George school" refers to the circle of conservative intellectuals around the poet Stefan George (1868–1933), whose high-modernist verse appeared in such volumes as *Das Jahr der Seele* (The Year of the Soul; 1897), and *Der siebente Ring* (The Seventh Ring; 1907). George's attempt to "purify" German language and culture exerted a powerful influence on younger poets. The Kaaba is the building in the Great Mosque at Mecca that houses the Black Stone, a meteorite that was the object of worship before Muhammad.
2. Friedrich Gundolf (pseudonym of Friedrich Gundelfinger; 1880–1931) was a prominent literary critic, a professor at Heidelberg, and a disciple of Stefan George. For Benjamin's attacks on Gundolf, see the essays "Comments on Gundolf's *Goethe*" and "Goethe's Elective Affinities" in Volume 1 of this edition.
3. Friedrich Heinrich Jacobi (1743–1819) was a novelist of the late Enlightenment whose best-known work is *Woldemar* (1779). Johann Gottfried von Herder (1744–1803), philosopher, historian, and theologian, first met Goethe in Strasbourg in the 1770s; he later became the court pastor in Weimar. Friedrich Gottlieb Klopstock was the most important lyricist of the eighteenth century before Goethe. His lyrical odes, composed between 1747 and 1780, remain widely influential.
4. Friedrich Wolters (1876–1930) was a German historian and an early member of George's circle.
5. Benjamin alludes here to Hölderlin's often-cited letter to his friend Böhlendorff, dated December 4, 1801.
6. Benjamin parodies the cult of old Germanness (a cult embraced by the George school) by using a series of archaic words that purport to evoke the Teutonic spirit.
7. Melchior Lechter (1865–1937), German painter and book illustrator, was the

member of the George school charged with overseeing the first editions of George's works.

8. Florens Christian Rang, *Deutsche Bauhütte: Ein Wort an uns Deutsche über mögliche Gerechtigkeit gegen Belgien und Frankreich und zur Philosophie der Politik* [German Master-Builder's Huts: A Word to Us Germans on the Possibility of Justice toward Belgium and France and on the Philosophy of Politics] (Leipzig: Eberhard Arnold, 1924), p. 51. Rang, a conservative intellectual, was one of Benjamin's most important conversational partners in the mid-1920s.

9. Johann Kaspar Lavater (1741–1801), preacher and theorist of physiognomy, was befriended by Goethe in 1794; Goethe broke off the relationship in 1786 and ridiculed his former friend in *Faust,* returning to a more balanced assessment only in *Dichtung und Wahrheit.*

10. Emil Ludwig (pseudonym of Emil Cohn; 1881–1948) blended empirical research and fictional narration in his popular biographies; his highly successful biography of Goethe appeared in 1920.

11. Marking the end of the first phase of the Franco-German war, the Battle of Sedan on September 1, 1870, led to the capture and fall of Napoleon III and the proclamation of a new French Republic.

12. The George circle thought of itself as the "secret Germany" that upheld properly German values against the onslaught of modernity. The slogan lasted down to the bomb plot of Count Stauffenberg against Hitler, and beyond.

Myslovice—Braunschweig—Marseilles

The Story of a Hashish Trance

This story is not mine. Whether the painter Eduard Scherlinger (whom I saw for the first and last time the evening he told it) was a great storyteller or not is not a matter I wish to enlarge on, since in this age of plagiarism there are always listeners prepared to ascribe a story to you when you have insisted that you are only reporting it faithfully. Nevertheless, this is a story I heard one evening at Lutter and Wegener's, one of Berlin's few classic locations for storytelling and listening. We were a small party, sitting comfortably at a round table, but the conversations had long since dried up and carried on only fitfully, in an undertone, in groups of two or three that paid no attention to each other. At one point (I never learned in what context), my friend Ernst Bloch, the philosopher, let fall the remark that there was no one who had not at some point in his life just missed becoming a millionaire. People laughed. They thought this was just one of his paradoxes. But then the conversation took a strange turn. The more we considered his remark, debating its pros and cons, the more each of us in turn began to take it seriously, until each person arrived at the point where he had come close to getting his hands on the millions. A number of curious stories then came to light, among them this one by the late lamented Scherlinger. I reproduce it here, as far as possible in his own words.

"Following my father's death," he began, "I inherited a not insignificant sum of money, and hastened to make arrangements for my departure for France. I was particularly fortunate to be able to go to Marseilles before the end of the 1920s, since that was the home of Monticelli,[1] to whom I owe everything in my art, not to mention all the other things that Marseilles symbolized to me at the time. I had left my funds invested in a small private bank that had advised my father to his satisfaction for decades on end, and whose junior director was, if not a close friend, at any rate someone with whom I was very well acquainted. Furthermore, he was emphatic in agreeing to keep a watchful eye on my capital; should a favorable opportunity to invest it arise, he would notify me immediately. 'The only point to remember,' he said, 'is that you must leave us a code name.' I looked at him blankly. 'We can carry out instructions per telegram only if we are able to protect ourselves against fraud. Suppose that we wire you and the telegram falls into the wrong hands. We can protect ourselves against the consequences by agreeing on a code name with you—a name you would use instead of your own for transmitting instructions by telegraph.' I understood, but was momentarily in some perplexity. It is not so easy to slip suddenly into a strange name as if it were a costume. There are countless thousands available; the realization that they are all arbitrary has a paralyzing effect, but even more paralyzing is the feeling—an almost unconscious feeling, scarcely capable of articulation—that the choice is irrational but may have grave consequences. Feeling like a chess player who is in a difficult situation and would rather not move at all, but who is finally forced to make a move, I said, 'Braunschweiger.' I knew no one of this name, and had never been to the town from which it derives.

"Around noon on a sultry day in July, I arrived at Saint-Louis Station in Marseilles after a four-week interlude in Paris. Friends had recommended the Hotel Regina, close to the harbor. I left myself just enough time to make sure I obtained a room, tried out the bedside lamp and the taps, and set out to explore. Since this was my first visit to the town, I faithfully followed my old rule for travelers. Unlike average tourists—who, as soon as they arrive in a city, begin hanging awkwardly around the alien city center—I make it my policy to head straight for the suburbs so as to learn my way around the outskirts. I soon discovered the rightness of this principle in the case of Marseilles. Never had the first hour been as profitable as the one I spent in and among the inner port and dock installations, the warehouses, the poorer neighborhoods, the scattered refuges of the destitute. The outlying districts represent, in fact, a town in a state of emergency; they are the terrain upon which the great decisive battles between town and country are continuously being fought out. These battles are nowhere more bitter than between Marseilles and the Provençal countryside. It is the hand-to-hand combat of telegraph poles with agaves, barbed wire with prickly palms, the stench of steamed-up corridors with the damp, sycamore-lined, brooding squares, short-winded flights of steps with overbearing hills. The long rue de Lyon is the road Marseilles blasted through the landscape, exploding it into Saint-Lazare, Saint-Antoine, Arenc, and Septèmes, burying it in the clouds of shrapnel created by the languages of every nation and business concern: Alimentation Moderne, Rue de Jamaïque, Comptoir de la Limite, Savon Abat-Jour, Minoterie de la Campagne, Bar du Gaz, Bar Facultatif. And over everything hang dust clouds comprising an amalgam of sea salt, lime, and mica. From there the road goes on to the most distant quays, which are used only by the largest oceangoing liners, beneath the piercing rays of the slowly setting sun, between the battlements of the Old Town on the left and the bare hills or quarries on the right, down to the towering Pont Transbordeur, which closes off the rectangular Old Port resembling a huge town square that the Phoenicians[2] had reserved for the sea. Up to now, I had followed my path quite alone amid the most densely populated suburbs. But from this point on, I found myself caught up in the procession of celebrating sailors, dockworkers returning home, and housewives out for a stroll, all interspersed with children, which wended its way past the bazaars and cafés, disappearing finally in the side streets, with only the occasional sailor or *flâneur,* such as myself, persevering to the great central artery, La Canebière, the center of commerce, the stock exchange, and tourism. Right through the bazaars, the mountain range of souvenirs extends from one end of the port to the other. Seismic forces have created this massif of paste, seashells, and enamel in which inkwells, steamers, anchors, mercury thermometers, and sirens are all jumbled together. To my mind, however, the pressure of a thousand atmospheres, beneath which this entire world of images crowds together and rears up and then arranges itself, appears to be the same force embodied in the sailors' calloused hands which fumble women's breasts and thighs after a long voyage; and the lust that brings forth a red or blue velvet heart from the geological world and fixes it to the little boxes made of seashells, so that it can be used as a pincushion, is the same force that reverberates through the streets on payday. Preoccupied with such thoughts, I had long since left La Canebière behind me; without really noticing much, I found myself walking beneath the trees of the allée de Meilhan, past the barred windows of the cours Puget, until at last chance, which was still guiding my steps on my first visit to the town, led me to the passage de Lorette, the town mortuary, the narrow courtyard where in the sleepy presence of a number of men and women the whole world seemed to shrink into a single Sunday afternoon. I was overcome by a feeling of sadness, like the sadness I love to this day in the light in Monticelli's paintings. I believe that, at such moments, the stranger experiences something that normally only the long-standing inhabitants can discern. For it is childhood that is able to seek out the sources of sadness and to understand the mournful side of such celebrated and radiant cities; it is necessary to have lived in them as a child.

"It would be a fine piece of romantic embroidery," Scherlinger said with a smile, "if I were to go on and describe how I landed up in some disreputable harbor dive and obtained some hashish from an Arab who worked in the boiler room of a freighter, or who was perhaps a porter. But such embroidering would be of no use to me, since I was probably closer in spirit to those Arabs than to the tourists whose journeys led them to such dives. Closer in one respect at least, since I carried my own hashish with me on my travels. I do not believe that what induced me to take some hashish at around seven o'clock in the evening, upstairs in my room, was the unworthy desire to escape my depressed mood. It is more likely that this was an attempt to yield entirely to the magic hand with which the city had gently taken hold of me by the scruff of the neck. As I have said, I was not a novice when it came to using poison; but whether it was my almost daily feelings of homesickness, or the paucity of human contact and the uncongenial localities, never before had I felt myself so at home in the community of cognoscenti whose records of their experiences—from Baudelaire's *Paradis artificiels* to Hermann Hesse's *Steppenwolf*—were perfectly familiar to me.[3] I lay on my bed, read, and smoked. Through the window opposite me, far below, I could see one of the narrow black streets of the port district that intersect the body of the city like the marks of a knife. I was thus able to enjoy the absolute certainty that I could surrender to my dreams quite undisturbed in this city of hundreds of thousands in which not a single soul knew of my existence. But the expected effects failed to appear. Three-quarters of an hour had already passed, and I began to feel suspicious about the quality of the drug. Or had I been carrying it around for too long? Suddenly there was a loud knock at my door. I was completely baffled. I was frightened out of my wits, but made no attempt to open the door, and instead asked who it was, without even changing my position. The servant: 'A gentleman wishes to speak to you.'—'Let him come up,' I said; I did not have the courage, or perhaps just the presence of mind, to ask his name. I stood where I was, leaning against the bedpost with my heart palpitating, and staring at the open door until a uniform appeared. The 'gentleman' was a telegram boy.

"'Advise purchase of 1,000 Royal Dutch STOP Friday opening price STOP Wire approval.'

"I looked at my watch; it was eight o'clock. An urgent telegram would reach the Berlin branch of my bank first thing the following morning. I dismissed the messenger with a tip. I felt my mood alternate between anxiety and irritation. Fear of having to deal with a business matter, a chore, at precisely this time; irritation because the drug was still not working. The wisest course seemed to me to set out for the main post office at once, since I knew it was open until midnight for telegrams. In view of my adviser's reliability in the past, I had no doubt that I should agree to his suggestion. On the other hand, I was afraid that the hashish might start to work after all and that I might forget my code name. It was better to waste no time.

"As I went downstairs, I thought about the last time I had taken hashish—it had been several months previously—and how I had been unable to still the pangs of hunger that had suddenly overwhelmed me late one night in my room. It seemed advisable to buy a bar of chocolate. In the distance a shopwindow beckoned, with candy jars, shiny tinfoil wrapping, and piles of beautiful *pâtisserie*. I entered the shop and was pulled up short. There was no one to be seen. But I was less struck by this than by the very strange chairs that compelled me to admit for good or ill that in Marseilles people drank chocolate while enthroned on high chairs that bore a remarkable resemblance to the chairs used to perform operations. At that moment the owner came running from across the street wearing a white coat, and I had just time enough to decline, with a loud laugh, his offer of a shave or a haircut. Only now did I realize that the hashish had begun to work, and if I had not been alerted by the way in which boxes of powder had changed into candy jars, nickel trays into chocolate bars, and wigs into cakes, my own loud laughter would have been warning enough. For the trance always begins with such laughter, or sometimes with a less noisy, more inward, but more joyful laugh. And now I recognized it by the infinite tenderness of the wind that was blowing the fringes of the curtains on the opposite side of the street.

"Then the hashish eater's demands on time and space came into force. As is well known, these are absolutely regal. For anyone who has taken hashish, Versailles is not too large, nor eternity too long. Against the background of these immense dimensions of inner experience, of absolute duration and immeasurable space, a wonderful beatific humor dwells all the more fondly on the limitless contingencies of all existence. Moreover, my steps became light and sure, so that the stony, uneven ground of the great square I was crossing seemed like the surface of a main road along which I strode at night, like an energetic hiker. At the end of this huge square, however, was an ugly, symmetrical hall-like building, with an illuminated clock over the door: the post office. I can say now that it is ugly; at the time, I would not have conceded this. Not just because we do not wish to hear of ugliness when we have taken hashish, but primarily because the post office aroused a profound feeling of gratitude in me—this gloomy building, waiting expectantly for me, its every nook and cranny ready to receive and transmit the priceless confirmation that would make me a rich man. I could not take my eyes off it; indeed, I felt how much would have escaped me if I had approached too closely and lost sight of the building as a whole and especially the welcoming beacon of its moon-like clock. At that moment I could hear the chairs and tables of a little bar, a truly disreputable one no doubt, being moved around in the darkness. I was still quite far away from dangerous districts, but even so, there were no middle-class customers; at most, alongside the proletarians were a few local shopkeepers' families. I went and sat down in the bar. It was the riskiest thing of this kind I could contemplate, and in my trance I estimated the danger with the same accuracy you display when you are very tired and try to fill a glass of water to the brim without spilling a drop—something you would never manage to do when you're in full control of your senses. But scarcely had the hashish felt me relax than its magic began to have an effect, with an elemental sharpness I have never experienced before or since. It turned me into a physiognomist. I am normally quite unable to recognize people I know only slightly, or to retain people's features in my memory. But on this occasion I positively fixed my gaze on the faces around me, faces I would normally have had a twofold reason to avoid. On the one hand, I would not have wished to attract their gaze; and on the other, I would have been unable to endure the brutality of their expressions. I suddenly understood how for a painter (isn't this the case with Leonardo and many others?) ugliness is the true reservoir of beauty, better than any treasure chest; it was a fissured mountain, with its entire inner deposits of gold flashing through wrinkles, glances, and features. I particularly recollect the unpleasant, infinitely bestial face of one man: I was deeply shaken when I suddenly perceived the 'furrow of resignation' in it. It was men's faces above all that interested me. Now began that game in which every new face seemed to be the face of someone I knew; often I knew his name, often not. The illusion faded again, as illusions do fade away in such dream states—that is to say, not with a feeling of shame, of indiscretion, but peaceably and amicably, like a being that has done its duty. The face of my neighbor, however—a petty bourgeois to judge by his appearance—kept changing in shape, expression, and fullness. His haircut and black-rimmed glasses gave him, by turns, a severe and a good-humored expression. Of course, I told myself that a man could not change so quickly, but it made no difference. And he had already experienced much of life when he suddenly changed into a high school boy in a tiny eastern European town. He had a pretty, cultivated study-room. I wondered how this young man could have acquired so much culture. What did his father do? Was he a cloth merchant? Corn trader? Suddenly, I realized that this was Myslovice.[4] I looked up. And then I saw, right at the end of the street—in fact, at the end of the town—the high school in Myslovice; and the school clock (had it stopped? it didn't seem to be moving) pointed to shortly after eleven. Classes must have started again. I became completely immersed in this image, but couldn't find firm ground again. The people who had captured my attention just before (or was it two hours before?) seemed to have been completely erased. 'From century to century, things grow more estranged'—this thought passed through my mind. I hesitated to taste the wine. It was a half-bottle of Cassis, a dry wine that I had ordered. A piece of ice was floating in the glass. I do not know how long I gazed at the images within it. But when I next looked up at the square, I saw that it tended to change with each person who entered it, just as if it formed a configuration for him that of course had nothing to do with the way he looked at it, but rather had to do with the view that the great portrait painters of the seventeenth century create by placing their dignitaries, according to their character, against the background of a colonnade or a window, so that the view is generated by this backdrop.

"I was suddenly aroused with a start from the deepest contemplation. I was completely alert, and was conscious of only one thing: the telegram. It had to be sent off at once. To stay awake, I ordered black coffee. An eternity seemed to pass before the waiter appeared with the cup. I greedily seized it; I smelled the aroma; the cup was almost at my lips, when my hand stopped suddenly—Who could say whether it was automatic or from astonishment? I suddenly saw through the instinctive haste of my arm; I became aware of the beguiling scent of the coffee, and only now recollected what makes this drink the high point of pleasure for every hashish eater—namely, the fact that it intensifies the effect of the drug like nothing else. This is why I wanted to stop, and I did stop in time. The cup did not touch my lips. Nor did it touch the tabletop. It remained suspended in mid-air before me, held by my arm, which began to go numb and clutched it in a rigid grip like an emblem, a sacred stone or bone. My gaze fell on the creases in my white beach trousers, I recognized them, the creases of a burnous. My gaze fell on my hand—I recognized it, a brown, Ethiopian hand. And while my lips stayed firmly sealed, refusing drink and speech in equal measure, from within me a smile rose up to them—a supercilious, African, Sardanapoline smile, the smile of a man about to see through the world and its destinies and for whom nothing remains a mystery anymore, either in objects or in names. Brown and silent, I saw myself sitting there. *Braunschweiger.*[5] The Open Sesame of this name, which was supposed to contain all the riches of the earth in its interior, had opened up. Smiling a smile of infinite compassion, I now began to think for the first time of the Braunschweigers who lived a wretched life in their little central German town, in complete ignorance of the magic powers they possess thanks to their name. At this moment, by way of confirmation, the bells of all the church towers of Marseilles rang out to signal midnight, like a solemn choir.

"It was now dark; the bar was closing. I wandered along the quayside, reading the names of the boats that were tied up there. An incomprehensible feeling of joy came over me and made me smile at the names of the girls of France that appeared in a row: Marguerite, Louise, Renée, Yvonne, Lucile. The promise of love that these boats seemed to have been given along with their names was wonderful, beautiful, and moving. Next to the last one, there was a stone bench: 'Bank,' I said to myself,[6] and felt disapproval that it too did not have its name in gold letters on a black background. This was the last lucid thought I had that night. The next one came from the midday papers, which I read sitting on a bench by the water in the hot noon sun: 'Sensational Rise in Royal Dutch.'

"Never," the narrator concluded, "have I felt so ebullient, clear, and festive after a hashish trance."

Published in *Uhu,* November 1930. *Gesammelte Schriften,* IV, 729–737. Translated by Rodney Livingstone.

Notes

1. Adolphe Monticelli (1824–1886) was a French painter known for his landscapes and his skill as a colorist.
2. Benjamin here confuses the Phoenicians with the Phoceans, a Greek tribe from Asia Minor that established Massilia as a trading post around 600 B.C.
3. Serving as a literary template for Benjamin's own hashish experiments, Baudelaire's essay on opium and hashish was first published in 1860. Hesse's portrayal of psychic fragmentation—understood as the key to a personal authenticity beyond bourgeois convention—appeared in 1927.
4. Myslovice is a town in Silesia about seventy miles southeast of Wroclaw, Poland.
5. Benjamin puns here on the German word *Braunschweig,* whose components mean "brown" and "silent."
6. In German, *Bank* means both "bench" and "bank."

A Critique of the Publishing Industry

Writers are among the most backward sectors of the population when it comes to exploiting their own social experience. They regard one another simply as colleagues; their readiness to form judgments and protect their own interests is, as in all people concerned with status, far prompter toward those beneath them than toward those higher up. They do sometimes manage to obtain a good deal from a publisher. But for the most part they are unable to give an account of the social function of their writing, and it follows that in their dealings with publishers they are no better able to reflect on their function to any effect. There are undoubtedly publishers who take a naive view of their own activities and who genuinely believe that their only moral task is to distinguish between good books and bad, and that their only commercial task is to distinguish books that will sell from those that will not. In general, however, a publisher has an incomparably clearer idea of the circles to whom he is selling than writers have of the audience for whom they write. This is why they are no match for him and are in no position to control him. And who else should do that? Certainly not the reading public; the activities of publishers fall outside their field of vision. This leaves the retailer as the only court of appeal. It is superfluous to remark how problematic retailers' control must be, if only because it is irresponsible and secret.

What is called for is obvious. That it cannot happen overnight, and that it can never be fully implemented in the capitalist economic system, should not prevent us from stating it. As a prerequisite for everything else, what is indispensable is a statistical survey of the capital at work in the publishing world. From this platform, the investigation should proceed in two directions. On the one hand, as a follow-up to the question: What is the source of these capital sums? In other words, how much capital has migrated into publishing from the banking, textile, coal, steel, and printing industries? On the other hand, what does publishing capital supply to the book market? It would be but a short step from there to combine these questions and investigate whether, when capital flows into publishing, it is directed at specific customer strata and trends that correspond, say, to coal and steel, as opposed to textiles. But the statistical foundations of this third area are too difficult to obtain for there to be any prospects of undertaking such a project soon. In contrast, the more unreliable opinion surveys of the public and of booksellers could easily be supplemented by information gathered at intervals from the publishers themselves about the sales figures in different markets for their main products. Since publishers already inform us about the size of editions, this should not prove to be such a perilous step, or so one might think. Of the very greatest interest, furthermore, would be statistical information about the relation between the size of an edition and advertising costs; likewise, a statistical picture of the relation between commercial success (sales figures) and literary success (critical reception in the press). Last, and the most difficult of all: the percentages of successful books and failures among all the titles issued annually by individual publishers and by the German book trade as a whole.

The objection that such methods would lead to thinking that commercial success is the only criterion relevant to books is as obvious as it is false. Of course, there are valuable books that fail to sell, and that a good publisher will nevertheless wish to sell not only as a matter of honor but on publishing principles. (In the same way, confectioners will put sugar-icing castles and candy towers in their shopwindows without any intention of selling them.) But of course the analysis we are calling for, and which has the additional benefit of being the most reliable method of making use of books to inquire into the spiritual currents of the nation, also has the particular merit of eliminating the most common—and most erroneous—view of publishing in vogue at present. According to this view, a publishing house is a combined operation, consisting of organized patronage on the one hand and a lottery on the other, in which every new book is a number and the reading public acts as banker. From the players' (in other words, the publishers') winnings, a part is used to bet on numbers that look splendid and significant but that scarcely figure in the roulette of the reading public. In short, this is the abstract view of publishing: on the one hand, the publisher as a broker between individual manuscripts; on the other, "the" reading public. But this view is false through and through, because the publisher is not in a position to form an opinion in a vacuum about either the ideal value or the commercial value of a book. In the final analysis, a publisher has to have a close relationship with specific literary fields—within which he does not need to follow any particular line—because this is the only way for him to maintain contact with his reading public, without which his business is doomed to failure. Obvious though this is, it is no less striking that in Germany, which possesses a number of physiognomically clearly defined publishing houses—Insel, Reclam, S. Fischer, Beck, and Rowohlt—no attempt has ever been made to undertake a sociological study, let alone a critique of these institutions. Yet this would be the only way to measure the gulf that divides our great publishing houses from those dilettantish private operations that disappear every year by the dozen, only to be replaced by similar firms that open up in their wake. Moreover, it would be hard to resist the observation that even the straightforward commercial satisfaction of demand would be, if not exactly laudable, at any rate far more respectable than a pretentious idealism that floods the market with meaningless books, tying up capital in them that could be much better invested for nonliterary purposes.

Only experience will enable us to discover the benefits of an annual critical survey of German publishing policy. Such a critique, in which literary standards would have to take a back seat to sociological ones—which, themselves, would be only one aspect—would lay bare the antinomy between what might be called constructive and organic publishing policies. A publisher may construct his operations so as to encompass and establish certain sectors. But he can also let his business develop organically out of loyalty to particular authors or schools. These two approaches cannot always go hand in hand. This very fact ought to lead a publisher to make a definite business plan and approach writers with specific projects. Not that such an approach is entirely unknown. But in an age in which both economic production and intellectual production have been rationalized, it should become the norm. One reason there is no sign of it at present lies in the general underestimation of the role of publishers' referees. The time when a Julius Elias or a Moritz Heimann could exercise a decisive influence on a publisher appears to be over.[1] But publishers are making a great mistake when they treat their referees merely as gatekeepers or else as naysayers, instead of as experts in publishing policy who are intelligent enough to solicit usable manuscripts rather than merely sifting through useless ones. And for their part, the editors are wrong to set their own idealism against publishers' materialism, instead of treating ideas in such a way that the publisher will be tied to them for the sake of his material interests. It may lend additional weight to these brief proposals if publishers come to see that the leaders among them will benefit more in terms of both honor and profit from a sound criticism of their activities than from a case-by-case opinion of their products or their sense of fair play.

Published in the *Literaturblatt der Frankfurter Zeitung,* November 1930. *Gesammelte Schriften,* II, 769–772. Translated by Rodney Livingstone.

Notes

1. Julius Elias (1861–1927), German historian of art and literature, was a champion of Impressionism and the editor of Ibsen's collected works. Moritz Heimann (1868–1925), senior editor at Fischer Verlag, furthered the careers of such authors as Gerhart Hauptmann, Hermann Hesse, and Thomas Mann.

Graphology Old and New

Today scientific graphology is a good thirty years old.[1] With certain reservations, it can undoubtedly be described as a German achievement; and 1897, when the German Graphological Society was founded in Munich, can be deemed the year of its birth. It is a striking fact that academic science still withholds recognition, even though this technique has been providing proofs of the precision of its principles for the past three decades. To this day, no German university has established a chair for the interpretation of handwriting. But it is worthy of note that one of the free colleges, the Lessing-Hochschule in Berlin, has now taken the step of adopting the Central Institute for Scientific Graphology (under the direction of Anja Mendelssohn). Evidently this fact has also been acknowledged abroad as a milestone in the history of graphology. At any rate, the oldest living representative of this science, Jules Crépieux-Jamin, arrived from Rouen to attend the opening of the institute.[2] We found him to be an elderly, somewhat unworldly gentleman who at first glance looked like a doctor. An important practical doctor, that is, rather than a pioneering researcher. And this would also be an apt description of Crépieux-Jamin and his disciples' position in graphology. He inherited the mantle of his teacher, Michon, who in 1872 had published his *Geheimnis der Handschrift* [Secret of Handwriting], in which the concept of graphology appears for the first time.[3] What teacher and pupil have in common is a sharp eye for handwriting and a large dose of healthy common sense, in conjunction with a gift for ingenious inference. All of this shows to advantage in their analyses, which for their part do more to satisfy the requirements of practical life than those of a science of character. The demands of the latter were first articulated by Ludwig Klages in his fundamental works *Prinzipien der Charakterologie* [The Principles of Characterology] and *Handschrift und Charakter* [Handwriting and Character].[4] Klages takes aim at the so-called sign theory of the French school, whose proponents linked qualities of character to quite specific written signs that they used as stereotypes on which to construct their interpretations. In contrast, Klages interprets handwriting basically as gesture, as expressive movement. In his writings, there is no talk of specific signs; he speaks only of the general characteristics of writing, which are not restricted to the particular form of individual letters. A special role is assigned to the analysis of the so-called formal level—a mode of interpretation in which all the characteristic features of a specimen of handwriting are susceptible to a dual evaluation—either a positive or a negative interpretation—and where it is the formal level of the script that decides which of the two evaluations should be applied in each case. The history of modern German graphology can be defined essentially by the debates surrounding Klages' theories. These debates have been initiated at two focal points. Robert Saudek criticized the lack of precision in Klages' findings concerning the physiological features of handwriting, as well as his arbitrary preoccupation with German handwriting style.[5] He himself has attempted to produce a more differentiated graphological analysis of the various national scripts, on the basis of exact measurements of handwriting motion. In Saudek, characterological problems recede into the background; whereas in a second trend, which has recently taken issue with Klages, they stand at the center of attention. This view objects to his definition of handwriting as expressive movement. Max Pulver and Anja Mendelssohn, its leading representatives, are seeking to create a space for an "ideographic" interpretation of handwriting—that is to say, a graphology that interprets script in terms of the unconscious graphic elements, the unconscious image fantasies, that it contains.[6] The background to Klages' graphology is the philosophy of life of the George circle, and behind Saudek's approach we can discern Wundt's psychophysics; whereas in Pulver's endeavors the influence of Freud's theory of the unconscious is undeniable.[7]

Published in the *Südwestdeutsche Rundfunkzeitung,* November 1930. *Gesammelte Schriften,* IV, 596–598. Translated by Rodney Livingstone.

Notes

1. Benjamin was himself an amateur graphologist. See also his review of the Mendelssohns' *Der Mensch in der Handschrift,* in this volume.
2. Jules Crépieux-Jamin (1858–1940) was the author of many graphological treatises, including *L'écriture et le caractère* (Handwriting and Character; 1892), which went through numerous editions and was translated into many languages.
3. The abbé Jean Hippolyte Michon (1806–1861) published several studies of graphology, as well as work in other "border zones" such as the psychology of banditry.

4. Ludwig Klages (1872–1956), philosopher and psychologist, attempted to found a "metaphysical psychology" that would study human beings in the context of their relationship to a reality that was, for Klages, made up of archetypal images.

5. Robert Saudek (1880–1935), German novelist, playwright, and graphologist, was the author of *Wissenschaftliche Graphologie* (Scientific Graphology; 1926) and the editor of the American journal *Character and Personality*. His edition of Otto Weininger's notorious *Gedanken über Geschlechtsprobleme* (Thoughts on Sexual Problems) was published in 1907.

6. Max Pulver (1889–1952), Swiss poet, playwright, and graphologist, published his *Symbolik der Handschrift* (Symbolism of Handwriting) in 1931.

7. Wilhelm Max Wundt (1832–1920), German physiologist and psychologist, founded the first laboratory for experimental psychology at Leipzig in 1878.

Characterization of the New Generation

1. These people make not the slightest attempt to base their activities on any theoretical foundations whatsoever. They are not only deaf to the so-called great questions, those of politics or world views; they are equally innocent of any fundamental reflection on questions of art.

2. They are uneducated. Not just in the sense that their knowledge is very limited, but above all because they are incapable of extending their diminishing knowledge in a systematic manner. Never has a generation of writers been so oblivious to the need to understand the techniques of scholarly work as this one.

3. Although these writers stride blithely on from one work to the next, it is impossible to discern any sort of development—and above all any consistency—in their work, except at the level of technique. Their efforts and their ambition seem to exhaust themselves in the acquisition of a new subject or a grateful theme, and this is enough for them.

4. Popular literature has always existed—that is to say, a literature that acknowledges no obligations to the age and the ideas that move it, except perhaps the desirability of presenting such ideas in an agreeable, fashionably packaged form for immediate consumption. Such consumer literature of course has the right to exist; in bourgeois society at least, it has its place and its justification. But never before, in bourgeois or any other society, has this literature of pure consumption and enjoyment ever been identical with the avant-

garde at its technically and artistically most advanced. This is precisely the pass to which the latest school has now brought us.

5. Give respect to economic necessity where it is due: it may well force the writer to produce much inferior work. The nuances of his writing will then show what stuff he is made of. However dubious much literary journalism may be, there is hardly anything so bad that it cannot be salvaged from the worst excesses by certain aspects of its content and especially its style. Where a writer succeeds, he owes it to his grasp of technique; where he fails, it is the moral or substantive foundation that is lacking. What is astonishing is how completely alien to members of the new school the salutary, protecting reservations are—not just the moral ones, but even the linguistic ones too. And how these new writers absolutely take for granted their right to display an infinitely pampered, narcissistic, unscrupulous—in short, journalistic—ego. And how their writing is imbued to the very last detail with the *arriviste* spirit!

Fragment written ca. 1930; unpublished in Benjamin's lifetime. *Gesammelte Schriften,* VI, 167–168. Translated by Rodney Livingstone.

The Need to Take the Mediating Character of Bourgeois Writing Seriously

The need to take the mediating character of bourgeois writing seriously. Such art does indeed blur the distinctions between political and nonpolitical literature, but it ensures that the differences between opportunist writing and radical writing emerge all the more clearly.

It should also be pointed out that in reality even the effect of "unmediated opinion" is indirect—which is true of everything written that has not grown out of political activity. The disadvantage of this involuntary mediatedness: it lacks a clear awareness of which class it is addressing. The advantages of voluntary mediatedness.

The claim to originality that the form of literary journalism imposes on *everyone.*

The New Objectivity and war books.[1]

Originality and, simultaneously, an uninhibited harmlessness is what these fellows lay claim to.

False criticism.

The entire account in this section will be examined in the light of the concept . . .

[Breaks off; continued in the fragment titled "False Criticism."]

Fragment written ca. 1930; unpublished in Benjamin's lifetime. *Gesammelte Schriften,* VI, 174–175. Translated by Rodney Livingstone.

Notes

1. *Neue Sachlichkeit* (New Objectivity) was the term originally applied by the museum curator G. F. Hartlaub to an emergent figuration in German postwar painting. It gradually came to designate the Weimar "period style" in art, architecture, design, literature, and film: cool, objective, and analytical.

False Criticism

The entire account in this section will be examined in the light of the concept of objective corruption and related to present-day conditions.[1]

The distinction between personal criticism and object-based criticism, which is used to bring polemics into discredit, is a principal instrument of objective corruption. The whole prescriptive section reaches its pinnacle in an apologia on polemics. This amounts to the assertion that, in our day, the image of Karl Kraus seems to be that of the only champion of the power and technique of the art of polemics. The precondition of his mastery in polemics is the fact that he attacks people less for what they are than for what they do, more for what they say than for what they write—and least of all for their books, which according to accepted notions of criticism constitute the only object of study. The polemicist engages his entire person. Kraus goes even further. He sacrifices himself. The significance of this should be further developed.

Expressionism as the basis of objective corruption. (Kraus was always intransigently opposed to it.) Expressionism is the mimicry of revolutionary gesture without any revolutionary foundation. In Germany it was overcome only through a change of fashion, not as the result of criticism. This is why all its perversions have managed to survive in a different form in the New Objectivity, which succeeded it. Both movements base their solidarity on their efforts to come to terms with the experience of the war from the standpoint of the bourgeoisie. Expressionism attempts this in the name of humanity; subsequently this was done in the name of objectivity. The works of the latest German writers are milestones on a road from which a left or a right turn can be taken at any moment. They are the works of a caste between the classes that is at the highest state of alert. This *tendancisme sans tendance,* which has left its mark on literature ever since Expressionism, is best defined by the fact that there are no longer any feuds between literary coteries. Every writer wants to prove only one thing: that he has mastered the latest fashion. This is why the new manifestos are constantly being signed by the old names. Rarely has there been an age in which the old tread so hard on the heels of the young.

No one is claiming that it is essential, or even useful, for criticism to be based directly on political ideas. But this is absolutely indispensable for polemical criticism. The more individually the personal is brought to the fore, the more necessary it is for the critic and his public to agree about the image of the age that serves as backdrop and foil. Every authentic picture of the age, however, is political. The wretched state of criticism in Germany results in the fact that even in the extreme case of Communism, political strategies do not coincide with literary ones. This is the misfortune of critical and perhaps also political thought.

If the personal note predominates in successful polemics, this is merely an extreme instance of the general truth that critical objectivity which can express only individual judgment—from case to case and without any larger conception—is always insignificant. This "objectivity" is no more than the obverse of the haphazard nature and lack of authority of the reviewing business, with which journalism has destroyed criticism.

It is consistent with this objectivity (which could be called "new" but also "unscrupulous") that, in its products, its so-called bona fides always turn out to be no more than the "temperamental" reaction of an "original" critical mind—that uninhibited, unprejudiced being of which bourgeois criticism is so proud, and whose gestural language, obtrusively embodied in Alfred Kerr,[2] is in reality nothing but the servile zeal with which the literary reviewer satisfies the demand for character sketches, temperaments, originals, and personalities. The integrity of the literary reviewer is just a straining for effects; and the deeper his tone of conviction, the more his breath stinks.

The reaction of Expressionism, on the other hand, was pathological rather than critical. It strove to overcome the age that had given birth to it by becoming its expression. The negativism of Dada was much more revolutionary. And down to the Dada movement, there prevailed a far greater solidarity of the German intelligentsia with the French. But whereas in France the Surrealist movement was born, in Germany thought was emasculated and the banner of the New Objectivity was unfurled.[3] The true tendencies of this last movement can be grasped only through a comparison with Surrealism. Both are manifestations of a regression to 1885. On the one hand, a regression to Sudermann; on the other, to Ravachol.[4] At any rate, there is a difference between the two.

"Quand on soutient un mouvement révolutionnaire, ce serait en compromettre le développement que d'en dissocier les divers éléments au nom du goût" (Guillaume Apollinaire).[5] With these words, Apollinaire has also condemned the journalistic criticism that continues to speak in the name of taste. For what characterizes the run-of-the-mill reviewing industry is its unrestrained indulgence in its own reactions (the result is the famous "opinion of one's own"), and its pretense that an aesthetics still exists, whereas there has long been none. In truth, the starting point of criticism must be the perception that aesthetic criteria are in all cases completely devalued. Nor can they be resurrected from the old aesthetics by any "updating," however ingenious. On the contrary, criticism must—initially, at any rate— base itself on a program which must be committed to revolutionary politics if it is to tackle the tasks that face it. (Apollinaire's assertion is nothing but a call for such a program.) Even the old aesthetics, such as Hegel's, contained the greatest insights into the contemporary world. But the modern critic thinks of these old conceptual schemes in absolute terms, much as he regards the works.

Attempt to illustrate the genuinely mediated effectiveness of revolutionary writing with reference to the works of Karl Kraus. The conservative semblance of such writing. Since it focuses on the best that has been produced by the bourgeois class, it shows in exemplary fashion that the most valuable things this class has created must be stifled among the bourgeoisie and can be conserved only through a revolutionary stance. But it also teaches that the methods with which the bourgeoisie built up its knowledge will overthrow that knowledge today, if they are applied rigorously and without opportunism.

With the New Objectivity, criticism has finally obtained the literature it deserves.

Nothing characterizes our literature industry better than the attempt to produce a great effect at small cost in terms of effort. Publishers' gambles replace literary responsibility. It is absurd to behave like the writers of the New Objectivity and claim political effects without individual commitment. This commitment may be practical and consist in disciplined action in a political party; it may also be literary and consist in the principled publicity of private life—a polemical omnipresence as practiced by the Surrealists in France and by Karl Kraus in Germany. The left-wing writers practice neither one nor the other. This is why it is important to stop competing with them for the right to own the program of "political literature." For everyone who approaches the mediating character—even more, the mediating effect—of serious bourgeois writing recognizes that the distinctions between political and nonpolitical writing become blurred at this point. Whereas the distinctions between the programs of opportunist and radical writing stand out all the more clearly.

We may say of every approach to art that any analysis which fails to uncover hidden relationships in the work, and hence those that are not contained in the work, misses the point of the object under scrutiny. To see inside the work means giving a more precise account of the ways in which the work's truth-content and material content interpenetrate. At all events, a form of criticism which at no point establishes its solidarity with the truth contained in the work, and which retains a hold only on externals, has no claim to our recognition. Unfortunately, however, this is the case with almost everything that goes by the name of Marxist criticism. In almost every example, what we find is a thick-skinned tracing out of the lines in the works themselves, where the social content—if not the social tendency—lies partly on the surface. But this leads in no way into the interior of the work—only to statements about it. In contrast, the Marxist's hope that he can look around inside the work with the gaze of the sociologist is doomed to disappointment. A deductivist aesthetic, which no one needs more urgently than the Marxist, has not yet been devised. Only in the interior of the work, where truth-content and material content meet, is the sphere of art definitively left behind. At its threshold, all aesthetic aporias disappear too—the quarrel about form and content, and so on.

The structure of the final section will be grouped around these theses: (1) the works live on; (2) the law governing their survival is that of shrinkage; (3) with the survival of the works, their character as art recedes; (4) a successful form of criticism breaks through the limits of the aesthetic realm; (5) the technique of magical criticism.

Opposition of the categories "totality" (*Gestalt*-quality) and "authenticity."

Fragment written in 1930 or 1931; unpublished in Benjamin's lifetime. *Gesammelte Schriften*, VI, 175–179. Translated by Rodney Livingstone.

Notes

1. Like many of Benjamin's fragments on literary criticism, this one was part of the planning stages for a book on the topic. See the Chronology in this volume.
2. Alfred Kerr (pseudonym of Alfred Klemperer; 1867–1948) was, in his day, Berlin's most prominent and influential theater critic.
3. *Neue Sachlichkeit* (New Objectivity) was the term originally applied by the museum curator G. F. Hartlaub to an emergent figuration in German postwar painting. It gradually came to designate the Weimar "period style" in art, architecture, design, literature, and film: cool, objective, analytical.
4. Hermann Sudermann (1857–1928) was a Naturalist dramatist whose reputation waned rapidly as he turned to symbolism and biblical tragedy. François-Claudius Koenigstein, known as Ravachol (1859–1892), was part of a group of anarchists responsible for a series of bombings; he was guillotined in 1892.
5. "When you support a revolutionary movement, you would compromise its development if you were to dissociate it from certain elements in the name of taste."

Antitheses

CRITICIZABLE		UNCRITICIZABLE	
Primacy of truth-content	{Judgment of taste	Primacy of material content	Table of contents
	Journalism	Inspired	Philistine
Truth-content as model [*Vorbild*]		Material content as primal image [*Urbild*]	Literary history
Gloss	Reaction	Quotation	Source of quotation
Strategic	Mass communi- cation		
Society (Platonic)	Originality	Nature (Goethean)	Convention
Dominant	Presumptive	Serving	Dependent
Polemics (mini- mum of representation)	Rules}	Representation (minimum of criticism)	Moderation

The negation of criticism that the antithesis expresses is in a sense the position of the work. Commentary represents the dialectical overcoming of

the antinomies in criticism. Only at this stage is the work fully criticizable—
and noncriticizable at the same time. Only at this stage, therefore, is criticism
the pure function of life, or, as the case may be, of the ongoing life of the
work. Only at this stage do quotation and gloss become part of the formal
characteristics of criticism. Whereas Goethe's theory coincides in all essentials with a mediated criticism, the relation of Platonic criticism to Romantic
criticism remains to be clarified.

Fragment written in 1930 or later; unpublished in Benjamin's lifetime. *Gesammelte
Schriften,* VI, 169–170. Translated by Rodney Livingstone.

The Destructive Character, 1931

Walter Benjamin in Saint-Paul de Vence, France, May 1931. Photo by Gert Wissing. Collection of the Werkbundarchiv Museum der Dinge, Berlin.

In Parallel with My Actual Diary

In parallel with my actual diary, my intention here is to put down some notes on gambling. I would like to begin with a thesis that tackles the matter from the outside but is nonetheless important. It is the assertion that the most primitive link (precondition) of a game that is successful over a longer period is the player's clear understanding about his own economic existence. Nothing is more common than for people to make gambling into a drug, which will enable them to escape the consciousness of their economic situation. These people must lose; it may be that, for them, losing is a stronger drug than winning. Since wealthy people find it easier than poor people to contemplate their economic situation dispassionately, it follows that, independently of all technical considerations about the actual game, their chances of winning are greater.

Certain cells have the peculiar ability to take on bodily forms as the need arises, so that fingers or nose, flippers or tail, can be formed from the same cells. In the same way, great passions have the ability to stand in vicariously for quite different forms of life. We can perhaps go even further than Anatole France in his profound understanding of these things and demonstrate that gambling may be a substitute not only for religion but also for love, and even for marriage, for a man's profession, and even for a creative life.[1] Most miraculous of all, however, is that gambling can take possession not only of the future—in the form of feverish expectation—but also of the past. Indeed, isn't its ability to alter the visage of the past the greatest expression of its power over the gambler's heart? I sometimes believe that most gamblers are the stepchildren of love, whether of parental or sexual love, and that here at the gaming tables they are looking to fate to provide them with an adoption that ennobles them more than the origins that repudiated them.

A short register of superstitions / psychological and ontological study of gambling / gambling at the seaside.

Why do anxious people have an irresistible tendency toward games of chance? Perhaps because their policy is to bury their heads in the sand, or because they are able to endure the prospect of the future only if it is grotesquely disguised.

Fragment written 1929–1931; unpublished in Benjamin's lifetime. *Gesammelte Schriften*, VI, 190–191. Translated by Rodney Livingstone.

Notes

1. Anatole France (1844–1924), French writer and ironic, skeptical, urbane critic, was widely regarded in his day as the ideal man of letters. He was elected to the French Academy in 1896 and won the Nobel Prize for Literature in 1921.

Criticism as the Fundamental Discipline of Literary History

Criticism as the fundamental discipline of literary history. In Franz Mehring, literature appears solely as documentary material.[1] The disadvantage of his popularizing treatment is that he chose to treat only works that lend themselves to this approach. In consequence, he ignores Romanticism almost entirely.

Magical criticism as a manifestation of the highest stage of criticism. Opposite it on the same plane is the scholarly (literary-historical) treatise.

Max Dessoir, *Gesammelte Abhandlungen* (properly: *Beiträge zur allgemeinen Kunstwissenschaft;* Stuttgart: Ferdinand Enke, 1929).—Contains an essay on criticism.

The fundamental distinction between literary history and criticism must be rejected.

The theory of the life of works should be explored with reference to the most important works of Wiesengrund[2]—on *Wozzeck,* "New Tempi," and so on. This theory is closely linked both to the fact that works cannot be judged, and to the strategically judging stance of criticism.

Two modes, if we may put it thus, of transcendental criticism: one directed at authors, the other at the public.

On the theory of the survival of works—see Wiesengrund's theory of shrinkage [*Schrumpfung*]. This shrinkage can be seen in a twofold context. (1) In connection with my theory of packaging [*Verpackung*]. The theory of the ruins created by time should be complemented by the process of deconstruction [*Abmontieren*], which is the task of the critic. (2) In connection with my work on [Goethe's] *Wahlverwandtschaften* [Elective Affinities], shrinkage should be defined as the entrance of truth-content into material content. This formula represents the "hallowed sobriety" of that continued life.[3]

The whole critique of materialist literary criticism turns on the argument that it lacks a "magical," nonjudging side—that it always (or almost always) gets to the bottom of the mystery.

On the theory of shrinkage, see Wiesengrund, "New Tempi."

The third section, the theory of the survival of works, is dominated by the idea that this survival unmasks the terrain of "art" as semblance [*Schein*].

Fragment written in 1930 or 1931; unpublished in Benjamin's lifetime. *Gesammelte Schriften*, VI, 173–174. Translated by Rodney Livingstone.

Notes

1. Franz Mehring (1846–1919) was a radical journalist, a historian of the German Social Democratic party, and a biographer of Karl Marx.
2. That is, the work of Theodor Wiesengrund Adorno. Adorno's essay on Alban Berg's opera *Wozzeck* was published in *Musikalische Schriften* 5 (1982): 472–479. His theory of "shrinkage" is found in his essay "Neue Tempi" (New Tempi), *Musikalische Schriften* 4 (1984): 66–73.
3. "Hallowed sobriety" alludes to the swans in Friedrich Hölderlin's poem "Hälfte des Lebens" (Halves of Life), who dip their heads into the "hallowed-sober water."

Critique of the New Objectivity

Critique of the New Objectivity.[1] Expressionism signaled the energetic politicization of the intelligentsia. It could be shown how the movement is both the expression of that politicization and also the attempt to give it an idealist turn, despite its desire to have an impact in practice. This idealist stance was revised, and the New Objectivity was the result. But there was also a corresponding revision of the revolutionary practice whose modest beginnings Expressionism had inaugurated (examples!). Needless to say, this revision could not take place openly. The practical impulses atrophied, in line with the "stabilization" of the day, and simultaneously the absolute political significance of left-wing writing was proclaimed. Moreover, it was believed that this significance could not be better demonstrated than by ascribing an immediate effect to this entire body of writing. The first consequence was that every theoretical consideration was thrown overboard. Theory and reflection both seem and actually are detrimental to any immediate effect. It is high time to acknowledge that the fashionable appeal to "facts" is a two-edged sword. On the one hand, it is undoubtedly hostile to fictions removed from reality—to *belles lettres*, in short. On the other hand, it attacks theory. Experience proves this. Never has a generation of young writers been less interested in the theoretical legitimation of its activities than the generation that exists today. Everything which goes beyond an *argumentatio ad hominem* lies beyond their horizon. And how are they to arrive at a theoretical analysis of their position when this position is so confused and precludes any penetrating insight into itself? Such an insight would be insight into the class situation of the writers themselves. It is circumvented from the outset by the claim these writers make about the immediate political impact of their writings. It is this claim that will be scrutinized here.

The claim to immediate political impact will not just turn out to be a bluff; it will also be exposed as the attempt to liquidate an almost hopeless situation by a series of completely hopeless maneuvers. In short, it resembles nothing so much as Baron Münchhausen's claim that he pulled himself out of a swamp by his own hair.[2] This left-radical wing of writing and reportage may posture as much as it likes—it will never succeed in eliminating the fact that the proletarianization of the intellectual hardly ever turns him into a proletarian. Why? Because from childhood on, the middle class gave him a means of production in the form of an education—a privilege that establishes his solidarity with it and, perhaps even more strongly, its solidarity with him. This solidarity may become blurred superficially, or even be undermined, but it almost always remains powerful enough to exclude the intellectual from the constant state of alert, the sense of living your life at the front, which is characteristic of anyone who has been politicized by the proletarian class. Hence, it also remains powerful enough to deny him the energies flowing from struggles that have been personally experienced in the course of political practice. These energies, which only direct participation in struggle can confer, are called theory and knowledge. It is from Lenin's writings that we can see most clearly the huge distance separating the literary yield of political practice from the crude factual, journalistic stuff which is forced on us today under the guise of political writing, and that we can learn to understand the preeminently theoretical nature of this literature.

Fragment written in 1930 or 1931; unpublished in Benjamin's lifetime. *Gesammelte Schriften*, VI, 179–180. Translated by Rodney Livingstone.

Notes

1. *Neue Sachlichkeit* (New Objectivity) was the term originally applied by the museum curator G. F. Hartlaub to an emergent figuration in postwar German painting. It gradually came to designate the Weimar "period style" in art, architecture, design, literature, and film: cool, objective, analytical.
2. Karl Friedrich Hieronymus, Baron von Münchhausen (1720–1797), was a German storyteller. Some of his tales passed into popular consciousness, becoming sayings and anecdotes.

We Ought to Reexamine the Link between Teaching and Research

We ought to reexamine the link between teaching and research on which traditional academic activity is based. Such a link is not always the most appropriate form for the learning that the academy still wishes to impart today. It is suitable for matters that stand at the center of modern life, and for fields that have just become the object of research and are only now about to become living constituents of contemporary culture. In contrast, subjects that have long been investigated and appropriated by scholars need to be emancipated from the forms in which such scholarly acquisition took place, if they are still to have any value and any defined character today. In other words, it is precisely here that teaching and research should again part company and that both should seek to establish rigorous new forms. The whole pernicious spectrum of critical methods must disappear to make way for more enterprising researchers, on the one hand, and above all for a less banal, more considered learning, on the other. In these areas, in short, we should not look to research to lead a revival in teaching; instead, it is more important to strive with a certain intransigence for an—albeit very indirect—improvement in research to emerge from the teaching. These are insights that in the case of literary history force themselves quite urgently on the attention of anyone who has studied the *Outline of German Literary History* and the *Philosophy of Literary Science*.[1] The first displays the sterility of the complacent total approach; the second, the failure of research to turn teaching at the present time and in its present state into a fruitful activity. And if the alternative approach adumbrated above will be able to deliver the goods, this will only be because in principle teaching is capable of adapting to new strata of students in such a way that a rearrangement of the subject matter would give rise to entirely new forms of knowledge.

Examine the sense in which "Outlines," "Guides," and so on are touchstones for the state of a discipline. Show that they are the most demanding of all, and how clearly even their phrasing betrays every half-measure.

Fragment written in 1930 or 1931; unpublished in Benjamin's lifetime. *Gesammelte Schriften*, VI, 172–173. Translated by Rodney Livingstone.

Notes

1. H. A. Korff and W. Linden, *Aufriss der deutschen Literaturgeschichte nach neueren Gesichtspunkten* (Leipzig, 1930); E. Ermatinger, *Philosophie der Literaturwissenschaft* (Berlin, 1930).

Hofmannsthal and Aleco Dossena

Establish a connection between Hofmannsthal and Aleco Dossena.[1] Dossena, too, made forgeries without knowing it. He did his thing, and then others turned up and said, "What a unique Giotto!" or "What an incomparable Greco-Roman torso!" And having ascribed authorship in this fashion, they would then proceed to expose the artist. Hofmannsthal produced forgeries without knowing it, but of course he was inspired by the works that blossomed anew within him. Nowhere are we confronted more urgently by the question of what really drives the forger; but there can be no doubt that the great masterpieces of the past filled him with that very drive. This is why "translation" is such an inadequate term to describe his treatment of *Oedipus, Electra, Venice Preserved, Everyman, Life Is a Dream,* and so much else.[2] He used these works much as he used Goethe's *Novelle* or the fairy tale of the woman without a shadow, which is anything but a translation. At the same time, it gives us an insight into what is happening here, and what all these works have in common. In every instance, they amount to an almost unbearable condensation of the most personal features of those works. No novella is as Goethean as *Die Frau ohne Schatten* [The Woman without a Shadow]; no play of Calderón's is as Calderonic as *Der Turm* [The Tower]. And if there is any way of expressing the peculiarly cool element in these works, their remoteness from life, it is this: they present us with all the materials of their originary images [*Urbilder*], and they do so in their most condensed and most highly sublimated forms; but they have not been truly assimilated. We may perhaps put it best by saying that they are nourishing, but not really edible. To call them edible would mean they were digestible, and very little of what Hofmannsthal wrote is digestible.—

His genius could be summed up in a single phrase as a genius for quoting; and this comes very close to defining what we meant by forging. The great forger who has little or nothing to do with forgery as a purely commercial activity cites the originary image. And this is Hofmannsthal's situation: he quotes not single lines, purple passages, or the like, but the entire great work, the originary image in its entirety. He elevates it to the status of a quotation, but also of a manifestation. For in fact the forger cites the work in that other sense: he conjures it up. For Hofmannsthal, the art of conjuring was inseparable from the idea of culture [*Bildung*], whose lost authority he hoped to reestablish on the foundation of the magic of the past. The enterprise of founding culture on magic powerfully expresses what is great about Hofmannsthal, but also what is chimerical. This culture was without doubt legitimate, but it was no longer viable. For as long as possible, all essential events could be preserved as reflections of tradition. He had an infallible instinct for the topical relevance of even the remotest cultural goods. But when the current reality failed to discover its own reflection in the "eternal possessions of culture," Hofmannsthal found himself deprived of his own authentic faculty of expression. His ideal of authority and culture acquired chimerical overtones, and his synthesis of Protestant humanism and Hapsburg imperialism gradually collapsed. The culture he conjured up in the political Palatinate of postwar Germany was a Helen of Troy whose beauty was essentially impotent.

Fragment written in 1930 or 1931; unpublished in Benjamin's lifetime. *Gesammelte Schriften*, VI, 145–146. Translated by Rodney Livingstone.

Notes

1. Aleco Dossena (1878–1937) was an Italian sculptor. In 1928 a number of supposed classical Greek sculptures, as well as works said to be from the Trecento and Quattrocento, were shown to be forgeries made by Dossena.
2. Hugo von Hofmannsthal made adaptations, often very free, of Sophocles' *Oedipus Rex* and *Electra;* the latter was one of the key works in Hofmannsthal's long collaboration with Richard Strauss. He also adapted Thomas Otway's *Venice Preserved*. The medieval parable of *Everyman* was produced for the Salzburg Festival in 1911. Hofmannsthal's late play *Der Turm* (The Tower; 1927) was inspired by Calderón's *La vida es sueño* (Life Is a Dream).

Left-Wing Melancholy

Today Kästner's poems are already available in three imposing volumes.[1] Anyone wishing to study the character of these verses, however, is advised to stick to the form in which they originally appeared. In books they are too crowded and somewhat stifling, but they dart through the daily papers like fish in water. If this water is not always the cleanest and has quite a lot of refuse floating in it, all the better for the author, whose poetic minnows can fatten themselves thereon.

The popularity of these poems is linked to the rise of a stratum which took unconcealed possession of its commercial positions of power and prided itself like none other on the nakedness, the unmasked character, of its economic physiognomy. This is not to say that this stratum, whose only aim was success and which recognized nothing else, had now conquered the strongest positions. Its ideal was too asthmatic for that. It was the ideal of childless agents, parvenus of insignificant origin, who, unlike financial magnates, did not provide for their families over decades but provided only for themselves, and that hardly beyond the end of the season. Who cannot see them—their dreamy baby eyes behind horn-rimmed spectacles, their broad, pale cheeks, their halting voices, their fatalism in gesture and mode of thought? From the beginning, it is to this stratum and to this stratum alone that the poet has something to say; it is this stratum that he flatters, insofar as from dawn to dusk he holds up a mirror less *to* them than *against* them. The gaps between his stanzas are the folds of fat in their necks, his rhymes their thick lips, his caesuras dimples in their flesh, his punchlines the pupils in their eyes. Subject matter and effect remain restricted to this stratum, and Kästner is as incapable of striking the dispossessed with his rebellious accents as he is of touching the industrialists with his irony. This is because, despite appearances, this lyricism protects above all the status interests of the middle stratum—agents, journalists, heads of departments. The hatred it proclaims meanwhile toward the petty bourgeoisie has itself an all-too-intimate petty-bourgeois flavor. On the other hand, it noticeably abandons any striking power against the big bourgeoisie, and betrays its yearning for patronage at last in the heartfelt sigh: "If only there were a dozen wise men with a great deal of money." No wonder Kästner, in settling accounts with the bankers in "A Hymn," is as obliquely familial as he is obliquely economic when he presents the nocturnal thoughts of a proletarian woman under the title "A Mother Takes Stock." Ultimately, home and income remain the strings with which a better-off class leads the mewling poet.

This poet is dissatisfied—indeed, heavy-hearted. But this heaviness of heart derives from routine. For to be in a routine means to have sacrificed one's idiosyncrasies, to have forfeited the gift of being disgusted. And that makes one heavy-hearted. It is this circumstance which gives this case a certain similarity with Heine's. The notes with which Kästner indents his poems, to give these lacquered children's balls the appearance of rugby balls, are routine. And nothing is more routine than the irony which, like baking powder, helps to raise the kneaded dough of private opinion. It is only unfortunate that his impertinence is as much out of all proportion to the ideological forces at his disposal as it is to the political ones. Not least does the grotesque underestimation of the opponent that underlies these provocations betray how much the position of this left-radical intelligentsia is a lost one. It has little to do with the labor movement. Rather, as a phenomenon of bourgeois dissolution, it is a counterpart to the mimicry of feudalism that the *Kaiserreich* admired in the reserve lieutenant. Left-radical publicists of the stamp of Kästner, Mehring, and Tucholsky are the decayed bourgeoisie's mimicry of the proletariat.[2] Their function is to give rise, politically speaking, not to parties but to cliques; literarily speaking, not to schools but to fashions; economically speaking, not to producers but to agents. And indeed, for the past fifteen years this left-wing intelligentsia has been continually the agent of all intellectual booms, from Activism, via Expressionism, to the New Objectivity.[3] Its political significance, however, was exhausted by the transposition of revolutionary reflexes (insofar as they arose in the bourgeoisie) into objects of distraction, of amusement, which can be supplied for consumption.

Thus was Activism able to impose the face of a quasi-classless sound common sense on the revolutionary dialectic. It was in some sense the sale week on this intelligentsia's department store. Expressionism exhibited the revolutionary gesture, the raised arm, the clenched fist in papier-mâché. After this advertising campaign, the New Objectivity, from which Kästner's poems spring, was added to the catalogue. What, then, does the "intellectual elite" discover as it begins to take stock of its feelings? Those feelings themselves? They have long since been remaindered. What is left is the empty spaces where, in dusty heart-shaped velvet trays, the feelings—nature and love, enthusiasm and humanity—once rested. Now the hollow forms are absentmindedly caressed. A know-all irony thinks it has much more in these supposed stereotypes than in the things themselves; it makes a great display of its poverty and turns the yawning emptiness into a celebration. For this is what is new about this objectivity—it takes as much pride in the traces of former spiritual goods as the bourgeois do in their material goods. Never have such comfortable arrangements been made in such an uncomfortable situation.

In short, this left-wing radicalism is precisely the attitude to which there is no longer, in general, any corresponding political action. It is not to the left of this or that tendency, but simply to the left of what is in general possible. For from the beginning all it has in mind is to enjoy itself in a negativistic quiet. The metamorphosis of political struggle from a compulsory decision into an object of pleasure, from a means of production into an article of consumption—that is this literature's latest hit. Kästner, who is a considerable talent, has all its means at his fingertips. By far the most important of these is an attitude expressed even in the titles of many of his poems. Among them are "Elegy with Egg," "Chemically Purified Christmas Carol," "Suicide in the Public Pool," "Fate of a Stylized Negro," and so on. Why these dislocations? Because criticism and knowledge are ready to intervene; but they would be spoilsports and should on no condition be allowed to speak. So the poet must gag them, and their desperate convulsions now have the same effect as the tricks of a contortionist—that is, they amuse a wide public, insecure in its taste. In Morgenstern, nonsense was only the obverse of a flight into theosophy.[4] But Kästner's nihilism conceals nothing, as little as a mouth that cannot close for yawning.

Poets early became acquainted with a curious variety of despair: tortured stupidity. For the truly political poetry of the past decades has for the most part hurried on ahead of things as a harbinger. It was in 1912 and 1913 that Georg Heym's poems anticipated the then inconceivable constitution of the masses that came into the open in August 1914, in repellent descriptions of never-glimpsed collectivities: of suicides, of prisoners, of the sick, of sailors, of the insane.[5] In his lines, the earth armed itself for its submergence in the red deluge. And long before the Ararat of the goldmark was the only peak sticking up above the flood—every inch of it besieged by Feeding Trough, Belly Liner, and Sweet Tooth—Alfred Lichtenstein, who fell in the first days of the war, had brought into view the sad and flabby figures for which Kästner has found the stereotypes.[6] Now, what distinguishes the bourgeois in this early, still pre-expressionist version from the later, post-expressionist one is his eccentricity. It was no accident that

Lichtenstein dedicated one of his poems to a clown. The clowning of despair was still deep in the bones of his bourgeois. They had not yet shifted eccentricity outside themselves as an object of urban amusement. They were not yet so totally satiated, nor had they so totally become agents, that they did not feel their obscure solidarity with a commodity whose sales crisis is already on the horizon. Then came peace—the collapse of the market for the human commodity, a collapse with which we have become familiar as unemployment. And the suicide for which Lichtenstein's poems are propaganda is like dumping—the disposal of a commodity at ruinous prices. Kästner's verses have forgotten all this. Their beat very precisely follows the notes according to which poor rich folk play the blues; they correspond to the mournfulness of the satiated man who can no longer devote all his money to his stomach. Tortured stupidity: this is the latest of two millennia of metamorphoses of melancholy.

Kästner's poems are for people in the higher income bracket, those mournful, melancholy dummies who trample anything and anyone in their path. With the rigidity of their armor, the slowness of their advance, the blindness of their action, they are the rendezvous that tank and bedbug have made in people. These poems teem with them like a city café after the stock exchange closes. Is it surprising that their function is to reconcile this type of person to himself, and to establish that identity of professional and private life which these men understand by the name "humanity" but which is in truth the genuinely bestial, since authentic humanity—under present conditions—can arise only from a tension between these two poles? In this tension, consciousness and deed are formed. To create it is the task of all political lyricism, and today this task is most strictly fulfilled by Bertolt Brecht's poems. In Kästner, it has to give way to complacency and fatalism. This is the fatalism of those who are most remote from the process of production and whose obscure courting of the state of the market is comparable to the attitude of a man who yields himself up entirely to the inscrutable accidents of his digestion. The rumbling in these lines certainly has more to do with flatulence than with subversion. Constipation and melancholy have always gone together. But since the juices began to dry up in the body social, stuffiness meets us at every turn. Kästner's poems do not improve the atmosphere.

Published in *Die Gesellschaft*, 1931. *Gesammelte Schriften*, III, 279–283. Translated by Ben Brewster.

Notes

1. Erich Kästner (1899–1974), best-known for the children's book *Emil und die Detektive* (Emil and the Detectives; 1928), was a well-regarded poet, novelist,

and journalist during the Weimar Republic. His mostly ironic light verse in the detached mode of the New Objectivity appealed to middle-class readers in the late 1920s.

2. Franz Mehring (1846–1919) was a radical journalist, an important historian of the German Social Democratic party, and author of a widely influential biography of Karl Marx (1918). Kurt Tucholsky (1890–1935) was a journalist, poet, and satirical essayist. He is best-known for his biting cabaret lyrics and his work for the leading left-liberal journal in Germany, *Die Weltbühne*.

3. Activism *(Aktivismus)* was a movement dating back to the World War I years. It called for the elite—that is, artists and intellectuals—to engage actively in a new kind of spiritual politics. *Neue Sachlichkeit* (New Objectivity) was the term originally applied by the museum curator G. F. Hartlaub to an emergent figuration in German postwar painting. It gradually came to designate the Weimar "period style" in art, architecture, design, literature, and film: cool, objective, analytical.

4. Christian Morgenstern (1871–1914) was a German poet and humorist best-known for his nonsense verse. His collection *Galgenlieder* (Gallows Songs) appeared in 1905.

5. Georg Heym (1887–1912) was one of the leading poets of early German Expressionism. Examples of his visionary and apocalyptic verse appeared in the volumes *Der ewige Tag* (Eternal Day; 1911) and *Umbra Vitae* (1912). He drowned while skating on the frozen Havel, in Berlin.

6. Alfred Lichtenstein (1889–1914) was an early Expressionist poet. His work, characterized by grotesque images, was published posthumously in 1919. He was killed in action on the western front.

Theological Criticism

Willy Haas, *Gestalten der Zeit* [Figures of the Age] (Berlin: Gustav Kiepenheuer Verlag, 1930), 247 pages.

In a man's life the truly productive experiences are like seeds, unprepossessing and encapsulated. The most fruitful things are enclosed within the hard shell of immediacy. Nothing separates genuine productivity so clearly from the deficient kind, and above all from the false kind, as the question: What befell that particular man early on in life, between the ages of fifteen and twenty-five? Did he experience things that silenced him, that made him taciturn, conscious, and reflective, that furnished him with experience for which he could vouch and that he would never betray, never blurt out? Among these "figures of the age" are two to whom the author of this book is indebted for such incommunicable experiences—experiences that oblige him to testify in public. These are figures with whom he has kept faith, and who now act as patron saints, presiding over his book on its path through the contemporary world: Franz Kafka and Hugo von Hofmannsthal. Both, the reader will find, were encountered at the very heart of danger. Kafka, in Prague, in the camp of the degenerate Jewish intelligentsia, where in the name of Judaism he renounced Judaism, turning his back on it with a threatening, enigmatic gesture. Hofmannsthal, at the heart of the collapsing Hapsburg monarchy, where, in a kind of posthistorical maturity, he entirely transformed the energy on which it had thrived into formal structures.

It would be anything but surprising if the author were to regard as arbitrary the emphases we have given to his text. It would indeed be far-fetched to dwell on what Hofmannsthal and Kafka might have in common. But the question of what the two might mean to an author like Haas is a very different matter. He has discussed them in two quite separate essays. But to have discussed them in this way—in such masterful fashion, so uninfluenced by his own sentences and yet in such complete harmony with them—this is something that a writer achieves only when tackling the subjects closest to his heart. It is by no means crucial to his writing that he was personally acquainted with both Kafka and Hofmannsthal. For all that, it is no run-of-the-mill spectacle to see how in a mere six pages he conjures up the spirit of Kafka with an account of the laconic, precisely noted words that passed in a brief encounter with the writer. And we touch only the surface of things if we observe that Hofmannsthal's works provide a concentrate of the world of Catholicism, while Kafka's synthesize the Jewish world. What Haas wrote in 1929 under the impact of the news of Hofmannsthal's death—it was almost the only piece in the entire German press that did anything like justice to the event—inserted him into the space of the old Catholic monarchy, as a sort of descendant of the mother country that had lost all her sons, as a poetic genius of the state who had come too late. The country no longer had a future. And so—this is what we find in his second essay on Hofmannsthal—the time that was yet to come was, as it were, all rolled up into the past, like a scroll, and became a sort of underworld of the future, one haunted by only the oldest of things. In that realm of the "unborn children" with which *Die Frau ohne Schatten* [The Woman without a Shadow] opens, Haas has discerned the nebulous core of Hofmannsthal's world of images. Max Mell, the poet's friend, has recently done the same thing.[1] In no other writer have the worlds of image and semblance become more intimately, dangerously, intertwined. Indeed, this hidden ambiguity in Hofmannsthal's image-world is what gives it its spiritual gloss—that ideal significance, that surplus, which gives it its distinguishing character. Or, as Haas expresses it, "Never has spirit so magically become poetic experience."

The surprising feature of all this is that the deeper the reader immerses himself in the world of this essayist, the more he realizes that the world of semblance [*Schein*] constantly demands its due in a hundred different ways, whatever is depicted—whether it be the semblance of the hermaphrodite, as in André Gide, the semblance of eternal recurrence, as in Anatole France, or the semblance of a mediated reality, as in Hermann Bahr.[2] In truth, however, what we discover in these studies is that theology has pitched its tent near semblance itself, one of its favorite objects. The book abounds in discussions of the Talmud and Kierkegaard, of Thomas Aquinas and Pascal, of Ignatius Loyola and Léon Bloy.[3] But what commands the author's complete attention is not the study of theologians proper, so much as the works of those who grant asylum to theological contents [*Gehalte*] at their moment of maximum jeopardy, in their most threadbare disguise. One of these disguises is semblance itself. Popular fiction, colportage, is another. This explains why, alongside the exemplary analyses of Hofmannsthal, we find the perhaps even more significant discussions of Kafka. They point the way to future exegeses of this writer through an interpretation that energetically presses forward to theological questions at every point. In so doing, the author occasionally comes close to a theory of colportage. What he discovers in Kafka is a theology on the run which lies at the base of a number of essays that explore the topic of colportage. This is how we should classify his "theology in the detective novel," his superb characterization of Luden-dorff,[4] and his analysis of the Jewish joke.

We thought it right to regard Hofmannsthal and Kafka as the presiding geniuses in this book, particularly since the most perfect essays in it are devoted to them. What the author sets out to do in this collection is so difficult and dangerous that even the most resolute might keep an eye out for assistance. For what has Haas undertaken here? He has attempted to beat a path to the work of art by destroying the theory of the "sphere" of art. The theological approach gains its full significance through an attack on art which is all the more destructive for being covert. The ground motif of this book is that the theological illumination of works provides an authentic model with which to interpret their political aspects as much as their fashionable ones, their economic features as much as their metaphysical ones. As can be seen, this is a basic stance that opposes historical materialism with a radicalism that turns it into its very antithesis. "Where everyone else can make progress only through a series of compromises," Haas writes, "the Church can still advance its thought in profoundly true syntheses." But there are cases when this Catholic splicing of thesis and antithesis can take a rather convoluted form. Haas walks this tightrope with dizzying assurance. Nevertheless, the sight might trigger anxiety in spectators, were there not present here a more reliable and higher-grade safety element: the art of knowing how to fall. "To be able to stake one's entire life on an expedition—an expedition that can't be precisely calculated in advance—against some minor detail of this world: this and nothing else is what is meant by 'thinking'." Is it only by chance that this profound definition which we encounter on the last page of the book is that of a man in free fall? The author will have learned the hard way, risking his neck. But when he once again touches terra firma after his breathtaking fall, he stands firmly on his own two feet.

There have never been a great many writers who could combine authorial substance with the stance of the virtuoso—or rather, the schooled man of letters—as successfully as here. It is easy to believe that such people were more frequently to be found on the right of the political spectrum than on the left. However this may be, Haas is the editor of a left-leaning weekly magazine that always intervenes actively in the literary controversies of the day.[5] But as a scholar, he is really much more of a disciple of Adam Müller, Burke, or de Maistre than of Voltaire, Gutzkow, or Lassalle.[6] Fundamentally, his lineage stretches back much further into the past. We should have to go back as far as the literature and chronicles of the seventeenth century in order to discover anything comparable to the framework of universal history characteristic of these essays, both as the expression of an overall metaphysical stance and as a form of virtuoso writing that mediates effectively, even though it does not always create a satisfactory synthesis. In his obituary for Hofmannsthal, Haas himself has given a definitive account of this method, which is his own. It creates a perspective, like the backdrop for a stage set. It strives for a plasticity comprised of thick layers of meaning superimposed on one another. "This never results in a corporeal plasticity, but it does produce a perspectival one." The phenomenal form of his figures corresponds to this. They are figures of the age—there can be no doubt about that. But their life is that of epic pasts that have not been carried to decision, and whose contestation reveals to the author the true image of his age.

Published in *Die neue Rundschau*, February 1931. *Gesammelte Schriften*, III, 275–278. Translated by Rodney Livingstone.

Notes

1. Max Mell (1882–1971) was an Austrian poet whose work reflects his ties to popular and conservative traditions, as well as to the Catholic Church.
2. Hermann Bahr (1863–1934), Austrian playwright and critic, was an important conduit for French modernist ideas; he championed (successively) Naturalism, Romanticism, and Symbolism.
3. Léon Bloy (1846–1917), French novelist, critic, and polemicist, was a devout Roman Catholic convert who advocated spiritual revival through suffering and poverty.
4. Erich Ludendorff (1865–1937) was a German general who served as chief of staff to Field Marshal Hindenburg in World War I; he bore primary responsibility for German military strategy. During the Weimar Republic he was an important supporter of the Nazis. His writings idealize the Aryan race and attack the pope, Jews, Jesuits, and Freemasons.
5. Willy Haas (1891–1973) was a well-known writer and critic. He was editor of *Die literarische Welt* and *Die Welt im Wort*.
6. Adam Müller (1779–1829) was a German political pamphleteer of strongly conservative and authoritarian views. Edmund Burke (1729–1797), British political writer and statesman, entered Parliament in 1765; his most famous work, *Reflections on the Revolution in France* (1790), expresses his opposition to the Revolution. Joseph de Maistre (1753–1821), French diplomat and writer, was

one of the leading intellectual opponents of the French Revolution. Karl Gutzkow (1811–1878) was a journalist associated with the liberal and radical Young Germany movement in the 1830s. He was jailed in 1836 for having brought the Christian religion into disrepute with his novel *Wally die Zweiflerin* (Wally the Doubter). Ferdinand Lassalle (1825–1864) was one of the founding fathers of German Social Democracy.

Karl Kraus

Dedicated to Gustav Glück

1. Cosmic Man [*Allmensch*]

How noisy everything grows.
—Kraus, *Words in Verse II*

In old engravings, there is a messenger who rushes toward us crying aloud, his hair on end, brandishing a sheet of paper in his hands—a sheet full of war and pestilence, of cries of murder and pain, of danger from fire and flood—spreading everywhere the Latest News. "News" in this sense, in the sense that the word has in Shakespeare, is disseminated by *Die Fackel* [The Torch].[1] Full of betrayal, earthquakes, poison, and fire from the *mundus intelligibilis*. The hatred with which it pursues the tribe of journalists that swarms into infinity is not only a moral hatred but a vital one, such as is hurled by an ancestor upon a race of degenerate and dwarfish rascals that has sprung from his seed. The very term "public opinion" outrages Kraus. Opinions are a private matter. The public has an interest only in judgments. Either it is a judging public, or it is none. But it is precisely the purpose of the public opinion generated by the press to make the public incapable of judging, to insinuate into it the attitude of someone irresponsible, uninformed. Indeed, what is even the most precise information in the daily newspapers in comparison to the hair-raising meticulousness observed by *Die Fackel* in the presentation of legal, linguistic, and political facts? *Die Fackel* need not trouble itself about public opinion, for the blood-steeped novelties of this "newspaper" demand a passing of judgment. And on nothing more impetuously, urgently, than on the press itself.

A hatred such as that which Kraus has heaped on journalists can never be founded simply on what they do—however obnoxious this may be; this hatred must have its reason in their very being, whether it be antithetical or akin to his own. In fact, it is both. His most recent portrait, in its very first sentence, characterizes the journalist as "a person who has little interest either in himself and his own existence, or in the mere existence of things, but who feels things only in their relationships, above all where these meet in events—and only in this moment become united, substantial, and alive." What we have in this sentence is nothing other than the negative of an image of Kraus. Indeed, who could have shown a more burning interest in himself and his own existence than the writer who is never finished with this subject? Who, a more attentive concern for the mere existence of things, their origin? Whom does that coincidence of the event with the date, the witness, or the camera cast into deeper despair than him? In the end, he brought together all his energies in the struggle against the empty phrase, which is the linguistic expression of the despotism with which, in journalism, topicality sets up its dominion over things.

This side of his struggle against the press is illuminated most vividly by the life's work of his comrade-in-arms, Adolf Loos. Loos found his providential adversaries in the arts-and-crafts mongers and architects who, in the ambit of the "Vienna Workshops," were striving to give birth to a new art industry. He sent out his rallying cry in numerous essays—particularly, in its enduring formulation, in the article "Ornamentation and Crime," which appeared in 1908 in the *Frankfurter Zeitung*. The lightning flash ignited by this essay described a curiously zigzag course. "On reading the words with which Goethe censures the way the philistine, and thus many an art connoisseur, run their fingers over engravings and reliefs, the revelation came to him that what may be touched cannot be a work of art, and that a work of art must be out of reach." It was therefore Loos's first concern to separate the work of art from the article of use, as it was that of Kraus to keep apart information and the work of art. The hack journalist is, in his heart, at one with the ornamentalist. Kraus did not tire of denouncing Heine as an ornamentalist, as one who blurred the boundary between journalism and literature, as the creator of the feuilleton in poetry and prose; indeed, he later placed even Nietzsche beside Heine as the betrayer of the aphorism to the impression. "It is my opinion," he says of the former, "that to the mixture of elements . . . in the decomposing European style of the last half century, he added psychology, and that the new level of language he created is the level of essayism, as Heine's was that of feuilletonism." Both forms appear as symptoms of the chronic sickness of which all attitudes and standpoints merely mark the temperature curve: inauthenticity. It is from the unmasking of the inauthentic that this battle against the press arose. "Who was it that brought into the world this great excuse: 'I can do what I am not'?"

The empty phrase. It, however, is an abortion of technology. "The newspaper industry, like a factory, demands separate areas for working and selling. At certain times of day—twice, three times in the bigger newspapers—a particular quantity of work has to have been procured and prepared for the machine. And not from just any material: everything that has happened in the meantime, anywhere, in any region of life—politics, economics, art, and so on—must by now have been reached and journalistically processed." Or, as Kraus so splendidly sums it up: "It ought to throw light on the way in which technology, while unable to coin new platitudes, leaves the spirit of mankind in the state of being unable to do without the old ones. In this duality of a changed life dragging on in unchanged forms, the world's ills grow and prosper." In these words, Kraus deftly tied the knot binding technology to the empty phrase. True, its untying would have to follow a different pattern, journalism being clearly seen as the expression of the changed function of language in the world of high capitalism. The empty phrase of the kind so relentlessly pursued by Kraus is the label that makes a thought marketable, the way flowery language, as ornament, gives a thought value for the connoisseur. But for this very reason the liberation of language has become identical with that of the empty phrase—its transformation from reproduction to productive instrument. *Die Fackel* itself contains models of this, even if not the theory: its formulas are the kind that tie up, never the kind that untie. The intertwining of biblical magniloquence with stiff-necked fixation on the indecencies of Viennese life—this is its way of approaching phenomena. It is not content to call on the world as witness to the misdemeanors of a cashier; it must summon the dead from their graves.—Rightly so. For the shabby, obtrusive abundance of these scandals in Viennese coffeehouses, the press, and society is only a minor manifestation of a foreknowledge that then, more swiftly than anyone could perceive, suddenly arrived at its true and original subject: two months after the outbreak of war, Kraus called this subject by its name in his speech "In These Great Times," with which all the demons that inhabited this possessed man passed into the herd of swine who were his contemporaries.

In these great times, which I knew when they were small, which will again be small if they still have time, and which, because in the field of organic growth such transformations are not possible, we prefer to address as fat times and truly also as hard times; in these times, when precisely what is happening could not be imagined, and when what must *happen* can no longer be *imagined,* and if it could it would not happen; in these grave times that have laughed themselves to death at the possibility of growing serious and, overtaken by their own tragedy, long for distraction and then, catching themselves in the act, seek words; in these loud times, booming with the fearful symphony of deeds that engender reports, and of reports that bear the blame for deeds; in these unspeakable times, you can expect no word of my own from me. None except this, which just preserves silence from misinterpretation. Too deeply am I awed by the unalterability of language, the subordination of language to misfortune. In the empires bereft of imagination, where man is dying of spiritual starvation though feeling no spiritual hunger, where pens are dipped in blood and swords in ink, that which is not thought must be done, but that which is only thought is inexpressible. Expect from me no word of my own. Nor should I be capable of saying anything new; for in the room where someone writes, the noise is great, and whether it comes from animals, from children, or merely from mortars shall not be decided now. He who addresses deeds violates both word and deed and is twice despicable. This profession is not extinct. Those who now have nothing to say because it is the turn of deeds to speak, talk on. Let him who has something to say step forward and be silent!

Everything Kraus wrote is like that: a silence turned inside out, a silence that catches the storm of events in its black folds and billows, its livid lining turned outward. Notwithstanding their abundance, each of the instances of this silence seems to have broken upon it with the suddenness of a gust of wind. Immediately, a precise apparatus of control is brought into play: through a meshing of oral and written forms, the polemical possibilities of every situation are totally exhausted. With what precautions this is surrounded can be seen from the barbed wire of editorial pronouncements that encircles each edition of *Die Fackel,* as from the razor-sharp definitions and provisos in the programs and lectures accompanying his readings from his own work. The trinity of silence, knowledge, and alertness constitutes the figure of Kraus the polemicist. His silence is a dam before which the reflecting basin of his knowledge is constantly deepened. His alertness permits no one to ask it questions, forever unwilling to conform to principles offered to it. Its first principle is, rather, to dismantle the situation, to discover the true question the situation poses, and to present this in place of any other to his opponents. If in Johann Peter Hebel we find, developed to the utmost, the constructive, creative side of tact, in Kraus we see its most destructive and critical face. But for both, tact is moral alertness—Stössl calls it "conviction refined into dialectics"—and the expression of an unknown convention more important than the acknowledged one.[2] Kraus lived in a world in which the most shameful act was still the faux pas; he distinguishes between degrees of the monstrous, and does so precisely because his criterion is never that of bourgeois respectability, which, once above the threshold of trivial misdemeanor, becomes so quickly short of breath that it can form no conception of villainy on a world-historical scale. Kraus knew this criterion from the first; moreover, there is no other criterion for true tact. It is a theological criterion. For tact is not—as narrow minds imagine it—the gift of allotting to each, on consideration of all relationships, what is socially befitting. On the contrary, tact is the capacity to treat social relationships, though not departing from them, as natural, even paradisal, relationships, and so not only to approach the king as if he had been born with the crown on his brow, but the lackey like an Adam in livery. Hebel possessed this *noblesse* in his priestly bearing; Kraus, in armor. His concept of creation contains the theological inheritance of speculations that last possessed contemporary validity for the whole of Europe in the seventeenth century. At the theological core of this concept, however, a transformation has taken place that has caused it, quite without constraint, to coincide with the cosmopolitan credo of Austrian worldliness, which made creation into a church in which nothing remained to recall the rite except an occasional whiff of incense in the mists. Stifter gave this creed its most authentic stamp, and his echo is heard wherever Kraus concerns himself with animals, plants, children. Stifter writes:

> The stirring of the air, the rippling of water, the growing of corn, the tossing of the sea, the verdure of the earth, the shining of the sky, the twinkling of the stars, I hold great. The thunderstorm approaching in splendor, the lightning flash that cleaves houses, the storm driving the surf, the mountains spewing fire, the earthquake laying waste to countries, I do not hold greater than the former phenomena; indeed, I believe them smaller, because they are only effects of far higher laws . . . When man was in his infancy, his spiritual eye not yet touched by science, he was seized by what was close at hand and obtrusive, and was moved to fear and admiration; but when his mind was opened, when his gaze began to be directed at the connections between things, particular phenomena sank from sight and the law rose even higher, miracles ceased, and wonder increased . . . Just as in nature the general laws act silently and incessantly, and conspicuous events are only single manifestations of these laws, so the moral law acts silently, animating the soul through the infinite intercourse of human beings, and the miracles of the moment when deeds are performed are merely small signs of this general power.[3]

Tacitly, in these famous sentences, the holy has given place to the modest yet questionable concept of law. But this nature of Stifter's and his moral universe are transparent enough to escape any confusion with Kant, and to be still recognizable in their core as creation. This insolently secularized thunder and lightning, storms, surf, and earthquakes—cosmic man has won them back for creation by making them its world-historical answer to the criminal existence of men. Only the span between Creation and the Last Judgment here finds no redemptive fulfillment, let alone a historical overcoming. For as the landscape of Austria fills unbroken the captivating expanse of Stifter's prose, so for him, Kraus, the terrible years of his life are not history but nature, a river condemned to meander through a landscape of hell. It is a landscape in which every day fifty thousand trees are felled for sixty newspapers. Kraus imparted this information under the title "The End." For the fact that mankind is losing the fight against the creaturely is to him just as certain as the fact that technology, once deployed against creation, will not stop short of its master, either. His defeatism is of a supranational—that is, planetary—kind, and history for him is merely the wilderness dividing his race from creation, whose last act is world conflagration. As a deserter to the camp of animal creation—so he measures out this wilderness. "And only the animal that is conquered by humanity is the hero of life": never was Adalbert Stifter's patriarchal credo given so gloomy and heraldic a formulation.

It is in the name of the creature that Kraus again and again inclines toward the animal and toward "the heart of all hearts, that of the dog," for him creation's true mirror of virtue, in which fidelity, purity, gratitude smile from times lost and remote. How lamentable that people usurp its place! These are his followers. More numerously and eagerly than about their master, they throng with unlovely sniffings about the mortally wounded opponent. Indeed, it is no accident that the dog is the emblematic beast of this author: the dog, the epitome of the follower, who is nothing except devoted creature. And the more personal and unfounded this devotion, the better. Kraus is right to put it to the hardest test. But if anything makes plain what is infinitely questionable in these creatures, it is that they are recruited solely from those whom Kraus himself first called intellectually to life, whom he conceived and convinced in one and the same act. His testimony can determine only those for whom it can never become generative.

It is entirely logical that the impoverished, reduced human being of our day, the contemporary, can seek sanctuary in the temple of living things only in that most withered form: the form of a private individual. How much renunciation and how much irony lie in the curious struggle for the "nerves"—the last root fibers of the Viennese to which Kraus could still find Mother Earth clinging. "Kraus," writes Robert Scheu, "discovered a great subject that had never before set in motion the pen of a journalist: the rights of the nerves. He found that they were just as worthy an object of impassioned defense as were property, house and home, political party, and constitution. He became the advocate of the nerves and took up the fight against petty, everyday imitations; but the subject grew under his hands, became the problem of private life. To defend this against police, press, morality, and concepts, and ultimately against neighbors in every form, constantly finding new enemies, became his profession." Here, if anywhere, is manifest the strange interplay between reactionary theory and revolutionary practice that we find everywhere in Kraus. Indeed, to secure private life against morality and concepts in a society that perpetrates the political radioscopy of sexuality and family, of economic and physical existence, in a society that is in the process of building houses with glass walls, and terraces extending far into the living rooms that are no longer living rooms— such a watchword would be the most reactionary of all, were not the private life that Kraus made it his business to defend precisely that which, unlike the bourgeois form, is in strict accordance with this social upheaval; in other words, the private life that is dismantling itself, openly shaping itself, that of the poor, from whose ranks came Peter Altenberg, the agitator, and Adolf Loos. In this fight—and only in this fight—his followers also have their uses, since it is they who most sublimely ignore the anonymity with which the satirist has tried to surround his private existence, and nothing holds them in check except Kraus's decision to step in person before his threshold and pay homage to the ruins in which he is a "private individual."

As decisively as he makes his own existence a public issue when the fight demands it, he has always just as ruthlessly opposed the distinction between personal and objective criticism—a distinction which has been used to discredit polemics, and which is a chief instrument of corruption in our literary and political affairs. That Kraus attacks people less for what they are than for what they do, more for what they say than for what they write, and least of all for their books, is the precondition of his polemical authority, which is able to lift the intellectual universe of an author—all the more surely the more worthless it is, with confidence in a truly prestabilized, reconciling harmony—whole and intact from a single fragment of sentence, a single word, a single intonation. But the coincidence of personal and objective elements, not only in his opponents but above all in himself, is best demonstrated by the fact that he never puts forward an opinion. For opinion is false subjectivity that can be separated from the person and incorporated in the circulation of commodities. Kraus has never offered an argument that did not engage his whole person. Thus, he embodies the secret of authority: never to disappoint. Authority has no other end than this: it dies or it disappoints. It is not in the least undermined by what others must avoid: its own despotism, injustice, inconsistency. On the contrary, it would be disappointing to observe how it arrived at its pronouncements—by fairness, for example, or even self-consistency. "For a man," Kraus once said, "being right is not an erotic matter, and he gladly prefers others' being right to his being wrong." To prove his manhood in this way is denied to Kraus; his existence demands that at most the self-righteousness of others is opposed to his wrongness, and how right he then is to cling to this. "Many will be right one day. But it will be a rightness resulting from my wrongness today." This is the language of true authority. Insight into its operations can reveal only one thing: that it is binding, mercilessly binding, toward itself in the same degree as toward others; that it does not tire of trembling before itself, though never before others; that it never does enough to satisfy itself, to fulfill its responsibility toward itself; and that this sense of responsibility never allows him to accept arguments derived from his private constitution or even from the limits of human capacity, but always only from the matter at hand, however unjust it may be from a private point of view.

The characteristic of such unlimited authority has for all time been the union of legislative and executive power. But it was never a more intimate union than in the theory of language. This is therefore the most decisive expression of Kraus's authority. Incognito like Haroun al Rashid, he passes by night among the sentence constructions of the journals, and, from behind the petrified façades of phrases, he peers into the interior, discovering in the orgies of "black magic" the violation, the martyrdom, of words:

> Is the press a messenger? No: it is the event. Is it speech? No: life. The press not only claims that the true events are its news of events, but it also brings about a sinister identification that constantly creates the illusion that deeds are reported before they are carried out, and frequently also the possibility of a situation (which in any case exists) that when war correspondents are not allowed to witness events, soldiers become reporters. I therefore welcome the charge that all my life I have overestimated the press. It is not a servant—How could a servant demand and receive so much? It is the event. Once again the instrument has run away with us. We have placed the person who is supposed to report outbreaks of fire, and who ought doubtless to play the most subordinate role in the State, in power over the world, over fire and over the house, over fact and over our fantasy.

Authority and word against corruption and magic—thus are the catchwords distributed in this struggle. It is not idle to offer a prognosis. No one, Kraus least of all, can leave the utopia of an "objective" newspaper, the chimera of an "impartial transmission of news," to its own devices. The newspaper is an instrument of power. It can derive its value only from the character of the power it serves; not only in what it represents, but also in what it does, it is the expression of this power. When, however, high capitalism defiles not only the ends but also the means of journalism, then a new blossoming of paradisal, cosmic humanity can no more be expected of a power that defeats it than a second blooming of the language of Goethe or Claudius.[4] From the one now prevailing, it will distinguish itself first of all by putting out of circulation ideals that debase the former. This is enough to give a measure of how little Kraus would have to win or lose in such a struggle, of how unerringly *Die Fackel* would illuminate it. To the ever-repeated sensations with which the daily press serves its public, he opposes the eternally fresh "news" of the history of creation: the eternally renewed, uninterrupted lament.

2. Demon

Have I slept? I am just falling asleep.
—Kraus, *Words in Verse IV*

It is deeply rooted in Kraus's nature, and the stigma of every debate concerning him, that all apologetic arguments miss their mark. The great work of Leopold Liegler springs from an apologetic posture. To certify Kraus as an "ethical personality" is his first objective. This cannot be done. The dark background from which Kraus's image detaches itself is not formed by his contemporaries, but is the primeval world [*Vorwelt*], or the world of the demon. The light of the day of Creation falls on him—thus he emerges from this darkness. But not in all parts; others remain that are more deeply immersed in it than one suspects. An eye that cannot adjust to this darkness will never perceive the outline of this figure. On it will be wasted all the gestures that Kraus tirelessly makes in his unconquerable need to be perceived. For, as in the fairy tale, the demon in Kraus has made vanity the expression of his being. The demon's solitude, too, is felt by him who gesticulates wildly on the hidden hill: "Thank God nobody knows my name is Rumpelstiltskin." Just as this dancing demon is never still, in Kraus eccentric reflection is in continuous uproar. "The patient of his gifts," Berthold Viertel called him. In fact, his capacities are maladies; and over and above the real ones, his vanity makes him a hypochondriac.

If he does not see his reflection in himself, he sees it in the adversary at his feet. His polemics have been, from the first, the most intimate intermingling of a technique of unmasking that works with the most advanced means, and a self-expressive art that works with the most archaic. But in this zone, too, ambiguity, the demon, is manifest: self-expression and unmasking merge in it as self-unmasking. Kraus has said, "Anti-Semitism is the mentality that offers up and means seriously a tenth of the jibes that the stock-exchange wit holds ready for his own blood"; he thereby indicates the nature of the relationship of his own opponents to himself. There is no reproach to him, no vilification of his person, that could not find its most legitimate formulation in his own writings, in those passages where self-reflection is raised to self-admiration. He will pay any price to get himself talked about, and is always justified by the success of these speculations. If style is the power to move freely in the length and breadth of linguistic thinking without falling into banality, it is attained chiefly by the cardiac strength of great thoughts, which drives the blood of language through the capillaries of syntax into the remotest limbs. While such thoughts are quite unmistakable in Kraus, the powerful heart of his style is nevertheless the image he bears of himself in his own breast and exposes in the most merciless manner. Yes, he is vain. As such he has been portrayed by Karin Michaelis, who describes how he crosses a room with swift, restless bounds to reach the lecture podium. And if he then offers a sacrifice to his vanity, he would not be the demon that he is were it not finally himself, his life and his suffering, that he exposes with all its wounds, all its nakedness. In this way his style comes into being, and with it the typical reader of *Die Fackel*, for whom in a subordinate clause, in a particle, indeed in a comma, fibers and nerves quiver; from the obscurest and driest fact, a piece of his mutilated flesh hangs. Idiosyncrasy as the highest critical organ—this is the hidden logic of that self-reflection and the hellish state known only to a writer for whom every act of gratification becomes at the same time a station of his martyrdom, a state experienced, apart from Kraus, by no one as deeply as by Kierkegaard.

"I am," Kraus has said, "perhaps the first instance of a writer who simultaneously writes and experiences his writing theatrically." Thus he shows his vanity its most legitimate place: in mime. His mimetic genius, imitating while it glosses, pulling faces in the midst of polemics, is festively unleashed in the readings of dramas whose authors, with good reason, occupy a peculiarly intermediate position: Shakespeare and Nestroy, dramatists and actors; Offenbach, composer and conductor. It is as if the demon in the man sought the tumultuous atmosphere of these dramas, shot through with all the lightning flashes of improvisation, because it alone offered him the thousand opportunities to break out, teasing, tormenting, threatening. In them his own voice tries out the abundance of personae inhabiting the performer ("per-sona": that through which sound passes), and about his fingertips dart the gestures of the figures populating his voice. But in his polemics, too, mimesis plays a decisive role. He imitates his subjects in order to insert the crowbar of his hate into the finest joints of their posture. This quibbler, probing between syllables, digs out the larvae that nest there in clumps. The larvae of venality and garrulity, ignominy and bonhomie, childishness and covetousness, gluttony and dishonesty. Indeed, the exposure of inauthenticity—more difficult than that of the merely bad—is here performed behavioristically. The quotations in *Die Fackel* are more than documentary proof: they are the props with which the quoter unmasks himself mimetically. Admittedly, what emerges in just this connection is how closely the cruelty of the satirist is linked to the ambiguous modesty of the interpreter, which in his public readings is heightened beyond comprehension. "To creep"—this is the term used, not without cause, for the lowest kind of flattery; and Kraus creeps into those he impersonates, in order to annihilate them. Has courtesy here become the mimicry of hate, hate the mimicry of courtesy? However that may be, both have attained perfection, absolute pitch. "Torment," of which there is so much talk in Kraus in such opaque allusions, here has its seat. His protests against letters, printed matter, documents are nothing but the defensive reaction of a man who is himself implicated. But what implicates him so deeply is more than deeds and misdeeds; it is the language of his fellow men. His passion for imitating them is at the same time the expression of and the struggle against this implication, and also the cause and the result of that ever-watchful guilty conscience in which alone the demon is in his element.

The economy of his errors and weaknesses—more a fantastic edifice than the totality of his gifts—is so delicately and precisely organized that all outward confirmation only disrupts it. Well it may, if this man is to be certified as the "pattern of a harmoniously and perfectly formed human type," if he is to appear—in a term as absurd stylistically as semantically—as a philanthropist, so that anyone listening to his "hardness" with "the ears of the soul" would find the reason for it in compassion. No! This incorruptible, piercing, resolute assurance does not spring from the noble poetic or humane disposition that his followers are so fond of attributing to him. How utterly banal, and at the same time how fundamentally wrong, is their derivation of his hatred from love, when it is obvious how much more elemental are the forces here at work: a humanity that is only an alternation of malice and sophistry, sophistry and malice, a nature that is the highest school of aversion to mankind and a pity that is alive only when interlaced with vengeance. "Oh, had I only been left the choice / to carve the dog or the butcher, / I should have chosen." Nothing is more perverse than to try to fashion him after the image of what he loves. Rightly, Kraus the "timeless world-disturber" has been confronted with the "eternal world-improver," on whom benign glances not infrequently fall.

"When the age laid hands upon itself, he was the hands," Brecht said. Few insights can stand beside this, and certainly not the comment of his friend Adolf Loos. "Kraus," he declares, "stands on the threshold of a new age." Alas, by no means.—For he stands on the threshold of the Last Judgment. Just as, in the most opulent examples of Baroque altar painting, saints hard-pressed against the frame extend defensive hands toward the breathtakingly foreshortened extremities of the angels, the blessed, and the damned floating before them, so the whole of world history presses in on Kraus in the extremities of a single item of local news, a single phrase, a single advertisement. This is the inheritance that has come down to him from the sermons of Abraham a Sancta Clara. Thence the overwhelming immediacy, the ready wit, of the wholly uncontemplative moment; and the inversion that allows his will only theoretical, his knowledge only practical, expression. Kraus is no historic type. He does not stand on the threshold of a new age. If he ever turns his back on creation, if he breaks off in lamentation, it is only to file a complaint at the Last Judgment.

Nothing is understood about this man until it has been perceived that, of necessity and without exception, everything—language and fact—falls, for him, within the sphere of justice. All his fire-eating, sword-swallowing philology in the newspapers pursues justice just as much as language. It is to misunderstand his theory of language to see it as other than a contribution to the linguistic rules of court, the word of someone else in his mouth as other than a *corpus delicti,* and his own as other than a judging word. Kraus knows no system. Each thought has its own cell. But each cell can in an instant, and apparently almost without cause, become a chamber, a legal chamber over which language presides. It has been said of Kraus that he has to "suppress the Jewishness in himself," even that he "travels the road from Jewishness to freedom"; nothing better refutes this than the fact that, for him, too, justice and language remain founded in each other. To worship the image of divine justice in language—even in the German language—this is the genuinely Jewish *salto mortale* by which he tries to break the spell of the demon. For this is the last official act of this zealot: to place the legal system itself under accusation. And not in a petty-bourgeois revolt against the enslavement of the "free individual" by "dead formulas." Still less in the posture of those radicals who storm the legal code without ever for a moment having taken thought of justice. Kraus accuses the law in its substance, not in its effect. His charge: high treason of the law against justice. More exactly, betrayal of the word by the concept, which derives its existence from the word: the premeditated murder of imagination, which dies of the absence of a single letter and for which, in his "Elegy on the Death of a Sound," he has sung the most moving lament. For over jurisdiction, right-saying, stands orthography, right-spelling, and woe to the former if the latter should be wanting. Here, too, therefore, he confronts the press; indeed, in this charmed circle he holds his fondest rendezvous with the *lemures*. He has seen through law as have few others. If he nevertheless invokes it, he does so precisely because his own demon is drawn so powerfully by the abyss it represents. By the abyss that, not without reason, he finds most gaping where mind and sexuality meet—in the trial for sexual offenses—and has sounded in these famous words: "A trial for sexual offenses is the deliberate development from an individual immorality to a general immorality, against which dark background the proven guilt of the accused stands out luminously."

Mind and sexuality move in this sphere with a solidarity whose law is ambiguity. The obsession of demonic sexuality is the ego that, surrounded by sweet feminine mirages "such as the bitter earth does not harbor," enjoys itself. And no different is the loveless and self-gratifying trope of the obsessed mind: the joke. Neither reaches its object: the ego does not attain women any more than the joke attains words. Decomposition has taken the place of procreation; stridency, that of secrecy. Now, however, they shimmer in the most winsome nuances: in repartee, lust comes into its own; and in onanism, the joke. Kraus portrayed himself as hopelessly subjugated to the demon; in the pandemonium of the age, he reserved for himself the most melancholy place in the icy wilderness lit by reflected flames. There he stands on the Last Day of Humankind[5]—the "grumbler" who has described the preceding days. "I have taken the tragedy, which disintegrates into scenes of disintegrating humanity, on myself, so that it might be heard by the spirit who takes pity on the victims, even though he may have renounced for all time his connection with a human ear. May he receive the keynote of this age, the echo of my bloodstained madness, through which I share the guilt for these noises. May he accept it as redemption!"

"I share the guilt . . ." Because this has the ring of the manifestos—even if they are finally self-accusations—of an intelligentsia seeking to call to mind the memory of an epoch that seemed to be turning away from it, there is something to be said about this guilt feeling in which private and historical consciousness so vividly meet. This guilt will always lead to Expressionism, from which his mature work was nourished by roots that cracked open their soil. The slogans are well known—with what scorn did not Kraus himself register them: *geballt, gestuft, gesteilt* [clenched, stepped, steeped]; stage sets, sentences, paintings were composed.—Unmistakable—and the Expressionists themselves proclaim it—is the influence of early medieval miniatures on the world of their imagination. But anyone who examines their figures—for example, in the Vienna Genesis[6]—is struck by something very mysterious, not only in their wide-open eyes, not only in the unfathomable folds of their garments, but also in their whole expression. As if falling sickness had overtaken them thus, in their running which is always headlong, they lean toward one another. "Inclination" may be seen, before all else, as the deep human affect tremulously pervading the world of these miniatures, as it does the manifestos of that generation of poets. But only one, as it were inwardly curved, aspect of this relation is revealed by the front of these figures. The same phenomenon appears quite different to someone who looks at their backs. These backs are piled—in the saints of the adorations, in the servants of the Gethsemane scene, in the witnesses of the entrance into Jerusalem— into terraces of human necks and human shoulders that, really clenched in steep steps, lead less toward heaven than downward to and even under the earth. It is impossible to find, for their pathos, an expression that ignores the fact that they could be climbed like heaped rocks or rough-hewn steps. Whatever powers may have fought out their spiritual battles on these shoulders, one of them, from our experience of the condition of the defeated masses immediately after the end of the war, we are able to call by its name. What finally remained of Expressionism, in which an originally human impulse was converted almost without residue into a fashion, was the experience and the name of that nameless power toward which the backs of people bent: guilt. "That obedient masses are led into danger not by an unknown will but by an unknown guilt makes them pitiable," Kraus wrote as early as 1912. As a "grumbler" he participates in their lot in order to denounce them, and denounces them in order to participate. To meet them through sacrifice, he one day threw himself into the arms of the Catholic Church.

In those biting minuets that Kraus whistled to the *chassé-croisé* of Justitia and Venus, the leitmotif—that the philistine knows nothing of love—is articulated with a sharpness and persistence that have a counterpart only in the corresponding attitude of *décadence,* in the proclamation of art for art's sake. For it was precisely art for art's sake, which for the decadent movement applies to love as well, that linked expertise as closely as possible to craftsmanship, to technique, and allowed poetry to shine at its brightest only against the foil of hack writing, as it made love stand out against perversion. "Penury can turn every man into a journalist, but not every woman into a prostitute." In this formulation Kraus betrayed the false bottom of his polemic against journalism. It is much less the philanthropist, the enlightened friend of man and nature, who unleashed this implacable struggle than the literary expert, artiste, indeed the dandy, whose ancestor is Baudelaire. Only Baudelaire hated, as Kraus did, the satiety of healthy common sense, and the compromise that intellectuals made with it in order to find shelter in journalism. Journalism is betrayal of the literary life, of mind, of the demon. Idle chatter is its true substance, and every feuilleton poses anew the insoluble question of the relationship between the forces of stupidity and malice, whose expression is gossip. It is, fundamentally, on the complete agreement of two forms of existence—life under the aegis of mere mind, and life under the aegis of mere sexuality—that the solidarity of the man of letters with the whore is founded, a solidarity to which Baudelaire's existence is once again the most inviolable testimony. So Kraus can call by their name the laws of his own craft, intertwined with those of sexuality, as he did in *Die Chinesische Mauer* [The Great Wall of China]. Man "has wrestled a thousand times with the other, who perhaps does not live but whose victory over him is certain. Not because he has superior qualities but because he is the other, the latecomer, who brings woman the joy of variety and who will triumph as the last in the sequence. But they wipe it from her brow like a bad dream, and want to be the first." Now, if language—this we read between the lines—is a woman, how far the author is removed, by an unerring instinct, from those who hasten to be the first with her; how multifariously he forms his thought, thus inciting her with intuition rather than slaking her with knowledge; how he lets hatred, contempt, malice ensnare one another; how he slows his step and seeks the detour of followership, in order finally to end her joy in variety with the last thrust that Jack holds in readiness for Lulu![7]

The life of letters is existence under the aegis of mere mind, as prostitution is existence under the aegis of mere sexuality. The demon, however, who leads the whore to the street exiles the man of letters to the courtroom. This is therefore, for Kraus, the forum that it has always been for the great journalist—for a Carrel, a Paul-Louis Courier, a Lassalle. Evasion of the genuine and demonic function of mere mind, to be a disturber of the peace; abstention from attacking the whore from behind—Kraus sees this double omission as defining the journalist.—Robert Scheu rightly perceived that for Kraus prostitution was a natural form, not a social deformation, of female sexuality. Yet it is only the interlacing of sexual with commercial intercourse that constitutes the character of prostitution. It is a natural phenomenon as much in terms of its natural economic aspect (since it is a manifestation of commodity exchange) as in terms of its natural sexuality. "Contempt for prostitution? / Harlots worse than thieves? / Learn this: not only is love paid, / but payment, too, wins love!" This ambiguity—this double nature as twofold naturalness—makes prostitution demonic. But Kraus "enlists with the power of nature." That the sociological realm never becomes transparent to him—no more in his attack on the press than in his defense of prostitution—is connected with this attachment to nature. That for him the fit state of man appears not as the destiny and fulfillment of nature liberated through revolutionary change, but as an element of nature per se, of an archaic nature without history, in its pristine, primeval state, throws uncertain, disquieting reflections even on his ideas of freedom and humanity. They are not removed from the realm of guilt that Kraus has traversed from pole to pole: from mind to sexuality.

But in the face of this reality, to which Kraus exposed himself more harrowingly than any other, the "pure mind" that his followers worship in the master's activity is revealed as a worthless chimera. For this reason, none of the motives for his development is more important than the constant curbing and checking of mind. *Nachts* [By Night] is the title he gives to the logbook of this control. For night is the mechanism by which mere mind is converted into mere sexuality, mere sexuality into mere mind, and where these two abstractions hostile to life find rest in recognizing each other. "I work day and night. So I have a lot of free time. In order to ask a picture in the room how it likes work; in order to ask the clock whether it is tired and the night how it has slept." These questions are sacrificial gifts that he throws to the demon while working. His night, however, is not a maternal night, or a moonlit, romantic night: it is the hour between sleeping and waking, the night watch, the centerpiece of his threefold solitude: that of the coffeehouse, where he is alone with his enemy; of the nocturnal room, where he is alone with his demon; of the lecture hall, where he is alone with his work.

3. Monster [*Unmensch*]

Already the snow falls.
—Kraus, *Words in Verse III*

Satire is the only legitimate form of regional art. This, however, was not what people meant by calling Kraus a Viennese satirist. Rather, they were attempting to shunt him for as long as possible onto this siding, where his work could be assimilated into the great store of literary consumer goods. The presentation of Kraus as a satirist can thus yield the deepest insight both into what he is and into his most melancholy caricatures. For this reason, he was at pains from the first to distinguish the genuine satirist from the scribblers who make a trade of mockery and who, in their invectives, have little more in mind than giving the public something to laugh about. In contrast, the great type of the satirist never had firmer ground under his feet than amid a generation about to mount tanks and put on gas masks, a mankind that has run out of tears but not of laughter. In him civilization prepares to survive, if it must, and communicates with him in the true mystery of satire, which consists in the devouring of the adversary. The satirist is the figure in whom the cannibal was received into civilization. His recollection of his origin is not without filial piety, so that the proposal to eat people has become an essential constituent of his inspiration, from Jonathan Swift's pertinent project concerning the use of the children of the less wealthy classes, to Léon Bloy's suggestion that landlords of insolvent lodgers be conceded a right to the sale of the lodgers' flesh. In such directives, great satirists have taken the measure of the humanity of their fellow men. "Humanity, culture, and freedom are precious things that cannot be bought dearly enough with blood, understanding, and human dignity"—thus Kraus concludes the dispute between the cannibal and human rights. One should compare his formulation with Marx's treatment of the "Jewish question," in order to judge how totally this playful reaction of 1909—the reaction against the classical ideal of humanity—was likely to become a confession of materialist humanism at the first opportunity. Admittedly, one would need to understand *Die Fackel* from the first number on, literally word for word, to predict that this aesthetically oriented journalism, without sacrificing or gaining a single motif, was destined to become the political prose of 1930. For this it had to thank its partner, the press, which disposed of humanity in the way to which Kraus alludes in these words: "Human rights are the fragile toy that grownups like to trample on and so will not give up." Thus, drawing a boundary between the private and public spheres, which in 1789 was supposed to inaugurate freedom, became a mockery. Through the newspaper, says Kierkegaard, "the distinction between public and private affairs is abolished in private-public prattle . . ."

To open a dialectical debate between the public and private zones that commingle demonically in prattle, to lead concrete humanity to victory— this is operetta's purpose, which Kraus discovered and which in Offenbach he raised to its most expressive level.[8] Just as prattle seals the enslavement of language through stupidity, so operetta transfigures stupidity through music. To fail to recognize the beauty of feminine stupidity was for Kraus always the blackest philistinism. Before its radiance the chimeras of progress evaporate. And in Offenbach's operettas the bourgeois trinity of the true, the beautiful, and the good is brought together, freshly rehearsed and with musical accompaniment, in its star turn on the trapeze of idiocy. Nonsense is true, stupidity beautiful, weakness good. This is Offenbach's secret: how in the deep nonsense of public discipline—whether it be that of the upper ten thousand, a dance floor, or a military state—the deep sense of private licentiousness opens a dreamy eye. And what, in the form of language, might have been judicial strictness, renunciation, discrimination, becomes cunning and evasion, obstruction and postponement, in the form of music.—Music as the preserver of the moral order? Music as the police of a world of pleasure? Yes, this is the splendor that falls on the old Paris ballrooms, on the Grande Chaumière, on the Clôserie des Lilas in Kraus's rendering of *La vie parisienne*. "And the inimitable duplicity of this music, which simultaneously puts a plus and a minus sign before everything it says, betraying idyll to parody, mockery to lyricism; the abundance of musical devices ready to perform all duties, uniting pain and pleasure—this gift is here developed to its purest pitch." Anarchy as the only international constitution that is moral and worthy of man becomes the true music of these operettas. The voice of Kraus speaks, rather than sings, this inner music. It whistles bitingly about the peaks of dizzying stupidity, reverberates shatteringly from the abyss of the absurd; and in Frescata's lines it hums, like the wind in the chimney, a requiem to the generation of our grandfathers.—Offenbach's work is touched by the pangs of death. It contracts, rids itself of everything superfluous, passes through the dangerous span of this existence and re-emerges saved, more real than before. For wherever this fickle voice is heard, the lightning flashes of advertisements and the thunder of the Métro cleave the Paris of omnibuses and gas jets. And the work gives him all this in return. For at moments it is transformed into a curtain, and with the wild gestures of a fairground showman with which he accompanies the whole performance, Kraus tears aside this curtain and suddenly reveals the interior of his cabinet of horrors. There they stand: Schober, Bekessy, Kerr, and the other skits, no longer enemies but curiosities, heirlooms from the world of Offenbach or Nestroy[9]—no, older, rarer still, *lares* of the troglodytes, household gods of stupidity from prehistoric times. Kraus, when he reads in public, does not speak the words of Offenbach or Nestroy: they speak from him. And now and then a breathtaking, half-blank, half-glittering whore-monger's glance falls on the crowd before him, inviting them to the unholy marriage with the masks in which they do not recognize themselves, and for the last time invokes the evil privilege of ambiguity.

It is only now that the satirist's true face, or rather true mask, is revealed. It is the mask of Timon the misanthrope. "Shakespeare had foreknowledge of everything"—yes. But above all of Kraus. Shakespeare portrays inhuman figures—Timon the most inhuman of them—and says: Nature would produce such a creature if she wished to create something befitting the world as your kind have fashioned it, something worthy of it. Such a creature is Timon; such is Kraus. Neither has, or wants, anything in common with men. "An animal feud is on, and so we renounce humanity"; from a remote village in the Swiss mountains Kraus throws down this challenge to mankind, and Timon wants only the sea to weep at his grave. Like Timon's verse, Kraus's poetry stands opposite the colon of the *dramatis persona,* of the role. A Fool, a Caliban, a Timon—no more thoughtful, no more dignified or better—but, nevertheless, his own Shakespeare. All the figures thronging about him should be seen as originating in Shakespeare. Always he is the model, whether Kraus is speaking with Otto Weininger about man or with Peter Altenberg about women, with Frank Wedekind about the stage or with Adolf Loos about food, with Else Lasker-Schüler about the Jews or with Theodor Haecker about the Christians. The power of the demon ends at this realm. His semihuman or subhuman traits are conquered by a truly inhuman being, a monster. Kraus hinted at this when he said, "In me a capacity for psychology is united with the greater capacity to ignore the psychological." It is the inhuman quality of the actor that he claims for himself in these words: the cannibal quality. For in each of his roles the actor assimilates bodily a human being, and in Shakespeare's baroque tirades—when the cannibal is unmasked as the better man, the hero as an actor, when Timon plays the rich man, Hamlet the madman—it is as if the actor's lips were dripping blood. So Kraus, following Shakespeare's example, wrote himself parts that let him taste blood. The endurance of his convictions is persistence in a role, in its stereotypes, its cues. His experiences are, in their entirety, nothing but this: cues. This is why he insists on them, demanding them from existence like an actor who never forgives a partner for denying him his cue.

Kraus's public readings of Offenbach, his recital of couplets from Nestroy, are bereft of all musical means. The word never gives way to the instrument; but by extending its boundaries further and further, it finally depotentiates itself, dissolving into a merely creaturely voice. A humming that is to the word what his smile is to the joke is the holy of holies of this performer's art. In this smile, this humming—in which, as in a crater lake amid the most monstrous crags and cinders, the world is peacefully and contentedly mirrored—irrupts the deep complicity with his listeners and models that Kraus has never allowed to enter his words. His service to the word permits no compromise. But as soon as the word turns its back, he is ready for anything. Then the tormenting, inexhaustible charm of these recitals makes itself felt: the charm of seeing the distinction between like and unlike minds annulled and the homogeneous mass of false friends created—the charm that sets the tone of these performances. Kraus confronts a world of enemies, seeks to coerce them to love, yet coerces them to nothing but hypocrisy. His defenselessness before the latter has a precise connection to the subversive dilettantism that is particularly prominent in his Offenbach renderings. Here Kraus confines music to limits narrower than were ever dreamed of in the manifestos of the George school.[10] This cannot, of course, obscure the antithesis between the linguistic gestures of the two men. Rather, an exact correlation exists between the factors which give Kraus access to both poles of linguistic expression—the enfeebled pole of humming and the armed pole of pathos—and those which forbid his sanctification of the word to take on the forms of the Georgean cult of language. To the cosmic rising and falling that for George "deifies the body and embodies the divine," language is simply a Jacob's ladder with ten thousand word-rungs. Kraus's language, by contrast, has done away with all hieratic moments. It is the medium neither of prophecy nor of domination. It is the theater of a sanctification of the name—with this Jewish certainty, it sets itself against the theurgy of the "word-body." Very late, with a decisiveness that must have matured in years of silence, Kraus entered the lists against the great partner whose work had arisen at the same time as his own, beneath the threshold of the century. George's first published book and the first volume of *Die Fackel* are dated 1899. And only retrospectively, in "After Thirty Years" (1929), did Kraus issue the challenge. There, as the zealot, he confronts George, the object of worship,

> who dwells in the temple from which
> he never had to drive the traders and the lenders,
> nor yet the pharisees and scribes,
> who therefore—camped about the place—describe it.
> The *profanum vulgus* praises this renouncer,
> who never told it what it ought to hate.
> And he who found the goal before the way
> did not come from the origin [*Ursprung*].

"You came from the origin—the origin is the goal" is received by the "Dying Man" as God's comfort and promise. To this Kraus alludes here, as does Berthold Viertel when, in the same way as Kraus, he calls the world a "wrong, deviating, circuitous way back to paradise." "And so," he continues in this most important passage of his essay on Kraus, "I attempt to interpret the development of this odd talent: intellectuality as a deviation . . . leading back to immediacy; publicity—a false trail back to language; satire—a detour to the poem." This "origin"—the seal of authenticity on the phenomenon—is the subject of a discovery that has a curious element of recognition. The theater of this philosophical recognition scene in Kraus's work is poetry, and its language is rhyme: "A word that never tells an untruth at its origin" and that, just as blessedness has its origin at the end of time, has its at the end of the line. Rhyme—two putti bearing the demon to its grave. It died at its origin because it came into the world as a hybrid of mind and sexuality. Its sword and shield—concept and guilt—have fallen from its hands to become emblems beneath the feet of the angel that killed it. This is a poetic, martial angel with a foil in his hand, as only Baudelaire knew him: "practicing alone fantastic swordsmanship,"

Flairant dans tous les coins les hasards de la rime,
Trébuchant sur les mots comme sur les pavés,
Heurtant parfois des vers depuis longtemps rêvés.

[Scenting rhyme's hazards in every corner,
Stumbling on words as on uneven pavements,
Jostling now and then long-dreamed-of lines.]

Also, to be sure, a licentious angel, "here chasing a metaphor that has just turned the corner, there coupling words like a procurer, perverting phrases, infatuated with similarities, blissfully abusing chiastic embraces, always on the lookout for adventure, impatient and hesitant to consummate in joy and torment." So, finally, the hedonistic impulse of the work finds its purest expression in this melancholy and fantastic relationship to existence in which Kraus, in the Viennese tradition of Raimund and Girardi, arrives at a conception of happiness that is as resigned as it is sensual.[11] This must be borne in mind if one is to understand the urgency with which he decried the dancing pose affected by Nietzsche—not to mention the wrath with which the monster [*Unmensch*] was bound to greet the Superman [*Übermensch*].

The child recognizes by rhyme that it has reached the ridge of language, from which it can hear the rushing of all springs at their origin. Up there, creaturely existence is at home; after so much dumbness in the animal and so much lying in the whore, it has found its tongue in the child. "A good brain must be capable of imagining each fiber of childhood with all its manifestations so intensely that the temperature is raised"—in statements such as this, Kraus aims further than it appears. He himself, at any rate, satisfied this requirement to the extent that he never envisaged the child as the object of education; rather, in an image from his own youth, he saw the child as the antagonist of education who is educated by this antagonism, not by the educator. "It was not the cane that should be abolished, but the teacher who uses it badly." Kraus wants to be nothing except the teacher who uses it better. The limit of his philanthropy, his pity, is marked by the cane, which he first felt in the same class at school to which he owes his best poems.

"I am only one of the epigones"—Kraus is an epigone of school anthologies. "The German Boy's Table Grace," "Siegfried's Sword," "The Grave in the Busento," "Kaiser Karl Inspects a School"—these were his models, poetically re-created by the attentive pupil who learned them. So "The Steeds of Gravelotte" became the poem "To Eternal Peace," and even the most incandescent of his hate poems were ignited by Hölty's "Forest Fire," whose glow pervaded the anthologies of our schooldays. And if on the last day not only the graves but the school anthologies open, to the tune of "How the Trumpets Blow, Hussars Away," the true Pegasus of the little folk will burst from them and, with a shriveled mummy, a puppet of cloth or yellowish ivory, hanging dead and withered from the shoulders of his horse, this unparalleled fashioner of verses will go careening off; but the two-edged saber in his hand, as polished as his rhymes and as incisive as on the First Day, will belabor the green woods, and blooms of style will bestrew the ground.

Language has never been more perfectly distinguished from mind, never more intimately bound to eros, than by Kraus in the observation, "The more closely you look at a word, the more distantly it looks back." This is a Platonic love of language. The only closeness from which the word cannot escape, however, is rhyme. So the primal erotic relationship between nearness and distance is, in his language, given voice as rhyme and name. As rhyme, language rises up from the creaturely world; as name, it draws all creatures up to it. In "The Forsaken" the most ardent interpenetration of language and eros, as Kraus experienced them, expresses itself with an innocent grandeur that recalls the perfect Greek epigrams and vase pictures. "The Forsaken" are forsaken by each other. But—this is their great solace— also with each other. On the threshold between dying and rebirth, they pause. With head turned back, joy "in unheard-of fashion" takes her eternal leave; turned from her, the soul "in unwonted fashion" silently sets foot in an alien world. Thus forsaken with each other are joy and soul, but also language and eros, also rhyme and name.—To "The Forsaken" the fifth volume of *Words in Verse* is dedicated. Only the dedication now reaches them, and this is nothing other than an avowal of Platonic love, which does not satisfy its desire in what it loves, but possesses and holds it in the name. This self-obsessed man knows no other self-renunciation than giving thanks. His love is not possession, but gratitude. Thanking and dedicating—for to thank is to put feelings under a name. How the beloved grows distant and lustrous, how her minuteness and her glow withdraw into name: this is the only experience of love known to *Words in Verse*. And, therefore, "To live without women, how easy. / To have lived without women, how hard."

From within the linguistic compass of the name, and only from within it, can we discern Kraus's basic polemical procedure: citation. To quote a word is to call it by its name. So Kraus's achievement exhausts itself at its highest level by making even the newspaper quotable. He transports it to his own sphere, and the empty phrase is suddenly forced to recognize that even in the deepest dregs of the journals it is not safe from the voice that swoops on the wings of the word to drag it from its darkness. How wonderful if this voice approaches not to punish but to save, as it does on the Shakespearean wings of the lines in which, before the town of Arras, someone sends word home of how in the early morning, on the last blasted tree beside the fortifications, a lark began to sing. A single line, and not even one of his, is enough to enable Kraus to descend, as savior, into this inferno, and insert a single italicization: "It was a nightingale and not a lark which sat there on the pome*granate* tree and sang."[12] In the quotation that both saves and punishes, language proves the matrix of justice. It summons the word by its name, wrenches it destructively from its context, but precisely thereby calls it back to its origin. It appears, now with rhyme and reason, sonorously, congruously, in the structure of a new text. As rhyme, it gathers the similar into its aura; as name, it stands alone and expressionless. In citation the two realms—of origin and destruction—justify themselves before language. And conversely, only where they interpenetrate—in citation—is language consummated. In it is mirrored the angelic tongue in which all words, startled from the idyllic context of meaning, have become mottoes in the book of Creation.

From its two poles—classical humanism and materialist humanism—the whole world of this man's culture is embraced by citation. Schiller, admittedly unnamed, stands beside Shakespeare: "There is also a moral nobility. Mean natures pay / With that which they do; noble, with that which they are"—this classical distich characterizes, in the convergence of manorial *noblesse* and cosmopolitan rectitude, the utopian vanishing point where Weimar humanism was at home, and which was finally fixed by Stifter. It is decisive for Kraus that he locates origin at exactly this vanishing point. It is his program to reverse the development of bourgeois-capitalist affairs to a condition that was never theirs. But he is nonetheless the last bourgeois to claim his justification from Being, and Expressionism was portentous for him because in it this attitude had for the first time to prove its worth in the face of a revolutionary situation. It was precisely the attempt to do justice to this situation not by actions but by Being that led Expressionism to its clenched, precipitous voice. So it became the last historical refuge of personality. The guilt that bowed it and the purity it proclaimed—both are part of the phantom of the unpolitical or "natural" man who emerges at the end of that regression and was unmasked by Marx. He writes:

Man as member of bourgeois society, unpolitical man, necessarily appears as natural man . . . Political revolution dissolves bourgeois life into its component parts without revolutionizing or criticizing these components themselves. It stands to bourgeois society, to the world of needs, work, private interests, private right, in the same relation as it does to the foundation of its existence . . . and therefore to its natural basis . . . The real man is acknowledged only in the form of the egoistical individual; the true man, only in the form of the abstract *citoyen* . . . Only when the really individual man takes back into himself the abstract citizen and, as an individual man, has become in his empirical life, in his individual work, in his individual circumstances a species-being . . . and therefore no longer separates social power from himself in the form of political power, only then is human emancipation complete.[13]

The materialist humanism which Marx here opposes to its classical counterpart manifests itself for Kraus in the child, and the developing human being raises his face against the idols of ideal man—the romantic child of nature as much as the dutiful citizen. For the sake of such development, Kraus revised the school anthology, investigated German education, and found it tossing helplessly on the waves of journalistic caprice. Hence his "Lyrik der Deutschen" [Lyric of the Germans]:

> He who *can* is their man and not he who *must;*
> they strayed from being to seeming.
> Their lyrical case was not Claudius
> but Heine.

The fact, however, that the developing man actually takes form not within the natural sphere but in the sphere of mankind, in the struggle for liberation, and that he is recognized by the posture which the fight with exploitation and poverty stamps upon him, that there is no idealistic but only a materialistic deliverance from myth, and that at the origin of creation stands not purity but purification—all this did not leave its trace on Kraus's materialist humanism until very late. Only when despairing did he discover in citation the power not to preserve but to purify, to tear from context, to destroy; the only power in which hope still resides that something might survive this age—because it was wrenched from it.

Here we find confirmation that all the martial energies of this man are innate civic virtues; only in the melee did they take on their combative aspect. But already no one recognizes them any more; no one can grasp the necessity that compelled this great bourgeois character to become a comedian, this guardian of Goethean linguistic values a polemicist, or why this irreproachably honorable man went berserk. This, however, was bound to happen, since he thought fit to change the world by beginning with his own class, in his own home, in Vienna. And when, admitting to himself the futility of his enterprise, he abruptly broke it off, he placed the matter back in the hands of nature—this time destructive not creative nature:

> Let time stand still! Sun, be consummate!
> Make great the end! Announce eternity!
> Rise up with menace, let your light boom thunder,
> that our strident death be silenced.

> You golden bell, melt in your own heat,
> Make yourself a gun against the cosmic foe!
> Shoot firebrands in his face! Had I but Joshua's power,
> I tell you, Gideon would be again![14]

On this unfettered nature Kraus's later political credo is founded, though in antithesis to Stifter's patriarchal code; it is a confession that is in every respect astonishing, but incomprehensible only in the fact that it has not been preserved in *Die Fackel*'s largest type, and that this most powerful of postwar bourgeois prose must be sought in the now-vanished issue of November 1920:

> What I mean is—and now for once I shall speak plainly to this dehumanized brood of owners of property and blood, and to all their followers, because they do not understand German and from my "contradictions" are incapable of deducing my true intention . . .—what I mean is, Communism as a reality is only the obverse of their own life-violating ideology, admittedly by the grace of a purer ideal origin, a deranged remedy with a purer ideal purpose: the devil take its practice, but God preserve it as a constant threat over the heads of those who have property and would like to compel all others to preserve it, driving them, with the consolation that worldly goods are not the highest, to the fronts of hunger and patriotic honor. God preserve it, so that this rabble who are beside themselves with brazenness do not grow more brazen still, and so that the society of those exclusively entitled to enjoyment, who believe they are loving subordinate humanity enough if they give it syphilis, may at least go to bed with a nightmare! So that at least they may lose their appetite for preaching morality to their victims, take less delight in ridiculing them!

A human, natural, noble language—particularly in the light of a noteworthy declaration by Loos: "If human work consists only of destruction, it is truly human, natural, noble work." For far too long, the accent was placed on creativity. People are only creative to the extent that they avoid tasks and supervision. Work as a supervised task—its model being political and technical work—is attended by dirt and detritus, intrudes destructively into matter, is abrasive to what is already achieved and critical toward its conditions, and is in all this opposite to the work of the dilettante luxuriating in creation. His work is innocent and pure, consuming and purifying masterliness. And therefore the monster stands among us as the messenger of a more real humanism. He is the conqueror of the empty phrase. He feels solidarity not with the slender pine but with the plane that devours it, not with the precious ore but with the blast furnace that purifies it. The average European has not succeeded in uniting his life with technology, because he has clung to the fetish of creative existence. One must have followed Loos in his struggle with the dragon "ornament," heard the stellar Esperanto of Scheerbart's creations, or seen Klee's *New Angel* (who preferred to free men by taking from them, rather than make them happy by giving to them) to understand a humanity that proves itself by destruction.[15]

Justice, therefore, is destructive in opposing the constructive ambiguities of law, and Kraus destructively did justice to his own work: "All my errors stay behind to lead." This is a sober language that bases its dominance on permanence. The writings of Kraus have already begun to last, so that he might furnish them with an epigraph from Lichtenberg, who dedicated one of his most profound works to "Your Majesty Forgetfulness." So his modesty now appears—bolder than his former self-assertion, which dissolved in demonic self-reflection. Neither purity nor sacrifice mastered the demon; but where origin and destruction come together, his reign is over. Like a creature sprung from the child and the cannibal, his conqueror stands before him: not a new man—a monster, a new angel. Perhaps one of those who, according to the Talmud, are at each moment created anew in countless throngs, and who, once they have raised their voices before God, cease and pass into nothingness. Lamenting, chastising, or rejoicing? No matter—on this evanescent voice the ephemeral work of Kraus is modeled. Angelus— that is the messenger in the old engravings.

Published in the *Frankfurter Zeitung und Handelsblatt,* March 1931. *Gesammelte Schriften,* II, 334–367. Translated by Edmund Jephcott.

Notes

1. Karl Kraus (1874–1936) edited and wrote for *Die Fackel* from 1899 to 1936.
2. Otto Stössl, *Lebensform und Dichtungsform* [Life Form and Poetic Form] (Munich, 1914). Johann Peter Hebel (1760–1826) was a journalist and author who developed a number of innovative short prose forms during his work as editor and chief writer at the *Badischer Landkalendar,* an annual publication not unlike the American *Old Farmer's Almanach.* See Benjamin's essays on Hebel in Volume 1 of this edition.
3. This quotation by Adalbert Stifter (1805–1868) comes from the introduction to his *Bunte Steine* (1853), a volume of short stories. Stifter's prose is characterized by an unusually graceful style and a reverence for natural processes. See Benjamin's essay "Stifter" in Volume 1 of this edition.
4. Matthias Claudius (1740–1815), German poet, was perhaps the most notable poetic voice between Klopstock and Goethe. He served as editor of the important journal *Der Wandsbecker Bote.*
5. *Die letzten Tage der Menschheit* (The Last Days of Humankind) is the title of Kraus's mammoth apocalyptic drama, which sought to expose the bureaucratic mediocrity and political criminality that he believed had brought Europe to the Great War. The play was published in its final form in 1923. Due to its length (it has 220 scenes and approximately 500 characters), it was first performed in Vienna only in 1964—and even then in a shortened version.
6. "Vienna Genesis" refers to an illuminated manuscript—a copy of the book of Genesis—in the collection of the Austrian National Library. Its dating (early Byzantine, perhaps 500–600 A.D.) and place of origin (Constantinople or Syria) are disputed. The linkage of Expressionism and late Antiquity had been a concern of Benjamin's from the time he read Alois Riegl's *Die spätrömische Kunst-Industrie* (The Late Roman Art Industry) during the years of the First World War; the linkage plays an important role in Benjamin's *Ursprung des deutschen Trauerspiels* (Origin of the German Trauerspiel).

7. Benjamin refers here to the "Lulu" cycle, two dramas by the German playwright Frank Wedekind (1864–1918). In *Erdgeist* (Earth Spirit; 1895) and *Die Büchse der Pandora* (Pandora's Box; 1904), the conflict of a desiccated, hypocritical bourgeois morality with a personal and above all sexual freedom is played out in the fate of the amoral femme fatale Lulu. Alban Berg based his opera *Lulu* on Wedekind's plays.

8. Kraus translated and edited the operetta *La vie parisienne* (music by Offenbach and libretto by Henri Meilhac and Ludovic Halévy). See "Karl Kraus Reads Offenbach," in this volume.

9. Johann Schober (1874–1932), a police official, was twice prime minister of Austria (1921–1922 and 1929–1930). He was best-known for his attempts to negotiate a union between Austria and Germany. Alfred Kerr (pseudonym of Alfred Klemperer; 1867–1948) was Berlin's most prominent and influential theater critic. Johann Nestroy (1801–1862), Austrian dramatist and character actor, used satire, irony, and parody as weapons against the newly rising bourgeoisie. His best-known work is *Einen Jux will er sich machen* (He Intends to Have a Fling; 1842), adapted by Thornton Wilder as *The Matchmaker* and later turned into the musical play and film *Hello, Dolly!*

10. "George school" refers to the circle of conservative intellectuals around the poet Stefan George (1868–1933), whose high-modernist verse appeared in such volumes as *Das Jahr der Seele* (The Year of the Soul; 1897) and *Der siebente Ring* (The Seventh Ring; 1907). George's attempt to "purify" German language and culture exerted a powerful influence on younger poets.

11. Ferdinand Raimund, Austrian comic dramatist, was—along with Johann Nestroy—among the preeminent playwrights of Vienna in the mid-nineteenth century.

12. Kraus cites this line in *Die Fackel* and attributes it to an anonymous Belgian soldier. *Granat* means "pomegranate"; *Granate*, "grenade" or "shell."

13. This is the conclusion of Karl Marx's 1844 review of Bruno Bauer's "On the Jewish Question."

14. Karl Kraus, *Worte in Versen II* (Words in Verse II).

15. The reference is to Paul Klee's ink wash drawing *Angelus Novus* (1920), which Benjamin owned for a time. See the discusssion under "1921" in the Chronology to Volume 1 of this edition.

Literary History and the Study of Literature

Scholars attempt again and again to present the history of individual disciplines in terms of one self-contained development. They like to speak of "autonomous disciplines." And even though this formulation initially refers only to the conceptual system of individual disciplines, the idea of autonomy easily spills over into the historical domain. It then leads to the attempt to portray the history of scholarship as an independent, separate process set apart from overall political and intellectual developments. There is no need to debate the rights and wrongs of this procedure here; independently of any judgment on this issue, one must, in a survey of the current situation in a particular discipline, consider any findings not just as a link in the autonomous historical development of the subject, but also as an element of the prevailing cultural situation at that point in time. If, as is maintained in what follows, literary history is in the depths of a crisis, this crisis must be seen as part of a much broader one. Literary history is not only a discipline in its own right; in its development, it is also a moment of history in general.

It certainly is the latter. But is it really the former? Is literary history a historical discipline? The following will clarify the sense in which this must be denied. It is fair to say in advance that despite what the term might lead us to expect, "literary history" did not make its initial appearance in the context of historical studies. In the eighteenth century it was a branch of aesthetic education, a kind of applied taxonomy of taste, and it stood halfway between a textbook of aesthetics and a bookseller's catalogue.

The first pragmatic historian of literature was Gervinus, the first volume of whose *Geschichte der poetischen Nationalliteratur der Deutschen* [History of the Poetic National Literature of the Germans] appeared in 1835.[1] He saw himself as a member of the historical school. In his eyes, great works are "historical events, poets are geniuses of activity, and judgments about them have far-reaching public effects . . . This analogy to world history is as much a part of Gervinus' own individual attitude as his method of filling the gap due to the absence of art-historical analysis by 'comparing' great works with 'related' ones."[2] The true relationship between literature and history—let alone the relationship between history and literary history—is something that this brilliant but methodologically naive work could not focus on. And if we survey the attempts made prior to the middle of the century, we see how the position of literary history, and the extent to which it was a part of history or something *outside* it but related to it, remained unclarified. With men like Michael Bernays, Richard Heinzel, and Richard Maria Werner, this epistemological perplexity was followed by a reaction.[3] With varying degrees of intention the link with history was abandoned in favor of a leaning toward the exact natural sciences. Whereas previously even bibliographic compilations tended to give an idea of the overall historical development, scholars now doggedly fell back on individual studies and on "collecting and cherishing." To be sure, this period of positivist doctrine brought forth a plethora of histories of literature for use by the layman, as a complement to scholarly research in the strict sense. But the panorama of universal history that they unfolded was nothing but a kind of narrative comforter for both writer and reader. Wilhelm Scherer's history of literature, with its factual underpinning and its great rhythmic periodization (three phases over each of three centuries), can be seen as a synthesis of the two great basic trends of scholarship at the time.[4] Commentators have been right to emphasize the cultural-political and organizational intentions which underlie this work, together with the Makart-like vision on which it is based[5]—that of a colossal triumphal procession of ideal German figures. Scherer's bold conception makes the dominant figures "arise sometimes from the political sphere and sometimes from the realm of literature, religion, or philosophy, without creating the impression of a higher necessity, or even of external consistency. He cancels out their effects with those of individual works, fetishized ideas, or literary giants, and the entire project ends up a colorful jumble that is the very antithesis of historical order."[6]

What we see emerging here is the false universalism of the methods of cultural history. It is a development that culminates logically in the concept of the "cultural sciences" [*Kulturwissenschaften*] as formulated by Rickert and Windelband.[7] Indeed, the victory of these cultural sciences was so complete that with Karl Lamprecht's *Deutsche Geschichte* [German History] it even went on to become the epistemological foundation of pragmatic history. With the proclamation of "values," history was distorted once and for all in the service of modernism, while research was demoted to the status of an auxiliary in a cult in which the "eternal values" were celebrated in accordance with a syncretist rite. It is always worth reflecting how short the path is from here to the wildest aberrations of the most recent forms of literary history, and what charms the castrated methodologies have succeeded in extracting from the repulsive neologisms that lurk behind the golden gates of the "values." "Just as all poetry ultimately aspires to a world of 'verbalizable' [wortbaren] values, so too in formal terms it signifies an ultimate intensification and interiorization of the immediate expressive powers of speech."[8] After this assertion the reader will have become anesthetized, for good or ill, to the shock of recognition with which the poet himself experiences this "ultimate intensification and interiorization" as "the pleasures of verbalizing" [Wortungs-Lust].[9] This is the same world in which the "verbal artwork" is at home. Rarely has a word that has been so much abused displayed so much nobility as the word "poetry." And with all that, this science throws its weight around while simultaneously betraying itself through the "breadth" of its object and through its "synthesizing" comportment. The profligate drive toward totalities is its misfortune. Just listen: "Spiritual values come to the fore with overwhelming power and purity . . . as 'ideas' which make the poet's soul soar aloft and impel him to create symbolic forms. Unsystematically, yet with complete clarity, the poet makes us feel at every moment which values or which value-strata he privileges; and also perhaps, what priority he gives to values in general."[10]

In this quagmire, the hydra of scholastic aesthetics is at home with its seven heads: creativity, empathy, freedom from time, imitation, sympathetic understanding, illusion, and aesthetic enjoyment. Whoever wishes to explore the world of its acolytes could not do better than to take a look at its latest, representative handbook—Philosophie der Literaturwissenschaft, edited by Emil Ermatinger—in which the German literary historians of the present attempt to give an account of their work and from which these quotations have been taken. This does not mean that all the contributors to this volume take responsibility for one another in a spirit of solidarity. Undoubtedly, writers like Gumbel, Cysarz, Muschg, and Nadler stand out from the chaotic background in which they appear.[11] It is all the more revealing, then, that even men who have notable scholarly achievements to their credit have brought few of the attitudes that ennobled the study of German literature in its early days into the community of their colleagues. For anyone who is at home in literature, the entire enterprise creates the uncanny impression that the beautiful, well-built house of poetry has been invaded by a company of mercenaries who clump around with their heavy boots in the ostensible desire to admire its treasures and wonders. At the sight of them, everything immediately becomes clear: these people do not give a damn for the order and inventory of the house. They have moved in because it is strategically situated and because it is a convenient vantage point from which to bombard a railway or bridgehead whose defense is important in the civil war. And this is how literary history has established itself in the house of literature: the "beautiful," the "worthwhile experience," the "ideal," and so on are all apertures from which it is easy to bombard the enemy.

It cannot be said that the troops caught up in this crossfire are adequately trained. They operate under the command of the materialist literary historians, among whom old Franz Mehring still stands head and shoulders above the rest.[12] What this man means can be seen anew from every attempt at materialist literary history since his death. Most clearly in Alfred Kleinberg's *Deutsche Dichtung in ihren sozialen, zeit- und geistesgeschichtlichen Bedingungen* [German Literature in Its Social, Historical, and Intellectual Context]—a work that slavishly colors all the stereotypes of a Leixner or a Koenig and then frames them with a few ornaments of free thought.[13] The whole thing is a real blessing for the ordinary man. For his part, Mehring is a materialist far more because of the scope of his general historical and economic knowledge than through his methodology. His ideology derives from Marx; his intellectual discipline, from Kant. The result is that the work of this man—who held unswervingly to the belief that "the noblest possessions of the nation" had to be preserved at all cost—is conservative in the best sense of the word, rather than revolutionary.

But the Fountain of Youth of history is fed by Lethe. Nothing is so rejuvenating as oblivion. With the crisis in education, the use of literary history for the creation of "representative examples" is growing, as can be seen most obviously in the many popular handbooks on the subject. It is always the same blurred text that makes its appearance in one format or another. Such achievements have long since ceased to have anything in common with scholarship; their function is limited to giving certain social strata the illusion that they are participating in the cultural and literary heritage. Only a discipline that abandons its museum characteristics can replace illusion with reality. That would call not just for the courage to omit much, but also for the ability to bring the entire business of literary history into an age in which the number of writers—and this means more than the poets and literati—is growing daily and has a much more urgent technical interest in the problems of writing than in those of edification. More recent scholars can take this into account, and have already begun to do so in part, with analyses of anonymous writing—calendar stories and colportage—as well as of the sociology of the reading public, writers' associations, and the history of the publishing industry. But this is perhaps a matter less of renewing teaching through research than of renewing research through teaching. For the crisis in education stands in precise correlation to the fact that literary history has now completely lost sight of its most important challenge—namely, its pedagogical task, the task with which it began its life as the "science of belles lettres."

So much for the social context. Just as modernism has flattened out the tension between knowledge and practice with its museum-like concept of culture, the same fate has afflicted the historical sphere: the distinction has fallen away between past and present—that is to say, between criticism and literary history. The literary history of modernism is not concerned with legitimating itself prematurely by a creative interaction with the past. It imagines that it can do this better with acts of patronage toward contemporary writing. It is astonishing to see how academic scholarship goes along with this trend. In former times, German literary scholars refused to regard the literature of their age as a suitable subject for research. This was not, as is believed today, a matter of prudence, but sprang from the ascetic attitudes of researchers who served their age directly by attempting to do justice to the past. The style and attitude of the Brothers Grimm testify to the fact that the regimen required for such work is no less demanding than that needed for great artistic creativity. This attitude has been replaced by the ambition of scholars to demonstrate that they are as well informed as the midday edition of any metropolitan newspaper.

Present-day German studies are eclectic—that is to say, unphilological through and through. This is to measure them not by the positivistic yardstick of the Scherer school but by that of the Brothers Grimm, who never sought to grasp material content except through words and who would have shuddered to hear contemporary talk of a literary analysis that was "transparent" or "pointed beyond itself." Needless to say, no later generation has been able to approach their talent for interweaving critical and historical analysis. True, there is some remarkable literary history emerging in a few isolated cases (Hellingrath, Kommerell) from the work of the George circle—history that does succeed in combining the literary with the academic.[14] But if this is so, it is because in their own way these writers breathe something of the same antiphilological spirit. The panoply of Alexandrian learning that is familiar from the works of the George circle—"genius" and "virtus," "kairos" and "daemon," Fortuna and Psyche—is really designed to exorcize the historical. And the ideal of this trend would really be to divide up the whole of German literature into sacred groves containing temples to poets of timeless worth. Last, the abandonment of the philological approach leads (not least in the George circle) to that fallacious question that is increasingly a source of confusion in the field of literary history—namely, whether, and to what extent, reason is ever capable of comprehending the work of art. We are now very far from grasping the fact that the existence of a work of art in time and the understanding of it are but two sides of the same thing. The task of opening literary history to reason has been consigned to the monographic treatment of works and forms.

"For the present," writes Walter Muschg, "we may say that in its essential works literary history is almost exclusively focused on monographs. Faith in the possibility of a comprehensive description has been almost entirely lost by the present generation. Instead it struggles with individuals and problems that it mostly found missing in the age of universal histories." It struggles with individuals and problems—this may well be accurate. The truth, however, is that it should struggle above all with the works. Their entire life and their effects [*Wirkung*] should have the right to stand alongside the history of their composition. In other words, their fate, their reception by their contemporaries, their translations, their fame. For with this the work is transformed inwardly into a microcosm, or indeed a microeon. What is at stake is not to portray literary works in the context of their age, but to represent the age that perceives them—our age—in the age during which they arose. It is this that makes literature into an organon of history; and to achieve this, and not to reduce literature to the material of history, is the task of the literary historian.

Published in *Die literarische Welt*, April 1931. *Gesammelte Schriften*, III, 283–290. Translated by Rodney Livingstone.

Notes

1. Georg Gottfried Gervinus (1805–1871), historian, literary historian, and politician, held professorships at Heidelberg and Göttingen and was a delegate to the German National Assembly in Frankfurt in 1848. His literary history broke new ground in its effort to embed the discussion of literature within a larger historical narrative.
2. Walter Muschg, "Das Dichterporträt in der Literaturgeschichte" [The Portrait of the Poet in Literary History], in Emil Ermatinger, ed., *Philosophie der Literaturwissenschaft* [Philosophy of Literary Scholarship] (Berlin: Junker und Dünnhaupt, 1930), p. 288.
3. Michael Bernays (1834–1897), German literary historian, was best-known for his work on Goethe and Shakespeare. Richard Heinzel (1835–1905), literary historian, attempted to bring the exactitude of the natural sciences to the study of language and literature. Richard Maria Werner (1854–1913), literary historian, was best-known for his work on the dramatist Hebbel.
4. Wilhelm Scherer (1841–1886), one of the nineteenth century's leading linguists and literary historians, sought to replace descriptive literary history with a comparative approach which emphasized the "genetic" development of a national literature.
5. Hans Makart (1840–1884) was an Austrian painter who made his reputation with vast historical and allegorical canvases that made his name a byword for empty monumentality.
6. Muschg, "Das Dichterporträt," p. 290.
7. The philosopher Heinrich Rickert (1863–1936) founded, together with Wilhelm Windelband, one of the principal schools of Neo-Kantian philosophy in Ger-

many. His work in epistemology emphasized the role of transcendental subjectivity in the acquisition of knowledge. Both Benjamin and Heidegger studied with Rickert. Wilhelm Windelband (1848–1915), also a philosopher, taught in Zürich, Freiburg, and Strasbourg before joining Rickert in Heidelberg. He is best-known for the way in which he differentiated the methods of the humanities from those of the natural sciences.

8. Robert Petsch, "Die Analyse des Dichtwerks" [Analysis of the Poetic Work], in Ermatinger, ed., *Philosophie,* p. 263.
9. Ibid., p. 255.
10. Ibid., p. 259.
11. Emil Julius Gumbel (1891–1966), literary scholar, was forced to resign his position at Heidelberg because of his pronounced republican and pacifist ideas. He emigrated first to France and then to the United States, where he ended his career at the New School for Social Research in New York. Herbert Cysarz (1896–1985), literary historian, concentrated much of his work on Baroque literature. Benjamin cites Cysarz extensively in his *Ursprung des deutschen Trauerspiels* (Origin of the German Trauerspiel). Walter Muschg (1898–1965) was a Swiss poet, dramatist, and literary historian. Josef Nadler (1884–1963) was a German literary historian.
12. Franz Mehring (1846–1919), radical journalist, was a historian of the German Social Democratic Party and the biographer of Karl Marx.
13. Otto Leixner von Grünberg (1847–1907), literary historian, editor, and author, was coeditor of the journal *Die Gegenwart,* which published several of Benjamin's articles.
14. Friedrich Norbert Theodor von Hellingrath (1888–1916), literary historian, caused a sensation in Germany with his historical-critical edition of the works of Friedrich Hölderlin. Benjamin's own early work on Hölderlin is indebted to Hellingrath. In the years before World War I, Hellingrath became associated with the circle around Stefan George; he died in the Battle of Verdun. Max Kommerell (1902–1944), literary critic, author, and translator, belonged intermittently to the George circle. He was a widely influential critical voice in the Weimar Republic. See also Benjamin's "Against a Masterpiece," in this volume.

German Letters

I

The series of German letters that is inaugurated here is not to be thought of as an anthology. However much the attentive reader may learn from it about the value and honor of the German language, and however clearly some of these letters enable him to glimpse a human being where previously he had perceived only an achievement, this is not the intention of the present writer—any more than he wishes to advance the general education of the reader.[1] The intention of this series is, rather, to reveal the lineaments of a "secret Germany" that people nowadays would much prefer to shroud in heavy mist. For a secret Germany really exists. It is merely that its secretness is not simply the expression of its inwardness and depth, but—albeit in a different sense—the product of raucous and brutal forces that have prevented it from playing an effective role in public life and have condemned it to a secret one. And these forces are the same ones that drove Georg Forster from his native land, that led Hölderlin to try to earn his living as a tutor in France, and that made Johann Seume play into the hands of the recruiting officers from Hesse, who then sent him to fight in America. Must we define these forces more precisely? Forster and Seume call them by name, and, in his greatest poems, Hölderlin confronts them as never before with the figure of the German genius. For none of these men—and this holds good for the others who will appear later in this sequence—has ever in his creative work sought an alibi that might enable him to evade the call of civic duty in an emergency. It is because these letters make this so clear that they have remained so unknown. This is as true of Forster as of Seume. And although Hölderlin's letters were read, they were misunderstood most in what they said to the Germans about Germany. One consolation in all this is that these letters have remained quite untouched. They were overlooked by public speakers and those who commemorate anniversaries. And if the latter occasionally managed to pervert the works of these men, as if they had no message to convey to us, or rather no witness to bear, a glance at their letters is sufficient to show where that Germany stands today—a Germany that unfortunately remains a secret one.

Georg Forster (1754–1794) died at the age of forty. He was, to vary a famous saying, at every moment of his life a man who dies at the age of forty. The age of manhood was the age of his maturity, and everything about him that became mature was manly. Forster was as familiar with the *misère* of the German intellectuals of his day as any Hölderlin or Seume. But he had a particular affinity with the latter because, like Seume's, his own misfortune did not derive from being a private tutor. Instead, the theater of his misfortune was Europe as a whole, which he came to know in the course of extensive traveling. This is why he was almost the only German who was destined to understand the European response to the prevailing conditions, which is how he interpreted the French Revolution. In 1795 he went to Paris as a delegate from the city of Mainz; and after the Germans reconquered the town and made his return there impossible by outlawing him, he remained in Paris until his death.

Hölderlin (1770–1843) can have entertained no doubts about the insignificance of the play that Böhlendorff sent him and for which he thanks him in the following letter. Yet it is not just tact that moved him to respond with such a magnanimous letter, but his consciousness of the superhuman difficulties that his friend faced in his life—difficulties that were so unfavorable to any poetic production and that were so similar to Hölderlin's own. The writing and the terrible fate of Schubart, who was imprisoned in a house of correction for eleven years by the duke of Württemberg, and who was never informed of the reason for this punishment, had a powerful influence on Hölderlin in his youth.[2] He hardly ever spoke out against despotism. But anyone who takes the measure of the profundity of his philosophical thoughts about everything German will be able also to gauge the depth of the silence about conditions in Germany that had been imposed on him.

Johann Gottfried Seume (1763–1810) was no great writer. Yet it is not this that distinguishes him from many others who occupy a position in the history of German literature, but his unfailingly irreproachable attitude at times of crisis and the imperturbability with which—after he had been press-ganged by Hessian recruiters and shipped off to America as a soldier—

he consistently stood for the dependable citizen long after he had shed his officer's uniform and had become a proofreader for the publisher Göschen. What the eighteenth century understood by the phrase *honnête homme* can be seen as clearly in Seume as in Tellheim.[3] The only difference is that for Seume the honor of an officer is not so far removed from that of the kind of highwayman his contemporaries revered in *Rinaldo Rinaldini*.[4] When at one point he has fallen into the deepest poverty and is on the verge of despair, he considers going back into the army, and the one thought which consoles him is that in no profession is the man of honor so sorely needed as in that of the soldier.

Written either in early April 1931 or after 1933; unpublished in Benjamin's lifetime. *Gesammelte Schriften*, IV, 945–947. Translated by Rodney Livingstone.

Notes

1. Benjamin's involvement with the publication of a series of German letters spans the years 1931–1936. In 1931 and 1932, the *Frankfurter Zeitung* published twenty-seven letters from the years 1783–1883; Benjamin had chosen and edited the letters, but his name was not mentioned in association with them. In the months leading up to and during the publication of the letters, he composed both a provisional introduction—the text at hand—and a text probably intended as a radio broadcast (see "On the Trail of Old Letters," in this volume). The twenty-seven letters, together with a foreword to the collection and a brief introduction to each selection, were published in book form in Switzerland in 1936 under the title *Deutsche Menschen*. The three letters Benjamin would have included here, by Forster, Hölderlin, and Seume, are not identical with the ones included in the later collection. The letters are: Georg Forster to his wife, July 26, 1793; Friedrich Hölderlin to Casimir Böhlendorff, December 4, 1801; and Johann Gottfried Seume to Karl Böttiger, November 1805.
2. Christian Friedrich Daniel Schubart was a poet and publicist, known for his outspoken religious, patriotic, and democratic views. The duke of Württemberg imprisoned him in the fortress of Hohenasperg from 1777 to 1787. Friedrich Schiller visited him there in 1781. After his release he was appointed Master of Music to the Württemberg court.
3. Tellheim is one of the two chief characters in Lessing's *Minna von Barnhelm*. He is a model of rectitude and dignity.
4. *Rinaldo Rinaldini* was a three-volume novel written in 1798 by Goethe's brother-in-law, Christian August Vulpius. It was widely read in its day.

May–June 1931

Juan-les-Pins, May 4, 12:45 in the morning. I'm going to save my remaining sheets of paper for a diary. On the assumption that what lies ahead of me is not worth making much of a fuss about, I will concentrate on the past. A number of factors have prompted this project. The most important, however, is that I feel tired. Tired above all of the struggle, the struggle for money, of which I now have enough in reserve to enable me to stay here. But tired also of aspects of my personal life with which strictly speaking— apart from my economic situation—I have no reason to be dissatisfied. But the very sense of tranquillity that has taken possession of me inwardly to a degree that has always been rare with me leads me to probe more deeply into the life I am now leading. And then this fatigue. It not only dredges up memories from the past; what is crucial is that of the events in my past which surface in my memory from time to time, it is the factors that make them moments of my life, make them mine, that have become clear, whereas previously I never gave them a thought. Last, this fatigue combines in a strange way with the causes of my dissatisfaction with my life. This dissatisfaction involves a growing aversion to, as well as a lack of confidence in, the methods I see chosen by people of my kind and my situation to assert control over the hopeless situation of cultural politics in Germany. What torments me is the lack of clarity and precision with which the few people close to me divide into factions. What disturbs my inner peace, which is also a peaceable attitude, is the disproportion between the bitterness with which they debate their differences of opinion in my presence—though they have long since ceased to do so among themselves—and the frequently minimal differences in substance. It is actually the consistent characters among the writers who are the worst of all; but in the interests of professional solidarity, they are hardly ever exposed. I have often wondered whether my particular irenic nature is not linked to the contemplative spirit engendered by the use of drugs. The universal reservations toward one's own way of life, which are forced upon every writer—without exception, I believe—by the contemplation of the situation in Western Europe, are related in a bitter way to the attitude toward other human beings that is induced in the drugtaker by the poison he takes. And to take the full measure of the ideas and impulses that preside over the writing of this diary, I need only hint at my growing willingness to take my own life. This willingness is not the product of a panic attack; but profound though its connection is with my exhaustion from my struggles on the economic front, it would not have been conceivable without my feeling of having lived a life whose dearest wishes had been granted, wishes that admittedly I have only now come to recognize as the original text on a page subsequently covered with the handwritten marks of my destiny.

The morning of the same day. Further thoughts about wishes. People would have fewer doubts about the assertion that everyone has his dearest wishes granted, if they would only realize that these wishes are almost always unconscious—in other words, are different from the wishes they know of and which (they may rightly complain) they have not been granted. Fairy tales make this very clear with the motif of the three wishes. We have no right to be astonished at the folly and shortsightedness of the use people make of those magic wishes. For we are those people. Except that our dearest wishes are never present in our minds, as they are to the lucky fairy-tale characters who have them granted; we become aware of them only as events in the past, and often we find that they have unfortunately come true and that we have been duped. The true characteristic of these wishes, however, was that no price was too high for what one desired; and in retrospect these wishes can best be recognized by the fact that this limitless willingness was actually exploited and by the actual cost of their fulfillment. Of the three greatest wishes of my life, the one I recognized soonest was the wish for distant and, above all, long journeys. This was also the wish I became aware of most quickly before it was granted, if only by the violence of my reaction. At first it may simply have been the irresistible impulse to flee Germany, a desire that gripped people during the war years with the same force as the wish for an automobile during the inflation and the period of reconstruction. Then came the moment when I had enough money to enable me, in an emergency, to spend some time abroad; I arranged to spend time in Capri with some friends. I have a very clear memory of the shock I received when I saw the headline in an evening paper in the hand of a woman selling newspapers on the corner of Friedrichsstrasse and Unter den Linden: "Ban on Foreign Travel." A regulation had been issued restricting foreign travel to those people who were able to deposit a sum that was perhaps tenfold what I had available. The regulation was due to come into force in two or three days' time. It was evident to me that, in the circumstances, I could not wait for the departure date that I had agreed on with my friends and that happened to fall just before the deadline. Only when I came to unpack my suitcase in Capri or Naples did I discover what a mad rush I'd been in: I had just packed whatever came immediately to hand. Many essentials were missing, while a hundred superfluous things had been brought along. Yet the real turning point of that trip was not my swift resolve to leave Berlin (my friends managed, with difficulty, to leave a few days later) but, five or six weeks later, when my financial resources were exhausted, my decision to put up with anything as long as I did not have to leave the island. I even considered in all seriousness the possibility of living in one of its large caves, and the images I still have of this are so vivid that today I no longer know whether they were mere fantasies or were based on one of the adventure stories that abound on the island. There have been similar reports of someone actually doing this during the war. In this way my wish was granted with my stay on the island, and later because of it. For I am convinced that to have lived for a long time on Capri gives you a claim on distant journeys, so strong is the belief of anyone who has long lived there that he has all the threads in his hand and that in the fullness of time everything he needs will come to him.

Juan-les-Pins, May 5, in the morning. Before continuing with my three wishes, I want to write down my thoughts about Hemingway. Entirely successful, entirely meaningful ventures can sometimes best be perceived when placed next to complete failures, things that are completely banal. Compare Hemingway with a bad writer. A bad writer is a writer who always says more than he thinks. A good writer—and here we must be careful if we wish to arrive at any real insight—is a writer who does not say more than he thinks. This definition will probably be read as a request for "clear and simple writing"; people will imagine that a good writer is one who says exactly what he thinks. But it is this obvious inference that must be avoided at all costs. The foundation of every insight into questions of style is the realization that there is no such thing as "saying what you think." The fact is that speech is not so much the expression as the making real of thought, a process that subjects thought to the profoundest modifications—much as running toward a goal is not just the expression of a wish to reach it, but a making real, a process that likewise subjects the wish to profound modification. Yet the way these modifications turn out—whether they ennoble the wish, refine it, or allow it to become too vague and general—depends on the writer's training regimen. The more he disciplines his body, and the more he limits his body to running and avoids superfluous, uncoordinated, or slack movements, the more his gait will itself become a criterion of the goal of his wish, will refine it, or drop it if it is not worth the trouble. The magic of Hemingway is his ability to make these phenomena, which normally only the practiced eye can discern in a rigorously and intelligently trained body, visible in his style. It would be a mistake to overemphasize individual technical achievements, such as his skill in knowing what to omit, or his talent for dialogue. His prose presents us with the great drama of an education in right thinking through correct writing. He does not say more than he thinks, and hence the whole power of his writing redounds to the benefit of what he really thinks.

As I returned, dead tired, from the Casino de la Lotée in Nice to Juanles-Pins by bus on the night of May 5, an illuminating etymological insight occurred to me. The French say *allure* [walk, gait, bearing]; we say *Haltung*. Both words come from the idea of walking. But in order to say the same thing (and just how little it is the "same" can be seen from this observation), the French emphasize the process of walking—*allure*—while the Germans talk of its interruption—*Haltung* [posture, stance, attitude].

On the way here, I spent the night with Egon in Basel.[1] We shared a room; and although it was after two or even three A.M. when we went to bed and our train was due to leave at seven in the morning, we stayed awake talking about this and that. It so happened that I expressed for the first time an idea that had struck me several times during the previous few weeks. Egon made a comment about the Bauhaus style that coincided with the negative opinions I used to hold. His criticism was based on his aesthetic reservations about the formal idiom of Bauhaus furniture, and this gave me my cue to indicate how—even though my views had not become fully clarified—it had given me a remarkable insight into the famous manorial style of the very rich. And in fact, the intentions of the Bauhaus people and their like can be seen far less well from the theories they proclaim than from the hidden laws that determined the architectural style of the immediately preceding generations. If you enter one of the bourgeois rooms of the 1880s, the main impression you receive, for all the "coziness" it may well radiate, is one that says, "You have no business here." You have no business there because there is not an inch on which the owner has not left a trace of his own. What this means is made clear enough by a fine phrase of Brecht's. "Erase the traces" is the refrain of the first poem in his *Lesebuch für Städtebewohner* [Reader for Citydwellers]. Here, in the bourgeois room the opposite behavior has become an ethos in the strictest sense—that is to say, a habit. Indeed, leaving traces is not just a habit, but the primal phenomenon of all the habits that are involved in inhabiting a place. What is possible among the pieces of furniture of the Bauhaus is no more than a bare lodging [*ein Hausen*] when compared with life in a bourgeois dwelling, whose interior compels the inhabitant to adopt a maximum number of habits; and indeed these habits are better calculated to celebrate the interior in which he lives than to do justice to himself. This will be readily understood by anyone who still remembers the absurd fuss people made in those days when anything was broken. Even their way of showing their anger—and this emotion, which is gradually starting to atrophy, was one they could turn on and off to spectacular effect—was, above all, the reaction of someone denied his habits. The modern style of building, whatever else may be said of it, has now created rooms in which it is hard to leave such traces (this is why glass and metal have become so important) and which make it almost impossible to acquire habits in the first place. This is why the rooms are empty and often adjustable at will.

May 6, evening. Lay around yesterday with Gert and Egon. We spoke about experiences of love, and in the course of this conversation I understood something for the first time in my life: every time I've experienced a great love, I've undergone a change so fundamental that I've amazed myself and have been forced to realize that the man who said such unexpected things and behaved in such unpredictable ways was myself. This is based on the fact that a genuine love makes me resemble the woman I love. I was delighted to hear Gert confirm this so emphatically, even though she did so by asserting that this was the true mark of feminine love in general. This transformation into the realm of the similar—which is so indispensable that in the view of the Church it has to be guaranteed by the sacrament of marriage, for nothing makes people resemble each other more than living together in marriage—was something I experienced most powerfully in my relationship with Asja, with the result that I discovered many things in myself for the first time. On the whole, however, the three great loves of my life have influenced me not just chronologically, in terms of periodization, but also in terms of experience. I have come to know three different women in the course of my life, and three different men in myself.[2] To write the story of my life would mean describing the rise and fall of these three men and the compromise among them—one could also say, the triumvirate—that represents my life.

Sanary, May 13, 1931. I wonder whether the enjoyment of the world of images isn't fed by a sullen defiance of knowledge. I gaze out over the landscape. Before me lies the sea, which in the bay is as smooth as a mirror; forests extend up to the hilltop, an immobile, silent mass; to one side, ruined castle walls stand there as they have for centuries; the sky is cloudless—a heavenly blue, as the phrase goes. This is what the dreamer who immerses himself in this landscape wants to see. The fact that the sea rises and falls in thousands upon thousands of waves every moment; that the forests tremble anew every second, from their roots to the very last leaf; that in the stones of the castle ruins, there is a constant crumbling and crashing; that in the sky, gases surge invisibly to and fro in conflict with each other before they condense into clouds; that science pursues all this movement into the innermost heart of matter, sees in atoms nothing but electron storms—all this he must forget and wishes to deny so as to surrender to the images that will give him peace, rest, eternity. Every gnat that hums in his ears, every gust of wind that makes him shiver, everything near that strikes him gives the lie to his dreams, but every distance rebuilds them again. They spring to life at every mountain ridge in the dusk, or every lighted window. And the dream appears at its most perfect when he succeeds in removing the sting from movement itself, in translating the trembling of the leaves above him into the top of a tree, the flitting and darting of the birds above his head into a flock of migrating birds. To command Nature herself to stand still in the name of faded images—this is the black magic of sentimentality. But to utter a call that will freeze it anew is the gift of poets.

In the evening, a brief conversation with Speyer sitting next to a fire in the hearth.[3] As I watched the flame licking around the logs just as we were talking about a novel, the two topics of conversation merged in my mind. I suddenly imagined that the way the logs were piled represented the true model of composition in the novel. The plot must be just as loosely arranged, and should be designed for consumability in just the same way. In other words, it must be completely opposed to architectonic—and, even more, monumental—construction. Of course, the Germans in their novels have never been able to free themselves from the idea of architecture. Even Gottfried Keller lacked the touch to pile up the logs of his story artistically like Balzac or Dostoevsky. The actual adversary of this novelistic technique—which produces books that can warm the reader as much as an open fire—is the great constructor Flaubert, whose works have the same impact on the reader as a splendid Delft stove in which there is no fire.

Juan-les-Pins, May 17, 1931. Attempted to set down some of what was said about Eva Hermann[4] in conversation partly with Wilhelm and partly with Maria Speyer.

May 21. Went with Speyer by car to Saint-Paul de Vence. One ought to spend ten days in this extraordinary place sometime. Unfortunately, however remote and self-contained a place may be, nowadays a chink in its armor will soon be discovered. I had no sooner said to Speyer—we were alone together briefly, since Wissing's and Speyer's wives had gone on ahead— "Quel bonheur que ça ne soit pas encore découvert par les cinéastes" [How lucky that the place has not yet been discovered by film enthusiasts], than Willy Fritsch and Lilian Harvey suddenly appeared in the marketplace with a large party.[5] Anyway, the place can't really be described as undiscovered;

otherwise, how would it have acquired a celebrated tea room run by two young girls, friends, lesbians, with candles lighting up the interior and old-fashioned copper kettles, ladles, and similar implements to give it cachet. Still, it is all very charming and tasteful. In addition, the tea salon is combined with the sale of postcards and an antique shop. And just outside the town, in front of the gates, there are two inns. Of these we saw the Colombe d'Or, a beautifully maintained hostelry, with gardens laid out in terraces going down to the valley floor, and tables standing ready for guests under blossoming orange trees surrounded by flower beds. Without seeing anything, the Berlin film company thundered around the market square, which satisfies all the requirements for show simply by the unsurpassable economy of a tiny arcade and a single Empire fountain, and whose very modesty succeeds in bringing out the very best in the tiny dimensions of the town. Of course, it unobtrusively takes its revenge, since, as I suddenly discovered, it has found room in the confined space for no fewer than two sundials. Neither of these has an inscription.—Some of this reminds me of San Gimignano, but the authority of the fortifications is greater here. It allows no space for the development of any splendor, or even leisureliness. Even the marketplace is tiny. And amid the network of crisscrossing streets, there is not a single spot that invites the visitor to linger—apart, that is, from one place in front of the church and the spaces around the fortifications. The strict, uninterrupted contrast between house and street completely dominates the architecture; all mediations are avoided, and even the presumably indispensable presence of shops has actually been rendered invisible. So unified is the row of house façades that you can scarcely tell whether they are inhabited, let alone whether they conceal stores or workshops. At most you catch a glimpse of a room with a man and a woman sorting orange blossoms, or laying them out to dry. The ten days I wished for in Saint-Paul would certainly be necessary to get to know the place. In such a town, there is hardly anything that does not lie concealed and would not be worth the trouble of discovering: the narrow shafts between the houses that frame the green depths of the landscape beyond like a chimney; the sundials affixed at right angles to two gabled walls on the market square; the view through the monumental arches of the gateways; the fringed profile of the ruins of the town ramparts. In a courtyard that made us pause in surprise as we passed by, and above which it was impossible to see the sky—we were standing at an angle, and the houses here were very tall—someone had put up a poster with the one word "Cinema" on it. The painter may have painted the word with a stencil, or perhaps had just designed it himself, since only this clumsy, rustic lettering would have matched the dull browns and grays of this shady neighborhood so perfectly. Even if it had been the courtyard of a Lyons monastery, the monks would scarcely have been able to fix a more inexorably styled pious motto over the portal. We stood around for a long time on the ancient ramparts and gazed down into the countryside lying beneath an overcast sky. In the even light, all the lines that human labor had incised in the landscape emerged more starkly. Hedges and furrows idiosyncratically drew their lines and angles. But one would have had to know all the plants by name in order to be able to decode their geometry. Indeed, faced with this supremely cultivated landscape, the untutored townsman stands baffled, like a Westerner confronted by a page of Chinese script. To think that such ignorance is the only common foundation of the majority of descriptions! In most cases, the further apart these Provençal farms are, the more admirably they are built, and the more you realize how snugly they fit into the landscape and how natural their forms are, compared to the inexorably geometric lines of the groves, beds, and fields. The town has the *grandezza* that work on the land confers on the villages: before nightfall hardly anyone is to be seen on the streets.

June 3, 1931. In front of the Potinière in Le Lavandou. A very cold wind is blowing. I am there with Brecht, Hesse-Burri, Elisabeth Hauptmann, the Brentanos, and Marie Grossmann.[6] Of course, I could record all sorts of things from my conversations with Brecht. The most diverse topics were touched on: the international society of materialist friends of the Hegelian dialectic; the idea of a detective play; the trial of Friedrich Schiller; and last of all Proust, in an hour-long conversation yesterday at which Marie Grossmann was present. But I prefer to describe a different scene, one in which my own behavior is quite inscrutable. I had gone for a walk on my own to Saint Clair. It was the first for a long time—the first walk, not just the first one on my own, for a long time. On the way, I was struck by the dog roses. I picked one; it did not disappoint me, since it had a wonderful fragrance. I removed the thorns from the end of the stalk and carried it in my hand. On the way back I passed a bush full of peonies. They reminded me vividly of the bunch of flowers Jula Cohn once gave me years ago for my birthday; that, too, had consisted entirely of peonies. With some difficulty I broke off a small twig and put it, together with the dog rose, between the pages of Jouhandeau's *Journal du Coiffeur,* which I was carrying. On the way, as I was passing the Villa Mar Belo, where Brecht and the others were staying, I thought I would stop in. I did so, even though I said to myself that they would still be at table. And in the somewhat labile state this first walk on my own for such a long time had induced in me, I probably did so at least partly because I had grown tired of following a pretty girl in a red beach-jacket and blue trousers who had been walking along the highroad in front of me in the twilight. The worst thing was that she suddenly stopped to talk to a man she had met, so that I would have been forced to walk on past her. So I went down the side path to the villa and entered the hall. They had seen me coming, and at the door to the dining room Brecht came out to meet me. Despite my protestations, he refused to go back to the table and took me into the next room. We stayed there and talked for about two hours, partly on our own, and partly with the others, mainly just with Frau Grossmann, until I felt it was time to go. As I picked up my book the flowers peeked out of it, and when someone joked about them my embarrassment grew, since even before I had entered the house I had been wondering why I was arriving bearing flowers and whether I shouldn't throw them away. But I hadn't done so, God knows why. There was undoubtedly an element of defiance in it. Needless to say, I realized there would be no opportunity to give my rose to Elisabeth Hauptmann, so I decided I would at least hoist it like a flag. But this idea was a complete failure. In the face of Brecht's ironic jokes, I no less ironically presented him with the peony, keeping a firm grip on the dog rose. Of course, Brecht refused to accept it. I ended up putting the peony unobtrusively into a large vase full of blue flowers next to me. The dog rose, however, I threw in among the blue flowers from above. There it stuck, looking as if it were growing out of the blue flowers—a veritable botanical curiosity. And there it remained quite clearly. So the bunch of flowers had hoisted my flag after all, and had to take the place of her for whom it was intended.

The previous evening, a conversation with Brecht, Brentano, and Hesse in the Café du Centre. The conversation turned to Trotsky; Brecht maintained there were good reasons for thinking that Trotsky was the greatest living European writer. We exchanged episodes from his books. Brecht contributed the following anecdote. It concerned a particular account of Lenin's first days in Leningrad, as reported in Trotsky's book. Trotsky tells how completely isolated Lenin was in the Communist party immediately after his arrival, and how finally there was to be a particularly important vote, at which Lenin declared that he would leave if he were outvoted. Brecht was talking to Brik about this, and asked him with some anxiety what he thought of such monstrous proceedings, and what he thought of Lenin's undisciplined reaction. And now Brik's reply—Brecht repeated it full of admiration: "That was like the tree trunk saying to the foliage, 'I'm leaving.'"[7]

June 6. Brecht regards Kafka as a prophetic writer. He says that he knows him as well as his own pocket. But what he means by this is not so easy to find out. So much is clear: he believes that Kafka has just one theme, and that the richness of Kafka as a writer is simply the rich variety of this one theme. According to Brecht, this theme, in its most general sense, is astonishment. The astonishment of a man who feels that huge shifts are in the offing in every aspect of life, without being able to find a niche for himself in the new order of things. For this new order—if I have understood Brecht correctly—is governed by the dialectical laws that dictate the life of the masses to themselves and to the individual. But the individual as such must react with astonishment tinged with panic-stricken horror to the almost incomprehensible deformations of life that are revealed by the emergence of these laws.—Kafka, it seems to me, is dominated by this to the point that he is quite incapable of portraying any event without distortion. In other words, everything he describes makes statements about something other than itself. The permanent, visionary presence of distorted things is met with the writer's own gaze, full of inconsolable earnestness and despair. As a result of this stance, Brecht is inclined to regard Kafka as the only authentic Bolshevist writer. Kafka's fixation on his one and only theme can give the reader an impression of obsessiveness. But in reality this impression is only a sign that Kafka has broken with the tradition of pure narrative prose. It may be that his prose proves nothing; but it is so constructed that it can be inserted into passages of argument at any time. This is reminiscent of the form of the Haggadah. That is what Jews call the stories and anecdotes in the Talmud that serve to elucidate and confirm the teachings—the Halachah.[8] Admittedly, the teachings as such are never enunciated by Kafka. The only possibility is to read them from the astonishing behavior of people—behavior that is either born of fear or that causes it in others.

One can gain some insight into Kafka by observing that he attributes the most interesting forms of behavior to animals. The reader follows these animal tales for a fair distance without even noticing that they do not deal with human beings at all. Then, when the animal is identified for the first time—as a mouse or a mole—you are suddenly jolted and realize how far you have drifted away from the continent of human beings. As far away from it as a future society will be. Incidentally, it is worth paying attention to the kinds of animals Kafka chooses to embody his ideas. They always dwell in the interior of the earth, or, like the beetle in "Die Verwandlung" [The Metamorphosis], they are creatures that hide away on the ground, in cracks and crannies. This scurrying away seems to the author the only appropriate behavior for the isolated members of his generation and their context, with their ignorance of the law.

Brecht contrasts Kafka—and the figure of K.—with Schweik: the man who is astonished by everything with the one who is astonished by nothing. Schweik puts to the test the monstrous nature of the existence into which he has been placed by making it seem as if nothing is impossible for him. In his experience, conditions are so completely bereft of laws that he has long since abandoned the expectation that laws might be found. Kafka, on the other hand, comes up against the law at every turn; indeed, one could even say that he bloodies his brow smashing up against the law (see the Mole, and see also p. 213);[9] but it is no longer the law governing the real world of things in which he lives, or any world of things whatsoever. It is the law of a new order in which all the things in which it expresses itself are misshapen, a law that deforms all things and all the people it touches.

June 7. In conversation with Brentano the other day, Brecht let fall a remark that seems to me to be worth preserving. Brentano was in the midst of one of his blustering speeches about the revolutionizing of the intellectual workers, the situation of the intelligentsia, and so forth, when Brecht interrupted rather fiercely. What was wrong with the position of the intellectuals, and what prospects could the revolution hold out to them? "The intelligentsia," he said, "is not overworked. And even if there are doctors and lawyers who are slaving away, what does that matter? It's a kind of work that suits them; it cannot be compared with the work of the proletariat by any stretch of the imagination. And so what if they ask themselves what they should do when they're sixty and haven't saved anything? That's really going too far!" he said angrily. "For God's sake, let them croak! It's far too late then, anyway. It would be better if they died right away." A day or so later, we touched on the same subject when I spoke about the lack of pretentiousness of the Surrealists—a trait that made it easier to form a grouping in France and that was precluded in Germany by the far-reaching demands made by German writers. To be sure, it is only right for a collective to moderate its demands; for the individual, it is mainly a mistake.

June 8. A truly unusual afternoon with Brecht. A discussion about "propositions"—the kind of propositions that one hears from Brecht almost every day—took a strange turn, thanks to an objection from me. I disagreed with his search for "ideas" [*Vorstellungen*] and instead called for a study of modes of behavior. I focused on my favorite topic, dwelling [*das Wohnen*]. Brecht entered into the discussion enthusiastically and produced an extraordinary account of his manner of dwelling—which I then followed up with a different one, without identifying it as my own. I kept a record of what was said and so can repeat it accurately. The two accounts were seen to be dialectical and were represented as polar opposites. Brecht's starting point was a "sympathetic" [*mitahmend*] dwelling.[10] This is a mode of dwelling that "shapes" its environment, arranges it in a suitable, adaptable, and compliant way—a world in which the dweller is at home in his own way. Brecht contrasted this with a different approach: the habit of always behaving like a guest. Such a person refuses to take responsibility for what he makes use of; he feels invited by the chair on which he sits, and when he gets up he feels himself to be disinvited. At this point, I set out to explain a different dialectic of living. I managed to convince Brecht that my account was not just a paraphrase of his own views. I made a distinction between a way of dwelling that gives the inhabitant a maximum of habits, and a way of dwelling that gives him a minimum. Both extremes are pathological. The probable difference between this approach and the one outlined by Brecht is that the attitudes he described tend to diverge, whereas those I defined tend to converge. The mode of dwelling that reinforces habits is the one imagined by the landladies of rented accommodations. For them, a human being becomes a function of the activities that the furnishings require of him. The person inhabiting a dwelling has a completely different relationship to the world of things from the relationship involved in "sympathetic" dwelling. The objects are taken seriously (whether or not they are "property" in the legal sense), whereas for "sympathetic" dwelling they have roughly the same meaning as a stage set. We might even say that one mode takes place in a stage set; the other, in an interior. What is less easily defined is the element of habit in "sympathetic" dwelling, whereas for living as a guest, it is completely captured by Nietzsche's statement, "I love ephemeral habits."[11] Last, the fourth mode of dwelling—the dwelling that gives you the fewest habits—is just simple lodging [Hausen]. This idea, too, appears best-developed in the mentality of landladies. At its center are the idea of the bad lodger and the concept of wear and tear. For simple lodging is destructive dwelling—a mode of dwelling that undoubtedly prevents the development of any habits, because it constantly clears away its basis: the objects.

June 10. A few days ago, a conversation with Speyer's wife, who reported this astounding statement by Eva Hermann from the period of her greatest depression: "The fact that I'm unhappy doesn't mean that I have to run around with a face full of wrinkles." This made a number of things clear to me. Above all, that my recently acquired peripheral contact with the world of these creatures—Gert, Eva Hermann, and so on—is only a belated and feeble echo of one of the fundamental experiences of my life: that of semblance [Schein]. I expressed this view yesterday in the course of a conversation with Speyer, who has also begun to reflect about these people, and who made the astonishing comment that they had no conception of honor—or, rather, that their code of honor was actually to say everything they thought. This is very true, and basically it is merely a proof of the obligation they feel to semblance. For this "saying everything" means destroying what has been said. Or, better: once these people have destroyed what has been said, it is turned into a subject of conversation. Only when it has become semblance-like are they able to digest it. Speyer and I also spoke about the fact that the stance of this circle is very much the complement of that attitude of pseudo-maturity, pseudo-knowledge, characteristic of people who have the answer to everything. The microcosm of a false childhood in which these people shield themselves from life is the other side of the coin from the would-be gigantic scale on which others (I'm thinking of Lawrence above all) experience life. Speyer's friend Max Mohr must be a person of this type.[12] For him, everything that followed Mycenae is decadence, and today tourism seems to him to represent the greatest guarantee of health.

June 12. Yesterday, with Speyer's wife up in Mar Belo. It was the first real contact between Brecht and Speyer, and I was very pleased that it went off so well. I had not actually been anxious about it, given Brecht's behavior during the past few days. But it was a stroke of luck that Brecht started talking about his childhood and hence about things to which Speyer feels especially sympathetic. Above all, he talked about the school of strategy from which he had graduated: the battles between different school classes at the bleaching grounds on the River Lech, and the battles with tin soldiers in the garden. The incidental stories he told about his school life reminded me very powerfully of Kraus's attitude toward school. "We learned," Brecht said, "everything we needed later on. In our eyes, the teacher was simply the human being as such: vigilant, bad-tempered, unjust. And the faking, cheating, and inventing excuses—all this had to be learned. We had to do our English homework during math class and our German homework during English class—all this had to be learned." But as already mentioned, he talked mainly about the battles with tin soldiers. "There were set-piece encounters with four or five thousand such soldiers. The battles had to follow strict rules: at every move the infantry was allowed to advance a distance equivalent to its own height, while the cavalry could move twice its own height. Of course, only soldiers were usable when you were on the attack. Other tin soldiers would have deprived the conflict of every illusion." Brecht told us about a march that had acquired historical fame: one of his friends had succeeded in moving a 300-strong body of troops over a meadow without any cover in such a way that 180 were still alive at the end of it. While these troops were advancing, they came under fire from cannons that pelted them with tiny missiles (crackers). The secret was to hit them broadside; otherwise they did not fall over. If we reflect that just moving the soldiers around manually on that march must have taken hours, this really was a great achievement. In these battles, villages were marked by strips of cardboard, rivers were crossed on pontoons, and tree roots represented mountains. Moreover, Brecht claimed that in those days he had learned by heart a whole series of the battles of world history—that he had studied *De Bello Gallico* and all the battles of Frederick the Great.[13] He believed that he could probably reconstruct the Battle of Waterloo even now.

This morning he made his appearance at nine, and, as luck would have it, he continued where he had left off with stories from his youth. Today, though, he talked about the later years. He was "very cheerful," as he said himself, because the political news from Berlin had shaken his conviction that Germany would have to wait for years for a revolutionary situation to arise. Everything could turn around very suddenly, he thought. And he based this prognosis on some very interesting theses about the masses, which I will simply set down here. The intelligence of the capitalists grows in proportion to their isolation; that of the masses, in proportion to their solidarity. The proletariat's sense of reality is incorruptible. You can give workers as many assurances as you wish, but if they come to the conclusion that the person giving these assurances cannot fulfill them, even if he wanted to, then they will simply proceed as if nothing had happened—very much in contrast to intellectuals. Moreover, capitalism had now reached the point where even its well-intentioned promises would find no credence with the masses.—The masses wished to be treated as individuals: this was the main dialectical proposition to bear in mind when dealing with them. For all these assertions Brecht appealed to the period at the outbreak of the revolution in Munich, when he had effectively been in charge of a military ward for patients with venereal disease, even though formally he was only a junior doctor.[14] Of all the wards, this was the only one in which patients were not allowed to leave the barracks—a regulation that could not be enforced anywhere else. Brecht was very funny in his description of the various methods he used to keep the patients where they were. He first tried to persuade the masses to organize, and to get the cleverest and strongest of their leaders on his side. He then tried to join with the masses in a united front of illegality: he procured blankets for them through deception, coal through a break-in, and so on. What helped him most was that he was better at giving injections than the other doctors. "I could do it skillfully—but I could also do it unskillfully." And he acted out a splendid solo scene for me, showing how, when he had to inject a patient who had pulled a fast one, he would gradually work himself into a state while preparing the injection, so that the patient began to worry about how deeply upset the doctor was and to realize how very unpleasant this procedure might be, just from the way the doctor washed out the syringe. Brecht sometimes took measures that affected the collective as a whole; one evening, for example, he confiscated all the blankets in one dormitory.—He also gave very curious reasons in favor of such collective measures, in our discussion about the German situation. If he were on the Berlin executive committee, he would devise a five-day plan according to which at least 200,000 Berliners would be eliminated within that period. Simply because this would ensure that "people get involved." "If this were done, I would know that at least 50,000 proletarians would have been made to participate actively."

June 17, 1931. The following emerged from several conversations with Brecht about the Epic Theater. Speyer was present at some of these conversations, and Carola Neher at others.[15] Brecht seems to regard Georg Kaiser (alongside Strindberg) as the greatest technician among modern dramatists, and thinks that *Der gerettete Alkibiades* [Alcibiades Saved], in particular, is one of the greatest achievements and models of the Epic Theater.[16] He describes Kaiser as the last idealist dramatist, but claims that in his works dramatic technique has reached a level that makes it unusable for idealist purposes. He is the last dramatist before the great change. Other examples of Epic Theater from Calderón and Shakespeare.[17] I referred him particularly to *El mayor monstruo, los celos* [The Greatest Monster, Jealousy], and *La gran Cenobia* [The Great Zenobia], and Brecht asked me if I would at some point prepare a description of these plays for publication. And then Shakespeare. He kept returning to his favorite passage—that great speech by a mother to her son, the speech that is supposed to induce Coriolanus to withdraw from Rome and that achieves its purpose even though it could hardly have been more wretched and incoherent. "It's a miracle," Brecht says of Shakespeare, "where he could have got this speech from; he must have spent enough time looking for it." And yet it is this speech that leads the mother to her goal. How this comes about is explained by Coriolanus in the sentence which sums up the situation: "I have sat too long," he says, and nothing more.[18] Further examples from Shakespeare. I talk about Gloucester's leap from the cliff that isn't a cliff;[19] it was this episode that first gave me an inkling of other possibilities for the stage than were contained in Freytag's *Die Technik des Dramas* [Dramatic Technique]. It might not be the worst idea to explicate the laws of Epic Theater by comparing them with that book. I also gleaned a very important idea from a remark made in the course of a conversation between Brecht and Neher on the journey from Le Lavandou to Marseilles. Brecht was saying that he would like little descriptions from people about human "behavior" taken from direct experience. It appears that Neher had been making similar experiments of this sort for some time. Brecht was keen to encourage her in this. She should simply write down what she had been able to discover. "And above all, no punch lines. That would ruin them." In my view, this would tell us a lot not only about the Epic Theater but also about Brecht. He seems to hate and abhor nothing so much as activities and modes of behavior that bring their own reward.—Very curious is what Brecht has to say about *Romeo and Juliet* in the context of a defense of the Epic Theater. The conversation was triggered by a comment that Speyer had made about the play years ago—about how very significant and also how bold it was of Shakespeare to have introduced Romeo as the most passionate lover of Rosaline in order to show how much he is in love with Juliet.[20] Brecht instantly added an astonishing variation to this theme by saying that Romeo was not just the most passionate but also the most fortunate lover—namely, a totally exhausted one, quite bereft of his manly powers. And if Brecht is to be believed, this really seemed to be the "epic" theme of the play—namely, that it was primarily for physiological reasons that the couple were unable to come together. For just as "it is well known" that the sexual act does not work if the partners have only sexual intentions, so too the love of Romeo and Juliet failed because they were trying too hard, were too eager.

June 21. On the last day of our journey from Marseilles to Paris, we paused for a break in the open air. The Brentanos stayed on the road, while I went higher, climbing up an embankment. I then lay down under a tree. There was a bit of a breeze; the tree was a willow or a poplar—in any case, a tree with very pliant, swaying boughs. As I looked up into the foliage and followed its movements, it suddenly occurred to me how many images and metaphors are nesting in a single tree. The branches and the treetop sway up and down reflectively, and bend away in rejection; the boughs, depending on the way the wind is blowing, lean toward you or fly upward; the mass of leaves resists the demands of the wind, recoils from them, or comes to meet them; the trunk has the solid ground on which it stands; and one leaf casts a shadow on another.

Postscript to Brecht's studies on dwelling and ideas in general: dwelling in a hotel—the idea that life is a novel.

Written May–June 1931; unpublished in Benjamin's lifetime. *Gesammelte Schriften,* VI, 422–441. Translated by Rodney Livingstone.

Notes

1. Egon Wissing, a physician, was Benjamin's cousin. They were neighbors on Prinzregentenstrasse in Berlin. In 1932, when Benjamin again contemplated taking his own life, he wrote a farewell letter to Wissing and made him the executor of his will. Egon's wife, Gert, died in 1933.
2. According to Gershom Scholem, the three women were presumably Dora Benjamin (Walter's wife), Jula Cohn, and, Asja Lacis. For more information on Benjamin's relations with them, see the Chronologies to volumes 1 and 2 of this edition.
3. Wilhelm Speyer (1887–1952) was a novelist and dramatist whom Benjamin accompanied on a motoring tour of Italy in 1929 and with whom he collaborated on a novel and several plays.
4. Eva Hermann (1901–1978) was a graphic artist friendly with Klaus and Erika Mann.
5. Willy Fritsch (1901–1973) and Lilian Harvey (1907–1968) were prominent German film actors who had recently appeared together in two popular films, *Die Drei von der Tankstelle* (1930) and *Der Kongreß tanzt* (1931).
6. Emil Hesse-Burri was a writer and producer who collaborated with Brecht on his *Saint Joan of the Stockyards.* Elisabeth Hauptmann (1897–1973) was a major

collaborator of Brecht's—on *The Threepenny Opera, Mahagonny,* and other works. Bernhard von Brentano (1901–1964) was a left-wing journalist and novelist.

7. Osip Maximovich Brik (1888–1945) was a friend and associate of the poet Vladimir Mayakovsky. Originally a Formalist writer, he later helped to found the Levy front iskusstva (Left Front of Art), known as LEF—a Marxist literary group.

8. The term *Lehre* figured prominently in Benjamin's discussions with Gershom Scholem during the World War I years. It signifies something between "religious doctrine" and "teachings."

9. K. is the protagonist of Kafka's novel *Das Schloß* (The Castle). Schweik is the protagonist of the satirical novel *The Good Soldier Schweik* (3 vols., 1920–1933), by the Czech writer Jaroslav Hašek (1883–1923). See also "The Burrow," in Franz Kafka, *The Collected Short Stories* (Harmondsworth: Penguin, 1983), p. 328; and "The Great Wall of China," ibid., p. 244. "The Mole" is Benjamin's name for the narrator of "The Burrow." His page reference is to Franz Kafka, *Beim Bau der Chinesischen Mauer* (Berlin: Kiepenheuer, 1931).

10. Brecht's word *mitahmend* is a coinage combining elements of *nachahmend* ("imitative") and *Mitgefühl* ("sympathy").

11. Nietzsche, *Die fröhliche Wissenschaft* (The Gay Science), aphorism 295.

12. Max Mohr (1891–1944) was a physician and the author of novels and plays. He emigrated to China in 1934.

13. Julius Caesar's *De Bello Gallico* (On the Gallic War) is his account of the Romans' conquest of Gaul in 58–50 B.C.

14. Brecht had in fact been a medical orderly. The reference is to the socialist revolution of 1918–1919 in Munich.

15. Carola Neher (1905–1942) was an actress who performed in many of Brecht's plays, including the original version of *The Threepenny Opera.* She emigrated to the USSR in 1933, was arrested in 1939, and was murdered in one of the camps three years later.

16. Georg Kaiser (1878–1945) was one of the leading dramatists of the German Expressionist theater. His most important works include *Die Bürger von Calais* (The Burghers of Calais; 1914), *Von Morgens bis Mitternachts* (From Morn to Midnight; 1916), and the *Gas* trilogy, consisting of *Die Koralle* (The Coral; 1917), *Gas I* (1918), and *Gas II* (1920).

17. Pedro Calderón de la Barca (1600–1681) was one of the premier dramatists and poets of Spain's Golden Age. His best-known secular dramas include *El médico de su honra* (The Surgeon of His Honor; 1635), *La vida es sueño* (Life Is a Dream; 1635), *El alcalde de Zalamea* (The Mayor of Zalamea; ca. 1640), and *La hija del aire* (The Daughter of the Air; 1653).

18. See *Coriolanus,* Act 5, scene 3, line 131.

19. See *King Lear,* Act 4, scene 6.

20. See *Romeo and Juliet,* Act 1, scene 2.

Unpacking My Library

A Talk about Collecting

I am unpacking my library. Yes, I am. The books are not yet on the shelves, not yet touched by the mild boredom of order. I cannot march up and down their ranks to pass them in review before a friendly audience. You need not fear any of that. Instead, I must ask you to join me in the disorder of crates that have been wrenched open, the air saturated with wood dust, the floor covered with torn paper, to join me among piles of volumes that are seeing daylight again after two years of darkness, so that you may be ready to share with me a bit of the mood—certainly not an elegiac mood but, rather, one of anticipation—which these books arouse in a genuine collector. For such a man is speaking to you, and on closer scrutiny he proves to be speaking only about himself. Would it not be presumptuous of me if, in order to appear convincingly objective and matter-of-fact, I enumerated for you the main sections or prize pieces of a library—if I presented you with their history, or even their usefulness to a writer? I, for one, have in mind something less obscure, something more palpable than that; what I am really concerned with is giving you some insight into the relationship between a collector and his possessions, into collecting rather than a collection. If I do this by elaborating on the various ways of acquiring books, this is something entirely arbitrary. This or any other procedure is merely a dam against the spring tide of memories which surges toward any collector as he contemplates his possessions. Every passion borders on the chaotic, but the collector's passion borders on the chaos of memories. More than that: the chance, the fate, which suffuse the past before my eyes are conspicuously present in the accustomed confusion of these books. For what else is this collection but a disorder to which habit has accommodated itself to such an extent that it can appear as order? You have all heard of people whom the loss of their books has turned into invalids, or of those who in order to acquire books became criminals. These are the very areas in which any order is nothing more than a hovering above the abyss. "The only exact knowledge there is," said Anatole France, "is the knowledge of the date of publication and the format of books."[1] And indeed, if there is a counterpart to the confusion of a library, it is the order of its catalogue.

Thus, the life of a collector manifests a dialectical tension between the poles of disorder and order.

Naturally, his existence is tied to many other things as well: to a very mysterious relationship to ownership (something about which we shall have more to say later); also, to a relationship to objects which does not emphasize their functional, utilitarian value—that is, their usefulness—but studies and loves them as the scene, the stage, of their fate. The most profound enchantment for the collector is the locking of individual items within a magic circle in which they are frozen as the final thrill, the thrill of acquisition, passes over them. Everything remembered and thought, everything conscious, becomes the pedestal, the frame, the base, the lock of his property. The period, the region, the craftsmanship, the former ownership—for a true collector, the whole background of an item adds up to a magic encyclopedia whose quintessence is the fate of his object. In this circumscribed area, then, it may be surmised how the great physiognomists—and collectors are the physiognomists of the world of things—turn into interpreters of fate. One has only to watch a collector handle the objects in his glass case. As he holds them in his hands, he seems to be seeing through them into their distant past, as though inspired. So much for the magical side of the collector—his old-age image, I might call it.—*Habent sua fata libelli.* These words may have been intended as a general statement about books.[2] So books like *The Divine Comedy,* Spinoza's *Ethics,* and *The Origin of Species* have their fates. A collector, however, interprets this Latin saying differently. For him, not only books but also *copies of books* have their fates. And in this sense, the most important fate of a copy is its encounter with him, with his own collection. I am not exaggerating when I say that to a true collector the acquisition of an old book is its rebirth. This is the childlike element which, in a collector, mingles with the element of old age. For children can accomplish the renewal of existence in a hundred unfailing ways. Among children, collecting is only one process of renewal; other processes are the painting of objects, the cutting out of figures, the application of decals—the whole range of childlike modes of acquisition, from touching things to giving them names. To renew the old world—this is the collector's deepest desire when he is driven to acquire new things, and this is why a collector of older books is closer to the wellsprings of collecting than the acquirer of luxury editions. How do books cross the threshold of a collection and become the property of a collector? The history of their acquisition is the subject of the following remarks.

Of all the ways of acquiring books, writing them oneself is regarded as the most praiseworthy method. At this point, many of you will remember with pleasure the large library which Jean Paul's poor little schoolmaster Wutz gradually acquired by writing, himself, all the works whose titles interested him in book-fair catalogues; after all, he could not afford to buy them.[3] Writers are really people who write books not because they are poor, but because they are dissatisfied with the books which they could buy but do not like. You, ladies and gentlemen, may regard this as a whimsical definition of a writer. But everything said from the angle of a real collector is whimsical.—Of the customary modes of acquisition, the one most appropriate to a collector would be the borrowing of a book and the subsequent failure to return it. The book borrower of real stature whom we envisage here proves himself an inveterate collector of books not so much by the fervor with which he guards his borrowed treasures and by the deaf ear which he turns to all reminders from the everyday world of legality as by his failure to read these books. If my experience may serve as evidence, a man is more likely now and then to return a borrowed book than to read it. And the nonreading of books, you will object, should be characteristic of collectors? This is news to me, you may say. It is not news at all. Experts will bear me out when I say that it is the oldest thing in the world. Suffice it to quote the answer which Anatole France gave to a philistine who admired his library and then finished with the standard question, "And you have read all these books, Monsieur France?" "Not one-tenth of them. I don't suppose you eat off of your Sèvres china every day?"

Incidentally, I have put the right to such an attitude to the test. For years, for at least the first third of its existence, my library consisted of no more than two or three shelves which increased only by inches each year. This was its militant age, when no book was allowed to enter it without the certification that I had not read it. Thus, I might never have acquired a library extensive enough to be worthy of the name if there had not been the inflation. Suddenly the emphasis shifted; books acquired real value, or, at any rate, were difficult to obtain. At least, this is how it seemed in Switzerland. At the eleventh hour I sent my first major book orders from there and in this way was able to secure such irreplaceable items as *Der blaue Reiter* and Bachofen's *Sage von Tanaquil,* which could still be obtained from the publishers at that time.—[4] Well (so you may say), after exploring all these byways we should finally reach the wide highway of book acquisition— namely, the purchasing of books. This is indeed a wide highway, but not a comfortable one. The purchasing done by a book collector has very little in common with that done in a bookshop by a student getting a textbook, a man of the world buying a present for his lady, or a businessman intending to while away his next train journey. I have made my most memorable purchases on trips, as a transient. Property and possession belong to the tactical sphere. Collectors are people with a tactical instinct; their experience teaches them that when they capture a strange city, the smallest antique shop can be a fortress, the most remote stationery store a key position. How many cities have revealed themselves to me in the marches I undertook in pursuit of books!

Many of the most important purchases, though, are not made on the premises of a dealer. Catalogues play a far greater part. And even though the purchaser may be thoroughly acquainted with the book ordered from a catalogue, the individual copy always remains a surprise and the order always a bit of a gamble. There are grievous disappointments, but also happy finds. I remember, for instance, that I once ordered a book with colored illustrations for my old collection of children's books only because it contained fairy tales by Albert Ludwig Grimm and was published at Grimma, Thuringia. Grimma was also the place of publication of a book of fables edited by the same Albert Ludwig Grimm. With its sixteen illustrations, my copy of this book of fables was the only extant example of the early work of the great German book illustrator Lyser, who lived in Hamburg around the middle of the last century. Well, my reaction to the consonance of the names had been correct. In this case, too, I discovered the work of Lyser—namely, *Linas Märchenbuch,* a book which has remained unknown to his bibliographers and which deserves a more detailed reference than this first one I am introducing here.[5]

The acquisition of books is by no means a matter of money or expert knowledge alone. Not even both factors together suffice for the establishment of a real library, which is always somewhat impenetrable and at the same time uniquely itself. Anyone who buys from catalogues must have flair in addition to the qualities I have mentioned. Dates, place names, formats, previous owners, bindings, and the like: all these details must tell him something—not as dry, isolated facts, but as a harmonious whole. From the quality and intensity of this harmony, he must be able to recognize whether a book is for him or not.—An auction requires yet another set of qualities in a collector. To the reader of a catalogue, the book itself must speak—or possibly its previous ownership, if the provenance of the copy has been established. A man who wishes to participate at an auction must pay equal attention to the book and to his competitors, in addition to keeping a cool enough head to avoid being carried away in the competition. It frequently happens that someone gets stuck with a high purchase price because he kept raising his bid—more to assert himself than to acquire the book. On the other hand, one of the finest memories of a collector is the moment when he rescued a book to which he might never have given a thought, much less a wishful look, because he found it lonely and abandoned in the marketplace and bought it to give it its freedom—the way the prince bought a beautiful slave girl in the *Thousand and One Nights*. To a book collector, you see, the true freedom of all books is somewhere on his shelves.

To this day, Balzac's *Peau de chagrin* stands out from long rows of French volumes in my library as a memento of my most exciting experience at an auction. This happened in 1915 at the Rümann auction held by Emil Hirsch, one of the greatest of book experts and most distinguished of dealers. The edition in question appeared in 1838 in Paris, place de la Bourse. When I pick up my copy, I see not only its number in the Rümann Collection, but even the label of the shop in which the first owner bought the book more than ninety years ago, for one-eightieth of today's price. "Papeterie I. Flanneau," it says. A fine age, in which it was still possible to buy such a de luxe edition at a stationery dealer's! The steel engravings of this book were designed by the foremost French graphic artist and executed by the foremost engravers. But I was going to tell you how I acquired this book. I had gone to Emil Hirsch's for an advance inspection and had handled forty or fifty volumes; that particular volume had inspired in me the ardent desire to hold on to it forever. The day of the auction came. As chance would have it, in the sequence of the auction this copy of *La peau de chagrin* was preceded by a complete set of its illustrations printed separately on India paper. The bidders sat at a long table; diagonally across from me sat the man who was the focus of all eyes at the first bid, the famous Munich collector Baron von Simolin. He was greatly interested in this set, but he had rival bidders; in short, there was a spirited contest which resulted in the highest bid of the entire auction—far in excess of three thousand marks. No one seemed to have expected such a high figure, and all those present were quite excited. Emil Hirsch remained unconcerned, and whether he wanted to save time or was guided by some other consideration, he proceeded to the next item, with no one really paying attention. He called out the price, and with my heart pounding and with the full realization that I was unable to compete with any of those big collectors I bid a somewhat higher amount. Without arousing the bidders' attention, the auctioneer went through the usual routine—"Do I hear more?" and three bangs of his gavel, with an eternity seeming to separate each from the next—and proceeded to add the auctioneer's charge. For a student like me, the sum was still considerable. What happened the following morning at the pawnshop is no longer part of this story. I prefer to speak about another incident, which I would like to call the negative of an auction. It occurred last year at a Berlin auction. The books offered were a motley collection in both quality and subject matter, and only a number of rare works on occultism and natural philosophy were worthy of note. I bid for a number of them, but each time I noticed a gentleman in the front row who seemed only to have waited for my bid to counter with his own, evidently prepared to top any offer. After this had been repeated several times, I gave up all hope of acquiring the book which I was most interested in that day. It was the rare *Fragmente aus dem Nachlass eines jungen Physikers* [Posthumous Fragments by a Young Physicist], which Johann Wilhelm Ritter had published in two volumes at Heidelberg in 1810. This work has never been reprinted, but I have always considered its preface, in which the author-editor tells the story of his life in the guise of an obituary for a supposedly deceased unnamed friend—with whom he is really identical—as the most important example of personal prose in German Romanticism. Just as the item came up, I had an illumination. It was simple enough: since my bid was bound to give the item to the other man, I must not bid at all. I controlled myself and remained silent. What I had hoped for came about: no interest, no bid, and the book was put aside. I deemed it wise to let several days go by; and when I appeared on the premises after a week, I found the book in the secondhand department, and profited from the lack of interest when I acquired it.

Once you have approached the mountains of crates in order to mine the books from them and bring them to the light of day—or, rather, of night— what memories crowd in upon you! Nothing highlights the fascination of unpacking more clearly than the difficulty of stopping this activity. I had started at noon, and it was midnight before I had worked my way to the last crates. Now I put my hands on two volumes, bound in faded boards, which—strictly speaking—do not belong in a bookcase at all: two albums with paste-in pictures which my mother had glued in as a child and which I inherited. They are the seeds of a collection of children's books which is growing steadily even today, though no longer in my garden.—There is no living library that does not harbor a number of booklike creations from fringe areas. They need not be paste-in albums or family albums, autograph books or portfolios containing pamphlets or religious tracts. Some people become attached to leaflets and prospectuses; others, to handwriting facsimiles or typewritten copies of unobtainable books. And certainly periodicals can form the prismatic fringes of a library. But to get back to those albums: Actually, inheritance is the soundest way of acquiring a collection. For a collector's attitude toward his possessions stems from an owner's feeling of responsibility toward his property. Thus it is, in the highest sense, the attitude of an heir, and the most distinguished trait of a collection will always be its heritability. You should know that, in saying this, I fully realize that my discussion of the mental climate of collecting will confirm many of you in your conviction that this passion is behind the times, in your distrust of the collector type. Nothing is further from my mind than to shake either your conviction or your distrust. But one thing should be noted: the phenomenon of collecting loses its meaning when it loses its subject. Even though public collections may be less objectionable socially and more useful academically than private collections, the objects get their due only in the latter. I do know that night is coming for the type that I am discussing here and have been representing before you a bit *ex officio*. But, as Hegel put it, only when it is dark does the owl of Minerva begin its flight.[6] Only in extinction is the collector comprehended.

Now I am on the last half-emptied crate, and it is way past midnight. Other thoughts fill me than the ones I am talking about—not thoughts but images, memories. Memories of the cities in which I found so many things: Riga, Naples, Munich, Danzig, Moscow, Florence, Basel, Paris; memories of Rosenthal's sumptuous rooms in Munich, of the Danzig Stockturm, where the late Hans Rhaue was domiciled, of Süssengut's musty book cellar in North Berlin; memories of the rooms where these books had been housed, of my student's den in Munich, of my room in Bern, of the solitude of Iseltwald on the Lake of Brienz, and finally of my boyhood room, the former location of only four or five of the several thousand volumes that are piled up around me. O bliss of the collector, bliss of the man of leisure! No one has had less expected of him and no one has had a greater sense of well-being than the man who has been able to carry on his disreputable existence in the guise of Spitzweg's "Bookworm."[7] For inside him there are spirits, or at least little genii, which have seen to it that for a collector—and I mean a real collector, a collector as he ought to be—ownership is the most intimate relationship that one can have to things. Not that they come alive in him; it is he who lives in them. So I have erected before you one of his dwellings, with books as the building stones; and now he is going to disappear inside, as is only fitting.

Published in *Die literarische Welt*, July 1931. *Gesammelte Schriften*, IV, 388–396. Translated by Harry Zohn.

Notes

1. Anatole France (pseudonym of Jacques-Anatole-François Thibault; 1844–1924), writer and ironic, skeptical, urbane critic, was widely regarded in his day as the ideal French man of letters. He was elected to the French Academy in 1896 and was awarded the Nobel Prize for Literature in 1921.
2. *Habent sua fata libelli:* "Books have their own fates," or "Every book has its fate."
3. The poor little schoolmaster Wutz, a perpetually happy figure, appears in Jean Paul's *Leben des vergnügten Schulmeisterlein Maria Wutz in Auenthal* (Life of the Contented Little Schoolmaster Maria Wutz in Auenthal; 1793).
4. *Der blaue Reiter* was edited by Wassily Kandinsky and Franz Marc and published in 1912. A compendium of reproductions of works of art and theoretical texts, it served as the manifesto of the group of artists known as Der blaue Reiter. *Die Sage von Tanaquil* [The Legend of Tanaquil] is a rare book by Johann Jakob

Bachofen (1815–1887), Swiss professor of law, historian, and anthropologist best-known for his study of matriarchal societies.

5. Johann Peter Lyser (1804–1870) was an author, graphic artist, and music critic. Benjamin admired his illustrations for children's books; see "Notes for a Study of the Beauty of Colored Illustrations in Children's Books" and "Old Forgotten Children's Books" in the first volume of this edition.

6. Hegel, introduction to *Grundlinien der Philosophie des Rechts* (Elements of the Philosophy of Right).

7. Carl Spitzweg (1808–1885), German painter, established himself with humorous and often satirical scenes from bourgeois life. "The Bookworm" depicts a collector on a ladder, examining his vast collection.

Franz Kafka: *Beim Bau der Chinesischen Mauer*

Let me begin by recounting a little story that has been taken from the collection with the title given above[1] and that will show you two things: the greatness of this writer and the difficulty of articulating it. Kafka purports to be retelling a Chinese legend:

> The emperor, so the story goes, has sent you a message—you, the individual, his paltry subject, the insignificant shadow cowering in the remotest distance before the imperial sun. The emperor, from his deathbed, has sent a message to you alone. He commanded the messenger to kneel down by his bedside and whispered the message to him. So important to the emperor was this message that he ordered the messenger to repeat it back in his ear. He confirmed the accuracy of the statement with a nod of his head. And in the presence of all those assembled to witness his death—all the obstructing walls having been broken down, the grandees of his empire had gathered round in a circle on the vast and lofty staircases—he dispatched the messenger. The messenger sets out without delay. A powerful, indefatigable man, he forces a path for himself through the crowd, thrusting out now one arm, now the other. If he encounters resistance he points to his chest, on which the symbol of the sun is emblazoned. He makes rapid progress, more so than anyone else would have done. But the throng is so vast, their dwellings have no end. If only he could reach the open fields, how he would fly! And soon you would hear the glorious sound of his fists hammering at your door. But instead, how vainly he labors—he is still struggling to make his way through the chambers of the innermost palace. Never will he get to the end of them. And even if he succeeded in this, nothing would be gained—he would still have to fight his way down the stairs. And even if he succeeded in this, nothing would be gained—he would still have the

courtyards to cross. And after the courtyards, came the second, outer palace; then more staircases and courtyards; then beyond them another palace; and so on for thousands of years. And even if he managed at long last to force a path through the outermost gateway—but never, never can this happen—he would find the imperial capital lying before him, the center of the world, crammed to bursting with its dregs. No one can fight his way through that, let alone with a message from a dead man.—But you sit at your window and dream it to yourself when evening comes.

I will not interpret this story for you. You need no guidance from me to realize that the person addressed here is, primarily, Kafka himself. But who, then, was Kafka? He has done everything in his power to bar the way to an answer. It is impossible to overlook the fact that he stands at the center of his novels, but what happens to him there is designed to reduce to insignificance the person who experiences it, to render him invisible by concealing him at the heart of banality. And the cipher "K.," which designates the protagonist of his novel *Das Schloß* [The Castle], tells us no more than the initials on a handkerchief or the lining of a hat, and is certainly not enough to enable us to recognize the person who has disappeared. The most we can do is weave a legend around this man Kafka. It is as if he had spent his entire life wondering what he looked like, without ever discovering that there are such things as mirrors.

But to return to the initial story: I would like at least to suggest how *not* to interpret Kafka, since unfortunately this is almost the only way to establish a link with what has been said about him up to now. Admittedly, to provide a religious interpretation of Kafka's books, as has been done, is plausible enough. And such ideas may very possibly be aroused or even confirmed by the sort of close acquaintance with the writer enjoyed by Max Brod, to whom we are indebted for the publication of Kafka's works. Nevertheless, this approach amounts to a particular way of evading—or, one might almost say, of dismissing—Kafka's world. Doubtless, it is impossible to refute the assertion that in his novel *Das Schloß* Kafka wished to depict the higher powers, the realm of grace, whereas in *Der Prozeß* [The Trial] his aim was to portray the lower world of the law courts, and in his last great work, *Amerika,* he described earthly existence—all of these topics to be understood in a theological sense. The only problem is that such methods are far less productive than the admittedly much more challenging task of interpreting a writer from the center of his image world. To give but one example: the case against Joseph K. is played out in an everyday world, in backyards or waiting rooms, but always in different and unexpected places which the accused does not so much enter as find himself in by mistake. One day, for instance, he finds himself in an uppermost gallery. The banks of seats are packed full of people who have crowded in to follow the proceedings. They have come expecting a lengthy session, but conditions up there are almost unbearable. The ceiling (ceilings are almost always low in Kafka) presses down on them. So they have even brought cushions with them to lean their heads on.—But this is an image that precisely copies the grotesque faces familiar to us from the capitals surmounting the pillars in so many medieval churches. Of course, this is not to imply that Kafka intended to imitate them. But if we think of his works as a reflecting surface, a long-forgotten capital of this sort might easily appear to be the actual unconscious object of such descriptions. In that case, the interpreter would have to look for its reflection at precisely the same distance from the mirror as the reflected model, only in the opposite direction. In other words, it would have to be sought in the future.

Kafka's work is prophetic. The precisely registered oddities that abound in the life it deals with must be regarded by the reader as no more than the little signs, portents, and symptoms of the displacements that the writer feels approaching in every aspect of life without being able to adjust to the new situation. His only reaction to the almost incomprehensible distortions of existence that betray the emergence of these new laws is a sense of astonishment, mixed with elements of panic-stricken horror. Kafka is so possessed by this that he is incapable of imagining any single event that would not be distorted by the mere act of describing it—though by "description" here we really mean "investigation." In other words, everything he describes makes statements about something other than itself. Kafka's fixation on the sole topic of his work—namely, the distortion of existence— may appear to the reader like obsessiveness. But this impression, as well as the inconsolable earnestness, the despair, in the writer's gaze, is merely a sign that Kafka has abandoned the idea of a purely poetic prose. His prose may prove nothing; but it is so constructed that it can be inserted into passages of argument at any time. We may remind ourselves here of the form of the Haggadah, the name Jews have given to the rabbinical stories and anecdotes that serve to explicate and confirm the teachings—the Halachah. Like the haggadic parts of the Talmud, these books, too, are stories; they are a Haggadah that constantly pauses, luxuriating in the most detailed descriptions, in the simultaneous hope and fear that it might encounter the halachic order, the doctrine itself, en route.

Indeed, procrastination is the true meaning of that noteworthy and often striking fullness of detail which according to Max Brod lay at the heart of Kafka's search for perfection and the true way. Brod observes: "Of all the aspects of life to be taken seriously, we may say what a girl in *Das Schloß* says of the enigmatic letters from the authorities—namely, that 'the reflections to which they give rise are interminable.'" But what Kafka enjoys about these interminable reflections is the very fear that they might come to an end. Hence, his love of detail has a quite different meaning from that of an episode in a novel. Novels are sufficient unto themselves. Kafka's books are never that; they are stories pregnant with a moral to which they never give birth. This is why Kafka learned—if we must discuss matters in these terms—not from the great novelists but from much more modest writers, from mere storytellers. The moralist Johann Peter Hebel and the enigmatic Swiss Robert Walser were among his favorite writers.[2]—We have drawn attention to the dubious religious interpretations of Kafka's work, according to which the Castle is to be seen as the seat of grace. Yet it is the fact that his books are incomplete which shows the true working of grace in his writings. The fact that the Law never finds expression as such—this and nothing else is the gracious dispensation of the fragment.

Whoever doubts this truth may be persuaded by Max Brod's account of what Kafka told him in conversation about the planned conclusion to the novel. After a long, restless life in the village, a life without rights, K. lies exhausted on his deathbed, exhausted by his struggles. Then, at last, at long last, the messenger arrives from the Castle, bringing the decisive piece of news: K. has indeed no legal right to live in the village, but because of various subsidiary factors he is to be allowed to stay and work there. At this point, however, K.'s life ebbs away.—You can see that this story inhabits the same mental world as the tale with which I began. We also learn from Max Brod that Kafka had a particular village in mind—Zürau, in the Erzgebirge—as a model for the village at the foot of the Castle hill. For my own part, I am reminded of the village referred to in a legend from the Talmud. It is a legend related by a rabbi in reply to the question why Jews prepare a festive meal on Friday evenings. He tells the story of a princess who is pining away in exile, far from her fellow countrymen, among a people whose language she does not understand. One day this princess receives a letter bearing the news that her fiancé has not forgotten her and has set out on the journey to see her. The fiancé, says the rabbi, is the Messiah, the princess is the soul, and the village to which she has been exiled is the body. And because she has no other way of communicating her joy to the people around her who do not know her language, the soul prepares a festive meal for the body.

It needs only a minute shift of emphasis in this story from the Talmud for us to find ourselves in Kafka's world. Modern man dwells in his body as K. does in the village: as a stranger, an outcast who is ignorant of the laws that connect this body to higher and vaster orders. Much light is shed on this aspect of his works by the fact that Kafka frequently places animals at the center of his tales. The reader follows these animal tales for a fair distance without even noticing that they do not deal with human beings at all. Then, when the animal is identified for the first time—as a mouse or a mole—you are suddenly jolted and realize how far you have drifted away from the continent of human beings. Incidentally, it is worth paying attention to the kinds of animals Kafka chooses to embody his ideas. They always dwell in the interior of the earth, or, like the beetle in "Die Verwandlung" [The Metamorphosis], they are creatures that hide away on the ground, in cracks and crannies. This scurrying away seems to the author the only appropriate behavior for the isolated members of his generation and their context, with their ignorance of the law. Yet this absence of law is the result of a process of development. Kafka never tires of describing his fictional realm as dust-laden, rotten, and outmoded. The dingy rooms in which the Trial is enacted are just like the regulations that hold sway in the Penal Colony, or the sexual habits of the women who lend K. moral support. But the depravity of this realm is palpable, and not just in the unbounded promiscuity of the women characters. The same uninhibited brazenness can be seen in the activities of the higher authorities, who have rightly been seen to play as cruel a game of cat and mouse with their victims as the one played by the lower organs of power. "Both worlds are a murky, dust-covered, poky, airless labyrinth of chancelleries, offices, waiting rooms, with an endless hierarchy of junior, senior, very senior, and quite unapproachable officials and subofficials, lawyers, clerks, and messenger boys who look outwardly like a parody of a ludicrous and senseless bureaucracy."[3] As we see, even the people in power are as lawless as those at the bottom of the pile, and creatures from every level of society mix indiscriminately; the only bond that unites them is a unique feeling of anxiety. This anxiety is not a reaction, but something organic. And we can readily specify what it is constantly and infallibly alert to. But before its object is defined, the remarkable dual nature of this organic fear should give us pause. For it is—and this takes us back to the mirror image with which we began—at one and the same time and in equal measure both fear of the primeval, the immemorial, and also fear of what is close by, the immediate future with all its urgency. In a word, it is fear of an unknown guilt and of the atonement, which brings only one blessing: it makes the guilt explicit.

For the clearest deformation that is characteristic of Kafka's world has its roots in the fact that what is great, new, and liberating here manifests itself as atonement, in cases where the past has not seen through itself, confessed, and been finished with. This is why Willy Haas was fully justified in decoding the unadmitted guilt that the trial of Joseph K. conjures up: it is guilt over forgetting. Kafka's writing is simply full of configurations of forgetting—of silent pleas to recall things to mind. And this holds good whether we think of "Die Sorge des Hausvaters" [The Cares of a Family Man]—of that strange talking spool called Odradek, whom no one can classify; or of the dung beetle, the hero of "Die Verwandlung," whom we know all too well to have been a human being; or of the "Kreuzung"

[Crossbreed], the animal that is half-kitten, half-lamb, and for which the butcher's knife might well come as salvation.

> If to my garden I go
> To water flowers among the trees,
> A little hunchback's standing there
> And he begins to sneeze.

These lines come from a mysterious folk song.[4] The little hunchback, too, is something that has been forgotten, something we once used to know; he was then at peace with himself, but now he blocks our way to the future. It is highly revealing that Kafka was able to recognize (though unable to create) the figure of a supremely religious man, a man who is in the right. And where did he find him? In none other than Sancho Panza, who has freed himself from a promiscuous relationship with his demon by directing the demon toward another object than himself, so that he might pursue a peaceful life in which he has no need to forget anything. As Kafka's brief but magnificent interpretation expresses it: "Sancho Panza succeeded in the course of the years, by feeding him with a great quantity of romances of chivalry and adventure during the evening and night hours, in diverting from himself his demon, whom he later called Don Quixote. This demon knew no restraint in carrying out the maddest exploits—which, however, for lack of a preordained object (one that should have been Sancho Panza himself), did no one any harm. A free man, Sancho Panza philosophically followed Don Quixote on his crusades, perhaps from a certain feeling of responsibility, and derived great and useful entertainment from them to the end of his days."

If the author's large-scale novels are the well-tended fields that he has bequeathed to us, the new volume of stories from which this interpretation has been taken is the sower's bag that is filled with seeds—ones which have the strength of the natural seeds that sprout from graves even after millennia, and that we know will still bear fruit.

Radio talk broadcast July 1931. *Gesammelte Schriften,* II, 676–683. Translated by Rodney Livingstone.

Notes

1. *Beim Bau der Chinesischen Mauer* (The Great Wall of China) is a posthumous collection of Kafka's short fiction edited by his friend Max Brod and published in 1931.
2. Johann Peter Hebel (1760–1826), German journalist and author, was much esteemed for his use of dialect in his writings. As editor and chief writer for the *Badischer Landkalendar,* an annual publication not unlike the American *Old*

Farmer's Almanac, he produced an enormous volume of poetry and prose. Robert Walser (1878–1956), Swiss poet, novelist, and short-story writer, was revered by Benjamin for his mastery of the brief impressionistic sketch. See Benjamin's essay "Robert Walser" (1929), in this volume.

3. Willy Haas, *Gestalten der Zeit* (Berlin: Kiepenheuer, 1930), p. 176. See also Benjamin's review of Haas (titled "Theological Criticism") in this volume.

4. The source is Achim von Arnim and Clemens Brentano, *Des Knaben Wunderhorn* (Munich: Winkler, 1966), pp. 824–825.

Diary from August 7, 1931, to the Day of My Death

This diary does not promise to become very long. Today I received a negative response from Anton Kippenberg,[1] and this gives my plan the relevance that only futility can guarantee. I need to discover "a method that is just as convenient but somewhat less definitive," I said to I. today.[2] My hope of making any such discovery is fast disappearing. But if anything can strengthen still further the determination, indeed the peace of mind, with which I think of my intention, it must be the shrewd, dignified use to which I put my last days or weeks. Those just past leave a lot to be desired in this respect. Incapable of action, I just lay on the sofa and read. Frequently, I fell into so deep a reverie that I forgot to turn the page. I was mainly preoccupied with my plan, with wondering whether or not it was unavoidable, whether it should best be implemented here in the studio or back at the hotel, and so on.

I read *Das Friedensfest* [The Peace Festival] and *Einsame Menschen* [Lonely People].[3] People really were uncivilized in that Friedrichshagen milieu. But the fact is that the members of Bruno Wille and Wilhelm Bölsche's "New Community" do indeed seem to have behaved childishly.[4] The modern reader cannot but ask himself whether he belongs to a new race of Spartans—so disciplined is he in comparison, and above all, so much better able to detach himself and to look beyond his own immediate interests. That Johannes Vockerat whom Hauptmann depicts with such evident sympathy is certainly a nasty piece of work: bad manners and lack of discretion seem to be the prerequisites of heroism in these plays.[5] At the same time, these figures enable us to see how the characters in a play can be invalidated, if the author listens to them too attentively. Anyone who turns to them after forty years and tries to enter into their spirit finds it impossible to gain entry, because from every window a word or a turn of phrase stares out at him; these characters are merely tenements full of worn-out reactions and sentiments. They enable us to formulate one of the laws governing the truly great characters of drama: they contain vacant cavities, uninteresting cells that ensure that they have a real life, chambers of silence or empty staterooms of pathos in which a guest can find accommodation or make himself at home after decades or even centuries.— A remarkable feature of a different kind in these Hauptmann plays is sickness. Here, as in Ibsen, the various illnesses seem to be a cover for the sickness of the turn of the century, the *mal du siècle*. In those half-failed Bohemians like Braun and Dr. Scholz, the yearning for freedom is at its most powerful; but on the other hand, it often seems as if it is the intense preoccupation with art, with social questions, and the like that is making people ill. In other words, illness here is like a social emblem, much like madness among the ancients. Sick people have a special insight into the state of society; their private casting off of inhibitions is converted into an inspired sensitivity to the atmosphere their "contemporaries" breathe. But the form taken by this conversion is "nerves." It might be important to establish whether this word had not become a fashionable concept in the Jugendstil [Art Nouveau] period. At any rate the nerves are inspired threads; they resemble those fiberlike lines that trailed around furniture and house façades, redolent of unsatisfied rejuvenations and curves full of yearning. As for the figures of the Bohemian and the emancipated woman, Naturalism liked to dwell on them in the shape of a Daphne pursued by reality and changing into a bundle of nerves, laid bare, plantlike, trembling in the fresh air of the now [*Jetztzeit*].

Yesterday evening, a meeting with Albert Salomon and Fritz Holborn.[6] The conversation turned on questions of methodology in history. Someone quoted an excellent remark by Johan Huizinga: run-of-the-mill history answers more questions than a wise man will ask. My attempt to explain a theory of history in which the concept of development is entirely supplanted by the concept of origins. Understood in this way, history cannot be sought in the riverbed of a process of development. Instead, as I have remarked elsewhere, the image of a riverbed is replaced by that of a whirlpool. In such a whirlpool earlier and later events—the prehistory and posthistory of an event, or, better, of a status, swirl around it. The actual objects of such a view of history are not specific events but specific unchanging *statuses* of a conceptual or sensual kind—for example, the Russian agrarian system, the city of Barcelona, population shifts in the Mark of Brandenburg, barrel vaulting, and so on. If this approach is determined by its firm rejection of the possibility of an evolutionary or universalist dimension in history, it is determined *internally* by a productive polarity. The twin poles of such a view are the historical and the political—or, to point up the distinction even more sharply, the historical and the event. These two factors occupy two completely different planes. We can never say, for example, that we experience history; nor can we maintain that a historical account brings the events so close to us that it has the same impact as a historical event (such an account would be worthless), or that we have experienced events that are destined to become history (since such a view is journalistic).

Before the closing of the gates, I shall confer on myself a title thought up by Lichtenberg: *professor philosophiae extraordinariae.*

August 12. In conversation with Gustav Glück,[7] I discovered the true reason for Kraus's reaction to my series of essays.[8] Kraus's attitude toward his followers undoubtedly played a role, but the real key to his behavior is surely to be found in "The Diebold Case" in the latest issue of *Die Fackel.* If my essays had only contained Diebold's name somewhere, however inconspicuously, and had alluded, however indirectly, to his denigration of Kraus, he would have overwhelmed the work with compliments. But as it was, he sought the name Diebold in vain throughout its length and breadth, and he was not willing to modify his negative attitude toward the *Frankfurter Zeitung* on my account—all the less as I failed to supply him with any ammunition.

The older you get as a writer, the more you're struck from time to time by a word that you've never written. Such a word can evoke an entire period. And it's not just the older you get the more you're struck, but you're also struck more frequently. For this openness to the glossy stamp of words comes only in later years, the more frequently you encounter worn-out words, indeed words that have become worn out by your own use.

August 16, at the home of Willy Haas.[9] On the little glass veranda built onto the house—present were his wife, Tritsch, Artur Rosen, and Peter Huchel—a conversation took place, some of which seems worth preserving.[10] I told them about the meeting that had been held on the thirteenth in the Schubert Rooms to protest the censorship. This led to the related topic of Marxism and art, which enabled me to discuss the dialectic of this relationship. I advanced two theses that have always—or rather, since the rise of capitalism—been in conflict with each other:

1. Art is for the people.
2. Art is for the connoisseurs.

It is obvious that on the surface everything speaks for the second thesis. Above all, it has always been the case that an artistic practice very quickly degenerates if it addresses itself more to the undifferentiated needs of consumers than to the critical collaboration of experts. In recent times, this is most strikingly borne out by the novel. The novel seems from the outset to be more evidently aimed at consumption, unproductive enjoyment, than other forms of art. Elsewhere, I have explored the analogy between the novel and food in greater depth.[11] The time when this type of food possessed any nutritional value has long since passed, and the "popularity" of art, something that today is represented by popular novels, has long since ceased to have anything productive or nourishing about it—unlike the novel at the time of the incipient emancipation of the bourgeoisie. Nowadays it is rather the expression of the complete integration of this kind of writing into the world of commodity circulation. Its sole purpose is to pander to the need for comfort. As long as a century ago, the Romantics made the most daring efforts to introduce expertise into the reading of the novel; but the only result was to deprive the novel of any popularity. Thus, at the very point at which bourgeois writing achieves its greatest productivity, the antinomy is at its starkest. On the other hand, however, in the long run every class and every social stratum will open the door to the forms of their life and language only to the person who is active on their behalf, and who reproduces in modified form for their benefit the themes that they make available to him. This means that every form of art that systematically sets out to dispense with popularity will rightly find itself consigned to the luxury segment of the market, and thus subject to the dictates of fashion. Of course, every flourishing literature has always undergone a whole series of transitions between the popular and the esoteric. The decisive factor, however, was that these intermediate products possessed a continuity—not just externally, in terms of commercial success or size of edition, but an internal continuity—between the specific provinces of writing in itself. In our day this continuity has been broken, meaning that precisely the most important tasks—namely, work on the new art forms on the basis of the entire arsenal of proletarian life and language—have become insoluble and, we might even say, incapable of formulation. This is the situation that has led to the so-called crisis of art and to calls for art's abolition, or even to the demand that it be replaced by journalism. Incomprehensible though such a demand is under the class hegemony of the bourgeoisie, the fact that it could be made is significant, as is its value as a prognosis of things to come. The complete takeover of literature by the newspaper—which by publishing fiction in serial form has even appropriated the novel, decisively modifying it in the process—is in fact a dialectical process. On the one hand, it spells the demise of literature in contemporary social conditions, but, on the other, it prepares the way for its reinstatement when conditions change. And since the contemporary situation and the changed circumstances are basically already having an impact on each other, the symptoms of future developments can already be discerned. Admittedly, the first result of the predominance of the newspaper is to expose the fact that literary production has been integrated into the production of commodities—to reveal this fact in every sphere where it had not previously been evident. But the second result stands in a dialectical relationship to the first. For as writing gains in breadth what art loses in depth, the separation between the author and the public—a separation that journalism maintains in a corrupt way—starts to be overcome in an admirable way. The reader is ready at any moment to become a writer—that is to say, a describer and prescriber. From every form of material knowledge, a path leads to the writing about it: in short, work itself finds a voice. And its representation in words becomes a part of the ability that is needed for its exercise. Literary competence is based not on consumption, but on working practices; in other words, it becomes a popular activity. The popular nature of writing is based not on consumption, but on production; it is part of an expertise. In a word, it is the literarization of living conditions, which becomes master of what are otherwise the insoluble antinomies that dominate all artistic activity in our age. And the stage on which we see enacted the profoundest debasement of the printed word—that is, the newspaper—will be the site of its regeneration in a new society. Moreover, this is not the most contemptible ruse of reason. It is poverty that compresses the creativity of our best talents today, with an enormous atmospheric pressure. In this way, talent finds a refuge in the belly of the cultural section of the newspaper—as if in the belly of a wooden horse, from which one day this creativity will emerge and set alight the Troy of the modern press.

Diary entries from late 1931; unpublished in Benjamin's lifetime. *Gesammelte Schriften*, VI, 441–446. Translated by Rodney Livingstone.

Notes

1. Anton Kippenberg was the head of the Insel publishing company. Benjamin had hoped that Insel would publish a book by him, commemorating Goethe's centenary.
2. "I." probably refers to Inge Buchholz, a close friend of Benjamin's in the early 1930s. Nothing else is known about her.
3. These are plays by Gerhart Hauptmann. *Das Friedensfest* (The Peace Festival; 1890) is an analysis of the troubled relations within a neurotic family. *Einsame Menschen* (Lonely People; 1891) describes the tragic end of an unhappy intellectual torn between his wife and a young woman with whom he can share his thoughts. Friedrichshagen lies on the outskirts of Berlin. For a slightly different version of this section, see "Thought Figures" (1933), in this volume.
4. Bruno Wille (1860–1928), German author, editor, and impresario, founded one of Berlin's most important theaters, the Freie Volksbühne Berlin, in 1901. He also

established, with Wilhelm Bölsche (1861–1939), an alternative school called the Freie Hochschule. Bölsche, poet and novelist, was a founder of Berlin Naturalism in the 1890s. The "New Community" was bound together by belief in Darwinism, positivism, and determinism; its members envisioned a harmonious, nonreligious, and scientifically based world.

5. Gerhart Hauptmann (1862–1946), German playwright, poet, and novelist, established himself as the leading voice in German Naturalism in the 1890s. In 1912 he received the Nobel Prize for Literature.

6. Albert Salomon (1891–1966), sociologist and political scientist, was editor of *Die Gesellschaft*. He left Germany in 1933 for Switzerland and then the United States, where he became a professor at the New School for Social Research in New York.

7. Gustav Glück (1902–1973), perhaps Benjamin's closest friend during the 1930s, was a director of the foreign section of the Reichskreditgesellschaft (Imperial Credit Bank) in Berlin until 1938. He was able to arrange the transfer to Paris of the fees Benjamin received from his occasional contributions to German newspapers until 1935. In 1938 Glück emigrated to Argentina; after World War II, he was a board member of the Dresdner Bank.

8. Benjamin's essay on Karl Kraus, included in this volume, appeared in four installments in the *Frankfurter Zeitung* in March 1931, with a dedication to Gustav Glück. Despite its positive view, it provoked an ironic response from Kraus which Benjamin attempts to explain here. Bernhard Diebold was a Nazi critic who had condemned the works of Kraus, Brecht, and Kurt Tucholsky as morally rootless, while he praised the "healthy" ideas of "artists" like Josef Goebbels. Kraus attacked Diebold on a number of occasions in *Die Fackel*. Following Kraus's response to his essay, Benjamin, who had been preoccupied with Kraus since around 1916, vowed to write nothing further about him. He was also deeply shocked by Kraus's endorsement of Engelbert Dollfuss's Austro-Fascism in 1932 as "the lesser evil."

9. Willy Haas (1891–1973) was a well-known writer and critic. He was editor of *Die literarische Welt* and *Die Welt im Wort*.

10. Artur Rosen was managing editor of *Die literarische Welt*. Peter Huchel (1903–1981), poet and editor, was the editor-in-chief of the important East German journal *Sinn und Form* from 1949 to 1962. He left the German Democratic Republic in 1971.

11. See the section "Reading Novels" in the piece entitled "Little Tricks of the Trade" (1933), in this volume.

Little History of Photography

The fog that surrounds the beginnings of photography is not quite as thick as that which shrouds the early days of printing; more obviously than in the case of the printing press, perhaps, the time was ripe for the invention, and was sensed by more than one—by men who strove independently for the same objective: to capture the images in the camera obscura, which had been known at least since Leonardo's time. When, after about five years of effort, both Niepce and Daguerre simultaneously succeeded in doing this, the state, aided by the patenting difficulties encountered by the inventors, assumed control of the enterprise and made it public, with compensation to the pioneers.[1] This paved the way for a rapid ongoing development which long precluded any backward glance. Thus it is that the historical or, if you like, philosophical questions suggested by the rise and fall of photography have gone unheeded for decades. And if they are beginning to enter into consciousness today, there is a definite reason for it. The latest writings on the subject point up the fact that the flowering of photography—the work of Hill and Cameron, Hugo and Nadar—came in its first decade.[2] But this was the decade which preceded its industrialization. Not that hucksters and charlatans did not appropriate the new techniques for gain, even in that early period; indeed, they did so en masse. But that was closer to the arts of the fairground, where photography is at home to this day, than to industry. Industry made its first real inroads with the visiting-card picture, whose first manufacturer, significantly, became a millionaire. It would not be surprising if the photographic methods which today, for the first time, are harking back to the preindustrial heyday of photography had an underground connection with the crisis of capitalist industry. But that does not make it any easier to use the charm of old photographs, available in fine recent publications,[3] for real insights into their nature. Attempts at theoretical mastery of the subject have so far been entirely rudimentary. And no matter how extensively it may have been debated in the last century, basically the discussion never got away from the ludicrous stereotype which a chauvinistic rag, the *Leipziger Stadtanzeiger,* felt it had to offer in timely opposition to this black art from France. "To try to capture fleeting mirror images," it said, "is not just an impossible undertaking, as has been established after thorough German investigation; the very wish to do such a thing is blasphemous. Man is made in the image of God, and God's image cannot be captured by any machine of human devising. The utmost the artist may venture, borne on the wings of divine inspiration, is to reproduce man's God-given features without the help of any machine, in the moment of highest dedication, at the higher bidding of his genius." Here we have the philistine notion of "art" in all its overweening obtuseness, a stranger to all technical considerations, which feels that its end is nigh with the alarming appearance of the new technology. Nevertheless, it was this fetishistic and fundamentally antitechnological concept of art with which the theoreticians of photography sought to grapple for almost a hundred years, naturally without the smallest success. For they undertook nothing less than to legitimize the photographer before the very tribunal he was in the process of overturning. Far different is the tone of the address which the physicist Arago, speaking on behalf of Daguerre's invention, gave in the Chamber of Deputies on July 3, 1839.[4] The beautiful thing about this speech is the connections it makes with all aspects of human activity. The panorama it sketches is broad enough not only to make the dubious project of authenticating photography in terms of painting—which it does anyway—seem beside the point; more important, it offers an insight into the real scope of the invention. "When inventors of a new instrument," says Arago, "apply it to the observation of nature, what they expect of it always turns out to be a trifle compared with the succession of subsequent discoveries of which the instrument was the origin." In a great arc Arago's speech spans the field of new technologies, from astrophysics to philology: alongside the prospects for photographing the stars and planets we find the idea of establishing a photographic record of the Egyptian hieroglyphs.

Daguerre's photographs were iodized silver plates exposed in the camera obscura, which had to be turned this way and that until, in the proper light, a pale gray image could be discerned. They were one of a kind; in 1839 a plate cost an average of 25 gold francs. They were not infrequently kept in a case, like jewelry. In the hands of many a painter, though, they became a technical adjunct. Just as seventy years later Utrillo painted his fascinating views of Paris not from life but from picture postcards,[5] so the highly regarded English portrait painter David Octavius Hill based his fresco of

Newhaven Fishwife. Photo by David Octavius Hill.

the first general synod of the Church of Scotland in 1843 on a long series of portrait photographs. But these pictures he took himself. And it is they, unpretentious makeshifts meant for internal use, that gave his name a place in history, while as a painter he is forgotten. Admittedly a number of his studies lead even deeper into the new technology than this series of portraits—anonymous images, not posed subjects. Such figures had long been the subjects of painting. Where the painting remained in the possession of a particular family, now and then someone would ask about the person portrayed. But after two or three generations this interest fades; the pictures, if they last, do so only as testimony to the art of the painter. With photography, however, we encounter something new and strange: in Hill's Newhaven fishwife, her eyes cast down in such indolent, seductive modesty, there remains something that goes beyond testimony to the photographer's art, something that cannot be silenced, that fills you with an unruly desire to know what her name was, the woman who was alive there, who even now is still real and will never consent to be wholly absorbed in "art."

> And I ask: How did the beauty of that hair,
> those eyes, beguile our forebears?
> How did that mouth kiss, to which desire
> curls up senseless as smoke without fire?[6]

Or you turn up the picture of Dauthendey the photographer, the father of the poet, from the time of his engagement to that woman whom he found one day, shortly after the birth of her sixth child, lying in the bedroom of his Moscow house with her veins slashed. Here she can be seen with him. He seems to be holding her, but her gaze passes him by, absorbed in an ominous distance. Immerse yourself in such a picture long enough and you will realize to what extent opposites touch, here too: the most precise technology can give its products a magical value, such as a painted picture can never again have for us. No matter how artful the photographer, no matter how carefully posed his subject, the beholder feels an irresistible urge to search such a picture for the tiny spark of contingency, of the here and now, with which reality has (so to speak) seared the subject, to find the inconspicuous spot where in the immediacy of that long-forgotten moment the future nests so eloquently that we, looking back, may rediscover it. For it is another nature which speaks to the camera rather than to the eye: "other" above all in the sense that a space informed by human consciousness gives way to a space informed by the unconscious. Whereas it is a commonplace that, for example, we have some idea what is involved in the act of walking (if only in general terms), we have no idea at all what happens during the fraction of a second when a person actually takes a step. Photography, with its devices of slow motion and enlargement, reveals the secret. It is through photography that we first discover the existence of this

Karl Dauthendey (Father of the Poet), with His Fiancée.
Photo by Karl Dauthendey.

optical unconscious, just as we discover the instinctual unconscious through psychoanalysis. Details of structure, cellular tissue, with which technology and medicine are normally concerned—all this is, in its origins, more native to the camera than the atmospheric landscape or the soulful portrait. Yet at the same time, photography reveals in this material physiognomic aspects, image worlds, which dwell in the smallest things—meaningful yet covert enough to find a hiding place in waking dreams, but which, enlarged and capable of formulation, make the difference between technology and magic visible as a thoroughly historical variable. Thus, Blossfeldt with his astonishing plant photographs[7] reveals the forms of ancient columns in horse willow, a bishop's crosier in the ostrich fern, totem poles in tenfold enlargements of chestnut and maple shoots, and gothic tracery in the fuller's thistle. Hill's subjects, too, were probably not far from the truth when they described "the phenomenon of photography" as still being "a great and mysterious experience"—even if, for them, this was no more than the consciousness of "standing before a device which in the briefest time could capture the visible environment in a picture that seemed as real and alive as nature itself." It has been said of Hill's camera that it kept a discreet distance. But his subjects, for their part, are no less reserved; they maintain a certain shyness before the camera, and the watchword of a later photographer from the heyday of the art, "Don't look at the camera," could be derived from their attitude. But that did not mean the "They're looking at you" of animals, people, and babies, which so distastefully implicates the buyer and to which there is no better counter than the way old Dauthendey talks about daguerreotypes: "We didn't trust ourselves at first," he reported, "to look long at the first pictures he developed. We were abashed by the distinctness of these human images, and believed that the little tiny faces in the picture could see *us*, so powerfully was everyone affected by the unaccustomed clarity and the unaccustomed fidelity to nature of the first daguerreotypes."

The first people to be reproduced entered the visual space of photography with their innocence intact—or rather, without inscription. Newspapers were still a luxury item which people seldom bought, preferring to consult them in the coffeehouse; photography had not yet become a journalistic tool, and ordinary people had yet to see their names in print. The human countenance had a silence about it in which the gaze rested. In short, the portraiture of this period owes its effect to the absence of contact between contemporary relevance and photography. Many of Hill's portraits were made in the Edinburgh Greyfriars cemetery—and nothing is more characteristic of this early period, except perhaps the way his subjects were at home there. And indeed the cemetery itself, in one of Hill's pictures, looks like an interior, a separate closed-off space where the gravestones propped against gable walls rise up from the grass, hollowed out like chimneypieces,

The Philosopher Schelling, ca. 1850. Photographer (German)
unknown.

with inscriptions inside instead of flames. But this setting could never have been so effective if it had not been chosen on technical grounds. The low light-sensitivity of the early plates made prolonged exposure outdoors a necessity. This in turn made it desirable to take the subject to some out-of-the-way spot where there was no obstacle to quiet concentration. "The synthetic character of the expression which was dictated by the length of time the subject had to remain still," says Orlik of early photography, "is the main reason these photographs, apart from their simplicity, resemble well-drawn or well-painted pictures and produce a more vivid and lasting impression on the beholder than more recent photographs."[8] The procedure itself caused the subject to focus his life in the moment rather than hurrying on past it; during the considerable period of the exposure, the subject (as it were) grew into the picture, in the sharpest contrast with appearances in a snapshot—which is appropriate to that changed environment where, as Kracauer has aptly noted, the split second of the exposure determines "whether a sportsman becomes so famous that photographers start taking his picture for the illustrated papers." Everything about these early pictures was built to last. Not only the incomparable groups in which people came together—and whose disappearance was surely one of the most precise symptoms of what was happening in society in the second half of the century—but the very creases in people's clothes have an air of permanence. Just consider Schelling's coat. It will surely pass into immortality along with him: the shape it has borrowed from its wearer is not unworthy of the creases in his face. In short, everything suggests that Bernard von Brentano was right in his view that "a photographer of 1850 was on a par with his instrument"—for the first time, and for a long while the last.[9]

To appreciate the full impact made by the daguerreotype in the age of its discovery, one should also bear in mind that *plein air* painting was then opening up entirely new perspectives for the most advanced painters. Conscious that in this very area photography had to take the baton from painting, even Arago, in his historical review of the early attempts of Giovanni Battista Della Porta, explicitly commented: "As regards the effect produced by the imperfect transparency of our atmosphere (which has been loosely termed 'atmospheric degradation'), not even experienced painters expect the camera obscura"—i.e., the copying of images appearing in it— "to help them to render it accurately."[10] At the moment when Daguerre succeeded in fixing the images of the camera obscura, painters parted company on this point with technicians. The real victim of photography, however, was not landscape painting but the portrait miniature. Things developed so rapidly that by 1840 most of the innumerable miniaturists had already become professional photographers, at first only as a sideline, but before long exclusively. Here the experience of their original livelihood stood them in good stead, and it is not their artistic background so much as their training as craftsmen that we have to thank for the high level of their photographic achievement. This transitional generation disappeared very gradually; indeed, there seems to have been a kind of biblical blessing on those first photographers: the Nadars, Stelzners, Piersons, Bayards all lived well into their eighties and nineties.[11] In the end, though, businessmen invaded professional photography from every side; and when, later on, the retouched negative, which was the bad painter's revenge on photography, became ubiquitous, a sharp decline in taste set in. This was the time photograph albums came into vogue. They were most at home in the chilliest spots, on occasional tables or little stands in the drawing room—leather-bound tomes with repellent metal hasps and those gilt-edged pages as thick as your finger, where foolishly draped or corseted figures were displayed: Uncle Alex and Aunt Riekchen, little Trudi when she was still a baby, Papa in his first term at university . . . and finally, to make our shame complete, we ourselves—as a parlor Tyrolean, yodeling, waving our hat before a painted snowscape, or as a smartly turned-out sailor, standing rakishly with our weight on one leg, as is proper, leaning against a polished door jamb. The accessories used in these portraits, the pedestals and balustrades and little oval tables, are still reminiscent of the period when, because of the long exposure time, subjects had to be given supports so that they wouldn't move. And if at first head clamps and knee braces were felt to be sufficient, "further impedimenta were soon added, such as were to be seen in famous paintings and therefore had to be 'artistic.' First it was pillars, or curtains." The most capable started resisting this nonsense as early as the 1860s. As an English trade journal of the time put it, "in painting the pillar has some plausibility, but the way it is used in photography is absurd, since it usually stands on a carpet. But anyone can see that pillars of marble or stone are not erected on a foundation of carpeting." This was the period of those studios—with their draperies and palm trees, their tapestries and easels—which occupied so ambiguous a place between execution and representation, between torture chamber and throne room, and to which an early portrait of Kafka bears pathetic witness. There the boy stands, perhaps six years old, dressed up in a humiliatingly tight child's suit overloaded with trimming, in a sort of greenhouse landscape. The background is thick with palm fronds. And as if to make these upholstered tropics even stuffier and more oppressive, the subject holds in his left hand an inordinately large broad-brimmed hat, such as Spaniards wear. He would surely be lost in this setting were it not for his immensely sad eyes, which dominate this landscape predestined for them.

This picture, in its infinite sadness, forms a pendant to the early photographs in which people did not yet look out at the world in so excluded and godforsaken a manner as this boy. There was an aura about them, a medium that lent fullness and security to their gaze even as it penetrated

Robert Bryson. Photo by David Octavius Hill.

that medium. And once again the technical equivalent is obvious: it consists in the absolute continuum from brightest light to darkest shadow. Here, too, we see in operation the law that new advances are prefigured in older techniques, for the earlier art of portrait painting, before its disappearance, had produced the strange flower of the mezzotint. The mezzotint process was of course a technique of reproduction, which was only later combined with the new photographic reproduction. The way light struggles out of darkness in the work of a Hill is reminiscent of mezzotint: Orlik talks about the "comprehensive illumination" brought about by the long exposure times, which "gives these early photographs their greatness."[12] And among the invention's contemporaries, Delaroche had already noted the "unprecedented and exquisite" general impression, "in which nothing disturbs the tranquillity of the composition."[13] So much for the technical determinedness of the auratic appearance. Many group photos in particular still preserve an air of animated conviviality for a brief time on the plate, before being ruined by the print. It was this breathy halo that was sometimes captured with delicacy and depth by the now old-fashioned oval frame. That is why it would be a misreading of these incunabula of photography to make too much of their "artistic perfection" or their "taste." These pictures were made in rooms where every client was confronted, in the person of the photographer, with a technician of the latest school; whereas the photographer was confronted, in the person of every client, with a member of a rising class equipped with an aura that had seeped into the very folds of the man's frock coat or floppy cravat. For this aura was by no means the mere product of a primitive camera. Rather, in this early period subject and technique were as exactly congruent as they become incongruent in the period of decline that immediately followed. For soon advances in optics made instruments available that wholly overcame darkness and recorded appearances as faithfully as any mirror. After 1880, though, photographers made it their business to simulate the aura which had been banished from the picture with the suppression of darkness through faster lenses, exactly as it was being banished from reality by the deepening degeneration of the imperialist bourgeoisie. They saw it as their task to simulate this aura using all the arts of retouching, and especially the so-called gum print. Thus, especially in Jugendstil [Art Nouveau], a penumbral tone, interrupted by artificial highlights, came into vogue. Notwithstanding this fashionable twilight, however, a pose was more and more clearly in evidence, whose rigidity betrayed the impotence of that generation in the face of technical progress.

And yet, what is again and again decisive for photography is the photographer's attitude to his techniques. Camille Recht has found an apt metaphor: "The violinist," he says, "must first produce the note, must seek it out, find it in an instant; the pianist strikes the key and the note rings out. The painter and the photographer both have an instrument at their disposal.

Drawing and coloring, for the painter, correspond to the violinist's production of sound; the photographer, like the pianist, has the advantage of a mechanical device that is subject to restrictive laws, while the violinist is under no such restraint. No Paderewski will ever reap the fame, ever cast the almost fabulous spell, that Paganini did."[14] There is, however—to continue the metaphor—a Busoni of photography, and that is Atget.[15] Both were virtuosos, but at the same time precursors. The combination of unparalleled absorption in their work and extreme precision is common to both. There was even a facial resemblance. Atget was an actor who, disgusted with the profession, wiped off the mask and then set about removing the makeup from reality too. He lived in Paris poor and unknown, selling his pictures for a trifle to photographic enthusiasts scarcely less eccentric than himself; he died recently, leaving behind an oeuvre of more than 4,000 pictures. Berenice Abbott from New York has gathered these together, and a selection has just appeared in an exceptionally beautiful volume published by Camille Recht.[16] The contemporary journals "knew nothing of the man, who for the most part hawked his photographs around the studios and sold them for next to nothing, often for the price of one of those picture postcards which, around 1900, showed such pretty town views, bathed in midnight blue, complete with touched-up moon. He reached the Pole of utmost mastery; but with the bitter modesty of a great craftsman who always lives in the shadows, he neglected to plant his flag there. Therefore many are able to flatter themselves that they have discovered the Pole, even though Atget was there before them." Indeed, Atget's Paris photos are the forerunners of Surrealist photography—an advance party of the only really broad column Surrealism managed to set in motion. He was the first to disinfect the stifling atmosphere generated by conventional portrait photography in the age of decline. He cleanses this atmosphere—indeed, he dispels it altogether: he initiates the emancipation of object from aura, which is the most signal achievement of the latest school of photography. When avant-garde periodicals like *Bifur* or *Variété* publish pictures that are captioned "Westminster," "Lille," "Antwerp," or "Breslau" but that show only details, here a piece of balustrade, there a treetop whose bare branches crisscross a gas lamp, or a gable wall, or a lamppost with a life buoy bearing the name of the town—this is nothing but a literary refinement of motifs that Atget discovered. He looked for what was unremarked, forgotten, cast adrift. And thus such pictures, too, work against the exotic, romantically sonorous names of the cities; they suck the aura out of reality like water from a sinking ship.—What is aura, actually? A strange weave of space and time: the unique appearance or semblance of distance, no matter how close it may be. While at rest on a summer's noon, to trace a range of mountains on the horizon, or a branch that throws its shadow on the observer, until the moment or the hour become part of their appearance—this is what it means to breathe

the aura of those mountains, that branch. Now, to bring things *closer* to us, or rather to the masses, is just as passionate an inclination in our day as the overcoming of whatever is unique in every situation by means of its reproduction. Every day the need to possess the object in close-up in the form of a picture, or rather a copy, becomes more imperative. And the difference between the copy, which illustrated papers and newsreels keep in readiness, and the original picture is unmistakable. Uniqueness and duration are as intimately intertwined in the latter as are transience and reproducibility in the former. The peeling away of the object's shell, the destruction of the aura, is the signature of a perception whose sense for the sameness of things has grown to the point where even the singular, the unique, is divested of its uniqueness—by means of its reproduction. Atget almost always passed by the "great sights and so-called landmarks." What he did not pass by was a long row of boot lasts; or the Paris courtyards, where from night to morning the handcarts stand in serried ranks; or the tables after people have finished eating and left, the dishes not yet cleared away—as they exist by the hundreds of thousands at the same hour; or the brothel at No. 5, Rue ——, whose street number appears, gigantic, at four different places on the building's façade. Remarkably, however, almost all these pictures are empty. Empty is the Porte d'Arceuil by the fortifications, empty are the triumphal steps, empty are the courtyards, empty, as it should be, is the Place du Tertre. They are not lonely, merely without mood; the city in these pictures looks cleared out, like a lodging that has not yet found a new tenant. It is in these achievements that Surrealist photography sets the scene for a salutary estrangement between man and his surroundings. It gives free play to the politically educated eye, under whose gaze all intimacies are sacrificed to the illumination of detail.

It is obvious that this new way of seeing stands to gain least in an area where there has been the greatest self-indulgence: commercial, conventional portrait photography. On the other hand, to do without people is for photography the most impossible of renunciations. And anyone who did not know it was taught by the best Russian films that milieu and landscape, too, reveal themselves most readily to those photographers who succeed in capturing their anonymous physiognomy, as it were presenting them at face value. Whether this is possible, however, depends very much on the subject. The generation that was not obsessed with going down to posterity in photographs, rather shyly drawing back into their private space in the face of such proceedings—the way Schopenhauer withdrew into the depths of his chair in the Frankfurt picture, taken about 1850—for this very reason allowed that space, the space in which they lived, to get onto the plate with them. That generation did not pass on its virtues. So the Russian feature film was the first opportunity in decades to put before the camera people who had no use for their photographs. And immediately the human face appeared on film with new and immeasurable significance. But it was no longer a portrait. What was it? It is the outstanding service of a German photographer to have answered this question. August Sander[17] has compiled a series of faces that is in no way inferior to the tremendous physiognomic gallery mounted by an Eisenstein or a Pudovkin, and he has done it from a scientific viewpoint.[18] "His complete work comprises seven groups which correspond to the existing social order, and is to be published in some forty-five folios containing twelve photographs each." So far we have a sample volume containing sixty reproductions, which offer inexhaustible material for study. "Sander starts off with the peasant, the earthbound man, takes the observer through every social stratum and every walk of life up to the highest representatives of civilization, and then goes back down all the way to the idiot." The photographer did not approach this enormous undertaking as a scholar, or with the advice of ethnographers and sociologists, but, as the publisher says, "from direct observation." It was assuredly a very impartial, indeed bold sort of observation, but delicate too, very much in the spirit of Goethe's remark: "There is a delicate empiricism which so intimately involves itself with the object that it becomes true theory." So it was quite in order for an observer like Döblin to have hit on precisely the scientific aspects of this work, commenting: "Just as there is comparative anatomy, which helps us to understand the nature and history of organs, so this photographer is doing comparative photography, adopting a scientific standpoint superior to that of the photographer of detail."[19] It would be a pity if economic considerations should prevent the continuing publication of this extraordinary body of work. Apart from this basic encouragement, there is a more specific incentive one might offer the publisher. Work like Sander's could overnight assume unlooked-for topicality. Sudden shifts of power such as are now overdue in our society can make the ability to read facial types a matter of vital importance. Whether one is of the Left or the Right, one will have to get used to being looked at in terms of one's provenance. And one will have to look at others the same way. Sander's work is more than a picture book. It is a training manual.

"In our age there is no work of art that is looked at so closely as a photograph of oneself, one's closest relatives and friends, one's sweetheart," wrote Lichtwark back in 1907, thereby moving the inquiry out of the realm of aesthetic distinctions into that of social functions.[20] Only from this vantage point can it be carried further. It is indeed significant that the debate has raged most fiercely around the aesthetics of photography-as-art, whereas the far less questionable social fact of art-as-photography was given scarcely a glance. And yet the impact of the photographic reproduction of artworks is of very much greater importance for the function of art than the greater or lesser artistry of a photography that regards all experience as fair game for the camera. The amateur who returns home with great piles of artistic shots is in fact no more appealing a figure than the hunter who comes back

Pastry Cook. Photo by August Sander.

Parliamentary Representative (a Democrat). Photo by August Sander.

with quantities of game that is useless to anyone but the merchant. And the day does indeed seem to be at hand when there will be more illustrated magazines than game merchants. So much for the snapshot. But the emphasis changes completely if we turn from photography-as-art to art-as-photography. Everyone will have noticed how much easier it is to get hold of a painting, more particularly a sculpture, and especially architecture, in a photograph than in reality. It is all too tempting to blame this squarely on the decline of artistic appreciation, on a failure of contemporary sensibility. But one is brought up short by the way the understanding of great works was transformed at about the same time the techniques of reproduction were being developed. Such works can no longer be regarded as the products of individuals; they have become a collective creation, a corpus so vast it can be assimilated only through miniaturization. In the final analysis, mechanical reproduction is a technique of diminution that helps people to achieve control over works of art—a control without whose aid they could no longer be used.

If one thing typifies present-day relations between art and photography, it is the unresolved tension between the two introduced by the photography of works of art. Many of those who, as photographers, determine the current face of this technology started out as painters. They turned their back on painting after attempts to bring its expressive resources into a living and unequivocal relationship with modern life. The keener their feel for the temper of the times, the more problematic their starting point became for them. For once again, as eighty years before, photography has taken the baton from painting. As Moholy-Nagy has said:

> The creative potential of the new is for the most part slowly revealed through old forms, old instruments and areas of design which in their essence have already been superseded by the new, but which under pressure from the new as it takes shape are driven to a euphoric efflorescence. Thus, for example, futurist (structural) painting brought forth the clearly defined problematic of the simultaneity of motion, the representation of the instant, which was later to destroy it—and this at a time when film was already known but far from being understood . . . Similarly, some of the painters (neoclassicists and verists) today using representational-objective methods can be regarded—with caution—as forerunners of a new representational optical form which will soon be making use only of mechanical, technical methods.[21]

And Tristan Tzara, 1922: "When everything that called itself art was stricken with palsy, the photographer switched on his thousand-candle-power lamp and gradually the light-sensitive paper absorbed the darkness of a few everyday objects. He had discovered what could be done by a pure and sensitive flash of light—a light that was more important than all the constellations arranged for the eye's pleasure."[22] The photographers who

Display Window. Photo by Germaine Krull.

Storefront. Photo by Germaine Krull.

went over from figurative art to photography not on opportunistic grounds, not by chance, not out of sheer laziness, today constitute the avant-garde among their colleagues, because they are to some extent protected by their background against the greatest danger facing photography today: the touch of the commercial artist. "Photography-as-art," says Sascha Stone, "is a very dangerous field."[23]

When photography takes itself out of context, severing the connections illustrated by Sander, Blossfeldt, or Germaine Krull, when it frees itself from physiognomic, political, and scientific interest, it becomes *creative*.[24] The lens now looks for interesting juxtapositions; photography turns into a sort of arty journalism. "The spirit that overcomes mechanics translates exact findings into parables of life." The more far-reaching the crisis of the present social order, and the more rigidly its individual components are locked together in their death struggle, the more the creative—in its deepest essence a variant (contradiction its father, imitation its mother)—becomes a fetish, whose lineaments live only in the fitful illumination of changing fashion. The creative in photography is its capitulation to fashion. *The world is beautiful*—that is its watchword.[25] In it is unmasked the posture of a photography that can endow any soup can with cosmic significance but cannot grasp a single one of the human connections in which it exists, even when this photography's most dream-laden subjects are a forerunner more of its salability than of any knowledge it might produce. But because the true face of this kind of photographic creativity is the advertisement or association, its logical counterpart is the act of unmasking or construction. As Brecht says: "The situation is complicated by the fact that less than ever does the mere reflection of reality reveal anything about reality. A photograph of the Krupp works or the AEG tells us next to nothing about these institutions.[26] Actual reality has slipped into the functional. The reification of human relations—the factory, say—means that they are no longer explicit. So something must in fact be *built up*, something artificial, posed." We must credit the Surrealists with having trained the pioneers of such photographic construction. A further stage in this contest between creative and constructive photography is typified by Russian film. It is not too much to say that the great achievements of Russian directors were possible only in a country where photography sets out not to charm or persuade, but to experiment and instruct. In this sense, and in this only, there is still some meaning in the grandiloquent salute offered to photography in 1855 by that uncouth painter of ideas Antoine Wiertz.[27]

For some years now the glory of our age has been a machine which daily amazes the mind and startles the eye. Before another century is out, this machine will be the brush, the palette, the colors, the craft, the experience, the patience, the dexterity, the sureness of touch, the atmosphere, the luster, the exemplar, the perfection, the very essence of painting . . . Let no one suppose that daguerreotype photography will be the death of art . . . When the daguerreotype, that infant prodigy, has grown to its full stature, when all its art and strength have been revealed, then will Genius seize it by the scruff of the neck and shout: "Come with me—you are mine now! We shall work together!'"

How sober—indeed, pessimistic—by contrast are the words in which Baudelaire announced the new technology to his readers, two years later, in his *Salon of 1857*. Like the preceding quotation, they can be read today only with a subtle shift of emphasis. But as a counterpart to the above, they still make sense as a violent reaction to the encroachments of artistic photography. "In these sorry days, a new industry has arisen that has done not a little to strengthen the asinine belief . . . that art is and can be nothing other than the accurate reflection of nature . . . A vengeful god has hearkened to the voice of this multitude. Daguerre is his messiah." And: "If photography is permitted to supplement some of art's functions, they will forthwith be usurped and corrupted by it, thanks to photography's natural alliance with the mob. It must therefore revert to its proper duty, which is to serve as the handmaiden of science and the arts."

One thing, however, both Wiertz and Baudelaire failed to grasp: the lessons inherent in the authenticity of the photograph. These cannot be forever circumvented by a commentary whose clichés merely establish verbal associations in the viewer. The camera is getting smaller and smaller, ever readier to capture fleeting and secret images whose shock effect paralyzes the associative mechanisms in the beholder. This is where inscription must come into play, which includes the photography of the literarization of the conditions of life, and without which all photographic construction must remain arrested in the approximate. It is no accident that Atget's photographs have been likened to those of a crime scene. But isn't every square inch of our cities a crime scene? Every passer-by a culprit? Isn't it the task of the photographer—descendant of the augurs and haruspices—to reveal guilt and to point out the guilty in his pictures? "The illiteracy of the future," someone has said, "will be ignorance not of reading or writing, but of photography." But shouldn't a photographer who cannot read his own pictures be no less accounted an illiterate? Won't inscription become the most important part of the photograph? Such are the questions in which the interval of ninety years that separate us from the age of the daguerreotype discharges its historical tension. It is in the illumination of these sparks that the first photographs emerge, beautiful and unapproachable, from the darkness of our grandfathers' day.

Published in *Die literarische Welt,* September–October 1931. *Gesammelte Schriften,* II, 368–385. Translated by Edmund Jephcott and Kingsley Shorter.

Notes

1. Joseph-Nicéphore Niepce (1765–1833), French inventor, succeeded in making the first permanent photographic image. In 1826–1827, he used a camera to produce a view from his studio that was captured on a pewter plate. His death cut off his collaboration with Louis Jacques Mandé Daguerre (1787–1851), French painter and physicist, who went on to refine Niepce's work. Daguerre reduced the exposure time from Niepce's eight hours to twenty minutes and invented a process that was widely applicable.

2. David Octavius Hill (1802–1870), Scottish painter and photographer, collaborated with the chemist Robert Adamson on a series of remarkable portraits. Julia Margaret Cameron (1815–1879), English photographer, was, unlike many of the most important early photographers, an amateur. She is considered one of the greatest portrait photographers of the nineteenth century. Victor Hugo (1802–1885), poet, novelist, and dramatist, was the most important of the French Romantic writers. Hugo and indeed his entire family were enthusiastic amateur photographers and produced a sizable body of work. Nadar (pseudonym of Gaspard-Félix Tournachon; 1820–1910), French writer, caricaturist, and photographer, emerged from a large group of Parisian studio portraitists as one of the great portraitists of the century. Among his many innovations are his natural posing of his subjects, a patent on the use of photographs in mapmaking and surveying, the first aerial photograph (from a balloon), and the first photographic interview: twenty-one images of the scientist Eugène Chevreul, accompanied by text.

3. Helmut Bossert and Heinrich Guttmann, *Aus der Frühzeit der Photographie, 1840–1870: Ein Bildbuch nach 200 Originalen* (Frankfurt: Societäts Verlag, 1930). Heinrich Schwarz, *David Octavius Hill: Der Meister der Photographie* (Leipzig: Insel, 1931), with 80 plates. [Benjamin's note]

4. Dominique François Jean Arago (1786–1853), French physicist, was active in the study of light. He devised an experiment that proved the wave theory of light and contributed to the discovery of the laws of light polarization.

5. Maurice Utrillo (1883–1955), French painter, was known for his Montmartre street scenes.

6. Stefan George, *Der Teppich des Lebens und die Lieder von Traum und Tod* (The Carpet of Life and the Songs of Dream and Death), "Standbilder, das Sechste," verses 13–16.

7. Karl Blossfeldt, *Urformen der Kunst: Photographische Pflanzenbilder,* edited and with an introduction by Karl Nierendorf (Berlin: Ernst Wasmuth, 1928), with 120 plates. [Benjamin's note. Blossfeldt, a professor of drawing and painting in Berlin, created a sensation in the 1920s with the publication of his magnified photos of plant parts; see "News about Flowers" (1928), in this volume.—*Trans.*]

8. Emil Orlik, *Kleine Aufsätze* (Berlin: Propyläen Verlag, 1924), pp. 38ff. Orlik (1870–1932) was a German graphic artist and painter whose work was influenced by Jugendstil (Art Nouveau).

9. Bernard von Brentano (1901–1964), leftist novelist and journalist, wrote for the *Frankfurter Zeitung* and the *Berliner Tageblatt*. He is perhaps best-known for the historical novel *Theodor Chindler,* which depicts the transition from the empire to the Weimar Republic.

10. Giovanni Battista (Giambattista) Della Porta (1535–1615) was an Italian physicist and dramatist whose works contain descriptions of the camera obscura, as well as of a special lens he developed for it.

11. Carl Ferdinand Stelzner (ca. 1805–1895) was a German painter and photographer who, like many miniaturist painters, turned to daguerreotypy; together with Hermann Biow, he shot some of the earliest news photographs. Pierre-Louis Pierson (1822–1913) was a prominent French studio portraitist; his firm, Mayer and Pierson, catered to high society and the court. In 1862 Pierson and his partners, the brothers Léopold Ernest Mayer and Louis Frédéric Mayer, were named official photographers to Napoleon III. Hippolyte Bayard (1801–1887), French photographer, was active as an inventor in the earliest days of photography. He is widely regarded as one of photography's first significant artists, and held the first known photographic exhibition, displaying thirty of his own works.

12. Orlik, *Kleine Aufsätze,* p. 38.

13. Paul Delaroche, cited in Schwarz, *David Octavius Hill,* p. 39. Delaroche (1757–1859) was a French academic painter who specialized in historical subjects.

14. Eugène Atget, *Lichtbilder,* with an introduction by Camille Recht (Paris and Leipzig, 1930), p. 10. [Benjamin's note]

15. Eugène Atget (1857–1927), French photographer, spent his career in obscurity making pictures of Paris and its environs. He is widely recognized as one of the leading photographers of the twentieth century.

16. Berenice Abbott (1898–1991), American photographer, preserved Atget's work and oversaw its earliest publication. She undertook, very much in the spirit of Atget, a photographic documentation of New York City in the 1930s and 1940s.

17. August Sander, *Das Antlitz der Zeit: Sechzig Aufnahmen deutscher Menschen des 20. Jahrhunderts,* with an introduction by Alfred Döblin (Munich, 1929). [Benjamin's note. Sander (1876–1964), a German photographer, sought to compile a photographic portrait of the German people; *Das Antlitz der Zeit* (The Face of Our Time) was the first precipitate of this sociologically oriented project, which included portraits of peasants, workers, artisans, capitalists, and artists, among many others.—*Trans.*]

18. Sergei Mikhailovich Eisenstein (1898–1948), Soviet film director and theorist, produced a large body of work. His best-known films include *Battleship Potemkin* (1925), *Alexander Nevsky* (1938), and *Ivan the Terrible* (released in two parts, 1944 and 1958). Vsevolod Illarionovich Pudovkin (1893–1953) was a Soviet film director and theorist whose work often focused on heroic figures caught in violent historical change. His films include *Mat* (Mother; 1926), based on Gorky's novel; *Konets Sankt-Peterburga* (The End of St. Petersburg; 1927);

Potomok Chingis-Khan (Heir to Genghis Khan, or Storm over Asia; 1928); and the sound films *Dezertir* (Deserter; 1933), *Suvorov* (General Suvorov; 1941), and *Admiral Nakhimov* (1946–1947).

19. Alfred Döblin, introduction to Sander, *Antlitz der Zeit,* p. vi.

20. Alfred Lichtwark, introduction to Fritz Matthies-Masuren, *Künstlerische Photographie: Entwicklung und Einfluss in Deutschland* [Artistic Photography: Development and Influence in Germany] (Berlin: Marrquardt, 1907), p. 16.

21. László Moholy-Nagy, *Malerei Fotographie Film* (Munich: Langen, 1925). Moholy-Nagy (1895–1946), Hungarian painter, photographer, and art teacher, emerged as a dominant figure at the Bauhaus, where he was responsible for the famous Preliminary Course. As a photographer, he moved freely between the abstract photogram and representational photography. He is arguably the most influential photographer of the 1920s in Europe.

22. Tristan Tzara, "La photographie à l'envers" (Photography from the Verso), translated by Benjamin as "Die Photographie von der Kehrseite," in *G: Zeitschrift für elementare Gestaltung,* July 1924, p. 30. Tzara (1896–1963), Romanian-born French poet and essayist, was one of the founders of Dada in Zurich. He carried Dada ideas to Paris after World War I.

23. Sascha Stone (pseudonym of Alexander Sergei Steinsapir; 1895–1940), German-Jewish photographer, worked as a professional photographer in Berlin, primarily for the illustrated magazines published by Ullstein Verlag. Stone was active at the borders of the group around the journal *G,* which included Moholy-Nagy, Mies van der Rohe, Hans Richter, El Lissitsky, and Benjamin. He created the photomontage for the book jacket of Benjamin's *One-Way Street* (see Volume 1 of this edition).

24. Germaine Krull (1897–1985), German photographer, emigrated to Paris in 1924, where she became known for her work in portraiture, as well as in architectural, industrial, and fashion photography.

25. *Die Welt ist schön* (The World Is Beautiful) is the title of a photo volume by Albert Renger-Patzsch; it became the most influential of all of the photo essays published in the Weimar Republic. Benjamin was involved in a long-standing polemic against Renger-Patzsch's work. See especially "The Author as Producer" (1934), in this volume.

26. The Krupp works at Essen was the original plant in the Krupp steel, armaments, and shipbuilding empire, which had been founded in 1811 by Friedrich Krupp. The AEG is the Allgemeine Elektricitäts Gesellschaft, or General Electric Company, founded in Berlin in 1833 by the industrialist Emil Rathenau; it was largely responsible for building the electrical infrastructure of modern Germany.

27. Antoine Wiertz (1806–1865), Belgian painter, was known for his large, frequently grotesque paintings. Wiertz plays an important role in Benjamin's *Passagen-Werk* (Arcades Project).

Paul Valéry

On His Sixtieth Birthday

O langage chargé de sel, et paroles véritablement marines![1]

Valéry once wanted to become a naval officer. Elements of this youthful dream can still be discerned in what he did become. First, there is his poetry with its sustained formal abundance, which language garners from thought as the sea does from a calm. Second, there is the thought itself, imbued with the spirit of mathematics—a thought that leans over its objects as if they were maritime charts and that, without indulging itself in contemplation of the "depths," is content if it can hold a safe course. The sea and mathematics: they come together in a captivating union in one of the most beautiful passages he has written, the one in which Socrates tells Phaedra of the discovery he has made on the shore. His find is puzzling. Is it ivory, or marble, or an animal bone? At any rate, the object washed up by the tide could almost be a head with the features of Apollo. And Socrates wonders whether it is the work of an artist or of the waves. He weighs it in his hand. How long would the ocean take to create this shape rather than millions of others, and how long the artist? Socrates may well assert "that an artist is worth a thousand centuries or a hundred thousand, or many more . . . This is an unusual measuring rod for works of art."[2] If the admirers of the author of this outstanding work, *Eupalinos, ou l'Architecte* [Eupalinos, or the Architect], had decided to honor his sixtieth birthday by making a surprise presentation of an Ex Libris, it might have taken the form of a giant compass, with one arm firmly anchored in the seabed and the other stretched out wide toward the horizon. It would be a metaphor for the broad span encompassed by this man. Tension is the dominating impression of his physical appearance; tension is in the expression of his face, whose deep-set eyes hint at a reverie that is remote from earthly images and that enables him to set the course of his interior life by them as well as by those of the stars. Solitude is the night out of which such images shine, and Valéry has had long experience with solitude. Having published his first poems and his first two essays at the age of twenty-five, he began a twenty-year hiatus in his public activities from which he emerged with glory in 1917 with the poem "La jeune Parque." Eight years later, a series of outstanding works and ingenious maneuverings in society brought him membership in the Académie Française. Not without malice, he was assigned the seat previously occupied by Anatole France. Valéry parried the thrust with an exceedingly elegant address—the obligatory eulogy of his predecessor—in which France's name did not occur once. Aside from that, the speech contains a survey of literature that is sufficiently out of the ordinary to provide a clue to its author. He talks there of the "Valley of Jehoshaphat"[3] which is crowded with the mass of writers past and present: "Everything new is lost in something else new. Every illusion of being original disappears. The soul is cast down and turns its thoughts, with pain, albeit mixed with irony and a profound compassion, to those millions of feathered creatures, those innumerable agents of the mind, each of whom appears to himself to be the man of the moment, a free creator, the first mover, the possessor of an irrefragable certainty, a unique, distinctive source; and he who has spent his days in toil and who has used up his best moments in preserving his distinctiveness finds himself annihilated by the multitudes and swallowed up in the ever-growing swarms of those like himself."[4] In Valéry, this entirely vain exercise of the will to distinguish oneself is replaced by another goal: the will to endure, the endurance of the written word. The endurance of the written word, however, is quite different from the immortality of the writer, and has often taken place without it. Endurance, not originality, is the mark of the classical in writing, and Valéry is indefatigable in his search for what makes it possible. "A classical writer," he remarks, "is a writer who conceals or absorbs the associations of his ideas."[5] In those passages where the author's inspiration soars to the heights and where he feels himself to be above the demands of construction, sees no joints, and (because he cannot see them) does not feel them—it is at these points that the mildew of old age sets in. In order to recognize the joints, the limits of thought, one needs self-criticism. Valéry sets out to explore the writer's and especially the poet's intelligence like an inquisitor, and calls for a break with the widely held view that it is self-evident that writers are intelligent, as well as with the even more widely held idea that intelligence is irrelevant to the poet. He himself possesses intelligence of a kind that is anything but self-evident. Nothing can be more disconcerting than its embodiment: Monsieur Teste. Again and again, from his earliest writings to his later ones, Valéry has recourse to this strange figure around whom a whole series of little writings has grown up—"La soirée avec Monsieur Teste," a letter to Teste's wife, a preface, and of course a logbook. Monsieur Teste ("Mr. Head") is a personification of the intellect that reminds us very strongly of the God conceived by the negative theology of Nicholas of Cusa.[6] Everything we learn about Teste ends up in negation. What is so very seductive about him is not theorems, but the tricks of a way of behaving that impinges as little as possible on nonbeing and follows the maxim, "Every sense of excitement, every feeling, is the sign of a failure of construction and adaptation."[7] However human Monsieur Teste feels himself to be, he has taken to heart Valéry's aperçu that the most important ideas are those that contradict our feelings. He represents, therefore, the negation of the "human." "Behold, the twilight of the approximate breaks in, and before the door stands the reign of the dehumanized that will emerge from precision, rigor, and purity in human affairs."[8] No expansive, pathos-filled gestures, nothing "human," comes into the ambit of this Valéryesque eccentric, for whom thought is the only substance from which perfection may arise. One of its attributes is continuity. Thus, art and science are a continuum through which Leonardo's method (Valéry's first work was his "Introduction à la méthode de Léonard de Vinci," and Leonardo may be seen as a forerunner of Monsieur Teste) opens up paths that must not be misunderstood as boundaries. It is this method that, when applied to poetry, led Valéry to the celebrated concept of *poésie pure,* an idea that was certainly not made to be dragged through the literary magazines of France for months on end by a belletristically minded abbé in order to force Valéry to admit that it was identical with the concept of prayer.[9] Time and again, and with a remarkable degree of success, Valéry himself has recorded the different stages in the history of poetic theory—from Poe down to Baudelaire and Mallarmé—in which the constructive and musical elements of lyric poetry sought to demarcate their particular domains, defining them against each other, until they culminated in reflections whose core is formed by his lyrical masterpieces "Le cimetière marin," "La jeune Parque," and "Le Serpent"—poems in which we find the perfect interplay of voice and intelligence. The ideas in his poems rise like islands out of the sea of the voice. This is what separates this "reflective poetry" [*Gedankenlyrik*] from everything that we Germans understand by the term: at no point does the idea it contains come into contact with "life" or "reality." The idea has no connection with anything but the voice: this is the essence of *poésie pure.* "Lyric poetry is that mode of literature which is predicated on the voice in action—the voice as it speaks spontaneously, or as it is awakened by the things we see or the things we feel in their presence."[10] Or again, "The strict requirements of prosody are the artistic device which confers on natural speech the qualities of a resistant material that is alien to our soul and remains deaf to our desires."[11] And this is the peculiar feature of pure intelligence. But this *intelligence pure* that in Valéry has taken up its winter quarters on the inhospitable mountain peaks of esoteric poetry is, after all, identical with the intelligence under whose aegis the European bourgeoisie embarked on its voyages of conquest in the Age of Discovery. The Cartesian doubts about knowledge have been extended in Valéry in an almost reckless but also profound manner, to the point where they become doubts about the questions themselves: "The realms of chance, the powers of the gods or Fate, are nothing but the symptoms of our own mental deficiencies. If we had an answer to everything—a precise answer, that is—these powers would not exist . . . We feel this ourselves, and this is why we end up turning against our own questions. But that should be just the beginning. We ought to be able to formulate a question for ourselves that precedes all others and tests them in turn to see what they are worth."[12] The strict return of such ideas to their context in the heroic period of the European bourgeoisie allows us to master the surprise at encountering once more the idea of progress at such an advanced stage of the old European humanism. It is, furthermore, the valid and genuine idea of a progress transferable at the level of "methodology"—a term that corresponds to Valéry's concept of "construction" as neatly as it conflicts with the *idée fixe* of inspiration. As one of his contemporaries has claimed, "The work of art is not a creation, but a construction in which analysis, calculation, and planning play the principal roles." The ultimate merit of the systematic process of leading the investigator to excel himself has proved its worth in Valéry. For who is Monsieur Teste except the individual who is ready to cross the threshold where he will vanish into history—but who, like a disappearing shade, answers the call one last time, only to become submerged once again where he enters into an order of things whose approach Valéry describes in these terms: "In the age of Napoleon, electricity had roughly the same significance as Christianity in the age of Tiberius. Gradually it became apparent that this general infusion of energy was of greater consequence and better able to change the future than any 'political' event from Ampère to the present day."[13] The gaze Valéry turns on this approaching world is no longer that of the officer, but simply that of the experienced sailor who feels the approach of the storm and has too clear-eyed a vision of the changed world-historical situation ("with the increase in precision and exactitude, a corresponding increase in effect") not to realize that today, "faced with these changes, the profoundest thoughts of a Machiavelli or a Richelieu have about the same value and efficacy as a stock market tip."[14] Thus he stands there, "upright, on the pinnacle of thought, keeping as sharp a lookout as he can for the limits of things or of his own vision."[15]

Published in *Die literarische Welt*, October 1931. *Gesammelte Schriften*, II, 386–390. Translated by Rodney Livingstone.

Notes

1. "O language filled with salt, and words that are truly of the sea!" From Paul Valéry, *Eupalinos, ou l'Architecte*, in Valéry, *Oeuvres*, ed. Jean Hytier (Paris: Pléiade, 1971), vol. 2, p. 117.
2. Ibid., p. 119.
3. The Valley of Jehoshaphat was the site of Jehovah's apocalyptic judgment upon the nations (Joel 4:14).
4. "Remerciement à l'Académie française," in Valéry, *Oeuvres*, vol. 1, p. 731.
5. Ibid., p. 793.
6. Nicholas of Cusa (1401–1464) propounded a theology that stressed the limitations of human knowledge of God, which must be content with conjecture or approximation to the truth. The absolute truth escapes man; his proper attitude is "learned ignorance."
7. *Mauvaises pensées et autres*, in Valéry, *Oeuvres*, vol. 2, p. 866.
8. *Rhumbs*, in Valéry, *Oeuvres*, vol. 2, p. 621.
9. The reference is to the abbé Henri Bremond, who presented a report to the Académie Française on October 24, 1925, entitled "Poésie pure: D'où s'élève une querelle entre poètes, critiques et esthéticiens."
10. "La Poésie," in Valéry, *Oeuvres*, vol. 2, p. 549.
11. "Au sujet d'Adonis," in Valéry, *Oeuvres*, vol. 1, p. 480.
12. "Rhumbs: Arrière-pensées," in Valéry, *Oeuvres*, vol. 2, p. 647.
13. *"Regards sur le monde actuel" et autres essais*, in Valéry, *Oeuvres*, vol. 2, pp. 919–920. Jean-Jacques Ampère (1800–1864), French historian and philologist, studied the origins of western European languages and mythology.
14. Ibid., p. 925.
15. "Extraits du log-book de *Monsieur Teste*," in Valéry, *Oeuvres*, vol. 2, p. 39.

The Lisbon Earthquake

Have you ever had to wait at the drug store, watching a prescription being made up? The pharmacist measures out on a scale all the substances and powders that are needed for the finished medicine, using a finely calibrated set of weights, gram by gram or ounce by ounce. I feel like a chemist when I talk to you over the radio. My weights are the minutes, and I have to measure them out very accurately: so much of this and so much of that, if the final mixture is going to come out right. "How come?" you will ask. "If you want to tell us about the Lisbon earthquake, begin by telling us how it started. And then you can go on to tell us what happened next." But if I followed this advice, I don't think the description would be much fun. One house after another collapses; one family after another loses their lives. The panic created by the spreading fire, the flood of water, the darkness, the plundering, the groans of the injured, and the cries of people searching for their loved ones—to hear of all this and nothing else would please no one. And besides, those are the very things that recur in more or less the same form in every natural disaster.

But the earthquake that destroyed Lisbon on November 1, 1755, was not a disaster like a thousand others. In many respects it was remarkable, even unique. And this is what I would like to tell you about. In the first place, it was one of the largest and most destructive earthquakes of all time. Yet it is not for this reason alone that it excited and preoccupied the entire world like few other events in that century. The destruction of Lisbon in 1755 was roughly equivalent to the destruction of London or Chicago today. In the middle of the eighteenth century, Portugal was at the height of its power as a colonial empire. Lisbon was one of the most prosperous trading cities in the world. Year in, year out, its port at the mouth of the Tagus was filled with ships, and its streets were lined with the great trading houses of English, French, and German—especially Hamburg—merchants. The city had 30,000 houses and well over 250,000 inhabitants, of whom roughly a fourth perished in the earthquake. The king's court was famous for its strictness and its pomp. The many accounts of the city that appeared in the period preceding the earthquake contain the most curious descriptions of the stiffness and solemnity that could be seen on summer evenings in the main square of the city, the Rucio, when the courtiers and their families congregated in their carriages and chatted together for a while without descending from their vehicles. Moreover, people had such an exalted conception of the king of Portugal that one of the many pamphlets which spread precise descriptions of the catastrophe throughout Europe was quite unable to come to terms with the fact that such a great king had been affected by it. This extraordinary reporter notes: "Just as the magnitude of a disaster can be fully appreciated only once it has been overcome, so too you can grasp the awful import of this dreadful catastrophe only when you reflect that a great king, together with his wife, spent the entire day in a carriage, in the most wretched state, abandoned by all." The pamphlets in which such accounts can be studied took the place of newspapers at that time. Whoever was able to do so obtained eyewitness descriptions in as much detail as possible, and then printed and sold them. In what follows, I shall read to you from such a report—one which records the experiences of an Englishman who was then residing in Lisbon.

There is a further, special reason that helps to explain why this event affected people's minds so powerfully—why countless pamphlets passed from hand to hand, and indeed why new descriptions continued to make their appearance almost a century later. The reason is that this earthquake was the most powerful on record. Its impact was felt throughout Europe and as far away as Africa. It has been calculated that, together with its most distant tremors, it affected two and a quarter million square kilometers—a huge area. Its most powerful shocks extended from the Moroccan coast to the shores of Andalusia and France. The cities of Cádiz, Jerez, and Algeciras were almost completely destroyed. An eyewitness in Seville claimed that the cathedral spires shook like reeds in the wind. But the most powerful tremors were transported by the sea. From Finland to the Dutch East Indies, mighty tidal waves were felt; and it was calculated that they moved with amazing speed—in a quarter of an hour!—from the Portuguese coast to the mouth of the Elbe. And these were just the events actually experienced at the time of the disaster. Even more significant is the way in which people's imaginations brooded on the strange phenomena of nature that had been observed in the weeks preceding the earthquake and that subsequently—and probably not always without justification—were regarded as portents of the catastrophe to come. In Locarno, in the south of Switzerland, for example, some two weeks before the disaster, steam was seen coming out of the earth; within a couple of hours it had transformed itself into a red mist, which, toward evening, fell as purple rain. From then on, people claimed to have observed terrible hurricanes, with cloudbursts and floods in western Europe. Eight days before the earthquake, the ground near Cádiz was found to be covered with a vast quantity of worms.

No one was more fascinated by these remarkable events than the great German philosopher Kant, whose name may be familiar to some of you. At the time of the earthquake he was a young man of twenty-four, who had never left his hometown of Königsberg—and who would never do so in the future. But he eagerly collected all the reports of the earthquake that he could find, and the slim book he wrote about it probably represents the beginnings of scientific geography in Germany. And certainly the beginnings of seismology. I would gladly tell you something of the route taken by this science from that description of the earthquake of 1755 down to the present day. But I must take care lest the Englishman whose first-hand account I still wish to read to you gets lost in the crowd. He is waiting impatiently, because after 150 years in which no one has taken any notice of him, he would welcome the opportunity to speak once again and hence will permit me to say only a few words about our present knowledge of earthquakes. A word to the wise: it is not what you imagine. I would wager that if I were to interrupt my talk briefly and ask you how you would go about explaining earthquakes, your first thoughts would be of volcanos. And the fact is that volcanic eruptions often are associated with earthquakes, or at least announced by them. And this is why people have imagined for two thousand years—from the ancient Greeks down to Kant, and indeed even longer, roughly until 1870—that earthquakes came from the fiery gases and steam arising from the interior of the earth and suchlike. But when people began to take measurements and to make calculations whose subtlety and precision you and I can scarcely conceive of—in short, when they started to look at the problem scientifically—the truth turned out to lie in quite a different direction, at least insofar as major earthquakes like the one in Lisbon were concerned. They arise not from the innermost core of the earth, which to this day is thought of as being liquid, or at least mudlike, a sort of seething sludge, but from events in the earth's crust. The earth's crust is a layer about 3,000 kilometers thick. It is in a state of permanent turmoil; the masses of matter it contains are constantly shifting and striving to achieve equilibrium. We know some of the factors that disturb this equilibrium, and are striving unceasingly to discover others. So much is clear: that the most important changes are caused by the constant cooling of the earth. This gives rise to huge tensions in the rock formations and ends up fracturing them, seeking a new equilibrium through a reconfiguration that we experience as an earthquake. Other changes arise from the erosion of the mountains, making them lighter, and accretions in the seabed, which thus becomes denser. Storms that rage around the globe, especially in autumn, have an impact on the earth's surface. And last, scientists are in the process of establishing what effect the gravitational pull of extraterrestrial bodies might have on the surface of the globe. "But," you might say, "in that case, the earth can never come to rest. There must be a continuous series of earth tremors!" You're quite right about that. The extremely sensitive instruments that we have nowadays—in Germany alone, there are thirteen earthquake-monitoring stations in various towns—these sensitive instruments are never entirely still. In other words, the earth experiences tremors all the time, but for the most part not so violently that we notice.

All the worse if suddenly, out of the blue, we feel a tremor. This "out of the blue" should be taken quite literally. "For," says our Englishman, who has at long last managed to have his say,

the sun now shone in its full glory. The sky was completely blue and clear, and there was not the least sign of any natural event. Then, between nine and ten in the morning, I was sitting at my desk when my table moved, and since I could not discern any reason, I felt some surprise. I was wondering what could possibly have been the cause when the house suddenly shook from top to bottom. From beneath the ground arose a sound of thunder, as if a storm were raging at a great distance. I put my pen down quickly and leaped to my feet. The danger was great, but I was still hopeful that the matter would pass without much ill effect; but the very next moment put an end to any doubts on that score. There was a shattering noise, as if all the buildings in town were collapsing at the same time. My house, too, was profoundly affected: the upper stories instantly collapsed, and the rooms I was staying in swayed so much that all the utensils came crashing down. I truly thought my last moment had arrived, for the walls were bursting apart and great stones were falling out of the joints—all the beams seemed to be supported by thin air. At this very moment the sky went dark, and it became possible to recognize any object. Everything was in Stygian gloom, either from the immeasurable amounts of dust caused by the collapsing buildings, or because of the volumes of sulphurous fumes that arose from the bowels of the earth. At last the night became light once more, and the force of the tremors abated. I regained some of my composure and began to look about me. I realized that my life had been spared up to then thanks to a trivial circumstance. Had I been fully clothed, I would surely have fled into the street, where I would have been buried beneath the buildings crashing all around. I threw on my coat and shoes and rushed out into the street in the direction of St. Paul's cemetery, convinced that the high ground on which it was situated would afford me some measure of safety. No one was able to recognize the street in which he lived; many were unable to describe what had happened to them. Everything was scattered, and no one knew what had happened to his family or possessions. From the heights of the cemetery, I now became witness to a terrifying spectacle: out on the ocean, as far as the eye could see, there was a throng of ships being tossed about by the waves and crashing into each other as if they were the playthings of a mighty storm. Suddenly the huge quay by the shore sank into the sea and vanished, together with all the people who had imagined that standing on it ensured their safety. At the same time, the boats and vehicles in which so many were trying to escape all suddenly became victims of the sea.

As we know from other reports, it was about an hour after the second and most destructive tremor that the vast wave—twenty meters high—which the Englishman could see from a distance came crashing down over the city. As the tide withdrew, the bed of the Tagus was suddenly left completely dry: the ebb was so powerful that it drained all the water from the river. The Englishman's account concludes as follows: "When evening settled on the desolate city, the landscape seemed to turn into a sea of fire; the brightness was such that you could have read a letter by it. At a hundred different points at least, the flames rose to the sky, and they blazed for six days. What the earthquake had spared, they now consumed. As if petrified by fear, thousands gazed at the flames, while women and children prayed to the saints and angels for help. The ground continued to tremble more or less violently, often for a quarter of an hour on end."

So much for that day of misfortune, November 1, 1755. The catastrophe it brought in its wake is one of the very few that can render men as impotent now as they were 170 years ago. But here, too, technology will find ways to combat it, even if in a roundabout way: by prediction. For the moment, however, the senses of some animals are still superior to our most sensitive instruments. Dogs, especially, are said to display unmistakable signs of agitation days before the eruption of an earthquake, so that people keep them as helpers in the lookout posts in earthquake-prone regions. This brings me to the end of my twenty minutes, and I hope they have not passed too slowly for you.

Children's narrative broadcast by Berliner Rundfunk, October 1931. *Gesammelte Schriften*, VII, 220–226. Translated by Rodney Livingstone.

The Destructive Character

It could happen to someone looking back over his life that he realized that almost all the deeper obligations he had endured in its course originated in people who everyone agreed had the traits of a "destructive character." He would stumble on this fact one day, perhaps by chance, and the heavier the shock dealt to him, the better his chances of representing the destructive character.

The destructive character knows only one watchword: make room. And only one activity: clearing away. His need for fresh air and open space is stronger than any hatred.

The destructive character is young and cheerful. For destroying rejuvenates, because it clears away the traces of our own age; it cheers, because everything cleared away means to the destroyer a complete reduction, indeed a rooting out, of his own condition. Really, only the insight into how radically the world is simplified when tested for its worthiness for destruction leads to such an Apollonian image of the destroyer. This is the great bond embracing and unifying all that exists. It is a sight that affords the destructive character a spectacle of deepest harmony.

The destructive character is always blithely at work. It is Nature that dictates his tempo, indirectly at least, for he must forestall her. Otherwise she will take over the destruction herself.

The destructive character sees no image hovering before him. He has few needs, and the least of them is to know what will replace what has been destroyed. First of all, for a moment at least, empty space—the place where the thing stood or the victim lived. Someone is sure to be found who needs this space without occupying it.

The destructive character does his work; the only work he avoids is creative. Just as the creator seeks solitude, the destroyer must be constantly surrounded by people, witnesses to his efficacy.

The destructive character is a signal. Just as a trigonometric sign is exposed on all sides to the wind, so he is exposed to idle talk. To protect him from it is pointless.

The destructive character has no interest in being understood. Attempts in this direction he regards as superficial. Being misunderstood cannot harm him. On the contrary, he provokes it, just as oracles, those destructive institutions of the state, provoked it. The most petty bourgeois of all phenomena, gossip, comes about only because people do not wish to be misunderstood. The destructive character tolerates misunderstanding; he does not promote gossip.

The destructive character is the enemy of the étui-man. The étui-man looks for comfort, and the case is its quintessence. The inside of the case is the velvet-lined trace that he has imprinted on the world. The destructive character obliterates even the traces of destruction.

The destructive character stands in the front line of traditionalists. Some people pass things down to posterity, by making them untouchable and thus conserving them; others pass on situations, by making them practicable and thus liquidating them. The latter are called the destructive.

The destructive character has the consciousness of historical man, whose deepest emotion is an insuperable mistrust of the course of things and a readiness at all times to recognize that everything can go wrong. Therefore, the destructive character is reliability itself.

The destructive character sees nothing permanent. But for this very reason he sees ways everywhere. Where others encounter walls or mountains, there, too, he sees a way. But because he sees a way everywhere, he has to clear things from it everywhere. Not always by brute force; sometimes by the most refined. Because he sees ways everywhere, he always stands at a crossroads. No moment can know what the next will bring. What exists he reduces to rubble—not for the sake of the rubble, but for that of the way leading through it.

The destructive character lives from the feeling not that life is worth living, but that suicide is not worth the trouble.

Published in the *Frankfurter Zeitung*, November 1931. *Gesammelte Schriften*, IV, 396–398. Translated by Edmund Jephcott.

Reflections on Radio

The crucial failing of this institution has been to perpetuate the fundamental separation between practitioners and the public, a separation that is at odds with its technological basis. A child can see that it is in the spirit of radio to put as many people as possible in front of a microphone on every possible occasion; the public has to be turned into the witnesses of interviews and conversations in which now this person and now that one has the opportunity to make himself heard. Whereas in Russia they are in the process of drawing out the logical implications of the different apparatuses, with us the mindless notion of the "offering," under whose aegis the practitioner presents himself to the public, still has the field to itself. What this absurdity has led to after long years of practice is that the public has become quite helpless, quite inexpert in its critical reactions, and has seen itself more or less reduced to sabotage (switching off). There has never been another genuine cultural institution that has failed to authenticate itself by taking advantage of its own forms or technology—using them to create in the public a new expertise. This was as true of the Greek theater as of the Meistersingers, as true of the French stage as of orators from the pulpit. But it was left to the present age, with its unrestrained development of a consumer mentality in the operagoer, the novel reader, the tourist, and other similar types to convert them into dull, inarticulate masses—and create a "public" (in the narrower sense of the word) that has neither yardsticks for its judgments nor a language for its feelings. This barbarism has reached its zenith in the attitude of the masses toward radio programs, and now seems on the point of reversing itself. Only one thing is needed for this: listeners must direct their reflections at their own real reactions, in order to sharpen and justify them. This task would of course be insoluble if their behavior really were—as radio managers and especially presenters like to imagine—more or less impossible to calculate, or simply dependent upon the content of the programs. But the most superficial reflection proves the opposite. No reader has ever closed a just-opened book with the finality with which the listener switches off the radio after hearing perhaps a minute and a half of a talk. The problem is not the remoteness of the subject matter; in many cases, this might be a reason to keep listening for a while before making up one's mind. It is the voice, the diction, and the language—in a word, the formal and technical side of the broadcast—that so frequently make the most desirable programs unbearable for the listener. Conversely, for the same reason but very rarely, programs that might seem totally irrelevant can hold the listener spellbound. (There are speakers who can hold your attention while reading weather forecasts.) Accordingly, it is the technical and formal aspects of radio that will enable the listener to train himself and to outgrow this barbarism. The matter is really quite obvious. We need only reflect that the radio listener, unlike every other kind of audience, welcomes the human voice into his house like a visitor. Moreover, he will usually judge that voice just as quickly and sharply as he would a visitor. Yet no one tells it what is expected of it, what the listener will be grateful for or will find unforgivable, and so on. This can be explained only with reference to the indolence of the masses and the narrowmindedness of broadcasters. Not that it would be an easy task to describe the way the voice relates to the language used—for this is what is involved. But if radio paid heed only to the arsenal of impossibilities that seems to grow by the day—if, for example, it merely provided from a set of negative assumptions a typology of comic errors made by speakers—it would not only improve the standard of its programs but would win listeners over to its side by appealing to them as experts. And this is the most important point of all.

Fragment written no later than November 1931; unpublished in Benjamin's lifetime. *Gesammelte Schriften*, II, 1506–1507. Translated by Rodney Livingstone.

Mickey Mouse

From a conversation with Gustav Glück and Kurt Weill.[1]—Property relations in Mickey Mouse cartoons: here we see for the first time that it is possible to have one's own arm, even one's own body, stolen.

The route taken by Mickey Mouse is more like that of a file in an office than it is like that of a marathon runner.

In these films, mankind makes preparations to survive civilization.

Mickey Mouse proves that a creature can still survive even when it has thrown off all resemblance to a human being. He disrupts the entire hierarchy of creatures that is supposed to culminate in mankind.

These films disavow experience more radically than ever before. In such a world, it is not worthwhile to have experiences.

Similarity to fairy tales. Not since fairy tales have the most important and most vital events been evoked more unsymbolically and more unatmospherically. There is an immeasurable gulf between them and Maeterlinck or Mary Wigman.[2] All Mickey Mouse films are founded on the motif of leaving home in order to learn what fear is.[3]

So the explanation for the huge popularity of these films is not mechanization, their form; nor is it a misunderstanding. It is simply the fact that the public recognizes its own life in them.

Fragment written in 1931; unpublished in Benjamin's lifetime. *Gesammelte Schriften*, VI, 144–145. Translated by Rodney Livingstone.

Notes

1. Gustav Glück (1902–1973), perhaps Benjamin's closest friend during the 1930s, was director of the foreign section of the Reichskreditgesellschaft (Imperial Credit Bank) in Berlin until 1938. He was able to arrange the transfer to Paris of the fees Benjamin received from his occasional contributions to German newspapers until 1935. In 1938 Glück emigrated to Argentina; after World War II, he was a board member of the Dresdner Bank.
2. Maurice Maeterlinck (1862–1949), Belgian writer and dramatist, was one of the leading figures of the Symbolist movement at the end of the nineteenth century. He was awarded the Nobel Prize in 1911. Mary Wigman (1886–1973) was one of the greatest German dancers of the twentieth century. A pupil of Emile Jaques-Dalcroze, she developed her own school in Dresden and Leipzig, creating expressionist solo and group dances that were mainly performed without music except for percussion accompaniment. The idea was that the shape of the dance would emerge from the dancer's own rhythmic movement.
3. This refers to a fairy tale by the Brothers Grimm—"The Boy Who Left Home in Order To Learn the Meaning of Fear"—which also served as a principal theme in Wagner's version of the Siegfried legend.

In Almost Every Example We Have of Materialist Literary History

In almost every example we have of materialist literary history, what we find is a thick-skinned tracing out of the lines in the works themselves, whose social content—if not social tendency—lies partly on the surface. In contrast, the sociologist's detective-like expectation, which this method above all others might be expected to satisfy, is almost always disappointed.

Literary history burdened by value judgment. The scientific value of my theory of the fame of great works.

The enjoyability of all works of art: not simply because they can be explained but because—thanks to these explanations—they become the repositories not only of abstract or specific truth-contents, but of truth-contents that are shot through with material contents.

For the true critic, the actual *judgment* is the ultimate step—something that comes with a struggle after everything else, never the basis of his activities. In the ideal case, he forgets to pass judgment.

On the point that criticism is internal to the work: in the case of great works, art is merely a transitional stage. They were something else (in the course of their gestation) and become something else again (in the state of criticism).

Fragment written in 1931; unpublished in Benjamin's lifetime. *Gesammelte Schriften,* VI, 172. Translated by Rodney Livingstone.

The Task of the Critic

Reading is only one of a hundred ways of gaining access to a book. Always ultimately essential (within limits) as a means of verification, but often no more than this. What does it mean to have a sense of the aura surrounding a book? Perhaps it means the ability to forget. To forget a word or conversation about a book, or a glance through its pages, means perhaps consigning it to the judgment of our unconscious. The unconscious—which has the power to turn impressions and images, however fleeting, into extracts we often recognize in our dreams. This explains why the true critic often has waking dreams about a book even before he comes to know it. Moreover, this is what he has in common with a good publisher. It was no accident that these connections occurred to us in the course of a conversation with a Berlin publisher.

Regarding the terrible misconception that the quality indispensable to the true critic is "his own opinion": it is quite meaningless to learn the opinion of someone about something when you do not even know who he is. The more important the critic, the more he will avoid baldly asserting his own opinion. And the more his insights will absorb his opinions. Instead of giving his own opinion, a great critic enables others to form *their* opinion on the basis of his critical analysis. Moreover, this definition of the figure of the critic should not be a private matter but, as far as possible, an objective, strategic one. What we should know about a critic is what he stands for. He should tell us this.

Investigate why the concept of taste is obsolete. It emerged in the early stages of capitalism. Now we are in the late stages. Lexicon of literary history.

The section "Critical Technique" will include a number of major topics: theory of the critical quotation. Praise and censure. Theory of polemics.

The section "The Task of the Critic" will include a critique of the great figures of today, a critique of the sects. Physiognomic criticism. Strategic criticism.

Dialectical criticism: judgment and the events within the work itself.

Max Dessoir, *Kunstphilosophische Studien* (properly: *Beiträge zur allgemeinen Kunstwissenschaft*, Stuttgart, 1929).

Fragment written ca. 1931; unpublished in Benjamin's lifetime. *Gesammelte Schriften*, VI, 171–172. Translated by Rodney Livingstone.

Ibizan Sequence, 1932

Walter Benjamin on Ibiza, ca. 1932. Photographer unknown. Courtesy of the Theodor W. Adorno Archiv, Frankfurt am Main.

Experience

The character type that learns by experience is the exact opposite of the gambler as a type.

Experiences are lived similarities.

There is no greater error than the attempt to construe experience—in the sense of life experience—according to the model on which the exact natural sciences are based. What is decisive here is not the causal connections established over the course of time, but the similarities that have been lived.

Most people have no wish to learn by experience. Moreover, their convictions prevent them from doing so.

That experience and observation are identical has to be shown. See the concept of "romantic observation" in my dissertation.[1]—Observation is based on self-immersion.

Fragment written in 1931 or 1932; unpublished in Benjamin's lifetime. *Gesammelte Schriften*, VI, 88–89. Translated by Rodney Livingstone.

Notes

1. See Volume 1 of the present edition, pp. 147–148.

On Ships, Mine Shafts, and Crucifixes in Bottles

On ships, mine shafts, and crucifixes in bottles, as well as panopticons.

"While reading Goethe's rebuke to philistines and many other art lovers who like to touch copper engravings and reliefs, the idea came to him that anything that can be touched cannot be a work of art, and anything that is a work of art should be placed out of reach." Franz Glück on Adolf Loos, in *Adolf Loos: Das Werk des Architekten* [Adolf Loos: The Architect's Works], edited by Heinrich Kulka (Vienna, 1931), p. 9.

Does this mean that these objects in bottles are works of art *because* they have been placed out of reach?

Fragment written no later than 1932; unpublished in Benjamin's lifetime. *Gesammelte Schriften*, VI, 127. Translated by Rodney Livingstone.

On the Trail of Old Letters

What I would like to tell you about today, Ladies and Gentlemen, has its focus in a number of documents—some old letters, in fact—and in the circumstances that led me to them.[1] I would like to confine myself here to a few brief words of introduction. I will not discuss the various bibliographic and library techniques that enable the researcher to find his way around the mass of letters that German history has bequeathed to us. About all this, let us say merely that in the case of many of the most valuable of these letters, the real work comes after they have been discovered; for they confront us with the challenge of making them comprehensible in their proper context and from every angle. No, what I would like to tell you about are the motives that guide me in my search. I won't say "the motives that guided me from the outset," since, as with so many enterprises (and not the least interesting among them), what triggered my search initially was no more than an idea, a whim, which contained little more than the dim outlines of what I perceive with greater clarity today. And if I am clearer about my own intentions now, I owe this in no small measure to the editors of the *Frankfurter Zeitung,* who were happy to place their trust in a casual suggestion and to make room for this small selection—the beginnings of a series for which I have already obtained many useful ideas.

Many of you will perhaps recall the stratification that Gundolf once proposed for analyzing the mountain of a great artist's life; we do not wish to adopt his scheme, but it is useful to describe it.[2] Any conversations that have survived form the foothills of the peak, which begin an almost imperceptible rise. This would be followed by the broad layer of the correspondence that has been handed down and is closer to the final shape, while the summit contains the genuinely creative achievement. Now if we can stick with this metaphor for a moment, the situation with the age of German Classicism, which was my starting point and to which we should confine ourselves, is that this mountain is covered by a glacier. For it cannot be denied that the canon of German Classicism has long been fixed and is no longer open to debate, and its rigid immobility threatens to be matched by its present lack of influence. Anyone who has become aware of this will also realize that the huge mass of correspondence we possess from that period represents (to continue the metaphor) something like the snow line. Not that there has been a dearth of attempts to extend the debilitating concept of Classicism to various collections of letters, to label them canonical and condemn them to impotence. I need only name the correspondence between Goethe and Schiller, Feuerbach's letters to his mother, and Wilhelm von Humboldt's letters to Karoline, his future wife—volumes that can even be acquired in gilt-edged editions. But this does not change the fact that the overwhelming mass of these great collections of letters has been ignored by schools, the press, and the speechifying industries and has for that reason been prevented from falling into the all-consuming and insatiable maw of culture. In other words, a knowledge of these letters has hitherto been the preserve of scholars—indeed, of specialists. But this means that, even among them, hardly anyone has turned his attention to the letters for their own intrinsic interest. In most cases they have remained evidence, treasure trove, source material, or whatever else you may care to call it. Hence, Gervinus is right to assert in the introduction to his extremely important study of Goethe's correspondence: "Literary historians have obviously extracted the chief benefits that these collections of letters can confer . . . They make possible a literary-historical pragmatism that was previously inconceivable and that in earlier times was neither known nor needed. For . . . desire and the pleasure of peeking through a writer's windows can result only from the author's desire to conceal the writer behind the man, or vice versa. But this effort is particularly characteristic of the modern age and its authors, even though it is as foolish and futile as the attempt to keep political matters a secret."[3] With these words Gervinus introduces his considered project of allowing an image of Goethe, and more especially the old Goethe, to emerge from his correspondence. This is one of the very few exhaustive and penetrating attempts to analyze a corpus of letters, an attempt that is as different from the scholarly industry that followed as it is from the misuse of important collections of letters to underpin a cult of the writer as hero.

But I do not commend this exemplary piece of research to you without reservation. It must not be overlooked that Gervinus published his study five years after Goethe's death, and that he lacked the necessary historical distance for a proper appraisal of the letters. Yet it is this very historical distance which dictates the laws governing our own examination, chief among them that of content: the fact that with the passage of time those distinctions between man and author, the private and the objective, the person and the thing, gradually lose their validity. To the point where it becomes clear that to do justice to a single significant letter, to illuminate it in all of its factual references, its allusions and details, means going to the very heart of the person's humanity. If this humanity does not amount to a striking character, a hero or genius, but instead to something that facilitates communication with his lesser contemporaries, this will merely make it the more noble, creditable, and rich in substance. We do not shy away from saying straight out: the more deeply the historian enters into the past, the more the psychology characteristic of someone like Emil Ludwig in his slick and cheap biographies becomes devalued, and the more the facts, the data, and the names come into their own—an achievement that need be no mere philological accretion, but a true human gain.[4]

What follows are some modest attempts to live up to these intentions.

[The typescript here contains a gap, which was presumably to be filled by a number of letters and the relevant commentaries.]

So much for today. It would give me great pleasure if the few letters that I now lay before you were to whet your appetite for a further series which the *Frankfurter Zeitung* proposes to publish shortly. And it would please me even more if I have managed to convince you that these publications are not intended to gratify either philological ambition or a dubious need for culture, but are meant instead to transmit a living tradition.

Undelivered talk written in late 1931 or early 1932. *Gesammelte Schriften*, IV, 942–944. Translated by Rodney Livingstone.

Notes

1. From April 1931 to May 1932, Benjamin published a series of twenty-seven letters from the period 1783–1883 in the *Frankfurter Zeitung*. The present talk, which may have been intended for radio broadcast, serves as a kind of introduction to the series, which did not bear Benjamin's name.

2. Friedrich Gundolf (pseudonym of Friedrich Gundelfinger; 1880–1931), a disciple of Stefan George, was a prominent literary critic and, after 1920, a professor at Heidelberg. Benjamin was engaged in a long polemic against Gundolf in the Teens and Twenties. See "Comments on Gundolf's *Goethe*" and "Goethe's Elective Affinities," in Volume 1 of this edition.

3. Georg Gottfried Gervinus, *Ueber den Göthischen Briefwechsel* [On Goethe's Correspondence] (Leipzig, 1836), pp. 2–3. Gervinus (1805–1871), a historian,

literary historian, and politician, held professorships at Heidelberg and Göttingen and was a delegate to the German National Assembly in Frankfurt in 1848. His literary history broke new ground in its effort to embed the discussion of literature within a larger historical narrative.

4. Emil Ludwig (1881–1948), German biographer, gained an international reputation for his popular biographies. His biography of Goethe (1925) established him as a writer in the "new school" of biography, which emphasized the personality of the subject.

A Family Drama in the Epic Theater

On the occasion of the world premiere of Brecht's play *Die Mutter* [The Mother].

Brecht has said of Communism that it is "the middle term." "Communism is not radical. It is capitalism that is radical." How radical it is can be seen in its attitude toward the family—as in every other matter. It insists upon the family at any price, even where intensification of family life can only aggravate the suffering already caused by conditions utterly unworthy of human beings. Communism is not radical. Therefore, it has no intention of simply abolishing family relations. It merely tests them to determine their capacity for change. It asks itself: Can the family be dismantled so that its components may be socially refunctioned? These components are not so much the family members themselves as their relationships with one another. Of these, it is clear that none is more important than the relationship between mother and child. Furthermore, the mother, among all family members, is the most unequivocally determined as to her social function: she produces the next generation. The question raised by Brecht's play is: Can this social function become a revolutionary one, and how? In a capitalist economic system, the more directly a person is engaged in production relations, the more he or she is subject to exploitation. Under today's conditions, the family is an organization for the exploitation of the woman as mother. Pelagea Vlassova, "widow of a worker and mother of a worker," is therefore someone who is doubly exploited: first, as a member of the working class, and, second, as a woman and mother. The doubly exploited childbearer represents the exploited in their most extreme oppression. If mothers are revolutionized, there is nothing left to revolutionize. Brecht's subject is a sociological experiment concerning the revolutionizing of a mother. This explains a number of simplifications which are not agitational but constructive. "Widow of a worker, mother of a worker"—here lies the first simplification. Pelagea Vlassova is the mother of only one worker, and for this reason she somewhat contradicts the original meaning of the word "proletarian woman" (*proles,* in Latin, means descendants). This mother has only one son. The one is enough. For it turns out that with this one lever she can operate the mechanism which channels her maternal energies toward the entire working class. Her first duty is to cook. Producer of a man, she becomes the reproducer of his working strength. But there is no longer enough to eat for such reproduction. The son looks with contempt at the food she puts in front of him. How easily this look can wound the mother. She cannot help herself because she does not yet know that "the decision about the meat lacking in the kitchen is not made in the kitchen." This, or something like it, is surely written in the leaflets she goes out to distribute. Not in order to help Communism, but in order to help her son, whose turn it is to distribute them. This is how her work for the party begins. And in this way she transforms the antagonism which threatened to develop between herself and her son into an antagonism against their mutual enemy. This attitude of a mother is the sole suitable form of help—followed here into its true, original housing, the folds of a mother's skirt—that can at the same time acquire a social validity (as the solidarity of the oppressed) which it possessed before only in an animal sense. The road which the mother travels is that from this first kind of help to the ultimate form, the solidarity of the working class. Her speech to the mothers who queue up to hand in their copper kitchenware is not a pacifist one; it is a revolutionary exhortation to the childbearers who, by betraying the cause of the weak, also betray the cause of their own young, their children. And so we see that the mother's way to the party starts first with helping, and comes to theory only afterward. This is the second constructive simplification. The purpose of these simplifications is to underline the simplicity of the lessons they teach. It is in the nature of Epic Theater to replace the undialectical opposition between the form and content of consciousness (which meant that a character can refer to his own actions only by reflections) by the dialectical one between theory and praxis (which meant that any action making a breakthrough opens up a clearer view of theory). Epic Theater, therefore, is the theater of the hero who is beaten. A hero who is not beaten never makes a thinker. "Spare the rod and spoil the hero," to modify one of our forefathers' pedagogical maxims. There is something special about the "lessons" with which the mother occupies herself, as if with commentary on her own behavior, during her times of defeat or of waiting (for Epic Theater, there is no difference between the two): she sings them. She sings, "What Are the Objections to Communism?" She sings, "Learn, Woman of Sixty!" She sings, "In Praise of the Third Cause." And she sings these songs as a mother. For they are lullabies. Lullabies for Communism, which is small and weak but irresistibly growing. This Communism she has taken unto herself as a mother. It becomes clear, too, that she is loved by Communism as only a mother is loved: she is loved not for the sake of her beauty or her fame or her excellence, but as the inexhaustible source of help. She represents help at its source, where it is still pure-flowing, where it is still practical and not false, from where it can still be channeled without reservation to that which, without reservation, needs help—namely, Communism. The mother is praxis incarnate. We see this when she makes tea, and we see it when she wraps up the piroshkis; when she is visiting her son in prison, we see that every single thing she does with her hands serves Communism; and when she is hit by stones and the policemen strike her with their rifle butts, we see that whenever a hand is raised against her it is in vain. The mother is praxis incarnate. This means that we shall find in her not enthusiasm but reliability. Yet she would not be reliable if she had not, at first, raised objections against Communism. But—and this is the decisive fact—her objections were not those of an interested party but those of common sense. "It's necessary, therefore it isn't dangerous"—she'll never accept statements like that. And she has just as little use for utopias. "Does Mr. Sukhlinov own his factory or doesn't he? Well, then!" You can explain to her, however, that his ownership of the factory is a limited one. And so, step by step, she travels along the path of ordinary common sense.—"If you've a disagreement with Mr. Sukhlinov, what has that got to do with the police?" This step-by-step advance of ordinary common sense, the opposite of radicalism, leads the mother to the head of the May Day demonstration, where she is beaten down. So much for the mother. It is time to turn the tables and ask: If the mother leads, what is happening to the son? It is the son, after all, who reads books and prepares himself for leadership. There are four characters—mother and son, theory and praxis—and they regroup themselves; they play a game of change and change about. Once the critical moment arrives when ordinary common sense becomes the leader, theory is only good enough to do the housework. The son must cut bread while the mother, who is illiterate, works the printing press; the necessity of life no longer catalogues people according to their sex. In the workers' room, space is made for a blackboard between the kitchen range and the bed. When the State is turned upside down for the sake of a kopeck, much will change within the family, too; and at that moment the place of the bride, who personifies the ideals of the future, will be taken by the mother, who, with all her forty years' experience, will confirm Marx and Lenin. The dialectic has no need of a far distance shrouded in mist. It is at home within the four walls of praxis, and it stands on the threshold of the moment to speak the closing words of the play: "And 'Never' becomes, 'Before the day is out!'"

Published in *Die literarische Welt,* February 1932. *Gesammelte Schriften,* II, 511–514. Translated by Anna Bostock.

The Railway Disaster at the Firth of Tay

When people first attempted to smelt iron and build steam engines at the beginning of the nineteenth century, that was a very different matter from what happens today when scientists and engineers go about developing a new airplane or even a space rocket or some other new machine. Today we know what technology is. Such scientists and engineers have the attention of the whole world; newspapers inform us of their achievements, and great industrial concerns provide them with money for their research. But as for the men who made those inventions at the turn of the past century and who transformed the face of the earth—the inventors of the mechanical loom or gaslighting, iron smelting or the steam engine—basically the average person had no idea what they were doing, and even they could form no conception of the implications of their own work. It is difficult to call any one of these major discoveries more important than the others. For people in our day, they can scarcely be thought of independently of their applications. Even so, we may say that the most striking alterations to the globe in the course of the previous century were all in some way or other connected with the railway. I am going to tell you today about a railway disaster. Not so much to recount a horrifying story, but rather to put the event in the context of the history of technology and more particularly of railway construction. A bridge plays a role in this story. The bridge collapsed. This was without doubt a catastrophe for the two hundred people who lost their lives, for their relatives, and for many others. Nevertheless, I wish to portray this disaster as no more than a minor episode in a great struggle from which human beings have emerged victorious and shall remain victorious unless they themselves destroy the work of their own hands once more.

As I was thinking about what to say to you today, I went back to one of my favorite books. It is a thick book, with illustrations, dating from around 1840, and is actually full of jokes and fanciful stories.[1] But we can acquire all sorts of curious knowledge from reading about what people in olden times found amusing and entertaining. For example, this book tells the adventures of a fantastic little imp who is trying to find his way about in the cosmos. When he arrives at the planets, he comes across a cast-iron bridge that links the countless heavenly bodies to one another. "A bridge whose two ends could not be glimpsed at the same time and whose piers rested on the various planets led, on a marvelously smooth asphalt surface, from one heavenly body to the next. The 333,000th pillar rested on Saturn. Then our imp noticed that the famous ring around this planet was nothing other than a balcony running entirely around the planet and on which the inhabitants of Saturn strolled in the evening to get a breath of fresh air." Do you see what I mean when I said that, at the time, people did not really know how they should react to technological advances? The latter were not without a comic side in their eyes. In particular, they thought it very funny that when iron buildings were constructed, only questions of form and matters of calculation should be taken into account. It was fitting, therefore, that there should have been a playful dimension in the first buildings of this kind to be built. Building in iron thus began with winter gardens and arcades—that is to say, with luxury buildings. But suitable technical applications were soon discovered, and this gave rise to buildings of a completely new type—constructions that had no precedent in the past. It was not just that they were founded on the new technology; they also satisfied quite new needs. It was at this time that the first exhibition palaces were built, the first covered markets, and above all the first train stations. They were still known then as "iron-railway stations" and they called up the strangest images in people's minds. Around the middle of the century a particularly audacious Belgian painter, Antoine Wiertz,[2] even put in an application to be allowed to paint the walls of these first stations with huge ceremonial pictures.

Before we take a look at the Firth of Tay—the vast, 3,000-meter-wide mouth of the River Tay in central Scotland—let's cast our minds back a little further into the past. In 1814 Stephenson built his first locomotive.[3] But it was not until 1820, when it became possible to manufacture the rails, that the first rail*way* became a possibility. You should not imagine, however, that all this was achieved systematically, step by step. On the contrary, a violent quarrel at once broke out on the subject of the rails. Under no circumstances, so it was claimed, would it ever be possible to provide enough iron for the English rail network—and at this time people thought in terms of a tiny network by today's standards. It would be necessary, according to many experts, to make the "steam carriages" run on granite tracks. Then, in 1825, the first railway line was opened, and even today

"Locomotive No. 1" can still be seen at one of the terminals—and if you were ever to go see it, you would undoubtedly be tempted to think it was a steamroller for smoothing pavement rather than a genuine locomotive. In Europe, on the Continent, they began with quite short stretches of line, over distances that could have been covered just as well by mail coach, or even on foot. You may have heard that the first two German towns to be linked by rail were Nuremberg and Fürth; they were followed by Berlin and Potsdam, and so on. But on balance these developments were regarded largely as a curiosity. When the Medical Faculty of Erlangen University was asked for an expert opinion about the proposed Nuremberg railway, they replied that it should not be permitted under any circumstances. The passengers' brains would be affected by the speed, and even the mere sight of these roaring trains might well cause people to faint. At the very least, it would be necessary to build fences three meters high on either side of the tracks. The second German railway, between Leipzig and Dresden, was the subject of legal proceedings brought by a miller who alleged it diverted the wind from his mill; and when it turned out that a tunnel would be required, physicians again protested on the grounds that elderly people might suffer a stroke as a result of the sudden change in air pressure. What people thought of the railroad in those days can best be seen from the comment of an English scholar, who in other respects was anything but a fool. He said that he could not regard going by rail as a form of travel; in reality, you were just being sent from one place to another, as if you were a package.

In addition to these arguments about the benefits or drawbacks of the railroad, there were also struggles associated with the building process itself. We find it difficult today to imagine the stamina required of these early engineers, or the huge timespans with which they were forced to reckon. In 1858, when they were constructing the twelve-kilometer-long tunnel through Mont Cenis, they calculated that the work would last seven years. It was similar with the bridge over the Tay. In the latter case, there was a further factor to be considered. They had to take into account not just the loads that the bridge had to bear, but also the terrible storms that rage around the Scottish coast, above all in autumn and spring. During the building of the bridge, which lasted from 1872 to 1878, there were whole months when the storms hardly ever ceased, and there were times when work could be done only five or six days in a month. In 1877, when the bridge was almost complete, a gale of unprecedented violence tore two iron girders, each forty-five meters in length, from their stone piers and at one fell swoop destroyed several years' worth of work. All the greater was the triumph, then, in May 1878, when the bridge was opened amid great celebration. Only one warning voice was to be heard, although that was the voice of J. Towler, one of the greatest of English bridge builders.[4] He expressed the view that it would be unable to withstand the storms for long and that people would soon be hearing of the Tay bridge once again.

A year and a half later, on December 28, 1879, at 4:00 in the afternoon, the regular passenger train left Edinburgh for Dundee, crowded with people. It was Sunday, and the six cars contained 200 passengers. Once again, it was one of those stormy Scottish days. The train was due to arrive in Dundee at 7:15 in the evening, but the time was already 7:14 when the signal box on the south side of the bridge announced its approach. I shall recount what happened next in the words of Theodor Fontane,[5] who describes the last that was heard of the train after that final signal. This is a passage from his poem "The Bridge over the Tay":

> It was the train. It chugs past
> the South Tower, the storm in its face,
> And Johnny says, "There's only the bridge!
> But it won't stop us—we'll win the race.
> A stout boiler, a great head of steam
> will carry the prize off in this fight.
> And though it may rage and batter and scream,
> We'll conquer the elements this very night.
>
> The bridge o'er the Tay is our pride and joy.
> It makes me laugh when I think of the past,
> with all of the trouble, the grief, and the woe
> the old ferryboat gave us right up to the last.
> Many and many a dear Christmas Eve
> Have I spent in the ferryman's cottage
> And gazed at our windows, lights burning so bright,
> And couldn't cross over there, wish though I might."
>
> On the northern shore, the bridge watchman's house,
> All the windows gaze out to the south,
> And the watchman's people full of alarm
> Anxiously gaze out through the storm.
> For the wind in furious play seemed to grow
> and down from the skies flames did glow,
> Bursting in glory as they descended
> to the water beneath . . . and all was ended.

There were no witnesses to the events of that night. Of those who were in the train, none was rescued. So to this very day no one knows what happened—perhaps the storm had blown away the middle of the bridge even before the train arrived, and the train simply plunged into the void. At all events, the storm is said to have raged so furiously that it drowned out all other sounds. But other engineers, especially those who actually built the bridge, maintained that the storm had blown the train off its tracks and hurled it against the parapet. It was this that caused a breach in the protective wall, and the bridge collapsed only much later.—So the first sign of the disaster was not the noise made by the falling train, but the flames that three fishermen noticed at the time, without suspecting that they came from the locomotive as it went hurtling down. These three men alerted the station on the south side, but when the latter tried to establish contact with the north station they received no response. The cables had been severed. They then contacted the stationmaster in Tay, who set out at once with a locomotive. He reached the spot a quarter of an hour later. Cautiously he inched the locomotive onto the bridge. He had barely reached the first central pier, about a kilometer out, when the driver applied the brakes so fiercely that the train almost leaped from the track. The moonlight had enabled him to see a gaping hole in the line. The central section of the bridge was gone.

If you look up the *Funkstunde* [Radio Times], you will find a picture of the damaged bridge that appeared at the time in the *Leipziger Illustrierte*. Even though the iron construction is evident at a glance, this bridge still had much in common with wooden bridges. Building in iron was in its infancy, and had not yet become fully confident of its own strengths. Of course, you are all familiar—from pictures, if from nowhere else—with the building in which iron first displayed itself with pride and utter self-confidence, a building which was also a monument to engineering calculation. I am referring to the tower that Eiffel completed for the World's Fair in Paris just ten years after the collapse of the Tay bridge. When the Eiffel Tower was built, it served no practical purpose of any kind; it was simply a landmark— a wonder of the world, as people say. But it was followed by the invention of radio telegraphy, and, at a stroke, the huge construction suddenly acquired a meaning. Today the Eiffel Tower is a Paris radio transmitter. Eiffel and his engineers had built the tower in seventeen months. Every rivet-hole had been precisely positioned in the workshops to within a tenth of a millimeter. Each of the twelve thousand metal fittings, each of the two and a half million rivets, had been machined to the millimeter. There was no sound of chisels on the work site; in the open air as much as in the builders' workshops, thought reigned over sheer muscle power, which it was able to transmit via cranes and secure scaffolding.[6]

Radio talk broadcast by Berliner Rundfunk, February 1932. *Gesammelte Schriften*, VII, 232–237. Translated by Rodney Livingstone.

Notes

1. The book in question is *Un Autre Monde* (Another World), first published in 1844, with satirical-oneiric drawings by the great illustrator Jean Ignace Isidore Gérard, known as Grandville (1803–1847).
2. Antoine Wiertz (1806–1865), a Belgian painter of colossal historical scenes, was lampooned by Baudelaire. See also Benjamin's comments in his *Passagen-Werk* (Arcades Project).
3. George Stephenson (1781–1848), English inventor and railroad pioneer, built and successfully demonstrated the first locomotive, at Killingworth, in 1814. He went on to invent a number of other locomotives and cofounded the locomotive works at Newcastle in 1823.
4. Benjamin surely means Sir John *Fowler* (1817–1898), English civil engineer, who designed the Pimlico Railway Bridge (1860) and, with Sir Benjamin Baker, the Forth Railway Bridge (1882–1890). He was also consulting engineer to Ismail Pasha, Khedive of Egypt.
5. Theodor Fontane (1819–1898), novelist, poet, and essayist, was Germany's greatest realist writer. He wrote his first novel when he was fifty-six. He is best-known in the English-language world for *Effi Briest* (1895).
6. The last two sentences are quoted without attribution from Alfred Gotthold Meyer, *Eisenbauten: Ihre Geschichte und Aesthetik* [Iron Constructions: Their History and Aesthetics] (Esslingen, 1907), p. 93. See Benjamin's *Passagen-Werk* (Arcades Project), F4a,2.

Privileged Thinking

On Theodor Haecker's *Virgil*

Virgil: Father of the West[1] is the title of a book in which Theodor Haecker presents us with the truths, teachings, and warnings from the works of Virgil that seem most relevant to him after the passing of two thousand years. The author, although a Catholic, is a disciple of Kierkegaard, not merely as a theologian but also as a polemicist. And his book must be considered in the light of its polemical intent. Haecker has two chief concerns: the overthrow of the traditional evaluation, which places Virgil in the shadow of Homer; and the demolition of every untheological—or, more exactly, un-Catholic— interpretation of the poet. This dual focus makes the book quite distinctive among the mass of commemorative writing, but it shares with other important works the goal of ascertaining Virgil's proper place beyond Homer, beyond Greek culture in general, and even beyond the realm of pure poetry. The radical nature of the change, undoubtedly the first for several hundred years, can be seen from a glance at any of the literary histories published around the turn of the century. "Virgil," we are told there quite baldly, "was no great poet." In contrast, the various writings that have appeared for the bimillennial celebration bespeak a very positive assessment of the poet, and also emphasize that his greatness is rooted in the religious. Vyacheslav Ivanov writes, for example,

> So what we have in Virgil's narrative of the wanderings and wartime toils of his *pater Aeneas* is not an old-style heroic saga, with tales of fame and suffering that amount to a mythological corroboration of the cult of the hero concerned, but a kind of hagiography reminiscent of Bible stories, inaugurating an endless series of deeds accomplished not by himself but by his successors, and serving as the launching pad for a vast destiny in the light of which the hero sees himself not so much as the enactor of those deeds but as the forerunner of the promised

salvation and as the instrument of God . . . In consequence of this, Virgil's view of history falls historically between the Bible and Saint Augustine's masterwork, *The City of God*.[2]

It so happens that these words provide a very useful paraphrase of Haecker's own basic conception. But the further development of this conception is linked to a very curious methodology. The majority of the chapters in Haecker's book bear epigraphs consisting of a Virgilian hemistich. These are then subjected to a process of interpretation. This means that the analysis largely becomes an exegesis of specific turns of phrase, or even single words—which of course can come as no surprise, in view of Haecker's language-mysticism. No interpretation—let alone a theological interpretation—can proceed without some violence. In order to penetrate to deeper reserves of substance, it may blast apart the poetic framework, at the same time allowing the most fruitful unfolding of the text from out of the core of the word; it can be theological without sacrificing philology. Haecker's interpretive practice, however, does violence to the text. It blasts apart the Roman context rather than the poetic one; it violates the philological sphere so that the words can unfold *ad majorem Dei gloriam*.[3] (If this were the place to explore Haecker's entire doctrinal system, his ahistorical, idealist language-mysticism would be a principal focus of attention. Even the present account cannot afford, in what follows, to ignore it entirely.) Haecker's mystical approach to interpretation gives his work the character of a tract, and this accords well with both the elevated language and the authoritarian assertiveness with which Christian dogmas and dicta are linked to every line or hemistich. In one instance, the last line of the *Aeneid* is given a Pascalian twist; in another, the famous "Sunt lacrimae rerum"[4] is made to invoke the idea of justification. Elsewhere the "richness of Virgil's humanity" is interpreted as the readiness to "venerate the mystery—in other words, to believe in a divine fate without any abatement of free will and human responsibility." Haecker even goes on to define it further as a double mystery, one that is fulfilled "by Christianity through the gracious pleasure of the trinitarian God who is Spirit and life, through the gracious pleasure of the God who is inscrutable, inaccessible, like the Fates of old, who is obscure not by virtue of the night but by virtue of the light, who brings suffering not through whim but from wisdom, and who brings not merely perfect justice but also the Passion and the flames of love." After further theological reflections, he reverts to aesthetic considerations: "God is true and good and beautiful; no sooner does the poet touch the hem of God's beauty, thereby touching also the hem of the true and the good, than his work instantly acquires something absolute and immortal." The book undoubtedly contains profounder and more rigorous statements about Virgil than these. But this does not alter the fact that Haecker's resolute neglect of any secular—in other words, authentic—philological study of Virgil prevents him from recognizing such theological arguments for what they are: clichés inherited from the aesthetics of Late Romanticism.

We may frequently applaud the invective that Haecker unleashes against the translations of Virgil by Rudolf Alexander Schröder—but there can be no doubt that the latter's "Marginal Notes by a Reader of Virgil," which appeared at roughly the same time as Haecker's book, have chosen a superior approach.[5] Schröder, too, recognizes the importance of *pietas* for Virgil. But he can place it in its rich historical context, and in so doing he develops a novel and fertile concept of syncretism. In addition to everything he has to say about Virgil's importance for posterity, he is able to say something about Virgil's own view of history—unlike Haecker, who quite significantly, but also quite irritatingly, never transcends the sphere of the poet's individual soul, the *anima naturaliter christiana*,[6] and never attains a view of Roman *religio*. Thus, according to Schröder,

> There can be no doubt that a religious view of the world, in which every terrestrial manifestation, all earthly activities, seem to be reduplicated at a scarcely higher level of spirituality, can easily degenerate into crude animism in the vulgar mind, or into a jumble of more or less absurd observances in minds incapable of faith. But behind this we also find an overarching concept of such profundity as can move and inspire whole worlds—namely, the idea that something sacred which commands respect inhabits even the most profane aspects of the phenomenal world . . . The divine service that dedicated wreaths and offerings not just to the *lares* and *penates*[7] but also to boundary stones, the labor of ploughing and sowing, the *genius* of opening and shutting doors, and to many other objectifications of fleeting moments of time . . . may not inspire every person on every occasion with the image of a fully spiritualized or divine universe. Despite this, the world view represented here was an immanent entelechy that was articulated in each and every one of its component parts.

See how dessicated and pallid Haecker is in comparison: "We no longer have any vital interest in the outward practices of the Roman state religion—this is of concern to scholarship alone—nor can we warm to the entire Roman pantheon, which for the most part (aside from the rustic gods) has no more than a poetic importance, a purely external symbolic significance, even in Virgil." And describing the distinction between state religion and piety in the same context, he says: "In the pure spirit there is no possible antagonism between external piety, which is no piety at all, and internal piety, which despises the external one or maligns it; for in the pure spirit everything is *within*, both form and content. In mankind, however, this antithesis is real." The unassuming concept of the "pure spirit," as manifest here, is worthy of note. For it is precisely this concept which is the holder of those curious privileges characteristic of the kind of thinking practiced by Haecker. We have already seen that this thinking is authoritarian. Now, authority is a strange thing. It must be strong and immovable—no doubt. Yet it must also be inviting and captivating. It must be visible from far off—a fortress, if you like, but with a thousand gates. Knowing better is also a mighty fortress, but the knower has the privilege of inhabiting it alone.

In Germany, there have always been many people—nowadays they are particularly numerous—who believe that *what* they know, and the fact that *they* know it, are the key to the situation and that from now on everything will have to change. But they have only the vaguest notion about how to give this knowledge any direction and how to bring it to the people. They imagine you just have to express it, stress it. They are miles away from the idea that knowledge which contains no indication of how it should be propagated is of little use, and that in truth it is no knowledge at all. And if you tell them that every true knowledge always begins by testing its truth historically, that it tries itself out on new people unfamiliar with it, this will simply unnerve them. Nothing is so characteristic of their helplessness, their lack of realism, as the spurious immediacy with which the "pure spirit" inside them addresses itself to "mankind." In their heads "spirit" and "man" have concluded a spectral alliance; and so united, they join together here too. The introduction to Haecker's book contains a perhaps superfluous defense of "mankind" or "the human"—terms that anyway enjoy all the privileges of fashionable phrases. He writes: "There is scarcely anyone who, observing the countless different species of plants and animals and paying particular attention to the differences between them, nevertheless overlooks, or wishes to deny, the fact that there is such a thing as *the* plant or *the* animal, with eternally immutable qualities. Whereas there are people today who appear to believe that there have been radical changes in the nature of mankind in the course of time." For someone schooled in the tradition of scholasticism, as Haecker obviously is, a statement of this kind requires an uncommon freedom from intellectual scruple. For the question whether such species-beings exist—whether they exist *ante rem*, as the Schoolmen put it—was nowhere fought out so bitterly as in the dispute over universals, which nominalists carried on against realists. The fact that the author has chosen to come down so firmly on one side, particularly in this context, will perhaps raise some eyebrows. But only until it is realized what this partisanship achieves on behalf of the above-mentioned privileges. And this brings us back to "mankind" as beheld by the "spirit." "We have to say," Haecker writes further on, "that for the last 2,000 years Western man has had the ascendancy over all other nations and races. What this ultimately means is that it is *in principle* possible for him (regardless of the fact that he has often failed to make use of it in reality) to *understand* all other human beings, and this entails both his actual and possible political domination over them. And what has given him this possibility and this reality is his 'faith'." It is not our fault if the author makes the political implications of his "idea of humanity" so painfully clear—namely, that radically privileged understanding of non-Western man which is characterized by a combination of exploitation and the missionary spirit. The fact is that this is how contraband looks when wrapped in the fine muslin of the pure spirit which travelers take with them to cloud-cuckoo-land.

Theology should be the last place to be such a cloud-cuckoo-land. In fact, there have been theological thinkers, even in our generation, who have declared war against all idolatry of the spirit: Franz Rosenzweig, a Jew, who has done so from a linguistic point of view, and Florens Christian Rang, a Christian, who has done so from the perspective of politics.[8] Now, Haecker of course regards himself as both a politician and a philosopher of language, even if he might prefer not to be known as such. But he must be denied a place in the ranks of authentic theological thinkers in view of the fact that, on the basis of spirit alone, he imagines he can be master of both the philosophy of language and of politics without becoming conversant either with philology or with economics. Of course—and here we see the matter in its proper light—Rosenzweig, and even more clearly Rang, were essentially heretics in their attitudes; they saw no difficulty in advancing tradition by carrying it on their backs, instead of simply administering it in a sedentary way. It is Haecker's very moderation that cheats him of the fruits of his endeavors. For however radical his rereading of the sources, however great the art with which he interprets the texts, what is the use of all that if his mind clings to convention—a convention that is revealed to us here by his amateurish questions about Virgil's meaning for us today. This corresponds precisely to the false immediacy with which spirit addresses itself to mankind. (The great political significance of the doctrine of original sin is that it does away with immediacy and inwardness of this type.)

If Haecker had only managed to arrive at the genuine, mediated form of the problem—namely, what we can learn from the history of Virgil's poem and research on it, at a time when both threaten to come to an untimely end—he would have been able to provide us with proof of his brilliant gifts as a writer, without directing our gaze to his very modest talent as a thinker. There is no lack of models for such a project. If we think of the scholarly austerity with which Bezold has researched the afterlife of the ancient gods in medieval humanism,[9] we shall better understand how much more meaningful it would have been to embed not just Virgil but also Scholasticism in the context of medieval writing, whereas Haecker's formulas basically only repeat those that had once been used to conjure up the image of "Virgil the Sorcerer."

"A humanism emptied of theology will not stand the test of time," the author claims. But to recommend Thomism as a cure for an age whose humanism is intellectually and actually compromised is to take the joke too far. Haecker lives in an ivory tower and spends his time gazing out of the topmost window, belittling things. And the worst of it is that the ground on which this tower has been built is giving way. How otherwise could anyone use the phrase "adventistic paganism" as if it were in common use, while not noticing that the future approaching him and all of us is perfectly "adventistic," even when it is on the march? How could he describe "a merely philological and aesthetic interpretation of Virgil" as "a false approach, an undermining of civilization, carried out by minds themselves undermined," yet find no words for the barbaric conditions to which humanism of every kind is tied nowadays? It is the arrogance and lack of integrity on the part of intellectuals that is to blame for this inconsistency—the same features that allow them to speak of "the spiritual" without blushing and for no other reason than that they are unable to give an account of their own place in the production process. For if they were, an essayist of Haecker's gifts could not avoid the problem of every truly contemporary interpretation of Virgil: the possibility of humanism in our age. And the sight of the privileges which still enable a man to remain a humanist would liberate him from their most calcified accretion: privileged knowledge of the true path—a knowledge that turns out to be the most lethal metamorphosis of cultural privilege.

Published in *Die literarische Welt*, February 1932. *Gesammelte Schriften*, III, 314–322. Translated by Rodney Livingstone.

Notes

1. Theodor Haecker, *Vergil: Vater des Abendlandes* (Leipzig: Jacob Hegner, 1931), 148 pages. [Benjamin's note]
2. Vyacheslav Ivanov, "Vergils Historiosophie," *Corona*, May 1, 1931, p. 769.
3. *Ad majorem Dei gloriam:* "to the greater glory of God."
4. "Sunt lacrimae rerum et mentem mortalia tagunt": *Aeneid*, Book 1, line 461. "Here [in Tyre] as well, there are tears for misfortune, and mortal sorrows touch the heart."
5. R. A. Schröder, "Marginalien eines Vergil-Lesers," *Corona*, May 1, 1931, p. 752.
6. *Anima naturaliter christiana:* "the natural Christian soul."
7. *Lares* and *penates:* tutelary deities in Roman religion. *Lares,* originally gods of the fields, eventually came to be worshiped in the household in association with the *penates,* the gods of the storeroom.
8. Franz Rosenzweig (1886–1929) was a German religious thinker whose magnum opus, *Der Stern der Erlösung* (The Star of Redemption; 1921), made him one of the most influential modern Jewish theologians. After 1922, he was afflicted by progressive paralysis, but pushed ahead with a number of projects, including a new German translation of the Hebrew Bible in collaboration with Martin Buber. Benjamin's friend Florens Christian Rang, a conservative intellectual, had published a book entitled *Deutsche Bauhütte: Ein Wort an uns Deutsche über mögliche Gerechtigkeit gegen Belgien und Frankreich und zur Philosophie der*

Politik [German Masons' Guilds: A Word to Us Germans on the Possibility of Justice toward Belgium and France and on the Philosophy of Politics] (Leipzig: Sannerz, 1924), which included "replies" from a number of well-known figures, including Martin Buber, Alfons Paquet, and Benjamin.

9. Friedrich Bezold, *Das Fortleben der antiken Götter in mittelalterlichen Humanismus* [The Afterlife of the Ancient Gods in Medieval Humanism] (Bonn: Schroeder, 1922).

Excavation and Memory

Language has unmistakably made plain that memory is not an instrument for exploring the past, but rather a medium. It is the medium of that which is experienced, just as the earth is the medium in which ancient cities lie buried. He who seeks to approach his own buried past must conduct himself like a man digging. Above all, he must not be afraid to return again and again to the same matter; to scatter it as one scatters earth, to turn it over as one turns over soil. For the "matter itself" is no more than the strata which yield their long-sought secrets only to the most meticulous investigation. That is to say, they yield those images that, severed from all earlier associations, reside as treasures in the sober rooms of our later insights—like torsos in a collector's gallery. It is undoubtedly useful to plan excavations methodically. Yet no less indispensable is the cautious probing of the spade in the dark loam. And the man who merely makes an inventory of his findings, while failing to establish the exact location of where in today's ground the ancient treasures have been stored up, cheats himself of his richest prize. In this sense, for authentic memories, it is far less important that the investigator report on them than that he mark, quite precisely, the site where he gained possession of them. Epic and rhapsodic in the strictest sense, genuine memory must therefore yield an image of the person who remembers, in the same way a good archaeological report not only informs us about the strata from which its findings originate, but also gives an account of the strata which first had to be broken through.

Written ca. 1932; unpublished in Benjamin's lifetime. *Gesammelte Schriften,* IV, 400–401. Translated by Rodney Livingstone, on the basis of a prior version by Edmund Jephcott.

Oedipus, or Rational Myth

It must have been shortly after the war that we heard about the English stage experiment *Hamlet in Tails*. At the time, this was highly controversial. Here it perhaps suffices to note the paradox that the play is too modern to be modernized. Of course, there have always been periods when similar things could be done without a conscious purpose in mind. It is well known that in the mystery plays of the Middle Ages, the characters appeared wearing the clothing of their time, just as they did in contemporary pictures.[1] But we can be sure that in modern times such an approach must be the product of very precise artistic reflection if it is to be anything more than a snobbish joke. And in fact it has been possible to observe how, in recent years, major—or at least thinking—artists have undertaken such "modernizations," in music and painting as well as in literature. The trend represented by Picasso's pictures around 1927, Stravinsky's *Oedipus Rex,* and Cocteau's *Orphée* has been given the name "Neoclassicism." Now, we have mentioned this name here not in order to link Gide with this trend (he would undoubtedly object to any such procedure, and rightly so), but to indicate how artists of very different kinds came to divest Greek characters of their traditional clothing, or rather to disguise them by clothing them in modern dress. In the first place, they could derive an advantage from harnessing figures for their experiments who were at once familiar to their audience and also remote from contemporary concerns. For all these cases are instances of outspoken constructivist experiments—studio works, so to speak. In the second place, nothing could suit the agenda of constructivism so well as to set up in competition with the works of the Greeks, whose canonical authority as embodiments of the natural and organic had endured for hundreds of years. And in the third place, there is also a covert or open intention involved: namely, the desire to make a genuine test—one grounded in the philosophy of history—of the eternal character of Greek art, which is to say, its constantly self-renewing relevance. With this third consideration the observer finds himself at the very heart of André Gide's latest work.[2] In any event, he will soon realize that the milieu of this Oedipus has its own story to tell. For we hear about Sunday, repression, Lorrainers, decadents, and vestal virgins. The author makes it impossible for his spectators to fasten on any details of locale or situation; he deprives them of the illusion, and with his very first words he calls the stage by its name. In short, whoever wishes to follow him must allow himself to float freely, to take in stride the peaks and troughs of the sea of saga, which has ebbed and flowed for over two thousand years. Only then will he realize what this Greek culture can mean for him, or he for it. And what is it? This is to be found in Oedipus himself—and of all the profound or playful transformations that the saga undergoes at his hands, this is the most curious of all: "But I understand, I alone have understood, that the only watchword that could protect a person from the claws of the Sphinx is 'man.' No doubt a certain courage was required to utter this word, but I already had it in reserve even before I heard the riddle, and my strength was that I wanted no truck with any other answer, whatever the question might be."[3]

Oedipus had known beforehand the word that would break the power of the Sphinx. Gide, too, had known in advance the word that would dispel the horror of the Sophoclean tragedy. More than twelve years earlier, he had published his "Reflections on Greek Mythology," in which he wrote: "'How was it possible to believe such things?' cries Voltaire. Yet it is reason above all—and reason alone—to which every myth turns; no myth has been understood unless it has been accepted by reason. The Greek myths are fundamentally rational, and for this very reason a man may say, without its making him a bad Christian, that they are much easier to grasp than the teachings of Paul."[4] Now it is important not to misunderstand this. Gide does not claim that reason produced Greek myths, nor even that for the Greeks the meaning of myth lay in its rationality. What is important, rather, is how the modern meaning gains a distance from the old, and how that distance from the old interpretation is just a new closeness to the myth itself, from which the modern meaning inexhaustibly offers itself up for renewed discovery. This is why Greek myths are like Philemon's pitcher, "which no thirst can empty while you drink in Jupiter's presence."[5] The right moment is also a Jupiter, and therefore Neoclassicism is able today to discover meanings in the myths that have never been found in them before: construction, logic, and reason.

We must pause here to counter an objection: that explanation has been replaced at this point by a truly vertiginous paradox. Can it be true that on the very site where the palace of Oedipus stood—the house that was surrounded by unparalleled darkness, horror, incest, parricide, doom, and guilt—we are asked to watch the temple of the Goddess of Reason be erected today? How can this be? What, then, has happened to Oedipus in twenty-three centuries—from the time Sophocles first put him on the Greek stage to the present day, when Gide has put him on the French stage? Very little. And what has this little achieved? Much. *Oedipus has learned to speak.* Sophocles' Oedipus is silent, or nearly so. A bloodhound after his own blood, screaming with the pain inflicted by his own hands—he utters speeches in which there can be no room for thought, for reflection. It is true that he is insatiable in his need to keep repeating the horrific events:

> Incestuous sin! Breeding where I was bred!
> Father, brother, and son; bride, wife, and mother;
> Confounded in one monstrous matrimony!
> All human filthiness in one crime compounded![6]

But it is this very speech that makes him fall silent inwardly; and in the same vein, he wishes to become like the night:

> Could I want sight to face this people's stare?
> No! Hearing neither! Had I any way
> To dam that channel too, I would not rest
> Till I had prisoned up this body of shame
> That I might be blind and deaf.[7]

And how could he not fall silent? How could thinking ever free him from the entanglement that makes it impossible to decide what is destroying him—the crime itself, Apollo's oracle, or the curse that he himself lays on the murderer of Laius? Moreover, this silence characterizes not just Oedipus alone, but the hero of Greek tragedy in general. This is why modern scholars tend to dwell on it. "The tragic hero has but one language that is wholly appropriate to him: silence."[8] Another writer claims that tragic heroes "tend to speak more superficially than they act."[9] And a third writes: "In tragedy, pagan man becomes aware that he is better than his gods, but the realization robs him of speech, remains unspoken. Without declaring itself, it seeks secretly to gather its forces . . . There is no question of the 'moral world order' being restored; instead, the moral hero, still dumb, not yet of age—as such he is called a hero—wishes to raise himself by shaking that tormented world. The paradox that genius is born in moral speechlessness, moral infantility, is the sublimity of tragedy."[10]

It is only from this vantage point that we can appreciate the boldness of Gide's attempt to endow the hero of tragedy with speech. Now we understand the magnificent words about "fate" that the author wrote in the above-mentioned essay long before he redeemed them in *Oedipe:* "With this repellent word, we concede much to chance—more than is merited. The dreadful workings of fate are in evidence wherever we dispense with explanations. I now maintain, however, that the deeper we drive fate back into the myths, the more instructive they are."[11] At the close of Act 2 in Sophocles (the tragedy has five acts in all), the role of Tiresias is at an end. Oedipus has needed two thousand years to reply to him in their great debate, in which he says what he did not even venture to think in Sophocles: "God imposed this crime on me. He held it hidden on my path. The trap into which I was to fall had been set even before my birth, for either your oracle lied or I could not save myself. I was surrounded."[12]

Thanks to this unsought superiority on the part of the hero, we now find that in Gide the satyr-play takes up residence in the precincts of the ancient horror, as it shimmers through from time to time in Creon's words or in those of the Chorus. And never more authoritatively than in the warning that Oedipus gives the children whose conversation he had overheard. A habitué of La Rotonde could not have replied more uninhibitedly.[13] It is as if there lay before him in the inextricable relationships of his household all the domestic miseries of the petty bourgeoisie (magnified on a monstrous scale). Oedipus turns his back on them to follow the trail of the emancipated people who have gone before—that is to say, the younger brother from *Le retour de l'enfant prodigue* [The Return of the Prodigal Son] and the Wanderer from *Les nourritures terrestres* [Fruits of the Earth]. Oedipus is the eldest of the great escapers who take their cue from the man who wrote, "Il faut toujours sortir n'importe d'où."[14]

Published in *Blätter des hessischen Landtheaters*, April 1932. *Gesammelte Schriften*, II, 391–395. Translated by Rodney Livingstone.

Notes

1. Mystery plays were one of the kinds of vernacular drama common to the European Middle Ages (along with the miracle play and the morality play). The plays were usually based on biblical material, such as the Creation, the Last Judgment, or the murder of Cain.
2. André Gide, *Oedipe* (Paris: Pléiade, 1931). Benjamin refers to the German translation by Ernst Robert Curtius, *Oedipus, oder Der vernünftige Mythos,* which appeared in the same year.
3. Gide, *Oedipus, oder Der vernünftige Mythos,* p. 62.
4. André Gide, *Incidences* (Paris: Nouvelle Revue Française, 1924), p. 62.
5. See the story of Philemon and Baucis in Ovid, *Metamorphoses,* Book 8, lines 620–725.
6. Sophocles, *King Oedipus,* in *The Theban Plays,* trans. E. F. Watling (Harmondsworth: Penguin, 1949), p. 64.

7. Sophocles, *King Oedipus*, p. 64.

8. Franz Rosenzweig, *Der Stern der Erlösung* [The Star of Redemption] (Frankfurt: J. Kauffmann, 1921), p. 98.

9. Friedrich Nietzsche, *Werke in drei Bänden*, ed. Karl Schlechta, vol. 1 (Munich: Hanser, 1954), p. 94.

10. Benjamin is quoting himself here. See "Fate and Character," in Volume 1 of this edition.

11. Gide, *Incidences*, p. 81.

12. Gide, *Oedipus, oder Der vernünftige Mythos*, p. 81.

13. La Rotonde was one of the cafés in the Montparnasse district in Paris that was frequented by artists and intellectuals in the 1920s and 1930s.

14. "One must always make a departure, no matter from where." This seems to be a free quote from the preface to André Gide, *Les nourritures terrestres*.

On Proverbs

Let us lay, at the foundation, the image of the women who carry full, heavy vessels on their heads without the aid of their hands.

The rhythm with which they do this is what the proverb teaches.

From the proverb speaks a *noli me tangere* of experience.

With this, it proclaims its ability to transform experience into tradition.

Proverbs cannot be applied to situations. Instead, they have a kind of magical character: they transform the situation. It is scarcely within the powers of the individual to purify the lessons of his life completely by purging them of his particular experience. But the proverb can do this by taking possession of them.

It turns the lesson that has been experienced into a wave in the living chain of innumerable lessons that flow down from eternity.

Jean Paulhan: *Expérience du proverbe.*

Fragment written April–May 1932 or later; unpublished in Benjamin's lifetime. *Gesammelte Schriften*, VI, 206–207. Translated by Rodney Livingstone.

Theater and Radio

The Mutual Control of Their Educational Program

Theater and radio: for the unprejudiced reader, the contemplation of these two institutions will not perhaps evoke an impression of harmony. It is true that the competition between them is not as acute as between radio and the concert hall. Nevertheless, we know too much about the ever-expanding activities of radio, on the one hand, and the ever-increasing problems of the theater, on the other, to find it easy to envisage a collaboration between the two. For all that, collaboration does exist. And has existed, moreover, for a considerable time. They could only work together in the realm of education—so much must be admitted from the outset. But this collaboration has just been initiated with particular energy by Südwestfunk [Southwest Radio]. Ernst Schoen,[1] the artistic director, has been one of the first to take note of the works that Bert Brecht and his literary and musical colleagues have been introducing to public discussion over the last few years. It is no accident that these works—*Der Lindberghflug, Das Badener Lehrstück, Der Jasager, Der Neinsager,*[2] among others—were unambiguously geared toward education. On the other hand, they also represent a highly original combination of theater and radio. These foundations would soon prove viable. Radio plays of a similar kind could be broadcast—*Ford*, by Elisabeth Hauptmann, is one such.[3] In addition, problems of everyday life—school and education, the techniques of success, marriage difficulties—could be debated in the form of example and counterexample. So-called radio-models [*Hörmodelle*]—written by Walter Benjamin and Wolf Zucker—were also promulgated by the Frankfurt-based radio station (in collaboration with Berlin). Such extensive activity provides a welcome occasion for a closer look at work of this kind, and simultaneously helps prevent misunderstandings about it.

But taking a closer look of this sort means being unable to ignore the most obvious aspect of radio—namely, its technological dimension. Here we would be well advised to put all touchiness aside and simply to affirm that, in comparison to the theater, radio represents not only a more advanced technical stage, but also one in which technology is more evident. Unlike the theater, it does not have a classical age behind it. The masses it grips are much larger; above all, the material elements on which its apparatus is based and the intellectual foundations on which its programming is based are closely intertwined in the interests of its audience. Confronted with this, what can the theater offer? The use of live people—and apart from this, nothing. The theater's future development out of this crisis may very well take its lead above all from this fact. What is the significance of the use of live people? There are two very distinct possible answers to this: one reactionary and one progressive.

The first sees absolutely no reason to take note of the crisis at all. According to this view, universal harmony remains intact, and man is its representative. Man is conceived to be at the height of his powers, the Lord of Creation, a personality (even if he is the meanest wage laborer). His stage is modern culture, and he holds sway over it in the name of "humanity." This proud, self-confident, big-city theater is as indifferent to its own crisis as to that of the world outside it (even though its best-known magnate recently abandoned it). And whether it presents dramas of the poor in the modern style or libretti by Offenbach, it will always produce itself as "symbol," as "totality," as *Gesamtkunstwerk* [total artwork].

What we have described here is a theater of education and of entertainment [*Zerstreuung*].[4] Both functions, however opposed to each other they may seem, are merely complementary phenomena in the realm of a saturated stratum which turns everything it touches into stimuli. But it is in vain that this theater attempts to use complex machinery and a vast horde of extras in order to compete with the attractions of the mass-market film; in vain that its repertoire is expanded to include all times and places, when, with a much smaller apparatus, radio and the cinema can create space in their studios for anything ranging from ancient Chinese drama to the latest Surrealist experiments. It is hopeless to try to compete with the technological resources available to radio and cinema.

But not hopeless to debate with them. This is the only thing that can be expected from the progressive stage. Brecht, the first to have developed its theory, calls it "epic." This Epic Theater is utterly matter-of-fact, not least in its attitude toward technology. This is not the place to expound on the theory of Epic Theater, let alone to show how its discovery and construction of *gestus* is nothing but a retranslation of the methods of montage—so crucial in radio and film—from a technological process to a human one. It is enough to point out that the principle of Epic Theater, like that of montage, is based on interruption. The only difference is that here interruption has a pedagogic function and not just the character of a stimulus. It brings the action to a halt, and hence compels the listener to take up an attitude toward the events on the stage and forces the actor to adopt a critical view of his role.

The Epic Theater brings the dramatic *Gesamtkunstwerk* into confrontation with the dramatic laboratory. It returns with a fresh approach to the grand old opportunity of theater—namely, to the focus on the people who are present. In the center of its experiments stands the human being in our crisis. It is the human being who has been eliminated from radio and film—the human being (to put it a little extremely) as the fifth wheel on the carriage of its technology. And this reduced, debarred human being is subjected to various trials and judged. What emerges from this approach is that events are alterable not at their climactic points, not through virtue and decisionmaking, but solely in their normal, routine processes, through reason and practice. What Epic Theater means is the attempt to take the smallest possible units of human behavior and use them to construct what was known as "action" in the Aristotelian theory of drama.

Thus, Epic Theater challenges the theater of convention. It replaces culture with training, distraction with group formation. As to this last, everyone who has followed the development of radio will be aware of the efforts made recently to bring together into coherent groups listeners who are similar to one another in terms of their social stratification, interests, and environment generally. In like fashion, Epic Theater attempts to attract a body of interested people who, independently of criticism and advertising, wish to see realized on the stage their most pressing concerns, including their political concerns, in a series of "actions" (in the above-mentioned sense). Remarkably enough, what this has meant in practice is that older plays—such as *Eduard II* [Edward II][5] and *Dreigroschenoper* [Threepenny Opera]—have been radically transformed, while more recent ones—such as *Der Jasager* and *Der Neinsager*—have been treated as if they were parts of ongoing controversies. This may shed light on what it means to say that culture (the culture of knowledge) has been replaced by training (the training of critical judgment). Radio, which has a particular duty to take up older cultural products, will best do this by means of adaptations that not only do justice to modern technology, but also satisfy the expectations of an audience that is contemporary with this technology. Only in this way will the apparatus be freed from the nimbus of a "gigantic machine for mass education" (as Schoen has described it) and reduced to a format that is worthy of human beings.

Published in *Blätter des hessischen Landestheaters*, May 1932. *Gesammelte Schriften*, II, 773–776. Translated by Rodney Livingstone.

Notes

1. Ernst Schoen (1894–1960), German musician, poet, and translator, was the artistic director of a major radio station in Frankfurt. Just as Benjamin's relationship with Jula Cohn was allegorized in the essay "Goethe's Elective Affinities," so too was Dora Benjamin's with Ernst Schoen. Schoen provided Benjamin with opportunities to present his work on the radio during the 1920s and early 1930s.

2. Works by Brecht. *Der Lindberghflug* is a cantata (with text by Brecht and music by Kurt Weill) based on Brecht's radio play *Der Flug der Lindberghs* (The Lindberghs' Flight), which was later renamed *Der Ozeanflug* (The Flight over the Ocean). *Das Badener Lehrstück* (The Baden-Baden Didactic Play of Acquiescence), *Der Jasager* (He Who Said Yes), and *Der Neinsager* (He Who Said No) are all didactic plays intended for performance by amateur, politically engaged troupes.

3. Elisabeth Hauptmann (1897–1973), dramatist and important collaborator of Brecht's, emigrated in 1933, first to France, and then to the United States.

4. *Zerstreuung* means not only "entertainment" but also "distraction," a sense to which Benjamin turns later in this essay.

5. Benjamin is referring to Brecht's play *Leben Eduards des Zweiten von England* (Life of Edward the Second of England; 1924).

Ibizan Sequence

Ibiza, April–May 1932

Politeness

It is well known that the recognized imperatives of ethics—honesty, humility, brotherly love, compassion, and many others—come off second-best in the daily clash of interests. It is all the more surprising, then, that people have so seldom reflected on the mediating factor that human beings have sought and found for thousands of years. The true mediator, the product of the conflict between morality and the struggle for existence, is politeness. Politeness is neither the one nor the other—neither moral imperative nor a weapon in the struggle—yet it is nevertheless both. In other words, it is nothing and everything, depending on the way it is regarded. It is nothing in its capacity as beautiful appearance [*Schein*], as form, as an agreeable way of enabling us to overlook the cruelty of the conflict raging between the opposing parties. And just as it is anything but a rigorous moral prescription (but merely the representation of a morality that has been annulled), so too its value in the struggle for existence is a fiction (the representation of the fact that this struggle is unresolved). Alternatively, the very same politeness is everything—namely, when it frees itself, and thus the events concerned, from convention. If a negotiating room is entirely surrounded by the barriers of convention, like the lists of a jousting tournament, then true politeness comes into its own, since it tears down these barriers; in other words, it widens the conflict past all bounds, while at the same time granting entry—as helpers, mediators, and conciliators—to all those forces and authorities that it had excluded. Anyone who allows himself to be dominated by the abstract picture of the relationship in which he finds himself with his opponent will never be able to make anything but violent attempts to gain the upper hand in this conflict. He has every opportunity to remain impolite. Whereas an alert openness to the extreme, the comic, the private, and the surprising aspects in a situation is the advanced school of politeness. Anyone who practices this will be able to seize the reins in a negotiation, and ultimately also gain control of the interests at stake. Finally, he will be able to astonish his opponent by manipulating the conflicting elements of the situation as if they were cards in a game of patience [solitaire]. Patience is in any case at the heart of politeness and, of all the virtues, is perhaps the only one that politeness adopts without modification. As to the others, which a godforsaken conventionality imagines could receive their due only in a "conflict of duties," politeness as the muse of the middle way has long since given them this due—that is to say, a real chance for the underdog.

Do Not Seek to Dissuade

Anyone who is asked for his advice would do well to begin by finding out the asker's own opinion and then endorsing it.[1] No one is easily persuaded of another's greater cleverness, and few people ask for advice with the intention of following someone else's. The fact is that they have already made up their minds and now wish to hear it from the outside, to accept it as the "advice" of another. This confirmation is what they seek, and they are right to do so. For it is very risky to set out to implement one's own decisions without passing them through the give-and-take of conversation, as if through a filter. This is why the person who seeks advice is already halfway to a decision; and if what he is planning to do is a mistake, it is better to lend it skeptical support than to contradict it with conviction.

Space for Precious Objects

In the little villages in southern Spain, through open doors whose bead curtains have been gathered to one side, you can obtain glimpses into interiors from whose shadows the dazzling white of the walls stands out.[2] These walls are whitewashed many times a year. And in front of the wall, to the rear, there are usually three or four chairs in a strict symmetrical arrangement. On their central axis, however, rests an invisible pair of scales in which Welcome and Rejection are equally balanced. Much can be gleaned from these chairs as they sit there, unpretentious in form but with strikingly beautiful wickerwork. No collector could hang rugs from Isphahan[3] or pictures by Van Dyck on his vestibule walls with greater pride than the farmer who puts out such chairs in the otherwise bare hallway. Moreover, they are not just chairs. They change their function instantly when a sombrero is hung on the back of one of them. And in this new arrangement the straw hat appears no less precious than the simple chair. In this way fishermen's nets and copper kettles, rudders and clay jars, come together and are ready, as the need arises, to change places and form new combinations a hundred times a day. They are all more or less precious. And the secret of their value is the sobriety, the austerity, of the living space they inhabit. It means that they do not simply occupy, visibly, the spot they belong in, but have enough space to take possession of whatever new positions they are called upon to fill. In the house, which has no bed, there is the rug with which the occupant covers himself at night; in the cart, where there is no upholstery, the cushion you set on its hard planking is precious. In our well-appointed houses, however, there is no space for precious objects, because there is no scope for their services.

First Dream

I was going somewhere with Jula—it was halfway between an ordinary walk and a mountain hike—and now we were getting close to the summit.[4] For some strange reason I imagined I could recognize the top by a very tall pole sticking straight up into the sky and standing out against the overhanging rock wall. When we reached the top, it turned out to be not a peak but a plateau, with a broad street stretching along it and lined with rather tall, old-fashioned houses on both sides. Suddenly we were no longer on foot but instead sitting in a car, next to each other in the back seat (or so it seemed to me), driving along this road. But it may be that the car changed direction while we were sitting in it. I leaned over to give Jula a kiss. She offered me her cheek instead of her mouth. And as I kissed her I noticed that her cheek was made of ivory, furrowed from one end to the other by black, skillfully scooped-out grooves, whose beauty moved me deeply.

The Compass of Success

It is a deeply rooted prejudice that willpower is the key to success. This would be true enough if success concerned only the individual—if it were not also an expression of the fact that an individual's life intervenes in the structure of the world as a whole. An expression admittedly full of reservations. Yet are reservations any the less valid vis-à-vis individual existence and the structure of the world? So we may say that success, which some people so readily dismiss as the blind activity of chance, is the deepest expression of the contingencies of this world. Success is a caprice in the workings of the universe. To this extent, it has very little to do with the willpower that pursues it. And in general what reveals the true nature of success is not the reasons that account for it, but the human figures it affects. These are its favorites, and it makes itself known in them. Its spoiled children—and its stepchildren. This caprice of the universe corresponds to idiosyncrasy in the individual. To account for this has always been the prerogative of comedy, whose justice is the work not of heaven but of countless mistakes that end up producing an exact result, thanks to one last little error. But where can we locate the idiosyncrasy of the subject? In conviction. The sober man who has no idiosyncrasies lives without convictions; life and thought have long since ground them into wisdom, as millstones grind corn to meal. The comic figure, however, is never wise; he is a rogue, a simpleton, a fool, a poor devil. But whatever he is, the world fits him like a glove. In his eyes success is no lucky star, failure no unlucky star. He is quite unconcerned about destiny, myth, or doom. The key to his nature is a mathematical figure that is constructed around the axes of success and conviction. The compass of success:

Success at the cost of abandoning every conviction. Normal success: Chlestakoff, or the confidence trickster.[5]—The confidence man lets himself be guided by the situation, like a medium. *Mundus vult decipi.*[6] He even chooses his name to please the world.

Success in testing every conviction. Genius of success. Schweik, or the lucky devil.—The lucky devil is an honest fellow who wants to please everyone. Lucky Hans changes places with anyone who asks him to.[7]

Lack of success in testing every conviction. Normal failure: Bouvard and Pécuchet, or the philistine.[8]—The philistine is the martyr of convictions of every kind, from Lao-tze to Rudolf Steiner.[9] But for each conviction "only a quarter of an hour."

Lack of success at the cost of abandoning every conviction. Genius of failure: Chaplin or Schlemihl.[10] The schlemihl takes offense at nothing; he just stumbles over his own feet. He is the only angel of peace who is suited to this world.

This, then, is the compass by which to determine all the winds, favorable and unfavorable, that play their games with human existence. Nothing remains but to define their heart, the point of intersection of the axes, the site of the complete identity of success and failure. At this center we find Don Quixote, *the man with a single conviction,* whose story teaches us that in this, the best or worst of all conceivable worlds (except that his world is inconceivable), the conviction that stories of chivalry are true can make a whipped fool happy, if it is his only conviction.

Practice

The fact that in the morning the pupil knows by heart the contents of the book he has put under his pillow the night before, that the Lord inspires His own in their sleep, and that a pause is creative—to make space for such things to happen is the alpha and omega of all mastery, its hallmark.[11] This, then, is the reward before which the gods have placed sweat. For work which achieves only modest success is child's play, compared to the success conjured up by luck. This is why Rastelli's[12] stretched-out little finger attracts the ball, which hops onto it like a bird. The decades' worth of practice that came before does not mean that either his body or the ball is "in his power," but it enables the two to reach an understanding behind his back. To weary the master to the point of exhaustion through diligence and hard work, so that at long last his body and each of his limbs can act in accordance with their own rationality: this is what is called "practice." It is successful because the will abdicates its power once and for all inside the body, abdicates in favor of the organs—the hand, for instance. This is why you can look for something for days, until you finally forget it; then, one day, when you are looking for something else, you suddenly find the first object. Your hand has, so to speak, taken the matter in hand and has joined forces with the object.

Do Not Forget the Best

A man of my acquaintance was at his most well-organized at the unhappiest period in his life. He forgot nothing. He registered his current activities down to the last detail, and if he had an appointment—and he never forgot them—he was punctuality itself. His life's way seemed to have been smoothly paved, and there was not even the smallest crack for time to run out of control. And so matters rested for a while. Then circumstances brought about a change in his life. It began with his getting rid of his watch. He practiced arriving late, and if the person he was going to meet had already left, he sat down to wait. If he had to do something with an object close at hand, he managed to mislay it, and if he was supposed to clear something up somewhere, the confusion elsewhere increased. When he sat down at his desk, it looked as if someone had been living in it. But it was he himself who was building his nest in the ruins. Whatever he did, he made a little house for himself out of it, as children do when they play. Similarly, just as children keep coming across things they have hidden away and then forgotten—in their pockets, in the sand, in a drawer—so it was with his mind, with his entire life. Friends visited him when he least expected them but needed them most, and the gifts he sent, which were not sumptuous, arrived as punctually as if he had the paths of heaven in his hands. Around this time, he liked to recall the tale of the shepherd who one Sunday was given permission to enter the mountain with his treasures, but who also received the mysterious instruction, "Do not forget the best." At this period in his life, he felt quite well. He settled few things and thought of nothing as settled.

Habit and Attentiveness

Foremost among the human capacities, according to Goethe, is attention. But it shares this primacy with habit, which from the outset vies with it for preeminence. All attentiveness has to flow into habit, if it is not to blow human beings apart, and all habit must be disrupted by attentiveness if it is not to paralyze the human being. To note something and to accustom oneself to it, to take offense and to put up with a thing—these are the peaks and troughs of the waves on the sea of the soul. But this sea has moments of calm. There can be no doubt that a person who is wholly concentrated on a thought that torments him, on a pain and its sudden twinges, can suddenly be disconcerted by a barely perceptible noise, an insect humming or flying, that might well have escaped the notice of a more attentive and sharper ear. It might be presumed that the soul can be more easily distracted, the more concentrated it is. Yet isn't this concentrated listening not just the furthest development of attention, but also its end—the moment when it gives birth to habit? That humming or fluttering is the threshold, and imperceptibly the soul has crossed it. It is as if it no longer wished to return to the accustomed world—as if it now inhabited a new world, one in which pain is the quartermaster. Attentiveness and pain are complementary. But even habit has its complement, and we cross its threshold in sleep. For what comes to us when we dream is a new and unprecedented attentiveness that struggles to emerge from the womb of habit. Everyday experiences, hackneyed expressions, the vestiges that remain in a glance, the pulsating of one's own blood—all this, hitherto unnoticed and in a distorted and overly sharp form, makes up the stuff of dreams. In dreams there is no astonishment and in pain there is no forgetting, because both bear their opposites within them, just as in a calm the peaks and troughs of the waves lie merged in one another.

Downhill

The word "shattered" [erschüttert] has been used ad nauseam. So perhaps something may be said in its defense. It will not distance itself from the sensual for an instant and will above all else cling to one fact: that shock leads to collapse. Do those who assure us after every theater premiere or every new book that they were "shattered" really wish to tell us that something inside them has collapsed? Unfortunately, the phrase that stood firm beforehand will also stand firm afterward. How could they allow themselves the pause which is the precondition of collapse? No one has ever felt this more clearly than Marcel Proust did when he learned of the death of his grandmother—an event which he found shattering but unreal, until the evening he burst into tears while taking off his shoes.[13] Why? Because he bent down. In this way, the body is what rouses a profound pain; and it can serve no less to arouse profound thought. Both require solitude. Anyone who has climbed a mountain on his own and arrived at the top exhausted, and then turns to walk down again with steps that shatter his entire body— for such a person, time hangs loose, the partition walls inside him collapse, and he pushes on through the rubble of the moment as if in a dream. Sometimes he tries to stop, but cannot. Who knows whether it is his thoughts that shatter him, or the roughness of the way? His body has become a kaleidoscope that at each step presents him with ever-changing figures of the truth.

Published in the *Frankfurter Zeitung,* June 1932. *Gesammelte Schriften,* IV, 402–409. Translated by Rodney Livingstone.

Notes

1. For a variant of this text, see "Spain, 1932," in this volume.
2. For a variant of this text, see "Spain, 1932," in this volume.
3. Isphahan (Isfahan) rugs, made in Iran, are brightly colored and opulent. Their patterns recall European Renaissance and Baroque decorative motifs.
4. For a variant of this text, see "Spain, 1932," in this volume. "Jula" is Benjamin's friend, Jula Radt, *neé* Cohn, a sculptor and the sister of Benjamin's schoolfriend Alfred Cohn. Benjamin's relationship with her precipitated the crisis in his marriage. The essay "Goethe's Elective Affinities" (see Volume 1 of this edition) allegorizes this relationship.
5. Chlestakoff is the protagonist of *The Inspector General,* by Nikolai Gogol, first published in 1836.
6. "The world wishes to be deceived." The statement is attributed to Pope Paul IV (d. 1559). He added, "So let it be deceived."
7. Schweik is the protagonist of the satirical novel *The Good Soldier Schweik* (1920–1923), by the Czech writer Jaroslav Hašek. In the fairy tale "Hans im Glück," sometimes translated as "Hans in Luck," Hans is persuaded to exchange a piece of silver "as big as his head"—a treasure that cost him seven years' work—for a horse, the horse for a cow, the cow for a pig, the pig for a goose, and, finally, the goose for an ordinary rough stone that is allegedly a grindstone.
8. Bouvard and Pécuchet are the heroes of Gustave Flaubert's unfinished satirical novel *Bouvard et Pécuchet* (published posthumously in 1881), which satirizes the propensity of the bourgeoisie to accumulate knowledge in encyclopedias and museums.
9. Lao-tze, the reputed founder of Taoism. Rudolf Steiner (1861–1925), Austrian-born scientist and editor, was the founder of anthroposophy, a movement based on the notion that there is a spiritual world accessible only to the highest faculties of mental knowledge.
10. See Adelbert von Chamisso, *Peter Schlemihls wundersame Geschichte* (The

Strange Tale of Peter Schlemihl; 1814), the story of a man who sells his shadow in the hope of gaining social acceptability, but who succeeds only in making himself an outcast.

11. For a variant of this text, see "Spain, 1932," in this volume.

12. Enrico Rastelli (1896–1931) was a famous juggler. See also Benjamin's essay "Rastelli erzählt" (Rastelli's Story).

13. The incident is described in Part 2, Chapter 1, of Proust's *Sodome et Gomorrhe* (translated as *Cities of the Plain*).

A Berlin Chronicle

For my dear Stefan

Now let me call back those who introduced me to the city. For although the child, in his solitary games, grows up in closest proximity to the city, he needs and seeks guides to its wider expanses, and the first of these—for a son of wealthy middle-class parents like me—are sure to have been nurse-maids. With them I went to the Zoo—although I recall it only from much later, with blaring military bands and "Scandal Avenue" (as the adherents of Jugendstil [Art Nouveau] dubbed this promenade)—or, if not to the Zoo, to the Tiergarten.[1] I believe the first "street" I thus discovered that no longer had anything habitable or hospitable about it, emanating forlornness between the shopfronts and even danger at the crossings, was Schillstrasse; I like to imagine that it has altered less than others in the West End and that it could even now accommodate a scene rising irresistibly from the mist: the saving of the life of "little brother." The way to the Tiergarten led over Herkules Bridge, whose gently sloping embankment must have been the first hillside the child encountered—accentuated by the fine stone flanks of the lion rising above. At the end of Bendlerstrasse, however, began the labyrinth, not without its Ariadne: the maze surrounding Frederick William III and Queen Louise, who, rising sheer from the flower beds on their illustrated, Empire-style plinths, seemed as if petrified by the runes that a little rivulet inscribed in the sand. Rather than the figures, my eyes sought the plinths, since the events taking place on them, if less clear in their ramifications, were closer in space. But that a particular significance attaches to this Hohenzollern labyrinth I find confirmed even now by the utterly uncon-cerned, banal appearance of the forecourt on Tiergartenstrasse, where nothing suggests that you stand but a few yards from the strangest place in the city. At that time, it is true, it must have corresponded more than closely to what was waiting behind it, for here, or not far away, were the haunts of that Ariadne in whose proximity I learned for the first time (and was never entirely to forget) something that was to make instantly comprehensible a word that, since I was scarcely three, I cannot have known: love. Here the nursemaid supervenes, a cold shadow driving away what I loved. It is likely that no one ever masters anything in which he has not known impotence; and if you agree, you will also see that this impotence comes not at the beginning of or before the struggle with the subject, but in the heart of it. Which brings me to the middle period of my life in Berlin, extending from the whole of my later childhood to my entrance to the university: a period of impotence before the city. This had two sources. The first was a very poor sense of direction; but if it was thirty years before the distinction between left and right had become visceral to me, and before I had acquired the art of reading a street map, I was far from appreciating the extent of my ineptitude; and if anything was capable of increasing my disinclination to perceive this fact, it was the insistence with which my mother thrust it under my nose. On her I lay the blame for my inability even today to make a cup of coffee; to her propensity for turning the most insignificant items of conduct into tests of my aptitude for practical life I owe the dreamy recalcitrance with which I accompanied her as we walked through the streets, rarely frequented by me, of the city center. But to this resistance, in turn, is due who knows how much that underlies my present intercourse with the city's streets. Above all, a gaze that appears to see not a third of what it takes in. I remember, too, how nothing was more intolerable to my mother than the pedantic care with which, on these walks, I always kept half a step behind her. My habit of seeming slower, more maladroit, more stupid than I am had its origin in such walks, and has the great attendant danger of making me think myself quicker, more dexterous, and shrewder than I am.

I have long, indeed for years, played with the idea of setting out the sphere of life—*bios*—graphically on a map. First I envisaged an ordinary map, but now I would incline to a general staff's map of a city center, if such a thing existed. Doubtless it does not, because of ignorance of the theater of future wars. I have evolved a system of signs, and on the gray background of such maps they would make a colorful show if I clearly marked the houses of my friends and girlfriends, the assembly halls of various collectives, from the "debating chambers" of the Youth Movement to the gathering places of Communist youth,[2] the hotel and brothel rooms that I knew for one night, the decisive benches in the Tiergarten, the ways to different schools and the graves that I saw filled, the sites of prestigious cafés whose long-forgotten names daily crossed our lips, the tennis courts where empty apartment blocks stand today, and the halls emblazoned with gold and stucco that the terrors of dancing classes made almost the equal of gymnasiums. And even without this map, I still have the encouragement provided by an illustrious precursor, the Frenchman Léon Daudet, exemplary at least in the title of one of his works, which exactly encompasses the best that I might achieve here: *Paris vécu*.[3] "Lived Berlin" doesn't sound as good, but is as real. And it is not just this title that concerns me here; Paris itself is the fourth in the series of voluntary or involuntary guides that began with my nursemaids. If I had to sum up in one word what I owe to Paris for these reflections, it would be "caution." I would scarcely be able to abandon myself to the shifting currents of these memories of my earliest city life, had not Paris set before me, strictly circumscribed, the two forms in which alone this can legitimately—that is, with a guarantee of permanence—be done; and had I not forsworn the attempt to equal the first as firmly as I hope one day to realize the second. The first form was created in the work of Marcel Proust, and the renunciation of any dalliance with related possibilities could scarcely be more bindingly embodied than in the translation of it that I have produced. Related possibilities—do they really exist? They would certainly permit no dalliance. What Proust began so playfully became awesomely serious. He who has once begun to open the fan of memory never comes to the end of its segments. No image satisfies him, for he has seen that it can be unfolded, and only in its folds does the truth reside—that image, that taste, that touch for whose sake all this has been unfurled and dissected; and now remembrance progresses from small to smallest details, from the smallest to the infinitesimal, while that which it encounters in these microcosms grows ever mightier. Such is the deadly game that Proust began so dilettantishly, in which he will hardly find more successors than he needed companions.

The most remarkable of all the street images from my early childhood, however—more so even than the arrival of the bears, which I witnessed by the side of a nursemaid, or it may have been my French governess, and more remarkable than the racecourse that passed Schillstrasse or ended there— was (this must have been about 1900) a completely deserted stretch of road upon which ponderous torrents of water continuously thundered down. I had been caught up in a local flood disaster, but in other ways, too, the idea of extraordinary events is inseparable from that day; possibly we had been sent home from school. In any case, this situation left behind an alarm signal; my strength must have been failing, and in the midst of the asphalt streets of the city I felt exposed to the powers of nature. In a primeval forest, among the giant trees, I would not have been more abandoned than here on Kurfürstenstrasse, between the columns of water. How I reached the mouths of the bronze lions on our front door, with their rings that were now lifebelts, I cannot remember.

Rides to the station in the rattling taxi, skirting the Landwehr Canal at night, while, among the dirty cushions, the weekly evening gathering in the drawing room or the living room of my parents' apartment, which had just neared its end (for a week at least), was revived with stricken violence. And so it was not what impended that weighed so terrifyingly upon me, or even the parting from what had been, but that which still continued, persisted, asserting itself even in this first stage of the journey. The destination of such rides would usually have been Anhalt Station—where you took the train to Suderode or Hahnenklee, to Bad Salzschlirf or—in later years—to Freuden-stadt. But now and again it was Arendsee, too, or Heiligendamm, and then you left from Stettin Station. I believe it is since that time that the dunes of the Baltic landscape have appeared to me like a *fata morgana* here on Chausseestrasse, supported only by the yellow, sandy colors of the station building and the boundless horizon opening in my imagination behind its walls.

The fourth guide. Not to find one's way in a city may well be uninteresting and banal. It requires ignorance—nothing more. But to lose oneself in a city—as one loses oneself in a forest—this calls for quite a different school-ing. Then, signboards and street names, passers-by, roofs, kiosks, and bars must speak to the wanderer like a twig snapping under his feet in the forest, like the startling call of a bittern in the distance, like the sudden stillness of a clearing with a lily standing erect at its center. Paris taught me this art of straying; it fulfilled a dream that had shown its first traces in the labyrinths on the blotting pages of my school exercise books. Nor is it to be denied that I penetrated to its innermost place, the Minotaur's chamber—the only difference being that *this* mythological monster had three heads: those of the occupants of the small brothel on the rue de la Harpe, in which, summoning my last reserves of strength (and not entirely without an Ariadne's thread), I set my foot. But if Paris thus answered my most uneasy expectations, from another side it surpassed my graphic fantasies. The city, as it disclosed itself to me in the footsteps of a hermetic tradition that I can trace back at least as far as Rilke and whose guardian at that time was Franz Hessel, was a maze not only of paths but also of tunnels. I cannot think of the underworld of the Métro and the North-South line opening their hun-dreds of shafts all over the city, without recalling my endless *flâneries*.

And then my fifth guide: Franz Hessel.[4] I do not mean his book *Spazieren in Berlin* [On Foot in Berlin], which was written later, but his *Nachfeier*

[Celebration]—the celebration that our walks together in Paris received in our native city, as if we were returning to harbor, the jetty still rising and falling as on waves under the feet of strolling seamen. The centerpiece of this celebration, however, was the "Green Meadow"—a bed that still stands high above the couches spreading all around, on which we composed a small, complaisant, orientally pallid epilogue to those great, sleeping feasts with which, a few years earlier in Paris, the Surrealists had unwittingly inaugurated their reactionary career, thus fulfilling the text that the Lord giveth unto his own in sleep. On this meadow we spread out such women as still amused us at home, but they were few. From beneath lowered lids, our gaze often encountered—better than on drafty stairways—the palms, caryatids, windows, and niches from which the "Tiergarten mythology" was evolving as the first chapter of a science of this city. It prospered, for we had been astute enough to gather to us girls from the most latinate quarter and, in general, to observe the Parisian custom of residing in the *quartier.* True, the *quartier* in Berlin is unfortunately an affair of the well-to-do, and neither Wedding nor Reinickendorf nor Tegel[5] bears comparison on this account with Ménilmontant, Auteuil, or Reuilly. All the more gratifying, therefore, were marauding Sunday-afternoon excursions on which we discovered an arcade in the Moabit neighborhood, the Stettin tunnel, or liberty in front of the Wallner Theater. A young woman, a photographer, was with us.[6] And it seems to me, as I think of Berlin, that only the side of the city that we explored at that time is truly receptive to photography. For the closer we come to its present-day, fluid, functional existence, the narrower draws the circle of what can be photographed. It has been rightly observed that photography records practically nothing of the essence of, for example, a modern factory. Such pictures can perhaps be compared to railway stations, which, in this age when railways are beginning to be out of date, are no longer, generally speaking, the true "gateways" through which the city unrolls its outskirts as it does along the approach roads for motorists. A station gives the order, as it were, for a surprise attack, but it is an outdated maneuver that confronts us with the archaic, and the same is true of photography, even the snapshot. Only the cinema commands optical approaches to the essence of the city, such as conducting the motorist into the new center.

But this vista would indeed be delusive if it did not make visible the medium in which alone such images take form, assuming a transparency in which, however mistily, the contours of what is to come are delineated like mountain peaks. The present in which the writer lives is this medium. And, dwelling in it, he now cuts another section through the sequence of his experiences. He detects in them a new and disturbing articulation. First, his early childhood, enclosing him in the district where he lived—the old or the new West End, where the class that had pronounced him one of its number resided in a posture compounded of self-satisfaction and resentment that turned the district into something like a ghetto held on lease. In any case, he was confined to this affluent neighborhood without knowing of any other. The poor? For rich children of his generation, they lived at the back of beyond. And if at this early age he could picture the poor, it was, without his knowing either name or origin, in the image of the tramp who is actually a rich man, though without money, since he stands—far removed from the process of production and the exploitation not yet abstracted from it—in the same contemplative relation to his destitution as the rich man to his wealth. The child's first excursion into the exotic world of abject poverty characteristically took written form (only by chance, perhaps, one of his first such excursions): the depiction of a leafleter and his humiliation at the hands of the public, who did not trouble even to take the pamphlets he held out to them, so that the wretched man—thus the story ended—secretly jettisoned his entire consignment. Certainly a wholly unfruitful solution to the problem, already announcing the flight into sabotage and anarchism that later makes it so difficult for the intellectual to see things clearly. Perhaps the same sabotage of real social existence is to be found even later, in my manner (already described) of walking in the city, in the stubborn refusal under any circumstances to form a united front, be it even with my own mother. There is no doubt, at any rate, that the feeling of crossing for the first time the threshold of one's class had a part in the almost unequaled fascination of publicly accosting a whore on the street. At the beginning, however, this was a crossing of frontiers not only social but topographic, in the sense that whole networks of streets were opened up under the auspices of prostitution. But was it really a crossing? Is it not, rather, an obstinate and voluptuous hovering on the brink, a hesitation that has its most cogent motive in the fact that beyond this frontier lies nothingness? But in great cities, there are countless places where one stands on the edge of the void; and the whores in the doorways of tenement blocks and on the less sonorous asphalt of railway platforms are like the household goddesses of this cult of nothingness. So on these erring paths the stations became my special habitat, each with its outskirts like a city: the Silesian, Stettin, Görlitz stations, and Friedrichstrasse.

Just as there are, for children, fairy tales in which a witch or even a fairy holds a whole forest in thrall, as a child I knew a street that was ruled and occupied entirely by a woman, even though she was always enthroned in her bay window, one minute's walk from the house in which I was born: Aunt Lehmann. She was the ruler of Steglitzer Strasse. The stairs rose steeply to her room from just behind the hall door; it was dark on the staircase, until the door opened and the brittle voice bid us a thin "Good morning" and directed us to place before us on the table the glass rhombus containing the mineworks, in which little men pushed wheelbarrows, labored with pickaxes, and shone lanterns into the shafts in which buckets were winched perpetually up and down. On account of this aunt and her mineworks, Steglitzer Strasse could henceforth, for me, never be named after the district of Steglitz. A goldfinch [*Stieglitz*] in its cage bore greater resemblance to this street harboring the aunt at her window than that Berlin suburb, which meant nothing to me. Where it joins Genthiner Strasse, it is one of the streets least touched by the changes of the past thirty years. In its back rooms and attics, as guardians of the past, numerous prostitutes have established themselves, who, during the inflation period, brought the district the reputation of being a theater of the most squalid diversions. Needless to say, no one could ever determine on which floors the impoverished opened their drawing rooms, and their daughters their skirts, to rich Americans.

Climbing the stairs in this fashion, with nothing before me but boots and calves, and the scraping of hundreds of feet in my ears, I was often seized—I seem to remember—by revulsion at being hemmed in by this multitude; and again, as on those walks in the city with my mother, solitude appeared to me as the only fit state of man. Very understandably—for such a mob of schoolchildren is among the most formless and ignoble of all masses, and betrays its bourgeois origin in representing, like every assembly of that class in our day, the most rudimentary organizational form that its individual members can give their reciprocal relationships. The corridors, and the classrooms that finally came into view, are among the horrors that have embedded themselves most ineradicably in me—that is to say, in my dreams; and these have taken revenge on the monotony, the cold torpor, that overcame me at each crossing of the classroom thresholds, by turning themselves into the arena of the most extravagant events. The backdrop was often the fear of having to take the *Abitur* again (under more unfavorable conditions),[7] a situation in which I had been placed by my own recklessness and folly. Undoubtedly, these rooms lend themselves to dreamlike representation; there is something nightmarish even in the sober recollection of the damp odor of sweat emitted by the stone steps that I had to hasten up five times or more each day. The school, outwardly in good repair, was, in its architecture and setting, among the most desolate. It matched its emblem, a plaster statue of the Emperor Frederick, which had been deposited in a remote corner of the playground (admittedly one favored by hordes engaged in martial games), puny and pitiful against a firewall. According to school legend, it was—if I am not mistaken—a donation. This monument, unlike the classrooms, was never washed, and had acquired over the years an admirable coat of dirt and soot. It still stands today in its appointed place. But soot descends upon it daily from the passing municipal railway. It is far

from impossible that my uncommon aversion to this railway dates from that
time, since all the people sitting at their windows seemed enviable to me.
They could afford to ignore the school clock that held sway above our heads,
and quite unawares they cut through the invisible bars of our timetable cage.
They could be seen only now and then, during the breaks, for the lower
panes of the classroom windows were of frosted glass. "Vagabond clouds,
sailors of the skies,"[8] had for us the same absolute precision that this line
of verse holds for prisoners. Moreover, little about the actual classrooms
has remained in my memory except these perfect emblems of imprisonment:
the frosted windows and the infamous carved wooden battlements over the
doors. It would not surprise me to hear that the cupboards, too, were
crowned with such adornments, not to mention the pictures of the kaiser
on the walls. Heraldic and chivalric obtuseness shone forth wherever possible. In the great hall, however, it was most ceremoniously united with
Jugendstil. A crude, extravagant ornament stretched with stiff gray-green
limbs across the paneling of the walls. References to objects were no more
to be found in it than references to history; nowhere did it offer the eye the
slightest refuge, while the ear was helplessly abandoned to the din of idiotic
harangues. All the same, one of these occasions is perhaps noteworthy for
the effect it continued to have on me for years afterward. It was the
leavetaking ceremony for those who had graduated. Here, as in several other
places, I find in my memory rigidly fixed words, expressions, verses that,
like a malleable mass which has later cooled and hardened, preserve in me
the imprint of the collision between a larger collective and myself. Just as,
when you awake, a certain kind of significant dream survives in the form
of words though all the rest of the dream-content has vanished, here isolated
words have remained in place as marks of catastrophic encounters. Among
them is one in which for me the whole atmosphere of the school is condensed; I heard it when, having previously received only private tutoring, I
was sent for my first morning, on a trial basis, to what was later to become
the Kaiser Friedrich School but at that time was still situated on Passauer-
strasse. This word, which still adheres in my mind to a phlegmatic, fat,
unbecoming figure of a boy, is "ringleader." Nothing else is left of this
earliest school experience. It was reenacted in similar form, however, some
six years later, when I spent my first day in alien and threatening circumstances in Haubinda[9] and was asked by a tall, hostile-seeming lout who
played a prominent part in the class whether my "old man" had already
left. This common piece of schoolboy parlance was entirely unfamiliar to
me. An abyss opened before me, which I sought to bridge with a laconic
protest. Here in the great hall, it was the verses with which the school choir
began the farewell song to the leavers—"Brother, now may we / your companions be / in the world so wide"—followed by something containing the
words "loyally by your side"; at any rate, these were the verses that enabled

me year by year to take the measure of my own weakness. For no matter how palpably the abominable goings-on at school were before my eyes every day, the melody of this song seemed to surround the departure from this hell with infinite melancholy. But by the time it was addressed to me and my class, it must have made little impression, for I remember nothing of it. More remarkable are some other verses that I heard once in the gymnasium dressing room after the lesson, and never forgot. Why? Perhaps because "Schulze"—as the impudent boy who knew the lines was called—was rather pretty, perhaps because I thought them true, but most probably because the situation in which they were spoken, one of frenetic, military hyperactivity, was so utterly appropriate. "Loitering at the rear / you never need fear / neurasthenia."

First of all, let no one think we were talking of a *Markt-Halle* [covered market]. No: it was pronounced *"Mark-Talle"*; and just as these words were eroded by the habit of speech until none retained its original "sense," so by the habit of this walk all the images it offered were worn away, to the point that none of them conforms to the original concept of buying and selling.

If I write better German than most writers of my generation, it is thanks largely to twenty years' observance of one little rule: never use the word "I" except in letters. The exceptions to this precept that I have permitted myself could be quickly counted. Now, this has had a curious consequence that is intimately connected to these notes. For when one day it was suggested that I should write, from day to day in a loosely subjective form, for a newspaper, a series of glosses on everything that seemed noteworthy in Berlin—and when I agreed—it became suddenly clear that this subject, accustomed for years to waiting in the wings, would not so easily be summoned to the limelight. But far from protesting, it relied on ruse—so successfully that I believed a retrospective glance at what Berlin had become for me over the years would be an appropriate "preface" to such glosses. If the preface has now far exceeded the space originally allotted to the glosses, this is not only the mysterious work of remembrance—which is really the capacity for endless interpolations into what has been—but also, at the same time, the precaution of the subject represented by the "I," which is entitled not to be sold cheap. Now, there is one district of Berlin with which this subject is more closely connected than any other that it has consciously experienced. To be sure, there are parts of the city in which it was destined to have equally deep and harrowing experiences, but in none of them was the place itself so much a part of the event. The part I am speaking of is the Tiergarten district. There, in a back wing of one of the houses standing nearest the municipal railway viaduct, was the "Meeting House." It was a small apartment that I had rented jointly with the student Ernst Joël. How we had agreed on this I no longer remember; it can hardly have been simple, for the student "Group for Social Work" led by Joël was, during the term in which I was president of the Berlin Free Students' Union, a chief target of my attacks, and it was precisely as leader of this group that Joël had signed the lease, while my contribution secured the rights of the "debating chamber" to the Meeting House. The allocation of the rooms between the two groups—in terms of both space and time—was very sharply defined, and in any case, for me at that time only the debating group mattered.

My cosignatory, Ernst Joël, and I were on less than cordial terms, and I had no inkling of the magical aspect of the city that this same Joël, fifteen years later, was to reveal to me.[10] So his image appears in me at this stage only as an answer to the question whether forty is not too young an age at which to evoke the most important memories of one's life. For this image is already now that of a dead man; and who knows how he might have been able to help me cross this threshold, with memories of even the most external and superficial things? To the other threshold he had no access, and of all those who once had it, I alone remain. I should never have thought that I would seek him by this topographic route. But if I call to mind the first trial run I made in this direction, more than ten years ago now, the earlier and more modest essay comes off better in the comparison. It was in Heidelberg, during work that I had undoubtedly undertaken so as to forget myself, that I tried to summon up, in a meditation on the nature of the lyric, the figure of my friend Fritz Heinle, around whom all the happenings in the Meeting House arrange themselves and with whom they vanish. Fritz Heinle was a poet, and the only one of them all whom I met not "in real life" but in his work. He died at nineteen, and could be known in no other way.[11] All the same, this first attempt to evoke the sphere of his life through that of poetry was unsuccessful, and the immediacy of the experience that gave rise to my lecture asserted itself irresistibly in the incomprehension and snobbery of the audience, who came to hear it at the house of Marianne Weber.[12] No matter how much memory has subsequently faded, or how indistinctly I can now give an account of the rooms in the Meeting House, it nevertheless seems to me today more legitimate to attempt to delineate the outward space the dead man inhabited, indeed the room where he was "announced," than the inner space in which he created. But perhaps that is only because, in this last and most crucial year of his life, he traversed the space in which I was born. Heinle's Berlin was the Berlin of the Meeting House. He lived at this period in closest proximity to it, in a fourth-floor room on Klopstockstrasse. I once visited him there. It was after a long separation resulting from a serious disagreement between us. But even today I remember the smile that lifted the whole weight of those weeks of separation, that turned a probably insignificant phrase into a magic formula which healed the wound. Later, after the morning when an express letter

woke me with the words, "You will find us lying in the Meeting House"—
when Heinle and his girlfriend were dead—this district remained for a
period the central meeting place of the living. Today, however, when I recall
its old-fashioned apartment houses, its many trees dust-covered in summer,
the cumbersome iron-and-stone constructions of the municipal railway cutting through it, the sparse streetcars spaced at great intervals, the sluggish
water of the Landwehr Canal that marked the district off from the proletarian neighborhood of Moabit, the splendid but wholly unfrequented clus-
ter of trees in the Schlosspark Bellevue, and the unspeakably crude hunting
groups flanking its approach at the star-shaped intersection of roads—today
this point in space where we happened to open our Meeting House is for
me the consummate pictorial expression of the point in history occupied by
this last true elite of bourgeois Berlin. It was as close to the abyss of the
Great War as the Meeting House was to the steep slope down to the
Landwehr Canal; it was as sharply divided from proletarian youth as the
houses of this *rentiers'* district were from those of Moabit; and the houses
were the last of their line, just as the occupants of those apartments were
the last who could appease the clamorous shades of the dispossessed with
philanthropic ceremonies. In spite—or perhaps because—of this, there is no
doubt that the city of Berlin was never again to impinge so forcefully on
my existence as it did in that epoch when we believed we could leave it
untouched, only improving its schools, only breaking the inhumanity of
their inmates' parents, only making a place in it for the words of Hölderlin
or George. It was a final, heroic attempt to change the attitudes of people
without changing their circumstances. We did not know that it was bound
to fail, but there was hardly one of us whose resolve such knowledge could
have altered. And today, as clearly as at that time, even if on the basis of
entirely different reasoning, I understand that the "language of youth" had
to stand at the center of our associations. Nor do I know today of any truer
expression of our impotence than the struggle that seemed the pinnacle of
our strength and our exuberance, even if the shadow of downfall, cast by
the incomprehension of the audience, was seldom more palpable than on
that evening. I think here of an altercation between Heinle and myself on
an evening at *Die Aktion*.[13] Originally only a speech by me entitled "Youth"
had been on the agenda. I took it for granted that its text should be known
to our closest circle before it was delivered. Scarcely had this happened,
however, when Heinle raised objections. Whether he wanted to speak himself, or to impose alterations on me that I refused, the upshot was an ugly
quarrel into which, as always happens on such occasions, the whole existence of each participant was drawn—Heinle's side being taken by the
youngest of the three sisters[14] around whom the most important events used
to gravitate, as if the fact that a Jewish widow was living with her three
daughters represented, for a group seriously intent upon the abolition of the

family, an appropriate base from which to launch an attack. In short, the young woman reinforced her friend's demands. But I was not prepared to yield, either. So it happened that on that evening at *Die Aktion*, before an astonished but less-than-captivated audience, two speeches with the same title and almost exactly identical texts were delivered; and in truth the latitude within which the Youth Movement had to maneuver was no larger than the area bounded by the nuances of those speeches. Thinking about the two speeches today, I like to compare them to the clashing islands in the legend of the Argonauts, the Symplegades, between which no ship can pass in safety and where, at that time, a sea of love and hatred roiled.—Assemblies of bourgeois intellectuals were then far commoner than nowadays, since they had not yet recognized their limits. We may say, however, that we felt those limits, even if much time was to pass before the realization matured that no one can improve his school or his parental home without first smashing the state that needs bad ones. We felt these limits when we held our discussions, at which the younger among us spoke of the brutalities they had to endure at home, in drawing rooms kindly made available by parents who at bottom thought no differently from those we wished to oppose. We felt them when we older members held our literary evenings in rooms at beerhouses that were never for a moment safe from the waiters; we felt them when we were obliged to receive our lady friends in furnished rooms with doors we were not at liberty to lock; we felt them in our dealings with owners of public rooms and with porters, with relations and guardians. And when, finally, after August 8, 1914, the days came when those among us who were closest to the dead couple did not want to part from one another until they were buried, we felt the limits in the shame of being able to find refuge only in a seedy railway hotel on Stuttgart Square. Even the graveyard demonstrated the boundaries set by the city to all that filled our hearts: it was impossible to procure for the pair who had died together graves in one and the same cemetery. But those were days that ripened a realization that was to come later, and that planted in me the conviction that the city of Berlin would also not be spared the scars of the struggle for a better order.—If I chance today to pass through the streets of the neighborhood, I set foot in them with the same uneasiness that one feels when entering an attic unvisited for years. Valuable things may be lying around, but nobody remembers where. And in truth this dead district with its tall apartment houses is today the junkroom of the West End bourgeoisie.

That was the time when the Berlin cafés played a part in our lives. I still remember the first that I took in consciously. This was much earlier, immediately after my graduation. The Viktoria Café, where our first communal jaunt ended at three in the morning, no longer exists. Its place—on the corner of Friedrichstrasse and Unter den Linden—has been taken by one of the noisiest luxury cafés of new Berlin, against which the earlier one, however luxurious it may have been in its day, stands out with all the magic of the age of chandeliers, mirrored walls, and plush comfort. This old Viktoria Café was on that occasion our last port of call, and we doubtless reached it a depleted group. It must have been more than half empty—at any rate I can discern, through the veils that mask the image today, no one apart from a few whores, who seemed to have the spacious café to themselves. We did not stay long, and I do not know whether I paid the Viktoria Café, which must have disappeared soon after, a second visit. The time had not yet arrived when the frequenting of cafés was a daily need, and it can hardly have been Berlin that fostered this vice in me, however well the vice later adapted itself to the establishments of that city, which leads far too strenuous and deliberate a life of pleasure to know real coffeehouses. Our first café, accordingly, was more a strategic base than a place of siesta. And I have thus unmistakably revealed its name: as is well known, the headquarters of bohemians until the onset of the war was the old West End Café. It was in this café that we sat together in those very first August days, choosing among the barracks that were being stormed by the rush of volunteers. We decided on the cavalry on Belle-Alliance Strasse, where I duly appeared on one of the following days, no spark of martial fervor in my breast. Yet however reserved I may have been in my thoughts, which were concerned only with securing a place among friends in the inevitable conscription, one of the bodies jammed in front of the barracks gates was mine. Admittedly only for two days: on August 8 came the event that was to banish for long afterward both the city and the war from my mind. I often saw Heinle in the West End Café. We usually met there late, about twelve. I cannot say that we had close relations with the literary Bohemia whose days, or nights, were spent there; we were a self-contained group, the world of our "movement" was different from that of the emancipated people around us, and contacts with them were only fleeting. A mediator between the two sides for a period was Franz Pfemfert, editor of *Die Aktion;* our relations with him were purely Machiavellian. Else Lasker-Schüler once drew me to her table; Wieland Herzfelde, then a young student, was to be seen there, as well as Simon Guttmann, to whom I shall return;[15] but the list here reaches the boundaries of our narrower world. I believe we were alien to the café; the feverish concentration induced by concern with so many rival actions, the organization of the Free Students' Union and the development of the debating chambers, the elaboration of our speeches in large assemblies of students, help for comrades in need, care for those imperiled by entanglements either of friendship or of love—all this set us apart from the sated, self-assured bohemians around us. Heinle was more closely acquainted with one or another of them, such as the painter Meidner,[16] who sketched him; but this connection remained unfruitful for us. Then, one day in Switzerland,

I read that the West End Café had been closed. I had never been much at home in it. At that time I did not yet possess that passion for waiting without which one cannot thoroughly appreciate the charm of a café. And if I see myself waiting one night amid tobacco smoke on the sofa that encircled one of the central columns, it was no doubt in feverish expectation of the outcome of some negotiation at the debating chamber, or of one of the mediators who were brought into play when tensions had once again reached an unbearable pitch. I came to be on much more intimate terms with the neighboring café, which had its beginning during the period I now refer to. This was the Princess Café. In an attempt to develop a "Physiology of Coffeehouses," one's first and most superficial classification would be into professional and recreational establishments. If, however, one leaves aside the most brazen entertainment places run along industrial lines, it becomes very noticeable that in the development of most hostelries the two functions coincide. A particularly telling example is the history of the Romanische Café from exactly the moment when the proprietor of the West End Café evicted his clientele. Very soon the Romanische Café accommodated the bohemians, who, in the years immediately after the war, were able to feel themselves masters of the house. The legendary, now-departed waiter Richard, distributor of newspapers—a hunchback who on account of his bad reputation enjoyed high esteem in these circles—was the symbol of their dominance. When the German economy began to recover, the bohemian contingent visibly lost the threatening nimbus that had surrounded them in the era of the Expressionist revolutionary manifestos. The bourgeois revised his relationship to the inmates of the Café Megalomania (as the Romanische Café soon came to be called), and found that everything was back to normal. At this moment the physiognomy of the Romanische Café began to change. The "artists" withdrew into the background, to become more and more a part of the furniture, while the bourgeois, represented by stock-exchange speculators, managers, film and theater agents, literary-minded clerks, began to occupy the place—as a site of relaxation. For one of the most elementary and indispensable diversions of the citizen of a great metropolis, wedged, day in, day out, in the structure of his office and family amid an infinitely variegated social environment, is to plunge into another world, the more exotic the better. Hence the bars haunted by artists and criminals. The distinction between the two, from this point of view, is slight. The history of the Berlin coffeehouses is largely that of different strata of the public, those who first conquered the floor being obliged to make way for others gradually pressing forward, and thus to ascend the stage.

Such a stage, for Heinle and me, was the Princess Café, which we were in the habit of patronizing as occupants of "private boxes." The latter phrase should be taken almost literally, for this café, designed by Lucian Bernhard, an interior decorator and poster artist much in demand at that time, offered its visitors an abundance of snug recesses, standing historically midway between the *chambres séparées* and the coffee parlors. The profession primarily served by this establishment is therefore clear. And when we visited it, indeed made it for a time our regular meeting place, it was certainly on account of the *cocottes*. Heinle wrote "Princess Café" at that time. "Doors draw coolness over through the song." We had no intention of making acquaintances in this café. On the contrary—what attracted us here was being enclosed in an environment that isolated us. Every distinction between us and the literary coteries of the city was welcome to us. This one, to be sure, more so than all others. And that certainly had to do with the *cocottes*. But this leads into a subterranean stratum of the Youth Movement, reached by way of an artist's studio in Halensee, to which we shall return. It is quite possible that Simon Guttmann, its occupant, met us here, too, from time to time. I have no recollection of it, just as in general, here more than elsewhere, the human figures recede before the place itself. None of them is as vividly present to me as a forlorn, approximately circular chamber in the upper story, hung with violet drapery and illuminated with a violet glow, in which many seats were always empty, while on others couples took up as little space as possible. I called this amphitheater the "anatomy school." Later, when this epoch was long since closed, I sat long evenings there, close to a jazz band, discreetly consulting sheets and slips of paper, writing my *Ursprung des deutschen Trauerspiels* [Origin of the German Trauerspiel]. When one day a new "renovation" set in, turning the Princess Café into Café Stenwyk, I gave up. Today it has sunk to the level of a beerhouse.

Never again has music possessed so dehumanized and shameless a quality as that of the two brass bands that tempered the flood of people surging torpidly along "Scandal Avenue" between the café restaurants of the Zoo. Today I perceive what gave this flow its elemental force. For the city dweller there was no higher school of flirtation than this, surrounded by the sandy precincts of gnus and zebras, the bare trees and clefts where vultures and condors nested, the stinking enclosures of wolves, and the hatcheries of pelicans and herons. The calls and screeches of these animals mingled with the noise of drums and percussion. This was the air in which the glance of a boy fell for the first time on a passing girl, while he talked all the more zealously to his friend. And such were his efforts to betray himself neither by his eyes nor his voice that he saw nothing of her.

At that time the Zoological Garden still had an entrance by the Lichtenstein Bridge. Of the three gates it was the least frequented, and gave access to the park's most deserted area: an avenue that, with the milk-white orbs of its candelabras, resembled some deserted promenade at Wiesbaden or Pyrmont.

And before the economic crisis had so depopulated these resorts that they seemed more ancient than Roman spas, this dead corner of the Zoological Garden was an image of what was to come, a prophesying place. It must be considered certain that there are such places; indeed, just as there are plants that primitive peoples claim confer the power of clairvoyance, so there are places endowed with such power: they may be deserted promenades, or treetops, particularly in towns, seen against walls, railway crossings, and above all the thresholds that mysteriously divide the districts of a town. The Lichtenstein gate was really such a threshold, between the two West End parks. It was as if in both, at the point where they were nearest, life paused. And this daily desertion was the more keenly felt by one who remembered the dazzling approach to be seen on festal nights for a number of years from a doorway of the Adler ballrooms, which has fallen now into just such disuse as has this long-closed gate.

How totally unlike this (the music at the Zoo) was some other park music that had begun to reach my ears at an earlier time. It came from Rousseau Island and drove the skaters looping and whirling on New Lake. I was among them long before I had any conception of the source of the island's name, not to mention the difficulty of Rousseau's style. Through its position this skating rink was comparable to no other, and still more by virtue of its life through the seasons. For what did summer make of the rest? Tennis courts. But here, under the overhanging branches of the trees along the bank, stretched a lake connected to labyrinthine waterways, and now one skated under the little arched bridges where in summer one had leaned on balustrades, or on chains held by lions' mouths, watching the boats gliding on the dark water. There were serpentine paths near the lake and, above all, the tender retreats of lonely old men, benches for "adults only" at the edge of the sand pit with its ditches, where toddlers dig or stand absorbed in thought until bumped by a playmate or roused by the voice of a nursemaid from the bench of command. There she sits, stern and studious, reading her novel and keeping the child in check while hardly raising an eyelid, until, her labor done, she changes places with the nurse at the other end of the bench, who is holding the baby between her knees and knitting. Old, solitary men found their way here, paying due honor—amid these scatterbrained womenfolk, among the shrieking children—to the serious side of life: the newspaper. Even if the girl I loved, after long tarrying on the paths of this garden, had left at last, there was nowhere I liked better to think of her than while sitting on a backless bench in one of those playgrounds, and I never swept the sand from where I was going to sit down. All these images I have preserved. But none would bring back New Lake and a few hours of my childhood so vividly as to hear once more the bars of music to which my feet, heavy with their skates after a lone excursion across the bustling ice, touched the familiar planks and stumbled past the chocolate-dispensing machines, and past the more splendid one with a hen laying candy-filled eggs, through the doorway behind which glowed the anthracite stove, to the bench where you now savored for a while the weight of the metal blades strapped to your feet, which did not yet reach the ground, before resolving to unbuckle them. If you then slowly rested one calf on the other knee and unfastened the skate, it was as if in its place you had suddenly grown wings, and you went out with steps that nodded to the frozen ground.

Language has unmistakably made plain that memory is not an instrument for exploring the past but its theater.[17] It is the medium of past experience, just as the earth is the medium in which dead cities lie buried. He who seeks to approach his own buried past must conduct himself like a man digging. This determines the tone and bearing of genuine reminiscences. They must not be afraid to return again and again to the same matter; to scatter it as one scatters earth, to turn it over as one turns over soil. For the matter itself is merely a deposit, a stratum, which yields only to the most meticulous examination what constitutes the real treasure hidden within the earth: the images, severed from all earlier associations, that stand—like precious fragments or torsos in a collector's gallery—in the sober rooms of our later insights. True, for successful excavations a plan is needed. Yet no less indispensable is the cautious probing of the spade in the dark loam, and it is to cheat oneself of the richest prize to preserve as a record merely the inventory of one's discoveries, and not this dark joy of the place of the finding, as well. Fruitless searching is as much a part of this as succeeding, and consequently remembrance must not proceed in the manner of a narrative or still less that of a report, but must, in the strictest epic and rhapsodic manner, assay its spade in ever-new places, and in the old ones delve to ever-deeper layers.

It is true that countless façades of the city stand exactly as they stood in my childhood. Yet I do not encounter my childhood in their contemplation. My gaze has brushed them too often since; too often they have been the decor and theater of my walks and concerns. And the few exceptions to this rule—above all, St. Matthew's Church on St. Matthew's Square—are perhaps only apparently so. For did I as a child really frequent the remote corner where it stands? Did I even know it? I cannot tell. What it says to me today it owes solely to the edifice itself: the church with the two pointed, gabled roofs over its two side aisles, and the yellow-and-ocher brick of which it is built. It is an old-fashioned church, of which the same is true of many an old-fashioned building: although they were not young with us and perhaps did not even know us when we were children, they have much knowledge of our childhood, and for this we love them. But I should confront myself at that age in quite a different way had I the courage to enter a certain front door that I have passed thousands upon thousands of times. A front door in the old West End. True, my eyes no longer see it, or the façade of the house. My soles would doubtless be the first to send me word, once I had closed the door behind me, that they had discovered in me myself the distance and the number of steps I had to cross on the stairs, that on this worn staircase they trod in ancient tracks, and if I no longer cross the threshold of that house it is for fear of an encounter with this stairway interior, which has conserved in seclusion the power to recognize me that the façade lost long ago. For with its colored windows it has stayed the same, even if within the living quarters all is changed. Bleak verses filled the intervals between our heartbeats, when we paused exhausted on the landing between floors. They glimmered or shone from a pane in which, like a Raphael Madonna, a woman with nut-brown eyebrows floated aloft with a goblet from a niche, and while the straps of my satchel cut into my shoulders I was forced to read, "Industry adorns the burgher; blessedness is toil's reward." Outside, it may have been raining. One of the colored windows was open, and to the drumming of the rain the upward march resumed.

Epigraph: O brown-baked column of victory
       With children's sugar from the winter days.

I never slept on the street in Berlin. I saw sunset and dawn, but between the two I found myself a shelter. Only those for whom poverty or vice turns the city into a landscape in which they stray from dark till sunrise know it in a way denied to me. I always found quarters, even though sometimes tardy and also unknown ones that I did not revisit and where I was not alone. If I paused thus late in a doorway, my legs had become entangled in the ribbons of the streets, and it was not the cleanest of hands that freed me.

Reminiscences, even extensive ones, do not always amount to an autobiography. And these quite certainly do not, even for the Berlin years that I am exclusively concerned with here. For autobiography has to do with time, with sequence and what makes up the continuous flow of life. Here, I am talking of a space, of moments and discontinuities. For even if months and years appear here, it is in the form they have at the moment of commemoration. This strange form—it may be called fleeting or eternal—is in neither case the stuff that life is made of. And this is shown not so much by the role that my own life plays here, as by that of the people closest to me in Berlin—whoever and whenever they may have been. The atmosphere of the city that is here evoked allots them only a brief, shadowy existence. They steal along its walls like beggars, appear wraithlike at windows, to vanish again, sniff at thresholds like a *genius loci,* and even if they fill whole neighborhoods with their names, it is as a dead man's name fills his gravestone. Noisy, matter-of-fact Berlin, the city of work and the metropolis of business, nevertheless has more—not less—than some other cities of those places and moments when it bears witness to the dead, shows itself full of dead; and the obscure awareness of these moments, these places, perhaps more than anything else, confers on childhood memories a quality that makes them at once as evanescent and as alluringly tormenting as half-forgotten dreams. For childhood, knowing no preconceived opinions, has none about life. It is as dearly attached (though with just as strong reservations) to the realm of the dead—where it juts into that of the living—as to life itself. How far a child has access to the past is difficult to tell, and depends on many things—time, environment, the child's nature and education. The limitation of my own feeling for the Berlin that is not circumscribed by a few facts about the Stratau Fair and King Frederick in 1848—that is, for the topographic tradition representing the connection with the dead of this ground—results entirely from the fact that neither of my parents' families was native to Berlin. This sets a limit to the child's memory—and it is this limit, rather than childhood experience itself, that is manifest in what follows. Wherever this boundary may have been drawn, however, the second half of the nineteenth century certainly lies within it, and to it belong the following images, not in the manner of general representations, but of images that, according to the teachings of Epicurus, constantly detach themselves from things and determine our perception of them.[18]

Behind us lay the forecourt, with its dangerous, heavy swinging-doors on their whiplash springs. We were now walking on the flagstones, which were slippery with fish water or swill and where you could so easily lose your footing on carrots or lettuce leaves. Behind wire partitions, each bearing a number, were ensconced the ponderous ladies, priestesses of Venal Ceres, purveyors of all the fruits of field and tree and of all edible birds, fishes, and mammals, procuresses, untouchable wool-clad colossi exchanging vibrant signs from booth to booth with a flash of their large mother-of-pearl buttons or a slap on their booming black aprons or their money-filled pouches. Didn't the earth bubble and seethe below the hems of their skirts, and wasn't this truly fertile ground? Didn't a god of the market himself cast the goods into their laps? Berries, crustaceans, mushrooms, chunks of meat and cabbage, invisibly cohabiting with the people who abandoned themselves as they languidly and mutely eyed the unsteady procession of housewives who, laden with baskets and bags, laboriously drove their brood before them along these slippery alleyways of ill repute. But when, in winter, the gas lamps went on in the early evening, you at once had a feeling of sinking, becoming aware, in this gentle gliding, of the ocean depths that heaved opaque and sluggish below the glassy surface of the waters.

The more frequently I return to these memories, the less fortuitous it seems to me how slight a role is played in them by people: I think of an afternoon in Paris to which I owe insights into my life that came in a flash, with the force of an illumination. It was on this very afternoon that my biographical relationships to people, my friendships and comradeships, my passions and love affairs, were revealed to me in their most vivid and hidden intertwinings. I tell myself it had to be in Paris, where the walls and quays, the asphalt surfaces, the collections and the rubbish, the railings and the squares, the arcades and the kiosks, teach a language so singular that our relations to people attain, in the solitude encompassing us in our immersion in that world of things, the depths of a sleep in which the dream image waits to show the people their true faces. I wish to write of this afternoon because it made so apparent what kind of regimen cities keep over imagination, and why the city—where people make the most ruthless demands on one another, where appointments and telephone calls, sessions and visits, flirtations and the struggle for existence grant the individual not a single moment of contemplation—indemnifies itself in memory, and why the veil it has covertly woven out of our lives shows images of people less often than those of the sites of our encounters with others or ourselves. Now, on the afternoon in question I was sitting inside the Café des Deux Magots in Saint-Germain-des-Prés, where I was waiting—I forget for whom. Suddenly, and with compelling force, I was struck by the idea of drawing a diagram of my life, and knew at the same moment exactly how it was to be done. With a very simple question I interrogated my past life, and the answers were inscribed, as if of their own accord, on a sheet of paper that I had with me. A year or two later, when I lost this sheet, I was inconsolable. I have never since been able to restore it as it arose before me then, resembling a series of family trees. Now, however, reconstructing its outline in thought without directly reproducing it, I would instead speak of a labyrinth. I am concerned here not with what is installed in the chamber at its enigmatic center, ego or fate, but all the more with the many entrances leading into the interior. These entrances I call "primal acquaintances"; each of them is a graphic symbol of my acquaintance with a person whom I met not through other people but through neighborhood, family relationships, school comradeship, mistaken identity, companionship on travels, or other such—hardly numerous—situations. So many primal relationships, so many entrances to the maze. But since most of them—at least those that remain in our memory—for their part open up new acquaintances, relations to new people, after a time they branch off these corridors (the male may be drawn to the right, the female to the left). Whether cross-connections are finally established between these systems also depends on the intertwinements of our path through life. More important, however, are the astonishing insights that a study of this plan provides into the differences among individual lives. What part is played in the primal acquaintanceships of different people's lives by profession and school, family and travel? And above all: Is the formation of the many offshoots governed in individual existence by hidden laws? Which ones start early in life, and which ones start late? Which are continued to the end of life, and which peter out? "If a man has character," says Nietzsche, "he will have the same experience over and over again."[19] Whether or not this is true on a large scale, on a small one there are perhaps paths that lead us again and again to people who have one and the same function for us: passageways that always, in the most diverse periods of life, guide us to the friend, the betrayer, the beloved, the pupil, or the master. This is what the sketch of my life revealed to me as it took shape before me on that Paris afternoon. Against the background of the city, the people who had surrounded me drew close together to form a figure. It was many years earlier, I believe at the beginning of the war, that in Berlin, against the background of the people then closest to me, the world of things contracted to a symbol similarly profound. It was an emblem of four rings. This takes me to one of the old Berlin houses on Kupfergraben. With their plain, genteel façades and their wide hallways, they may have stemmed from the Schinkel period.[20] In one of them lived at that time a prominent antique dealer. He had no display window. You had to go into his apartment to admire, in a number of showcases, a selection of prehistoric brooches and clasps, Lombard earrings, Late Roman neck chains, medieval coins, and many similar valuables. How my friend A.C. had tracked him down I do not know.[21] But I remember distinctly the engrossment with which, under the impression of Alois Riegl's *Die spätrömische Kunst-Industrie*,[22] which I had recently studied, I contemplated the sheet-gold breastplates and garnet-studded bracelets. There were, if I am not mistaken, three of us: my friend, his fiancée at that time or Frau Dorothea J., and me. C. asked to see rings—Greek and Renaissance cameos, rings from the imperial period, work usually carved in semiprecious stone. Each of the four that he finally purchased is imprinted unforgettably on my mind. Except for one that I have lost sight of, they are still today with those for whom they were intended that morning. One, a bright-yellow smoky topaz, was chosen by Dorothea J. The workmanship was Grecian and depicted in a tiny space Leda receiving the swan between her parted thighs. It was most graceful. I was less able to admire the amethyst that the donor, Ernst S.,[23] selected for our mutual friend: a fifteenth- or sixteenth-century Italian had carved a profile in it which Lederer[24] claimed was that of Pompey. I was quite differently affected, however, by the last two rings. One was intended for me, but only as a very temporary owner; it was really destined to reach, through me, my then fiancée, Grete R.[25] It was the most fascinating ring I have ever seen. Cut in a dark, solid garnet, it portrayed Medusa's head. It was a work from the Roman imperial period. The proustite mounting was not the original. Worn on the finger, the ring seemed merely the most perfect of signet rings. You entered its secret only by taking it off and contemplating the head against the light. As the different strata of the garnet were unequally translucent, and the thinnest so transparent that it glowed with rose hues, the somber bodies of the snakes seemed to rise above the two deep, glowing eyes, which looked out from a face that, in the purple-black portions of the cheeks, receded once more into the night. Later I tried more than once to stamp a seal with this stone, but it proved easy to crack and in need of the utmost care. Shortly after giving it away, I broke off my relationship with its new owner. My heart had already gone with the last of the four rings, which the giver had reserved for his sister. And certainly this girl was the true center of the circle's fate, though years were to elapse before we realized it. For apart from her beauty—itself not dazzling, but inconspicuous and without luster—she had nothing that seemed to destine her for center stage. And in fact she was the center never of people but, in the strictest sense, of fates, as if her plantlike passivity and inertia had arranged the latter—which, of all human things, seem the most subject to vegetal laws—concentrically about her. Many years were needed before what at that time was in part beginning to unfold in its seed, and in part still dormant, emerged in its ramifications to the light of day: the fate by virtue of which she, who had a relationship with her brother that by its tenderness filled to the very edge the capacities of sisterly love, was to form a liaison with her brother's two closest friends—with the recipient of the ring depicting the head of Pompey and with me—and ultimately find her husband in the brother of the woman who married her own brother as her second husband.[26] She it was, on the day I am speaking of, who received from me the ring with the Medusa's head. It cannot have been many days later that I sent—after the lapis lazuli with the lute wreathed in foliage engraved in it, after the fourth ring and to its wearer—this sonnet: "To your finger constantly encircled [text breaks off]

The treasure-dispensing giant in the green pine forest[27] or the fairy who grants one wish—they appear to each of us at least once in a lifetime. But only Sunday's children remember the wish they made, and so it is only a few who recognize its fulfillment in their own lives. I know of such a wish that was fulfilled for me, and would not claim it to be any wiser than those of children in fairy tales. It goes back to my early childhood, and arose in me in connection with the lamp that on dark winter mornings at half past six was carried through my doorway and cast the shadow of our nursemaid on the ceiling. The fire was lit in the stove, and soon, amid reddish reflections, the grating was marked out on the bare floor. When the temperature—the night warmth from my bed and the morning warmth from the fire—had made me doubly drowsy, it was time to get up. Then I had no other wish than to finish my sleep. This wish accompanied me throughout the whole of my schooldays. Its inseparable attendant, however, was fear of being late. I can still feel today, when I pass the Savignyplatz, the dread with which, stepping into Carmerstrasse, where I lived, I read my judgment in the spellbound space between the ten and the twelve on the repulsive clock-face. The wish that animated me on such winter days, and even later, when, in an extremity of fatigue, I rose from the couch in the afternoon because of a gymnastics class, had been fulfilled. Only I did not always recognize this fulfillment when yet another of my attempts to find a professional "place," in the bourgeois sense of the word, had come to grief.

There is one other sound that, thanks to the decades in which it neither passed my lips nor reached my ears, has preserved the unfathomable mystery that certain words from the language of adults possess for children. It was not long ago that I rediscovered it, and indeed a number of indivisible finds of this nature have played a large part in my decision to write down these memories. My parents being wealthy, we moved every year, before I went to school and perhaps later, too, notwithstanding other occasional summer trips, to summer residences not far from home. First it was Potsdam, later Neubabelsberg. Whereas the latter period still survives in a number of images, of which I may perhaps have more to tell—the night of the great burglary when my parents locked themselves in my room, the hours I stood fishing beside my father on the bank of Lake Griebnitz, the visit to Peacock Island that brought the first great disappointment of my life, because I could not find peacock feathers in the grass as I had been promised—by contrast, the summer months in Potsdam have wholly vanished, unless I may situate the asparagus cutting (my first and only agricultural passion) as far back as the garden on the Brauhausberg. And I have thus divulged the word in which, like countless rose petals in a drop of Rose Malmaison, hundreds of summer days, forfeiting their form, their color, and their multiplicity, are preserved in their scent. The word is "Brauhausberg." To approach what it enfolds is almost impossible. These words that exist on the frontier between two linguistic regions, that of children and that of adults, are comparable to the words of Mallarmé's poems, which the conflict between the poetic and the profane word has, as it were, consumed and made evanescent, airy. Likewise, the word "Brauhausberg" has lost all heaviness, no longer contains any trace of a brewery [Brauhaus], and is at most a hill swathed in blue that rose up each summer to give lodging to me and my parents.

The economic basis on which the finances of my parents rested was surrounded, long past my childhood and adolescence, by deepest secrecy. Probably not only for me, the eldest child, but also for my mother. And it is certain that such a state of affairs was the rule in Jewish families, and no doubt in a great many Christian ones as well. More curious is the fact that consumption, too, was wrapped in some of the mystery that so deeply shrouded income and fortune. I remember, at any rate, that the mention of certain suppliers—"sources," as they were called—always took place with the solemnity befitting an initiation. There are, it is true, distinctions to be drawn. The purveyors who met the daily household needs no more belonged to that secret circle than did the Berlin firms of long-standing repute that my mother visited when she took me and the younger children "downtown." On such occasions it was as certain that our suits would be bought at Arnold Müller's, our shoes at Stiller's, and our suitcases at Mädler's, as that at the end of these commissions our hot chocolate with whipped cream would be ordered at Hillbrich's. These shopping places were strictly preordained by tradition—quite unlike the connections with traders, which were my father's responsibility. My father possessed at bottom, along with a number of inhibitions stemming not only from his decency but also from a certain civic worthiness, the entrepreneurial nature of a big-business man. Unfavorable influences brought about his very premature retirement from an enterprise that was probably by no means ill-suited to his capacities, the Lepke art-auction house, which at that time was still located on Kochstrasse and in which he was a partner. After he had relinquished his share in the firm, he concerned himself increasingly with speculative investments of his capital, and it would not surprise me if the interest he took in household transactions was far keener from this time on. What is certain is that a good many of the suppliers he henceforth searched out were indirectly connected with his investments. If, therefore, from my mother's shopping excursions, a traditional and as it were official image of the Berlin commercial world emerged, the hints and instructions of my father gave rise to an unknown and slightly sinister one, whose prestige derived as much from the authoritarian resonance that these names carried at the family table as from the fact that these firms, unlike the others, were never seen by me. At their head, so to speak, was the Lepke auction room itself, with which my father not only had connections but from which, from time to time, he also brought home a purchase. I doubt that this commerce was an altogether happy one, with the exception perhaps of his carpet buying. Shortly before his death, he told me that he could distinguish the quality of a carpet's pile with the ball of his foot, if his soles were suitably thin. In my childhood, however, what impressed me most was to imagine the gavel blows with which my father accompanied the auction. Later, when he had withdrawn from Lepke's, this gavel always lay on his desk. Even if I never heard the rap of this gavel, there is another sound that became indissoluble from the image of my father's power and grandeur—or, rather, from those of a man in his profession. It is (implausible as this may seem) the noise made by the knife that my mother used to butter the rolls that my father took to work in the morning, when it was scraped for the last time, to remove the butter still adhering to it, against the crisp surface of the cut roll. This signal preluding the labor of my father's day was no less exciting to me than, in later years, the sound of the bell that announced the start of a performance at the theater. Apart from this, the real token of my father's profession in our apartment was a Moor, almost life-size, who stood on a gondola reduced to one-thirtieth of its size, holding with one hand an oar that could be taken out, and lifting on the other a golden bowl. This work of art was made of wood, the Moor black, the gondola and oar glowing in many colors beneath the varnish. The whole, however, was so urgently oriented toward its companion piece that I cannot tell today whether a second Moor, whom I imagine with it, really stood there originally or is a figment of my imagination. So much for Lepke's auction house. There was, besides, a further purveyor of artwork—at least as far as bronzes were concerned; this was the firm of Gladenbeck. Whether the choice was affected here, too, by more intimate commercial ties, I do not know. Such was certainly the case, however, with our supply of mouthwash, hydrogen peroxide obtained in huge bottles from the "Medicinal Stores," of which my father was a director. Less transparent, on the other hand, was the state of affairs regarding the Stabernack firm, which for years held an uncontested monopoly on installations in our apartment. Here the intermediate party was perhaps a certain company of building contractors, one of whose directors, Herr Altgelt, filled the role of partner in countless telephone conversations with my father, and whose name has stayed in my memory because his son was a member, and one of the most inglorious, of my class. Leaving aside mealtime conversations, it was only the telephone that intimated to us the occult world of business and traders. My father telephoned a great deal. He, whose outward manner seems to have been almost always courteous and pliable, possessed perhaps only on the telephone the bearing and decisiveness corresponding to his sometimes great wealth. In conversations with mediating agencies, this energy not infrequently grew vociferous; and the "serious side of life," which was embodied tangibly in my father's activity, found in the altercations with telephone operators its true symbol. The telephone first came into use during my childhood. I have therefore known it nailed in some corner of the corridor, whence, shrilling from the darkness, it augmented the terrors of that Berlin apartment with the endless passage leading from the half-lit dining room to the back bedrooms. It became a truly infernal machine when my school friends phoned in the prohibited period between two and four. But not all my father's mysterious transactions were carried out by telephone. From earliest times he had had—like many husbands who do not always find life easy in marriage—a tendency to address himself independently to certain branches of the domestic economy. Thus, he had connections in the provinces, principally in the vicinity of Hamburg, which frequently called him away on business. Our house was regularly plied from this source with Holstein butter, and in autumn with duck. Wine, on the other hand, was furnished by a Berlin firm, whose share certificates were also in my father's possession: this was the Central Wine Distributors, who were trying out new methods of calculation in the wine business. Finally these names became entwined, in parental discussions, with others in which the traditions of the middle-class Berlin of that time converged from both sides: for notarial attestation, Oberneck was consulted; surgical operations were performed by Rinne; dancing instruction was entrusted to Quaritsch; the family doctor was Renvers, at least as long as he lived in the same building;[28] Joseph Goldschmidt was our banker. But as for me, I was most lastingly affected by a reckless attempt that my father embarked upon one evening to bring even the family's amusements into the harmony with his business enterprises that he had been able to establish for all its other needs. For when, about 1910, on Lutherstrasse in the West End, a consortium erected a building (the one that now houses the Scala) as an "Ice Palace," my father, with a sizable stake, was among their number. Now, one evening—I don't know whether it was the opening date or later—my father conceived the idea of taking me there. The Ice Palace, however, was not only the first skating rink in Berlin, but also a thriving nightclub. So it happened that my attention was held far less by the convolutions in the arena than by the apparitions at the bar, which I was able to survey at my ease from a box in the circle. Among these was a prostitute in a very tight-fitting white sailor's suit, who, though I was unable to exchange a word with her, determined my erotic fantasies for years to come.

In those early years I got to know "downtown" only as the theater of purchases, on which occasions it first became apparent how my father's money could cut a path for us between the shop counters and assistants and mirrors, and the appraising eyes of our mother, whose muff lay on the counter. In the ignominy of a "new suit" we stood there, our hands peeping from the sleeves like dirty price tags, and it was only in the confectioner's that our spirits rose with the feeling of having escaped the false worship that humiliated our mother before idols bearing the names of Mannheimer, Herzog and Israel, Gerson, Adam, Esders and Mädler, Emma Bette, Bud and Lachmann. An impenetrable chain of mountains—no, caverns—of commodities: this was "downtown."

There are people who think they find the key to their destinies in heredity, others in horoscopes, others again in education. For my part, I believe that I would gain numerous insights into my later life from my collection of picture postcards, if I were able to leaf through it again today. The main contributor to this collection was my maternal grandmother, a decidedly enterprising lady, from whom I believe I have inherited two things: my delight in giving presents and my love of travel. If it is unclear what the Christmas holidays—which cannot be thought of without the Berlin of my childhood—meant for the first of these passions, it is certain that none of my boys' adventure books kindled my love of travel as did the postcards with which she supplied me in abundance from her far-flung travels. And because the longing we feel for a place determines it as much as does its outward image, I shall say something about these postcards. And yet—was what they awakened in me longing? Didn't they have far too magnetic an attraction to leave room for a wish to travel to the places they showed? For I was there—in Tabarz, Brindisi, Madonna di Campiglio, Westerland— when I gazed, unable to tear myself away, at the wooded slopes of Tabarz covered with glowing red berries, the yellow-and-white-daubed quays at Brindisi, the cupolas of Madonna di Campiglio printed bluish on blue, and the bows of the "Westerland" slicing high through the waves. Visiting the old lady in her carpeted window alcove, ornamented with a little balustrade and looking out onto the Blumeshof, it was hard to imagine how she had undertaken long sea voyages or even camel rides with the guidance of Stangel's Travel Bureau. She was a widow; three of her daughters were already married when I was small. I can tell nothing about the fourth, but a good deal about the room that she occupied in her mother's apartment. Yet perhaps I should first say something about the apartment as a whole. With what words am I to describe the almost immemorial feeling of bourgeois security that emanated from these rooms? Paradoxical as it may sound, the idea of that particular protectedness seems to relate most directly to their shortcomings. The inventory that filled these many rooms—twelve or fourteen—could today be accommodated without incongruity in the shabbiest of secondhand furniture shops. And if these ephemeral forms were so much more solid than those of the Jugendstil that superseded them—what made you feel at home, at ease, comfortable, and comforted in them was the nonchalance with which they attached themselves to the sauntering passage of years and days, entrusting their future to the durability of their material alone, and nowhere to rational calculation. Here reigned a species of things that was, no matter how compliantly it bowed to the minor whims of fashion, in the main so wholly convinced of itself and its permanence that it took no account of wear, inheritance, or moves, remaining forever equally near to and far from its ending, which seemed the ending of all things. Poverty could have no place in these rooms where even death had none. They had no space for dying—which is why their owners died in a sanatorium, while the furniture went straight to the secondhand dealer. Death was not provided for in them—that is why they were so cozy by day, and by night the theater of our most oppressive dreams. It is for this reason that, when I think of this house (it was number 10 or 12 Blumeshof)—in which were spent so many of my childhood's happiest hours, such as when I was allowed, to the sound of piano études, to browse in *Herzblättchens Zeitvertreib* in an armchair—I am met on its threshold by a nightmare. My waking existence has preserved no image of the staircase. But in my memory it remains today the scene of a haunting dream that I once had in just those happy years. In this dream the stairway seemed under the power of a ghost that awaited me as I mounted, though without barring my way, making its presence felt when I had only a few more stairs to climb. On these last stairs it held me spellbound.—The rooms in this apartment on the Blumeshof were not only numerous but also in some cases very large. To reach my grandmother at her window, I had to cross the huge dining room and attain the farthest end of the living room. Only feast days, and above all Christmas Day, could give an idea of the capaciousness of these rooms. But if, when this day came, it seemed as though it had been awaited all year long in the front rooms, there were other occasions that brought other parts of the apartment to life: a visit by a married daughter unlocked a long-disused wardrobe; another back room opened to us children when the grownups wished to take their afternoon nap at the front of the house; and another part again was animated by the piano lessons received by the last daughter remaining at home. The most important of these remote, less-frequented rooms, however, was the loggia. Perhaps this was because, being the least furnished, it was least suited to the sojourn of adults, or because muted street noises drifted in, or finally because it opened onto back courtyards with children, domestic servants, hurdy-gurdy men, and porters. But of these it was more often the voices than the forms that were to be described from the loggia. Moreover, the courtyards of a residential neighborhood as genteel as this never really bustled with activity; something of the composure of the rich people whose work was being done there seemed to have permeated this work itself, and everything seemed to await the Sleeping Beauty slumber that descended here on Sundays. For this reason Sunday was properly the day of the loggia—Sunday, which none of the other rooms could ever quite contain, as if they were damaged. Sunday seeped out of them. Only our loggia, looking out onto the yard (with its racks where the carpets were beaten), and the other loggias (with their bare walls of Pompeian red) could hold it. And not a chime of its cargo of bell-peals, with which the churches—the Twelve Apostles, St. Matthew's, and the Kaiser Wilhelm Memorial Church—slowly loaded it throughout the afternoon, slipped over its balustrade; all remained piled high till evening. As I have already indicated, this grandmother did not die in the Blumeshof; nor did the other one, who lived opposite her in the same street and was older and more severe—my father's mother. So the Blumeshof has become for me an Elysium, a vague realm of the shades of deceased but immortal grandmothers. And just as imagination, having once cast its veil over a district, is apt to adorn its edges with incomprehensible, capricious frills, so, in the course of decades and to this day, it turned a long-established grocery store situated near this house but on Magdeburgerstrasse (to someone driving past without ever having set foot inside) into a monument to an early-departed grandfather, solely because the first name of its owner, like his, was Georg.

But isn't this, too, the city—the strip of light under the bedroom door on evenings when we were "entertaining"? Didn't Berlin itself find its way into the expectant childhood night, as later the world of William Tell or Julius Caesar invaded the night of an audience? The dream ship that came to fetch us on those evenings must have rocked at our bedside on the waves of conversation, or under the spray of clattering plates; and in the early morning it set us down on the ebb of the carpet beating that came in at the window with the moist air on rainy days, and engraved itself more indelibly in the child's memory than the voice of the beloved in that of the man—this carpet beating that was the language of the nether world, of servant girls, the real grownups, a language that sometimes took its time, languid and muted under the gray sky, breaking at other times into an inexplicable gallop, as if the servants were pursued by phantoms. The courtyard was one of the places where the city opened itself to the child; others, admitting him or letting him go, were railway stations. On departure, their openings were a panorama, the frame of a *fata morgana*. No distance was more remote than the place where the rails converged in the mist. On the return home, however, all was different. For within us still burned the melancholy lamps that had shone in isolation from courtyard windows often without curtains, from staircases bristling with filth, from cellar windows hung with rags. These were the backyards that the city showed me as I returned from Hahnenklee or Sylt, only to close upon them once more, never to let me see or enter them. But those five last fearful minutes of the journey before everyone got out of the train have been converted into the gaze of my eyes, and there are those perhaps who look into them as into courtyard windows in damaged walls, in which at early evening a lamp stands.

Among the postcards in my album, there are a number whose written side has lasted better in my memory than their picture. All bear the handsome, legible signature "Helene Pufahl." She was my first teacher. Long before I knew of classes at school, I was brought by her into close relationship to the children of my "class," in the sense of the word that I would not become acquainted with until two decades later. And that it was high on the social scale I can infer from the names of the two girls from the little circle that remain in my memory: Ilse Ullstein and Luise von Landau. What order of nobility these Landaus belonged to I do not know. But their name had an immense attraction for me and—I have grounds to suppose—for my parents. Yet this is hardly the reason their name has remained undimmed in my mind until today; rather, it happens that this was the first name on which I consciously heard fall the accent of death. This occurred, as far as I know, not long after I had grown out of the little private circle. Later, each time I passed the Lützow quay, my eyes sought her house; and when, toward the end of my schooldays, I wrote my first philosophical essay, entitled "Reflections on the Nobility," the alluring name of my first schoolmate—beside that of Pindar, with which I had begun—stood unuttered. Fräulein Pufahl was succeeded by Herr Knoche, whom I had to confront quite alone. He was the preschool teacher from the school for which my parents later intended me. His instruction does not appear to have entirely agreed with me. At any rate, I performed on occasion magical rites directed against his person, and I still remember the feeling of omnipotence that came over me one day on Herkules Bridge on receiving the news that Herr Knoche had canceled the next day's class. At that time I knew to what I might attribute this, but today, sadly, I have forgotten the magic formula. More than in his private appearances, Herr Knoche impressed me in the classroom lessons I had with him later, when I had started school. They were enlivened by frequent intermezzi for thrashing. Herr Knoche was a zealous exponent of the cane. He was also entrusted with our singing instruction. And it was in a singing lesson that he showed me one of the shut gates that we all know from our childhood, behind which, we were assured, the way to later, real life lay open. We were practicing the cuirassier's song from *Wallensteins Lager*.[29]

> To horse, trusty friends, to horse and away
> to the field of freedom and valiance,
> where a man's worth more than dust and clay
> and the heart's still weighed in the balance.

Herr Knoche wanted the class to tell him what these last words actually meant. No one, of course, could give an answer. It was one of those artful questions that make children obtuse. Our discomfiture seemed most agreeable to Herr Knoche, who said pointedly, "You'll understand this when you are grown up." Now I am grown up; I am today inside the gate that Herr Knoche showed me; but it is still firmly shut. I was not to make my entrance through that portal.

Just as lights on a foggy night are surrounded by gigantic rings, my earliest theatrical impressions emerge from the mist of my childhood with great aureoles. At the very beginning is a "monkey theater" that performed perhaps on Unter den Linden and at which I appeared, as I remember, heavily escorted, since neither parents nor grandmother was prepared to forgo witnessing the effect on me of my first theatrical performance. True, the source of the light, the actual happening on the stage, I can no longer discern in so much luminous haze. A pinkish-gray cloud of seats, lights, and faces has obliterated the pranks of the poor little monkeys on the stage. And while I can recount the sequence of theatrical events in the following six or seven years, I can say nothing more of them—neither of the *Veilchenfresser* I saw at the Spa Theater at Suderode; nor of the *Wilhelm Tell* that, as is customary, initiated me to the Berlin stage; nor of the *Fiesko*, with Matkowsky, that I saw at the Schauspielhaus; nor of the *Carmen*, with Destinn, at the Opera.[30] The latter two performances my grandmother had assumed responsibility for; hence not only the dazzling program but also the imposing dress-circle seats. And yet, more fondly than to them, my mind goes back to the *Wilhelm Tell,* because of the event that preceded it, the highly hermetic nature of which is still undimmed, while nothing remains in my memory of the same evening's performance. It must have been in the afternoon that a difference of opinion arose between myself and my mother. Something was to be done that I did not like. Finally, my mother had recourse to coercion. She threatened that unless I did her bidding I would be left at home in the evening. I obeyed. But the feeling with which I did so, or rather, with which, the threat hardly uttered, I measured the two opposed forces and instantly perceived how enormous was the preponderance of the other side, and thus my silent indignation at so crude and brutal a procedure, which put at stake something totally disproportionate to the end—for the end was momentary, whereas the stake, the gratitude for the evening that my mother was about to give me, as I know today and anticipated then, was deep and permanent—this feeling of misused and violated trust has outlived in me all that succeeded it that day. Many years afterward it was proved a second time how much more significant and enduring the anticipation of an event can be than what actually ensues. As a boy, I longed for nothing more than to see Kainz.[31] But his guest performances in Berlin were during school time. Since the advance bookings in the morning offered the only possibility of procuring seats at prices commensurate with my pocket money, my wish was denied for years. My parents, at any rate, did nothing to advance its fulfillment. One day— whether because the advance bookings were on a Sunday or for another reason—I was able after all to be one of the first at the ticket office, which was already that of the theater on Nollendorfplatz. I see myself standing at the box office and—as if memory wanted to prelude the approaching main theme—waiting there, sure enough, but not buying my ticket. At this point memory pauses, and picks up its thread again only when I am mounting the stairs to the dress-circle in the evening, before the performance of

Richard II. What is it that imposes once again on memory, at the door of the auditorium, a "so far and no further"? True, I see before me a scene from the drama, but entirely cut off, without my knowing whether it is really from this performance or from another, any more than I know whether I saw Kainz or not—whether his appearance was canceled or whether the disappointment of finding him less great than I had believed him annulled, with the image of his acting, the whole evening. So I confront uncertainty wherever I follow my earliest theatrical memories, and in the end I can no longer even distinguish dream from reality. This is true of a dark winter evening when I went with my mother to a production of *Die lustigen Weiber von Windsor*.[32] I really saw this opera, in a kind of people's theater. It was a noisy, cheerful evening, but all the more silent was the journey there, through a snow-covered, unknown Berlin spreading about me in the gaslight. It stood in the same relation to the city I knew as that most jealously guarded of my postcards, the depiction of the Halle Gate in pale blue on a darker blue background. The Belle-Allianceplatz was to be seen, with the houses that frame it; the full moon was in the sky. From the moon and the windows in the façades, however, the top layer of card had been removed; their contrasting white disrupted the picture, and one had to hold it against a lamp or a candle to see, by the light of windows and a lunar surface parading in exactly the same illumination, the whole scene regain its composure. Perhaps that evening the opera we were approaching was the source of light that made the city suddenly gleam so differently, but perhaps it was only a dream that I had later of this walk, the memory of which has displaced what previously stood in for reality.

The architect of the Kaiser Friedrich School must have had something on the order of Brandenburg brick Gothic in mind. At any rate, it is constructed of red brick and displays a preference for motifs commonly found at Stendal or Tangermünde. The whole, however, gives a narrow-chested, high-shouldered impression. Rising close by the precincts of the municipal railway, the building exudes a sad, spinsterish primness. Even more than to the experiences I had within, it is probably to this exterior that I should attribute the fact that I have not retained a single cheerful memory of it. Nor, since leaving, have I ever had the idea of going back. Of the walk to school I have already spoken. But if the portal had been reached just in time, or there was no longer sufficient time (and the nightmarish things to come did not weigh too heavily) to allow me to buy at the adjoining stationer's another piece of plasticine, a protractor, or, at the very beginning, wafers and the little ribbons used to attach blotting sheets to exercise-book covers—if finally the wrought-iron door, which the janitor was allowed to open only ten minutes before school started, was still closed—how melancholy and oppressed must this wait at the door have been, under the arch of the municipal railway, which crossed Knesebeckstrasse at this point, if nothing of it comes back to me besides the compulsion incessantly to remove my cap, to pay attention to myself, when I saw passing before me one of the teachers, who were permitted to enter, of course, anytime they pleased.

Only today, it seems to me, am I able to appreciate how much hatefulness and humiliation lay in the obligation to raise my cap to teachers. The necessity of admitting them by this gesture into the sphere of my private existence seemed presumptuous. I would have had no objection to a less intimate and in some way military display of respect. But to greet a teacher as one would a relation or a friend seemed inordinately unfitting, as if they had wanted to hold classes in my home. From this alone it can be seen how little school was ever able to win me over. And if I experienced the antiquated forms of school discipline—caning, change of seats, or detention—only in the lower forms, nevertheless the terror and the pall they placed me under in those years never lifted from me. I find this not only in the importance attached to promotion to the next grade and to the four report cards brought home each year, but also in smaller but more telling details. Above all in the unfathomable shock or, rather, bewilderment into which I was plunged by interruptions in the continuity of teaching—such as excursions to the country, games, and especially the great annual competition between the schools of Greater Berlin to decide the best team at prisoner's base. Needless to say, I never belonged to the school team, which seldom met with success. But in the mobilization of the whole school that took place on such occasions, I, too, was involved. The matches were normally played in May or June, on some field or drill ground in the vicinity of the Lehrter station. As a rule, the weather was blazing hot. Nervously I would alight at the Lehrter station. Uncertainly I would set off in the direction I vaguely remembered, and would find myself at last, with mixed feelings of relief and repugnance, amid some alien troop of schoolboys. From now on, my bewilderment was uninterrupted—whether I had to look for my own school party, or sought a resting place in the shade, whether I had to reach a stall without crossing the field in order to buy fruit for breakfast, or congregate, while avoiding any appearance of indifference, around one of the gentlemen who made known the day's results, or finally, although I had not understood these results, exchange with my schoolfellows during the homeward journey observations on the course of the game. Yet what made these sporting occasions most hated and most repellent of all was not the multitudes they attracted but their site. The broad, unfrequented avenues leading to it were flanked by barracks; barracks bordered the playing field; the field was a parade ground. And on those days the feeling never left me that if I relaxed my vigilance for only a moment, permitted myself only the briefest well-being in the shade of a tree or before a sausage vendor's stand, I would fall in ten years' time irredeemably into the power of this place: I would have to become a soldier.—The Kaiser Friedrich School stands close by the municipal railway yard on Savignyplatz. At Savignyplatz station you can look down into its playground. And because, once liberated from it, I frequently took the opportunity to do this, it now stands before me quite uselessly, like one of those Mexican temples that were excavated much too early and inexpertly, their frescoes having been long effaced by rain by the time the excavation of the ceremonial implements and papyri, which might have thrown some light on these images, could at last seriously begin. So I have to make do with what is resurrected only today—isolated pieces of interior that have broken away yet contain the whole within them, while the whole, standing there before me, has lost its details without trace. The first fragment to reappear is what was certainly, throughout my whole time at school, the idlest of my perceptions: the molding, crowned with crenelations, above the classrooms. And perhaps this is not so difficult to explain. For everything else that came within my visual field sooner or later became of use to me, became associated with a thought or a notion that swept it along into the sea of oblivion. The exception was this narrow molding, cast out innumerable times by the healthy beat of everyday waves until it was left stranded like a shell on the shore of my daydreaming. And there I now come across it. I pick it up and question it like Hamlet addressing the skull. It is, as I have said, a molding representing a row of battlements. Thus, what is visible between them is not empty space but the same wood, only beveled and notched. The intention was certainly to remind the onlooker of a castle. What he was to do with the recollection was another question. In any event, this molding reinforced the idea of the dense mass divined in the morning behind the closed doors: the class at lessons. Over the doors leading to the arts-and-crafts rooms it became the emblem of a certain guildlike solidarity. On the classroom cupboard I encountered it again—but how much more emphasis it had on the identically shaped cupboards standing along the faculty-room wall! In the first, second, and third grades, in the vicinity of the many little coats and caps on their racks, its impact was lost; but in the upper classes it acquired an allusion to the *Abitur* that was soon to crown the labors of their members. Yet never more than a shadow of meaning and reason passed across it in such places, and it remained, with the unspeakable gray-green ornaments adorning the wall of the auditorium, and with the absurd bosses and scrolls of the cast-iron balustrades, the refuge of all my minutes of terror and my nightmares. Nothing, however, could compare with the molding, unless it was the bell that shrilly marked the beginning and end of lessons and breaks. The timbre and duration of this signal never varied. Yet how different it sounded at the beginning of the first and at the end of the last period! To describe this difference would be to lift the veil that seven years of school cast ever more tightly over each of the days that composed them. In winter the lamps were often still on when it rang, but the light they cast was bereft of coziness, offering as little shelter as the light the dentist shines into the mouth on which he is about to work. Between two peals of the bell lay the break, the second precipitating the shuffling, chattering uproar with which the mass of pupils, streaming through only two doors, surged up the narrow stairway from floor to floor. These staircases I have always hated: hated when I was forced to climb them amid the herd, a forest of calves and feet before me, defenselessly exposed to the bad odors emanating from all the bodies pressing so closely against mine; hated no less when, arriving late, passing deserted corridors, I hastened up them quite alone to the very top, arriving breathless in the classroom. If that happened before the teacher's hand was on the door handle, even though he might be quite near, you got in unseen. But woe if the door was already shut! However wide open those next to it might still be—and even if above or below some time passed before the bang of a shutting door announced the start of a lesson, and no matter how harmlessly the eye of a strange teacher approaching along the corridor brushed you—the judgment was ineluctable within, once you had plucked up the courage to open it.

"Cease your sewing, little mother, on that sarafan; useless will your labors be, so strain no more." "Earthward sink the evening shadows over wood and dale, and silent grows the world." "I am Doctor Eisenbart; hosanna, shout for joy! I serve the people faithfully; hosanna, shout for joy!" "Drink up the sparkling wine, dear friends; farewell, 'tis time to part." "As clouds go wand'ring o'er heaven's brow, so I shall cross the wide, wide world."— These and many other lieder from the songbook of Ludwig Erk,[33] which, in the form of two thick green-and-gold-bound volumes, rested on the music stand, my mother used to play for me. I did not join in the singing, but I listened with pleasure. These melodies belonged to the household, just like the jingling of the basket of keys when my mother searched impatiently through it for the purse or notebook that lay at the very bottom; like the dull pop with which, at dusk, the gas mantle of the chandelier that hung above the dining-room table responded to the match; like the creaking of the dumbwaiter that brought up food and tableware from the kitchen; like the stir made by my father's returning home at noon, as he unlocked the front door and let his stick fall into the umbrella stand.

Many years earlier, in one of the streets I passed along on my endless wanderings, I was surprised by the first stirring of my sexual urge, under the oddest circumstances. It was on the Jewish New Year's Day, and my parents had made arrangements for me to attend some religious celebration. Probably it was a service at the Reformed synagogue, which my mother, on grounds of family tradition, held in some sympathy, whereas my father's upbringing inclined him more to the Orthodox rite. But he had to give way. For this visit to the synagogue I had been entrusted to a relative, whom I had to fetch on my way. But whether because I had forgotten his address or because I was unfamiliar with the district, it grew later and later without my drawing nearer to my goal. To make my way independently to the synagogue was out of the question, since I had no idea where it was. This bewilderment, forgetfulness, and embarrassment were doubtless chiefly due to my dislike of the impending service, in its familial no less than its divine aspect. While I was wandering thus, I was suddenly and simultaneously overcome, on the one hand, by the thought, "Too late, time was up long ago, you'll never get there"—and, on the other, by a sense of the insignificance of all this, of the benefits of letting things take what course they would. And these two streams of consciousness converged irresistibly in an immense pleasure that filled me with blasphemous indifference toward the service, but exalted the street in which I stood, as if it had already intimated to me the services of procurement it was later to render to my awakened drive.

We had our "summer residences" first at Potsdam, then at Babelsberg. They were outside, from the point of view of the city; but from that of the summer, inside: we were ensconced within it, and I must disengage my memories of it—like moss that one plucks at random in the dark from the walls of a cave—from its sultry, humid glimmer. There are memories that are especially well preserved because, although not themselves affected, they are isolated by a shock from all that followed. They have not been worn away by contact with their successors and remain detached, self-sufficient. The first such memory appears when I speak of these summer days: it is an evening in my seventh or eighth year. One of our maidservants stands a long while at the wrought-iron gate, which opens onto I know not what tree-lined walk. The big garden, where I have been roaming in overgrown border regions, is already closed to me. It is time to go to bed. Perhaps I have sated myself with my favorite game: shooting with the rubber bolts of my "Eureka" pistol, somewhere in the bushes by the wire fence, at the wooden birds, which, struck by a bolt, fell backward out of the green-painted foliage, to which they were attached by strings. The whole day I had been keeping a secret to myself: the dream of the previous night. It had been an eerie one. A ghost had appeared to me. The site of its operations did not, in truth, really exist, but nevertheless bore a very strong resemblance to one that was known, tantalizing, and inaccessible to me—namely, the corner of my parents' bedroom which was separated from the rest of the chamber by an arch draped with a heavy, faded-violet curtain, and in which my mother's dressing gowns, house dresses, and shawls were hung. The darkness behind the curtain was impenetrable, and this corner was the sinister, nocturnal counterpart of that bright, beatific realm that opened occasionally with my mother's linen cupboard, in which, piled up on the shelves, edged with white trimming and bearing a blue-embroidered text from "Die Glocke,"[34] lay the sheets, tablecloths, napkins, and pillowcases. A sweet lavender scent came from the brightly colored silk sachets hanging on the inside of the cupboard doors. These were the hell and paradise into which the ancient magic of hearth and home, which had once been lodged in the spinning wheel, had been sundered. Now my dream had risen from the evil world: a ghost busying itself at a trestle draped with a profusion of silken fabrics, one covering another. These silks the ghost was stealing. It did not snatch them up or carry them away; it did nothing with or to them that was actually visible and distinguishable. Yet I knew it stole them, just as in legends people who discover a spirits' banquet know that these dead beings are feasting, without seeing them eat or drink. It was this dream that I had kept secret. And in the night that followed it I noticed, half asleep, my mother and father coming quietly into my room at an unusual hour. I did not see them lock themselves in. When I got up next morning, there was nothing for breakfast. The house had been stripped of everything. At midday my grandmother arrived from Berlin with the bare necessities. A large band of burglars had descended on the house in the night. Fortunately the noise they made gave an indication of their number, so that my mother had succeeded in restraining my father, who, armed only with a pocketknife, had wanted to confront them. The dangerous visit had lasted almost until morning. In vain my parents had stood at the window in the first light, signaling to the outside world: the band had departed at their leisure with the baskets. Much later they were caught, and it emerged that their organizer, a murderer and criminal with many previous convictions, was a deaf-mute. It made me proud that I was questioned about the events of the previous evening—for a complicity was suspected between the housebreakers and the maidservant who had stood at the gate. What made me even prouder, however, was the question why I had kept silent about my dream, which I now, of course, narrated at length as a prophecy.

What my first books were to me—to remember this I should first have to forget all other knowledge of books. It is certain that all I know of them today rests on the readiness with which I then opened myself to books; but whereas now content, theme, and subject matter are extraneous to the book, earlier they were solely and entirely in it, being no more external or independent of it than are today the number of its pages or its paper. The world that revealed itself in the book and the book itself were never, at any price, to be divided. So with each book its content, too, its world, was palpably there, at hand. But, equally, this content and world transfigured every part of the book. They burned within it, blazed from it; located not merely in its binding or its pictures, they were enshrined in chapter headings and opening letters, paragraphs and columns. You did not read books through; you dwelt, abided between their lines, and, reopening them after an interval, surprised yourself at the spot where you had halted. The rapture with which you received a new book, scarcely venturing a fleeting glance between its pages, was that of the guest invited for a few weeks to a mansion and hardly daring to dart a glance of admiration at the long suites of ceremonial rooms through which he must pass to reach his quarters. He is all the more impatient to be allowed to withdraw. And so, each year, scarcely had I found on the Christmas table the latest volume of the *Neuer deutscher Jugend-freund* [New Companion of German Youth] when I retreated completely behind the ramparts of its cover, which was adorned with coats of arms, and felt my way into the spy or hunting story in which I was to spend the first night. There was nothing finer than to sniff out, on this first tentative expedition into the labyrinth of stories, the various atmospheres, scents, brightnesses, and sounds that came from its different chambers and corridors. For in reality the longer stories, interrupted many times to reappear as continuations, extended through the whole like subterranean passages. And what did it matter if the aromas that rose from the tunnels high into the air, where we saw globes or waterwheels glisten, mingled with the smell of gingerbread, or if a Christmas carol wove its halo around the head of Stephenson[35] glimpsed between two pages like an ancestral portrait through a door crack, or if the smell of gingerbread joined with that of a Sicilian sulfur mine that suddenly burst upon us in a full-page illustration as in a fresco. But if I had sat for a while immersed in my book and then went back to the table bearing the presents, it no longer stood almost imperiously over me as it had when I first entered the Christmas room; rather, I seemed to be walking on a small platform that led down to it from my fairy castle.

With this joy that I remember, however, another is fused: that of possession in memory. Today I can no longer distinguish them: it is as if it were only a part of the gift of the moment I am now relating, that it, too, received the gift of never again being wholly lost to me—even if decades have passed between the seconds in which I think of it.

Anyone can observe that the length of time during which we are exposed to impressions has no bearing on their fate in memory. Nothing prevents our keeping rooms in which we have spent twenty-four hours more or less clearly in our memory, and forgetting others in which we passed months. It is not, therefore, due to insufficient exposure time if no image appears on the plate of remembrance. More frequent, perhaps, are the cases when the half-light of habit denies the plate the necessary light for years, until one day from an alien source it flashes as if from burning magnesium powder, and now a snapshot transfixes the room's image on the plate. It is we ourselves, however, who are always standing at the center of these rare images. Nor is this very mysterious, since such moments of sudden illumination are at the same time moments when we separated from ourselves, and while our waking, habitual, everyday self is involved actively or passively in what is happening, our deeper self rests in another place and is touched by the shock, as is the little heap of magnesium powder by the flame of the match. It is to this immolation of our deepest self in shock that our memory owes its most indelible images. So the room in which I slept at the age of six would have been forgotten, had not my father come in one night—I was already in bed—with the news of a death. It was not really the news itself that so affected me: the deceased with a distant cousin. But in the way in which my father told me, there lay [text breaks off]

The first great disappointment of my life reached me one afternoon on Peacock Island. I had been told, on the way there, that I would find peacock feathers in the grass. Scarcely had I heard this when, with the speed of a spark leaping between two charged systems, a close connection must have been formed in me between the name of these islands and the peacock feathers. It was not that the spark took a roundabout path by way of the image of the peacock. This had no part in the process. And so my reproachful dismay as I scoured the turf so vainly was directed not against the peacocks that I saw strutting up and down, but, rather, against the soil of the island itself, which was a peacock island yet bore no peacock earth. Had I found the feather I craved in the grass. I would have felt expected and welcome at this spot. Now the island seemed to have broken a promise. Certainly the peacocks could not console me. Weren't they there for everybody to see? But I was to have had something intended only for me, concealed from all others, to be found in the grass only by me. This disappointment would not have been so great had it not been Mother Earth herself who inflicted it on me. Similarly, the bliss at having, after much toil, at last learned to ride a bicycle would have been less sweet had not Mother Earth herself let me feel her praise. One learned to ride in those days—it was the heyday of bicycle racing—in large indoor arenas specially established for the purpose. These arenas did not, however, have the snobbish character of the later ice palaces or indoor tennis courts; rather, they resembled skating rinks or gymnasiums, and bespoke a mentality for which sport and open air were not inseparable, as they are today. It was the era of "sporting costumes" that, unlike our present sports attire, sought not to adapt the body to immediate needs but rather to define the particular sport as sharply as possible and isolate it from all others, just as those arenas cut it off from nature and other exercises. The sport, as it was practiced in those arenas, still had about it all the eccentricities of its beginnings. On the asphalt floor, moving under the supervision of trainers among the ordinary bicycles for gentlemen, ladies, and children, were constructions with front wheels ten times larger than their small rear wheels, their airy seats probably occupied by artistes rehearsing a number.

The orchard at Glienicke, the broad, ceremonious promenade of Schloss Babelsberg, the narrow, concealed pathways of our summer garden, the shady ways through the foliage leading down to Lake Griebnitz at the places where there were jetties—all this I annexed to my domain, completing in an instant in fantasy the work of countless walks, games, and outings, kneeling in my nuptials with the billowing ground as a dynast conquers endless territories by means of a single felicitous union.

I have talked of the courtyards. Even Christmas was fundamentally a festival of the courtyards. There it began with the barrel organs, which continued the week before the festival with chorales, and there it ended with the Christmas trees, which, bereft of feet, leaned in the snow or glistened in the rain. But Christmas came, and all at once, before the eyes of the bourgeois child, it divided his city into two mighty camps. These were not the genuine ones, in which the exploited and their rulers lie irreconcilably opposed. No, it was a camp posed and arranged almost as artificially as the crèches made of paper or the wooden figures, but also as old and as honorable: Christmas came and divided the rich from the poor. Christmas came and divided the children into those who shuffled past the booths on Potsdam Square with their parents and those who, alone, indoors, offered their dolls and lambkins for sale to children of their age. Christmas came and with it a whole, unknown world of wares, [text breaks off]

The *déjà vu* effect has often been described. But I wonder whether the term is actually well chosen, and whether the metaphor appropriate to the process would not be far better taken from the realm of acoustics. One ought to speak of events that reach us like an echo awakened by a call, a sound that seems to have been heard somewhere in the darkness of past life. Accordingly, if we are not mistaken, the shock with which moments enter consciousness as if already lived usually strikes us in the form of a sound. It is a word, a tapping, or a rustling that is endowed with the magic power to transport us into the cool tomb of long ago, from the vault of which the present seems to return only as an echo. But has the counterpart of this entranced removal ever been investigated—the shock with which we come across a gesture or a word the way we suddenly find in our house a forgotten glove or reticule? And just as they cause us to surmise that a stranger has been there, there are words or gestures from which we infer this invisible stranger, the future, who left them in our keeping. I was perhaps five years old. One evening—I was already in bed—my father appeared, probably to say good night. It was half against his will, I thought, that he told me the news of a relative's death. The deceased was a cousin, a grown man who scarcely concerned me. But my father gave the news with details, took the opportunity to explain, in answer to my question, what a heart attack was, and was communicative. I did not take in much of the explanation. But that evening I must have memorized my room and my bed, the way you observe with great precision a place where you feel dimly that you'll later have to search for something you've forgotten there. Many years afterward I discovered what it was. Here in this room, my father had "forgotten" part of the news about the deceased: the illness was called syphilis.

Diabolo / The desk at which I did my schoolwork / Neubabelsberg railroad station / Schloss Neubabelsberg.

Fragment written during the first half of 1932; unpublished in Benjamin's lifetime. *Gesammelte Schriften,* VI, 465–519. Translated by Edmund Jephcott.

Notes

1. The Tiergarten is a district of central Berlin that includes the 630-acre, labyrinthine Tiergarten Park, a deer preserve until the eighteenth century. The park was destroyed in World War II but afterward restored, along with the Berlin Zoo and the zoological gardens at its southwest corner.
2. Benjamin himself had been a prominent member of the German Youth Movement. "Youth Movement" refers collectively to a broad range of attempts to establish a new culture of youth in Germany. It had its origins in the 1890s with groups of young boys, known as the Wandervögel, who tramped through the open countryside around Berlin and indulged in a kind of primitive nature worship. In the early years of the twentieth century, the elements within the movement ran the gamut from bland pedagogical reforms through vaguely philosophical programs for cultural change to the virulent nationalism and anti-Semitism of the radical Right. The "debating chambers" mentioned in this passage were the meeting place of the Freie Studentenschaft (Berlin Free Students' Union), the Youth Movement's organ at the University of Berlin. Benjamin had been the president of this organization. It was also in these chambers that his friends Friedrich Heinle and Rika Seligson committed suicide in protest against the onset of war in 1914. See the Chronology in Volume 1 of this edition, and the references to the couple later in this essay.
3. Léon Daudet (1867–1942), writer and journalist, was a cofounder of the royalist journal *L'Action Française* (1907). *Paris vécu* had been published in 1930.
4. Franz Hessel (1880–1941), German writer and journalist, collaborated with

Benjamin in translating Proust; see also Benjamin's review of his book *Heim-liches Berlin* (Unknown Berlin; 1927), in this volume. Hessel and his wife inspired two of the three figures in Henri Roché's novel *Jules et Jim,* which formed the basis of François Truffaut's film of the same title.

5. Wedding, Reinickendorf, and Tegel are all working-class districts of Berlin.

6. Probably Germaine Krull.

7. The *Abitur* is the final comprehensive exam in German secondary school *(Gym-nasium)*—the exam that qualifies students for university study.

8. From Act 3, scene 1 (line 2098) of Schiller's *Maria Stuart* (1800).

9. From 1905 to 1907, Benjamin attended the Landerziehungsheim Haubinda, a distinctly progressive country boarding school in Thuringia. One of the directors of the school at this time was Gustav Wyneken. Wyneken's program of school reform became the first major intellectual influence on Benjamin, and his ideas on the role of youth in national cultural affairs left a lifelong imprint on Benjamin's thinking. See the Chronology in Volume 1 of this edition.

10. Ernst Joël became a physician in Berlin. He supervised Benjamin's experiments with hashish.

11. Friedrich (Fritz) Heinle, German poet and friend of Benjamin's, committed suicide on August 8, 1914.

12. Marianne Weber (1870–1954), author and feminist activist, was from 1919 to 1923 the head of the Union of German Women's Organizations. She wrote extensively on the professional role and development of women, especially in the university. She was the wife of Max Weber.

13. *Die Aktion,* a political journal founded in 1911 by Franz Pfemfert, was dedicated to revolution in literature and the visual arts.

14. The reference is to Rika (1891–1914), Carla (1892–1956), and Traute (1895–1915) Seligson.

15. Franz Pfemfert (1879–1954) was the founder and editor of the journal *Die Aktion.* Else Lasker-Schüler (1869–1945), German poet, short-story writer, playwright, and novelist, was one of the most widely recognized Expressionists. Wieland Herzfelde (1896–1988), German writer and publisher, was associated with the Dada movement in Berlin; he founded Malik Verlag, the main organ of Berlin Dada. He was the brother of John Heartfield, a prominent Berlin Dadaist and graphic artist. Simon Guttmann was a German photographer. In 1928, in Berlin, he founded the Deutsche Photodienst (German Photo Service), known as "Dephot" for short.

16. Ludwig Meidner (1884–1966), Expressionist painter and writer, was best-known for his playfully apocalyptic canvases of the years immediately before World War I.

17. Compare "Excavation and Memory" (1932), in this volume.

18. Epicurus (341 B.C.–270 B.C.) was a Greek philosopher, whose ideas initiated the direction in philosophy known as Epicureanism. Its adherents view pleasure as the sole good and as the first goal of morality.

19. See Nietzsche, *Beyond Good and Evil,* Aphorism 70.

20. Karl Schinkel (1781–1841), German architect, is best-known for his adaptations of classical Greek forms to modern structures.

21. The reference is to Alfred Cohn (1892–1954), a friend from Benjamin's youth

and the brother of Jula Cohn. Benjamin's relationship with Jula Cohn precipitated the crisis in his marriage. The essay "Goethe's Elective Affinities" (see Volume 1 of this edition) allegorizes their relationship.

22. Alois Riegl (1858–1905) was an Austrian art historian. His book *Die spätrömische Kunst-Industrie* (The Late Roman Art Industry) appeared in 1901. This work exerted an enormous influence on Benjamin; he counted it as one of the seminal works of the century. See "The Rigorous Study of Art," in this volume.

23. The reference is to Ernst Schoen (1894–1960), a German musician, poet, and translator, and the artistic director of a major radio station in Frankfurt. Just as Benjamin's relationship with Jula Cohn was allegorized in the essay "Goethe's Elective Affinities," so too was Dora Benjamin's with Ernst Schoen. Schoen continued to provide Benjamin with opportunities to present his work on the radio into the early 1930s.

24. Emil Lederer (1882–1939), German economist, emigrated to the United States in 1934. He was the first dean of the New School for Social Research, in New York.

25. The reference is to Grete Radt, Benjamin's first fiancée, who later married Alfred Cohn.

26. This cryptic passage refers to a complex series of relationships centering around Jula Cohn (see note 21 above). Jula married Fritz Radt (brother of Grete Radt, Benjamin's first fiancée, who married Alfred Cohn, Jula's brother).

27. A reference to the fairy tale "Das kalte Herz" (The Cold Heart), by Wilhelm Hauff (1802–1827).

28. According to Gershom Scholem, Professor R. Renvers lived at 24 Nettelbeckstrasse in Berlin.

29. *Wallensteins Lager* (Wallenstein's Camp) is a play by Schiller of 1799; see scene 11.

30. *Der Veilchenfresser* (The Ladies' Man; 1874) is a comedy by Gustav Moser. *Wilhelm Tell* (William Tell; 1804) is a drama by Schiller. *Fiesko* (1783) is a tragedy by Schiller. *Carmen* (1875) is an opera by Bizet. Adalbert Matkowsky (1857–1909) was a German actor. Emmy Destinn (1878–1930) was a Czech operatic soprano.

31. Josef Kainz (1858–1910) was a German actor.

32. *Die lustigen Weiber von Windsor* (The Merry Wives of Windsor; 1849) is a comic opera by the German composer Otto Nicolai.

33. Ludwig Erk (1807–1883) was a German singing teacher and editor who collected and popularized German folk songs.

34. The reference is to Schiller's poem "Das Lied der Glocke" (The Song of the Bell; 1800).

35. George Stephenson (1781–1848), English inventor and railroad pioneer, built and successfully demonstrated a series of locomotives.

Spain, 1932

The first images worth pondering in San Antonio: the interiors that can be glimpsed through open doors whose bead curtains have been gathered to one side. Defying the shadows, the gleaming white of the walls stands out. And in front of the wall, to the rear, there are usually two to four chairs in a strict symmetrical arrangement. Much can be gleaned from them as they sit there, unpretentious in form but with strikingly beautiful wickerwork, all highly presentable. No collector could hang expensive rugs or pictures on his hallway walls with greater pride than the farmer who puts out his chairs in the otherwise bare room. Moreover, they are not just chairs. They change their function instantly when a sombrero is hung on the back of one of them. And in this new arrangement the straw hat appears no less precious than the chair. And it will no doubt generally be the case that in our well-furnished rooms, equipped with every conceivable comfort, there will be no place for what is truly precious, because there is no room for utensils. Chairs and clothes, locks and rugs, swords and planes can all be precious. And the true secret of their value is the sobriety, the austerity, of the living space they inhabit. It means that they do not simply occupy, visibly, the space they belong in, but have the scope to perform a variety of unforeseen functions which enables them constantly to surprise us anew. This is what makes them precious and elevates them above the level of a common object.[1]

A dream from the first or second night of my stay in Ibiza. I went home late—it was not actually my house, but rather a splendid apartment house in which, in my dream, I had put up the Seligmanns. Suddenly, close to the building's entrance, a woman came out of a side street toward me, and as she passed she whispered, as quickly as she was walking, "I'm going to tea! I'm going to tea!" I did not yield to the temptation to follow her but instead went into the Seligmanns' apartment, where an unpleasant scene took place, in the course of which their son pulled me by the nose. Protesting vigorously, I slammed the door behind me. Scarcely was I outside again than the same woman darted up to me from the same side street, with the same words, and this time I followed her. To my disappointment, however, she ignored my approach and kept hurrying down a rather steep alleyway until she reached an iron grille, where she joined a whole group of prostitutes who were obviously standing around in front of their quarters. Not far away a policeman had taken up his post. In the midst of all these embarrassments, I awoke. It then occurred to me that the girl's exciting silk blouse with the unusual stripes had shone brightly in green and violet: the colors of Fromm's nude (see Notebook 1, illustration 22).[2]

Another dream (this time in Berlin, some time before setting off on my journey). I was going somewhere with Jula[3]—it was halfway between an ordinary walk and a mountain hike—and now we were getting close to the summit. For some strange reason I imagined I could recognize the top by a very tall pole sticking straight up into the sky and standing out against the overhanging rock wall. When we reached the top, it turned out to be not a peak but a plateau, with a broad street stretching along it and lined with rather tall, old-fashioned houses on both sides. Suddenly we were no longer on foot but instead sitting in a car, next to each other in the back seat (or so it seemed to me), driving along this road. But it may be that the car changed direction while we were sitting in it. I leaned over to give Jula a kiss. She offered me her cheek instead of her mouth. And as I kissed her I noticed that her cheek was made of ivory, furrowed from one end to the other by black, skillfully scooped-out grooves, whose beauty moved me deeply.[4]

The economy on the island is quite archaic. Fifty years ago bread was quite unknown; the staple food was maize. Even today there are no more than four to six cows, some say because of the absence of fodder, although Don Rossiglio, a fishery owner and deputy, blames it on the backwardness of the inhabitants. How long will this backwardness continue? The fields are still irrigated using old Arab methods: bucket wheels drawn by mules. The grain is still threshed by the hooves of horses driven around the threshing floor on long reins. But we can also see half-built hotels in San Antonio and Ibiza which, for tourists, hold out the promise of running water. The time remaining before their completion has become precious. The paths are still unfrequented; the rambler (who is startled by the lizards) and the lizards (who are startled by the ramblers) still have the countryside to themselves for the moment. Nevertheless, it is with these unpretentious lizards that the modern trend began. We can all recall the terraria that made their appearance some years ago in the cactus niche of ladies' boudoirs or in winter gardens. Lizards started to become an international fashion item. Among present-day pet shop owners, these islands, the Balearics, are just as famous for their lizards as they were among generals in Antiquity for their adepts at the slingshot. And so, at some point, a man settled here and decided to make a living with the aid of a small mail-order business in lizards. There are many methods for catching lizards, but all of them seem to be based on the great curiosity of these creatures. Who knows what biological instinct led to this curiosity? It can scarcely be hunger. For on the one hand they are able to survive three or even four weeks without eating (and this makes it easy to transport them), while on the other they never tire of gazing at even the most inedible objects, such as a hand, if they find it remarkable. People rely on this curiosity when setting traps. The simplest is a deep, open tin can containing strong-smelling bait—cheese, fish, sausage. The can is then buried up to its lip in the ground. After a few days you find that it contains a number of animals that are unable to clamber up its smooth walls. Other, less trusting lizards have to be caught using a fine snare, likewise smeared with some strong-smelling substance to attract them. The strangest method, though, is said to have been practiced in Antiquity. A large bubble of saliva was dropped into a snare, and this was then held out in front of the lizard like a mirror. The moment the animal put its head through the noose, the string was pulled tight. But it was not that first trapper who knew how to tell about such things. He appears to have revealed his professional secrets only in exchange for money. At any rate, this is what can be gleaned from the franchise history of the second trapper. For one day it turned out that the fashion for keeping lizards as household ornaments had been put to rest by the crisis on the Continent. At around the same time—this was in 1922—an unemployed sculptor in Stuttgart who had lost his money in the inflation sat down full of gloomy thoughts to listen to the rarely used radio. This sculptor was a restless spirit, one of those people who have escaped from their parents at an early age. By the time he was fifteen he was already living as the only white man in an Indian village in South America. The ship on which he had served as cabin boy had been wrecked and the rest of the crew had been taken back to Germany, but his family wanted to prevent him from ever going to sea again. Because this did not suit him, he stayed with the Indians, ignoring the warnings of the German consul in Pernambuco about the multitudes of fleas in the Indian villages. So, having started out young, he was now listening to the radio. The talk he heard was being given by a German who had once been interned in Spain, but who, thanks to the generosity of the Spaniards during the war, had come to know the country very well. He had also been to Ibiza, and was now speaking about this "forgotten island." This is what brought the sculptor J. to the island, initially just to reconnoiter. Having discovered that conditions were favorable, lizards in plentiful supply, and the natives friendly, he came a second time and prepared to settle down. He paid his predecessor one thousand marks for his client list and for agreeing not to engage in any further trade in animals on the island. In the meantime, however, the world crisis had taken its course and eliminated the lizards from winter gardens and boudoirs. Orders for lizards failed to materialize, except from traders whose prices were too low to make catching them profitable. For every trip to one of the isolated, uninhabited islands on which the rarer and to some extent still unknown species were to be found meant two or three days' work, as well as a risk for the boat, which could not find anywhere to drop anchor. J., however, once installed, saw his dream of earning a living on the island in a more civilized and even emancipated way dissolve. With its ancient traditions and its archaic way of life, the island had the last word. J. became a fisherman. And when today he lights up a cigarette, he uses a flintstone and a fuse, like everyone else. "In a boat," he says, "that is the best way. The wind blows matches out, but the harder it blows, the more the fuse glows."

It is raining, and the light that here so relentlessly lays claim to all things under heaven retreats and gives them back to the earth.—The white houses behind their cactus hedges are pressed hard by a throng of stormy green spirits.

On the honesty of the natives and its opposite. Two stories.[5] A stranger who had spent several months on the island, during which time he had gained the friendship and trust of the inhabitants, saw the last day of his stay arrive. It happened to be a very hot day, and, having finished his travel preparations, he decided to banish his worries about his possessions as quickly as possible so that he could spend a couple of hours enjoying the shade on the terrace of an Ibizan wine merchant. The people on the boat promised to look after his luggage as well as his jacket, and, noticeably lighter, he went off to the wine merchant's, who welcomed him heartily even though he was only in his shirtsleeves. He effortlessly knocked back the first few *copitas* [mugs] of the local white wine. But the more time passed and the more he drank, the harder he found it to take his leave, especially in such an unfestive manner. Questions occurred to him. He wanted to know about the beautiful porch of the cathedral in Ibiza; about the strange customs of abduction, about which no one knew anything precise; about the origins of those curious names that the fishermen used for the mountains—names quite different from those used by the farmers. Soon he recollected that he had once heard his host described as an authority on the island's history. He thought he would like to clear up a few matters at the last moment, and in this way could perhaps survive the loneliness of his last evening. He ordered a bottle of the best wine, and even as his host uncorked it before his eyes, they were already deep in conversation. Now, in the past weeks the stranger had had ample opportunity to become acquainted with the fanatical hospitality of the islanders. He knew that if he wished to have the honor of inviting them, this had to be properly prepared and made into a quasi-legal stipulation. Accordingly, his first task was to invite his host to be his guest. He insisted on this during the second bottle and the third, all the more since it meant he could take brief notes about this or that piece of information with a good conscience. And (to dwell a little on these notes) there are some that can compete in vividness with those of Stendhal's Italian tales.[6] What an image! The marriageable girl, surrounded by suitors on holiday, but whose father sets strict limits to the time the suitors can have to plead their cause: an hour, an hour and a half at most, even if there are thirty of them or more, so that each one must compress what he has to say into a few brief minutes.—During the conversation, the weather had turned cool; his host would not be denied and insisted on lending him one of his own jackets. The last bottle was opened. A good half of it still remained, when they were interrupted by a siren. It was the steamer lying out at the breakwater, ten minutes away, ready to depart and with the stranger's luggage on board. In the pale evening light, you could see its top light. Even his host could perceive that there wasn't much time left for compliments, so he handed his guest the bill without much resistance, in accord with their agreement. But the latter felt a sudden panic even before he had looked at it. His wallet, which he always kept in his back trouser pocket, was gone. He cast a swift glance at his host. The latter's honest face was filled with consternation. It was inconceivable that he could have the wallet. With the most courteous expressions of concern, the merchant asked the stranger not to take the matter to heart. He maintained that he had felt uncomfortable at being the stranger's guest in his own house. And as for the wallet, it would undoubtedly turn out to have been in his jacket on board the boat. The stranger, however, was only partly consoled by this. The banknotes it contained were not small, and they were quite numerous. Once he was on board, his worst fears were confirmed. His jacket pockets were empty, and he now knew what to think of the celebrated honesty of the island's people. Faced with the choice of suspecting the ship's crew or the wine merchant, he spent a sleepless night before deciding on the crew. But he was wrong. It was the wine merchant who had his wallet. Scarcely had he arrived back in Germany than he received proof of this in the form of the following telegram: "Wallet found in jacket you borrowed from me. Payment on its way."

Never dissuade a person from a course of action.[7] Anyone who is asked for his advice would do well to begin by finding out the asker's own opinion and then endorsing it. No one is easily persuaded of another's greater cleverness, and few people ask for advice with the intention of following someone else's. The fact is that they have already made up their minds and now wish to hear it from the outside, to accept it as the "advice" of another. This confirmation is what they seek, and they are right to do so. For it is very risky to set out to implement one's own decisions without passing them through the filter of conversation. This is why the person who seeks advice is already halfway to a decision; and if what he is planning to do is a mistake, it is better to lend it skeptical support than to contradict it with conviction.

The fact that in the morning the pupil knows by heart the contents of the book he has put under his pillow the night before, that the Lord inspires His own in their sleep, and that a pause is creative—to make space for such things to happen is the alpha and omega of all mastery, its hallmark.[8] This, then, is the reward before which the gods have placed sweat. For work which achieves only modest success is child's play, compared to the success conjured up by luck. This is why Rastelli's[9] stretched-out little finger attracts the ball, which hops onto it like a bird. The decades' worth of practice that came before does not mean that either his body or the ball is "in his power," but it enables the two to reach an understanding behind his back. To weary the master to the point of exhaustion through diligence and hard work, so that at long last his body and each of his limbs can act in accordance with their own rationality: this is what is called "practice." It is a form of post-hypnotic suggestion that starts to work inside the body, as it were, at the moment the will abdicates its power once and for all in favor of the organs—the hand, for instance. This is why you can look for something for days, until you finally forget it; then, one day, when you are looking for something else, you suddenly find the first object. Your hand has, so to speak, taken the matter in hand and has joined forces with the object which had successfully resisted the dogged efforts of the will.

A strange obsession has made travel writers become fixated on the idea of "fulfillment"—the desire to preserve for every country the blue haze that distance surrounds it with, or for every station in life the glamor that the imagination of the idler endows it with. The leveling of the globe through industry and technology has made such great strides that, by rights, each description should take place against a black backdrop of disillusionment, from which the truly strange incommensurability of the near at hand—of human beings in communication with one another and with the land—could then stand out more sharply. It has to be admitted that reportage in Germany, insofar as it can be regarded as a sort of inverted travelogue, does give expression to this. It is nothing more than a matter of time and study to make even the most distant lands appear immediately familiar. And naturally discipline is also required, of a sort which prevents the author from directly exploiting his first impressions; for if instead he allows them to fall like seeds into the womb of habit, they can subsequently give rise to the marvelous tree whose fruits have the scent of the near at hand.

Brief notes about the island.—Occasionally, when out walking, you hear a hollow sound. Perhaps there are hollow places in the lava (if indeed the island really is volcanic); but some say that there are graves.

There is a special breed of dog here that is said not to occur elsewhere. Dogs of this type are called galybs.

Very pretty, Jokisch's story about the way Customs treated his furniture shipper. Since Jokisch had influence from somewhere, they took the furniture apart as far as was possible, and made him pay duty only on the boards. When I was with him, he also told me how he had discovered that ants eat lizards. For some time after he had set his lizard traps, there was an uninterrupted spell of stormy weather. When he went back to his traps, he found one can full of lizards that had been able to survive cheerfully without food for three or four weeks on end. But others had been invaded by ants, which had killed off all the animals. Sometimes the lizards bite each other, and even themselves. On another occasion he lost some good customers when the lizards that he had kept segregated in various compounds at home all got mixed up. Since then he has ceased to keep a stock of them.

A book on the Balearics by Archduke Johann Salvator.[10]

The history of solitude. "How much land does a man need to live?" asks Tolstoy in one of his stories. The anchorites provided an answer: their way of life, restricted to the smallest speck of land possible, spread throughout the globe. The names of all the angels and devils that thronged around their souls or their camps descended from Athos or Montserrat, and spread throughout the world that once receded before the threshold of their hermitage. Throughout the still-unexplored globe, they asserted the claims of their faith to still-undiscovered climes and untutored creatures. They were the magical forerunners of the missionaries. But solitude is not so timeless that it does not change over time, albeit slowly. Today it is no more than a waste product of community. Hermits no longer exist, and whoever cuts himself off discovers no new community, but only the old one. Thus, there was one man who could not come to terms with the world and had retreated to the heart of a remote island. Few people came to disturb him, but those few were amazed to discover how well informed he was about the events and intrigues of the inhabitants of the coastal region. It was as if isolation had sharpened his ear and as if the wind had brought him news of the latest scandals that townsfolk learn about on the telephone. When they took their leave of him they would ask themselves, "How much gossip does a man need to live?"

There is nothing new about the fact that confidence men often find it easy to carry off their swindles once they have assumed a name that, as it were, dulls the senses of the people they are targeting. Rarely does it happen, however, that this is not the name of some ruling family or former ruling family ("They have all ruled at one time or another," as Fontane remarks), but the name of a remote island. To be sure, this too is not unprecedented; it goes back to the time of Marco Polo or Athanasius Kircher,[11] when one could gain an astonishing reputation through one's extensive travels and knowledge of distant lands. But the fact that an impoverished Mediterranean island can become the center of operations for a confidence man—and "in the name of global commerce"—perhaps deserves a more detailed account. Of course, there may be other minds that succumb to the magic of the name "Ibiza" [illegible phrase omitted]. But they must have two things in common: imagination and a lack of patience—in short, a passionate desire to escape from the conditions in which they live. This was the case with two friends, a writer and a publisher, who had no professional relationship with each other. [text incomplete]

The *Ciudad de Valencia,* which maintains communications between Barcelona and Ibiza, departs every Monday at six o'clock in the evening from the mainland and sails during the night. It is a fine new steamship to which one would like to assign a greater destiny than that of providing a ferry service for this small island. And in fact the image of the boat seemed to shrink before my eyes when I saw it the next day at the breakwater in Ibiza, waiting for the return voyage, for I had imagined that it would go on from there to the Canaries. In any case, toward six o'clock in the evening I stood on the empty promenade deck next to the wheelhouse, piecing together all the parts of the incomparable picture that large towns present to an observer gazing down from the heights of a ship. The sun was setting over the city, which seemed to have fallen silent. All life had retreated to the imperceptible transitions between the foliage on the trees, the cement of the buildings, and the rocks of the distant mountains. I stood and thought of Horace's famous truism, "What exile fleeing from his native land would ever flee his own mind?"[12]—and how questionable it is. For isn't traveling a purification, the overcoming of settled passions that are attached to one's accustomed environment, and hence an opportunity to develop new ones—something that in fact amounts to a metamorphosis? At any rate, I had just become conscious of a new passion, and the ten days at sea that now lay behind me had been sufficient to ignite it. This time I wanted to explore the epic vein—collect whatever facts and stories I could find, and test out my journey to see what it might yield once it was purified of all vague impressions. This should not be thought of as a travel account; rather, it is a matter of travel technique, one with a respectable pedigree—a technique, incidentally, that was the rule before journalism took over. I was standing thinking these thoughts when far below me on the quay I saw, or rather recognized, a stocky man with the most massive head that ever wore a captain's cap. It was Captain V., from the cargo boat on which I had arrived in port here ten hours previously. Anyone who is accustomed to a lonely departure from foreign towns will know what it means to encounter a familiar face—even if it is not a face one especially wants to see—at a moment when imminent departure sweeps aside all the difficulties of a prolonged conversation, but at the same time provides you with a handkerchief, a hand, or a hat in which the unaccommodated gaze may find refuge before venturing out over the sea. Here, however, few sights could have been more welcome to me than that of this captain, on whose boat I had begun to feel at home and who had provided me with the first of my collection of stories. That there was something unusual about him, something not altogether pleasant, had become clear to me very soon after we had left Hamburg. He had the sort of relationship with Tom, a dog he had borrowed from a German in Genoa, that is normally encountered only among eccentrics. It was strange to imagine his daily routine: he ignored breakfast and dinner, so that his working day really went from one lunch to the next, for when the sea is rough a nighttime's rest is a precarious business for a sea captain. And on leaving Hamburg, we had had stormy weather for over four days. Apart from this, he was never unfriendly, for all his reserve; and once he had produced the obligatory sailor's jokes even before we were clear of the estuary of the Elbe (to a somewhat unsympathetic audience, it must be said, since of the three passengers only one was a first-time traveler), he was occasionally not above spending five minutes in a more serious chat. In this way I obtained hints enough to be able to reconstruct for myself, all the way back to the time of the slave trade, the history of the shipping company in whose boat we were traveling. I learned about its beginnings as a ship broker, its trade with the first steamers, not to forget the later migrant transports—those masses of wretched passengers who meant far more to German shipping than the guests on luxury boats like the *Bremen* or the *Europa*. But these were no more than isolated highlights. It was not in such conversations that I heard so much about the history of the boat, and about the forces and interests that governed its voyage through timeless waves, that when I disembarked in Barcelona there seemed to be a whole seething mass of facts and figures in my mind. These included the original cost of the boat, its tonnage, the officers' wages, the year it was built, the cargo rates, and loading and unloading fees, right down to the salary of the most insignificant ship's boy, who was paid off on the day the boat arrived home and not signed on again until the day of the next sailing. Just to mention the first and last of these figures: in 1922 this boat had cost the buyer (who was not the person who had commissioned it) just a bit more than 25,000 marks; and twenty-five marks was a month's wages for a ship's boy. But even the captain of such a ship hasn't got much to laugh about. Indeed, it had been a different story in the days when the cargo business was still handled by sailing ships and when the ships' captains themselves negotiated the cost of transport in the harbors. Nowadays, however, the captain's position is less important, in relation not just to the shipowner but even to the inspector. And concerning the opportunities of rising to what is still a desirable post, an American officer seems to have spoken for many of his German colleagues when he complained about a certain kind of writer who described life on the sea as exciting and painted it in the rosiest of colors. It is of course true that the sailors on our steamships have a greater degree of comfort and their lives are significantly more pleasant than on the old sailing ships. In those says, the old sailor's joke could often be heard: Give up sailing and join a steamship! "But to get down to brass tacks. What are the prospects in the sailing business today? I guess we can assume that in recent years every shipowner has simply been overrun by young men who want to go to sea. But what work do they actually do on board? Scrub the deck, wash the paintwork, and polish the brass! The only chance they get to do anything a little more unusual is when they have to fetch some object that has torn loose on deck or been washed from its moorings and fix it back where it belongs. Only a minute proportion of these youths can stay the course and perhaps get as far as receiving their officer's commissions— and then they discover that supply exceeds demand even at sea. In this world where machines are making people redundant, the sailor's profession is marked by the same competition, the same desperate struggle for existence, as there is on land." I made them tell me about the entire process—from the training in a sailing ship to the helmsman's examination, from ship's boy to ship's officer, in all their various stages. I have also seen the textbook you have to study to prepare for the examinations; it is probably the only book in all the sciences that can claim to be in constant use. The first edition goes back to 1854. Nor is it easy to fom a picture of the world of books that a steamer like this carries with it, from *Quo vadis?* to the logarithmic tables.[13] Above all, there are the practical navigation books—alongside the sea charts, whose tiny clusters of figures reveal the presence of steep underwater mountains. Then there are the handbooks for all the coasts that the boat will, or conceivably could, encounter on its voyage. These are the Baedekers of places which are seldom visited by those who use the books. For here every peak and every promontory, every tower and settlement, is above all a signal, a reference point by which to locate a ship, as well as one for the officers who often find nothing in the examination but a set of data for taking their bearings, for which they have to provide so and so many hundred examples in their exercise books by way of proof if they want to pass the helmsman's examination. When darkness comes these are replaced by navigational beacons, which are likewise listed in the manuals, together with their colors and the intervals at which they flash; alternatively, the ship simply sails by the stars along "roads" that are as well worn as tracks across fields. Then come the best hours, the long ones during which the only diversion is a change of posture while you stand leaning on the bridge railing, or the steps you take walking up and down in front of the helm, which is tended by an ordinary seaman who is relieved by a comrade every three hours. None has remained so firmly in my memory as the one who had been to Iceland and who had been watching me with some resentment for a few nights, which I had spent listening to everything the third mate could tell me about his voyages. While the mate was gazing into the distance over the railing, the seaman suddenly erupted and a small cataract of names and numbers burst out of him: the 2 percent share he'd been given because he was on the Iceland run, the millions he possessed at the time (this was 1922), the vexation that was involved in earning his money, and how they were all so tired sometimes that they fell asleep over their food. I passed him a cigarette, but that was as far as it went. It was usually toward ten when I emerged from the radio operator's cabin. The deck had been cleared; the stars were in the sky. The conversation progressed slowly, but, like a fuse, it always burned its way toward an adventure or a story. My partner and I had discovered the best way of making the time pass quickly, and I never went back to my cabin without enjoying his hospitality for a while in the chart room over a cup of coffee or Van Houten's cocoa. The discussion of freeport dues was succeeded by an account of adventures on the coast of Panama or Schleswig. My host had left home young. At seventeen he had finished his apprenticeship on one of the sailing ships that Leist sent to Chile to bring back saltpeter and that sailed around Tierra del Fuego and Cape Horn, with their storms. At eighteen he got engaged, because he wanted to make use of a ring he had bought onshore. This turned out to be a good investment: he lodged for two weeks with his future mother-in-law, and whether, when he disappeared, his bride had any cause for complaint, even according to strict bourgeois criteria, did not become clear to me that night. For it was not just on topics of this kind that too many questions were impermissible. In this instance, curiosity might have excused my tactlessness; but nothing could have excused my ignorance, had I omitted to have explained to me the ins and outs of nautical maneuvers, the sailors' language, the meaning of the different ranks, or the names of the people and implements I did not understand. But this was not the right time for questions. The nights that week were dark; we couldn't see one another clearly; and the contours of the stories were just as fuzzy, like those of ships that crossed the path of our boat by night. I'm unable to retell them—least of all the one about the voyage of the *Prival,* which would most reward the telling. But since sailors' yarns are on the agenda, perhaps we could take up one particular comic subject with which few others, even from recent history, can compare. It was in 1919, when a number of Hamburg shipowners decided to try and repatriate some sailing ships, saltpeter cargo boats, that had been surprised by the outbreak of hostilities somewhere in Chile some five years previously. The legal position was quite straightforward: the ships had remained German property, and the only problem now was to procure the necessary crews to take possession of them in Rio de Janeiro. There were plenty of seamen available in German ports waiting for employment. But there was one little problem. How were the crews to be transported to Rio? This much was clear: they could travel from Hamburg only as passengers and could be put into service only at the various destinations. It was just as clear that the crews consisted of people who could not readily be managed with the kind of authority that the law of the sea gives captains over his passengers. Moreover, the date must be borne in mind: in 1919 the revolutionary mood of the Kiel uprising still permeated the navy, and much else besides.[14] The shipowners themselves knew this perfectly well, and had filled the higher ranks of the *Prival* with their most able and determined officers. They had gone even further, and the actual course of the voyage proved that their caution had been justified. For barely twelve hours after leaving the North Sea, there were signs that an alliance was being forged among the new recruits that might easily take on a threatening aspect in a voyage lasting over three weeks. On deck, in the cabins, in the crews' quarters, the officers' mess, and on the stairways, there were meetings from early until late of the most varied kinds of circles and associations. Off Finisterre, there were three gambling clubs and two boxing rings, with matches in constant progress. In the officers' mess, whose walls had been decorated with primitive but graphic drawings, the gentlemen from the audience tap-danced to a gramophone; on the steps a ship's exchange had been set up, where, as a sign of the approaching inflation, a lively barter trade had developed in boxes of cigars, dollar notes, binoculars, nude photos, and knives. In short, the boat had been transformed into a floating Magic City, and it would be easy to believe that even without women it was possible to conjure up all the depravity of harbor life. The captain—one of those people who combine a minimum of education and book learning with a maximum of true culture—managed to keep cool in this situation. Nor did he lose his composure when one fine afternoon off Dover, Frieda, a well-built girl from St. Pauli with a poor reputation, was found strolling up and down the stern with a cigarette in her mouth. No doubt there were people on board who knew where she had been hiding till then, and these were the same people who had agreed what measures to take if those in command made the slightest attempt to put the extra passenger back on shore. From then on the nightlife on board became even livelier, and anyone who insisted on his night's rest amid the din created by the 150 "passengers" would have fumed in vain. But it would not have been 1919 if, in addition to everything else, a political element had not appeared. This was no laughing matter, since it would have been easy for the mood to spread contagiously from the "passengers" to the "crew." Voices could already be heard claiming that this expedition would be the start of a new life in a new world; they wanted nothing to do with any work in the port they were heading for, let alone with any talk of returning home. Others saw the longed-for moment approach when there would be a grand reckoning with the rulers. There was no mistaking the fact that a harsher wind was blowing. It soon became plain where it was coming from. There was a certain Richard Schwenke, a tall fellow of slack demeanor who wore his red hair parted; the only thing known about him was that he had served as steward on various shipping lines. On the very first night he could be seen everywhere. He entered the bar, where the dancing was going on, and drew various people into such a loud quarrel that as soon as the record had come to an end, everyone gathered around him. In the boxing ring he provocatively inquired into the political opinions of the fighters, and the Reddest was always his man. And so he went to work, laboring tirelessly at the politicization of the ship, while the masses went in search of their primitive pleasures. By the fourth day, he had succeeded in organizing a general assembly; by the following evening, election fever was raging. And there was no lack of things to elect: a catering committee, a special inspection team, a political tribunal, a ship's secretariat—in short, an entire revolutionary apparatus was created in a few days out of nothing, without any bloodshed and without any serious conflict with the ship's command. Unfortunately, intrigues among the revolutionary leadership were all the more frequent. And they were all the more irritating because the closer you looked, the more apparent it became that in fact everybody belonged to the leadership. Anyone who did not yet have a post could expect one from the approaching elections; in fact, not an evening passed without there being a vote to verify here or there, or a report on various new abuses. When finally the action committee was asked to produce a plan for a coup for discussion in the general assembly, the *Mascot* had already passed Callao.[15] And on the morning of the day for which the final preparations had been set, the pilot from Rio came up the gangway. The last bearings noted in the ship's logbook turned out to be false. Forty-eight hours before the arrival date that the committee had reckoned on, the three-master was berthed at the breakwater as if nothing had happened. With this, my friend's story came to an end. The first week passed. We went into the chart room, where the cocoa already awaited us in two deep stoneware mugs. I had fallen silent, and only after a short interval did I realize that my nocturnal companion had asked me a question. I looked at him. "Yes, as I was saying. Surely you've understood?"—and when I said nothing, since I did not know what to say, he added, "You're right. I myself understood it only later on. One day I happened to go to the ship owner's office in Hamburg, and there I met Schwenke at the door. He still held in his hand the big cigar he had started to smoke in the boss's office. It was only then that I properly understood the story of the *Mascot*." Many of those stories I could never retell; but as I went down the steps to exchange a few words with the captain before the ship's departure, there wasn't one which failed to evoke a name or an image in my mind's eye. I had not formed a completely clear image of the man until the previous few hours—more precisely, until the previous evening, when I had sat with him in the cabin in Alicante before our departure, sharing a bottle, and he had told me the story of his son, who had started out as a sailor and now owned a little cigar shop. What lay between those two livelihoods was the kind of moment that anyone can experience who has stood and watched how a boat that has unloaded its cargo makes ready to cast off. I do not know the name of the large iron crossbeams that are then replaced in the frame that encloses the upper edge of the hold. But I know that they are not more than twenty centimeters wide and that the sailors who balance on them over the thirty-meter-deep hold have to be able to do so without feeling dizzy. And so they are for the most part; but every now and then one does fall, and this is what had happened to his son. He now moves about his shop with the aid of an artificial limb.

Once you've gone a good two hours in the direction of San Antonio, you'll come to a low hill among the last remote *fincas* [farms] that the road passes, up above San Antonio, which you can see lying down below by the bay. There you will see a peaceful farmhouse which seems to have been built in a style quite different from that of the other *fincas*—although at first sight you'd be hard put to say what this difference was.

Written April–July 1932; unpublished in Benjamin's lifetime. *Gesammelte Schriften*, VI, 446–464. Translated by Rodney Livingstone.

Notes

1. See also "Ibizan Sequence" (section entitled "Space for Precious Objects"), in this volume.
2. This notebook has never been found.

3. "Jula" is Benjamin's friend the German sculptor Jula Radt, neé Cohn, sister of Benjamin's schoolfriend Alfred Cohn. Benjamin's relationship with her precipitated the crisis in his marriage. The essay "Goethe's Elective Affinities" (in Volume 1 of this edition) allegorizes this relationship.

4. See also "Ibizan Sequence" (section entitled "First Dream"), in this volume.

5. A later version of this story can be found in this volume under the title "The Eve of Departure." The second story referred to here was never written or has not survived.

6. Stendhal based his *Chroniques italiennes* on unpublished accounts of crimes of passion and grim executions set in the Renaissance—accounts that he discovered in Rome during his consulate in the nearby port of Civitavecchia.

7. See also "Ibizan Sequence" (section entitled "Do Not Seek to Dissuade"), in this volume.

8. See also "Ibizan Sequence" (section entitled "Practice"), in this volume.

9. Enrico Rastelli (1896–1931) was a famous juggler. See also Benjamin's essay "Rastelli Erzählt" (Rastelli's Story).

10. Better-known as Ludwig Salvator, Archduke of Austria. He wrote *Die balearen geschildert in Wort und Bild* [The Balearics Depicted in Words and Pictures] (Leipzig, 1896).

11. Athanasius Kircher (1602–1680) was a Jesuit priest and a polymath. His astounding knowledge embraced archaeology, languages, science, alchemy, Egyptian hieroglyphs, mathematics, and philosophy.

12. "Patriae quis exsul / quoque fugit?" Horace, *Carmina*, Book 2, 16.

13. *Quo vadis?* is the best-known work of the Polish novelist Henryk Sienkiewicz (1846–1916). It deals with Rome under Nero, and was published in 1896.

14. The sailors' mutiny at Kiel in October 1918 was the first in the series of revolutionary actions that brought down the German Empire and led directly to the founding of the Weimar Republic.

15. This unfinished story about the *Prival* contains passages from another story, "Das Taschentuch" (The Handkerchief; see below in this volume), but also represents an early version of yet another story, "Die Fahrt der *Mascotte*" (The Voyage of the *Mascot*). Here the ship is introduced as the *Prival*, but is transformed into the *Mascot* in the course of the narrative.

Light from Obscurantists

Hans Liebstoeckl, *Die Geheimwissenschaften im Lichte unserer Zeit* [The Occult Sciences in the Light of Our Age] (Zurich: Amalthea Verlag, 1932), 432 pages.

In the realm of the occult sciences, the progress of the daily press is relatively slow and tentative. Its grasp of change in this area is usually belated. Rather like the husband who is the last to learn of his wife's infidelity, it is still very inadequately informed about the nature of suprasensual knowledge, in complete contrast to its journalistic quickness and competence in general.
—Liebstoeckl, *Die Geheimwissenschaften,* p. 9

There has always existed a literature that, alongside the need for education, also satisfies the desire of broad sections of the people for happiness. It was to be found in the newspaper shops of small towns just as much as in those of densely populated cities. It inducted its readers into "The Secrets of the Art of Love," "The Seventh Book of Moses," "The Key to Success," or "The Egyptian Interpretation of Dreams." Over the last few decades it has found its way from anonymous obscurity into the brightly lit window displays of more expensive shops that have made a specialty of selling occult writings. This improvement in status brought some changes in its train. The little magazines that attracted us as boys were destined for the classes of people who were excluded from higher education and who therefore aspired to better themselves at a stroke through some sort of magical divination or by mastering the art of winning a prize in the lottery. But the new magazines are addressed to people who have lost their faith in education. The stupidity, low cunning, and coarseness that are common to both types of writing do not prevent them from making a very clear distinction between the kinds of promise they hold out to their two very different readerships. What they promise the ordinary person is his elevation to a higher social class, whereas those who are already there are assured of the exclusive reality of the spirit and the meaninglessness of economic struggle. Not everyone, it must be said, is bold enough to go into such detail on this score as the author of *Die Geheimwissenschaften im Lichte unserer Zeit,* who declares:

> Now that the revival of spiritualism has enabled mankind to rediscover the occult, it has become possible for a poor proletarian—bound to Bolshevism and the comrades' shared store of funds by his compulsory subscriptions—to hear once more the knock on the door in his wretched little room . . . And since that day, the knock on the wall of the poor man has not ceased to make itself heard. Even worse, and most uncannily, when you ask a question of the spirit that is knocking, it answers quite precisely with a yes or a no . . . In broad daylight it plucks at your sleeve, pulls you by the ear, or suddenly hurls objects that miss you by a hair; tables float in the air, despite all the scientific talk of the force of gravity; a book opens of its own accord; a light suddenly shines; the footsteps of an invisible person shuffle through the room; a door opens by itself; and there is a scrabbling at the door, as if a poodle were asking to be let in. If our comrade secretly consults a wise woman or a fortuneteller, . . . he will mainly be given an answer he does not understand . . . But the shop steward will burst into laughter; of course he will soon laugh on the other side of his face, since even the most enlightened shop steward, who has effortlessly passed all the courses in freethinking, will be forced to admit that the supernatural is at work, even though it is broad daylight and he is in complete control of his faculties. I have met workers—loyal socialists and party members—who secretly attended spiritualist meetings and who were not to be deterred from informing me when new phenomena and messages were observed. (pp. 351–352)

The boss will not have many illusions about the reliability of the spirits summoned to besiege the shop steward in his tenement block. Rather, he will be inclined to quietly mutter to himself Wolfskehl's melancholy question, "Shouldn't we say that the spiritualists are fishing in the next world?"[1] This is done with even greater dexterity by the followers of Rudolf Steiner, who regard the author of these remarkable lines as one of themselves.[2] They presuppose a higher level of education than do the straightforward spiritualists, and for this very reason have had far more success in recent years among those who are placing their hopes in the occult. For if the "magic" of the good old penny magazines was the last pitiful by-product of more significant cultural traditions, "anthroposophy," with its associated swindles, is more closely linked to the "general education" of recent times. It is, in fact, the product of its dissolution.

Anyone who undertakes to account for the crisis which has befallen general education in the past few decades will become aware that the process is inadequately described in terms of the alienation of Europe from the works and traditions of its heyday, the withering of the humanities, the collapse of knowledge of the classical languages. For general education is not simply vanishing without a trace. Looked at more closely, it is being undermined. At this point in time, it has reached the stage where one can identify the products which have resulted from its decline and with which it is saturating the spiritual climate. The magic of blood and glitter in its manifold variants is just one of the two elements, neither of which is comprehensible in the absence of the other, that have appeared amid the decline. The oleaginous gibberish of the false prophets (to dwell on them for a moment) can easily be understood as a residue of the great philosophy of humanism that had formerly constituted an integral part of general education, along with the hard sciences. Among these prophets the adherents of anthroposophy are by far the most ambitious. They are concerned not just with the world of spirits, like spiritualists, or with supernatural ways of seeing, like mystics, or even with the stars, like astrologers. They regard the whole gamut of the sciences as their own realm. And it is undeniable that they have made new discoveries all along the line. As anthropologists, for example: "If, under the old Saturn, man's physical body was a body of heat, under the old sun-time it became an air-body that, like a gas, represents a new stage of density" (p. 61). Or as historians: "It cannot be maintained that the displacement of migrant nations (in the barbarian migrations) and the search for a new space was without meaning, if only because they were linked with the distribution of aether throughout the globe" (p. 228). Or as physicists: "Einstein slammed the doors of physics to it [i.e., the aether], but the presence of molecules—which Einstein, Smoluchowski, and Svedberg[3] regard as proven—does little credit to those who expelled the aether from physics, at least insofar as their capacity for logical thought is concerned" (p. 297). Even though we find these skirmishes a recurring feature, as here with Einstein, or again with Eduard Meyer, and Dessoir,[4] the essential thing for Steiner, as with Krishnamurti or Bo Yin Ra,[5] is the great universal harmony in which all individual details are subsumed. If we wish to gain a purchase on these details in the bizarre forms to which they have been condemned by the decay of general education, we have to look at their opposite pole. That the latter has just as powerful a magnetic attraction for the masses as the various essays in magic can be deduced from the popular "Ask Me" columns or the items along the lines of "Did you know . . . ?" that have been a permanent feature of certain daily papers for years now. The chaotic scattering of pieces of factual information that characterizes such diversions is not as senseless as might appear at first sight. At any rate, there is one great branch of economic activity that makes use of them—namely, advertising. Look through the advertising section of the illustrated weeklies. On every page, you'll find pictures of famous men and landscapes, cultural, historical, and technical information, classical rules on how to live, statistical tables, and chemical and physiological data. Commodities thus drape themselves in the world of knowledge and the human spirit, in order to stand out more alluringly. No wonder it was a trade-minded America that took the first great step here, by hiring its radio stations out by the hour to individual large companies and concerns, who are happy to sponsor at their own expense the greatest virtuosi and the most popular comedians to enhance the reputation of their products. In Europe the producers of commodities make do, for the time being at least, with less costly endeavors: they enlist general education in their service so as to anchor their products in the intellectual life of their customers, as well as in their needs. So much for the subterranean interplay between the newer techniques of advertising and the occult sciences, both of which have profited from the collapse of general education. If one of them has mastered the art of transforming the commodity into an arcanum, the other is able to sell the arcanum as a commodity. Just as a cigarette can be regarded as the best healer of the soul, so Steiner's "Goetheanum"[6] can be thought of as a solid business venture, and the occult science it purveys can be packaged as a brand-name product that does not hesitate to enlist the whole of world history as a marketing device.

All this may shed some light on what is at first glance the astonishing zeal with which the occult movement watches over its coverage in the press. We begin to understand why the master took time to reflect on "the press and its significance for the humanities," and on the extent to which "journalists were strong enough to liberate themselves from prejudices and their interest in ephemera" (p. 369). And now that, with this book, we see entering the stage a man who, as the publisher's blurb says, "enjoys a Europe-wide reputation as a music and theater critic," occult science should make the most of him. The reader, however, will think back with some nostalgia to the now-superseded brochures that offered for a few cents good luck at gambling or in love, and will confess how much purer they seemed than writings that summon up Ophir and Atlantis, Buddha and Christ, *The Book of the Dead* and the *Zohar,* merely to establish barbarism in the place occupied by culture a century ago.[7]

Published in the *Frankfurter Zeitung,* August 1932. *Gesammelte Schriften,* III, 356–360. Translated by Rodney Livingstone.

Notes

1. Karl Wolfskehl (1869–1948), a German-Jewish philosopher, was a friend of Stefan George and Ludwig Klages. He fled Germany in 1933.
2. Rudolf Steiner (1861–1925), Austrian-born scientist and editor, was the founder of anthroposophy, a movement based on the notion that there is a spiritual world

accessible only to the highest faculties of mental knowledge. His ideas exerted a broad influence on education in the early part of the twentieth century.

3. Maryan von Smoluchowski (1872–1917) was a Polish physicist. In 1906 he explained the movement of molecules suspended in fluid ("Brownian motion"). Theodor Svedberg (1884–1971) was a Swedish chemist who specialized in the study of colloids. He won the Nobel Prize for Chemistry in 1926.

4. Eduard Meyer (1855–1930) was a well-known classical historian. Max Dessoir (1867–1947) was a philosopher and psychologist. He coined the term "parapsychology."

5. Jiddu Krishnamurti (1895–1986), Indian mystic, enjoyed a prolonged career of writing and teaching. Beginning in the 1920s he spent much time in the United States and Europe, where his books have enjoyed considerable popularity. Bo Yin Ra (pseudonym of Joseph Anton Schneiderfranken; 1876–1943), German painter and writer, left behind thirty-two volumes of mystical writings. A self-described "medium of spiritual insights," his writings portray the world as a realm of spiritual powers inaccessible to the human senses, and the human task as the rediscovery of this divine realm.

6. The "Goetheanum" is the headquarters and the university of the anthroposophist movement. It was established near Basel in 1913.

7. Ophir was an area famous in Old Testament times for its fine gold; biblical texts offer contradictory information on its exact location. *The Book of the Dead* is an ancient Egyptian collection of funerary texts made up of spells and magic formulas, which were placed in tombs and were believed to protect and aid the deceased in the hereafter. The *Zohar*, or *Sefer ha-zohar* (Hebrew: "Book of Splendor"), dates from the thirteenth century; it is the central text of the esoteric system of interpretation known as the Kaballah.

The Handkerchief

Why is storytelling on the decline?—This is a question I often asked myself when I sat with other guests around a table for an entire evening feeling bored. One afternoon, however, when I was standing on the promenade deck of the *Bellver* next to the wheelhouse, surveying with the aid of my excellent binoculars every facet of the incomparable picture that Barcelona offers when viewed from the heights of a ship, I thought I had found the answer. The sun was setting over the city and seemed to be melting it. All life had retreated to the light-gray transitions between the foliage on the trees, the cement of the buildings, and the rocks of the distant mountains. The *Bellver* is a fine, spacious steamship that one would like to think deserved a greater destiny than providing a ferry service to the Balearics. And in fact the image before my eyes really did seem to shrink when, the following day, I saw her tied up at the breakwater in Ibiza, waiting for the return voyage, for I had imagined that it would go on from there to the Canaries. So I was standing there thinking of Captain O., from whom I had taken my leave a few hours before, the first and perhaps the last storyteller I ever met in my life. For, as I have said, the art of storytelling is coming to an end. And when I thought back to the many hours that Captain O. spent walking back and forth on the afterdeck, looking up idly from time to time and gazing into the distance, I realized that people who are not bored cannot tell stories. But there is no longer any place for boredom in our lives. The activities that were covertly and inwardly bound up with it are dying out. A second reason, then, for the decline in storytelling is that people have ceased to weave and spin, tinker and scrape, while listening to stories. In short, if stories are to thrive, there must be work, order, and subordination.

Storytelling is not just an art; it is a kind of dignity—if not, as in the East, an office. It culminates in wisdom, just as, for its part, wisdom often substantiates itself as story. For this reason the storyteller is always someone who knows what has to be done. And to receive such counsel, you yourself have to tell him something. But we know only how to moan and groan about our worries, not how to tell a story. And third, I called to mind the captain's pipe, a pipe that he knocked the ash out of when he started and again when he had finished; but in between, he would let it go out. It had an amber mouthpiece, while its bowl was made of horn with heavy silver mountings. It had come to him from his grandfather, and I think it was the storyteller's talisman. For another reason no proper stories can be heard today is that things no longer last the way they should. Anyone who wears a leather belt until it falls to pieces will always find that at some point in the course of time a story has attached itself to it. The captain's pipe must have known quite a number of them.

Thus I was dreaming, when far below me on the quay I caught sight of a stocky man with the most massive head that ever wore a captain's cap. It was Captain O., from the cargo boat on which I had arrived in port. Anyone who is accustomed to a lonely departure from foreign towns will know what it means to encounter a familiar face—even if it is not that of a close friend—at a moment when imminent departure sweeps aside all the difficulties of a prolonged conversation, but at the same time provides you with a hat, a hand, or a handkerchief in which the unaccommodated gaze may find refuge before venturing out over the sea. And here, then, was the captain, as if my thinking about him had made him appear. At fifteen he had left home, had spent three years on a training ship cruising around in the Pacific and the Atlantic, and had subsequently ended up on one of the steamers of the Lloyd Line on the America run. He had soon left this, however, although he did not say why. Nor could I discover more about him. There seemed to be a shadow lying over his life, but he did not wish to discuss it. And that, of course, means that he appeared to lack the most marvelous feature of a storyteller: the ability to narrate his own life, to allow that wick to be consumed in the gentle flame of the telling. Be that as it may, his life appeared poor compared with that of the ship, every one of whose ribs and spars he was able to bring to life. This was the ship I had before me when I went on board that morning. I was as well informed about the year it was built, the cargo rates, the size of its hold, and its tonnage as I was about the wages of the ship's boys and the worries of its officers. Indeed, those were the days when the cargo business was still handled by the sailing ships and when the ships' captains themselves negotiated the cost of transport in the harbors. In those days, the old sailor's joke could often be heard: "Give up sailing and join a steamship!" Now, however, . . . and there followed a string of sentences from which you could learn how radically things had been changed here too by the economic crisis.

On such occasions Captain O. sometimes let fall some remarks on politics.

But I never saw him with a newspaper. I have never forgotten his reply when one day I brought the matter up. "You can learn nothing from the papers," he said. "They always want to explain everything to you." And in fact isn't it half the art of journalism to keep the news free of explanations? And didn't the ancients set an example for us by presenting events, as it were, dry, draining them entirely of psychological explanations and opinions of every sort? It must be admitted that his own stories kept quite free of superfluous explanations, without losing anything in consequence—or so it seemed to me. There were some strange tales among them, but none that confirms this characterization more than the story below, which was to be followed that very afternoon on the breakwater off Barcelona by a most surprising sequel.

"It was many years ago," the captain had begun as we sailed off Cádiz, "on one of my first voyages to America, during which I was serving as the most junior officer. We'd been sailing for seven days and were due to reach Bremerhaven the following noon. I was making my rounds on the promenade deck as usual, pausing now and then to exchange a few words with the passengers, when suddenly I was startled to see that the sixth deckchair in the row was empty. A feeling of oppression overcame me, yet I fancy that on the previous days I had gone past it feeling even more apprehensive when I had turned with a silent greeting to the young lady who sat in it, her hands folded behind her head, gazing motionlessly before her. She was very beautiful, but her reserve was as striking as her beauty. This went so far that one seldom had the opportunity of hearing her voice—the most marvelous voice I can recollect hearing: soft, husky, dark, metallic. Once, when I had picked up her handkerchief (I can still remember how struck I'd been by the mark embroidered on it: a tripartite coat-of-arms with three stars in each field), I'd heard her say 'Thank you' in a tone that suggested I'd just saved her life. On this occasion, I finished my tour of the deck and was just looking around to see if I could see the ship's doctor to inquire whether she had been taken ill, when I was suddenly enveloped in a whirl of white scraps of paper. I looked up and saw the missing woman leaning over the railing on the sundeck, absentmindedly watching a mass of papers being tossed about by the wind and waves. The next day at noon—I'd taken up my post on deck and was watching the landing maneuver—I again saw the unknown woman, out of the corner of my eye. The ship was about to dock, and the keel was slowly edging closer to the quay to which the stern was already made fast. You could clearly see the faces of the people who were waiting; she scrutinized them feverishly. I was distracted by the sight of the anchor cables being let out. Then, suddenly, I heard shouts and screams. I turned around and saw that the unknown woman had disappeared; you could tell from the commotion of the crowd that she had fallen overboard. Every effort to rescue her seemed futile. If only the engine could have stopped the boat dead—the stern was not more than three meters from the quay and it was unstoppable. Anyone who came between the ship and the quay was lost. Then the implausible actually happened. There was someone who was willing to make the superhuman effort. You could see him straining every muscle, his eyebrows drawn together as if he were taking aim; then he leaped over the rail. And while—to the horror of the onlookers—the whole length of the steamer moved to starboard and came to rest against the quay, the rescuer suddenly surfaced with the woman in his arms on the port side, which was so abandoned that at first no one noticed him. He had in fact taken aim with his entire weight and borne her down with him under the water and beneath the keel before coming back to the surface. 'As I held her,' he told me later, 'she whispered "Thank you," as if I'd just picked up her handkerchief.'"

I could still hear the tone of voice with which the storyteller had uttered these last words. If I wanted to shake hands with him one last time, there was no time to be lost. I was just about to hurry down the steps when I noticed how the granaries, sheds, and cranes had begun to recede. We were under way. With my binoculars raised to my eyes, I let Barcelona pass in review before me one last time. I then lowered them toward the quay. There stood the captain among the crowd; he must have seen me, too. He lifted his hand in greeting; I waved mine. By the time I'd raised the binoculars to my eyes again, he had unfolded a handkerchief and waved. I could clearly see the mark in its corner: a tripartite coat-of-arms with three stars in each field.

Published in the *Frankfurter Zeitung*, November 1932. *Gesammelte Schriften*, IV, 741–745. Translated by Rodney Livingstone.

In the Sun

There are, so it is said, seventeen kinds of figs on the island. One ought—the man told himself as he walked in the sun—to know their names. Indeed, not only ought one to have seen the grasses and the animals that give the island its face, its sound, and its scent; not only ought one to have seen the strata of the mountains and the different kinds of soil, which vary from a dusty yellow to a violet brown, from the cinnabar; above all, one ought to know their names. Isn't every region governed by a unique confluence of plants and animals, and isn't every local name a cipher behind which flora and fauna meet for the first and last time? The farmer, however, has the key to this code. He knows their names. Yet it is not in his power to say anything about his domain. Is it that the names have made him taciturn? Would this mean that the cornucopia of language falls only to the man who has the knowledge without the names; and the cornucopia of silence, to the man who has nothing *but* the names?

It was evident that the man walking along deep in thought was not from here; and if, when he was at home, thoughts came to him in the open air, it was always night. With astonishment he would recall that entire nations—Jews, Indians, Moors—had built their schools beneath a sun that seemed to make all thinking impossible for him. This sun was burning into his back. Resin and thyme impregnated the air in which he felt he was struggling for breath. A bumble bee brushed his ear. Hardly had he registered its presence than it was already sucked away into the vortex of silence. The message of many summers that he had heedlessly let slip by unnoticed (for the first time, his ears were receptive), and now it had ceased to transmit. The nearly obliterated path broadened; tracks led to a charcoal kiln. Behind it the mountains, to which the gaze of the climber was drawn, cowered in the haze.

He felt something cold on his cheek. Thinking it was a fly, he struck at it. But it was only the first droplet of sweat. Soon he felt thirsty. The thirst came not from his palate but from his stomach. From there it spread everywhere, instructing his body, large as it was, in its ability to absorb and drink up the slightest breath of air with all its pores. His shirt had long since slipped from his shoulders, and when he hitched it up to protect them from sunburn, it felt like a damp shawl. In a hollow, almond trees cast their shadows straight down to the base of their trunks. Almonds are the wealth of the country. No other fruit brings the farmer a better price. At this time of year it is the only one ripe, and it is a pleasure to reach out for it among the branches as one walks. The hand is reluctant to part with the shells once the kernel has been removed. It continues to hold them for a while, and then lets them float away in a brook, which carries it along as well. The kernels are ripe, but not entirely ripe; the juice in them is fresher than it is later, when their skin is brown and can no longer be easily removed. At present it was still ivory-colored, like goat's cheese and women's silk shifts. Their taste is ivory, too. Whoever has them between his teeth can tranquilly hear creeks murmuring through the foliage of the fig trees. But the figs were green and hard, and were nestling, barely visible, in the axils. The moment had come when only the trees seemed alive. Amid the pines, you could hear the shrill chirping of cicadas; the noise they made echoed back from the dusty fields. The fields had been stripped of their harvest and now lay bare, with the expression of people who have given away everything. Their last possession—their shadows—lay shrunken, gathered in, at the foot of the tall haystacks. For this was the hour for gathering.

The forests themselves lay around the hilltops, as if harvested by the rake of summer. Only willows stood singly in the stubble, and their foliage gleamed black with white streaks, like tula metal. None was more decked out with bunting, yet more brittle, richer in signs—which were barely noticed. Nevertheless, one of them attracted the attention of the passer-by. He recalled the day he had felt at one with a tree. On that occasion, it had required only the woman he loved—she had stood, quite unconcerned about him, on the lawn—and his sadness or tiredness. So he had leaned with his back against the trunk, and the tree had taken his feelings in hand. He had learned to breathe in when the tree began to sway, and to breathe out when the trunk sprang back. Of course, that had been merely the well-tended trunk of an ornamental tree; it was impossible to imagine the life of a man who could learn from this gnarled willow trunk, deeply split three ways, leaning toward an unexplored world that spread out over the terrain in three directions. No pathway opened them up. But as he paused, uncertain whether or not to proceed along one that threatened to betray him at any moment—seeming now to peter out into a field path, now to come to a stop in a thorny hedge—he found he had himself under control once again as a man: stone blocks rose up in steps to form terraces, and cart tracks made their appearance, pointing to a farmstead in the vicinity.

No sound gives a clue to the neighboring environment of such settlements. Around them the intensity of noonday stillness appears redoubled. But now the fields thinned out, opening up the district with a second and even a third pathway; and while the walls and barns lay hidden behind trees or a ridge, a crossroads suddenly became visible in the abandoned stretch of fields and established the midpoint. There were no highways or mail routes leading here, but neither were these just paths made by animals. Instead, here in the open countryside converged the pathways on which farmers and their wives and children and herds, through the centuries, had moved from field to field, from house to house, from pasture to pasture, rarely in such a way that they did not return to sleep under their own roof at night. The ground here sounded hollow; the sound with which it responded to every step brought comfort to anyone walking this way. With this sound, the solitude of the passer-by laid the land at his feet. If he came to places where he felt good, he knew that solitude had brought him to that point; it had given him this stone to sit on, this hollow as a nest for his limbs. But he was already too tired to pause. Losing control of his feet, which carried him forward much too quickly, he became aware that his imagination had made itself independent of him and, poised against the broad slope that paralleled his path in the distance, had begun to operate on him of its own accord. Does imagination shift rocks and hilltops? Or does it just touch them with its breath? Does it leave no stone unturned, or does it leave everything as it was?

The Hasidim have a saying about the world to come. Everything there will be arranged just as it is with us. The room we have now will be just the same in the world to come; where our child lies sleeping, it will sleep in the world to come. The clothes we are wearing we shall also wear in the next world. Everything will be the same as here—only a little bit different. Thus it is with imagination. It merely draws a veil over the distance. Everything remains just as it is, but the veil flutters and everything changes imperceptibly beneath it.

Things change, and trade places; nothing remains and nothing disappears. From all this activity, however, names suddenly emerge; wordlessly they enter the mind of the passer-by, and as his lips shape them, he recognizes them. They come to the surface. And what further need has he of this landscape? They drift past him on the nameless distant horizon, without leaving a trace. The names of islands that rose out of the sea like marble sculptures, of steep rocks whose craggy peaks broke up the sky, of stars that surprised him in the boat when they came on guard duty in the early darkness. The chirping of the cicadas has fallen silent; the man's thirst has vanished; the day is waning. A sound rises up from somewhere down below. Is it a barking dog, some falling rocks, or a person calling from afar? As he listens, trying to identify it, a peal of bells wells up within him, note by note. Then it ripens and expands in his blood. Lilies blossom at the corner of the cactus hedge. In the distance a cart trundles silently across the fields between the olive and almond trees; and when the wheels vanish behind the foliage, women, larger than life, their faces turned toward him, seem to float motionlessly through the motionless countryside.

Published in the *Kölnische Zeitung,* December 1932. *Gesammelte Schriften,* IV, 417–420. Translated by Rodney Livingstone.

The Rigorous Study of Art

On the First Volume of the *Kunstwissenschaftliche Forschungen*

In the foreword to his 1898 study *Die klassische Kunst* [Classic Art], Heinrich Wölfflin made a gesture that cast aside the history of art as it was then understood by Richard Muther.[1] "Contemporary public interest" he declared, "seems nowadays to want to turn toward more specifically artistic questions. One no longer expects an art-historical book to give mere biographical anecdotes or a description of the circumstances of the time; rather, one wants to learn something about those things which constitute the value and the essence of a work of art . . . The natural thing would be for every art-historical monograph to contain some aesthetics as well." A bit further on, one reads: "In order to be more certain of attaining this goal, the first, historical, section has been furnished with a second, systematic, section as a counterpart."[2] This arrangement is all the more indicative because it reveals not only the aims but also the limits of an endeavor which was so epoch-making in its time. And, in fact, Wölfflin did not succeed in his attempt to use formal analysis (which he placed at the center of his method) to remedy the bleak condition in which his discipline found itself at the end of the nineteenth century. He identified a dualism—a flat, universalizing history of the art of "all cultures and times," on the one hand, and an academic aesthetic, on the other—without, however, being able to overcome it entirely.

Only from the perspective of the current situation does it become evident to what extent the understanding of art history as universal history—under whose aegis eclecticism had free play—fettered authentic research. And this is true not only for the study of art. In a programmatic explanation, the literary historian Walter Muschg writes: "It is fair to say that the most essential work being done at present is almost exclusively oriented toward the monograph. To a great extent, today's generation no longer believes in the significance of an all-encompassing presentation. Instead it is grappling with figures and problems which it sees marked primarily by gaps during that era of universal histories."[3] Indeed, the "turn away from an uncritical realism in the contemplation of history and the shriveling up of macroscopic constructions"[4] are the most important hallmarks of the new research. Sedlmayr's programmatic article "Toward a Rigorous Study of Art," the opening piece in the recently published yearbook *Kunstwissenschaftliche Forschungen* [Research Essays in the Study of Art], is entirely in accord with this position:

> The currently evolving phase in the study of art will have to emphasize, in a heretofore unknown manner, the *investigation of individual works*. Nothing is more important at the present stage than an improved knowledge of the individual artwork, and it is in just this task, above all, that the extant study of art manifests its incompetence ... Once the individual artwork is perceived as a still unmastered task specific to the study of art, it appears powerfully new and close. Formerly a mere means to knowledge, a trace of something else which was to be disclosed through it, the artwork now appears as a self-contained *small world* of its own, particular sort.[5]

In accordance with these introductory remarks, the three essays which follow are thus rigorously monographic studies. G. A. Andreades presents the Hagia Sophia as a synthesis between Orient and Occident; Otto Pächt develops the historical task posed by Michael Pacher; and Carl Linfert explores the foundations of the architectural drawing.[6] What these studies share is a convincing love for—and a no less convincing mastery of—their subject. The three authors have nothing in common with the type of art historian "who, really convinced that artworks were meant not to be studied (but only 'experienced'), studied them nevertheless—only badly."[7] Furthermore, these authors know that headway can be made only if one considers contemplation of one's own activity—a new awareness—not as a constraint but as an impetus to rigorous study. This is particularly so because such study is not concerned with objects of pleasure, with formal problems, with giving form to experience, or any other clichés inherited from a belletristic consideration of art. Rather, this sort of studious work considers the formal incorporation of the given world by the artist

> not as a selection but rather always as an advance into a field of knowledge which did not yet "exist" prior to the moment of this formal conquest ... This approach becomes possible only through a frame of mind that recognizes that the realm of perception itself changes over time and in accordance with shifts in cultural and intellectual [*geistig*] direction. Such a frame of mind, however, in no way presumes objects that are always present in an unvarying manner such that their formal makeup is merely determined by a changing "stylistic drive" within perceptual surroundings that remain constant.

For "we should never be interested in 'problems of form' as such, as if a form ever arose out of formal problems alone or, to put it in other words, as if a form ever came into existence for the sake of the stimulus it would produce."

Also characteristic of this manner of approaching art is the "esteem for the insignificant" (which the Brothers Grimm practiced in their incomparable expression of the spirit of true philology).[8] But what animates this esteem, if not the willingness to push research forward to the point where even the "insignificant"—no, *precisely* the insignificant—becomes significant? The bedrock that these researchers come up against is the concrete bedrock of past historical existence [*geschichtliches Gewesenseins*]. The "insignificance" with which they are concerned is neither the nuance of new stimuli nor the characteristic trait, which was formerly employed to identify column forms much the way Linné taxonomized plants.[9] Instead it is the inconspicuous aspect—or this *and* the offensive aspect (the two together are not a contradiction)—which survives in true works and which constitutes the point where the content reaches the breaking point for an authentic researcher. One need only read a study such as the one on the Sistine Madonna published years ago by Hubert Grimme (who does not belong to this group) in order to observe how much such an inquiry, based on the most inconspicuous data of an object, can wrest from even the most worn-out things. And thus, because of the focus on materiality in such work, the precursor of this new type of art scholar is not Wölfflin but Riegl. Pächt's investigation of Pacher "is a new attempt at that grand form of presentation exemplified in Riegl's masterly command of the transition from the individual object to its cultural and intellectual [*geistig*] function, as can be seen especially in his study 'Das holländische Gruppenportrait.'"[10] One could just as well refer to Riegl's book *Die spätrömische Kunst-Industrie* [The Late Roman Art Industry], particularly since this work demonstrates in exemplary fashion the fact that sober and simultaneously undaunted research never misses the vital concerns of its time.[11] The reader who reads Riegl's major work today, recalling that it was written at almost the same time as the work by Wölfflin cited in the opening paragraph, will recognize retrospectively how forces that are already stirring subterraneously in *Die spätrömische Kunst-Industrie* will surface a decade later in expressionism. Thus, one can assume that sooner or later contemporaneity will catch up with the studies by Pächt and Linfert as well.

There are some methodological reservations, however, regarding the advisability of the move that Sedlmayr attempts in his introductory essay, juxtaposing the rigorous study of art as a "secondary" field of study against a primary (that is, positivist) study of art. The kind of research undertaken in this volume is so dependent upon auxiliary fields of study—painting technique and painting media, the history of motifs, iconography—that it can be confusing to constitute these as a somehow separate "primary study of art." Sedlmayr's essay also demonstrates how difficult it is for a particular course of research (such as the one represented here) to establish purely methodological definitions without reference to any concrete examples whatsoever. This is difficult; but is it necessary? Is it appropriate to place this new aspiration [*Wollen*] so assiduously under the patronage of phenomenology and *Gestalt* theory? It could easily be that, in the process, one loses nearly as much as one gains. Admittedly, the references to "levels of meaning" in the works, to their "physiognomic character," to their "sense of orientation," can be useful in the polemic against positivist art chatter and even in the polemic against formalist analysis. But they are of little help to the self-definition of the new type of research. This type of study stands to gain from the insight that the more crucial the works are, the more inconspicuously and intimately their meaning-content [*Bedeutungsgehalt*] is bound up with their material content [*Sachgehalt*]. It is concerned with the correlation that gives rise to reciprocal illumination between, on the one hand, the historical process and radical change and, on the other hand, the accidental, external, and even strange aspects of the artwork. For if the most meaningful works prove to be precisely those whose life is most deeply embedded in their material contents—one thinks of Giehlow's interpretation of Dürer's *Melancolia*[12]—then over the course of their historical duration these material contents present themselves to the researcher all the more clearly the more they have disappeared from the world.

   It would be difficult to find a better clarification of the implications of this train of thought than Linfert's study located at the end of the volume. As the text explains, its very subject matter, the architectural drawing, "is a marginal case."[13] But it is precisely in the investigation of the marginal case that material contents reveal their key position most decisively. If one examines the abundant plates accompanying Linfert's study, one discovers names in the captions that are unfamiliar to the layman and, to some extent, to the professional as well. As regards the images themselves, one cannot say that they *re*-produce architecture. They *produce* it in the first place, a production which less often benefits the reality of architectural planning than it does dreams. One sees, to take a few examples, Babel's heraldic, ostentatious portals, the fairy-tale castles which Delajoue has conjured into a shell, Meissonier's knickknack architecture, Boullée's conception of a library that looks like a train station, and Juvara's ideal views ["Prospettiva ideale"] that look like glances into the warehouse of a building dealer:[14] a completely new and untouched world of images, which Baudelaire would have ranked higher than all painting. In Linfert's work, however, the images are submitted to a descriptive technique that succeeds in establishing the most revealing facts in this unexplored marginal realm. There is, as is commonly known, a manner of representing buildings using purely painterly means. The architectural drawing is sharply distinguished from images of this sort and is found to have the closest affinity to nonrepresentational [*unbildmässige*] work—that is, the supposedly authentically architectonic presentations of buildings in topographic designs, prospects, and vedutas. Since in these, too, certain "errors" have survived up through the late eighteenth century despite all the progress in naturalism, Linfert takes this to be a peculiar imaginary world [*Vorstellungswelt*] of architecture, which is markedly different from that of the painters. There are various indications that confirm the existence of this world, the most important one being that such architecture is not primarily "seen," but rather is imagined as an objective entity [*Bestand*] and is sensed by those who approach or even enter it as a surrounding space [*Umraum*] *sui generis*—that is, without the distancing effect of the edge of the image space [*Bildraum*]. Thus, what is crucial in the consideration of architecture is not seeing but the apprehension [*durchspüren*] of structures. The objective effect of the buildings on the imaginative being [*vorstellungsmässige Sein*] of the viewer is more important than their "being seen." In short, the most essential characteristic of the architectural drawing is that "it does not take a pictorial detour."

So much for the formal aspects. In Linfert's analyses, however, formal questions are very closely tied to historical circumstances. His investigation deals with "a period during which the architectural drawing began to lose its principal and decisive expression."[15] But how transparent this "process of decay" becomes here! How the architectural prospects open up in order to take into their core allegories, stage designs, and monuments! And each of these forms in turn points to unrecognized aspects which appear to the researcher Linfert in their full concreteness: Renaissance hieroglyphics; Piranesi's visionary fantasies of ruins; the temples of the Illuminati, such as we know them from *Die Zauberflöte*.[16] Here it becomes evident that the hallmark of the new type of researcher is not the eye for the "all-encompassing whole" or the eye for the "comprehensive context" (which mediocrity has claimed for itself), but rather the capacity to be at home in marginal domains. The men whose work is contained in this yearbook represent the most rigorous of this new type of researcher. They are the hope of their field of study.

Written July–December 1932; abridged version published in the *Literaturblatt der Frankfurter Zeitung*, July 1933 (under the pseudonym Detlef Holz). *Gesammelte Schriften*, III, 363–369. Translated by Thomas Y. Levin.

Notes

1. Richard Muther (1860–1909) was an art historian and critic who is often cited as paradigmatic of the "old school" of nineteenth-century art history. His work was a mixture of religiosity, sentimentality, and eroticism.

2. Heinrich Wölfflin, *Die klassische Kunst: Eine Einführung in die italienische Renaissance* (Munich: F. Bruckmann, 1899), pp. vii–viii; translated by Linda Murray and Peter Murray as *Classic Art: An Introduction to the Italian Renaissance* (London: Phaidon, 1952), pp. xi–xii.

3. Walter Muschg, "Das Dichterporträt in der Literaturgeschichte" [The Writer's Portrait in Literary History], in Emil Ermatinger, ed. *Philosophie der Literaturwissenschaft* (Berlin: Junker und Dünnhaupt, 1930), p. 311. Compare also Benjamin's citation of the same passage in his essay "Literaturgeschichte und Literaturwissenschaft" (Literary History and the Study of Literature), *Gesammelte Schriften,* vol. 3, pp. 289–290. Walter Muschg (1898–1965) was a Swiss literary historian, poet, and dramatist.

4. Muschg, "Das Dichterportrait," p. 314.

5. Hans Sedlmayr, "Zu einer strengen Kunstwissenschaft" (Toward a Rigorous Study of Art), in Otto Pächt, ed., *Kunstwissenschaftliche Forschungen,* vol. 1 (Berlin: Frankfurter Verlags-Anstalt, 1931), pp. 19–20. Hans Sedlmayr (1896–1984) was a German art historian. Otto Pächt (1902–1988), Austrian art historian, was a leading figure in the "second Viennese school" of art history (the first school having formed around Alois Riegl at the turn of the century).

6. G. A. Andreades, "Die Sophienkathedrale von Konstantinopel" (The Hagia Sophia in Constantinople), in Pächt, ed., *Kunstwissenschaftliche Forschungen,* pp. 33–94; Otto Pächt, "Die historische Aufgabe Michael Pachers" (The Historical Task of Michael Pacher), ibid., pp. 95–132; Carl Linfert, "Die Grundlagen der Architektur-zeichnung" (Fundamentals of Architectural Drawing), ibid., pp. 133–246.

7. Pächt, ed., *Kunstwissenschaftliche Forschungen,* p. 31.

8. The phrase comes not from the Brothers Grimm but from Sulpiz Boisserée, who used it, in a letter to Goethe, to describe August Wilhelm Schlegel's review of the Grimms' book *Altdeutsche Wälder* (Old-German Woods).

9. Carl von Linné, also known as Carolus Linnaeus (1707–1778), was a Swedish naturalist credited with the founding of modern systematic botany. He based his classification of each genus and its species on the system of binomial scientific nomenclature, which he developed.

10. Alois Riegl (1858–1905) was an Austrian art historian. His book *Die spätrömische Kunst-Industrie* (The Late Roman Art Industry; 1901) effected a revolution in the study of artistic epochs previously held to be degenerate. Benjamin counted this text as one of the four most important books of the young century. Alois Riegl, "Das holländische Gruppenportrait" [The Dutch Group Portrait], *Jahrbuch der Kunsthistorischen Sammlungen des Allerhöchsten Kaiserhauses,* vol. 23, parts 3–4 (Vienna: F. Tempsky, 1902), pp. 71–278.

11. Alois Riegl, *Die spätrömische Kunst-Industrie nach den Funden in Oesterreich-Ungarn,* Part 1 (Vienna: K.K. Hof- und Staatsdruckerei, 1901); translated by

Rolf Winks as *Late Roman Art Industry* (Rome: Giorgio Bretschneider Editore, 1985).

12. Karl Giehlow, "Dürers Stich *Melancolia I* und der maximilianische Humanistenkreis" [Dürer's Engraving *Melancholy I* and the Humanist Circle under Maximilian], in *Mitteilungen der Gesellschaft für vervielfältigende Kunst: Beilage der "Graphischen Künste"* (Vienna, 1903). Giehlow (1863–1913) was a German art historian and a leading Dürer scholar.

13. Linfert, "Architektur-zeichnung," p. 153.

14. Paul Emile Babel (1720–1770), French designer and engraver, worked in a rococo style. Jacques Delajoue (1686–1761; also spelled "de Lajoue") did elegant drawings and paintings of rococo architecture, often in fanciful pastoral settings. Juste-Aurèle Meissonnier (1675–1750) was a French painter, sculptor, and architect whose work was characterized by fantasy and arabesque. Etienne-Louis Boullée (1728–1799) was a French visionary architect, theorist, and teacher. Filippo Juvara (1678–1736) was an Italian architect and stage designer.

15. Linfert, "Architektur-zeichnung," p. 231.

16. Benjamin is probably referring to the epoch-making stage sets for Mozart's opera *Die Zauberflöte* (The Magic Flute), produced in 1816 by the eminent architect Karl Friedrich Schinkel (1781–1841), whose neoclassical exoticism became a model for many subsequent stagings. Benjamin might even have seen a performance of *Die Zauberflöte* with these Schinkel sets, since they were still being used by the Berlin State Opera as late as 1937.

Hashish in Marseilles

Preliminary remark: One of the first signs that hashish is beginning to take effect is

a dull feeling of foreboding; something strange, ineluctable, is approaching . . . Images and chains of images, long-submerged memories appear; whole scenes and situations are experienced. At first they arouse interest, now and then enjoyment, and finally, when there is no turning away from them, weariness and torment. By everything that happens, and by what he says and does, the subject is surprised and overwhelmed. His laughter, all his utterances, happen to him like external events. He also attains experiences that approach inspiration, illumination . . . Space can expand, the ground tilt steeply, atmospheric sensations occur: vapor, an opaque heaviness of the air. Colors grow brighter, more luminous; objects more beautiful, or else lumpy and threatening. . . . All this does not occur in a continuous development; rather, it is typified by a continual alternation of dreaming and waking states, a constant and finally exhausting oscillation between totally different worlds of consciousness. In the middle of a sentence these transitions can take place . . . All this the subject reports in a form that usually diverges very widely from the norm. Connections become difficult to perceive, owing to the frequently sudden rupture of all memory of past events; thought is not formed into words; the situation can become so compulsively hilarious that the hashish eater for minutes on end is capable of nothing except laughing . . . The memory of the intoxication is surprisingly clear.

"It is curious that hashish poisoning has not yet been experimentally studied. The most admirable description of the hashish trance is by Baudelaire *(Les paradis artificiels).*" From Joël and Fränkel, "Der Haschisch-Rausch," *Klinische Wochenschrift,* 5 (1926), p. 37.

Marseilles, July 29. At seven o'clock in the evening, after long hesitation, I took hashish. During the day, I had been in Aix. With the absolute certainty (in this city of hundreds of thousands where no one knows me) of not being disturbed, I lie on the bed. Yet I am disturbed, by a little child crying. I think three-quarters of an hour have already passed. But it is only twenty minutes . . . So I lie on the bed, reading and smoking. Opposite me always this view of the belly of Marseilles. The street I have so often seen is like a knife cut.

At last I left the hotel, the effects seeming nonexistent or so weak that the precaution of staying at home was unnecessary. My first port of call was the café on the corner of the Cannebière and the Cours Belsunce. Seen from the harbor, the one on the right; therefore not my usual café. What now? Only a certain benevolence, the expectation of being received kindly by people. The feeling of loneliness is very quickly lost. My walking stick begins to give me a special pleasure. One becomes so tender, fears that a shadow falling on the paper might hurt it. The nausea disappears. One reads the notices on the urinals. It would not surprise me if this or that person came up to me. But when no one does I am not disappointed, either. But it's too noisy for me here.

Now the hashish eater's demands on time and space come into force. As is known, these are absolutely regal. Versailles, for one who has taken hashish, is not too large, or eternity too long. Against the background of these immense dimensions of inner experience, of absolute duration and immeasurable space, a wonderful, beatific humor dwells all the more fondly on the contingencies of the world of space and time. I feel this humor infinitely when I am told at the Restaurant Basso that the kitchen has just been closed, while I have just sat down to feast into eternity. Afterward, despite this, the feeling that all this is indeed bright, frequented, animated, and will remain so. I must note how I found my seat. What mattered to me was the view of the old port that one got from the upper floors. Walking past below, I had spied an empty table on the balcony of the second story. Yet in the end, I reached only the first. Most of the window tables were occupied, so I went up to a very large one that had just been vacated. As I was sitting down, however, the disproportion of seating myself at so large a table caused me such shame that I walked across the entire floor to the opposite end to sit at a smaller table that became visible to me only as I reached it.

But the meal came later. First, the little bar on the harbor. I was again just on the point of retreating in confusion, for a concert—indeed, a brass band—seemed to be playing there. I only just managed to explain to myself that it was nothing more than the blaring of car horns. On the way to the

Vieux Port, I already had this wonderful lightness and sureness of step that transformed the stony, unarticulated earth of the great square that I was crossing into the surface of a country road along which I strode at night like an energetic hiker. For at this time I was still avoiding the Cannebière, not yet quite sure of my regulatory functions. In that little harbor bar, the hashish then began to exert its canonical magic with a primitive sharpness that I had scarcely felt until then. For it made me into a physiognomist, or at least a contemplator of physiognomies, and I underwent something unique in my experience: I positively fixed my gaze on the faces that I had around me, some of which were of remarkable coarseness or ugliness. Faces that I would normally have avoided for a twofold reason: I would neither have wished to attract their gaze nor have endured their brutality. It was a very advanced post, this harbor tavern. (I believe it was the farthest accessible to me without danger—a circumstance I had gauged, in the trance, with the same accuracy with which, when utterly weary, one is able to fill a glass exactly to the brim without spilling a drop, something one can never do with sharp senses.) It was still sufficiently far from the rue Bouterie, yet no bourgeois sat there; at the most, besides the true port proletariat, a few petty-bourgeois families from the neighborhood. I now suddenly understood how, to a painter (hadn't it happened to Rembrandt and many others?), ugliness could appear as the true reservoir of beauty—or better, as its treasure chest: a jagged mountain with all the inner gold of beauty gleaming from the wrinkles, glances, features. I especially remember an infinitely bestial, vulgar male face in which the "line of renunciation" struck me with sudden violence. It was, above all, men's faces that had begun to interest me. Now began the game, which I played for quite a while, of recognizing someone I knew in every face. Often I knew the name, often not. The deception vanished as deceptions vanish in dreams: not in shame, not compromised, but peacefully and amiably, like a being who has performed his service. Under these circumstances, there was no question of loneliness. Was I my own company? Surely not so undisguisedly. I doubt whether that would have made me so happy. More likely this: I became my own most skillful, fond, shameless procurer, gratifying myself with the ambiguous assurance of one who knows from profound study the wishes of his employer.—Then it began to take half an eternity until the waiter reappeared. Or, rather, I could not wait for him to appear. I went into the barroom and paid at the counter. Whether tips are usual in such taverns I do not know. But under other circumstances, I should have given something in any case. Under the influence of hashish yesterday, however, I was on the stingy side; for fear of attracting attention by extravagance, I succeeded in making myself really conspicuous.

Similarly at Basso's. First I ordered a dozen oysters. The man wanted me to order the next course at the same time. I named some local dish. He came back with the news that none was left. I then pointed to a place on the menu in the vicinity of this dish, and was on the point of ordering each item, one after another, but then the name of the one above it caught my attention, and so on, until I finally reached the top of the list. This was not just from greed, however, but from an extreme politeness toward the dishes, which I did not wish to offend by a refusal. In short, I came to a stop at a *pâté de Lyon*. "Lion paste," I thought with a witty smile, when it lay clean on a plate before me; and then, contemptuously: "This tender rabbit or chicken meat—whatever it may be." To my lionish hunger, it would not have seemed inappropriate to satisfy itself on a lion. Moreover, I had tacitly decided that as soon as I had finished at Basso's (it was about half past ten) I would go elsewhere and dine a second time.

But first, back to the walk to Basso's. I strolled along the quay and read, one after another, the names of the boats tied up there. As I did so, an incomprehensible gaiety came over me, and I smiled in turn at all the Christian names of France. The love promised to these boats by their names seemed wonderfully beautiful and touching to me. Only one of them, *Aero II*, which reminded me of aerial warfare, I passed by without cordiality, exactly as, in the bar that I had just left, my gaze had been obliged to pass over certain excessively deformed countenances.

Upstairs at Basso's, when I looked down, the old games began again. The square in front of the harbor was my palette, on which my imagination mixed the qualities of the place, trying them out now this way, now that, without concern for the result, like a painter daydreaming on his palette. I hesitated before ordering wine. It was a half bottle of Cassis. A piece of ice was floating in the glass. Yet it went excellently with my drug. I had chosen my seat on account of the open window, through which I could look down on the dark square. And when I did so from time to time, I noticed that it had a tendency to change with everyone who stepped onto it, as if it formed a figure about him that, clearly, had nothing to do with the square as he saw it but, rather, had to do with the view that the great portrait painters of the seventeenth century—in accordance with the character of the dignitary whom they placed before a colonnade or a window—threw into relief with this colonnade, this window. Later I noted as I looked down, "From century to century, things grow more estranged."

Here I must observe in general: the solitude of such trances has its dark side. To speak only of the physical aspect, there was a moment in the harbor tavern when a violent pressure in my diaphragm sought relief through humming. And there is no doubt that truly beautiful, illuminating visions were not awakened. On the other hand, solitude works in these states as a filter. What one writes down the following day is more than an enumeration of impressions. In the night, the trance cuts itself off from everyday reality with fine, prismatic edges. It forms a kind of figure, and is more easily memorable. I would say: it shrinks and takes on the form of a flower.

To begin to solve the riddle of the ecstasy of trance, one ought to meditate on Ariadne's thread. What joy in the mere act of unrolling a ball of thread! And this joy is very deeply related to the joy of intoxication, just as it is to the joy of creation. We go forward; but in so doing, we not only discover the twists and turns of the cave, but also enjoy this pleasure of discovery against the background of the other, rhythmic bliss of unwinding the thread. The certainty of unrolling an artfully wound skein—isn't that the joy of all productivity, at least in prose? And under the influence of hashish, we are enraptured prose-beings raised to the highest power.

A deeply submerged feeling of happiness that came over me afterward, on a square off the Cannebière where the rue Paradis opens onto a park, is more difficult to recall than everything that went before. Fortunately I find in my newspaper the sentence, "One should scoop sameness from reality with a spoon." Several weeks earlier I had noted another, by Johannes V. Jensen,[1] which appeared to say something similar: "Richard was a young man with understanding for everything in the world that was of the same kind." This sentence had pleased me very much. It enabled me now to bring the political, rational sense it had had for me earlier into juxtaposition with the individual, magical meaning of my experience the day before. Whereas Jensen's sentence amounted (as I had understood it) to saying that things are, as we know them to be, thoroughly mechanized and rationalized, since the particular is confined today solely to nuances, my new insight was entirely different. For I saw only nuances, yet these were the same. I immersed myself in contemplation of the sidewalk before me, which, through a kind of unguent with which I glided over it, could have been—precisely like these very stones—also the sidewalk of Paris. One often speaks of stones instead of bread. These stones were the bread of my imagination, which was suddenly seized by a ravenous hunger to taste what is the same in all places and countries. Yet I thought with immense pride of sitting here in Marseilles in a hashish trance; of who else might be sharing my intoxication this evening, and of how few actually were. Of how I was incapable of fearing future misfortune, future solitude, for hashish would always remain. The music from a nearby nightclub that I had been following played a part in this stage. G. rode past me in a cab. It happened suddenly, exactly as, earlier, from the shadows of the boat, U. had suddenly detached himself in the form of a harbor loafer and pimp. But there were not only known faces. Here, while I was in the state of deepest trance, two figures (citizens, vagrants, what do I know?) passed me as "Dante and Petrarch." "All men are brothers." So began a train of thought that I am no longer able to pursue. But its last link was certainly much less banal than its first, and led on perhaps to images of animals.

"Barnabe," read the sign on a streetcar that stopped briefly at the square where I was sitting. And the sad confused story of Barnabas seemed to me no bad destination for a streetcar going into the outskirts of Marseilles.[2]

Something very beautiful was going on around the door of the dance hall. Now and then a Chinese man in blue silk trousers and a glowing pink silk jacket stepped outside. He was the doorman. Girls displayed themselves in the doorway. My mood was free of all desire. It was amusing to see a young man with a girl in a white dress coming toward me, and to be immediately obliged to think: "She got away from him in there in her shift, and now he is fetching her back. Well, well." I felt flattered by the thought of sitting here in a center of dissipation, and by "here" I meant not the town but the little, not-very-eventful spot where I found myself. But events took place in such a way that the appearance of things touched me with a magic wand, and I sank into a dream of them. At such hours, people and things behave like those little stage sets and figurines made of elder pith in the glazed tin-foil box, which, when the glass is rubbed, become electrically charged and fall at every movement into the most unusual relationships.

The music, which meanwhile kept rising and falling, I called the "rush switches of jazz." I have forgotten on what grounds I permitted myself to mark the beat with my foot. This is against my education, and it did not happen without inner disputation. There were times when the intensity of acoustic impressions blotted out all others. In the little bar, above all, everything was suddenly submerged in the noise of voices, not of streets. What was most peculiar about this din of voices was that it sounded entirely like dialect. The people of Marseilles suddenly did not speak good enough French for me. They were stuck at the level of dialect. The phenomenon of alienation that may be involved in this—which Kraus has formulated in the fine dictum, "The more closely you look at a word, the more distantly it looks back"—appears to extend to the optical.[3] At any rate, I find among my notes the surprised comment: "How things withstand the gaze!"

The trance abated when I crossed the Cannebière and at last turned the corner to have a final ice cream at the little Café des Cours Belsunce. It was not far from the first café of the evening, in which, suddenly, the amorous joy dispensed by the contemplation of some fringes blown by the wind had convinced me that the hashish had begun its work. And when I recall this state, I would like to believe that hashish persuades nature to permit us—for less egoistic purposes—that squandering of our own existence that we know in love. For if, when we love, our existence runs through Nature's fingers like golden coins that she cannot hold and lets fall so that they can thus purchase new birth, she now throws us, without hoping or expecting anything, in ample handfuls toward existence.

Published in the *Frankfurter Zeitung,* December 1932. *Gesammelte Schriften,* IV, 409–416. Translated by Edmund Jephcott.

Notes

1. Johannes Vilhelm Jensen (1873–1950) was a Danish novelist, poet, and essayist. He received the Nobel Prize for Literature in 1944.
2. The story of Barnabas is told in the New Testament (Acts 15).
3. Karl Kraus (1874–1936) was an Austrian journalist, critic, playwright, and poet. See the essays on Kraus in this volume.

The Eve of Departure

The economy on the island is archaic.[1] They do not mow, but cut the grain with sickles. In some places the women pull it up with their hands, so there is no stubble left. When it is harvested, the corn is brought to the threshing floor, where a horse, urged on by a farmer who stands in the middle of the floor holding the reins, separates with trudging hooves the grain from the ears. Sixty years ago bread was unknown here; the staple food was maize. And even today the fields are irrigated using an old-fashioned method: bucket wheels drawn by mules. There are only a few cows on the island. Some say because of the absence of fodder; but Don Rosello, the deputy and wine merchant, who represents progress here, blames it on the backwardness of the inhabitants. Not so long ago, a new arrival in Ibiza could learn from the first inhabitant he met: "Now we have so-and-so-many foreigners on the island." From that time dates the following story, which was told at Don Rosello's table:

"A stranger who had spent several months on the island, during which time he had gained the friendship and trust of the inhabitants, saw the last day of his stay arrive. It happened to be a very hot day, and, having finished his travel preparations, he decided to banish his worries about his possessions as quickly as possible so that he could spend a couple of hours enjoying the shade on the terrace of an Ibizan wine merchant. The people on the boat promised to look after his luggage as well as his jacket, and, noticeably lighter, he went off to the *tienda* [store] belonging to the wine merchant, who welcomed him heartily even though he was only in his shirtsleeves. He effortlessly knocked back the first few *copitas* [mugs] of the local white wine. But the more time passed and the more he drank, the harder he found it to take his leave, especially in such an unfestive manner. Questions occurred to him. He wanted to know about the history of the beautiful Galgos, the descendants of the dogs of the Pharaohs that roam the island without a master; about the old customs of courtship and abduction, about which he could never obtain any precise information; about the origins of those curious names that the fishermen used for the mountains—names quite different from those used by the farmers. Soon he recollected that he had once heard the owner of this little *tienda* described as an authority on the island's history. He thought he would like to clear up a few matters at the last moment, and in this way could perhaps get over the loneliness of his last evening. He ordered a bottle of the best wine, and even as his host uncorked it before his eyes, they were already deep in conversation. Now, in the past weeks the stranger had had ample opportunity to become acquainted with the fanatical hospitality of the islanders. He knew that if he wished to have the honor of inviting them, this had to be properly prepared and made into a quasi-legal stipulation. Accordingly, his first task was to invite his host to be his guest. He insisted on this during the second bottle and the third, all the more since it meant he could take brief notes about this or that piece of information with a good conscience. And as he leafed through his notebook by the light of the candle, he came across sketches (he was something of a draftsman) that he had made in the first few days after his arrival. There was the blind man with the red leg of goat or mutton who always walked around the streets led by a boy; on another page were the living profiles of the walls that had been built without any reference to standard measurements; then came the tiled steps with the mysterious numbers that he had seen at the very beginning when he was looking for a place to live. His host looked on with interest over his shoulder. Of course, he knew the story of the leg of mutton; he had himself been responsible for helping the blind man obtain permission to run a meagre little lottery and give out tickets whose only prize was this same leg of mutton. And he had himself seen the mysteriously numbered tiles on a street in which they had served as the house numbers. Even more, he knew the meaning of the white crosses that stood at the foot of a number of houses and that were so puzzling to outsiders. They were a kind of altar of rest. Each marked one of the places where the processions suddenly paused in their progress through the streets. And now the visitor suddenly remembered vaguely that he had come across something similar in Westphalian villages. During the conversation, the weather had turned cool; his host would not be denied and insisted on lending him one of his own jackets. The last bottle was opened.—But to return to those notes by the stranger: Where can you find in Stendhal's Italian tales a motif that could compete with this one from Ibiza?[2] The marriageable girl, surrounded by suitors on holiday, while her father sets strict limits to the time the suitors can have to plead their cause:

an hour, an hour and a half at most, even if there are thirty of them or more, so that each one must compress what he has to say into a few brief minutes.—A good half of the bottle still awaited them, when they were interrupted by a siren. It was the *Ciudad de Mahon* lying out at the breakwater, ten minutes away, ready to depart and with the stranger's luggage on board. Above the roofs you could see its top light piercing the darkness. Even his host could perceive that there wasn't much time left for compliments, so he handed his guest the bill without much resistance, in accord with their agreement. The visitor, however, felt a sudden panic even before glancing down at the bill. His money was gone. He cast a swift glance at his host. The latter's honest face was filled with consternation. It was inconceivable that he could have the envelope with the banknotes. With the most courteous expressions of concern, he asked the stranger not to take the matter to heart. He maintained that he had felt uncomfortable at being the stranger's guest in his own house. And as for the money, it would undoubtedly turn out to have been in his jacket on board the boat. The stranger, however, was only partly consoled by this. The banknotes he was missing were not small, and they were quite numerous. Once he was on board, his worst fears were confirmed. His jacket pockets were empty, and he now knew what to think of the celebrated honesty of the island's people. Faced with the choice of suspecting the steward or the wine merchant, he spent a sleepless night in his cabin before deciding on the steward. But he was wrong. It was the wine merchant who had his money. Scarcely had he arrived back home than he received proof of this in the form of the following telegram: 'Money found in jacket you borrowed from me. Payment on its way.'"

"As for the telegram," Don Rosello said, having listened with an obliging smile, "it must have been the first he'd ever sent."—"And what difference does that make?"—"I know what point you want to make," he replied. "You want to make me believe in the innocence of the inhabitants. In the Golden Age. Rousseauesque platitudes. Seven years ago the prison in an old Moorish castle was opened up, and has in fact not been needed since. But do you know why? I'll tell you in the words of the old warder, whom we had to dismiss at the time: 'Our people—they've all seen so much of the world nowadays. They've learned to distinguish between good and evil.' World travel promotes morality. That's the entire secret."

Written ca. 1932; unpublished in Benjamin's lifetime. *Gesammelte Schriften*, IV, 745–748. Translated by Rodney Livingstone.

Notes

1. An earlier version of this story appears in the autobiographical essay "Spain, 1932," in this volume.
2. Stendhal based his *Chroniques italiennes* on unpublished accounts of crimes of passion and grim executions set in the Renaissance—accounts that he discovered in Rome during his consulate in the nearby port of Civitavecchia.

On Astrology

An attempt to procure a view of astrology from which the doctrine of magical "influences," of "radiant energies," and so on has been excluded. Such an attempt may be provisional, if you like. It is very important because it would purify the aura surrounding these investigations. And we necessarily come across such research if we inquire into the historical origins of the concepts of a scientific humanism. Nowhere more pervasively, perhaps, than in astrology. I have shown the intensity it conferred on the concept of melancholy. Something along these lines could be adduced for many other concepts.

The approach looks like this: We start with "similarity." We then try to obtain clarity about the fact that the resemblances we can perceive, for example, in people's faces, in buildings and plant forms, in certain cloud formations and skin diseases, are nothing more than tiny prospects from a cosmos of similarity. We can go beyond this and attempt to clarify for ourselves the fact that not only are these resemblances imported into things by virtue of chance comparisons on our part, but that all of them—like the resemblances between parents and children—are the effects of an active, mimetic force working expressly inside things. Furthermore, not only are the objects of this mimetic force innumerable, but the same thing may be said of subjects, of the mimetic centers that may be numerous within every being. On top of all this, it must be remembered that neither the mimetic centers nor their objects, the mimetic objects, can have remained unchanged through time, and that in the course of the centuries both the mimetic force and the mimetic mode of vision may have vanished from certain spheres, perhaps only to surface in others. For example, there can be no doubt that people in Antiquity had a much sharper mimetic sense for physiognomic resemblances than does modern man, who really only recognizes facial similarities, and no longer has much ability to recognize bodily similarities. We may further reflect that in Antiquity, physiognomy was based on animal resemblances.

If these considerations bring us close to astrology, the decisive factor is still lacking. As students of ancient traditions, we have to reckon with the possibility that manifest configurations, mimetic resemblances, may once have existed where today we are no longer in a position even to guess at them. For example, in the constellations of the stars. The horoscope must above all be understood as an originary totality that astrological interpretation merely subjects to analysis. The panorama of the heavenly bodies presents a characteristic unity, and the characters of the individual planets, for example, are recognized only through their function within the constellation. (The word "character" is provisional here. We should really say "essence.") We must reckon with the fact that, in principle, events in the heavens could be imitated by people in former ages, whether as individuals or groups. Indeed, this imitation may be seen as the only authority that gave to astrology the character of experience. Modern man can be touched by a pale shadow of this on southern moonlit nights in which he feels, alive within himself, mimetic forces that he had thought long since dead, while nature, which possesses them all, transforms itself to resemble the moon. Nevertheless, these rare moments furnish no conception of the nascent promises that lay in constellations of the stars.

But if mimetic genius really was a life-determining force in Antiquity, then it is more or less unavoidable that the full possession of this gift, the most consummate expression of cosmic meaning, should be given to the newborn infant, who even today in the early years of his life will evidence the utmost mimetic genius by learning language.

This, then, is the complete prolegomenon of every rational astrology.

Fragment written probably in 1932; unpublished in Benjamin's lifetime. *Gesammelte Schriften*, VI, 192–193. Translated by Rodney Livingstone.

"Try to Ensure That Everything in Life Has a Consequence"

"Try to ensure that everything in life has a consequence."—This is without doubt one of the most detestable of maxims, one that you would not expect to run across in Goethe.[1] It is the imperative of progress in its most dubious form. It is not the case that the consequence leads to what is fruitful in right action, and even less that the consequence is its fruit. On the contrary, bearing fruit is the mark of evil acts. The acts of good people have no "consequence" that could be ascribed (or ascribed exclusively) to them. The fruits of an act are, as is right and proper, internal to it. To enter into the interior of a mode of action is the way to test its fruitfulness. But how to do this?

Fragment written probably in 1932; unpublished in Benjamin's lifetime. *Gesammelte Schriften,* VI, 205–206. Translated by Rodney Livingstone.

Notes

1. The precise source of this quotation is unknown, but there are similar formulations in Goethe. For example: "From this we can see that a man's life is worth something only insofar as it has a consequence." *Sankt-Rochus-Fest zu Bingen,* in J. W. von Goethe, *Gedenkausgabe der Werke, Briefe und Gespräche,* ed. Ernst Beutler (Zurich: Artemis Verlag, 1961–1966), vol. 12, p. 482.

Notes (IV)

I ought to investigate the way in which my concept of origin, as it is developed in the work on *Trauerspiel* and in the Kraus essay, relates to Rosenzweig's concept of revelation.[1]

To have presence of mind means to let oneself go at the moment of danger.

Feeble creativity: he created [*schuf*], but only in that he ousted [*schaffte fort*].

The great majority of intellectuals—particularly in the arts—are in a desperate plight.[2] The problem, however, is not one of character, pride, or inaccessibility. The journalists, novelists, and literati are for the most part ready for every compromise. It is just that they do not realize it. And this is the explanation of their failures. Because they do not know, or want to know, that they are venal, they do not understand that they should separate out those parts of their opinions, experiences, modes of behavior that might be of interest to the market. Instead they make it a point of honor to be wholly themselves on every issue. Because they want to be sold, so to speak, only "in one piece," they are as unsalable as a calf that the butcher will sell to the housewife only as an undivided whole.

The market will accept even the worst goods. But from each provider it will accept only his best.

Two mottos on Brecht:

"Methinks that was your good angel who inspired you to treat the drama in more epic fashion." Hölderlin, *Sämtliche Werke* [Complete Works], edited by Norbert von Hellingrath et al., volume 5 (Munich and Leipzig, 1913), p. 316, Letter to Böhlendorff, December 4, 1801.

"When thinking stops, the pointed heads have won, just as surely as they have when crooked thinking starts." Oskar Planer and Camillo Reissmann, *Johann Gottfried Seume* (Leipzig, 1898), p. 538. From the preface to *Mein Sommer 1805* [My Summer of 1805].[3]

As long as there is a single beggar, there will still be myth.

Fragment written 1931–1932 or later; unpublished in Benjamin's lifetime. *Gesammelte Schriften,* VI, 207–208. Translated by Rodney Livingstone.

Notes

1. See Franz Rosenzweig, *Der Stern der Erlösung* [The Star of Redemption] (Frankfurt: J. Kauffmann, 1921).
2. See also "Venal but Unusable" (1934), in this volume.
3. Benjamin is alluding to Brecht's play *Rundköpfe und Spitzköpfe* (Roundheads and Squareheads).

Thought Figures, 1933

The Lamp

"In this way the marks on the bottom of a pewter plate tell the story of all the meals it has been used for. In the same way, the form of every piece of land—the shape of its sand dunes and rocks—contains in natural script the history of the earth; every rounded pebble that the ocean casts on the shore could tell that story to a soul that is chained to it, as our soul is chained to our brain." Said to be found in Lichtenberg, *Schriften* [Writings], volume 1, p. 223.[1]

What is certain is that childhood chains us to things in this way; indeed, it may be that in childhood we wander through the world of things like the stations of a journey of whose extent we can form no conception. Couldn't it be the case that childhood makes a start with the most remote things? At first, at the moment of birth, it makes itself similar to the most distant things in the deepest, most unconscious stratum of its own existence, so as subsequently to enable the objects of the world around to accrete, layer by layer. Hence, what education and human influence do is only one factor in a field of many active forces—forces the child responds to with that gift of mimesis which was the natural heritage of mankind in its early stages and which continues to function nowadays only in children. The gift we possess for seeing similarity is nothing but a feeble vestige of the formerly powerful compulsion to be similar and to behave mimetically. And the now-vanished ability to become similar reached far beyond the narrow world of perception in which we are still able to perceive similarity. Millennia ago, the effect of the stars on a man's life at the moment of his birth was woven into his life, on the basis of the similarity by virtue of which the spirits and forces of life were shaped in accordance with a model that was inscribed in the cosmos.

It is possible, or even probable, that the formative powers familiar to recent generations are no longer able to extend their influence so far. And am I mistaken when I maintain that they have formed in me the image of chairs, stairwells, cupboards, net curtains, and even a lamp—objects that surrounded me in my childhood?

Thus, we must reckon with the fact that, basically, even events in the sky could be imitated by people in former times. Modern man can be touched by a pale shadow of this when he looks through a mask, or when, on southern moonlit nights, he feels mimetic forces alive in himself that he had thought long since dead, while nature, which possesses them all, transforms itself to resemble the moon. But he is transported into this very force field by his memories of childhood.

Here the lamp is fixed in position. Yet it was portable. And unlike our lighting systems, with their cables, cords, and electrical contacts, you could carry it through the entire apartment, accompanied always by the clatter of the tube in its casing and the glass globe on its metal ring—a clinking that is part of the dark music of the surf which slumbers in the laborious toil of the century. When I bring the lamp close to my ear, I do not hear the noise of field artillery, or the sounds of Offenbach's gala music, or factory sirens.[2]

Now the nineteenth century is empty. It lies there like a large, dead, cold seashell. I pick it up and hold it up to my ear. What do I hear? I do not hear the noise of field artillery or of Offenbach's gala music; nor do I hear the howling of factory sirens or the cry that goes up at midday on the stock exchange—not even the din of soldiers on parade or the long-drawn-out whistle of a train. I can of course imagine all these things. But what I hear when I put the shell up to my ear is something else: it is the rattling noise of the anthracite that is emptied from the coal scuttle into the furnace; it is the dull pop with which the flame lights up the gas mantle; it is the jangling of my mother's keys in her basket, the clatter of the tube in its casing, the clink of the glass globe on its metal ring when the lamp is carried from one room to another.

Has this lamp ever been lit? The little cap I see on top of the tube leads me to believe it has. For it was intended as a safety device that would protect the room from soot when it smoked. I undoubtedly had greater pleasure painting it than anything else. For I had intended it as a present for my grandmother on Christmas or on her birthday—long before it occurred to me to use it as a model. I had sown some brightly colored wool onto the upper section, and had then glued it onto cardboard. But just because it was a present it may have been put in a place of honor instead of having to suffer the indignity of being used. Thus, the picture reveals as little about the place the lamp stood as about the use to which it was put or which it was spared. And undoubtedly the light that was able to penetrate the globe of molded glass, with its blazing ornaments, must have been feeble and dim at best.

The hunting scenes depicted on this lamp, and on cake tins; birds on branches, with the golden orb of the sun—bisque, cloisonné, marquetry.

The gift we possess for seeing similarity is nothing but a feeble vestige of the formerly powerful compulsion to become similar and to behave mimetically. Even our parents still practiced it on us. Nowhere more painfully than at the photographer's. There we would stand, wearing a loden jacket, in front of a screen depicting an Alpine scene; and our right hand, which holding a little hat made of chamois leather, cast a shadow on the clouds and the snowfields depicted on the backdrop. Of this, nothing has remained. For the forced smile with which the little alpinist gazes out at us no longer concerns us. Unlike the other gaze—the one that falls on us from the earnest face in the shadow of the potted palm. I stand there bareheaded; in my hand, a large straw hat that I am holding nonchalantly, with carefully rehearsed gracefulness. My elbow leans anxiously on the edge of the little mahogany table. Behind me, but at a great distance, next to the heavy curtain covering the door, stands my mother, her narrow waist in a tight-fitting dress that matches my jacket, which is embroidered with naval emblems.

For this was the torture: we had to display ourselves, even though nothing lay further from our wishes. Thus, we made ourselves more like the embroidered cushion that someone had pushed toward us, or the ball we had been given to hold, than like a moment from our real lives.

Fragment written in early 1933; unpublished in Benjamin's lifetime. *Gesammelte Schriften*, VII, 792–794. Translated by Rodney Livingstone.

Notes

1. This text represents a transitional formulation of Benjamin's late mimetic theory of language; it was sketched during the final stages of the writing of "Berliner Kindheit um Neunzehnhundert" (Berlin Childhood around 1900; to appear in Volume 3 of this edition) and stands as a preliminary version of many of the ideas set down in "Doctrine of the Similar" (included in this volume). Georg Christoph Lichtenberg (1742–1799), German author and experimental psychologist, was a feared satirist in his time. Yet he is best-remembered today as the first great German aphorist. More than 1,500 pages of his notes were published posthumously; alongside jokes, linguistic paradoxes, puns, metaphors, and excerpts from other writers, they contain thousands of memorable aphorisms.
2. Jacques Offenbach (1819–1880), French composer, created the light comic opera we know as the operetta.

Doctrine of the Similar

Insight into the realms of the "similar" is of fundamental significance for the illumination of major sectors of occult knowledge. Such insight, however, is gained less by demonstrating found similarities than by replicating the processes which generate such similarities. Nature produces similarities—one need only think of mimicry. The very greatest capacity for the generation of similarities, however, belongs to human beings. Indeed, there may be no single one of their higher functions that is not codetermined by the mimetic faculty. This faculty has a history, however, in both the phylogenetic and the ontogenetic sense. As regards the latter, play is to a great extent its school. Children's play is everywhere permeated by mimetic modes of behavior, and its realm is by no means limited to what one person can imitate in another. The child plays at being not only a shopkeeper or teacher but also a windmill and a train. The question on which this turns, however, is the following: What advantage does this schooling in mimetic conduct bring to a human being?

The answer presupposes pointed thinking about the phylogenetic significance of mimetic conduct. To determine this, it is not enough to think, for example, of what we understand today by the concept of similarity. As is known, the sphere of life that formerly seemed to be governed by the law of similarity was much larger. This sphere was the microcosm and the macrocosm, to name only one version of many that the experience of similarity found over the course of history. It can still be claimed of our contemporaries that the cases in which they consciously perceive similarities in everyday life make up a tiny proportion of those numberless cases unconsciously determined by similarity. The similarities perceived consciously—for instance, in faces—are, compared to the countless similarities perceived unconsciously or not at all, like the enormous underwater mass of an iceberg in comparison to the small tip one sees rising out of the water.

These natural correspondences assume decisive importance, however, only in light of the consideration that they are all, fundamentally, stimulants and awakeners of the mimetic faculty which answers them in man. It must be borne in mind that neither mimetic powers nor mimetic objects have remained unchanged over time; and that, in the course of centuries, the mimetic power, and with it the gift of mimetic perception, have disappeared from certain fields—perhaps in order to flow into others. The supposition may not be too bold that, on the whole, a unified direction is perceptible in the historical development of this mimetic faculty.

This direction could, at first sight, lie solely in the increasing fragility of this mimetic faculty. For clearly the perceptual world [*Merkwelt*] of modern human beings seems to contain far fewer of those magical correspondences than did that of the ancients or even that of primitive peoples. The question is simply: Are we dealing with a dying out of the mimetic faculty, or rather perhaps with a transformation that has taken place within it? Of the direction in which the latter might lie, some indications could be derived, even if indirectly, from astrology. As researchers into old traditions, we must take account of the possibility that sensuous shape-giving took place—meaning that objects had a mimetic character—where we are today no longer capable even of suspecting it. For example, in the constellations of the stars.

In order to grasp this, we must above all understand the horoscope as an originary totality which astronomical interpretation merely analyzes. (The state of the stars represents a characteristic unity, and the character of the individual planets can be recognized only by the way they function in relation to this state of the stars.) We must assume in principle that processes in the sky were imitable, both collectively and individually, by people who lived in earlier times; indeed, that this imitability contained instructions for mastering an already present similarity. In this imitability by humans, or, as the case may be, in this mimetic faculty that humans have, we must discern what is for the time being the basis for astrology's experiential character. If, however, mimetic genius was really a life-determining force for the ancients, then we have little choice but to attribute full possession of this gift, and in particular its perfect adaptation to the form of cosmic being, to the newborn.

The moment of birth, which is decisive here, is but an instant. This directs our attention to another peculiarity in the realm of similarity. The perception of similarity is in every case bound to a flashing up. It flits past, can possibly be won again, but cannot really be held fast as can other perceptions. It offers itself to the eye as fleetingly and transitorily as a constellation of stars. The perception of similarities thus seems to be bound to a moment in time. It is like the addition of a third element—the astrologer—to the conjunction of two stars; it must be grasped in an instant. Otherwise the astrologer is cheated of his reward, despite the sharpness of his observational tools.

The reference to astrology may already suffice to make comprehensible the concept of a nonsensuous similarity. This concept is, obviously enough, a relative one: it indicates that we no longer possess in our perception whatever once made it possible to speak of a similarity which might exist between a constellation of stars and a human. Yet we, too, possess a canon, on whose basis we can attain more clarity regarding the obscurity which clings to the concept of nonsensuous similarity. And that canon is language.

From time immemorial, the mimetic faculty has been conceded some influence on language. But this was done without foundation—without serious consideration of a further meaning, still less a history, of the mimetic faculty. Above all, such considerations remained closely tied to the common-place (sensuous) realm of similarity. All the same, imitative behavior in language formation was acknowledged as an onomatopoetic element. Now, if language, as is evident, is not an agreed-upon system of signs, we will be constantly obliged to have recourse to the kind of thoughts that appear in their rawest, most primitive form as the onomatopoetic mode of explanation. The question is whether this can be developed and accommodated to an improved understanding.

In other words, the question is whether one can establish an underlying meaning for Rudolf Leonhard's assertion in his instructive work, *Das Wort* [The Word]: "Every word—indeed, the whole language—is onomatopoetic." The key which finally makes this thesis fully transparent lies concealed in the concept of a nonsensuous similarity. For if words meaning the same thing in different languages are arranged about that signified as their center, we have to inquire how they all—while often possessing not the slightest similarity to one another—are similar to the signified at their center. Such an understanding is of course related in the most intimate way to mystical or theological theories of language, without, however, being alien to empirical philology. Yet it is well known that mystical language teachings do not content themselves with drawing the spoken word into the space of their considerations. They certainly also deal likewise with script. And here it is worth noting that script, perhaps even more than certain combinations of sound in language, clarifies—in the relationship of the written form [*Schriftbild*] of words or letters to the signified, or, as the case may be, to the one who gives the name—the nature of nonsensuous similarity. Thus, for instance, the letter *beth* [in Hebrew] is the root for the word meaning "house." It is thus nonsensuous similarity that establishes the ties not only between what is said and what is meant, but also between what is written and what is meant, and equally between the spoken and the written. And every time, it does so in a completely new, original, and underivable way.

The most important of these ties may, however, be the one mentioned last—that between what is written and what is said. For the similarity which reigns here is comparatively the most nonsensuous. It is also the one which takes the longest to be reached. And the attempt to represent the actual essence of this similarity can hardly be undertaken without a glance into the history of its birth, however impenetrable the darkness that is still spread over it today. The most recent graphology has taught us to recognize, in handwriting, images—or, more precisely, picture puzzles—that the unconscious of the writer conceals in his writing. It may be supposed that the mimetic process which expresses itself in this way in the activity of the writer was, in the very distant times in which script originated, of utmost importance for writing. Script has thus become, like language, an archive of nonsensuous similarities, of nonsensuous correspondences.

But this, if you will, magical aspect of language, as well as of script, does not develop in isolation from its other, semiotic aspect. Rather, everything mimetic in language is an intention which can appear at all only in connection with something alien as its basis: precisely the semiotic or communicative element of language. Thus, the literal text of the script is the sole basis on which the picture puzzle can form itself. Thus, the nexus of meaning which resides in the sounds of the sentence is the basis from which something similar can become apparent out of a sound, flashing up in an instant. Since this nonsensuous similarity, however, exerts its effects in all reading, at this deep level access opens to a peculiar ambiguity of the word "reading," in both its profane and magical senses. The schoolboy reads his ABC book, and the astrologer reads the future in the stars. In the first clause, reading is not separated out into its two components. Quite the opposite in the second, though, which clarifies the process at both its levels: the astrologer reads the constellation from the stars in the sky; simultaneously, he reads the future or fate from it.

If, at the dawn of humanity, this reading from stars, entrails, and coincidences was reading per se, and if it provided mediating links to a newer kind of reading, as represented by runes, then one might well assume that this mimetic gift, which was earlier the basis for clairvoyance, very gradually found its way into language and writing in the course of a development over thousands of years, thus creating for itself in language and writing the most perfect archive of nonsensuous similarity. In this way, language is the highest application of the mimetic faculty—a medium into which the earlier perceptual capacity for recognizing the similar had, without residue, entered to such an extent that language now represents the medium in which objects encounter and come into relation with one another. No longer directly, as they once did in the mind of the augur or priest, but in their essences, in their most transient and delicate substances, even in their aromas. In other words: it is to script and language that clairvoyance has, over the course of history, yielded its old powers.

So tempo, that swiftness in reading or writing which can scarcely be separated from this process, would then become, as it were, the effort, or gift, or mind to participate in that measure of time in which similarities flash up fleetingly out of the stream of things only in order to sink down once more. Thus, even profane reading, if it is not to forsake understanding altogether, shares this with magical reading: that it is subject to a necessary tempo, or rather a critical moment, which the reader must not forget at any cost lest he go away empty-handed.

Addendum

Our gift for seeing similarity is nothing but a weak rudiment of the once powerful compulsion to become similar and also to behave mimetically. And the lost faculty of becoming similar extended far beyond the narrow perceptual world in which we are still capable of seeing similarities. What the state of the stars—millennia ago, at the moment of their birth—wrought with one human existence was woven there on the basis of similarity.

Written January–February 1933; unpublished in Benjamin's lifetime. *Gesammelte Schriften,* II, 204–210. Translated by Michael Jennings, on the basis of prior versions by Knut Tarnowski and Edmund Jephcott.

Short Shadows (II)

Secret Signs. A word of Schuler's has been preserved for us.[1] Every piece of knowledge, he said, contains a dash of nonsense, just as in ancient carpet patterns or ornamental friezes it was always possible to find somewhere or other a minute deviation from the regular pattern. In other words, what is decisive is not the progression from one piece of knowledge to the next, but the leap implicit in any one piece of knowledge. This is the inconspicuous mark of authenticity which distinguishes it from every kind of standard product that has been mass produced.

A Saying of Casanova's. "She knew," Casanova says of a procuress, "that I would not have the strength to leave without giving her something." A strange statement. What strength was needed to cheat the procuress of her reward? Or, more precisely, what is the weakness on which she can always rely? It is shame. The procuress is venal—in contrast to the customer employing her services, who is ashamed. Filled with shame, he seeks a hiding place and finds one in the most hidden place of all: in money. Insolence throws the first coin down on the table. Shame follows it up with a hundred, in order to cloak it.

The Tree and Language. I climbed up an embankment and lay down under a tree. The tree was a poplar or an alder. Why have I not remembered which? Because while I was gazing up into the foliage, following its movements with my eyes, I suddenly found that, within me, language was so gripped by it that momentarily the age-old marriage with the tree was suddenly reenacted once again in my presence. The branches and the treetop swayed to and fro reflectively, or leaned over in rejection; the twigs bent down toward me or leaped upward; the foliage braced itself against a sharp gust of wind, shuddered, or met it halfway; the trunk was firmly planted in the solid ground; and one leaf cast its shadow over another. A gentle breeze signaled the start of a wedding and soon carried throughout the world the children who had quickly sprung from this bed, like an image speech.

Gambling. Gambling, like every other passion, can be recognized by the way in which the spark leaps within the body from one point to the next, imparting movement now to this organ, now to that one, concentrating the whole of existence and delimiting it. It is condensed to the time allowed to the right hand before the ball has fallen into the slot. The hand sweeps over the rows like a plane, spreading the seeds—the chips—into their furrows. The announcing of this time limit is a moment reserved exclusively for the ear, when the ball is poised to go into a whirl and the gambler listens for Lady Luck to tune her bass viols. Gambling addresses itself to all the senses, not excluding the atavistic sense of clairvoyance; hence, the eye has its turn as well. All the numbers wink at it. But because it has utterly forgotten the language of winking, it mainly leads astray those who still rely on it. On the other hand, these are the very people who are most deeply devoted to gambling. For a few moments, the stake that they have now forfeited remains on the table, before their eyes. It is kept there by the rules. Just as a lover is momentarily held by the displeasure of the person he adores. He sees her hand near his; but he will make no move to take it. Gambling has passionate devotees, who love it for its own sake and not for what it brings them. Indeed, if it strips them of everything, they tend to blame themselves: they say, "I played badly." And this love contains its own reward, to the point where they even love their losses because this enables them to demonstrate their capacity for self-sacrifice. The prince de Ligne was just such an irreproachable Knight of Fortune in the years following Napoleon's defeat, when he frequented the Paris clubs and was celebrated for the *sang froid* he displayed in the face of huge losses.[2] Day in, day out, he behaved in the same way. His right hand, which constantly wagered vast stakes on the tables, hung slackly. His left hand, however, was immobile, held horizontally across his right breast beneath his jacket. Later it became known, through his valet, that there were three scars on his chest—the precise imprint of the nails of the three fingers that had lain there so motionlessly.

Distance and Images. I wonder whether enjoyment of the world of images isn't fed by a sullen defiance of knowledge. I gaze out over the landscape. Before me lies the sea, smooth as a mirror in the bay; forests extend up to the hilltop—an immobile, silent mass; to one side, ruined castle walls lie there as they have for centuries; the sky is cloudless, a heavenly blue. This is what the dreamer wants to see. The fact that the ocean rises and falls in thousands and thousands of waves every moment; that the forests tremble anew at every instant, from their roots to the very last leaf; that in the stones of the castle ruins there is a constant crumbling and crashing; that, in the sky, gases surge invisibly to and fro in conflict with each other, and then condense into clouds—all this he must forget, so he can surrender to the images. These will give him peace, eternity. Every bird's wing that brushes past, every gust of wind that makes him shiver, everything he sees from up close gives the lie to his dreams. But every view from a distance rebuilds them again. They spring to life at every bank of clouds, at every lighted window. And the dream appears at its most perfect when he succeeds in removing the sting from movement itself—in translating the gust of wind into a rustling, and the flitting and darting of the birds above his head into a migratory flock. To command nature herself to stand still in this way in the name of faded images is the dreamer's delight. But to utter a call that will freeze it anew is the gift of poets.

To Live without Leaving Traces.[3] If you enter a bourgeois room of the 1880s, for all the coziness it radiates, the strongest impression you receive may well be, "You've got no business here." And in fact you have no business in that room, for there is no spot on which the owner has not left his mark—the ornaments on the mantlepiece, the monogrammed antimacassars on the armchairs, the transparencies in the windows, the screen in front of the fire. A neat phrase by Brecht helps us out here: "Erase the traces!" is the refrain in the first poem of his *Lesebuch für Städtebewohner* [Reader for City-Dwellers].[4] Here in the bourgeois room, the opposite behavior became the norm. And conversely, the *intérieur* forces the inhabitant to adopt the greatest possible number of habits. They are assembled in the image of the "furnished gentleman" as imagined by landladies. Living in these plush compartments was nothing more than leaving traces made by habits. Even the rage expressed when the least little thing broke was perhaps merely the reaction of a person who felt that someone had obliterated "the traces of his days on earth."[5] The traces that he had left in cushions and armchairs, that his relatives had left in photos, and that his possessions had left in linings and étuis and that sometimes made these rooms look as overcrowded as halls full of funerary urns. This is what has now been achieved by the new architects, with their glass and steel: they have created rooms in which it is hard to leave traces. "It follows from the foregoing," Scheerbart declared a good twenty years ago, "that we can surely talk about a 'culture of glass.' The new glass-milieu will transform humanity utterly.

And now it remains only to be wished that the new glass-culture will not encounter too many enemies."

Short Shadows. Toward noon, shadows are no more than the sharp, black edges at the feet of things, preparing to retreat silently, unnoticed, into their burrow, into their secret. Then, in its compressed, cowering fullness, comes the hour of Zarathustra—the thinker in "the noon of life," in "the summer garden." For it is knowledge that gives objects their sharpest outline, like the sun at its zenith.

Published in the *Kölnische Zeitung,* February 1933. *Gesammelte Schriften,* IV, 425–428. Translated by Rodney Livingstone.

Notes

1. Alfred Schuler (1865–1923) was a member of the George circle. He was a believer in ritual magical cults, through which he sought to establish communion with the dead. George broke with him in 1903 because of the "muddiness" and eccentricity of his thinking.
2. Charles-Joseph, prince de Ligne (1735–1814), Belgian military officer, diplomat, and man of letters, was a favorite at many European courts. His memoirs and his correspondence with figures such as Rousseau and Voltaire established him as an important literary voice in Belgium.
3. See also "Experience and Poverty" (1933), in this volume.
4. Brecht's text was published in Berlin in 1926–1927.
5. J. W. von Goethe, *Faust, Part II,* line 11,583: "The trace of my days on earth cannot perish in eons."

Kierkegaard

The End of Philosophical Idealism

The last attempt to take over or develop Kierkegaard's intellectual world in toto was that of Karl Barth's "dialectical theology."[1] At their outer limits the waves of this theological movement make contact with the concentric circles set in motion by Heidegger's existentialist philosophy. The present work—Theodor Wiesengrund Adorno's *Kierkegaard*[2]—approaches the subject from quite a different angle. Here Kierkegaard is taken not forward but back—back into the inner core of philosophical idealism, within whose enchanted circle the ultimately theological nature of his thought remained doomed to impotence.

Wiesengrund's approach can be called historical. But in its execution he shows how his cautious method actually springs from highly topical interests. It leads to a critique of German idealism, which he decodes from the point of view of its later developments. For Kierkegaard is a latecomer. Wiesengrund gives an illuminating description of the hybrid nature of his writings, and shows that his works are frequently the bastard offspring of poetry and knowledge. In so doing, he sheds light on the hidden elements of idealism that are still at work in them. For in the aesthetic idealism of Romanticism, the mythic elements of absolute idealism make their appearance. And the logical and historical description of these elements forms the centerpiece of Wiesengrund's account.

The author demonstrates the presence of myth not just in Kierkegaard's existential philosophy, but in "every idealism of Absolute Spirit." Yet nowhere, not even in the later Schelling or Baader,[3] is it given such an original, illuminating formulation, so completely true to its age, as in Kierkegaard. The extremely precise and exhaustive analysis and description of these formulations gives many pages of this study the character of a phantasma-goria. But Wiesengrund's insight and power of expression are never achieved at the cost of critical accuracy—as is so often the case in cultural history. And no cultural history of the nineteenth century will be able to compete with the vividness with which, from the very center of his thinking, Kierkegaard is here linked now with Hegel, now with Wagner, now with Poe, now with Baudelaire. The panorama of the century which Wiesengrund spreads out before us is as broad as his perspective on the past is deep. Pascal and the allegorical Hell of the Baroque are presented here as the vestibule to that cell in which Kierkegaard abandons himself to melancholy and which he shares with Irony, his false mistress.

This world of images whose labyrinths and halls of mirrors contain Kierkegaard's innermost experiences is something he himself considered insignificant, arbitrary, and idiosyncratic. All the arrogant pretensions of his existentialist philosophy rest on his conviction that he had found the realm of "inwardness," of "pure spirituality," which had enabled him to overcome appearance through "decision," through existential resolve—in short, through a religious stance. It is at this juncture that Wiesengrund's penetrat-ing analysis of the concept of existence turns him into an incorruptible critic of Kierkegaard. He unmasks the "fraudulent theology of an existence based on paradox." In his view, "Kierkegaard's profundity (if we wish to retain this much abused concept) does not consist in his ability to reinstate an absolute, religious primal meaning disguised as idealist forms of thought." Instead, "in the historical decline of idealism" Kierkegaard discerned an underlying mythic content, which he declared "its primal meaning and at the same time its historical truth."

In this way, Kierkegaard's inward spirituality is assigned a specific place in history and society. Its model is the bourgeois interior, in which historical and mythical elements merge. Wiesengrund, with a sure hand, draws a whole series of fascinating descriptions of such interior spaces from Kierkegaard's writings. In these interiors, Kierkegaard's inwardness proves itself "the historical prison of a primordial humanity." And it is not, as Kierkegaard believed, the "leap" that will liberate mankind from this incar-ceration with the magical power of "paradox." Nowhere does Wiesen-grund's insight go deeper than where he ignores the stereotypes of Kierkegaardian philosophy and where he looks instead for the key to Kierkegaard's thought in its apparently insignificant relics, in its images, similes, and allegories. He discerns the ultimate statement of this philosophy in the image of (a painter's) vanishing in a picture (painted by himself)—an image borrowed from the tradition of Chinese folktales. The self is "some-thing vanishing that is rescued by a process of reduction." This entry into and dissolution in [*Eingehen in*] the image is not redemption but consola-tion—the consolation whose source is the imagination, "which is the organ by means of which the seamless transition from the mythic-historical into reconciliation can be effected."

This book contains much in a small space. The author's subsequent writings may someday emerge from it. It is, in any case, one of those rare first books in which inspiration manifests itself in the guise of criticism.

Published in the *Vossische Zeitung*, April 1933. *Gesammelte Schriften*, III, 380–383. Translated by Rodney Livingstone.

Notes

1. Karl Barth (1886–1968), Swiss theologian, was perhaps the most influential theologian of the twentieth century. The turn in Protestant thought that followed from his assertion that God is "wholly other" can still be felt today. His *Letters to the Romans* and monumental *Church Dogmatics* stand out among his many works.
2. Theodor Wiesengrund Adorno, *Kierkegaard: Konstruktion des Ästhetischen* [Kierkegaard: The Construction of the Aesthetic] (Tübingen: J. C. B. Mohr, 1933).
3. Friedrich Wilhelm Joseph von Schelling (1775–1854), German philosopher and educator, lent major impulses to the post-Kantian development of German idealism. His work incorporates mystical and pantheistic elements. Franz Xaver von Baader (1765–1841) was a Roman Catholic layman who became an influential mystical theologian and ecumenicist. Benjamin himself read Baader early in his career.

Stefan George in Retrospect

On a New Study of the Poet

Willi Koch, *Stefan George: Weltbild, Naturbild, Menschenbild* [Stefan George: His Image of the World, Nature, and Man] (Halle/Saale: Max Niemeyer Verlag, 1933), 114 pages.

Stefan George has been silent for years. With the passage of time, we have acquired a new ear for his voice. We recognize it as the voice of a prophet. This does not mean that George foresaw historical developments, and even less that he understood their causes—an ability which distinguishes the politician, not the prophet. Prophecy is a process in the moral world. What the prophet foresees is the wrath of God. This is what George has predicted for the race of "hurriers and gapers" in whose midst he has found himself. The night of the world, whose approach has darkened his days, arrived for him in 1914. And the fact that, in his view, its end has not yet come is indicated in his last collection of poems, in a title that speaks volumes: "Einem jungen Führer im ersten Weltkrieg" [To a Young Leader in the First World War]. New lights and shadows have migrated into his deeply furrowed features. But we do not yet know the aureole with which history will illuminate those features on the day they receive their expression for eternity.

Within this poet, however, there also lives an opponent of the prophet. The more audible the latter's voice becomes, the more the other voice—the reformer's voice—sinks into impotence. George, whose foreknowledge of the catastrophe springs from his strict discipline and innate sense of the powers of darkness, was, as leader and teacher, able to prescribe only feeble rules or courses of action, remote from the realities of life. In his eyes, art was that "Seventh Ring"[1] with which an order that was collapsing on all fronts was to be bound together one more time. This art has indisputably shown itself to be rigorous and valid, the ring well-fitting and precious. But what it binds together was the same order that was concerned to maintain the old powers that be—with far less noble methods than his. This is why George failed to extricate his poetry from the enchanted circle of symbols that—unlike those of Hölderlin—did not come to the surface like springs emerging from the rich soil of a great tradition. In his case, the symbolic work is the most fragile part of his oeuvre. At its core, it is not really different from the array of symbolic ideas and images derived from the church and the nation that were being proclaimed in France by Barrès at the same time that the "circle" was being formed around the Master. George's own array of symbols is defensive in character, often with a note of desperation. This is why the treasure of secret signs in his poetry already has the appearance of being the impoverished, anxiously preserved property of "style."

In his great review of *Der siebente Ring* [The Seventh Ring] in the *Hesperus* annual, Rudolf Borchardt was the first to attempt a general assessment of George's achievement as a poet.[2] And without ascribing to this question more importance than it deserves in the larger context of his work, he did focus attention on a significant number of feeble and failed stanzas. In the twenty-five years that have passed since the publication of the volume, such lapses strike us even more painfully. But basically we are saying the same thing if we note that in George's poems something like the "style" forces itself upon our attention in a way that overwhelms and eclipses the meaning. Poems in which his energy fails him are mainly those in which the style is triumphant. The style is that of Jugendstil—in other words, the style in which the old bourgeoisie disguises the premonition of its own impotence by indulging in poetic flights of fancy on a cosmic scale and abusing the word "youth" as a magic incantation with which to conjure up intoxicated visions of the future. Here, for the first time, and initially only as a program, we find regression migrating from the social sphere into the natural and biological world—a process which has since been increasingly confirmed as a symptom of the crisis. In the mind of the George circle, the biological and cosmic idols merge. This subsequently gives birth to the idea of the mythic ideal, Maximin.[3] Concerning the tortured ornamentation that was typical of the furniture and façades of the day, it has been said that they represented the attempt to translate forms which first made their appearance in modern technology back into the language of the arts and crafts. Jugendstil does in fact involve a great and quite conscious act of regression. What is expressed in its formal idiom is the will to evade imminent developments and the presentiments that rise up to confront it. The same may be said of that "spiritual movement" that aspired to the renewal of human existence without paying heed to politics. It, too, amounted to a retrospective transformation of societal contradictions into those hopeless, tragic tensions and convulsions that are so typical of the life of small conventicles.

Only historical reflection which goes far beyond the framework of literary history can lead to insights into George's figure and work that summoned the "spiritual movement" into life forty years ago. It is indisputable that Koch's study, too, stands well outside that framework. He is nowhere indebted to those dire stereotypes that are so often encountered in literary histories, particularly in their treatment of George. Nevertheless, a historical point of view is quite foreign to this book. It approaches George's work gingerly, fully accepting the "eternal" validity of the meanings that condition it. Yet this is done with such circumspection and methodological conscientiousness as to earn it a place of honor from which it will not easily be ousted.

The method underlying this study is "the analysis of a poetic work that aspires only to explicate the mode of expression, because it believes that it has understood the deeper meaning." And its achievement is an illuminating periodization of George's works, based on the phases—which are of course closely intertwined—in which George's view of the world has developed. The foundation of Koch's discussion is the terrible pervasiveness of chaos in George's deeper experience of nature. Chaos appears as the basic force of history:

> Unlovely, not wholly shapened forces;
> All-hearing time that entered in the book
> every feeble hubbub and every blast of dust,
> But heard not your subterranean stirrings.[4]

Yet this poet heard them from early on. The essence of Koch's account is to trace George's efforts to break the hostile spell—vainly at first with the aid of Christian symbolism, but then with the appearance of Maximin, when he feels that the spell has been lifted and reconciliation has been offered to him as a gift. Following the theological trend of rewriting the objects of religion, Koch classifies George's experience of nature under the concept of "the other." It is not difficult for him to provide some convincing evidence of the gloomy, chthonic elements that originally seemed to the poet to be dominant forces. At the same time, this starting point provides him with a link to problems that call on the latest developments in scholarly knowledge. He takes as his reference point the fact that, particularly since the later Romantic movement, the gaze of many poets has been fixed on opening up the world from its chthonic aspect. "The poetic treatment of this problem is still one for which the groundwork is lacking. The cause lies in the fact that, up to now, literary scholarship has been mainly concerned with formal aesthetics, focusing either on the *Gestalt* as an individual, sociological, or ideological factor, or else on the 'artistic' as an application of language. The factual 'ground' of a literary work, and with it the discipline for scrutinizing it, must always be sought in the religious sphere, which is the source of a writer's ideas, motifs, form, and language." A formulation in which a writer's language appears as the "product" of the religious—whereas in reality it is its medium—sets limits to even the most conscientious research. And the abrupt way in which Koch's study breaks off underlines the fact that the larger their object, the narrower these limits will prove to be. But this cannot detract from the very valuable insights he obtains in the process.

These involve constant variations on the theme of George's struggle with his experience of nature. "George's view that nature is a demonic being," Koch writes, "is rooted in his peasant feeling for the natural world." With these words, the author touches on the factors that might have given him insight into the historical workshop in which George's poetry was created. George is the son of a peasant who regards nature as a superior power "that he can never conquer, from whom he can at most copy a few habits, with which he lives in constant struggle and against which he must defend himself." And even though he is a writer and an inhabitant of big cities, nature is constantly present in his mind, with all its power and terrors. The hand that has ceased to grip the plow is still clenched in rage against nature. In this gesture of irreconcilability, the forces of his origins and those of his later life, far from his roots, meet and mingle. Nature appears to him "depraved—it has arrived at the point of being completely 'de-spiritualized' [*Entgottung*]. For this reason we are living in the 'night of the world,' in which formative forces are 'rigid and exhausted' and can be only feebly perceived." The author is quite right to see a chief source of George's poetic energies in the two famous stanzas from *Der siebente Ring*:

And when the great seamstress in rage
Stands to one side, leans at the lower bourn
In a world-night, rigid and tired, knocks:
So can only one man who always fought

And vanquished her, and never according to her rules,
Press her hand, seize her braid;
So that she compliantly continues her work:
Deifies the body and embodies the god.

But the possibility that this braid of *natura naturans* can be grasped only via the ordering and reordering of human conditions—certainly not through the cult of Maximin—is the insight needed to liberate the critical faculties of the investigator.

For knowledge of every kind, and not just criticism, contains the salt of negation—as Hegel insisted. It is possible to act from a stance of unreserved affirmation, but not to think. Hence, the "approach to his work" that

Eduard Lachmann has just published, under the title *Die ersten Bücher Stefan Georges* [Stefan George's First Books], does not get very far.[5] One cannot compare this book with Koch's valuable study. To a degree remarkable even for writings on George, the book lacks detachment and the ability to evaluate the poet's works as anything but perfect, or even to approach them with any other assumption in mind. The empty ceremonies once performed in verse by a Lothar Treuge, at the altar of the George circle, now turn up in prose at the end of the movement.[6] But this unstinting praise forms a barrier even for the reflective observer. In Koch's study the critical debate about the poetic figure of Maximin, who serves as the guardian angel at the threshold of George's late work, fails to take place. Instead, the author does not hesitate to comment on the Maximin experience as the "kernel of George's *religiosity*": "The history of ideas and the psychological approach must be complemented by a phenomenology of religious consciousness; indeed, everything must be based on this. *For the religious sense of responsibility is the impulse underlying the Maximin myth and is not explicable in psychological and historical terms.*"

Thus, we see once again that during the period dominated by George his great work has drawn to a close without attracting the genuine critic he merits. It approaches the judgment seat of history, almost unrecognizable amid a swarm of disciples, yet without an advocate. But not without witnesses. What manner of people are they? They are found among the young people who lived in those poems. Not among those who have ascended university chairs in the name of their master, nor among those who have used his teachings to strengthen their own positions in the power struggles between political parties, but rather among those who—the best of whom, at any rate—can serve as witnesses before the judgment seat of history because they are dead. The verses that hovered on their lips were not from *Der Stern des Bundes,*[7] and rarely from *Der siebente Ring.* In the priestly science of poetry, as this had been formulated in *Blätter für die Kunst,* they discovered no echo of the voice that had spoken "Das Lied des Zwergen" [The Song of the Dwarf], or the "Die Entführung" [The Abduction]. For these young people, George's poems were a song of consolation. Consolation in distress for which today he is unlikely to have a heart, a song of a kind for which today he is unlikely to have an ear.

"By making a hero of himself and of those who truly understand his work, George has rid the world of the purely aesthetic stance"—or so Koch asserts, ambiguously enough. For at the same time as he eliminated the aesthetic stance, he also eliminated life. The great regression of Jugendstil means that even youth shrinks to the size of a mummy, and its features are those of Eilert Lövborg as much as of Maximin. Both die in beauty.[8] The generation for whom George's most beautiful and perfect poems provided something of a refuge was doomed. The darkness that with the war had gathered above its head only what had long since been brewing in its heart seemed to that generation, as to the poet whose verses fulfilled it, to be the epitome of all the forces of nature. George was by no means the "prophet" [*Künder*] of "instructions," but a minstrel who moved the young as the wind moves the "flowers of the childhood home" that smilingly issue an invitation to the long summer. George was the great poet in the eyes of that generation, and he was so as the perfecter of the decadence whose playfulness he rejected in order to create for death the space it was to claim for itself at this crucial turning point. He stands at the end of an intellectual line that began with Baudelaire. It may well be that this statement once belonged to the history of literature. In the meantime, it has become part of history proper, and comes to claim its due.

Published in the *Frankfurter Zeitung*, July 1933. *Gesammelte Schriften*, III, 392–399. Translated by Rodney Livingstone.

Notes

1. *Der siebente Ring* (The Seventh Ring; 1907) was the title of one of George's collections of poems.
2. *Hesperus: Ein Jahrbuch*, ed. Rudolf Borchardt, Hugo von Hofmannsthal, and Rudolf Alexander Schröder (Leipzig: Insel, 1909). Rudolf Borchardt (1877–1945), a conservative author and essayist, promoted the literary models of classical Antiquity and the Middle Ages.
3. Maximin (pseudonym of Maximilian Kronberger; 1888–1904) was a youth of fifteen whom George regarded as an incarnation of the divine. In *Der siebente Ring*, inspired by Maximin, George celebrated the new youthful elite that would lead to the renewal of civilization.
4. Stefan George, *Der Stern des Bundes* (The Star of the Covenant), in *Werke* (Munich: H. Kupper, 1958), vol. 1, p. 366.
5. Eduard Lachmann, *Die ersten Bücher Stefan Georges: Eine Annäherung an das Werk* (Berlin: G. Bondi, 1933). [Benjamin's note]
6. Lothar Treuge (1877–1920), German poet, was a minor member of the circle around George. His poetry appeared frequently in George's journal, *Blätter für die Kunst*, which appeared from 1892 to 1919.
7. *Der Stern des Bundes* (The Star of the Covenant) was George's volume of poetry published in 1914.
8. Eilert Lövborg was the failed Dionysian poet in Henrik Ibsen's *Hedda Gabler* (1890). He is supposed to die beautifully, "with vine leaves in his hair" (though, in the event, his death by his own hand is rather messier).

Agesilaus Santander (First Version)

When I was born, it occurred to my parents that I might perhaps become a writer.[1] If that happened, it would be a good idea if people did not immediately notice I was a Jew. This is why they gave me two very unusual names, in addition to my first name. I do not wish to reveal them. It is enough to say that forty years ago it would have been very difficult for parents to be more prescient. What they regarded as a remote possibility has come to pass. But the precautions that were supposed to combat fate were nullified by the very person they concerned most. Instead of making the two prophylactic names public with his works, he kept them to himself. He watched over them as the Jews used to watch over the secret name that they gave to each of their children. These children did not learn of it until the day of their maturity. But because this day can come more than once in a lifetime, and perhaps because not every secret name can remain the same and untransformed, its transformation may well become manifest with a new maturity. Thus, it remains the name which gathers all the forces of life unto itself, and by which these forces can be conjured up and protected against outsiders.

But this name is by no means an enrichment of the person who bears it. It deprives him of many things—above all, of the gift of appearing entirely as the person he was before. In the room I was last living in, even before that person had emerged fully armored and accoutered from the old name, he had displayed his image: New Angel.[2] The Kaballah relates that, at every moment, God creates a whole host of new angels, whose only task before they return to the void is to appear before His throne for a moment and sing His praises. Mine had been interrupted in the process; his features had nothing human about them. Aside from that, he has made me pay for having disturbed him at his work. By turning to his advantage the fact that I was born under the sign of Saturn—the planet of slow revolution, the star of hesitation and delay—he sent his feminine aspect after the masculine one reproduced in the picture, and did so by the most circuitous, most fatal detour, even though the two had been such close neighbors.

He may have been unaware that in doing this he brought out the strength of the man against whom he was proceeding. For nothing can overcome my patience. Its pinions resemble those of the angel: they need but a few movements to hold it stationary in the face of the woman whom it is determined to await. But my patience has claws like the angel and razor-sharp pinions, and makes no attempt to pounce on her whom it has sighted. It learns from the angel and sees how he embraces his partner with a glance, but then retreats in a series of spasms, inexorably. He draws the angel after him on that flight into a future from which he has emerged. He hopes for nothing new from that future, other than the gaze of the person to whom he keeps his face turned.

And so, scarcely had I seen you the first time than I returned with you to where I had come from.

Ibiza, August 12, 1933

Written August 1933; unpublished in Benjamin's lifetime. *Gesammelte Schriften,* VI, 520–521. Translated by Rodney Livingstone.

Notes

1. The two autobiographical texts entitled "Agesilaus Santander" have provoked much speculation. There is now general agreement that the title does not refer to the Spartan king Agesilaos II (444–360 B.C.), who is mentioned by Xenophon, Cornelius Nepos, and Plutarch: no parallel between Benjamin and Agesilaos has been discovered. Nor is it now thought to refer to the name of the ferry linking Barcelona and Ibiza. Gershom Scholem has speculated that, if we set aside the extra *i* as an ornamental flourish, the name is an anagram of *Der Engel Satanas,* "Satan's angel."

2. Sometime in the spring of 1921, Benjamin bought a small ink wash drawing by Paul Klee entitled *Angelus Novus,* which was to become his best-known possession (see *Selected Writings,* vol. 1, p. 215). The image plays a role here and, in the last years of his life, was the inspiration for his meditation on the angel of history in "Über den Begriff der Geschichte" (On the Concept of History; 1940).

Agesilaus Santander (Second Version)

When I was born, it occurred to my parents that I might perhaps become a writer.[1] If that happened, it would be a good idea if people did not immediately notice I was a Jew. This is why they gave me two names in addition to my first name—eccentric names which showed neither that a Jew bore them, nor even that they were his first names. Forty years ago, it was impossible for parents to be more prescient. What they regarded as a remote possibility has come to pass. But the precautions that were supposed to combat fate were nullified by the very person they concerned most. Instead of making the names public with his works, he followed the Jewish custom of keeping them secret. Jews tell their children about a secret name only when the children reach maturity. Because this day can come more than once in a lifetime, and perhaps because even the secret name can remain the same and untransformed only for the pious, the man who is not pious may experience its transformation at a stroke with this new manhood. This was my situation. Thus, it remains the name that binds together all the forces of life and that is to be protected against outsiders.

But this name is by no means an enrichment of the person it designates. On the contrary, much of his image falls away when the name is heard. He loses, above all, the gift of appearing human. In the room I occupied in Berlin, even before that person had emerged fully armored and accoutered from my name, he had fixed his image to the wall: New Angel.[2] The Kaballah relates that, at every moment, God creates a whole host of angels, whose only task before they return to the void is to appear before His throne for a moment and sing His praises. The new angel presented himself as such before naming himself. I only fear that I had kept him excessively long from his hymn. Aside from that, he has paid me back. By turning to his advantage the fact that I was born under the sign of Saturn—the planet of the slowest revolution, the star of hesitation and delay—he sent his feminine aspect after the masculine one reproduced in the picture, and did so by the most circuitous, most fatal detour, even though the two had once (while remaining unknown to each other) been such close neighbors.

He may have been unaware that in doing this he brought out the strength of the man against whom he was proceeding—namely, his ability to wait. Whenever this man encountered a woman who held him in thrall, he at once determined to lie in wait for her on her journey through life and to wait until she fell into his hands, ill, aged, and in ragged clothes. In short, nothing could overcome the man's patience. And its pinions resembled those of the angels: they needed but a few movements to hold him stationary in the face of the woman whom he was determined not to abandon.

But the angel resembles everything from which I have had to part: the people, and especially the things. He dwells in the things I no longer possess. He makes them transparent, and behind each of them appears the figure of the person for whom they are intended. This is why no one can surpass me when it comes to giving presents. Indeed, the angel may have been attracted by a person who gives but who goes away empty-handed himself. For he, too, has claws and pointed, razor-sharp pinions, and makes no attempt to fall upon whomever he has his eye on. He looks him steadily in the eye, for a long time, and then retreats—in a series of spasms, but inexorably. Why? To draw him after himself on that road to the future along which he came, and which he knows so well that he can traverse it without turning round and letting him whom he has chosen out of his sight. He wants happiness—that is to say, the conflict in which the rapture of the unique, the new, the yet unborn is combined with that bliss of experiencing something once more, of possessing once again, of having lived. This is why he has nothing new to hope for on any road other than the road home, when he takes a new person with him. Just like myself; for scarcely had I seen you the first time than I returned with you to where I had come from.

Ibiza, August 13, 1933

Written August 1933; unpublished in Benjamin's lifetime. *Gesammelte Schriften*, VI, 521–523. Translated by Rodney Livingstone.

Notes

1. The two autobiographical texts entitled "Agesilaus Santander" have provoked much speculation. There is now general agreement that the title does not refer to the Spartan king Agesilaos II (444–360 B.C., who is mentioned by Xenophon,

Cornelius Nepos, and Plutarch: no parallel between Benjamin and Agesilaos has been discovered. Nor is it now thought to refer to the name of the ferry linking Barcelona and Ibiza. Gershom Scholem has speculated that, if we set aside the extra *i* as an ornamental flourish, the name is an anagram of *Der Engel Satanas,* "Satan's angel."

2. Sometime in the spring of 1921, Benjamin bought a small ink drawing by Paul Klee entitled *Angelus Novus,* which was to become his best-known possession (see *Selected Writings,* vol. 1, p. 215). The image plays a role here and, in the last years of his life, was the inspiration for his meditation on the angel of history in "Über den Begriff der Geschichte" (On the Concept of History; 1940).

Antitheses Concerning Word and Name

Word in the supreme sense[1]

The creative word of God.
Its likeness: the human proper name.
Its residue: mute nature.
Man is not created from the word.
"The more existent and real the mind, the more it is inexpressible and unexpressed." [Vol. 1, pp. 66–67]

Name, or the Adamite spirit of language

"All human language is only the reflection of the word in name. The name is no closer to the word than knowledge is to creation." [Vol. 1, p. 68]
The name is the translation of the mute into sound and of the nameless into the name.
The foundation of the name: communication of matter in its magic community.
"God made things knowable in their names. Man, however, names them according to knowledge." [Vol. 1, p. 68]

The human word

"The name no longer lives in [the *human word*] intact.
It has stepped out of . . . its own immanent magic, in order to become expressly, as it were externally, magic. [Vol. 1, p. 71]

Similarity

"The communication of matter in its magical community takes place through similarity."
Are "to measure" [*ahmen*] and "to have a presentiment" [*ahnen*] related?[2]

The atonement for damaging the name lies in the word of judgment, which is also the root of abstraction.

The character of the name is damaged by that of the sign.

The magic of nature

In the things from which it shines back silently and in the mute magic of nature, God's word has become the communication of matter in magical community.

"Moreover, the communication of things is certainly communal in a way that grasps the world as such as an undivided whole." [Vol. 1, p. 73]

The fleeting appearance of a similarity in sound corresponds to the fleeting appearance of a similarity in the object.

Historically, the fleeting appearance of similarity has the character of an anamnesis—that is to say, of a lost similarity, free from the tendency to become dissipated. This lost similarity, which existed in time, prevails in the Adamite spirit of language. Song holds fast to the image of such a past.

The determinate empirical (albeit nonsensuous) similarity always appears fleetingly in a heterogeneous substratum—namely, in the sign character of the word.

Selection [*herauslesen*]—on the basis of similarity—as the primal form of reading [*lesen*].[3] Runes as a transitional form between treetops, clouds, entrails, on the one hand, and letters, on the other. The magical function of the alphabet: to provide the nonsensuous similarity with the enduring semiotic ground on which it can appear.

The symbol is definable as a sign by means of which no similarity can appear.

Fragment written summer 1933; unpublished in Benjamin's lifetime. *Gesammelte Schriften*, VII, 795–796. Translated by Rodney Livingstone.

Notes

1. This fragment, a preliminary study for the essay "On the Mimetic Faculty," contains Benjamin's comparison of the theory of language he had recently set down in the essay "Doctrine of the Similar" and that formulated in the 1916 essay "On Language as Such and on the Language of Man." References in brackets are to Volume 1 of this edition.

2. *Ahmen*, a rare word meaning "to measure" or "to mark" (as in "to measure a ship's draught") is also the root of the common verb *nachahmen*, "to initiate"

or "to copy." It is etymologically distinct from *ahnen,* "to suspect," "to have a presentiment or foreboding," although the two words are close phonetically.

3. In Latin, reading was a "picking out" or selecting of letters. In contrast to English, German retains this Latin root in the words *lesen* ("to read") and *herauslesen* ("to gather," "to pick out," "to read into").

On the Mimetic Faculty

Nature produces similarities; one need only think of mimicry. The highest capacity for producing similarities, however, is man's. His gift for seeing similarity is nothing but a rudiment of the once powerful compulsion to become similar and to behave mimetically. There is perhaps not a single one of his higher functions in which his mimetic faculty does not play a decisive role.

This faculty has a history, however, in both the phylogenetic and the ontogenetic sense. As regards the latter, play is to a great extent its school. Children's play is everywhere permeated by mimetic modes of behavior, and its realm is by no means limited to what one person can imitate in another. The child plays at being not only a shopkeeper or teacher, but also a windmill and a train. Of what use to him is this schooling of his mimetic faculty?

The answer presupposes an understanding of the phylogenetic significance of the mimetic faculty. Here it is not enough to think of what we understand today by the concept of similarity. As is known, the sphere of life that formerly seemed to be governed by the law of similarity was comprehensive; it ruled both microcosm and macrocosm. But these natural correspondences are given their true importance only if we see that they, one and all, are stimulants and awakeners of the mimetic faculty which answers them in man. It must be borne in mind that neither mimetic powers nor mimetic objects remain the same in the course of thousands of years. Rather, we must suppose that the gift for producing similarities (for example, in dances, whose oldest function this is), and therefore also the gift of recognizing them, have changed in the course of history.

The direction of this change seems determined by the increasing fragility of the mimetic faculty. For clearly the perceptual world [*Merkwelt*] of modern man contains only minimal residues of the magical correspondences and analogies that were familiar to ancient peoples. The question is whether we are concerned with the decay of this faculty or with its transformation. Of the direction in which the latter might lie, some indications may be derived, even if indirectly, from astrology.

We must assume in principle that in the remote past the processes considered imitable included those in the sky. In dance, on other cultic occasions, such imitation could be produced, such similarity dealt with. But if the mimetic genius was really a life-determining force for the ancients, it is not difficult to imagine that the newborn child was thought to be in full possession of this gift, and in particular to be perfectly adapted to the form of cosmic being.

Allusion to the astrological sphere may supply a first reference point for an understanding of the concept of nonsensuous similarity. True, our existence no longer includes what once made it possible to speak of this kind of similarity: above all, the ability to produce it. Nevertheless we, too, possess a canon according to which the meaning of nonsensuous similarity can be at least partly clarified. And this canon is language.

From time immemorial, the mimetic faculty has been conceded some influence on language. Yet this was done without foundation—without consideration of a further meaning, still less a history, of the mimetic faculty. But above all, such considerations remained closely tied to the commonplace, sensuous realm of similarity. All the same, imitative behavior in language formation was acknowledged under the name of onomatopoeia. Now if language, as is evident to the insightful, is not an agreed-upon system of signs, we will, in attempting to approach language, be constantly obliged to have recourse to the kind of thoughts that appear in their most primitive form as the onomatopoeic mode of explanation. The question is whether this can be developed and adapted to improved understanding.

"Every word—and the whole of language," it has been asserted, "is onomatopoeic." It is difficult to conceive in any detail the program that might be implied by this proposition. But the concept of nonsensuous similarity is of some relevance. For if words meaning the same thing in different languages are arranged about that signified as their center, we have to inquire how they all—while often possessing not the slightest similarity to one another—are similar to the signified at their center. Yet this kind of similarity cannot be explained only by the relationships between words meaning the same thing in different languages, just as, in general, our reflections cannot be restricted to the spoken word. They are equally concerned with the written word. And here it is noteworthy that the latter—in some cases perhaps more vividly than the spoken word—illuminates, by the relation of its written form [*Schriftbild*] to the signified, the nature of nonsensuous similarity. In brief, it is nonsensuous similarity that establishes the ties not only between what is said and what is meant but also between what is written and what is meant, and equally between the spoken and the written.

Graphology has taught us to recognize in handwriting images that the unconscious of the writer conceals in it. It may be supposed that the mimetic process which expresses itself in this way in the activity of the writer was, in the very distant times in which script originated, of utmost importance for writing. Script has thus become, like language, an archive of nonsensuous similarities, of nonsensuous correspondences.

But this aspect of language, as well as of script, does not develop in isolation from its other, semiotic aspect. Rather, the mimetic element in language can, like a flame, manifest itself only through a kind of bearer. This bearer is the semiotic element. Thus, the nexus of meaning of words or sentences is the bearer through which, like a flash, similarity appears. For its production by man—like its perception by him—is in many cases, and particularly the most important, tied to its flashing up. It flits past. It is not improbable that the rapidity of writing and reading heightens the fusion of the semiotic and the mimetic in the sphere of language.

"To read what was never written." Such reading is the most ancient: reading prior to all languages, from entrails, the stars, or dances. Later the mediating link of a new kind of reading, of runes and hieroglyphs, came into use. It seems fair to suppose that these were the stages by which the mimetic gift, formerly the foundation of occult practices, gained admittance to writing and language. In this way, language may be seen as the highest level of mimetic behavior and the most complete archive of nonsensuous similarity: a medium into which the earlier powers of mimetic production and comprehension have passed without residue, to the point where they have liquidated those of magic.

Written April–September 1933; unpublished in Benjamin's lifetime. *Gesammelte Schriften*, II, 210–213. Translated by Edmund Jephcott.

Thought Figures

Death of an Old Man

The loss that a much younger person may feel directs his gaze, perhaps for the first time, to the laws that govern the relationship between people who are separated by a great distance in terms of age, but who may nevertheless be linked by bonds of affection. The dead man was a partner with whom the majority of things that concerned you, and the most important ones, could not possibly be discussed. Yet conversation with him had a freshness and a peaceful quality that could never be achieved with someone of the same age. This had two causes. First, any confirmation, however faint or uneffusive, that was forthcoming and that succeeded in bridging the gulf between the generations was far more convincing than confirmation between equals. Second, the younger partner found something that quite disappears later on, when the old have left him and until he himself grows old—namely, a dialogue that is free of calculation of every kind and the need to spare anyone's feelings, because neither has any expectations of the other and neither comes up against any feelings, except one that is rarely encountered: benevolence without admixture of any kind.

The Good Writer

The good writer says no more than he thinks.[1] And much depends on that. For speech is not simply the expression but also the making real of thought. In the same way that running is not just the expression of the desire to reach a goal, but also the realization of that goal. But the kind of realization—

whether it is precisely adapted to the goal, or whether it loosely and wantonly wastes itself on the desire—depends on the training of the person who is running. The more he has himself in hand and avoids superfluous, exaggerated, and uncoordinated movements, the more self-sufficient his position will be and the more economical his use of his body. The bad writer has many ideas which he lets run riot, just like the bad, untrained runner with his slack, overenthusiastic body action. And for that very reason, he can never say soberly just what he thinks. The talent of the good writer is to make use of his style to supply his thought with a spectacle of the kind provided by a well-trained body. He never says more than he has thought. Hence, his writing redounds not to his own benefit, but solely to the benefit of what he wants to say.

Dream

The O——s showed me their house in the Dutch East Indies. The room I found myself in was paneled in dark wood and gave the impression of affluence. But that was nothing, said my guides. What I must admire was the view from the upper story. I thought it must overlook the expanse of sea that was nearby, and so I climbed the stairs. At the top I stood at a window. I looked down. There before my eyes was the very same warm, paneled cozy-looking room I had just left.

Storytelling and Healing

The child is sick. His mother puts him to bed and sits down beside him. And then she begins to tell him stories. How are we to understand this? The answer dawned on me when N. told me about the strange healing powers of his wife's hands. What he said about her hands was this. "Their movements are highly expressive. But it is not possible to describe their expression . . . It is as if they were telling a story." We have learned about the healing powers of storytelling from the Merseburg magic spells.[2] It is not simply that they repeat Wotan's formula;[3] in addition, they explain the situation which led him to use it in the first place. We know, too, that the story a sick man tells the doctor at the start of his treatment can become the first stage in the healing process. And this provokes the question of whether storytelling may not provide the right climate and the most favorable precondition for many a healing—indeed, of whether every illness might be cured if it could only float along the river of narrative—until it reached the mouth. If we reflect that pain is a dam that offers resistance to the current of narrative, it is evident that the dam will be pierced when the gradient is steep enough for everything that crosses its path to be swept into an ocean of blissful oblivion. Stroking marks out a bed for this torrent.

Dream

Berlin. I sat in a coach in the company of two highly dubious girls. Suddenly the sky darkened. "Sodom," said a woman of a certain age in a bonnet who was suddenly in the coach too. In this way, we arrived at a railroad station where the tracks emerged from beyond the station roof. Here a court was in session, the two opposing parties sitting opposite each other on two street corners. I pointed to the outsize bleached moon low down in the sky, as a symbol of justice. Then I was part of a small expedition that was moving down a ramp of the sort you find in freight stations (and I was, and remained, in the precincts of the station). We stopped in front of a narrow rivulet. The rivulet flowed between two rows of porcelain slabs that seemed to be not fixed but floating, and that gave way like buoys under your feet. Whether the second row was really porcelain, I'm not certain. More like glass. At any rate, they were all filled with flowers—like onions in glass jars, only round and brightly colored ones, which gently bumped up against each other in the water, once again like buoys. I stepped into the flowerbed of the furthermost row for a moment. At the same time I could hear the explanations of a little junior official who was showing us the way. In this channel, he was saying, the suicides kill themselves, the poor devils who own nothing more than the flower they hold between their teeth. A light now fell on the flowers. An Acheron,[4] you might think; but in the dream nothing was said about that. As I stepped backward, someone told me where to put my foot on the first slabs. The porcelain at this point was white and full of grooves. Deep in conversation, we made our way out of the depths of the freight station. I drew attention to the strange pattern on the tiles that we were still walking on, and to their usefulness in a film. But no one wanted such projects to be spoken about so openly. Suddenly a boy all in rags came toward us. The others seemed to let him pass without comment, but I searched feverishly in all my pockets. I was looking for a five-mark piece. I could not find it. As he crossed my path—for he did not break his stride—I thrust a smaller coin at him, and awoke.

The "New Community"

I read *Das Friedensfest* [The Peace Festival] and *Einsame Menschen* [Lonely People].[5] People really were uncivilized in that Friedrichshagen milieu.[6] But the fact is that the members of Bruno Wille's and Wilhelm Bölsche's "New Community," which was so much talked about in Gerhart Hauptmann's youth, do indeed seem to have behaved childishly.[7] The modern reader cannot but ask himself whether he belongs to a new race of Spartans—so disciplined is he in comparison. That Johannes Vockerat, whom Hauptmann depicts with such evident sympathy, is certainly a nasty piece of work: bad manners and lack of discretion seem to be the prerequisites of heroism in these plays. In reality, however, the true prerequisite is nothing other than sickness.[8] Here, as in Ibsen, the various illnesses seem to be a cover for the sickness of the turn of the century, the *mal du siècle*. In those half-failed bohemians like Braun and Dr. Scholz, the yearning for freedom is at its most powerful; but on the other hand, it often seems as if it is the intense preoccupation with art, with social questions, and the like that is making them ill. In other words, illness here resembles a social emblem, much like madness among the ancients. Sick people have a special insight into the state of society; their private casting off of inhibitions is converted into an inspired sensitivity to the atmosphere their "contemporaries" breathe. But the form taken by this conversion is "nerves." The nerves are inspired threads; they resemble those fiber-like lines that trailed around furniture and house façades, redolent of unsatisfied rejuvenations and curves full of yearning. Jugendstil [Art Nouveau] liked to dwell on the figure of the Bohemian in the shape of a Daphne pursued by reality and changing into a bundle of nerves, laid bare, plantlike, trembling in the fresh air of the now [*Jetztzeit*].

Pretzel, Feather, Pause, Lament, Clowning

Such unconnected words are the starting point of a game that was very popular during the Biedermeier period.[9] What you had to do was link them up meaningfully, without changing their order. The shorter the sentence and the fewer the intervening clauses, the more the solution was admired. This game produced the most wonderful discoveries, especially among children. To children, words are still like caverns, with the strangest corridors connecting them. Now, however, imagine this game being turned back to front: think of a sentence as if it had been constructed according to these rules. This would, at a stroke, give it a strange, exciting meaning for us. In reality, something of this perspective is contained in every act of reading. It is not just ordinary people who read novels in this way—that is to say, for the names or formulas that leap out of the text at the reader. The educated person, too, is constantly on the lookout for turns of phrase or striking expressions, and the meaning is merely the background on which rests the shadow that they cast, like figures in relief. This is particularly apparent with texts that are regarded as sacred. The commentaries designed to serve such texts fix on particular words, as if they had been chosen according to the rules of the game and assigned to the reader as a task. And in fact the sentences that a child will compose from a group of words during a game really do have more in common with those in sacred texts than with the everyday language of grownups. Here is an example that shows how a child of twelve joined up some prescribed words: "Time sweeps through nature like a pretzel. The feather paints the landscape, and if a pause ensues, it is filled with rain. No lament is heard, for there is no clowning around."

Published in *Die literarische Welt,* November 1933, under the pseudonym Detlef Holz. *Gesammelte Schriften,* IV, 428–433. Translated by Rodney Livingstone.

Notes

1. See also "Little Tricks of the Trade" and "May–June 1931," in this volume.
2. The two Merseburg magic spells *(Zaubersprüche)* date back to the tenth century and are clearly of pre-Christian origin. They consist of a magical imperative formula, preceded by a narrative in which a similar past occurrence is described. The second spell describes the healing of a lame horse.
3. Wotan, the sovereign god of Germanic myth, was regarded as the divine founder of the Germanic dynasties in England and in Scandinavia. In the Merseburger Zaubersprüche, Wotan figures as the master of the most powerful spells.
4. The Acheron is a river in Epirus, Greece, that was thought in ancient times to go to Hades because it flowed through dark gorges and went underground in several places; an oracle of the dead was located on its banks. In Greek mythology it is a river in Hades, and the name sometimes refers to the Underworld generally.
5. These are plays by Gerhart Hauptmann (1862–1946), German playwright, poet, and novelist who was one of the founders of German Naturalism in Berlin in the 1890s; in 1912 he was awarded the Nobel Prize for Literature. *Das Friedensfest* (The Peace Festival; 1890) is an analysis of the troubled relations within a neurotic family. *Einsame Menschen* (Lonely People; 1891) describes the tragic end of an unhappy intellectual torn between his wife and a young woman with whom he can share his thoughts. For a slightly different version of this passage, see "Diary from August 7, 1931, to the Day of My Death," in this volume.
6. Friedrichshagen lies on the outskirts of Berlin.
7. Bruno Wille (1860–1928), German author, editor, and impresario, founded one of Berlin's most important theaters, the Freie Volksbühne Berlin, in 1901. He also established, with Wilhelm Bölsche (1861–1939), an alternative school called the Freie Hochschule. Bölsche, poet and novelist, was a founder of Berlin Naturalism in the 1890s.
8. Johannes Vockerat is a character in Hauptmann's *Einsame Menschen.* Vockerat is a hypersensitive scholar who suffers under the conservative and Christian ideas of his wife and parents.
9. "Biedermeier" refers to the German provincial style in interior decoration, furniture, and architecture of the first half of the nineteenth century. Originally a pejorative term stressing parochialism and apoliticism, Biedermeier came in the twentieth century to be esteemed for its sober, modest, and dignified qualities.

Little Tricks of the Trade

Good Writing

The good writer says no more than he thinks.[1] And much depends on that. For speech is not simply the expression but also the making real of thought. In the same way that running is not just the expression of the desire to reach a goal, but also the realization of that goal. But the kind of realization, whether it is precisely adapted to the goal, or whether it loosely and wantonly wastes itself on the desire—depends on the training of the person who is running. The more he has himself in hand and avoids superfluous, exaggerated, and uncoordinated movements, the more self-sufficient his position will be and the more economical his use of his body. The bad writer has many ideas which he lets run riot, just like the bad, untrained runner with his slack, overenthusiastic body action. And for that very reason, he can never say soberly just what he thinks. The talent of the good writer is to make use of his style to supply his thought with a spectacle of the kind provided by a well-trained body. He never says more than he has thought. Hence, his writing redounds not to his own benefit, but solely to the benefit of what he wants to say.

Reading Novels

Not all books are to be read in the same way. Novels, for example, are there to be devoured. To read them is a pleasure of consumption [*Einverleibung*]. This is not empathy. The reader does not put himself in the place of the hero; he absorbs what befalls the hero into himself. The vivid report on those events, however, is the enticing form in which a nourishing meal is presented at the table. Now, there is of course a raw, healthy form of experience, just as there is raw, healthy food for the stomach—namely, experiencing something for oneself. But the art of the novel, like the art of cooking, begins where the raw products end. There are many nourishing foodstuffs that are inedible when raw. Just as there are any number of experiences that are better read about than personally undergone. They affect many people so strongly that individuals would not survive them if they were to experience them in the flesh. In short, if there is a Muse of the novel—it would be the tenth—it must bear the features of a kitchen fairy. She raises the world from its raw state in order to produce something edible, something tasty. Read a newspaper while eating, if you must. But never a novel. For that involves two sets of conflicting obligations.

The Art of Storytelling

Every morning brings us news from all over the world.[2] Yet we are poor in remarkable stories. Why is that? It is because no events reach us without being permeated by explanations. In other words, hardly anything redounds to the advantage of the story; nearly everything, to that of information. In fact, half the art of storytelling is that of keeping it free of all explanations during the telling. In this respect the ancients, Herodotus above all, were masters. In Chapter 14 of Book III of his *Histories,* he tells the story of Psammenitus. The Egyptian king Psammenitus had been defeated and taken prisoner by the Persian king Cambyses; Cambyses was bent on humbling his captive. He gave orders to place Psammenitus on the road on which the Persian triumphal procession was to pass. And he further arranged that the prisoner should see his daughter as a serving girl, taking her pitcher to the well. While all the Egyptians stood lamenting and bewailing this spectacle, Psammenitus alone stood silent and motionless, his eyes fixed on the ground. And when soon after he saw his son in the procession, being led to execution, he likewise remained unmoved. But when he saw one of his old servants, an old man, reduced to beggary, in the ranks of the prisoners, he beat his head with his fists and gave every sign of the profoundest grief.— From this story we can see the nature of true storytelling. The value of information does not survive the moment when it was new. It lives only at that moment. It has to surrender to it completely and explain itself to the moment without loss of time. A story is different; it does not expend itself. It preserves its strength concentrated within itself and is capable of releasing it even after a long time. Thus, Montaigne referred to the story of this Egyptian king, and asked himself why the king mourned only when he caught sight of his servant and not before. Montaigne answers: "Since he was already overwhelmed by grief, it took only the smallest addition for the dam to burst." The story can be understood in this way. But there is room for other explanations, too. Anyone can find out what these reasons are by asking Montaigne's question in a circle of friends. For example, one of mine said, "The king is unmoved by the fate of those of royal blood, for it is his own." And another: "We are moved by much on the stage that does not move us in real life. To the king, this servant is only an actor." And a third: "Great suffering builds up and only breaks forth with relaxation. The sight of his servant was the relaxation."—"If this story had taken place today," said a fourth, "all the papers would claim that Psammenitus loved his servant more than his children." What is certain is that every reporter would find an explanation at the drop of a hat. Herodotus offers no explanations. His report is the driest. That is why this story from ancient Egypt is still capable of arousing astonishment and thought even after thousands of years. It resembles the seeds of grain that have lain hermetically sealed in the chambers of the Pyramids for thousands of years, and have retained their power to germinate to this very day.

After Completion

The origin of great works has often been conceptualized in terms of the image of birth. This image is dialectical; it embraces the process from two sides. One is concerned with creative conception and affects the feminine side of genius. This feminine aspect comes to an end with the completion of the work. It sets the work in motion and then it dies. What dies in the master with the finished creation is that part of him in which it was conceived. Now, however—and this is the other side of the coin—the completion of the work is no dead thing. It is not achievable from outside; filing and tinkering does not bring it about. It is perfected in the interior of the work itself. And here, too, we may speak of giving birth. In the act of completion, the created thing gives birth once more to its creator. Not in its feminine aspect, in which it was conceived, but on its masculine side. Ecstatic, the creator overtakes nature, for he will now be indebted to a brighter source for the existence that he received for the first time from the dark depths of the maternal womb. His home is not where he was born; rather, he comes into the world where his home is. He is the masculine firstborn of the work that he had once conceived.

Written 1928–1933; unpublished in Benjamin's lifetime. *Gesammelte Schriften,* IV, 435–438. Translated by Rodney Livingstone.

Notes

1. See also the essay "Thought Figures" (section entitled "The Good Writer") in this volume.
2. See also sections VI and VII of Benjamin's essay "Der Erzähler" (The Storyteller).

Experience and Poverty

Our childhood anthologies used to contain the fable of the old man who, on his deathbed, fooled his sons into believing that there was treasure buried in the vineyard. They would only have to dig. They dug, but found no treasure. When autumn came, however, the vineyard bore fruit like no other in the whole land. They then perceived that their father had passed on a valuable piece of experience: the blessing lies in hard work and not in gold. Such lessons in experience were passed on to us, either as threats or as kindly pieces of advice, all the while we were growing up: "Still wet behind the ears, and he wants to tell us what's what!" "You'll find out [*erfahren*] soon enough!" Moreover, everyone knew precisely what experience was: older people had always passed it on to younger ones. It was handed down in short form to sons and grandsons, with the authority of age, in proverbs; with an often long-winded eloquence, as tales; sometimes as stories from foreign lands, at the fireside.—Where has it all gone? Who still meets people who really know how to tell a story? Where do you still hear words from the dying that last, and that pass from one generation to the next like a precious ring? Who can still call on a proverb when he needs one? And who will even attempt to deal with young people by giving them the benefit of their experience?

No, this much is clear: experience has fallen in value, amid a generation which from 1914 to 1918 had to experience some of the most monstrous events in the history of the world. Perhaps this is less remarkable than it appears. Wasn't it noticed at the time how many people returned from the front in silence? Not richer but poorer in communicable experience? And what poured out from the flood of war books ten years later was anything but the experience that passes from mouth to ear. No, there was nothing remarkable about that. For never has experience been contradicted more thoroughly: strategic experience has been contravened by positional warfare; economic experience, by the inflation; physical experience, by hunger; moral experiences, by the ruling powers. A generation that had gone to school in horse-drawn streetcars now stood in the open air, amid a landscape in which nothing was the same except the clouds and, at its center, in a force field of destructive torrents and explosions, the tiny, fragile human body.

With this tremendous development of technology, a completely new poverty has descended on mankind. And the reverse side of this poverty is the oppressive wealth of ideas that has been spread among people, or rather has swamped them entirely—ideas that have come with the revival of astrology and the wisdom of yoga, Christian Science and chiromancy, vegetarianism and gnosis, scholasticism and spiritualism. For this is not a genuine revival but a galvanization. We need to remind ourselves of Ensor's magnificent paintings,[1] in which the streets of great cities are filled with ghosts; philistines in carnival disguises roll endlessly down the streets, wearing distorted masks covered in flour and cardboard crowns on their heads. These paintings are perhaps nothing so much as the reflection of the ghastly and chaotic renaissance in which so many people have placed their hopes. But here we can see quite clearly that our poverty of experience is just a part of that larger poverty that has once again acquired a face—a face of the same sharpness and precision as that of a beggar in the Middle Ages. For what is the value of all our culture if it is divorced from experience? Where it all leads when that experience is simulated or obtained by underhanded means is something that has become clear to us from the horrific mishmash of styles and ideologies produced during the last century—too clear for us not to think it a matter of honesty to declare our bankruptcy. Indeed (let's admit it), our poverty of experience is not merely poverty on the personal level, but poverty of human experience in general. Hence, a new kind of barbarism.

Barbarism? Yes, indeed. We say this in order to introduce a new, positive concept of barbarism. For what does poverty of experience do for the barbarian? It forces him to start from scratch; to make a new start; to make a little go a long way; to begin with a little and build up further, looking neither left nor right. Among the great creative spirits, there have always been the inexorable ones who begin by clearing a tabula rasa. They need a drawing table; they were constructors. Such a constructor was Descartes, who required nothing more to launch his entire philosophy than the single certitude, "I think, therefore I am." And he went on from there. Einstein, too, was such a constructor; he was not interested in anything in the whole wide world of physics except a minute discrepancy between Newton's equations and the observations of astronomy. And this same insistence on start-ing from the very beginning also marks artists when they followed the example of mathematicians and built the world from stereometric forms, like the Cubists, or modeled themselves on engineers, like Klee.[2] For just like any good car, whose every part, even the bodywork, obeys the needs above all of the engine, Klee's figures too seem to have been designed on the drawing board, and even in their general expression they obey the laws of their interior. Their interior, rather than their inwardness; and this is what makes them barbaric.

Here and there, the best minds have long since started to think in these terms. A total absence of illusion about the age and at the same time an unlimited commitment to it—this is its hallmark. It makes no difference whether the poet Bert Brecht declares that Communism is the just distribu-tion of poverty, not of wealth, or whether Adolf Loos, the forerunner of modern architecture,[3] states, "I write only for people who possess a modern sensibility . . . I do not write for people consumed by nostalgia for the Renaissance or the Rococo." A complex artist like the painter Paul Klee and a programmatic one like Loos—both reject the traditional, solemn, noble image of man, festooned with all the sacrificial offerings of the past. They turn instead to the naked man of the contemporary world who lies scream-ing like a newborn babe in the dirty diapers of the present. No one has greeted this present with greater joy and hilarity than Paul Scheerbart.[4] There are novels by him that from a distance look like works by Jules Verne.[5] But quite unlike Verne, who always has ordinary French or English gentle-men of leisure traveling around the cosmos in the most amazing vehicles, Scheerbart is interested in inquiring how our telescopes, our airplanes, our rockets can transform human beings as they have been up to now into completely new, lovable, and interesting creatures. Moreover, these creatures talk in a completely new language. And what is crucial about this language is its arbitrary, constructed nature, in contrast to organic language. This is the distinctive feature of the language of Scheerbart's human beings, or rather "people"; for humanlikeness—a principle of humanism—is some-thing they reject. Even in their proper names: Peka, Labu, Sofanti, and the like are the names of the characters in the book *Lesabéndio,* titled after its hero. The Russians, too, like to give their children "dehumanized" names: they call them "October," after the month of the Revolution; "Pyatiletka," after the Five-Year Plan; or "Aviakhim," after an airline. No technical renovation of language, but its mobilization in the service of struggle or work—at any rate, of changing reality instead of describing it.

To return to Scheerbart: he placed the greatest value on housing his "people"—and, following this model, his fellow citizens—in buildings befit-ting their station, in adjustable, movable glass-covered dwellings of the kind since built by Loos and Le Corbusier.[6] It is no coincidence that glass is such a hard, smooth material to which nothing can be fixed. A cold and sober material into the bargain. Objects made of glass have no "aura." Glass is, in general, the enemy of secrets. It is also the enemy of possession. The great writer André Gide once said, "Everything I wish to own becomes opaque to me." Do people like Scheerbart dream of glass buildings because they are the spokesmen of a new poverty? But a comparison will perhaps reveal more than theory.[7] If you enter a bourgeois room of the 1880s, for all the coziness it radiates, the strongest impression you receive may well be, "You've got no business here." And in fact you have no business in that room, for there is no spot on which the owner has not left his mark—the ornaments on the mantlepiece, the antimacassars on the armchairs, the transparencies in the windows, the screen in front of the fire. A neat phrase by Brecht helps us out here: "Erase the traces!" is the refrain in the first poem of his *Lesebuch für Städtebewohner* [Reader for City-Dwellers]. Here in the bourgeois room, the opposite behavior became the norm. And conversely, the *intérieur* forces the inhabitant to adopt the greatest possible number of habits—habits that do more justice to the interior he is living in than to himself. This is understood by everyone who is familiar with the absurd attitude of the inhabitants of such plush apartments when something broke. Even their way of showing their annoyance—and this affect, which is gradually starting to die out, was one that they could produce with great virtuosity—was above all the reaction of a person who felt that someone had obliterated "the traces of his days on earth."[8] This has now been achieved by Scheerbart, with his glass, and by the Bauhaus, with its steel. They have created rooms in which it is hard to leave traces. "It follows from the foregoing," Scheerbart declared a good twenty years ago, "that we can surely talk about a 'culture of glass.' The new glass-milieu will transform humanity utterly. And now it remains only to be wished that the new glass-culture will not encounter too many enemies."

Poverty of experience. This should not be understood to mean that people are yearning for new experience. No, they long to free themselves from experience; they long for a world in which they can make such pure and decided use of their poverty—their outer poverty, and ultimately also their inner poverty—that it will lead to something respectable. Nor are they ignorant or inexperienced. Often we could say the very opposite. They have "devoured" everything, both "culture and people," and they have had such a surfeit that it has exhausted them. No one feels more caught out than they by Scheerbart's words: "You are all so tired, just because you have failed to concentrate your thoughts on a simple but ambitious plan." Tiredness is followed by sleep, and then it is not uncommon for a dream to make up for the sadness and discouragement of the day—a dream that shows us in its realized form the simple but magnificent existence for which the energy is lacking in reality. The existence of Mickey Mouse is such a dream for contemporary man.[9] His life is full of miracles—miracles that not only surpass the wonders of technology, but make fun of them. For the most extraordinary thing about them is that they all appear, quite without any machinery, to have been improvised out of the body of Mickey Mouse, out of his supporters and persecutors, and out of the most ordinary pieces of furniture, as well as from trees, clouds, and the sea. Nature and technology, primitiveness and comfort, have completely merged. And to people who have grown weary of the endless complications of everyday living and to whom the purpose of existence seems to have been reduced to the most distant vanishing point on an endless horizon, it must come as a tremendous relief to find a way of life in which everything is solved in the simplest and most comfortable way, in which a car is no heavier than a straw hat and the fruit on the tree becomes round as quickly as a hot-air balloon. And now we need to step back and keep our distance.

We have become impoverished. We have given up one portion of the human heritage after another, and have often left it at the pawnbroker's for a hundredth of its true value, in exchange for the small change of "the contemporary." The economic crisis is at the door, and behind it is the shadow of the approaching war. Holding on to things has become the monopoly of a few powerful people, who, God knows, are no more human than the many; for the most part, they are more barbaric, but not in the good way. Everyone else has to adapt—beginning anew and with few resources. They rely on the men who have adopted the cause of the absolutely new and have founded it on insight and renunciation. In its buildings, pictures, and stories, mankind is preparing to outlive culture, if need be. And the main thing is that it does so with a laugh. This laughter may occasionally sound barbaric. Well and good. Let us hope that from time to time the individual will give a little humanity to the masses, who one day will repay him with compound interest.

Published in *Die Welt im Wort* (Prague), December 1933. *Gesammelte Schriften*, II, 213–219. Translated by Rodney Livingstone.

Notes

1. James Sydney Ensor (1860–1949) was a Belgian painter and printmaker whose works are known for their troubling fantasy, explosive colors, and subtle social commentary.
2. Paul Klee (1879–1940), Swiss painter, was associated in the teens with the group Der Blaue Reiter, which formed around Wassily Kandinsky. Klee was an instructor in the painting workshop at the Bauhaus between 1921 and 1931.
3. Adolf Loos (1870–1933), Austrian architect, was an important precursor of the

International Style. An influential essayist and social commentator, his attack on ornament drew broad attention in Europe before World War I.

4. Paul Scheerbart (1863–1915), German author, produced poetry and prose oriented toward a gently fantastic science fiction. In 1919, Benjamin wrote an unpublished review of his novel *Lesabéndio* (1913). Scheerbart's book *Glasarchitektur* (Glass Architecture), produced in collaboration with the architect Bruno Taut, was one of the inspirations for the present essay.

5. Jules Verne (1828–1905), French author, wrote remarkably popular novels which laid much of the foundation for modern science fiction.

6. Le Corbusier (pseudonym of Charles-Edouard Jeanneret; 1887–1965) was a Swiss architect and city planner whose designs combine the functionalism of the modernist movement with a bold, sculptural expressionism.

7. Compare the following passage with "Short Shadows (II)," in this volume.

8. J. W. von Goethe, *Faust, Part II*, lines 11,583–84: "The trace of my days on earth cannot perish in eons."

9. Compare the fragment "Mickey Mouse" (1931), in this volume.

The Author as Producer, 1934

Walter Benjamin (center), with lobster-fisherman and (in foreground) Paul Gauguin, off Ibiza, May 1933. Photographer unknown. Collection of Marga Noeggerath, Munich.

Once Is as Good as Never

While writing, you sometimes pause over a purple passage—one which is more successful than everything else and after which you suddenly do not know how to go on. Something has gone awry. It is as if there were such a thing as a bad or unfruitful success; and perhaps you have to have a concept of precisely such a thing in order to grasp what a good success might be. Basically, there are two opposed adages that apply here: "Once and for all," and "Once is as good as never" [*Einmal ist keinmal*]. Of course, there are cases where "Once and for all" is entirely apt—in games, for example, or in examinations, or in a duel. But never at work. With work, "Once is as good as never" comes into its own. Only not everyone is eager to uncover the innermost nature of the practices and arrangements by which this wisdom can put down roots. Trotsky did so in a few sentences in which he erects a monument to his father's labor in the cornfields. He writes: "Touched, I watch him. My father moves simply and economically. You wouldn't think he was at work. His steps are measured; they're practice steps, as if he were looking for a spot where he could really make a start. His sickle makes its way without any artificial show of naturalness. You might be tempted to think he was not very sure of it—yet it cuts sharply and close to the ground, and throws off to the left in regular ribbons what it has cut down."[1] Here we have the work habits of the experienced man who has learned every day and with every swing of the scythe to make a fresh start. He does not pause to look at what he has achieved; indeed, what he has done seems to evaporate under his hands and to leave no trace. Only hands like those will succeed in difficult things as if they were child's play, because they are cautious when dealing with easy ones. "Never profit from an acquired élan," says Gide.[2] He is one of the writers in whose works "purple passages" are extremely rare.

Written ca. 1932; published in *Der öffentliche Dienst* (Zürich), February 1934. *Gesammelte Schriften*, IV, 433–434. Translated by Rodney Livingstone.

Notes

1. This citation differs from the corresponding passage in the German translation of Trotsky's autobiography, *Mein Leben* (Berlin: S. Fischer, 1930), p. 80. Benjamin may have translated the passage himself from the French edition: *Ma Vie* (Paris, 1930).
2. André Gide, *Journal des "Faux-monnayeurs"* (Paris: Gallimard, 1929), p. 89.

The Newspaper

In our writing, opposites that in happier ages fertilized one another have become insoluble antinomies.[1] Thus, science and belles lettres, criticism and literary production, culture and politics, fall apart in disorder and lose all connection with one another. The scene of this literary confusion is the newspaper; its content, "subject matter" that denies itself any other form of organization than that imposed on it by the reader's impatience. For impatience is the state of mind of the newspaper reader. And this impatience is not just that of the politician expecting information, or of the speculator looking for a stock tip; behind it smolders the impatience of people who are excluded and who think they have the right to see their own interests expressed. The fact that nothing binds the reader more tightly to his paper than this all-consuming impatience, his longing for daily nourishment, has long been exploited by publishers, who are constantly inaugurating new columns to address the reader's questions, opinions, and protests. Hand in hand, therefore, with the indiscriminate assimilation of facts goes the equally indiscriminate assimilation of readers, who are instantly elevated to collaborators. Here, however, a dialectical moment lies concealed: the decline of writing in this press turns out to be the formula for its restoration in a different one. For since writing gains in breadth what it loses in depth, the conventional distinction between author and public that the press has maintained (although it is tending to loosen it through routine) is disappearing in a socially desirable way. The reader is at all times ready to become a writer—that is, a describer or even a prescriber. As an expert—not perhaps in a discipline, but perhaps in a post that he holds—he gains access to authorship. Work itself has its turn to speak. And its representation in words becomes a part of the ability that is needed for its exercise. Literary competence is no longer founded on specialized training but is now based on polytechnical education, and thus becomes public property. It is, in a word, the literarization of the conditions of living that masters the otherwise insoluble antinomies. And it is at the scene of the limitless debasement of the word—the newspaper, in short—that its salvation is being prepared.

Published in *Der öffentliche Dienst* (Zürich), March 1934. *Gesammelte Schriften*, II, 628–629. Translated by Rodney Livingstone, on the basis of a prior version by Edmund Jephcott.

Notes

1. The following passage is a modification of similar ideas expressed in "Diary from August 7, 1931, to the Day of My Death," in this volume. Benjamin also cites from this essay in "The Author as Producer," also in this volume.

Venal but Unusable

The great majority of intellectuals—particularly in the arts—are in a desperate plight.[1] The fault lies, however, not with their character, pride, or inaccessibility. Journalists, novelists, and literati are for the most part ready for every compromise. It's just that they do not realize it. And this is the reason for their failures. Because they do not know, or want to know, that they are venal, they do not understand that they should separate out those aspects of their opinions, experiences, modes of behavior that might be of interest to the market. Instead they make it a point of honor to be wholly themselves on every issue. Because they want to be sold, so to speak, only "in one piece," they are as unsalable as a calf that the butcher will sell to the housewife only as an undivided whole.

Published in *Der öffentliche Dienst* (Zürich), April 1934. *Gesammelte Schriften,* II, 630. Translated by Rodney Livingstone.

Notes

1. See also "Notes (IV)" (1932), in this volume.

The Present Social Situation of the French Writer

When war broke out in 1914, a book by Guillaume *Apollinaire—Le poète assassiné* [The Poet Assassinated]—was in press.[1] Apollinaire has been called the Bellachini of literature.[2] Both his way of life and his style of writing contain all the theories and slogans whose time was ripe. He drew them out of his own nature just as a magician pulls objects out of a hat: pancakes, goldfish, ball gowns, pocket watches. As long as this man lived—he died on Armistice Day—no radical or eccentric fashion appeared, whether in painting or literature, that he had not created or at least launched. Together with Marinetti, he was the first to proclaim the main keywords of Futurism; he followed this up by making propaganda for Dada; then came the latest wave of painting, from Picasso to Max Ernst; and last, there was Surrealism, which he gave its name.[3] In the title story of the volume *Le poète assassiné,* Apollinaire prints an apocryphal article that allegedly appeared "on January 26 of this year" in *The Voice,* a paper published in Adelaide, Australia. The article, supposedly written by a German chemist, includes these words:

> True glory has abandoned literature in favor of science, philosophy, acrobatics, philanthropy, sociology, and so on. Nowadays, the only task of poets is to draw on money that they no longer earn, because they scarcely do any work; and the vast majority of them (with a few exceptions, such as cabaret artists) have not the slightest talent and hence not the slightest excuse. As for those who are not wholly without ability, they are even more pernicious, because they neither receive anything nor turn their hand to anything, yet they make more noise than an entire regiment . . . All these people have forfeited their right to exist. The prizes that are conferred on them have been purloined from workers, inventors, scholars, philosophers, acrobats, philanthropists, sociologists, and

so on. Poets have to go. Lycurgus drove them out of the republic; they should be driven from the face of the earth.

In the evening edition, the author is said to have published a postscript in which he argued: "You have to choose, O world, between literature and your own life; unless serious steps are taken to deal with literature, it will mean the end of civilization. This is no time for procrastination. The new age begins tomorrow. There will no longer be any poetry . . . Writers will be exterminated."[4]

These words do not look as if they had been written twenty years ago. Not that they are unmarked by the passing of twenty years. But their effect has been to transform a whim, an exuberant improvisation, and to lay bare the truth it contained. The landscape that is illuminated by these words as if by a lightning flash, and that at the time could barely be discerned in the distance, is one we have since become familiar with. It is the social climate of imperialism, in which the position of intellectuals has become increasingly intractable. The process of selection that has since taken place at the hands of the ruling classes has assumed forms that are scarcely less inexorable than the process Apollinaire described. Subsequent attempts to define the function of the intellectual in society are vivid testimony to the crisis in which he lives. Few people have had the wit or the resoluteness to perceive that this process of attrition, which has so undermined the intellectual's moral basis in society, if not his economic one, is predicated on the most radical changes in society itself. If this insight is unambiguously expressed by André Gide[5] and a number of other, younger writers, its value can be enhanced only by a scrutiny of the difficult conditions under which it was acquired.

The lightning shafts of Apollinaire's prophecies serve to discharge a stifling atmosphere. It is the atmosphere which gave birth to the work of Maurice *Barrès,* who had a decisive influence on the intelligentsia of the prewar years.[6] Barrès was a romantic nihilist. The disorientation of the intellectuals who succeeded him must have been great indeed if they could approve the utterances of a man who had said, "What do I care about the truth of ideas—it is the enthusiasm with which they are advanced that I respect." Barrès profoundly believed, and made a point of declaring, that "everything amounts to the same thing, with the exception of the excitement which we and people like us derive from certain ideas; for those who have managed to adopt the right point of view, there are no great events but only magnificent spectacles." The more thoroughly we become acquainted with his ideas, the more closely they seem to be related to the doctrines which the present age has everywhere brought forth. They consist of the same basic nihilistic outlook, the same set of idealistic gestures, and the same conformism that result from the synthesis of nihilism and idealism. La Rochefoucauld said that education can do nothing more than teach a man to peel a peach with decorum. In the same spirit, the entire romantic and ultimately political apparatus that Barrès sets in motion to propagate "the cult of the earth and the dead" ends up by subserving no higher purpose than "to transform chaotic feelings into more cultivated ones." These cultivated feelings never deny that they originate in an aestheticism which is merely the obverse side of nihilism. And just as modern Italian nationalism harks back to Imperial Rome and the Germans hark back to Teutonic paganism, Barrès believes that the time is ripe "for a reconciliation of the saints and the defeated gods." He wishes to salvage the pure springs and dense forests of France, as well as its cathedrals, on whose behalf he wrote a celebrated pamphlet in 1914. "And in order to preserve the spiritual vitality of the race, I call for an alliance between Catholic feeling and the spirit of the soil."

Barrès made his greatest impact with his novel *Les Déracinés* [Men without Roots], which follows the fortunes of seven Lorrainers who pursue their studies in Paris. The critic Thibaudet has made an illuminating comment on this novel: "As if by chance, four members of the group make something of their lives and become respectable people. They are the ones who have money. Of the two that receive scholarships, however, one becomes a blackmailer and the other a murderer. This is no accident. Barrès tells us that the great precondition of respectability is independence—in other words, wealth."[7]

Barrès' philosophy is the philosophy of inheritance. Significantly, one of the main figures in this weighty novel, in which he works out this philosophy, is a character study of one of his teachers, Jules *Lagneau*.[8] In real life, the two men failed to understand each other, and came from radically different parts of the social spectrum. Lagneau was genuinely without roots. He hailed from Metz; his family was ruined after they sided with France in 1871.[9] For the young Lagneau, France was the very opposite of a legacy. At the age of twenty, the philosopher had to assume the burden of supporting his family. At the same age, Barrès came into an inheritance that gave him the leisure to write *Le culte du moi*.[10]

Lagneau left few writings. But in the intellectual history of the last few decades, he is an important signpost. He produced two important students—two intellectuals whose work gives a more or less complete picture of the bourgeois ideology of France. What Barrès' work did for the ideologies of the Right, his other pupil, Emile Chartier,[11] did for the Left. Alain's political statement of faith, *Eléments d'une doctrine radicale* (the title refers to the doctrines of the Radical party),[12] are a kind of intellectual legacy of Jules Lagneau. The Radicals are, at least as far as their leaders are concerned, a party of professors and teachers. Lagneau was a very typical representative of this stratum. "We renounce," he writes, "every bid for popularity, every ambition to represent anything; we also deny ourselves the right to entertain or create any untruth, however slight, or any misguided opinions about what might be possible, whether in speech or in writing." He adds, "We will not store up any wealth: we renounce all claim to savings, to provision for ourselves and our families. This virtue, which shall be the death of us, needs no recommendation." The features of this intellectual—however real their basis in life—represent such a definite and deeply ingrained ideal of the bourgeois elites in the "republic of professors" that we would do well to shed as much light on them as possible. This can perhaps be achieved with the aid of a paragraph by Jacques *Chardonne,* in which this type of bourgeois intellectual is seen as the epitome of the petty bourgeois himself.[13] The fact that this depiction is stereotyped and exaggerated makes it all the more useful for our purposes:

> The bourgeois—and it is the petty bourgeois we have specifically in mind—is an artist. He is an educated character, but sufficiently independent of books to have his own ideas. Whether from experience or from close proximity, he has known enough wealth to enable him not to have to think about it constantly; he is fundamentally indifferent to indifferent matters, and was made for poverty like no one else. He is without prejudices, even exalted ones; without illusions and without hope. He is the first person to demand justice for others, and the first to suffer it, if need be. On earth, where he has received everything but his just deserts, he expects nothing more, nor does he expect to fare better in the world to come. Yet he takes pleasure in his unpretentious life, and is able to enjoy what it offers without maligning it. The world that has brought forth such people has not failed in its task. The path that leads to such wisdom is not an evil one. This is why there is still hope for the disinherited. This is why we must not dispute in advance a person's right to whatever society can offer.

As a political party, the Radicals have taken Barrès literally. He and they pose the problems in the same way, only his answers are diametrically opposed to theirs. To the inherited rights of the traditionalists he opposes the rights of the child; to the privileges of birth and wealth, the personal merits of the individual and success in state examinations. "And why not?" concludes Thibaudet. "Chinese civilization maintained itself for thousands of years as an examinocracy." Strange though the comparison with China may seem, it provides some insight. It has long since formed part of essayists' stock in trade. Paul *Morand* has used it to point out the striking similarities between the Chinese and the French petty bourgeois.[14] Both display the same "fanatical thrift, the art of constantly repairing things to prolong their usefulness . . . , distrust, a centuries-old politeness, a deep-rooted but passive hatred of foreigners, a conservatism punctuated by social squalls, an absence of public spirit, and the toughness of old people who have outlived their illnesses. One is tempted to think that all old civilizations resemble one another." The social subsoil on which the largest party in France has grown—for this is what the Radical party is—is far from being identical with the structure of the country as a whole. But the clubs and organizations (the so-called cadres) that this party possesses throughout the land undoubtedly constitute the climate in which the most important ideologies of the intelligentsia have been shaped, and from which only the most progressive have fully developed. The book that André Siegfried wrote three years ago under the title *Tableau des partis en France* [Portrait of the Parties in France] is a valuable tool for the study of these cadres.[15] Alain is by no means their leader, but he is the shrewdest interpreter of these groups. He defines their activities as "a constant battle of the small against the great." And in fact it has been asserted that the entire economic program of Radicalism consists in creating an aureole around the little word "small" and in defending the interests of the small farmer, the small businessman, the small property owner, the small depositor. So much for Alain. He is an interpreter more than a fighter. It is in the nature of the social substructure on which the activities of bourgeois intellectuals take place that any more determined course of action at once threatens to slip into Romantic sectarianism. The ideologies of Benda and Péguy are proof of this.[16]

In the intellectual situation fostered by Barrès and Maurras[17] and sanctioned by postwar developments, the appearance of Julien *Benda*'s book *La trahison des clercs* [The Treason of the Intellectuals] five years ago was like a bombshell. Here, Benda is concerned with the way in which intellectuals have begun to respond to politics over the past few decades. According to him, ever since intellectuals came into being, their world-historical task has been to teach the universal, abstract values of mankind: freedom, justice, and humanity. But now, with Maurras and Barrès, d'Annunzio and Marinetti, Kipling and Conan Doyle, Rudolf Borchardt and Spengler, they have begun to betray these values, whose guardians they have been for centuries. This new turn of events is marked by two signs. First, the unprecedented immediate relevance that politics has acquired for the writer. Wherever you look, you see political novelists, political poets, political historians, political reviewers.—But it is not just political passions that he finds incredible and unprecedented. Even more disconcerting and damaging is the direction this political activity is taking: he is shocked by the slogans of an intelligentsia that defends the cause of nations against that of mankind, of parties against justice, and of power against the mind. The bitter necessities of reality, the maxims of *Realpolitik,* were defended by the *clercs* in earlier times, but not even Machiavelli tried to embellish them with the pathos of ethical precepts.

Benda's general stance is prescribed by Catholicism. The thesis which underlies his book formally asserts a dual morality: that of force for states and peoples, and that of Christian humanism for intellectuals. His complaint is less that the norms of Christian humanism have no decisive effect on the world events than that they must forgo their claims to do so, because the intellectuals who defended them in the past have now gone over to the party of power. We cannot but admire the virtuosity Benda displays in confining his attention to the foreground of the problem. The decline of the independent intelligentsia is determined crucially, if not exclusively, by economic factors. The author understands as little of the economic basis of their crisis as he does of the crisis in the sciences—the undermining of the dogma of an objective research free from preconceptions. And he seems not to understand that the attachment of intellectuals to the political prejudices of classes and nations is for the most part no more than a disastrous, short-sighted attempt to break free of idealistic abstractions and come closer, closer than ever before, to reality. Admittedly, this entire movement was, in the end, violent and desperate. But instead of seeking an appropriate form for it, reversing it, and attempting to return intellectuals to the seclusion of their utopian idealism, he reveals—and no appeal to the ideals of democracy can disguise the fact—a thoroughly Romantic outlook. Benda recently proclaimed this openly in his *Discours à la nation européenne,* in which he gives an enticing description of a unified world whose economic forms have survived unaltered:

> This Europe will be scientific rather than literary, intellectual rather than artistic, philosophical rather than picturesque. And to more than a few of us it will come as a bitter lesson. For aren't poets more attractive than scholars? Aren't artists more captivating than thinkers? Here, however, we have to be more modest: either Europe will be serious, or it will not come into being. It will be far less entertaining than the various nations, which had been far less entertaining in their turn than the provinces. So we must choose: either we shall create Europe, or we shall remain eternal children. The nations have been lovable Clorindas; they will rejoice in the knowledge that they have been sensuous, passionately adored creatures. But Europe will come to resemble those youthful scholars of the thirteenth century who taught mathematics at the University of Bologna and who appeared before their audience veiled, so as not to confuse them with their beauty.[18]

It is not hard to discern in this very utopian Europe a disguised and, as it were, oversize monk's cell, to which intellectuals—"the spiritual"—retreat in order to weave the text of a sermon, undaunted by the thought that it will be delivered to rows of empty seats, if indeed it is delivered at all. This is why Berl is unanswerable when he says, "Revolt of the spirit? When Benda uses the word 'spirit,' isn't he thinking really of priests who minister to souls and see to earthly goods? . . . Doesn't his voice echo with nostalgia for the monastery, the Benedictines . . . a nostalgia that has become so powerful in the modern world? Must we continue to lament their loss?"[19]

The "spirit" to which Benda appeals so beseechingly, in an effort to counter the crisis, shows itself quickly enough in its true colors. It is nothing more than the manifestation of a figure from the past: the medieval cleric in his cell. But there has been no lack of attempts to breathe life into this notion of the "spirit," and no one has striven more fervently to give it flesh and bones than Charles *Péguy,* who appealed to the forces of the soil and of faith to assign intellectuals a place in the life of the nation and of history, although—unlike Barrès—he does not renounce the libertarian and anarchic elements they drew from the traditions of the French Revolution. Péguy fell early in the war. His life's work is still important today, thanks to the lucidity and energy with which he sought to define the role of the intellectual. Péguy might well be thought to fit the picture that Benda sketched of the *clerc trahissant,* the intellectual as traitor. But a closer inspection reveals that this is not the case. "You can say of Péguy what you will, but not that he is a traitor. And why? Because a particular attitude becomes treachery only when it is dictated by fear or indolence. The treason of intellectuals lies in their willingness to submit to prevailing moods and prejudices. Péguy does nothing of the sort. He was a nationalist, yet a supporter of Dreyfus. He was a Catholic, but was banned from taking Communion."[20] And when Berl, alluding to the title of a book by Barrès, sums up a certain type of writer with the words, "Enemy of the laws, indeed, but friend of the powers that be," this applies least of all to Péguy. He came from Orléans. There, according to the Tharauds, who describe their friend's origins, "he grew up surrounded by an ancient civilization, whose original complexion was determined by local traditions and a centuries-old history with no (or barely any) foreign element, in the womb of a population that was close to the earth and belonged to a peasant type . . . In short, he was surrounded by an ancient world that was closer to the France of the ancien régime than to the present."[21]

Péguy's great reform efforts bore in all respects the stamp of his origins. Even before he had established the *Cahiers de la Quinzaine* (acting as his own publisher and his own printer so as to create a vehicle for his own ideas), he had already consciously tried to maintain the traditions of his home, while he was still at the Ecole Normale. For the first time since the Renaissance, the generation he belonged to gave France great writers of peasant stock, with accompanying rustic language and way of thinking: Claudel, Jammes, Ramuz.[22] "Péguy was the first to provide the repellent spectacle of a student who had attended the Ecole Normale but who failed to exhibit the slightest evidence of a cultivated, classical, traditional style." On the contrary, Péguy's style comes from the soil; the long, coarse sentences that characterize it have been compared with long, coarse furrows intended for seed.

Thus, the forces to which Péguy appeals in order to form the type of the revolutionary intellectual are of prerevolutionary origin. According to André Siegfried, "the peasant and the French craftsman have come down to us from the Middle Ages; and if we gaze deeply into ourselves, we will have to confess that for good or ill, everything important in us was shaped before the Revolution. We are not a youthful nation."[23] This must be borne in mind if we are to understand that Péguy directed his appeal not to the young (as would be customary nowadays) but to those in their forties. The revolutionary task he set them was not of the defensive sort whose spirit was succinctly formulated by Alain when he said, "The attitude of the Left is that of a controlling authority." On the contrary, he urged his supporters to go on the attack, and his onslaught was directed not just at the rulers, but also at the cohorts of academics and intellectuals who had betrayed the people from whom they sprang. "I shall found the great party of forty-year-olds. Someone recently included me in that category, impulsively putting me in the class of forty-year-olds. I shall make use of this for my own purposes. An old politician makes use of everything. I will found the party of forty-year-olds."[24] That was in 1914. But those to whom Péguy was making his appeal were twenty in 1894; and that was the year in which Dreyfus was courtmartialed and demoted. So the controversy about Dreyfus had the same importance for Péguy's contemporaries as the Great War had for the generation that followed. With regard to the Dreyfus Affair, however, Péguy sought to distinguish between two aspects that point to the way in which he and his friends were to be cheated of the fruits of their victory. He speaks of "two Dreyfus Affairs, one good and one bad. The first is pure; the second, reprehensible. The first is religious; the second, political." And Péguy decisively repudiated the political struggle over Dreyfus. He opposed his allies on the left, accusing them of "Combes-like demagogy," and changed camps the moment the victors turned against the religious orders.[25] So before the bar of history it is Zola, not Péguy, who delivered the judgment of the intellectuals on the Dreyfus case.

And in this and other respects, it is *Zola* who provides the standard by which we must judge the historical outcome. The same may be said of great tracts of his fiction. It is well known that Zola's work is not based on a directly political theory. But it is a theory in the full sense of the word to the extent that Naturalism not only determined the subject of Zola's novels, and their form, but also supplied some of the basic ideas—such as the project of representing the heredity and social development of a single family. In contrast to this, what characterizes the social novel to which more than a few left-wing writers today have been devoting their energies is the absence of a theoretical foundation of any kind. As has been remarked by a sympathetic critic, the sheer impersonality and simplistic nature of the characters of the so-called *roman populiste* make them resemble characters in the popular fairy plays of times past, and their expressive power is so limited that it recalls the childish babble of those forgotten puppet-like figures.[26] It is the fatal, old confusion—we find it first, perhaps, in Rousseau—according to which the interior life of the disinherited and the oppressed is distinguished by a simplicity all its own, one to which authors often like to add an element of moral edification. It is obvious that such books have a very meagre yield. In fact, the *roman populiste* represents not so much an advance for the proletarian novel as a retreat on the part of bourgeois aesthetics. What is more, this corresponds to its origins. The fashion—if not the term—goes back to Thérive, the current critic for *Le Temps*.[27] But despite the enthusiasm with which he has sought to promote the new trend, its products—not least his own—show that what we are dealing with is just the old philanthropic impulses in a new form. The genre's only chance lies in choosing subjects that halfway conceal the author's lack of insight and education. It is no accident that the genre's first great success—*Voyage au bout de la nuit* [Journey to the End of Night], by *Céline*—is concerned with the *Lumpenproletariat*.[28] Like the *Lumpenproletariat,* which has no class consciousness that might enable it to fight for a life worthy of human beings, Céline, in his description of it, is quite unable to make visible this defect in his subject. Hence, the monotony in which the plot is veiled is fundamentally ambiguous. He succeeds in vividly portraying the sadness and sterility of a life in which the distinctions between workday and holiday, sex and love, war and peace, town and country have been obliterated. But he is quite incapable of showing us the forces that have shaped the lives of these outcasts. Even less is he able to convey how these people might begin to react against such forces. This is why nothing can be more treacherous than the judgment on Céline's book delivered by Dabit, who is himself a respected representative of the genre:[29] "We are confronted here with a work in which revolt does not proceed from aesthetic or symbolic discussions, and in which what is at issue is not art, culture, or God, but a cry of rage against the conditions of life that human beings can impose on a majority of other human beings." Bardamu—this is the name of the hero of the novel—"is made of the same stuff as the masses. He is made from their cowardice, their panic-stricken horror, their desires, and their outbursts of violence." So far so good. Were it not for the fact that the essence of revolutionary training and experience is to recognize the class structure of the masses and to exploit it.

If Zola was able to portray the France of the 1860s, this was because he rejected it. He rejected Haussmann's urban planning, La Païva's palace,[30] and Rouher's eloquence.[31] And if modern French novelists are unable to portray the France of our own day, this is because they are inclined to accept it at its face value. "Imagine," says Berl, "a reader in the year 2200 who tries to picture to himself the France of our day on the basis of our best novels. He would not even learn about the housing shortage. The financial crises of these years would be barely discernible. And there is no immediate prospect that our writers will begin to concern themselves with money matters."[32] This conformism turns a blind eye to the world in which it lives.

And it is the product of fear. Writers know that for the bourgeoisie the function of the intelligentsia is no longer that of defending its most human interests over the long term. For the second time in the bourgeois age, its intellectuals have entered a militant phase. But whereas between 1789 and 1848 they occupied a leading position as part of the bourgeois offensive, now their role is defensive. The less rewarding such a stance frequently is, the more urgent is the demand that intellectuals demonstrate their class reliability.

The novel is such an outstanding test of this reliability that the different attitudes displayed by authors in the process of adapting to society bring something resembling an ordered point of view into the chaos of producing literature. This does not mean, of course, that such literary production will automatically lend ideological support to the bourgeoisie. On the contrary, a large number of writers are much more likely to stand aloof from the middle class, at least in appearance. The position of a humanistic anarchism that seemed to hold sway for half a century or so—and in a real sense actually did so—has been irrevocably lost. Hence, the fata morgana of a new emancipation beckons, of a freedom between the classes—that is to say, the freedom of the *Lumpenproletariat*. The intellectual mimics the external appearance of proletarian existence without being even remotely connected to the working class. He thereby seeks the illusory state of standing outside the class system. While a Francis Carco could become the sensitive portrayer, the Richardson, of this new independence, a MacOrlan could become its ironic moralist, its Sterne.[33]

But conformism has even more elusive hiding places. And since even the greatest writer cannot be truly understood without defining the role of his works in society, and since, on the other hand, it is often those with the greatest talent who display a tendency to escape the consciousness of this role, even if they have to retreat to Hell to do so, this is the proper place to speak of Julien *Green*.[34] Green is undoubtedly one of the most important of the younger generation of writers, and he really has made the descent into Hell. His works are night-paintings of the passions. They burst the confines of the psychological novel in every respect. The antecedents of this writer take us back to the great Catholic and ultimately even the heathen depicters and interpreters of *passio*—to Calderón and even Seneca. But however deeply Green buries his characters in the provinces, and however subterranean the forces that move them, he does not always succeed in insulating them so completely from our own world that we should not expect them to make some sort of statement about it. Yet it is precisely at this point that we encounter the silence which is the expression of his conformism. I may perhaps be permitted to explore the traces of this attitude in his latest work, *Epaves* [Flotsam], if only because its conception makes it one of his greatest achievements.[35]

At the opening of the story, we encounter the hero taking a solitary evening walk along the banks of the Seine in the capital. In a remote corner of Passy, down by the waterside, he becomes the involuntary witness of a street fight between an old woman and a drunkard. It is a quite ordinary family scene, "but the man had been drinking and the woman was obviously afraid that he would throw her into the Seine." And further, "The man held her by the arm and shook her, loudly abusing her all the while. But she didn't take her eyes off Philippe"—this is the hero's name—"and shouted to him, 'Mister!' Her voice was coarse, but at the same time so subdued that he was transfixed with terror. He remained motionless." After this, he steps back. Then he goes home. "He arrived back home almost at the same time as usual."—That is all. Green's book now shows how this encounter begins to ferment inside his hero. It leads him, in the author's eyes, to a process of self-knowledge; it compels him to confront his cowardice, and it eventually undermines his entire life, over which the Seine increasingly gains a mysterious power. But he does not take his own life in the river.—Because this novel was written by a man of Green's qualities, it offers a pitiless example of the destruction of a great idea by conformism. No one will deny that the incident Green describes at the opening of his book is typical of life in our big cities. For this very reason, it clearly tells us nothing about the psychology of the man who refused to heed the cry for help. But it helps us understand his social character. For the involuntary witness who turns a blind eye is a bourgeois. An open quarrel between two bourgeois would scarcely take such a form in the street, in full view of the public. So what paralyzes Green's hero is the abyss that opens up in front of the bourgeois, while beyond it two members of the class of outcasts conduct their quarrel. It is not really the critic's task to make suggestions about how the author might have depicted this hidden meaning of the scene—the meaning that is actually its authentic one. The crass circumstance that unceremoniously opens the eyes of the bourgeois to the abyss that surrounds his class exist-ence—the same crass circumstance might equally cause him to slip over the edge into madness, which could turn the abandonment and loneliness of his class into the abandonment and loneliness of his individual existence. The uncertainty about the fate of the woman who had appealed to him for help and of whom he hears nothing further seems to contain the seeds of such a development in Green.

Green's problem is old-fashioned, and no less old-fashioned is the stand-point of most of these novelists on questions of technique: "Most of these writers have an unshakable faith in their characters' statements, or pretend they do—even though, since Freud, this faith must be seen as misplaced. They refuse to see that a report which someone gives about his own past reveals more about his present state than about the past that is the report's ostensible subject. They insist on seeing the life of a character in a novel as an isolated process that has been fixed in advance within the framework of an empty time. They refuse to take cognizance of behaviorism, or even of psychoanalysis."[36] Thus writes Berl. In a word, it is characteristic of the present state of French literature that we are beginning to see a separation between leading intellectuals and novelists. The exceptions—Proust and Gide above all—confirm the rule. For both have made more or less crucial modifications to the technique of the novel. But neither Alain nor Péguy, neither Valéry nor Aragon, have published novels;[37] and those that we have from Barrès and Benda are really illustrations of theses. For the mass of writers today, however, we may venture this generalization: the more mediocre an author is, the greater his desire to use his activity as a novelist as an excuse to evade his responsibilities as a writer.

For this reason, it makes sense to inquire what the novel of the last decade has achieved for freedom. It is difficult to conceive of any answer, other than to note the defense of homosexuality that *Proust* has been the first to undertake. However, even though such a comment does justice to the meager revolutionary fruits of literature, it by no means exhausts the meaning of homosexuality in *A la recherche du temps perdu*. On the contrary, homosexuality appears in his work because both the most remote and the most primitive memories of the productive forces of nature are banished from the world he is concerned with. The world Proust depicts excludes everything that is involved in production. The attitude of the snob that predominates throughout is nothing other than the consistent, organized, and hardened observation of existence from the standpoint of the pure consumer. His work conceals a merciless and penetrating critique of contemporary society, and up to now criticism has scarcely done more than scratch the surface of his analysis. Still, this much is clear. Starting with the work's structure, which combines poetry, memoir, and commentary, down to the syntax of the overflowing sentences (the Nile of language pouring out over the plains of truth, fertilizing them in the process), the writer is everywhere present, adopting a point of view, giving an account of himself, and constantly placing himself at the disposition of the reader. In no instance can an author have any claim to making an impact on the public, unless he begins by asserting his claim to be regarded as a writer. France is fortunate that the highly suspect confrontation between "poetry" and writing has never really gained much currency there. Today, more than ever, what is decisive is the idea a writer forms of his work. And it is even more decisive if it is a true poet who attempts to make this concept a reality.

These remarks pertain to Paul *Valéry*. He has a symptomatic importance for the function of the writer in society. And this symptomatic importance is intimately connected with the unquestionable high quality of his work.

Among contemporary French writers, Valéry possesses the greatest technical expertise. He has reflected on the nature of technique in writing like no one else. And the unique position he occupies can perhaps best be summed up in the statement that, in his eyes, writing is primarily a matter of technique.

But it is equally important to note that writing, in his sense, includes poetry. He has appeared before the public, in a decisive capacity, both as essayist and lyric poet, and in neither case has he failed to provide repeated explanations of his technique. Valéry sets out to explore the writer's and especially the poet's intelligence like an inquisitor; he calls for a break with the widely held view that it is self-evident that writers are intelligent, as well as with the even more widely held idea that intellect is irrelevant to the poet. He himself possesses great intelligence, of a kind that is anything but self-evident. Nothing can be more disconcerting than its embodiment, Monsieur Teste. In his appearance, Monsieur Teste is a philistine; in his way of life, he is a man with a private income. He sits at home; he does not really mix with people; he is looked after by his wife. Monsieur Teste—in English, "Mr. Head"—is a personification of the intellect that reminds us very strongly of God as conceived by the negative theology of Nicholas of Cusa.[38] Everything we learn about Teste ends up in negation. "Every sense of excitement, every feeling is the sign of a failure of construction and adaptation." However human Monsieur Teste feels himself to be, he has taken to heart Valéry's aperçu that the most important ideas are those that contradict our feelings. He represents therefore the negation of the "human." "Behold, the twilight of the approximate is setting in; and before the door stands the reign of the dehumanized, which will emerge from the precision, rigor, and purity in human affairs."[39] No expansive, pathos-filled gestures, nothing "human," comes into the ambit of this Valéryesque eccentric, in whose image the pure writer is to be formed. Thought is the only substance from which the perfect can be created. "A classical writer," Valéry says, "is a writer who conceals or absorbs his associations of ideas."

But within the framework of the French bourgeoisie, Monsieur Teste represents nothing but the experience that Valéry attempted to trace on a human scale in a number of great artists. It was with this aim that he wrote one of his earliest works, *Introduction à la méthode de Léonard de Vinci*. Leonardo appears there as the artist who never in his work renounces his claim to give the most precise account possible of his activity and his methods. Valéry has said that he would prefer a mediocre page in which he was able to give an exact account of every word that flowed from his pen to a perfect work for which he was indebted to the power of chance and inspiration. Similarly, at another point, he writes: "The realms of chance, the powers of the gods, and Fate are nothing but the symptoms of our own mental deficiency. If we had an answer to everything—a precise answer, that is—these powers would not exist . . . We feel this ourselves, and this is why we end up turning against our own questions. But that should be just the beginning. We ought to be able to formulate a question within ourselves that precedes all others and tests them in turn to see what they are worth."[40]

The strict return of such ideas to their context in the heroic period of the European bourgeoisie allows us to master our surprise at encountering once more the idea of progress at such an advanced stage of the old European humanism. It is, furthermore, the valid and genuine idea of a progress transferable at the level of methodology, a term that corresponds to Valéry's concept of "construction" as neatly as it conflicts with the *idée fixe* of inspiration. As one of his interpreters has claimed, "The work of art is not a creation, but a construction in which analysis, calculation, and planning play the principal roles." The ultimate merit of the systematic process of leading the investigator to go beyond himself has proved its worth in Valéry. For who is Monsieur Teste if not the human subject who is ready to cross the historical threshold marking the dividing line between the harmoniously educated, self-sufficient individual and the technician and specialist who is ready to assume a place within a much larger plan? Valéry failed to extend the idea of planning from the realm of art to the sphere of the human community. That threshold he did not cross. The intellectual remains a private person, and this is the melancholy secret of Monsieur Teste. Two or three decades earlier, Lautréamont had said: "Poetry must be made by all. Not by a single person."[41] These words have not reached Monsieur Teste.

The threshold that constituted such a barrier for Valéry has recently been crossed by *Gide*. He has joined the Communists. This is a matter of significance for the development of the problems in the advanced intelligentsia in France that we are attempting to portray. It may be said that Gide has not missed any of its vital phases of the past forty years. The first stage could be seen in his critique of Barrès' *Déracinés*. It contained more than a sharp repudiation of his hymn to roots. It contained a reinterpretation. Of the four main characters in the novel who are made to exemplify Barrès' thesis about the nation, Gide can interest himself only in the one who has sunk furthest in the social scale and has become a murderer. "If Racadot had never left Lorraine, he would never have become a murderer. In that case, he would have been of absolutely no interest to me."[42] Being "deprived of his roots" forces Racadot into originality. In Gide's view, this is the true subject of the book. It was in the name of originality that Gide undertook to explore the entire range of possibilities that disposition and development had opened up for him. And the more astonishing these possibilities were, the more ruthlessly he fought to make room for them in his life—in the full glare of the public gaze, moreover. Self-contradictions were the last consideration that might have deterred him. "In every direction I started out in, I went right to the very end, so that I might turn round and pursue the opposite course with just as much determination." This fundamental rejection of the golden mean, this commitment to extremes, is dialectics—not as an intellectual method, but as life's blood and passion. Even at its extremes, the world is still whole, still healthy, still nature. And what drives him toward these extremes is not curiosity or apologetic zeal, but dialectical passion.

It has been said that Gide's nature is not rich. This is a judgment that is not just valid but decisive. And Gide's own attitude suggests he is not unaware of this himself. In his book on Dostoevsky, he writes: "At the origins of every great ethical reform we always encounter a small, physiological secret, a failing of the flesh, a restlessness, an anomaly . . . The discomfort from which the reformer suffers stems from the absence of inner equilibrium. The moral givens, positions, and values are in contradiction with one another, and he is laboring to bring them all under one roof; what he wants is a new equilibrium. His work is nothing but an attempt, with the aid of logic and reason, to sort out the confusion he feels within himself and to replace it with a new order . . . An action in which I do not recognize all the contradictions inside me betrays me."[43] The attitude that is expressed in these and similar statements has been questioned countless times. The critic Massis calls Gide "demonic."[44] But rather more illuminating is the fact that Gide has never claimed for himself that other kind of demonism which the bourgeoisie is always happy to concede to the artist—namely, the freedom of the genius. Just as Valéry succeeded in integrating his entire production into his intellectual life, Gide integrated his into his moral life. It is to this that he owes his pedagogical influence. After Barrès, he is the greatest leader the French intelligentsia has found. As Malraux writes: "It is perhaps incorrect to regard André Gide as a philosopher. I think he is something quite different: an advisor on matters of conscience. That is a highly important and unusual profession . . . For a long time, Maurice Barrès dedicated himself to the same cause. Gide likewise. It is certainly no small matter to influence the mindset of an entire epoch. But while Barrès could only give advice, Gide has drawn attention to the gulf between our desires and our dignity, between our aspirations and our wish to master or exploit them . . . He has awakened the intellectual conscience of half the people we call 'the young generation.'"

The effect described here can be closely linked to a particular character in Les caves du Vatican [The Vatican Cellars]. The novel appeared just before the outbreak of the Great War, when, for the first time in the younger generation, intellectual currents began to appear that would later flow, via Expressionism and Dadaism, into Surrealism. Gide had every reason to reprint in his selected writings, Pages choisis, which he has dedicated to the youth of France, the page from Les caves du Vatican in which Lafcadio's decision to commit murder is described. Traveling in a train, Gide's young hero is irritated by the ugliness of an old man who is sharing a compartment alone with him. It occurs to Lafcadio to do away with him. "Who would see?" he muses. "There within reach of my hand is this double lock that I can easily undo. The door would suddenly give way and he would topple over; the least push would do it; he would fall out like a stone; you wouldn't even hear a scream . . . It is not so much the events I am curious about, as about myself. Some people imagine themselves capable of anything, but when it comes to acting, they hold back . . . What a gulf between intention and deed. And you have no more right to take it all back than in chess. No matter; if you knew all the risks in advance, the game would lose all its interest."[45] And slowly, cold-bloodedly, Lafcadio counts to ten and then pushes his traveling companion out, for no reason—purely from curiosity about himself. In the Surrealists Lafcadio has found his most eager pupils. Like him they began with a series of *actes gratuits*—groundless or almost idle scandals. But the path taken by subsequent developments is well designed to shed a retrospective light on Lafcadio. For the Surrealists showed themselves increasingly intent on bringing scenes that had originally been initiated in a playful spirit or out of curiosity into harmony with the slogans of the Communist International. And if there could still be any doubt about the meaning of that extreme individualism under whose banner Gide's work was launched, it has lost all validity in the face of his recent statements. For these make clear how, once this extreme individualism had tested itself on the world around it, it inevitably became transformed into Communism.

"All things considered, what strikes one most immediately about the spirit of democracy is that it is asocial." This was written not by Gide, but by Alain.[46] Gide came late to this insight into the spirit of democracy. It was only at a late date that he prepared himself intellectually to recognize it. After his various travels into the interior of Africa, his descriptions of the living conditions of the indigenous populations under colonial rule created some unease among the political public. A few years earlier, when he had put himself forward as the advocate of homosexuals, he had caused offense, but now, as the champion of black people, he threatened to create an uproar.[47] For him, as for those who followed him, the factors that provided the occasion for his intervention were exclusively political. The war in Morocco has a special importance in this context, particularly for the younger generation.

Surrealism would have been spared many enemies (from which, incidentally, it derived enormous benefit) had it originated unambiguously in politics. But this was far from the case. Surrealism came to maturity in the confined space of the literary circle around Apollinaire. Aragon showed, in his *Vague de rêves* [Wave of Dreams] of 1924, in what an unprepossessing, homegrown substance the dialectical nucleus of Surrealism was originally found. At that time, the movement broke over its founders in an inspirational dream wave. Life appeared worth living only where the threshold between sleeping and waking had been eroded, as if by the footsteps of images ebbing and flowing by the thousand. Language was itself only where, with automatic exactitude, sound and image, image and sound, had merged with each other so utterly that there was no space left for "meaning," not even the smallest fissure. To enlist "the forces of intoxication for the revolution"—that was the real program. The dialectical development of the movement, however, was such that the image space which it had so boldly opened up for itself proved more and more to be identical with the image space of political praxis. It was within this space, at any rate, that the members of the group located the home of a classless society. It may well be that the promise of such a society owed less to the dialectical materialism of a Plekhanov or a Bukharin[48] than to an anthropological materialism derived from their own experiences, and from the earlier experiences of Lautréamont and Rimbaud.[49] However that may be, under the leadership of Breton and Aragon, this world of ideas established the rules that governed the actions and literary production of the group, until political developments permitted them to formulate their ideas in a simpler, more concrete way.

Since the end of the war the left-wing intellectuals, the revolutionary artists, have set the tone for a major segment of the public. It has now turned out, all too clearly, that this public esteem was not matched by any profounder impact on society. From this we may conclude, in Berl's words, that "an artist, however much he may have revolutionized the arts, is no more revolutionary than Poiret, who in his day revolutionized the world of fashion."[50] The most advanced and daring products of the avant-garde in all the arts have had only the haute bourgeoisie as their public—in France and Germany alike. This fact does not necessarily imply a judgment on their work, but it does point to the political uncertainty of the groups that stood behind these manifestations. Again and again we see the decisive influence of anarchism on the literary movements of the 1930s: the gradual displacement of anarchism characterizes the trajectory of Surrealism from its beginnings to the present. The crucial turning point came in the mid-1920s. In 1926 Blaise *Cendrars'* book *Moravagine* appeared.[51] In the type of revolutionary terrorist depicted in those pages, left-wing intellectuals could see the reflection of their former ideal, one they were in the process of discarding:

> What impulse did we obey when we undertook the assassination of the czar, and what was our frame of mind? I often asked myself this question when observing my comrades . . . Everything in them had withered and died. Feelings fell away from them like scales and became waste products. Their brittle senses had become fragile and were no longer capable of enjoyment; they disintegrated into dust at the merest attempt to enjoy anything. Inwardly we were all singed as if by a blazing fire, and our hearts were no more than a heap of ashes. Our souls had been laid waste. We had long since ceased to believe in anything, or

even in nothing. The nihilists of 1880 were a sect of mystics, dreamers, agents of a universal happiness. But we were the antithesis of these merry fellows and their opaque theories. We were men of action, technicians, specialists, the pioneers of a new generation who had dedicated our souls even unto death, the harbingers of world revolution . . . Angels or demons? No; in a word, we were automata . . . We dwelled not in the shadow of a guardian angel or in the folds of his robe, but rather at the feet of our own *Doppelgänger,* who gradually detached themselves from us to find a new shape of their own and to take on bodily form. As the alien projections of ourselves, these new beings absorbed us into them so that we imperceptibly slipped into their skin and became identical with them. And our final preparations were very similar to the final stages of production of those terrible, arrogant automata that are known to magic as Teraphim. Like them, we set about destroying a city, laying waste a whole country and crushing the imperial family between our fearsome jaws.[52]

The civil war in Russia is now part of history. In the meantime, civil wars have broken out elsewhere. And the fact that the climate and problems of Russia's civil war are of greater concern to the literary intelligentsia of the West than the evidence about the construction of society in Soviet Russia reflects not just the primitive nature of the political education in Western Europe, but also the situation there. *Malraux*'s work is symptomatic here.[53] The setting of his latest book—like that of his earlier novel *Les Conquérants* [The Conquerors]—is China during its civil war period. In *La condition humaine* [The Human Condition] Malraux forestalls neither the historian nor even the chronicler.[54] The episode of the revolutionary uprising in Shanghai that was successfully put down by Chiang Kai Shek is neither politically nor economically transparent. It serves as a backdrop for the depiction of a group of people who play an active role in these events. Different though their roles are, and different though these people are in character and background, and hostile to the ruling class as they may be, they have one thing in common: they all spring from it. They work either for that class or against it; they may have left it behind them or been expelled from it; they represent it or see through it. But whatever their situation, that ruling class is in their bones. This is equally true of the professional revolutionaries who are in the foreground in the book.

Malraux does not say this in so many words. Does he know it? He proves it, at any rate. For the work, which is laden with the dialectical tension from which the revolutionary activity of the intelligentsia is born, feeds on this secret homogeneity of his characters. The fact that these intellectuals have abandoned their own class in order to make common cause with the proletariat does not mean that the latter have accepted them into their ranks. Nor have they. Hence the dialectic in which Malraux's heroes move. They live for the proletariat; but they do not act as proletarians. At the very least, they act far less from their consciousness of class than from their consciousness of their own isolation. That is the torment that none of these people escapes. It is also the source of their dignity. "There is no dignity not based on suffering."[55] Suffering makes people lonely, and it feeds on the loneliness that it creates. To escape it is the fanatical desire of those who have the decisive say in this book. The pathos of the book owes much more to its nihilism than might be thought.

What human need is satisfied by revolutionary action? This question arises simply and solely from the special situation of the intellectual. His solitude is a major factor here. But when the intellectual elevates this to the essence of *la condition humaine,* the human condition, as Malraux does here, it prevents him from seeing quite different preconditions of revolutionary mass action—preconditions eminently worthy of study. The masses have quite different needs, and elicit quite different reactions—reactions that seem primitive only to primitive psychologists. Malraux's analysis is limited by its inability to explain the actions of the proletarian masses for whom revolutions are part of their experimental historical agenda. But (it will be objected) if his analysis is limited, his story is likewise. Without doubt. But we may legitimately ask how much freedom an author has when constructing a plot on this subject. Can he really afford not to anticipate the historian? Is there a genuine revolutionary literature without didacticism?

These questions highlight the crisis that besets literature, and their clarification remains the preserve of the Surrealists. The preconditions for a solution have been fulfilled, even if there is little to show for it at present. They lay in the emergence of the new nationalism that made manifest the true features of the "spiritual" which had been delineated by Barrès. They lay in the crisis of parliamentarianism that made the entry of young intellectuals into the ranks of those who adopted Alain's ideas increasingly precarious. They lay, furthermore, in the fact that internationalism, as a cultural concern, as Benda understands it, was about to undergo a series of very demanding trials. They lay in the speed with which the image of Péguy became the stuff of legend; in the impossibility of discovering in his writings any practical lessons for the situation in which intellectuals find themselves today. They lay in the insight that gradually imposed itself on the conscientious—namely, that they would have to learn to renounce a public which could not reconcile the satisfaction of its needs with its own better judgment. An indirect indication of these preconditions, however, can be found in an important writer like Valéry, who is a problematic figure only insofar as he lacked the strength to make clear to himself the contradiction between his technique and the society to which he was making it available. Last, these preconditions could be found in the example provided by André Gide.

What is crucial about all this is that the Surrealists approached the problem in a way that enabled them to exploit these preconditions to the full. Thus, they variously imitated Lafcadio's playful action before they tackled more serious ones. They lent a more pointed meaning to what appears as "pure poetry" in Valéry when they started to view literature as a key to the psychoses. In the same vein, they found a place for the intellectual as technologist by acknowledging the proletariat's right to make use of his technology, because only the proletariat depends on technology at its most advanced. In a word—and this is the decisive factor—they attained their achievements without compromise and as a result of constantly reexamining their own position. They reached their goal as intellectuals—that is to say, via the longest route possible. For the intellectual's path to the radical critique of the social order is the longest, just as that of the proletariat is the shortest. Hence their attack on Barbusse[56] and others who were concerned to shorten it by appealing to conviction. And this, too, is why they have no room for depictions of poverty and deprivation.

The petty bourgeois who means business with his libertarian and erotic aspirations ceases to provide the idyllic picture that Chardonne welcomes in him. The more uninhibitedly and resolutely he asserts his claims, the greater the certainty that he will find himself on the road to politics—albeit via the most circuitous route, the only one viable for him. At the same moment, he will cease to be the petty bourgeois he once was. "Revolutionary writers," Aragon maintains, "if they are of bourgeois stock, are essentially and crucially traitors to the class of their origins." They become militant politicians. As such, they are the only ones able to interpret that dark prophecy of Apollinaire's with which we began. They know from experience why literature—the only literature they still think worthy of the name—is dangerous.

Written April–June 1933 and January 1934; published in the *Zeitschrift für Sozialforschung,* spring 1934. *Gesammelte Schriften,* II, 776–803. Translated by Rodney Livingstone.

Notes

1. This collection of stories by Guillaume Apollinaire (1880–1918) was in fact first published in Paris in 1916, following his recovery from head wounds incurred in World War I.
2. Bellachini (1828–1885) was a well-known conjuror.
3. The first Futurist Manifesto, of which Filippo Tommas Marinetti (1876–1944) was the principal author, was published in *Le Figaro* on February 20, 1909. The first use of the term "surrealist" occurred in the subtitle of Apollinaire's play *Les mamelles de Tirésias: Drame surréaliste.*
4. These citations are from Barrès' *La grande pitié des églises de France* (Paris: Emile Paul Frères, 1914).

5. André Gide (1869–1951), French writer, humanist, and moralist, received the Nobel Prize for Literature in 1947. See "André Gide and Germany" and "Conversation with André Gide," in this volume.

6. Maurice Barrès (1862–1923) was a French writer and politician whose fervent individualism and nationalism made his ideas a rallying point for the Right.

7. Albert Thibaudet (1874–1936) was an eminent French literary historian. Benjamin here cites *La république des professeurs* (Paris: B. Grasset, 1927).

8. Jules Lagneau (1851–1894), French philosopher, is known for the idealist-spiritualist influence he exerted on a number of his students who later achieved prominence.

9. Metz, in the Lorraine, was lost to the Germans in October 1870. The defeat marked a turning point in the Franco-Prussian War.

10. While studying literature in Paris, Barrès embarked on a solitary project of self-analysis, through a rigorous method described in the trilogy of novels entitled *Le culte du moi* (The Cult of the Self). This work comprises *Sous l'oeil des barbares* (Under the Eye of the Barbarians; 1888), *Un homme libre* (A Free Man; 1889), and *Le jardin de Bérénice* (The Garden of Bérénice; 1891).

11. Emile Chartier (1868–1951), French essayist, took his pseudonym, Alain, from a fifteenth-century poet. His collected essays, *Propos,* found a primarily youthful audience.

12. The Parti Radical (the name is an abbreviation of Parti Républicain Radical et Radical-Socialiste) was founded in 1901 as a coalition of various socialist and republican forces that had been brought together by their support for Dreyfus. Alain was a leading spokesman for the party. His *Eléments d'une doctrine radicale* appeared in Paris in 1925.

13. Jacques Chardonne (pseudonym of Jacques Boutelleau; 1884–1968), French novelist, detailed the tribulations of (mostly hopeless) marriages.

14. Paul Morand (1883–1976), French diplomat, novelist, and biographer, served as the Vichy government's ambassador to Romania and Switzerland.

15. André Siegfried (1875–1976) was a distinguished French sociologist and historian.

16. Julien Benda (1867–1956) and Charles Péguy (1873–1914) collaborated on the journal of politics and letters *Les Cahiers de la Quinzaine* (1900–1914). Both writers came to intellectual maturity during the Dreyfus Affair as champions of Dreyfus' innocence. After 1910, Benda emerged as an outspoken opponent of Henri Bergson and of what he saw as philosophical and political irrationalism in general; his most famous and influential work, *La trahison des clercs* (1927), condemns the European intelligentsia for their submission to the irrationalist temptation. Péguy, in contrast, favored Bergson and campaigned against "scientific" socialism and positivism.

17. Charles Maurras (1868–1952) was a French writer and political theorist whose "integral nationalism" anticipated some of the ideas of fascism.

18. Julien Benda, *Discours à la nation européenne* (Paris: Gallimard, 1933), pp. 70–71. Clorinda is a virgin warrior-maiden in Tasso's *Gerusalemme liberata*.

19. Emmanuel Berl, *Mort de la pensée bourgeoise* (Paris: B. Grasset, 1929), p. 32.

20. Ibid., pp. 45, 49–50.

21. Jérome Tharaud and Jean Tharaud, *Notre cher Péguy,* vol. 1 (Paris: Plon-Nourrit, 1926), pp. 19–20.

22. Paul Claudel (1868–1955), poet and dramatist, spent his childhood in the village of Villeneuve-sur-Fère, in northeastern France. Francis Jammes (1868–1938), poet, spent much of his life in villages in the French Pyrenees. Charles Ferdinand Ramuz (1878–1947), poet, came from a village in Switzerland's Vaud canton.

23. André Siegfried, *Tableau des partis en France* (Paris: B. Grasset, 1930), p. 10.

24. Charles Péguy, "Victor-Marie, Comte Hugo," *Oeuvres en prose, 1910–1914* (Paris: Gallimard, 1957), p. 838.

25. A reference to Emile Combes (1835–1921), a radical politician and minister. His anticlerical views helped enact the law separating Church and State.

26. Fairy plays, a genre established in the eighteenth century by the Venetian playwright Carlo Gozzi (1720–1806), were dramatizations of fairy tales, fables, puppet plays, and oriental stories. They were deliberately naive in characterization and expression. Gozzi, a defender of traditional dramatic forms such as the *commedia dell'arte*, was opposed to the innovations of such realist playwrights as Carlo Goldoni. His dramas were quite successful for a time, and formed the basis of many subsequent theatrical and musical works—especially in Germany, where he was admired by Goethe, Schiller, Lessing, and the Schlegels.

27. André Thérive (pseudonym of Roger Puthoste; 1891–1967) was a novelist whose work exemplifies the populist genre under discussion here. *Le Temps* (founded 1861) was one of France's most distinguished newspapers until its demise in 1942, on the day of the occupation of Lyon.

28. A German translation has just been published by Julius Kittl in Mährisch-Ostrau. [Benjamin's note. Louis-Ferdinand Céline's famous first novel, whose bleak vision and linguistic brilliance powerfully affected a generation of writers, was published in Paris in 1922.—*Trans.*]

29. Eugène Dabit (1898–1936), novelist, was the author of the popular novel *Hôtel du Nord,* which depicts life in a proletarian hotel. It was made into a film by Marcel Carné in 1938.

30. Thérèse Lachmann, known as La Païva, was a celebrated courtesan married to the Marquis de Païva, the Portuguese ambassador in Paris. The palace in question—which was built with money provided by her later husband, Count Henckel de Donnersmarck, and which still stands on the Champs-Elysées—is famous for such features as its monumental entrance and an onyx staircase.

31. Eugène Rouher (1814–1884), conservative politician, was one of the leading figures in the Bonapartist party during the Third Republic.

32. Berl, *Mort de la pensée bourgeoise*, p. 107.

33. Francis Carco (1886–1953) was a writer of memoirs and novels known for their realistic descriptions of low-life milieux. Pierre MacOrlan was the nom de plume of Pierre Dumarchey (1882–1970), a novelist who worked in the group around Apollinaire and Max Jacob. His novels are notable for their mixture of fantasy and reality, and for their sensitive portrayals of the marginalized and vagabond.

34. Julien Hartridge Green (1900–1998), French-American novelist, wrote bleak stories that were influenced by the gothic novel of the southern United States. His characters are typically neurotic and compulsive small-town figures. Green was elected to the Académie Française in 1971.

35. Green's novel *Epaves* appeared in Paris in 1932. An English translation, under the title *The Strange River,* appeared the same year.

36. Berl, *Mort de la pensée bourgeoise,* pp. 89–90.

37. Paul Valéry (1871–1945) was a French poet, essayist, and theorist. Louis Aragon (1897–1982) was a French poet, novelist, and essayist associated with the circle of Surrealists around André Breton. Aragon's *Paysan de Paris* and *Vague des rêves* were important stimuli in Benjamin's initial work on *Das Passagen-Werk* (The Arcades Project).

38. Nicholas of Cusa (1401–1464) propounded the idea that God is the "coincidence of opposites." Because God is infinite, He embraces all things in perfect unity; He is at once the maximum and the minimum. As for man's knowledge of the infinite God, he must be content with conjecture or approximation to the truth. Absolute truth escapes man; his proper attitude is "learned ignorance."

39. Paul Valéry, *Rhumbs,* in Valéry, *Oeuvres,* ed. Jean Hytier (Paris: Pléiade, 1971), vol. 2, p. 621.

40. Ibid., p. 647.

41. Comte de Lautréamont, "Poésies II," in Lautréamont, *"Maldoror" and the Complete Works* (Cambridge, Mass.: Exact Change, 1994), p. 244. "Lautréamont" was the pseudonym of Isidore Ducasse (1846–1870), whose work is notable for the violence, and the violent juxtaposition, of its images. He was a major influence on the Surrealists.

42. André Gide, *Prétextes* (Paris: Mercure de France, 1903), p. 56.

43. André Gide, *Dostoïevsky: Articles et causeries* (Paris: Plon, 1930), pp. 265–266.

44. Henri Massis (1886–1970), author and critic, was aligned with Péguy's Catholic nationalism. He attacked Gide for representing an anarchy supposedly originating in the East (and thought to comprise communism).

45. André Gide, *The Vatican Cellars* (Harmondsworth: Penguin, 1982), p. 139.

46. Alain, *Eléments d'une doctrine radicale* (Paris: Gallimard, 1925), p. 139.

47. See André Gide, *Corydon* (Paris: Nouvelle Revue Française, 1924); and idem, *Le retour du Tchad* (Paris: Gallimard, 1928).

48. Georgy Valentinovich Plekhanov (1856–1918), Marxist theorist, was the founder and for many years the leading exponent of the Marxist movement in Russia. A Menshevik, he opposed the Bolshevik seizure of power in Russia in 1917 and died in exile. Nikolai Ivanovich Bukharin (1888–1938), Bolshevik and Marxist theoretician and economist, was a prominent leader of the Communist International (Comintern).

49. Arthur Rimbaud (1854–1891) was a French poet and adventurer whose Symbolist poetry had a profound influence on modern literature.

50. Paul Poiret (1879–1944), couturier and decorator, is best-known for helping to eliminate the corset from feminine fashion.

51. This novel by Blaise Cendrars (pseudonym of Frédéric Sauser; 1887–1961) is, like much of his work, marked by striking images and an intense focus on rendering immediate experience.

52. Blaise Cendrars, *Moravagine* (Paris: Le Club Français du Livre, 1926), pp. 122–124, 134.

53. André Malraux (1901–1976) was a novelist, art historian, and statesman. His major works include the novel *La condition humaine* (The Human Condition, translated as *Man's Fate;* 1933); *Les voix du silence* (The Voices of Silence; 1951), a history and philosophy of world art; and *Le musée imaginaire* (The Imaginary Museum, translated as *Museum without Walls;* 1952–1954). Mal-

raux became an active supporter of General Charles de Gaulle and, after de Gaulle was elected president in 1958, served for ten years as France's minister of cultural affairs.

54. André Malraux, *Les Conquérants* (Paris: B. Grasset, 1928); *La condition humaine* (Paris: Gallimard, 1933).
55. Malraux, *La condition humaine,* p. 399.
56. Henri Barbusse (1874–1935), French writer and journalist, published novels, poems, and essays infused with pacifist and socialist views. His novels include *L'Enfer* (1908), *Le Feu* (1916), and *Clarté* (1919).

The Author as Producer

Address at the Institute for the Study of Fascism,
Paris, April 27, 1934[1]

The task is to win over the intellectuals to the working class by making them
aware of the identity of their spiritual enterprises and of their conditions as
producers.
—Ramón Fernandez

You will remember how Plato deals with poets in his ideal state: he banishes
them from it in the public interest. He had a high conception of the power
of poetry, but he believed it harmful, superfluous—in a *perfect* community,
of course. The question of the poet's right to exist has not often, since then,
been posed with the same emphasis; but today it poses itself. Probably it is
only seldom posed in this *form,* but it is more or less familiar to you all as
the question of the autonomy of the poet, of his freedom to write whatever
he pleases. You are not disposed to grant him this autonomy. You believe
that the present social situation compels him to decide in whose service he
is to place his activity. The bourgeois writer of entertainment literature does
not acknowledge this choice. You must prove to him that, without admitting
it, he is working in the service of certain class interests. A more advanced
type of writer does recognize this choice. His decision, made on the basis
of class struggle, is to side with the proletariat. This puts an end to his
autonomy. His activity is now decided by what is useful to the proletariat
in the class struggle. Such writing is commonly called *tendentious.*

Here you have the catchword around which has long circled a debate
familiar to you. Its familiarity tells you how unfruitful it has been, for it has
not advanced beyond the monotonous reiteration of arguments for and
against: *on the one hand,* the correct political line is demanded of the poet;

on the other, one is justified in expecting his work to have quality. Such a formulation is of course unsatisfactory as long as the connection between the two factors, political line and quality, has not been *perceived.* Of course, the connection can be asserted dogmatically. You can declare: a work that shows the correct political tendency need show no other quality. You can also declare: a work that exhibits the correct tendency must of necessity have every other quality.

This second formulation is not uninteresting, and, moreover, it is correct. I adopt it as my own. But in doing so I abstain from asserting it dogmatically. It must be *proved.* And it is in order to attempt to prove it that I now claim your attention. This is, you will perhaps object, a very specialized, out-of-the-way theme. And do I intend to promote the study of fascism with such a proof? This is indeed my intention. For I hope to be able to show you that the concept of political tendency, in the summary form in which it usually occurs in the debate just mentioned, is a perfectly useless instrument of political literary criticism. I would like to show you that the tendency of a literary work can be politically correct only if it is also literarily correct. That is to say, the politically correct tendency includes a literary tendency. And I would add straightaway: this literary tendency, which is implicitly or explicitly contained in every *correct* political tendency of a work, alone constitutes the quality of that work. The correct political tendency of a work thus includes its literary quality *because* it includes its literary *tendency.*

This assertion—I hope I can promise you—will soon become clearer. For the moment, I would like to interject that I might have chosen a different starting point for my reflections. I started from the unfruitful debate on the relationship between tendency and quality in literature. I could have started from an even older and no less unfruitful debate: What is the relationship between form and content, particularly in political poetry? This kind of question has a bad name; rightly so. It is the textbook example of the attempt to explain literary connections undialectically, with clichés. Very well. But what, then, is the dialectical approach to the same question?

The dialectical approach to this question—and here I come to the heart of the matter—has absolutely no use for such rigid, isolated things as work, novel, book. It has to insert them into the living social contexts. You rightly declare that this has been done time and again among our friends. Certainly. Only they have often done it by launching at once into large, and therefore necessarily often vague, questions. Social conditions are, as we know, determined by conditions of production. And when a work was subjected to a materialist critique, it was customary to ask how this work stood vis-à-vis the social relations of production of its time. This is an important question, but also a very difficult one. Its answer is not always unambiguous. And I would like now to propose to you a more immediate question, a question that is somewhat more modest, somewhat less far-reaching, but that has, it seems to me, more chance of receiving an answer. Instead of asking, "What is the attitude of a work to the relations of production of its time? Does it accept them, is it reactionary? Or does it aim at overthrowing them, is it revolutionary?"—instead of this question, or at any rate before it, I would like to propose another. Rather than asking, "What is the attitude of a work *to* the relations of production of its time?" I would like to ask, "What is its position *in* them?" This question directly concerns the function the work has within the literary relations of production of its time. It is concerned, in other words, directly with the literary *technique* of works.

In bringing up technique, I have named the concept that makes literary products accessible to an immediately social, and therefore materialist, analysis. At the same time, the concept of technique provides the dialectical starting point from which the unfruitful antithesis of form and content can be surpassed. And furthermore, this concept of technique contains an indication of the correct determination of the relation between tendency and quality, the question raised at the outset. If, therefore, we stated earlier that the correct political tendency of a work includes its literary quality, because it includes its literary tendency, we can now formulate this more precisely by saying that this literary tendency can consist either in progress or in regression of literary technique.

You will certainly approve if I now pass, with only an appearance of arbitrariness, to very concrete literary conditions. Russian conditions. I would like to direct your attention to Sergei Tretiakov, and to the type (which he defines and embodies) of the "operating" writer.[2] This operating writer provides the most tangible example of the functional interdependence that always, and under all conditions, exists between the correct political tendency and progressive literary technique. I admit, he is only one example; I hold others in reserve. Tretiakov distinguishes the operating writer from the informing writer. His mission is not to report but to struggle; not to play the spectator but to intervene actively. He defines this mission in the account he gives of his own activity. When, in 1928, at the time of the total collectivization of agriculture, the slogan "Writers to the *kolkhoz!*" was proclaimed, Tretiakov went to the "Communist Lighthouse" commune and there, during two lengthy stays, set about the following tasks: calling mass meetings; collecting funds to pay for tractors; persuading independent peasants to enter the *kolkhoz* [collective farm]; inspecting the reading rooms; creating wall newspapers and editing the *kolkhoz* newspaper; reporting for Moscow newspapers; introducing radio and mobile movie houses; and so on. It is not surprising that the book *Commanders of the Field*, which Tretiakov wrote following these stays, is said to have had considerable influence on the further development of collective agriculture.

You may have a high regard for Tretiakov, yet still be of the opinion that his example does not prove a great deal in this context. The tasks he performed, you will perhaps object, are those of a journalist or a propagandist; all this has little to do with literature. But I cited the example of Tretiakov deliberately, in order to point out to you how comprehensive the horizon is within which we have to rethink our conceptions of literary forms or genres, in view of the technical factors affecting our present situation, if we are to identify the forms of expression that channel the literary energies of the present. There were not always novels in the past, and there will not always have to be; there have not always been tragedies or great epics. Not always were the forms of commentary, translation, indeed even so-called plagiarism playthings in the margins of literature; they had a place not only in the philosophical but also in the literary writings of Arabia and China. Rhetoric has not always been a minor form: in Antiquity, it put its stamp on large provinces of literature. All this is to accustom you to the thought that we are in the midst of a mighty recasting of literary forms, a melting down in which many of the opposites in which we have been used to think may lose their force. Let me give an example of the unfruitfulness of such opposites, and of the process of their dialectical transcendence. And we shall remain with Tretiakov. For this example is the newspaper.

One left-wing author has declared:[3]

> In our writing, opposites that in happier ages fertilized one another have become insoluble antinomies. Thus, science and belles lettres, criticism and literary production, education and politics, fall apart in disorder and lose all connection with one another. The scene of this literary confusion is the newspaper; its content, "subject matter" that denies itself any other form of organization than that imposed on it by readers' impatience. And this impatience is not just that of the politician expecting information, or of the speculator looking for a stock tip; behind it smolders the impatience of people who are excluded and who think they have the right to see their own interests expressed. The fact that nothing binds the reader more tightly to his paper than this all-consuming impatience, his longing for daily nourishment has long been exploited by publishers, who are constantly inaugurating new columns to address the reader's questions, opinions, and protests. Hand in hand, therefore, with the indiscriminate assimilation of facts goes the equally indiscriminate assimilation of readers, who are instantly elevated to collaborators. Here, however, a dialectical moment lies concealed: the decline of writing in the bourgeois press proves to be the formula for its revival in the press of Soviet Russia. For as writing gains in breadth what it loses in depth, the conventional distinction between author and public, which is upheld by the bourgeois press, begins in the Soviet press to disappear. For there the reader is at all times ready to become a writer—that is, a describer, or even a prescriber. As an expert—not perhaps in a discipline but perhaps in a post that he holds—he gains access to authorship. Work itself has its turn to speak. And its representation in words

becomes a part of the ability that is needed for its exercise. Literary competence is no longer founded on specialized training but is now based on polytechnical education, and thus becomes public property. It is, in a word, the literarization of the conditions of living that masters the otherwise insoluble antinomies. And it is at the scene of the limitless debasement of the word—the newspaper, in short—that its salvation is being prepared.

I hope I have shown, by means of this quotation, that the description of the author as producer must extend as far as the press. For through the press, at any rate through the Soviet Russian press, one realizes that the mighty process of recasting that I spoke of earlier not only affects the conventional distinction between genres, between writer and poet, between scholar and popularizer, but also revises even the distinction between author and reader. Of this process the press is the decisive example, and therefore any consideration of the author as producer must include it.

It cannot, however, stop at this point. For in Western Europe the newspaper does not constitute a serviceable instrument of production in the hands of the writer. It still belongs to capital. Since, on the one hand, the newspaper, technically speaking, represents the most important literary position, but, on the other, this position is controlled by the opposition, it is no wonder that the writer's understanding of his dependent social position, his technical possibilities, and his political task has to grapple with the most enormous difficulties. It has been one of the decisive processes of the last ten years in Germany that a considerable proportion of its productive minds, under the pressure of economic conditions, have passed through a revolutionary development in their attitudes, without being able simultaneously to rethink their own work, their relation to the means of production, or their technique in a really revolutionary way. I am speaking, as you see, of so-called left-wing intellectuals, and will limit myself to the bourgeois Left. In Germany the leading politico-literary movements of the last decade have emanated from this left-wing intelligentsia. I shall mention two of them. Activism and New Objectivity [*Neue Sachlichkeit*], using these examples to show that a political tendency, however revolutionary it may seem, has a counterrevolutionary function so long as the writer feels his solidarity with the proletariat only in his attitudes, not as a producer.[4]

The catchword in which the demands of Activism are summed up is "logocracy"; in plain language, "rule of the mind." This is apt to be translated as "rule of the intellectuals." In fact, the concept of the intellectual, with its attendant spiritual values, has established itself in the camp of the left-wing intelligentsia, and dominates its political manifestos from Heinrich Mann to Döblin.[5] It can readily be seen that this concept has been coined without any regard for the position of intellectuals in the process of production. Hiller, the theoretician of Activism, means intellectuals to be understood not as "members of certain professions" but as "representatives of a certain characterological type."[6] This characterological type naturally stands as such between the classes. It encompasses any number of private individuals without offering the slightest basis for organizing them. When Hiller formulates his denunciation of party leaders, he concedes them a good deal. They may be "better informed in important matters . . . , have more popular appeal . . . , fight more courageously" than he, but of one thing he is sure: they "think more defectively." Probably. But where does this lead him, since politically it is not private thinking but, as Brecht once expressed it, the art of thinking in other people's heads that is decisive? Activism attempted to replace materialistic dialectics by the notion of common sense—a notion that in class terms is unquantifiable.[7] Activism's intellectuals represent at best a social group. In other words, the very principle on which this collective is formed is reactionary. No wonder its effect could never be revolutionary.

Yet the pernicious principle of such collectivization continues to operate. This could be seen three years ago, when Döblin's *Wissen und Verändern* came out.[8] As is known, this pamphlet was written in reply to a young man—Döblin calls him Herr Hocke—who had put to the famous author the question, "What is to be done?" Döblin invites him to join the cause of socialism, but with reservations. Socialism, according to Döblin, is "freedom, a spontaneous union of people, the rejection of all compulsion, indignation at injustice and coercion, humanity, tolerance, a peaceful disposition." However that may be, on the basis of this socialism he sets his face against the theory and practice of the radical workers' movement. "Nothing," Döblin declares, "can come out of anything that was not already in it—and from a murderously exacerbated class war, justice can come but not socialism." Döblin formulates the recommendation that, for these and other reasons, he gives Herr Hocke: "You, my dear sir, cannot put into effect your agreement in principle with the struggle [of the proletariat] by joining the proletarian front. You must be content with an agitated and bitter approval of this struggle. But you also know that if you do more, an immensely important post will remain unmanned . . . : the original communistic position of human individual freedom, of the spontaneous solidarity and union of men . . . It is this position, my dear sir, that alone falls to you." Here it is quite palpable where the conception of the "intellectual"—as a type of person defined by his opinions, attitudes, or dispositions, but not by his position in the process of production—leads. He must, as Döblin puts it, find his place *beside* the proletariat. But what kind of place is this? That of a benefactor, of an ideological patron—an impossible place. And so we return to the thesis stated at the outset: the place of the intellectual in the class struggle can be identified—or, better, chosen—only on the basis of his position in the process of production.

To signify the transformation of the forms and instruments of production in the way desired by a progressive intelligentsia—that is, one interested in freeing the means of production and serving the class struggle—Brecht coined the term *Umfunktionierung* [functional transformation]. He was the first to make of intellectuals the far-reaching demand not to supply the apparatus of production without, to the utmost extent possible, changing it in accordance with socialism. "The publication of the *Versuche*," the author writes in his introduction to the series of writings bearing this title, "occurred at a time when certain works ought no longer to be individual experiences (have the character of works) but should, rather, concern the use (transformation) of certain institutes and institutions."⁹ It is not spiritual renewal, as fascists proclaim, that is desirable: technical innovations are suggested. I shall come back to these innovations. Here I would like to content myself with a reference to the decisive difference between the mere supplying of a productive apparatus and its transformation. And I would like to preface my discussion of the "New Objectivity" with the proposition that to supply a productive apparatus without—to the utmost extent possible—changing it would still be a highly censurable course, even if the material with which it is supplied seemed to be of a revolutionary nature. For we are faced with the fact—of which the past decade in Germany has furnished an abundance of examples—that the bourgeois apparatus of production and publication can assimilate astonishing quantities of revolutionary themes—indeed, can propagate them without calling its own existence, and the existence of the class that owns it, seriously into question. This remains true at least as long as it is supplied by hack writers, even if they are revolutionary hacks. I define "hack writer" as a writer who abstains in principle from alienating the productive apparatus from the ruling class by improving it in ways serving the interests of socialism. And I further maintain that a considerable proportion of so-called left-wing literature possessed no other social function than to wring from the political situation a continuous stream of novel effects for the entertainment of the public. This brings me to the New Objectivity. Its stock in trade was reportage. Let us ask ourselves to whom this technique was useful.

For the sake of clarity I will place its photographic form in the foreground, but what is true of this can also be applied to its literary form. Both owe the extraordinary increase in their popularity to the technology of publication: radio and the illustrated press. Let us think back to Dadaism. The revolutionary strength of Dadaism consisted in testing art for its authenticity. A still life might have been put together from tickets, spools of cotton, and cigarette butts, all of which were combined with painted elements. The whole thing was put in a frame. And thereby the public was shown: Look, your picture frame ruptures time; the tiniest authentic fragment of daily life says more than painting. Just as the bloody fingerprint of a murderer on the page of a book says more than the text. Much of this revolutionary content has gone into photomontage. You need only think of the work of John

Heartfield, whose technique made the book cover into a political instrument.[10] But now follow the path of photography further. What do you see? It becomes ever more *nuancé,* ever more modern; and the result is that it can no longer record a tenement block or a refuse heap without transfiguring it. Needless to say, photography is unable to convey anything about a power station or a cable factory other than, "What a beautiful world!" *The World Is Beautiful*—this is the title of the well-known picture anthology by Renger-Patzsch, in which we see New Objective photography at its peak.[11] For it has succeeded in transforming even abject poverty—by apprehending it in a fashionably perfected manner—into an object of enjoyment. For if it is an economic function of photography to restore to mass consumption, by fashionable adaptation, subjects that had earlier withdrawn themselves from it (springtime, famous people, foreign countries), it is one of its political functions to renew from within—that is, fashionably—the world as it is.

Here we have a flagrant example of what it means to supply a productive apparatus without changing it. To change it would have meant overthrowing another of the barriers, transcending another of the antitheses, that fetter the production of intellectuals—in this case, the barrier between writing and image. What we require of the photographer is the ability to give his picture a caption that wrenches it from modish commerce and gives it a revolutionary use value. But we will make this demand most emphatically when we—the writers—take up photography. Here, too, therefore, technical progress is for the author as producer the foundation of his political progress. In other words, only by transcending the specialization in the process of intellectual production—a specialization that, in the bourgeois view, constitutes its order—can one make this production politically useful; and the barriers imposed by specialization must be breached jointly by the productive forces that they were set up to divide. The author as producer discovers—even as he discovers his solidarity with the proletariat—his solidarity with certain other producers who earlier seemed scarcely to concern him. I have spoken of the photographer; here I will very briefly insert a word of Eisler's on the musician:[12]

> In the development of music, too, both in production and in reproduction, we must learn to recognize an ever-increasing process of rationalization . . . The phonograph record, the sound film, jukeboxes can purvey top-quality music . . . canned as a commodity. The consequence of this process of rationalization is that musical reproduction is consigned to ever-diminishing but also ever more highly qualified groups of specialists. The crisis of the commercial concert is the crisis of an antiquated form of production made obsolete by new technical inventions.

The task, therefore, consisted of an *Umfunktionierung* of the form of the concert that had to fulfill two conditions: it had to eliminate the antithesis, first, between performers and listeners and, second, between technique and content. On this, Eisler makes the following illuminating observation: "One must beware of overestimating orchestral music and considering it the only high art. Music without words attained its great importance and its full extent only under capitalism." This means that the task of changing the concert is impossible without the collaboration of the word. It alone can effect the transformation, as Eisler formulates it, of a concert into a political meeting. But that such a transformation does indeed represent a peak of musical and literary technique, Brecht and Eisler prove with their didactic play *Die Massnahme* [The Measures Taken].

If you look back from this vantage point on the recasting of literary forms that I spoke of earlier, you can see how photography and music, and whatever else occurs to you, are entering the growing, molten mass from which the new forms are cast. You will find this confirmed: only the literarization of all the conditions of life provides an accurate conception of the range of this melting-down process, just as the state of the class struggle determines the temperature at which—more or less perfectly—it is accomplished.

I spoke of the process of a certain modish photography whereby poverty is made an object of consumption. In turning to New Objectivity as a literary movement, I must take a step further and say that it has made the *struggle against poverty* an object of consumption. The political importance of the movement was indeed exhausted in many cases by the conversion of revolutionary impulses, insofar as they occurred among bourgeoisie, into objects of distraction, of amusement, which found their way without difficulty into the big-city cabaret business. The transformation of the political struggle from a call-to-decision into an object of contemplative enjoyment, from a means of production into a consumer article, is the defining characteristic of this literature. A perceptive critic has explained this, using the example of Erich Kästner, as follows:[13]

> With the workers' movement, this left-wing radical intelligentsia has nothing in common. It is, rather, a phenomenon of bourgeois decomposition, a counterpart of the feudalistic mimicry that the Second Empire admired in the reserve officer. The radical-left publicists of the stamp of Kästner, Mehring, or Tucholsky are the proletarian mimicry of decayed bourgeois strata.[14] Their function is to produce, from the political standpoint, not parties but cliques; from the literary standpoint, not schools but fashions; from the economic standpoint, not producers but agents—agents or hacks who make a great display of their poverty, and a banquet out of yawning emptiness. One could not be more cozily accommodated in an uncozy situation.

This school, I said, made a great display of its poverty. It thereby shirked the most urgent task of the present-day writer: to recognize how poor he is and how poor he has to be in order to begin again from the beginning. For this is what is involved. The Soviet state will not, it is true, banish the poet, as Plato did; but it will—and this is why I evoked Plato's republic at the outset—assign him tasks that do not permit him to display in new master-pieces the long-since-counterfeit wealth of creative personality. To expect a renewal in terms of such personalities and such works is a privilege of fascism, which gives rise to such asinine formulations as that with which Günther Gründel, in his *Mission of the Young Generation,* rounds off the section on literature: "We cannot better conclude this . . . survey and prog-nosis than with the observation that the *Wilhelm Meister* and the *Green Henry* of our generation have not yet been written."[15] Nothing will be further from the author who has reflected deeply on the conditions of present-day production than to expect, or desire, such works. His work will never be merely work on products but always, at the same time, work on the means of production. In other words, his products must have, over and above their character as works, an organizing function, and in no way must their organizational usefulness be confined to their value as propaganda. Their political tendency alone is not enough. The excellent Lichtenberg has said, "What matters is not a man's opinions, but the kind of man these opinions make of him."[16] Now, it is true that opinions matter greatly, but the best are of no use if they make nothing useful out of those who hold them. The best political tendency is wrong if it does not demonstrate the attitude with which it is to be followed. And this attitude the writer can demonstrate only in his particular activity—that is, in writing. A political tendency is a necessary but never sufficient condition for the organizing function of a work. This further requires a directing, instructing stance on the part of the writer. And today this must be demanded more than ever before. *An author who teaches writers nothing teaches no one.* What mat-ters, therefore, is the exemplary character of production, which is able, first, to induce other producers to produce, and, second, to put an improved apparatus at their disposal. And this apparatus is better, the more consumers it is able to turn into producers—that is, readers or spectators into collabo-rators. We already possess such an example, to which, however, I can only allude here. It is Brecht's Epic Theater.

Tragedies and operas are constantly being written that apparently have a well-tried theatrical apparatus at their disposal, but in reality do nothing but supply a derelict one. "The lack of clarity about their situation that prevails among musicians, writers, and critics," says Brecht, "has immense consequences that are far too little considered. For, thinking that they are in possession of an apparatus that in reality possesses them, they defend an apparatus over which they no longer have any control and that is no longer, as they still believe, a means for the producers, but has become a means against the producers."[17] This theater, with its complicated machinery, its gigantic supporting staff, its sophisticated effects, has become a "means against the producers" not least in seeking to enlist them in the hopeless competitive struggle in which film and radio have enmeshed it. This theater (whether in its educating or its entertaining role; the two are complementary)[18] is that of a sated class for which everything it touches becomes a stimulant. Its position is lost. Not so that of a theater that, instead of competing with newer instruments of publication, seeks to use and learn from them—in short, to enter into debate with them. This debate the Epic Theater has made its own affair. It is, measured by the present state of development of film and radio, the contemporary form.

In the interest of this debate, Brecht fell back on the most primitive elements of the theater. He contented himself, by and large, with a podium. He dispensed with wide-ranging plots. He thus succeeded in changing the functional connection between stage and public, text and performance, director and actor. Epic Theater, he declared, had to portray situations, rather than develop plots. It obtains such situations, as we shall see presently, by interrupting the plot. I remind you here of the songs, which have their chief function in interrupting the action. Here—according to the principle of interruption—Epic Theater, as you see, takes up a procedure that has become familiar to you in recent years from film and radio, literature and photography. I am speaking of the procedure of montage: the superimposed element disrupts the context in which it is inserted. But here this procedure has a special right, perhaps even a perfect right, as I will briefly show. The interruption of action, on account of which Brecht described his theater as "epic," constantly counteracts illusion on the part of the audience. For such illusion is a hindrance to a theater that proposes to make use of elements of reality in experimental rearrangements. But it is at the end, not the beginning, of the experiment that the situation appears—a situation that, in this or that form, is always ours. It is not brought home to the spectator but distanced from him. He recognizes it as the real situation—not with satisfaction, as in the theater of Naturalism, but with astonishment. Epic Theater, therefore, does not reproduce situations; rather, it discovers them. This discovery is accomplished by means of the interruption of sequences. Yet interruption here has the character not of a stimulant but of an organizing function. It arrests the action in its course, and thereby compels the listener to adopt an attitude vis-à-vis the process, the actor vis-à-vis his role. I would like to show you, through an example, how Brecht's discovery and use of the *gestus* is nothing but the restoration of the method of montage decisive in radio and film, from an often merely modish procedure to a human event. Imagine a family scene: the wife is just about to grab a bronze sculpture and throw it at her daughter; the father is opening the window to call for help. At this moment a stranger enters. The process is interrupted. What appears in its place is the situation on which the stranger's eyes now fall: agitated faces, open window, disordered furniture. There are eyes, however, before which the more usual scenes of present-day existence do not look very different: the eyes of the epic dramatist.

To the total dramatic artwork he opposes the dramatic laboratory. He makes use in a new way of the great, ancient opportunity of the theater: to expose what is present. At the center of his experiment stands the human being. Present-day man; a reduced man, therefore, chilled in a chilly environment. But since this is the only one we have, it is in our interest to know him. He is subjected to tests, examinations. What emerges is this: events are alterable not at their climaxes, not by virtue and resolution, but only in their strictly habitual course, by reason and practice. To construct from the smallest elements of behavior what in Aristotelian dramaturgy is called "action" is the purpose of Epic Theater. Its means are therefore more modest than those of traditional theater; likewise its aims. It is concerned less with filling the public with feelings, even seditious ones, than with alienating it in an enduring way, through thinking, from the conditions in which it lives. It may be noted, incidentally, that there is no better trigger for thinking than laughter. In particular, convulsion of the diaphragm usually provides better opportunities for thought than convulsion of the soul. Epic Theater is lavish only in occasions for laughter.

It has perhaps struck you that the train of thought which is about to be concluded presents the writer with only one demand: the demand *to think*, to reflect on his position in the process of production. We may depend on it: this reflection leads, sooner or later, for the writers who *matter* (that is, for the best technicians in their field), to observations that provide the most factual foundation for solidarity with the proletariat. Thus, I would like to conclude by adducing a topical illustration in the form of a small extract from a journal published here, *Commune*. *Commune* circulated a questionnaire asking, "For whom do you write?" I quote from the reply of René Maublanc and from the comment added by Aragon.[19] "Unquestionably," says Maublanc, "I write almost exclusively for a bourgeois public. First, because I am obliged to" (here Maublanc is alluding to his professional duties as a grammar-school teacher), "second, because I have bourgeois origins and a bourgeois education and come from a bourgeois milieu, and so am naturally inclined to address myself to the class to which I belong, which I know and understand best. This does not mean, however, that I write in order to please or support it. I am convinced, on the one hand, that the proletarian revolution is necessary and desirable and, on the other, that it will be the more rapid, easy, and successful, and the less bloody, the weaker the opposition of the bourgeoisie . . . The proletariat today needs allies from the camp of the bourgeoisie, exactly as in the eighteenth century the bourgeoisie needed allies from the feudal camp. I wish to be among those allies."

On this Aragon comments:

> Our comrade here touches on a state of affairs that affects a large number of present-day writers. Not all have the courage to look it in the face . . . Those who see their own situation as clearly as René Maublanc are few. But precisely from them more must be required . . . It is not enough to weaken the bourgeoisie from within; it is necessary to fight them *with* the proletariat . . . René Maublanc, and many of our friends among the writers who are still hesitating, are faced with the example of the Soviet Russian writers who came from the Russian bourgeoisie and nevertheless became pioneers in the building of socialism.

Thus Aragon. But how did they become pioneers? Certainly not without very bitter struggles, extremely difficult debates. The considerations I have put before you are an attempt to draw some conclusions from these struggles. They are based on the concept to which the debate on the attitude of Russian intellectuals owes its decisive clarification: the concept of the specialist. The solidarity of the specialist with the proletariat—herein lies the beginning of this clarification—can only be a mediated one. Proponents of Activism and of the New Objectivity could gesticulate as they pleased, but they could not do away with the fact that even the proletarianization of an intellectual hardly ever makes a proletarian. Why? Because the bourgeois class gave him, in the form of education, a means of production that, owing to educational privilege, makes him feel solidarity with it, and still more it with him. Aragon was thereby entirely correct when, in another connection, he declared, "The revolutionary intellectual appears first and foremost as the betrayer of his class of origin." In the case of the writer, this betrayal consists in conduct that transforms him from a supplier of the productive apparatus into an engineer who sees it as his task to adapt this apparatus to the purposes of the proletarian revolution. This is a mediating activity, yet it frees the intellectual from that purely destructive task to which Maublanc and many of his comrades believe it necessary to confine him. Does he succeed in promoting the socialization of the intellectual means of production? Does he see how he himself can organize intellectual workers in the production process? Does he have proposals for the *Umfunktionierung* of the novel, the drama, the poem? The more completely he can orient his activity toward this task, the more correct the political tendency of his work will be, and necessarily also the higher its technical quality. And at the same time, the more exactly he is thus informed about his position in the process of production, the less it will occur to him to lay claim to "spiritual" qualities. The spirit that holds forth in the name of fascism *must* disappear. The spirit that, in opposing it, trusts in its own miraculous powers *will* disappear. For the revolutionary struggle is not between capitalism and spirit; it is between capitalism and the proletariat.

Written spring 1934; unpublished in Benjamin's lifetime. *Gesammelte Schriften,* II, 683–701. Translated by Edmund Jephcott.

Notes

1. That the date given in the subtitle is erroneous can be gathered from a letter that Benjamin wrote to Adorno the following day (April 28, 1934), in which he mentions that the address has not yet been presented (*Gesammelte Schriften,* vol. 2, pp. 1460–1461). Gershom Scholem claims that the twenty-seventh was the date of Benjamin's *completion* of the text, which was *never* presented; see *The Correspondence of Walter Benjamin and Gershom Scholem, 1932–1940* (New York: Schocken, 1989), p. 111n. The Institute for the Study of Fascism was a Communist front organization.
2. Sergei Tretiakov (1892–1939) was a Russian writer whose work, based on a "literature of facts," was agitational and propagandistic. His book *Commanders of the Field* (1931) comprised two volumes of diaries and sketchbooks.
3. The "left-wing author" is Benjamin himself. See "The Newspaper" (1934), in this volume.
4. Centered around the yearbook *Das Ziel* (The Goal), "Activism" was a political stance that fused Nietzschean ideals with a pacifist socialism; it stood opposed to German Expressionism. Prominent figures associated with the movement included the German author and editor Kurt Hiller (1885–1972), who edited the yearbook; the theater critic Alfred Kerr; and the novelist Heinrich Mann. The young Benjamin had been a vocal opponent of Hiller's ideas. "New Objectivity" (Neue Sachlichkeit) was the term coined by the museum curator G. F. Hartlaub for a new tendency toward figuration in postwar German painting. It gradually came to designate the Weimar "period style" in art, architecture, design, literature, and film: cool, objective, analytical.
5. Heinrich Mann (1871–1950), German novelist and essayist, was the brother of Thomas Mann. Many of the disputes between the brothers over the years stemmed from Heinrich's left-liberal activism. Alfred Döblin (1878–1957), German novelist, is best-known for the novel *Berlin Alexanderplatz* (1929). He, too, was a prominent left-liberal voice in Weimar.
6. Kurt Hiller, *Der Sprung ins Helle* (Leipzig: Lindner, 1932), p. 314.
7. In place of this sentence, the original manuscript contained a different one, which was deleted: "Or, in Trotsky's words, 'If enlightened pacifists attempt to abolish war by means of rational argument, they simply make fools of themselves, but if the armed masses begin to use the arguments of reason against war, this means the end of war.'"
8. *Wissen und Verändern* (Know and Change; 1931) was Döblin's apology for his humane, party-independent, and frankly mystical socialism.
9. Bertolt Brecht, *Versuche 1–3* (Berlin: Kiepenheuer, 1930).
10. John Heartfield (pseudonym of Helmut Herzfelde; 1891–1968), German graphic artist, photographer, and designer, was one of the founders of Berlin Dada. He went on to reinvent photomontage as a political weapon.

11. Albert Renger-Patzsch, *Die Welt ist schön: Einhundert photographische Aufnahmen* (Munich: K. Wolff, 1928). Renger-Patzsch (1897–1966) was a German photographer who espoused a straight photographic realism, rejecting both the romanticism of photographers who tried to imitate painting and the photography that tried to gain its effects through startling techniques. His book *Die Welt ist schön* (The World Is Beautiful; 1928) established him as one of the leading European photographers.

12. Hanns Eisler (1898–1962) was a German composer best-known for his collaborations with Brecht. He became the leading composer in the German Democratic Republic, for which he wrote the national anthem.

13. The "perceptive critic" is Benjamin himself, in his essay "Left-Wing Melancholy," in this volume. Erich Kästner (1899–1974) was a German satirist, poet, and novelist who is especially known for his children's books. He was the most durable practitioner of the style of witty, laconic writing associated with the highbrow cabaret, the Berlin weekly *Die Weltbühne* (The World Stage), and the Neue Sachlichkeit (New Objectivity) movement of the mid-1920s.

14. Franz Mehring (1846–1919), German socialist historian and pamphleteer, is best-known for his biography of Karl Marx. Kurt Tucholsky (1890–1935) was a German satirist and journalist whose work is emblematic of the wit and savage irony of the Berlin cabaret.

15. E. Günther Gründel, *Die Sendung der jungen Generation: Versuch einer umfassenden revolutionären Sinndeutung der Krise* (Munich: Beck, 1932), p. 116. Gründel is referring to novels by Goethe and Gottfried Keller, respectively.

16. Georg Christoph Lichtenberg (1742–1799) was a German satirist and experimental psychologist. Although he was a feared satirist in his time, he is remembered today as the first great German aphorist.

17. Brecht, *Versuche 4–7* (Berlin: Kiepenheuer, 1930), p. 107.

18. See "Theater and Radio," in this volume.

19. René Maublanc (1891–1960) was a French Marxist historian whose books include *Fourier* (1937) and *Le Marxisme et la liberté* (1945). Louis Aragon (pseudonym of Louis Andrieux; 1897–1982) was a French poet, novelist, and essayist who, as a prominent Surrealist, was a political activist and spokesman for Communism. Benjamin's earliest work on *Das Passagen-Werk* (The Arcades Project) was inspired by Aragon's books *Vague de rêves* and *Paysan de Paris*.

Notes from Svendborg, Summer 1934

July 4. Long conversation in Brecht's sickroom in Svendborg yesterday.[1] It centered on my essay "The Author as Producer," in which I develop the theory that a decisive criterion of a revolutionary function of literature lies in the extent to which technical advances lead to a transformation of artistic forms and hence of intellectual means of production. Brecht was willing to concede the validity of this thesis only for a single type—namely, the upper-middle-class writer, a type he thought included himself. "Such a writer," he said, "experiences solidarity with the interests of the proletariat at a single point: the issue of the development of his means of production. But if solidarity exists at this single point, he is, as producer, totally proletarianized. This total proletarianization at a single point leads to a solidarity all along the line." Brecht thought my criticism of proletarian writers of the Becher type too abstract.[2] He tried to improve it with an analysis of a poem by Becher entitled "I Say Quite Openly . . . ," a poem that had appeared recently in one of the official proletarian literary reviews. Brecht compared it, on the one hand, with his didactic poem on acting, written for Carola Neher, and, on the other hand, with "Le bateau ivre."[3] "I have taught Carola Neher a variety of things," he explained. "She has not only learned to act, but, for example, she has learned how to wash herself. Up to then, she had washed so as not to be dirty. That was completely beside the point. I taught her how to wash her face. She acquired such skill in this that I wanted to make a film of her doing it. But nothing came of it because I was not making a picture at the time, and she did not want to be filmed by anyone else. That didactic poem was a model. Every learner was expected to take the place of his 'self.' When Becher says 'I,' he regards himself (since he's president of the Union of the Proletarian Revolutionary Writers of Germany) as exemplary. The only thing is that no one wants to emulate him. They simply conclude that he's pleased with himself." Brecht added that he had intended for a long time to write a number of model poems for various professions, such as engineering and writing.—On the other hand, Brecht compared Becher's poem with Rimbaud's. In the latter, he maintained that Marx and Lenin—if they had read it—would have detected the great historical movement of which it is an expression. They would have realized very clearly that it describes not just the eccentric stroll of an individual but the flight, the vagabondage, of a human being who can no longer bear to be confined within the limits of a class which—with the Crimean War and the Mexican adventure—has started to open up exotic parts of the globe to its own commercial interests. It was completely impossible to import into the model of the proletarian fighter the gesture of the footloose vagabond who leaves his own concerns to chance and turns his back on society.

July 6. Brecht said, in the course of yesterday's conversation, "I often imagine being interrogated by a tribunal: 'Tell us the truth. Are you in earnest?' I would have to confess that I am not completely in earnest. I think too much about artistic matters, about what might work on the stage, for me to be completely serious. But having uttered this disclaimer, I would go on to add an even more important claim—namely, that my behavior is *legitimate*." Of course, this is a statement that came somewhat later in the course of the conversation. Brecht had begun by doubting not the legitimacy of his methods but their efficacy. In particular, with the statement provoked by some comments I had made about Gerhart Hauptmann: "I occasionally wonder whether they aren't the only writers who really achieve something— the *substance writers,* I mean." By this, Brecht means writers who are completely serious. And to explain this idea, he begins by imagining that Confucius had written a tragedy, or Lenin a novel. We would regard that as improper, he claims, and as an act unworthy of them. "Let's assume that you read an excellent political novel and discover subsequently that it was by Lenin. You'd change your opinion about both Lenin and the novel; they'd both go down in your estimation. Nor could Confucius have written a tragedy like those of Euripides; it would have seemed unworthy of him. But the same thing couldn't be said about his parables." In short, all this amounts to a distinction between two types of writers: the visionary, who is in earnest, and the reflective writer, who is not quite serious. And this leads me to raise the question of Kafka. Which group does he belong to? I realize that the question cannot be answered. And the very fact that it cannot be decided is, in Brecht's eyes, proof that Kafka (whom he regards as a great writer) is a failure, like Kleist and Grabbe, or Büchner.[4] His starting point is really the parable, the allegory, which is answerable to reason and hence cannot be entirely in earnest on the literal plane. But Kafka then develops the parable. It grows up into a novel. And a closer look reveals that it has contained the seed of the novel from the outset. It was never completely transparent. Furthermore, Brecht is convinced that Kafka would never have discovered his own proper form without Dostoevsky's Grand Inquisitor and that other parabolic passage in *The Brothers Karamazov*, where the corpse of the holy Staretz begins to stink. In Kafka, then, parable is in conflict with the visionary. But Brecht adds that, as a visionary, Kafka saw what was to come, without seeing what exists now. Brecht emphasizes the prophetic element in Kafka's works, as he did earlier, in Le Lavandou, and even more explicitly to me. Kafka had only one problem, that of organization. What gripped his imagination was his fear of a society of ants: the way in which people become alienated from each other by the forms of their life together. And he foresaw certain forms of this alienation, such as the methods of the Russian Secret Police. But he did not find any solution and has never awoken from his nightmare. Brecht added that Kafka's precision was the precision of an imprecise man, a dreamer.

July 12. Yesterday, after a game of chess, Brecht said: "When Karl Korsch comes, we ought to work out a new game with him.[5] A game in which the positions do not always remain constant, in which the functions of the pieces change after they have stood in the same place for a certain length of time. They would then become either stronger or weaker. At present, there is no development; things stay as they are for too long."

July 23. Yesterday, a visit from Karin Michaelis, who has just returned from a trip to Russia and is full of enthusiasm.[6] Brecht remembers being shown around by Sergei Tretiakov, who gave him a tour of Moscow and was proud of everything his visitor saw, no matter what. "That's not a bad thing," Brecht said. "It shows that what he showed me belongs to him. No one is proud of what belongs to someone else." After a while, he added: "But in the end, I did become a bit tired of it all. I couldn't admire everything, nor did I want to. After all, they are his soldiers and his trucks. Unfortunately, they are not mine."

July 24. On a horizontal beam supporting the roof of Brecht's study, there is a painted inscription: "The truth is concrete." On a window ledge stands a little wooden donkey that can nod its head. Brecht has hung a little notice round its neck with the words: "I, too, must understand it."

August 5. Three weeks ago I gave Brecht my essay on Kafka to read. He doubtless read it, but did not allude to it of his own accord; and on the two occasions when I brought the subject up, he responded evasively. Finally, I took the manuscript back without comment. Yesterday, he suddenly referred to the essay. With a somewhat abrupt and forced transition in the conversation, he remarked that I, too, could not entirely escape the charge of writing in diary form, in the style of Nietzsche. My Kafka essay, for example. It was interested in Kafka only as a phenomenon; looked at the work as if it—and likewise the author—were a product of nature and isolated it from every possible context, even the author's life. I was always interested exclusively in the question of *essence*. But how should such matters be addressed? The questions to be raised about Kafka are: What is he doing? How does he behave? And you should start with the general rather than the particular. What then emerges is that he lived, in Prague, in an unfortunate milieu of journalists and self-important literati. In that milieu, literature was the principal reality, if not the only one. And this view of things was inseparable from Kafka's own strengths and weaknesses—his artistic value, but also his uselessness in many respects. He was a Jewboy (you could also coin the term "Aryan-boy")—a feeble, unattractive figure, a bubble on the iridescent surface of the swamp of Prague's cultural life, and nothing more. But then, in this perspective, there were certain definite and highly interesting aspects. They could be made visible. One can imagine a conversation between Lao-tze[7] and his disciple Kafka: "'Very well then, Disciple Kafka, is it true that the organizations, the legal and economic institutions, around you have begun to give you the creeps?' 'Yes.' 'You cannot find your way around them any more?' 'No.' 'A stock certificate terrifies you?' 'Yes.' 'And now you are longing for a leader you can rely on, Disciple Kafka.'" "Of course, that is reprehensible," Brecht comments. "I reject Kafka." And he goes on to relate the parable told by a Chinese philosopher, concerning "the sufferings of usefulness." "In the forest, there are trees of different sorts. The thickest trunks are used for the beams of ships; the less massive but still quite serviceable trunks are used to make crates and coffins; the much thinner ones are used to make canes. But the twisted ones are not used for anything at all—they escape the sufferings of usefulness. You have to look around in Kafka's writings as if it were such a forest. You will find a number of very useful things. The images are good. The rest is just mystery-mongering. It is nonsense. You must ignore it. You cannot make progress with depth. Depth is simply a dimension; it is just depth—in which nothing can be seen." I end up telling Brecht that descending into the depths is my way of journeying to the antipodes. In my essay on Kraus, I had in fact managed to arrive there. I knew that the Kafka piece was less successful. I could not refute the criticism that it was a diary-like set of notes. In fact, I felt at home in the marginal space marked out by Kraus and, in a different way, by Kafka. Ultimately I had not yet fully managed to explore this space in the case of Kafka. I was well aware that his writings contained a lot of debris and rubbish—a lot of real mystery-mongering. But other things were crucial, and my study had touched on some of them. Brecht's judgment would have to be tested on particular works. I suggested "Das nächste Dorf" [The Next Village]. I saw right away the conflict that this suggestion produced in Brecht. He flatly rejected Hanns Eisler's assertion that this story was "worthless."[8] On the other hand, he was quite unable to define its value. "It has to be studied closely," he said. The discussion broke off at this point. It was ten o'clock—time for the news from Vienna on the radio.

August 31. The day before yesterday, a long, heated debate about my Kafka. Its foundation: the accusation that the essay promoted Jewish fascism. It increased and spread confusion about him, instead of dissipating it. Whereas the real task was to shed light on Kafka, and that meant formulating the practical proposals that could be distilled from his stories. One must assume that proposals can be distilled from them, if only because of the sovereign calm that characterizes the stance of the narrator. These proposals must be sought in the vicinity of the great evils that beset mankind today. Brecht attempted to point to their imprint on Kafka's writing. He concentrated mainly on *Der Prozess* (The Trial). What you find there above all, he said, is fear of the inexorable and never-ending growth of big cities. From his own intimate experience, he knows of the nightmare force with which this idea weighs on mankind. The incalculable mediations, dependencies, and complications that human beings find themselves in, thanks to modern forms of life, find expression in these cities. On the other hand, they also find expression in the longing for a "leader," for that *Führer* who—especially in the eyes of the petty bourgeois—can be held to account for all the latter's misfortunes in a world where everyone points the finger at someone else and everyone denies responsibility. Brecht calls *Der Prozess* a prophetic book. "You can see from the Gestapo what could become of the Cheka."[9] Kafka's perspective: that of a man who has fallen under the wheels. Symptomatic of this is Odradek: Brecht interprets "Die Sorge des Hausvaters" [The Cares of a Family Man] as those of the homeowner. The petty bourgeois necessarily gets it in the neck. His situation is Kafka's. But whereas the type of the petty bourgeois familiar today—the fascist, in other words—resolves to combat this situation by means of his invincible iron will, Kafka offers scarcely any resistance; he is wise. Where the fascist brings heroism into play, Kafka asks questions. He asks for guarantees of his situation. But his situation is such that the guarantees would have to exceed the bounds of reason. It is a Kafkaesque irony that the man was an insurance agent who appeared to be convinced of nothing more surely than the invalidity of all guarantees. Incidentally, his boundless pessimism is free from every tragic sense of fate. For not only is his expectation of disaster based entirely on empirical realities (although there it is total), but, in addition, the criteria of ultimate success are attached with incorrigible naïveté to the most trivial and commonplace activities, such as the visit of a commercial traveler or an inquiry addressed to a governmental department.—The discussion kept coming back to "Das nächste Dorf." Brecht said it was a companion piece to the story of Achilles and the tortoise. A rider can never reach the next village if he divides the journey up into its smallest components—even aside from any incidents en route. Because life is too short for such a journey. But the error lies in the concept of "a rider." For you have to divide up the traveler, as well as the journey. And since in doing this you abolish the unity of life, you likewise do away with its brevity. However short it may be. This doesn't matter, because the man who started out on his journey is different from the man who arrives.—For my part, I proposed the following interpretation: the true measure of life is memory. Looking back, it runs through life like lightning. The speed with which you can turn back a few pages is the same as the speed with which memory flies from the next village back to the place from which the rider decided to leave. Whoever, like the Ancients, has seen his life transformed into writing, let him read this writing backward. Only in this way will he encounter himself, and only in this way—in full flight from the present—will he be able to understand it.

September 27; Dragør. During an evening conversation a few days ago, Brecht displayed the strange indecisiveness that prevents him from making definite plans at the moment. The underlying cause of this indecisiveness is—as he himself emphasizes—the advantages that distinguish his personal situation from that of the majority of émigrés. Because in general he scarcely acknowledges the emigration as the foundation of plans and enterprises, it seems a fortiori to have no relevance for him. His plans operate on a larger scale. This presents him with alternatives. On one side, there are prose projects awaiting him. The smaller one about Ui—a satire on Hitler in the style of Renaissance historiography[10]—and the larger project of *Der Tui-Roman* [The Tui Novel]. *Der Tui-Roman* is intended to provide an encyclopedic survey of the follies of the Tellectuall-Ins (the intellectuals); it is set, partly at least, in China. A brief first draft of this work is finished. Alongside these prose plans, he is also preoccupied with projects that go back to very old studies and ideas. Whereas the reflections that arose in the context of the Epic Theater could be defined at a pinch in the notes and introductions to the *Versuche* [Experiments], ideas that originated in the same interests outgrew this narrow framework once they had been joined by the study of Leninism, on the one hand, and scientific empiricism, on the other. They have been concentrated for years now under one label or another, so that, in turn, non-Aristotelian logic, behavior theory, the new encyclopedia, and the critique of ideas became the focal point of his preoccupations. These different concerns are converging at present in the idea of a philosophical didactic poem. Brecht's misgivings revolve around the question whether he will have enough credit with the public for such a work—in the light of his entire past production, especially its satirical parts and above all *Der Drei-groschenroman* [The Threepenny Novel]. Such doubts are the meeting point of two different lines of thought. On the one hand, there are misgivings that concern his satirical and especially his ironic stance as such—the more so, the closer Brecht's involvement with the problems and methods of proletarian class struggle becomes. Such misgivings—which are essentially practical in nature—might be comprehensible, but not if they are identified with other, deeper-lying doubts. These deeper-lying reservations concern the artistic and playful aspect of art—above all, those impulses that from time to time make art resistant to reason. Brecht's sustained efforts to legitimate art vis-à-vis rationality have driven him again and again to the parable, a form in which artistic mastery is demonstrated by the fact that, in the end, the artistic elements cancel one another out. And these efforts to make use of the parable are at present emerging in a more radical form in the ideas connected with the didactic poem. In the course of this discussion, I tried to persuade Brecht that a didactic poem did not have to win over a bourgeois audience so much as a proletarian one, and that a proletarian audience was less likely to take its standards from Brecht's earlier, partly bourgeois-oriented works than from the dogmatic and theoretical content of the didactic poem itself. "If this didactic poem succeeds in mobilizing the authority of Marxism in its own cause," I told him, "the facts about your previous work are unlikely to undermine it."

October 4, 1934. Yesterday Brecht left for London.—Whether he sometimes feels especially challenged by me, or whether such behavior comes more easily to him now than it used to, what he himself thinks of as the inflammatory side of his thought comes to the fore in discussion much more often now than it did formerly. Indeed, I have been struck by a special vocabulary that turns up in his speech, in conjunction with this attitude. The concept of the *Würstchen* [little sausage] is a particular favorite of his in this respect. In Dragør I was reading Dostoevsky's *Crime and Punishment*. Brecht began by claiming that reading this novel was the main cause of my illness. And by way of proof he told me how, when he was young, a chronic illness whose germ had been latent in him for a long time broke out one afternoon when a schoolfriend played Chopin on the piano, at a time when Brecht was already too enfeebled to protest. He ascribes to Chopin and Dostoevsky particularly dire effects on health. Furthermore, on every possible occasion he took exception to the books I was reading, and since he was himself reading *The Good Soldier Schweik* he did not pass up the opportunity to compare the merits of the two writers. It turned out that Dostoevsky was no match for Hašek, and was relegated to the *Würstchen* without more ado. It would not have required much for Brecht to extend to Dostoevsky's writings the epithet that lately he has been ready to apply to any works that lack an enlightened tendency, or whose enlightened tendency he denies. He calls them a *Klump* [junk].

Written July–October 1934; unpublished in Benjamin's lifetime. *Gesammelte Schriften,* VI, 523–532. Translated by Rodney Livingstone.

Notes

1. Southern Funen Island, Denmark, on Svendborg Sound, Brecht's home in exile until 1939.
2. Johannes R. Becher (1891–1958) was a leading Expressionist poet who subsequently became a major force in Marxist literary circles, both as an émigré in Russia and, after 1945, in the German Democratic Republic, where he became minister of culture and president of the East German Academy of Arts.
3. Carola Neher (1905–ca. 1940) was one of Weimar's most gifted actresses. She played, among many other roles, Lulu in Frank Wedekind's *Büchse der Pandora* (Pandora's Box) and Eliza Doolittle in G. B. Shaw's *Pygmalion.* After she had played the role of Polly in the second cast of Brecht's *Dreigroschenoper* (Threepenny Opera), he wrote the play *Heilige Johanna der Schlachthofe* (Saint Joan of the Slaughterhouse) for her. She emigrated to the Soviet Union in 1933, was arrested in 1939, and died in a Soviet prison sometime thereafter. "Le bateau ivre" (The Drunken Boat; 1871) is perhaps the finest work by the French poet Arthur Rimbaud (1854–1891). He produced most of his writings before 1875, when, following an intense and violent relationship with Paul Verlaine, he began to wander through Europe and Africa.
4. Heinrich von Kleist (1777–1811), the first of the great German dramatists and short-story writers of the nineteenth century, wrote three plays that, although they received little acclaim in their time, have proven to be enduring classics: *Penthesilea* (1808), *Der zerbrochene Krug* (The Broken Pitcher; 1808), and *Prinz Friedrich von Homburg* (published posthumously in 1821 by Ludwig Tieck). His dramas combine remarkable intensity, psychological acuity, and a unique poetic voice. Christian Dietrich Grabbe (1801–1836), German dramatist, produced a number of plays that exceeded the capacities of the contemporary stage. Both *Napoleon, oder Die Hundert Tage* (Napoleon, or The Hundred Days; 1831) and *Don Juan und Faust* (1829) avoid continuous action in their use of rapidly changing, highly vivid scenes. Georg Büchner (1813–1837), German dramatist, produced two landmarks of the European theater, *Dantons Tod* (Danton's Death; 1835) and *Woyzeck* (1836). They combine harsh psychological realism with a fragmentary but highly suggestive dramatic technique.
5. Karl Korsch (1892–1939), German legal and Marxist theorist, had been one of Brecht's teachers. He was an outspoken opponent of Stalinist Russia, and settled in the United States after the Nazis rose to power. Benjamin used his work extensively in *Das Passagen-Werk* (The Arcades Project).

6. Karin Michaelis (1872–1950) was a celebrated Danish writer. In works such as *The Dangerous Age,* she addressed women's sexual needs.

7. Lao-tze (fl. sixth century B.C.) was the first philosopher of Chinese Taoism and the alleged author of the Tao-te Ching. Modern scholars discount the possibility that the text was written by one person but acknowledge the influence of Taoism on the development of Buddhism.

8. Hanns Eisler (1898–1962) was a German composer best-known for his collaborations with Brecht. He became the leading composer in the German Democratic Republic, for which he composed the national anthem.

9. The Cheka—also called the Vecheka—was an early Soviet secret-police agency and a forerunner of the KGB.

10. The "smaller one about Ui" is not the play about Arturo Ui, but *Die Geschichte des Giacomo Ui* (The History of Giacomo Ui).

Hitler's Diminished Masculinity

Hitler's diminished masculinity—
  to be compared with the feminine cast of the little tramp portrayed by
  Chaplin
So much luster surrounding so much shabbiness
Hitler's following
  to be compared with Chaplin's public
Chaplin—the plowshare that cuts through the masses; laughter loosens up
  the mass
  the ground of the Third Reich is stamped down hard and firm, and no
  more grass grows there
Ban on puppets in Italy, on Chaplin's films in the Third Reich—
  every puppet can put on Mussolini's chin, and every inch of Chaplin can
  become the Führer
The poor devil wants to be taken seriously, and instantly must call upon all
  hell
Chaplin's docility is apparent to all eyes; Hitler's, only to those of his bosses
Chaplin shows up the comedy of Hitler's gravity; when he acts the well-
  bred man, then we know how things stand with the Führer
Chaplin has become the greatest comic because he has incorporated into
  himself the deepest fears of his contemporaries
The fashion keynote for Hitler is not the image of the military man, but
  that of the gentleman in easy circumstances. The feudal emblems of authority are out of date; there remained only men's fashions. Chaplin, too,
  looks to men's fashions. He does this in order to take the master caste at
  its word. His cane is the rod around which the parasite creeps (the

vagabond is no less a parasite than the gent), and his bowler hat, which no longer sits so securely on his head, betrays the fact that the rule of the bourgeoisie is tottering.

It would be wrong to interpret the figure of Chaplin in a purely psychological light. Rarely do such popular figures fail to carry with them sundry properties or emblems that, from without, set the proper tone for them. In Chaplin's case, this role is played by his accoutrements—the cane and bowler hat.

"That happens only once, and never comes again." Hitler did not accept the title of president of the Reich;[1] his aim was to impress upon the people the singularity of his appearance. This singularity works in favor of his magically transposed prestige.

Fragment written ca. August 1934; unpublished in Benjamin's lifetime. *Gesammelte Schriften*, VI, 103–104. Translated by Howard Eiland, on the basis of a prior version by Lieven De Cauter.

Notes

1. After the death of Paul von Hindenburg on August 2, 1934, Hitler took over the office of Reichspräsident though officially renouncing the title. Chaplin's film parodying Hitler, *The Great Dictator,* was not released until 1940.

Franz Kafka

On the Tenth Anniversary of His Death

Potemkin

It is said that Potemkin suffered from states of depression which recurred more or less regularly.[1] At such times no one was allowed to go near him, and access to his room was strictly forbidden. This malady was never mentioned at court, and in particular it was known that any allusion to it would incur the disfavor of Empress Catherine. One of the chancellor's depressions lasted for an extraordinary length of time and caused serious difficulties; in the offices documents piled up that required Potemkin's signature, and the empress pressed for their completion. The high officials were at their wits' end. One day, an unimportant little clerk named Shuvalkin happened to enter the anteroom of the chancellor's palace and found the councillors of state assembled there, moaning and groaning as usual. "What is the matter, Your Excellencies?" asked the obliging Shuvalkin. They explained things to him and regretted that they could not use his services. "If that's all it is," said Shuvalkin, "I beg you gentlemen to let me have those papers." Having nothing to lose, the councillors of state let themselves be persuaded to do so, and with the sheaf of documents under his arm, Shuvalkin set out, through galleries and corridors, for Potemkin's bedroom. Without knocking or even stopping, he turned the door handle; the room was not locked. In semidarkness Potemkin was sitting on his bed, in a threadbare nightshirt, biting his nails. Shuvalkin stepped up to the writing desk, dipped a pen in ink, and without saying a word pressed it into Potemkin's hand while putting one of the documents on his knees. Potemkin gave the intruder a vacant stare; then, as though in his sleep, he started to sign—first one paper, then a second, finally all of them. When the last signature had been affixed, Shuvalkin took the papers under his arm and left the room without further ado, just as he had entered it. Waving the papers triumphantly, he stepped into the anteroom. The councillors of state rushed toward him and tore the documents out of his hands. Breathlessly they bent over them. No one spoke a word; the whole group seemed paralyzed. Again Shuvalkin came closer and solicitously asked why the gentlemen seemed so upset. At that point he noticed the signatures. One document after another was signed Shuvalkin . . . Shuvalkin . . . Shuvalkin . . .

This story is like a herald of Kafka's work, storming two hundred years ahead of it. The enigma which beclouds this story is Kafka's enigma. The world of offices and registries, of musty, shabby, dark rooms, is Kafka's world. The obliging Shuvalkin, who takes everything so lightly and is finally left empty-handed, is Kafka's K. Potemkin, on the other hand, who vegetates, somnolent and unkempt, in a remote, inaccessible room, is an ancestor of those holders of power in Kafka's works who live in the attics as judges or in the castle as secretaries. No matter how highly placed they may be, they are always fallen or falling men, although even the lowest and seediest of them, the doorkeepers and the decrepit officials, may abruptly and strikingly appear in the fullness of their power. Why do they vegetate? Could they be the descendants of those figures of Atlas that support globes with their shoulders? Perhaps this is why each has his head "so deep on his chest that one can hardly see anything of his eyes," like the Castellan in his portrait, or Klamm when he is alone. But it is not the globe they are carrying; it is just that even the most everyday things have their weight. "His fatigue is that of the gladiator after a fight; his job was to whitewash a corner of the office of an official!"[2]—Georg Lukács once said that in order to make a decent table nowadays, a man must have the architectural genius of a Michelangelo.[3] If Lukács thinks in terms of historical ages, Kafka thinks in terms of cosmic epochs. The man who whitewashes has epochs to move, even in his most insignificant gesture. On many occasions, and often for strange reasons, Kafka's figures clap their hands. Once, the casual remark is made that these hands are "really steam hammers" ["Auf der Galerie"].

We meet these holders of power in constant, slow movement, rising or falling. But they are at their most terrible when they rise from the deepest decay—from the fathers. The son in "Das Urteil" [The Judgment] calms his spiritless, senile father whom he has just gently put to bed:

"Don't worry, you are well covered up."
"No," cried his father, cutting short the answer. He threw the blanket off with such strength that it unfolded fully as it flew, and he stood up in bed. Only one hand lightly touched the ceiling to steady him.

"You wanted to cover me up, I know, my little scamp, but I'm not all covered up yet. And even if this is all the strength I have left, it's enough for you—too much for you . . . But thank goodness a father does not need to be taught how to see through his son" . . . And he stood up quite unsupported and kicked his legs out. He beamed with insight . . .

"So now you know what else there was in the world besides yourself; until now, you have known only about yourself! It is true, you were an innocent child, but it is even more true that you have been a devilish person!"

As the father throws off the burden of the blanket, he also throws off a cosmic burden. He has to set cosmic ages in motion in order to turn the age-old father-son relationship into a living and consequential thing. But what consequences! He sentences his son to death by drowning. The father is the one who punishes; he is drawn to guilt, just as the court officials are. There is much to indicate that the world of officials and the world of fathers are the same to Kafka. The similarity does not redound to this world's credit; it consists of dullness, decay, and filth. The father's uniform is stained all over; his underwear is dirty. Filth is the element of officials. "She could not understand why there were office hours for the public in the first place. 'To get some dirt on the front staircase'—this is how her question was once answered by an official, who was probably annoyed, but it made a lot of sense to her" [*Das Schloß*]. Uncleanness is so much the attribute of officials that one could almost regard them as enormous parasites. This, of course, refers not to the economic context, but to the forces of reason and humanity from which this clan makes a living. In the same way, the fathers in Kafka's strange families batten on their sons, lying on top of them like giant parasites. They not only prey upon their strength, but gnaw away at the sons' right to exist. Fathers punish, but they are at the same time accusers. The sin of which they accuse their sons seems to be a kind of original sin. The definition of it which Kafka has given applies to the sons more than to anyone else: "Original sin, the old injustice committed by man, consists in the complaint unceasingly made by man that he has been the victim of an injustice, the victim of original sin" ["Er"]. But who is accused of this inherited sin—the sin of having produced an heir—if not the father by the son? Accordingly, the son would be the sinner. But one must not conclude from Kafka's definition that the accusation is sinful because it is false. Nowhere does Kafka say that it is made wrongfully. A never-ending process is at work here, and no cause can appear in a worse light than the one for which the father enlists the aid of these officials and court offices. A boundless corruptibility is not their worst feature, for their essence is such that their venality is the only hope held out to the human spirit facing them. The courts, to be sure, have lawbooks at their disposal, but people are not allowed to see them. "It is characteristic of this legal system," conjectures K. in *Der Prozeß* [The Trial], "that one is sentenced not only in innocence but also in ignorance." Laws and definite norms remain unwritten in the prehistoric world. A man can transgress them without suspecting it and then must strive for atonement. But no matter how hard it may hit the unsuspecting, the transgression in the sense of the law is not accidental but fated, a destiny which appears here in all its ambiguity. In a side-glance at the idea of fate in Antiquity, Hermann Cohen came to a "conclusion that becomes inescapable": "The very rules of fate seem to be what causes and brings about the breaking away from them, the defection."[4] It is the same way with the legal authorities whose proceedings are directed against K. It takes us back, far beyond the time of the giving of the Law on twelve tablets, to a prehistoric world, written law being one of the first victories scored over this world. In Kafka the written law is contained in lawbooks, but these are secret; by basing itself on them, the prehistoric world exerts its rule all the more ruthlessly.

In Kafka's works, the conditions in offices and in families have multifarious points of contact. In the village at the foot of Castle Hill, people quote an illuminating saying. "'We have a saying here that you may be familiar with: Official decisions are as shy as young girls.' 'That's a sound observation,' said K., 'a sound observation. Decisions may have even other characteristics in common with girls.'" The most remarkable of these qualities is the willingness to lend oneself to anything, like the shy girls whom K. meets in *Das Schloß* [The Castle] and *Der Prozeß*—girls who indulge in unchaste behavior in the bosom of their family as they would in a bed. He encounters them at every turn; the rest give him as little trouble as the conquest of the barmaid.

> They embraced each other; her little body burned in K.'s hands. In a state of unconsciousness which K. tried to master constantly but fruitlessly, they rolled a little way, hit Klamm's door with a thud, and then lay in the little puddles of beer and the other refuse that littered the floor. Hours passed . . . in which K. constantly had the feeling that he was losing his way or that he had wandered farther than anyone had ever wandered before, to a place where even the air had nothing in common with his native air, where all this strangeness might choke one, yet a place so insanely enchanting that one could not help going on and losing oneself even further [*Das Schloß*].

We shall have more to say about this strange place. The remarkable thing is that these whorelike women never seem to be beautiful. Rather, beauty appears in Kafka's world only in the most obscure places—among accused persons, for example. "This, to be sure, is a strange phenomenon, a natural law, as it were . . . It cannot be guilt that makes them attractive . . . nor can it be the just punishment which makes them attractive in anticipation . . . So it must be the mere charges brought against them that somehow show on them."

From *Der Prozeß*, it may be seen that these proceedings are usually hopeless for those accused—hopeless even when they have hopes of being acquitted. It may be this hopelessness that brings out the beauty in them—the only creatures in Kafka thus favored. At least, this would be very much in keeping with the fragment of a conversation which Max Brod has related.

> I remember a conversation with Kafka which began with present-day Europe and the decline of the human race.
>
> "We are nihilistic thoughts, suicidal thoughts, that come into God's head," Kafka said. This reminded me at first of the Gnostic view of life: God as the evil demiurge, the world as his Fall.
>
> "Oh no," said Kafka, "our world is only a bad mood of God, a bad day of his."
>
> "Then there is hope outside this manifestation of the world that we know."
>
> He smiled. "Oh, plenty of hope, an infinite amount of hope—but not for us."⁵

These words provide a bridge to those extremely strange figures in Kafka, the only ones who have escaped from the family circle and for whom there may be hope. These are not the animals, not even those hybrids or imaginary creatures like the Cat Lamb or Odradek; they all still live under the spell of the family. It is no accident that Gregor Samsa wakes up as a bug in his parental home and not somewhere else, and that the peculiar animal which is half-kitten, half-lamb, is inherited from the father; Odradek likewise is the concern of the father of the family. The "assistants," however, are outside this circle.⁶

These assistants belong to a group of figures which recurs through Kafka's entire work. Their tribe includes the confidence man who is unmasked in *Betrachtung* [Meditation]; the student who appears on the balcony at night as Karl Rossmann's neighbor [in *Amerika*]; and the fools who live in that town in the south and never get tired [in "Kinder auf der Landstrasse"]. The twilight in which they exist is reminiscent of the uncertain light that surrounds the figures in the short prose pieces of Robert Walser—the author of *Der Gehülfe* [The Assistant], a contemporary novel of which Kafka was very fond.⁷ In Indian mythology there are the *gandharvas*, mist-bound creatures, beings in an unfinished state. Kafka's assistants are of that kind: neither members of, nor strangers to, any of the other groups of figures, but, rather, messengers busy moving between them. Kafka tells us that they resemble Barnabas, who is a messenger. They have not yet been completely released from the womb of nature, and that is why they have "settled down on two old skirts on the floor in a corner. It was . . . their ambition . . . to use up as little space as possible. To that end they kept making various experiments, folding their arms and legs, huddling close together; in the darkness, all one could see in their corner was one big ball" [*Das Schloß*].

It is for them and their kind, the unfinished and the hapless, that there is hope.

What may be discerned, more tenderly subdued, in the activities of these messengers is the Law that reigns, in an oppressive and gloomy way, over this whole group of creatures. None has a firm place in the world, or firm, inalienable outlines. There is not one that is not either rising or falling, none that is not trading qualities with its enemy or neighbor, none that has not completed its period of time and yet is unripe, none that is not deeply exhausted and yet is only at the beginning of a long existence. To speak of any order or hierarchy is impossible here. Even the world of myth, which comes to mind in this context, is incomparably younger than Kafka's world, which has been promised redemption by myth. But if we can be sure of one thing, it is this: Kafka did not succumb to its temptation. A latter-day Ulysses, he let the Sirens pass before "his gaze, which was fixed on the distance; the Sirens disappeared, as it were, before his determination, and at the very moment when he was closest to them he was no longer aware of them." Among Kafka's ancestors in the ancient world, the Jews and the Chinese (whom we shall encounter later), this Greek one should not be forgotten. Ulysses, after all, stands at the dividing line between myth and fairy tale. Reason and cunning have inserted tricks into myths; their forces cease to be invincible. Fairy tales are the traditional stories about victory over these forces, and fairy tales for dialecticians are what Kafka wrote when he went to work on legends. He inserted little tricks into them; then he used them as proof "that inadequate, even childish measures may also serve as a means of rescue." With these words, he begins his story "Das Schweigen der Sirenen" [The Silence of the Sirens]. For Kafka's Sirens are silent; they have "an even more terrible weapon than their song . . . their silence." This they used on Ulysses. But he, so Kafka tells us, "was so full of guile, was such a fox, that not even the goddess of fate could pierce his armor. Perhaps he had really noticed (although here human understanding is out of its depth) that the Sirens were silent, and he opposed the aforementioned pretense to them and the gods merely as a sort of shield."

Kafka's Sirens are silent. Perhaps because for Kafka music and singing are an expression or at least a token of escape, a token of hope which comes to us from that intermediate world—at once unfinished and everyday, comforting and silly—in which assistants are at home. Kafka is like the lad who set out to learn what fear was. He has got into Potemkin's palace and finally, in the depths of its cellar, has encountered Josephine, the singing mouse, whose tune he describes: "Something of our poor, brief childhood is in it, something of lost happiness which can never be found again, but also something of active present-day life, of its small gaieties, unaccountable and yet real and unquenchable" ["Josefine, die Sängerin; oder, Das Volk der Mäuse"].

A Childhood Photograph

There is a childhood photograph of Kafka, a supremely touching portrayal of his "poor, brief childhood." It was probably made in one of those nineteenth-century studios whose draperies and palm trees, tapestries and easels, placed them somewhere between a torture chamber and a throne room. At the age of about six the boy is presented in a sort of greenhouse setting, wearing a tight, heavily lace-trimmed, almost embarrassing child's suit. Palm branches loom in the background. And as if to make these upholstered tropics still more sultry and sticky, the subject holds in his left hand an oversized, wide-brimmed hat of the type worn by Spaniards. Immensely sad eyes dominate the landscape arranged for them, and the auricle of a large ear seems to be listening for its sounds.

The ardent "wish to be a Red Indian" may have consumed this great sadness at some point. "If one were only an Indian, instantly alert, and on a galloping horse, leaning into the wind, kept on quivering briefly over the quivering ground, until one shed one's spurs, for there were no spurs, threw away the reins, for there were no reins, and barely saw the land before one as a smoothly mown plain, with the horse's neck and head already gone." A great deal is contained in this wish. Its fulfillment, which he finds in America, yields up its secret. That *Amerika* is a very special case is indicated by the name of its hero. While in the earlier novels the author never addressed himself otherwise than with a mumbled initial, here, on a new continent, he undergoes a rebirth and acquires a full name. He has this experience in the Nature Theater of Oklahoma.

> On a street corner, Karl saw a poster with the following announcement: "Today, from 6 A.M. until midnight, at Clayton Racetrack, the Oklahoma Theater will be hiring members for its company. The great Theater of Oklahoma calls you! The one and only call is today! If you miss your chance now, you miss it forever! If you think of your future, you belong with us! Everyone is welcome! If you want to be an artist, come forward! Our theater can use everyone and find the right place for everyone! If you decide to join us, we congratulate you here and now! But hurry, so that you get in before midnight! At twelve o'clock the doors will be shut and never opened again! A curse on those who do not believe in us! Set out for Clayton!"

The reader of this announcement is Karl Rossmann, the third and happiest incarnation of K., the hero of Kafka's novels. Happiness awaits him at the Nature Theater of Oklahoma, which is really a racetrack, just as "unhappiness" had once beset him on the narrow rug in his room on which he ran about "as on a racetrack." Ever since Kafka had written his "Nachdenken für Herrenreiter" [Reflections for Gentleman Jockeys]; ever since he had made the "new advocate" mount the courthouse steps, lifting his legs high, with a tread that made the marble ring; ever since he had made his "children on a country road" amble through the countryside with large steps and folded arms—this figure had been familiar to him. Even Karl Rossmann, "distracted by his sleepiness," may often make "leaps that are too high, too time-consuming, and useless." Thus, it can only be a racetrack on which he attains the object of his desire.

This racetrack is at the same time a theater, and this poses a puzzle. But the mysterious place and the entirely unmysterious, transparent, pure figure of Karl Rossmann are congruous. For Karl Rossmann is transparent, pure, without character, as it were, in the same sense in which Franz Rosenzweig says in his *Stern der Erlösung* [Star of Redemption] that in China people are—so far as their spiritual aspects are concerned—"devoid of individual character, as it were. The idea of the wise man, of which Confucius is the classic incarnation, blurs any individuality of character; he is the truly characterless man—namely, the average man . . . What distinguishes a Chinese is something quite different from character: a very elemental purity of feeling."[8] No matter how one conveys it intellectually, this purity of feeling may be a particularly sensitive gauge of gestural behavior. In any case, the Nature Theater of Oklahoma harks back to Chinese theater, which is a theater of gesture. One of the most significant functions of this theater is to dissolve events into their gestural components. One can go even further and say that a good number of Kafka's shorter studies and stories are seen in their full light only when they are, so to speak, put on as acts in the "Nature Theater of Oklahoma." Only then will one come to the certain realization that Kafka's entire work constitutes a code of gestures which surely had no definite symbolic meaning for the author from the outset; rather, the author tried to derive such a meaning from them in ever-changing contexts and experimental groupings. The theater is the logical place for such groupings. In an unpublished commentary on the story "Ein Brudermord" [A Fratricide], Werner Kraft perceptively identified the events in this little story as scenic events. "The play is ready to begin, and it is actually announced by a bell. This comes about in a very natural way. Wese leaves the building in which his office is located. But this doorbell (we are expressly told) is 'too loud for a doorbell; it rings out over the town and up to heaven.'"[9] Just as this bell, which is too loud for a doorbell, rings out toward heaven, the gestures of Kafka's figures are too powerful for our accustomed surroundings and break out into wider areas. The greater Kafka's mastery became, the more frequently he avoided adapting these gestures to common situations or explaining them. "It is strange behavior," we read in "Die Verwandlung" [The Metamorphosis], "to sit on the desk and talk down at the employee, who, furthermore, must come quite close because his boss is hard of hearing." *Der Prozeß* has already left such motivations far behind. In the penultimate chapter, K. stops at the first rows in the cathedral, "but the priest seemed to consider the distance still too great; he stretched out an arm and pointed with his sharply bent forefinger to a spot right in front of the pulpit. K. followed this direction, too; in that spot, he had to bend his head far back to see the priest at all."

Max Brod has said: "The world of those realities that were important for him was unfathomable." What Kafka could fathom least of all was the *gestus*. Each gesture is an event—one might even say a drama—in itself. The stage on which this drama takes place is the World Theater, which opens up toward heaven. On the other hand, this heaven is only background; to explore it according to its own laws would be like framing the painted backdrop of a stage and hanging it in a picture gallery. Like El Greco, Kafka tears open the sky behind every gesture; but as with El Greco—who was the patron saint of the Expressionists—the gesture remains the decisive thing, the center of the event. In "Der Schlag ans Hoftor" [The Knock at the Gate], the people who hear the knock double up with fright. This is how a Chinese actor would portray terror, but no one would give a start. Elsewhere, K. himself does a bit of acting. Without being fully conscious of it, "slowly, . . . with his eyes not looking down but cautiously raised upward, he took one of the papers from the desk, put it on the palm of his hand, and gradually raised it up to the gentlemen while getting up himself. He had nothing definite in mind, but acted only with the feeling that this was what he would have to do once he had completed the big petition which was to exonerate him completely" [*Der Prozeß*]. This animal gesture combines the utmost mysteriousness with the utmost simplicity. You can read Kafka's animal stories for quite a while without realizing that they are not about human beings at all. When you finally come upon the name of the creature—monkey, dog, mole—you look up in fright and realize that you are already far away from the continent of man. But it is always Kafka; he divests human gesture of its traditional supports, and then has a subject for reflection without end.

Strangely enough, these reflections are endless even when their point of departure is one of Kafka's philosophical tales. Take, for example, the parable "Vor dem Gesetz" [Before the Law]. The reader who read it in *Ein Landarzt* [A Country Doctor] may have been struck by the cloudy spot at its interior. But would it have led him to the never-ending series of reflections traceable to this parable at the spot where Kafka undertakes to interpret it? This is done by the priest in *Der Prozeß*, and at such a significant moment that it looks as if the novel were nothing but the unfolding of the parable. The word "unfolding" has a double meaning. A bud unfolds into a blossom, but the boat which one teaches children to make by folding paper unfolds into a flat sheet of paper. This second kind of "unfolding" is really appropriate to parable; the reader takes pleasure in smoothing it out so that he has the meaning on the palm of his hand. Kafka's parables, however, unfold in the first sense, the way a bud turns into a blossom. That is why their effect is literary. This does not mean that his prose pieces belong entirely in the tradition of Western prose forms; they have, rather, a relationship to religious teachings similar to the one Haggadah has to Halachah. They are not parables, yet they do not want to be taken at their face value; they lend themselves to quotation and can be recounted for purposes of clarification. But do we have the teachings which Kafka's parables accompany and which K.'s postures and the gestures of his animals clarify? It does not exist; all we can say is that here and there we have an allusion to it. Kafka might have said that these are relics transmitting the teachings, although we could just as well regard them as precursors preparing the teachings. In every case, it is a question of how life and work are organized in human society. This question increasingly occupied Kafka, even as it became impenetrable to him. If Napoleon, in his famous conversation with Goethe at Erfurt, substituted politics for fate, Kafka, in a variation of this dictum, could have defined organization as destiny. He faces it not only in the extensive hierarchy of officialdom in *Der Prozeß* and *Das Schloß*, but even more concretely in the difficult and incalculable construction plans whose venerable model he dealt with in "Beim Bau der Chinesischen Mauer" [The Great Wall of China].

> The wall was to be a protection for centuries; accordingly, the most scrupulous care in the construction, the application of the architectural wisdom of all known ages and peoples, and a constant sense of personal responsibility on the part of the builders were indispensable prerequisites for the work. To be sure, for the menial tasks, ignorant day laborers from the populace—men, women, and children, whoever offered his services for good money—could be used. But for the supervision of every four day laborers, a man trained in the building trade was required . . . We—and here I speak in the name of many people—did not really know ourselves until we had carefully scrutinized the decrees of the high command; then we discovered that, without this leadership, neither our book learning nor our common sense would have sufficed for the humble tasks which we performed in the great whole.

This organization resembles fate. Metchnikoff, who has outlined this in his famous book *La civilisation et les grands fleuves historiques* [Civilization and the Great Historical Rivers], uses language that could be Kafka's:

> The canals of the Yangtze and the dams of the Yellow River are in all likelihood the result of the skillfully organized joint labor of . . . generations. The slightest carelessness in the digging of a ditch or the buttressing of a dam, the least bit of negligence or selfish behavior on the part of an individual or a group in the maintenance of the common hydraulic wealth becomes, under such unusual circumstances, the source of social evils and far-reaching social calamity. Consequently, a life-giving river requires on pain of death a close and permanent solidarity among groups of people that frequently are alien or even hostile to one another; it sentences everyone to labors whose common usefulness is

revealed only by time and whose design quite often remains utterly incomprehensible to an ordinary man.[10]

Kafka wished to be numbered among ordinary men. He was pushed to the limits of understanding at every turn, and he liked to push others to them as well. At times he seems to come close to saying, with Dostoevsky's Grand Inquisitor: "So we have before us a mystery which we cannot comprehend. And precisely because it is a mystery we have had the right to preach it, to teach the people that what matters is neither freedom nor love, but the riddle, the secret, the mystery to which they have to bow—without reflection and even against their conscience." Kafka did not always evade the temptations of a modish mysticism. There is a diary entry concerning his encounter with Rudolf Steiner;[11] in its published form, at least, it does not reflect Kafka's attitude toward him. Did Kafka avoid taking a stand? His way with his own writings certainly does not exclude this possibility. Kafka had a rare capacity for creating parables for himself. Yet his parables are never exhausted by what is explainable; on the contrary, he took all conceivable precautions against the interpretation of his writings. One has to find one's way in them circumspectly, cautiously, and warily. One must keep in mind Kafka's way of reading, as exemplified in his interpretation of the above-mentioned parable. The text of his will is another case in point. Given its background, the directive in which Kafka ordered the destruction of his literary remains is just as unfathomable, to be weighed just as carefully as the answers of the doorkeeper in "Vor dem Gesetz." Perhaps Kafka, whose every day on earth brought him up against insoluble modes of behavior and imprecise communications, in death wished to give his contemporaries a taste of their own medicine.

Kafka's world is a world theater. For him, man is on stage from the very beginning. The proof is the fact that everyone is hired by the Nature Theater of Oklahoma. What the standards for admission are cannot be determined. Dramatic talent, the most obvious criterion, seems to be of no importance. But this can be expressed in another way: all that is expected of the applicants is the ability to play themselves. It is no longer within the realm of possibility that they could, if necessary, be what they claim to be. With their roles, these people look for a position in the Nature Theater the way Pirandello's six characters seek an author. For all of them this place is the last refuge, which does not preclude it from being their salvation. Salvation is not a premium on existence, but the last way out for a man whose path, as Kafka puts it in "Er" [He], is "blocked . . . by his own frontal bone." The law of this theater is contained in a sentence tucked away in "Ein Bericht für eine Akademie" [A Report to an Academy]: "I imitated people because I was looking for a way out, and for no other reason." Before the end of his trial, K. seems to have an intimation of these things. He suddenly turns to the two gentlemen wearing top hats who have come for him and asks them: "'What theater are you playing at?' 'Theater?' asked one, the corners of his mouth twitching as he looked for advice to the other, who acted as if he were a mute struggling to overcome a stubborn disability." The men do not answer this question, but there is much to indicate that it has hit home.

At a long bench which has been covered with a white cloth, all those who will henceforth be with the Nature Theater are fed. "They were all happy and excited." By way of celebration, extras act as angels. They stand on high pedestals that are covered with flowing drapery and have stairs inside— the makings of a country church fair, or perhaps a children's festival, which may have eliminated the sadness from the eyes of the tightly laced, dressed-up boy we discussed above.—But for the fact that their wings are tied on, these angels might be real. They have forerunners in Kafka's works. One of them is the impresario who climbs up on the luggage rack next to the trapeze artist beset by his "first sorrow," caresses him, and presses his face against his, "so that he was bathed by the trapeze artist's tears" ["Erstes Leid"]. Another, a guardian angel or guardian of the law, takes care of Schmar the murderer following the "fratricide" and leads him away, stepping lightly, with Schmar's "mouth pressed against the policeman's shoulder" ["Ein Brudermord"].—Kafka's *Amerika* ends with the rustic ceremonies of Oklahoma. "In Kafka," said Soma Morgenstern, "there is the air of a village, as with all great founders of religions."[12] Lao-tze's presentation of piousness is all the more pertinent here because Kafka has supplied its most perfect description in "Das nächste Dorf" [The Next Village].[13] "Neighboring countries may be within sight, so that the sounds of roosters and dogs may be heard in the distance. Yet people are said to die at a ripe old age without having traveled far." Thus Lao-tze. Kafka was also a writer of parables, but he did not found a religion.

Let us consider the village at the foot of Castle Hill, whence K.'s alleged employment as a land surveyor is so mysteriously and unexpectedly confirmed. In his postscript to *Das Schloß,* Brod mentioned that in depicting this village at the foot of Castle Hill, Kafka had in mind a specific place: Zürau in the Erzgebirge.[14] We may, however, also recognize another village in it. It is the village in a Talmudic legend told by a rabbi in answer to the question why Jews prepare a festive evening meal on Fridays. The legend is about a princess languishing in exile, in a village whose language she does not understand, far from her compatriots. One day this princess receives a letter saying that her fiancé has not forgotten her and is on his way to her. —The fiancé, so says the rabbi, is the Messiah; the princess is the soul; the village in which she lives in exile is the body. She prepares a meal for him because this is the only way in which she can express her joy in a village whose language she does not know. —This village of the Talmud is right in

Kafka's world. For just as K. lives in the village on Castle Hill, modern man lives in his own body: the body slips away from him, is hostile toward him. It may happen that a man wakes up one day and finds himself transformed into vermin. Strangeness—his own strangeness—has gained control over him. The air of this village blows about Kafka, and that is why he was not tempted to found a religion. The pigsty which houses the country doctor's horses; the stuffy back room in which Klamm, a cigar in his mouth, sits over a glass of beer; the manor gate which brings ruin to anyone who knocks on it—all these are part of this village. The air in this village is permeated with all the abortive and overripe elements that form such a putrid mixture. This is the air that Kafka had to breathe throughout his life. He was neither mantic nor the founder of a religion. How was he able to survive in this air?

The Little Hunchback

Some time ago it became known that Knut Hamsun was in the habit of expressing his views in an occasional letter to the editor of the local paper in the small town near which he lived.[15] Years ago, that town was the scene of the jury trial of a young woman who had killed her infant child. She was sentenced to prison. Soon thereafter the local paper printed a letter from Hamsun in which he announced his intention of leaving a town which did not impose the supreme punishment on a mother who killed her newborn child—the gallows, or at least a life term of hard labor. A few years passed. *Growth of the Soil* appeared, and it contained the story of a young woman who committed the same crime, suffered the same punishment, and, as is made clear to the reader, surely deserved no more severe one.

Kafka's posthumous reflections, which are contained in *Beim Bau der Chinesischen Mauer,* recall this episode to mind. Hardly had this volume appeared when the reflections served as the basis for a body of Kafka criticism which concentrated on an interpretation of these reflections to the neglect of his actual works. There are two ways to miss the point of Kafka's works. One is to interpret them naturally; the other is to interpret them from a supernatural perspective. Both the psychoanalytic and the theological interpretations miss the essential points. The first kind is represented by Hellmuth Kaiser; the second, by numerous writers, such as H. J. Schoeps, Bernhard Rang, and Bernhard Groethuysen.[16] To these last also belongs Willy Haas, although he has made revealing comments on Kafka in other contexts which we shall discuss later; such insights have not prevented him from interpreting Kafka's work after a theological pattern. "The powers above, the realm of grace," Haas writes, "Kafka has depicted in his great novel *Das Schloß;* the powers below, the realm of the courts and of damnation, he has dealt with in his equally great novel *Der Prozeß*. The earth between the two, earthly fate and its arduous demands, he attempted to present in strictly stylized form in a third novel, *Amerika*."[17] The first third of this interpretation has, since Brod, become a commonplace of Kafka criticism. Bernhard Rang writes in a similar vein: "To the extent that one may regard the Castle as the seat of grace, precisely these vain efforts and attempts mean, theologically speaking, that God's grace cannot be attained or forced by man willfully and deliberately. Unrest and impatience only impede and confound the exalted stillness of the divine."[18] This interpretation is a convenient one; but the further it is carried, the more we realize that it is untenable. This is perhaps seen most clearly in a statement by Willy Haas. "Kafka goes back . . . to Kierkegaard as well as to Pascal; one may call him the only legitimate heir of these two. In all three, there is an excruciatingly harsh basic religious theme: man is always in the wrong before God . . . Kafka's upper world, his so-called Castle, with its immense, complex staff of petty and rather lecherous officials, his strange heaven, plays a horrible game with people . . . yet man is very much in the wrong even before this god."[19] This theology, lagging far behind the doctrine of justification formulated by Saint Anselm of Canterbury, falls into barbaric speculations which do not even seem consistent with the text of Kafka's works.[20] "Can an individual official forgive?" we read in *Das Schloß*. "This could be a matter only for the supreme authorities, but even they can probably not forgive but only judge." This road soon leads into a blind alley. "All this," says Denis de Rougemont, "is not the wretched situation of man without a god, but the wretched state of a man who is bound to a god he does not know, because he does not know Christ."[21]

It is easier to draw speculative conclusions from Kafka's posthumous collection of notes than to explore even one of the motifs that appear in his stories and novels. Yet only these give some clue to the prehistoric forces that dominated Kafka's creativeness—forces which, to be sure, may justifiably be regarded as belonging to our world as well. Who can say under what names they appeared to Kafka himself? Only this much is certain: he did not know them and failed to get his bearings among them. In the mirror which the prehistoric world held up to him in the form of guilt, he merely saw the future emerging in the form of judgment. Kafka, however, did not say what it was like. Wasn't it the Last Judgment? Doesn't it turn the judge into the defendant? Isn't the trial the punishment? Kafka gave no answer. Did he expect anything of this punishment? Or wasn't he, rather, concerned to postpone it? In the stories which Kafka left us, narrative art regains the significance it had in the mouth of Scheherazade: its ability to postpone the future. In *Der Prozeß*, postponement is the hope of the accused man only if the proceedings do not gradually turn into the judgment. The patriarch

Abraham himself could benefit by postponement, even though he may have to trade his place in tradition for it.

> I could conceive of another Abraham (to be sure, he would never get to be a patriarch or even an old-clothes dealer), an Abraham who would be prepared to satisfy the demand for a sacrifice immediately, with the promptness of a waiter, but would be unable to bring it off, because he cannot get away, being indispensable; the household needs him, there is always something or other to take care of, the house is never ready. But without having his house ready, without having something to fall back on, he cannot leave—this the Bible also realized, for it says: "He set his house in order."[22]

This Abraham appears "with the promptness of a waiter." Kafka could understand things only in the form of a *gestus,* and this *gestus* which he did not understand constitutes the cloudy part of the parables. Kafka's writings emanate from it. The way he withheld them is well known. His will orders their destruction. This document, which no one interested in Kafka can disregard, says that the writings did not satisfy their author, that he regarded his efforts as failures, that he counted himself among those who were bound to fail. He did fail in his grandiose attempt to convert poetry into teachings, to turn it into a parable and restore to it that stability and unpretentiousness which, in the face of reason, seemed to him the only appropriate thing for it. No other writer has obeyed the commandment "Thou shalt not make unto thee a graven image" so faithfully.

"It was as if the shame of it were to outlive him." With these words *Der Prozeß* ends. Shame—corresponding as it does to his "elemental purity of feeling"[23]—is Kafka's strongest gesture. It has a dual aspect, however. Shame is an intimate human reaction, but at the same time it has social claims. Shame is not only shame in the presence of others, but can also be shame one feels *for* others. Kafka's shame, then, is no more personal than the life and thought which govern it and which he has described thus: "He does not live for the sake of his own life; he does not think for the sake of his own thought. He feels as though he were living and thinking under the constraint of a family . . . Because of this unknown family, . . . he cannot be released" ["Er"]. We do not know the makeup of this unknown family, which is composed of human beings and animals. But this much is clear: it is this family that forces Kafka to move cosmic ages in his writings. Doing this family's bidding, he moves the mass of historical happenings the way Sisyphus rolled the stone. As he does so, its nether side comes to light; it is not a pleasant sight, but Kafka is capable of bearing it. "To believe in progress is not to believe that progress has already taken place. That would be no belief."[24] Kafka did not consider the age in which he lived as an advance over the beginnings of time. His novels are set in a swamp world. In his works, the creature appears at the stage which Bachofen has termed the hetaeric stage.[25] The fact that this stage is now forgotten does not mean that it does not extend into the present. On the contrary: it is present by virtue of this very oblivion. An experience deeper than that of the average person can make contact with it. "I have experience [*Erfahrung*]," we read in one of Kafka's earliest notes, "and I am not joking when I say that it is a seasickness on dry land."[26] It is no accident that the first "Meditation" ["Kinder auf der Landstrasse"] was conceived on a swing. And Kafka does not tire of expressing himself on the fluctuating nature of experiences. Each gives way and mingles with its opposite. "It was summer, a hot day": so begins "Der Schlag ans Hoftor." "Walking home with my sister, I was passing the gate of a great house. I don't remember whether she knocked on the gate out of mischief or in a fit of absentmindedness, or merely shook her fist at it and did not knock at all." The very possibility of the third alternative puts the other two, which at first seemed harmless, in a different light. It is from the swampy soil of such experiences that Kafka's female characters rise. They are swamp creatures—like Leni, "who stretches out the middle and ring fingers of her right hand, between which the connecting web of skin reached almost to the top joint, short as the fingers were" [*Der Prozeß*]. "Fine times," the ambiguous Frieda reminisces about her earlier life; "You never asked me about my past" [*Das Schloß*]. This past takes us back to the dark, deep womb, the scene of the mating "whose untrammeled voluptuousness," to quote Bachofen, "is hateful to the pure forces of heavenly light and which justifies the term used by Arnobius, *luteae voluptates* [dirty voluptuousness]."[27]

Only from this vantage point can the technique of Kafka the storyteller be comprehended. Whenever figures in the novels have anything to say to K., no matter how important or surprising it may be, they do so casually and with the implication that he must really have known it all along. It is as though nothing new were being imparted, as though the hero were just being subtly invited to recall to mind something he had forgotten. This is how Willy Haas has interpreted the course of events in *Der Prozeß*, and justifiably so: "The object of the trial—indeed, the real hero of this incredible book—is forgetting, whose main characteristic is the forgetting of itself . . . Here it has actually become a mute figure in the shape of the accused man, a figure of the most striking intensity." It probably cannot be denied that "this mysterious center . . . derives from the Jewish religion." "Memory plays a very mysterious role as piousness. It is not an ordinary quality but . . . the most profound quality of Jehovah that He remembers, that He retains, an infallible memory 'to the third and fourth, even to the hundredth, generation.' The most sacred . . . act of the . . . ritual is the erasing of sins from the book of memory."[28]

What has been forgotten—and with this insight we stand before another threshold of Kafka's work—is never something purely individual. Everything forgotten mingles with what has been forgotten of the prehistoric world, forms countless uncertain and changing compounds, yielding a constant flow of new, strange products. Oblivion is the container from which the inexhaustible intermediate world in Kafka's stories presses toward the light. "Here the very fullness of the world is considered the only reality. All spirit must be concrete, particularized, in order to have its place and *raison d'être*. The spiritual, if it plays a role at all, turns into spirits. These spirits become definite individuals, with names and a very special connection with the name of the worshiper . . . Unhesitatingly, the fullness of the world is filled to overflowing with their fullness . . . Unconcernedly, the crowd of spirits is swelled . . . New ones are constantly added to the old ones, and each is distinguished from the others by its own name." All this refers not to Kafka, but to—China. This is how Franz Rosenzweig describes the Chinese ancestor cult in his book *Der Stern der Erlösung*.[29] To Kafka, the world of his ancestors was as unfathomable as the world of realities was important, and we may be sure that, like the totem poles of primitive peoples, the world of ancestors took him down to the animals. Incidentally, Kafka is not the only writer for whom animals are the receptacles of the forgotten. In Tieck's profound story *Der blonde Eckbert* [Fair Eckbert],[30] the forgotten name of a little dog, Strohmi, stands for a mysterious guilt. One can understand, then, why Kafka never tired of hearing about the forgotten from animals. They are not the goal, to be sure, but one cannot do without them. A case in point is the hunger artist, who, "strictly speaking, was only an impediment on the way to the menagerie" ["Ein Hungerkünstler"]. Can't one see the animal in *Der Bau* [The Burrow] or the giant mole ["Der Riesenmaulwurf"] ponder as they dig in? Yet this thinking is extremely flighty. Irresolutely, it flits from one worry to the next; it nibbles at every anxiety with the fickleness of despair. Thus, there are butterflies in Kafka, too. The guilt-ridden hunter Gracchus, who refuses to acknowledge his guilt, "has turned into a butterfly" ["Der Jäger Gracchus"]. "Don't laugh," says the hunter Gracchus. This much is certain: of all of Kafka's creatures, the animals have the greatest opportunity for reflection. What corruption is in the law, anxiety is in their thinking. It messes a situation up, yet it is the only hopeful thing about it. But because the most forgotten source of strangeness is our body—one's own body—one can understand why Kafka called the cough that erupted from within him "the animal." It was the vanguard of the great herd.

In Kafka's work, the most singular bastard which the prehistoric world has begotten with guilt is Odradek ["Die Sorge des Hausvaters"]. "At first sight it looks like a flat, star-shaped spool for thread, and it really seems to have thread wound around it; to be sure, this is probably just old, broken-off bits of thread that are knotted and tangled together, of all sorts and colors. But the object is not just a spool, for a small wooden crossbar sticks out of the middle of the star, and another small rod is joined to it at right angles. With the aid of this latter rod on one side and one of the extensions of the star on the other, the whole thing can stand upright as if on two legs." Odradek "stays alternately in the attic, on the staircase, in the corridors, and in the hall." So it prefers the same places as the court of law which investigates guilt. Attics are the places of discarded, forgotten objects. Perhaps having to appear before a court of justice gives rise to a feeling similar to that with which one approaches trunks in the attic which have been locked up for years. One would like to put off this chore till the end of time, just as K. regards his written defense as suitable "for occupying one's senile mind someday during retirement."

Odradek is the form which things assume in oblivion. They are distorted. The "cares of a family man," which no one can identify, are distorted; the bug, which we know all too well represents Gregor Samsa, is distorted; the big animal, half-lamb, half-kitten, for which "the butcher's knife" might be "a release," is distorted. These Kafka figures are connected by a long series of figures with the prototype of distortion: a hunched back. Among the images in Kafka's stories, none is more frequent than that of the man who bows his head far down on his chest: the fatigue of the court officials, the noise affecting the doormen in the hotel, the low ceiling facing the visitors in the gallery. In the penal colony, those in power use an archaic apparatus which engraves letters with curlicues on the back of every guilty man, multiplying the stabs and piling up the ornaments to the point where the back of the guilty man becomes clairvoyant and is able to decipher the script from which he must derive the nature of his unknown guilt. It is the back on which this is incumbent. It was always this way with Kafka. Compare this early diary entry: "In order to make myself as heavy as possible, which I believe is an aid to falling asleep, I had crossed my arms and put my hands on my shoulders, so that I lay there like a soldier with his pack."[31] Quite palpably, being loaded down is here equated with forgetting—the forgetting of a sleeping man. The same symbol occurs in the folksong "The Little Hunchback." This little man is at home in distorted life; he will disappear with the coming of the Messiah, who (a great rabbi once said) will not wish to change the world by force but will merely make a slight adjustment in it.

When I come into my room,
My little bed to make,
A little hunchback is in there,
With laughter he does shake.

This is the laughter of Odradek, which is described as sounding "something like the rustling of falling leaves."

When I kneel upon my stool
And I want to pray,
A hunchbacked man is in the room
And he starts to say:
My dear child, I beg of you,
Pray for the little hunchback too.[32]

So ends the folksong. In his depths, Kafka touches ground which neither "mythical divination" nor "existential theology" supplied him with. It is the ground of folk tradition, German as well as Jewish. Even if Kafka did not pray—and this we do not know—he still possessed in the highest degree what Malebranche called "the natural prayer of the soul": attentiveness.[33] And in this attentiveness he included all creatures, as saints include them in their prayers.

Sancho Panza

In a Hasidic village, so the story goes, Jews were sitting together in a shabby inn one Sabbath evening. They were all local people, with the exception of one person no one knew, a very poor, ragged man who was squatting in a dark corner at the back of the room. All sorts of things were discussed, and then it was suggested that everyone should tell what wish he would make if one were granted him. One man wanted money; another wished for a son-in-law; a third dreamed of a new carpenter's bench; and so each spoke in turn. After they had finished, only the beggar in his dark corner was left. Reluctantly and hesitantly he answered the question. "I wish I were a powerful king reigning over a big country. Then, some night while I was asleep in my palace, an enemy would invade my country, and by dawn his horsemen would penetrate to my castle and meet with no resistance. Roused from my sleep, I wouldn't have time even to dress and I would have to flee in my shirt. Rushing over hill and dale and through forests day and night, I would finally arrive safely right here at the bench in this corner. This is my wish." The others exchanged uncomprehending glances. "And what good would this wish have done you?" someone asked. "I'd have a shirt," was the answer.[34]

This story takes us deep into the household that is Kafka's world. No one says that the distortions which it will be the Messiah's mission to set right someday affect only our space; surely they are distortions of our time as well. Kafka must certainly have thought this. And in this certainty he made the grandfather in "Das nächste Dorf" say: "Life is astonishingly short. As I look back over it, life seems so foreshortened to me that I can hardly understand, for instance, how a young man can decide to ride over to the next village without being afraid that, quite apart from accidents, even the span of a normal life that passes happily may be totally insufficient for such a ride." This old man's brother is the above-mentioned beggar, whose "normal" life that "passes happily" does not even leave him time for a wish, but who is exempted from this wish in an abnormal, unhappy life (that is, the flight which he attempts in his story) and who exchanges the wish for its fulfillment.

Among Kafka's creations, there is a clan which reckons with the brevity of life in a peculiar way. It comes from the "city in the south . . . of which it was said: 'People live there who—imagine!—don't sleep!' 'And why not?' 'Because they don't get tired.' 'Why don't they?' 'Because they are fools.' 'Don't fools get tired?' 'How could fools get tired?'" ["Kinder auf der Landstrasse"]. One can see that the fools are akin to the indefatigable assistants. But there is more to this clan. It is casually remarked of the assistants' faces that they seem to be those of "grown-ups, perhaps even students" [Das Schloß]. Actually, the students who appear in the strangest places in Kafka's works are the spokesmen for and leaders of this clan. "'But when do you sleep?' asked Karl, looking at the student in surprise. 'Oh, sleep!' said the student. 'I'll get some sleep when I'm finished with my studies.'" This reminds one of the reluctance with which children go to bed; after all, while they are asleep, something might happen that concerns them. "Don't forget the best!" We are familiar with this remark "from a nebulous bunch of old stories, although it may not occur in any of them."[35] But forgetting always involves the best, for it involves the possibility of redemption. "The idea of helping me is an illness and requires bed rest for a cure," ironically says the restlessly wandering ghost of the hunter Gracchus.— While they study, the students are awake, and perhaps their being kept awake is the best thing about their studies. The hunger artist fasts, the doorkeeper is silent, and the students are awake. This is the veiled way in which the great rules of asceticism operate in Kafka.

The crowning achievement of asceticism is study. Reverently Kafka unearths it from long-lost boyhood. "In a way not very different from this—a long time ago—Karl had sat at home at his parents' table doing his homework, while his father read the newspaper or did bookkeeping and correspondence for some organization and his mother was busy sewing, drawing the thread high out of the fabric in her hand. To avoid disturbing his father, Karl would put only his exercise book and his writing materials on the table, while he arranged the books he needed on chairs to the right and left of him. How quiet it had been there! How seldom strangers had entered that room!" [Amerika]. Perhaps these studies had amounted to nothing. But they are very close to that nothing which alone makes it possible for a something to be useful—that is, they are very close to the Tao. This is what Kafka was after with his desire "to hammer a table together with painstaking craftsmanship and, at the same time, to do nothing—not in such a way that someone could say 'Hammering is nothing to him,' but 'To him, hammering is real hammering and at the same time nothing,' which would have made the hammering even bolder, more determined, more real, and, if you like, more insane" ["Er"]. This is the resolute, fanatical mien which students have when they study; it is the strangest mien imaginable. The scribes, the students, are out of breath; they fairly race along. "Often the official dictates in such a low voice that the scribe cannot even hear it sitting down; he has to jump up, catch the dictated words, quickly sit again and write them down, then jump up again, and so forth. How strange that is! It is almost incomprehensible!" [*Das Schloß*]. It may be easier to understand this if one thinks of the actors in the Nature Theater. Actors have to catch their cues in a flash, and they resemble those assiduous students in other ways as well. Truly, for them "hammering is real hammering and at the same time nothing"—provided that this is part of their role. They study this role, and only a bad actor would forget a word or a gesture from it. For the members of the Oklahoma troupe, however, the role is their earlier life; hence the "nature" in this Nature Theater. Its actors have been redeemed. But this is not true of the student whom Karl watches silently at night on the balcony as the student reads his book, "turning the pages, occasionally looking something up in another book which he always snatched up quick as a flash, and frequently making notes in a notebook, which he always did with his face surprisingly close to the paper."

Kafka does not grow tired of making the *gestus* present in this fashion, but he invariably does so with astonishment. K. has rightly been compared with the Good Soldier Schweik: the one is astonished at everything; the other, at nothing.[36] The invention of motion pictures and the phonograph came in an age of maximum alienation of men from one another, of unpredictably intervening relationships which have become their only ones. Experiments have proved that a man does not recognize his own gait on film or his own voice on the phonograph. The situation of the subject in such experiments is Kafka's situation; this is what leads him to study, where he may encounter fragments of his own existence—fragments that are still within the context of the role. He might catch hold of the lost *gestus* the way Peter Schlemihl caught hold of the shadow he had sold.[37] He might understand himself, but what an enormous effort would be required! It is a tempest that blows from forgetting, and study is a cavalry attack against it. Thus, the beggar on the corner bench rides toward his past in order to catch hold of himself in the figure of the fleeing king. This ride, which is long enough for a life, corresponds to life, which is too short for a ride— "until one shed one's spurs (for there were no spurs), threw away the reins (for there were no reins), and barely saw the land before one as a smoothly mown plain, with the horse's neck and head already gone." This is the fulfillment of the fantasy about the blessed horseman who rushes toward the past on an untrammeled, happy journey, no longer a burden on his galloping horse. But accursed is the rider who is chained to his nag because he has set himself a future goal, even though it is as close as the coal cellar—accursed is his animal, accursed are both of them: bucket and rider. "Seated on the bucket, my hands up on the handle, with the simplest kind of bridle, I propel myself with difficulty down the stairs. But once I am down below, my bucket ascends, superbly, superbly; camels lying flat on the ground do not rise any more handsomely as they shake themselves under the sticks of their drivers" ["Der Kübelreiter"]. There is no more hopeless vista than that of "the regions of ice mountains" in which the bucket rider drops out of sight forever. From the "nethermost regions of death" blows the wind that is favorable to him—the same wind which so often blows from the prehistoric world in Kafka's works, and which also propels the boat of the hunter Gracchus. "At mysteries and sacrifices, among Greeks as well as barbarians," writes Plutarch, "it is taught that there must be two primary essences and two opposing forces, one of which points to the right and straight ahead, whereas the other turns around and drives back."[38] Reversal is the direction of study which transforms existence into script. Its teacher is Bucephalus, "the new advocate," who takes the road back without the powerful Alexander—which means, rid of the onrushing conqueror. "His flanks free and unhampered by the thighs of a rider, under a quiet lamp far from the din of Alexander's battles, he reads and turns the pages of our old books."—Werner Kraft once wrote an interpretation of this story. After giving careful attention to every detail of the text, Kraft notes: "Nowhere else in literature is there such a powerful and penetrating criticism of myth in its full scope."[39] According to Kraft, Kafka does not use the word "justice," yet it is justice which serves as the point of departure for his critique of myth.—But once we have reached this point, we are in danger of missing Kafka by stopping here. Is it really the law which could thus be invoked against myth in the name of justice? No, as a legal scholar Bucephalus remains true to his origins, except that he does not seem to be practicing law—and this is probably something new, in Kafka's sense, for both Bucephalus and the bar. The law which is studied but no longer practiced is the gate to justice.

The gate to justice is study. Yet Kafka doesn't dare attach to this study the promises which tradition has attached to the study of the Torah. His assistants are sextons who have lost their house of prayer; his students are pupils who have lost the Holy Writ [Schrift]. Now there is nothing to support them on their "untrammeled, happy journey."[40] Kafka, however, has found the law of his journey: on at least one occasion, he succeeded in bringing its breathtaking speed in line with the slow narrative pace that he presumably sought all his life. He expressed this in a little prose piece which is his most perfect creation—and not only because it is an interpretation.

Without ever boasting of it, Sancho Panza succeeded over the years, by supplying a lot of romances of chivalry and adventure for the evening and night hours, in so diverting from him his demon, whom he later called Don Quixote, that his demon thereupon freely performed the maddest exploits—which, however, lacking a preordained object, which Sancho Panza himself was supposed to have been, did no one any harm. A free man, Sancho Panza philosophically followed Don Quixote on his crusades, perhaps out of a sense of responsibility, and thus enjoyed great and profitable entertainment to the end of his days." ["Die Wahrheit über Sancho Pansa"]

Sancho Panza, a sedate fool and a clumsy assistant, sent his rider on ahead; Bucephalus outlived his. Whether it is a man or a horse is no longer so important, if only the burden is taken off the back.

Published in *Jüdische Rundschau,* December 1934. *Gesammelte Schriften,* II, 409–438. Translated by Harry Zohn.

Notes

1. Grigori Potemkin (1739–1791) was a Russian soldier and statesman who became the chief favorite of Catherine II. The immediate source of Benjamin's story is Aleksandr Pushkin, *Anecdotes and Tabletalk,* no. 24.
2. Kafka, *Beim Bau der Chinesischen Mauer* (Berlin: Kiepenheuer, 1931), p. 231: "Betrachtungen über Sünde, Leid, Hoffnung und den wahren Weg" (Observations on Sin, Suffering, Hope and the True Way), aphorism 34. See also Benjamin's essay "Franz Kafka: *Beim Bau der Chinesischen Mauer,* in this volume. The Castellan and Klamm are officials in the castle in Kafka's novel *Das Schloß* (The Castle).
3. Cited in Ernst Bloch, *Geist der Utopie* (Munich: Duncker und Humblot, 1918), p. 22.
4. Hermann Cohen, *Ethik des reinen Willens* (Berlin: Cassirer, 1907), p. 362. Cohen (1842–1918) did important work that combined philosophy (he was the cofounder of the Marburg school of neo-Kantianism and published books on ethics, epistemology, and aesthetics) and Jewish theology. His work figures prominently in Benjamin's essay "Goethe's Elective Affinities" (see Volume 1 of this edition).
5. Max Brod, "Der Dichter Franz Kafka," *Die neue Rundschau* 11 (1921): 1213. Brod (1884–1968) was a Czech-born, German-language novelist and essayist known primarily as Kafka's friend and as the editor of his major works, most of which were first published after Kafka's death. Brod had a major influence on the first wave of Kafka interpretations, many of which were religiously oriented.
6. For the Cat Lamb, Odradek, and Gregor Samsa, see the stories "Eine Kreuzung" (A Crossbreed), "Die Sorge des Hausvaters" (The Cares of a Family Man), and "Die Verwandlung" (The Metamorphosis), respectively.
7. Robert Walser (1878–1956), Swiss prose writer, was much cherished by Benjamin (as well as by Kafka and Robert Musil) for his literary miniatures, which mix keen observation of detail with wit, irony, and a sense of paradox.
8. Franz Rosenzweig, *Der Stern der Erlösung* (Frankfurt: J. Kauffmann, 1921), p. 96: Part 1, Book 3. Rosenzweig (1886–1929) was a German-Jewish religious

Existentialist who, through his fresh handling of traditional religious themes, became one of the most influential modern Jewish theologians. While on active service in World War I, he began his magnum opus, *Der Stern der Erlösung* (The Star of Redemption; 1921). From 1922 he was afflicted with progressive paralysis but continued work on numerous projects, including a new German translation of the Hebrew Bible in collaboration with Martin Buber.

9. Werner Kraft, *Franz Kafka: Durchdringung und Geheimnis* (Frankfurt: Suhrkamp, 1968), p. 24. Kraft (1896–1991), German essayist, poet, and novelist, was a friend of Benjamin's. He emigrated to Palestine in 1933.

10. Léon Metchnikoff, *La civilisation et les grands fleuves historiques* (Paris: Hachette, 1889), p. 189.

11. See Kafka, *Tagebücher, 1910–1923* (New York: Schocken, 1951), pp. 54–58: entry for March 26, 1911. Rudolf Steiner (1861–1925) was an Austrian-born scientist and editor, and the founder of anthroposophy, a movement based on the notion that there is a spiritual world comprehensible to pure thought but accessible only to the highest faculties of mental knowledge. Steiner's ideas exerted a remarkable influence on educational philosophy in the early years of the twentieth century.

12. Conversation with Benjamin (ms. 334 in the Benjamin archive).

13. Lao-tze (fl. sixth century B.C.) was the first philosopher of Chinese Taoism and the alleged author of the Tao-te Ching. Modern scholars discount the possibility that the text was written by one person but acknowledge the influence of Taoism on the development of Buddhism.

14. Brod's remark is not in the postscript to *Das Schloß*, but was recorded by Willy Haas in *Gestalten der Zeit* (Berlin: Kiepenheuer, 1930), pp. 183ff.

15. Knut Hamsun (pseudonym of Knut Pedersen; 1859–1952) was a Norwegian writer. *Growth of the Soil* appeared in 1917.

16. Hans Joachim Schoeps (1901–1980) was a German historian who published widely on Jewish religious history. Bernhard Groethuysen (1880–1946), German cultural historian, was a student of Wilhelm Dilthey and applied Dilthey's method of "intellectual history" to studies of the intellectual development of the European bourgeoisie.

17. Haas, *Gestalten der Zeit*, p. 175. Willy Haas (1891–1973), German critic and essayist, founded (along with Ernst Rowohlt) the weekly journal *Die literarische Welt*, which he edited until 1933 and in which he published numerous pieces by his friend Benjamin.

18. Bernhard Rang, "Franz Kafka," *Die Schildgenossen* (Augsburg) 12, nos. 2–3 (1932).

19. Haas, *Gestalten der Zeit*, p. 176.

20. Saint Anselm of Canterbury (1033/34–1109) was the founder of Scholasticism, the school of thought that dominated the Middle Ages. Anselm first proposed the ontological argument for the existence of God. His satisfaction theory of redemption was based on the feudal notion of making satisfaction or recompense according to the status of the person against whom the offense had been committed. According to Anselm's notion, God was the offended party and man the offender.

21. Denis de Rougemont, "*Le Procès*, par Franz Kafka," *Nouvelle Revue Française* 22 (May 1934): 869.

22. Kafka, *Briefe, 1902–1924* (New York: Fischer, 1958), p. 333: letter of June 1921 to Robert Klopstock.
23. Rosenzweig, *Der Stern der Erlösung,* p. 96.
24. Kafka, *Beim Bau der Chinesischen Mauer,* p. 234: "Betrachtungen," aphorism 48.
25. Johann Jakob Bachofen (1815–1887) was a Swiss anthropologist and jurist, best-known as the author of *Das Mutterrecht* (1861) and *Urreligion und antike Symbole* (1861). See Benjamin's review of Bernoulli's book on Bachofen, in Volume 1 of this edition.
26. Kafka, in *Hyperion* 2, no. 1 (1909).
27. Bachofen, *Urreligion und antike Symbole* (Leipzig: Reclam, 1926), vol. 1, p. 386. Arnobius (fl. A.D. 300) was an early Christian apologist.
28. Haas, *Gestalten der Zeit,* pp. 195, 196–197.
29. Rosenzweig, *Der Stern der Erlösung,* pp. 76–77: Part 1, Book 2.
30. Ludwig Tieck (1773–1853) was a German Romantic writer, critic, and translator. His novella *Der blonde Eckbert* appeared in 1797.
31. Kafka, *Tagebücher, 1910–1923,* p. 76: entry for October 3, 1911.
32. *Des Knaben Wunderhorn: Alte deutsche Lieder* (1808; rpt. Meersburg, 1928), p. 297: "Das buckliche Männlein."
33. Nicolas de Malebranche (1638–1715) was a French metaphysician whose work sought a synthesis of Cartesianism, Neoplatonism, and the thought of Augustine.
34. This joke was current in books of Jewish humor around 1900.
35. Kafka, *Beim Bau der Chinesischen Mauer,* p. 248: "Betrachtungen," aphorism 108.
36. *The Good Soldier Schweik* (1920–1923) is an unfinished sequence of satirical novels by the Czech writer Jaroslav Hašek (1883–1923).
37. In the 1814 prose tale *Peter Schlemihl,* by the German Romantic writer Adalbert von Chamisso, a man sells his shadow to the Devil for an inexhaustible purse of gold, but then regrets the bargain.
38. Plutarch, *On Isis and Osiris;* cited in Bachofen, *Urreligion und antike Symbole,* vol. 1, p. 253.
39. Kraft, *Franz Kafka: Durchdringung und Geheimnis,* pp. 13–14.
40. Kafka, *Beim Bau der Chinesischen Mauer,* p. 233: "Betrachtungen," aphorism 45.

A Note on the Texts · Chronology, 1927–1934 · Index

A Note on the Texts

Most of the texts included in this second volume of Benjamin's selected writings were published during his lifetime. In the years 1927–1933, Benjamin established himself as a public intellectual in the Weimar Republic; this volume, with its mix of essays, critical glosses, travel writings, reviews, and radio talks, documents that emergence. The volume also offers a rich selection of the form Benjamin had pioneered in *One-Way Street* (reprinted in Volume 1): the "thought figure" [*Denk-bild*], a prose form which combines aspects of the aphorism and the Romantic fragment with a decidedly materialist interest in things. Benjamin published dozens of these short texts in the period under scrutiny here. Alongside this array of texts that Benjamin succeeded in publishing, the volume also includes a representative selection of unpublished writings from the period. Some, like the "Introductory Remarks on a Series for *L'Humanité*," are simply parts of projects that were never completed. Others are fragments found in Benjamin's notebooks long after his death; many of these fragments, such as "Mickey Mouse" or "Notes on a Theory of Gambling," articulate important stages and aspects of his thought, and provide much of what we know about Benjamin's ideas on a wide range of topics. But the bulk of these posthumously published texts are autobiographical. They range from résumés through protocols of hashish experiments and on to extensive journals ("Diary of My Journey to the Loire") and intensive self-examination ("Agesilaus Santander").

The German edition of Benjamin's collected writings groups texts generically (volumes of essays, of reviews, of fragments, and so on). In the present volume, all texts are arranged chronologically by date of composition; if this differs markedly from the date of publication, both dates are given. Each text is accompanied by the following information: date of composition; place of publication, or a statement that the piece was unpublished during Benjamin's lifetime; and the word "Fragment" if the text is designated as such in the German edition. All endnotes other than Benjamin's were produced by the editors in collaboration with the translators.

The *Selected Writings* aims to present to English-language readers a very broad and representative selection from Benjamin's oeuvre. Every major text published during Benjamin's lifetime is included in this edition. We have attempted to supplement these major texts with examples of every *form* in which Benjamin worked: thought figures, radio plays, autobiographical writings, book reviews, letter collections, essays, fragments, cultural histories, travel accounts. Examples of each of the remarkable number of *fields* to which Benjamin contributed are likewise included: cultural theory; epistemology; art history; toys; the French avant-garde, especially Surrealism; the new Soviet Union; cinema; radical pedagogy; contemporary writers ranging from André Gide and Julien Green through Karl Kraus and Hugo von Hofmannsthal (to say nothing of Proust and Kafka, the subjects of two of Benjamin's most famous essays); graphology; political and social analysis; media theory; the theory of experience; marginalized popular forms such as novels by the mentally ill and penny romances; photography; and the theory of language. We hope that the English-language reader will for the first time be able to assess the remarkable breadth and intensity of Benjamin's achievement.

All translations are based on the text of the standard German edition: Walter Benjamin, *Gesammelte Schriften,* seven volumes (Frankfurt: Suhrkamp Verlag, 1972–1989), edited by Rolf Tiedemann and Hermann Schweppenhäuser. The editors of the present volume are indebted to Benjamin's German editors for the meticulous dating and preparation of his texts.

The editors would like to thank a number of friends, colleagues, and collaborators who provided information and assistance at crucial stages of the project. Above all, an immense debt of gratitude is due two research assistants, Joel Golb in Berlin and Daniel Magilow in Princeton, whose vigorous research formed the basis for a number of the notes to the text. Eduardo Cadava, Stanley Corngold, Michael Curschmann, James Eggleston, Barbara Hahn, Thomas Levin, Michael Wachtel, and Christian Wildberg answered our questions with patience and generosity. Hans Puttnies gave us his time and energy as we sought to procure images of Benjamin from the period in question. Very special thanks are due our colleagues at Harvard University Press. The idea for an expanded edition of Benjamin's writings came from Lindsay Waters, and without his now patient, now insistent godfathering, the edition would certainly never have been completed. And Maria Ascher, through her consistently insightful and meticulous editing—based on a brilliant ear for the sound of English prose—of the final manuscript, improved not just the texts themselves but the conception and the apparatus of this second volume of the edition.

Chronology, 1927–1934

1927

On New Year's Day Benjamin was in Moscow, where the long winter of the Stalinization of Soviet cultural policy was beginning. He had arrived some three weeks earlier, after learning that the Latvian-born Bolshevik actress and educator Asja Lacis—his "holiday love" from a vacation on Capri—had suffered a nervous breakdown. Benjamin had financed the trip by securing an advance from the journal *Die Kreatur* for an article on Moscow. He found the city in ferment, rundown yet extremely expensive—"an improvised metropolis," as he calls it in the extensive diary he kept during his two-month stay there.[1] A letter written at the end of December reflects his own excitement: "In the current state of affairs, the present—though fleeting—is of extraordinary value. Everything is being built or rebuilt, and almost every moment poses very critical questions. The tensions of public life—which, for the most part, are actually of a theological sort—are so great that they block off all private life to an unimaginable degree . . . It remains to be seen to what extent I'll be able to establish concrete relations with developments here" (*MD*, 127). In this matter of establishing contacts, Benjamin, who did not speak Russian, was almost entirely dependent on the good graces of his Moscow host, the German-born Bernhard Reich, a prominent theater critic then living in Moscow and a rather tolerant rival for the affections of Asja Lacis. (She and Reich would remain together through banishment and imprisonment during the Stalin era, and after the war would write about and produce the plays of Bertolt Brecht.) Benjamin's position as a freelance writer, "without party or profession," was a subject of conversation among his friends in Moscow, and to Reich he admitted that he "was in a critical situation" insofar as his "activity as an author was concerned" (*MD*, 60, 47).

Benjamin was weighing the advantages and disadvantages of becoming a professional fellow traveler. In his diary, at the beginning of January, he wrote about the choice that was facing him: either join the Communist party and gain a solid institutional framework and mandate, at the sacrifice of his private independence; or seek to consolidate a marginal position as "a left-wing outsider," and organize his existence on "this narrow base" (*MD*, 72–73). At issue, of course, was the continuation of his scholarly work, "with its formal and metaphysical grounding"—something that in itself might have a revolutionary function. He asked himself whether his "illegal incognito among bourgeois authors makes any sense," and whether, for the sake of his work, he should "avoid certain extremes of 'materialism'" (73). "As long as I continue to travel," he concluded, "joining the party is obviously something fairly inconceivable" (73).

Benjamin was intent on observing a wide variety of the daily affairs—as well as the cultural and political affairs—of Moscow, for, as he believed, "one knows a spot only after one has experienced it in as many dimensions as possible" (*MD*, 25). He visited shops (toy shops were his delight), restaurants, pubs, museums, offices, a factory manufacturing Christmas tree decorations, a children's clinic, a famous monastery. He took in life on the streets—beggars, children, street vendors, shop signs and posters, the relative absence of cars and church bells, the clothing and idiosyncrasies of the inhabitants. He went to plays, films, and ballets. He saw Sergei Eisenstein's film *Potemkin*, and the ballet *Petrushka*, set to Igor Stravinsky's music. He saw a shortened production (still more than four hours long) of Vsevolod Meyerhold's adaptation of Gogol's *Inspector General*, whose extravagant staging—involving a series of tableaux—he compared to the architecture of a Muscovite cake. And he was present at the Meyerhold Theater for a crowded public debate involving writers such as Vladimir Mayakovsky, Andrei Bely, Anatoly Lunacharsky, and Meyerhold himself. He was interviewed by a Moscow newspaper as an expert on literature and the plastic arts. Everywhere in the city he witnessed the "thoroughgoing politicization of life" (*MD*, 71). His observations on these particulars, and on more general features of Russian society as it pursued its grand experiment, were recorded in his Moscow diary, which he then mined, over the next four years, for articles and radio scripts. And throughout all the organized *flânerie* in the stunning cold, there was the lure of Asja Lacis, as mercurial and difficult of access as the city itself.

On his return, at the beginning of February, from Moscow to Berlin, where he was living with his wife and son in an apartment in his parents' villa, Benjamin found that the translation of Proust's *Within a Budding Grove*, which he had undertaken together with Franz Hessel, had just appeared and was getting generally respectful reviews. Hessel was editor-in-chief of the Rowohlt publishing house, which was due to bring out Benjamin's books *One-Way Street* and *Origin of the German Trauerspiel* (though their publication was on hold for the moment; they would not appear until 1928). Meanwhile, and amid "a great deal of idleness,"[2] Benjamin was busy on a number of fronts. Through Reich he had obtained a commission for a compendious article on Goethe for the *Great Soviet Encyclopedia*, although in February he heard from Reich that the editorial board was balking at his synopsis. (The article would eventually be written the following year and would appear, in 1929, drastically modified by the editors.) The article on Moscow for *Die Kreatur* was now claiming his attention. To Martin Buber, who ran the journal, he wrote of his intention to allow the "creatural" to speak for itself; in his picture of Moscow, he said (adapting Goethe), "everything factual is already theory" (Letters,

313). This statement seems prophetic for the direction of much of his future activity as an author, as does what he wrote to Siegfried Kracauer on the same day: his presentation of Moscow would take the form of "small, disparate notes, and for the most part the reader will be left to his own devices."[3] The critic Kracauer, with whom Benjamin had become friendly in 1923, was cultural affairs editor at the *Frankfurter Zeitung;* this newspaper, along with *Die literarische Welt* (published by Rowohlt under the editorship of Willy Haas), was to become a mainstay of Benjamin's work for the duration of the Weimar Republic.

It was at this point, in the second half of the Weimar Republic's brief life, that Walter Benjamin emerged as a public intellectual. In 1927 he not only brought out a number of articles stemming from his visit to Moscow—articles on the city itself, on Russian literature, and on Russian film—but he also published the first results of his intense involvement with French culture. And he made his debut at the microphone of a radio station on March 23, when he broadcast a talk entitled "Young Russian Writers." Regular work in this medium would begin for him two years later; between 1929 and 1932, he would be heard more than eighty times on Frankfurt and Berlin radio stations, usually presenting material he himself had written or was improvising. In an overview of the work he had undertaken in 1931, Benjamin could in fact write that he had succeeded in getting every word he had written published. This commercial activity—along with that of his wife, Dora, who in 1926 had become editor of a Berlin fashion magazine—helped to fund his few independent projects of these years, especially his work on the Paris arcades, begun in the summer of 1927.

In April, Benjamin traveled to Paris for what he expected would be a two- or three-month stay, to assess new developments in French literature. Much of the time he was reading Proust. At the end of the month, he met for a few days with his old friend Gershom Scholem, who had become a lecturer in Jewish mysticism at the newly founded Hebrew University in Jerusalem and was visiting libraries in England and France to research kabbalist texts. Benjamin remarked to Scholem that he wanted to settle permanently in Paris because he found the city's "atmosphere" suited him.[4] In mid-May he was joined by Dora and his son, Stefan; they went on to the Riviera and Monte Carlo, where Benjamin won enough money in the casinos to finance a week's vacation in Corsica on his own. He took a plane back from Corsica to Antibes, "and this brought me up to date on the latest means of human transportation" (Scholem, 132).

At the beginning of June, Benjamin sent a letter to the Austrian writer Hugo von Hofmannsthal, whose journal, *Neue deutsche Beiträge,* had published Benjamin's essay "Goethe's Elective Affinities" in 1924–1925 and would publish a chapter on melancholy from the forthcoming *Trauerspiel* book in August. The letter describes his current projects, including the essay on Moscow, in which he claims to have concentrated on "rhythmic experiences" more than on purely visual ones. At the moment, he says, his work is mainly devoted to consolidating his position in Paris, to gaining proximity "to the French spirit in its modern form," given that "it incessantly preoccupies me in its historical form" (Letters, 315). In Germany, he adds, he feels "completely isolated" among those of his generation (315). He mentions that he is writing a piece on the Swiss poet and novelist Gottfried Keller, covering matters that have long run through his mind. This work would continue into July, and the piece would appear in *Die literarische Welt* in August, inaugurating a series of major essays on important literary figures for the German newspapers. The Keller essay announces a characteristic set of motifs, ranging from the revaluation of the nineteenth century to the concepts of image space and mirror world, from the interfusion of humor and choler to the efflorescence of Antiquity within the smallest cell of the present day.

Another trip, in August, took him to Orléans, Blois, and Tours, where he visited some of the châteaus on the Loire. In a travel diary he noted the peace, the "immediate sense of presence," that comes with gazing at great works of architecture; he also felt gloom at being stood up by "a Parisian woman . . . with whom he had fallen in love—something he did rather easily and frequently in those years" (Scholem, 133). In mid-August, Scholem again came to Paris to examine manuscripts at the Bibliothèque Nationale and often met with Benjamin, mostly in cafés around the Boulevard Montparnasse. On one occasion, he visited Benjamin's "shabby, tiny, ill-kept room, which contained hardly more than an iron bedstead and a few other furnishings" (133). They went to the movies (Benjamin especially admired the American actor Adolphe Menjou) and took part in violent mass demonstrations in the boulevards against the execution of Sacco and Vanzetti on August 23. Benjamin spoke of his plans for an (unrealized) anthology of Wilhelm von Humboldt's writings on the philosophy of language, and he read to Scholem from the early drafts of *The Arcades Project,* which at that epoch wore the guise of an essay that would number "about fifty printed pages" (135). After parting in Paris, he and Scholem would see each other only one more time, in February 1938, when they met for a few days, again in Paris.

Benjamin's letters of the period point to his rapidly growing interest in photography. In October, Benjamin attended an International Exhibition of Photography in Paris but was disappointed in the selection of early photographs of that city. In a letter to his old schoolmates Grete and Alfred Cohn, he comments that photos of persons mean more than those of localities, because fashions in clothing provide such a reliable temporal index (*GB*, III, 291). He was reading Flaubert's *Sentimental Education* and, under the great impression which this novel was making on him, felt unable to focus on contemporary French literature (291–292). And "with fear and trembling" in his heart, he was giving himself up to "a new work that deals with Paris," on which he was spending every available hour in documentation at the Bibliothèque Nationale (292–293).

Benjamin returned from Paris to Berlin in November, and soon afterward came down with a case of jaundice. A letter of November 18, to Scholem, mentions that he was reading Kafka's novel *The Trial* in bed. It also comments on the cover for the upcoming Rowohlt edition of *One-Way Street,* with its collage by Sasha Stone; he calls it "one of the most effective covers ever" (*GB*, III, 203). At the end of this letter he adds a short allegorical spinoff of Kafka's novel—a piece entitled "The Idea of a Mystery," in which history itself is represented as a trial. While he was ailing, Benjamin received a visit from the poet and philosopher Karl Wolfskehl, a friend of Stefan George and Ludwig Klages: "It's a good thing I've hardly read a line of his; it enabled me to follow his wonderful conversation without any scruples" (312). An account of this visit would appear in *Die literarische Welt* in 1929. In November and December, Benjamin stepped up his efforts to gain entry into the circle surrounding the German art historian Aby Warburg, but Warburg's Hamburg associate Erwin Panofsky, to whom Hofmannsthal had written at Benjamin's request, was put off by his work. On December 12, he wrote to Alfred and Grete Cohn that he had finished *The Trial* in a state verging on agony, "so overwhelming is the unpretentious abundance of this book" (312).

Soon after this, Benjamin made his first experiment with hashish, which he took orally under the supervision of two doctors with whom he was friendly. Baudelaire's writings on hashish and opium, as well as the influence of Surrealism, played a part in this experiment, which he repeated at various times over the next seven years or so. It would seem that he owed his idea of the aura, at least in part, to his experience with hashish. Benjamin was particularly interested in what he called the "colportage phenomenon of space," a kind of spatiotemporal palimpsest effect afforded by the drug. This played a role in the concept of the *flâneur,* which he was developing in connection with *The Arcades Project.* Over the next few years his letters sometimes refer to a book on hashish intoxication, but he never managed to write the work; it was only in 1972, under the title *On Hashish,* that the protocols he kept for the experiments, along with related texts, were first collected and published.

1928

The competing claims on Benjamin's attention continued to intensify during 1928. His unflagging efforts as strategist in the literary wars were balanced by greater immersion in his independent study of the Paris arcades, while his engagement with Marxism, in part mediated through Asja Lacis (with whom he would live in Berlin at the end of the year), and later through Brecht, was carried on in conjunction with constantly revamped plans to emigrate to Palestine. In August of the previous year, in Paris, Scholem had introduced Benjamin to the chancellor of the Hebrew University in Jerusalem, Rabbi Judah L. Magnes, who listened with emotion to Benjamin's description of his career in the philosophy of language. Their two-hour conversation, in which Benjamin maintained that he "had already done what he could as a critic of significant texts" and "that his position had found virtually no response in Germany," so that the interpretation of Hebrew literature remained his only viable option (Scholem, 138), led to Magnes' request for letters of recommendation as a first step in considering Benjamin for a teaching position in Jerusalem. Naturally, such a position would require that he learn Hebrew. Benjamin therefore set about collecting copies of his published work to send to Magnes and requesting academic references (including one from Hofmannsthal) attesting to his scholarly qualifications; these reached Magnes in the spring and were pronounced excellent. His immediate goal was to secure some sort of financial support from Jerusalem.

In January, at long last, *One-Way Street* and the *Trauerspiel* book were published by Rowohlt Verlag. Among the reviews which appeared in Germany, France, Switzerland, Holland, and Hungary, the most important for Benjamin were those by Kracauer, Willy Haas, Franz Hessel, Ernst Bloch, and Marcel Brion (a friend of Hofmannsthal's who was associated with the *Cahiers du Sud*). He also found it noteworthy that Hermann Hesse wrote very favorably to Rowohlt about *One-Way Street.* He was bothered, however, by a rather catty review by Werner Milch (later a specialist in Romanticism at Marburg) which appeared in a Berlin daily. Yet this review, despite its unpleasant tone, nevertheless made the fundamental point that what unites these two texts, outwardly so different, is a formal predisposition, reminiscent of Friedrich Schlegel, for the collection of fragments.

One incident gives some indication of Benjamin's growing recognition. When André Gide came to Berlin in January, he took part in a two-hour interview with Benjamin, who was the only German journalist he agreed to see. This encounter, which Benjamin found "enormously interesting" and "delightful," resulted in two articles on Gide, published soon afterward in the *Deutsche allgemeine Zeitung* and *Die literarische Welt*.

At the end of January, Benjamin wrote to Scholem outlining his need for a subsidy of 300 marks a month if he was "now to jump off the cart that, although slow-moving, is traveling the career path of a German writer" (Letters, 322). He declared himself ready to take up the study of Hebrew just as soon as he completed his current project—"the highly remarkable and extremely precarious essay 'Paris Arcades: A Dialectical Fairy Scene' . . . [with which] one cycle of work, that of *One-Way Street*, will have come to a close for me in much the same way in which the *Trauerspiel* book concluded the German cycle. The profane motifs of *One-Way Street* will march past in this project, hellishly intensified" (322). At this point Benjamin could not have known that the project initially conceived as a newspaper article (to be written in collaboration with Hessel) would expand exponentially during the subsequent decade, coming eventually to fill two fat, posthumously published volumes.

Early 1928 was a period in which Benjamin cultivated a number of old and new intellectual relationships. In February, Theodor Wiesengrund Adorno spent some weeks in Berlin, and he and Benjamin were able to resume the discussions they had begun in Frankfurt in 1923. Benjamin reported to Kracauer in mid-February that he was "often and profitably together with Wiesengrund," who had just met Ernst Bloch (*GB*, III, 334). Adorno and Benjamin would see each other again in Königstein in early June and, a month after that, would begin their historic twelve-year correspondence. Earlier in the year, Benjamin had come to know Margarete (Gretel) Karplus, later Adorno's wife, another important correspondent of his in the Thirties and a provider of financial aid in 1933. Also that February, Benjamin became personally acquainted with the critic Ernst Robert Curtius, and he had his first meetings with Hofmannsthal, to whom he had sent his two books. The *Trauerspiel* book carried the dedication: "For Hugo von Hofmannsthal, / who cleared the way for this book, / with thanks, / February 1, 1928, WB" (333n), a sentence clarified by his remark to Marcel Brion that Hofmannsthal had been the first reader of the work (336). About *One-Way Street* he wrote to Hofmannsthal—echoing here the Baudelairean concept of *modernité*—that its object was "to grasp topicality [*Aktualität*] as the reverse of the eternal in history and to make an impression of this, the side of the medallion hidden from view" (Letters, 325). His conversation with Hofmannsthal touched on his own relation to his Jewishness and to Hebrew, as well as on his ideas about "Paris Arcades"—"an essay," he told Scholem, "that might turn out to be more extensive than I had thought" (327). To Scholem he described "an almost senile tendency" in Hofmannsthal, moments "when he sees himself completely misunderstood by everybody" (328).

Although Dora had been hard at work translating a detective novel by G. K. Chesterton, giving radio lectures on the education of children, and contributing book reviews to *Die literarische Welt* (including one that concerned Joyce's "Work in Progress"—*Finnegans Wake*), Benjamin told Scholem that their current situation was "gloomy" (*GB*, III, 348). He himself had just completed an essay, "Old Toys," which at the end of February he had sent to Kracauer, along with a routine request for a book to review. In his accompanying letter he observes that this essay (which would appear in the *Frankfurter Zeitung* in March) stands in close proximity to his study of the Paris arcades. About the latter he says that he knows one thing: what it's like, "for weeks on end, to be carrying around a subject in one's head and, for the present, enjoying its only success in the fact that I am totally incapable of occupying myself with anything else whatsoever" (359). The emerging intellectual centrality of his work on the arcades, which he liked to call the *Passagen-Werk*, is further indicated by the investigations he was now undertaking into the philosophical significance of fashion—"into the question of what this natural and wholly irrational temporal measure of historical process is all about" (Letters, 329)—and by his response to Karl Kraus's reading of Offenbach's *La vie parisienne* at the end of March, which set in motion, as he remarks to Alfred Cohn, "a whole mass of ideas" connected to the arcades project (*GB*, III, 358). His account of Kraus's performance was published the following month in *Die literarische Welt*.

In April, Benjamin moved into a new room located "in the deepest, most forgotten section of the Tiergarten," where "nothing but trees peer at me through two high windows" (Letters, 335). For the two months that he lived there, before subletting it to Ernst Bloch, he took advantage of the easy access it provided to the Prussian State Library, where he pursued his research on the arcades. He characterized the project in a pointed manner to Scholem: "The work on the Paris arcades is taking on an ever more mysterious and insistent mien, and howls into my nights like a small beast if I have failed to water it at the most distant springs during the day. God knows what it will do when . . . I set it free. But this will not happen for a long time, and though I may already be constantly staring into the abode in which it does what comes naturally, I let hardly anyone else have a look inside" (335). This beast of his was inhabiting "an old and somewhat rebellious quasi-apocryphal province of my thought," and what he had in mind with its subjugation was a testing of "the extent to which it is possible to be 'concrete' in the context of the philosophy of history" (333). An advance which he had received from Rowohlt for "a projected book on Kafka, Proust, and so on" (335–336) was helping to maintain the *Passagen-Werk*.

In his letter of May 24, he announced to Scholem: "I have firmly put an autumn visit to Palestine on my agenda for the coming year. I hope that, before then, Magnes and I will have reached an agreement about the financial terms of my apprenticeship" (Letters, 335). A few weeks later he met with Magnes in Berlin, and the latter "promised, on his own and without further ado," to provide him with a stipend to study Hebrew (338). Meanwhile, he interrupted his research on the arcades to resume work on his Goethe article for the *Soviet Encyclopedia;* this would occupy him until October. At the same time, he was working on a translation of part of Louis Aragon's *Paris Peasant* for *Die literarische Welt;* on an article eventually entitled "The Path to Success, in Thirteen Theses," which would appear in the *Frankfurter Zeitung* in September (and which bears a close relation to the theory of gambling elaborated in *The Arcades Project*); and on a short meditative piece called simply "Weimar," to be published in the *Neue schweizer Rundschau* in October. This last was a by-product of his encyclopedia article on Goethe, which in June had taken him to the Goethe house in Weimar to check his documentation. There, quite unexpectedly, he had suddenly found himself alone for twenty minutes in the great author's study, without even the shadow of a guard to disturb him. "And thus it happens," he wrote to Alfred and Grete Cohn, drawing the moral, "that the more cold-bloodedly one accosts things, the more tenderly they sometimes respond" (*GB*, III, 386).

Amid "all the deadlines" for articles long and short, including "some long articles about French literary currents" (Letters, 335), and amid drawn-out, ultimately fruitless negotiations in May regarding the transfer of rights for the Proust translation to Piper Verlag (a development that led to his and Hessel's abandonment of any further work on this project which had had such "an intense effect on my own writing"; 340), Benjamin characteristically began, that summer, to meditate an escape from Berlin: "I sit and brood—a penguin on the barren rocks of my thirty-seven [*sic*] years—on the possibility of a lonely Scandinavian cruise. But it is probably too late in the year" (*GB*, III, 399). In fact, this plan would have to wait two years for its realization. Meanwhile, he had received news of Asja Lacis' transfer to the Soviet Embassy in Berlin, where she was to work as a trade representative for Soviet films, and so he wrote to Scholem at the beginning of August that the trip to Palestine was "a settled matter" and that he would be staying in Jerusalem "for at least four months," but that his departure "may have to be delayed until mid-December. This will depend, first of all, on whether I can make up my mind to complete the arcades project before I leave Europe. Second, on whether I get together with a Russian woman friend in Berlin in the fall" (Letters, 339). He goes on to mention that Dora has no fixed income of any kind at the moment, while there is nothing presently in the works at Rowohlt for him; "therefore, please have Magnes send something on September 1" (339). In this matter, too, he would have to wait a little longer.

His alleged lack of funds did not stand in the way of a trip to Italy in September. From Lugano, whence he would travel to Marseilles at the end of the month, he wrote to Scholem that the encyclopedia article on Goethe was nearly finished and that he would be returning soon to the arcades project. "It would be splendid," he affirms, "if the ignominious writing I do for profit did not, for its part, need to be maintained at a certain level, so as not to become disgusting to me. I cannot say that I have lacked the opportunity to publish bad stuff; what I have always lacked, despite everything, is only the courage to compose it" (*GB*, III, 414). After this rueful boast, he put off his arrival in Palestine to January.

In October, Benjamin received a check from Magnes for 3,642 marks. The thank-you would come only eight months later, after he finally got around to arranging some Hebrew lessons. On October 22, he wrote to Alfred Cohn of the leisure he had been enjoying "for the past few weeks" since finishing the Goethe article (*GB*, III, 418). Soon, though, he was immersed in a new round of reviewing and feuilleton work. This included reviews of Kraus's reading and of a novel by Julien Green, for the Dutch journal *Internationale Revue;* a series of sketches of Marseilles, for the *Neue schweizer Rundschau;* reviews of a new edition of Goethe's book on color theory and of a startling volume of botanical photographs by Karl

Blossfeldt, for *Die literarische Welt;* and the essay "Hashish in Marseilles," for the *Frankfurter Zeitung.* But the most important of the journalistic projects undertaken at this time was the essay "Surrealism," which would appear in three installments in *Die literarische Welt* in February 1929. The preoccupation with Surrealism had a particular bearing on his ideas for the *Passagen-Werk.* He spoke of this in a letter to Scholem at the end of October: "An all too ostentatious proximity to the Surrealist movement might become fatal to the project, . . . well-founded though this proximity might be. In order to extricate the project from this situation, I have had to expand my ideas of it . . . , making it so universal within its most particular and minute framework that it will take possession of the inheritance of Surrealism . . . Enough of it exists now . . . for me to be able to accept the great risk entailed in slowing the pace of the work while expanding the subject matter" (Letters, 342–343). From this, of course, it followed that his trip to Palestine would have to be postponed again: "I now think I will be coming in the spring of next year" (343).

In November, Asja Lacis came to Berlin in the company of Bernhard Reich (who was there for a short visit only, while Brecht was finishing *The Threepenny Opera*). Before she returned to Moscow in 1930, she would try to arrange for Benjamin's emigration to the Soviet Union, in another of her vain attempts to find something for her friend there. According to Scholem, she advised Benjamin against moving to Palestine. Through her, he would get to meet Brecht in the course of the following year, along with a number of "revolutionary proletarian" authors. And for two months, from December 1928 through January 1929, he would live with her in an apartment at 42 Düsseldorfer Strasse.

1929

At the end of January, Benjamin moved back into his parents' villa on Delbrück-strasse in the Grunewald section of Berlin West—a wealthy haven from Berlin's poverty and misery—where Dora and Stefan were living with his mother. In the spring, after a series of turbulent scenes, he asked his wife for a divorce so that he could marry Asja Lacis and provide her with German citizenship. In August, Dora would insist that he leave his parents' house, which he described rather pathetically as his home of "ten or twenty years," and he would go to live for a while with the Hessels. The legal process that began on June 29 and ended on March 27, 1930, the date of their divorce, would prove financially draining (he would sign over his entire inheritance—including his cherished collection of children's books—to cover the 40,000 marks he owed her). It was because of this, and also to escape the nervous exhaustion of the entire process, that Benjamin flew to his writing desk. In 1929 he would produce more writings (including many newspaper reviews and radio scripts) than in any year before or after. "The year 1929 constituted a distinct turning point in his intellectual life," writes Scholem, "as well as a high point of intensive literary and philosophical activity. It was a visible turning point, which nevertheless did not exclude the continuity of his thought . . .—something that is more clearly discernible now than it was then" (Scholem, 159).

Benjamin was working on his Surrealism essay and also thinking about Proust. To Max Rychner, editor of the *Neue schweizer Rundschau,* which was practically the only German-language periodical to have published articles on Proust on a regular basis, he wrote: "German Proust scholarship is sure to have a different look to it, when compared to its French counterpart. There is so much to Proust that is greater and more important than the 'psychologist,' who, as far as I can tell, is almost the exclusive topic of conversation in France" (Letters, 344). His essay "Surrealism," which he described as "an opaque screen placed before the arcades" (347), began appearing in *Die literarische Welt* on February 1. It, too, announced a movement beyond psychology: "Language takes precedence. / Not only before meaning. Also before the self." The priority of language was, of course, a longstanding concern of Benjamin's—indeed, the hallmark of his thought. And reaching just as far back in his thinking was the emphasis on an expanded concept of experience, which, in Surrealism, takes the form of a "profane illumination" of the world of things, a recognition of mystery within the orders of the everyday. Occupying "its highly exposed position between an anarchistic *Fronde* and a revolutionary discipline," Surrealism, in Benjamin's presentation, discloses a crisis of the intellect, or, more specifically, of "the humanistic concept of freedom."

That the question of revolution was, for Benjamin, necessarily a question of tradition is nicely indicated by a letter of February 15 to the Swiss art historian Sigfried Giedion, whose 1928 study *Architecture in France* had had an "electrifying" effect on Benjamin and was to figure prominently in the pages of *The Arcades Project*. "As I read through your book (together with so many others claiming my attention at the moment), I am struck by the heart-quickening difference between a radical attitude and radical knowing. What you exemplify is the latter, and therefore you are capable of highlighting tradition—or rather, discovering it—within the present day itself" (*GB*, III, 144). The present day had become a kind of well from which tradition could be drawn, or a ground in which mystery was embedded. This was the logic of his work on the Paris arcades, which was aimed at excavating the everyday life of the nineteenth century in France. Benjamin touched on this conception in a letter to Scholem in March: "The issue here is . . . to attain the most extreme concreteness for an era, as it occasionally manifested itself in children's games, in a building, or in a particular situation. A perilous, breathtaking enterprise, repeatedly put off over the course of the winter—not without reason" (Letters, 348).

In the same letter, Benjamin informed Scholem of his latest projects and personal contacts. He had been seeing the political philosopher Leo Strauss, whom he found "sympathetic," and Martin Buber, to whom he detailed his plans for visiting Palestine, and he had received "a delightful, delighted, even enthusiastic letter from Wolfskehl" praising his Surrealism article, "as well as one or two friendly notices" (Letters, 349). He had recently completed a piece called "Marseilles," which would be coming out in April in the *Neue schweizer Rundschau* (of all his cityscapes, he found this one the most difficult to write), and he was working on a piece called "Short Shadows," which would form part of the sequence "Thought Figures" published in November in the same periodical. And he had begun an essay entitled "On the Image of Proust": "I have produced a pack of reviews for the next French issue of *Die literarische Welt,* and am currrently hatching some arabesques on Proust" (349). This "very provisional but cunning essay on Proust," he later tells Scholem, was "begun from a thousand and one different angles" (*GB*, III, 462)—in this respect it resembled *The Arcades Project,* which he had been working "toward, not nearly on" (459). He wanted to know which of all these things, or of his other things, Scholem considered part of the Benjaminian "experimental demonology" (Letters, 349). To borrow a moment from Thomas Mann: he was playing Leverkühn to Scholem's Zeitblom.

A quite different sort of relationship developed in May, when Asja Lacis introduced Benjamin to Brecht. Benjamin was nearly thirty-seven at the time; Brecht, thirty-one. Together with Lacis, they met for long discussions in Brecht's apartment near the zoo—discussions on the crucial importance of winning over the petty bourgeoisie to the side of the Left before Hitler appropriated it first; or on the instructive example afforded by Charlie Chaplin, whose film *The Circus* had opened in Berlin at the beginning of 1929 and had impressed Benjamin as "the first work of maturity in the art of film." Brecht encouraged Benjamin's efforts in radio and introduced him to fellow Marxists, such as the philosopher Karl Korsch, whom Benjamin would cite extensively in *The Arcades Project*. Scholem's portrait is just: "Brecht brought an entirely new element, an elemental force in the truest sense of the word, into his life . . . As early as June 6, he informed me of his rather close acquaintance with Brecht: 'There is a lot to say about him and about it' . . . Three weeks later he wrote: 'You will be interested to know that a very friendly relationship between Bert Brecht and me has recently developed, based less on what he has produced (I know only *The Threepenny Opera* and his ballads) than on the well-founded interest one must take in his present plans'" (Scholem, 159). During the years of exile, Benjamin would find at Brecht's house near Svendborg, Denmark, one of his oases, and with Brecht he would continue the sort of personal confrontation with German thinking that he had begun with Fritz Heinle and Florens Christian Rang. It was also around this time that his relationship with Adorno became closer.

From Scholem's point of view, Benjamin seemed to be Janus-faced: turned simultaneously toward Moscow and Jerusalem. On May 22, he had written to Scholem that his daily Hebrew lessons were beginning the next week, although "inwardly" he was preoccupied with the historical significance of the movement in art and literature known as Jugendstil, partly in the context of the *Passagen-Werk*, partly as a subject for the collection of essays he was planning with Rowohlt (but which never materialized). On June 6 he wrote to Magnes, apologizing for the long delay in thanking him for the stipend, and announcing that his study of Hebrew with the Orthodox rabbi Max Mayer of the *Jüdische Rundschau* had been going on "for a month." He reassured Magnes of his own earnestness, as witnessed in their Paris conversation of 1927, and he went on to express the hope that he would be in Palestine in the fall. To Scholem, the same day, he wrote that his "coming in the fall depends strictly on my material circumstances" (Letters, 350). He countered his friend's "reproaches" by admitting that he was up against "a truly pathological inclination to procrastinate in this matter," although he would "absolutely go on with Hebrew" (350). He even declared that he kept his Hebrew grammar book with him at all times. In fact, the Hebrew lessons were discontinued in July, when Benjamin went off on a trip to Italy with an old friend, and they never resumed.

Before this, he had taken a two-day trip with the same friend—the dramatist and novelist Wilhelm Speyer, with whom he had been a pupil at Haubinda twenty-three years earlier, and with whom he was now collaborating on a detective play. On June 24, from Bansin, France, he wrote to Scholem of his satisfaction with his current literary relations (a feature article on *One-Way Street* had just appeared in a Rotterdam newspaper), and of his dissatisfaction with his friend Ernst Bloch. Back in February, he had complained to Scholem of Bloch's shameless, if subtle, pilferings of his ideas and terminology; now he announced the appearance of "two new books by Bloch, *Traces* and *Essays,* in which a not insubstantial proportion of my immortal works, in part somewhat damaged, has been transmitted to posterity" (*GB,* III, 469). On his return to Berlin he wrote to Hofmannsthal, enclosing some of his recent publications, of which the essay on Proust then appearing in *Die literarische Welt* was to serve as the showpiece. Benjamin's "synthetic interpretation" of Proust underscores the novelist's "impassioned cult of similarity" and his unprecedented revelation of the world of things, arguing that the Proustian idea of happiness transforms existence into "a preserve of memory." As it happened, these were all key motifs of Benjamin's own writing at that period.

Hofmannsthal died on Benjamin's birthday, July 15, and a couple of weeks later Benjamin wrote to Scholem from Italy to express his sadness at the event. He was busy with a number of other articles in July and August, including a review entitled "The Return of the *Flâneur*" (concerning his friend Hessel's book about Berlin) and "a hostile essay" on the Swiss prose writer Robert Walser (Letters, 357). At the end of August, he published in *Die literarische Welt* a piece entitled "Conversation with Ernst Schoen," in which he and the composer Schoen—one of his oldest friends, who had just become director-general of the radio station Südwestdeutscher Rundfunk in Frankfurt—discussed the educational possibilities of radio and television. Benjamin renounced the use of these media for any specific propaganda purposes, although he was interested in combating "false consciousness" among the bourgeoisie. In the latter half of 1929, he began to do radio broadcasts (lectures and readings) more regularly.

In September, Benjamin sent a telegram to Scholem announcing his upcoming arrival in Palestine on November 4—this at a time when his financial situation had stabilized with his steady work for the newspapers, when his relationship with Brecht was blossoming, and when Asja Lacis (as he informed Scholem in a letter of September 18) had suddenly fallen ill again and he had put her on a train to Frankfurt to see a neurologist. He visited her often in Frankfurt during September and October. In the course of these visits, Benjamin also met with Adorno, Gretel Karplus, and Max Horkheimer for intensive discussions of the key theoretical elements of his work. Benjamin now read early drafts of his *Arcades Project,* including "the magnificently improvised theory of the gambler," as Adorno later described it. These "Königstein conversations" left a deep imprint on the thought and writings of all concerned; an important strand of the Frankfurt School's thinking on cultural theory had its beginnings here.

On November 1 Benjamin wrote to Scholem of the unexpectedly "cruel" dimensions that the divorce process was assuming, of Dora's "relentless bitterness," and of the help she was getting from "one of the most cunning and dangerous lawyers in Germany" (*GB,* III, 489). Dora—and the judges—saw the matter rather differently. She had already written, in 1915 (two years before their marriage), "If you love him, then you already know that his words are grand and divine, his thoughts and works significant, his feelings petty and cramped, and his actions of a sort to correspond to all of this."[5] Now, deeply embittered by Benjamin's initiation of divorce proceedings (which centered on accusations of her infidelity) and by his behavior toward her and his son, Stefan (Benjamin had by his own admission lived for years on Dora's earnings as a journalist; he now refused to repay her the 40,000 marks from her inheritance that he had borrowed, and in addition refused all requests to assist in the support of his son), Dora became even more explicit in a letter to Scholem: "The thing with Asja began as early as April 1924, on Capri. Since then he has always made his pacts: with Bolshevism, which he was unwilling to negate, so as not to lose his last excuse (for in the moment of denial he would have had to admit that it is not the sublime principles of this lady that bind him to her, but rather only sexual things); with Zionism, partly for your sake, partly (don't be angry, but these are his own words) 'because his home lies there, where someone can give him the possibility of spending money'; . . . with the literary life (not with literature), for he is naturally ashamed to admit his Zionist leanings in front of Hessel and in front of the little ladies that Hessel brings him during the breaks in his affair with Asja."[6] The judges, in granting a divorce, found that the fault in the marriage lay unequivocally on Benjamin's side. The text of their decision confirms that the accuser "had denied the accused marital intercourse since 1921 (aside from a brief period in 1923) and since then had had sexual relations with other women, in particular with a Frau Lacis. He has, furthermore, repeatedly conceded, orally and in writing, the same freedom to the accused that he, the accuser, has for years claimed for himself in the sexual realm."[7] Benjamin naturally spared Scholem such details, merely remarking that, aside from this all-consuming process (which had even brought on a ten-day nervous collapse), nothing was keeping him in Germany. Nevertheless, he could not for the moment think of leaving.

At the end of December, however, he did leave the country—not for Jerusalem, but for Paris. *Die literarische Welt* was covering his traveling expenses. In return, the periodical expected him to write a "Paris Diary," based on his interviews with literary celebrities.

1930

Benjamin's deepening friendship with Brecht was an important motivating factor in a good deal of his writing during the years 1930–1933; although his political convictions had gradually deepened, he had up to now produced little that could be called engaged writing. In 1930 and 1931, though, Benjamin overtly sought to claim for himself a role as "strategist in the literary struggle." He first issued a series of challenges to the political Right. On the cultural front, he published a long review of "the most astonishing publication to have come out of the George circle in the past few years": Max Kommerell's *The Poet as Leader in German Classicism*. Benjamin's review, "Against a Masterpiece," is his most detailed encounter with the conservative forces that dominated the German cultural scene. And the long review "Theories of German Fascism" offers a devastating critique of the war mysticism that characterized the writings of Ernst Jünger and his circle. If Benjamin was uncompromising in his critique of the Right, however, he was positively merciless in his attacks on left-liberal intellectuals. The review "Left-Wing Melancholy," with Erich Kästner's poems as its ostensible topic, accuses such moderate-left writers as Kästner, Kurt Tucholsky, and Walter Mehring of providing not ammunition in the class struggle but commodities for the entertainment industry. The tone of this review was sufficiently bitter to cause its rejection by the *Frankfurter Zeitung;* like many of Benjamin's political writings of the period, it finally appeared in the social-democratic periodical *Die Gesellschaft.*

In Paris, Benjamin met with acquaintances of Proust and with various Surrealists, including Louis Aragon and Robert Desnos. He was able to follow at first hand the quarrel that had just erupted in the Surrealist group after the publication of André Breton's second *Surrealist Manifesto* in December 1929 and its rejection by the dissidents gathered around Desnos. He interviewed Julien Green, Marcel Jouhandeau, Emmanuel Berl, and the bookseller Adrienne Monnier, who told him that all methods of mechanical reproduction were basically techniques of reduction. Benjamin's "Paris Diary," a kind of supplement to the essays on Proust and Surrealism which he extracted from the actual diary kept during his trip, would appear in *Die literarische Welt* in three installments from April to June.

From his hotel on the Boulevard Raspail, Benjamin wrote to Marcel Brion, at the beginning of January, that he had had "to abandon, at least provisionally," his plans for going to Palestine (*GB*, III, 498). His communication to Scholem was less bald. Ending a silence of nearly three months, during which Asja Lacis had returned to Moscow, he wrote, on January 20, an extraordinary letter in French, beginning "Cher Gerhard."[8]

"You will probably think me crazy," the letter begins, "but I find it immensely difficult to end my silence and write you about my projects. I find it so difficult that I may never manage it without resorting to this mode of alibi that French is for me.

"I cannot delude myself any longer that the question I have been putting off for so long threatens to turn into one of my life's most serious failures. Let me begin by saying that I will not be able to think about my trip to Palestine at all until my divorce becomes final. It does not look like this will happen very soon. You will understand that this subject is so painful to me that I do not want to speak about it" (Letters, 358–359). He added that he had to give up all hope of learning Hebrew as long as he remained in Germany.

On the one hand, requests for contributions were coming in "from all quarters"; on the other—and here he sounded a note that would become a constant refrain through the next decade—his economic situation was "too precarious" for him to think of ignoring such opportunities. Of course, it was not in itself the worsening economic situation of the country (the number of unemployed would reach three million by March) but rather the change in political climate that would spell the end of his career as a man of letters in Germany.

This career was the real subject of his letter to Scholem: "I have already carved out a reputation for myself in Germany, although of modest proportions . . . The goal is that I be considered the foremost critic of German literature. The problem is that literary criticism is no longer considered a serious genre in Germany, and has not been for more than fifty years . . . One must thus recreate criticism as a genre [*le créer comme genre*]. Others have made some progress in doing this, but myself especially" (Letters, 359). His expression of confidence in a positive reception of his work by his contemporaries, if it did not give the lie to his assertions to Magnes of two and a half years earlier, at least signaled his sense of accomplishment since his last stay in Paris. For not only was he the author of two respected, and highly original books of criticism, but he was now publishing regularly with the two most important literary journals of the day. Furthermore, there was the negotiation with Rowohlt for a collection of his essays, on which he laid particular emphasis to Scholem. In 1930 and 1931 Benjamin sought to further solidify this position by publishing a major statement on the theory of literary criticism. A rich variety of preliminary studies and partial drafts of this planned work are included in this volume under titles such as "Program for Literary Criticism" and "Criticism as the Fundamental Discipline of Literary History." The work would never appear, although central ideas that emerged from this process found their way into two little-noticed reviews, "The Rigorous Study of Art" and "Literary History and the Study of Literature."

But he was founding his hopes, above all, on his study of the Paris arcades. "This book," he told Scholem, "is the theater of all my struggles and all my ideas" (Letters, 359). His plan was to pursue the project on "a different plane," in comparison to what, under the influence of Surrealism, he had conceived in 1927 and 1928. Faced with the problem of "documentation" on one side, and of "metaphysics" on the other, he was looking to Hegel and Marx to provide "a solid scaffolding" for his work. An explicit discussion of the theory of historical knowledge would be necessary: "This is where I will find Heidegger on my path, and I expect sparks will fly from the shock of the confrontation between our two very different ways of looking at history" (359–360). In actual fact, though, Benjamin now put his arcades work on the back burner for the next four years. Other projects, in combination with the rapidly worsening political situation in Germany, began to intervene. Not until late 1934 would Benjamin again turn to the arcades and begin to follow the direction he was laying out here.

In February, Scholem wrote a tart letter to Benjamin seeking an end to all equivocation. He accused his friend of "indulging in false illusions" and of lacking candor. He demanded to know where Benjamin really stood vis-à-vis Palestine and Hebrew, and whether or not he was serious about a "true confrontation with Judaism . . . outside the medium of our friendship" (Letters, 363–364). He was also upset about Benjamin's securing a stipend from Magnes under what now appeared to be false pretenses. He would have to wait another two months for Benjamin's response, on April 25, in which he again vaguely suggested that he would be coming to Palestine "before the end of the year" (365). Benjamin offered a direct rejoinder to Scholem's challenge in the matter of Judaism ("I have come to know living Judaism in absolutely no form other than you"; 364), but otherwise sidestepped the issues Scholem had raised by alluding to "that procrastination . . . which is second nature to me in the most important situations of my life" (364), and by shifting attention to his recent divorce with Dora and the "makeshift existence" into which he had been forced as a result. Benjamin, of course, had long since spent the stipend granted him from Jerusalem, and he had no intention of paying it back. When Scholem's wife brought the matter up again in June, while Benjamin was visiting her in Berlin, he once more changed the subject.

That April, Benjamin signed a contract with Rowohlt for the collection of essays he had been meditating. In addition to already published articles—"The Task of the Translator" and "Surrealism," as well as essays on Keller, Hebel, Hessel, Walser, Green, Gide, and Proust—the book was to contain pieces entitled "The Task of the Critic," "Novelist and Storyteller," and "On Jugendstil."

Benjamin was also busy with his broadcasts for radio stations in Berlin and Frankfurt. In February and March, he had presented a series of talks for young listeners on the city of Berlin, and these were followed by lectures on E. T. A. Hoffmann and on Bertolt Brecht, among others. With the journalist Wolf Zucker, he was working on a series of "radio models" (*Hörmodelle*), which consisted of dialogues and short scenes on everyday situations, followed by spontaneous discussions. He was planning an article (unrealized) on the political aspects of radio for the *Frankfurter Zeitung;* it was to incorporate ideas of his colleague Ernst Schoen on the feasibility of transforming radio from a medium of entertainment to one with educational and political significance as well—one that would work against "the limitless spread of a consumer mentality" (as he put it in a sketch of 1930–1931, "Reflections on Radio") and would serve as a model for a new "people's art." On April 4, he wrote to Schoen, listing some thirteen points to be discussed in his proposed article. These include the trivialization of radio as a consequence, in part, of the failure of a liberal and demagogic press and, in part, of the failure of Wilhelminian ministers; the domination of radio by trade unionism; radio's indifference to things literary; and the corruption in the relations between radio and the press (*GB*, III, 515–517).

Among his publications that spring was a review of Kracauer's book *White-Collar Workers*, in *Die Gesellschaft*. Entitled "An Outsider Makes His Mark," it suggests something of Benjamin's own conception of himself as a left-wing outsider, alienated from the "morally rosy" adaptation of the white-collar workers to "the inhuman side of the contemporary social order," yet sufficiently aware—in pointed contrast to Brecht's position—that "the proletarianization of the intellectual hardly ever turns him into a proletarian." Rejecting both the depoliticized "sensation seeking of the snobs" and the depoliticized subordination of white- and blue-collar workers, the writer "rightly stands alone." At the conclusion of the piece, Benjamin compares the writer to a "ragpicker, at daybreak, picking up rags of speech and verbal scraps with his stick." If Benjamin here outlines a materialist criticism in terms of the unmasking of false consciousness among the bourgeoisie, his essay "Food," which appeared in the *Frankfurter Zeitung* at the end of May, is a small masterpiece of materialism in a very different vein, one more personal and, above all, bodily oriented. What he would call "anthropological materialism" was centered in the body as understood philosophically.

His divorce had left him, after he had finally found the "strength" to end his marriage, "at the threshold of my forties, without property or position, dwelling or resources," as he wrote, somewhat exaggerating, to Scholem in June (*GB*, III, 530). Applying himself diligently to labors that (in writing to Scholem) he often derided as "tomfoolery" or "stupidities," he felt overworked and exhausted. He was longing for some sort of "relaxation" (531). The idea of a trip to Scandinavia, first broached some two years earlier, now came to his rescue. At the end of July, he set sail on a voyage that took him over the Arctic Circle into northern Finland. On board ship, he translated a novel by Jouhandeau and read Ludwig Klages, whom he considered, despite Klages' "clumsy metaphysical dualism" and his suspect political tendencies, a great philosopher (Letters, 366). Benjamin's spirits, as he indicated in a letter to Gretel Karplus, were restored: "Once Berlin has been left behind, the world becomes spacious and beautiful, and it even has room on a 2,000-ton steamer, swarming with assorted tourists, for your quietly exhilarated servant" (*GB*, III, 534). An account of his trip would appear in the *Frankfurter Zeitung* in September.

In October, Benjamin moved into a quiet two-room studio apartment in the Wilmersdorf section of Berlin, opposite his cousin Egon Wissing. Sublet from the artist Eva Boy, it would remain his home until he emigrated from Germany in 1933. He had a large study, with space for his 2,000-volume library and for Paul Klee's drawing *Angelus Novus*. Someone had given him a gramophone and he was putting together a record collection, which he enjoyed with his son, Stefan. As Scholem remarks, "it was the last time he had all his possessions together in one place" (Scholem, 178). Pressured by money worries, he was busy, as usual, on several fronts. A major essay on Karl Kraus was nearing completion, and he was working on the review essay "Left-Wing Melancholy." He was preparing his sparkling radio script "Myslovice—Braunschweig—Marseilles" for publication in the humor periodical *Uhu*. He had been present at a conference of the National Socialists' Strasser group (a branch of the Sturmabteilung, or SA—the Storm Troopers) and had witnessed a "debate that was in part fascinating" (*GB*, III, 546–547). He was reading Karl Korsch's *Marxism and Philosophy*, and he would soon be quite absorbed in a German translation of Charles Dickens' *Old Curiosity Shop*.

With Brecht, who had now become the *enfant terrible* of the Berlin theater world, he was engaged in long conversations about a plan for a new journal to be published by Rowohlt, one oriented toward the recognition of a crisis in art and science. "Its formal stance," he told Scholem, "will be scholarly, even academic, rather than journalistic, and it will be called *Krisis und Kritik*. I have completely won Rowohlt over to the plan . . . Beyond this is the difficulty inherent in working with Brecht. I of course assume that I am the one who will be able to deal with that, if anyone can" (Letters, 368). The journal was to be edited by the theater critic and dramatist Herbert Ihering, with Benjamin and Brecht as coeditors. Potential contributors included Adorno, Kracauer, Korsch, Georg Lukács, Robert Musil, and Alfred Döblin. Benjamin's own first contribution was to be an essay on Thomas Mann.

Furthermore, Benjamin was planning, with Adorno and Horkheimer, to deliver a lecture at the end of 1930 entitled "The Philosophy of Literary Criticism" at Frankfurt's Institut für Sozialforschung, of which Horkheimer had become the director in October. On November 2, however, Benjamin's mother died after a long illness (his father had died in 1926), and he asked for a postponement of the lecture, which then was never rescheduled. At this time, he was helping to support himself by working as a publisher's reader for Rowohlt. His translation of Proust's *The Guermantes Way* appeared about a month later, from Piper Verlag.

In December, Benjamin wrote a brief letter accompanying the delivery of his *Trauerspiel* book to the conservative political philosopher Carl Schmitt, whose treatise *Political Theology* had been a principal source. "You will quickly notice how much this book, in its exposition of the doctrine of sovereignty in the seventeenth century, owes to you" (*GB*, III, 558). He referred to Schmitt's recent work in political philosophy as a confirmation of his own work in the philosophy of art. Schmitt would later make use of Benjamin's book in his *Hamlet or Hecuba* of 1956. A different sort of influence is indicated in a letter of mid-December to the literary historian Franz Glück, who had sent Benjamin a volume of the selected writings of the Viennese architect Adolf Loos. To Glück, Benjamin speaks of the importance of

Loos's work to his present studies in particular (559). Loos would be cited at pivotal moments in the essay on Kraus.

1931

Unusually for the peripatetic Benjamin, he spent much of 1931 in Berlin. The pleasure he derived from the security of his apartment in Berlin-Wilmersdorf is a recurrent theme in his letters: "The study is pleasant and livable. All of my books are here now and, even given these times, their number has increased gradually from 1,200—although I certainly have not kept all of them, by a long shot—to 2,000. The study . . . has a panoramic view of the old filled-in bog, or, as it is also called, Lake Schramm—almost *l'atelier qui chante et qui bavarde;* and now that the weather is cold, a view of the ice-skating rinks and a clock is in sight at all seasons. As time goes by, this clock, especially, becomes a luxury it is difficult to do without" (Letters, 387). The lovely essay "Unpacking My Library" is the result of this sentiment. Yet the apartment was not merely the kind of bourgeois refuge Benjamin depicted with such glee throughout his work; if his thought was, as he described it, a "contradictory and mobile whole," then this apartment certainly mirrored that configuration. Benjamin wrote to Scholem with self-mocking irony: "To my horror, I already have to answer for the fact that only saints' pictures are hanging on the walls of my communist cell" (Letters, 386).

The security and continuity of this Berlin existence had a marked effect on Benjamin's self-conception. He could write in October: "I feel like an adult for the first time in my life. Not just no longer young, but grown up, in that I have almost realized one of the many modes of existence inherent in me" (Letters, 385). This state of mind was highly productive. In 1931 he published two of his most important essays, "Karl Kraus" and "Little History of Photography," as well as a number of fine literary and political essays, some radio talks, and several autobiographical pieces. And this was only the completed work. In February, Benjamin mentioned to Scholem that he was at work on what he hoped would be his definitive statement on literary criticism, "The Task of the Critic" (which would stand as the preface to his collection of literary essays), as well as on a "major essay on Jugendstil" (Scholem, 167). A letter to Scholem from October 28 gives an indication of the "ridiculous variety of projects" on which he typically worked: "The series of letters is to be continued;[9] there is a somewhat more detailed physiognomic attempt to describe the connections between Kant's feeblemindedness (in old age) and his philosophy; additionally, a shattering review of Haecker's Virgil;[10] a position as a judge in an open competition for sound-film scripts, for which I am reading and judging approximately 120 drafts a week; a short study of Paul Valéry . . . and I do not know whether the list is complete" (Letters, 385). This diversity in his writing was complemented by the diversity in his reading at the time: Shmarya Levin's *Childhood in Exile,* a life of Johann Heinrich Pestalozzi, Brecht's *Versuche,* and works by Nikolai Bukharin.

From his base in Wilmersdorf, Benjamin made sorties into the social world of the Berlin intelligentsia. He continued to meet frequently with Ernst Bloch and Franz Hessel and discuss ideas; he formed a close friendship with the bank official Gustav Glück; and he continued to frequent the company of journalists such as Willy Haas and Albert Salomon. Max Rychner, editor of the *Neue schweizer Rundschau,* dined with Benjamin in November 1931 and left us a portrait of him in this period: "I observed the massive head of the man across from me and couldn't break free from this observation: of the eyes—hardly visible, well fortified behind the glasses—which now and then seemed to awaken; of the moustache, obliged to deny the youthful character of the face and functioning like two small flags of some country I couldn't quite identify."[11]

But of all of Benjamin's social and intellectual contacts at this time, it was the ones with Brecht that had the most obvious and immediate impact. The two writers debated the relative merits of Stalin and Trotsky, and Benjamin was keen to collaborate on a study of Heidegger's *Being and Time,* which had appeared in 1927. "We were planning to annihilate Heidegger here in the summer," he reported to Scholem, "in the context of a very close-knit circle of readers led by Brecht and me. Unfortunately, Brecht . . . will be leaving soon, and I will not do it on my own" (Letters, 365).

In early 1931, though, the plans for *Krisis und Kritik,* the journal they had hoped to coedit, foundered. It was not merely the foreseeable financial difficulties that brought the journal to a halt before it had begun; differences between Brecht's conception of the work and Benjamin's soon arose. Benjamin had placed enormous weight on the project, not only because of its potential for solidifying the increasingly important relationship with Brecht, but also because it would have embodied the strongest form of Benjamin's now overtly political criticism. Feeling that his intellectual independence would be compromised by further participation, though, Benjamin withdrew from the enterprise in February 1931. Notes on the discussions between Brecht and Benjamin have survived, as has a programmatic memorandum written by Benjamin in October or November.

But the contact with Brecht and his circle was by no means the only manifestation of Benjamin's political will. Just as characteristic is his great essay on Karl Kraus, which appeared in March 1931. Kraus himself, who may well have met Benjamin through a common acquaintance, the composer Ernst Krenek, judged the essay with his own very typical irony: "I can only express the hope that other readers have understood his writings better than I have. (Perhaps it is psychoanalysis.)"[12] The essay, which intertwines a radical politics and a no less radical theology, provoked a series of queries and attacks from friendly quarters and a series of highly revealing defenses and justifications from Benjamin. In a letter of March 7, 1931, to Max Rychner, Benjamin offered a direct apology for the mixture of political and theological elements in his work. He described himself as "a scholar to whom the stance of the materialist seems scientifically and humanely more productive in everything that moves us than does that of the idealist. If I might express it in brief: I have never been able to do research and think in any sense other than, if you will, a theological one—namely, in accord with the talmudic teaching about the forty-nine levels of meaning in every passage of Torah. That is: in my experience, the most trite Communist platitude possesses more hierarchies of meaning than does contemporary bourgeois profundity" (Letters, 372–373). Scholem, in a letter of March 30, delivered what can only be described as a frontal assault on the position Benjamin now occupied: he asserted that Benjamin was "engaging in an unusually intent kind of self-deception" based on a "disconcerting alienation and disjuncture between your *true* way of thinking and your *alleged* way of thinking." Scholem objected to what he saw as a tendency in the Kraus essay to conflate "the metaphysician's insights into the language of the bourgeois" with the insights "of the materialist into the economic dialectic of society" (Letters, 374–375). Benjamin's reply was a model of restraint—and of no little evasion: he finally, much later, sent Scholem a copy of the letter to Rychner, as a kind of belated answer. If he did not defend his politics, though, he did issue Scholem an apology for his continued failure to make good on his promise to learn Hebrew and come to Palestine. "Where is my productive base? It is—and I have not the slightest illusion about this—in Berlin W[ilmersdorf-West]. WW, if you will. The most advanced civilization and the most 'modern' culture not only are part of my private comforts but are, in part, simply the means of my production" (Letters, 378).

In late spring, Benjamin made an extended trip to the south of France, in the company of his friends the Speyers and his cousins the Wissings; they stayed in Juan-les-Pins, Saint-Paul de Vence, Sanary, Marseilles, and Le Lavandou, where they met Brecht, Carola Neher, Emil Hesse-Burri, Elisabeth Hauptmann, Marie Gross-man, and Bernhard and Margot von Brentano. As always when he was together with Brecht, Benjamin engaged in a series of long and heated discussions on a wide range of problems and writers—from the Hegelian dialectic and Trotsky to Proust, Kafka, and Schiller.

During this trip, Benjamin's letters and diaries began to show signs that his new stability and self-confidence were being increasingly punctuated—and not for the first time in his life—by periods of deep depression and thoughts of suicide.

"I feel tired. Tired above all of the struggle, the struggle for money, of which I now have enough in reserve to enable me to stay here. But tired also of aspects of my personal life with which, strictly speaking—apart from my economic situation—I have no reason to be dissatisfied . . . This dissatisfaction involves a growing aversion to and also a lack of confidence in the methods I see chosen by people of my kind and my situation to assert control over the hopeless situation of cultural politics in Germany . . . And to take the full measure of the ideas and impulses that preside over the writing of this diary, I need only hint at my growing willingness to take my own life."[13]

This "growing willingness" is most evident in a diary Benjamin kept in August, 1931—a diary on whose first page he wrote "Diary from August 7, 1931, to the Day of My Death."

"This diary does not promise to become very long. Today there came the negative response from [Anton] Kippenberg, and this gives my plan the relevance that only futility can guarantee. I need to discover 'a method that is just as convenient, but somewhat less definitive,' I said to I[nge] today. The hope of any such discovery is fast disappearing. But if anything can strengthen still further the determination—indeed, the peace of mind—with which I think of my intention, it must be the shrewd, dignified use to which I put my last days or weeks. Those just past leave a lot to be desired in this respect. Incapable of action, I just lay on the sofa and read. Frequently, I fell into so deep a reverie at the end of each page that I forgot to turn the page. I was mainly preoccupied with my plan—with wondering whether or not it was unavoidable, whether it should best be implemented here in the studio or back at the hotel, and so on."

Suicide—whether thoughts of his own or that of people close to him—had played a remarkable role in his work starting as early as 1914, with the writing of "Two Poems by Friedrich Hölderlin" and its commemoration of the suicide of his friends Fritz Heinle and Rika Seligson. An attempted suicide emerges as the "secret" that organizes his reading of Goethe's *Elective Affinities*. And the problem of suicide informs one of Benjamin's most provocative short texts, "The Destructive Character" of 1931. Now, however, despite his deepening depression, Benjamin failed to carry through on his plan; but thoughts of taking his life would never be far from him in the years to come.

Benjamin returned to Berlin in July 1931 and remained there until April 1932. In August he published his "Little History of Photography." Benjamin here establishes himself as an early and significant theorist of photography; the essay contains, in addition, an important early formulation of his concept of the aura. His letters from these months are full of capsule descriptions of the political situation and, naturally, of foreboding. "The economic order of Germany has as firm a footing as the high seas, and emergency decrees collide with each other like the crests of waves. Unemployment is about to make revolutionary programs just as obsolete as economic and political programs already are. To all appearances, the National Socialists have actually been delegated to represent the unemployed masses here; the Communists have not as yet established the necessary contact with these masses and, consequently, the possibility of revolutionary action" (Letters, 382).

It was in late 1931 that Benjamin began to sense the end of his career as a public intellectual in Germany. "The constriction of the space in which I live and write (not to mention the space I have for thought) is becoming increasingly difficult to bear. Long-range plans are totally impossible" (Letters, 384). This is one of the first soundings of what will be the dominant theme of his letters in the years to come: the progressive elimination of all but a very few sites for the publication of his work, and with that elimination, his gradual reduction to abject poverty.

1932

Benjamin's long preoccupation with the bourgeois letter as a literary form bore fruit in early 1932. First in a radio talk called "On the Trail of Old Letters," delivered in January, and then in a series of letters called "From World Citizen to Haut Bourgeois," coedited with Willy Haas, Benjamin began to explore possibilities for grouping and commenting on a series of letters that he hoped would have revelatory and potentially revolutionary potential. This line of his thought would culminate in the pseudonymously published *Deutsche Menschen* of 1936, one of the keystones of Benjamin's work in the 1930s.

In January and February 1932, he also began to set down the first drafts of the recollections of his childhood and youth that Scholem would eventually publish as *Berlin Chronicle*. The short texts, for which he had received a contract from *Die literarische Welt* in the fall, took advantage of the form Benjamin had first developed in *One-Way Street:* often aphoristic but always dense and allusive meditations on things and places. He would continue to refine his drafts in the months to come. But no longer in Berlin.

Driven by the bleakness of his long-term economic prospects and the short-term presence of a bit of cash, Benjamin boarded a ship in Hamburg on April 7, bound for Barcelona. From there he took the mail boat to Ibiza, the Balearic island on which he would spend important parts of the coming years. While on the island, he shared lodgings with Felix Noeggerath (a friend from the days of the Youth Movement) and Noeggerath's family. His first remarks on Ibiza, contained in a letter to Scholem of April 22, reflect a subdued hope. He was prepared to do without "any kind of comfort" because of the "composure the landscape provides; the most untouched landscape I have ever come across" (Letters, 390). In a letter to Gretel Karplus written early in his stay, he elaborated on the particular forms of "deprivation" he had to endure. After rising early, swimming, and sunbathing, he faced "a long day of doing without countless things, less so because they shorten life than because none of them is available, or, when they are, they are in such bad condition that you are glad to do without them—electric light and butter, liquor and running water, flirting and reading the paper" (Letters, 393). Nothing, of course, could deter Benjamin from reading (Stendhal's *Charterhouse of Parma*—an already familiar text; Theodor Fontane's *Der Stechlin;* Trotsky's autobiography and his history of the February Revolution). Or, apparently, from flirting. While on Ibiza, he proposed marriage to a German-Russian woman named Olga Parem, who turned him down. In subsequent months, Benjamin saw a number of other women, including the divorced wife of a Berlin physician.

While on the island, he pushed forward with his autobiographical project. He brought *Berlin Chronicle* to a provisional conclusion, though he remained unsure of just what to do with it. The short form that he was developing there, which he now came to call a "thought figure," found other uses. "Ibizan Sequence," a series of these short texts, was published in June. Benjamin also used the time on Ibiza to produce an unusual number of novellas, travel reports, and landscape sketches. "Spain, 1932," "The Handkerchief," and "In the Sun" all date from this period. He complained, meanwhile, of the island's relative lack of detective novels, which were always a passion with him; and he commented on his reading of Thornton Wilder's novel *The Cabala* and Proust.

Although Benjamin had planned to extend his stay on Ibiza at least through August, on July 17 he boarded a ship for the French mainland. His departure was undoubtedly comical: "When we finally arrived at the quay, the gangplank had been taken away and the ship had already begun to move . . . After calmly shaking hands with my companions, I began to scale the hull of the moving vessel and, aided by curious Ibizans, managed to clamber over the rail successfully."[14] His reasons for leaving Ibiza were considerably less comical: he planned to take his life in a hotel in Nice. In a letter to Scholem of July 26, written in Nice, Benjamin spoke of his "profound fatigue" and of his horror and disgust at events in Germany. On July 20, 1932, Franz von Papen, who had been German chancellor for only a month, suspended the democratically elected Prussian government, naming himself "Imperial Commissar for Prussia" and preparing the way for Hitler's assumption of power. Benjamin was all too aware of the immediate and possibly future results of Germany's political demise. By the end of July he had already, as a Jew, received a letter from the building-safety authorities ordering him to abandon his apartment because of alleged code violations; his radio work had also been brought to a halt by the dismissal of the left-leaning directors of the Berlin and Frankfurt stations. The tone of the July 26 letter, in which he compiles a retrospective assessment of his accomplishments and failures, leaves little to the imagination. "The literary forms of expression that my thought has forged for itself over the last decade have been utterly conditioned by the preventive measures and antidotes with which I had to counter the disintegration constantly threatening my thought as a result of such contingencies. And though many—or a sizable number—of my works have been small-scale victories, they are offset by large-scale defeats." He goes on to name the "four books that mark off the real site of ruin or catastrophe" in his life: the unfinished work on the arcades of Paris, his collected essays on literature, the edited series of old letters, and a truly exceptional book about hashish (Letters, 396).[15]

Now, in the Hôtel du Petit Parc, he prepared to put an end to his life. He wrote out a will, leaving his manuscripts and those of his friends Fritz and Wolf Heinle to Scholem as executor, and he drafted farewell letters to Egon Wissing, Ernst Schoen, Franz Hessel, and Jula (Cohn) Radt. Whether it was a change of heart or a failure of will that led Benjamin to stop short of suicide itself will undoubtedly remain a mystery (Scholem, 185–188).

From Nice, Benjamin went to join the Speyers in Povoremo, Italy, in order to collaborate with Speyer on a detective play. "I live away from all the bustle, in a simple but quite satisfactory room, and I am rather content, insofar as conditions and prospects allow me to be" (Scholem Letters, 16). In Povoremo, Benjamin turned again to the series of short autobiographical texts he had completed on Ibiza three months before, and the project underwent a decisive conceptual change. In the early texts finished on Ibiza that Scholem would later publish as *Berlin Chronicle,* the autobiographical element of the project had been predominant. But in Italy, Benjamin began to turn the texts toward the poetical and philosophical form of the "thought figure"—an attempt to capture the essence of a place and a time. He soon began referring to this project as *A Berlin Childhood around 1900.* Benjamin worked hard on the project, and was able to send a provisionally completed text to Scholem from Berlin in December. That mailing inaugurated the long and troubled publication history of the *Childhood.* The version of December 1932 contains thirty sections; the version published in 1972, in the fourth volume of the Suhrkamp edition of Benjamin's writings, contains forty-one sections, in a different order; and the "definitive" version, published in Volume 7 of the Suhrkamp edition and based on a manuscript long believed lost, contains thirty again, but in a still different order.

The collaboration with Speyer at least held out some prospect of eventual remuneration; all other prospects seemed to be vanishing. Just as his radio contracts had disappeared during the summer, his two major publishing venues were rendered inaccessible. The *Frankfurter Zeitung* left his letters unanswered, and *Die literarische Welt* asked explicitly that he submit no more work. Even the few hopes that dangled from Berlin were to prove futile. Rowohlt again hinted at the publication of the volume of literary essays that he had hoped, in 1931, would make his career and that was now seen only as a source of a few marks; but this, too, led to nothing. Benjamin was now destitute, totally dependent upon Speyer's generosity. "I am now engulfed in [the economic crisis] like a fish in water, but I am hardly as well off as the fish" (Scholem Letters, 20). Scholem had been in Europe, working at a series of archives on kabbalistic texts, since early in the year; Benjamin had avoided a meeting for reasons he never articulated, but which undoubtedly were bound up with his commitments to Brecht and his politics. Now, in the fall, when Benjamin expressed an interest in seeing Scholem, he was unable to afford the return fare to Berlin, where Scholem stayed until mid-October. Benjamin returned only when Speyer—along with his automobile—was ready, in mid-November. While Benjamin wrote and worried, he read Arthur Rosenberg's *A History of Bolschevism* and Rudolf Leonhard's *The Word.*

Returning directly from Italy to Berlin, Benjamin had to turn down a gratifying invitation to visit, in Frankfurt, the first university seminar devoted to his work. The young *Privatdozent* Theodor Wiesengrund Adorno was offering a seminar to selected students on Benjamin's *Origin of the German Trauerspiel.* In turning down Adorno's invitation, Benjamin affirmed that he was "less than ever the master of my decisions . . . As such, the temptation to stay in Germany for any length of time is not very great" (Letters, 398).

In Berlin, Benjamin detailed to Scholem the way in which intellectuals were continuing to betray one another. He had been stung by a letter from his former collaborator Willy Haas, the editor of *Die literarische Welt,* one of his central organs of publication. "In order to know how someone fares who deals with such 'intellectuals,' in the form of editors or newspaper owners, you need only remember that the 'intellectuals' among our 'coreligionists' are the first to offer the oppressors hecatombs from their own circles, so as to remain spared themselves. True, I have been able to stem the boycott led against me simply by showing up. But whether the energy I invested over these first few weeks will avert the worst cannot yet be judged" (Scholem Letters, 23).

1933

In early 1933, Benjamin made the acquaintance of a woman who would figure prominently in his correspondence with Scholem in the coming years: Kitty Marx (who would soon become Kitty Marx-Steinschneider, after her marriage to Scholem's friend Karl Steinschneider). Unusually for Benjamin, a deep and lasting friendship sprang up between them almost immediately; their subsequent correspondence is filled with a courtly irony that borders on long-distance flirtation. This new friendship represented, though, only a temporary respite from concerns that were becoming more pressing every day.

Benjamin was experiencing first-hand the preparations for the "opening ceremonies of the Third Reich" that he had already prophesied in spring of 1932. The persecution of political opponents, the book burnings, the unleashing of the Brownshirts—all this was part of daily life in Germany's capital. "The little composure that people in my circles were able to muster in the face of the new regime was rapidly spent, and one realizes that the air is hardly fit to breath anymore—a condition which of course loses significance as one is being strangled anyway" (Scholem Letters, 27). After the night of February 27, 1933, when the Reichstag was burned, Benjamin's friends began to disappear: Ernst Schoen and Fritz Fränkel into hastily erected concentration camps; Brecht, Bloch, Kracauer, and Speyer into exile. Benjamin was prescient regarding the implications for his own work. "I don't know how I will be able to make it through [the coming months], either inside or outside Germany. There are places where I could earn a minimal income, and places where I could live on a minimal income, but not a single place where these two conditions coincide" (Letters, 402).

What is perhaps most remarkable about these months is Benjamin's ability to suppress the ugly clamor in the streets outside his window and push on with his work. While still in Berlin, he completed a radio play on the German aphorist Lichtenberg (long one of his heroes), began an essay on Kafka, and, above all, finished one of his most important "private" essays, intended only for his own use and the eyes of a few adepts. This essay, "Doctrine of the Similar," represented a "new theory of language," an important building on the foundations of his language essay of 1916, "On Language as Such and on the Language of Man." In a letter of this period to Scholem, he continued to press his friend to read two texts about which Scholem has a host of reservations: Adorno's *Kierkegaard* and Brecht's *Versuche*.

On about March 18, Benjamin left Berlin. From Paris, his first stop, he wrote to Scholem: "I can at least be certain that I did not act on impulse, out of panic: the German atmosphere in which you look first at people's lapels, and after that usually do not want to look them in the face anymore, is unbearable. Rather, it was pure reason which bid all possible haste" (Letters, 406). Another letter sounded a note that would become recurrent: Benjamin's concern for friends and family who, for various reasons, delayed their departure from Germany. He was anxious first and foremost about the safety of his son. "All of this . . . would be bearable, if only Stefan weren't where he still is. In my first letter from here, I urged Dora to send him to Palestine, where her brother owns a plantation" (Scholem Letters, 36). In Paris, where Benjamin stayed only a short time, he met acquaintances from his stay on Ibiza in 1932: Jean Selz and his wife. He left Paris for the island in their company on April 5, arriving ten days later after a stay of several days in Barcelona.

On Ibiza, Benjamin returned to his former, remarkably simple lifestyle. He lodged with acquaintances (including the Noeggeraths) or in rented accommodations; for a good part of his stay, he lived in an isolated house that was half finished and devoid of any conveniences. Ibiza represented for Benjamin a reduction of his living expenses to "the European minimum of about sixty or seventy reichsmarks a month." He was able to raise this sum through a combination of income from his writings, income from the slow selling-off of the most valuable contents of his library, and regular contributions from friends such as Gretel Adorno and Fritz and Jula Radt (Letters, 410). But even Ibiza had begun to change, with many new residents, many new buildings, and not a few Nazis. Without knowing how long he would—or could—remain there, Benjamin began to learn Spanish. His reports from the island contrast markedly with those from his stay in 1932, which had been so idyllic in tone; now he gave way to irritation with the "blastings and hammer blows, the gossip and debates that constitute the atmosphere of San Antonio" (Scholem Letters, 58). Only on occasional rambles in the interior of the island, some of them in the company of Paul Gauguin, a grandson of the famous painter, could he escape the tumult and recover some of the earlier sense of place. Benjamin's account of one such walk takes even this encounter with a more primitive side of the island and organizes it around a symbol of death: "A man came walking toward us, carrying a tiny white child's coffin under his arm" (Letters, 420).

News from Germany persistently added to his sense of despair. In early May, he learned that his brother Georg, who had been active in Germany's Communist party, had been arrested. First reports had him in the hands of the SA, tortured, and blinded in one eye. Benjamin soon learned that his brother was in fact in "preventive detention" in a regular prison, and relatively healthy; better news, but hardly the sort to allay his fears. Dora and Stefan remained in Berlin. And a new source of anxiety soon made itself felt: his passport would expire at the end of the summer, and he was doubtful that he would be allowed to reenter France without one.

Among his most pressing personal concerns was, naturally, the problem of finding new sources of income. He was surprised to learn that Germany was, at first, not as closed to him as he had feared. Both the *Vossische Zeitung* and the *Frankfurter Zeitung* continued to publish reviews and short prose (including individual sections of *A Berlin Childhood*). These and other efforts were published under a series of pseudonyms, "Detlev Holz" remaining his favorite. The first major statement from his time of exile to appear in Germany was his final reckoning with an author who had preoccupied him since his earliest encounters with literature: Stefan George. "Stefan George in Retrospect" is predictably cautious in its political assessment of George, the most important figure in the conservative literary world in the first half of the twentieth century. Benjamin's remarks on this aspect of George are more direct in a letter to Scholem: "If ever God has smitten a prophet by fulfilling his prophecies, then this is the case with George" (Scholem Letters, 59). Benjamin's published critique takes on George, instead, in the coded language he had developed in his own work: the terms "nature," "daemonic," and "hero" carry with them philosophical and theological associations first developed in the 1921 essay "Goethe's Elective Affinities." The George essay was followed by a commission to write a piece commemorating the two hundredth anniversary of the birth of Christoph Martin Wieland, one of the chief literary figures of the German Enlightenment.

Older journals now in exile represented further publishing outlets. One of the first such opportunities was a commission from the Institut für Sozialforschung, which had managed to transfer its endowment from Germany to Switzerland. Benjamin agreed to produce a very substantial review of the current state of French letters, although he repeatedly expressed reservations about his ability to carry out this task on Ibiza, with no scholarly library and few books; early in the process, he called the essay "sheer fakery" (Scholem Letters, 41). By late May, however, when he had finished "The Present Social Situation of the French Writer," he accorded himself grudging approval: "It wasn't possible to produce something definitive. Nonetheless, I believe that the reader will gain insight into connections that until now have not been brought out so clearly" (Scholem Letters, 54). And late in the year in Paris, with the Bibliothèque Nationale at his disposal, he began to work on two further commissions from the Institut: a major essay on the collector and historian Eduard Fuchs, and a collective review of recent publications on the philosophy and sociology of language.

But the paths to the exile journals were often tortuous. At Scholem's urging, Benjamin overcame a strong personal disinclination and submitted two pieces to Max Brod for publication in the *Prager Tageblatt*. Brod not only rejected the pieces, but gave them without the author's permission to Willy Haas, editor of the periodical *Die Welt im Wort*. Haas, now an object of Benjamin's scorn, agreed to publish both "Experience and Poverty" (Benjamin's important reflection on the thoroughly positive reduction of modern experience to a "new barbarism") and a small piece on Johann Peter Hebel. Before they appeared, and certainly before Benjamin had been paid, *Die Welt im Wort* failed—an event which Benjamin described as "gratifying" (Scholem Letters, 100). Brod eventually published both pieces in the *Tageblatt.*

Despite isolated successes, most of Benjamin's efforts to find new venues failed. A review of Brecht's *Threepenny Novel* had initially been accepted and indeed typeset by the journal *Die Sammlung,* edited by Klaus Mann; Benjamin was bold enough to ask for 250 francs rather than the offered 150, and Mann returned the piece without comment. And an attempt late in the year to find a home for some longer works with an émigré press planned in Jerusalem by Shoshanah Persitz came to nothing.

By late May, Benjamin's isolation and the poor nutrition that resulted from his lack of funds began to take effect. He reported to Scholem that his health was not good and that he saw no hope of relief. Unable to work on "what matters most to me"—the continuation of *A Berlin Childhood*—he began to work with Jean Selz on a French translation of his text. Selz knew no German, but Benjamin paraphrased in French, leading to results that Benjamin deemed excellent. And he continued to think about his new language theory; he asked Scholem to forward a copy of the 1916 essay, so that he could compare it with the new writings.

With the increasing desperation of exile and poverty, Benjamin again began to weigh a possibility he had discarded with seeming finality early in the decade: emigration to Palestine. Scholem had written him a few mildly discouraging sentences regarding possibilities for work for European professionals and intellectuals. Benjamin now responded with a long, circuitous account of his current state of mind.

"Thousands of intellectuals have made their way to you. One thing distinguishes them from me—and this seems to work in my favor at first glance. But thereafter—as you well know—the advantage becomes theirs. Precisely this: they represent blank pages. Nothing would have more fateful consequences than an attitude on my part that could be construed as though I were attempting to cover up a private calamity with a public one . . . I would be glad and fully prepared to come to Palestine if you, or others concerned, assume that I could do so without provoking such a situation . . . Is there more room for me—for what I know and what I can do—there than in Europe? If there is not more, then there is less . . . If I could improve upon my knowledge and my abilities there without abandoning what I have already accomplished, then I would not be the least bit indecisive in taking that step" (Scholem Letters, 59–60).

Translated into the plain language which Benjamin was incapable of using with Scholem on this topic, the letter indicates that Benjamin was at this point willing neither to give up his engagement with European ideas, nor to use Palestine as a mere base for that engagement. Scholem, long a shrewd reader of Benjaminian prose, understood immediately. He replied that he found it "questionable whether a person could possibly feel well in this country without directly participating in the life here, whether . . . this would not rapidly bring about a morally unbearable state of estrangement in which life cannot be sustained" (Scholem Letters, 66).

Late spring and early summer brought an intense fascination with the work of Arnold Bennett. Benjamin recommended the novel *Clayhanger* to each of his correspondents, wrote a review of the German translation of *Constance and Sophie,* and described Bennett as a kind of Benjaminian alter ego. He recognized in Bennett "a man whose stance is very much akin currently to my own and who serves to validate it—that is to say, a man for whom a far-reaching lack of illusion and a fundamental mistrust of where the world is going lead neither to moral fanaticism nor to embitterment but to an extremely cunning, clever, and subtle art of living. This leads him to wrest from his own misfortune the chances, and from his own wickedness the few respectable ways to conduct himself, that amount to a human life" (Letters, 422).

In mid-July the first of a series of illnesses overtook Benjamin. Upon his return from Majorca, where he had succeeded in obtaining a new passport, a leg wound became inflamed while he was visiting friends in the town of Ibiza, and the resultant fever combined with bouts of intense summer heat to keep Benjamin from returning to his room in San Antonio. Even so, he managed during his illness to write one of the most compelling sections of A Berlin Childhood, "Loggias," which he described as a "kind of self-portrait" (Letters, 427). And a glimmer of hope revealed itself to him when, through Wilhelm Speyer's intervention, he received an invitation to live, free of charge, in a house in Paris funded by the Baroness Goldschmidt-Rothschild for refugee Jewish intellectuals.

A relationship with a woman to whom Benjamin alluded only in the vaguest terms in his letters seems to have been a dominant element in his life during these months. By the end of the summer, he could pay her the highest of compliments—calling her the female counterpart to the Angelus Novus—while continuing to conceal her identity. Whether or not this relationship played a role, during the summer Benjamin produced two of his most important "private" writings of the period of exile: "On the Mimetic Faculty" (the later version of his new theory of language) and two pieces entitled "Agesilaus Santander" (versions of a highly esoteric meditation on naming and identity). Scholem speculates that the lovely last line of "Agesilaus Santander"—"And so, scarcely had I seen you the first time than I returned with you to where I had come from"—could well refer to the unnamed woman of the summer. During the summer Benjamin was also able to arrange for the transfer of part of his "archive" (his own writings and those of the Heinles) from Berlin; he continued to be anxious about the fate of his library, whose packing and shipping he simply could not afford.

By early September, Benjamin's condition had not improved; he continued to run a fever, and experienced prolonged periods of exhaustion during which he was bedridden in an isolated country house. He realized that his recovery was made difficult by his sparse diet and his emotional state. Ill as he was, Benjamin retained his sense of humor, at least when it came to reading. Commenting to Scholem on their shared interest in Christian theology (he had just finished a book on Luther), Benjamin claimed: "I have now grasped for the fifth or sixth time in my life what is meant by justification through faith. But I have the same trouble here as I have with infinitesimal calculus: as soon as I have mastered it for a few hours, it vanishes again for just as many years" (Scholem Letters, 77).

He planned to return to Paris when he had regained his health, but even Paris seemed to be less a superior haven for an exile than a marginally preferable place of suffering. "It hardly needs to be stated that I am facing my stay in Paris with the utmost reserve. The Parisians are saying, 'Les émigrés sont pires que les boches' [The émigrés are worse than the Krauts]" (Scholem Letters, 72). When he finally did make the trip to the French capital in early October, it was under "unimaginable conditions" (82): he was diagnosed on his arrival with malaria and treated with a course of quinine. Exactly when the lingering illness related to his leg wound gave way to this far more serious disease remains unclear.

Paris was all he had feared. The lodging in the house provided by the baroness proved to be "by no means free of charge" (83); it soon revealed itself as no option at all. And the possibility of earning a living from his writings in French was just as hopeless. "I am faced here with as many question marks as there are street corners in Paris. Only one thing is certain: that I have no intention of making a futile attempt to earn my living by writing for French journals" (82). He would eventually receive a commission from *Le Monde* for a piece on Baron Haussmann, but this was never completed; like so much of Benjamin's work, the research for the newspaper article found its way into *The Arcades Project*.

By the end of the year, Paris had begun to present difficulties to which Benjamin had no solution. "Life among the émigrés is unbearable, life alone is no more bearable, and a life among the French cannot be brought about" (Scholem Letters, 93). And although the city was far too expensive, he had no other place to go. Brecht had invited him to follow in his footsteps and emigrate to Denmark, luring him with attractive estimates of living costs. "But I am horrified by the winter, the travel costs, and the idea of being dependent on him and him alone" (Scholem Letters, 93). Dora and Stefan were still in Berlin; his brother Georg had been released from the Sonnenburg concentration camp, but refused to flee Germany. It was the beginning of a Parisian exile that would, with a few interruptions, extend to the end of Benjamin's life.

1934

Material hardship and intellectual isolation remained the key elements in Benjamin's existence in Paris. "I have hardly ever been as lonely as I am here," he wrote to Scholem in January. "If I were seeking opportunities to sit in a café with émigrés, they would be easy to find. But I avoid them" (Letters, 434). He wandered into Sylvia Beach's bookshop, and lingered over the portraits and autographs of British and American writers; he strolled the boulevards as a latter-day *flâneur;* and trapped by day, he dreamed at night. "In these times, when my imagination is preoccupied with the most unworthy problems between sunrise and sunset, I experience at night, more and more often, its emancipation in dreams, which nearly always have a political subject . . . They represent a pictorial atlas of the secret history of National Socialism" (Scholem Letters, 100).

Benjamin's first letters in the new year inaugurated what would be the dominant theme for the year as a whole: Franz Kafka. In a letter to Scholem, he expressed the hope that he would some day be able to lecture on Kafka and S. J. Agnon, the Jewish writer whose story "The Great Synagogue" would have figured prominently in the first issue of Benjamin's planned journal *Angelus Novus* in 1921. Discussions on Kafka also opened the way for Benjamin to take up new, albeit cautious, relations with his old friend Werner Kraft, with whom he had broken in 1921. Kraft had, until 1933, been a librarian in Hannover; he now shared Benjamin's exile and experienced the same dilemmas that confronted the émigré intellectual.

Rejections and disappointments continued to frustrate Benjamin's attempts to find venues for his work. He placed great hopes in some talks on the German avant-garde, to be delivered in French—a series of subscription lectures that he was to hold in a Parisian art salon; aside from the funds they would have brought, Benjamin hoped that they might establish a bridgehead on the French intellectual scene. The talks, which would have included an introduction on the German reading public and individual lectures on Kafka, Bloch, Brecht, and Kraus, were canceled when their sponsor, a prominent gynecologist, fell ill. Similarly, a commission from the *Nouvelle Revue Française* for an article on Johann Jakob Bachofen led to much research, a completed essay, and a rejection. And a major project intended for the *Zeitschrift für Sozialforschung* fell prey not to rejection but to Benjamin's failure to complete it. He devoted months to the preparation of this "retrospective recapitulation of the cultural politics of *Die neue Zeit*" (Scholem Letters, 139), the ideological organ of Germany's Social Democratic party; he hoped to "demonstrate for once how collective literary products are particularly suited to materialist treatment and analysis and, indeed, can be rationally evaluated only when treated in such a way" (Letters, 456). Though he mentioned the project in nearly every letter he wrote in the late summer and early fall, the project simply disappeared. One notable exception to this pattern of frustration and failure was the championing of *A Berlin Childhood* by Hermann Hesse, who approached two publishers, S. Fischer and Albert Langen, in an effort to find a home for the text. His efforts ultimately came to nothing, but Benjamin was gratified by the attention paid to his work by the prominent novelist.

In addition to the small gifts of money from friends, Benjamin was able to supplement his income through stipends paid by various organizations and by the ongoing sale of his books. In the spring, he began to receive 700 francs a month from the Israélite Alliance Universelle; at about the same time, the Institut für Sozialforschung initiated a stipend of 500 francs per month that would continue throughout the 1930s. And the institute, in the person of Friedrich Pollack, performed another important service: it funded the transfer of Benjamin's books—"about half the library, but the more important half"—from Berlin to Denmark, care of Brecht (Letters, 437). This transfer not only put the library at Benjamin's disposal for his writing, but allowed him to make important sales, foremost among them a tortuously negotiated sale of the complete works of Franz von Baader to the library of the Hebrew University in Jerusalem.

In March, his fortunes had so declined that he was forced to move from his cheap hotel in the sixth arrondissement. Fortunately, his sister Dora had recently moved to Paris. Benjamin's relations with his sister had long been troubled, but now, in Paris, they improved, and Benjamin moved into her small apartment on a temporary basis. Sometime that month, Benjamin also broke with one of his few remaining French acquaintances, Jean Selz, under circumstances that remain clouded. His family in Germany was still an object of intense concern. Dora and Stefan remained in Berlin, while Benjamin's brother Georg, freed from prison, returned to Berlin from a trip to Switzerland and Italy and immediately resumed his clandestine political work.

Despite these conditions, Benjamin continued to write. He finished the long review essay "Problems of the Sociology of Language" for the *Zeitschrift für Sozialforschung,* and a review of Max Kommerell's book on Jean Paul, which he published under the pseudonym K. A. Stempflinger in the *Frankfurter Zeitung.* In late spring, he finished a long piece on literary politics, "The Author as Producer." The text, as published twenty-six years after Benjamin's death, indicates that it was delivered as a lecture at the "Institute for the Study of Fascism" in Paris on April 27. This institute, with Arthur Koestler at its head, was a research group controlled by the Comintern but financed by French workers and intellectuals. The essay is one of Benjamin's most significant analyses of the relations between literary form and politics; whether it was ever delivered remains a mystery.

Once again, he sat in the Bibliothèque Nationale and took up his work on the Paris arcades. "The arcades project is the *tertius gaudens* these days between fate and me. I have not only been able to do much more research recently, but also—for the first time in a long while—to imagine ways in which that research might be put to use. That this image diverges greatly from the first, original one is quite understandable" (Scholem Letters, 100).

A letter from Scholem of April 19 opened the way for one of Benjamin's most significant essays, "Franz Kafka." Scholem had approached Robert Weltsch—editor of the *Jüdische Rundschau,* the largest-circulation Jewish publication still allowed in Germany—regarding the possibility of Benjamin's contributing an essay on Kafka. When Weltsch followed up Scholem's suggestion with an invitation, Benjamin on May 9 accepted enthusiastically, while warning Weltsch that his essay would not conform to the "straightforward theological explication of Kafka" (Letters, 442). And this was not the only activity on Benjamin's behalf that his friend had undertaken: he also asked Moritz Spitzer, editor of the Schocken Library (a series of small, somewhat popular volumes with a largely German-Jewish readership), to solicit "one or more small books" from Benjamin (Scholem Letters, 106). Despite Benjamin's willingness, this plan, too, foundered, as the German exchange office soon stopped all payments to Schocken authors living abroad.

Scholem's important letter also rekindled the old, uncomfortable debate between the friends regarding Benjamin's politics. After reading the relatively mild and straightforward essay "The Present Social Situation of the French Writer," Scholem claimed that he was unable to understand it and asked Benjamin if the essay was a "Communist credo" (107). Scholem wanted to know where Benjamin stood, and reminded him that he had been unwilling to give clear answers to this question in the past. Scholem's letter elicited an important and highly revealing response from Benjamin. A draft later found in East Berlin reads: "I have always written according to my convictions—with perhaps a few minor exceptions—but I have never made the attempt to express the contradictory and mobile whole that my convictions represent in their multiplicity" (109). In the letter he finally sent, he defined his communism as "absolutely nothing other than the expression of certain experiences I have undergone in my thinking and in my life. That it is a drastic, not infertile expression of the fact that the present intellectual industry finds it impossible to accommodate my life; that it represents the obvious, reasoned attempt on the part of a man who is completely or almost completely deprived of any means of production to proclaim his right to them, both in his thinking and in his life . . . Is it really necessary to say all this to you?" (110). Benjamin continued with a passage on Brecht that showed he was all too aware of the real stakes here: Scholem's objection to his incorporation of a Brechtian, engaged politics alongside both his theological inclinations and the carefully considered, though still markedly leftist social analyses that allied him with the Institut für Sozialforschung. In a letter written that summer, Benjamin again alluded to this controversy while also claiming that he could not send Scholem the much more provocative essay "The Author as Producer," because he had failed to have enough copies made; when Scholem asked for a copy in person in 1938, Benjamin said (as Scholem later recalled), "I think I had better not let you read it" (113).

In early summer 1934, Benjamin undertook the trip to Skovsbostrand (near Svendborg), where Brecht and Helene Weigel were living in an isolated farmhouse; it was to be the first of three such extended summer visits, the others coming in 1936 and 1938. Shortly before leaving Paris for Denmark, Benjamin had suggested to Brecht that a series of affinities exist between his plays and the game of Go, with its initially empty board and its strategy of placing, rather than moving, pieces. "You place each of your figures and formulations on the right spot, whence they fulfill their proper strategic function on their own and without having to act" (443). He now took a room in a neighboring house in the countryside, which limited his social relations to Brecht and Weigel. His entertainment consisted of his customary walks (solitary, because neither of his hosts was interested) and evenings in front of Brecht's radio. "Thus, I was able to listen to Hitler's Reichstag speech, and because it was the very first time I had ever heard him, you can imagine the effect" (Scholem Letters, 130).

Despite the manifest difference in their personalities, Brecht and Benjamin shared a remarkable friendship. As Ruth Berlau, a member of Brecht's circle, remembers: "Whenever Benjamin and Brecht were together in Denmark, an atmosphere of confidence and trust immediately arose between them. Brecht had an enormous liking for Benjamin; in fact, he loved him. I think they understood each other without saying a word. They played chess wordlessly, and when they stood up, they had had a conversation."[16] When they did speak, the conversations were extensive and memorable. In the summer of 1934, they discussed Rimbaud and Johannes R. Becher, Confucius and Euripides, Gerhart Hauptmann and Dostoevsky. But most of their conversations concerned Kafka and the essay Benjamin was writing (see "Notes from Svendborg," in this volume).

An odd, three-part conversation on this topic soon arose, with Scholem the silent partner in Palestine. His frequent letters challenged Benjamin to answer a series of explicitly theological questions. Benjamin's replies are noteworthy. In reflecting on the question as to how one is to conceive, "in Kafka's sense, the Last Judgment's projection into world history," Benjamin emphasized not the answers to such questions, but rather Kafka's failure. "I endeavoured to show how Kafka sought—on the nether side of that 'nothingness,' in its inside lining, so to speak—to feel his way toward redemption. This implies that any kind of victory over that nothingness . . . would have been an abomination for him" (Scholem Letters, 129). A few weeks later, Benjamin admitted a "small, nonsensical hope" intended for Kafka's creatures and helpers, so memorably portrayed in the essay. "That I do not deny the component of revelation in Kafka's work already follows from my appreciation—by declaring the work to be 'distorted'—of its messianic aspect. Kafka's messianic category is the 'reversal' or 'study'" (135). Just as the great essay on Karl Kraus had done, the essay on Kafka marked a point of crystallization in Benjamin's thought. In a letter of November 12 to Werner Kraft, he asserted that "the study brought me to a crossroads in my thoughts and reflections. Devoting additional thought to it promises to do for me precisely what using a compass would do to orient a person on uncharted terrain" (Letters, 462).

The world and its politics penetrated, if somewhat slowly, to Skovsbostrand. In September, Benjamin was dismayed by what he saw as Kraus's "capitulation to Austro-fascism, the glossing-over of the white terror instituted against the Viennese workers, the admiration of the rhetoric . . . of Starhemberg." He was led to ask, "Who can still give in?" (Letters, 458). By October, Benjamin was clearly desperate to leave Denmark, and this despite continuing productive and cordial relations with Brecht. He badly wished to return to his arcades work, an undertaking impossible on an isolated farm with no access to a library. This to some extent explains Benjamin's enthusiastic response to a proposal by Horkheimer that he follow the Institut für Sozialforschung, which was moving to New York. "I would most gratefully welcome the chance to work in America, regardless of whether it is to do research at your institute or at an institute associated with yours. Indeed, allow me to say that you have my prior consent to any arrangement that seems appropriate to you" (Letters, 460).

In late October, Benjamin left Denmark for Italy. After a layover of a few days in Paris, he continued on to San Remo, where Dora had bought and was running a pension, the Villa Verde. In the years since the divorce, her relations with her former husband had gradually improved. She had actively sought publication possibilities for him while she remained in Berlin, and she now offered him food and shelter in Italy, and not for the last time. As one can imagine, Benjamin was acutely aware of the ambiguous position in which his acceptance of Dora's hospitality placed him. In a moment of self-laceration, he said it was "pitiful and a disgrace to nest, as it were, in the ruins of my own past" (465). But in the relative peace and security of the Italian countryside, he returned to his habits of long walks, much reading, and a good deal of writing. Aside from the customary detective novels (Somerset Maugham and the ever-present Simenon), he read Julien Green's latest book, *Visionnaire* (which he found quite disappointing) and Karl Thieme's *The Old Truth: A Cultural History of the West*, a gift from the author. He also told each of his correspondents of his esteem for Robert Louis Stevenson's *Master of Ballantrae*, which he ranked "ahead of almost all great novels, and right behind *The Charterhouse of Parma*" (Letters, 464).

In December, his sense of isolation was relieved by a visit from Stefan, who intended to return to Berlin and his schooling at least until he could be registered in the Italian school system in the spring. Benjamin found his son composed, confident, and rather too serious. Even this visit was not enough, though, to lend Benjamin a sense of rootedness, and he continued to cast about for opportunities for movement. Scholem, having abandoned all hope of bringing Benjamin back onto the path of a fully committed Judaism, now proposed for the first time that Benjamin pay a short, three-to-four-week visit to Palestine. As the year came to an end, Benjamin responded to this idea with the same enthusiasm he had expressed at Horkheimer's theoretical invitation to visit America.

Notes

1. Walter Benjamin, *Moscow Diary,* ed. Gary Smith, trans. Richard Sieburth (Cambridge, Mass.: Harvard University Press, 1986), p. 31. Subsequent references to this work will appear in the text as *MD.*
2. *The Correspondence of Walter Benjamin,* trans. Manfred R. Jacobson and Evelyn M. Jacobson (Chicago: University of Chicago Press, 1994), p. 312. Subsequent references to this work will appear in the text as Letters.
3. Walter Benjamin, *Gesammelte Briefe,* vol. 3, 1925–1930, ed. Christoph Gödde and Henri Lonitz (Frankfurt: Suhrkamp, 1997), p. 233. Subsequent references to this work will appear in the text as *GB.*
4. Gershom Scholem, *Walter Benjamin: The Story of a Friendship,* trans. Harry Zohn (Philadelphia: Jewish Publication Society of America, 1981), p. 130. Subsequent references to this work will appear in the text as Scholem.
5. Dora Pollak to Herbert Blumenthal and Carla Seligson, June 29, 1915. Cited in Hans Puttnies and Gary Smith, *Benjaminiana* (Giessen: Anabas Verlag, 1991), p. 140.
6. Dora Benjamin to Gerhard Scholem, July 24, 1929. Cited in Puttnies and Smith, *Benjaminiana,* p. 150.
7. Divorce Decree, April 24, 1930. Cited in Puttnies and Smith, *Benjaminiana,* p. 159.
8. Benjamin always addressed Scholem as "Gerhard," using his original name. (Scholem took the name "Gershom" only after moving to Palestine.
9. See the essay "German Letters," in this volume.
10. See the essay "Privileged Thinking," in this volume.
11. Puttnies and Smith, *Benjaminiana,* p. 33.
12. Karl Kraus in *Die Fackel* 33, nos. 852–856 (1931): 27.
13. See "May–June 1931," in this volume.
14. Gershom Scholem, ed., *The Correspondence of Walter Benjamin and Gershom Scholem, 1932–1940,* trans. Gary Smith and André Lefevere (New York: Schocken, 1989), p. 13. Subsequent references to this work will appear in the text as Scholem Letters.
15. Benjamin refers here to (1) an early conception of *The Arcades Project;* (2) a book of his collected criticism on which he had pinned the greatest hopes; (3) a series of selected examples of bourgeois prose that would eventually be published pseudonymously in Switzerland as *Deutsche Menschen;* and (4) a book that would include his hashish protocols and commentary.
16. Ruth Berlau, *Brechts Lai-tu* (Darmstadt, 1985); cited in Momme Brodersen, *Spinne im eigenen Netz* (Bühl-Moos: Elster Verlag, 1990), p. 233.

Index